RAPID REVIEW
Chapter Content

BUDGETS (Chapter 9)

Components of the Master Budget

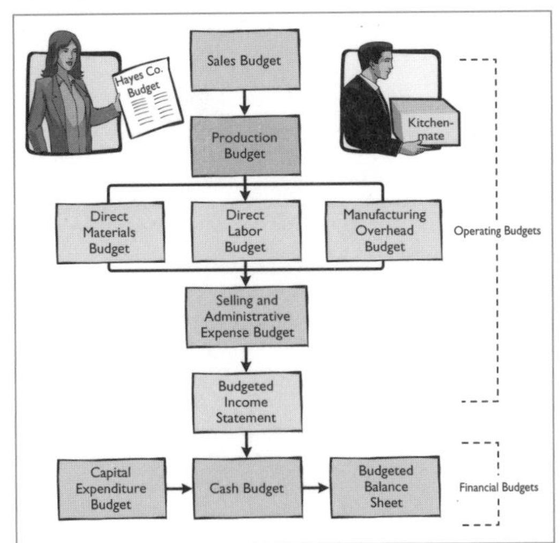

RESPONSIBILITY ACCOUNTING (Chapter 10)

Types of Responsibility Centers

Cost	Profit	Investment
Expenses only	Expenses and Revenues	Expenses and Revenues and ROI

Return on Investment

Return on investment (ROI) = Investment center controllable margin ÷ Average investment center operating assets

STANDARD COSTS (Chapter 11)

Standard Cost Variances

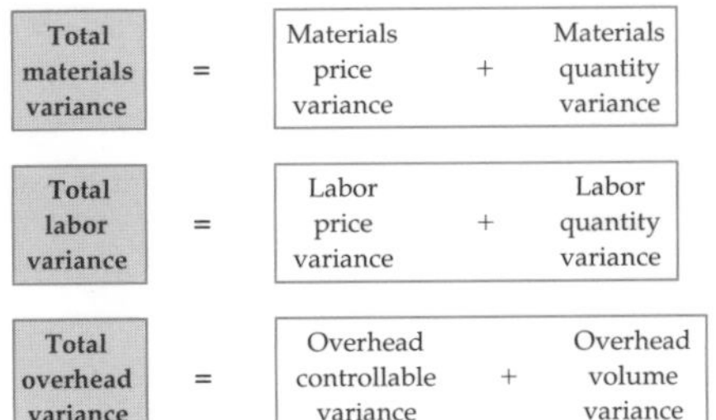

Total materials variance = Materials price variance + Materials quantity variance

Total labor variance = Labor price variance + Labor quantity variance

Total overhead variance = Overhead controllable variance + Overhead volume variance

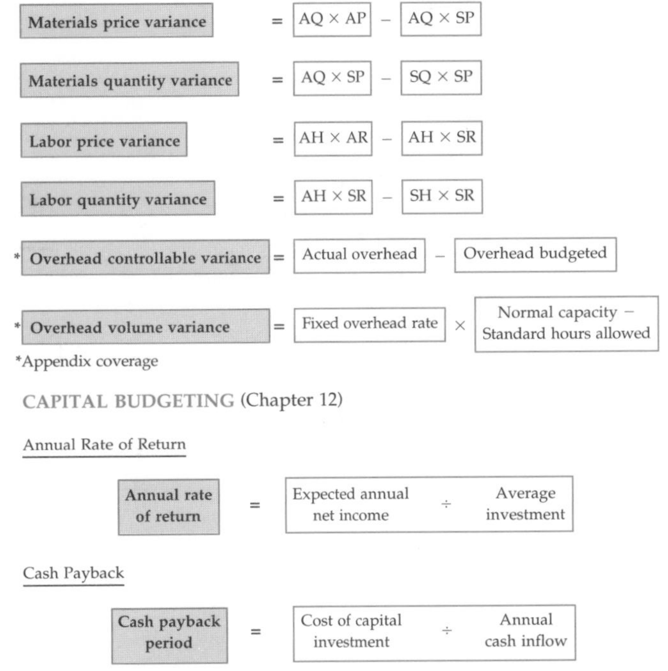

Materials price variance = AQ × AP – AQ × SP

Materials quantity variance = AQ × SP – SQ × SP

Labor price variance = AH × AR – AH × SR

Labor quantity variance = AH × SR – SH × SR

***Overhead controllable variance** = Actual overhead – Overhead budgeted

***Overhead volume variance** = Fixed overhead rate × Normal capacity – Standard hours allowed

*Appendix coverage

CAPITAL BUDGETING (Chapter 12)

Annual Rate of Return

Annual rate of return = Expected annual net income ÷ Average investment

Cash Payback

Cash payback period = Cost of capital investment ÷ Annual cash inflow

Discounted Cash Flow Approaches

Net Present Value	Internal Rate of Return
Compute net present value (a dollar amount). If net present value is zero or positive, accept the proposal. If net present value is negative, reject the proposal.	Compute internal rate of return (a percentage). If internal rate of return is equal to or greater than the minimum required rate of return, accept the proposal. If internal rate of return is less than the minimum rate, reject the proposal.

STATEMENT OF CASH FLOWS (Chapter 13)

Cash flows from operating activities (**indirect method**)

Net income			
Add:	Losses on disposals of assets	$ X	
	Amortization and depreciation	X	
	Decreases in noncash current assets	X	
	Increases in current liabilities	X	
Deduct:	Gains on disposals of assets	(X)	
	Increases in noncash current assets	(X)	
	Decreases in current liabilities	(X)	
Net cash provided (used) by operating activities			$ X

Cash flows from operating activities (**direct method**)

Cash receipts		
(Examples: from sales of goods and services to customers, from receipts of interest and dividends on loans and investments)	$ X	
Cash payments		
(Examples: to suppliers, for operating expenses, for interest, for taxes)	(X)	
Cash provided (used) by operating activities		$ X

Balanced Scorecard

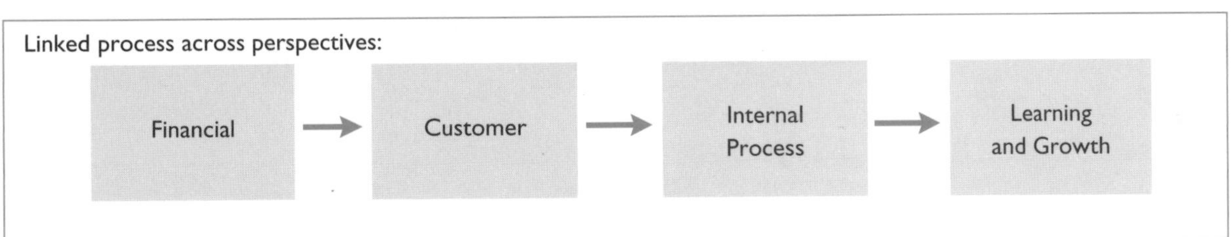

RAPID REVIEW
Chapter Content

FINANCIAL STATEMENT ANALYSIS (Chapter 14)

	Ratio	Formula	Purpose or Use
	Liquidity Ratios		
1.	Current ratio	$\frac{\text{Current assets}}{\text{Current liabilities}}$	Measures short-term debt-paying ability.
2.	Acid-test (quick) ratio	$\frac{\text{Cash + Short-term investments + Receivables (net)}}{\text{Current liabilities}}$	Measures immediate short-term liquidity.
3.	Receivables turnover	$\frac{\text{Net credit sales}}{\text{Average net receivables}}$	Measures liquidity of receivables.
4.	Inventory turnover	$\frac{\text{Cost of goods sold}}{\text{Average inventory}}$	Measures liquidity of inventory.
	Profitability Ratios		
5.	Profit margin	$\frac{\text{Net income}}{\text{Net sales}}$	Measures net income generated by each dollar of sales.
6.	Asset turnover	$\frac{\text{Net sales}}{\text{Average assets}}$	Measures how efficiently assets are used to generate sales.
7.	Return on assets	$\frac{\text{Net income}}{\text{Average total assets}}$	Measures overall profitability of assets.
8.	Return on common stockholders' equity	$\frac{\text{Net income}}{\text{Average common stockholders' equity}}$	Measures profitability of stockholders' investment.
9.	Earnings per share (EPS)	$\frac{\text{Net income}}{\text{Weighted average common shares outstanding}}$	Measures net income earned on each share of common stock.
10.	Price-earnings (P-E) ratio	$\frac{\text{Market price per share of stock}}{\text{Earnings per share}}$	Measures the ratio of the market price per share to earnings per share.
11.	Payout ratio	$\frac{\text{Cash dividends}}{\text{Net income}}$	Measures percentage of earnings distributed in the form of cash dividends.
	Solvency Ratios		
12.	Debt to total assets ratio	$\frac{\text{Total debt}}{\text{Total assets}}$	Measures percentage of total assets provided by creditors.
13.	Times interest earned	$\frac{\text{Income before income taxes and interest expense}}{\text{Interest expense}}$	Measures ability to meet interest payments as they come due.
14.	Free cash flow	Cash provided by operating activities − Capital expenditures − Cash dividends	Measures the amount of cash generated during the current year that is available for the payment of additional dividends or for expansion.

The Wiley Bicentennial–Knowledge for Generations

Each generation has its unique needs and aspirations. When Charles Wiley first opened his small printing shop in lower Manhattan in 1807, it was a generation of boundless potential searching for an identity. And we were there, helping to define a new American literary tradition. Over half a century later, in the midst of the Second Industrial Revolution, it was a generation focused on building the future. Once again, we were there, supplying the critical scientific, technical, and engineering knowledge that helped frame the world. Throughout the 20th Century, and into the new millennium, nations began to reach out beyond their own borders and a new international community was born. Wiley was there, expanding its operations around the world to enable a global exchange of ideas, opinions, and know-how.

For 200 years, Wiley has been an integral part of each generation's journey, enabling the flow of information and understanding necessary to meet their needs and fulfill their aspirations. Today, bold new technologies are changing the way we live and learn. Wiley will be there, providing you the must-have knowledge you need to imagine new worlds, new possibilities, and new opportunities.

Generations come and go, but you can always count on Wiley to provide you the knowledge you need, when and where you need it!

William J. Pesce
President and Chief Executive Officer

Peter Booth Wiley
Chairman of the Board

Managerial Accounting

Tools for Business Decision Making

Jerry J. Weygandt PhD, CPA
Arthur Andersen Alumni Professor of Accounting
University of Wisconsin
Madison, Wisconsin

Paul D. Kimmel PhD, CPA
Associate Professor of Accounting
University of Wisconsin—Milwaukee
Milwaukee, Wisconsin

Donald E. Kieso PhD, CPA
KPMG Emeritus Professor of Accounting
Northern Illinois University
DeKalb, Illinois

John Wiley & Sons, Inc.

Dedicated to
our former students and our colleagues,
past and present, and to our wives
Enid, Donna, and Merlynn

Executive Publisher Donald Fowley
Executive Editor Christopher DeJohn
Senior Marketing Manager Julia Flohr
Development Editor Ann Torbert
Project Editor Ed Brislin
Production Services Manager Dorothy Sinclair
Senior Production Editor Valerie A. Vargas
Senior Media Editor Allison Morris
Production Management Ingrao Associates
Associate Editor Brian Kamins
Senior Photo Editor Elle Wagner
Senior Illustration Editor Sandra Rigby
Cover Photo Superstudio/Reportage/Getty Images
Text & Cover Design Madelyn Lesure
Cover Design Superstudio/Reportage/Getty Images
Editorial Assistant Kathryn Fraser

This book was set in New Aster by Aptara, Inc. and printed and bound by RR Donnelley & Sons, Inc.—Jefferson City.
The cover was printed by RR Donnelley & Sons, Inc.—Jefferson City.

This book is printed on acid-free paper.

ISBN-13 digit U.S. Edition 978-0470-11726-2
Printed in the United States of America
10 9 8 7 6 5 4 3 2 1

ABOUT THE AUTHORS

Jerry J. Weygandt, PhD, CPA, is Arthur Andersen Alumni Professor of Accounting at the University of Wisconsin—Madison. He holds a Ph.D. in accounting from the University of Illinois. Articles by Professor Weygandt have appeared in the *Accounting Review. Journal of Accounting Research, Accounting Horizons, Journal of Accountancy*, and other academic and professional journals. These articles have examined such financial reporting issues as accounting for price-level adjustments, pensions, convertible securities, stock option contracts, and interim reports. Professor Weygandt is author of other accounting and financial reporting books and is a member of the American Accounting Association, the American Institute of Certified Public Accountants, and the Wisconsin Society of Certified Public Accountants. He has seved on numerous committees of the American Accounting Association and as a member of the editorial board of the *Accounting Review*; he also has served as President and Secretary-Treasurer of the American Accounting Association. In addition, he has been actively involved with the American Institute of Certified Public Accountants and has been a member of the Accounting Standards Executive Committee (AcSEC) of that organization. He has served on the FASB task force that examined the reporting issues related to accounting for income taxes and served as a trustee of the Financial Accounting Foundation. Professor Weygandt has received the Chancellor's Award for Excellence in Teaching and the Beta Gamma Sigma Dean's Teaching Award. He is on the board of directors of M & I Bank of Southern Wisconsin. He is the recipient of the Wisconsin Institute of CPA's Outstanding Educator's Award and the Lifetime Achievement Award. In 2001 he received the American Accounting Association's Outstanding Accounting Educator Award.

Paul D. Kimmel, PhD, CPA, received his bachelor's degree from the University of Minnesota and his doctorate in accounting from the University of Wisconsin. He is an Associate Professor at the University of Wisconsin—Milwaukee, and has public accounting experience with Deloitte & Touche (Minneapolis). He was the recipient of the UWM School of Business Advisory Council Teaching Award, the Reggie Taite Excellence in Teaching Award. and a three-time winner of the Outstanding Teaching Assistant Award at the University of Wisconsin. He is also a recipient of the Elijah Watts Sells Award for Honorary Distinction for his results on the CPA exam. He is a member of the American Accounting Association and the Institute of Management Accountants and has published articles in *Accounting Review, Accounting Horizons, Advances in Management Accounting, Managerial Finance, Issues in Accounting Education, Journal of Accounting Education*, as well as other journals. His research interests include accounting for financial instruments and innovation in accounting education. He has published papers and given numerous talks on incorporating critical thinking into accounting education, and helped prepare a catalog of critical thinking resources for the Federated Schools of Accountancy.

Donald E. Kieso, PhD, CPA, received his bachelor's degree from Aurora University and his doctorate in accounting from the University of Illinois. He has served as chairman of the Department of Accountancy and is currently the KPMG Emeritus Professor of Accountancy at Northern Illinois University. He has public accounting experience with Price Waterhouse & Co. (San Francisco and Chicago) and Arthur Andersen & Co. (Chicago) and research experience with the Research Division of the American Institute of Certified Public Accountants (New York). He has done postdoctorate work as a Visiting Scholar at the University of California at Berkeley and is a recipient of NIU's Teaching Excellence Award and four Golden Apple Teaching Awards. Professor Kieso is the author of other accounting and business books and is a member of the American Accounting Association, the American Institute of Certified Public Accountants, and the Illinois CPA Society. He has served as a member of the Board of Directors of the Illinois CPA Society, the AACSB's Accounting Accreditation Committees, the State of Illinois Comptroller's Commission, as Secretary-Treasurer of the Federation of Schools of Accountancy, and as Secretary-Treasurer of the American Accounting Association. Professor Kieso is currently serving on the Board of Trustees and Executive Committee of Aurora University, as a member of the Board of Directors of Kishwaukee Community Hospital, and as Treasurer and Director of Valley West Community Hospital. From 1989 to 1993 he served as a charter member of the national Accounting Education Change Commission. He is the recipient of the Outstanding Accounting Educator Award from the Illinois CPA Society, the FSA's Joseph A. Silvoso Award of Merit, the NIU Foundation's Humanitarian Award for Service to Higher Education, a Distinguished Service Award from the Illinois CPA Society, and in 2003 an honorary doctorate from Aurora University.

PREFACE

In this Fourth Edition of *Managerial Accounting: Tools for Business Decision Making*, we strove to build on those things that made the earlier editions a success in the classroom. Our goals are straightforward: We want this book to present the fundamental concepts of managerial accounting in an easy-to-understand fashion. We want to present only those concepts that students need to know. And we want students to leave the course confident that they will be able to apply the basic decision skills that they learned in this course when they enter the workforce.

As you read through the list of changes to this edition and review the text, the common theme you will notice is that we made changes intended to demonstrate to students that knowledge of managerial accounting is important for their future careers as well as useful for their personal financial decisions. We believe features such as the new All About You boxes and All About You Activities will generate student interest in the course and consequently increase the likelihood of student success. We are very excited about this edition of the text.

As in the earlier editions, our efforts were driven by the following key beliefs:

"Less is more."

Our instructional objective is to provide students with an understanding of those concepts that are fundamental to the use of managerial accounting. Most students will forget procedural details within a short period of time. On the other hand, concepts—if well taught—should be remembered for a lifetime. Concepts are especially important in a world where the details are constantly changing.

"Don't just sit there—do something."

Students learn best when they are actively engaged. The overriding pedagogical objective of this book is to provide students with continual opportunities for active learning. One of the best tools for active learning is strategically placed questions. Our discussions are framed by questions, often beginning with rhetorical questions and ending with review questions. Our analytical devices, called *Decision Tools*, use key questions to emphasize the purpose of each tool. Technology also offers many opportunities to enhance the learning environment. Through our *WileyPLUS* website, students can access a wide array of learning resources to support every learning style. At the book's companion website, at *www.wiley.com/college/weygandt*, we offer many opportunities for active learning. In addition, both in the homework and at the website, we offer opportunities to employ spreadsheet templates, another form of active learning for students.

"I'll believe it when I see it."

Students will be most willing to commit time and energy to a topic when they believe that it is relevant to their future careers. There is no better way to demonstrate relevance than to ground discussion in the real world. By using high-profile companies like Starbucks, Microsoft, Ben & Jerry's, and Intel to frame our discussion of accounting issues, we demonstrate the relevance of accounting while teaching students about companies with which they are familiar. In addition, because the economy has shifted toward service industries, many of the companies used as examples are service-based. This shift is emphasized by our homework feature that highlights service-company exercises. In addition, we provide many references to service companies such as American Express, Federal Express, and Union Pacific Railroad in text discussion and boxed stories throughout the book.

"You'll need to make a decision."

All business people must make decisions. Decision making involves critical evaluation and analysis of the information at hand, and this takes practice. To provide opportunities for practice, we have integrated important analytical tools throughout the book. After each new decision tool is presented, we summarize the key features of that tool in a *Decision Toolkit.* At the end of each chapter, the *Using the Decision Toolkit* activity provides a comprehensive demonstration of an analysis of a real-world problem using the decision tools presented in the chapter. Also, the *Broadening Your Perspective* homework activities require the student to employ these decision tools. Finally, seven *Cases for Management Decision Making*, provided at the end of the text, require students to employ decision-making skills in rich, realistic business settings.

New in This Edition

NEW FEATURES

An exciting new feature of this edition is titled "All About You." This high-interest feature links a specific aspect of the chapter's topic to students' personal lives. Each *All About You* box presents a topic, offers some facts about it, poses a situation for students to think about, and offers alternative answers as a starting place for further discussion. For example, in Chapter 5 we evaluate the financial aspects of the decision to purchase a hybrid car, and in Chapter 9 we demonstrate the usefulness of a personal budget. As a feedback mechanism at the end of the chapter, we offer our own comments and opinions about the *All About You* situation. Also, linked to the *All About You* box in each chapter is an *All About You Activity* (located in the *Broadening Your Perspective* section); it offers further opportunity to explore aspects of the topic in a homework assignment. The *All About You* boxes and related materials are intended to promote financial literacy by getting students to think about how accounting concepts impact their personal lives.

In this edition of the text we have continued our efforts to incorporate real-world companies and situations to pique student interest through *Insight* and *Accounting Across the Organization* boxes. The *Accounting Across the Organization* boxes are a new feature intended to demonstrate use of accounting information by people in non-accounting functions (e.g. marketing, finance, management). The *Insight* boxes focus on management issues, international companies, ethics, and service companies.

To boost student interest and provide more feedback to increase student interaction with content, we have added critical thinking questions at the end of both the *Insight* and *Accounting Across the Organization* boxes. Guideline answers to these critical thinking questions appear at the end of the chapter.

Further, to give you more choice of homework opportunities, we have added several new assignment features. At the end of the Problem section, we have added a new continuing problem, using the business activities of a fictional company called Waterways Corporation. This problem applies the topics covered in each chapter to the same company. Its purpose is to capture student interest in a realistic entrepreneurial situation. In addition, as discussed above, we have added a *Broadening Your Perspective* activity related to the *All About You* feature. Finally, at the book's companion website there are new B Exercises and C Problems for each chapter.

CHAPTER-BY-CHAPTER CHANGES IN THE FOURTH EDITION

Chapter 1: Managerial Accounting

New *All About You* feature on outsourcing and jobs.

Three new Exercises.

New Waterways Continuing Problem.

New *All About You Activity* that has students find personal situations to which managerial accounting techniques apply.

Chapter 2: Job Order Costing

New *Accounting Across the Organization* box on types of job order costs in service companies.

New *All About You* feature on calculating costs for a small business.

New Waterways Continuing Problem.

New *All About You Activity* asks students to investigate success characteristics required of small business owners

Chapter 3: Process Costing

New *All About You* feature on calculating production costs for a small company that has been offered an opportunity to sell its product to Wal-Mart.

Four new Exercises.

New Waterways Continuing Problem.

New *All About You Activity* asks students to explore aspects of activity-based costing in a service company.

Chapter 4: Activity-Based Costing

New *All About You* feature on employing the concepts of ABC to identify value-added and non-value-added activities in your own life.

New Waterways Continuing Problem.

New *All About You Activity* on identifying cost drivers in a local hospital.

Chapter 5: Cost-Volume-Profit

New *All About You* feature on calculating cost tradeoffs of hybrid vehicles.

Four new Exercises.

Two new Problems.

New Waterways Continuing Problem.

New *All About You Activity* asks students to compute costs of hybrid vehicle purchase.

Chapter 6: Cost-Volume-Profit Analysis: Additional Issues

Begins with a new comprehensive review of basic CVP concepts.

Moved variable costing discussion to appendix.

Expanded and reorganized discussion of sales mix and break-even analysis.

Moved discussion of sales mix and limited resources from incremental analysis chapter to Chapter 6.

New *All About You* feature on the evaluation of alternative electrical-plant energy sources.

Three new Exercises.

One new Problem.

New Waterways Continuing Problem.

New *All About You Activity* asks students to apply break-even analysis techniques to the decision whether to open a workout (fitness) center franchise.

Chapter 7: Incremental Analysis

New *All About You* feature evaluates the incremental benefits of post-high-school education.

New Waterways Continuing Problem.

New *All About You Activity* applies incremental analysis to the problem of chronic homelessness.

Chapter 8: Pricing

New *All About You* feature on pricing of fair-trade products and prescription drugs.

New Waterways Continuing Problem.

New *All About You Activity* on websites that help consumers compare product prices.

Chapter 9: Budgetary Planning

New *All About You* feature on personal budgeting for college students.

Four new Exercises.

New Waterways Continuing Problem.

New *All About You Activity* asks students to compute and analyze a student's budget.

Chapter 10: Budgetary Control and Responsibility Accounting

New *Accounting Across the Organization* box on budgeting at the San Diego Zoo.

New *All About You* feature on budgeting for housing costs.

Four new Exercises.

New Waterways Continuing Problem.

New *All About You Activity* that explores the strategy of "envelope budgeting."

Chapter 11: Standard Costs and Balanced Scorecard

New *All About You* feature on the balance between cost and quality in health care.

Five new Exercises.

New Waterways Continuing Problem.

New *All About You Activity* addresses the idea of imposing standards by way of standardized tests to measure college learning.

Chapter 12: Planning for Capital Investments

New *All About You* feature on the risk of financing home purchases with adjustable-rate mortgages.

New Waterways Continuing Problem.

New *All About You Activity* focusing on early-warning signals of personal debt troubles.

Chapter 13: The Statement of Cash Flows

Significantly revised chapter: shortened coverage of the operating activities section, for both methods, and condensed the presentation from two years to one.

Moved the direct method into an end-of-chapter appendix.

New *Accounting Across the Organization* box on sales level and cash provided by operations.

New *All About You* feature on personal cash budgeting.

Four new Exercises.

New Waterways Continuing Problem.

New *All About You Activity* asks students to calculate how much to set aside for short-term needs.

Chapter 14: Financial Statement Analysis

Replaced Sears with J.C. Penney as featured company throughout the chapter.

Added quality of earnings discussion.

Shortened section on changes in accounting principle.

New *Investor Insight* box on effects of large restructuring costs.

New *All About You* feature on when to begin investing in the stock market.

One new Self-Study Question, one new Question, and one new Brief Exercise.

One new Exercise.

New Waterways Continuing Problem.

New *All About You Activity* asks students to complete questionnaire on mutual funds.

Appendix A: Time Value of Money

Added new section on using financial calculators for time value of money calculations, with five related Brief Exercises.

Proven Pedagogical Framework

In this book we have used many proven pedagogical tools to help students learn accounting concepts and procedures and apply them to the business world. This pedagogical framework emphasizes the processes that students undergo as they learn. Turn to the **Student Owner's Manual** on page xx to see all of the learning tools in detail. These tools help students learn how to use the textbook, understand the context, learn the material, "put it all together," develop skills through practice, and expand and apply knowledge. Here are a few key features.

LEARNING HOW TO USE THE TEXTBOOK

- The **Student Owner's Manual**, p. xx, and **notes in blue** in Chapter 1, explain how to use the text's learning tools to help achieve success in the course.

- A **Learning Styles Quiz** includes tips on learning styles and strategies.
- **The Navigator** guides students through each chapter by pulling all the learning tools together into a learning system. **The Navigator** box on the chapter-opening page lays out a study framework; throughout the chapter, **Navigator** icons prompt students to use the learning aids and to set priorities as they study.

UNDERSTANDING THE CONTEXT

- **Study Objectives**, listed at the beginning of each chapter, reappear in the margins and again in the **Summary of Study Objectives**.
- A **Feature Story** helps students picture how the chapter topic relates to the real world of accounting and business and serves as a recurrent example.
- A **Chapter Preview** links the Feature Story to the major topics of the chapter and provides a road map to the chapter.

LEARNING THE MATERIAL

- Financial statement excerpts emphasize accounting experiences of **real companies throughout**.
- **Insight** and **Accounting Across the Organization** boxes give students glimpses into how real companies use accounting in practice. **Accounting Across the Organization** specifically addresses non-accounting business functions. Both types of boxes now include critical thinking questions, with guideline answers provided at the end of the chapter.
- **Color illustrations**, including **infographics**, help students visualize and apply accounting concepts to the real world.
- **Before You Go On** sections provide learning checks **(Review It)** and mini demonstration problems **(Do It)**.
- **Helpful Hints, Alternative Terminology**, and highlighted **key terms and concepts** help focus students on key concepts as they study the material.
- **Ethics Notes** help sensitize students to some of the ethical issues of accounting.
- Each chapter presents **decision tools** that are useful for analyzing and solving the business problems discussed in that chapter. At the end of the text discussion relating to the decisions tools, a **Decision Toolkit** summarizes the key features of the decision tools and reinforces their purpose.
- A **Using the Decision Toolkit** exercise, which follows the final Before You Go On section in the chapter, shows students how to use the decision tools presented in the chapter.

PUTTING IT TOGETHER

- The new **All About You** feature links some aspect of the chapter topic to students' personal lives. These high-interest boxes promote financial literacy and are intended to get students thinking and talking about how accounting impacts their personal lives.

At the end of each chapter are several additional features useful for review and reference.

- A **Summary of Study Objectives** reviews the main points of the chapter. The **Decision Toolkit Summary** presents in one place the decision tools used through the chapter.
- A **Glossary** of key terms gives definitions with page references to the text.
- A **Demonstration Problem** with an **Action Plan** gives students an opportunity to see a detailed solution to a representative problem before they do homework assignments.

DEVELOPING SKILLS THROUGH PRACTICE

Each chapter is supported by a full complement of homework material. **Self-Study Questions, Questions, Brief Exercises, two sets of Exercises (one online)**, and three sets of **Problems (one online)** are all keyed to the Study Objectives. Certain exercises and problems, marked with a pencil icon, help students practice business writing skills. Exercises relating to service companies are marked with an identifying icon. ***Check figures*** for selected Problems appear in the students' textbook.

In addition:

- New in this edition, the **Waterways Continuing Problem** follows the continuing saga of accounting for a small manufacturing and service company.
- Certain Exercises and Problems can be solved using the Excel supplement that is available to accompany the text and are identified by these icons.

EXPANDING AND APPLYING KNOWLEDGE

The **Broadening Your Perspective** section at the end of each chapter offers a wealth of resources for those instructors who want to broaden the learning experience by bringing in more real-world decision making, analysis, and critical thinking activities.

- **Decision Making Across the Organization Cases** help promote group collaboration and build decision-making and business communication skills by requiring teams of students to evaluate a manager's decision.
- **Managerial Analysis** assignments build analytical and decision-making skills in situations encountered by managers.
- **Real-World Focus** problems ask students to apply techniques and concepts presented in the chapter to specific situations faced by actual companies.

- **Exploring the Web** exercises guide students to Internet sites from which they can mine and analyze information related to the chapter topic.
- **Communication Activities** provide practice in written communication and presentation—skills much in demand among employers.
- **Ethics Cases** ask students to analyze situations, identify the stakeholders and the ethical issues involved, and decide on an appropriate course of action.
- **"All About You" Activities** offers further opportunities to explore aspects of the *All About You* topic in an activity-based homework assignment. These assignments may involve such matters as evaluating an article, doing research on a subject, answering a series of questions, or stating an opinion and providing rationale.
- Finally, on the last page(s) of the chapter, to give students a way to check their thinking and learning, we provide guideline answers and answer feedback to the following in-chapter items: Answers to Insight and Accounting Across Organization Questions; Authors' Comments on the *All About You* feature; and answers to the Self-Study Questions.

*

Managerial Accounting, Fourth Edition, features a full line of teaching and learning resources. Driven by the same basic beliefs as the textbook, these supplements provide a consistent and well-integrated learning system. This hands-on, real-world package guides *instructors* through the process of active learning and gives them the tools to create an interactive learning environment. With its emphasis on activities, exercises, and the Internet, the package encourages *students* to take an active role in the course and prepares them for decision making in a real-world context.

WEYGANDT'S INTEGRATED TECHNOLOGY SOLUTIONS HELPING TEACHERS TEACH AND STUDENT LEARN—*www.wiley.com/college/weygandt*

WileyPLUS—For Instructors. **WileyPLUS** is an online suite of resources that contains online homework, drill, and practice activities with access to a complete online version of the textbook. *WileyPLUS* gives you the technology to create an environment where students reach their full potential and experience academic success. Instructor resources include a wealth of presentation and preparation tools, easy-to-navigate assignment and assessment tools, and a complete system to administer and manage your course exactly as you wish. In addition, *WileyPLUS* includes selected problems powered by new General Ledger Software and Excel Working Papers.

WileyPLUS is built around the activities you regularly perform:

- **Prepare and present class presentations** using relevant Wiley resources such as PowerPoint™ slides, image galleries, animations, and other WileyPLUS materials. You can also upload your own resources or web pages to use in conjunction with Wiley materials.
- **Create assignments** by choosing from end-of-chapter exercises, problems, and test bank questions organized by chapter, study objective, level of difficulty, and source—or add your own questions. Algorithmic versions are available for each exercise and problems, allowing for additional drill and practice. *WileyPLUS* automatically grades students' homework and quizzes and records the results in your gradebook.
- **Offer context-sensitive help to students, 24/7.** When you assign homework or quizzes, you decide if and when students get access to hints, solutions, or answers where appropriate. Or students can be linked to relevant sections of their complete, online text for additional help whenever and wherever they need it most.
- **Track student progress.** You can analyze students' results and assess their level of understanding on an individual and class level using the *WileyPLUS* gradebook, and you can export data to your own personal gradebook.
- **Seamlessly integrate** all of the rich *WileyPLUS* content and resources with the power and convenience of your **WebCT or Blackboard course**—with a single sign-on.

WileyPLUS—For Students. *WileyPLUS* for students offers "**Read, Study, and Practice**" resources that can include the entire online textbook, select interactive, and end-of-chapter demonstration problems. Additional resources can include interactive chapter reviews, web-based tutorials, multi-media demo problems and other problem-solving resources.

- **An "Assignment"** area helps students stay "on task" by containing all homework assignments in one location. Many homework problems contain a link to the relevant sections of the ebook, providing students with context-sensitive help that allows them to conquer problem-solving obstacles.
- **A Personal Gradebook** for each student will allow students to view their results from past assignments at any time.

Book Companion Site—For Instructors. On this website instructors will find electronic versions of the Solutions Manual, Test Bank, Instructor's Manual, Computerized Test Bank, and other resources.

Book Companion Site—For Students. The *Managerial Accounting* student website provides a wealth of support materials that will help students develop their conceptual understanding of class material and increase their ability to solve problems. On this website students will find Excel templates, PowerPoint presentations, web quizzing, and other resources. In addition, students can access the new B Exercises and C Problems at this site. Finally, full versions of the Waterways Continuing Problem are included at the student website. Besides showing the data needed to complete these exercises, the website offers Excel templates that encourage completion of the Waterways problem tasks.

Wiley Faculty Network. When it comes to improving the classroom experience, there is no better source of ideas and inspiration than your fellow colleagues. The Wiley Faculty Network connects teachers with technologies, facilitates the exchange of best practices, and helps to enhance instructional efficiency and effectiveness. Faculty Network activities include technology training and tutorials, virtual seminars, peer-to-peer exchanges of experiences and ideas, personal consulting, and sharing of resources. For details visit *www.wherefacultyconnect.com.*

INSTRUCTOR'S ACTIVE-TEACHING AIDS

An extensive support package, including print and technology tools, helps you maximize your teaching effectiveness. We offer useful supplements for instructors with varying levels of experience and different instructional circumstances.

Instructor's Resource CD. The Instructor's Resource CD (IR CD) contains an electronic version of all instructor supplements. The IR CD gives you the flexibility to access and prepare instructional materials based on your individual needs.

Solutions Manual. The Solutions Manual contains detailed solutions to all questions, brief exercises, exercises, and problems in the textbook as well as suggested answers to the questions and cases. Each chapter includes an *assignment classification table*, an *assignment characteristics table*, and a *Bloom's taxonomy table.* Print is large and bold for easy readability in lecture settings. A team of independent accuracy checkers has carefully verified the Solutions Manual.

Solution Transparencies. The solution transparencies feature detailed solutions to brief exercises, exercises, problems, and Broadening Your Perspectives activities. They feature large, bold type for better projection and easy readability in large classroom settings. Transparencies can be easily ordered from the Instructor's Book Companion Site at *www.wiley.com/college/weygandt.*

Instructor's Manual. Included in each chapter are lecture outlines with teaching tips, chapter reviews, illustrations, and review quizzes.

Teaching Transparencies. The teaching transparencies are 4-color acetate images of the illustrations found in the Instructor's Manual. Transparencies can be easily ordered from the Instructor's Book Companion Site at *www.wiley.com/college/weygandt.*

Test Bank. With *over 400 new questions*, the test bank allows instructors to tailor examinations according to study objectives and Bloom's taxonomy. Achievement tests, comprehensive examinations, and a final exam are included.

Algorithmic Computerized Test Bank. The algorithmic feature of the new computerized test bank allows instructors to assign different values to a particular question, ensuring each student can receive a different version of the same exam. The computerized test bank also allows instructors to add questions, scramble the order of questions, and scramble the order of possible answers in multiple-choice questions.

PowerPoint™ Presentation Material. The new PowerPoint™ presentations contain a combination of key concepts, images and problems from the textbook. Review exercises and "All About You" summaries are included in each chapter to encourage classroom participation.

WebCT and Desire2Learn. WebCT or Desire2Learn offer an integrated set of course management tools that enable instructors to easily design, develop, and manage Web-based and Web-enhanced courses.

STUDENT ACTIVE-LEARNING AIDS

The *Managerial Accounting* Website. The student website at *www.wiley.com/college/weygandt* provides a wealth of support materials that will help students develop their conceptual understanding of course concepts and increase their ability to solve problems. On this website students will find PowerPoint™ presentations, Excel workbook and templates, web quizzing, and other resources.

Study Guide. Each study guide chapter contains a detailed chapter review, demonstration problems, true/false, multiple-choice, and matching questions, as well as comprehensive exercises. Solutions are provided.

Working Papers. Working Papers are templates for end-of-chapter brief exercises, exercises, problems, and cases. A convenient resource for organizing and completing homework assignments, they demonstrate how to correctly present homework solutions.

Excel Working Papers. An electronic version of the print working papers, these Excel-formatted templates help students properly format and present end-of-chapter textbook solutions. Available on CD or within *WileyPLUS.*

Excel Templates. This online manual and collection of Excel templates allow students to complete select end-of-chapter exercises and problems identified by a spreadsheet icon in the textbook.

Acknowledgments

In the course of developing *Managerial Accounting*, we have benefited greatly from the input of focus group participants, manuscript reviewers, users of the first three editions, ancillary authors, and proofers and problem checkers. We greatly appreciate the constructive suggestions, innovative ideas, and careful thought that these talented teachers and accounting practitioners have offered. We wish to express our ongoing gratitude to the following people.

REVIEWERS AND FOCUS GROUP PARTICIPANTS FOR THE FOURTH EDITION

Robert Bromley, *Central Michigan University*
Vernon Kwiatkowski, *Central Michigan University*
Lisa Capozzoli, *College of DuPage*
Maureen McBeth, *College of DuPage*
Deborah Most, *Dutchess Community College*
Natalie Allen, *Texas A&M University*
Kermit Keeling, *Loyola College Maryland*
Jayne Maas, *Loyola College Maryland*
Hong Zhu, *Loyola College Maryland*
Bill Johnstone, *Montgomery College Rockville*
Brian Baick, *Montgomery College Rockville*
Bill Talbot, *Montgomery College Rockville*
Richard Lenet, *Montgomery College Rockville*
Philip Ringeisen, *Montgomery College Germantown*
Sherry Mirbod, *Montgomery College Germantown*
Joyce Mauro, *Westchester Community College*
Doris Warmflash, *Westchester Community College*
Carolyn Perricone, *Westchester Community College*
Sal Marino, *Westchester Community College*
Nancy Uddin, *Monmouth University*
Gilda Agacer, *Monmouth University*
Norris Dorsey, *California State University, Northridge*
Denise Guithues-Amrhein, *Saint Louis University*

REVIEWERS AND FOCUS GROUP PARTICIPANTS FOR PRIOR EDITIONS

Victoria Beard, *University of North Dakota*
Kelly A. Blacker, *Mercy College*
Nancy Boyd, *Middle Tennessee State University*
Joan Cook, *Milwaukee Area Technical College*
Ken Coubillion, *San Joaquin Delta College*
Linda Denning, *Jefferson Community College*
'Denise M. English, *Boise State University*
Cecelia Fewox, *Trident Technical College*
Albert Fisher, *Community College of Southern Nevada*
Jeannie Folk, *College of DuPage*
George Gardner, *Bemidji State University*
Jane Grange, *Chicago State University*
Marc Giullian, *University of Louisiana—Lafayette*
John J. Goetz, *University of Texas—Arlington*
Thomas Hofmeister, *Northwestern Business School*
Kathy Horton, *College of DuPage*
Sharon Johnson, *Kansas City Community College*
David Karmon, *Central Michigan University*
J. Suzanne King, *University of Charleston*
Shirly Kleiner, *Johnson County Community College*
Terry Kubichan, *Old Dominion University*
Chor Lau, *California State University—Los Angeles*
Robyn Lawrence, *University of Scranton*
Melanie Mackey, *Ocean County College*
Jamie O'Brien, *South Dakota State University*
Shelly Ota, *Leeward Community College*
Deanne Pannell, *Pellissippi State Technical College*
Kenneth R. Pelfrey, *Ohio State University*
Peter J. Poznanski, *Cleveland State University*
David Ravetch, *University of California—Los Angeles*
Jill Russell, *Camden County College*
Paul J. Shinal, *Cayuga Community College*
Jerome Spallino, *Westmoreland County Community College*
Ellen Sweatt, *Georgia Perimeter College*
Cynthia Tomes, *Des Moines Area Community College*
Michael F. van Breda, *Southern Methodist University*
Chris Widmer, *Tidewater Community College*
Dawn Addington, *St. Louis University*
Peter Aghimien, *Indiana University—South Bend*
Walter Baggett, *Manhattan College*
Kevan Bloomgrem, *Fairleigh Dickinson University*
Angela Brandt, *University of Wisconsin—Madison*
Christy Burge, *University of Louisville*
Jacqueline Calderone, *Monmouth University*
Charles Carmen, *Delso Community College*
D. Constable, *Georgia Perimeter College*
Constance Cooper, *University of Cincinnati*
Patti Fedje, *Minor State University*
Ron Flinn, *Creighton University*
Lisa Gillespie, *Loyola University of Chicago*
Linda Graves, *John A. Logan College*
Kevin Green, *Washington and Lee University*
Mary Haley, *Cumberland University*
Kermilt Keeling, *Loyola College*
Mehmet Kocakulah, *University of Southern Indiana*
Laura Jean Kreissl, *University of Wisconsin—Parkside*
Mike Labalokie, *Penn State—Mt. Alto*
Ira Landis, *University of Judaism*

Adena LeJuene, *Louisiana State University—Alexandria*
Bernard McNeal, *Bowie State University*
Mike Metzcar, *Indiana Wesleyan University*
Lee Nicholas, *University of Northern Iowa*
Roger Reynolds, *University of Dayton*
Martin Rudoff, *Community College of Philadelphia*
Karen Senecal, *Washington College*
William Serafin, *Community College of Allegheny*
Robbie Sheffy, *Tarrant County Junior College* NW
Jeff Storm, *Lincolnland Community College*
Paul Swanson, *Bradley University*
Leslie Vaughan, *St. Louis University*
Lin Zheng, *Northeastern Illinois University*

ANCILLARY AUTHORS, CONTRIBUTORS, AND PROOFERS

John Borke, *University of Wisconsin—Platteville:* Text and Solutions Manual Proofer

James M. Emig, *Villanova University:* Solutions Manual, Test Bank, and Study Guide proofer

Larry R. Falcetto, *Emporia State University:* Instructor's Manual and Check Figures author, Text and Solutions Manual Proofer

Douglas W. Kieso, *Aurora University:* Study Guide author

Laura McNally, *Black Hills State University:* WileyPLUS author and proofer

Charles J. Russo, *Bloomsburg University:* Test Bank author

Rex Schildhouse, *University of Phoenix, San Diego:* Excel Templates and Workbook author

Teresa Speck, *St. Mary's University:* Text and Solutions Manual proofer

Diane Tanner, *University of North Florida:* Test Bank author

Sheila Viel, *University of Wisconsin—Milwaukee:* Problem material contributor and text proofer

Dan R. Ward, *University of Louisiana at Lafayette:* PowerPoint author

Suzanne Ward, *University of Louisiana at Lafayette:* PowerPoint author

Dick D. Wasson, *Southwestern College:* Working Papers and Excel Working Papers author, Text and Solutions Manual proofer

We appreciate the exemplary support and professional commitment given to us by executive editor Chris DeJohn, marketing manager Julia Flohr, project editor Ed Brislin, senior associate editor Brian Kamins, editorial assistant Katie Fraser, senior media editor Allie Morris, vice president of higher education production and manufacturing Ann Berlin, designer Maddy Lesure, illustration editor Anna Melhorn, photo editor Elle Wagner, development editor Ann Torbert, permissions editor Karyn Morrison, project editor Suzanne Ingrao of Ingrao Associates, indexer Steve Ingle, product manager Jane Shifflet at Aptara, and project manager Kim Nichols at Elm Street Publishing Services. All of these professionals provided innumerable services that helped the book take shape.

Finally, our thanks to Amy Scholz, Susan Elbe, Don Fowley, Joe Heider, Bonnie Lieberman, and Will Pesce, for their support and leadership in Wiley's College Division.

We will appreciate suggestions and comments from users—instructors and students alike. You can send your thoughts and ideas about the book to us via email at:

AccountingAuthors@yahoo.com

Jerry J. Weygandt
Madison, Wisconsin

Paul D. Kimmel
Milwaukee, Wisconsin

Donald E. Kieso
DeKalb, Illinois

STUDENT OWNER'S MANUAL

How to Use the Study Aids in This Book

Chapter 6

Cost-Volume-Profit Analysis: Additional Issues

STUDY OBJECTIVES

After studying this chapter, you should be able to:

1. Describe the essential features of a cost-volume-profit income statement.
2. Apply basic CVP concepts.
3. Explain the term sales mix and its effects on break-even sales.
4. Determine sales mix when a company has limited resources.
5. Understand how operating leverage affects profitability.

The Navigator

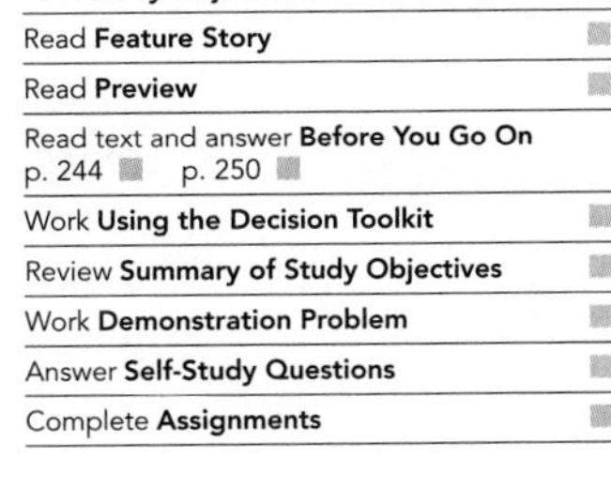

The Navigator

Scan **Study Objectives**

Read **Feature Story**

Read **Preview**

Read text and answer **Before You Go On** p. 244 p. 250

Work **Using the Decision Toolkit**

Review **Summary of Study Objectives**

Work **Demonstration Problem**

Answer **Self-Study Questions**

Complete **Assignments**

The Navigator is a learning system designed to guide you through the chapter and help you succeed in learning the material. It consists of (1) a checklist at the beginning of the chapter, which outlines text features and study aids you will need, and (2) a series of check boxes that prompt you to use the chapter's learning aids and set priorities as you study.

Feature Story

WHAT GOES UP (*FAST*), MUST COME DOWN (*FAST*)

During the late 1990s many people marveled at the efficiency of the so-called "New Economy," which uses digital technologies to improve business processes. Some managers were actually startled by their own success. The New Economy had created a new formula for profit. For example, David Peterschmidt, chief executive at software developer Inktomi, noted that the company had incurred considerable fixed costs in developing new software, but its variable costs were minor. As a consequence, once sales had covered the fixed costs, every additional sale was basically pure profit. When sales were booming, he happily stated, "Next to the federal government, this is the only business that's allowed to print money." But that was then. When the economy lagged, the new profit formula went sour. The company's sales

234

The **Feature Story** helps you picture how the chapter topic relates to the real world of accounting and business. References to the Feature Story throughout the chapter will help you put new ideas in context, organize them, and remember them.

disappeared, but its fixed costs did not. In no time, Inktomi went from record profits to staggering losses.

Many other companies have had similar experiences. As their manufacturing plants have become more automated, their fixed costs have become increasingly high. For example, during a five-year period, the average cost of a typical Intel semiconductor plant rose from $500 million to $2 billion as its manufacturing processes became increasingly sophisticated. These high fixed costs have made Intel very dependent on producing a high volume of computer chips. It needs high volume so that it can spread its fixed costs across a lot of units, thereby reducing the fixed cost per unit. As one Intel employee put it, "You have high fixed costs, so you want to minimize those fixed costs and keep factories running 24 hours a day."

However, when management focuses too heavily on keeping volume high to reduce fixed costs per unit, it sometimes produces more inventory than the market wants. When this happens, companies have to cut prices sharply. High-tech firms, like Intel, whose products rapidly become obsolete, have occasionally been stuck with inventory that nobody wanted. Thus, while the huge outlays for new equipment have made these companies exceptionally efficient, such outlays have also increased their exposure to economic swings. In fact, because so many companies now have cost structures that rely heavily on fixed costs, many economists worry that swings in the entire economy will be more volatile than in the past.

Source: Greg Ip, "As Profits Swoon, Companies Blame A Marked Change in Cost Structure," *Wall Street Journal*, May 16, 2001.

The Navigator

Study Objectives at the beginning of each chapter give you a framework for learning the specific concepts in the chapter. Each study objective reappears in the margin where the concept is discussed. You can review the study objectives in the **Summary** at the end of the chapter text.

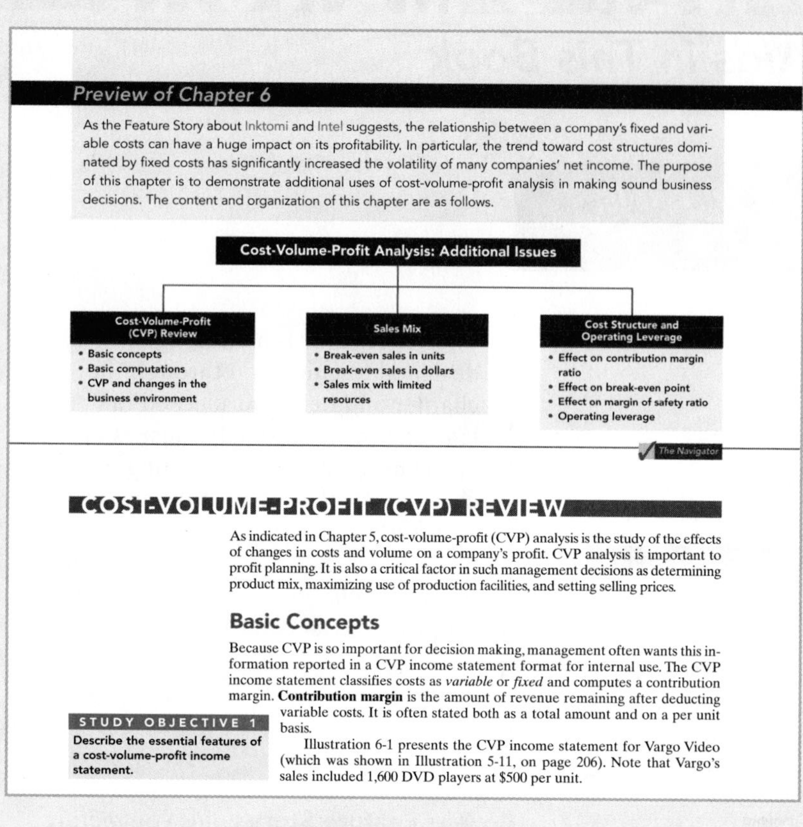

Preview of Chapter 6

As the Feature Story about Inktomi and Intel suggests, the relationship between a company's fixed and variable costs can have a huge impact on its profitability. In particular, the trend toward cost structures dominated by fixed costs has significantly increased the volatility of many companies' net income. The purpose of this chapter is to demonstrate additional uses of cost-volume-profit analysis in making sound business decisions. The content and organization of this chapter are as follows.

COST-VOLUME-PROFIT (CVP) REVIEW

As indicated in Chapter 5, cost-volume-profit (CVP) analysis is the study of the effects of changes in costs and volume on a company's profit. CVP analysis is important to profit planning. It is also a critical factor in such management decisions as determining product mix, maximizing use of production facilities, and setting selling prices.

Basic Concepts

Because CVP is so important for decision making, management often wants this information reported in a CVP income statement format for internal use. The CVP income statement classifies costs as *variable* or *fixed* and computes a contribution margin. **Contribution margin** is the amount of revenue remaining after deducting variable costs. It is often stated both as a total amount and on a per unit basis.

STUDY OBJECTIVE 1

Describe the essential features of a cost-volume-profit income statement.

Illustration 6-1 presents the CVP income statement for Vargo Video (which was shown in Illustration 5-11, on page 206). Note that Vargo's sales included 1,600 DVD players at $500 per unit.

The **Preview** links the Feature Story with the major topics of the chapter and describes the purpose of the chapter.

A **graphic outline** provides a visual preview of the chapter topics. Together, the narrative and visual previews help you organize the information you are learning.

Study Objectives reappear in the margins next to the text discussion of the related topic. End-of-chapter assignments are keyed to study objectives.

Helpful Hints in the margins further clarify concepts being discussed. They are like having an instructor with you as you read.

HELPFUL HINT

Approvals are an important part of a materials requisition slip because they help to establish individual accountability over inventory.

Companies assign raw materials costs when their materials storeroom issues the materials. Requests for issuing raw materials are made on a prenumbered **materials requisition slip.** The materials issued may be used directly on a job, or they may be considered indirect materials. As Illustration 2-6 shows, the requisition should indicate the quantity and type of materials withdrawn and the account to be charged. The company will charge direct materials to Work in Process Inventory, and indirect materials to Manufacturing Overhead.

The names of real companies are highlighted in red type.

Ethics Notes point out ethical issues related to the nearby text discussion.

JUST-IN-TIME INVENTORY METHODS

Many companies have significantly lowered inventory levels and costs using **just-in-time (JIT) inventory** methods. Under a just-in-time method, goods are manufactured or purchased just in time for use. As noted in the Feature Story, Dell is famous for having developed a system for making computers in response to individual customer requests. Even though each computer is custom-made to meet each customer's particular specifications, it takes Dell less than 48 hours to assemble the computer and put it on a truck. By integrating its information systems with those of its suppliers, Dell reduced its inventories to nearly zero. This is a huge advantage in an industry where products become obsolete nearly overnight.

ETHICS NOTE

Does just-in-time inventory justify "just-in-time" employees obtained through temporary employment services?

MANAGEMENT INSIGHT

Don't Just Look—Buy Something

When analyzing an Internet business, analysts closely watch the so-called "conversion rate." This rate is calculated by dividing the number of people who actually take action at an Internet site (buy something) by the total number of people who visit the site. Average conversion rates are from 3% to 5%. A rate below 2% is poor, while a rate above 10% is great.

Conversion rates have an obvious effect on the break-even point. Suppose you spend $10,000 on your site, and you attract 5,000 visitors. If you get a 2% conversion rate (100 purchases), your site costs $100 per purchase ($10,000 ÷ 100). A 4% conversion rate gets you down to a cost of $50 per transaction, and an 8% conversion rate gets you down to $25. Studies show that conversion rates increase if the site has an easy-to-use interface, fast-performing screens, a convenient ordering process, and advertising that is both clever and clear.

Source: J. William Gurley, "The One Internet Metric That Really Counts," *Fortune*, March 6, 2000, p. 392.

? Besides increasing their conversion rates, what steps can online merchants use to lower their break-even points?

***Insight* boxes** offer a glimpse into how actual companies make decisions using accounting information. These high-interest boxes focus on various themes—ethics, international, investor concerns, and management. *Guideline answers* to the critical thinking questions appear at the end of the chapter.

A **critical thinking question** asks you to apply your accounting learning to the story in the example.

Accounting Across the Organization boxes show the use of accounting by people in non-accounting functions—such as finance, marketing, or management.

Guideline Answers to the critical thinking questions in Accounting Across the Organization boxes and the Insight boxes appear at the end of the chapter.

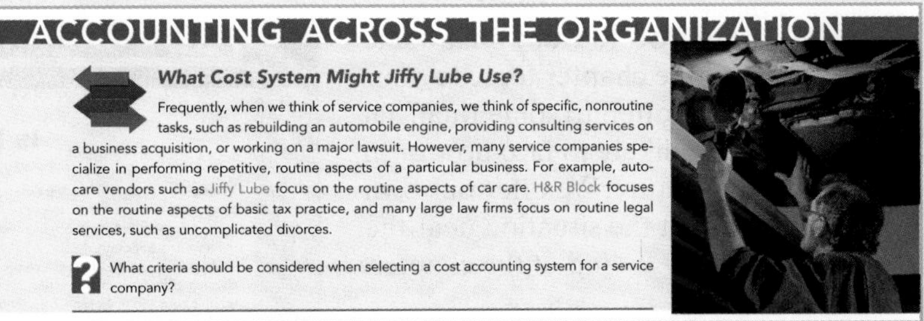

ACCOUNTING ACROSS THE ORGANIZATION

What Cost System Might Jiffy Lube Use?

Frequently, when we think of service companies, we think of specific, nonroutine tasks, such as rebuilding an automobile engine, providing consulting services on a business acquisition, or working on a major lawsuit. However, many service companies specialize in performing repetitive, routine aspects of a particular business. For example, auto-care vendors such as Jiffy Lube focus on the routine aspects of car care. H&R Block focuses on the routine aspects of basic tax practice, and many large law firms focus on routine legal services, such as uncomplicated divorces.

? What criteria should be considered when selecting a cost accounting system for a service company?

Key terms and concepts are printed in blue where they are first explained in the text. They are listed and defined again in the end-of- chapter **Glossary.**

Key formulas that you will need to know and use are boxed off.

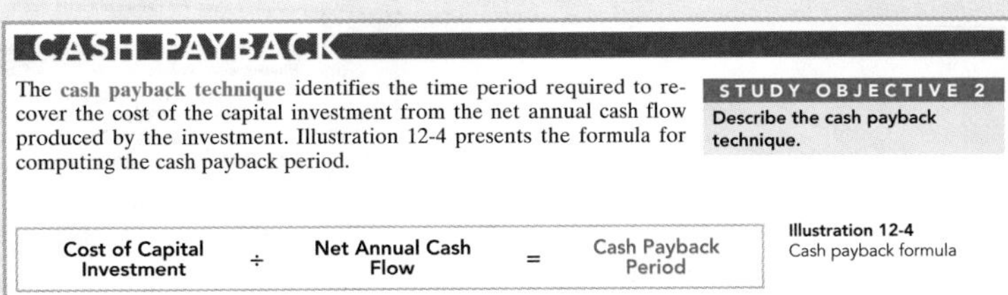

CASH PAYBACK

The **cash payback technique** identifies the time period required to recover the cost of the capital investment from the net annual cash flow produced by the investment. Illustration 12-4 presents the formula for computing the cash payback period.

STUDY OBJECTIVE 2

Describe the cash payback technique.

Cost of Capital Investment ÷ Net Annual Cash Flow = Cash Payback Period

Illustration 12-4
Cash payback formula

Color illustrations, such as this **infographic,** help you visualize and apply information as you study. They reinforce important concepts and therefore often contain material that may appear on exams.

Illustration 1-13
A manufacturer's value chain

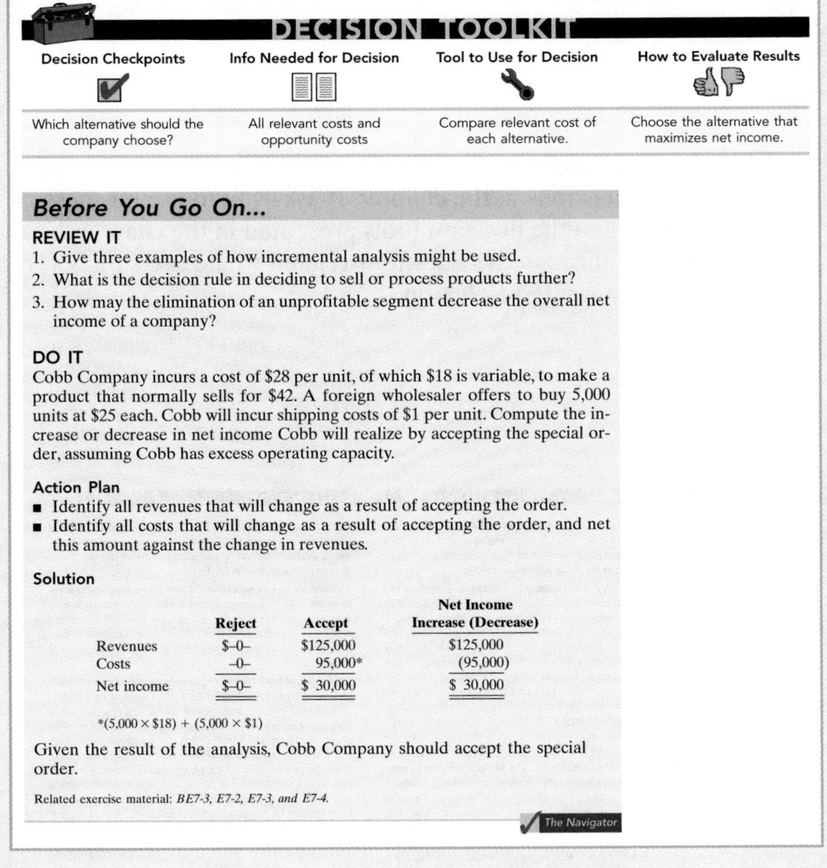

DECISION TOOLKIT

Decision Checkpoints	Info Needed for Decision	Tool to Use for Decision	How to Evaluate Results
Which alternative should the company choose?	All relevant costs and opportunity costs	Compare relevant cost of each alternative.	Choose the alternative that maximizes net income.

Before You Go On...

REVIEW IT

1. Give three examples of how incremental analysis might be used.
2. What is the decision rule in deciding to sell or process products further?
3. How may the elimination of an unprofitable segment decrease the overall net income of a company?

DO IT

Cobb Company incurs a cost of $28 per unit, of which $18 is variable, to make a product that normally sells for $42. A foreign wholesaler offers to buy 5,000 units at $25 each. Cobb will incur shipping costs of $1 per unit. Compute the increase or decrease in net income Cobb will realize by accepting the special order, assuming Cobb has excess operating capacity.

Action Plan

- Identify all revenues that will change as a result of accepting the order.
- Identify all costs that will change as a result of accepting the order, and net this amount against the change in revenues.

Solution

	Reject	Accept	Net Income Increase (Decrease)
Revenues	$-0-	$125,000	$125,000
Costs	-0-	95,000*	(95,000)
Net income	$-0-	$ 30,000	$ 30,000

*(5,000 × $18) + (5,000 × $1)

Given the result of the analysis, Cobb Company should accept the special order.

Related exercise material: *BE7-3, E7-2, E7-3, and E7-4.*

The Navigator

Each chapter presents **Decision Tools** that help decision makers analyze and solve business problems. At the end of a topic discussion, a **Decision Toolkit** summarizes the key features of a decision tool and reviews why and how you would use it.

Before You Go On sections follow each key topic. ***Review It*** questions prompt you to stop and review the key points you have just studied. If you cannot answer these questions, you should go back and read the section again.

Brief ***Do It*** exercises ask you to put to work your newly acquired knowledge. They outline an ***Action Plan*** necessary to complete the exercise, and they show a ***Solution.***

An **All About You feature** links some aspect of the chapter topic to your personal life, and often to some financial situation you are likely to face now or in the near future. We offer our own *opinions* about the situation near the end of the chapter.

all about YOU

Is the Price Right?

The right price can make a big difference to companies. For example, at Coca-Cola a 4% increase in the price received for its products would increase net income significantly.

As indicated in the chapter, a company has to choose a price for its products that will cover its variable costs and make some contribution to fixed overhead in the short run. In the long run, the company must price its products to cover all costs. But pricing products to achieve these objectives is complex, given the nature of consumer behavior.

Some Facts

* Prices come in all forms such as tuition for school, fees for medical care, premiums for insurance, user fees for tolls. In some cases we can influence the price by our behavior (e.g., buying airplane tickets online rather than through a travel agent); in other cases, it is more difficult to influence price (e.g., the price of cable TV).
* In one survey, marketing managers rated pricing as their biggest problem. Other issues such as new competition, product differentiation, and selling expenses were not as stressful. Reasons for the stress are the importance of getting the price right to ensure overall profitability and the difficulty of getting it right.
* Do you buy products based on expected savings from rebates? If so, do you actually file for the rebate? Some 40% of rebates do not get redeemed. Many people do not bother to fill out the form and process the receipts. And some companies do not make it easy: They make up complex rules, demand original copies of bills, set short expiration periods, and delay sending checks. In some cases, the companies send the check with another company's name on the envelope in hope you will not recognize it and tear it up.
* Retailers use price-optimization software to assess difficult situations. For example: In a store with a variety of paintbrushes, the best seller was the cheapest one, at $1. But after inputting many variables, the store stopped selling the $1 brushes, which enabled it to sell more high-priced (and more profitable) paintbrushes. Why? The key factor in whether a customer bought a paintbrush was whether he or she was buying paint, not the price of the brush.

Some useful sites for pricing information are

About the Numbers

At your local grocery store, you may see items that are identified as fair-traded. Fair-traded means that the retailer paid a minimum price to the producer to ensure a fair profit for the producer. Most individuals believe that by paying the fair-trade price, you are helping some struggling farmer, often in a less-developed country.

To better understand how pricing works in a fair-trade situation, here is an example of how the price is set for one pound of fair-trade coffee computed by wholesaler roaster Dean's Beans.

$1.41 Price paid to grower, includes 5-cent fair-trade premium
0.39 Administrative costs and shipping
0.36 Shrinkage during roasting
2.50 Operating and maintenance costs
0.14 Packaging and misc. cost
$4.80 Wholesale roaster cost

The price at which Dean's sells to the grocery store is $5.00, for a profit of $0.20 to the wholesaler. The retailer sells the pound of coffee to you for $8.49, for a profit of $3.49 profit before expenses. So next time you are considering a fair-traded product, you might ask, How much does that poor struggling farmer receive in relation to the markup that the retailer receives when the product is fair-traded?

Source: Steve Stecklow and Erin White, "What Price Virtue? At Some Retailers, 'Fair Trade' Carries a Very High Cost: Stores Charge Big Markups on Goods Intended to Help Farmers in Poor Countries; Bananas at $2.74 a Bunch," *Wall Street Journal*, June 8, 2004, p. Al.

What Do You Think?

One issue that always raises many questions is the pricing of medical drugs. For example, we often hear about the fact that certain drugs sold by U.S. companies cost much less overseas than in the United States. And there are certain drugs in the United States that seem extremely expensive. For example, Avantis is a cancer-reducing drug that costs patients $55,000 a year. Congress continues to study the issue of drug pricing. Do you think that high pricing of pharmaceuticals is fair?

YES: Drug companies have to spend substantial amounts of money to create new therapies. In addition to the heavy research and development costs involved, the lead time from discovery to actual use of new drugs on patients can exceed 10 years. In short, the drug companies must recover these costs by charging high prices.

NO: The drug companies are profitable. How can they expect individuals to pay very high prices for some of these live-saving drugs? Furthermore, how can a drug sold in the United States often sell for much less in another part of the world?

Sources: Brian Bergstein, "It's Buyer Beware in Stores," Wisconsin State Journal, April 28, 2007.

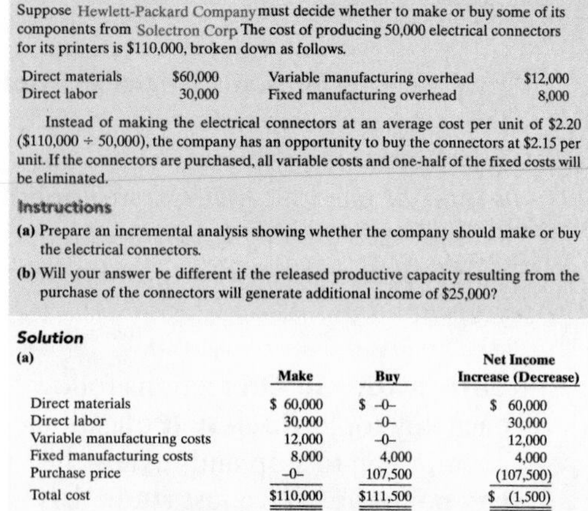

Using the Decision Toolkit

Suppose Hewlett-Packard Company must decide whether to make or buy some of its components from Solectron Corp. The cost of producing 50,000 electrical connectors for its printers is $110,000, broken down as follows.

Direct materials	$60,000	Variable manufacturing overhead	$12,000
Direct labor	30,000	Fixed manufacturing overhead	8,000

Instead of making the electrical connectors at an average cost per unit of $2.20 ($110,000 ÷ 50,000), the company has an opportunity to buy the connectors at $2.15 per unit. If the connectors are purchased, all variable costs and one-half of the fixed costs will be eliminated.

Instructions

(a) Prepare an incremental analysis showing whether the company should make or buy the electrical connectors.

(b) Will your answer be different if the released productive capacity resulting from the purchase of the connectors will generate additional income of $25,000?

Solution

(a)

	Make	Buy	Net Income Increase (Decrease)
Direct materials	$ 60,000	$ -0-	$ 60,000
Direct labor	30,000	-0-	30,000
Variable manufacturing costs	12,000	-0-	12,000
Fixed manufacturing costs	8,000	4,000	4,000
Purchase price	-0-	107,500	(107,500)
Total cost	$110,000	$111,500	$ (1,500)

This analysis indicates that Hewlett-Packard will incur $1,500 of additional costs if it buys the electrical connectors. H-P therefore would choose to make the connectors.

A **Using the Decision Toolkit** exercise follows the final set of ***Review It*** questions in the chapter. It asks you to use business information and the decision tools presented in the chapter. You should think through the questions related to the decision before you study the printed ***Solution.***

The **Summary of Study Objectives** reviews the main points related to the study objectives. It provides you with an opportunity to review what you have learned and to see how the key topics within the chapter fit together.

In some chapters, **appendixes** that follow the summary of the main part of the chapter offer expanded coverage of accounting procedures or further discussion of certain topics.

SUMMARY OF STUDY OBJECTIVES

1 **Describe the essential features of a cost-volume-profit income statement.** The CVP income statement classifies costs and expenses as variable or fixed and reports contribution margin in the body of the statement.

2 **Apply basic CVP concepts.** Contribution margin is the amount of revenue remaining after deducting variable costs. It can be expressed as a per unit amount or as a ratio. The break-even point in units is fixed costs divided by contribution margin per unit. The break-even point in dollars is fixed costs divided by the contribution margin ratio. These formulas can also be used to determine units or sales dollars needed to achieve target net income, simply by adding target net income to fixed costs before dividing by the contribution margin. Margin of safety indicates how much sales can decline before the company is operating at a loss. It can be expressed in dollar terms or as a percentage.

3 **Explain the term sales mix and its effects on break-even sales.** Sales mix is the relative proportion in which each product is sold when a company sells more than one product. For a company with a small number of products, break-even sales in units is determined by using the weighted-average unit contribution margin of all the products. If the company sells many different products, then calculating the break-even point using unit information is not practical. Instead, in a company with many products, break-even sales in dollars is calculated using the weighted-average contribution margin ratio.

4 **Determine sales mix when a company has limited resources.** When a company has limited resources, it is necessary to find the contribution margin per unit of limited resource. This amount is then multiplied by the units of limited resource to determine which product maximizes net income.

5 **Understand how operating leverage affects profitability.** Operating leverage refers to the degree to which a company's net income reacts to a change in sales. Operating leverage is determined by a company's relative use of fixed versus variable costs. Companies with high fixed costs relative to variable costs have high operating leverage. A company with high operating leverage will experience a sharp increase (decrease) in net income with a given increase (decrease) in sales. The degree of operating leverage can be measured by dividing contribution margin by net income.

At the end of each chapter, the **Decision Toolkit—A Summary** reviews the context and techniques useful for decision making that were covered in the chapter.

The **Glossary** defines all the **key terms** and **concepts** introduced in the chapter. Page references help you find any terms you need to study further.

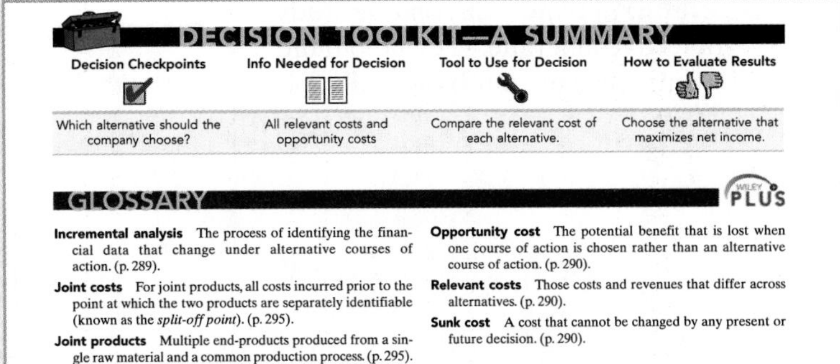

DECISION TOOLKIT—A SUMMARY

Decision Checkpoints	Info Needed for Decision	Tool to Use for Decision	How to Evaluate Results
Which alternative should the company choose?	All relevant costs and opportunity costs	Compare the relevant cost of each alternative.	Choose the alternative that maximizes net income.

GLOSSARY

Incremental analysis The process of identifying the financial data that change under alternative courses of action. (p. 289).

Joint costs For joint products, all costs incurred prior to the point at which the two products are separately identifiable (known as the *split-off point*). (p. 295).

Joint products Multiple end-products produced from a single raw material and a common production process. (p. 295).

Opportunity cost The potential benefit that is lost when one course of action is chosen rather than an alternative course of action. (p. 290).

Relevant costs Those costs and revenues that differ across alternatives. (p. 290).

Sunk cost A cost that cannot be changed by any present or future decision. (p. 290).

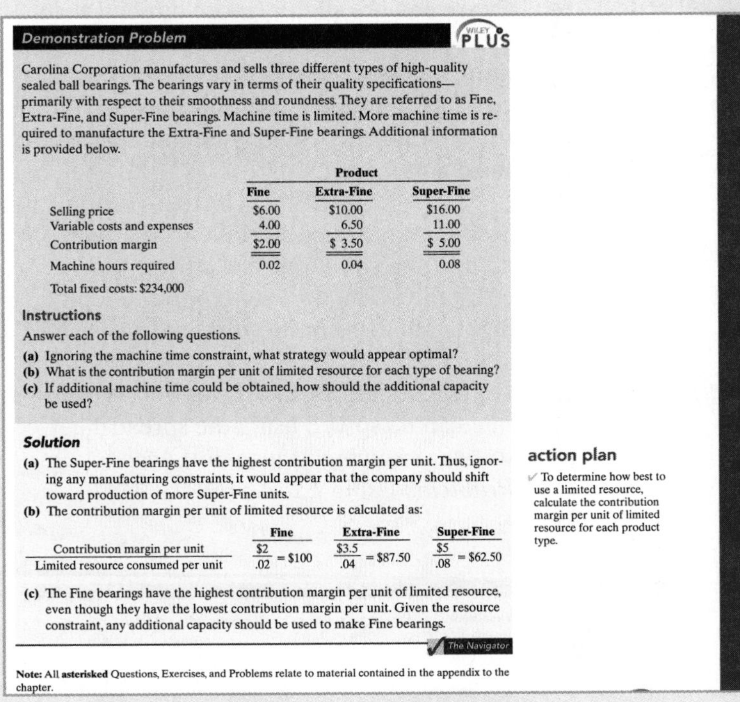

Demonstration Problem

Carolina Corporation manufactures and sells three different types of high-quality sealed ball bearings. The bearings vary in terms of their quality specifications—primarily with respect to their smoothness and roundness. They are referred to as Fine, Extra-Fine, and Super-Fine bearings. Machine time is limited. More machine time is required to manufacture the Extra-Fine and Super-Fine bearings. Additional information is provided below.

	Product		
	Fine	Extra-Fine	Super-Fine
Selling price	$6.00	$10.00	$16.00
Variable costs and expenses	4.00	6.50	11.00
Contribution margin	$2.00	$ 3.50	$ 5.00
Machine hours required	0.02	0.04	0.08

Total fixed costs: $234,000

Instructions

Answer each of the following questions.

(a) Ignoring the machine time constraint, what strategy would appear optimal?

(b) What is the contribution margin per unit of limited resource for each type of bearing?

(c) If additional machine time could be obtained, how should the additional capacity be used?

Solution

(a) The Super-Fine bearings have the highest contribution margin per unit. Thus, ignoring any manufacturing constraints, it would appear that the company should shift toward production of more Super-Fine units.

(b) The contribution margin per unit of limited resource is calculated as:

	Fine	Extra-Fine	Super-Fine
$\frac{\text{Contribution margin per unit}}{\text{Limited resource consumed per unit}}$	$\frac{\$2}{.02} = \$100$	$\frac{\$3.5}{.04} = \$87.50$	$\frac{\$5}{.08} = \$62.50$

(c) The Fine bearings have the highest contribution margin per unit of limited resource, even though they have the lowest contribution margin per unit. Given the resource constraint, any additional capacity should be used to make Fine bearings.

The Navigator

action plan

✓ To determine how best to use a limited resource, calculate the contribution margin per unit of limited resource for each product type.

Note: All **asterisked** Questions, Exercises, and Problems relate to material contained in the appendix to the chapter.

A **Demonstration Problem** is a review of key concepts and a warm-up before you begin homework. These sample problems provide you with an **Action Plan** in the margin that lists the strategies needed to approach and solve the problem.

The **Solution to the Demonstration Problem** demonstrates both the form and content of complete answers.

The ***WileyPLUS* icon** here and throughout the end-of-chapter material identifies resources for further reading, study, and practice that can be accessed via *WileyPLUS*.

Self-Study Questions provide a practice test, keyed to study objectives, with which you can check your knowledge of important chapter topics. *Answers* appear on the last page of the chapter.

SELF-STUDY QUESTIONS

Answers are at the end of the chapter.

(SO 1) 1. Which one of the following is the format of a CVP income statement?

a. Sales − Variable costs = Fixed costs + Net income.

b. Sales − Fixed costs − Variable costs − Operating expenses = Net income.

c. Sales − Cost of goods sold − Operating expenses = Net income.

d. Sales − Variable costs − Fixed costs = Net income.

(SO 1, 2) 2. Croc Catchers calculates its contribution margin to be less than zero. Which statement is true?

a. Its fixed costs are less than the variable cost per unit.

b. Its profits are greater than its total costs.

c. The company should sell more units.

d. Its selling price is less than its variable costs.

3. Which one of the following describes the break-even point? (SO 2)

a. It is the point where total sales equals total variable plus total fixed costs.

b. It is the point where the contribution margin equals zero.

c. It is the point where total variable costs equal total fixed costs.

d. It is the point where total sales equals total fixed costs.

Questions focus your study on understanding concepts and relationships from the chapter. Use them to help prepare for class discussion and tests.

QUESTIONS

1. What steps are frequently involved in management's decision-making process?
2. Your roommate, Mike Myer, contends that accounting contributes to most of the steps in management's decision-making process. Is your roommate correct? Explain.
3. "Incremental analysis involves the accumulation of information concerning a single course of action." Do you agree? Why?
4. Sara Gura asks for your help concerning the relevance of variable and fixed costs in incremental analysis. Help Sara with her problem.
5. What data are relevant in deciding whether to accept an order at a special price?
6. Son Ly Company has an opportunity to buy parts at $7 each that currently cost $10 to make. What manufacturing costs are relevant to this make-or-buy decision?
7. Define the term "opportunity cost." How may this cost be relevant in a make-or-buy decision?
8. What is the decision rule in deciding whether to sell a product or process it further?
9. What are joint products? What accounting issue results from the production process that creates joint products?
10. How are allocated joint costs treated when making a sell-or-process-further decision?
11. Your roommate, Vanessa Hunt, is confused about sunk costs. Explain to your roommate the meaning of sunk costs and their relevance to a decision to retain or replace equipment.
12. Erm Paris Inc. has one product line that is unprofitable. What circumstances may cause overall company net income to be lower if the unprofitable product line is eliminated?

Brief Exercises focus on one study objective at a time. They help build confidence in your basic skills and knowledge.

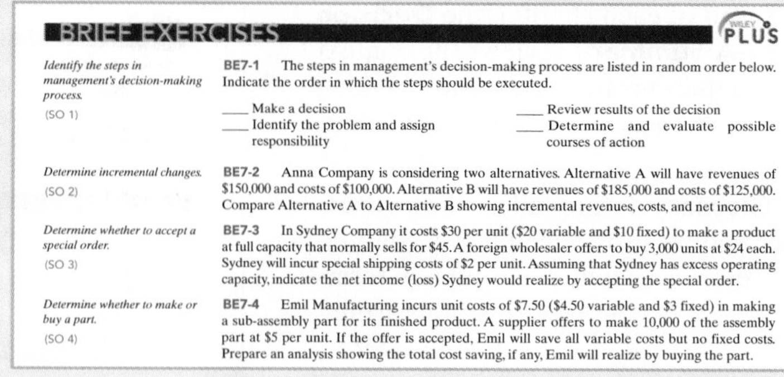

BRIEF EXERCISES

WILEY PLUS

Identify the steps in management's decision-making process. (SO 1)

BE7-1 The steps in management's decision-making process are listed in random order below. Indicate the order in which the steps should be executed.

____ Make a decision
____ Identify the problem and assign responsibility
____ Review results of the decision
____ Determine and evaluate possible courses of action

Determine incremental changes. (SO 2)

BE7-2 Anna Company is considering two alternatives. Alternative A will have revenues of $150,000 and costs of $100,000. Alternative B will have revenues of $185,000 and costs of $125,000. Compare Alternative A to Alternative B showing incremental revenues, costs, and net income.

Determine whether to accept a special order. (SO 3)

BE7-3 In Sydney Company it costs $30 per unit ($20 variable and $10 fixed) to make a product at full capacity that normally sells for $45. A foreign wholesaler offers to buy 3,000 units at $24 each. Sydney will incur special shipping costs of $2 per unit. Assuming that Sydney has excess operating capacity, indicate the net income (loss) Sydney would realize by accepting the special order.

Determine whether to make or buy a part. (SO 4)

BE7-4 Emil Manufacturing incurs unit costs of $7.50 ($4.50 variable and $3 fixed) in making a sub-assembly part for its finished product. A supplier offers to make 10,000 of the assembly part at $5 per unit. If the offer is accepted, Emil will save all variable costs but no fixed costs. Prepare an analysis showing the total cost saving, if any, Emil will realize by buying the part.

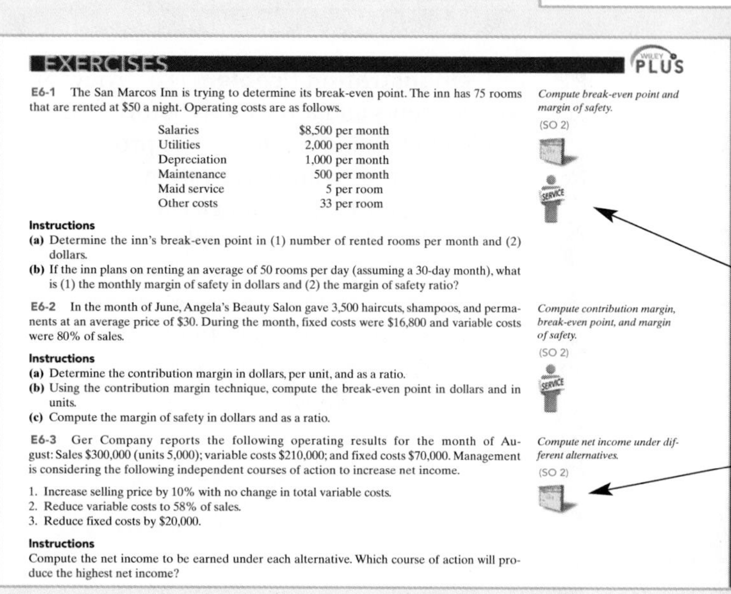

EXERCISES

WILEY PLUS

E6-1 The San Marcos Inn is trying to determine its break-even point. The inn has 75 rooms that are rented at $50 a night. Operating costs are as follows.

Compute break-even point and margin of safety. (SO 2)

Salaries	$8,500 per month
Utilities	2,000 per month
Depreciation	1,000 per month
Maintenance	500 per month
Maid service	5 per room
Other costs	33 per room

Instructions

(a) Determine the inn's break-even point in (1) number of rented rooms per month and (2) dollars.
(b) If the inn plans on renting an average of 50 rooms per day (assuming a 30-day month), what is (1) the monthly margin of safety in dollars and (2) the margin of safety ratio?

E6-2 In the month of June, Angela's Beauty Salon gave 3,500 haircuts, shampoos, and permanents at an average price of $30. During the month, fixed costs were $16,800 and variable costs were 80% of sales.

Compute contribution margin, break-even point, and margin of safety. (SO 2)

Instructions

(a) Determine the contribution margin in dollars, per unit, and as a ratio.
(b) Using the contribution margin technique, compute the break-even point in dollars and in units.
(c) Compute the margin of safety in dollars and as a ratio.

E6-3 Ger Company reports the following operating results for the month of August: Sales $300,000 (units 5,000); variable costs $210,000; and fixed costs $70,000. Management is considering the following independent courses of action to increase net income.

Compute net income under different alternatives. (SO 2)

1. Increase selling price by 10% with no change in total variable costs.
2. Reduce variable costs to 58% of sales.
3. Reduce fixed costs by $20,000.

Instructions

Compute the net income to be earned under each alternative. Which course of action will produce the highest net income?

Exercises are slightly more difficult than Brief Exercises, and may combine two or more study objectives. They help you continue to build confidence in your ability to combine and use the material learned in the chapter.

Some Exercises and Problems focus on accounting situations faced by service companies. The **service-company icon** highlights these homework materials.

An icon identifies **Exercises** and **Problems** that can be solved using the spreadsheet software *Solving Managerial Accounting Problems Using Excel.*

A set of **B Exercises**, closely related to the Exercises in the book, appears at the book's *Companion Website*, for additional practice.

Each **Problem** helps you pull together and apply several concepts from the chapter.

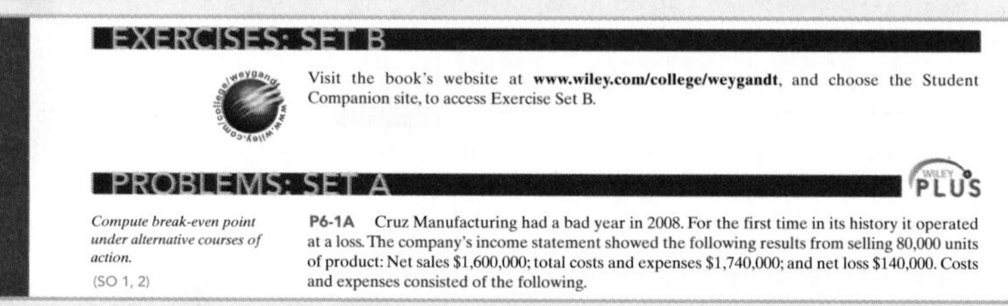

EXERCISES: SET B

Visit the book's website at **www.wiley.com/college/weygandt**, and choose the Student Companion site, to access Exercise Set B.

PROBLEMS: SET A

WILEY PLUS

Compute break-even point under alternative courses of action. (SO 1, 2)

P6-1A Cruz Manufacturing had a bad year in 2008. For the first time in its history it operated at a loss. The company's income statement showed the following results from selling 80,000 units of product: Net sales $1,600,000; total costs and expenses $1,740,000; and net loss $140,000. Costs and expenses consisted of the following.

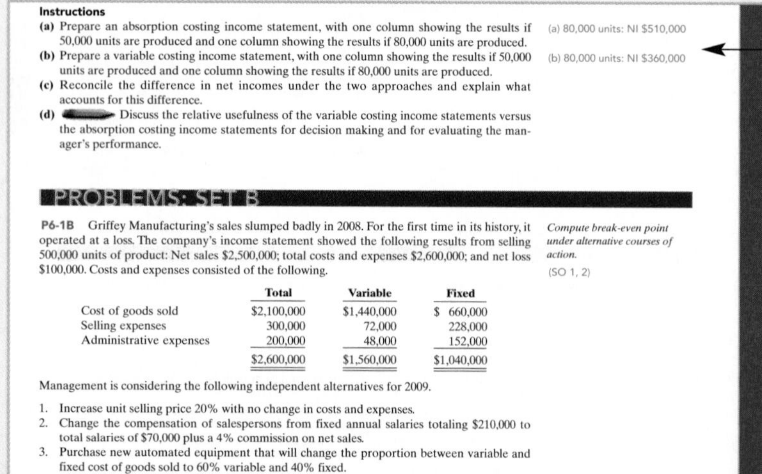

Instructions

(a) Prepare an absorption costing income statement, with one column showing the results if 50,000 units are produced and one column showing the results if 80,000 units are produced.
(b) Prepare a variable costing income statement, with one column showing the results if 50,000 units are produced and one column showing the results if 80,000 units are produced.
(c) Reconcile the difference in net incomes under the two approaches and explain what accounts for this difference.
(d) Discuss the relative usefulness of the variable costing income statements versus the absorption costing income statements for decision making and for evaluating the manager's performance.

(a) 80,000 units: NI $510,000

(b) 80,000 units: NI $360,000

PROBLEMS: SET B

P6-1B Griffey Manufacturing's sales slumped badly in 2008. For the first time in its history, it operated at a loss. The company's income statement showed the following results from selling 500,000 units of product: Net sales $2,500,000; total costs and expenses $2,600,000; and net loss $100,000. Costs and expenses consisted of the following.

Compute break-even point under alternative courses of action. (SO 1, 2)

	Total	Variable	Fixed
Cost of goods sold	$2,100,000	$1,440,000	$ 660,000
Selling expenses	300,000	72,000	228,000
Administrative expenses	200,000	48,000	152,000
	$2,600,000	$1,560,000	$1,040,000

Management is considering the following independent alternatives for 2009.

1. Increase unit selling price 20% with no change in costs and expenses.
2. Change the compensation of salespersons from fixed annual salaries totaling $210,000 to total salaries of $70,000 plus a 4% commission on net sales.
3. Purchase new automated equipment that will change the proportion between variable and fixed cost of goods sold to 60% variable and 40% fixed.

Instructions

(a) Compute the break-even point in dollars for 2008.
(b) Compute the break-even point in dollars under each of the alternative courses of action. (Round to the nearest dollar.) Which course of action do you recommend?

(b) (1) $2,166,667

Check figures in the margin provide key numbers to let you know you're on the right track as you work the problems.

In the book, two similar sets of **Problems—A and B**—are keyed to the same study objectives.

An additional set of **C Problems** appears at the book's companion website.

The **Waterways Continuing Problem** uses the business activities of a fictional company called Waterways Corporation. Its purpose is to apply the chapter topic to a realistic entrepreneurial situation.

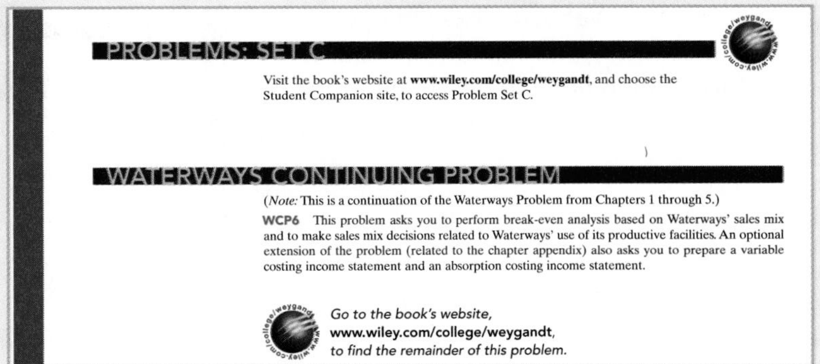

PROBLEMS: SET C

Visit the book's website at **www.wiley.com/college/weygandt**, and choose the Student Companion site, to access Problem Set C.

WATERWAYS CONTINUING PROBLEM

(*Note:* This is a continuation of the Waterways Problem from Chapters 1 through 5.)

WCP6 This problem asks you to perform break-even analysis based on Waterways' sales mix and to make sales mix decisions related to Waterways' use of its productive facilities. An optional extension of the problem (related to the chapter appendix) also asks you to prepare a variable costing income statement and an absorption costing income statement.

Go to the book's website,
www.wiley.com/college/weygandt,
to find the remainder of this problem.

The **Broadening Your Perspective** section helps you pull together concepts from the chapter and apply them to real-world business situations.

Decision Making Across the Organization helps you build decision-making skills by analyzing accounting information in a less structured situation. These cases require teams of students to evaluate a manager's decision or lead to a decision among alternative courses of action.

Managerial Analysis assignments build analytical and decision-making skills in situations encountered by managers. They also will require you to apply and practice business communication skills.

Broadening Your Perspective 281

BROADENING YOUR PERSPECTIVE

DECISION MAKING ACROSS THE ORGANIZATION

BYP6-1 ComfortCraft manufactures swivel seats for customized vans. It currently manufactures 10,000 seats per year, which it sells for $480 per seat. It incurs variable costs of $180 per seat and fixed costs of $2,200,000. It is considering automating the upholstery process, which is now largely manual. It estimates that if it does so, its fixed costs will be $3,200,000, and its variable costs will decline to $80 per seat.

Instructions

With the class divided into groups, answer the following questions.

(a) Prepare a CVP income statement based on current activity.
(b) Compute contribution margin ratio, break-even point in dollars, margin of safety ratio, and degree of operating leverage based on current activity.
(c) Prepare a CVP income statement assuming that the company invests in the automated upholstery system.
(d) Compute contribution margin ratio, break-even point in dollars, margin of safety ratio, and degree of operating leverage assuming the new upholstery system is implemented.
(e) Discuss the implications of adopting the new system.

MANAGERIAL ANALYSIS

BYP6-2 For nearly 20 years Custom Coatings has provided painting and galvanizing services for manufacturers in its region. Manufacturers of various metal products have relied on the quality and quick turnaround time provided by Custom Coatings and its 20 skilled employees. During the last year, as a result of a sharp upturn in the economy, the company's sales have increased by 30% relative to the previous year. The company has not been able to increase its capacity fast enough, so Custom Coatings has had to turn work away because it cannot keep up with customer requests.

Top management is considering the purchase of a sophisticated robotic painting booth. The booth would represent a considerable move in the direction of automation versus manual labor. If Custom Coatings purchases the booth, it would most likely lay off 15 its skilled painters. To analyze the decision, the company compiled production information from the most recent year and then prepared a parallel compilation assuming that the company would purchase the new equipment and lay off the workers. Those data are shown below. As you can see, the company projects that during the last year it would have been far more profitable if it had used the automated approach.

	Current Approach	Automated Approach
Sales	$2,000,000	$2,000,000
Variable costs	1,200,000	400,000
Contribution margin	800,000	1,600,000
Fixed costs	200,000	600,000
Net income	$ 600,000	$1,000,000

Instructions

(a) Compute and interpret the contribution margin ratio under each approach.
(b) Compute the break-even point in sales dollars under each approach. Discuss the implications of your findings.
(c) Using the current level of sales, compute the margin of safety ratio under each approach and interpret your findings.
(d) Determine the degree of operating leverage for each approach at current sales levels. How much would the company's net income decline under each approach with a 10% decline in sales?
(e) At what level of sales would the company's net income be the same under either approach?
(f) Discuss the issues that the company must consider in making this decision.

Real-World Focus problems ask you to apply techniques and concepts presented in the chapter to specific situations faced by actual companies. These problems often have a global focus.

REAL-WORLD FOCUS

BYP6-3 In its 2003 annual report the Del Monte Foods Company reported three separate operating segments: consumer products (which includes a variety of canned foods including tuna, fruit, and vegetables); pet products (which includes pet food and snacks and veterinary products); and soup and infant-feeding products (which includes soup, broth, and infant feeding and pureed products).

In its annual report Del Monte uses absorption costing. As a result, information regarding the relative composition of its fixed and variable costs is not available. We have assumed that $860.3 million of its total operating expenses of $1,920.3 million are fixed and have allocated the remaining variable costs across the three divisions. Sales data, along with assumed expense data, are provided below.

Exploring the Web exercises guide you to websites where you can find and analyze information related to the chapter topic.

EXPLORING THE WEB

BYP6-4 The external financial statements published by publicly traded companies are based on absorption cost accounting. As a consequence, it is very difficult to gain an understanding of the relative composition of the companies' fixed and variable costs. It is possible, however, to learn about a company's sales mix and the relative profitability of its various divisions. This exercise looks at the financial statements of FedEx Corporation.

Address: www.fedex.com/us/investorrelations, or go to **www.wiley.com/college/weygandt**

Steps
1. Go to the site above.
2. Under "Financial Information," choose "Annual Reports."
3. Choose "2006 Annual Report."

Instructions
(a) Read page 38 of the report under the heading "Description of Business." What are the three primary product lines of the company? What does the company identify as the key factors af-

COMMUNICATION ACTIVITY

BYP6-5 Westfield Corporation makes two different boat anchors—a traditional fishing anchor and a high-end yacht anchor—using the same production machinery. The contribution margin of the yacht anchor is three times as high as that of the other product. The company is currently operating at full capacity and has been doing so for nearly two years. Ralph Sampson, the company's CEO, want to cut back on production of the fishing anchor so that the company can make more yacht anchors. He says that this is a "no-brainer" because the contribution margin of the yacht anchor is so much higher.

Communication Activities help you build business communication skills by asking you to engage in real-world business situations using writing, speaking, or presentation skills.

ETHICS CASE

***BYP6-6** Scott Bestor was hired during January 2008 to manage the home products division of Advanced Techno. As part of his employment contract, he was told that he would get $5,000 of additional bonus for every 1% increase that the division's profits exceeded those of the previous year.

Soon after coming on board, Scott met with his plant managers and explained that he wanted the plants to be run at full capacity. Previously the plant had employed just-in-time inventory practices and had consequently produced units only as they were needed. Scott stated that under previous management the company had missed out on too many sales opportunities because it didn't have enough inventory on hand. Because previous management had employed just-in-time inventory practices, when Scott came on board there was virtually no beginning inventory. The selling price and variable cost per unit remained the same from 2007 to 2008. Additional information is provided below.

Ethics Cases ask you to reflect on typical ethical dilemmas analyze the stakeholders and the issues involved, and decide on an appropriate course of action.

The **"All About You" Activity** offers another opportunity to explore the All About You topic in a homework assignment.

"ALL ABOUT YOU" ACTIVITY

BYP8-7 In the "All About You" feature in this chapter, you learned that pricing is a difficult and complex task both from the seller's and the consumer's sides. One issue that you will face is making sure that you receive a fair price for the goods that you are interested in buying. In some cases, price is not necessarily the deciding factor. Your wealth level, the quality of the product, the convenience of the product, the warranty, and the reputation of the manufacturer all may play an important role in your decision. As a result, it often is important to do solid research before you make your decision. Fortunately there are now a number of services that provide comparisons on price and quality for many products.

Instructions
Suppose you are interested in golf and want to buy a new driver and three dozen golf balls. (Hopefully that number of golf balls will last the season.) Go to *www.golfdigest.com/hotlist/* and see whether you can find any information that will help you make a decision on the driver and golf balls you might purchase.

Answers to Insight and Accounting Across the Organization questions offer guideline answers for questions in the boxed-real-world examples.

Answers to Business Insight and Accounting Across the Organization Questions

What's the Price on the Internet? p. 325
Q: How does the Internet affect product prices?
A: *The Internet can result in lower product prices because it is easier for customers to compare prices across different retailers. However, the Internet also makes it possible for companies to*

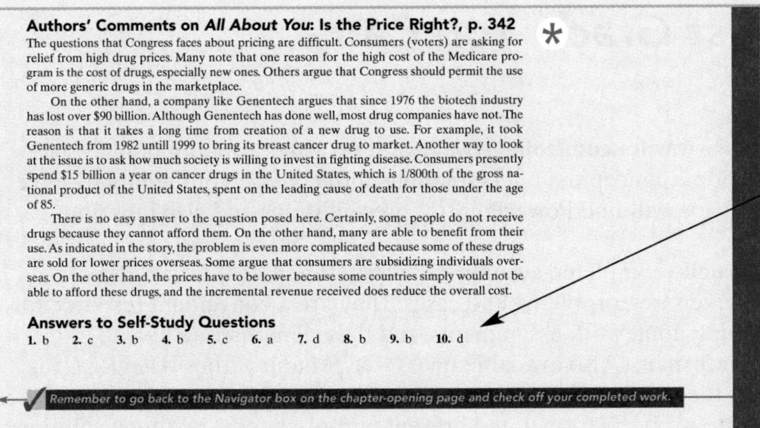

Authors' Comments on *All About You*: Is the Price Right?, p. 342

The questions that Congress faces about pricing are difficult. Consumers (voters) are asking for relief from high drug prices. Many note that one reason for the high cost of the Medicare program is the cost of drugs, especially new ones. Others argue that Congress should permit the use of more generic drugs in the marketplace.

On the other hand, a company like Genentech argues that since 1976 the biotech industry has lost over $90 billion. Although Genentech has done well, most drug companies have not. The reason is that it takes a long time from creation of a new drug to use. For example, it took Genentech from 1982 untill 1999 to bring its breast cancer drug to market. Another way to look at the issue is to ask how much society is willing to invest in fighting disease. Consumers presently spend $15 billion a year on cancer drugs in the United States, which is 1/800th of the gross national product of the United States, spent on the leading cause of death for those under the age of 85.

There is no easy answer to the question posed here. Certainly, some people do not receive drugs because they cannot afford them. On the other hand, many are able to benefit from their use. As indicated in the story, the problem is even more complicated because some of these drugs are sold for lower prices overseas. Some argue that consumers are subsidizing individuals overseas. On the other hand, the prices have to be lower because some countries simply would not be able to afford these drugs, and the incremental revenue received does reduce the overall cost.

Answers to Self-Study Questions

1. b 2. c 3. b 4. b 5. c 6. a 7. d 8. b 9. b 10. d

✓ Remember to go back to the Navigator box on the chapter-opening page and check off your completed work.

Authors' Comments on All About You provide the author's opinions and further discussion about financial literacy topic in the chapter.

Answers to Self-Study Questions provide feedback on your understanding of the chapter's basic concepts.

After you complete your homework assignments, it's a good idea to go back to **The Navigator** checklist at the start of the chapter to see if you have used all the chapter's study aids.

Case 1

Greetings Inc.: Job Order Costing

Developed by Thomas L. Zeller, Loyola University Chicago, and Paul D. Kimmel, University of Wisconsin–Milwaukee

The Business Situation

Greetings Inc. has operated for many years as a nationally recognized retailer of greeting cards and small gift items. It has 1,500 stores throughout the United States located in high-traffic malls.

As the stock price of many other companies soared, Greetings' stock price remained flat. As a result of a heated 2007 shareholders' meeting, the president of Greetings, Robert Burns, came under pressure from shareholders to grow Greetings' stock value. As a consequence of this pressure, in 2008 Mr. Burns called for a formal analysis of the company's options with regard to business opportunities.

Location was the first issue considered in the analysis. Greetings stores are located in high-traffic malls where rental costs are high. The additional rental cost was justified, however, by the revenue that resulted from these highly visible locations. In recent years, though, the intense competition from other stores in the mall selling similar merchandise has become a disadvantage of the mall locations.

Mr. Burns felt that to increase revenue in the mall locations, Greetings would need to attract new customers and sell more goods to repeat customers. In order to do this, the company would need to add a new product line. However, to keep costs down, the product line should be one that would not require much additional store space. In order to improve earnings, rather than just increase revenues, Greetings would have to carefully manage the costs of this new product line.

After careful consideration of many possible products, the company's management found a product that seemed to be a very good strategic fit for its existing products: high-quality unframed and framed prints. The critical element of this plan was that customers would pick out prints by viewing them on wide-screen computer monitors in each store. Orders would be processed and shipped from a central location. Thus, store size would not have to increase at all. To offer these products, Greetings established a new e-business unit called Wall Décor. Wall Décor is a "profit center"; that is, the manager of the new business unit is responsible for decisions affecting both revenues and costs.

Wall Décor was designed to distribute unframed and framed print items to each Greetings store on a just-in-time (JIT) basis. The system works as follows: The Wall Décor website allows customers to choose from several hundred prints. The print can be purchased in various forms: unframed, framed with a metal frame and no matting, or framed with a wood frame and matting. When a customer purchases an

Cases for Management Decision Making, provided at the end of the text, ask you to use the decision tools presented in the chapters in realistic business situations. Your instructor can assign cases as a comprehensive capstone activity at the end of the course or as a recurring activity during the course.

Sweats Galore

Developed by Jessica Johnson Frazier, Eastern Kentucky University, and Patricia H. Mounce, Mississippi College

The Business Situation

After graduating with a degree in business from Eastern University in Campus Town, USA, Michael Woods realized that he wanted to remain in Campus Town. After a number of unsuccessful attempts at getting a job in his discipline, Michael decided to go into business for himself. In thinking about his business venture, Michael determined that he had four criteria for the new business:

1. He wanted to do something that he would enjoy.
2. He wanted a business that would give back to the community.
3. He wanted a business that would grow and be more successful every year.
4. Realizing that he was going to have to work very hard, Michael wanted a business that would generate a minimum net income of $25,000 annually.

While reflecting on the criteria he had outlined, Michael, who had been president of his fraternity and served as an officer in several other student organizations, realized that there was no place in Campus Town to have custom sweatshirts made using a silk-screen process. When student organizations wanted sweatshirts to give to their members or to market on campus, the officers had to make a trip to a city 100 miles away to visit "Shirts and More."

Michael had worked as a part-time employee at Shirts and More while he was in high school and had envisioned owning such a shop. He realized that a sweatshirt shop in Campus Town had the potential to meet all four of his criteria. Michael set up an appointment with Jayne Stoll, the owner of Shirts and More, to obtain information useful in getting his shop started. Because Jayne liked Michael and was intrigued by his entrepreneurial spirit, she answered many of Michael's questions.

In addition, Jayne provided information concerning the type of equipment Michael would need for his business and its average useful life. Jayne knows a competitor who is retiring and would like to sell his equipment. Michael can purchase the equipment at the beginning of 2008, and the owner is willing to give him terms of 50% due upon purchase and 50% due the quarter following the purchase. Michael decided to purchase the following equipment as of January 1, 2008.

SPECIAL STUDENT SUPPLEMENTS

That Help You Get the Best Grade You Can

The Managerial Accounting Website

The book's website at **www.wiley.com/college/weygandt** provides a wealth of materials that will help you develop a conceptual understanding and increase your ability to solve problems. For example, you will find PowerPoint™ presentations and web quizzing.

Working Papers

Working papers are partially completed accounting forms (templates) for all end-of-chapter brief exercises, exercises, problems, and cases. They are a convenient resource for organizing and completing homework assignments, and they demonstrate how to correctly set up solution formats. Also available on CD-ROM and within *WileyPLUS* is an electronic version of the print working papers, which are Excel-formatted templates that will help you learn to properly format and present end-of-chapter textbook solutions.

Study Guide

The Study Guide is a comprehensive review of accounting. It guides you through chapter content, tied to study objectives. Each chapter of the Study Guide includes a chapter review (20 to 30 key points); a demonstration problem; and for extra practice, true/false, multiple-choice, and matching questions, and additional exercises, with solutions. The Study Guide is an excellent tool for use on a regular basis during the course and also when preparing for exams.

Problem-Solving Survival Guide

This tutorial is designed to improve your success rates in solving homework assignments and exam questions. Each chapter includes an overview of key topics; a purpose statement and link to study objectives for each homework assignment; numerous review tips to alert you to common pitfalls and misconceptions; and reminders to concepts and principles. Multiple-choice exercises and cases similar to common homework assignments or exam questions enhance your problem-solving proficiency. Solutions not only explain answers but also discuss an approach to similar types of accounting problems.

Solving Managerial Accounting Problems Using Excel

A manual guides you step-by-step from an introduction to computers and Excel, to completion of preprogrammed spreadsheets, to design of your own spreadsheets. Accompanying spreadsheet templates allow you to complete selected end-of-chapter exercises and problems, identified by the icon shown here.

For more information on any of these student supplements, check with your professor or bookstore, or go to the book's Student Companion site at **www.wiley.com/college/weygandt**.

HOW DO I LEARN BEST?

This questionnaire aims to find out something about your preferences for the way you work with information. You will have a preferred learning style, and one part of that learning style is your preference for the intake and output of ideas and information.

Choose the answer which best explains your preference. You can select more than one response if a single answer does not match your perception. Leave blank any question that does not apply.

1. You are about to give directions to a person who is standing with you. She is staying in a hotel in town and wants to visit your house later. She has a rental car. You would:
- **a.** draw or provide a map on paper.
- **b.** tell her the directions.
- **c.** write down the directions (without a map).
- **d.** pick her up from the hotel in a car.

2. You are not sure whether a word should be spelled "dependent" or "dependant." You would:
- **c.** look it up in the dictionary.
- **a.** see the word in your mind and choose by the way it looks
- **b.** sound it out in your mind.
- **d.** write both versions down on paper and choose one.

3. You have just received a copy of your itinerary for a world trip. This is of interest to some friends. You would:
- **b.** phone, text, or email them and tell them about it.
- **c.** send them a copy of the printed itinerary.
- **a.** show them on a map of the world.
- **d.** describe what you plan to do at each place on the itinerary.

4. You are going to cook something as a special treat for your family. You would:
- **d.** cook something familiar without the need for instructions.
- **a.** thumb through the cookbook looking for ideas from the pictures.
- **c.** refer to a specific cookbook where there is a good recipe.

5. A group of tourists has been assigned to you to find out about wildlife reserves or parks. You would:
- **d.** drive them to a wildlife reserve or park.
- **a.** show them slides and photographs.
- **c.** give them pamphlets or a book on wildlife reserves or parks.
- **b.** give them a talk on wildlife reserves or parks.

6. You are about to purchase a new CD player. Other than price, what would most influence your decision?
- **b.** The salesperson telling you what you want to know.
- **c.** Reading the details about it.
- **d.** Playing with the controls and listening to it.
- **a.** It looks really smart and fashionable.

7. Recall a time in your life when you learned how to do something like playing a new board game. Try to avoid choosing a very physical skill, e.g. riding a bike. You learned best by:
- **a.** visual clues–pictures, diagrams and charts.
- **c.** written instructions.
- **b.** listening to somebody explaining it.
- **d.** doing it or trying it.

8. You have a knee problem. You would prefer that the doctor:
- **b.** told you what was wrong.
- **a.** showed you a diagram of what was wrong.
- **d.** used a model of a knee to show you what was wrong.

9. You are about to learn to use a new program on a computer. You would:
- **d.** sit down at the keyboard and experiment with the program.
- **c.** read the manual that came with the program.
- **b.** telephone or text a friend and ask questions about the program.

10. You are staying in a hotel and have a rental car. You would like to visit friends whose address/location you do not know. You would like them to:
- **a.** draw you a map on paper or provide a map from the Internet.
- **b.** tell you the directions.
- **c.** write down the directions (without a map).
- **d.** pick you up from the hotel in a car.

11. Apart from the price, what would most influence your decision to buy a particular textbook?
- **d.** You have used a copy before.
- **b.** A friend talking about it.
- **c.** Quickly reading parts of it.
- **a.** The way it looks is appealing.

12. A new movie has arrived in town. What would most influence your decision to go (or not go)?
- **b.** You heard a review about it on the radio.
- **c.** You read a review about it.
- **a.** You saw a preview of it.

13. You prefer a teacher who likes to use:
- **c.** a textbook, handouts, and reading.
- **a.** flow diagrams, charts, and graphs.
- **d.** field trips, models, laboratories, and practical sessions.
- **b.** class or email discussion, online chat groups, and guest speakers.

	a.	**b.**	**c.**	**d.**
Count your choices:	❑	❑	❑	❑
	V	**A**	**R**	**K**

Now match the letter or letters you have recorded most to the same letter or letters in the Learning Styles Chart. You may have more than one learning style preference—many people do. Next to each letter in the chart are suggestions that will refer you to different learning aids throughout this text.

LEARNING STYLES CHART

	Intake: To take in the information	To make a study package
Visual **V**	• Pay close attention to charts, drawings, and handouts your instructors use. • Underline. • Use different colors. • Use symbols, flow charts, graphs, different arrangements on the page, white spaces.	Convert your lecture notes into "page pictures." To do this: • Use the "Intake" strategies. • Reconstruct images in different ways. • Redraw pages from memory. • Replace words with symbols and initials. • Look at your pages.
Aural 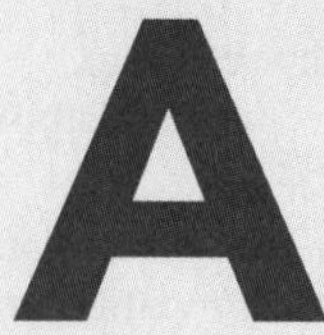	• Attend lectures and tutorials. • Discuss topics with students and instructors. • Explain new ideas to other people. • Use a tape recorder. • Leave spaces in your lecture notes for later recall. • Describe overheads, pictures, and visuals to somebody who was not in class.	You may take poor notes because you prefer to listen. Therefore: • Expand your notes by talking with others and with information from your textbook. • Tape-record summarized notes and listen. • Read summarized notes out loud. • Explain your notes to another "aural" person.
Reading/ Writing 	• Use lists and headings. • Use dictionaries, glossaries, and definitions. • Read handouts, textbooks, and supplementary library readings. • Use lecture notes.	• Write out words again and again. • Reread notes silently. • Rewrite ideas and principles into other words. • Turn charts, diagrams, and other illustrations into statements.
Kinesthetic 	• Use all your senses. • Go to labs, take field trips. • Listen to real-life examples. • Pay attention to applications. • Use hands-on approaches. • Use trial-and-error methods.	You may take poor notes because topics do not seem concrete or relevant. Therefore: • Put examples in your summaries. • Use case studies and applications to help with principles and abstract concepts. • Talk about your notes with another "kinesthetic" person. • Use pictures and photographs that illustrate an idea.

Source: Adapted from VARK pack. © Copyright 2001–2006 Neil D. Fleming. This material may be used for faculty or student development if attribution is given. It may not be published in either paper or electronic form without consent of the authors. There is a VARK website at **www.vark-learn.com.**

Text features that may help you the most	Output: To do well on exams	
The Navigator/Feature Story/Preview Infographics/Illustrations Highlighted words Decision Toolkits Graph in *All About You* Demonstration Problem/Action Plan Questions/Exercises/Problems Real-World Focus Exploring the Web	• Recall your "page pictures." • Draw diagrams where appropriate. • Practice turning your visuals back into words.	***Visual*** **V**
Preview Insight Boxes Review It/Do It/Action Plan "What Do You Think?" in *All About You* Summary of Study Objectives Glossary Demonstration Problem/Action Plan Self-Study Questions Questions/Exercises/Problems Managerial Analysis Exploring the Web Decision Making Across the Organization Communication Activity Ethics Case	• Talk with the instructor. • Spend time in quiet places recalling the ideas. • Practice writing answers to old exam questions. • Say your answers out loud.	***Aural*** 
The Navigator/Feature Story/Study Objectives/Preview Review It/Do It/Action Plan Summary of Study Objectives Glossary/Self-Study Questions Questions/Exercises/Problems Writing Problems Managerial Analysis Real-World Focus *"All About You"* Activity Exploring the Web Decision Making Across the Organization Communication Activity	• Write exam answers. • Practice with multiple-choice questions. • Write paragraphs, beginnings and endings. • Write your lists in outline form. • Arrange your words into hierarchies and points.	***Reading/ Writing*** **R**
The Navigator/Feature Story/Preview Infographics/Illustrations Review It/Do It/Action Plan Summary of Study Objectives Demonstration Problem/Action Plan Self-Study Questions Questions/Exercises/Problems Exploring the Web Decision Making Across the Organization Communication Activity *"All About You"* Activity	• Write practice answers. • Role-play the exam situation.	***Kinesthetic*** **K**

For all learning styles: Be sure to use the book's website to enhance your understanding of the concepts and procedures of the text.

BRIEF CONTENTS

COST CONCEPTS FOR DECISION MAKERS

DECISION-MAKING CONCEPTS

PLANNING AND CONTROL CONCEPTS

PERFORMANCE EVALUATION CONCEPTS

APPENDICES

CONTENTS

PHOTO CREDITS

Chapter 1 Page 3: Justin Sullivan/Getty Images, Inc. Page 6: Peter Kramer/Getty Images, Inc. Page 11: iStockphoto. Page 21: Octavio Campos/iStockphoto.

Chapter 2 Page 53: PhotoDisc, Inc./Getty Images. Page 56: iStockphoto. Page 67: Photodisc/Getty Images, Inc. Page 71: Marcin Balcerzak/iStockphoto.

Chapter 3 Page 95: Lon C. Diehl/PhotoEdit. Page 100: iStockphoto. Page 104: Yoshikazu Tsuno/Getty Images, Inc. Page 111: PhotoDisc, Inc./Getty Images.

Chapter 4 Page 147: iStockphoto. Page 155: Paul Chesley/Stone/Getty Images. Page 161: Jason Lugo/iStockphoto. Page 158: PhotoDisc.

Chapter 5 Page 197: Tad Denson/iStockphoto. Page 200: Kirill Zdorov/iStockphoto. Page 210: Digital Vision/Getty Images. Page 214: Yael/Retna.

Chapter 6 Page 235: Charles O Rear/Corbis Images. Page 240: Ingvald Kaldhussaeter/iStockphoto. Page 244: PhotoDisc, Inc. Page 247: iStockphoto. Page 250: Digital Vision.

Chapter 7 Page 287: Dragan Trifunovic/iStockphoto. Page 298: Max Blain/iStockphoto. Page 300: Mitch Kezar/Stone/Getty Images.

Chapter 8 Page 323: Photodisc/Getty Images, Inc. Page 325: Dan Brandenburg/iStockphoto. Page 326: Paul Hart/iStockphoto. Page 330: Oleg Prikhodko/iStockphoto. Page 341: ©2000 Artville, Inc.

Chapter 9 Page 371: ©2000 Artville, Inc. Page 374: Dar Yang Yan/iStockphoto. Page 376: Onur Dongel/iStockphoto. Page 386: Popperfoto/Alamy Images.

Chapter 10 Page 415: ©EyeWire. Page 425: Derek Dammann/iStockphoto. Page 428: Digital Vision/Getty Images, Inc. Page 438: Sandy Jones/iStockphoto. Page 469: Dick Luria/Taxi/Getty Images.

Chapter 11 Page 472: Wally McNamee/Corbis Images. Page 475: Hywit Dimyadi/iStockphoto. Page 487: PhotoDisc, Inc./Getty Images.

Chapter 12 Page 519: Thomas Perkins/iStockphoto. Page 521: iStockphoto. Page 531: Christopher O Driscoll/iStockphoto. Page 534: Rebecca Ellis/iStockphoto. Page 535: Johanna Goodyear/iStockphoto.

Chapter 13 Page 557: ny1/NewsCom. Page 561: Lisa Gee and Elle Wagner/John Wiley & Sons. Page 564: Corbis Digital Stock. Page 575: PhotoDisc, Inc./Getty Images.

Chapter 14 Page 619: Jeremy Edwards/iStockphoto. Page 622: Don Wilkie/iStockphoto. Page 622: Don Wilkie/iStockphoto. Page 630: Nora Good/Masterfile. Page 638: Royalty-Free/Corbis Images. Page 643: Martina Misar/iStockphoto. Page 648: iStockphoto. Page 648: iStockphoto.

all about YOU quick guide

The new ***All About You*** features promote financial literacy. They are intended to get students thinking and talking about how accounting impacts their personal lives. Students are more likely to understand the accounting concept being made within the textbook when accounting material is linked to a familiar topic. Each *All About You* box, one in each chapter, presents a high-interest issue related to the chapter topic, offers facts about it, poses a situation for students to think about, and offers brief opposing answers as a starting place for further discussion. As a feedback mechanism, the authors' comments and opinions about the situation appear at the end of the chapter.

An ***"All About You" Activity,*** located in the *Broadening Your Perspective* section near the end of the assignment material, offers further opportunity to explore aspects of the topic in a homework assignment.

CHAPTER 1 Managerial Accounting
Outsourcing and Jobs (p. 23)
Discusses trends in outsourcing. Presents facts about outsourcing by U.S. companies and top foreign employers in the U.S. Asks students to assess the outsourcing tax-prep services overseas. *AAY Activity* has students identify personal situations to which managerial accounting techniques apply.

CHAPTER 2 Job Order Costing
Minding Your Own Business (p. 72)
Focuses on how small business owners calculate product costs. Presents facts about sole proprietorships and franchises. Poses a start-up business idea and asks students to evaluate the cost of labor input. *AAY Activity* sends students to SBA website to take quiz on readiness to start a small business.

CHAPTER 3 Process Costing
Wal-Mart Is on the Phone (p. 112)
Describes cost accounting for a small company with a possible Wal-Mart deal. Presents facts about Wal-Mart's desirability as an outlet and potential risks for its suppliers. Ask students to evaluate whether a small company should accept a distribution offer. *AAY Activity* asks students to identify activities and cost drivers in a service company.

CHAPTER 4 Activity-Based Costing
Where Does the Time Go? (p. 167)
Uses the concepts of ABC to identify value-added and non-value-added activities in one's own life. Presents facts about time-wasting activities on the job and at school. Asks students to consider application of time-management techniques in order to minimize non-value-added activities. *AAY Activity* asks students to identify cost drivers in a local hospital.

CHAPTER 5 Cost-Volume-Profit
A Hybrid Dilemma (p. 215)
Explores the cost tradeoffs of hybrid vehicles. Presents facts about sales, costs, and fuel efficiency of hybrid vehicles. Asks students to evaluate the pros and cons of buying a hybrid vehicle. *AAY Activity* asks students to do a break-even analysis on the decision to buy a hybrid car.

CHAPTER 6 Cost-Volume-Profit Analysis: Additional Issues
Big Decisions for Your Energy Future (p. 251)
Evaluates alternative electrical-plant energy sources. Presents facts about energy sources and their use. Asks students to consider whether environmental costs should be included in decision making for capital asset purchases. *AAY Activity* asks students to apply break-even analysis techniques to the decision whether to open a fitness center.

CHAPTER 7 Incremental Analysis
What Is a Degree Worth? (p. 301)
Explores the decision to stay in college as an example of incremental analysis. Presents facts about cost of college, and benefits of college education. Asks students to consider the value of a college education. *AAY Activity* applies incremental analysis to the problem of chronic homelessness.

CHAPTER 8 Pricing
Is the Price Right? (p. 342)
Considers additional aspects of pricing for products and services. Presents facts about the pricing of fair-traded products at a grocery store. Asks students to consider fairness issues relating to pricing of pharmaceuticals. *AAY Activity* asks students to explore some online services that compare product prices and quality.

CHAPTER 9 Budgetary Planning
Avoiding Personal Financial Disaster (p. 392)
Explores personal budgets for college students. Presents facts about the average family budget. Asks students to look at a budgeting calculator and consider whether student loans should be considered a source of income. *AAY Activity* has students compute and analyze a personal budget, using assumed data.

CHAPTER 10 Budgetary Control and Responsibility Accounting
Budgeting for Housing Costs (p. 440)
Applies performance evaluation to personal budgeting, via control of routine expenses, especially housing costs. Presents facts about expenses for childrearing, medical, and housing costs. Asks students to consider the pros and cons of buying a house immediately out of college. *AAY Activity* explores the strategy of "envelope budgeting."

CHAPTER 11 Standard Costs and Balanced Scorecard
Balancing Costs and Quality in Health Care (p. 488)
Applies the concept of standard costs to balancing cost and quality in health care. Presents facts about medical costs and incentives for physicians to reduce costs and maintain quality care. Asks students to consider whether doctors should have to meet standard-cost targets. *AAY Activity* addresses the idea of imposing standards by way of standardized tests to measure college students' learning.

CHAPTER 12 Planning for Capital Investments

The Risks of Adjustable Rates (p. 539)

Describes benefits and drawbacks of adjustable-rate mortgages (ARMs). Presents facts about use of ARMs and fixed-rate mortgages. Asks students to evaluate a home-buying scenario and whether to use adjustable-rate financing. AAY Activity has students research articles about early-warning signs of personal debt troubles.

CHAPTER 13 Statement of Cash Flows

Where Does the Money Go? (p. 577)

Discusses the need to know how one spends one's cash. Presents facts about college students' spending patterns. Asks students to analyze a personal cash flow statement and decide whether, and where, cuts should be made. *AAY Activity* has students read an article at The Motley Fool website and discuss how much money to set aside for short-term needs.

CHAPTER 14 Financial Statement Analysis

Should I Play the Market Yet? (p. 656)

Discusses when to begin investing in the stock market. Presents facts about stock ownership in the U.S. Asks students to decide whether a young working person should invest in her employer's stock. *AAY Activity* asks students to complete a questionnaire about appropriate types of mutual fund.

Chapter 1

Managerial Accounting

STUDY OBJECTIVES

After studying this chapter, you should be able to:

1. Explain the distinguishing features of managerial accounting.
2. Identify the three broad functions of management.
3. Define the three classes of manufacturing costs.
4. Distinguish between product and period costs.
5. Explain the difference between a merchandising and a manufacturing income statement.
6. Indicate how cost of goods manufactured is determined.
7. Explain the difference between a merchandising and a manufacturing balance sheet.
8. Identify trends in managerial accounting.

The Navigator

Study Objectives *give you a framework for learning the specific concepts covered in the chapter.*

The Navigator

Scan **Study Objectives**	☐
Read **Feature Story**	☐
Read **Preview**	☐
Read text and answer **Before You Go On** p. 9 ☐ p. 12 ☐ p. 18 ☐ p. 22	☐
Work **Using the Decision Toolkit**	☐
Review **Summary of Study Objectives**	☐
Work **Demonstration Problem**	☐
Answer **Self-Study Questions**	☐
Complete **Assignments**	☐

The Navigator *is a learning system designed to prompt you to use the learning aids in the chapter and to help you set priorities as you study.*

Feature Story

The ***Feature Story*** *helps you picture how the chapter topic relates to the real world of business and accounting. You will find references to the story throughout the chapter.*

WHAT A DIFFERENCE A DAY MAKES

In January 1998 Compaq Computer (*www.compaq.com*) had just become the largest seller of personal computers, and it was *Forbes* magazine's "company of the year." Its chief executive, Eckhard Pfeiffer, was riding high. But during the next two years Compaq lost $2 billion. The company was in chaos, and Mr. Pfeiffer was out of a job. What happened?

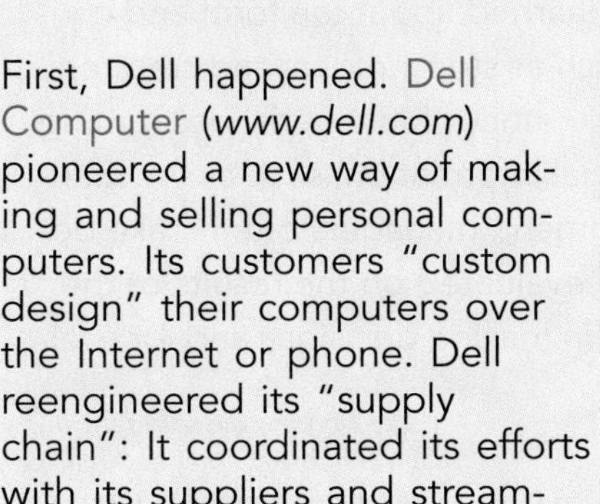

First, Dell happened. Dell Computer (*www.dell.com*) pioneered a new way of making and selling personal computers. Its customers "custom design" their computers over the Internet or phone. Dell reengineered its "supply chain": It coordinated its efforts with its suppliers and streamlined its order-taking and production process. It can ship a computer within two days of taking an order. Personal computers lose 1 percent of their value every week they sit on a shelf. Thus, having virtually no inventory is a great advantage to Dell. Compaq tried to adopt Dell's approach, but with limited success.

The second shock to Compaq came when it acquired a company even larger than itself—Digital Equipment. Mr. Pfeiffer believed that the purchase of Digital, with its huge and respected technical sales force, opened new opportunities for Compaq as a global service company. But combining the two companies proved to be hugely expensive and extremely complicated. Ultimately Compaq decided to merge with Hewlett-Packard (HP) (*www.hp.com*) in order to survive.

After this merger, HP lost significant market share to Dell because its higher cost structure made it hard to compete with Dell on price. Dell created a buzz in the financial press when it decided to enter the computer printing business—a segment that HP had long dominated. Many predicated that Dell would soon take over printers as well. But just when it appeared that Dell could not be beat, HP regained its footing and Dell stumbled. HP reduced its costs by adopting many of Dell's "lean" practices. Thus Dell lost much of its competitive advantage. In addition, computer purchasing habits changed, and Dell wasn't able to adjust fast enough.

✓ *The Navigator*

Inside Chapter 1

*"**Inside Chapter**" lists boxes in the chapter that should be of special interest to you.*

Preview of Chapter 1

This chapter focuses on issues illustrated in the Feature Story about Compaq Computer, Hewlett-Packard, and Dell. These include determining and controlling the costs of material, labor, and overhead and the relationship between costs and profits. In a financial accounting course, you learned about the form and content of **financial statements for external users** of financial information, such as stockholders and creditors. These financial statements represent the principal product of financial accounting. Managerial accounting focuses primarily on the preparation of **reports for internal users** of financial information, such as the managers and officers of a company. In today's rapidly changing global environment, managers often make decisions that determine their company's fate—and their own. Managers are evaluated on the results of their decisions. Managerial accounting provides tools for assisting management in making decisions and for evaluating the effectiveness of those decisions.

The content and organization of this chapter are as follows.

*The **Preview** describes the purpose of the chapter and outlines the major topics and subtopics you will find in it.*

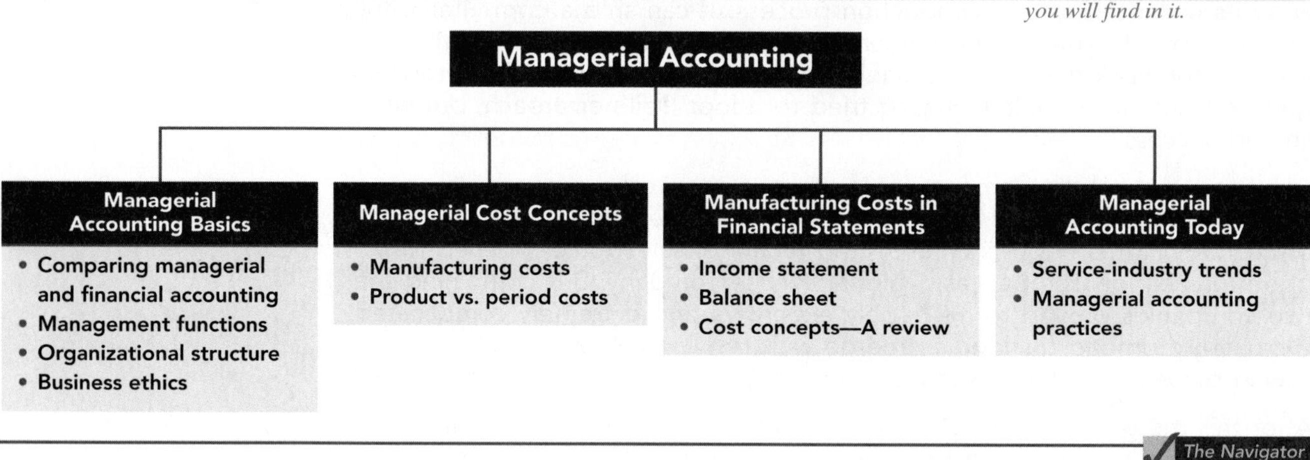

The Navigator

MANAGERIAL ACCOUNTING BASICS

__Essential terms__ and concepts are printed in blue where they first appear and are defined in the end-of-chapter Glossary.

Managerial accounting, also called **management accounting**, is a field of accounting that provides economic and financial information for managers and other internal users. The activities that are part of managerial accounting (and the chapters in which they are discussed in this textbook) are as follows.

1. Explaining manufacturing and nonmanufacturing costs and how they are reported in the financial statements (Chapter 1).
2. Computing the cost of providing a service or manufacturing a product (Chapters 2, 3, and 4).
3. Determining the behavior of costs and expenses as activity levels change and analyzing cost–volume–profit relationships within a company (Chapters 5 and 6).
4. Accumulating and presenting data for management decision making (Chapter 7).
5. Determining prices for external and internal transactions (Chapter 8).
6. Assisting management in profit planning and formalizing these plans in the form of budgets (Chapter 9).
7. Providing a basis for controlling costs and expenses by comparing actual results with planned objectives and standard costs (Chapters 10 and 11).
8. Accumulating and presenting data for capital expenditure decisions (Chapter 12).

Managerial accounting applies to all types of businesses—service, merchandising, and manufacturing. It also applies to all forms of business organizations—

proprietorships, partnerships, and corporations. Not-for-profit entities as well as profit-oriented enterprises need managerial accounting.

In the past, managerial accountants were primarily engaged in cost accounting—collecting and reporting costs to management. Recently that role has changed significantly. First, as the business environment has become more automated, methods to determine the amount and type of cost in a product have changed. Second, managerial accountants are now held responsible for strategic cost management; that is, they assist in evaluating how well the company is employing its resources. As a result, managerial accountants now serve as team members alongside personnel from production, marketing, and engineering when the company makes critical strategic decisions.

Opportunities for managerial accountants to advance within the company are considerable. Financial executives must have a background that includes an understanding of managerial accounting concepts. Whatever your position in the company—marketing, sales, or production, knowledge of managerial accounting greatly improves your opportunities for advancement. As the CEO of Microsoft noted: "If you're supposed to be making money in business and supposed to be satisfying customers and building market share, there are numbers that characterize those things. And if somebody can't sort of speak to me quantitatively about it, then I'm nervous."

Comparing Managerial and Financial Accounting

STUDY OBJECTIVE 1

Explain the distinguishing features of managerial accounting.

There are both similarities and differences between managerial and financial accounting. First, each field of accounting deals with the economic events of a business. Thus, their interests overlap. For example, *determining* the unit cost of manufacturing a product is part of managerial accounting. *Reporting* the total cost of goods manufactured and sold is part of financial accounting. In addition, both managerial and financial accounting require that a company's economic events be quantified and communicated to interested parties.

Illustration 1-1 summarizes the principal differences between financial accounting and managerial accounting. The need for various types of economic data is responsible for many of the differences.

Illustration 1-1
Differences between financial and managerial accounting

Financial Accounting		Managerial Accounting
• External users: stockholders, creditors, and regulators.	**Primary Users of Reports**	• Internal users: officers and managers.
• Financial statements. • Quarterly and annually.	**Types and Frequency of Reports**	• Internal reports. • As frequently as needed.
• General-purpose.	**Purpose of Reports**	• Special-purpose for specific decisions.
• Pertains to business as a whole. • Highly aggregated (condensed). • Limited to double-entry accounting and cost data. • Generally accepted accounting principles.	**Content of Reports**	• Pertains to subunits of the business. • Very detailed. • Extends beyond double-entry accounting to any relevant data. • Standard is relevance to decisions.
• Audit by CPA.	**Verification Process**	• No independent audits.

Management Functions

STUDY OBJECTIVE 2

Identify the three broad functions of management.

Managers' activities and responsibilities can be classified into three broad functions:

1. Planning.
2. Directing.
3. Controlling.

In performing these functions, managers make decisions that have a significant impact on the organization.

Planning requires managers to look ahead and to establish objectives. These objectives are often diverse: maximizing short-term profits and market share, maintaining a commitment to environmental protection, and contributing to social programs. For example, Hewlett-Packard, in an attempt to gain a stronger foothold in the computer industry, has greatly reduced its prices to compete with Dell. A key objective of management is to **add value** to the business under its control. Value is usually measured by the trading price of the company's stock and by the potential selling price of the company.

Directing involves coordinating a company's diverse activities and human resources to produce a smooth-running operation. This function relates to implementing planned objectives and providing necessary incentives to motivate employees. For example, manufacturers such as Campbell Soup Company, General Motors, and Dell must coordinate purchasing, manufacturing, warehousing, and selling. Service corporations such as American Airlines, Federal Express, and AT&T must coordinate scheduling, sales, service, and acquisitions of equipment

MANAGEMENT INSIGHT

Insight boxes illustrate interesting situations in real companies and show how managers make decisions using accounting information. Guideline answers to the critical thinking questions appear on the last page of the chapter.

Even the Best Have to Get Better

Louis Vuitton is a French manufacturer of high-end handbags, wallets, and suitcases. Its reputation for quality and style allows it to charge extremely high prices—for example, $700 for a tote bag. But often in the past, when demand was hot, supply was nonexistent—shelves were empty, and would-be buyers left empty-handed.

Luxury-goods manufacturers used to consider stock-outs to be a good thing, but recently Louis Vuitton changed its attitude. The company adopted "lean" processes used by car manufacturers and electronics companies to speed up production of "hot" products. Work is done by flexible teams, with jobs organized based on how long a task takes. By reducing wasted time and eliminating bottlenecks, what used to take 20 to 30 workers eight days to do now takes 6 to 12 workers one day. Also, production employees who used to specialize on a single task on a single product are now multiskilled. This allows them to quickly switch products to meet demand.

To make sure that the factory is making the right products, within a week of a product launch, Louis Vuitton stores around the world feed sales information to the headquarters in France, and production is adjusted accordingly. Finally, the new production processes have also improved quality. Returns of some products are down by two-thirds, which makes quite a difference to the bottom line when the products are pricey.

Source: Christina Passariello, "Louis Vuitton Tries Modern Methods on Factory Lines," *Wall Street Journal*, October 9, 2006.

What are some of the steps that this company has taken in order to ensure that production meets demand?

and supplies. Directing also involves selecting executives, appointing managers and supervisors, and hiring and training employees.

The third management function, **controlling**, is the process of keeping the company's activities on track. In controlling operations, managers determine whether planned goals are being met. When there are deviations from targeted objectives, managers must decide what changes are needed to get back on track. Recent scandals at companies like Enron, Lucent, and Xerox attest to the fact that companies must have adequate controls to ensure that the company develops and distributes accurate information.

How do managers achieve control? A smart manager in a small operation can make personal observations, ask good questions, and know how to evaluate the answers. But using this approach in a large organization would result in chaos. Unless there is some record of what has happened and what is expected to occur, imagine the president of Dell attempting to determine whether the company is meeting its planned objectives. Thus, large businesses typically use a formal system of evaluation. These systems include such features as budgets, responsibility centers, and performance evaluation reports—all of which are features of managerial accounting.

Decision making is not a separate management function. Rather, it is the outcome of the exercise of good judgment in planning, directing, and controlling.

Organizational Structure

In order to assist in carrying out management functions, most companies prepare **organization charts** to show the interrelationships of activities and the delegation of authority and responsibility within the company. Illustration 1-2 shows a typical organization chart, which outlines the delegation of responsibility.

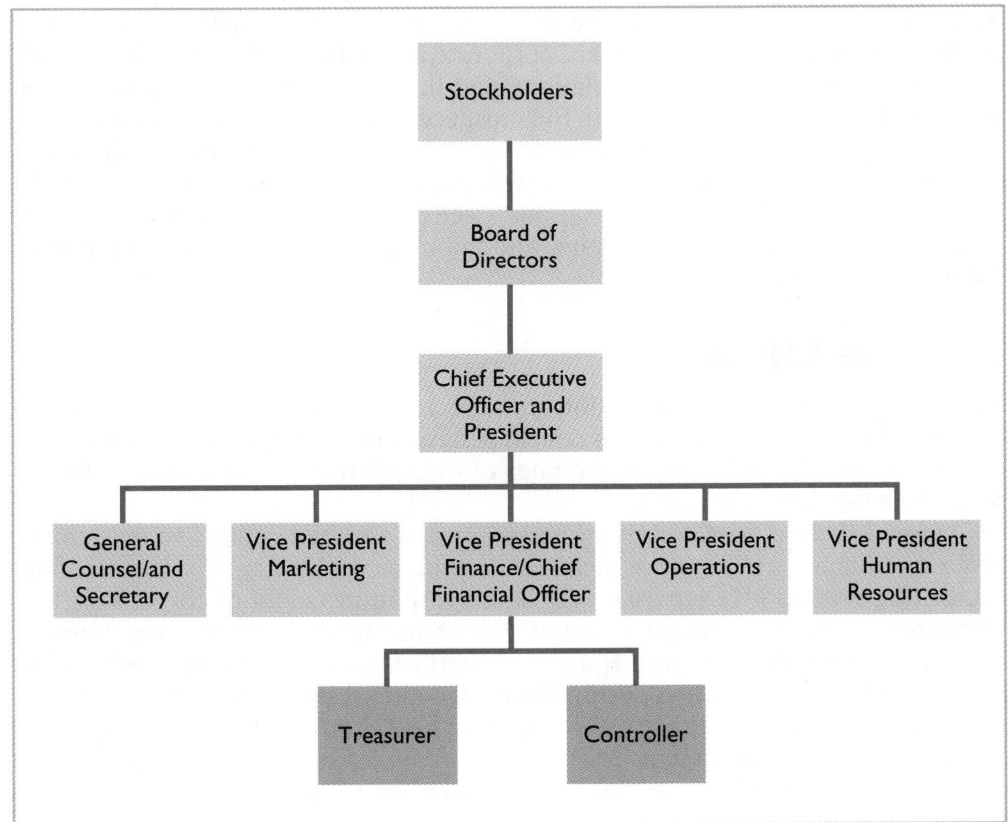

Illustration 1-2
Corporation's organization chart

Stockholders own the corporation, but they manage it indirectly through a **board of directors** they elect. Even not-for-profit organizations have boards of directors. The board formulates the operating policies for the company or organization. The board also selects officers, such as a president and one or more vice presidents, to execute policy and to perform daily management functions.

The **chief executive officer (CEO)** has overall responsibility for managing the business. Obviously, even in a small business, in order to accomplish organizational objectives, the company relies on delegation of responsibilities. As the organization chart on page 7 shows, the CEO delegates responsibilities to other officers. Each member of the organization has a clearly defined role to play.

Responsibilities within the company are frequently classified as either line or staff positions. Employees with **line positions** are directly involved in the company's primary revenue-generating operating activities. Examples of line positions include the vice president of operations, vice president of marketing, plant managers, supervisors, and production personnel. Employees with **staff positions** are involved in activities that support the efforts of the line employees. In a firm like General Electric or ExxonMobil, employees in finance, legal, and human resources have staff positions. While activities of staff employees are vital to the company, these employees are nonetheless there to serve the line employees who engage in the company's primary operations.

The **chief financial officer (CFO)** is responsible for all of the accounting and finance issues the company faces. The CFO is supported by the **controller** and the **treasurer**. The controller's responsibilities include (1) maintaining the accounting records, (2) maintaining an adequate system of internal control, and (3) preparing financial statements, tax returns, and internal reports. The treasurer has custody of the corporation's funds and is responsible for maintaining the company's cash position.

Also serving the CFO is the internal audit staff. The staff's responsibilities include reviewing the reliability and integrity of financial information provided by the controller and treasurer. Staff members also ensure that internal control systems are functioning properly to safeguard corporate assets. In addition, they investigate compliance with policies and regulations, and in many companies they determine whether resources are being used in the most economical and efficient fashion.

The vice president of operations oversees employees with line positions. For example, the company might have multiple plant managers, each of whom would report to the vice president of operations. Each plant would also have department managers, such as fabricating, painting, and shipping, each of whom would report to the plant manager.

Business Ethics

All employees within an organization are expected to act ethically in their business activities. Given the importance of ethical behavior to corporations and their owners (stockholders), an increasing number of organizations provide codes of business ethics for their employees.

Despite these efforts, recent business scandals resulted in massive investment losses and numerous employee layoffs. A recent survey of fraud by international accounting firm KPMG reported a 13% increase in instances of corporate fraud compared to five years earlier. It noted that while employee fraud (such things as expense-account abuse, payroll fraud, and theft of assets) represented 60% of all instances of fraud, financial reporting fraud (the intentional misstatement of financial reports) was the most costly to companies. That should not be surprising given the long list of companies such as Enron, Global Crossing, WorldCom, and others that engaged in massive financial frauds which led to huge financial losses and thousands of lost jobs.

CREATING PROPER INCENTIVES

Companies like Motorola, IBM, and Nike use complex systems to control and evaluate the actions of managers. They dedicate substantial resources to monitor and effectively evaluate the actions of employees. Unfortunately, these systems and controls sometimes unwittingly create incentives for managers to take unethical actions. For example, companies prepare budgets to provide direction. Because the budget is also used as an evaluation tool, some managers try to "game" the budgeting process by underestimating their division's predicted performance so that it will be easier to meet their performance targets. On the other hand, if the budget is set at unattainable levels, managers sometimes take unethical actions to meet the targets in order to receive higher compensation or, in some cases, to keep their jobs.

For example, in recent years, airline manufacturer Boeing was plagued by a series of scandals including charges of over-billing, corporate espionage, and illegal conflicts of interest. Some long-time employees of Boeing blame the decline in ethics on a change in the corporate culture that took place after Boeing merged with McDonnell Douglas. They suggest that evaluation systems implemented after the merger to monitor results and evaluate employee performance made employees believe they needed to succeed no matter what actions were required to do so.

As another example, manufacturing companies need to establish production goals for their processes. Again, if controls are not effective and realistic, problems develop. To illustrate, Schering-Plough, a pharmaceutical manufacturer, found that employees were so concerned with meeting production standards that they failed to monitor the quality of the product, and as a result the dosages were often wrong.

CODE OF ETHICAL STANDARDS

In response to corporate scandals in 2000 and 2001, the U.S. Congress enacted legislation to help prevent lapses in internal control. This legislation, referred to as the **Sarbanes-Oxley Act of 2002 (SOX)** has important implications for the financial community. One result of SOX was to clarify top management's responsibility for the company's financial statements. CEOs and CFOs must now certify that financial statements give a fair presentation of the company's operating results and its financial condition. In addition, top managers must certify that the company maintains an adequate system of internal controls to safeguard the company's assets and ensure accurate financial reports.

Another result of Sarbanes-Oxley is that companies now pay more attention to the composition of the board of directors. In particular, the audit committee of the board of directors must be comprised entirely of independent members (that is, non-employees) and must contain at least one financial expert.

Finally, to increase the likelihood of compliance with the rules that are part of the new legislation, the law substantially increases the penalties for misconduct.

To provide guidance for managerial accountants, the Institute of Management Accountants (IMA) has developed a code of ethical standards, entitled *IMA Statement of Ethical Professional Practice.* Management accountants should not commit acts in violation of these standards. Nor should they condone such acts by others within their organizations. We include the IMA code of ethical standards in Appendix B at the end of the book. Throughout the book, we will address various ethical issues managers face.

Before You Go On...

REVIEW IT

1. Compare financial accounting and managerial accounting and identify the principal differences.
2. Identify and discuss the three broad functions of management.

Before You Go On . . . Review It *questions at the end of major text sections offer an opportunity to stop and re-examine the key points you have studied.*

3. What are staff positions? What are line positions? Give examples.
4. What were some of the regulatory changes enacted under the Sarbanes-Oxley Act?

MANAGERIAL COST CONCEPTS

In order for managers at companies like Dell or Hewlett-Packard to plan, direct, and control operations effectively, they need good information. One very important type of information is related to costs. Managers should ask questions such as the following.

1. What costs are involved in making a product or providing a service?
2. If we decrease production volume, will costs decrease?
3. What impact will automation have on total costs?
4. How can we best control costs?

To answer these questions, managers need reliable and relevant cost information. We now explain and illustrate the various cost categories that companies use.

Manufacturing Costs

STUDY OBJECTIVE 3
Define the three classes of manufacturing costs.

Manufacturing consists of activities and processes that convert raw materials into finished goods. Contrast this type of operation with merchandising, which sells merchandise in the form in which it is purchased. Manufacturing costs are typically classified as shown in Illustration 1-3.

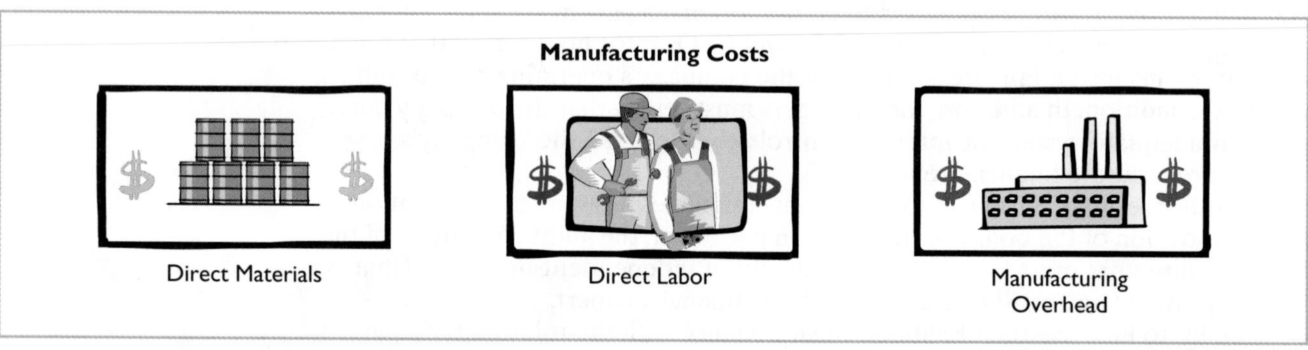

Illustration 1-3
Classifications of manufacturing costs

DIRECT MATERIALS

To obtain the materials that will be converted into the finished product, the manufacturer purchases raw materials. **Raw materials** are the basic materials and parts used in the manufacturing process. For example, auto manufacturers such as General Motors, Ford, and Toyota use steel, plastic, and tires as raw materials in making cars.

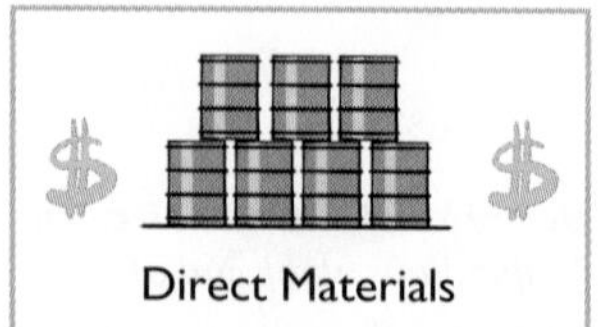

Raw materials that can be physically and directly associated with the finished product during the manufacturing process are **direct materials**. Examples include flour in the baking of bread, syrup in the bottling of soft drinks, and steel in the making of automobiles. Direct materials for Hewlett-Packard and Dell Computer (in the Feature Story) include plastic, glass, hard drives, and processing chips.

But some raw materials cannot be easily associated with the finished product. These are called indirect materials. **Indirect materials** have one of two characteristics: (1) They do not physically become part of the finished product (such as lubricants and polishing compounds). Or, (2) they cannot be traced because their physical association with the finished product is too small in terms of cost (such as cotter pins and lock washers). Companies account for indirect materials as part of **manufacturing overhead**.

DIRECT LABOR

The work of factory employees that can be physically and directly associated with converting raw materials into finished goods is **direct labor**. Bottlers at Coca-Cola, bakers at Sara Lee, and typesetters at Aptara Corp. are employees whose activities are usually classified as direct labor. **Indirect labor** refers to the work of employees that has no physical association with the finished product, or for which it is impractical to trace costs to the goods produced. Examples include wages of maintenance people, time-keepers, and supervisors. Like indirect materials, companies classify indirect labor as **manufacturing overhead**.

MANAGEMENT INSIGHT

How Many Labor Hours to Build a Car?

Nissan and Toyota were number 1 and 2 in a recent annual study of labor productivity in the auto industry. But U.S. auto manufacturers showed improvements. Labor represents about 15% of the total cost to make a vehicle. Since Nissan required only 28.46 labor hours per vehicle, it saves about $300 to $450 in labor costs to build a car relative to Ford, the least-efficient manufacturer. General Motors (GM) has shown steady improvement over the years. In 1998 it needed almost 17 more hours of labor than Toyota to build a car; it now needs only 4 more hours than Toyota. Chrysler says that much of its improvement in labor productivity has come from designing cars that are easier to build.

Source: Rick Popely, "Japanese Automakers Lead Big Three in Productivity Review," *Knight Ridder Tribune News Service*, June 1, 2006, p. 1.

Why might Nissan production require significantly fewer labor hours?

MANUFACTURING OVERHEAD

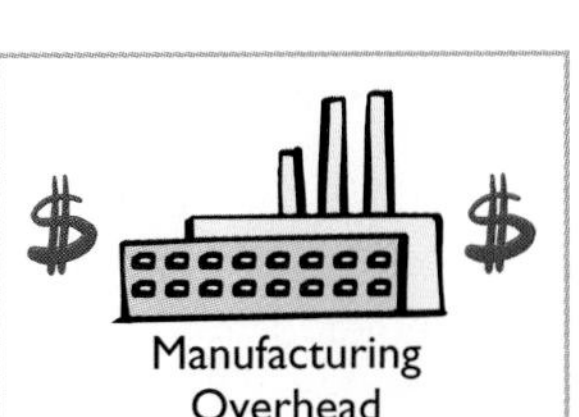

Manufacturing overhead consists of costs that are indirectly associated with the manufacture of the finished product. These costs may also be manufacturing costs that cannot be classified as direct materials or direct labor. Manufacturing overhead includes indirect materials, indirect labor, depreciation on factory buildings and machines, and insurance, taxes, and maintenance on factory facilities.

Alternative Terminology notes present synonymous terms used in practice.

One study found the following magnitudes of the three different product costs as a percentage of the total product cost: direct materials 54%, direct labor 13%, and manufacturing overhead 33%. Note that the direct labor component is the smallest. This component of product cost is dropping substantially because of automation. In some companies, direct labor has become as little as 5% of the total cost.

Allocating materials and labor costs to specific products is fairly straightforward. Good record keeping can tell a company how much plastic it used in making each type of gear, or how many hours of factory labor it took to assemble a part. But allocating overhead costs to specific products presents problems. How much of the purchasing agent's salary is attributable to the hundreds of different products made in the same plant? What about the grease that keeps the machines humming, or the computers that make sure paychecks come out on time? Boiled down to its simplest form, the question becomes: Which products cause the incurrence of which costs? In subsequent chapters we show various methods of allocating overhead to products.

ALTERNATIVE TERMINOLOGY

Some companies use terms such as *factory overhead, indirect manufacturing costs,* and *burden* instead of manufacturing overhead.

Product versus Period Costs

STUDY OBJECTIVE 4

Distinguish between product and period costs.

ALTERNATIVE TERMINOLOGY

Product costs are also called *inventoriable* costs.

Each of the manufacturing cost components—direct materials, direct labor, and manufacturing overhead—are product costs. As the term suggests, **product costs** are costs that are a necessary and integral part of producing the finished product. Companies record product costs, when incurred, as inventory. Under the matching principle, these costs do not become expenses until the company sells the finished goods inventory. At that point, the company records the expense as cost of goods sold.

Period costs are costs that are matched with the revenue of a specific time period rather than included as part of the cost of a salable product. These are nonmanufacturing costs. Period costs include selling and administrative expenses. In order to determine net income, companies deduct these costs from revenues in the period in which they are incurred.

Illustration 1-4 summarizes these relationships and cost terms. Our main concern in this chapter is with product costs.

Illustration 1-4
Product versus period costs

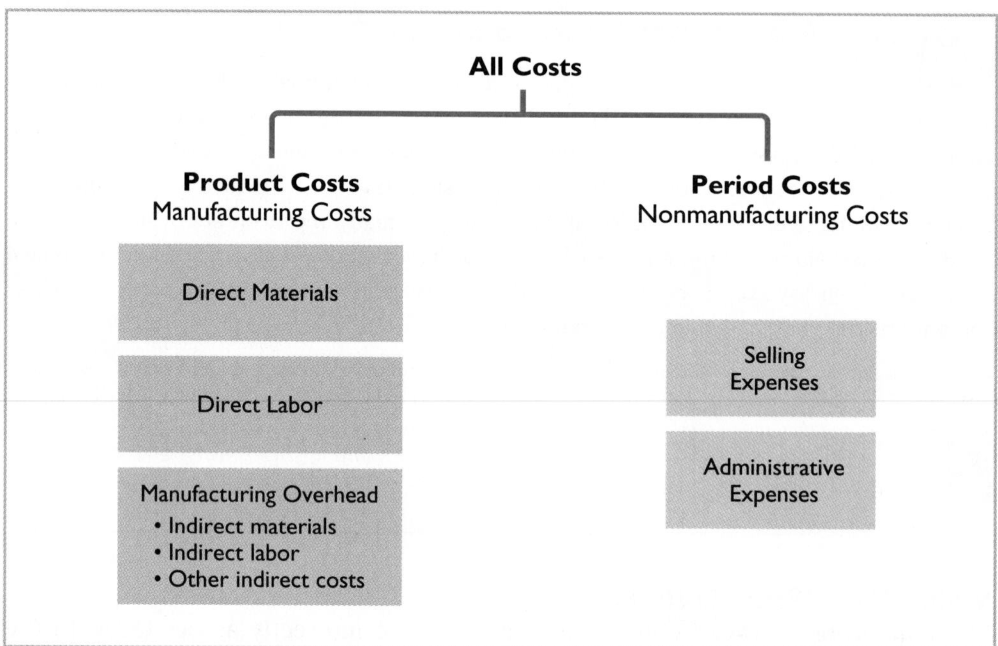

Before You Go On...

REVIEW IT

1. What are the major cost classifications involved in manufacturing a product?
2. What are product and period costs, and what is their relationship to the manufacturing process?

DO IT

A bicycle company has these costs: tires, salaries of employees who put tires on the wheels, factory building depreciation, wheel nuts, spokes, salary of factory manager, handlebars, and salaries of factory maintenance employees. Classify each cost as direct materials, direct labor, or overhead.

*Before You Go On . . . Do It exercises ask you to put to work newly acquired knowledge. The **Action Plan** outlines the reasoning necessary to complete the exercise. The accompanying **Solution** (next page) shows how the exercise should be solved.*

Action Plan

- Classify as direct materials any raw materials that can be physically and directly associated with the finished product.

- Classify as direct labor the work of factory employees that can be physically and directly associated with the finished product.
- Classify as manufacturing overhead any costs that are indirectly associated with the finished product.

Solution Tires, spokes, and handlebars are direct materials. Salaries of employees who put tires on the wheels are direct labor. All of the other costs are manufacturing overhead.

Related exercise material: BE1-4, BE1-5, BE1-6, BE1-7, E1-2, E1-3, E1-4, E1-5, E1-6, and E1-7.

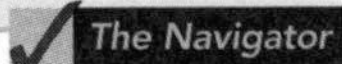

MANUFACTURING COSTS IN FINANCIAL STATEMENTS

STUDY OBJECTIVE 5
Explain the difference between a merchandising and a manufacturing income statement.

The financial statements of a manufacturer are very similar to those of a merchandiser. For example, you will find many of the same sections and same accounts in the financial statements of Procter & Gamble that you find in the financial statements of Dick's Sporting Goods. The principal differences between their financial statements occur in two places: the cost of goods sold section in the income statement and the current assets section in the balance sheet.

Income Statement

Under a periodic inventory system, the income statements of a merchandiser and a manufacturer differ in the cost of goods sold section. Merchandisers compute cost of goods sold by adding the beginning merchandise inventory to the **cost of goods purchased** and subtracting the ending merchandise inventory. Manufacturers compute cost of goods sold by adding the beginning finished goods inventory to the **cost of goods manufactured** and subtracting the ending finished goods inventory. Illustration 1-5 shows these different methods.

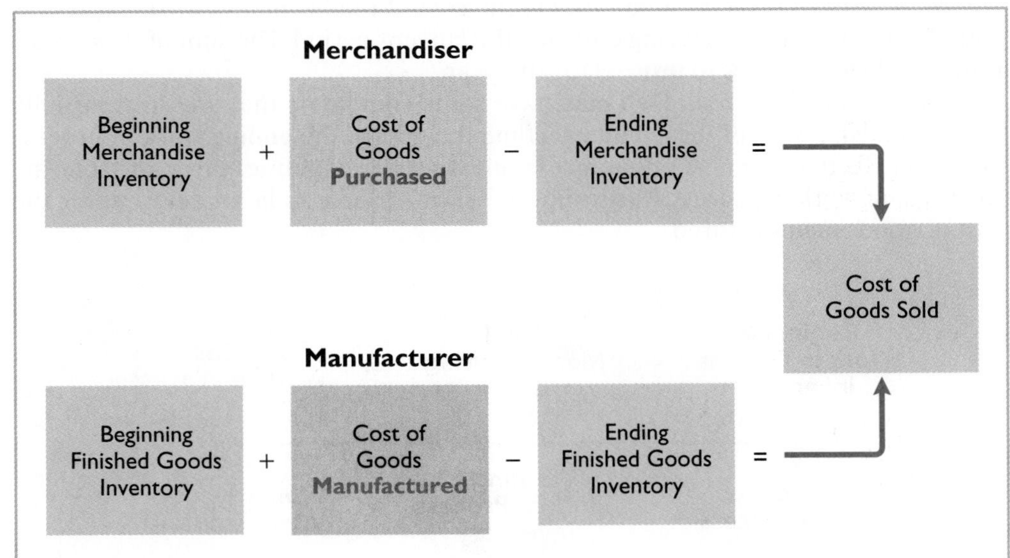

Illustration 1-5
Cost of goods sold components

***Helpful Hints** clarify concepts being discussed.*

HELPFUL HINT
We assume a periodic inventory system in this illustration.

A number of accounts are involved in determining the cost of goods manufactured. To eliminate excessive detail, income statements typically show only the total cost of goods manufactured. A separate statement, called a Cost of Goods Manufactured Schedule, presents the details. (For more information, see the discussion on page 15 and Illustration 1-8.)

Illustration 1-6 shows the different presentations of the cost of goods sold sections for merchandising and manufacturing companies. The other sections of an income statement are similar for merchandisers and manufacturers.

Illustration 1-6
Cost of goods sold sections of merchandising and manufacturing income statements

MERCHANDISING COMPANY Income Statement (partial) For the Year Ended December 31, 2008		MANUFACTURING COMPANY Income Statement (partial) For the Year Ended December 31, 2008	
Cost of goods sold		Cost of goods sold	
Merchandise inventory, January 1	$ 70,000	**Finished goods inventory, January 1**	$ 90,000
Cost of goods purchased	650,000	**Cost of goods manufactured (see Illustration 1-8)**	370,000
Cost of goods available for sale	720,000	Cost of goods available for sale	460,000
Merchandise inventory, December 31	400,000	**Finished goods inventory, December 31**	80,000
Cost of goods sold	$320,000	Cost of goods sold	$380,000

DETERMINING THE COST OF GOODS MANUFACTURED

STUDY OBJECTIVE 6
Indicate how cost of goods manufactured is determined.

An example may help show how companies determine the cost of goods manufactured. Assume that on January 1 Dell has a number of computers in various stages of production. In total, these partially completed units are called **beginning work in process inventory**. The costs the company assigns to beginning work in process inventory are based on the **manufacturing costs incurred in the prior period.**

Dell first uses the manufacturing costs incurred in the current year to complete the work that was in process on January 1. It then incurs manufacturing costs for production of new orders. The sum of the direct materials costs, direct labor costs, and manufacturing overhead incurred in the current year is the **total manufacturing costs** for the current period.

We now have two cost amounts: (1) the cost of the beginning work in process and (2) the total manufacturing costs for the current period. The sum of these costs is the **total cost of work in process** for the year.

At the end of the year, Dell may have some computers that are only partially completed. The costs of these units become the cost of the **ending work in process inventory**. To find the **cost of goods manufactured**, we subtract this cost from the total cost of work in process. Illustration 1-7 shows the formula for determining the cost of goods manufactured.

Illustration 1-7
Cost of goods manufactured formula

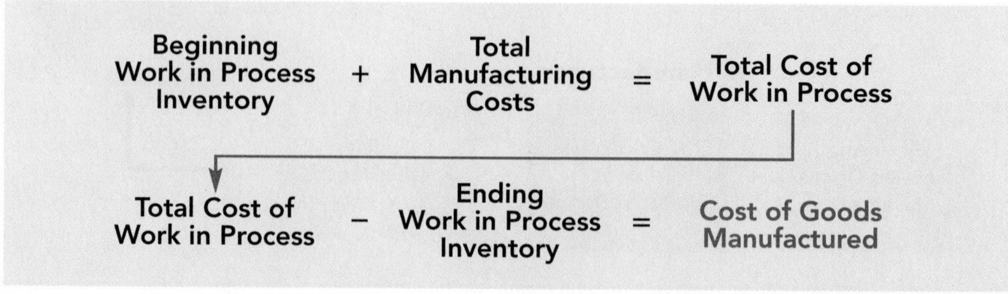

COST OF GOODS MANUFACTURED SCHEDULE

The **cost of goods manufactured schedule** reports cost elements used in calculating cost of goods manufactured. Illustration 1-8 shows the schedule for Olsen Manufacturing Company (using assumed data). The schedule presents detailed data for direct materials and for manufacturing overhead.

Review Illustration 1-7 and then examine the cost of goods manufactured schedule in Illustration 1-8. You should be able to distinguish between "Total manufacturing costs" and "Cost of goods manufactured." The difference is the effect of the change in work in process during the period.

Illustration 1-8
Cost of goods manufactured schedule

OLSEN MANUFACTURING COMPANY Cost of Goods Manufactured Schedule For the Year Ended December 31, 2008			
Work in process, January 1			**$ 18,400**
Direct materials			
Raw materials inventory, January 1	$ 16,700		
Raw materials purchases	152,500		
Total raw materials available for use	169,200		
Less: Raw materials inventory, December 31	22,800		
Direct materials used		$146,400	
Direct labor		175,600	
Manufacturing overhead			
Indirect labor	14,300		
Factory repairs	12,600		
Factory utilities	10,100		
Factory depreciation	9,440		
Factory insurance	8,360		
Total manufacturing overhead		54,800	
Total manufacturing costs			**376,800**
Total cost of work in process			395,200
Less: Work in process, December 31			**25,200**
Cost of goods manufactured			**$370,000**

Often, numbers or categories in the financial statements are highlighted in ***red type*** *to draw your attention to key information.*

Each chapter presents useful information about how decision makers analyze and solve business problems. ***Decision Toolkits*** *summarize the key features of a decision tool and review why and how to use it.*

DECISION TOOLKIT

Decision Checkpoints	Info Needed for Decision	Tool to Use for Decision	How to Evaluate Results
Is the company maintaining control over the costs of production?	Cost of material, labor, and overhead	Cost of goods manufactured schedule	Compare the cost of goods manufactured to revenue expected from product sales.

Balance Sheet

The balance sheet for a merchandising company shows just one category of inventory. In contrast, the balance sheet for a manufacturer may have three inventory accounts, as shown in Illustration 1-9 (page 16).

Illustration 1-9
Inventory accounts for a manufacturer

Raw Materials Inventory

Shows the cost of raw materials on hand.

Work in Process Inventory

Shows the cost applicable to units that have been started into production but are only partially completed.

Finished Goods Inventory

Shows the cost of completed goods on hand.

STUDY OBJECTIVE 7
Explain the difference between a merchandising and a manufacturing balance sheet.

Finished Goods Inventory is to a manufacturer what Merchandise Inventory is to a merchandiser. Each of these classifications represents the goods that the company has available for sale.

The current assets sections presented in Illustration 1-10 contrast the presentations of inventories for merchandising and manufacturing companies. Manufacturing companies generally list their inventories in the order of their liquidity—the order in which they are expected to be realized in cash. Thus, finished goods inventory comes first. The remainder of the balance sheet is similar for the two types of companies.

Illustration 1-10
Current assets sections of merchandising and manufacturing balance sheets

MERCHANDISING COMPANY
Balance Sheet
December 31, 2008

Current assets	
Cash	$100,000
Receivables (net)	210,000
Merchandise inventory	400,000
Prepaid expenses	22,000
Total current assets	$732,000

MANUFACTURING COMPANY
Balance Sheet
December 31, 2008

Current assets		
Cash		$180,000
Receivables (net)		210,000
Inventories		
Finished goods	$80,000	
Work in process	25,200	
Raw materials	22,800	128,000
Prepaid expenses		18,000
Total current assets		$536,000

For expanded coverage, see the appendix at the end of the chapter.

Each step in the accounting cycle for a merchandiser applies to a manufacturer. For example, prior to preparing financial statements, manufacturers make adjusting entries. The adjusting entries are essentially the same as those of a merchandiser. The closing entries are also similar for manufacturers and merchandisers.

DECISION TOOLKIT

Decision Checkpoints 	Info Needed for Decision	Tool to Use for Decision 	How to Evaluate Results 
What is the composition of a manufacturing company's inventory?	Amount of raw materials, work in process, and finished goods inventories	Balance sheet	Determine whether there are sufficient finished goods, raw materials, and work in process inventories to meet forecasted demand.

Cost Concepts—A Review

You have learned a number of cost concepts in this chapter. Because many of these concepts are new, here we provide an extended example for review.

Assume that Northridge Company manufactures and sells pre-hung metal doors. Recently, it also has decided to start selling pre-hung wood doors. The company will use an old warehouse that it owns to manufacture the new product. Northridge identifies the following costs associated with manufacturing and selling the pre-hung wood doors.

1. The material cost (wood) for each door is $10.
2. Labor costs required to construct a wood door are $8 per door.
3. Depreciation on the factory equipment used to make the wood doors is $25,000 per year.
4. Property taxes on the factory building used to make the wood doors are $6,000 per year.
5. Advertising costs for the pre-hung wood doors total $2,500 per month or $30,000 per year.
6. Sales commissions related to pre-hung wood doors sold are $4 per door.
7. Salaries for employees who maintain the factory facilities are $28,000.
8. The salary of the plant manager in charge of pre-hung wood doors is $70,000.
9. The cost of shipping pre-hung wood doors is $12 per door sold.

Illustration 1-11 shows how Northridge would assign these manufacturing and selling costs to the various categories.

Illustration 1-11
Assignment of costs to cost categories

	Product Costs			
Cost Item	**Direct Materials**	**Direct Labor**	**Manufacturing Overhead**	**Period Costs**
1. Material cost ($10) per door	X			
2. Labor costs ($8) per door		X		
3. Depreciation on factory equipment ($25,000 per year)			X	
4. Property taxes on factory building ($6,000 per year)			X	
5. Advertising costs ($30,000 per year)				X
6. Sales commissions ($4 per door)				X
7. Maintenance salaries (factory facilities) ($28,000 per year)			X	
8. Salary of plant manager ($70,000)			X	
9. Cost of shipping pre-hung doors ($12 per door)				X

Remember that total manufacturing costs are the sum of the **product costs—** direct materials, direct labor, and manufacturing overhead. If Northridge Company produces 10,000 pre-hung wood doors the first year, the total manufacturing costs would be $309,000 as shown in Illustration 1-12.

Illustration 1-12
Computation of total manufacturing costs

Cost Number and Item	Manufacturing Cost
1. Material cost ($10 × 10,000)	$100,000
2. Labor cost ($8 × 10,000)	80,000
3. Depreciation on factory equipment	25,000
4. Property taxes on factory building	6,000
7. Maintenance salaries (factory facilities)	28,000
8. Salary of plant manager	70,000
Total manufacturing costs	**$309,000**

Knowing the total manufacturing costs, Northridge can compute the manufacturing cost per unit. Assuming 10,000 units, the cost to produce one pre-hung wood door is $30.90 ($309,000 ÷ 10,000 units).

In subsequent chapters, we will use extensively the cost concepts discussed in this chapter. Study Illustration 1-11 carefully. If you do not understand any of these classifications, go back and reread the appropriate section in this chapter.

Before You Go On...

REVIEW IT

1. How does the content of an income statement for a merchandiser differ from that for a manufacturer?
2. How do companies report the work in process inventories in the cost of goods manufactured schedule?
3. How does the content of the balance sheet for a merchandiser differ from that for a manufacturer?

MANAGERIAL ACCOUNTING TODAY

STUDY OBJECTIVE 8
Identify trends in managerial accounting.

In recent years, the competitive environment for U.S. business has changed significantly. For example, the airline, financial services, and telecommunications industries have been deregulated. Global competition has intensified. The world economy now has the European Union, NAFTA, and ASEAN. Countries like China and India are becoming economic powerhouses. As indicated earlier, managerial accountants must be forward-looking, acting as advisors and information providers to different members of the organization. Some of the issues they face are discussed below.

Ethics Notes help sensitize you to some of the ethical issues in accounting.

Service-Industry Trends

ETHICS NOTE
Do telecommunications companies have an obligation to provide service to remote or low-user areas for a fee that may be less than the cost of the service?

The Feature Story notes that at the peak of its success as a personal computer manufacturer, Compaq purchased Digital Equipment. Its management believed that the future of computing was in providing computer services, rather than in manufacturing computer hardware. In fact, the U.S. economy in general has shifted toward an emphasis on providing services, rather than goods. Today over 50% of U.S. workers work in service companies, and that percentage is projected to increase in coming years. Much of this chapter focused on manufacturers, but most of the techniques that you will learn in this course apply equally to service companies.

Managers of service companies look to managerial accounting to answer many questions. In some instances the managerial accountant may need to develop new systems for measuring the cost of serving individual customers. In others, companies may need new operating controls to improve the quality and efficiency of specific services. Many of the examples we present in subsequent chapters will be based on service companies.

Managerial Accounting Practices

As discussed earlier, the practice of managerial accounting has changed significantly in recent years to better address the needs of managers. The following sections explain some recent managerial accounting practices.

THE VALUE CHAIN

The **value chain** refers to all activities associated with providing a product or service. For a manufacturer these include research and development, product design, acquisition of raw materials, production, sales and marketing, delivery, customer relations, and subsequent service. Illustration 1-13 depicts the value chain for a manufacturer. In recent years, companies have made huge strides in analyzing all stages of the value chain in an effort to improve productivity and eliminate waste. Japanese automobile manufacturer Toyota pioneered many of these innovations.

Illustration 1-13
A manufacturer's value chain

In the 1980s many companies purchased giant machines to replace humans in the manufacturing process. These machines were designed to produce large batches of products. In recent years these large-batch manufacturing processes have been recognized as very wasteful. They require vast amounts of inventory storage capacity and considerable movement of materials. Consequently, many companies have reengineered their manufacturing processes. As one example, the manufacturing company Pratt and Whitney has replaced many large machines with smaller, more flexible ones and has begun reorganizing its plants for more efficient flow of goods. Pratt and Whitney was able to reduce the time that its turbine engine blades spend in the grinding section of its factory from 10 days down to 2 hours. It cut the total amount of time spent making a blade from 22 days to 7 days. Analysis of the value chain has made companies far more responsive to customer needs and has improved profitability.

TECHNOLOGICAL CHANGE

Technology has played a large role in the value chain. Computerization and automation have permitted companies to be more effective in streamlining production and thus enhancing the value chain. For example, many companies now employ **enterprise resource planning (ERP)** software systems to manage their value chain. ERP systems provide a comprehensive, centralized, integrated source of information that companies can use to manage all major business processes, from purchasing to manufacturing to human resources.

In large companies, an ERP system might replace as many as 200 individual software packages. For example, an ERP system can eliminate the need for individual software packages for personnel, inventory management, receivables, and payroll. Because the value chain extends beyond the walls of the company, ERP systems enable a two-way flow of information between a company and its major suppliers, customers, and business partners. Such systems both collect and disperse information throughout the value chain. The largest ERP provider, German corporation SAP AG, has more than 36,000 customers worldwide.

Another example of technological change is **computer-integrated manufacturing (CIM)**. Using CIM, many companies can now manufacture products that are untouched by human hands. An example is the use of robotic equipment in the steel and automobile industries. Workers monitor the manufacturing process by watching instrument panels. Automation significantly reduces direct labor costs in many cases.

Also, the widespread use of computers has greatly reduced the cost of accumulating, storing, and reporting managerial accounting information. Computers now make it possible to do more detailed costing of products, processes, and services than was possible under manual processing.

Technology is also affecting the value chain through business-to-business (B2B) e-commerce on the Internet. The Internet has dramatically changed the way corporations do business with one another. Interorganizational information systems connected over the Internet enable suppliers to share information nearly instantaneously. The Internet has also changed the marketplace, often having the effect of cutting out intermediaries. Industries such as the automobile, airline, hotel, and electronics industries have made commitments to purchase some or all of their supplies and raw materials in the huge B2B electronic marketplaces. For example, Hilton Hotels recently agreed to purchase as much as $1.5 billion of bed sheets, pest control services, and other items from an online supplier, PurchasePro.com.

JUST-IN-TIME INVENTORY METHODS

Many companies have significantly lowered inventory levels and costs using **just-in-time (JIT) inventory** methods. Under a just-in-time method, goods are manufactured or purchased just in time for use. As noted in the Feature Story, Dell is famous for having developed a system for making computers in response to individual customer requests. Even though each computer is custom-made to meet each customer's particular specifications, it takes Dell less than 48 hours to assemble the computer and put it on a truck. By integrating its information systems with those of its suppliers, Dell reduced its inventories to nearly zero. This is a huge advantage in an industry where products become obsolete nearly overnight.

ETHICS NOTE

Does just-in-time inventory justify "just-in-time" employees obtained through temporary employment services?

QUALITY

JIT inventory systems require an increased emphasis on product quality. If products are produced only as they are needed, it is very costly for the company to have to stop production because of defects or machine breakdowns. Many companies have installed **total quality management (TQM)** systems to reduce defects in finished products. The goal is to achieve zero defects. These systems require timely data on defective products, rework costs, and the cost of honoring warranty contracts. Often, companies use this information to help redesign the product in a way that makes it less prone to defects. Or they may use the information to reengineer the production process to reduce setup time and decrease the potential for error. TQM systems also provide information on nonfinancial measures such as customer satisfaction, number of service calls, and time to generate reports. Attention to these measures, which employees can control, leads to increased profitability.

MANAGEMENT INSIGHT

Bananas Receive Special Treatment

When it comes to total quality management, few companies can compare with Chiquita Brands International. Grocery store customers are very picky about bananas—bad bananas are consistently the number one grocery store complaint. Because bananas often account for up to 3% of a grocery store's sales, Chiquita goes to great lengths to protect the popular fruit. While bananas are in transit from Central America, "black box" recording devices attached to shipping crates ensure that they are kept in an environment of 90% humidity and an unvarying 55-degree temperature. Upon arrival in the U.S., bananas are ripened in airtight warehouses that use carefully monitored levels of ethylene gas. Regular checks are made of each warehouse using ultrasonic detectors that can detect leaks the size of a pinhole. Says one grocery store executive, "No other item in the store has this type of attention and resources devoted to it."

Source: Devon Spurgeon, "When Grocers in U.S. Go Bananas Over Bad Fruit, They Call Laubenthal," *Wall Street Journal*, August 14, 2000, p. A1.

Why is it important to keep track of costs that are incurred to improve product quality?

ACTIVITY-BASED COSTING

As discussed earlier, overhead costs have become an increasingly large component of product and service costs. By definition, overhead costs cannot be directly traced to individual products. But to determine each product's cost, overhead must be **allocated** to the various products. In order to obtain more accurate product costs, many companies now allocate overhead using **activity-based costing (ABC)**. Under ABC, companies allocate overhead based on each product's use of activities in making the product. For example, companies can keep track of their cost of setting up machines for each batch of a production process. Then companies can allocate part of the total set-up cost to a particular product based on the number of set-ups that product required.

Activity-based costing is beneficial because it results in more accurate product costing and in more careful scrutiny of all activities in the value chain. For example, if a product's cost is high because it requires a high number of set-ups, management will be motivated to determine how to produce the product using the optimal number of machine set-ups. Both manufacturing and service companies now widely use ABC. Allied Signal and Coca-Cola have both enjoyed improved results from ABC. Fidelity Investments uses ABC to identify which customers cost the most to serve.

THEORY OF CONSTRAINTS

All companies have certain aspects of their business that create "bottlenecks"—constraints that limit the company's potential profitability. An important aspect of managing the value chain is identifying these constraints. The **theory of constraints** is a specific approach used to identify and manage constraints in order to achieve the company's goals. Automobile manufacturer General Motors has implemented the theory of constraints in all of its North American plants. GM has found that it is most profitable when it focuses on fixing bottlenecks, rather than worrying about whether all aspects of the company are functioning at full capacity. It has greatly improved the company's ability to effectively use overtime labor while meeting customer demand. Chapter 6 discusses an application of the theory of constraints.

BALANCED SCORECARD

As companies implement various business practice innovations, managers sometimes focus too enthusiastically on the latest innovation, to the detriment of other areas of the business. For example, in focusing on improving quality, companies sometimes have lost sight of cost/benefit considerations. Similarly, in focusing on reducing inventory levels through just-in-time, companies sometimes have lost sales due to inventory shortages. The **balanced scorecard** is a performance-measurement approach that uses both financial and nonfinancial measures to evaluate all aspects of a company's operations in an **integrated** fashion. The performance measures are linked in a cause-and-effect fashion to ensure that they all tie to the company's overall objectives.

For example, the company may desire to increase its return on assets, a common financial performance measure (calculated as net income divided by average total assets). It will then identify a series of linked goals. If the company accomplishes each goal, the ultimate result will be an increase in return on assets. For example, in order to increase return on assets, sales must increase. In order to increase sales, customer satisfaction must be increased. In order to increase customer satisfaction, product defects must be reduced. In order to reduce product defects, employee training must be increased. Note the linkage, which starts with employee training and ends with return on assets. Each objective will have associated performance measures.

The use of the balanced scorecard is widespread among well-known and respected companies. For example, Hilton Hotels Corporation uses the balanced scorecard to evaluate the performance of employees at all of its hotel chains. Wal-Mart employs the balanced scorecard, and actually extends its use to evaluation of its suppliers. For example, Wal-Mart recently awarded Welch Company the "Dry Grocery Division Supplier of the Year Award" for its balanced scorecard results. We discuss the balanced scorecard further in Chapter 11.

Before You Go On...

REVIEW IT

1. Describe, in sequence, the main components of a manufacturer's value chain.
2. Why is product quality important for companies that implement a just-in-time inventory system?
3. Explain what is meant by "balanced" in the balanced scorecard approach.

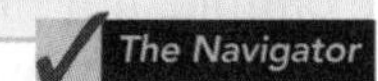

*An **All About You** feature (next page) links some aspect of the chapter topic to your personal life or a financial situation you are likely to face.*

Be sure to read **ALL ABOUT YOU: *Outsourcing and Jobs*** on the next page for information on how topics in this chapter apply to you.

all about YOU

Outsourcing and Jobs

As noted in this chapter, because of global competition, companies have become increasingly focused on reducing costs. To reduce costs, and remain competitive, many companies are turning to outsourcing. *Outsourcing* means hiring an outside supplier to provide elements of a product rather than producing them internally.

In many instances, companies outsource jobs to foreign suppliers. This practice has caused considerable concern about the loss of U.S. jobs. Until recently, most of the debate about outsourcing related to manufacturing. Now outsourcing is also taking place in professional services like engineering and accounting. This is occurring because high-speed transmission of large amounts of data over the Internet is now cheap and easy. As a consequence, jobs that once seemed safe from foreign competition are now condidates for outsourcing.

Some Facts

* IBM has expanded beyond information technology into providing advisory services related to outsourcing, which it believes will be a $500 billion market.
* A U.S. professional association of certified public accountants requires that its members notify clients before they share confidential client information with an outside contractor as part of an outsourcing arrangement.
* During a recent two-year period Ford Motor Co. inspected the working conditions at about 160 of the more than 2,000 foreign-owned plants in low-cost countries that supply it with outsourced parts.
* The McKinsey Global Institute predicts that white-collar overseas outsourcing will increase at a rate of 30% to 40% over the next five years. By 2015, the consultancy group Forrester predicts roughly 3.3 million service jobs will have moved offshore, including 1.7 million "back-office" jobs such as payroll processing and accounting, and 473,000 jobs in the information technology industry.
* On the other hand, Hewlett-Packard has begun to "insource" (bring back inhouse) many of the manufacturing operations that it previously outsourced.

About the Numbers

Interestingly, foreign firms doing business in the United States also hire a lot of Americans. In a recent year, U.S. subsidiaries of foreign companies employed approximately 5.3 million Americans. In comparison, in that same year 134,000 Americans lost their jobs due to outsourcing. The following graph shows which countries are the top foreign employers in the United States.

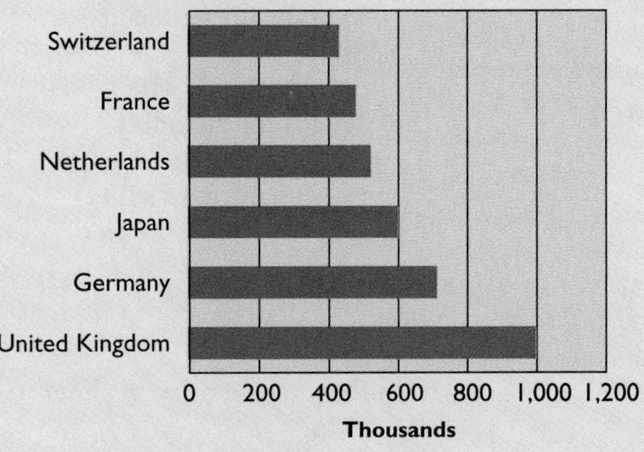

Source for graph: Darren Dahl, "Insourcing 101," *Inc.* Magazine, April 2006, p. 50.

What Do You Think?

Suppose you are the managing partner in a CPA firm with 30 full-time staff. Larger firms in your community have begun to outsource basic tax-return preparation work to India. Should you outsource your basic tax return work to India as well? You estimate that you would have to lay off six staff members if you outsource the work.

YES: The wages paid to Indian accountants are very low relative to U.S. wages. You will not be able to compete unless you outsource.

NO: Tax-return data is highly sensitive. Many customers will be upset to learn that their data is being emailed around the world.

Sources: Jonathan Weil, "Accountants Scrutinize Outsourcing," *Wall Street Journal*, August 11, 2004, p. A2; Jeffrey McCracken, "Ford Probes Work Conditions at Part Makers in China, Mexico," *Wall Street Journal*, April 5, 2006, p. A12; Council on Foreign Affairs, "Backgrounder, Trade: Outsourcing Jobs," February 20, 2004, *www.cfr.org/publication* (accessed June 2006).

The authors' comments on this situation appear on page 51.

Using the Decision Toolkit exercises ask you to use business information and the decision tools presented in the chapter. We encourage you to think through the questions related to the decision before you study the Solution.

Using the Decision Toolkit

Giant Manufacturing Co. Ltd. specializes in manufacturing many different models of bicycles. Assume that the market has responded enthusiastically to a new model, the Jaguar. As a result, the company has established a separate manufacturing facility to produce these bicycles. The company produces 1,000 bicycles per month. Giant's monthly manufacturing cost and other expenses data related to these bicycles are as follows.

1. Rent on manufacturing equipment (lease cost)	$2,000/month	8. Miscellaneous materials (lubricants, solders, etc.)	$1.20/bicycle
2. Insurance on manufacturing building	$750/month	9. Property taxes on manufacturing building	$2,400/year
3. Raw materials (frames, tires, etc.)	$80/bicycle	10. Manufacturing supervisor's salary	$3,000/month
4. Utility costs for manufacturing facility	$1,000/month	11. Advertising for bicycles	$30,000/year
5. Supplies for administrative office	$800/month	12. Sales commissions	$10/bicycle
6. Wages for assembly line workers in manufacturing facility	$30/bicycle	13. Depreciation on manufacturing building	$1,500/month
7. Depreciation on office equipment	$650/month		

Instructions

(a) Prepare an answer sheet with the following column headings.

	Product Costs			
Cost Item	**Direct Materials**	**Direct Labor**	**Manufacturing Overhead**	**Period Costs**

Enter each cost item on your answer sheet, placing an "X" mark under the appropriate headings.

(b) Compute total manufacturing costs for the month.

Solution

(a)

	Product Costs			
Cost Item	**Direct Materials**	**Direct Labor**	**Manufacturing Overhead**	**Period Costs**
1. Rent on manufacturing equipment ($2,000/month)			X	
2. Insurance on manufacturing building ($750/month)			X	
3. Raw materials ($80/bicycle)	X			
4. Manufacturing utilities ($1,000/month)			X	
5. Office supplies ($800/month)				X
6. Wages for workers ($30/bicycle)		X		

Cost Item	Product Costs: Direct Materials	Product Costs: Direct Labor	Manufacturing Overhead	Period Costs
7. Depreciation on office equipment ($650/month)				X
8. Miscellaneous materials ($1.20/bicycle)			X	
9. Property taxes on manufacturing building ($2,400/year)			X	
10. Manufacturing supervisor's salary ($3,000/month)			X	
11. Advertising cost ($30,000/year)				X
12. Sales commissions ($10/bicycle)				X
13. Depreciation on manufacturing building ($1,500/month)			X	

(b)

Cost Item	Manufacturing Cost
Rent on manufacturing equipment	$ 2,000
Insurance on manufacturing building	750
Raw materials ($80 × 1,000)	80,000
Manufacturing utilities	1,000
Labor ($30 × 1,000)	30,000
Miscellaneous materials ($1.20 × 1,000)	1,200
Property taxes on manufacturing building ($2,400 ÷ 12)	200
Manufacturing supervisor's salary	3,000
Depreciation on manufacturing building	1,500
Total manufacturing costs	$119,650

The Navigator

*The **Summary of Study Objectives** reiterates the main points related to the Study Objectives. It provides you with an opportunity to review what you have learned.*

SUMMARY OF STUDY OBJECTIVES

1 **Explain the distinguishing features of managerial accounting.** The *primary users* of managerial accounting reports are internal users, who are officers, department heads, managers, and supervisors in the company. Managerial accounting issues internal reports as frequently as the need arises. The purpose of these reports is to provide special-purpose information for a particular user for a specific decision. The content of managerial accounting reports pertains to subunits of the business, may be very detailed, and may extend beyond the double-entry accounting system. The reporting standard is relevance to the decision being made. No independent audits are required in managerial accounting.

2 **Identify the three broad functions of management.** The three functions are planning, directing, and controlling. Planning requires management to look ahead and to establish objectives. Directing involves coordinating the diverse activities and human resources of a company to produce a smooth-running operation. Controlling is the process of keeping the activities on track.

3 **Define the three classes of manufacturing costs.** Manufacturing costs are typically classified as either (1) direct materials, (2) direct labor, or (3) manufacturing overhead. Raw materials that can be physically and directly associated with the finished product during the manufacturing process are called direct materials. The work of factory employees that can be physically and directly associated with converting raw materials into finished goods is considered direct labor. Manufacturing overhead consists of costs that are indirectly associated with the manufacture of the finished product.

4 **Distinguish between product and period costs.** Product costs are costs that are a necessary and integral part of producing the finished product. Product costs are also called inventoriable costs. Under the matching principle, these costs do not become expenses until the company sells the finished goods inventory. Period costs are costs that are identified with a specific time period rather than with a salable product. These costs relate to nonmanufacturing costs and therefore are not inventoriable costs.

5 **Explain the difference between a merchandising and a manufacturing income statement.** The difference between a merchandising and a manufacturing income statement is in the cost of goods sold section. A manufacturing cost of goods sold section shows beginning and ending finished goods inventories and the cost of goods manufactured.

6 **Indicate how cost of goods manufactured is determined.** Companies add the cost of the beginning work in process to the total manufacturing costs for the current year to arrive at the total cost of work in process for the year. They then subtract the ending work in process from the total cost of work in process to arrive at the cost of goods manufactured.

7 **Explain the difference between a merchandising and a manufacturing balance sheet.** The difference between a merchandising and a manufacturing balance sheet is in the current assets section. The current assets section of a manufacturing company's balance sheet presents three inventory accounts: finished goods inventory, work in process inventory, and raw materials inventory.

8 **Identify trends in managerial accounting.** Managerial accounting has experienced many changes in recent years. Among these are a shift toward addressing the needs of service companies and improving practices to better meet the needs of managers. Improved practices include a focus on managing the value chain through techniques such as just-in-time inventory and technological applications such as enterprise resource management, computer-integrated manufacturing, and B2B e-commerce. In addition, techniques such as just-in-time inventory, total quality management, activity-based costing, and theory of constraints are improving decision making. Finally, the balanced scorecard is now used by many companies in order to attain a more comprehensive view of the company's operations.

The Navigator

*The **Decision Toolkit—A Summary** reviews the contexts and techniques useful for decision making that were covered in the chapter.*

DECISION TOOLKIT—A SUMMARY

Decision Checkpoints	Info Needed for Decision	Tool to Use for Decision	How to Evaluate Results
Is the company maintaining control over the costs of production?	Cost of material, labor, and overhead	Cost of goods manufactured schedule	Compare the cost of goods manufactured to revenue expected from product sales.
What is the composition of a manufacturing company's inventory?	Amount of raw materials, work in process, and finished goods inventories	Balance sheet	Determine whether there are sufficient finished goods, raw materials, and work in process inventories to meet forecasted demand.

APPENDIX Accounting Cycle for a Manufacturing Company

STUDY OBJECTIVE 9

Prepare a worksheet and closing entries for a manufacturing company.

The accounting cycle for a manufacturing company is the same as for a merchandising company when companies use a periodic inventory system. The journalizing and posting of transactions is the same, except for the additional manufacturing inventories and manufacturing cost accounts. Similarly, the preparation of a trial balance and the journalizing and posting of adjusting entries are the same. Some changes, however, occur in using a worksheet and in preparing closing entries.

To illustrate the changes in the worksheet, we will use the cost of goods manufactured schedule for Olsen Manufacturing presented in Illustration 1-8, along with other assumed data. For convenience, we reproduce the cost of goods manufactured schedule in Illustration 1A-1.

Illustration 1A-1
Cost of goods manufactured schedule

OLSEN MANUFACTURING COMPANY Cost of Goods Manufactured Schedule For the Year Ended December 31, 2008			
Work in process, January 1			$ 18,400
Direct materials			
Raw materials inventory, January 1	$ 16,700		
Raw materials purchases	152,500		
Total raw materials available for use	169,200		
Less: Raw materials inventory, December 31	22,800		
Direct materials used		$146,400	
Direct labor		175,600	
Manufacturing overhead			
Indirect labor	14,300		
Factory repairs	12,600		
Factory utilities	10,100		
Factory depreciation	9,440		
Factory insurance	8,360		
Total manufacturing overhead		54,800	
Total manufacturing costs			376,800
Total cost of work in process			395,200
Less: Work in process, December 31			25,200
Cost of goods manufactured			$370,000

Worksheet

When a company uses a worksheet in preparing financial statements, it needs two additional columns for the cost of goods manufactured schedule. As illustrated in the worksheet in Illustration 1A-2 (page 28), we insert debit and credit columns for this schedule before the income statement columns.

In completing the cost of goods manufactured columns, you would enter the beginning inventories of raw materials and work in process as debits. In addition, you would enter all of the manufacturing costs as debits. The reason is that each of these amounts increases cost of goods manufactured. In contrast, you would enter ending inventories for raw materials and work in process as credits in the cost of goods manufactured columns because they have the opposite effect—they decrease cost of goods manufactured. The balancing amount for these columns is the cost of goods manufactured. Note that the amount ($370,000) agrees with the amount reported for cost of goods manufactured in Illustration 1A-1. This amount is also entered in the income statement debit column.

The income statement and balance sheet columns for a manufacturing company are basically the same as for a merchandising company. For example, the treatment of the finished goods inventories is identical with the treatment of merchandise inventory: The beginning inventory appears in the debit column of the income statement, and the ending finished goods inventory appears in the income statement credit column as well as in the balance sheet debit column.

As in the case of a merchandising company, manufacturing companies can prepare financial statements from the statement columns of the worksheet. They also can prepare the cost of goods manufactured schedule directly from the worksheet.

Illustration 1A-2
Partial worksheet

Olsen Manufacturing Company.xls

File Edit View Insert Format Tools Data Window Help

	A	B	C	D	E	F	G	H	I
1–3	OLSEN MANUFACTURING COMPANY Worksheet (Partial) For theYear Ended December 31, 2008								
4		Adjusted Trial Balance		**Cost of Goods Manufactured**		Income Statement		Balance Sheet	
5		Dr.	Cr.	**Dr.**	**Cr.**	Dr.	Cr.	Dr.	Cr.
6	Cash	42,500						42,500	
7	Accounts Receivable (Net)	71,900						71,900	
8	Finished Goods Inventory	24,600				24,600	19,500	19,500	
9	Work in Process Inventory	18,400		**18,400**	**25.200**			25,200	
10	Raw Material Inventory	16,700		**16,700**	**22,800**			22,800	
11	Plant Assets	724.000						724,000	
12	Accumulated Depreciation		278,400						278,400
13	Notes Payable		100,000						100,000
14	Accounts Payable		40,000						40,000
15	Income Taxes Payable		5,000						5,000
16	Common Stock		200,000						200,000
17	Retained Earnings		205,100						205,100
18	Sales		680,000				680,000		
19	Raw Materials Purchases	152,500		**152,500**					
20	Direct Labor	175,600		**175,600**					
21	Indirect Labor	14,300		**14,300**					
22	Factory Repairs	12,600		**12,600**					
23	Factory Utilities	10,100		**10,100**					
24	Factory Depreciation	9,440		**9,440**					
25	Factory Insurance	8,360		**8,360**					
26	Selling Expenses	114,900				114,900			
27	Administrative Expenses	92,600				92,600			
28	Income Tax Expense	20,000				20,000			
29	Totals	1,508,500	1,508,500	**418,000**	**48,000**				
30	**Cost of Goods Manufactured**				**370,000**	**370,000**			
31	Totals			**418,000**	**418,000**	622,100	699,500	905,900	828,500
32	Net Income					77,400			77,400
33	Totals					699,500	699,500	905,900	905,900
34									

Closing Entries

The closing entries are different for manufacturing and merchandising companies. Manufacturing companies use a Manufacturing Summary account to close all accounts that appear in the cost of goods manufactured schedule. The balance of the Manufacturing Summary account is the Cost of Goods Manufactured for the period. Manufacturing Summary is then closed to Income Summary.

Companies can prepare the closing entries from the worksheet. As illustrated below, they first prepare the closing entries for the manufacturing accounts. The closing entries for Olsen Manufacturing are as follows.

Dec. 31	Work in Process Inventory (Dec. 31)	25,200	
	Raw Materials Inventory (Dec. 31)	22,800	
	Manufacturing Summary		**48,000**
	(To record ending raw materials and work in process inventories)		

(The closing entries continue on the next page.)

Date	Account Titles and Explanation	Debit	Credit
Dec. 31	**Manufacturing Summary**	**418,000**	
	Work in Process Inventory (Jan. 1)		18,400
	Raw Materials Inventory (Jan. 1)		16,700
	Raw Materials Purchases		152,500
	Direct Labor		175,600
	Indirect Labor		14,300
	Factory Repairs		12,600
	Factory Utilities		10,100
	Factory Depreciation		9,440
	Factory Insurance		8,360
	(To close beginning raw materials and work in process inventories and manufacturing cost accounts)		
31	Finished Goods Inventory (Dec. 31)	19,500	
	Sales	680,000	
	Income Summary		699,500
	(To record ending finished goods inventory and close sales account)		
31	Income Summary	622,100	
	Finished Goods Inventory (Jan. 1)		24,600
	Manufacturing Summary		**370,000**
	Selling Expenses		114,900
	Administrative Expenses		92,600
	Income Tax Expense		20,000
	(To close beginning finished goods inventory, manufacturing summary, and expense accounts)		
31	Income Summary	77,400	
	Retained Earnings		77,400
	(To close net income to retained earnings)		

After posting, the summary accounts will show the following.

Illustration 1A-3
Summary accounts for a manufacturing company, after posting

Manufacturing Summary

Date		Debit	Date		Credit
Dec. 31	Close	418,000	Dec. 31	Close	48,000
			31	Close	370,000

Income Summary

Date		Debit	Date		Credit
Dec. 31	Close	622,100	Dec. 31	Close	699,500
31	Close	77,400			

SUMMARY OF STUDY OBJECTIVE FOR APPENDIX

9 **Prepare a worksheet and closing entries for a manufacturing company.** The worksheet for the cost of goods manufactured needs two additional columns. In these columns, manufacturing companies enter the beginning inventories of raw materials and work in process as debits, and the ending inventories as credits. All manufacturing costs are entered as debits. To close all of the accounts that appear in the cost of goods manufactured schedule, manufacturers use a Manufacturing Summary account.

GLOSSARY

Activity-based costing (ABC) A method of allocating overhead based on each product's use of activities in making the product. (p. 21).

Balanced scorecard A performance-measurement approach that uses both financial and nonfinancial measures, tied to company objectives, to evaluate a company's operations in an integrated fashion. (p. 22).

Board of directors The group of officials elected by the stockholders of a corporation to formulate operating policies, select officers, and otherwise manage the company. (p. 8)

Chief executive officer (CEO) Corporate officer who has overall responsibility for managing the business and delegates responsibilities to other corporate officers. (p. 8)

Chief financial officer (CFO) Corporate officer who is responsible for all of the accounting and finance issues of the company. (p. 8)

Controller Financial officer responsible for a company's accounting records, system of internal control, and preparation of financial statements, tax returns, and internal reports. (p. 8)

Cost of goods manufactured Total cost of work in process less the cost of the ending work in process inventory. (p. 14).

Direct labor The work of factory employees that can be physically and directly associated with converting raw materials into finished goods. (p. 11).

Direct materials Raw materials that can be physically and directly associated with manufacturing the finished product. (p. 10).

Enterprise resource planning (ERP) system Software that provides a comprehensive, centralized, integrated source of information used to manage all major business processes. (p. 19).

Indirect labor Work of factory employees that has no physical association with the finished product, or for which it is impractical to trace the costs to the goods produced. (p. 11).

Indirect materials Raw materials that do not physically become part of the finished product or cannot be traced because their physical association with the finished product is too small. (p. 10).

Just-in-time (JIT) inventory Inventory system in which goods are manufactured or purchased just in time for use. (p. 20).

Line positions Jobs that are directly involved in a company's primary revenue-generating operating activities. (p. 8).

Managerial accounting A field of accounting that provides economic and financial information for managers and other internal users. (p. 4).

Manufacturing overhead Manufacturing costs that are indirectly associated with the manufacture of the finished product. (p. 11).

Period costs Costs that are matched with the revenue of a specific time period and charged to expense as incurred. (p. 12).

Product costs Costs that are a necessary and integral part of producing the finished product. (p. 12).

Sarbanes-Oxley Act of 2002 (SOX) Law passed by Congress in 2002 intended to reduce unethical corporate behavior. (p. 9).

Staff positions Jobs that support the efforts of line employees. (p. 8).

Theory of constraints A specific approach used to identify and manage constraints in order to achieve the company's goals. (p. 21).

Total cost of work in process Cost of the beginning work in process plus total manufacturing costs for the current period. (p. 14).

Total manufacturing costs The sum of direct materials, direct labor, and manufacturing overhead incurred in the current period. (p. 14).

Total quality management (TQM) Systems implemented to reduce defects in finished products with the goal of achieving zero defects. (p. 20).

Treasurer Financial officer responsible for custody of a company's funds and for maintaining its cash position. (p. 8).

Value chain All activities associated with providing a product or service. (p. 19).

Demonstration Problem

*Demonstration Problems are a final review before you begin homework. An **Action Plan** that appears in the margin gives you tips about how to approach the problem, and the **Solution** provided demonstrates both the form and content of complete answers.*

Superior Manufacturing Company has the following cost and expense data for the year ending December 31, 2008.

Raw materials, 1/1/08	$ 30,000	Insurance, factory	$ 14,000
Raw materials, 12/31/08	20,000	Property taxes, factory building	6,000
Raw materials purchases	205,000	Sales (net)	1,500,000
Indirect materials	15,000	Delivery expenses	100,000
Work in process, 1/1/08	80,000	Sales commissions	150,000
Work in process, 12/31/08	50,000	Indirect labor	90,000
Finished goods, 1/1/08	110,000	Factory machinery rent	40,000
Finished goods, 12/31/08	120,000	Factory utilities	65,000
Direct labor	350,000	Depreciation, factory building	24,000
Factory manager's salary	35,000	Administrative expenses	300,000

Instructions

(a) Prepare a cost of goods manufactured schedule for Superior Company for 2008.

(b) Prepare an income statement for Superior Company for 2008.

(c) Assume that Superior Company's ledgers show the balances of the following current asset accounts: Cash $17,000, Accounts Receivable (net) $120,000, Prepaid Expenses $13,000, and Short-term Investments $26,000. Prepare the current assets section of the balance sheet for Superior Company as of December 31, 2008.

Solution

(a)

SUPERIOR MANUFACTURING COMPANY
Cost of Goods Manufactured Schedule
For the Year Ended December 31, 2008

Work in process, 1/1			$ 80,000
Direct materials			
Raw materials inventory, 1/1	$ 30,000		
Raw materials purchases	205,000		
Total raw materials available for use	235,000		
Less: Raw materials inventory, 12/31	20,000		
Direct materials used		$215,000	
Direct labor		350,000	
Manufacturing overhead			
Indirect labor	90,000		
Factory utilities	65,000		
Factory machinery rent	40,000		
Factory manager's salary	35,000		
Depreciation on building	24,000		
Indirect materials	15,000		
Factory insurance	14,000		
Property taxes	6,000		
Total manufacturing overhead		289,000	
Total manufacturing costs			854,000
Total cost of work in process			934,000
Less: Work in process, 12/31			50,000
Cost of goods manufactured			$884,000

action plan

- ✔ Start with beginning work in process as the first item in the cost of goods manufactured schedule.
- ✔ Sum direct materials used, direct labor, and total manufacturing overhead to determine total manufacturing costs.
- ✔ Sum beginning work in process and total manufacturing costs to determine total cost of work in process.
- ✔ Cost of goods manufactured is the total cost of work in process less ending work in process.
- ✔ In the cost of goods sold section of the income statement, show beginning and ending finished goods inventory and cost of goods manufactured.
- ✔ In the balance sheet, list manufacturing inventories in the order of their expected realization in cash, with finished goods first.

(b)

SUPERIOR MANUFACTURING COMPANY
Income Statement
For the Year Ended December 31, 2008

Sales (net)		$1,500,000
Cost of goods sold		
Finished goods inventory, January 1	$110,000	
Cost of goods manufactured	884,000	
Cost of goods available for sale	994,000	
Less: Finished goods inventory, December 31	120,000	
Cost of goods sold		874,000
Gross profit		626,000
Operating expenses		
Administrative expenses	300,000	
Sales commissions	150,000	
Delivery expenses	100,000	
Total operating expenses		550,000
Net income		$ 76,000

(c)

SUPERIOR MANUFACTURING COMPANY
Balance Sheet (partial)
December 31, 2008

Current assets		
Cash		$ 17,000
Short-term investments		26,000
Accounts receivable (net)		120,000
Inventories		
Finished goods	$120,000	
Work in process	50,000	
Raw materials	20,000	190,000
Prepaid expenses		13,000
Total current assets		$366,000

The Navigator

This would be a good time to return to the ***Student Owner's Manual*** *at the beginning of the book (or look at it for the first time if you skipped it before) to read about the various types of homework materials that appear at the ends of chapters. Knowing the purpose of different assignments will help you appreciate what each contributes to your accounting skills and competencies.*

Note: All asterisked Questions, Exercises, and Problems relate to material in the appendix to the chapter.

SELF-STUDY QUESTIONS

Answers are at the end of the chapter.

(SO 1) **1.** Managerial accounting:
a. is governed by generally accepted accounting principles.
b. places emphasis on special-purpose information.
c. pertains to the entity as a whole and is highly aggregated.
d. is limited to cost data.

(SO 2) **2.** The management of an organization performs several broad functions. They are:
a. planning, directing, and selling.
b. planning, directing, and controlling.
c. planning, manufacturing, and controlling.
d. directing, manufacturing, and controlling.

3. Direct materials are a: (SO 3)

	Product Cost	Manufacturing Overhead	Period Cost
a.	Yes	Yes	No
b.	Yes	No	No
c.	Yes	Yes	Yes
d.	No	No	No

(SO 4) 4. Indirect labor is a:
a. nonmanufacturing cost.
b. raw material cost.
c. product cost.
d. period cost.

(SO 3) 5. Which of the following costs would a computer manufacturer include in manufacturing overhead?
a. The cost of the disk drives.
b. The wages earned by computer assemblers.
c. The cost of the memory chips.
d. Depreciation on testing equipment.

(SO 3) 6. Which of the following is *not* an element of manufacturing overhead?
a. Sales manager's salary.
b. Plant manager's salary.
c. Factory repairman's wages.
d. Product inspector's salary.

(SO 5) 7. For the year, Redder Company has cost of goods manufactured of $600,000, beginning finished goods inventory of $200,000, and ending finished goods inventory of $250,000. The cost of goods sold is:
a. $450,000.
b. $500,000.
c. $550,000.
d. $600,000.

8. A cost of goods manufactured schedule shows beginning and ending inventories for: (SO 6)
a. raw materials and work in process only.
b. work in process only.
c. raw materials only.
d. raw materials, work in process, and finished goods.

9. A manufacturer may report three inventories on its balance sheet: (1) raw materials, (2) work in process, and (3) finished goods. Indicate in what sequence these inventories generally appear on a balance sheet. (SO 7)
a. (1), (2), (3)
b. (2), (3), (1)
c. (3), (1), (2)
d. (3), (2), (1)

10. Which of the following managerial accounting techniques attempts to allocate manufacturing overhead in a more meaningful fashion? (SO 8)
a. Just-in-time inventory.
b. Total-quality management.
c. Balanced scorecard.
d. Activity-based costing.

Go to the book's website, **www.wiley.com/college/weygandt**, for Additional Self-Study questions.

QUESTIONS

1. **(a)** "Managerial accounting is a field of accounting that provides economic information for all interested parties." Do you agree? Explain.
   (b) Mary Barett believes that managerial accounting serves only manufacturing firms. Is Mary correct? Explain.
2. Distinguish between managerial and financial accounting as to (a) primary users of reports, (b) types and frequency of reports, and (c) purpose of reports.
3. How does the content of reports and the verification of reports differ between managerial and financial accounting?
4. In what ways can the budgeting process create incentives for unethical behavior?
5. Karen Fritz is studying for the next accounting mid-term examination. Summarize for Karen what she should know about management functions.
6. "Decision making is management's most important function." Do you agree? Why or why not?
7. Explain the primary difference between line positions and staff positions, and give examples of each.
8. What new rules were enacted under the Sarbanes-Oxley Act to address unethical accounting practices?
9. Stan Kaiser is studying for his next accounting examination. Explain to Stan what he should know about the differences between the income statements for a manufacturing and for a merchandising company.
10. Terry Lemay is unclear as to the difference between the balance sheets of a merchandising company and a manufacturing company. Explain the difference to Terry.
11. How are manufacturing costs classified?
12. Matt Litkee claims that the distinction between direct and indirect materials is based entirely on physical association with the product. Is Matt correct? Why?
13. Megan Neill is confused about the differences between a product cost and a period cost. Explain the differences to Megan.
14. Identify the differences in the cost of goods sold section of an income statement between a merchandising company and a manufacturing company.
15. The determination of the cost of goods manufactured involves the following factors: (A) beginning work in process inventory, (B) total manufacturing costs, and (C) ending work in process inventory. Identify the meaning of x in the following formulas:
   (a) $A + B = x$
   (b) $A + B - C = x$
16. Ohmie Manufacturing has beginning raw materials inventory $12,000, ending raw materials inventory $15,000, and raw materials purchases $170,000. What is the cost of direct materials used?
17. Neff Manufacturing Inc. has beginning work in process $26,000, direct materials used $240,000, direct labor $200,000, total manufacturing overhead $180,000, and ending work in process $32,000. What are total manufacturing costs?
18. Using the data in Q17, what are (a) the total cost of work in process and (b) the cost of goods manufactured?

19. In what order should manufacturing inventories be listed in a balance sheet?
20. What is the value chain? Describe, in sequence, the main components of a manufacturer's value chain.
21. What is an enterprise resource planning (ERP) system? What are its primary benefits?
22. Why is product quality important for companies that implement a just-in-time inventory system?
23. Explain what is meant by "balanced" in the balanced scorecard approach.
24. What is activity-based costing, and what are its potential benefits?

*25. How, if at all, does the accounting cycle differ between a manufacturing company and a merchandising company?

*26. What typical account balances are carried into the cost of goods manufactured columns of the manufacturing worksheet?

*27. Prepare the closing entries for (a) ending work in process and raw materials inventories and (b) manufacturing summary. Use XXXs for amounts.

BRIEF EXERCISES

Distinguish between managerial and financial accounting.
(SO 1)

BE1-1 Complete the following comparison table between managerial and financial accounting.

	Financial Accounting	Managerial Accounting
Primary users		
Types of reports		
Frequency of reports		
Purpose of reports		
Content of reports		
Verification		

Identify important regulatory changes.
(SO 2)

BE1-2 The Sarbanes-Oxley Act of 2002 (SOX) has important implications for the financial community. Explain two implications of SOX.

Identify the three management functions.
(SO 2)

BE1-3 Listed below are the three functions of the management of an organization.

1. Planning 2. Directing 3. Controlling

Identify which of the following statements best describes each of the above functions.

(a) ____ requires management to look ahead and to establish objectives. A key objective of management is to add value to the business.
(b) ____ involves coordinating the diverse activities and human resources of a company to produce a smooth-running operation. This function relates to the implementation of planned objectives.
(c) ____ is the process of keeping the activities on track. Management must determine whether goals are being met and what changes are necessary when there are deviations.

Classify manufacturing costs.
(SO 3)

BE1-4 Determine whether each of the following costs should be classified as direct materials (DM), direct labor (DL), or manufacturing overhead (MO).

(a) ____Frames and tires used in manufacturing bicycles.
(b) ____Wages paid to production workers.
(c) ____Insurance on factory equipment and machinery.
(d) ____Depreciation on factory equipment.

Classify manufacturing costs.
(SO 3)

BE1-5 Indicate whether each of the following costs of an automobile manufacturer would be classified as direct materials, direct labor, or manufacturing overhead.

(a) ____Windshield.
(b) ____Engine.
(c) ____Wages of assembly line worker.
(d) ____Depreciation of factory machinery.
(e) ____Factory machinery lubricants.
(f) ____Tires.
(g) ____Steering wheel.
(h) ____Salary of painting supervisor.

Identify product and period costs.
(SO 4)

BE1-6 Identify whether each of the following costs should be classified as product costs or period costs.

(a) ____Manufacturing overhead.
(b) ____Selling expenses.
(c) ____Administrative expenses.
(d) ____Advertising expenses.
(e) ____Direct labor.
(f) ____Direct material.

BE1-7 Presented below are Lang Company's monthly manufacturing cost data related to its personal computer products.

Classify manufacturing costs.
(SO 3)

(a) Utilities for manufacturing equipment	$116,000
(b) Raw material (CPU, chips, etc.)	$ 85,000
(c) Depreciation on manufacturing building	$880,000
(d) Wages for production workers	$191,000

Enter each cost item in the following table, placing an "X" under the appropriate headings.

	Product Costs		
	Direct Materials	**Direct Labor**	**Factory Overhead**
(a)			
(b)			
(c)			
(d)			

BE1-8 Francum Manufacturing Company has the following data: direct labor $229,000, direct materials used $180,000, total manufacturing overhead $208,000, and beginning work in process $25,000. Compute (a) total manufacturing costs and (b) total cost of work in process.

Compute total manufacturing costs and total cost of work in process.
(SO 6)

BE1-9 In alphabetical order below are current asset items for Dieker Company's balance sheet at December 31, 2008. Prepare the current assets section (including a complete heading).

Prepare current assets section.
(SO 7)

Accounts receivable	$200,000
Cash	62,000
Finished goods	71,000
Prepaid expenses	38,000
Raw materials	73,000
Work in process	87,000

BE1-10 Presented below are incomplete manufacturing cost data. Determine the missing amounts for three different situations.

Determine missing amounts in computing total manufacturing costs.
(SO 6)

	Direct Materials Used	Direct Labor Used	Factory Overhead	Total Manufacturing Costs
(1)	$25,000	$61,000	$ 50,000	?
(2)	?	$75,000	$140,000	$296,000
(3)	$55,000	?	$111,000	$310,000

BE1-11 Use the same data from BE1–10 above and the data below. Determine the missing amounts.

Determine missing amounts in computing cost of goods manufactured.
(SO 6)

	Total Manufacturing Costs	Work in Process (1/1)	Work in Process (12/31)	Cost of Goods Manufactured
(1)	?	$120,000	$82,000	?
(2)	$296,000	?	$98,000	$321,000
(3)	$310,000	$463,000	?	$715,000

***BE1-12** Table Manufacturing Company uses a worksheet in preparing financial statements. The following accounts are included in the adjusted trial balance: Finished Goods Inventory $28,000, Work in Process Inventory $21,600, Raw Materials Purchases $175,000, and Direct Labor $140,000. Indicate the worksheet column(s) to which each account should be extended.

Identify worksheet columns for selected accounts.
(SO 9)

EXERCISES

Identify distinguishing features of managerial accounting.
(SO 1)

E1-1 Chris Martin has prepared the following list of statements about managerial accounting and financial accounting.

1. Financial accounting focuses on providing information to internal users.
2. Analyzing cost-volume-profit relationships is part of managerial accounting.
3. Preparation of budgets is part of financial accounting.
4. Managerial accounting applies only to merchandising and manufacturing companies.
5. Both managerial accounting and financial accounting deal with many of the same economic events.
6. Managerial accounting reports are prepared only quarterly and annually.
7. Financial accounting reports are general-purpose reports.
8. Managerial accounting reports pertain to subunits of the business.
9. Managerial accounting reports must comply with generally accepted accounting principles.
10. Although managerial accountants are expected to behave ethically, there is no code of ethical standards for managerial accountants.

Instructions
Identify each statement as true or false. If false, indicate how to correct the statement.

Classify costs into three classes of manufacturing costs.
(SO 3)

E1-2 Presented below is a list of costs and expenses usually incurred by Burrand Corporation, a manufacturer of furniture, in its factory.

1. Salaries for assembly line inspectors.
2. Insurance on factory machines.
3. Property taxes on the factory building.
4. Factory repairs.
5. Upholstery used in manufacturing furniture.
6. Wages paid to assembly line workers.
7. Factory machinery depreciation.
8. Glue, nails, paint, and other small parts used in production.
9. Factory supervisors' salaries.
10. Wood used in manufacturing furniture.

Instructions
Classify the above items into the following categories: (a) direct materials, (b) direct labor, and (c) manufacturing overhead.

Identify types of cost and explain their accounting.
(SO 3, 4)

E1-3 Coldplay Corporation incurred the following costs while manufacturing its product.

Materials used in product	$100,000	Advertising expense	$45,000
Depreciation on plant	60,000	Property taxes on plant	14,000
Property taxes on store	7,500	Delivery expense	21,000
Labor costs of assembly-line workers	110,000	Sales commissions	35,000
Factory supplies used	13,000	Salaries paid to sales clerks	50,000

Instructions
(a) Identify each of the above costs as direct materials, direct labor, manufacturing overhead, or period costs.
(b) Explain the basic difference in accounting for product costs and period costs.

Determine the total amount of various types of costs.
(SO 3, 4),

E1-4 Caroline Company reports the following costs and expenses in May.

Factory utilities	$ 11,500	Direct labor	$69,100
Depreciation on factory equipment	12,650	Sales salaries	46,400
Depreciation on delivery trucks	3,800	Property taxes on factory building	2,500
Indirect factory labor	48,900	Repairs to office equipment	1,300
Indirect materials	80,800	Factory repairs	2,000
Direct materials used	137,600	Advertising	18,000
Factory manager's salary	8,000	Office supplies used	2,640

Instructions
From the information, determine the total amount of:

(a) Manufacturing overhead.
(b) Product costs.
(c) Period costs.

E1-5 Sota Company is a manufacturer of personal computers. Various costs and expenses associated with its operations are as follows.

Classify various costs into different cost categories.
(SO 3, 4)

1. Property taxes on the factory building.
2. Production superintendents' salaries.
3. Memory boards and chips used in assembling computers.
4. Depreciation on the factory equipment.
5. Salaries for assembly line quality control inspectors.
6. Sales commissions paid to sell personal computers.
7. Electrical components used in assembling computers.
8. Wages of workers assembling personal computers.
9. Soldering materials used on factory assembly lines.
10. Salaries for the night security guards for the factory building.

The company intends to classify these costs and expenses into the following categories: (a) direct materials, (b) direct labor, (c) manufacturing overhead, and (d) period costs.

Instructions
List the items (1) through (10). For each item, indicate the cost category to which it belongs.

E1-6 The administrators of San Diego County's Memorial Hospital are interested in identifying the various costs and expenses that are incurred in producing a patient's X-ray. A list of such costs and expenses in presented below.

Classify various costs into different cost categories.
(SO 3)

Homework materials related to service companies are indicated by this icon.

1. Salaries for the X-ray machine technicians.
2. Wages for the hospital janitorial personnel.
3. Film costs for the X-ray machines.
4. Property taxes on the hospital building.
5. Salary of the X-ray technicians' supervisor.
6. Electricity costs for the X-ray department.
7. Maintenance and repairs on the X-ray machines.
8. X-ray department supplies.
9. Depreciation on the X-ray department equipment.
10. Depreciation on the hospital building.

The administrators want these costs and expenses classified as: (a) direct materials, (b) direct labor, or (c) service overhead.

Instructions
List the items (1) through (10). For each item, indicate the cost category to which the item belongs.

E1-7 Rapid Delivery Service reports the following costs and expenses in June 2008.

Classify various costs into different cost categories.
(SO 4)

Indirect materials	$ 5,400	Drivers' salaries	$11,000
Depreciation on delivery equipment	11,200	Advertising	1,600
Dispatcher's salary	5,000	Delivery equipment repairs	300
Property taxes on office building	870	Office supplies	650
CEO's salary	12,000	Office utilities	990
Gas and oil for delivery trucks	2,200	Repairs on office equipment	180

Instructions
Determine the total amount of (a) delivery service (product) costs and (b) period costs.

Compute cost of goods manufactured and sold.
(SO 5, 6)

E1-8 Coldplay Corporation incurred the following costs while manufacturing its product.

Materials used in product	$100,000	Advertising expense	$45,000
Depreciation on plant	60,000	Property taxes on plant	14,000
Property taxes on store	7,500	Delivery expense	21,000
Labor costs of assembly-line workers	110,000	Sales commissions	35,000
Factory supplies used	23,000	Salaries paid to sales clerks	50,000

Work-in-process inventory was $12,000 at January 1 and $15,500 at December 31. Finished goods inventory was $60,000 at January 1 and $55,600 at December 31.

Instructions
(a) Compute cost of goods manufactured.
(b) Compute cost of goods sold.

Determine missing amounts in cost of goods manufactured schedule.
(SO 6)

E1-9 An incomplete cost of goods manufactured schedule is presented below.

CEPEDA MANUFACTURING COMPANY
Cost of Goods Manufactured Schedule
For the Year Ended December 31, 2008

Work in process (1/1)			$210,000
Direct materials			
Raw materials inventory (1/1)	$?		
Add: Raw materials purchases	158,000		
Total raw materials available for use	?		
Less: Raw materials inventory (12/31)	12,500		
Direct materials used		$190,000	
Direct labor		?	
Manufacturing overhead			
Indirect labor	$ 18,000		
Factory depreciation	36,000		
Factory utilities	68,000		
Total overhead		122,000	
Total manufacturing costs			?
Total cost of work in process			?
Less: Work in process (12/31)			81,000
Cost of goods manufactured			$510,000

Instructions
Complete the cost of goods manufactured schedule for Cepeda Manufacturing Company.

Determine the missing amount of different cost items.
(SO 6)

E1-10 Manufacturing cost data for Criqui Company are presented below.

	Case A	Case B	Case C
Direct materials used	(a)	$58,400	$130,000
Direct labor	$ 57,000	86,000	(g)
Manufacturing overhead	46,500	81,600	102,000
Total manufacturing costs	185,650	(d)	253,700
Work in process 1/1/08	(b)	16,500	(h)
Total cost of work in process	221,500	(e)	337,000
Work in process 12/31/08	(c)	11,000	70,000
Cost of goods manufactured	185,275	(f)	(i)

Instructions
Indicate the missing amount for each letter (a) through (i).

Determine the missing amount of different cost items, and prepare a condensed cost of goods manufactured schedule.
(SO 6)

E1-11 Incomplete manufacturing cost data for Ikerd Company for 2008 are presented as follows for four different situations.

	Direct Materials Used	Direct Labor Used	Manufacturing Overhead	Total Manufacturing Costs	Work in Process 1/1	Work in Process 12/31	Cost of Goods Manufactured
(1)	$127,000	$140,000	$ 77,000	(a)	$33,000	(b)	$360,000
(2)	(c)	200,000	132,000	$450,000	(d)	$40,000	470,000
(3)	80,000	100,000	(e)	245,000	60,000	80,000	(f)
(4)	70,000	(g)	75,000	288,000	45,000	(h)	270,000

Instructions

(a) Indicate the missing amount for each letter.

(b) Prepare a condensed cost of goods manufactured schedule for situation (1) for the year ended December 31, 2008.

Prepare a cost of goods manufactured schedule and a partial income statement.

(SO 5, 6)

E1-12 Aikman Corporation has the following cost records for June 2008.

Indirect factory labor	$ 4,500	Factory utilities	$ 400
Direct materials used	20,000	Depreciation, factory equipment	1,400
Work in process, 6/1/08	3,000	Direct labor	30,000
Work in process, 6/30/08	3,800	Maintenance, factory equipment	1,800
Finished goods, 6/1/08	5,000	Indirect materials	2,200
Finished goods, 6/30/08	7,500	Factory manager's salary	3,000

Instructions

(a) Prepare a cost of goods manufactured schedule for June 2008.

(b) Prepare an income statement through gross profit for June 2008 assuming net sales are $87,100.

Classify various costs into different categories and prepare cost of services provided schedule.

(SO 4, 5, 6)

E1-13 Sara Collier, the bookkeeper for Danner, Cheney, and Howe, a political consulting firm, has recently completed a managerial accounting course at her local college. One of the topics covered in the course was the cost of goods manufactured schedule. Sara wondered if such a schedule could be prepared for her firm. She realized that, as a service-oriented company, it would have no Work-in-Process inventory to consider.

Listed below are the costs her firm incurred for the month ended August 31, 2008.

Supplies used on consulting contracts	$ 1,200
Supplies used in the administrative offices	1,500
Depreciation on equipment used for contract work	900
Depreciation used on administrative office equipment	1,050
Salaries of professionals working on contracts	12,600
Salaries of administrative office personnel	7,700
Janitorial services for professional offices	400
Janitorial services for administrative offices	500
Insurance on contract operations	800
Insurance on administrative operations	900
Utilities for contract operations	1,400
Utilities for administrative offices	1,300

Instructions

(a) Prepare a schedule of cost of contract services provided (similar to a cost of goods manufactured schedule) for the month.

(b) For those costs not included in (a), explain how they would be classified and reported in the financial statements.

Prepare a cost of goods manufactured schedule and a partial income statement.

(SO 5, 6, 7)

E1-14 The following information is available for Sassafras Company.

	January 1, 2008	2008	December 31, 2008
Raw materials inventory	$ 21,000		$30,000
Work in process inventory	13,500		17,200
Finished goods inventory	27,000		21,000
Materials purchased		$150,000	
Direct labor		200,000	
Manufacturing overhead		180,000	
Sales		900,000	

Instructions

(a) Compute cost of goods manufactured.
(b) Prepare an income statement through gross profit.
(c) Show the presentation of the ending inventories on the December 31, 2008 balance sheet.
(d) How would the income statement and balance sheet of a merchandising company be different from Sassafras's financial statements?

Indicate in which schedule or financial statement(s) different cost items will appear.

(SO 5, 6, 7)

E1-15 Corbin Manufacturing Company produces blankets. From its accounting records it prepares the following schedule and financial statements on a yearly basis.

(a) Cost of goods manufactured schedule.
(b) Income statement.
(c) Balance sheet.

The following items are found in its ledger and accompanying data.

1. Direct labor
2. Raw materials inventory, 1/1
3. Work in process inventory, 12/31
4. Finished goods inventory, 1/1
5. Indirect labor
6. Depreciation on factory machinery
7. Work in process, 1/1
8. Finished goods inventory, 12/31
9. Factory maintenance salaries
10. Cost of goods manufactured
11. Depreciation on delivery equipment
12. Cost of goods available for sale
13. Direct materials used
14. Heat and electricity for factory
15. Repairs to roof of factory building
16. Cost of raw materials purchases

Instructions

List the items (1)–(16). For each item, indicate by using the appropriate letter or letters, the schedule and/or financial statement(s) in which the item will appear.

Prepare a cost of goods manufactured schedule, and present the ending inventories of the balance sheet.

(SO 6, 7)

E1-16 An analysis of the accounts of Chamberlin Manufacturing reveals the following manufacturing cost data for the month ended June 30, 2008.

Inventories	Beginning	Ending
Raw materials	$9,000	$13,100
Work in process	5,000	7,000
Finished goods	9,000	6,000

Costs incurred: Raw materials purchases $54,000, direct labor $57,000, manufacturing overhead $19,900. The specific overhead costs were: indirect labor $5,500, factory insurance $4,000, machinery depreciation $4,000, machinery repairs $1,800, factory utilities $3,100, miscellaneous factory costs $1,500. Assume that all raw materials used were direct materials.

Instructions

(a) Prepare the cost of goods manufactured schedule for the month ended June 30, 2008.
(b) Show the presentation of the ending inventories on the June 30, 2008, balance sheet.

Determine the amount of cost to appear in various accounts, and indicate in which financial statements these accounts would appear.

(SO 5, 6, 7)

E1-17 Todd Motor Company manufactures automobiles. During September 2008 the company purchased 5,000 head lamps at a cost of $9 per lamp. Todd withdrew 4,650 lamps from the warehouse during the month. Fifty of these lamps were used to replace the head lamps in autos used by traveling sales staff. The remaining 4,600 lamps were put in autos manufactured during the month.

Of the autos put into production during September 2008, 90% were completed and transferred to the company's storage lot. Of the cars completed during the month, 75% were sold by September 30.

Instructions

(a) Determine the cost of head lamps that would appear in each of the following accounts at September 30, 2008: Raw Materials, Work in Process, Finished Goods, Cost of Goods Sold, and Selling Expenses.
(b) Write a short memo to the chief accountant, indicating whether and where each of the accounts in (a) would appear on the income statement or on the balance sheet at September 30, 2008.

E1-18 The following is a list of terms related to managerial accounting practices.

Identify various managerial accounting practices.
(SO 8)

1. Activity-based costing.
2. Just-in-time inventory.
3. Balanced scorecard.
4. Value chain.

Instructions
Match each of the terms with the statement below that best describes the term.

(a) ____ A performance-measurement technique that attempts to consider and evaluate all aspects of performance using financial and nonfinancial measures in an integrated fashion.
(b) ____ The group of activities associated with providing a product or service.
(c) ____ An approach used to reduce the cost associated with handling and holding inventory by reducing the amount of inventory on hand.
(d) ____ A method used to allocate overhead to products based on each product's use of the activities that cause the incurrence of the overhead cost.

***E1-19** Data for Chamberlin Manufacturing are presented in E1-16.

Prepare a partial worksheet for a manufacturing firm.
(SO 9)

Instructions
Beginning with the adjusted trial balance, prepare a partial worksheet for Chamberlin Manufacturing using the format shown in Illustration 1A-2.

EXERCISES: SET B

Visit the book's website at **www.wiley.com/college/weygandt**, and choose the Student Companion site, to access Exercise Set B.

PROBLEMS: SET A

P1-1A Bjerg Company specializes in manufacturing a unique model of bicycle helmet. The model is well accepted by consumers, and the company has enough orders to keep the factory production at 10,000 helmets per month (80% of its full capacity). Bjerg's monthly manufacturing cost and other expense data are as follows.

Classify manufacturing costs into different categories and compute the unit cost.
(SO 3, 4)

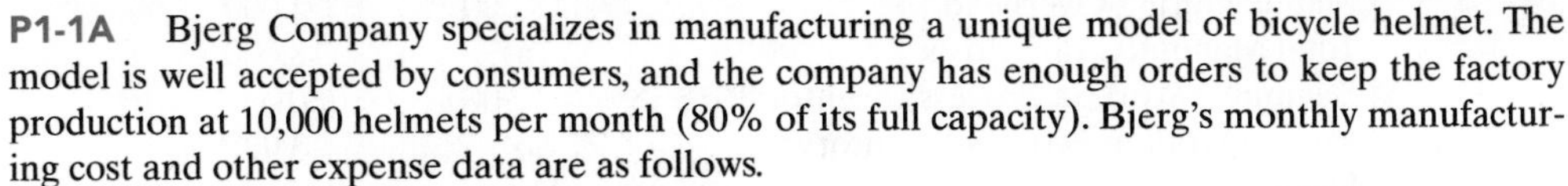

Rent on factory equipment	$ 7,000
Insurance on factory building	1,500
Raw materials (plastics, polystyrene, etc.)	75,000
Utility costs for factory	900
Supplies for general office	300
Wages for assembly line workers	43,000
Depreciation on office equipment	800
Miscellaneous materials (glue, thread, etc.)	1,100
Factory manager's salary	5,700
Property taxes on factory building	400
Advertising for helmets	14,000
Sales commissions	7,000
Depreciation on factory building	1,500

Marginal check figures for parts of some problems, in most chapters, provide key numbers to confirm that you are on the right track in your computations.

(a) DM $75,000
DL $43,000
MO $18,100
PC $22,100

Instructions

(a) Prepare an answer sheet with the following column headings.

Cost Item	Direct Materials	Direct Labor	Manufacturing Overhead	Period Costs
	Product Costs			

Enter each cost item on your answer sheet, placing the dollar amount under the appropriate headings. Total the dollar amounts in each of the columns.

(b) Compute the cost to produce one helmet

Classify manufacturing costs into different categories and compute the unit cost.

(SO 3, 4)

P1-2A Copa Company, a manufacturer of stereo systems, started its production in October 2008. For the preceding 3 years Copa had been a retailer of stereo systems. After a thorough survey of stereo system markets, Copa decided to turn its retail store into a stereo equipment factory.

Raw materials cost for a stereo system will total $74 per unit. Workers on the production lines are on average paid $12 per hour. A stereo system usually takes 5 hours to complete. In addition, the rent on the equipment used to assemble stereo systems amounts to $4,900 per month. Indirect materials cost $5 per system. A supervisor was hired to oversee production; her monthly salary is $3,000.

Factory janitorial costs are $1,300 monthly. Advertising costs for the stereo system will be $8,500 per month. The factory building depreciation expense is $7,200 per year. Property taxes on the factory building will be $9,000 per year.

(a) DM $96,200
DL $78,000
MO $17,050
PC $ 8,500

Instructions

(a) Prepare an answer sheet with the following column headings.

Cost Item	Direct Materials	Direct Labor	Manufacturing Overhead	Period Costs
	Product Costs			

Assuming that Copa manufactures, on average, 1,300 stereo systems per month, enter each cost item on your answer sheet, placing the dollar amount per month under the appropriate headings. Total the dollar amounts in each of the columns.

(b) Compute the cost to produce one stereo system.

Indicate the missing amount of different cost items, and prepare a condensed cost of goods manufactured schedule, an income statement, and a partial balance sheet.

(SO 5, 6, 7)

P1-3A Incomplete manufacturing costs, expenses, and selling data for two different cases are as follows.

	Case 1	Case 2
Direct Materials Used	$ 7,600	$ (g)
Direct Labor	5,000	8,000
Manufacturing Overhead	8,000	4,000
Total Manufacturing Costs	(a)	18,000
Beginning Work in Process Inventory	1,000	(h)
Ending Work in Process Inventory	(b)	3,000
Sales	24,500	(i)
Sales Discounts	2,500	1,400
Cost of Goods Manufactured	17,000	22,000
Beginning Finished Goods Inventory	(c)	3,300
Goods Available for Sale	18,000	(j)
Cost of Goods Sold	(d)	(k)
Ending Finished Goods Inventory	3,400	2,500
Gross Profit	(e)	7,000
Operating Expenses	2,500	(l)
Net Income	(f)	5,000

Instructions

(a) Indicate the missing amount for each letter.

(b) Ending WIP $4,600

(b) Prepare a condensed cost of goods manufactured schedule for Case 1.

(c) Prepare an income statement and the current assets section of the balance sheet for Case 1. Assume that in Case 1 the other items in the current assets section are as follows: Cash $4,000, Receivables (net) $15,000, Raw Materials $600, and Prepaid Expenses $400.

(c) Current assets $28,000

P1-4A The following data were taken from the records of Stellar Manufacturing Company for the fiscal year ended June 30, 2008.

Prepare a cost of goods manufactured schedule, a partial income statement, and a partial balance sheet.

(SO 5, 6, 7)

Raw Materials Inventory 7/1/07	$ 48,000	Factory Insurance	$ 4,600
Raw Materials Inventory 6/30/08	39,600	Factory Machinery Depreciation	16,000
Finished Goods Inventory 7/1/07	96,000	Factory Utilities	27,600
Finished Goods Inventory 6/30/08	95,900	Office Utilities Expense	8,650
Work in Process Inventory 7/1/07	19,800	Sales	554,000
Work in Process Inventory 6/30/08	18,600	Sales Discounts	4,200
Direct Labor	149,250	Plant Manager's Salary	29,000
Indirect Labor	24,460	Factory Property Taxes	9,600
Accounts Receivable	27,000	Factory Repairs	1,400
		Raw Materials Purchases	96,400
		Cash	32,000

Instructions

(a) Prepare a cost of goods manufactured schedule. (Assume all raw materials used were direct materials.)

(b) Prepare an income statement through gross profit.

(c) Prepare the current assets section of the balance sheet at June 30, 2008.

(a) CGM $367,910

(b) Gross profit $181,790

(c) Current assets $213,100

P1-5A Tombert Company is a manufacturer of computers. Its controller resigned in October 2008. An inexperienced assistant accountant has prepared the following income statement for the month of October 2008.

Prepare a cost of goods manufactured schedule and a correct income statement.

(SO 5, 6)

TOMBERT COMPANY
Income Statement
For the Month Ended October 31, 2008

Sales (net)		$780,000
Less: Operating expenses		
Raw materials purchases	$264,000	
Direct labor cost	190,000	
Advertising expense	90,000	
Selling and administrative salaries	75,000	
Rent on factory facilities	60,000	
Depreciation on sales equipment	45,000	
Depreciation on factory equipment	31,000	
Indirect labor cost	28,000	
Utilities expense	12,000	
Insurance expense	8,000	803,000
Net loss		$(23,000)

Prior to October 2008 the company had been profitable every month. The company's president is concerned about the accuracy of the income statement. As his friend, you have been asked to review the income statement and make necessary corrections. After examining other manufacturing cost data, you have acquired additional information as follows.

1. Inventory balances at the beginning and end of October were:

	October 1	October 31
Raw materials	$18,000	$34,000
Work in process	16,000	14,000
Finished goods	30,000	48,000

2. Only 70% of the utilities expense and 60% of the insurance expense apply to factory operations. The remaining amounts should be charged to selling and administrative activities.

(a) CGM $572,200
(b) NI $ 9,000

Instructions

(a) Prepare a schedule of cost of goods manufactured for October 2008.
(b) Prepare a correct income statement for October 2008.

Complete a worksheet; prepare a cost of goods manufactured schedule, an income statement, and a balance sheet; journalize and post the closing entries.

(SO 9)

***P1-6A** Medina Manufacturing Company uses a simple manufacturing accounting system. At the end of its fiscal year on August 31, 2008, the adjusted trial balance contains the following accounts.

Debits		Credits	
Cash	$ 16,700	Accumulated Depreciation	$353,000
Accounts Receivable (net)	62,900	Notes Payable	45,000
Finished Goods Inventory	56,000	Accounts Payable	36,200
Work in Process Inventory	27,800	Income Taxes Payable	9,000
Raw Materials Inventory	37,200	Common Stock	352,000
Plant Assets	890,000	Retained Earnings	205,300
Raw Materials Purchases	236,500	Sales	998,000
Direct Labor	283,900		$1,998,500
Indirect Labor	27,400		
Factory Repairs	17,200		
Factory Depreciation	16,000		
Factory Manager's Salary	40,000		
Factory Insurance	11,000		
Factory Property Taxes	14,900		
Factory Utilities	13,300		
Selling Expenses	96,500		
Administrative Expenses	115,200		
Income Tax Expense	36,000		
	$1,998,500		

Physical inventory accounts on August 31, 2008, show the following inventory amounts: Finished Goods $50,600, Work in Process $23,400, and Raw Materials $44,500.

Instructions

(a) Enter the adjusted trial balance data on a worksheet in financial statement order and complete the worksheet.
(b) Prepare a cost of goods manufactured schedule for the year.
(c) Prepare an income statement for the year and a balance sheet at August 31, 2008.
(d) Journalize the closing entries.
(e) Post the closing entries to Manufacturing Summary and to Income Summary.

(b) CGM $657,300
(c) NI $ 87,600

PROBLEMS: SET B

Classify manufacturing costs into different categories and compute the unit cost.

(SO 3, 4)

P1-1B Hite Company specializes in manufacturing motorcycle helmets. The company has enough orders to keep the factory production at 1,000 motorcycle helmets per month. Hite's monthly manufacturing cost and other expense data are as follows.

Maintenance costs on factory building	$ 600
Factory manager's salary	4,000
Advertising for helmets	8,000
Sales commissions	3,000
Depreciation on factory building	700
Rent on factory equipment	6,000
Insurance on factory building	3,000
Raw materials (plastic, polystyrene, etc.)	20,000
Utility costs for factory	800
Supplies for general office	200
Wages for assembly line workers	44,000
Depreciation on office equipment	500
Miscellaneous materials (glue, thread, etc.)	2,000

Instructions

(a) Prepare an answer sheet with the following column headings.

	Product Costs			
Cost Item	Direct Materials	Direct Labor	Manufacturing Overhead	Period Costs

Enter each cost item on your answer sheet, placing the dollar amount under the appropriate headings. Total the dollar amounts in each of the columns.

(b) Compute the cost to produce one motorcycle helmet.

(a) DM $20,000
DL $44,000
MO $17,100
PC $11,700

not part of pdction cost

Classify manufacturing costs into different categories and compute the unit cost.

(SO 3, 4)

P1-2B Ladoca Company, a manufacturer of tennis rackets, started production in November 2008. For the preceding 5 years Ladoca had been a retailer of sports equipment. After a thorough survey of tennis racket markets, Ladoca decided to turn its retail store into a tennis racket factory.

Raw materials cost for a tennis racket will total $23 per racket. Workers on the production lines are paid on average $13 per hour. A racket usually takes 2 hours to complete. In addition, the rent on the equipment used to produce rackets amounts to $1,300 per month. Indirect materials cost $3 per racket. A supervisor was hired to oversee production; her monthly salary is $3,500.

Factory janitorial costs are $1,400 monthly. Advertising costs for the rackets will be $6,000 per month. The factory building depreciation expense is $8,400 per year. Property taxes on the factory building will be $5,400 per year.

Instructions

(a) Prepare an answer sheet with the following column headings.

	Product Costs			
Cost Item	Direct Materials	Direct Labor	Manufacturing Overhead	Period Costs

Assuming that Ladoca manufactures, on average, 2,000 tennis rackets per month, enter each cost item on your answer sheet, placing the dollar amount per month under the appropriate headings. Total the dollar amounts in each of the columns.

(b) Compute the cost to produce one racket.

(a) DM $46,000
DL $52,000
MO $13,350
PC $ 6,000

Indicate the missing amount of different cost items, and prepare a condensed cost of goods manufactured schedule, an income statement, and a partial balance sheet.

(SO 5, 6, 7)

P1-3B Incomplete manufacturing costs, expenses, and selling data for two different cases are as follows.

	Case 1	Case 2
Direct Materials Used	$ 8,300	$ (g)
Direct Labor	3,000	4,000
Manufacturing Overhead	6,000	5,000
Total Manufacturing Costs	(a)	18,000
Beginning Work in Process Inventory	1,000	(h)
Ending Work in Process Inventory	(b)	2,000
Sales	22,500	(i)
Sales Discounts	1,500	1,200
Cost of Goods Manufactured	15,800	20,000
Beginning Finished Goods Inventory	(c)	4,000
Goods Available for Sale	17,300	(j)
Cost of Goods Sold	(d)	(k)
Ending Finished Goods Inventory	1,200	2,500
Gross Profit	(e)	6,000
Operating Expenses	2,700	(l)
Net Income	(f)	3,200

Instructions

(a) Indicate the missing amount for each letter.

(b) Prepare a condensed cost of goods manufactured schedule for Case 1.

(c) Prepare an income statement and the current assets section of the balance sheet for Case 1. Assume that in Case 1 the other items in the current assets section are as follows: Cash $3,000, Receivables (net) $10,000, Raw Materials $700, and Prepaid Expenses $200.

(c) Current assets $17,600

Prepare a cost of goods manufactured schedule, a partial income statement, and a partial balance sheet.

(SO 5, 6, 7)

P1-4B The following data were taken from the records of Ruiz Manufacturing Company for the year ended December 31, 2008.

Raw Materials Inventory 1/1/08	$ 47,000	Factory Insurance	$ 7,400
Raw Materials Inventory 12/31/08	44,200	Factory Machinery Depreciation	7,700
Finished Goods Inventory 1/1/08	85,000	Factory Utilities	12,900
Finished Goods Inventory 12/31/08	77,800	Office Utilities Expense	8,600
Work in Process Inventory 1/1/08	9,500	Sales	475,000
Work in Process Inventory 12/31/08	8,000	Sales Discounts	2,500
Direct Labor	145,100	Plant Manager's Salary	30,000
Indirect Labor	18,100	Factory Property Taxes	6,100
Accounts Receivable	27,000	Factory Repairs	800
		Raw Materials Purchases	67,500
		Cash	28,000

Instructions

(a) CGM $299,900

(b) Gross profit $165,400

(c) Current assets $185,000

(a) Prepare a cost of goods manufactured schedule. (Assume all raw materials used were direct materials.)

(b) Prepare an income statement through gross profit.

(c) Prepare the current assets section of the balance sheet at December 31.

Prepare a cost of goods manufactured schedule and a correct income statement.

(SO 5, 6)

P1-5B Agler Company is a manufacturer of toys. Its controller, Joyce Rotzen, resigned in August 2008. An inexperienced assistant accountant has prepared the following income statement for the month of August 2008.

AGLER COMPANY
Income Statement
For the Month Ended August 31, 2008

Sales (net)		$675,000
Less: Operating expenses		
Raw materials purchases	$200,000	
Direct labor cost	160,000	
Advertising expense	75,000	
Selling and administrative salaries	70,000	
Rent on factory facilities	60,000	
Depreciation on sales equipment	50,000	
Depreciation on factory equipment	35,000	
Indirect labor cost	20,000	
Utilities expense	10,000	
Insurance expense	5,000	685,000
Net loss		$(10,000)

Prior to August 2008 the company had been profitable every month. The company's president is concerned about the accuracy of the income statement. As her friend, you have been asked to review the income statement and make necessary corrections. After examining other manufacturing cost data, you have acquired additional information as follows.

1. Inventory balances at the beginning and end of August were:

	August 1	August 31
Raw materials	$19,500	$30,000
Work in process	25,000	21,000
Finished goods	40,000	64,000

2. Only 60% of the utilities expense and 70% of the insurance expense apply to factory operations; the remaining amounts should be charged to selling and administrative activities.

Instructions

(a) Prepare a cost of goods manufactured schedule for August 2008.

(b) Prepare a correct income statement for August 2008.

(a) CGM $478,000
(b) NI $ 20,500

PROBLEMS: SET C

Visit the book's website at **www.wiley.com/college/weygandt**, and choose the Student Companion site, to access Problem Set C.

WATERWAYS CONTINUING PROBLEM

(*Note:* The Waterways Problem begins in Chapter 1 and continues in every chapter. You can also find this problem at the book's Student Companion site.)

The ***Waterways Problem*** *starts in this chapter and continues in every chapter. You will find the complete problem for each chapter at the book's companion website.*

WCP1 Waterways Corporation is a private corporation formed for the purpose of providing the products and the services needed to irrigate farms, parks, commercial projects, and private lawns. It has a centrally located factory in a U.S. city that manufactures the products it markets to retail outlets across the nation. It also maintains a division that provides installation and warranty servicing in six metropolitan areas.

The mission of Waterways is to manufacture quality parts that can be used for effective irrigation projects that also conserve water. By that effort, the company hopes to satisfy its customers, provide rapid and responsible service, and serve the community and the employees who represent them in each community.

The company has been growing rapidly, so management is considering new ideas to help the company continue its growth and maintain the high quality of its products.

Waterways was founded by Will Winkman, who is the company president and chief executive officer (CEO). Working with him from the company's inception was Will's brother, Ben, whose sprinkler designs and ideas about the installation of proper systems have been a major basis of the company's success. Ben is the vice president who oversees all aspects of design and production in the company.

The factory itself is managed by Todd Senter who hires his line managers to supervise the factory employees. The factory makes all of the parts for the irrigation systems. The purchasing department is managed by Hector Hines.

The installation and training division is overseen by vice president Henry Writer, who supervises the managers of the six local installation operations. Each of these local managers hires his or her own local service people. These service employees are trained by the home office under Henry Writer's direction because of the uniqueness of the company's products.

There is a small human resources department under the direction of Sally Fenton, a vice president who handles the employee paperwork, though hiring is actually performed by the separate departments. Sam Totter is the vice president who heads the sales and marketing area; he oversees 10 well-trained salespeople.

The accounting and finance division of the company is headed by Abe Headman, who is the chief financial officer (CFO) and a company vice president; he is a member of the Institute of Management Accountants and holds a certificate in management accounting. He has a small staff of Certified Public Accountants, including a controller and a treasurer, and a staff of accounting input operators who maintain the financial records.

A partial list of Waterway's accounts and their balances for the month of November follows.

Accounts Receivable	$295,000
Advertising Expenses	54,000
Cash	260,000
Depreciation—Factory Equipment	16,800
Depreciation—Office Equipment	2,500
Direct Labor	22,000
Factory Supplies Used	16,850

(*Continued*)

Factory Utilities	10,200
Finished Goods Inventory, November 30	68,300
Finished Goods Inventory, October 31	72,550
Indirect Labor	48,000
Office Supplies Expense	1,400
Other Administrative Expenses	72,000
Prepaid Expenses	41,250
Raw Materials Inventory, November 30	52,700
Raw Materials Inventory, October 31	38,000
Raw Materials Purchases	185,400
Rent—Factory Equipment	47,000
Repairs—Factory Equipment	4,200
Salaries	325,000
Sales	1,350,000
Sales Commissions	40,500
Work in Process Inventory, October 31	52,900
Work in Process Inventory, November 30	42,000

Instructions

(a) Based on the information given, construct an organizational chart of Waterways Corporation

(b) A list of accounts and their values are given above. From this information, prepare a cost of goods manufactured schedule, an income statement, and a partial balance sheet for Waterways Corporation for the month of November.

BROADENING YOUR PERSPECTIVE

DECISION MAKING ACROSS THE ORGANIZATION

BYP1-1 Mismatch Manufacturing Company specializes in producing fashion outfits. On July 31, 2008, a tornado touched down at its factory and general office. The inventories in the warehouse and the factory were completely destroyed as was the general office nearby. Next morning, through a careful search of the disaster site, however, Ross Clarkson, the company's controller, and Catherine Harper, the cost accountant, were able to recover a small part of manufacturing cost data for the current month.

"What a horrible experience," sighed Ross. "And the worst part is that we may not have enough records to use in filing an insurance claim."

"It was terrible," replied Catherine. "However, I managed to recover some of the manufacturing cost data that I was working on yesterday afternoon. The data indicate that our direct labor cost in July totaled $240,000 and that we had purchased $345,000 of raw materials. Also, I recall that the amount of raw materials used for July was $350,000. But I'm not sure this information will help. The rest of our records are blown away."

"Well, not exactly," said Ross. "I was working on the year-to-date income statement when the tornado warning was announced. My recollection is that our sales in July were $1,260,000 and our gross profit ratio has been 40% of sales. Also, I can remember that our cost of goods available for sale was $770,000 for July."

"Maybe we can work something out from this information!" exclaimed Catherine. "My experience tells me that our manufacturing overhead is usually 60% of direct labor."

"Hey, look what I just found," cried Catherine. "It's a copy of this June's balance sheet, and it shows that our inventories as of June 30 are Finished goods $38,000, Work in process $25,000, and Raw materials $19,000."

"Super," yelled Ross. "Let's go work something out."

In order to file an insurance claim, Mismatch Company must determine the amount of its inventories as of July 31, 2008, the date of the tornado touchdown.

Instructions

With the class divided into groups, determine the amount of cost in the Raw Materials, Work in Process, and Finished Goods inventory accounts as of the date of the tornado touchdown.

MANAGERIAL ANALYSIS

BYP1-2 Love All is a fairly large manufacturing company located in the southern United States. The company manufactures tennis rackets, tennis balls, tennis clothing, and tennis shoes, all bearing the company's distinctive logo, a large green question mark on a white flocked tennis ball. The company's sales have been increasing over the past 10 years.

The tennis racket division has recently implemented several advanced manufacturing techniques. Robot arms hold the tennis rackets in place while glue dries, and machine vision systems check for defects. The engineering and design team uses computerized drafting and testing of new products. The following managers work in the tennis racket division.

Andre Agassi, Sales Manager (supervises all sales representatives).
Serena Williams, technical specialist (supervises computer programmers).
Pete Sampras, cost accounting manager (supervises cost accountants).
Andy Roddick, production supervisor (supervises all manufacturing employees).
Venus Williams, engineer (supervises all new-product design teams).

Instructions

(a) What are the primary information needs of each manager?
(b) Which, if any, financial accounting report(s) is each likely to use?
(c) Name one special-purpose management accounting report that could be designed for each manager. Include the name of the report, the information it would contain, and how frequently it should be issued.

REAL-WORLD FOCUS

BYP1-3 Anchor Glass Container Corporation, the third largest manufacturer of glass containers in the U.S., supplies beverage and food producers and consumer products manufacturers nationwide. Parent company Consumers Packaging Inc. (*Toronto Stock Exchange:* CGC) is a leading international designer and manufacturer of glass containers.

The following management discussion appeared in a recent annual report of Anchor Glass.

ANCHOR GLASS CONTAINER CORPORATION
Management Discussion

Cost of Products Sold Cost of products sold as a percentage of net sales was 89.3% in the current year compared to 87.6% in the prior year. The increase in cost of products sold as a percentage of net sales principally reflected the impact of operational problems during the second quarter of the current year at a major furnace at one of the Company's plants, higher downtime, and costs and expenses associated with an increased number of scheduled capital improvement projects, increases in labor, and certain other manufacturing costs (with no corresponding selling price increases in the current year). Reduced fixed costs from the closing of the Streator, Illinois, plant in June of the current year and productivity and efficiency gains partially offset these cost increases.

Instructions

What factors affect the costs of products sold at Anchor Glass Container Corporation?

EXPLORING THE WEB

BYP1-4 The Institute of Management Accountants (IMA) is an organization dedicated to excellence in the practice of management accounting and financial management.

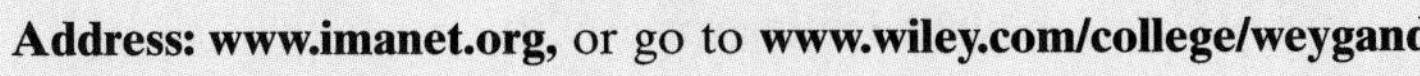
Address: www.imanet.org, or go to **www.wiley.com/college/weygandt**

Instructions

At the IMA's home page, locate the answers to the following questions.

(a) How many members does the IMA have, and what are their job titles?
(b) What are some of the benefits of joining the IMA as a student?
(c) Use the chapter locator function to locate the IMA chapter nearest you, and find the name of the chapter president.

COMMUNICATION ACTIVITY

BYP1-5 Refer to Problem 1–5A and add the following requirement.

Prepare a letter to the president of the company, Sue Tombert, describing the changes you made. Explain clearly why net income is different after the changes. Keep the following points in mind as you compose your letter.

1. This is a letter to the president of a company, who is your friend. The style should be generally formal, but you may relax some requirements. For example, you may call the president by her first name.
2. Executives are very busy. Your letter should tell the president your main results first (for example, the amount of net income).
3. You should include brief explanations so that the president can understand the changes you made in the calculations.

ETHICS CASE

BYP1-6 Wayne Terrago, controller for Robbin Industries, was reviewing production cost reports for the year. One amount in these reports continued to bother him—advertising. During the year, the company had instituted an expensive advertising campaign to sell some of its slower-moving products. It was still too early to tell whether the advertising campaign was successful.

There had been much internal debate as how to report advertising cost. The vice president of finance argued that advertising costs should be reported as a cost of production, just like direct materials and direct labor. He therefore recommended that this cost be identified as manufacturing overhead and reported as part of inventory costs until sold. Others disagreed. Terrago believed that this cost should be reported as an expense of the current period, based on the conservatism principle. Others argued that it should be reported as Prepaid Advertising and reported as a current asset.

The president finally had to decide the issue. He argued that these costs should be reported as inventory. His arguments were practical ones. He noted that the company was experiencing financial difficulty and expensing this amount in the current period might jeopardize a planned bond offering. Also, by reporting the advertising costs as inventory rather than as prepaid advertising, less attention would be directed to it by the financial community.

Instructions

(a) Who are the stakeholders in this situation?
(b) What are the ethical issues involved in this situation?
(c) What would you do if you were Wayne Terrago?

"ALL ABOUT YOU" ACTIVITY

BYP1-7 The primary purpose of managerial accounting is to provide information useful for management decisions. Many of the managerial accounting techniques that you learn in this course will be useful for decisions you make in your everyday life.

Instructions

For each of the following managerial accounting techniques, read the definition provided and then provide an example of a personal situation that would benefit from use of this technique.

(a) Break-even analysis (page 208).
(b) Budgeting (page 372).
(c) Balanced scorecard (page 485).
(d) Capital budgeting (page 520).

Answers to Insight and Accounting Across the Organization Questions

Even the Best Have to Get Better, p. 6

Q: What are some of the steps that this company has taken in order to ensure that production meets demand?

A: *The company has organized flexible teams, with jobs arranged by the amount of time a task takes. Employees now are multiskilled, so they can switch between tasks and products. Also, the stores now provide sales data more quickly to the manufacturing facility, so that production levels can be changed more quickly to respond to demand.*

How Many Labor Hours to Build a Car?, p. 11

Q: Why might Nissan production require significantly fewer labor hours?

A: *Nissan's U.S. factories are probably newer than those of Daimler-Chrysler and Ford. Newer factories tend to be more highly automated with less reliance on production-line employees.*

Bananas Receive Special Treatment, p. 21

Q: Why is it important to keep track of costs that are incurred to improve product quality?

A: *Most companies are concerned about product quality, but managers need to consider the cost/benefit tradeoff. If you spend too much on improving product quality, your customers might not be willing to pay the price needed to recover costs. Therefore it is very important that Chiquita closely track all of the costs that it incurs to protect the bananas, to ensure that these costs are factored into the price that it ultimately charges for the bananas.*

Authors' Comments on *All About You*: Outsourcing and Jobs, p. 23

This is a difficult decision. While the direct costs of outsourced tax return preparation may in fact be lower, you must also consider other issues: Will the accuracy of the returns be as high? Will your relationships with your customers suffer due to the loss of direct contact? Will customers resent having their personal information shipped overseas? While you may not want to lay off six employees, you also don't want to put your firm at risk by not remaining competitive.

Perhaps one solution would be to outsource the most basic tasks, and then provide training to the six employees so they can perform higher-skilled services such as tax planning. Many of the techniques that you learn in the remaining chapters of this text will help you evaluate the merits of your various options.

Answers to Self-Study Questions

1. b **2.** b **3.** b **4.** c **5.** d **6.** a **7.** c **8.** a **9.** d **10.** d

Remember to go back to the Navigator box on the chapter-opening page and check off your completed work.

Chapter 2

Job Order Costing

STUDY OBJECTIVES

After studying this chapter, you should be able to:

1 Explain the characteristics and purposes of cost accounting.

2 Describe the flow of costs in a job order costing system.

3 Explain the nature and importance of a job cost sheet.

4 Indicate how the predetermined overhead rate is determined and used.

5 Prepare entries for jobs completed and sold.

6 Distinguish between under- and overapplied manufacturing overhead.

The Navigator

The Navigator

- Scan **Study Objectives**
- Read **Feature Story**
- Read **Preview**
- Read text and answer **Before You Go On** p. 56 p. 65 p. 71
- Work **Using the Decision Toolkit**
- Review **Summary of Study Objectives**
- Work **Demonstration Problem**
- Answer **Self-Study Questions**
- Complete **Assignments**

Feature Story

". . . AND WE'D LIKE IT IN RED"

Western States Fire Apparatus, Inc., of Cornelius, Oregon, is one of the few U.S. companies that makes fire trucks. The company builds about 25 trucks per year. Founded in 1941, the company is run by the children and grandchildren of the original founder.

"We buy the chassis, which is the cab and the frame," says Susan Scott, the company's bookkeeper. "In our computer, we set up an account into which all of the direct material that is purchased for that particular job is charged." Other direct materials include the water pump—which can cost $10,000—the lights, the siren, ladders, and hoses.

As for direct labor, the production workers fill out time tickets that tell what jobs they worked on. Usually, the company is building four trucks at any one time. On payday, the controller allocates the payroll to the appropriate job record.

The company allocates indirect materials, such as nuts and bolts, wiring, lubricants, and abrasives, to each job in proportion to direct material dollars. It allocates other costs, such as insurance and supervisors' salaries, based on direct labor hours. "We need to allocate overhead in order to know what kind of price we have to charge when we submit our bids," she says.

Western gets orders through a "blind-bidding" process. That is, Western submits its bid without knowing the bid prices made by its competitors. "If we bid too low, we won't make a profit. If we bid too high, we don't get the job."

Regardless of the final price for the truck, the quality had better be first-rate. "The fire departments let you know if they don't like what you did, and you usually end up fixing it."

The Navigator

Inside Chapter 2

Preview of Chapter 2

The Feature Story about Western States Fire Apparatus describes the manufacturing costs used in making a fire truck. It demonstrates that accurate costing is critical to the company's success. For example, in order to submit accurate bids on new jobs and to know whether it profited from past jobs, the company needs a good costing system. This chapter illustrates how these manufacturing costs are assigned to specific jobs, such as the manufacture of individual fire trucks. We begin the discussion in this chapter with an overview of the flow of costs in a job order cost accounting system. We then use a case study to explain and illustrate the documents, entries, and accounts in this type of cost accounting system.

The content and organization of Chapter 2 are as follows.

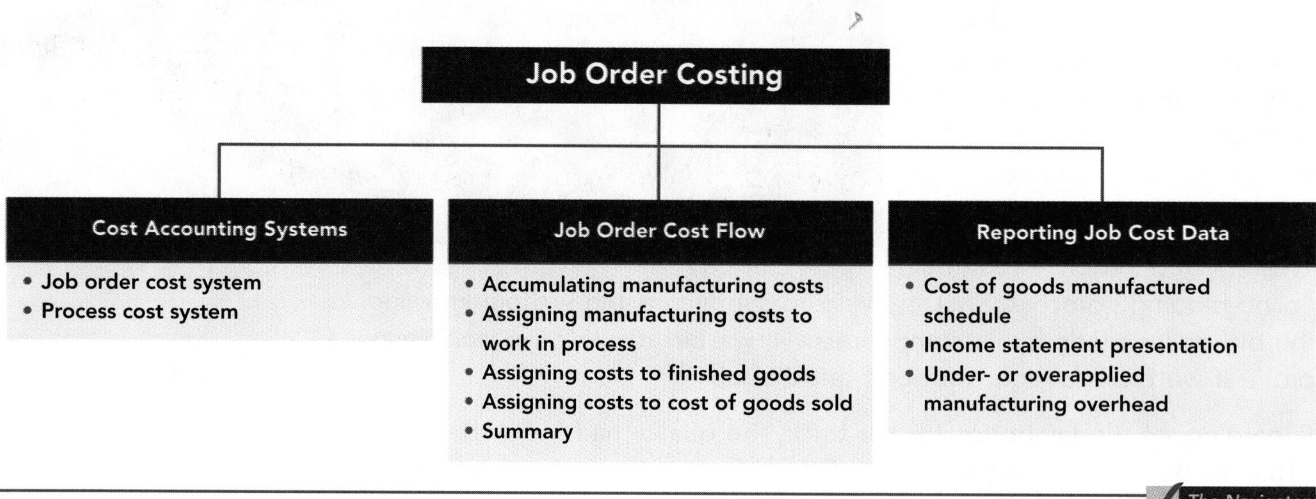

COST ACCOUNTING SYSTEMS

STUDY OBJECTIVE 1

Explain the characteristics and purposes of cost accounting.

Cost accounting involves the measuring, recording, and reporting of product costs. From the data accumulated, companies determine both the total cost and the unit cost of each product. The accuracy of the product cost information produced by the cost accounting system is critical to the success of the company. Companies use this information to determine which products to produce, what price to charge, and the amounts to produce. Accurate product cost information is also vital for effective evaluation of employee performance.

A **cost accounting system** consists of accounts for the various manufacturing costs. These accounts are fully integrated into the general ledger of a company. An important feature of a cost accounting system is the use of **a perpetual inventory system.** Such a system **provides immediate, up-to-date information on the cost of a product**.

There are two basic types of cost accounting systems: (1) a job order cost system and (2) a process cost system. Although cost accounting systems differ widely from company to company, most involve one of these two traditional product costing systems.

Job Order Cost System

Under a **job order cost system**, the company assigns costs to each **job** or to each **batch** of goods. An example of a job is the manufacture of a mainframe computer by IBM, the production of a movie by Disney, or the making of a fire truck by Western States. An example of a batch is the printing of 225 wedding invitations by a local print shop, or the printing of a weekly issue of *Fortune* magazine by a hi-tech printer such as Quad Graphics. Companies may complete jobs or batches to fill a specific customer order or to replenish inventory.

An important feature of job order costing is that each job or batch has its own distinguishing characteristics. For example, each house is custom built, each consulting engagement by a CPA firm is unique, and each printing job is different. **The objective is to compute the cost per job.** At each point in manufacturing a product or providing a service, the company can identify the job and its associated costs. A job order cost system measures costs for each completed job, rather than for set time periods. Illustration 2-1 shows the recording of costs in a job order cost system.

Illustration 2-1
Job order cost system

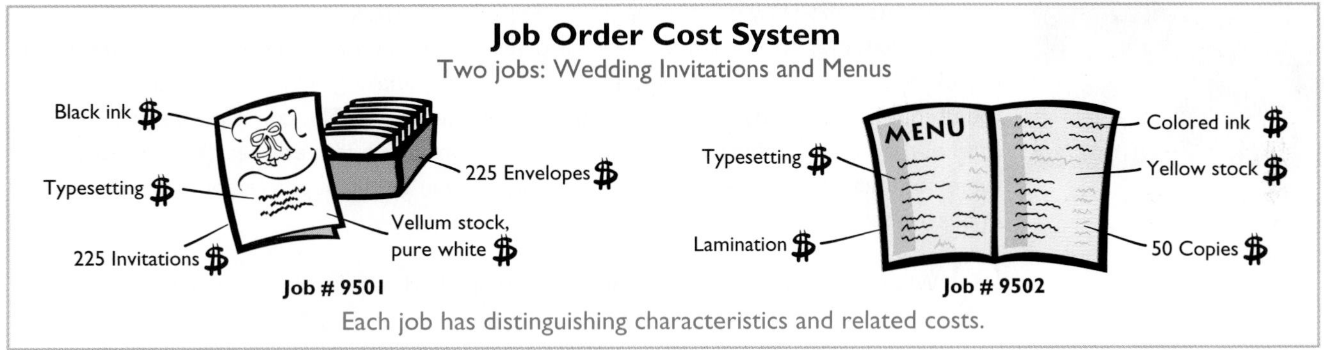

Process Cost System

A company uses a **process cost system** when it manufactures a large volume of similar products. Production is continuous. Examples of a process cost system are the manufacture of cereal by Kellogg, the refining of petroleum by ExxonMobil, and the production of automobiles by General Motors. Process costing accumulates product-related costs **for a period of time** (such as a week or a month) instead of assigning costs to specific products or job orders. In process costing, companies assign the costs to departments or processes for the specified period of time. Illustration 2-2 shows examples of the use of a process cost system. We will discuss the process cost system further in Chapter 3.

Illustration 2-2
Process cost system

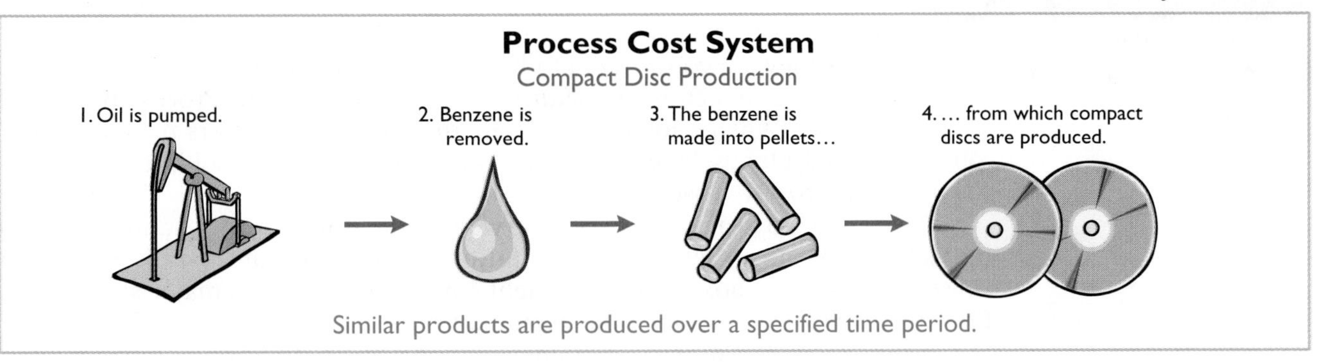

Can a company use both types of cost systems? Yes. For example, General Motors uses process cost accounting for its standard model cars, such as Saturns and Corvettes, and job order cost accounting for a custom-made limousine for the President of the United States.

The objective of both cost accounting systems is to provide unit cost information for product pricing, cost control, inventory valuation, and financial statement presentation.

MANAGEMENT INSIGHT

Jobs Won, Money Lost

Many companies suffer from poor cost accounting. As a result, they sometimes make products they should not be selling at all, or they buy other products that they could more profitably make themselves. Also, inaccurate cost data leads companies to misallocate capital and frustrates efforts by plant managers to improve efficiency.

For example, consider the case of a diversified company in the business of rebuilding diesel locomotives. The managers thought they were making money, but a consulting firm found that the company had seriously underestimated costs. The company bailed out of the business, and not a moment too soon. Says the consultant who advised the company, "The more contracts it won, the more money it lost." Given that situation, a company cannot stay in business very long!

? What type of costs do you think the company had been underestimating?

Before You Go On...

REVIEW IT

1. What is cost accounting?
2. What does a cost accounting system consist of?
3. How does a job order cost system differ from a process cost system?

JOB ORDER COST FLOW

STUDY OBJECTIVE 2

Describe the flow of costs in a job order costing system.

The flow of costs (direct materials, direct labor, and manufacturing overhead) in job order cost accounting parallels the physical flow of the materials as they are converted into finished goods. As shown in Illustration 2-3, companies assign manufacturing costs to the Work in Process Inventory account. When a job is completed, the company transfers the cost of the job to Finished Goods Inventory. Later when the goods are sold, the company transfers their cost to Cost of Goods Sold.

Illustration 2-3 provides a basic overview of the flow of costs in a manufacturing setting. A more detailed presentation of the flow of costs is shown in Illustration 2-4. The box in its lower right corner indicates two major steps in the flow of costs: (1) *accumulating* the manufacturing costs incurred, and (2) *assigning* the accumulated costs to the work done. As shown, the company accumulates manufacturing costs incurred in entries 1–3 by debits to Raw Materials Inventory, Factory Labor, and Manufacturing Overhead. When the company incurs these costs, it does not attempt to associate the costs with specific jobs. The remaining entries

Manufacturing Costs
Raw Materials
Factory Labor
Manufacturing Overhead
Assigned to
Work in Process Inventory
Completed
Finished Goods Inventory
Sold
Cost of Goods Sold

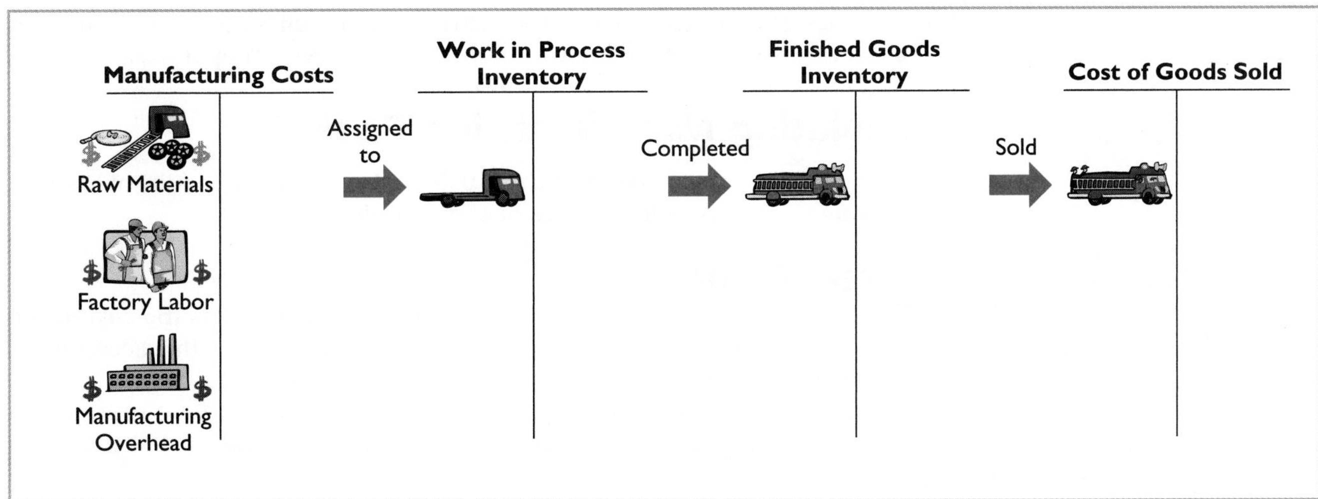

Illustration 2-3
Flow of costs in job order costing

Illustration 2-4
Job order costing system

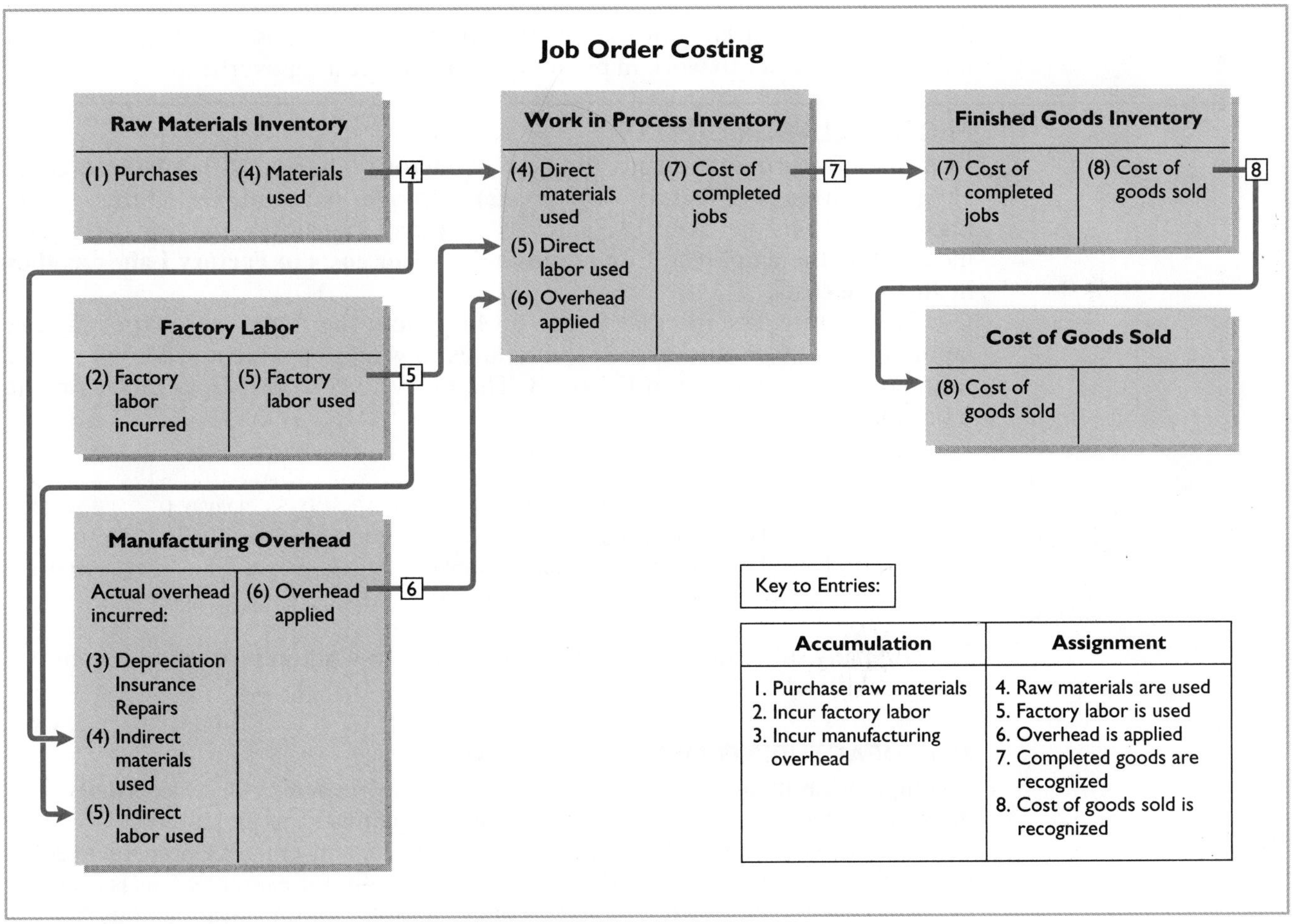

Job Order Costing
Raw Materials Inventory
(1) Purchases
(4) Materials used
Factory Labor
(2) Factory labor incurred
(5) Factory labor used
Manufacturing Overhead
Actual overhead incurred:
(3) Depreciation Insurance Repairs
(4) Indirect materials used
(5) Indirect labor used
(6) Overhead applied
Work in Process Inventory
(4) Direct materials used
(5) Direct labor used
(6) Overhead applied
(7) Cost of completed jobs
Finished Goods Inventory
(7) Cost of completed jobs
(8) Cost of goods sold
Cost of Goods Sold
(8) Cost of goods sold
4
5
6
7
8
Key to Entries:
Accumulation
1. Purchase raw materials
2. Incur factory labor
3. Incur manufacturing overhead
Assignment
4. Raw materials are used
5. Factory labor is used
6. Overhead is applied
7. Completed goods are recognized
8. Cost of goods sold is recognized

(entries 4–8) assign manufacturing costs incurred. In the remainder of this chapter, we will use a case study to explain how a job order cost system operates.

Accumulating Manufacturing Costs

To illustrate a job order cost system, we will use the January transactions of Wallace Manufacturing Company, which makes machine tools.

RAW MATERIALS COSTS

When Wallace receives the raw materials it has purchased, **it debits the cost of the materials to Raw Materials Inventory**. The company would debit this account for the invoice cost of the raw materials and freight costs chargeable to the purchaser. It would credit the account for purchase discounts taken and purchase returns and allowances. Wallace makes **no effort at this point to associate the cost of materials with specific jobs or orders.**

To illustrate, assume that Wallace Manufacturing purchases 2,000 handles (Stock No. AA2746) at $5 per unit ($10,000) and 800 modules (Stock No. AA2850) at $40 per unit ($32,000) for a total cost of $42,000 ($10,000 + $32,000). The entry to record this purchase on January 4 is:

	(1)		
Jan. 4	Raw Materials Inventory	42,000	
	Accounts Payable		42,000
	(Purchase of raw materials on account)		

As we will explain later in the chapter, the company subsequently assigns raw materials inventory to work in process and manufacturing overhead.

FACTORY LABOR COSTS

In a manufacturing company, the cost of factory labor consists of three costs: (1) gross earnings of factory workers, (2) employer payroll taxes on these earnings, and (3) fringe benefits (such as sick pay, pensions, and vacation pay) incurred by the employer. **Companies debit labor costs to Factory Labor as they incur those costs.**

To illustrate, assume that Wallace Manufacturing incurs $32,000 of factory labor costs. Of that amount, $27,000 relates to wages payable and $5,000 relates to payroll taxes payable in February. The entry to record factory labor for the month is:

	(2)		
Jan. 31	Factory Labor	32,000	
	Factory Wages Payable		27,000
	Employer Payroll Taxes Payable		5,000
	(To record factory labor costs)		

The company subsequently assigns factory labor to work in process and manufacturing overhead.

MANUFACTURING OVERHEAD COSTS

A company has many types of overhead costs. It may recognize these costs **daily**, as in the case of machinery repairs and the use of indirect materials and indirect labor. Or, it may record overhead costs **periodically** through adjusting entries. Companies record property taxes, depreciation, and insurance periodically, for example. This is done using a **summary entry**, which summarizes the totals from multiple transactions.

Using assumed data, the summary entry for manufacturing overhead in Wallace Manufacturing Company is:

	(3)		
Jan. 31	Manufacturing Overhead	13,800	
	Utilities Payable		4,800
	Prepaid Insurance		2,000
	Accounts Payable (for repairs)		2,600
	Accumulated Depreciation		3,000
	Property Taxes Payable		1,400
	(To record overhead costs)		

The company subsequently assigns manufacturing overhead to work in process.

Assigning Manufacturing Costs to Work in Process

STUDY OBJECTIVE 3

Explain the nature and importance of a job cost sheet.

As Illustration 2-4 (page 57) shows, assigning manufacturing costs to work in process results in the following entries:

1. **Debits** made to Work in Process Inventory.
2. **Credits** made to Raw Materials Inventory, Factory Labor, and Manufacturing Overhead.

An essential accounting record in assigning costs to jobs is a **job cost sheet**, as shown in Illustration 2-5. A **job cost sheet** is a form used to record the costs chargeable to a specific job and to determine the total and unit costs of the completed job.

Illustration 2-5
Job cost sheet

Job Cost Sheet

Job No. ____________ Quantity ____________
Item ____________ Date Requested ____________
For ____________ Date Completed ____________

Date	Direct Materials	Direct Labor	Manufacturing Overhead

Cost of completed job
  Direct materials $ ____________
  Direct labor ____________
  Manufacturing overhead ____________
Total cost $ ____________
Unit cost (total dollars ÷ quantity) $ ____________

HELPFUL HINT

In today's electronic environment, companies typically maintain job cost sheets as computer files.

Companies keep a separate job cost sheet for each job. The job cost sheets constitute the subsidiary ledger for the Work in Process Inventory account. A **subsidiary ledger** consists of individual records for each individual item—in this case, each job. The Work in Process account is referred to as a **control account** because it summarizes the detailed data regarding specific jobs contained in the job cost sheets. **Each entry to Work in Process Inventory must be accompanied by a corresponding posting to one or more job cost sheets.**

RAW MATERIALS COSTS

HELPFUL HINT
Approvals are an important part of a materials requisition slip because they help to establish individual accountability over inventory.

Companies assign raw materials costs when their materials storeroom issues the materials. Requests for issuing raw materials are made on a prenumbered **materials requisition slip**. The materials issued may be used directly on a job, or they may be considered indirect materials. As Illustration 2-6 shows, the requisition should indicate the quantity and type of materials withdrawn and the account to be charged. The company will charge direct materials to Work in Process Inventory, and indirect materials to Manufacturing Overhead.

Illustration 2-6
Materials requisition slip

Wallace Manufacturing Company
Materials Requisition Slip

Deliver to: Assembly Department — Req. No. R247
Charge to: Work in Process–Job No. 101 — Date: 1/6/08

Quantity	Description	Stock No.	Cost per Unit	Total
200	Handles	AA2746	$5.00	$1,000

Requested by Bruce Howart — Received by Herb Crowley
Approved by Kap Shin — Costed by Heather Remmers

ETHICS NOTE
The internal control principle of documentation includes prenumbering to enhance accountability.

The company may use any of the inventory costing methods (FIFO, LIFO, or average-cost) in costing the requisitions **to the individual job cost sheets.**

Periodically, the company journalizes the requisitions. For example, if Wallace Manufacturing uses $24,000 of direct materials and $6,000 of indirect materials in January, the entry is:

(4)

Jan. 31	Work in Process Inventory	24,000	
	Manufacturing Overhead	6,000	
	Raw Materials Inventory		30,000
	(To assign materials to jobs and overhead)		

Direct Materials
Indirect materials

Illustration 2-7 shows the posting of requisition slip R247 to Job No. 101 and other assumed postings to the job cost sheets for materials. The requisition slips provide the basis for total direct materials costs of $12,000 for Job No. 101, $7,000 for Job No. 102, and $5,000 for Job No. 103. After the company has completed all postings, the sum of the direct materials columns of the job cost sheets (the subsidiary accounts) should equal the direct materials debited to Work in Process Inventory (the control account).

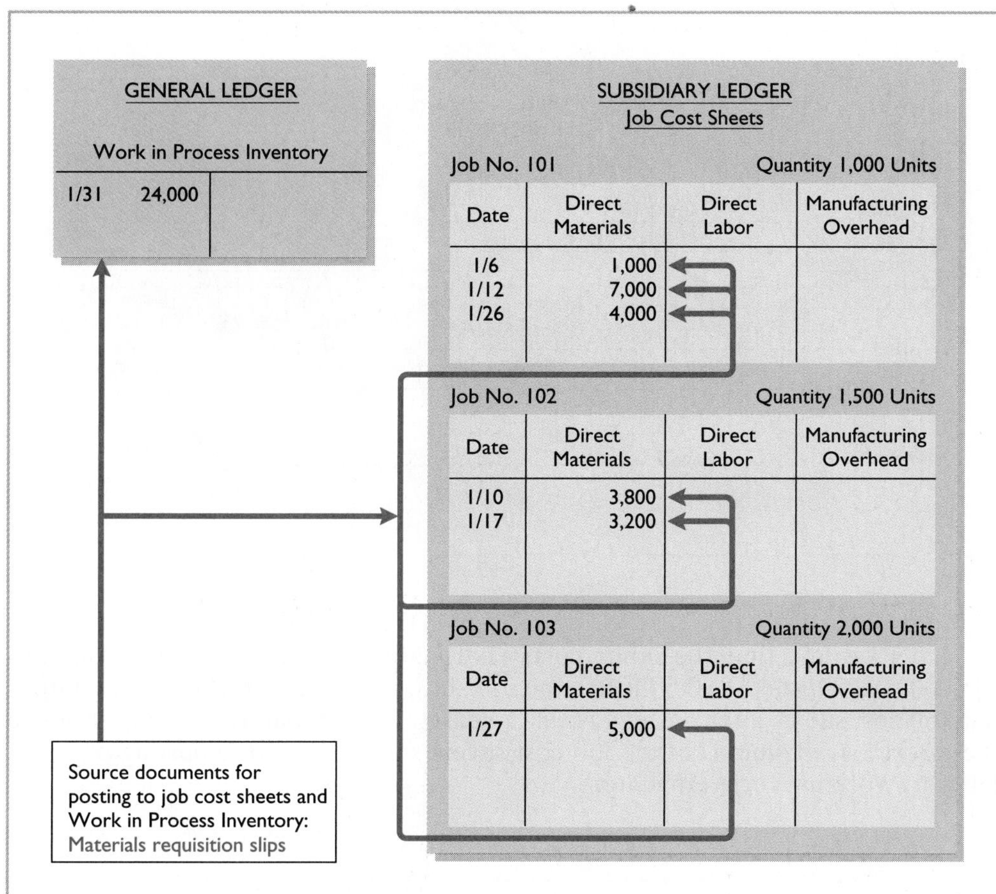

Illustration 2-7
Job cost sheets—direct materials

HELPFUL HINT

Companies post to control accounts monthly, and post to job cost sheets daily.

FACTORY LABOR COSTS

Companies assign factory labor costs to jobs on the basis of time tickets prepared when the work is performed. The time ticket indicates the employee, the hours worked, the account and job to be charged, and the total labor cost. Many companies accumulate these data through the use of bar coding and scanning devices. When they start and end work, employees scan bar codes on their identification badges and bar codes associated with each job they work on. When direct labor is involved, the time ticket must indicate the job number, as shown in Illustration 2-8 (page 62). The employee's supervisor should approve all time tickets.

The time tickets are later sent to the payroll department, which applies the employee's hourly wage rate and computes the total labor cost. Finally, the company journalizes the time tickets. It debits the account Work in Process Inventory for direct labor and debits Manufacturing Overhead for indirect labor. For example, if the $32,000 total factory labor cost consists of $28,000 of direct labor and $4,000 of indirect labor, the entry is:

	(5)		
Jan. 31	Work in Process Inventory	28,000	
	Manufacturing Overhead	4,000	
	Factory Labor		32,000
	(To assign labor to jobs and overhead)		

As a result of this entry, Factory Labor has a zero balance, and gross earnings are assigned to the appropriate manufacturing accounts.

Illustration 2-8
Time ticket

Wallace Manufacturing Company
Time Ticket

Date: 1/6/08

Employee: John Nash — Employee No. 124

Charge to: Work in Process — Job No. 101

Time			Hourly Rate	Total Cost
Start	Stop	Total Hours		
0800	1200	4	10.00	40.00

Approved by *Bob Kadler*   Costed by *M Chen*

Let's assume that the labor costs chargeable to Wallace's three jobs are $15,000, $9,000, and $4,000. Illustration 2-9 shows the Work in Process Inventory and job cost sheets after posting. As in the case of direct materials, the postings to the direct labor columns of the job cost sheets should equal the posting of direct labor to Work in Process Inventory.

Illustration 2-9
Job cost sheets—direct labor

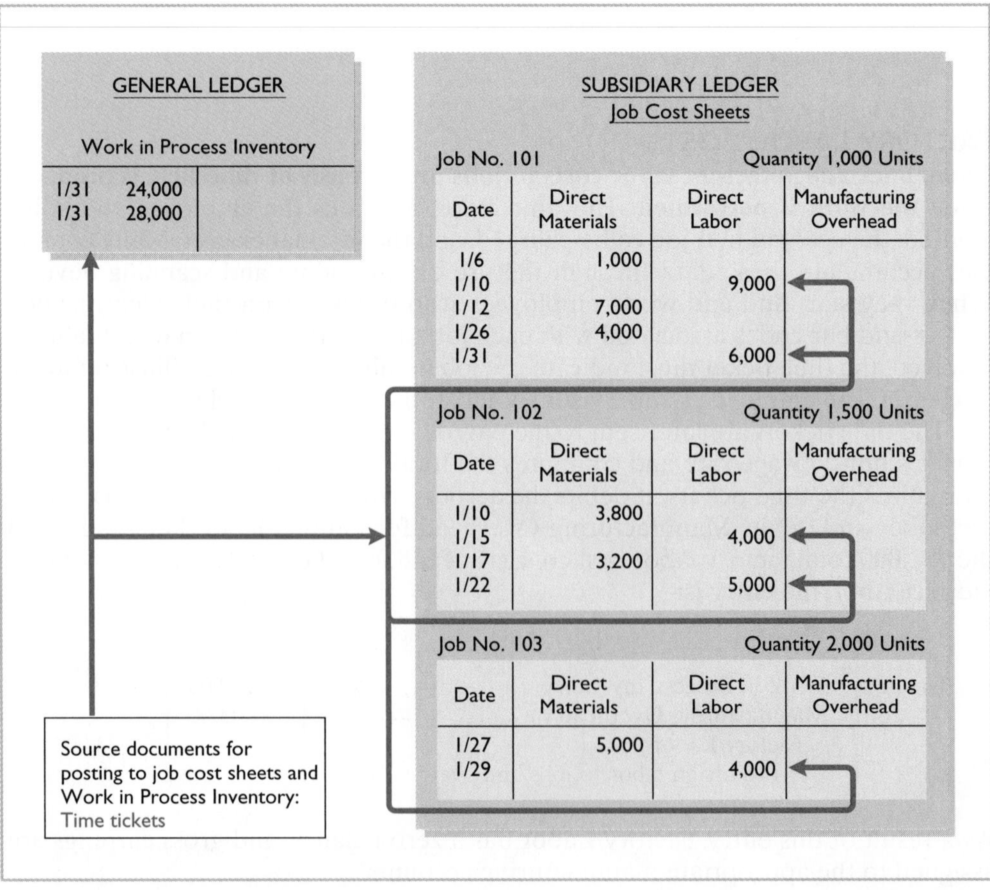

HELPFUL HINT

Prove the $28,000 direct labor charge to Work in Process Inventory by totaling the charges by jobs:

101	$15,000
102	9,000
103	4,000
	$28,000

MANUFACTURING OVERHEAD COSTS

STUDY OBJECTIVE 4

Indicate how the predetermined overhead rate is determined and used.

Companies charge the actual costs of direct materials and direct labor to specific jobs. In contrast, manufacturing **overhead** relates to production operations **as a whole**. As a result, overhead costs cannot be assigned to specific jobs on the basis of actual costs incurred. Instead, companies assign manufacturing overhead to work in process and to specific jobs **on an estimated basis through the use of a predetermined overhead rate**.

The **predetermined overhead rate** is based on the relationship between estimated annual overhead costs and expected annual operating activity, expressed in terms of a common **activity base**. The company may state the activity in terms of direct labor costs, direct labor hours, machine hours, or any other measure that will provide an equitable basis for applying overhead costs to jobs. Companies establish the predetermined overhead rate at the beginning of the year. Small companies often use a single, company-wide predetermined overhead rate. Large companies often use rates that vary from department to department. The formula for a predetermined overhead rate is as follows.

Estimated Annual Overhead Costs ÷ **Expected Annual Operating Activity** = **Predetermined Overhead Rate**

Illustration 2-10
Formula for predetermined overhead rate

Overhead relates to production operations as a whole. To know what "the whole" is, the logical thing is to wait until the end of the year's operations. At that time the company knows all of its costs for the period. As a practical matter, though, managers cannot wait until the end of the year. To price products accurately, they need information about product costs of specific jobs completed during the year. Using a predetermined overhead rate enables a cost to be determined for the job immediately. Illustration 2-11 indicates how manufacturing overhead is assigned to work in process.

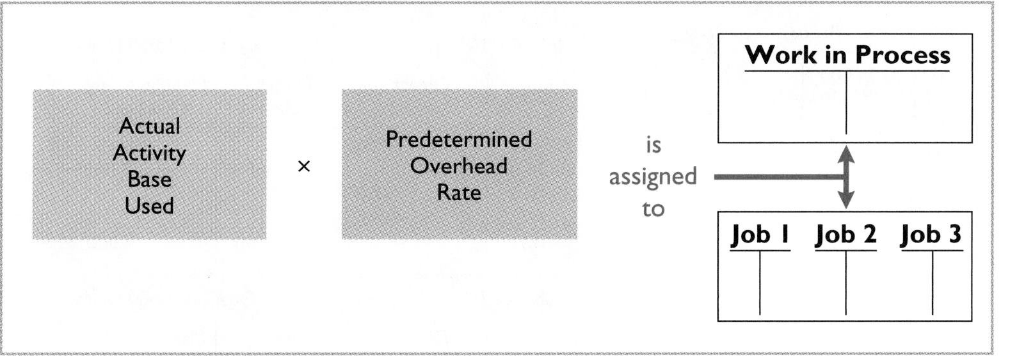

Illustration 2-11
Using predetermined overhead rates

Wallace Manufacturing uses direct labor cost as the activity base. Assuming that the company expects annual overhead costs to be \$280,000 and direct labor costs for the year to be \$350,000, the overhead rate is 80%, computed as follows:

$$\$280{,}000 \div \$350{,}000 = 80\%$$

This means that for every dollar of direct labor, Wallace will assign 80 cents of manufacturing overhead to a job. The use of a predetermined overhead rate enables the company to determine the approximate total cost of each job **when it completes the job**.

Historically, companies used direct labor costs or direct labor hours as the activity base. The reason was the relatively high correlation between direct labor and manufacturing overhead. Today more companies are using **machine hours as the activity**

base, due to increased reliance on automation in manufacturing operations. Or, as mentioned in Chapter 1 (and discussed more fully in Chapter 4), many companies now use activity-based costing to more accurately allocate overhead costs based on the activities that give rise to the costs.

A company may use more than one activity base. For example, if a job is manufactured in more than one factory department, each department may have its own overhead rate. In the Feature Story about fire trucks, Western States Fire Apparatus uses two bases in assigning overhead to jobs: direct materials dollars for indirect materials, and direct labor hours for such costs as insurance and supervisors' salaries.

Wallace Manufacturing applies manufacturing overhead to work in process when it assigns direct labor costs. It also applies manufacturing overhead to specific jobs at the same time. For January, Wallace applied overhead of \$22,400 (direct labor cost of \$28,000 × 80%). The following entry records this application.

	(6)		
Jan. 31	Work in Process Inventory	22,400	
	Manufacturing Overhead		22,400
	(To assign overhead to jobs)		

The overhead that Wallace applies to each job will be 80% of the direct labor cost of the job for the month. Illustration 2-12 shows the Work in Process Inventory account and the job cost sheets after posting. Note that the debit of \$22,400 to Work in Process Inventory equals the sum of the overhead applied to jobs: Job 101 \$12,000 + Job 102 \$7,200 + Job 103 \$3,200.

Illustration 2-12
Job cost sheets—manufacturing overhead applied

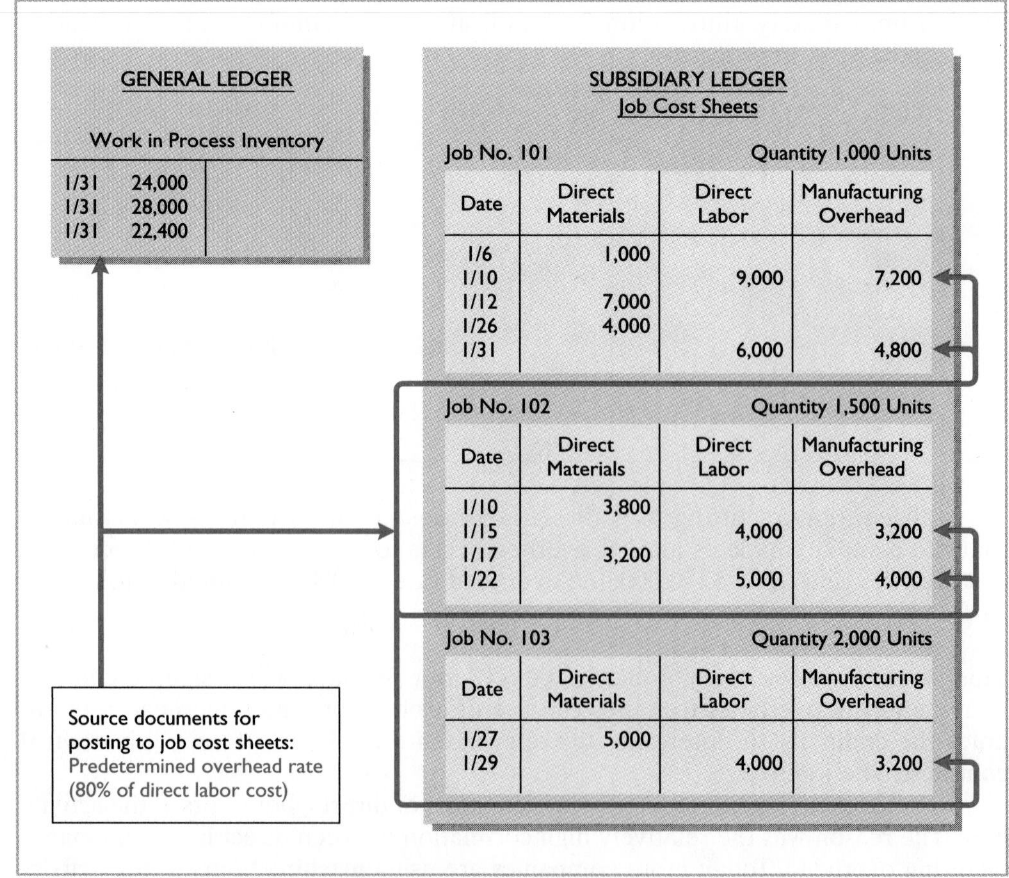

At the end of each month, **the balance in Work in Process Inventory should equal the sum of the costs shown on the job cost sheets of unfinished jobs**. Illustration 2-13 presents proof of the agreement of the control and subsidiary accounts in Wallace Manufacturing. (It assumes that all jobs are still in process.)

Work in Process Inventory			Job Cost Sheets	
Jan. 31	24,000		No. 101	$39,000
31	28,000		102	23,200
31	22,400		103	12,200
	74,400	←		**$74,400**

Illustration 2-13
Proof of job cost sheets to work in process inventory

DECISION TOOLKIT

Decision Checkpoints	Info Needed for Decision	Tool to Use for Decision	How to Evaluate Results
What is the cost of a job?	Cost of material, labor, and overhead assigned to a specific job	Job cost sheet	Compare costs to those of previous periods and to those of competitors to ensure that costs are in line. Compare costs to expected selling price or service fees charged to determine overall profitability.

Before You Go On...

REVIEW IT

1. What source documents do companies use in assigning manufacturing costs to Work in Process Inventory?
2. What is a job cost sheet, and what is its primary purpose?
3. What is the formula for computing a predetermined overhead rate?

DO IT

Danielle Company is working on two job orders. The job cost sheets show the following:

Direct materials—Job 120 $6,000; Job 121 $3,600
Direct labor—Job 120 $4,000; Job 121 $2,000
Manufacturing overhead—Job 120 $5,000; Job 121 $2,500

Prepare the three summary entries to record the assignment of costs to Work in Process from the data on the job cost sheets.

Action Plan

- Recognize that Work in Process Inventory is the control account for all unfinished job cost sheets.
- Debit Work in Process Inventory for the materials, labor, and overhead charged to the job cost sheets.
- Credit the accounts that were debited when the manufacturing costs were accumulated.

Solution

The three summary entries are:

Work in Process Inventory ($6,000 + $3,600)	9,600	
Raw Materials Inventory		9,600
(To assign materials to jobs)		
Work in Process Inventory ($4,000 + $2,000)	6,000	
Factory Labor		6,000
(To assign labor to jobs)		
Work in Process Inventory ($5,000 + $2,500)	7,500	
Manufacturing Overhead		7,500
(To assign overhead to jobs)		

Related exercise material: *BE2-3, BE2-4, and BE2-7.*

The Navigator

Assigning Costs to Finished Goods

STUDY OBJECTIVE 5

Prepare entries for jobs completed and sold.

When a job is completed, Wallace summarizes the costs and completes the lower portion of the applicable job cost sheet. For example, if we assume that Wallace completes Job No. 101 on January 31, the job cost sheet appears as shown in Illustration 2-14.

Illustration 2-14
Completed job cost sheet

Job Cost Sheet

Job No. 101   Quantity 1,000
Item Magnetic Sensors   Date Requested February 5
For Tanner Company   Date Completed January 31

Date	Direct Materials	Direct Labor	Manufacturing Overhead
1/6	$ 1,000		
1/10		$ 9,000	$ 7,200
1/12	7,000		
1/26	4,000		
1/31		6,000	4,800
	$12,000	$15,000	$12,000

Cost of completed job	
Direct materials	$ 12,000
Direct labor	15,000
Manufacturing overhead	12,000
Total cost	$ 39,000
Unit cost ($39,000 ÷ 1,000)	$ 39.00

When a job is finished, Wallace makes an entry to transfer its total cost to finished goods inventory. The entry is as follows:

(7)

Jan. 31	Finished Goods Inventory	39,000	
	Work in Process Inventory		39,000
	(To record completion of Job No. 101)		

Finished Goods Inventory is a control account. It controls individual finished goods records in a finished goods subsidiary ledger. The company posts directly from completed job cost sheets to the receipts columns. Illustration 2-15, below, shows the finished goods inventory record for Job No. 101.

Assigning Costs to Cost of Goods Sold

Companies recognize cost of goods sold when each sale occurs. To illustrate the entries a company makes when it sells a completed job, assume that on January 31 Wallace Manufacturing sells on account Job 101. The job cost $39,000, and it sold for $50,000. The entries to record the sale and recognize cost of goods sold are:

	(8)		
Jan. 31	Accounts Receivable	50,000	
	Sales		50,000
	(To record sale of Job No. 101)		
31	Cost of Goods Sold	39,000	
	Finished Goods Inventory		39,000
	(To record cost of Job No. 101)		

As Illustration 2-15 shows, Wallace records, in the issues section of the finished goods record, the units sold, the cost per unit, and the total cost of goods sold for each job sold.

Illustration 2-15
Finished goods record

Finished Goods.xls

File Edit View Insert Format Tools Data Window Help

	A	B	C	D	E	F	G	H	I	J
1–2	**Item: Magnetic Sensors**									**Job No: 101**
3			**Receipts**			**Issues**			**Balance**	
4	Date	Units	Cost	Total	Units	Cost	Total	Units	Cost	Total
5	1/31	1,000	$39	$39,000				1,000	$39	$39,000
6	1/31				1,000	$39	$39,000			– 0 –
7										

ACCOUNTING ACROSS THE ORGANIZATION

What About Service Companies?

Many of you will work for service companies. Service companies like the Mayo Clinic (health care), PriceWaterhouseCoopers (accounting firm), and Merrill Lynch (financial services firm) also use job order costing systems. The major difference in a job order costing system between a manufacturing company such as Western States Fire Apparatus and a service company such as Massachusetts General Hospital involves inventory. Service companies do not have raw materials nor finished goods inventory.

Because service industries use job order costing systems extensively, we provide exercises in the end-of-chapter material to help you understand how to cost various types of services.

What types of costs will service companies report in job order cost systems?

Summary of Job Order Cost Flows

Illustration 2-16 (below) shows a completed flow chart for a job order cost accounting system. All postings are keyed to entries 1–8 in Wallace Manufacturing's accounts presented in the cost flow graphic in Illustration 2-4 (page 57).

The cost flows in the diagram can be categorized as one of four types:

- **Accumulation:** The company first accumulates costs by (1) purchasing raw materials, (2) incurring labor costs, and (3) incurring manufacturing overhead costs.
- **Assignment to Jobs:** Once the company has incurred manufacturing costs, it must assign them to specific jobs. For example, as it uses raw materials on specific jobs (4), it assigns them to work in process, or treats them as manufacturing overhead if the raw materials cannot be associated with a specific job. Similarly, it either assigns factory labor (5) to work in process, or treats it as manufacturing overhead if the factory labor cannot be associated with a specific job. Finally it assigns manufacturing overhead (6) to work in process using a *predetermined overhead rate*. This deserves emphasis: **Do not assign overhead using actual overhead costs, but instead use a predetermined rate.**
- **Completed Jobs:** As jobs are completed (7), the company transfers the cost of the completed job out of work in process inventory into finished goods inventory.
- **When Goods Are Sold:** As specific items are sold (8), the company transfers their cost out of finished goods inventory into cost of goods sold.

Illustration 2-17 (next page) summarizes the flow of documents in a job order cost system.

Illustration 2-16
Flow of costs in a job order cost system

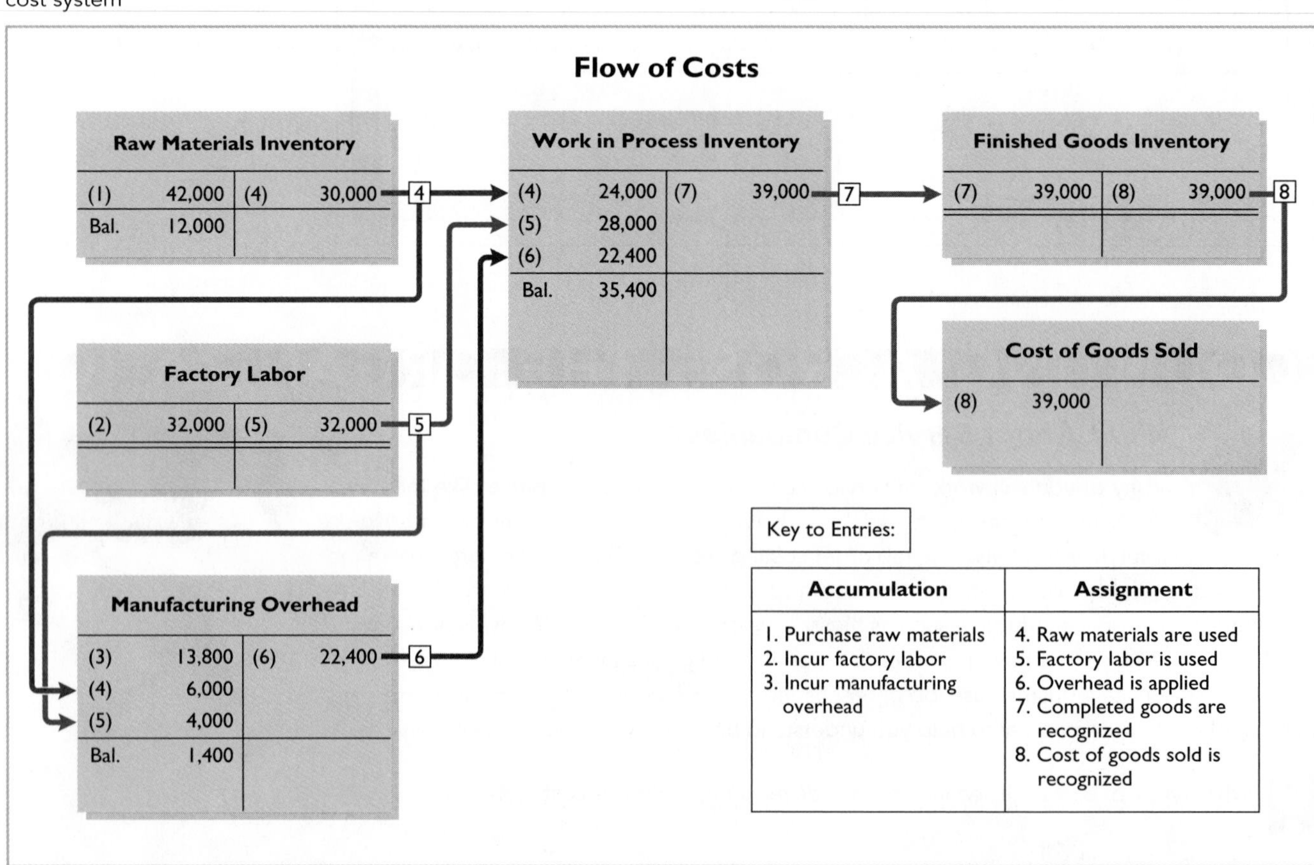

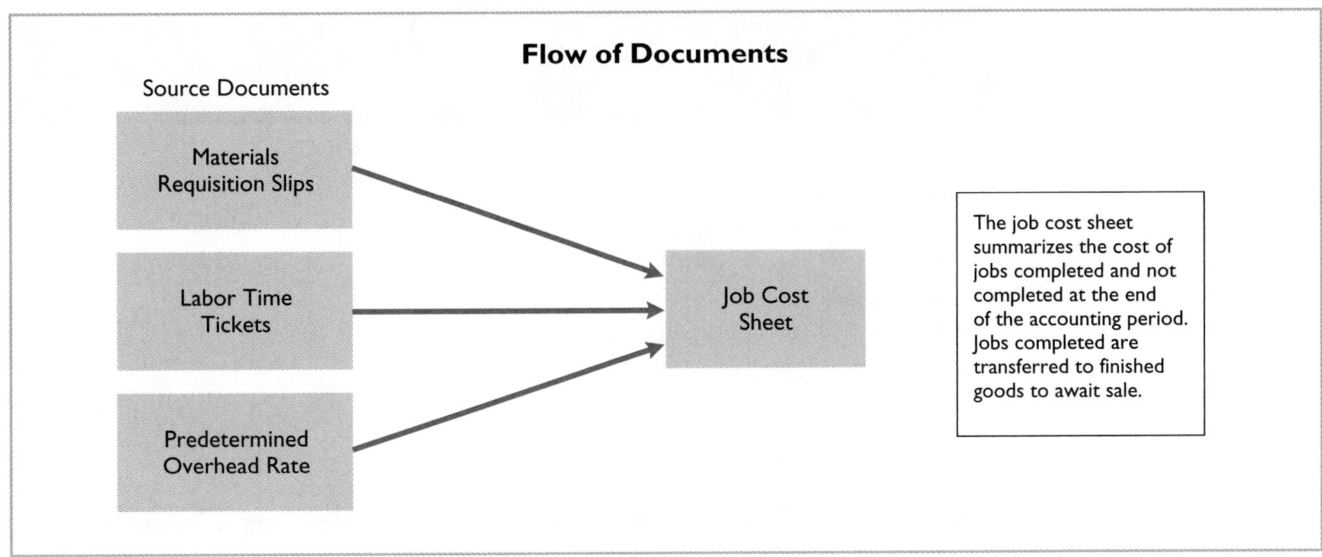

Illustration 2-17
Flow of documents in a job order cost system

REPORTING JOB COST DATA

At the end of a period, companies prepare financial statements that present aggregate data on all jobs manufactured and sold. The cost of goods manufactured schedule in job order costing is the same as in Chapter 1 with one exception: **The schedule shows manufacturing overhead applied, rather than actual overhead costs. The company adds this amount to direct materials and direct labor to determine total manufacturing costs.**

Companies prepare the cost of goods manufactured schedule directly from the Work in Process Inventory account. Illustration 2-18 shows a condensed schedule for Wallace Manufacturing Company for January.

HELPFUL HINT
Companies usually prepare monthly financial statements for management use only.

Illustration 2-18
Cost of goods manufactured schedule

WALLACE MANUFACTURING COMPANY
Cost of Goods Manufactured Schedule
For the Month Ended January 31, 2008

Work in process, January 1		$ -0-
Direct materials used	$24,000	
Direct labor	28,000	
Manufacturing overhead applied	**22,400**	
Total manufacturing costs		74,400
Total cost of work in process		74,400
Less: Work in process, January 31		35,400
Cost of goods manufactured		$39,000

Note that the cost of goods manufactured ($39,000) agrees with the amount transferred from Work in Process Inventory to Finished Goods Inventory in journal entry No. 7 in Illustration 2-16 (page 68).

The income statement and balance sheet are the same as those illustrated in Chapter 1. For example, Illustration 2-19 (page 70) shows the partial income statement for Wallace Manufacturing for the month of January.

Illustration 2-19
Partial income statement

WALLACE MANUFACTURING COMPANY
Income Statement (partial)
For the Month Ending January 31, 2008

Sales		$50,000
Cost of goods sold		
Finished goods inventory, January 1	$ -0-	
Cost of goods manufactured (See Illustration 2-18)	**39,000**	
Cost of goods available for sale	39,000	
Less: Finished goods inventory, January 31	-0-	
Cost of goods sold		39,000
Gross profit		$11,000

Under- or Overapplied Manufacturing Overhead

STUDY OBJECTIVE 6
Distinguish between under- and overapplied manufacturing overhead.

When Manufacturing Overhead has a **debit balance**, overhead is said to be underapplied. **Underapplied overhead** means that the overhead assigned to work in process is less than the overhead incurred. Conversely, when manufacturing overhead has a **credit balance**, overhead is overapplied. **Overapplied overhead** means that the overhead assigned to work in process is greater than the overhead incurred. Illustration 2-20 shows these concepts.

Illustration 2-20
Under- and overapplied overhead

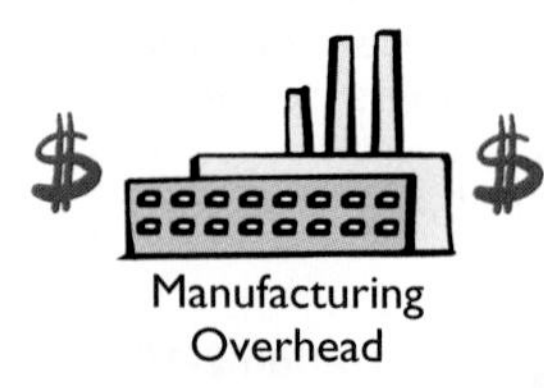

Manufacturing Overhead	
Actual (Costs incurred)	Applied (Costs assigned)

If actual is ***greater*** than applied, manufacturing overhead is underapplied.

If actual is ***less*** than applied, manufacturing overhead is overapplied.

YEAR-END BALANCE

At the end of the year, all manufacturing overhead transactions are complete. There is no further opportunity for offsetting events to occur. At this point, Wallace eliminates any balance in Manufacturing Overhead by an adjusting entry. It considers under- or overapplied overhead to be an **adjustment to cost of goods sold**. Thus, Wallace **debits underapplied overhead to Cost of Goods Sold**. It **credits overapplied overhead to Cost of Goods Sold**.

To illustrate, assume that Wallace Manufacturing has a $2,500 credit balance in Manufacturing Overhead at December 31. The adjusting entry for the overapplied overhead is:

Dec. 31	Manufacturing Overhead	2,500	
	Cost of Goods Sold		2,500
	(To transfer overapplied overhead to cost of goods sold)		

After Wallace posts this entry, Manufacturing Overhead has a zero balance. In preparing an income statement for the year, Wallace reports cost of goods sold **after adjusting it** for either under- or overapplied overhead.

Conceptually, some argue, under- or overapplied overhead at the end of the year should be allocated among ending work in process, finished goods, and cost of goods sold. The discussion of this possible allocation approach is left to more advanced courses.

ETHICS INSIGHT

Working a 25-Hour Day

In some industries, companies bill jobs on a "cost plus profit" basis. For example, law offices bill their customers based upon the "billable hours" incurred by their legal staff. This creates an incentive for law offices to pad their bills—that is, to overstate the costs incurred on particular jobs so as to inflate their bills. In one survey, two-thirds of attorneys reported knowledge of bill padding.

Similarly, suppliers to the government have often been accused of overbilling by misstating their cost accounting records. For example, the government recently filed a lawsuit against Northrop Grumman. This suit accused the company of intentionally concealing cost-accounting and material-tracking problems related to radar-jamming devices that the company made for the U.S. government more than 20 years before.These problems, the suit alleged, resulted in the government overpaying by $27 million. Company memos discussed strategies for training cost-accounting managers on how to conceal the problem from the government. One memo stated, "We can't tell the truth."

Sources: Nathan Koppel, "Lawyer's Charge Opens Window on Bill Padding," *Wall Street Journal*, August 30, 2006; and Andy Pasztor and Jonathan Karp, "Northrup Papers Indicate Coverup," *Wall Street Journal*, April 19, 2004.

? What feature of these businesses creates an incentive to misstate cost accounting data on particular jobs? What can customers do to protect themselves from overbilling?

DECISION TOOLKIT

Decision Checkpoints 	Info Needed for Decision 	Tool to Use for Decision 	How to Evaluate Results 
Has the company over- or underapplied overhead for the period?	Actual overhead costs and overhead applied	Manufacturing overhead account	If the account balance is a credit, overhead applied exceeded actual overhead costs. If the account balance is a debit, overhead applied was less than actual overhead costs.

Before You Go On...

REVIEW IT

1. When do companies make entries to record the completion and sale of a job?
2. What costs are included in total manufacturing costs in the cost of goods manufactured schedule?

Be sure to read **ALL ABOUT YOU: *Minding Your Own Business*** on page 72 for information on how topics in this chapter apply to you.

Minding Your Own Business

After graduating, you might decide to start a small business. As discussed in this chapter, owners of any business need to know how to calculate the cost of their products. In fact, many small businesses fail because they do not accurately calculate their product costs, so they don't know if they are making money or losing money—until it is too late.

Some Facts

* There are about 17.6 million sole proprietorships in the U.S. The most common type of sole proprietorship is construction contractor.
* During a recent year, 25% of all sole proprietorships reported losses. The safest business is surveying and mapping, with only 6% of firms reporting losses. The riskiest business is hunting and trapping, with 76% of firms reporting losses.
* *Inc.* Magazine ranked the following as the top ten best places to start a business in 2006: Yuma, AZ; St. George, UT: Cape Coral–Fort Myers, FL; Fort Walton Beach–Crestview–Destin, FL; Coeur d'Alene, ID; Bellingham, WA; Port St. Lucie–Fort Pierce, FL; Naples–Marco Island, FL: Las Vegas–Paradise, NV; Idaho Falls, ID.
* About.com ranked the top ten business opportunities for 2005: business coach (motivates managers); business broker (brings together buyers and sellers of businesses); garage-organizing service; designing and producing smart (customized) clothes; medical transcription; trash removal; anti-aging spas; college admissions consulting; translation services; gaming-related businesses.

About the Numbers

Instead of starting your own business from scratch, perhaps you think it makes more sense to purchase a franchise. Initial investment varies, and annual franchise fees range from about $20,000 up to $80,000. The nearby chart of some well-known franchises shows the investment you typically need to make for these franchises. As you can see, you have to generate considerable revenue to cover the investment and related franchise fees. That's a lot of overhead.

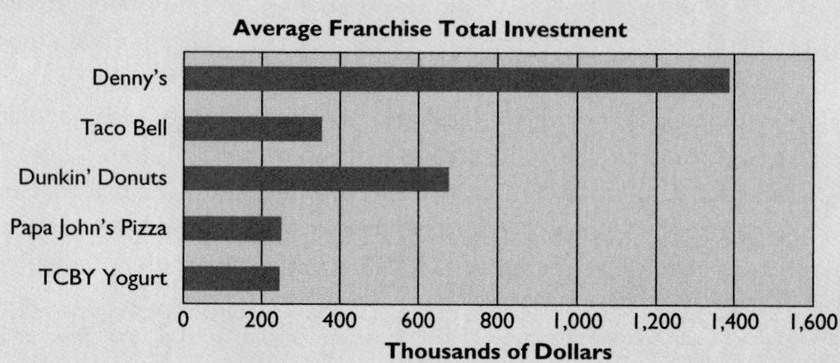

Source for graph: AllBusiness.com, *www.allbusiness.com/franchise/listings.asp?cat=4933&sub=4970* (accessed June 2006).

What Do You Think?

Suppose that you decide to start a landscape business. You use an old pickup truck that you've fully paid for. You store the truck and other equipment in your parents' barn, and you store trees and shrubs on their land. Your parents will not charge you for the use of these facilities for the first two years, but beginning in the third year they will charge a reasonable rent. Your mother helps you by answering phone calls and providing customers with information. She doesn't charge you for this service, but she plans on doing it for only your first two years in business.

In pricing your services, should you include charges for the truck, the barn, the land, and your mother's services when calculating your product cost?

YES: If you don't include charges for these costs, your costs are understated and your profitability is overstated.

NO: At this point you are not actually incurring costs related to these activities, therefore you shouldn't record charges.

Sources: *www.bizstats.com;* Darrel Zahorsky, "10 Best Small Business Opportunities for 2005," *sbinformation.about.com* (accessed June 2006); Joel Kotkin, "Boomtowns '06," *Inc.* Magazine, May 2006, p. 97.

The authors' comments on this situation appear on page 93.

Using the Decision Toolkit

Martinez Building Products Company is one of the largest manufacturers and marketers of unique, custom-made residential garage doors in the U.S. It also is a major supplier of industrial and commercial doors, grills, and counter shutters for the new-construction, repair, and remodel markets. Martinez has developed plans for continued expansion of a network of service operations that sell, install, and service manufactured fireplaces, garage doors, and related products.

Martinez uses a job cost system and applies overhead to production on the basis of direct labor cost. In computing a predetermined overhead rate for the year 2008, the company estimated manufacturing overhead to be $24 million and direct labor costs to be $20 million. In addition, it developed the following information.

Actual Costs Incurred During 2008	
Direct materials used	$30,000,000
Direct labor cost incurred	21,000,000
Insurance, factory	500,000
Indirect labor	7,500,000
Factory maintenance	1,000,000
Rent on factory building	11,000,000
Depreciation on factory equipment	2,000,000

Instructions

Answer each of the following.

(a) Why is Martinez Building Products Company using a job order costing system?

(b) On what basis does Martinez allocate its manufacturing overhead? Compute the predetermined overhead rate for 2008.

(c) Compute the amount of the under- or overapplied overhead for 2008.

(d) Martinez had balances in the beginning and ending work in process and finished goods accounts as follows.

	1/1/08	12/31/08
Work in process	$ 5,000,000	$ 4,000,000
Finished goods	13,000,000	11,000,000

Determine the (1) cost of goods manufactured and (2) cost of goods sold for Martinez during 2008. Assume that any under- or overapplied overhead should be included in the cost of goods sold.

(e) During 2008, Job G408 was started and completed. Its cost sheet showed a total cost of $100,000, and the company prices its product at 50% above its cost. What is the price to the customer if the company follows this pricing strategy?

Solution

(a) The company is using a job order system because it custom-makes garage doors. Each job has its own distinguishing characteristics. For example, each garage door would be different, and therefore a different cost per garage door can be assigned.

(b) The company allocates its overhead on the basis of direct labor cost. The predetermined overhead rate is 120%, computed as follows.

$$\$24{,}000{,}000 \div \$20{,}000{,}000 = 120\%$$

(c)

Actual manufacturing overhead	$22,000,000
Applied overhead cost ($21,000,000 × 120%)	25,200,000
Overapplied overhead	$ 3,200,000

(d) (1)	Work in process, 1/1/08		$ 5,000,000
	Direct materials used	$30,000,000	
	Direct labor	21,000,000	
	Manufacturing overhead applied	25,200,000	
	Total manufacturing costs		76,200,000
	Total cost of work in process		81,200,000
	Less: Work in process, 12/31/08		4,000,000
	Cost of goods manufactured		$77,200,000
(2)	Finished goods inventory, 1/1/08	$13,000,000	
	Cost of goods manufactured (see above)	77,200,000	
	Cost of goods available for sale	90,200,000	
	Finished goods inventory, 12/31/08	11,000,000	
	Cost of goods sold (unadjusted)	79,200,000	
	Less: Overapplied overhead	3,200,000	
	Cost of goods sold	$76,000,000	
(e)	G408 cost	$ 100,000	
	Markup percentage	× 50%	
	Profit	$ 50,000	

Price to customer: $150,000 ($100,000 + $50,000)

The Navigator

SUMMARY OF STUDY OBJECTIVES

1 **Explain the characteristics and purposes of cost accounting.** Cost accounting involves the procedures for measuring, recording, and reporting product costs. From the data accumulated, companies determine the total cost and the unit cost of each product. The two basic types of cost accounting systems are job order cost and process cost.

2 **Describe the flow of costs in a job order costing system.** In job order costing, companies first accumulate manufacturing costs in three accounts: Raw Materials Inventory, Factory Labor, and Manufacturing Overhead. They then assign the accumulated costs to Work in Process Inventory and eventually to Finished Goods Inventory and Cost of Goods Sold.

3 **Explain the nature and importance of a job cost sheet.** A job cost sheet is a form used to record the costs chargeable to a specific job and to determine the total and unit costs of the completed job. Job cost sheets constitute the subsidiary ledger for the Work in Process Inventory control account.

4 **Indicate how the predetermined overhead rate is determined and used.** The predetermined overhead rate is based on the relationship between estimated annual overhead costs and expected annual operating activity. This is expressed in terms of a common activity base, such as direct labor cost. Companies use this rate to assign overhead costs to work in process and to specific jobs.

5 **Prepare entries for jobs completed and sold.** When jobs are completed, companies debit the cost to Finished Goods Inventory and credit it to Work in Process Inventory. When a job is sold, the entries are: (a) Debit Cash or Accounts Receivable and credit Sales for the selling price; and (b) debit Cost of Goods Sold and credit Finished Goods Inventory for the cost of the goods.

6 **Distinguish between under- and overapplied manufacturing overhead.** Underapplied manufacturing overhead indicates that the overhead assigned to work in process is less than the overhead incurred. Overapplied overhead indicates that the overhead assigned to work in process is greater than the overhead incurred.

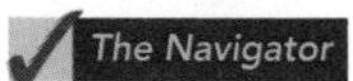

DECISION TOOLKIT—A SUMMARY

Decision Checkpoints 	Info Needed for Decision 	Tool to Use for Decision 	How to Evaluate Results 
What is the cost of a job?	Cost of material, labor, and overhead assigned to a specific job	Job cost sheet	Compare costs to those of previous periods and to those of competitors to ensure that costs are in line. Compare costs to expected selling price or service fees charged to determine overall profitability.
Has the company over- or underapplied overhead for the period?	Actual overhead costs and overhead applied	Manufacturing overhead account	If the account balance is a credit, overhead applied exceeded actual overhead costs. If the account balance is a debit, overhead applied was less than actual overhead costs.

GLOSSARY

Cost accounting An area of accounting that involves measuring, recording, and reporting product costs. (p. 54)

Cost accounting system Manufacturing-cost accounts that are fully integrated into the general ledger of a company. (p. 54)

Job cost sheet A form used to record the costs chargeable to a specific job and to determine the total and unit costs of the completed job. (p. 59)

Job order cost system A cost accounting system in which costs are assigned to each job or batch. (p. 54)

Materials requisition slip A document authorizing the issuance of raw materials from the storeroom to production. (p. 60)

Overapplied overhead A situation in which overhead assigned to work in process is greater than the overhead incurred. (p. 70)

Predetermined overhead rate A rate based on the relationship between estimated annual overhead costs and expected annual operating activity, expressed in terms of a common activity base. (p. 63)

Process cost system A cost accounting system used when a company manufactures a large volume of similar products. (p. 55)

Summary entry A journal entry that summarizes the totals from multiple transactions. (p. 58)

Time ticket A document that indicates the employee, the hours worked, the account and job to be charged, and the total labor cost. (p. 61)

Underapplied overhead A situation in which overhead assigned to work in process is less than the overhead incurred. (p. 70)

Demonstration Problem

During February, Cardella Manufacturing works on two jobs: A16 and B17. Summary data concerning these jobs are as follows.

Manufacturing Costs Incurred

Purchased $54,000 of raw materials on account.
Factory labor $76,000, plus $4,000 employer payroll taxes.
Manufacturing overhead exclusive of indirect materials and indirect labor $59,800.

Assignment of Costs

Direct materials:	Job A16 $27,000, Job B17 $21,000
Indirect materials:	$3,000
Direct labor:	Job A16 $52,000, Job B17 $26,000
Indirect labor:	$2,000

Manufacturing overhead rate: 80% of direct labor costs.

The company completed Job A16 and sold it on account for $150,000. Job B17 was only partially completed.

Instructions

(a) Journalize the February transactions in the sequence followed in the chapter.
(b) What was the amount of under- or overapplied manufacturing overhead?

action plan

- ✓ In accumulating costs, debit three accounts: Raw Materials Inventory, Factory Labor, and Manufacturing Overhead.
- ✓ When Work in Process Inventory is debited, credit one of the three accounts listed above.
- ✓ Debit Finished Goods Inventory for the cost of completed jobs. Debit Cost of Goods Sold for the cost of jobs sold.
- ✓ Overhead is underapplied when Manufacturing Overhead has a debit balance.

Solution

(a)

	1.		
Feb. 28	Raw Materials Inventory	54,000	
	Accounts Payable		54,000
	(Purchase of raw materials on account)		
	2.		
28	Factory Labor	80,000	
	Factory Wages Payable		76,000
	Employer Payroll Taxes Payable		4,000
	(To record factory labor costs)		
	3.		
28	Manufacturing Overhead	59,800	
	Accounts Payable, Accumulated Depreciation, and Prepaid Insurance		59,800
	(To record overhead costs)		
	4.		
28	Work in Process Inventory	48,000	
	Manufacturing Overhead	3,000	
	Raw Materials Inventory		51,000
	(To assign raw materials to production)		
	5.		
28	Work in Process Inventory	78,000	
	Manufacturing Overhead	2,000	
	Factory Labor		80,000
	(To assign factory labor to production)		
	6.		
28	Work in Process Inventory	62,400	
	Manufacturing Overhead		62,400
	(To assign overhead to jobs— 80% × $78,000)		
	7.		
28	Finished Goods Inventory	120,600	
	Work in Process Inventory		120,600
	(To record completion of Job A16: direct materials $27,000, direct labor $52,000, and manufacturing overhead $41,600)		
	8.		
28	Accounts Receivable	150,000	
	Sales		150,000
	(To record sale of Job A16)		
28	Cost of Goods Sold	120,600	
	Finished Goods Inventory		120,600
	(To record cost of sale for Job A16)		

(b) Manufacturing Overhead has a debit balance of $2,400 as shown below.

Manufacturing Overhead

(3)	59,800	(6)	62,400
(4)	3,000		
(5)	2,000		
Bal.	2,400		

Thus, manufacturing overhead is underapplied for the month.

SELF-STUDY QUESTIONS

Answers are at the end of the chapter.

(SO 1) **1.** Cost accounting involves the measuring, recording, and reporting of:
a. product costs.
b. future costs.
c. manufacturing processes.
d. managerial accounting decisions.

(SO 2) **2.** In accumulating raw materials costs, companies debit the cost of raw materials purchased in a perpetual system to:
a. Raw Materials Purchases.
b. Raw Materials Inventory.
c. Purchases.
d. Work in Process.

(SO 2) **3.** When incurred, factory labor costs are debited to:
a. Work in Process.
b. Factory Wages Expense.
c. Factory Labor.
d. Factory Wages Payable.

(SO 3) **4.** The source documents for assigning costs to job cost sheets are:
a. invoices, time tickets, and the predetermined overhead rate.
b. materials requisition slips, time tickets, and the actual overhead costs.
c. materials requisition slips, payroll register, and the predetermined overhead rate.
d. materials requisition slips, time tickets, and the predetermined overhead rate.

(SO 3) **5.** In recording the issuance of raw materials in a job order cost system, it would be *incorrect* to:
a. debit Work in Process Inventory.
b. debit Finished Goods Inventory.
c. debit Manufacturing Overhead.
d. credit Raw Materials Inventory.

(SO 3) **6.** The entry when direct factory labor is assigned to jobs is a debit to:
a. Work in Process Inventory and a credit to Factory Labor.
b. Manufacturing Overhead and a credit to Factory Labor.
c. Factory Labor and a credit to Manufacturing Overhead.
d. Factory Labor and a credit to Work in Process Inventory.

7. The formula for computing the predetermined manufacturing overhead rate is estimated annual overhead costs divided by an expected annual operating activity, expressed as: (SO 4)
a. direct labor cost.
b. direct labor hours.
c. machine hours.
d. any of the above.

8. In Crawford Company, the predetermined overhead rate is 80% of direct labor cost. During the month, Crawford incurs $210,000 of factory labor costs, of which $180,000 is direct labor and $30,000 is indirect labor. Actual overhead incurred was $200,000. The amount of overhead debited to Work in Process Inventory should be: (SO 4)
a. $200,000.
b. $144,000.
c. $168,000.
d. $160,000.

9. Mynex Company completes Job No. 26 at a cost of $4,500 and later sells it for $7,000 cash. A correct entry is: (SO 5)
a. Debit Finished Goods Inventory $7,000 and credit Work in Process Inventory $7,000.
b. Debit Cost of Goods Sold $7,000 and credit Finished Goods Inventory $7,000.
c. Debit Finished Goods Inventory $4,500 and credit Work in Process Inventory $4,500.
d. Debit Accounts Receivable $7,000 and credit Sales $7,000.

10. Manufacturing overhead is underapplied if: (SO 6)
a. actual overhead is less than applied.
b. actual overhead is greater than applied.
c. the predetermined rate equals the actual rate.
d. actual overhead equals applied overhead.

Go to the book's website, **www.wiley.com/college/weygandt**, for Additional Self-Study questions.

QUESTIONS

1. (a) Joe Delong is not sure about the difference between cost accounting and a cost accounting system. Explain the difference to Joe. (b) What is an important feature of a cost accounting system?

2. (a) Distinguish between the two types of cost accounting systems. (b) May a company use both types of cost accounting systems?

3. What type of industry is likely to use a job order cost system? Give some examples.
4. What type of industry is likely to use a process cost system? Give some examples.
5. Your roommate asks your help in understanding the major steps in the flow of costs in a job order cost system. Identify the steps for your roommate.
6. There are three inventory control accounts in a job order system. Identify the control accounts and their subsidiary ledgers.
7. What source documents are used in accumulating direct labor costs?
8. "Entries to Manufacturing Overhead normally are only made daily." Do you agree? Explain.
9. Tony Andres is confused about the source documents used in assigning materials and labor costs. Identify the documents and give the entry for each document.
10. What is the purpose of a job cost sheet?
11. Indicate the source documents that are used in charging costs to specific jobs.
12. Explain the purpose and use of a "materials requisition slip" as used in a job order cost system.
13. Mel Finney believes actual manufacturing overhead should be charged to jobs. Do you agree? Why or why not?
14. What relationships are involved in computing a predetermined overhead rate?
15. How can the agreement of Work in Process Inventory and job cost sheets be verified?
16. Tina Birk believes that the cost of goods manufactured schedule in job order cost accounting is the same as shown in Chapter 1. Is Tina correct? Explain.
17. Jeff Gillum is confused about under- and overapplied manufacturing overhead. Define the terms for Jeff, and indicate the balance in the manufacturing overhead account applicable to each term.
18. "At the end of the year, under- or overapplied overhead is closed to Income Summary." Is this correct? If not, indicate the customary treatment of this amount.

BRIEF EXERCISES

Prepare a flowchart of a job order cost accounting system, and identify transactions.
(SO 2)

BE2-1 Reyes Tool & Die begins operations on January 1. Because all work is done to customer specifications, the company decides to use a job order costing system. Prepare a flow chart of a typical job order system with arrows showing the flow of costs. Identify the eight transactions.

Prepare entries in accumulating manufacturing costs.
(SO 2)

BE2-2 During January, its first month of operations, Reyes Tool & Die accumulated the following manufacturing costs: raw materials $4,000 on account, factory labor $5,000 of which $4,200 relates to factory wages payable and $800 relates to payroll taxes payable, and utilities payable $2,000. Prepare separate journal entries for each type of manufacturing cost.

Prepare entry for the assignment of raw materials costs.
(SO 2)

BE2-3 In January, Reyes Tool & Die requisitions raw materials for production as follows: Job 1 $900, Job 2 $1,200, Job 3 $700, and general factory use $600. Prepare a summary journal entry to record raw materials used.

Prepare entry for the assignment of factory labor costs.
(SO 2)

BE2-4 Factory labor data for Reyes Tool & Die is given in BE2-2. During January, time tickets show that the factory labor of $5,000 was used as follows: Job 1 $1,200, Job 2 $1,600 Job 3 $1,400, and general factory use $800. Prepare a summary journal entry to record factory labor used.

Prepare job cost sheets.
(SO 3)

BE2-5 Data pertaining to job cost sheets for Reyes Tool & Die are given in BE2-3 and BE2-4. Prepare the job cost sheets for each of the three jobs. (*Note*: You may omit the column for Manufacturing Overhead.)

Compute predetermined overhead rates.
(SO 4)

BE2-6 Marquis Company estimates that annual manufacturing overhead costs will be $800,000. Estimated annual operating activity bases are: direct labor cost $500,000, direct labor hours 50,000, and machine hours 100,000. Compute the predetermined overhead rate for each activity base.

Assign manufacturing overhead to production.
(SO 4)

BE2-7 During the first quarter, Diaz Company incurs the following direct labor costs: January $40,000, February $30,000, and March $50,000. For each month, prepare the entry to assign overhead to production using a predetermined rate of 90% of direct labor cost.

Prepare entries for completion and sale of completed jobs.
(SO 5)

BE2-8 In March, Hollaway Company completes Jobs 10 and 11. Job 10 cost $25,000 and Job 11 $30,000. On March 31, Job 10 is sold to the customer for $35,000 in cash. Journalize the entries for the completion of the two jobs and the sale of Job 10.

Prepare adjusting entries for under- and overapplied overhead.
(SO 6)

BE2-9 At December 31, balances in Manufacturing Overhead are: Lott Company—debit $1,500, Perez Company—credit $900. Prepare the adjusting entry for each company at December 31, assuming the adjustment is made to cost of goods sold.

EXERCISES

Prepare entries for factory labor.
(SO 2, 3)

E2-1 The gross earnings of the factory workers for Brantley Company during the month of January are $60,000. The employer's payroll taxes for the factory payroll are $8,000. The fringe benefits to be paid by the employer on this payroll are $4,000. Of the total accumulated cost of factory labor, 85% is related to direct labor and 15% is attributable to indirect labor.

Instructions

(a) Prepare the entry to record the factory labor costs for the month of January.
(b) Prepare the entry to assign factory labor to production.

Prepare journal entries for manufacturing costs.
(SO 2, 3, 4, 5)

E2-2 Milner Manufacturing uses a job order costing system. On May 1, the company has a balance in Work in Process Inventory of $3,200 and two jobs in process: Job No. 429 $2,000, and Job No. 430 $1,200. During May, a summary of source documents reveals the following.

Job Number	Materials Requisition Slips		Labor Time Tickets	
429	$2,500		$1,900	
430	3,500		3,000	
431	4,400	$10,400	7,600	$12,500
General use		800		1,200
		$11,200		$13,700

Milner Manufacturing applies manufacturing overhead to jobs at an overhead rate of 80% of direct labor cost. Job No. 429 is completed during the month.

Instructions

(a) Prepare summary journal entries to record: (i) the requisition slips, (ii) the time tickets, (iii) the assignment of manufacturing overhead to jobs, and (iv) the completion of Job No. 429.
(b) Post the entries to Work in Process Inventory, and prove the agreement of the control account with the job cost sheets.

Analyze a job cost sheet and prepare entries for manufacturing costs.
(SO 2, 3, 4, 5)

E2-3 A job order cost sheet for Rolen Company is shown below.

Job No. 92			For 2,000 Units
Date	Direct Materials	Direct Labor	Manufacturing Overhead
Beg. bal. Jan. 1	5,000	6,000	4,500
8	6,000		
12		8,000	6,400
25	2,000		
27		4,000	3,200
	13,000	18,000	14,100
Cost of completed job:			
Direct materials			$13,000
Direct labor			18,000
Manufacturing overhead			14,100
Total cost			$45,100
Unit cost ($45,100 ÷ 2,000)			$22.55

Instructions

(a) On the basis of the foregoing data answer the following questions.
(1) What was the balance in Work in Process Inventory on January 1 if this was the only unfinished job?
(2) If manufacturing overhead is applied on the basis of direct labor cost, what overhead rate was used in each year?
(b) Prepare summary entries at January 31 to record the current year's transactions pertaining to Job No. 92.

Analyze costs of manufacturing and determine missing amounts.

(SO 2, 5)

E2-4 Manufacturing cost data for Pena Company, which uses a job order cost system, are presented below.

	Case A	Case B	Case C
Direct materials used	$ (a)	$ 83,000	$ 63,150
Direct labor	50,000	120,000	(h)
Manufacturing overhead applied	42,500	(d)	(i)
Total manufacturing costs	155,650	(e)	213,000
Work in process 1/1/08	(b)	15,500	18,000
Total cost of work in process	201,500	(f)	(j)
Work in process 12/31/08	(c)	11,800	(k)
Cost of goods manufactured	192,300	(g)	222,000

Instructions

Indicate the missing amount for each letter. Assume that in all cases manufacturing overhead is applied on the basis of direct labor cost and the rate is the same.

Compute the manufacturing overhead rate and under- or overapplied overhead.

(SO 4, 6)

E2-5 Renteria Company applies manufacturing overhead to jobs on the basis of machine hours used. Overhead costs are expected to total $305,000 for the year, and machine usage is estimated at 125,000 hours.

For the year, $322,000 of overhead costs are incurred and 130,000 hours are used.

Instructions

(a) Compute the manufacturing overhead rate for the year.
(b) What is the amount of under- or overapplied overhead at December 31?
(c) Prepare the adjusting entry to assign the under- or overapplied overhead for the year to cost of goods sold.

Analyze job cost sheet and prepare entry for completed job.

(SO 2, 3, 4, 5)

E2-6 A job cost sheet of Nilson Company is given below.

Job Cost Sheet

JOB NO. 469 — Quantity 2,000
ITEM White Lion Cages — Date Requested 7/2
FOR Tesla Company — Date Completed 7/31

Date	Direct Materials	Direct Labor	Manufacturing Overhead
7/10	825		
12	900		
15		440	550
22		380	475
24	1,600		
27	1,500		
31		540	675

Cost of completed job:	
Direct materials	____
Direct labor	____
Manufacturing overhead	____
Total cost	____
Unit cost	____

Instructions

(a) Answer the following questions.
(1) What are the source documents for direct materials, direct labor, and manufacturing overhead costs assigned to this job?
(2) What is the predetermined manufacturing overhead rate?
(3) What are the total cost and the unit cost of the completed job? (Round unit cost to nearest cent.)
(b) Prepare the entry to record the completion of the job.

E2-7 Elder Corporation incurred the following transactions.

Prepare entries for manufacturing costs.

(SO 2, 3, 4, 5)

1. Purchased raw materials on account $46,300.
2. Raw Materials of $36,000 were requisitioned to the factory. An analysis of the materials requisition slips indicated that $6,800 was classified as indirect materials.
3. Factory labor costs incurred were $53,900, of which $49,000 pertained to factory wages payable and $4,900 pertained to employer payroll taxes payable.
4. Time tickets indicated that $48,000 was direct labor and $5,900 was indirect labor.
5. Overhead costs incurred on account were $80,500.
6. Manufacturing overhead was applied at the rate of 150% of direct labor cost.
7. Goods costing $88,000 were completed and transferred to finished goods.
8. Finished goods costing $75,000 to manufacture were sold on account for $103,000.

Instructions

Journalize the transactions. (Omit explanations.)

E2-8 Garnett Printing Corp. uses a job order cost system. The following data summarize the operations related to the first quarter's production.

Prepare entries for manufacturing costs.

(SO 2, 3, 4, 5)

1. Materials purchased on account $192,000, and factory wages incurred $87,300.
2. Materials requisitioned and factory labor used by job:

Job Number	Materials	Factory Labor
A20	$ 35,240	$18,000
A21	42,920	22,000
A22	36,100	15,000
A23	39,270	25,000
General factory use	4,470	7,300
	$158,000	$87,300

3. Manufacturing overhead costs incurred on account $39,500.
4. Depreciation on machinery and equipment $14,550.
5. Manufacturing overhead rate is 80% of direct labor cost.
6. Jobs completed during the quarter: A20, A21, and A23.

Instructions

Prepare entries to record the operations summarized above. (Prepare a schedule showing the individual cost elements and total cost for each job in item 6.)

E2-9 At May 31, 2008, the accounts of Hannifan Manufacturing Company show the following.

Prepare a cost of goods manufactured schedule and partial financial statements.

(SO 2, 5)

1. May 1 inventories—finished goods $12,600, work in process $14,700, and raw materials $8,200.
2. May 31 inventories—finished goods $9,500, work in process $17,900, and raw materials $7,100.
3. Debit postings to work in process were: direct materials $62,400, direct labor $32,000, and manufacturing overhead applied $40,000.
4. Sales totaled $200,000.

Instructions

(a) Prepare a condensed cost of goods manufactured schedule.
(b) Prepare an income statement for May through gross profit.
(c) Indicate the balance sheet presentation of the manufacturing inventories at May 31, 2008.

E2-10 Tomlin Company begins operations on April 1. Information from job cost sheets shows the following.

Compute work in process and finished goods from job cost sheets.

(SO 3, 5)

Job Number	Manufacturing Costs Assigned: April	May	June	Month Completed
10	$5,200	$4,400		May
11	4,100	3,900	$3,000	June
12	1,200			April
13		4,700	4,500	June
14		4,900	3,600	Not complete

Job 12 was completed in April. Job 10 was completed in May. Jobs 11 and 13 were completed in June. Each job was sold for 25% above its cost in the month following completion.

Instructions

(a) What is the balance in Work in Process Inventory at the end of each month?
(b) What is the balance in Finished Goods Inventory at the end of each month?
(c) What is the gross profit for May, June, and July?

Prepare entries for costs of services provided.
(SO 2, 4, 5)

E2-11 Shown below are the job cost related accounts for the law firm of Barnes, King, and Morton and their manufacturing equivalents:

Law Firm Accounts	Manufacturing Firm Accounts
Supplies	Raw Materials
Salaries Payable	Factory Wages Payable
Operating Overhead	Manufacturing Overhead
Work in Process	Work in Process
Cost of Completed Work	Cost of Goods Sold

Cost data for the month of March follow.

1. Purchased supplies on account $1,500.
2. Issued supplies $1,200 (60% direct and 40% indirect).
3. Time cards for the month indicated labor costs of $50,000 (80% direct and 20% indirect).
4. Operating overhead costs incurred for cash totaled $40,000.
5. Operating overhead is applied at a rate of 90% of direct attorney cost.
6. Work completed totaled $70,000.

Instructions

(a) Journalize the transactions for March. Omit explanations.
(b) Determine the balance of the Work in Process account. Use a T account.

Determine cost of jobs and ending balance in work in process and overhead accounts.
(SO 3, 4, 6)

E2-12 Pedro Morales and Associates, a C.P.A. firm, uses job order costing to capture the costs of its audit jobs. There were no audit jobs in process at the beginning of November. Listed below are data concerning the three audit jobs conducted during November.

	Gonzalez	Navarro	Rojas
Direct materials	$600	$400	$200
Auditor labor costs	$5,400	$6,600	$3,375
Auditor hours	72	88	45

Overhead costs are applied to jobs on the basis of auditor hours, and the predetermined overhead rate is $55 per auditor hour. The Gonzalez job is the only incomplete job at the end of November. Actual overhead for the month was $12,000.

Instructions

(a) Determine the cost of each job.
(b) Indicate the balance of the Work in Process account at the end of November.
(c) Calculate the ending balance of the Manufacturing Overhead account for November.

Determine predetermined overhead rate, apply overhead and determine whether balance under- or overapplied.
(SO 4, 6)

E2-13 Easy Decorating uses a job order costing system to collect the costs of its interior decorating business. Each client's consultation is treated as a separate job. Overhead is applied to each job based on the number of decorator hours incurred. Listed below are data for the current year.

Estimated overhead	$960,000
Actual overhead	$982,800
Estimated decorator hours	40,000
Actual decorator hours	40,500

The company uses Operating Overhead in place of Manufacturing Overhead.

Instructions

(a) Compute the predetermined overhead rate.
(b) Prepare the entry to apply the overhead for the year.
(c) Determine whether the overhead was under- or overapplied and by how much.

EXERCISES: SET B

Visit the book's website at **www.wiley.com/college/weygandt**, and choose the Student Companion site, to access Exercise Set B.

PROBLEMS: SET A

Prepare entries in a job cost system and job cost sheets.

(SO 2, 3, 4, 5, 6)

P2-1A Garcia Manufacturing uses a job order cost system and applies overhead to production on the basis of direct labor costs. On January 1, 2008, Job No. 50 was the only job in process. The costs incurred prior to January 1 on this job were as follows: direct materials $20,000, direct labor $12,000, and manufacturing overhead $16,000. As of January 1, Job No. 49 had been completed at a cost of $90,000 and was part of finished goods inventory. There was a $15,000 balance in the Raw Materials Inventory account.

During the month of January, Garcia Manufacturing began production on Jobs 51 and 52, and completed Jobs 50 and 51. Jobs 49 and 50 were also sold on account during the month for $122,000 and $158,000, respectively. The following additional events occurred during the month.

1. Purchased additional raw materials of $90,000 on account.
2. Incurred factory labor costs of $65,000. Of this amount $16,000 related to employer payroll taxes.
3. Incurred manufacturing overhead costs as follows: indirect materials $17,000; indirect labor $15,000; depreciation expense $19,000, and various other manufacturing overhead costs on account $20,000.
4. Assigned direct materials and direct labor to jobs as follows.

Job No.	Direct Materials	Direct Labor
50	$10,000	$ 5,000
51	39,000	25,000
52	30,000	20,000

Instructions

(a) Calculate the predetermined overhead rate for 2008, assuming Garcia Manufacturing estimates total manufacturing overhead costs of $1,050,000, direct labor costs of $700,000, and direct labor hours of 20,000 for the year.

(b) Open job cost sheets for Jobs 50, 51, and 52. Enter the January 1 balances on the job cost sheet for Job No. 50.

(c) Prepare the journal entries to record the purchase of raw materials, the factory labor costs incurred, and the manufacturing overhead costs incurred during the month of January.

(d) Prepare the journal entries to record the assignment of direct materials, direct labor, and manufacturing overhead costs to production. In assigning manufacturing overhead costs, use the overhead rate calculated in (a). Post all costs to the job cost sheets as necessary.

(e) Total the job cost sheets for any job(s) completed during the month. Prepare the journal entry (or entries) to record the completion of any job(s) during the month.

(e) Job 50, $70,500
Job 51, $101,500

(f) Prepare the journal entry (or entries) to record the sale of any job(s) during the month.

(g) What is the balance in the Finished Goods Inventory account at the end of the month? What does this balance consist of?

(h) What is the amount of over- or underapplied overhead?

Prepare entries in a job cost system and partial income statement.

(SO 2, 3, 4, 5, 6)

P2-2A For the year ended December 31, 2008, the job cost sheets of DeVoe Company contained the following data.

Job Number	Explanation	Direct Materials	Direct Labor	Manufacturing Overhead	Total Costs
7640	Balance 1/1	$25,000	$24,000	$28,800	$ 77,800
	Current year's costs	30,000	36,000	43,200	109,200
7641	Balance 1/1	11,000	18,000	21,600	50,600
	Current year's costs	43,000	48,000	57,600	148,600
7642	Current year's costs	48,000	55,000	66,000	169,000

Other data:

1. Raw materials inventory totaled $15,000 on January 1. During the year, $140,000 of raw materials were purchased on account.
2. Finished goods on January 1 consisted of Job No. 7638 for $87,000 and Job No. 7639 for $92,000.
3. Job No. 7640 and Job No. 7641 were completed during the year.
4. Job Nos. 7638, 7639, and 7641 were sold on account for $530,000.
5. Manufacturing overhead incurred on account totaled $120,000.
6. Other manufacturing overhead consisted of indirect materials $14,000, indirect labor $20,000, and depreciation on factory machinery $8,000.

Instructions

(a) $169,000; Job 7642: $169,000

(a) Prove the agreement of Work in Process Inventory with job cost sheets pertaining to unfinished work. *Hint:* Use a single T account for Work in Process Inventory. Calculate each of the following, then post each to the T account: (1) beginning balance, (2) direct materials, (3) direct labor, (4) manufacturing overhead, and (5) completed jobs.

(b) Amount = $4,800

(b) Prepare the adjusting entry for manufacturing overhead, assuming the balance is allocated entirely to Cost of Goods Sold.

(c) $156,600

(c) Determine the gross profit to be reported for 2008.

Prepare entries in a job cost system and cost of goods manufactured schedule.

(SO 2, 3, 4, 5)

P2-3A Enos Inc. is a construction company specializing in custom patios. The patios are constructed of concrete, brick, fiberglass, and lumber, depending upon customer preference. On June 1, 2008, the general ledger for Enos Inc. contains the following data.

Raw Materials Inventory	$4,200	Manufacturing Overhead Applied	$32,640
Work in Process Inventory	$5,540	Manufacturing Overhead Incurred	$31,650

Subsidiary data for Work in Process Inventory on June 1 are as follows.

Job Cost Sheets

	Customer Job		
Cost Element	**Fowler**	**Haines**	**Krantz**
Direct materials	$ 600	$ 800	$ 900
Direct labor	320	540	580
Manufacturing overhead	400	675	725
	$1,320	$2,015	$2,205

During June, raw materials purchased on account were $3,900, and all wages were paid. Additional overhead costs consisted of depreciation on equipment $700 and miscellaneous costs of $400 incurred on account.

A summary of materials requisition slips and time tickets for June shows the following.

Customer Job	Materials Requisition Slips	Time Tickets
Fowler	$ 800	$ 450
Elgin	2,000	800
Haines	500	360
Krantz	1,300	1,600
Fowler	300	390
	4,900	3,600
General use	1,500	1,200
	$6,400	$4,800

Overhead was charged to jobs at the same rate of $1.25 per dollar of direct labor cost. The patios for customers Fowler, Haines, and Krantz were completed during June and sold for a total of $18,900. Each customer paid in full.

Instructions

(a) Journalize the June transactions: (i) for purchase of raw materials, factory labor costs incurred, and manufacturing overhead costs incurred; (ii) assignment of direct materials, labor, and overhead to production; and (iii) completion of jobs and sale of goods.

(b) Post the entries to Work in Process Inventory.

(c) Reconcile the balance in Work in Process Inventory with the costs of unfinished jobs.
(d) Prepare a cost of goods manufactured schedule for June.

(d) Cost of goods manufactured $14,740

Compute predetermined overhead rates, apply overhead and calculate under- or overapplied overhead.

(SO 4, 6)

P2-4A Mabry Manufacturing Company uses a job order cost system in each of its three manufacturing departments. Manufacturing overhead is applied to jobs on the basis of direct labor cost in Department D, direct labor hours in Department E, and machine hours in Department K.

In establishing the predetermined overhead rates for 2008 the following estimates were made for the year.

	Department		
	D	E	K
Manufacturing overhead	$1,050,000	$1,500,000	$840,000
Direct labor costs	$1,500,000	$1,250,000	$450,000
Direct labor hours	100,000	125,000	40,000
Machine hours	400,000	500,000	120,000

During January, the job cost sheets showed the following costs and production data.

	Department		
	D	E	K
Direct materials used	$140,000	$126,000	$78,000
Direct labor costs	$120,000	$110,000	$37,500
Manufacturing overhead incurred	$ 89,000	$124,000	$74,000
Direct labor hours	8,000	11,000	3,500
Machine hours	34,000	45,000	10,400

Instructions

(a) Compute the predetermined overhead rate for each department.
(b) Compute the total manufacturing costs assigned to jobs in January in each department.
(c) Compute the under- or overapplied overhead for each department at January 31.

(a) 70%, $12, $7.00
(b) $344,000, $368,000 $188,300
(c) $5,000, $(8,000), $1,200

Analyze manufacturing accounts and determine missing amounts.

(SO 2, 3, 4, 5, 6)

P2-5A Vargas Corporation's fiscal year ends on November 30. The following accounts are found in its job order cost accounting system for the first month of the new fiscal year.

Raw Materials Inventory

Dec. 1	Beginning balance	(a)	Dec. 31	Requisitions	18,850
31	Purchases	19,225			
Dec. 31	Ending balance	7,975			

Work in Process Inventory

Dec. 1	Beginning balance	(b)	Dec. 31	Jobs completed	(f)
31	Direct materials	(c)			
31	Direct labor	8,800			
31	Overhead	(d)			
Dec. 31	Ending balance	(e)			

Finished Goods Inventory

Dec. 1	Beginning balance	(g)	Dec. 31	Cost of goods sold	(i)
31	Completed jobs	(h)			
Dec. 31	Ending balance	(j)			

Factory Labor

Dec. 31	Factory wages	12,465	Dec. 31	Wages assigned	(k)

Manufacturing Overhead

Dec. 31	Indirect materials	1,900	Dec. 31	Overhead applied	(m)
31	Indirect labor	(l)			
31	Other overhead	1,245			

Other data:

1. On December 1, two jobs were in process: Job No. 154 and Job No. 155. These jobs had combined direct materials costs of $9,750 and direct labor costs of $15,000. Overhead was applied at a rate that was 80% of direct labor cost.
2. During December, Job Nos. 156, 157, and 158 were started. On December 31, Job No. 158 was unfinished. This job had charges for direct materials $3,800 and direct labor $4,800, plus manufacturing overhead. All jobs, except for Job No. 158, were completed in December.
3. On December 1, Job No. 153 was in the finished goods warehouse. It had a total cost of $5,000. On December 31, Job No. 157 was the only job finished that was not sold. It had a cost of $4,000.
4. Manufacturing overhead was $230 overapplied in December.

(c) $16,950
(f) $57,100
(i) $58,100

Instructions

List the letters (a) through (m) and indicate the amount pertaining to each letter.

PROBLEMS: SET B

Prepare entries in a job cost system and job cost sheets.

(SO 2, 3, 4, 5, 6)

P2-1B Lowry Manufacturing uses a job order cost system and applies overhead to production on the basis of direct labor hours. On January 1, 2008, Job No. 25 was the only job in process. The costs incurred prior to January 1 on this job were as follows: direct materials $10,000; direct labor $6,000; and manufacturing overhead $9,000. Job No. 23 had been completed at a cost of $45,000 and was part of finished goods inventory. There was a $5,000 balance in the Raw Materials Inventory account.

During the month of January, the company began production on Jobs 26 and 27, and completed Jobs 25 and 26. Jobs 23 and 25 were sold on account during the month for $67,000 and $74,000, respectively. The following additional events occurred during the month.

1. Purchased additional raw materials of $45,000 on account.
2. Incurred factory labor costs of $31,500. Of this amount $7,500 related to employer payroll taxes.
3. Incurred manufacturing overhead costs as follows: indirect materials $10,000; indirect labor $7,500; depreciation expense $12,000; and various other manufacturing overhead costs on account $8,000.
4. Assigned direct materials and direct labor to jobs as follows.

Job No.	Direct Materials	Direct Labor
25	$ 5,000	$ 3,000
26	20,000	12,000
27	15,000	9,000

5. The company uses direct labor hours as the activity base to assign overhead. Direct labor hours incurred on each job were as follows: Job No. 25, 200; Job No. 26, 800; and Job No. 27, 600.

Instructions

(a) Calculate the predetermined overhead rate for the year 2008, assuming Lowry Manufacturing estimates total manufacturing overhead costs of $440,000, direct labor costs of $300,000, and direct labor hours of 20,000 for the year.

(b) Open job cost sheets for Jobs 25, 26, and 27. Enter the January 1 balances on the job cost sheet for Job No. 25.

(c) Prepare the journal entries to record the purchase of raw materials, the factory labor costs incurred, and the manufacturing overhead costs incurred during the month of January.

(d) Prepare the journal entries to record the assignment of direct materials, direct labor, and manufacturing overhead costs to production. In assigning manufacturing overhead costs, use the overhead rate calculated in (a). Post all costs to the job cost sheets as necessary.

(e) Job 25, $37,400
Job 26, $49,600

(e) Total the job cost sheets for any job(s) completed during the month. Prepare the journal entry (or entries) to record the completion of any job(s) during the month.

(f) Prepare the journal entry (or entries) to record the sale of any job(s) during the month.

(g) What is the balance in the Work in Process Inventory account at the end of the month? What does this balance consist of?

(h) What is the amount of over- or underapplied overhead?

P2-2B For the year ended December 31, 2008, the job cost sheets of Mazzone Company contained the following data.

Prepare entries in a job cost system and partial income statement.

(SO 2, 3, 4, 5, 6)

Job Number	Explanation	Direct Materials	Direct Labor	Manufacturing Overhead	Total Costs
7650	Balance 1/1	$18,000	$20,000	$25,000	$ 63,000
	Current year's costs	32,000	30,000	37,500	99,500
7651	Balance 1/1	12,000	18,000	22,500	52,500
	Current year's costs	28,000	40,000	50,000	118,000
7652	Current year's costs	40,000	68,000	85,000	193,000

Other data:

1. Raw materials inventory totaled $20,000 on January 1. During the year, $100,000 of raw materials were purchased on account.
2. Finished goods on January 1 consisted of Job No. 7648 for $98,000 and Job No. 7649 for $62,000.
3. Job No. 7650 and Job No. 7651 were completed during the year.
4. Job Nos. 7648, 7649, and 7650 were sold on account for $490,000.
5. Manufacturing overhead incurred on account totaled $126,000.
6. Other manufacturing overhead consisted of indirect materials $12,000, indirect labor $18,000 and depreciation on factory machinery $19,500.

Instructions

(a) Prove the agreement of Work in Process Inventory with job cost sheets pertaining to unfinished work. (*Hint*: Use a single T account for Work in Process Inventory.) Calculate each of the following, then post each to the T account: (1) beginning balance, (2) direct materials, (3) direct labor, (4) manufacturing overhead, and (5) completed jobs.

(b) Prepare the adjusting entry for manufacturing overhead, assuming the balance is allocated entirely to cost of goods sold.

(c) Determine the gross profit to be reported for 2008.

(a) (1) $115,500
(4) $172,500
Unfinished job 7652, $193,000

(b) Amount = $3,000

(c) $164,500

P2-3B Chris Duncan is a contractor specializing in custom-built jacuzzis. On May 1, 2008, his ledger contains the following data.

Prepare entries in a job cost system and cost of goods manufactured schedule.

(SO 2, 3, 4, 5)

Raw Materials Inventory	$30,000
Work in Process Inventory	12,400
Manufacturing Overhead	2,500 (dr.)

The Manufacturing Overhead account has debit totals of $12,500 and credit totals of $10,000. Subsidiary data for Work in Process Inventory on May 1 include:

Job Cost Sheets

Job by Customer	Direct Materials	Direct Labor	Manufacturing Overhead
Looper	$2,500	$2,000	$1,500
Carpenter	2,000	1,200	900
Ingle	900	800	600
	$5,400	$4,000	$3,000

During May, the following costs were incurred: (a) raw materials purchased on account $5,000, (b) labor paid $7,600, (c) manufacturing overhead paid $1,400.

A summary of materials requisition slips and time tickets for the month of May reveals the following.

Job by Customer	Materials Requisition Slips	Time Tickets
Looper	$ 500	$ 400
Carpenter	600	1,000
Ingle	2,300	1,300
Bennett	2,400	2,900
	5,800	5,600
General use	1,500	2,000
	$7,300	$7,600

Overhead was charged to jobs on the basis of $0.75 per dollar of direct labor cost.

The jacuzzis for customers Looper, Carpenter, and Ingle were completed during May. Each jacuzzi was sold for $12,500 cash.

Instructions

(d) Cost of goods manufactured $20,525

(a) Prepare journal entries for the May transactions: (i) for purchase of raw materials, factory labor costs incurred, and manufacturing overhead costs incurred; (ii) assignment of direct materials, labor, and overhead to production; and (iii) completion of jobs and sale of goods.
(b) Post the entries to Work in Process Inventory.
(c) Reconcile the balance in Work in Process Inventory with the costs of unfinished jobs.
(d) Prepare a cost of goods manufactured schedule for May.

Compute predetermined overhead rates, apply overhead, and calculate under- or overapplied overhead.

(SO 4, 6)

P2-4B Eckstein Manufacturing uses a job order cost system in each of its three manufacturing departments. Manufacturing overhead is applied to jobs on the basis of direct labor cost in Department A, direct labor hours in Department B, and machine hours in Department C.

In establishing the predetermined overhead rates for 2008 the following estimates were made for the year.

	Department		
	A	**B**	**C**
Manufacturing overhead	$900,000	$800,000	$750,000
Direct labor cost	$600,000	$400,000	$600,000
Direct labor hours	50,000	40,000	40,000
Machine hours	100,000	120,000	125,000

During January, the job cost sheets showed the following costs and production data.

	Department		
	A	**B**	**C**
Direct materials used	$92,000	$86,000	$64,000
Direct labor cost	$48,000	$35,000	$50,400
Manufacturing overhead incurred	$76,000	$75,000	$72,100
Direct labor hours	4,000	3,500	4,200
Machine hours	8,000	10,500	12,600

(a) 150%, $20, $6
(b) $212,000, $191,000 $190,000
(c) $4,000, $5,000, $(3,500)

Instructions

(a) Compute the predetermined overhead rate for each department.
(b) Compute the total manufacturing costs assigned to jobs in January in each department.
(c) Compute the under- or overapplied overhead for each department at January 31.

Analyze manufacturing accounts and determine missing amounts.

(SO 2, 3, 4, 5, 6)

P2-5B Spivey Company's fiscal year ends on June 30. The following accounts are found in its job order cost accounting system for the first month of the new fiscal year.

Raw Materials Inventory

July 1	Beginning balance	19,000	July 31	Requisitions	(a)
31	Purchases	90,400			
July 31	Ending balance	(b)			

Work in Process Inventory

July 1	Beginning balance	(c)	July 31	Jobs completed	(f)
31	Direct materials	70,000			
31	Direct labor	(d)			
31	Overhead	(e)			
July 31	Ending balance	(g)			

Finished Goods Inventory

July 1	Beginning balance	(h)	July 31	Cost of goods sold	(j)
31	Completed jobs	(i)			
July 31	Ending balance	(k)			

Factory Labor

July 31	Factory wages	(l)	July 31	Wages assigned	(m)

Manufacturing Overhead

July 31	Indirect materials	8,900	July 31	Overhead applied	104,000
31	Indirect labor	16,000			
31	Other overhead	(n)			

Other data:

1. On July 1, two jobs were in process: Job No. 4085 and Job No. 4086, with costs of $19,000 and $8,200, respectively.
2. During July, Job Nos. 4087, 4088, and 4089 were started. On July 31, only Job No. 4089 was unfinished. This job had charges for direct materials $2,000 and direct labor $1,500, plus manufacturing overhead. Manufacturing overhead was applied at the rate of 130% of direct labor cost.
3. On July 1, Job No. 4084, costing $135,000, was in the finished goods warehouse. On July 31, Job No. 4088, costing $143,000, was in finished goods.
4. Overhead was $3,000 underapplied in July.

(d) $ 80,000
(f) $275,750
(l) $ 96,000

Instructions

List the letters (a) through (n) and indicate the amount pertaining to each letter. Show computations.

PROBLEMS: SET C

Visit the book's website at **www.wiley.com/college/weygandt**, and choose the Student Companion site, to access Problem Set C.

WATERWAYS CONTINUING PROBLEM

(*Note:* This is a continuation of the Waterways Problem from Chapter 1.)

WCP2 Waterways has two major public-park projects to provide with comprehensive irrigation in one of its service locations this month. Job J57 and Job K52 involve 15 acres of landscaped terrain which will require special-order sprinkler heads to meet the specifications of the project. This problem asks you to help Waterways use a job cost system to account for production of these parts.

Go to the book's website, **www.wiley.com/college/weygandt,** *to find the remainder of this problem.*

BROADENING YOUR PERSPECTIVE

DECISION MAKING ACROSS THE ORGANIZATION

BYP2-1 Pine Products Company uses a job order cost system. For a number of months there has been an ongoing rift between the sales department and the production department concerning a special-order product, TC-1. TC-1 is a seasonal product that is manufactured in batches of 1,000 units. TC-1 is sold at cost plus a markup of 40% of cost.

The sales department is unhappy because fluctuating unit production costs significantly affect selling prices. Sales personnel complain that this has caused excessive customer complaints and the loss of considerable orders for TC-1.

The production department maintains that each job order must be fully costed on the basis of the costs incurred during the period in which the goods are produced. Production personnel maintain that the only real solution to the problem is for the sales department to increase sales in the slack periods.

Regina Newell, president of the company, asks you as the company accountant to collect quarterly data for the past year on TC-1. From the cost accounting system, you accumulate the following production quantity and cost data.

	Quarter			
Costs	**1**	**2**	**3**	**4**
Direct materials	$100,000	$220,000	$ 80,000	$200,000
Direct labor	60,000	132,000	48,000	120,000
Manufacturing overhead	105,000	123,000	97,000	125,000
Total	$265,000	$475,000	$225,000	$445,000
Production in batches	5	11	4	10
Unit cost (per batch)	$ 53,000	$ 43,182	$ 56,250	$ 44,500

Instructions

With the class divided into groups, answer the following questions.

(a) What manufacturing cost element is responsible for the fluctuating unit costs? Why?

(b) What is your recommended solution to the problem of fluctuating unit cost?

(c) Restate the quarterly data on the basis of your recommended solution.

MANAGERIAL ANALYSIS

BYP2-2 In the course of routine checking of all journal entries prior to preparing year-end reports, Diane Riser discovered several strange entries. She recalled that the president's son Ron had come in to help out during an especially busy time and that he had recorded some journal entries. She was relieved that there were only a few of his entries, and even more relieved that he had included rather lengthy explanations. The entries Ron made were:

1.

Work in Process Inventory	25,000	
Cash		25,000

(This is for materials put into process. I don't find the record that we paid for these, so I'm crediting Cash, because I know we'll have to pay for them sooner or later.)

2.

Manufacturing Overhead	12,000	
Cash		12,000

(This is for bonuses paid to salespeople. I know they're part of overhead, and I can't find an account called "Non-factory Overhead" or "Other Overhead" so I'm putting it in Manufacturing Overhead. I have the check stubs, so I know we paid these.)

3.

Wages Expense	120,000	
Cash		120,000

(This is for the factory workers' wages. I have a note that payroll taxes are $15,000. I still think that's part of wages expense, and that we'll have to pay it all in cash sooner or later, so I credited Cash for the wages and the taxes.)

4.

Work in Process Inventory	3,000	
Raw Materials Inventory		3,000

(This is for the glue used in the factory. I know we used this to make the products, even though we didn't use very much on any one of the products. I got it out of inventory, so I credited an inventory account.)

Instructions

(a) How should Ron have recorded each of the four events?

(b) If the entry was not corrected, which financial statements (income statement or balance sheet) would be affected? What balances would be overstated or understated?

REAL-WORLD FOCUS

BYP2-3 Founded in 1970, Parlex Corporation is a world leader in the design and manufacture of flexible interconnect products. Utilizing proprietary and patented technologies, Parlex produces custom flexible interconnects including flexible circuits, polymer thick film, laminated cables, and value-added assemblies for sophisticated electronics used in automotive, telecommunications, computer, diversified electronics, and aerospace applications. In addition to manufacturing sites in Methuen, Massachusetts; Salem, New Hampshire; Cranston, Rhode Island; San Jose, California; Shanghai, China; Isle of Wight, UK; and Empalme, Mexico, Parlex has logistic support centers and strategic alliances throughout North America, Asia, and Europe.

The following information was provided in the company's annual report.

PARLEX COMPANY
Notes to the Financial Statements

The Company's products are manufactured on a job order basis to customers' specifications. Customers submit requests for quotations on each job, and the Company prepares bids based on its own cost estimates. The Company attempts to reflect the impact of changing costs when establishing prices. However, during the past several years, the market conditions for flexible circuits and the resulting price sensitivity haven't always allowed this to transpire. Although still not satisfactory, the Company was able to reduce the cost of products sold as a percentage of sales to 85% this year versus 87% that was experienced in the two immediately preceding years. Management continues to focus on improving operational efficiency and further reducing costs.

Instructions

(a) Parlex management discusses the job order cost system employed by their company. What are several advantages of using the job order approach to costing?

(b) Contrast the products produced in a job order environment, like Parlex, to those produced when process cost systems are used.

EXPLORING THE WEB

BYP2-4 The Institute of Management Accountants sponsors a certification for management accountants, allowing them to obtain the title of Certified Management Accountant.

Address: www.imanet.org, or go to **www.wiley.com/college/weygandt**

Steps

1. Go to the site shown above.
2. Choose **Certification**, and then, **Getting Started**.

Instructions

(a) What is the experience qualification requirement?

(b) How many hours of continuing education are required, and what types of courses qualify?

COMMUNICATION ACTIVITY

BYP2-5 You are the management accountant for Newberry Manufacturing. Your company does custom carpentry work and uses a job order costing system. Newberry sends detailed job cost sheets to its customers, along with an invoice. The job cost sheets show the date materials were used, the dollar cost of materials, and the hours and cost of labor. A predetermined overhead application rate is used, and the total overhead applied is also listed.

Donna Werly is a customer who recently had custom cabinets installed. Along with her check in payment for the work done, she included a letter. She thanked the company for including the detailed cost information but questioned why overhead was estimated. She stated that she would be interested in knowing exactly what costs were included in overhead, and she thought that other customers would, too.

Instructions

Prepare a letter to Ms. Werly (address: 123 Cedar Lane, Altoona, Kansas 66651) and tell her why you did not send her information on exact costs of overhead included in her job. Respond to her suggestion that you provide this information.

ETHICS CASE

BYP2-6 SEK Printing provides printing services to many different corporate clients. Although SEK bids most jobs, some jobs, particularly new ones, are negotiated on a "cost-plus" basis. Cost-plus means that the buyer is willing to pay the actual cost plus a return (profit) on these costs to SEK.

Betty Keiser, controller for SEK, has recently returned from a meeting where SEK's president stated that he wanted her to find a way to charge most costs to any project that was on a cost-plus basis. The president noted that the company needed more profits to meet its stated goals this period. By charging more costs to the cost-plus projects and therefore fewer costs to the jobs that were bid, the company should be able to increase its profit for the current year.

Betty knew why the president wanted to take this action. Rumors were that he was looking for a new position and if the company reported strong profits, the president's opportunities would be enhanced. Betty also recognized that she could probably increase the cost of certain jobs by changing the basis used to allocate manufacturing overhead.

Instructions

(a) Who are the stakeholders in this situation?
(b) What are the ethical issues in this situation?
(c) What would you do if you were Betty Keiser?

"ALL ABOUT YOU" ACTIVITY

BYP2-7 Many of you will work for a small business. As noted in the "All About You" feature in this chapter, some of you will even own your own business. In order to operate a small business, you will need a good understanding of managerial accounting, as well as many other skills. Much information is available to assist people who are interested in starting a new business. A great place to start is the website provided by the Small Business Administration which is an agency of the federal government whose purpose is to support small business.

Instructions

Go to **www.sba.gov** and in the Small Business Planner, Plan Your Business link, review the material under "Get Ready" Answer the following questions.

(a) What are some of the characteristics required of a small business owner?
(b) What are the top 10 reasons given for business failure?

Answers to Insight and Accounting Across the Organization Questions

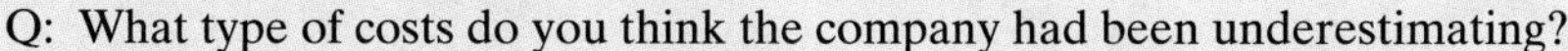

Jobs Won, Money Lost, p. 56

Q: What type of costs do you think the company had been underestimating?

A: *It is most likely that the company failed to estimate and track overhead. In a highly diversified company, overhead associated with the diesel locomotive jobs may have been "lost" in the total overhead pool for the entire company.*

What About Service Companies?, p. 67

Q: What types of costs will service companies report in job order cost systems?

A: *Like a manufacturing company, a service company will report direct labor and overhead charges. Although service companies do not produce inventory, many have significant material costs that are charged to each job. For example, a health-care provider would track medication and treatment supplies used by each patient.*

Working a 25-Hour Day, p. 71

Q: What feature of these businesses creates an incentive to misstate cost accounting data on particular jobs? What can customers do to protect themselves from overbilling?

A: *In these business situations the compensation to the supplier depends on the costs incurred by the supplier. This so-called "cost plus" arrangement creates an incentive for the supplier to overstate costs. Customers should stipulate that they have the right to have the suppliers' records audited.*

Authors' Comments on *All About You:* Minding Your Own Business, p. 72

The situation presented is a difficult one because you are presently receiving some help for free. It would seem that the best strategy is to price your services based on what it would cost you to do the landscape business without any free help. In the long run, it is going to be impossible to continue unless you can cover these costs. In addition, if you underprice your services today, your customers may expect your prices will remain as low in the future. That probably cannot happen, given that your costs will increase substantially after the first two years. However, we should note that it is not unusual to start a small business with some assets available to you. Then, as your business grows, you acquire additional assets to meet your needs. After all, you may need a low price to get started, and as you gain experience you will be able to charge more or become more efficient.

So what to do? Let's address your old truck first. You should treat the truck as an asset owned by your business. Put it on your books at its fair value, and depreciate it over a reasonable life. This will result in an overhead charge. You need to cover the cost of that truck, as you will have to buy another one some day.

The land, barn, and your mother's services are a little more difficult. If you rented the land and barn and if you paid an assistant, all of these costs would be charged to overhead. (The assistant would be indirect labor.) You are currently getting all these services for free. This is a good situation now, and you may need this situation early in your business to help you get started. But you should recognize that even if you run your business profitably for the first two years, you may have problems beginning in the third year. Thus, it would seem prudent to establish a budget based on both scenarios for the first two years. If you can charge based on your expected costs in the future, do so. If that is not realistic, because you need to establish yourself and get more experience, then charge less. But be sure from the start to cover a reasonable amount of your costs, or the business does not make sense for you financially.

Answers to Self-Study Questions

1. a **2.** b **3.** c **4.** d **5.** b **6.** a **7.** d **8.** b **9.** c **10.** b

Remember to go back to the Navigator box on the chapter-opening page and check off your completed work.

Chapter 3

Process Costing

STUDY OBJECTIVES

After studying this chapter, you should be able to:

1 Understand who uses process cost systems.
2 Explain the similarities and differences between job order cost and process cost systems.
3 Explain the flow of costs in a process cost system.
4 Make the journal entries to assign manufacturing costs in a process cost system.
5 Compute equivalent units.
6 Explain the four steps necessary to prepare a production cost report.
7 Prepare a production cost report.

The Navigator

- Scan **Study Objectives**
- Read **Feature Story**
- Read **Preview**
- Read text and answer **Before You Go On** p. 101 p. 110 p. 111
- Work **Using the Decision Toolkit**
- Review **Summary of Study Objectives**
- Work **Demonstration Problem**
- Answer **Self-Study Questions**
- Complete **Assignments**

Feature Story

BEN & JERRY'S TRACKS ITS MIX-UPS

Ben & Jerry's Homemade, Inc. (*www.benjerry.com*) is one of the "hottest" and "coolest" U.S. companies. Based in Waterbury, Vermont, the ice cream company that started out of a garage in 1978 is now a public company.

Making ice cream is a process—a movement of product from a mixing department to a prepping department to a pint department. The mixing department is where the ice cream is created. In the prep area, the

production process adds extras such as cherries and walnuts to make plain ice cream into "Cherry Garcia," Ben & Jerry's most popular flavor, or fudge-covered waffle cone pieces and a swirl of caramel for "Stephen Colbert's Americone Dream," Ben & Jerry's newest flavor. The pint department is where the ice cream is actually put into containers. As the product is processed from one department to the next, the appropriate materials, labor, and overhead are added to it.

"The incoming ingredients from the shipping and receiving departments are stored in certain locations, either in a freezer or dry warehouse," says Beecher Eurich, staff accountant. "As ingredients get added, so do the costs associated with them." How much ice cream is produced? Running plants around the clock, the company produces 18 million gallons a year.

With the company's process costing system, Eurich can tell you how much a certain batch of ice cream costs to make—its materials, labor, and overhead in each of the production departments. She generates reports for the production department heads, but makes sure not to overdo it. "You can get bogged down in numbers," says Eurich. "If you're generating a report that no one can use, then that's a waste of time."

It's more likely, though, Ben & Jerry's production people want to know how efficient they are. Why? Many own stock in the company.

✓ The Navigator

Inside Chapter 3

Preview of Chapter 3

The cost accounting system used by companies such as Ben & Jerry's is **process cost accounting**. In contrast to job order cost accounting, which focuses on the individual job, process cost accounting focuses on the *processes* involved in mass-producing products that are identical or very similar in nature. The primary objective of the chapter is to explain and illustrate process costing.

The content and organization of this chapter are as follows.

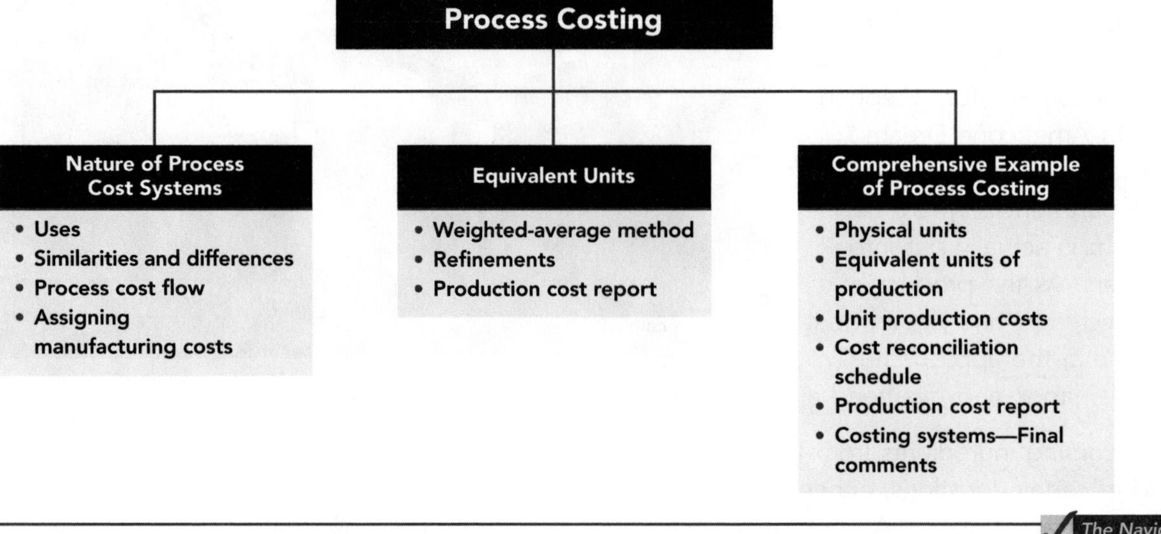

The Navigator

THE NATURE OF PROCESS COST SYSTEMS

Uses of Process Cost Systems

STUDY OBJECTIVE 1

Understand who uses process cost systems.

Companies use **process cost systems** to apply costs to similar products that are mass-produced in a continuous fashion. Ben & Jerry's uses a process cost system: Production of the ice cream, once it begins, continues until the ice cream emerges, and the processing is the same for the entire run—with precisely the same amount of materials, labor, and overhead. Each finished pint of ice cream is indistinguishable from another.

A company such as USX uses process costing in the manufacturing of steel. Kellogg and General Mills use process costing for cereal production; ExxonMobil uses process costing for its oil refining. Sherwin Williams uses process costing for its paint products. At a bottling company like Coca-Cola, the manufacturing process begins with the blending of ingredients. Next, automated machinery moves the bottles into position and fills them. The production process then caps, packages, and forwards the bottles to the finished goods warehouse. Illustration 3-1 shows this process.

Illustration 3-1
Manufacturing processes

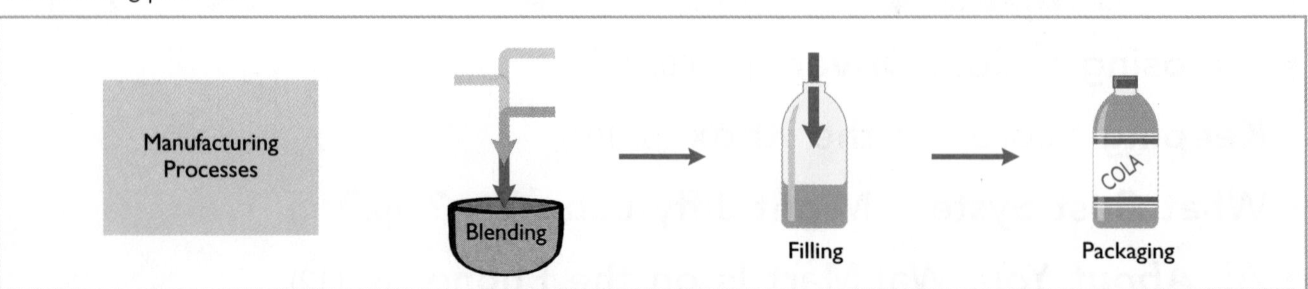

For Coca-Cola, as well as the other companies just mentioned, once the production begins, it continues until the finished product emerges, and each unit of finished product is like every other unit.

In comparison, in a job order cost system companies assign costs to a *specific job*. Examples are the construction of a customized home, the making of a motion picture, or the manufacturing of a specialized machine. Illustration 3-2 provides examples of companies that primarily use either a process cost system or a job order cost system.

Illustration 3-2
Process cost and job order cost companies and products

Process Cost System Company	Product	Job Order Cost System Company	Product
Coca-Cola, PepsiCo	Soft drinks	Young & Rubicam, J. Walter Thompson	Advertising
ExxonMobil, Royal Dutch Shell	Oil	Walt Disney, Warner Brothers	Motion pictures
Intel, Advanced Micro Devices	Computer chips	Center Ice Consultants, Ice Pro	Ice rinks
Dow Chemical, DuPont	Chemicals	Kaiser, Mayo Clinic	Patient health care

Similarities and Differences Between Job Order Cost and Process Cost Systems

STUDY OBJECTIVE 2
Explain the similarities and differences between job order cost and process cost systems.

In a job order cost system, companies assign costs to each job. In a process cost system, companies track costs through a series of connected manufacturing processes or departments, rather than by individual jobs. Thus, companies use process cost systems when they produce a large volume of uniform or relatively homogeneous products. Illustration 3-3 shows the basic flow of costs in these two systems.

Illustration 3-3
Job order cost and process cost flow

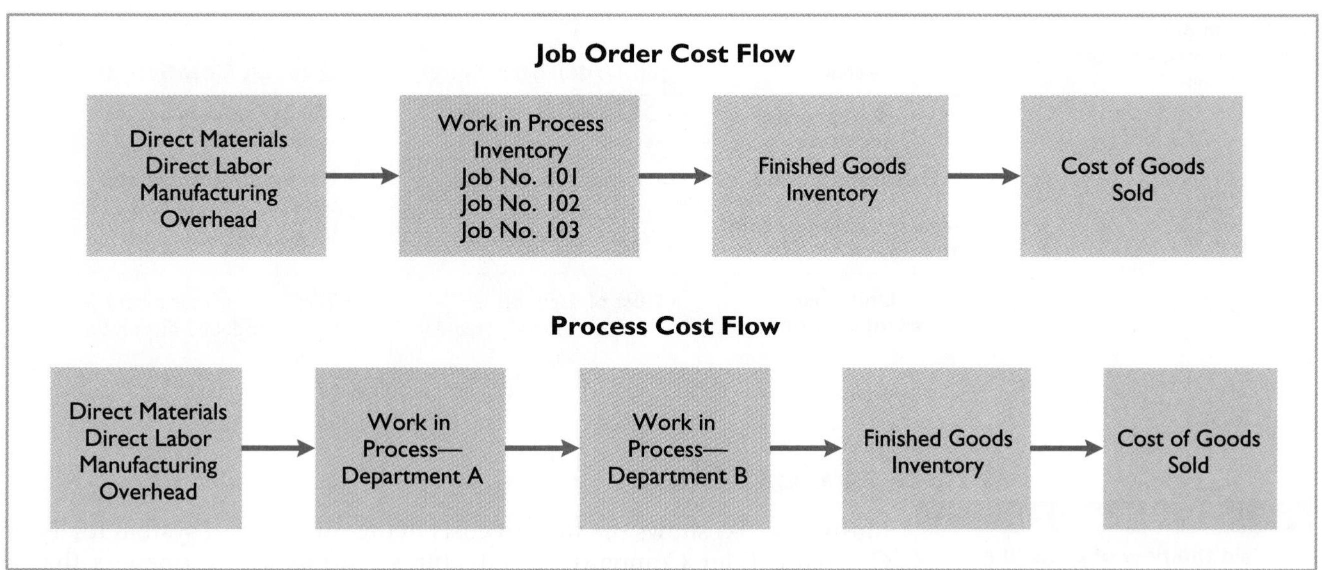

The following analysis highlights the basic similarities and differences between these two systems.

SIMILARITIES

Job order cost and process cost systems are similar in three ways:

1. **The manufacturing cost elements.** Both costing systems track three manufacturing cost elements—direct materials, direct labor, and manufacturing overhead.
2. **The accumulation of the costs of materials, labor, and overhead.** Both costing systems debit raw materials to Raw Materials Inventory; factory labor to Factory Labor; and manufacturing overhead costs to Manufacturing Overhead.
3. **The flow of costs.** As noted above, both systems accumulate all manufacturing costs by debits to Raw Materials Inventory, Factory Labor, and Manufacturing Overhead. Both systems then assign these costs to the same accounts—Work in Process, Finished Goods Inventory, and Cost of Goods Sold. **The methods of assigning costs, however, differ significantly.** These differences are explained and illustrated later in the chapter.

DIFFERENCES

The differences between a job order cost and a process cost system are as follows.

1. **The number of work in process accounts used.** A job order cost system uses only one Work in Process account. A process cost system uses multiple work in process accounts.
2. **Documents used to track costs.** A job order cost system charges costs to individual jobs and summarizes them in a job cost sheet. A process cost system summarizes costs in a production cost report for each department.
3. **The point at which costs are totaled.** A job order cost system totals costs when the job is completed. A process cost system totals costs at the end of a period of time.
4. **Unit cost computations.** In a job order cost system, the unit cost is the total cost per job divided by the units produced. In a process cost system, the unit cost is total manufacturing costs for the period divided by the units produced during the period.

Illustration 3-4 summarizes the major differences between a job order cost and a process cost system.

Illustration 3-4
Job order versus process cost systems

Features	Job Order Cost System	Process Cost System
Work in process accounts	• One work in process account	• Multiple work in process accounts
Documents used	• Job cost sheets	• Production cost reports
Determination of total manufacturing costs	• Each job	• Each period
Unit-cost computations	• Cost of each job ÷ Units produced for the job	• Total manufacturing costs ÷ Units produced during the period

Process Cost Flow

STUDY OBJECTIVE 3
Explain the flow of costs in a process cost system.

Illustration 3-5 shows the flow of costs in the process cost system for Tyler Company. Tyler Company manufactures automatic can openers that it sells to retail outlets. Manufacturing consists of two processes: machining and assembly. The Machining Department shapes, hones, and drills the raw materials. The Assembly Department assembles and packages the parts.

Illustration 3-5
Flow of costs in process cost system

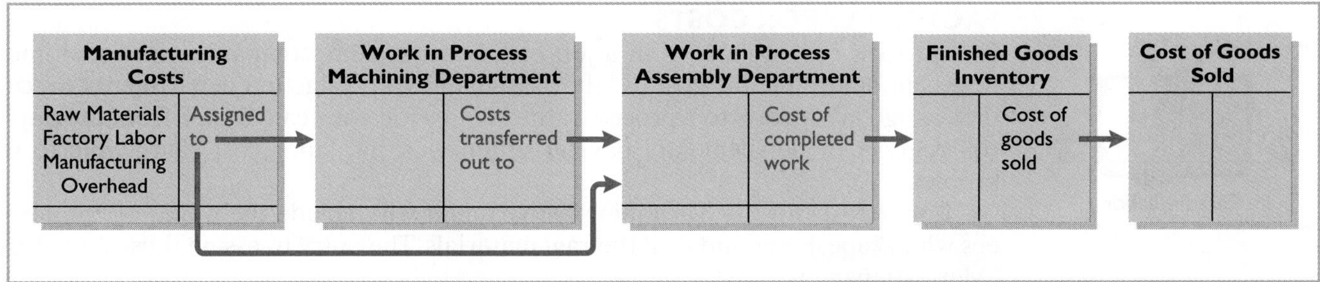

As the flow of costs indicates, the company can add materials, labor, and manufacturing overhead in both the Machining and Assembly departments. When it finishes its work, the Machining Department transfers the partially completed units to the Assembly Department. The Assembly Department finishes the goods and then transfers them to the finished goods inventory. Upon sale, Tyler removes the goods from the finished goods inventory. Within each department, a similar set of activities is performed on each unit processed.

Assigning Manufacturing Costs—Journal Entries

STUDY OBJECTIVE 4
Make the journal entries to assign manufacturing costs in a process cost system.

As indicated, the accumulation of the costs of materials, labor, and manufacturing overhead is the same in a process cost system as in a job order cost system. That is, both systems follow these procedures:

- Companies debit all raw materials to Raw Materials Inventory at the time of purchase.
- They debit all factory labor to Factory Labor as the labor costs are incurred.
- They debit overhead costs to Manufacturing Overhead as these costs are incurred.

However, the assignment of the three manufacturing cost elements to Work in Process in a process cost system is different from a job order cost system. Here we'll look at how companies assign these manufacturing cost elements in a process cost system.

MATERIALS COSTS

All raw materials issued for production are a materials cost to the producing department. A process cost system may use materials requisition slips, but **it generally requires fewer requisitions than in a job order cost system, because the materials are used for processes rather than for specific jobs** and therefore typically are for larger quantities.

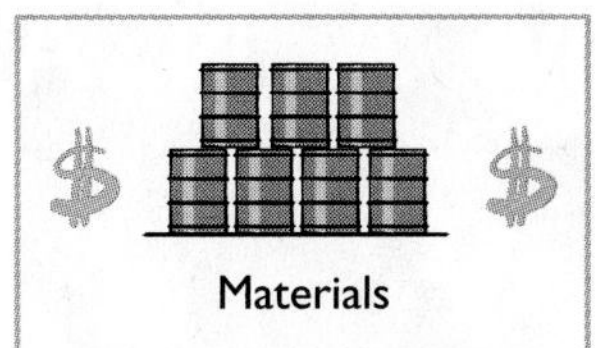

At the beginning of the first process, a company usually adds most of the materials needed for production. However, other materials may be added at various points. For example, in the manufacture of Hershey candy bars, the chocolate and other ingredients are added at the beginning of the first process, and the wrappers and cartons are added at the end of the packaging process. Tyler Company adds materials at the beginning of each process. Tyler makes the following entry to record the materials used:

Work in Process—Machining	XXXX	
Work in Process—Assembly	XXXX	
Raw Materials Inventory		XXXX
(To record materials used)		

Ice cream maker Ben & Jerry's adds materials in three departments: milk and flavoring in the mixing department; extras such as cherries and walnuts in the prepping department; and cardboard containers in the pinting (packaging) department.

FACTORY LABOR COSTS

In a process cost system, as in a job order cost system, companies may use time tickets to determine the cost of labor assignable to production departments. Since they assign labor costs to a process rather than a job, they can obtain, from the payroll register or departmental payroll summaries, the labor cost chargeable to a process.

Labor costs for the Machining Department will include the wages of employees who shape, hone, and drill the raw materials. The entry to assign these costs for Tyler Company is:

Work in Process—Machining	XXXX	
Work in Process—Assembly	XXXX	
Factory Labor		XXXX
(To assign factory labor to production)		

MANUFACTURING OVERHEAD COSTS

Manufacturing Overhead

The objective in assigning overhead in a process cost system is to allocate the overhead costs to the production departments on an objective and equitable basis. That basis is the activity that "drives" or causes the costs. A primary driver of overhead costs in continuous manufacturing operations is **machine time used**, not direct labor. Thus, companies **widely use machine hours** in allocating manufacturing overhead costs. Tyler's entry to allocate overhead to the two processes is:

Work in Process—Machining	XXXX	
Work in Process—Assembly	XXXX	
Manufacturing Overhead		XXXX
(To assign overhead to production)		

MANAGEMENT INSIGHT

Choosing a Cost Driver

In one of its automated cost centers, Caterpillar feeds work into the cost center, where robotic machines process it and transfer the finished job to the next cost center without human intervention. One person tends all of the machines and spends more time maintaining machines than operating them. In such cases, overhead rates based on direct labor hours may be misleading. Surprisingly, some companies continue to assign manufacturing overhead on the basis of direct labor despite the fact that there is no cause-and-effect relationship between labor and overhead.

What is the result if a company uses the wrong "cost driver" to assign manufacturing overhead?

TRANSFER TO NEXT DEPARTMENT

At the end of the month, Tyler needs an entry to record the cost of the goods transferred out of the Machining department. In this case, the transfer is to the Assembly Department, and Tyler makes the following entry.

Work in Process—Assembly	XXXXX	
Work in Process—Machining		XXXXX
(To record transfer of units to the Assembly Department)		

TRANSFER TO FINISHED GOODS

When the Assembly Department completes the units, it transfers them to the finished goods warehouse. The entry for this transfer is as follows.

Finished Goods Inventory	XXXXX	
Work in Process—Assembly		XXXXX
(To record transfer of units to finished goods)		

TRANSFER TO COST OF GOODS SOLD

When Tyler sells the finished goods, it records the cost of goods sold as follows.

Cost of Goods Sold	XXXXX	
Finished Goods Inventory		XXXXX
(To record cost of units sold)		

Before You Go On...

REVIEW IT

1. What type of manufacturing companies might use a process cost accounting system?
2. What are the principal similarities and differences between a job order cost system and a process cost system?

DO IT

Ruth Company manufactures ZEBO through two processes: blending and bottling. In June, raw materials used were Blending $18,000 and Bottling $4,000. Factory labor costs were Blending $12,000 and Bottling $5,000. Manufacturing overhead costs were Blending $6,000 and Bottling $2,500. The company transfers units completed at a cost of $19,000 in the Blending Department to the Bottling Department. The Bottling Department transfers units completed at a cost of $11,000 to Finished Goods. Journalize the assignment of these costs to the two processes and the transfer of units as appropriate.

Action Plan

- In process cost accounting, keep separate work in process accounts for each process.
- When the costs are assigned to production, debit the separate work in process accounts.
- Transfer cost of completed units to the next process or to Finished Goods.

Solution The entries are:

Work in Process—Blending	18,000	
Work in Process—Bottling	4,000	
Raw Materials Inventory		22,000
(To record materials used)		
Work in Process—Blending	12,000	
Work in Process—Bottling	5,000	
Factory Labor		17,000
(To assign factory labor to production)		
Work in Process—Blending	6,000	
Work in Process—Bottling	2,500	
Manufacturing Overhead		8,500
(To assign overhead to production)		
Work in Process—Bottling	19,000	
Work in Process—Blending		19,000
(To record transfer of units to the Bottling Department)		
Finished Goods Inventory	11,000	
Work in Process—Bottling		11,000
(To record transfer of units to finished goods)		

Related exercise material: *BE3-1, BE3-2, BE3-3, E3-2, and E3-4.*

✓ The Navigator

EQUIVALENT UNITS

STUDY OBJECTIVE 5
Compute equivalent units.

Suppose you have a work-study job in the office of your college's president, and she asks you to compute the cost of instruction per full-time equivalent student at your college. The college's vice president for finance provides the following information.

Illustration 3-6
Information for full-time student example

Costs:	
Total cost of instruction	$9,000,000
Student population:	
Full-time students	900
Part-time students	1,000

Part-time students take 60% of the classes of a full-time student during the year. To compute the number of full-time equivalent students per year, you would make the following computation.

Illustration 3-7
Full-time equivalent unit computation

Full-time Students	+	Equivalent Units of Part-time Students	=	Full-time Equivalent Students
900	+	(60% × 1,000)	=	1,500

The cost of instruction per full-time equivalent student is therefore the total cost of instruction ($9,000,000) divided by the number of full-time equivalent students (1,500), which is $6,000 ($9,000,000 ÷ 1,500).

A process cost system uses the same idea, called equivalent units of production. **Equivalent units of production** measure the work done during the period, expressed in fully completed units. Companies use this measure to determine the cost per unit of completed product.

Weighted-Average Method

The formula to compute equivalent units of production is as follows.

Units Completed and Transferred Out	+	Equivalent Units of Ending Work in Process	=	Equivalent Units of Production

Illustration 3-8
Equivalent units of production formula

To better understand this concept of equivalent units, consider the following two separate examples.

Example 1: In a specific period the entire output of Sullivan Company's Blending Department consists of ending work in process of 4,000 units which are 60% complete as to materials, labor, and overhead. The equivalent units of production for the Blending Department are therefore 2,400 units (4,000 × 60%).

Example 2: The output of Kori Company's Packaging Department during the period consists of 10,000 units completed and transferred out, and 5,000 units in ending work in process which are 70% completed. The equivalent units of production are therefore 13,500 [10,000 + (5,000 × 70%)].

This method of computing equivalent units is referred to as the **weighted-average method**. It considers the degree of completion (weighting) of the units completed and transferred out and the ending work in process.

Refinements on the Weighted-Average Method

Kellogg Company has produced Eggo® Waffles since 1970. Three departments produce these waffles: Mixing, Baking, and Freezing/Packaging. The Mixing Department combines dry ingredients, including flour, salt, and baking powder, with liquid ingredients, including eggs and vegetable oil, to make waffle batter. Illustration 3-9 provides information related to the Mixing Department at the end of June.

Illustration 3-9
Information for Mixing Department

MIXING DEPARTMENT

		Percentage Complete	
	Physical Units	Materials	Conversion Costs
Work in process, June 1	100,000	100%	70%
Started into production	800,000		
Total units	900,000		
Units transferred out	700,000		
Work in process, June 30	200,000	100%	60%
Total units	900,000		

Illustration 3-9 indicates that the beginning work in process is 100% complete as to materials cost and 70% complete as to conversion costs. **Conversion costs are the sum of labor costs and overhead costs.** In other words, Kellogg adds both the dry and liquid ingredients (materials) at the beginning of the waffle-making process, and the conversion costs (labor and overhead) related to the mixing of these ingredients are incurred uniformly and are 70% complete. The ending work in process is 100% complete as to materials cost and 60% complete as to conversion costs.

HELPFUL HINT

Question: When are separate unit cost computations needed for materials and conversion costs? Answer: Whenever the two types of costs do not occur in the process at the same time.

We then use the Mixing Department information to determine equivalent units. **In computing equivalent units, the beginning work in process is not part of the equivalent-units-of-production formula.** The units transferred out to the Baking Department are fully complete as to both materials and conversion costs. The ending work in process is fully complete as to materials, but only 60% complete as to conversion costs. We therefore need to make **two equivalent unit computations:** one for materials, and the other for conversion costs. Illustration 3-10 shows these computations.

Illustration 3-10
Computation of equivalent units—Mixing Department

MIXING DEPARTMENT

	Equivalent Units	
	Materials	**Conversion Costs**
Units transferred out	700,000	700,000
Work in process, June 30		
200,000 × 100%	200,000	
200,000 × 60%		120,000
Total equivalent units	900,000	820,000

We can refine the earlier formula used to compute equivalent units of production (Illustration 3-8) (page 103) to show the computations for materials and for conversion costs, as follows.

Illustration 3-11
Refined equivalent units of production formula

Units Completed and Transferred Out—Materials	+	**Equivalent Units of Ending Work in Process—Materials**	=	**Equivalent Units of Production—Materials**
Units Completed and Transferred Out—Conversion Costs	+	**Equivalent Units of Ending Work in Process—Conversion Costs**	=	**Equivalent Units of Production—Conversion Costs**

MANAGEMENT INSIGHT

Keeping Score for the Xbox

When you are as big and as profitable as Microsoft, you get to a point where continued rapid growth is very difficult. For example, many believe it is unlikely that Microsoft will see much growth in software sales. As a result, the company is looking for new markets, such as the video game market with its Xbox player.

Profitability in the video-game hardware market has been elusive. Microsoft has struggled to control the costs of both manufacturing and distribution. One analyst predicted that Microsoft's "snowballing" costs in the next period could exceed budget by $2.4 billion. Microsoft's Chief Financial Officer blamed the high costs on unexpectedly high volumes, saying, "We pushed market volumes very high in the Xbox business. As a result of that we incurred some costs in the supply chain." Given these issues and, despite its incredible success as a software company, some observers question whether Microsoft will be able to make the changes that are required to become a successful hardware manufacturer.

Source: Rober A. Guth, "Microsoft Net Rises 16%, but Costs Damp Results," *Wall Street Journal*, April 28, 2006.

? In what ways has cost accounting probably become more critical for Microsoft in recent years?

Production Cost Report

As mentioned earlier, companies prepare a production cost report for each department. A **production cost report** is the key document that management uses to understand the activities in a department; it shows the production quantity and cost data related to that department. For example, in producing Eggo® Waffles, Kellogg Company uses three production cost reports: Mixing, Baking, and Freezing/Packaging. Illustration 3-12 shows the flow of costs to make an Eggo® Waffle and the related production cost reports for each department.

Illustration 3-12
Flow of costs in making Eggo® Waffles

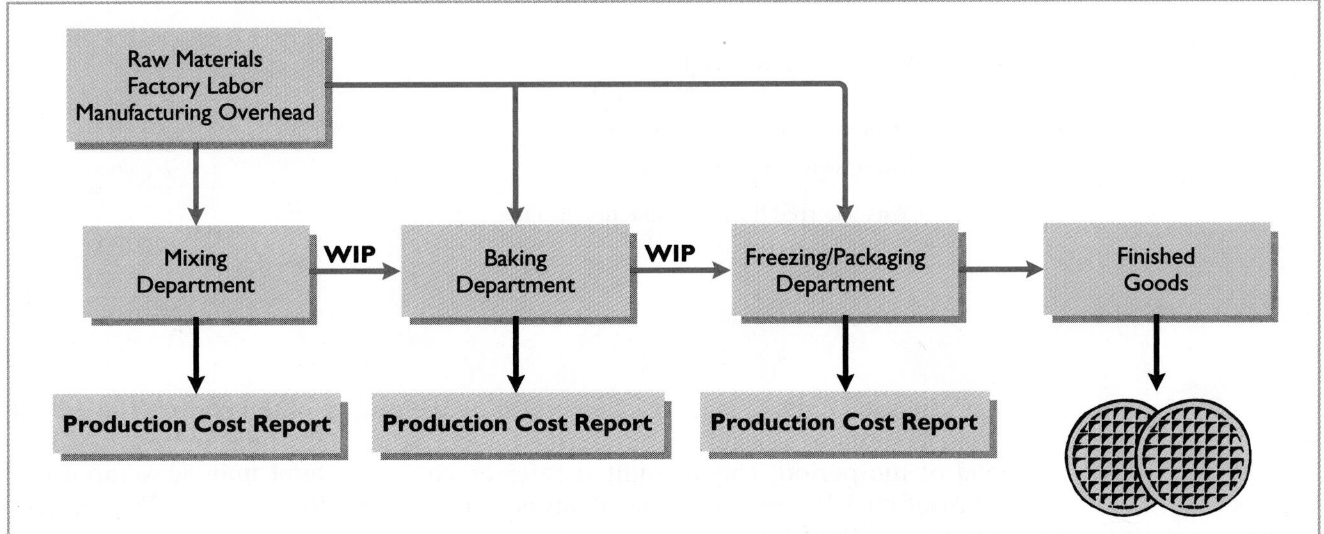

STUDY OBJECTIVE 6
Explain the four steps necessary to prepare a production cost report.

In order to complete a production cost report, the company must perform four steps, which as a whole, make up the process costing system.

1. Compute the physical unit flow.
2. Compute the equivalent units of production.
3. Compute unit production costs.
4. Prepare a cost reconciliation schedule.

The next section explores these steps in an extended example.

COMPREHENSIVE EXAMPLE OF PROCESS COSTING

Illustration 3-13 (page 106) shows assumed data for the Mixing Department at Kellogg Company for the month of June. We will use this information to complete a production cost report for the Mixing Department.

Compute the Physical Unit Flow (Step 1)

Physical units are the actual units to be accounted for during a period, irrespective of any work performed. To keep track of these units, add the units started (or transferred) into production during the period to the units in process at the beginning of the period. This amount is referred to as the **total units to be accounted for.**

Illustration 3-13
Unit and cost data—Mixing Department

MIXING DEPARTMENT

Units	
Work in process, June 1	100,000
Direct materials: 100% complete	
Conversion costs: 70% complete	
Units started into production during June	800,000
Units completed and transferred out to Baking Department	700,000
Work in process, June 30	200,000
Direct materials: 100% complete	
Conversion costs: 60% complete	
Costs	
Work in process, June 1	
Direct materials: 100% complete	$ 50,000
Conversion costs: 70% complete	35,000
Cost of work in process, June 1	$ 85,000
Costs incurred during production in June	
Direct materials	$400,000
Conversion costs	170,000
Costs incurred in June	$570,000

The total units then are accounted for by the output of the period. The output consists of units transferred out during the period and any units in process at the end of the period. This amount is referred to as the **total units accounted for.** Illustration 3-14 shows the flow of physical units for Kellogg's Mixing Department for the month of June.

Illustration 3-14
Physical unit flow—Mixing Department

MIXING DEPARTMENT

	Physical Units
Units to be accounted for	
Work in process, June 1	100,000
Started (transferred) into production	800,000
Total units	**900,000**
Units accounted for	
Completed and transferred out	700,000
Work in process, June 30	200,000
Total units	**900,000**

The records indicate that the Mixing Department must account for 900,000 units. Of this sum, 700,000 units were transferred to the Baking Department and 200,000 units were still in process.

Compute Equivalent Units of Production (Step 2)

HELPFUL HINT
Materials are not always added at the beginning of the process. For example, materials are sometimes added uniformly during the process.

Once the physical flow of the units is established, Kellogg must measure the Mixing Department's productivity in terms of equivalent units of production. The Mixing Department adds materials at the beginning of the process, and it incurs conversion costs uniformly during the process. Thus, we need two computations of equivalent units: one for materials and one for conversion costs. The equivalent unit computation is as follows.

	Equivalent Units	
	Materials	**Conversion Costs**
Units transferred out	700,000	700,000
Work in process, June 30		
200,000 × 100%	200,000	
200,000 × 60%		120,000
Total equivalent units	**900,000**	**820,000**

Illustration 3-15
Computation of equivalent units—Mixing Department

HELPFUL HINT
Remember that we ignore the beginning work in process in this computation.

Compute Unit Production Costs (Step 3)

Armed with the knowledge of the equivalent units of production, we can now compute the unit production costs. **Unit production costs** are costs expressed in terms of equivalent units of production. When equivalent units of production are different for materials and conversion costs, we compute three unit costs: (1) materials, (2) conversion, and (3) total manufacturing.

The computation of total materials cost related to Eggo® Waffles is as follows.

Work in process, June 1	
Direct materials cost	$ 50,000
Costs added to production during June	
Direct materials cost	400,000
Total materials cost	**$450,000**

Illustration 3-16
Total materials cost computation

The computation of unit materials cost is as follows.

Total Materials Cost	÷	Equivalent Units of Materials	=	Unit Materials Cost
$450,000	÷	900,000	=	$0.50

Illustration 3-17
Unit materials cost computation

Illustration 3-18 shows the computation of total conversion costs.

Work in process, June 1	
Conversion costs	$ 35,000
Costs added to production during June	
Conversion costs	170,000
Total conversion costs	**$205,000**

Illustration 3-18
Total conversion costs computation

The computation of unit conversion cost is as follows.

Total Conversion Costs	÷	Equivalent Units of Conversion Costs	=	Unit Conversion Cost
$205,000	÷	820,000	=	$0.25

Illustration 3-19
Unit conversion cost computation

Total manufacturing cost per unit is therefore computed as shown in Illustration 3-20 (page 108).

Illustration 3-20
Total manufacturing cost per unit

Unit Materials Cost	+	Unit Conversion Cost	=	Total Manufacturing Cost per Unit
$0.50	+	$0.25	=	$0.75

Prepare a Cost Reconciliation Schedule (Step 4)

We are now ready to determine the cost of goods transferred out of the Mixing Department to the Baking Department and the costs in ending work in process. Kellogg charged total costs of $655,000 to the Mixing Department in June, calculated as follows.

Illustration 3-21
Costs charged to Mixing Department

Costs to be accounted for	
Work in process, June 1	$ 85,000
Started into production	570,000
Total costs	**$655,000**

The company then prepares a cost reconciliation schedule to assign these costs to (a) units transferred out to the Baking Department and (b) ending work in process.

Illustration 3-22
Cost reconciliation schedule—Mixing Department

MIXING DEPARTMENT
Cost Reconciliation Schedule

Costs accounted for		
Transferred out (700,000 × $0.75)		$ 525,000
Work in process, June 30		
Materials (200,000 × $0.50)	$100,000	
Conversion costs (120,000 × $0.25)	30,000	130,000
Total costs		**$655,000**

Kellogg uses the total manufacturing cost per unit, $0.75, in costing the **units completed** and transferred to the Baking Department. In contrast, the unit cost of materials and the unit cost of conversion are needed in costing **units in process**. The **cost reconciliation schedule** shows that the **total costs accounted for** (Illustration 3-22) equal the **total costs to be accounted for** (see Illustration 3-21).

Preparing the Production Cost Report

STUDY OBJECTIVE 7
Prepare a production cost report.

At this point, Kellogg is ready to prepare the production cost report for the Mixing Department. As indicated earlier, this report is an internal document for management that shows production quantity and cost data for a production department.

There are four steps in preparing a production cost report. They are:

1. Prepare a physical unit schedule.
2. Compute equivalent units.
3. Compute unit costs.
4. Prepare a cost reconciliation schedule.

Illustration 3-23 shows the production cost report for the Mixing Department. The report identifies the four steps.

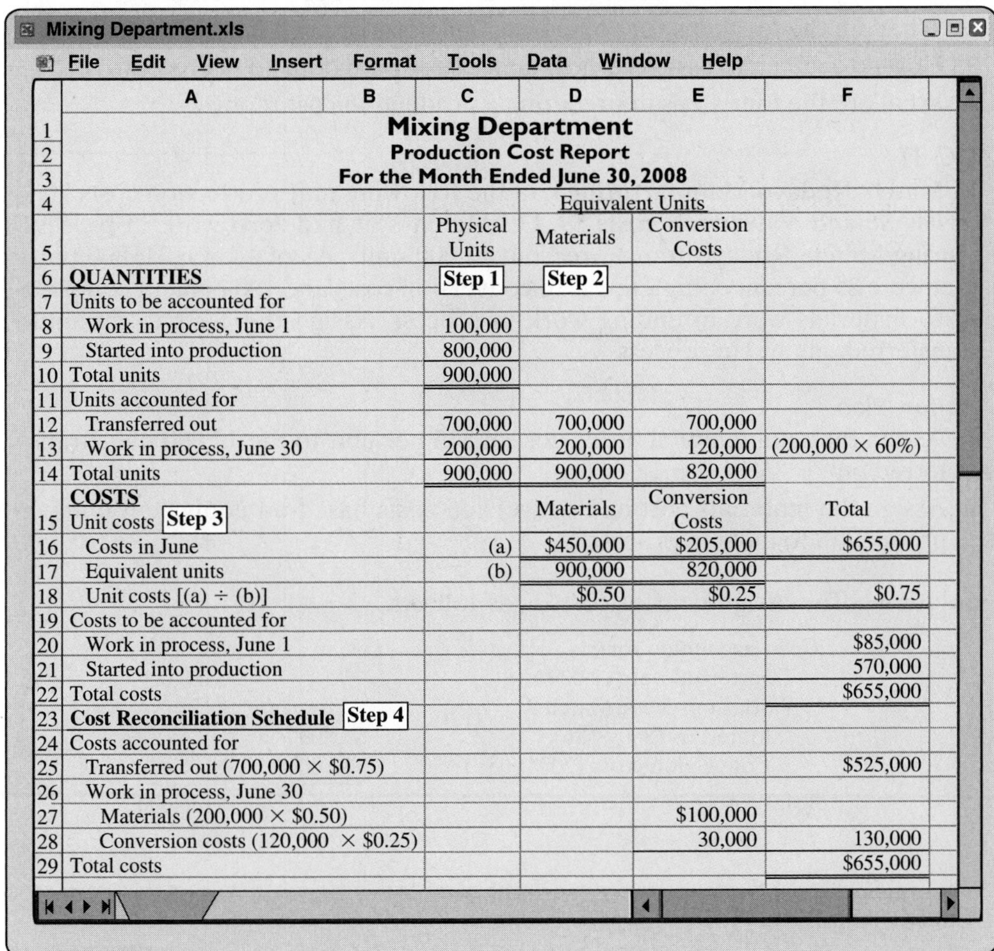

Mixing Department.xls

File Edit View Insert Format Tools Data Window Help

Mixing Department
Production Cost Report
For the Month Ended June 30, 2008

	A	B	C	D	E	F
4				Equivalent Units		
5			Physical Units	Materials	Conversion Costs	
6	**QUANTITIES**		Step 1	Step 2		
7	Units to be accounted for					
8	Work in process, June 1		100,000			
9	Started into production		800,000			
10	Total units		900,000			
11	Units accounted for					
12	Transferred out		700,000	700,000	700,000	
13	Work in process, June 30		200,000	200,000	120,000	(200,000 × 60%)
14	Total units		900,000	900,000	820,000	
15	**COSTS** Unit costs Step 3			Materials	Conversion Costs	Total
16	Costs in June		(a)	$450,000	$205,000	$655,000
17	Equivalent units		(b)	900,000	820,000	
18	Unit costs [(a) ÷ (b)]			$0.50	$0.25	$0.75
19	Costs to be accounted for					
20	Work in process, June 1					$85,000
21	Started into production					570,000
22	Total costs					$655,000
23	**Cost Reconciliation Schedule** Step 4					
24	Costs accounted for					
25	Transferred out (700,000 × $0.75)					$525,000
26	Work in process, June 30					
27	Materials (200,000 × $0.50)				$100,000	
28	Conversion costs (120,000 × $0.25)				30,000	130,000
29	Total costs					$655,000

Illustration 3-23
Production cost report

Production cost reports provide a basis for evaluating the productivity of a department. In addition, managers can use the cost data to assess whether unit costs and total costs are reasonable. By comparing the quantity and cost data with predetermined goals, top management can also judge whether current performance is meeting planned objectives.

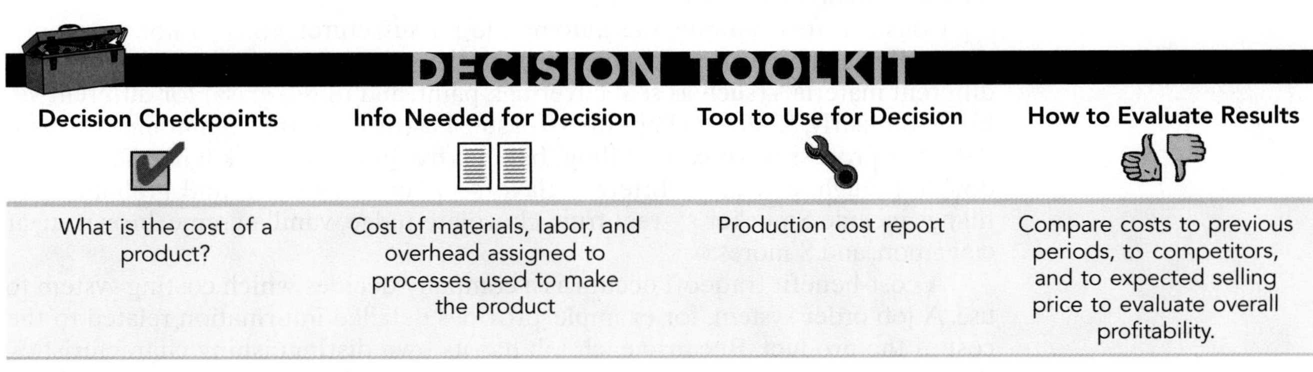

DECISION TOOLKIT

Decision Checkpoints	Info Needed for Decision	Tool to Use for Decision	How to Evaluate Results
What is the cost of a product?	Cost of materials, labor, and overhead assigned to processes used to make the product	Production cost report	Compare costs to previous periods, to competitors, and to expected selling price to evaluate overall profitability.

Before You Go On...

REVIEW IT

1. How do physical units differ from equivalent units of production?
2. What are the formulas for computing unit costs of production?
3. How do companies assign costs to units transferred out and in process?
4. What are the four steps in preparing a production cost report?

DO IT

In March, Rodayo Manufacturing had the following unit production costs: materials \$6 and conversion costs \$9. On March 1, it had zero work in process. During March, Rodayo transferred out 12,000 units. As of March 31, 800 units that were 25 percent completed as to conversion costs and 100 percent complete as to materials were in ending work in process. Assign the costs to the units transferred out and in process.

Action Plan

- Assign the total manufacturing cost of \$15 per unit to the 12,000 units transferred out.
- Assign the materials cost and conversion costs based on equivalent units of production to units in process.

Solution The assignment of costs is as follows.

Costs accounted for		
Transferred out (12,000 × \$15)		\$180,000
Work in process, March 31		
Materials (800 × \$6)	\$4,800	
Conversion costs (200[a] × \$9)	1,800	6,600
Total costs		\$186,600

[a]800 × 25%

Related exercise material: *BE3-4, BE3-5, BE3-6, BE3-7, BE3-8, BE3-9, BE3-10, E3-3, E3-5, E3-6, E3-7, E3-8, E3-9, E3-10, E3-11, E3-12, and E3-14.*

Costing Systems—Final Comments

Companies often use a combination of a process cost and a job order cost system. Called **operations costing**, this hybrid system is similar to process costing in its assumption that standardized methods are used to manufacture the product. At the same time, the product may have some customized, individual features that require the use of a job order cost system.

Consider, for example, the automobile manufacturer Ford Motor Company. Each vehicle at a given plant goes through the same assembly line, but Ford uses different materials (such as seat coverings, paint, and tinted glass) for different vehicles. Similarly, Kellogg's Pop-Tarts Toaster Pastries® go through numerous standardized processes—mixing, filling, baking, frosting, and packaging. The pastry dough, though, comes in different flavors—plain, chocolate, and graham—and fillings include Smucker's® real fruit, chocolate fudge, vanilla creme, brown sugar cinnamon, and S'mores.

A cost-benefit tradeoff occurs as a company decides which costing system to use. A job order system, for example, provides detailed information related to the cost of the product. Because each job has its own distinguishing characteristics, the system can provide an accurate cost per job. This information is useful in controlling costs and pricing products. However, the cost of implementing a job order cost system is often expensive because of the accounting costs involved.

On the other hand, for a company like Intel, which makes computer chips, is there a benefit in knowing whether the cost of the one hundredth chip produced is different from the one thousandth chip produced? Probably not. An average cost of the product will suffice for control and pricing purposes.

In summary, when deciding to use one of these systems, or a combination system, a company must weigh the costs of implementing the system against the benefits from the additional information provided.

ACCOUNTING ACROSS THE ORGANIZATION

What Cost System Might Jiffy Lube Use?

Frequently, when we think of service companies, we think of specific, nonroutine tasks, such as rebuilding an automobile engine, providing consulting services on a business acquisition, or working on a major lawsuit. However, many service companies specialize in performing repetitive, routine aspects of a particular business. For example, auto-care vendors such as Jiffy Lube focus on the routine aspects of car care. H&R Block focuses on the routine aspects of basic tax practice, and many large law firms focus on routine legal services, such as uncomplicated divorces.

? What criteria should be considered when selecting a cost accounting system for a service company?

DECISION TOOLKIT

Decision Checkpoints	Info Needed for Decision	Tool to Use for Decision	How to Evaluate Results
What costing method should be used?	Type of product or service produced	Cost of accounting system; benefits of additional information	The benefits of providing the additional information should exceed the costs of the accounting system needed to develop the information.

Before You Go On...

REVIEW IT

1. In what circumstances would a manufacturer use operations costing instead of process costing?
2. Describe the cost-benefit tradeoff involved in deciding what costing system to use.

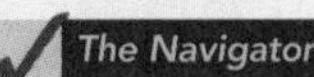

Be sure to read **ALL ABOUT YOU: *Wal-Mart Is on the Phone*** on page 112 for information on how topics in this chapter apply to you.

all about Y❁U

Wal-Mart Is on the Phone

If you own a small business that produces a consumer product, and if **Wal-Mart** decides to stock your product on its shelves, it is a big, big deal. But those companies lucky enough to have this happen often find themselves in a precarious situation. The same deal that might make them fabulously wealthy might also cause the failure of the business. Suppliers to Wal-Mart sell lots of units, but Wal-Mart demands extremely low prices. As the owner of such a company, you must learn to exist on razor-thin margins. Your cost accounting system had better be accurate, or you may soon be broke.

Some Facts

* Wal-Mart has 138 million weekly customers.
* In 2006 Wal-Mart had annual sales of $312 billion and net income of more than $11.2 billion.
* There are about 5,300 Wal-Mart stores worldwide. During a single recent year, it planned on adding 500 more stores, and it believes that the U.S. has room for at least 4,000 more "supercenters."
* During a recent year, 10,000 companies applied to be new suppliers to Wal-Mart. Of those, some 200 (about 2%) were accepted.
* Wal-Mart doesn't like to account for more than 30% of a supplier's total business for fear that changing an order can destroy the supplier.
* As shown in the "About the Numbers" section in the next column, Wal-Mart's "kingdom" spreads across many different countries. Recently, however, it sold all of its stores in Germany because they could not meet its desired profitability goals.

About the Numbers

Wal-Mart continues to grow across the world, but its success varies across countries. The following chart shows total store count in various countries.

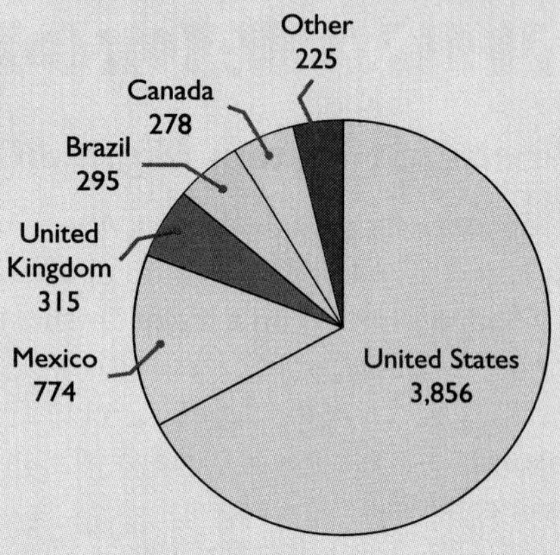

Source: Based on data from Wal-Mart 2006 Annual Report, p. 51.

What Do You Think?

Suppose that you were Colin Roche, whose PenAgain pen was recently offered a 30-day trial period at 500 Wal-Mart stores. In order for the product to pass the trial, in one month Wal-Mart needs to sell 85% of the 48,000 pens that it ordered. If it does, it will then order pens for a much wider distribution at many more of its stores. If it doesn't, the deal is off.

The PenAgain company gets between $6.49 and $12 from other retailers for the PenAgain pen, but Wal-Mart is willing to pay only $3.76. Last year total sales of PenAgain were $2,000,000. If you were Colin Roche would you accept Wal-Mart's offer?

YES: Are you kidding? If only a tiny fraction of Wal-Mart customers buy a pen, the company's sales will go through the roof. You have to take a shot at it.

NO: The risks are high on two counts. First, the company has to dramatically increase its operations in order to meet the production requirements. What will it do with this excess capacity if the deal falls through? Second, the company risks alienating the retailers that it currently supplies with pens. It could lose both Wal-Mart *and* its existing customers.

Sources: Gwendolyn Bounds, "One Month to Make It," *Wall Street Journal*, May 30, 2006, p. B1; Gwendolyn Bounds, "The Long Road to Wal-Mart," *Wall Street Journal*, September 19, 2005, p. R1; John Anderson, "Running the Gauntlet at Wal-Mart," *Inc.* Magazine, November 2003, p. 93.

The authors' comments on this situation appear on page 144.

Using the Decision Toolkit

Essence Company manufactures a high-end after-shave lotion, called Eternity, in 10-ounce plastic bottles. Because the market for after-shave lotion is highly competitive, the company is very concerned about keeping its costs under control. Eternity is manufactured through three processes: mixing, filling, and corking. Materials are added at the beginning of the process, and labor and overhead are incurred uniformly throughout each process. The company uses a weighted-average method to cost its product. A partially completed production cost report for the month of May for the Mixing Department is shown below.

ESSENCE COMPANY
Mixing Department
Production Cost Report
For the Month Ended May 31, 2008

		Equivalent Units	
Quantities	**Physical Units**	**Materials**	**Conversion Costs**
Units to be accounted for	Step 1	Step 2	
Work in process, May 1	1,000		
Started into production	2,000		
Total units	3,000		
Units accounted for			
Transferred out	2,200	?	?
Work in process, May 31	800	?	?
Total units	3,000	?	?

Costs		**Materials**	**Conversion Costs**	**Total**
Unit costs Step 3				
Costs in May	(a)	?	?	?
Equivalent units	(b)	?	?	
Unit costs [(a) ÷ (b)]		?	?	?
Costs to be accounted for				
Work in process, May 1				$ 56,300
Started into production				119,320
Total costs				$175,620
Cost Reconciliation Schedule Step 4				
Costs accounted for				
Transferred out				?
Work in process, May 31				
Materials			?	
Conversion costs			?	?
Total costs				?

Additional information:

Work in process, May 1, 1000 units		
Materials cost, 1,000 units (100% complete)	$49,100	
Conversion costs, 1,000 units (70% complete)	7,200	$ 56,300
Materials cost for May, 2,000 units		$100,000

Work in process, May 31, 800 units, 100% complete as to materials and 50% complete as to conversion costs.

Instructions

(a) Prepare a production cost report for the Mixing Department for the month of May.
(b) Prepare the journal entry to record the transfer of goods from the Mixing Department to the Filling Department.
(c) Explain why Essence Company is using a process cost system to account for its costs.

action plan

- ✔ Compute the physical unit flow—that is, the total units to be accounted for.
- ✔ Compute the equivalent units of production.
- ✔ Compute the unit production costs, expressed in terms of equivalent units of production.
- ✔ Prepare a cost reconciliation schedule, which shows that the total costs accounted for equal the total costs to be accounted for.

Solution

(a) A completed production cost report for the Mixing Department is shown below. Computations to support the amounts reported follow the report.

ESSENCE COMPANY
Mixing Department
Production Cost Report
For the Month Ended May 31, 2008

		Equivalent Units		
Quantities	**Physical Units**	**Materials**	**Conversion Costs**	
Units to be accounted for	Step 1	Step 2		
Work in process, May 1	1,000			
Started into production	2,000			
Total units	3,000			
Units accounted for				
Transferred out	2,200	2,200	2,200	
Work in process, May 31	800	800	400	(800 × 50%)
Total units	3,000	3,000	2,600	

Costs			**Conversion**	
Unit costs Step 3		**Materials**	**Costs**	**Total**
Costs in May*	(a)	$149,100	$26,520	$175,620
Equivalent units	(b)	3,000	2,600	
Unit costs [(a) ÷ (b)]		$49.70	$10.20	$59.90
Costs to be accounted for				
Work in process, May 1				$ 56,300
Started into production				119,320
Total costs				$175,620

*Additional computations to support production cost report data:
Materials cost—$49,100 + $100,000
Conversion costs—$7,200 + $19,320 ($119,320 − $100,000)

Cost Reconciliation Schedule Step 4

Costs accounted for		
Transferred out (2,200 × $59.90)		$131,780
Work in process, May 31		
Materials (800 × $49.70)	$39,760	
Conversion costs (400 × $10.20)	4,080	43,840
Total costs		$175,620

(b) Work in Process—Filling	131,780	
Work in Process—Mixing		131,780

(c) Companies use process cost systems to apply costs to similar products that are mass-produced in a continuous fashion. Essence Company uses a process cost system because production of the after-shave lotion, once it begins, continues until the after-shave lotion emerges. The processing is the same for the entire run—with precisely the same amount of materials, labor, and overhead. Each bottle of Eternity after-shave lotion is indistinguishable from another.

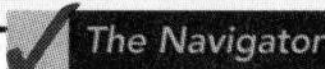

SUMMARY OF STUDY OBJECTIVES

1 **Understand who uses process cost systems.** Companies that mass-produce similar products in a continuous fashion use process cost systems. Once production begins, it continues until the finished product emerges. Each unit of finished product is indistinguishable from every other unit.

2 **Explain the similarities and differences between job order cost and process cost systems.** Job order cost systems are similar to process cost systems in three ways: (1) Both systems track the same cost elements—direct materials, direct labor, and manufacturing overhead. (2) Both accumulate costs in the same accounts—Raw Materials Inventory, Factory Labor, and Manufacturing Overhead. (3) Both assign accumulated costs to the same accounts—Work in Process, Finished Goods Inventory, and Cost of Goods Sold. However, the method of assigning costs differs significantly.

There are four main differences between the two cost systems: (1) A process cost system uses separate accounts for each department or manufacturing process, rather than only one work in process account used in a job order cost system. (2) A process cost system summarizes costs in a production cost report for each department. A job cost system charges costs to individual jobs and summarizes them in a job cost sheet. (3) Costs are totaled at the end of a time period in a process cost system, but at the completion of a job in a job cost system. (4) A process cost system calculates unit cost as: Total manufacturing costs for the period ÷ Units produced during the period. A job cost system calculates unit cost as: Total cost per job ÷ Units produced.

3 **Explain the flow of costs in a process cost system.** A process cost system assigns manufacturing costs for raw materials, labor, and overhead to work in process accounts for various departments or manufacturing processes. It transfers the costs of partially completed units from one department to another as those units move through the manufacturing process. The system transfers the costs of completed work to Finished Goods Inventory. Finally, when inventory is sold, the system transfers the costs to Cost of Goods Sold.

4 **Make the journal entries to assign manufacturing costs in a process cost system.** Entries to assign the costs of raw materials, labor, and overhead consist of a credit to Raw Materials Inventory, Factory Labor, and Manufacturing Overhead, and a debit to Work in Process for each department. Entries to record the cost of goods transferred to another department are a credit to Work in Process for the department whose work is finished and a debit to the department to which the goods are transferred. The entry to record units completed and transferred to the warehouse is a credit to Work in Process for the department whose work is finished and a debit to Finished Goods Inventory. The entry to record the sale of goods is a credit to Finished Goods Inventory and a debit to Cost of Goods Sold.

5 **Compute equivalent units.** Equivalent units of production measure work done during a period, expressed in fully completed units. Companies use this measure to determine the cost per unit of completed product. Equivalent units are the sum of units completed and transferred out plus equivalent units of ending work in process.

6 **Explain the four steps necessary to prepare a production cost report.** The four steps to complete a production cost report are: (1) Compute the physical unit flow—that is, the total units to be accounted for. (2) Compute the equivalent units of production. (3) Compute the unit production costs, expressed in terms of equivalent units of production. (4) Prepare a cost reconciliation schedule, which shows that the total costs accounted for equal the total costs to be accounted for.

7 **Prepare a production cost report.** The production cost report contains both quantity and cost data for a production department. There are four sections in the report: (1) number of physical units, (2) equivalent units determination, (3) unit costs, and (4) cost reconciliation schedule.

The Navigator

DECISION TOOLKIT—A SUMMARY

Decision Checkpoints	Info Needed for Decision	Tool to Use for Decision	How to Evaluate Results
What is the cost of a product?	Costs of materials, labor, and overhead assigned to processes used to make the product	Production cost report	Compare costs to previous periods, to competitors, and to expected selling price to evaluate overall profitability.
Which costing method should be used?	Type of product or service produced	Cost of accounting system; benefits of additional information	The benefits of providing the additional information should exceed the costs of the accounting system needed to develop the information.

APPENDIX FIFO Method

In this chapter we demonstrated the weighted-average method of computing equivalent units. Some companies use a different method, referred to as the **first-in, first-out (FIFO) method**, to compute equivalent units. The purpose of this appendix is to illustrate how companies use the FIFO method to prepare a production cost report.

Equivalent Units Under FIFO

STUDY OBJECTIVE 8

Compute equivalent units using the FIFO method.

Under the FIFO method, companies compute equivalent units on a first-in, first-out basis. Some companies favor the FIFO method because the FIFO cost assumption usually corresponds to the actual physical flow of the goods. Under the FIFO method, companies therefore assume that the beginning work in process is completed before new work is started.

Using the FIFO method, equivalent units are the sum of the work performed to:

1. Finish the units of beginning work in process inventory.
2. Complete the units started into production during the period (referred to as the **units started and completed**).
3. Start, but only partially complete, the units in ending work in process inventory.

Normally, in a process costing system, some units will always be in process at both the beginning and end of the period.

ILLUSTRATION

Illustration 3A-1 shows the physical flow of units for the Assembly Department of Shutters Inc. In addition, it indicates the degree of completion of the work in process accounts in regard to conversion costs.

Illustration 3A-1
Physical unit flow—Assembly Department

ASSEMBLY DEPARTMENT	
	Physical Units
Units to be accounted for	
Work in process, June 1 (40% complete)	500
Started (transferred) into production	8,000
Total units	**8,500**
Units accounted for	
Completed and transferred out	8,100
Work in process, June 30 (75% complete)	400
Total units	**8,500**

In Illustration 3A-1, the units completed and transferred out (8,100) plus the units in ending work in process (400) equal the total units to be accounted for (8,500). Using FIFO, we then compute equivalent units as follows.

1. The 500 units of beginning work in process were 40 percent complete. Thus, 300 equivalent units (60% × 500 units) were required to complete the beginning inventory.
2. The units started and completed during the current month are the units transferred out minus the units in beginning work in process. For the Assembly Department, units started and completed are 7,600 (8,100 − 500).
3. The 400 units of ending work in process were 75 percent complete. Thus, equivalent units were 300 (400 × 75%).

Equivalent units for the Assembly Department are 8,200, computed as follows.

Illustration 3A-2
Computation of equivalent units—FIFO method

ASSEMBLY DEPARTMENT

Production Data	Physical Units	Work Added This Period	Equivalent Units
Work in process, June 1	500	60%	**300**
Started and completed	7,600	100%	**7,600**
Work in process, June 30	400	75%	**300**
Total	8,500		**8,200**

Comprehensive Example

To provide a complete illustration of the FIFO method, we will use the data for the Mixing Department at Kellogg Company for the month of June, as shown in Illustration 3A-3 (page 118).

COMPUTE THE PHYSICAL UNIT FLOW (STEP 1)

Illustration 3A-4 (page 118) shows the physical flow of units for Kellogg for the month of June for the Mixing Department.

Under the FIFO method, companies often expand the physical units schedule, as shown in Illustration 3A-5 (page 118) to explain the transferred-out section. As a result, this section reports the beginning work in process and the units started and completed. These two items further explain the completed and transferred out section.

Illustration 3A-3
Unit and cost data—Mixing Department

MIXING DEPARTMENT

Units	
Work in process, June 1	100,000
Direct materials: 100% complete	
Conversion costs: 70% complete	
Units started into production during June	800,000
Units completed and transferred out to Baking Department	700,000
Work in process, June 30	200,000
Direct materials: 100% complete	
Conversion costs: 60% complete	
Costs	
Work in process, June 1	
Direct materials: 100% complete	$ 50,000
Conversion costs: 70% complete	35,000
Cost of work in process, June 1	$ 85,000
Costs incurred during production in June	
Direct materials	$400,000
Conversion costs	170,000
Costs incurred in June	$570,000

Illustration 3A-4
Physical unit flow—Mixing Department

MIXING DEPARTMENT

	Physical Units
Units to be accounted for	
Work in process, June 1	100,000
Started (transferred) into production	800,000
Total units	**900,000**
Units accounted for	
Completed and transferred out	700,000
Work in process, June 30	200,000
Total units	**900,000**

Illustration 3A-5
Physical unit flow (FIFO)—Mixing Department

MIXING DEPARTMENT

	Physical Units
Units to be accounted for	
Work in process, June 1	100,000
Started (transferred) into production	800,000
Total units	**900,000**
Units accounted for	
Completed and transferred out	
Work in process, June 1	**100,000**
Started and completed	**600,000**
	700,000
Work in process, June 30	200,000
Total units	**900,000**

The records indicate that the Mixing Department must account for 900,000 units. Of this sum, 700,000 units were transferred to the Baking Department and 200,000 units were still in process.

COMPUTE EQUIVALENT UNITS OF PRODUCTION (STEP 2)

As with the method presented in the chapter, once they determine the physical flow of the units, companies need to determine equivalent units of production. The Mixing Department adds materials at the beginning of the process, and it incurs conversion costs uniformly during the process. Thus, Kellogg must make two computations of equivalent units: one for materials and one for conversion costs.

HELPFUL HINT
Materials are not always added at the beginning of the process. For example, companies sometimes add materials uniformly during the process.

Equivalent Units for Materials Since Kellogg adds materials at the beginning of the process, no additional materials costs are required to complete the beginning work in process. In addition, 100 percent of the materials costs has been incurred on the ending work in process. Thus, the computation of equivalent units for materials is as follows.

Illustration 3A-6
Computation of equivalent units—materials

MIXING DEPARTMENT—MATERIALS

Production Data	Physical Units	Materials Added This Period	Equivalent Units
Work in process, June 1	100,000	-0-	**-0-**
Started and finished	600,000	100%	**600,000**
Work in process, June 30	200,000	100%	**200,000**
Total	900,000		**800,000**

Equivalent Units for Conversion Costs The 100,000 units of beginning work in process were 70 percent complete in terms of conversion costs. Thus, the Mixing Department required 30,000 equivalent units (30% × 100,000 units) of conversion costs to complete the beginning inventory. In addition, the 200,000 units of ending work in process were 60 percent complete in terms of conversion costs. Thus, the equivalent units for conversion costs is 750,000, computed as follows.

Illustration 3A-7
Computation of equivalent units—conversion costs

MIXING DEPARTMENT—CONVERSION COSTS

Production Data	Physical Units	Work Added This Period	Equivalent Units
Work in process, June 1	100,000	30%	**30,000**
Started and finished	600,000	100%	**600,000**
Work in process, June 30	200,000	60%	**120,000**
Total	900,000		**750,000**

COMPUTE UNIT PRODUCTION COSTS (STEP 3)

Armed with the knowledge of the equivalent units of production, Kellogg can now compute the unit production costs. Unit production costs are costs expressed in terms of equivalent units of production. When equivalent units of production are different for materials and conversion costs, companies compute three unit costs: (1) materials, (2) conversion, and (3) total manufacturing.

Under the FIFO method, the unit costs of production are based entirely on the production costs incurred during the month. Thus, the costs in the beginning work in process are not relevant, because they were incurred on work done in the preceding month. As Illustration 3A-3 (page 118) indicated, the costs incurred during production in June were:

Illustration 3A-8
Costs incurred during production in June

Direct materials	$400,000
Conversion costs	170,000
Total costs	$570,000

Illustration 3A-9 shows the computation of unit materials cost, unit conversion costs, and total unit cost related to Eggo® Waffles.

Illustration 3A-9
Unit cost formulas and computations—Mixing Department

(1)	**Total Materials Cost**	÷	**Equivalent Units of Materials**	=	**Unit Materials Cost**
	$400,000	÷	800,000	=	$0.50
(2)	**Total Conversion Costs**	÷	**Equivalent Units of Conversion Costs**	=	**Unit Conversion Cost**
	$170,000	÷	750,000	=	$0.227 (rounded)*
(3)	**Unit Materials Cost**	+	**Unit Conversion Cost**	=	**Total Manufacturing Cost per Unit**
	$0.50	+	$0.227	=	$0.727

**For homework problems, round unit costs to three decimal places.*

As shown, the unit costs are $0.50 for materials, $0.227 for conversion costs, and $0.727 for total manufacturing costs.

PREPARE A COST RECONCILIATION SCHEDULE (STEP 4)

Kellogg is now ready to determine the cost of goods transferred out of the Mixing Department to the Baking Department and the costs in ending work in process. The total costs charged to the Mixing Department in June are $655,000, calculated as follows.

Illustration 3A-10
Costs charged to Mixing Department

Costs to be accounted for	
Work in process, June 1	$ 85,000
Started into production	570,000
Total costs	$655,000

Kellogg next prepares a cost reconciliation to assign these costs to (1) units transferred out to the Baking Department and (2) ending work in process. Under the FIFO method, the first goods to be completed during the period are the units in beginning work in process. Thus, the cost of the beginning work in process is always assigned to the goods transferred to the next department (or finished goods, if processing is complete). Under the FIFO method, ending work in process also will be assigned only the production costs incurred in the current period. Illustration 3A-11 shows a cost reconciliation schedule for the Mixing Department.

Illustration 3A-11
Cost reconciliation report

MIXING DEPARTMENT
Cost Reconciliation Schedule

Costs accounted for		
Transferred out		
Work in process, June 1		$ 85,000
Costs to complete beginning work in process		
Conversion costs (30,000 × $0.227)		6,810
Total costs		91,810
Units started and completed (600,000 × $0.727)		435,950*
Total costs transferred out		527,760
Work in process, June 30		
Materials (200,000 × $0.50)	$100,000	
Conversion costs (120,000 × $0.227)	27,240	127,240
Total costs		$655,000

*Any rounding errors should be adjusted in the "Units started and completed" calculation.

As you can see, the total costs accounted for ($655,000 from Illustration 3A-11) equal the total costs to be accounted for ($655,000 from Illustration 3A-10).

PREPARING THE PRODUCTION COST REPORT

At this point, Kellogg is ready to prepare the production cost report for the Mixing Department. This report is an internal document for management that shows production quantity and cost data for a production department.

As discussed on page 108, there are four steps in preparing a production cost report:

1. Prepare a physical unit schedule.
2. Compute equivalent units.
3. Compute unit costs.
4. Prepare a cost reconciliation schedule.

Illustration 3A-12 (page 122) shows the production cost report for the Mixing Department, with the four steps identified in the report.

As indicated in the chapter, production cost reports provide a basis for evaluating the productivity of a department. In addition, managers can use the cost data to assess whether unit costs and total costs are reasonable. By comparing the quantity and cost data with predetermined goals, top management can also judge whether current performance is meeting planned objectives.

FIFO and Weighted-Average

The weighted-average method of computing equivalent units has **one major advantage:** It is simple to understand and apply. In cases where prices do not fluctuate significantly from period to period, the weighted-average method will be very similar to the FIFO method. In addition, companies that have been using just-in-time procedures effectively for inventory control purposes will have minimal inventory balances, and therefore differences between the weighted-average and the FIFO methods will not be material.

Conceptually, the FIFO method is superior to the weighted-average method because it measures **current performance** using only costs incurred in the current

Mixing Department.xls

File Edit View Insert Format Tools Data Window Help

	A	B	C	D	E	F	G
1	**Mixing Department**						
2	**Production Cost Report**						
3	**For the Month Ended June 30, 2008**						
4				Equivalent Units			
5			Physical Units	Materials	Conversion Costs		
6	QUANTITIES		Step 1	Step 2			
7	Units to be accounted for						
8	Work in process (WIP), June 1		100,000				
9	Started into production		800,000				
10	Total units		900,000				
11							
12	Units accounted for						
13	Completed and transferred out						
14	Work in process, June 1		100,000	0	30,000		
15	Started and completed		600,000	600,000	600,000		
16	Work in process, June 30		200,000	200,000	120,000		
17	Total units		900,000	800,000	750,000		
18							
19	COSTS						
20	Unit costs Step 3			Materials	Conversion Costs	Total	
21	Costs in June (excluding beginning WIP)		(a)	$400,000	$170,000	$570,000	
22	Equivalent units		(b)	800,000	750,000		
23	Unit costs [(a) ÷ (b)]			$0.50	$0.227	$0.727	
24							
25	Costs to be accounted for						
26	Work in process, June 1					$85,000	
27	Started into production					570,000	
28	Total costs					$655,000	
29							
30	Cost Reconciliation Schedule Step 4						
31	Costs accounted for						
32	Transferred out						
33	Work in process, June 1					$85,000	
34	Costs to complete beginning work in process						
35	Conversion costs (30,000 × $0.227)					6,810	
36	Total costs					91,810	
37	Units started and completed (600,000 × $0.727)**					435,950	**Any rounding errors should be adjusted in the "Units started and completed"
38	Total costs transferred out					527,760	
39	Work in process, June 30						
40	Materials (200,000 × $0.50)				$100,000		
41	Conversions costs (120,000 × $0.227)				27,240	127,240	
42	Total costs					$655,000	
43							

Illustration 3A-12
Production cost report—FIFO method

period. Managers are, therefore, not held responsible for costs from prior periods over which they may not have had control. In addition, the FIFO method **provides current cost information**, which the company can use to establish **more accurate pricing strategies** for goods manufactured and sold in the current period.

HELPFUL HINT

What are the two self-checks in the report? Answer: (1) Total physical units accounted for must equal the total units to be accounted for. (2) Total costs accounted for must equal the total costs to be accounted for.

SUMMARY OF STUDY OBJECTIVE FOR APPENDIX

8 **Compute equivalent units using the FIFO method.** Equivalent units under the FIFO method are the sum of the work performed to: (1) Finish the units of beginning work in process inventory, if any; (2) complete the units started into production during the period; and (3) start, but only partially complete, the units in ending work in process inventory.

GLOSSARY

Conversion costs The sum of labor costs and overhead costs. (p. 103).

Cost reconciliation schedule A schedule that shows that the total costs accounted for equal the total costs to be accounted for. (p. 108).

Equivalent units of production A measure of the work done during the period, expressed in fully completed units. (p. 102).

Operations costing A combination of a process cost and a job order cost system, in which products are manufactured primarily by standardized methods, with some customization. (p. 110).

Physical units Actual units to be accounted for during a period, irrespective of any work performed. (p. 105).

Process cost systems An accounting system used to apply costs to similar products that are mass-produced in a continuous fashion. (p. 96).

Production cost report An internal report for management that shows both production quantity and cost data for a production department. (p. 105).

Total units (costs) accounted for The sum of the units (costs) transferred out during the period plus the units (costs) in process at the end of the period. (pp. 106, 108).

Total units (costs) to be accounted for The sum of the units (costs) started (or transferred) into production during the period plus the units (costs) in process at the beginning of the period. (pp. 105, 108).

Unit production costs Costs expressed in terms of equivalent units of production. (p. 107).

Weighted-average method Method of computing equivalent units of production which considers the degree of completion (weighting) of the units completed and transferred out and the ending work in process. (p. 103).

Demonstration Problem

Karlene Industries produces plastic ice cube trays in two processes: heating and stamping. All materials are added at the beginning of the Heating Department process. Karlene uses the weighted-average method to compute equivalent units.

On November 1, the Heating Department had in process 1,000 trays that were 70% complete. During November, it started into production 12,000 trays. On November 30, 2008, 2,000 trays that were 60% complete were in process.

The following cost information for the Heating Department was also available.

Work in process, November 1:		Costs incurred in November:	
Materials	$ 640	Material	$3,000
Conversion costs	360	Labor	2,300
Cost of work in process, Nov. 1	$1,000	Overhead	4,050

Instructions

(a) Prepare a production cost report for the Heating Department for the month of November 2008, using the weighted-average method.

(b) Journalize the transfer of costs to the Stamping Department.

action plan

- Compute the physical unit flow—that is, the total units to be accounted for.
- Compute the equivalent units of production.
- Compute the unit production costs, expressed in terms of equivalent units of production.
- Prepare a cost reconciliation schedule, which shows that the total costs accounted for equal the total costs to be accounted for.

Solution

(a)

KARLENE INDUSTRIES
Heating Department
Production Cost Report
For the Month Ended November 30, 2008

	Physical Units	Equivalent Units: Materials	Equivalent Units: Conversion Costs	
	Step 1	Step 2		
Quantities				
Units to be accounted for				
Work in process, November 1	1,000			
Started into production	12,000			
Total units	13,000			
Units accounted for				
Transferred out	11,000	11,000	11,000	
Work in process, November 30	2,000	2,000	1,200	
Total units	13,000	13,000	12,200	
Costs				
Unit costs Step 3		**Materials**	**Conversion Costs**	**Total**
Costs in November	(a)	$ 3,640	$ 6,710	$10,350
Equivalent units	(b)	13,000	12,200	
Unit costs [(a) ÷ (b)]		$0.28	$0.55	$0.83
Costs to be accounted for				
Work in process, November 1				$ 1,000
Started into production				9,350
Total costs				$10,350
Cost Reconciliation Schedule Step 4				
Costs accounted for				
Transferred out (11,000 × $0.83)				$ 9,130
Work in process, November 30				
Materials (2,000 × $0.28)			$ 560	
Conversion costs (1,200 × $0.55)			660	1,220
Total costs				$10,350

(b)

	Debit	Credit
Work in Process—Stamping	9,130	
Work in Process—Heating		9,130
(To record transfer of units to the Stamping Department)		

The Navigator

Note: All asterisked Questions, Exercises, and Problems relate to material in the appendix to the chapter.

SELF-STUDY QUESTIONS

Answers are at the end of the chapter.

(SO 1) 1. Which of the following items is *not* characteristic of a process cost system?

a. Once production begins, it continues until the finished product emerges.

b. The products produced are heterogeneous in nature.
c. The focus is on continually producing homogeneous products.
d. When the finished product emerges, all units have precisely the same amount of materials, labor, and overhead.

(SO 2) **2.** Indicate which of the following statements is *not* correct.
a. Both a job order and a process cost system track the same three manufacturing cost elements—direct materials, direct labor, and manufacturing overhead.
b. A job order cost system uses only one work in process account, whereas a process cost system uses multiple work in process accounts.
c. Manufacturing costs are accumulated the same way in a job order and in a process cost system.
d. Manufacturing costs are assigned the same way in a job order and in a process cost system.

(SO 3) **3.** In a process cost system, the flow of costs is:
a. work in process, cost of goods sold, finished goods.
b. finished goods, work in process, cost of goods sold.
c. finished goods, cost of goods sold, work in process.
d. work in process, finished goods, cost of goods sold.

(SO 4) **4.** In making the journal entry to assign raw materials costs, a company
a. debits Finished Goods Inventory.
b. often debits two or more work in process accounts.
c. generally credits two or more work in process accounts.
d. credits Finished Goods Inventory.

(SO 5) **5.** The Mixing Department's output during the period consists of 20,000 units completed and transferred out, and 5,000 units in ending work in process 60% complete as to materials and conversion costs. Beginning inventory is 1,000 units, 40% complete as to materials and conversion costs. The equivalent units of production are:
a. 22,600. **c.** 24,000.
b. 23,000. **d.** 25,000.

(SO 6) **6.** In RYZ Company, there are zero units in beginning work in process, 7,000 units started into production, and 500 units in ending work in process 20% completed. The physical units to be accounted for are:
a. 7,000. **c.** 7,500.
b. 7,360. **d.** 7,340.

(SO 6) **7.** Mora Company has 2,000 units in beginning work in process, 20% complete as to conversion costs, 23,000 units transferred out to finished goods, and 3,000 units in ending work in process $33\frac{1}{3}$% complete as to conversion costs.

The beginning and ending inventory is fully complete as to materials costs. Equivalent units for materials and conversion costs are, respectively:
a. 22,000, 24,000.
b. 24,000, 26,000.
c. 26,000, 24,000.
d. 26,000, 26,000.

(SO 6) **8.** Fortner Company has no beginning work in process; 9,000 units are transferred out and 3,000 units in ending work in process are one-third finished as to conversion costs and fully complete as to materials cost. If total materials cost is $60,000, the unit materials cost is:
a. $5.00.
b. $5.45 rounded.
c. $6.00.
d. No correct answer is given.

9. Largo Company has unit costs of $10 for materials and $30 for conversion costs. If there are 2,500 units in ending work in process, 40% complete as to conversion costs, and fully complete as to materials cost, the total cost assignable to the ending work in process inventory is: (SO 6)
a. $45,000. **c.** $75,000.
b. $55,000. **d.** $100,000.

10. A production cost report (SO 7)
a. is an external report.
b. shows both the production quantity and cost data related to a department.
c. shows equivalent units of production but not physical units.
d. contains six sections.

***11.** Hollins Company uses the FIFO method to compute equivalent units. It has 2,000 units in beginning work in process, 20% complete as to conversion costs, 25,000 units started and completed, and 3,000 units in ending work in process, 30% complete as to conversion costs. All units are 100% complete as to materials. Equivalent units for materials and conversion costs are, respectively: (SO 8)
a. 28,000 and 26,600.
b. 28,000 and 27,500.
c. 27,000 and 26,200.
d. 27,000 and 29,600.

***12.** KLM Company uses the FIFO method to compute equivalent units. It has no beginning work in process; 9,000 units are started and completed and 3,000 units in ending work in process are one-third completed. All material is added at the beginning of the process. If total materials cost is $60,000, the unit materials cost is: (SO 8)
a. $5.00.
b. $6.00.
c. $6.67 (rounded).
d. No correct answer given.

***13.** Toney Company uses the FIFO method to compute equivalent units. It has unit costs of $10 for materials and $30 for conversion costs. If there are 2,500 units in ending work in process, 100% complete as to materials and 40% complete as to conversion costs, the total cost assignable to the ending work in process inventory is: (SO 8)
a. $45,000. **c.** $75,000.
b. $55,000. **d.** $100,000.

Go to the book's website, **www.wiley.com/college/weygandt**, for Additional Self-Study questions.

The Navigator

QUESTIONS

1. Identify which costing system—job order or process cost—the following companies would primarily use: (a) Quaker Oats, (b) Ford Motor Company, (c) Kinko's Print Shop, and (d) Warner Bros. Motion Pictures.
2. Contrast the primary focus of job order cost accounting and of process cost accounting.
3. What are the similarities between a job order and a process cost system?
4. Your roommate is confused about the features of process cost accounting. Identify and explain the distinctive features for your roommate.
5. Mel Storrer believes there are no significant differences in the flow of costs between job order cost accounting and process cost accounting. Is Storrer correct? Explain.
6. (a) What source documents are used in assigning (1) materials and (2) labor to production in a process cost system?
   (b) What criterion and basis are commonly used in allocating overhead to processes?
7. At Ace Company, overhead is assigned to production departments at the rate of $5 per machine hour. In July, machine hours were 3,000 in the Machining Department and 2,400 in the Assembly Department. Prepare the entry to assign overhead to production.
8. Gary Weiss is uncertain about the steps used to prepare a production cost report. State the procedures that are required in the sequence in which they are performed.
9. Rich Mordica is confused about computing physical units. Explain to Rich how physical units to be accounted for and physical units accounted for are determined.
10. What is meant by the term "equivalent units of production"?
11. How are equivalent units of production computed?
12. Mason Company had zero units of beginning work in process. During the period, 9,000 units were completed, and there were 600 units of ending work in process. What were the units started into production?
13. Mendle Co. has zero units of beginning work in process. During the period 12,000 units were completed, and there were 800 units of ending work in process one-fifth complete as to conversion cost and 100% complete as to materials cost. What were the equivalent units of production for (a) materials and (b) conversion costs?
14. Reyes Co. started 3,000 units for the period. Its beginning inventory is 500 units one-fourth complete as to conversion costs and 100% complete as to materials costs. Its ending inventory is 200 units one-fifth complete as to conversion costs and 100% complete as to materials costs. How many units were transferred out this period?
15. Kiner Company transfers out 14,000 units and has 2,000 units of ending work in process that are 25% complete. Materials are entered at the beginning of the process and there is no beginning work in process. Assuming unit materials costs of $3 and unit conversion costs of $6, what are the costs to be assigned to units (a) transferred out and (b) in ending work in process?
16. **(a)** Eve Adams believes the production cost report is an external report for stockholders. Is Eve correct? Explain.
    (b) Identify the sections in a production cost report.
17. What purposes are served by a production cost report?
18. At Frank Company, there are 800 units of ending work in process that are 100% complete as to materials and 40% complete as to conversion costs. If the unit cost of materials is $4 and the costs assigned to the 800 units is $6,000, what is the per-unit conversion cost?
19. What is the difference between operations costing and a process costing system?
20. How does a company decide whether to use a job order or a process cost system?

*21. Silva Co. started and completed 2,000 units for the period. Its beginning inventory is 600 units 25% complete and its ending inventory is 400 units 20% complete. Silva uses the FIFO method to compute equivalent units. How many units were transferred out this period?

*22. Ortiz Company transfers out 12,000 units and has 2,000 units of ending work in process that are 25% complete. Materials are entered at the beginning of the process and there is no beginning work in process. Ortiz uses the FIFO method to compute equivalent units. Assuming unit materials costs of $3 and unit conversion costs of $9, what are the costs to be assigned to units (a) transferred out and (b) in ending work in process?

BRIEF EXERCISES

Journalize entries for accumulating costs.
(SO 4)

BE3-1 Sanchez Manufacturing purchases $45,000 of raw materials on account, and it incurs $50,000 of factory labor costs. Journalize the two transactions on March 31 assuming the labor costs are not paid until April.

Journalize the assignment of materials and labor costs.
(SO 4)

BE3-2 Data for Sanchez Manufacturing are given in BE3-1. Supporting records show that (a) the Assembly Department used $24,000 of raw materials and $30,000 of the factory labor, and (b) the Finishing Department used the remainder. Journalize the assignment of the costs to the processing departments on March 31.

BE3-3 Factory labor data for Sanchez Manufacturing are given in BE3-2. Manufacturing overhead is assigned to departments on the basis of 200% of labor costs. Journalize the assignment of overhead to the Assembly and Finishing Departments.

Journalize the assignment of overhead costs.
(SO 4)

BE3-4 Bowyer Manufacturing Company has the following production data for selected months.

Compute physical units of production.
(SO 6)

			Ending Work in Process	
Month	**Beginning Work in Process**	**Units Transferred Out**	**Units**	**% Complete as to Conversion Cost**
January	–0–	30,000	10,000	40%
March	–0–	40,000	8,000	75
July	–0–	40,000	16,000	25

Compute the physical units for each month.

BE3-5 Using the data in BE3-4, compute equivalent units of production for materials and conversion costs, assuming materials are entered at the beginning of the process.

Compute equivalent units of production.
(SO 5)

BE3-6 In Montego Company, total material costs are $32,000, and total conversion costs are $54,000. Equivalent units of production are materials 10,000 and conversion costs 12,000. Compute the unit costs for materials, conversion costs, and total manufacturing costs.

Compute unit costs of production.
(SO 6)

BE3-7 Hindi Company has the following production data for April: units transferred out 40,000, and ending work in process 5,000 units that are 100% complete for materials and 40% complete for conversion costs. If unit materials cost is $4 and unit conversion cost is $9, determine the costs to be assigned to the units transferred out and the units in ending work in process.

Assign costs to units transferred out and in process.
(SO 6)

BE3-8 Production costs chargeable to the Finishing Department in June in Castilla Company are materials $15,000, labor $29,500, overhead $18,000. Equivalent units of production are materials 20,000 and conversion costs 19,000. Compute the unit costs for materials and conversion costs.

Compute unit costs.
(SO 6)

BE3-9 Data for Castilla Company are given in BE3-8. Production records indicate that 18,000 units were transferred out, and 2,000 units in ending work in process were 60% complete as to conversion cost and 100% complete as to materials. Prepare a cost reconciliation schedule.

Prepare cost reconciliation schedule.
(SO 6)

BE3-10 The Smelting Department of Massaro Manufacturing Company has the following production and cost data for November.

Compute equivalent units of production.
(SO 5)

> Production: Beginning work in process 2,000 units that are 100% complete as to materials and 20% complete as to conversion costs; units transferred out 8,000 units; and ending work in process 5,000 units that are 100% complete as to materials and 40% complete as to conversion costs.

Compute the equivalent units of production for **(a)** materials and **(b)** conversion costs for the month of November.

***BE3-11** Mora Company has the following production data for March: no beginning work in process, units started and completed 30,000, and ending work in process 5,000 units that are 100% complete for materials and 40% complete for conversion costs. Mora uses the FIFO method to compute equivalent units. If unit materials cost is $8 and unit conversion cost is $12, determine the costs to be assigned to the units transferred out and the units in ending work in process. The total costs to be assigned are $664,000.

Assign costs to units transferred out and in process.
(SO 8)

***BE3-12** Using the data in BE3-11, prepare the cost section of the production cost report for Mora Company.

Prepare a partial production cost report.
(SO 7, 8)

***BE3-13** Production costs chargeable to the Finishing Department in May at Bell Company are materials $8,000, labor $20,000, overhead $18,000, and transferred-in costs $62,000. Equivalent units of production are materials 20,000 and conversion costs 19,000. Bell uses the FIFO method to compute equivalent units. Compute the unit costs for materials and conversion costs. Transferred-in costs are considered materials costs.

Compute unit costs.
(SO 8)

EXERCISES

Understand process cost accounting.
(SO 1, 2)

E3-1 Doc Gibbs has prepared the following list of statements about process cost accounting.

1. Process cost systems are used to apply costs to similar products that are mass-produced in a continuous fashion.
2. A process cost system is used when each finished unit is indistinguishable from another.
3. Companies that produce soft drinks, motion pictures, and computer chips would all use process cost accounting.
4. In a process cost system, costs are tracked by individual jobs.
5. Job order costing and process costing track different manufacturing cost elements.
6. Both job order costing and process costing account for direct materials, direct labor, and manufacturing overhead.
7. Costs flow through the accounts in the same basic way for both job order costing and process costing.
8. In a process cost system, only one work in process account is used.
9. In a process cost system, costs are summarized in a job cost sheet.
10. In a process cost system, the unit cost is total manufacturing costs for the period divided by the units produced during the period.

Instructions
Identify each statement as true or false. If false, indicate how to correct the statement.

Journalize transactions.
(SO 4)

E3-2 Fernando Company manufactures pizza sauce through two production departments: Cooking and Canning. In each process, materials and conversion costs are incurred evenly throughout the process. For the month of April, the work in process accounts show the following debits.

	Cooking	Canning
Beginning work in process	$ -0-	$ 4,000
Materials	21,000	6,000
Labor	8,500	7,000
Overhead	29,500	25,800
Costs transferred in		53,000

Instructions
Journalize the April transactions.

Answer questions on costs and production.
(SO 3, 5, 6)

E3-3 The ledger of Molindo Company has the following work in process account.

Work in Process—Painting

5/1	Balance	3,590	5/31	Transferred out	?
5/31	Materials	5,160			
5/31	Labor	2,740			
5/31	Overhead	1,650			
5/31	Balance	?			

Production records show that there were 400 units in the beginning inventory, 30% complete, 1,100 units started, and 1,200 units transferred out. The beginning work in process had materials cost of $2,040 and conversion costs of $1,550. The units in ending inventory were 40% complete. Materials are entered at the beginning of the painting process.

Instructions
(a) How many units are in process at May 31?
(b) What is the unit materials cost for May?
(c) What is the unit conversion cost for May?
(d) What is the total cost of units transferred out in May?
(e) What is the cost of the May 31 inventory?

E3-4 Douglas Manufacturing Company has two production departments: Cutting and Assembly. July 1 inventories are Raw Materials $4,200, Work in Process—Cutting $2,900, Work in Process—Assembly $10,600, and Finished Goods $31,000. During July, the following transactions occurred.

Journalize transactions for two processes.

(SO 4)

1. Purchased $62,500 of raw materials on account.
2. Incurred $56,000 of factory labor. (Credit Wages Payable.)
3. Incurred $70,000 of manufacturing overhead; $40,000 was paid and the remainder is unpaid.
4. Requisitioned materials for Cutting $15,700 and Assembly $8,900.
5. Used factory labor for Cutting $29,000 and Assembly $27,000.
6. Applied overhead at the rate of $15 per machine hour. Machine hours were Cutting 1,680 and Assembly 1,720.
7. Transferred goods costing $67,600 from the Cutting Department to the Assembly Department.
8. Transferred goods costing $134,900 from Assembly to Finished Goods.
9. Sold goods costing $150,000 for $200,000 on account.

Instructions

Journalize the transactions. (Omit explanations.)

E3-5 In Ramirez Company, materials are entered at the beginning of each process. Work in process inventories, with the percentage of work done on conversion costs, and production data for its Sterilizing Department in selected months during 2008 are as follows.

Compute physical units and equivalent units of production.

(SO 5, 6)

	Beginning Work in Process			Ending Work in Process	
Month	**Units**	**Conversion Cost%**	**Units Transferred Out**	**Units**	**Conversion Cost%**
January	–0–	—	7,000	2,000	60
March	–0–	—	12,000	3,000	30
May	–0–	—	16,000	5,000	80
July	–0–	—	10,000	1,500	40

Instructions

(a) Compute the physical units for January and May.

(b) Compute the equivalent units of production for (1) materials and (2) conversion costs for each month.

E3-6 The Cutting Department of Groneman Manufacturing has the following production and cost data for July.

Determine equivalent units, unit costs, and assignment of costs.

(SO 5, 6)

Production

1. Transferred out 9,000 units.
2. Started 3,000 units that are 60% complete as to conversion costs and 100% complete as to materials at July 31.

Costs	
Beginning work in process	$ –0–
Materials	45,000
Labor	16,200
Manufacturing overhead	18,900

Materials are entered at the beginning of the process. Conversion costs are incurred uniformly during the process.

Instructions

(a) Determine the equivalent units of production for (1) materials and (2) conversion costs.

(b) Compute unit costs and prepare a cost reconciliation schedule.

E3-7 The Sanding Department of Ortiz Furniture Company has the following production and manufacturing cost data for March 2008, the first month of operation.

Prepare a production cost report.

(SO 5, 6, 7)

Production: 12,000 units finished and transferred out; 3,000 units started that are 100% complete as to materials and 20% complete as to conversion costs.

Manufacturing costs: Materials $33,000; labor $27,000; overhead $36,000.

Instructions

Prepare a production cost report.

Determine equivalent units, unit costs, and assignment of costs.

(SO 5, 6)

E3-8 The Blending Department of Hancock Company has the following cost and production data for the month of April.

Costs:	
Work in process, April 1	
Direct materials: 100% complete	$100,000
Conversion costs: 20% complete	70,000
Cost of work in process, April 1	$170,000
Costs incurred during production in April	
Direct materials	$ 800,000
Conversion costs	362,000
Costs incurred in April	$1,162,000

Units transferred out totaled 14,000. Ending work in process was 1,000 units that are 100% complete as to materials and 40% complete as to conversion costs.

Instructions

(a) Compute the equivalent units of production for (1) materials and (2) conversion costs for the month of April.
(b) Compute the unit costs for the month.
(c) Determine the costs to be assigned to the units transferred out and in ending work in process.

Determine equivalent units, unit costs, and assignment of costs.

(SO 5, 6)

E3-9 Podsednik Company has gathered the following information.

Units in beginning work in process	-0-
Units started into production	36,000
Units in ending work in process	6,000
Percent complete in ending work in process:	
Conversion costs	40%
Materials	100%
Costs incurred:	
Direct materials	$72,000
Direct labor	$81,000
Overhead	$97,200

Instructions

(a) Compute equivalent units of production for materials and for conversion costs.
(b) Determine the unit costs of production.
(c) Show the assignment of costs to units transferred out and in process.

Determine equivalent units, unit costs, and assignment of costs.

(SO 5, 6)

E3-10 Pink Martini Company has gathered the following information.

Units in beginning work in process	20,000
Units started into production	72,000
Units in ending work in process	24,000
Percent complete in ending work in process:	
Conversion costs	60%
Materials	100%
Costs incurred:	
Direct materials	$101,200
Direct labor	$164,800
Overhead	$123,600

Instructions

(a) Compute equivalent units of production for materials and for conversion costs.
(b) Determine the unit costs of production.
(c) Show the assignment of costs to units transferred out and in process.

Compute equivalent units, unit costs, and costs assigned.

(SO 5, 6)

E3-11 The Polishing Department of Estaban Manufacturing Company has the following production and manufacturing cost data for September. Materials are entered at the beginning of the process.

Production: Beginning inventory 1,600 units that are 100% complete as to materials and 30% complete as to conversion costs; units started during the period are 18,400; ending inventory of 5,000 units 10% complete as to conversion costs.

Manufacturing costs: Beginning inventory costs, comprised of $20,000 of materials and $43,180 of conversion costs; materials costs added in Polishing during the month, $177,200; labor and overhead applied in Polishing during the month, $102,680 and $257,140, respectively.

Instructions

(a) Compute the equivalent units of production for materials and conversion costs for the month of September.
(b) Compute the unit costs for materials and conversion costs for the month.
(c) Determine the costs to be assigned to the units transferred out and in process.

Explain the production cost report.

(SO 7)

E3-12 Stan Maley has recently been promoted to production manager, and so he has just started to receive various managerial reports. One of the reports he has received is the production cost report that you prepared. It showed that his department had 2,000 equivalent units in ending inventory. His department has had a history of not keeping enough inventory on hand to meet demand. He has come to you, very angry, and wants to know why you credited him with only 2,000 units when he knows he had at least twice that many on hand.

Instructions

Explain to him why his production cost report showed only 2,000 equivalent units in ending inventory. Write an informal memo. Be kind and explain very clearly why he is mistaken.

Prepare a production cost report.

(SO 5, 6, 7)

E3-13 The Welding Department of Batista Manufacturing Company has the following production and manufacturing cost data for February 2008. All materials are added at the beginning of the process.

Manufacturing Costs			Production Data	
Beginning work in process			Beginning work in process	15,000 units
Materials	$18,000			1/10 complete
Conversion costs	14,175	$32,175	Units transferred out	49,000
Materials		180,000	Units started	60,000
Labor		32,780	Ending work in process	26,000 units
Overhead		61,445		1/5 complete

Instructions

Prepare a production cost report for the Welding Department for the month of February.

Compute physical units and equivalent units of production.

(SO 5, 6)

E3-14 Container Shipping, Inc. is contemplating the use of process costing to track the costs of its operations. The operation consists of three segments (departments): receiving, shipping, and delivery. Containers are received at Container's docks and sorted according to the ship they will be carried on. The containers are loaded onto a ship, which carries them to the appropriate port of destination. The containers are then off-loaded and delivered to the receiving company.

Container Shipping wants to begin using process costing in the shipping department. Direct materials represent the fuel costs to run the ship, and "Containers in transit" represents work in process. Listed below is information about the shipping department's first month's activity.

Containers in transit, April 1	0
Containers loaded	800
Containers in transit, April 30	350, 40% of direct materials and 30% of conversion costs

Instructions

(a) Determine the physical flow of containers for the month.
(b) Calculate the equivalent units for direct materials and conversion costs.

Determine equivalent units, unit costs, and assignment of costs.

(SO 5, 6)

E3-15 Hi-Tech Mortgage Company uses a process costing system to accumulate costs in its loan application department. When an application is completed it is forwarded to the loan department for final processing. The following processing and cost data pertain to September.

1. Applications in process on September 1, 100
2. Applications started in September, 900
3. Completed applications during September, 800
4. Applications still in process at September 30 were 100% complete as to materials (forms) and 60% complete as to conversion costs.

Beginning WIP:	
Direct materials	$ 1,000
Conversion costs	4,000
September costs:	
Direct materials	$ 4,000
Direct labor	12,000
Overhead	9,400

Materials are the forms used in the application process, and these costs are incurred at the beginning of the process. Conversion costs are incurred uniformly during the process.

Instructions

(a) Determine the equivalent units of service (production) for materials and conversion costs.
(b) Compute the unit costs and prepare a cost reconciliation schedule.

Compute equivalent units, unit costs, and costs assigned.

(SO 6, 8)

***E3-16** Using the data in E3-15, assume Hi-Tech Mortgage Company uses the FIFO method. Also assume that the applications in process on September 1 were 100% complete as to materials (forms) and 40% complete as to conversion costs.

Instructions

(a) Determine the equivalent units of service (production) for materials and conversion costs.
(b) Compute the unit costs and prepare a cost reconciliation schedule.

Determine equivalent units, unit costs, and assignment of costs.

(SO 6, 8)

***E3-17** The Cutting Department of Chan Manufacturing has the following production and cost data for August.

Production

1. Started and completed 8,000 units.
2. Started 1,000 units that are 40% completed at August 31.

Costs	
Beginning work in process	$ –0–
Materials	45,000
Labor	14,700
Manufacturing overhead	18,900

Materials are entered at the beginning of the process. Conversion costs are incurred uniformly during the process. Chan Manufacturing uses the FIFO method to compute equivalent units.

Instructions

(a) Determine the equivalent units of production for (1) materials and (2) conversion costs.
(b) Compute unit costs and show the assignment of manufacturing costs to units transferred out and in work in process.

Compute equivalent units, unit costs, and costs assigned.

(SO 6, 8)

***E3-18** The Smelting Department of Amber Manufacturing Company has the following production and cost data for September.

Production: Beginning work in process 2,000 units that are 100% complete as to materials and 20% complete as to conversion costs; units started and finished 11,000 units; and ending work in process 1,000 units that are 100% complete as to materials and 40% complete as to conversion costs.

Manufacturing costs: Work in process, September 1, $15,200; materials added $60,000; labor and overhead $143,000.

Amber uses the FIFO method to compute equivalent units.

Instructions

(a) Compute the equivalent units of production for (1) materials and (2) conversion costs for the month of September.

(b) Compute the unit costs for the month.
(c) Determine the costs to be assigned to the units transferred out and in process.

***E3-19** The ledger of Platt Company has the following work in process account.

Answer questions on costs and production.
(SO 6, 8)

Work in Process—Painting

3/1	Balance	3,680	3/31	Transferred out	?
3/31	Materials	6,600			
3/31	Labor	2,500			
3/31	Overhead	1,280			
3/31	Balance	?			

Production records show that there were 800 units in the beginning inventory, 30% complete, 1,000 units started, and 1,300 units transferred out. The units in ending inventory were 40% complete. Materials are entered at the beginning of the painting process. Platt uses the FIFO method to compute equivalent units.

Instructions
Answer the following questions.

(a) How many units are in process at March 31?
(b) What is the unit materials cost for March?
(c) What is the unit conversion cost for March?
(d) What is the total cost of units started in February and completed in March?
(e) What is the total cost of units started and finished in March?
(f) What is the cost of the March 31 inventory?

***E3-20** The Welding Department of Hirohama Manufacturing Company has the following production and manufacturing cost data for February 2008. All materials are added at the beginning of the process. Hirohama uses the FIFO method to compute equivalent units.

Prepare a production cost report for a second process.
(SO 8)

Manufacturing Costs		Production Data	
Beginning work in process	$ 32,175	Beginning work in process	15,000 units, 10% complete
Costs transferred in	135,000		
Materials	57,000	Units transferred out	50,000
Labor	35,100	Units transferred in	60,000
Overhead	71,900	Ending work in process	25,000, 20% complete

Instructions
Prepare a production cost report for the Welding Department for the month of February. Transferred-in costs are considered materials costs.

EXERCISES: SET B

Visit the book's website at **www.wiley.com/college/weygandt**, and choose the Student Companion site, to access Exercise Set B.

PROBLEMS: SET A

P3-1A Kasten Company manufactures bowling balls through two processes: Molding and Packaging. In the Molding Department, the urethane, rubber, plastics, and other materials are molded into bowling balls. In the Packaging Department, the balls are placed in cartons and sent to the finished goods warehouse. All materials are entered at the beginning of each process.

Complete four steps necessary to prepare a production cost report.
(SO 5, 6, 7)

Labor and manufacturing overhead are incurred uniformly throughout each process. Production and cost data for the Molding Department during June 2008 are presented below.

Production Data	June
Beginning work in process units	–0–
Units started into production	20,000
Ending work in process units	2,000
Percent complete—ending inventory	60%
Cost Data	
Materials	$198,000
Labor	50,400
Overhead	112,800
Total	$361,200

(c) Materials $9.90
CC $8.50
(d) Transferred out $331,200
WIP $ 30,000

Instructions

(a) Prepare a schedule showing physical units of production.
(b) Determine the equivalent units of production for materials and conversion costs.
(c) Compute the unit costs of production.
(d) Determine the costs to be assigned to the units transferred and in process for June.
(e) Prepare a production cost report for the Molding Department for the month of June.

Complete four steps necessary to prepare a production cost report.
(SO 5, 6, 7)

P3-2A Ortega Industries Inc. manufactures in separate processes furniture for homes. In each process, materials are entered at the beginning, and conversion costs are incurred uniformly. Production and cost data for the first process in making two products in two different manufacturing plants are as follows.

	Cutting Department	
Production Data—July	**Plant 1 T12-Tables**	**Plant 2 C10-Chairs**
Work in process units, July 1	–0–	–0–
Units started into production	20,000	16,000
Work in process units, July 31	3,000	500
Work in process percent complete	60	80
Cost Data—July		
Work in process, July 1	$ –0–	$ –0–
Materials	380,000	288,000
Labor	234,400	125,900
Overhead	104,000	96,700
Total	$718,400	$510,600

(a) (1) T12:
Transferred out 17,000 units
WIP 3,000 units
(2) T12:
Materials 20,000 e.u.
CC 18,800 e.u.
(3) T12:
Materials $19
CC $18
(4) T12:
Transferred out $629,000
WIP $ 89,400

Instructions

(a) For each plant:
 (1) Compute the physical units of production.
 (2) Compute equivalent units of production for materials and for conversion costs.
 (3) Determine the unit costs of production.
 (4) Show the assignment of costs to units transferred out and in process.
(b) Prepare the production cost report for Plant 1 for July 2008.

Journalize transactions.
(SO 3, 4)

P3-3A Fiedel Company manufactures its product, Vitadrink, through two manufacturing processes: Mixing and Packaging. All materials are entered at the beginning of each process. On October 1, 2008, inventories consisted of Raw Materials $26,000, Work in Process—Mixing $0, Work in Process—Packaging $250,000, and Finished Goods $289,000. The beginning inventory for Packaging consisted of 10,000 units that were 50% complete as to conversion costs and fully complete as to materials. During October, 50,000 units were started into production in the Mixing Department and the following transactions were completed.

1. Purchased $300,000 of raw materials on account.
2. Issued raw materials for production: Mixing $210,000 and Packaging $45,000.
3. Incurred labor costs of $248,900.

4. Used factory labor: Mixing $182,500 and Packaging $66,400.
5. Incurred $790,000 of manufacturing overhead on account.
6. Applied manufacturing overhead on the basis of $22 per machine hour. Machine hours were 28,000 in Mixing and 6,000 in Packaging.
7. Transferred 45,000 units from Mixing to Packaging at a cost of $979,000.
8. Transferred 53,000 units from Packaging to Finished Goods at a cost of $1,315,000.
9. Sold goods costing $1,604,000 for $2,500,000 on account.

Instructions

Journalize the October transactions.

P3-4A Cavalier Company has several processing departments. Costs charged to the Assembly Department for November 2008 totaled $2,229,000 as follows.

Assign costs and prepare production cost report.

(SO 5, 6, 7)

Work in process, November 1		
Materials	$69,000	
Conversion costs	48,150	$ 117,150
Materials added		1,548,000
Labor		225,920
Overhead		337,930

Production records show that 35,000 units were in beginning work in process 30% complete as to conversion costs, 700,000 units were started into production, and 25,000 units were in ending work in process 40% complete as to conversion costs. Materials are entered at the beginning of each process.

Instructions

(a) Determine the equivalent units of production and the unit production costs for the Assembly Department.

(b) Determine the assignment of costs to goods transferred out and in process.

(c) Prepare a production cost report for the Assembly Department.

(b) Transferred out $2,165,500
WIP $ 63,500

P3-5A Chen Company manufactures basketballs. Materials are added at the beginning of the production process and conversion costs are incurred uniformly. Production and cost data for the month of July 2008 are as follows.

Determine equivalent units and unit costs and assign costs.

(SO 5, 6, 7)

Production Data—Basketballs		**Units**	**Percent Complete**
Work in process units, July 1		500	60%
Units started into production		1,000	
Work in process units, July 31		600	30%
Cost Data—Basketballs			
Work in process, July 1			
Materials	$750		
Conversion costs	600	$1,350	
Direct materials		2,400	
Direct labor		1,580	
Manufacturing overhead		1,060	

Instructions

(a) Calculate the following.

(1) The equivalent units of production for materials and conversion costs.

(2) The unit costs of production for materials and conversion costs.

(3) The assignment of costs to units transferred out and in process at the end of the accounting period.

(b) Prepare a production cost report for the month of July for the basketballs.

(a) Materials:
(1) 1,500 e.u.
(2) $2.10
(3) Transferred out $4,590
WIP $1,800

P3-6A Luther Processing Company uses a weighted-average process costing system and manufactures a single product—a premium rug shampoo and cleaner. The manufacturing activity for the month of October has just been completed. A partially completed production cost report for the month of October for the mixing and cooking department is shown on page 136.

Compute equivalent units and complete production cost report.

(SO 5, 7)

(a) Materials $1.50

(b) Transferred out $286,000
WIP $ 59,000

Instructions

(a) Prepare a schedule that shows how the equivalent units were computed so that you can complete the "Quantities: Units accounted for" equivalent units section shown in the production cost report, and compute October unit costs.

(b) Complete the "Cost Reconciliation Schedule" part of the production cost report below.

LUTHER PROCESSING COMPANY
Mixing and Cooking Department
Production Cost Report
For the Month Ended October 31

		Equivalent Units	
Quantities	**Physical Units**	**Materials**	**Conversion Costs**
Units to be accounted for			
Work in process, October 1 (all materials, 70% conversion costs)	20,000		
Started into production	160,000		
Total units	180,000		
Units accounted for			
Transferred out	130,000	?	?
Work in process, October 31 (60% materials, 40% conversion costs)	50,000	?	?
Total units accounted for	180,000	?	?

Costs	**Materials**		**Conversion Costs**		**Total**
Unit costs					
Costs in October	$240,000		$105,000		$345,000
Equivalent units	?		?		
Unit costs	$?	+	$?	=	$?
Costs to be accounted for					
Work in process, October 1					$ 30,000
Started into production					315,000
Total costs					$345,000

Cost Reconciliation Schedule		
Costs accounted for		
Transferred out		$?
Work in process, October 31		
Materials	?	
Conversion costs	?	?
Total costs		?

Determine equivalent units and unit costs and assign costs for processes; prepare production cost report.

(SO 8)

***P3-7A** National Company manufactures bicycles and tricycles. For both products, materials are added at the beginning of the production process, and conversion costs are incurred uniformly. National Company uses the FIFO method to compute equivalent units. Production and cost data for the month of March are as follows.

Production Data—Bicycles	**Units**	**Percent Complete**
Work in process units, March 1	200	80%
Units started into production	1,000	
Work in process units, March 31	200	40%

Cost Data—Bicycles	Units	Percent Complete
Work in process, March 1	$19,280	
Direct materials	50,000	
Direct labor	25,200	
Manufacturing overhead	30,000	

Production Data—Tricycles	Units	Percent Complete
Work in process units, March 1	100	75%
Units started into production	800	
Work in process units, March 31	60	25%

Cost Data—Tricycles	
Work in process, March 1	$ 6,125
Direct materials	38,400
Direct labor	15,100
Manufacturing overhead	20,000

Instructions

(a) Calculate the following for both the bicycles and the tricycles.

(1) The equivalent units of production for materials and conversion costs.

(2) The unit costs of production for materials and conversion costs.

(3) The assignment of costs to units transferred out and in process at the end of the accounting period.

(b) Prepare a production cost report for the month of March for the bicycles only.

(a) Bicycles:
(1) Materials 1,000
(2) Materials $50
(3) Transferred out $109,680
WIP $14,800

PROBLEMS: SET B

Complete four steps necessary to prepare a production cost report.

(SO 5, 6, 7)

P3-1B Bicnell Corporation manufactures water skis through two processes: Molding and Packaging. In the Molding Department fiberglass is heated and shaped into the form of a ski. In the Packaging Department, the skis are placed in cartons and sent to the finished goods warehouse. Materials are entered at the beginning of both processes. Labor and manufacturing overhead are incurred uniformly throughout each process. Production and cost data for the Molding Department for January 2008 are presented below.

Production Data	January
Beginning work in process units	-0-
Units started into production	35,000
Ending work in process units	5,000
Percent complete—ending inventory	40%

Cost Data	
Materials	$595,000
Labor	96,000
Overhead	224,000
Total	$915,000

Instructions

(a) Compute the physical units of production.

(b) Determine the equivalent units of production for materials and conversion costs.

(c) Compute the unit costs of production.

(c) Materials $17.00
CC $10.00

(d) Transferred out $810,000
WIP $105,000

(d) Determine the costs to be assigned to the units transferred out and in process.
(e) Prepare a production cost report for the Molding Department for the month of January.

Complete four steps necessary to prepare a production cost report.
(SO 5, 6, 7)

P3-2B Atkins Corporation manufactures in separate processes refrigerators and freezers for homes. In each process, materials are entered at the beginning and conversion costs are incurred uniformly. Production and cost data for the first process in making two products in two different manufacturing plants are as follows.

	Stamping Department	
Production Data—June	**Plant A R12 Refrigerators**	**Plant B F24 Freezers**
Work in process units, June 1	-0-	-0-
Units started into production	20,000	18,000
Work in process units, June 30	4,000	2,500
Work in process percent complete	75	60
Cost Data—June		
Work in process, June 1	$ -0-	$ -0-
Materials	840,000	684,000
Labor	245,000	251,000
Overhead	420,000	191,000
Total	$1,505,000	$1,126,000

(1) Plant A: Transferred out 16,000 units
WIP 4,000 units
(2) Plant A:
Materials 20,000 e.u.
CC 19,000 e.u.
(3) Plant A:
Materials $42
CC $35
(4) Plant A:
Transferred out $1,232,000
WIP $273,000

Instructions
(a) For each plant:
(1) Compute the physical units of production.
(2) Compute equivalent units of production for materials and for conversion costs.
(3) Determine the unit costs of production.
(4) Show the assignment of costs to units transferred out and in process.
(b) Prepare the production cost report for Plant A for June 2008.

Journalize transactions.
(SO 3, 4)

P3-3B McNally Company manufactures a nutrient, Everlife, through two manufacturing processes: Blending and Packaging. All materials are entered at the beginning of each process. On August 1, 2008, inventories consisted of Raw Materials $5,000, Work in Process—Blending $0, Work in Process—Packaging $3,945, and Finished Goods $7,500. The beginning inventory for Packaging consisted of 500 units, two-fifths complete as to conversion costs and fully complete as to materials. During August, 9,000 units were started into production in Blending, and the following transactions were completed.

1. Purchased $25,000 of raw materials on account.
2. Issued raw materials for production: Blending $18,930 and Packaging $7,140.
3. Incurred labor costs of $20,770.
4. Used factory labor: Blending $13,320 and Packaging $7,450.
5. Incurred $41,500 of manufacturing overhead on account.
6. Applied manufacturing overhead at the rate of $20 per machine hour. Machine hours were Blending 900 and Packaging 300.
7. Transferred 8,200 units from Blending to Packaging at a cost of $44,940.
8. Transferred 8,600 units from Packaging to Finished Goods at a cost of $67,490.
9. Sold goods costing $62,000 for $90,000 on account.

Instructions
Journalize the August transactions.

P3-4B Crosby Company has several processing departments. Costs charged to the Assembly Department for October 2008 totaled $1,354,400 as follows.

Assign costs and prepare production cost report.

(SO 5, 6, 7)

Work in process, October 1		
Materials	$29,000	
Conversion costs	26,200	$ 55,200
Materials added		1,071,000
Labor		90,000
Overhead		138,200

Production records show that 25,000 units were in beginning work in process 40% complete as to conversion cost, 415,000 units were started into production, and 40,000 units were in ending work in process 60% complete as to conversion costs. Materials are entered at the beginning of each process.

Instructions

(a) Determine the equivalent units of production and the unit production costs for the Assembly Department.

(b) Determine the assignment of costs to goods transferred out and in process.

(c) Prepare a production cost report for the Assembly Department.

(b) Transferred out $1,240,000
WIP $114,400

P3-5B Kiley Company manufactures bicycles and tricycles. For both products, materials are added at the beginning of the production process, and conversion costs are incurred uniformly. Production and cost data for the month of May are as follows.

Determine equivalent units and unit costs and assign costs.

(SO 5, 6, 7)

Production Data—Bicycles	**Units**	**Percent Complete**
Work in process units, May 1	500	80%
Units started in production	1,000	
Work in process units, May 31	600	10%

Cost Data—Bicycles		
Work in process, May 1		
Materials	$10,000	
Conversion costs	9,280	$ 19,280
Direct materials		50,000
Direct labor		18,320
Manufacturing overhead		30,000

Instructions

(a) Calculate the following.

(1) The equivalent units of production for materials and conversion costs.

(2) The unit costs of production for materials and conversion costs.

(3) The assignment of costs to units transferred out and in process at the end of the accounting period.

(b) Prepare a production cost report for the month of May for the bicycles.

(a) (1) Materials 1,500 e.u.
(2) Materials $40
(3) Transferred out $90,000
WIP $27,600

P3-6B Windsor Cleaner Company uses a weighted-average process costing system and manufactures a single product—an all-purpose liquid cleaner. The manufacturing activity for the month of March has just been completed. A partially completed production cost report for the month of March for the mixing and blending department is shown on page 140.

Compute equivalent units and complete production cost report.

(SO 5, 7)

WINDSOR CLEANER COMPANY
Mixing and Blending Department
Production Cost Report
For the Month Ended March 31

Quantities	Physical Units	Equivalent Units: Materials	Equivalent Units: Conversion Costs
Units to be accounted for			
Work in process, March 1 (40% materials, 20% conversion costs)	10,000		
Started into production	100,000		
Total units	110,000		
Units accounted for			
Transferred out	95,000	?	?
Work in process, March 31 (2/3 materials, 1/3 conversion costs)	15,000	?	?
Total units accounted for	110,000	?	?

Costs	Materials		Conversion Costs		Total
Unit costs					
Costs in March	$210,000		$90,000		$300,000
Equivalent units	?		?		
Unit costs	$?	+	$?	=	$?
Costs to be accounted for					
Work in process, March 1					$ 15,000
Started into production					284,300
Total costs					$300,000

Cost Reconciliation Schedule		
Costs accounted for		
Transferred out		$?
Work in process, March 31		
Materials	?	
Conversion costs	?	?
Total costs		?

(a) Materials $2.00
(b) Transferred out $275,500
WIP $24,500

Instructions

(a) Prepare a schedule that shows how the equivalent units were computed so that you can complete the "Quantities: Units accounted for" equivalent units section shown in the production cost report above, and compute March unit costs.

(b) Complete the "Cost Reconciliation Schedule" part of the production cost report above.

Determine equivalent units and unit costs and assign costs for processes; prepare production cost report.

(SO 8)

***P3-7B** Maloney Company manufactures basketballs and soccer balls. For both products, materials are added at the beginning of the production process and conversion costs are incurred uniformly. Maloney uses the FIFO method to compute equivalent units. Production and cost data for the month of August are as shown on page 141.

Production Data—Basketballs	Units	Percent Complete
Work in process units, August 1	500	60%
Units started into production	1,600	
Work in process units, August 31	600	50%

Cost Data—Basketballs	
Work in process, August 1	$1,125
Direct materials	1,600
Direct labor	1,175
Manufacturing overhead	1,000

Production Data—Soccer Balls	Units	Percent Complete
Work in process units, August 1	200	80%
Units started into production	2,000	
Work in process units, August 31	150	70%

Cost Data—Soccer Balls	
Work in process, August 1	$ 450
Direct materials	2,600
Direct labor	1,000
Manufacturing overhead	995

Instructions

(a) Calculate the following for both the basketballs and the soccer balls.

(1) The equivalent units of production for materials and conversion costs.

(2) The unit costs of production for materials and conversion costs.

(3) The assignment of costs to units transferred out and in process at the end of the accounting period.

(b) Prepare a production cost report for the month of August for the basketballs only.

(a) Basketballs:	
(1) Materials	1,600
(2) Materials	$1
(3) Transferred out	$3,865
WIP	$1,035

PROBLEMS: SET C

Visit the book's website at **www.wiley.com/college/weygandt**, and choose the Student Companion site, to access Problem Set C.

WATERWAYS CONTINUING PROBLEM

(*Note:* This is a continuation of the Waterways Problem from Chapters 1 and 2.)

WCP3 Because most of the parts for its irrigation systems are standard, Waterways handles the majority of its manufacturing as a process cost system. There are multiple process departments. Three of these departments are the Molding, Cutting, and Welding departments. All items eventually end up in the Packaging department which prepares items for sale in kits or individually. This problem asks you to help Waterways calculate equivalent units and prepare a production cost report.

Go to the book's website,
www.wiley.com/college/weygandt,
to find the remainder of this problem.

BROADENING YOUR PERSPECTIVE

DECISION MAKING ACROSS THE ORGANIZATION

BYP3-1 Sunshine Beach Company manufactures suntan lotion, called Surtan, in 11-ounce plastic bottles. Surtan is sold in a competitive market. As a result, management is very cost-conscious. Surtan is manufactured through two processes: mixing and filling. Materials are entered at the beginning of each process and labor and manufacturing overhead occur uniformly throughout each process. Unit costs are based on the cost per gallon of Surtan using the weighted-average costing approach.

On June 30, 2008, Jill Ritzman, the chief accountant for the past 20 years, opted to take early retirement. Her replacement, Sid Benili, had extensive accounting experience with motels in the area but only limited contact with manufacturing accounting. During July, Sid correctly accumulated the following production quantity and cost data for the Mixing Department.

Production quantities: Work in process, July 1, 8,000 gallons 75% complete; started into production 91,000 gallons; work in process, July 31, 5,000 gallons 20% complete. Materials are added at the beginning of the process.

Production costs: Beginning work in process $88,000, comprised of $21,000 of materials costs and $67,000 of conversion costs; incurred in July: materials $573,000, conversion costs $769,000.

Sid then prepared a production cost report on the basis of physical units started into production. His report showed a production cost of $15.71 per gallon of Surtan. The management of Sunshine Beach was surprised at the high unit cost. The president comes to you, as Jill's top assistant, to review Sid's report and prepare a correct report if necessary.

Instructions

With the class divided into groups, answer the following questions.

(a) Show how Sid arrived at the unit cost of $15.71 per gallon of Surtan.
(b) What error(s) did Sid make in preparing his production cost report?
(c) Prepare a correct production cost report for July.

MANAGERIAL ANALYSIS

BYP3-2 Guion Furniture Company manufactures living room furniture through two departments: Framing and Upholstering. Materials are entered at the beginning of each process. For May, the following cost data are obtained from the two work in process accounts.

	Framing	Upholstering
Work in process, May 1	$ -0-	$?
Materials	420,000	?
Conversion costs	280,000	330,000
Costs transferred in	-0-	600,000
Costs transferred out	600,000	?
Work in process, May 31	100,000	?

Instructions

Answer the following questions.

(a) If 3,000 sofas were started into production on May 1 and 2,500 sofas were transferred to Upholstering, what was the unit cost of materials for May in the Framing Department?
(b) Using the data in (a) above, what was the per unit conversion cost of the sofas transferred to Upholstering?
(c) Continuing the assumptions in (a) above, what is the percentage of completion of the units in process at May 31 in the Framing Department?

REAL-WORLD FOCUS

BYP3-3 The May 10, 2004, edition of the *Wall Street Journal* includes an article by Evan Ramstad titled "A Tight Squeeze" (page R9).

Instructions

Read the article and answer the following questions.

(a) What is **Proview**'s profit margin on computer monitors? Why is the profit margin so thin on computer monitors?
(b) What are some of the steps that Proview International has taken to control costs?
(c) Why does the company continue to build tube-based monitors even as many consumers are moving away from them?
(d) Mr. Wang's final comment is, "Every aspect of the business is important, but the most important is cost." Why does he feel this way?

EXPLORING THE WEB

BYP3-4 Search the Internet and find the websites of two manufacturers that you think are likely to use process costing. Are there any specifics included in their websites that confirm the use of process costing for each of these companies?

COMMUNICATION ACTIVITY

BYP3-5 Carol Gorden was a good friend of yours in high school and is from your home town. While you chose to major in accounting when you both went away to college, she majored in marketing and management. You have recently been promoted to accounting manager for the Snack Foods Division of Koonce Enterprises, and your friend was promoted to regional sales manager for the same division of Koonce. Carol recently telephoned you. She explained that she was familiar with job cost sheets, which had been used by the Special Projects division where she had formerly worked. She was, however, very uncomfortable with the production cost reports prepared by your division. She faxed you a list of her particular questions:

1. Since Koonce occasionally prepares snack foods for special orders in the Snack Foods Division, why don't we track costs of the orders separately?
2. What is an equivalent unit?
3. Why am I getting four production cost reports? Isn't there one Work in Process account?

Instructions

Prepare a memo to Carol. Answer her questions, and include any additional information you think would be helpful. You may write informally, but do use proper grammar and punctuation.

ETHICS CASE

BYP3-6 R. B. Patrick Company manufactures a high-tech component that passes through two production processing departments, Molding and Assembly. Department managers are partially compensated on the basis of units of products completed and transferred out relative to units of product put into production. This was intended as encouragement to be efficient and to minimize waste.

Sue Wooten is the department head in the Molding Department, and Fred Barando is her quality control inspector. During the month of June, Sue had three new employees who were not yet technically skilled. As a result, many of the units produced in June had minor molding defects. In order to maintain the department's normal high rate of completion, Sue told Fred to pass through inspection and on to the Assembly Department all units that had defects nondetectable to the human eye. "Company and industry tolerances on this product are too high anyway," says Sue. "Less than 2% of the units we produce are subjected in the market to the stress tolerance we've designed into them. The odds of those 2% being any of this month's units are even less. Anyway, we're saving the company money."

Instructions

(a) Who are the potential stakeholders involved in this situation?

(b) What alternatives does Fred have in this situation? What might the company do to prevent this situation from occurring?

"ALL ABOUT YOU" ACTIVITY

BYP3-7 Some of you may ultimately own or manage a small manufacturing company. Suppose you manage Logan Company, which manufactures bird houses in four departments. The first department is Sawing. It is responsible for cutting the pieces of lumber to be used to manufacture the houses. The second department is Construction. In the Construction department the houses are nailed together; no other materials are added in the Construction department. The third department is Painting. In the Painting department, each house receives a primer and then two coats of weather-resistant paint. The fourth and last department is Finishing. Workers in the Finishing department add trim and pack the bird houses for shipment. Data for March follow.

Started by Sawing	10,000 units
Transferred to Construction	11,000
Transferred to Painting	12,000
Transferred to Finishing	10,000
Transferred to Finished Goods warehouse	11,000

Each department had 2,000 bird houses on hand at the beginning of the month, which were 25% complete as to conversion costs. Each department's ending inventory was 50% complete as to conversion costs.

Instructions

Compute the physical units for each department or for only one of the departments, as your instructor directs.

Answers to Insight and Accounting Across the Organization Questions

Choosing a Cost Driver, p. 100

Q: What is the result if a company uses the wrong "cost driver" to assign manufacturing overhead?

A: *Incorrect assignment of manufacturing overhead will result in some products receiving too much overhead and others receiving too little.*

Keeping Score for the Xbox, p. 104

Q: In what ways has cost accounting probably become more critical for Microsoft in recent years?

A: *In the past Microsoft enjoyed very high profit margins on its software sales. As a consequence, it could afford to be less cost-conscious than most companies. In addition, in producing software, manufacturing costs represented a very small part of its total product cost. But the video-game hardware market is very competitive. In order to achieve its profitability goals, Microsoft will have to manufacture its product efficiently in order to meet its cost targets to ensure adequate margins. The information provided by process cost accounting will be critical to its efforts.*

What Cost System Might Jiffy Lube Use?, p. 111

Q: What criteria should be considered when selecting a cost accounting system for a service company?

A: *Companies that provide specific, non-routine services will probably benefit from using a job order cost system. Those that perform routine, repetitive services will probably be better off with a process cost system. In fact, since there may be little or no work in process at the end of an accounting period, applying process costing may be even easier for a service company than for a manufacturer.*

Authors' Comments on All About You: Wal-Mart Is on the Phone, p. 112

It will come as a surprise to some of you that some companies would decline this offer. The production requirements will be extreme, the necessary new investments will be high, and there is no guarantee of continued orders from Wal-Mart. While there eventually should be production efficiencies that result from the increased scale, there will certainly be many growing pains in the short run. Wal-Mart's price does not allow for any error.

By accepting Wal-Mart's order, you would be changing the nature of your company from a producer of a high-price, high-margin, lower-volume product to that of a low-price, low-margin, high-volume product. Very few companies are able to continue to sell their products at a high price in one outlet and a low price in another. As noted, because margins will be razor-thin, the company will now have to be incredibly cost-conscious. Its cost accounting system will become far more critical to its success.

See the article at the following site for a discussion of how things didn't work out well for one company that tried to be a Wal-Mart supplier: *www.inc.com/magazine/20031101/walmart.html.*

Answers to Self-Study Questions

1. b **2.** d **3.** d **4.** b **5.** b **6.** a **7.** c **8.** a **9.** b **10.** b ***11.** b ***12.** a ***13.** b

Remember to go back to the Navigator box on the chapter-opening page and check off your completed work.

Chapter 4

Activity-Based Costing

STUDY OBJECTIVES

After studying this chapter, you should be able to:

1. Recognize the difference between traditional costing and activity-based costing.
2. Identify the steps in the development of an activity-based costing system.
3. Know how companies identify the activity cost pools used in activity-based costing.
4. Know how companies identify and use cost drivers in activity-based costing.
5. Understand the benefits and limitations of activity-based costing.
6. Differentiate between value-added and non–value-added activities.
7. Understand the value of using activity levels in activity-based costing.
8. Apply activity-based costing to service industries.

The Navigator

The Navigator

Scan **Study Objectives**	
Read **Feature Story**	
Read **Preview**	
Read text and answer **Before You Go On** p. 155 p. 163 p. 166	
Work **Using the Decision Toolkit**	
Review **Summary of Study Objectives**	
Work **Demonstration Problem**	
Answer **Self-Study Questions**	
Complete **Assignments**	

Feature Story

THE ABCs OF DOUGHNUT MAKING—VIRTUAL-REALITY STYLE

Super Bakery, Inc., created in 1990 by former Pittsburgh Steelers' running back Franco Harris, is a nationwide supplier of mineral-, vitamin-, and protein-enriched doughnuts and other baked goods to the institutional food market, primarily school systems. Super Bakery is a *virtual corporation,* in which only the core, strategic functions of the business are performed inside

the company. The remaining activities—selling, manufacturing, warehousing, and shipping—are outsourced to a network of external companies.

Super Bakery draws these cooperating companies together and organizes the work flow. The goal is to add maximum value to the company while making the minimum investment in permanent staff, fixed assets, and working capital. The results are notable: Super Bakery's sales have grown at an average annual rate of approximately 20% during most of its existence.

One of Super Bakery's challenges has been to control the cost of the outsourced activities. Management suspected a wide variation in the cost of serving customers in different parts of the country. Yet its traditional costing methods were spreading costs over the entire customer base. Each customer's order *appeared* to cost the same amount to complete. In actuality, orders with high profit margins were subsidizing orders with low profit margins. Super Bakery desired a system that would more accurately assign the costs of each order. With such a system, pricing could be improved.

The company looked at and eventually changed to a system that could identify the costs associated with the *activities* performed in the business—manufacturing, sales, warehousing, and shipping. The new activity-based costing system showed that the costs and profit margins on each sale vary significantly. Super Bakery is now able to track the profitability of each customer's account and the performance of outsourced activities. This doughnut maker, as a result, even knows the cost of the doughnut holes!

Source: Based on Tom R. V. Davis and Bruce L. Darling, "ABC in a Virtual Corporation," *Management Accounting* (October 1996), pp. 18–26.

The Navigator

Inside Chapter 4

Preview of Chapter 4

As indicated in the Feature Story about Super Bakery, Inc., the traditional costing systems described in earlier chapters are not the best answer for every company. Because Super Bakery suspected that the traditional system was masking significant differences in its real cost structure, it sought a new method of assigning costs. Similar searches by other companies for ways to improve operations and gather more accurate data for decision-making have resulted in the development of powerful new management tools, including **activity-based costing (ABC).** The primary objective of this chapter is to explain and illustrate this concept.

The content and organization of this chapter are as follows.

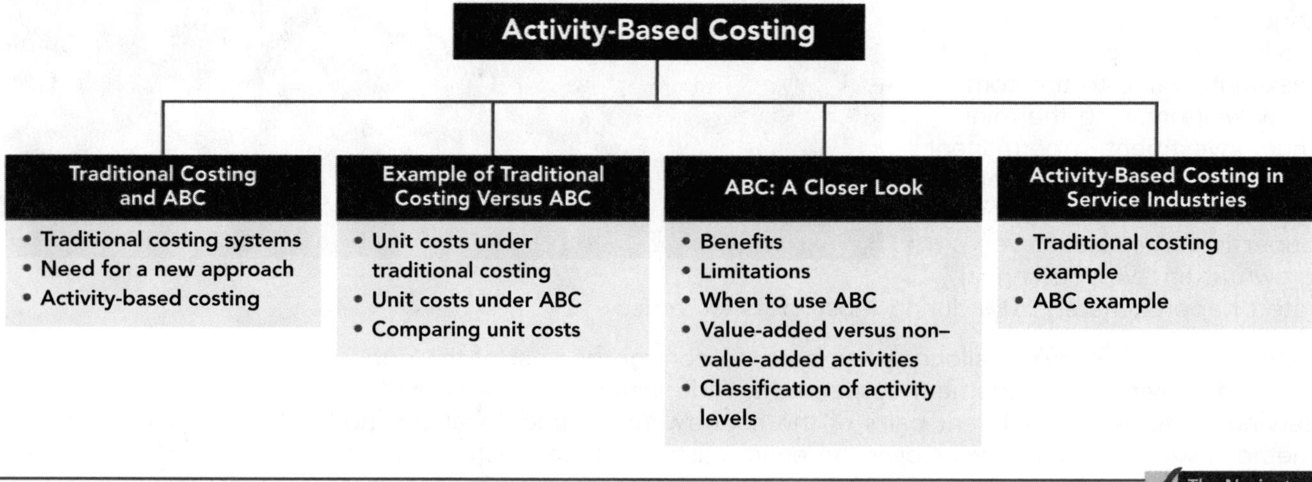

The Navigator

TRADITIONAL COSTING AND ACTIVITY-BASED COSTING

Traditional Costing Systems

STUDY OBJECTIVE 1

Recognize the difference between traditional costing and activity-based costing.

It is probably impossible to determine the *exact* cost of a product or service. However, in order to achieve improved management decisions, companies strive to provide decision makers with the most accurate cost estimates they can. The most accurate estimate of product cost occurs when the costs are traceable directly to the product produced or the service provided. Direct material and direct labor costs are the easiest to trace directly to the product through the use of material requisition forms and payroll time sheets. Overhead costs, on the other hand, are an indirect or common cost that generally cannot be easily or directly traced to individual products or services. Instead, companies use estimates to assign overhead costs to products and services.

Often the most difficult part of computing accurate unit costs is determining the proper amount of **overhead cost** to assign to each product, service, or job. In our coverage of job order costing in Chapter 2 and of process costing in Chapter 3, we used a single or plantwide overhead rate throughout the year for the entire factory operation. That rate was called the **predetermined overhead rate**. For job order costing we assumed that **direct labor cost** was the relevant activity base for assigning all overhead costs to jobs. For process costing, we assumed that **machine hours** was the relevant activity base for assigning all overhead to the process or department.

The use of direct labor as the activity base made sense when overhead cost allocation systems were first developed. At that time, direct labor made up a large portion of total manufacturing cost. Therefore, it was widely accepted that there was a high correlation between direct labor and the incurrence of overhead cost. As a result, direct labor became the most popular basis for allocating overhead.

Even in today's increasingly automated environment, direct labor is sometimes the appropriate basis for assigning overhead cost to products. It is appropriate to use direct labor when (a) direct labor constitutes a significant part of total product cost and (b) a high correlation exists between direct labor and changes in the amount of overhead costs. Illustration 4-1 displays a simplified (one-stage) traditional costing system relying on direct labor to assign overhead.

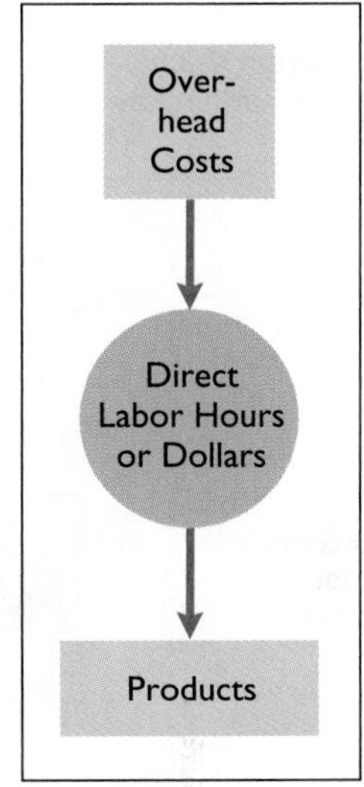

Illustration 4-1
Traditional one-stage costing system

The Need for a New Approach

In recent years manufacturers and service providers have experienced tremendous change. Advances in computerized systems, technological innovation, global competition, and automation have changed the manufacturing environment drastically. As a result, the amount of direct labor used in many industries has greatly decreased, and total overhead costs resulting from depreciation on expensive equipment and machinery, utilities, repairs, and maintenance have significantly increased. When there is not a correlation between direct labor and overhead, it is inappropriate to use plantwide predetermined overhead rates based on direct labor. Companies that use overhead rates based on direct labor, even though this correlation does not exist, experience significant product-cost distortions.

To avoid such distortions, many companies now use machine hours as the basis on which to allocate overhead in an automated manufacturing environment. But even machine hours may not suffice as the only plantwide basis for allocating all overhead. If the manufacturing process is complex, then only multiple allocation bases can result in more accurate product-cost computations. In such situations, managers need to consider an overhead cost allocation method that uses *multiple* bases. That method is **activity-based costing**.

Activity-Based Costing

Broadly, **activity-based costing (ABC)** is an approach for allocating overhead costs. More specifically, ABC allocates overhead to multiple activity cost pools, and it then assigns the activity cost pools to products and services by means of cost drivers. To understand more clearly what that means, you need to apply some new meanings to the rather common-sounding words that make up the definition: In activity-based costing, an **activity** is any event, action, transaction, or work sequence that incurs cost when producing a product or providing a service. An **activity cost pool** is the overhead cost attributed to a distinct type of activity (e.g., ordering materials or setting up machines). A **cost driver** is any factor or activity that has a direct cause-effect relationship with the resources consumed. The reasoning behind ABC cost allocation is simple: **Products consume activities, and activities consume resources.**

These definitions of terms will become clearer as we look more closely at how ABC works. ABC allocates overhead in a two-stage process. The first stage allocates overhead costs to activity cost pools. (Traditional costing systems, in contrast, allocate these costs to departments or to jobs.) Examples of overhead cost pools are ordering materials, setting up machines, assembling products, inspecting products.

The second stage assigns the overhead allocated to the activity cost pools to products, using cost drivers. The cost drivers measure the number of individual activities undertaken or performed to produce products or provide services.

Examples are number of purchase orders, number of setups, labor hours, or number of inspections. Illustration 4-2 shows examples of activities, and possible cost drivers to measure them, for a company that manufactures two products—axles and steering wheels.

Illustration 4-2
Activities and related cost drivers

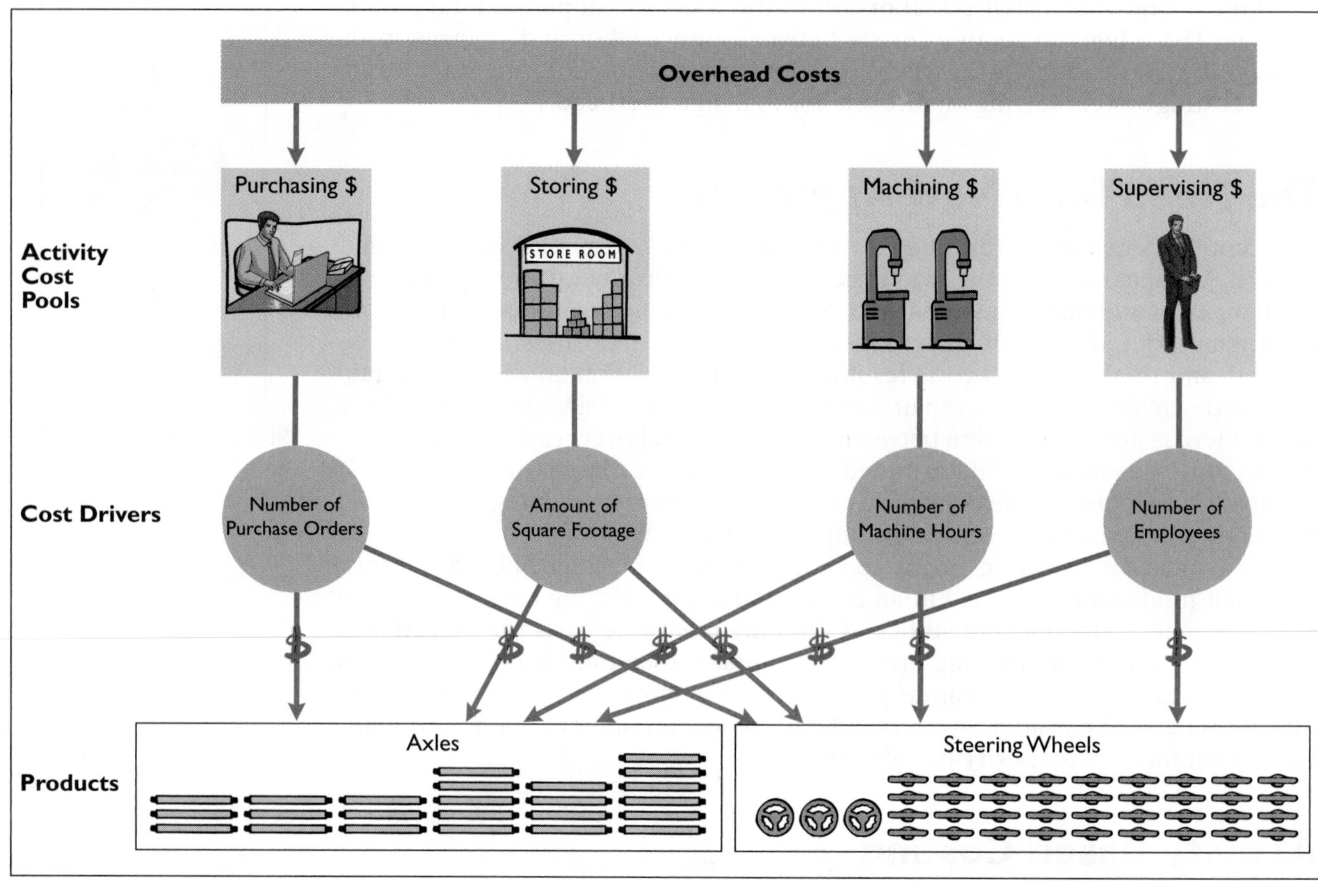

In the first step (as shown at the top of Illustration 4-2), the company allocates overhead costs to activity cost pools. In this simplified example, the company has identified four activity cost pools: purchasing, storing, machining, and supervising. After the costs are allocated to the activity cost pools, the company uses cost drivers to determine the costs to assign to the individual products (either axles or steering wheels) based on each product's use of each activity. For example, if axles require more activity by the purchasing department, as measured by the number of required purchase orders, then more of the overhead cost from the purchasing pool will be allocated to the axles.

The more complex a product's manufacturing operation, the more activities and cost drivers it is likely to have. If there is little or no correlation between changes in the cost driver and consumption of the overhead cost, inaccurate product costs are inevitable.

Illustration 4-3 shows the design of a more complex activity-based costing system with seven activity cost pools for Lift Jack Company. Lift Jack Company manufactures two automotive jacks—an automobile scissors jack and a truck hydraulic jack.

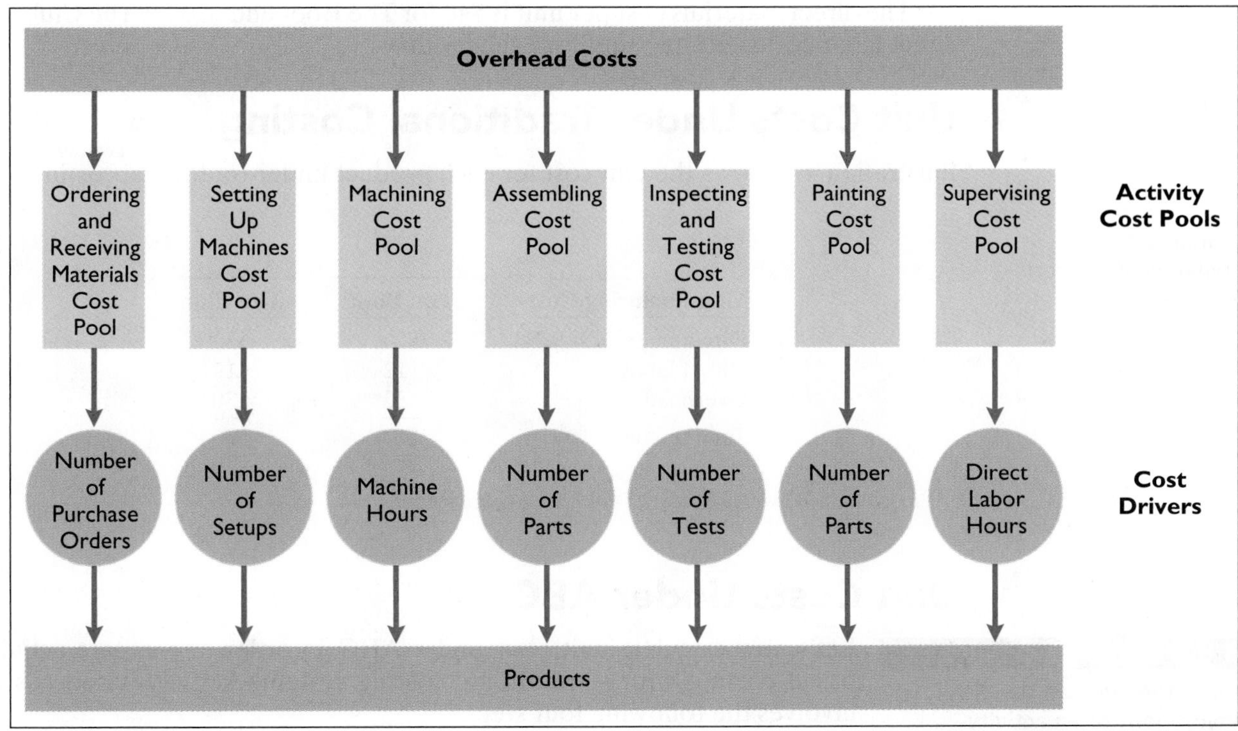

Illustration 4-3
ABC system design—Lift Jack Company

The Lift Jack Company illustration contains seven activity cost pools. In some companies the number of activities related to a cost pool can be substantial. For example, Clark-Hurth (a division of Clark Equipment Company), a manufacturer of axles and transmissions, identified over 170 activities. Compumotor (a division of Parker Hannifin) identified over 80 activities in just the procurement function of its Material Control Department.

EXAMPLE OF TRADITIONAL COSTING VERSUS ABC

In this section we present a simple case example that compares traditional costing and activity-based costing. It illustrates how ABC eliminates the distortion that can occur in traditional overhead cost allocation. As you study this example, you should understand that ABC does not *replace* an existing job order or process costing system. What ABC does is to segregate overhead into various cost pools in an effort to provide more accurate cost information. As a result, ABC supplements—not replaces—the traditional cost systems.

Assume that Atlas Company produces two automobile antitheft devices, The Boot and The Club. The Boot is a high-volume item totaling 25,000 units annually. The Club is a low-volume item totaling only 5,000 units per year. Each product requires one hour of direct labor for completion. Therefore, total annual direct labor hours are 30,000 (25,000 + 5,000). Expected annual manufacturing overhead costs are \$900,000. Thus, the predetermined overhead rate is \$30 (\$900,000 ÷ 30,000) per direct labor hour.

The direct materials cost per unit is $40 for The Boot and $30 for The Club. The direct labor cost is $12 per unit for each product.

Unit Costs Under Traditional Costing

Illustration 4-4 shows the unit cost for each product under traditional costing.

Illustration 4-4
Computation of unit costs—traditional costing

	Products	
Manufacturing Costs	**The Boot**	**The Club**
Direct materials	$40	$30
Direct labor	12	12
Overhead	30*	30*
Total unit cost	$82	$72

*Predetermined overhead rate × Direct labor hours = $30 × 1 hr. = $30

Unit Costs Under ABC

STUDY OBJECTIVE 2
Identify the steps in the development of an activity-based costing system.

Let's now calculate unit costs under ABC, in order to compare activity-based costing with a traditional costing system. Activity-based costing involves the following four steps.

1. Identify and classify the major activities involved in the manufacture of specific products, and allocate manufacturing overhead costs to the appropriate cost pools.
2. Identify the cost driver that has a strong correlation to the costs accumulated in the cost pool.
3. Compute the overhead rate for each cost driver.
4. Assign manufacturing overhead costs for each cost pool to products, using the overhead rates (cost per driver).

IDENTIFY AND CLASSIFY ACTIVITIES AND ALLOCATE OVERHEAD TO COST POOLS (STEP 1)

STUDY OBJECTIVE 3
Know how companies identify the activity cost pools used in activity-based costing.

A well-designed activity-based costing system starts with an analysis of the activities performed to manufacture a product or provide a service. This analysis should identify all resource-consuming activities. It requires a detailed, step-by-step walk-through of each operation, documenting every activity undertaken to accomplish a task. Atlas Company identified three activity-cost pools: setting up machines, machining, and inspecting.

Next, the system assigns overhead costs directly to the appropriate activity cost pool. For example, all overhead costs directly associated with Atlas Company's machine setups (such as salaries, supplies, and depreciation) would be assigned to the machine setup cost pool. Illustration 4-5 shows the three cost pools, along with the estimated overhead allocated to each cost pool.

Illustration 4-5
Activity cost pools and estimated overhead

Activity Cost Pools	**Estimated Overhead**
Setting up machines	$ 300,000
Machining	500,000
Inspecting	100,000
Total	$ 900,000

IDENTIFY COST DRIVERS (STEP 2)

STUDY OBJECTIVE 4

Know how companies identify and use cost drivers in activity-based costing.

After costs are allocated to the activity cost pools, the company must identify the cost drivers for each cost pool. The cost driver must accurately measure the actual consumption of the activity by the various products. To achieve accurate costing, a **high degree of correlation** must exist between the cost driver and the actual consumption of the overhead costs in the cost pool.

Illustration 4-6 shows the cost drivers identified by Atlas and their total expected use per activity cost pool.

Illustration 4-6 Cost drivers and their expected use

Activity Cost Pools	Cost Drivers	Expected Use of Cost Drivers per Activity
Setting up machines	Number of setups	**1,500** setups
Machining	Machine hours	**50,000** machine hours
Inspecting	Number of inspections	**2,000** inspections

Availability and ease of obtaining data relating to the cost driver is an important factor that must be considered in its selection.

COMPUTE OVERHEAD RATES (STEP 3)

Next, the company computes an **activity-based overhead rate** per cost driver by dividing the estimated overhead per activity by the number of cost drivers expected to be used per activity. Illustration 4-7 shows the formula for this computation.

Illustration 4-7 Formula for computing activity-based overhead rate

$$\frac{\text{Estimated Overhead Per Activity}}{\text{Expected Use of Cost Drivers Per Activity}} = \text{Activity-Based Overhead Rate}$$

Atlas Company computes its activity-based overhead rates by using estimated overhead per activity cost pool, shown in Illustration 4-5, and the expected use of cost drivers per activity, shown in Illustration 4-6. These computations are presented in Illustration 4-8.

Illustration 4-8 Computation of activity-based overhead rates

Activity Cost Pools	Estimated Overhead	÷	Expected Use of Cost Drivers per Activity	=	Activity-Based Overhead Rates
Setting up machines	$300,000		1,500 setups		**$200** per setup
Machining	500,000		50,000 machine hours		**$10** per machine hour
Inspecting	100,000		2,000 inspections		**$50** per inspection
Total	$900,000				

ASSIGN OVERHEAD COSTS TO PRODUCTS (STEP 4)

In assigning overhead costs, it is necessary to know the expected use of cost drivers **for each product**. Because of its low volume, The Club requires more setups and inspections than The Boot. Illustration 4-9 (page 154) shows the expected use of cost drivers per product for each of Atlas's products.

Illustration 4-9
Expected use of cost drivers per product

Activity Cost Pools	Cost Drivers	Expected Use of Cost Drivers per Activity	Expected Use of Cost Drivers per Product: The Boot	Expected Use of Cost Drivers per Product: The Club
Setting up machines	Number of setups	1,500 setups	500	1,000
Machining	Machine hours	50,000 machine hours	30,000	20,000
Inspecting	Number of inspections	2,000 inspections	500	1,500

To assign overhead costs to each product, Atlas multiplies the activity-based overhead rates per cost driver (Illustration 4-8) by the number of cost drivers expected to be used per product (Illustration 4-9). Illustration 4-10 shows the amount of overhead cost assigned to each product for Atlas Company.

Illustration 4-10
Assignment of activity cost pools to products

Atlas Company.xls

File Edit View Insert Format Tools Data Window Help

ATLAS COMPANY

	The Boot					The Club				
Activity Cost Pools	Expected Use of Cost Drivers per Product	×	Activity-Based Overhead Rates	=	Cost Assigned	Expected Use of Cost Drivers per Product	×	Activity-Based Overhead Rates	=	Cost Assigned
Setting up machines	500		$200		$100,000	1,000		$200		$200,000
Machining	30,000		$10		300,000	20,000		$10		200,000
Inspecting	500		$50		25,000	1,500		$50		75,000
Total costs assigned [(a)]					$425,000					$475,000
Units produced [(b)]					25,000					5,000
Overhead cost per unit [(a) ÷ (b)]					$17					$95

These data show that under ABC, overhead costs are shifted from the high-volume product (The Boot) to the low-volume product (The Club). This shift results in more accurate costing for two reasons:

1. Low-volume products often require more special handling, such as more machine setups and inspections, than high-volume products. This is true for Atlas Company. Thus, the low-volume product frequently is responsible for more overhead costs per unit than is a high-volume product.[1]
2. Assigning overhead using ABC will usually increase the cost per unit for low-volume products as compared to a traditional overhead allocation. Therefore, traditional cost drivers such as direct labor hours are usually not appropriate for assigning overhead costs to low-volume products.

Comparing Unit Costs

A comparison of unit manufacturing costs under traditional costing and ABC shows the following significant differences.

[1]Robin Cooper and Robert S. Kaplan, "How Cost Accounting Distorts Product Costs," *Management Accounting* 69, No. 10 (April 1988), pp. 20–27.

Illustration 4-11
Comparison of unit product costs

	The Boot		The Club	
Manufacturing Costs	**Traditional Costing**	**ABC**	**Traditional Costing**	**ABC**
Direct materials	$40	$40	$30	$ 30
Direct labor	12	12	12	12
Overhead	30	17	30	95
Total cost per unit	**$82**	**$69**	**$72**	**$137**
	Overstated $13		Understated $65	

The comparison shows that unit costs under traditional costing are significantly distorted. The cost of producing The Boot is overstated $13 per unit ($82 − $69), and the cost of producing The Club is understated $65 per unit ($137 − $72). These differences are attributable entirely to how Atlas Company assigns manufacturing overhead. A likely consequence of the differences in assigning overhead is that Atlas has been overpricing The Boot and possibly losing market share to competitors. It also has been sacrificing profitability by underpricing The Club.

INTERNATIONAL INSIGHT

The Origins of ABC

Activity-based costing was pioneered in the United States: John Deere Company coined the term about 25 years ago. Numerous well-known U.S. companies, including IBM, AT&T, Hewlett-Packard, Procter & Gamble, Tektronix, Hughes Aircraft, Caterpillar, and American Express, have adopted ABC. Its use outside the United States is limited. The cost of implementation may discourage some foreign companies.

In Japan, where activity-based costing is less widely used, companies prefer volume measures such as direct labor hours to assign overhead cost to products. Japanese managers are convinced that reducing direct labor is essential to continuous cost reduction. Using direct labor as the basis for overhead allocation forces Japanese companies to watch direct labor more closely. Possibly, Japanese management believes that labor cost reduction is more of a priority than developing more accurate product costs.

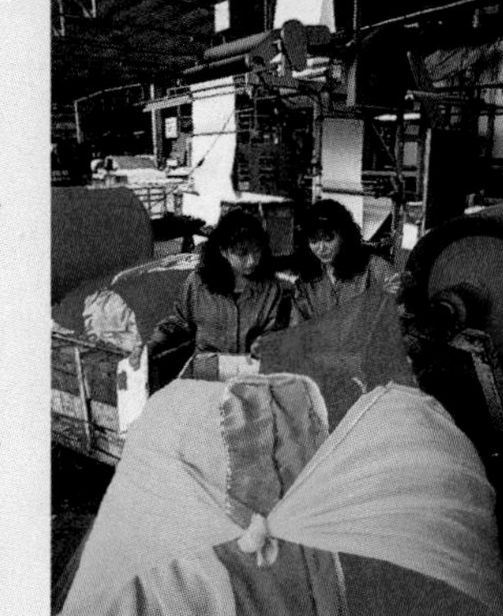

Why does using direct labor as the basis for overhead allocation result in lower direct labor costs for Japanese companies?

Before You Go On...

REVIEW IT

1. Historically, why has direct labor hours been the most popular basis for allocating overhead costs to products?
2. What changes have occurred in the industrial environment to diminish the appeal of traditional volume-based overhead allocation systems?
3. What four steps are involved in developing an ABC system?

DO IT

Lift Jack Company, as shown in Illustration 4-3, page 151, has seven activity cost pools and two products. It expects to produce 200,000 units of its automobile scissors jack and 80,000 units of its truck hydraulic jack. Having identified its activity cost pools and the cost drivers for each cost pool, Lift Jack Company accumulated the following data relative to those activity cost pools and cost drivers.

Annual Overhead Data				Expected Use of Cost Drivers per Product	
Activity Cost Pools	**Cost Drivers**	**Estimated Overhead**	**Expected Use of Cost Drivers per Activity**	**Scissors Jacks**	**Hydraulic Jacks**
Ordering and receiving	Purchase orders	$ 200,000	2,500 orders	1,000	1,500
Machine setup	Setups	600,000	1,200 setups	500	700
Machining	Machine hours	2,000,000	800,000 hours	300,000	500,000
Assembling	Parts	1,800,000	3,000,000 parts	1,800,000	1,200,000
Inspecting and testing	Tests	700,000	35,000 tests	20,000	15,000
Painting	Parts	300,000	3,000,000 parts	1,800,000	1,200,000
Supervising	Direct labor hours	1,200,000	200,000 hours	130,000	70,000
		$6,800,000			

Using the above data, do the following:

(a) Prepare a schedule showing the computations of the activity-based overhead rates per cost driver.

(b) Prepare a schedule assigning each activity's overhead cost to the two products.

(c) Compute the overhead cost per unit for each product.

(d) Comment on the comparative overhead cost per unit.

Action Plan

- Determine the activity-based overhead rate by dividing the estimated overhead per activity by the expected use of cost drivers per activity.
- Assign the overhead of each activity cost pool to the individual products by multiplying the expected use of cost driver per product times the activity-based overhead rate.
- Determine overhead cost per unit by dividing the overhead assigned to each product by the number of units of that product.

Solution

(a) Computations of activity-based overhead rates per cost driver:

Activity Cost Pools	Estimated Overhead	÷	Expected Use of Cost Drivers per Activity	=	Activity-Based Overhead Rates
Ordering and receiving	$ 200,000		2,500 purchase orders		$80 per order
Machine setup	600,000		1,200 setups		$500 per setup
Machining	2,000,000		800,000 machine hours		$2.50 per machine hour
Assembling	1,800,000		3,000,000 parts		$0.60 per part
Inspecting and testing	700,000		35,000 tests		$20 per test
Painting	300,000		3,000,000 parts		$0.10 per part
Supervising	1,200,000		200,000 direct labor hours		$6 per direct labor hour
	$6,800,000				

(b) Assignment of each activity's overhead cost to products using ABC:

	Scissors Jacks						Hydraulic Jacks					
Activity Cost Pools	**Expected Use of Cost Drivers per Product**	×	**Activity-Based Overhead Rates**	=	**Cost Assigned**		**Expected Use of Cost Drivers per Product**	×	**Activity-Based Overhead Rates**	=	**Cost Assigned**	
Ordering and receiving	1,000		$80		$ 80,000		1,500		$80		$ 120,000	
Machine setup	500		$500		250,000		700		$500		350,000	
Machining	300,000		$2.50		750,000		500,000		$2.50		1,250,000	
Assembling	1,800,000		$0.60		1,080,000		1,200,000		$0.60		720,000	
Inspecting and testing	20,000		$20		400,000		15,000		$20		300,000	
Painting	1,800,000		$0.10		180,000		1,200,000		$0.10		120,000	
Supervising	130,000		$6		780,000		70,000		$6		420,000	
Total assigned costs					$3,520,000						$3,280,000	

(c) Computation of overhead cost per unit:

	Scissors Jack	**Hydraulic Jack**
Total costs assigned	$3,520,000	$3,280,000
Total units produced	200,000	80,000
Overhead cost per unit	$17.60	$41.00

(d) These data show that the total overhead assigned to 80,000 hydraulic jacks is nearly as great as the overhead assigned to 200,000 scissors jacks. However, the overhead cost per hydraulic jack is $41. It is only $17.60 per scissors jack.

Related exercise material: BE4-5, BE4-6, BE4-7, E4-1, E4-2, E4-3, E4-4, E4-5, E4-6, and E4-11.

✓ The Navigator

ACTIVITY-BASED COSTING: A CLOSER LOOK

STUDY OBJECTIVE 5

Understand the benefits and limitations of activity-based costing.

As the use of activity-based costing has grown, both its practical benefits and its limitations have become apparent.

Benefits of ABC

The primary benefit of ABC is **more accurate product costing.** Here's why:

1. **ABC leads to more cost pools** being used to assign overhead costs to products. Instead of one plantwide pool (or even departmental pools) and a single cost driver, companies use numerous activity cost pools with more relevant cost drivers. Costs are assigned more directly on the basis of the cost drivers used to produce each product.
2. **ABC leads to enhanced control over overhead costs.** Under ABC, companies can trace many overhead costs directly to activities—allowing some indirect costs to be identified as direct costs. Thus, managers have become more aware of their responsibility to control the activities that generate those costs.

3. **ABC leads to better management decisions.** More accurate product costing should contribute to setting selling prices that can help achieve desired product profitability levels. In addition, more accurate cost data could be helpful in deciding whether to make or buy a product part or component, and sometimes even whether to eliminate a product.

Activity-based costing does not change the amount of overhead costs. What it does do is allocate those overhead costs in a more accurate manner. Furthermore, if the score-keeping is more realistic and more accurate, managers should be able to better understand cost behavior and overall profitability.

Limitations of ABC

Although ABC systems often provide better product cost data than traditional volume-based systems, there are limitations:

1. **ABC can be expensive to use.** The increased cost of identifying multiple activities and applying numerous cost drivers discourages many companies from using ABC. Activity-based costing systems are more complex than traditional costing systems—sometimes significantly more complex. So companies must ask, is the cost of implementation greater than the benefits of greater accuracy? Sometimes it may be. For some companies there may be no need to consider ABC at all because their existing system is sufficient. If the costs of ABC outweigh the benefits, then the company should not implement ABC.
2. **Some arbitrary allocations continue.** Even though more overhead costs can be assigned directly to products through ABC's multiple activity cost pools, certain overhead costs remain to be allocated by means of some arbitrary volume-based cost driver such as labor or machine hours.

SERVICE COMPANY INSIGHT

Using ABC to Aid in Employee Evaluation

Although most publicized ABC applications are in manufacturing companies or large service firms, very small service businesses can apply it also. Mahany Welding Supply, a small family-run welding service business in Rochester, N.Y., used ABC to determine the cost of servicing customers and to identify feasible cost reduction opportunities.

Application of ABC at Mahany Welding's operations provided information about the five employees who were involved in different activities of revenue generation—i.e., delivery of supplies (rural versus city), welding services, repairs, telephone sales, field or door-to-door sales, repeat business sales, and cold-call sales. Managers applied activity cost pools to the five revenue-producing employees using relevant cost drivers. ABC revealed annual net income (loss) by employee as follows:

Employee #1	$65,431	Employee #4	$(10,957)
Employee #2	$35,154	Employee #5	$(46,180)
Employee #3	$13,731		

This comparative information was an eye-opener to the owner of Mahany Welding— who was Employee #5!

Source: Michael Krupnicki and Thomas Tyson, "Using ABC to Determine the Cost of Servicing Customers," *Management Accounting* (December 31, 1997), pp. 40–46.

What positive implications does application of ABC have for the employees of this company?

When to Use ABC

How does a company know when to use ABC? The presence of one or more of the following factors would point to its possible use:

1. Product lines differ greatly in volume and manufacturing complexity.
2. Product lines are numerous and diverse, and they require differing degrees of support services.
3. Overhead costs constitute a significant portion of total costs.
4. The manufacturing process or the number of products has changed significantly—for example, from labor-intensive to capital-intensive due to automation.
5. Production or marketing managers are ignoring data provided by the existing system and are instead using "bootleg" costing data or other alternative data when pricing or making other product decisions.

The redesign and installation of a product-costing system is a significant decision that requires considerable cost and a major effort to accomplish. Therefore, financial managers need to be very cautious and deliberate when initiating changes in costing systems. A key factor in implementing a successful ABC system is the support of top management.

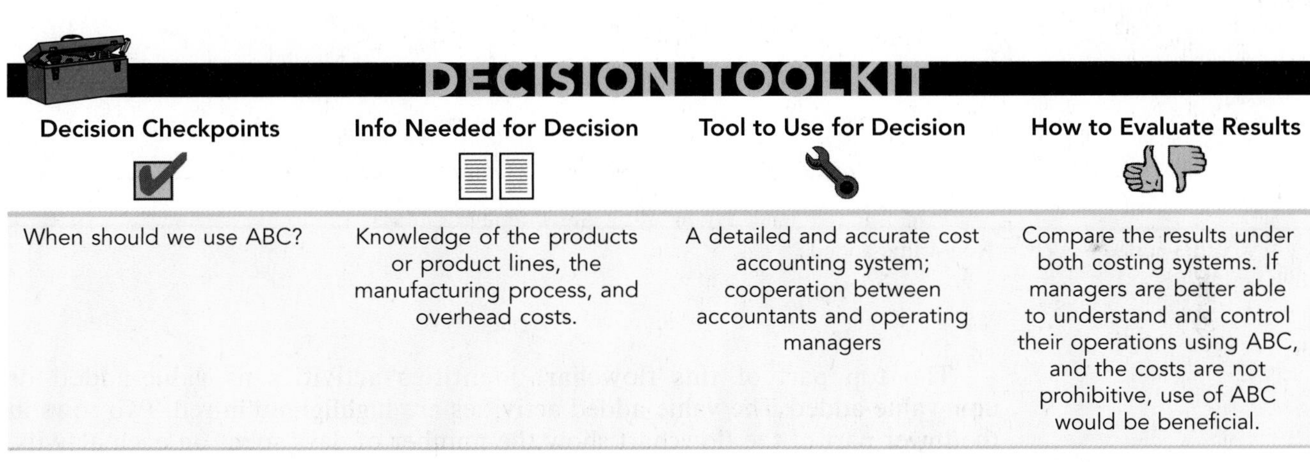

DECISION TOOLKIT

Decision Checkpoints	Info Needed for Decision	Tool to Use for Decision	How to Evaluate Results
When should we use ABC?	Knowledge of the products or product lines, the manufacturing process, and overhead costs.	A detailed and accurate cost accounting system; cooperation between accountants and operating managers	Compare the results under both costing systems. If managers are better able to understand and control their operations using ABC, and the costs are not prohibitive, use of ABC would be beneficial.

Value-Added versus Non–Value-Added Activities

STUDY OBJECTIVE 6

Differentiate between value-added and non–value-added activities.

Some companies that have experienced the benefits of activity-based costing have applied it to a broader range of management activities. **Activity-based management (ABM)** extends the use of ABC from product costing to a comprehensive management tool that focuses on reducing costs and improving processes and decision making. A refinement of activity-based costing used in ABM is the classification of activities as either value-added or non–value-added.

Value-added activities increase the worth of a product or service to customers. Such activities involve resource usage and related costs that customers are willing to pay for. Value-added activities are the activities of actually manufacturing a product or performing a service. Examples of value-added activities in a manufacturing operation are engineering design, machining, assembly, painting, and packaging. Examples of value-added activities in a service company would be performing surgery, providing legal research for legal services, or delivering packages by a delivery service.

Non–value-added activities are production- or service-related activities that simply **add cost to or increase the time spent on a product or service without increasing its market value.** Examples of non–value-added activities in a manufacturing operation include the repair of machines; the storage of inventory; the moving of raw materials, assemblies, and finished product within the factory; building maintenance; inspections; and inventory control. Examples of non–value-added activities in service enterprises might include taking appointments, reception, bookkeeping, billing, traveling, ordering supplies, advertising, cleaning, and computer repair.

Companies often use **activity flowcharts** to help identify the ABC activities. Illustration 4-12 shows an activity flowchart.

Illustration 4-12
Flowchart showing value-added and non–value-added activities

HEARTLAND MANUFACTURING COMPANY
Activity Flowchart

Activities

	NVA	NVA	NVA	NVA	VA		NVA	NVA	VA	NVA	NVA	NVA	VA
	Receive and Inspect Materials	Move and Store Materials	Move Materials to Production and Wait	Set up Machines	Machining: Drill	Machining: Lathe	Inspect	Move and Wait	Assembly	Inspect and Test	Move to Storage	Store Finished Goods	Package and Ship
Current Days	1	12	2.5	1.5	2	1	0.2	6	2	0.3	0.5	14	1
	Total Current Average Time = 44 days												
Proposed Days	1	4	1.5	1.5	2	1	0.2	2	2	0.3	0.5	10	1
	Total Proposed Average Time = 27 days												

Proposed reduction in non–value-added time = 17 days

VA = Value-added NVA = Non–value-added

The top part of this flowchart identifies activities as value-added or non–value-added. The value-added activities are highlighted in red. Two rows in the lower part of the flowchart show the number of days spent on each activity. The first row shows the number of days spent on each activity under the current manufacturing process. The second row shows the number of days expected to be spent on each activity under management's proposed reengineered manufacturing process.

The proposed changes would reduce time spent on non–value-added activities by 17 days. This 17-day improvement would be due entirely to moving inventory more quickly through the non–value-added processes—that is, by reducing inventory time in moving, storage, and waiting. The appendix at the end of this chapter discusses a just-in-time inventory system, which some companies use to eliminate non–value-added activities related to inventory.

Not all activities labeled non–value-added are totally wasteful, nor can they be totally eliminated. For example, although inspection time is a non–value-added activity from a customer's perspective, few companies would eliminate their quality control functions. Similarly, moving and waiting time is non–value-added, but it would be impossible to completely eliminate. Nevertheless, when managers recognize the non–value-added characteristic of these activities, they are motivated to minimize them as much as possible. Attention to such matters is part of the growing practice of activity-based management which helps managers concentrate on **continuous improvement** of operations and activities.

MANAGEMENT INSIGHT

What Does NASCAR Have to Do with Breakfast Cereal?

Often the best way to improve a process is to learn from observing a different process. Production line technicians from giant food producer General Mills were flown to North Carolina to observe first-hand how race-car pit crews operate. In a NASCAR race, the value-added activity is driving toward the finish-line; any time spent in the pit is non–value-added. Every split second saved in the pit increases the chances of winning. From what the General Mills technicians learned at the car race, as well as other efforts, they were able to reduce setup time from 5 hours to just 20 minutes.

? What are the benefits of reducing setup time?

DECISION TOOLKIT

Decision Checkpoints	Info Needed for Decision	Tool to Use for Decision	How to Evaluate Results

How can activity-based management help managers manage the business?	Activities classified as value-added and non–value-added	The activity analysis flowchart extended to identify each activity as value-added or non–value-added	The flowchart should motivate managers to minimize non–value-added activities. Managers should better understand the relationship between activities and the resources they consume.

Classification of Activity Levels

STUDY OBJECTIVE 7

Understand the value of using activity levels in activity-based costing.

As mentioned earlier, traditional costing systems are volume-driven—driven by unit-based cost drivers such as direct labor or machine hours. Some activity costs are strictly variable and are caused by the production or acquisition of a single unit of product or the performance of a single unit of service. However, the recognition that other activity costs are not driven by unit-based cost drivers has led to the development of a classification of ABC activities consisting of four levels, as follows:

1. **Unit-level activities.** Activities performed for each unit of production.
2. **Batch-level activities.** Activities performed for each batch of products rather than each unit.
3. **Product-level activities.** Activities performed in support of an entire product line, but not always performed every time a new unit or batch of products is produced.
4. **Facility-level activities.** Activities required to support or sustain an entire production process.

Companies may achieve greater accuracy in overhead cost allocation by recognizing these four different levels of activities and, from them, developing specific

Illustration 4-13
Hierarchy of activity levels

Four Levels	Types of Activities	Examples of Cost Drivers
Unit-Level Activities	Machine-related Drilling, cutting, milling, trimming, pressing	Machine hours
	Labor-related Assembling, painting, sanding, sewing	Direct labor hours or cost
Batch-Level Activities	Equipment setups	Number of setups or setup time
	Purchase ordering	Number of purchase orders
	Inspection	Number of inspections or inspection time
	Material handling	Number of material moves
Product-Level Activities	Product design	Number of product designs
	Engineering changes	Number of changes
Facility-Level Activities	Plant management salaries	Number of employees managed
	Plant depreciation	Square footage
	Property taxes	Square footage
	Utilities	Square footage

activity cost pools and their related cost drivers. Illustration 4-13 graphically displays this four-level activity hierarchy, along with the types of activities and examples of cost drivers for those activities at each level.

This classification provides managers a structured way of thinking about the relationships between activities and the resources they consume. In contrast, traditional volume-based costing recognizes only unit-level costs. **Failure to recognize this classification of activities is one of the reasons that volume-based cost allocation causes distortions in product costing.**

As indicated earlier, allocating all overhead costs by unit-based cost drivers can send false signals to managers: Dividing batch-, product-, or facility-level costs by the number of units produced gives the mistaken impression that these costs vary with the number of units. **The resources consumed by batch-, product-, and facility-level supporting activities do not vary at the unit level,** nor can managers control them at the unit level. The number of activities performed at the batch level goes up as the *number of batches* rises—not as the number of units within the batches changes. Similarly, the number of product-level activities performed depends on the *number of different products*—not on how many units or batches are produced. Furthermore facility-sustaining activity costs are not dependent upon the number of products, batches, or units produced. Companies can control batch-, product-, and facility-level costs only by modifying batch-, product-, and facility-level activities.

Before You Go On...

REVIEW IT

1. What are the benefits of activity-based costing?
2. What are the limitations of activity-based costing?
3. What company factors would indicate ABC as the superior costing system?
4. What is the benefit of classifying activities as value-added and non–value-added?
5. How is the classification of activities into unit-level, batch-level, product-level, and facility-level important to managers?

DO IT

Morgan Toy Company manufactures six primary product lines in its Morganville plant. As a result of an activity analysis, the accounting department has identified eight activity cost pools. Each of the toy products is produced in large batches, with the whole plant devoted to one product at a time. Classify each of the following activities as either unit-level, batch-level, product-level, or facility-level: (a) engineering design, (b) machine setup, (c) inventory management, (d) plant cafeteria, (e) inspections after each setup, (f) polishing parts, (g) assembling parts, (h) health and safety.

Action Plan

- Recall that:
  Unit-level activities are performed for each individual unit of product.
  Batch-level activities are performed each time a batch of a product is produced.
  Product-level activities are performed to support an entire product line.
  Facility-level activities support the production process across the entire range of products.

Solution (a) Product-level, (b) batch-level, (c) product-level, (d) facility-level, (e) batch-level, (f) unit-level, (g) unit-level, (h) facility-level.

Related exercise material: BE4-10, BE4-11, BE4-12, E4-17, and E4-18.

✓ The Navigator

ACTIVITY-BASED COSTING IN SERVICE INDUSTRIES

STUDY OBJECTIVE 8

Apply activity-based costing to service industries.

Although initially developed and implemented by manufacturers, activity-based costing has been widely adopted in service industries as well. ABC has been a useful tool in such diverse industries as airlines, railroads, hotels, hospitals, banks, insurance companies, telephone companies, and financial services firms. The overall objective of ABC in service firms is no different than it is in a manufacturing company. That objective is to identify the key activities that generate costs and to keep track of how many of those activities are performed for each service provided (by job, service, contract, or customer).

The general approach to identifying activities, activity cost pools, and cost drivers is the same for service companies and for manufacturers. Also, the labeling of activities as value-added and non–value-added, and the attempt to reduce or eliminate non–value-added activities as much as possible, is just as valid in service industries as in manufacturing operations. What sometimes makes implementation of activity-based costing difficult in service industries is that **a larger proportion of**

overhead costs are company-wide costs that cannot be directly traced to specific services provided by the company.

To illustrate the application of activity-based costing to a service enterprise, contrasted to traditional costing, we use a public accounting firm. This illustration is equally applicable to a law firm, consulting firm, architect, or any service firm that performs numerous services for a client as part of a job.

Traditional Costing Example

Assume that the public accounting firm of Check and Doublecheck prepares the condensed annual budget shown in Illustration 4-14.

Illustration 4-14
Condensed annual budget of a service firm under traditional costing

CHECK AND DOUBLECHECK, CPAs
Annual Budget

Revenue		$2,000,000
Direct labor	$ 600,000	
Overhead (expected)	1,200,000	
Total costs		1,800,000
Operating income		$ 200,000

$$\frac{\text{Estimated overhead}}{\text{Direct labor cost}} = \text{Predetermined overhead rate}$$

$$\frac{\$1{,}200{,}000}{\$600{,}000} = 200\%$$

Under *traditional costing,* direct labor is the professional service performed, and it is the basis for overhead application to each audit job. To determine the operating income earned on any job, Check and Doublecheck applies overhead at the rate of 200% of actual direct professional labor costs incurred. For example, assume that Check and Doublecheck records $70,000 of actual direct professional labor cost during its audit of Plano Molding Company, which was billed an audit fee of $260,000. Under traditional costing, using 200% as the rate for applying overhead to the job, Check and Doublecheck would compute applied overhead and operating income related to the Plano Molding Company audit as shown in Illustration 4-15.

Illustration 4-15
Overhead applied under traditional costing system

CHECK AND DOUBLECHECK, CPAs
Plano Molding Company Audit

Revenue		$260,000
Less: Direct professional labor	$ 70,000	
Applied overhead (200% × $70,000)	140,000	210,000
Operating income		$ 50,000

This example, under traditional costing, uses only one direct cost item and one overhead application rate.

Activity-Based Costing Example

Under *activity-based costing,* Check and Doublecheck distributes its estimated annual overhead costs of $1,200,000 to several activity cost pools. The firm computes activity-based overhead rates per cost driver by dividing each activity overhead cost pool by the expected number of cost drivers used per activity. Illustration 4-16 shows an annual overhead budget using an ABC system.

Illustration 4-16
Condensed annual budget of a service firm under activity-based costing

CHECK AND DOUBLECHECK, CPAs
Annual Overhead Budget

Activity Cost Pools	Cost Drivers	Estimated Overhead	÷	Expected Use of Cost Drivers per Activity	=	Activity-Based Overhead Rates
Secretarial support	Direct professional hours	$210,000		30,000		$7 per hour
Direct labor fringe benefits	Direct labor cost	240,000		$600,000		$0.40 per $1 labor cost
Printing and photocopying	Working paper pages	20,000		20,000		$1 per page
Computer support	CPU minutes	200,000		50,000		$4 per minute
Telephone and postage	None (Traced directly)	71,000		N/A		Based on usage
Legal support	Hours used	129,000		860		$150 per hour
Insurance (professional liability, etc.)	Revenue billed	120,000		$2,000,000		$0.06 per $1 revenue
Recruiting and training	Direct professional hours	210,000		30,000		$7 per hour
		$1,200,000				

Note that some of the overhead costs can be directly assigned (see telephone and postage).

The assignment of the individual overhead activity rates to the actual number of activities used in the performance of the Plano Molding audit results in total overhead assigned of $165,100 as shown in Illustration 4-17.

Illustration 4-17
Assigning overhead in a service company

Check and Doublecheck CPA.xls

File Edit View Insert Format Tools Data Window Help

Check and Doublecheck, CPAs
Plano Molding Company Audit

	A	B	C	D	E
4	Activity Cost Pools	Cost Drivers	Actual Use of Drivers	Activity-Based Overhead Rates	Cost Assigned
5	Secretarial support	Direct professional hours	3,800	$7.00	$ 26,600
6	Direct labor fringe benefits	Direct labor cost	$70,000	$0.40	28,000
7	Printing and photocopying	Working paper pages	1,800	$1.00	1,800
8	Computer support	CPU minutes	8,600	$4.00	34,400
9	Telephone and postage	None (traced directly)			8,700
10	Legal support	Hours used	156	$150.00	23,400
11	Insurance (professional liability, etc)	Revenue billed	$260,000	$0.06	15,600
12	Recruiting and training	Direct professional hours	3,800	$7.00	26,600
13					$165,100

Under activity-based costing, Check and Doublecheck assigns overhead costs of $165,100 to the Plano Molding Company audit, as compared to $140,000 under traditional costing. Illustration 4-18 compares total costs and operating margins under the two costing systems.

Illustration 4-18
Comparison of traditional costing with ABC in a service company

CHECK AND DOUBLECHECK, CPAs
Plano Molding Company Audit

	Traditional Costing		ABC	
Revenue		$260,000		$260,000
Expenses				
Direct professional labor	$ 70,000		$ 70,000	
Applied overhead	140,000		165,100	
Total expenses		210,000		235,100
Operating income		**$ 50,000**		**$ 24,900**
Profit margin		**19.2%**		**9.6%**

The comparison shows that the assignment of overhead costs under traditional costing is distorted. The total cost assigned to performing the audit of Plano Molding Company is greater under activity-based costing by $25,100, and the profit margin is only half as great. Traditional costing gives the false impression of an operating profit of $50,000. This is more than double the operating income of $24,900 using ABC.

Before You Go On...

REVIEW IT

1. What is the primary barrier to effectively implementing ABC in a service-company environment?
2. What is the main advantage to be gained by using ABC in a service-company environment?

Be sure to read **ALL ABOUT YOU: *Where Does the Time Go?*** on the next page for information on how topics in this chapter apply to you.

Where Does the Time Go?

As discussed in the chapter, the principles underlying activity-based costing have evolved into the broader approach known as activity-based management. As you learned in this chapter, one of the common practices of activity-based management is to identify all business activities, classify each activity as either a value-added or a non–value-added activity, and then try to reduce or eliminate the time spent on non–value-added activities.

Consider the implications of applying this same approach to your everyday life, at work and at school. How do you spend your time each day? How much of your day is spent on activities that help you accomplish your objectives, and how much of your day is spent on activities that do not add value?

Some Facts

* The average worker wastes about 2.1 hours per eight-hour workday. This does not include lunch and scheduled breaks. According to human resources managers, companies assume that employees will waste about one hour per day.
* The top time-wasting activities cited by employees are surfing the Internet, socializing with coworkers, and conducting personal business.
* Older people waste less time at work than younger people. Men and women waste about the same amount of time.
* The average worker earns $19.13 per hour. If, as stated above, the average worker wastes about 1.1 hours more per day than employers expect, then the total lost salary dollars is about $759 billion per year.
* A third (33%) of survey respondents said that they waste time at work because they do not have enough work to do. About a quarter (23%) of respondents said they waste time at work because they are not paid enough.

Source: Dan Malachowski, "Wasted Time at Work Costing Companies Billions," *SFGate.com* (accessed February 24, 2007).

About the Numbers

The information provided in the "Some Facts" section suggests that the average American worker spends a significant portion of the day "wasting" time. How well does the average student fare? A recent survey found that only about 11% of full-time students spend more than 25 hours a week preparing for class (which is about the number of hours that instructors say is needed to do well in college). About 44% of the students in the survey said that they spend less than 10 hours per week. The table below provides additional information from that survey.

How Students Spend Time Each Week (in hours)	First-Year Students		Seniors	
	Part-time	Full-time	Part-time	Full-time
Studying	9	13	10	14
Working on-campus	2	3	3	4
Working off-campus	18	5	20	10
Participating in co-curricular activities	1	5	2	5
Relaxing and socializing	10	12	10	11
Caring for dependents	13	2	12	4
Commuting to class	5	4	5	5

Source: National Survey of Student Engagement—Annual Report 2004, Center for Postsecondary Research, Indiana University, School of Education, Table 2.

What Do You Think?

Many "self-help" books and websites offer suggestions on how to improve your time management. Should you minimize the "non–value-added" hours in your life by adopting the methods suggested by these sources?

YES: There are a limited number of hours in a day. You should try to maximize your chances of achieving your goals by eliminating the time that you waste.

NO: Life is about more than working yourself to death. Being an efficiency expert doesn't guarantee that you will be happy. Schedules and daily planners are too constraining.

The authors' comments on this situation appear on page 195.

Using the Decision Toolkit

Precor Company manufactures a line of high-end exercise equipment of commercial quality. Assume that the chief accountant has proposed changing from a traditional costing system to an activity-based costing system. The financial vice-president is not convinced, so she requests that the next large order for equipment be costed under both systems for purposes of comparison and analysis. An order from Slim-Way Salons, Inc., for 150 low-impact treadmills is received and is identified as the order to be subjected to dual costing. The following cost data relate to the Slim-Way order.

Data relevant to both costing systems

Direct materials	$55,500
Direct labor hours	820
Direct labor rate per hour	$ 18.00

Data relevant to the traditional costing system

Predetermined overhead rate is 300% of direct labor cost.

Data relevant to the activity-based costing system

Activity Cost Pools	Cost Drivers	Activity-Based Overhead Rate	Expected Use of Cost Drivers for Treadmill Order
Engineering design	Engineering hours	$30 per hour	330
Machine setup	Setups	$200 per setup	22
Machining	Machine hours	$25 per hour	732
Assembly	Number of subassemblies	$8 per subassembly	1,500
Packaging and shipping	Packaging/shipping hours	$15 per hour	152
Building occupancy	Machine hours	$6 per hour	732

Instructions

Compute the total cost of the Slim-Way Salons, Inc. order under (a) the traditional costing system and (b) the activity-based costing system. (c) As a result of this comparison, which costing system is Precor likely to adopt? Why?

Solution

(a) Traditional costing system:

Direct materials	$ 55,500
Direct labor (820 × $18)	14,760
Overhead assigned ($14,760 × 300%)	44,280
Total costs assigned to Slim-Way order	$114,540
Number of low-impact treadmills	150
Cost per unit	$763.60

(b) Activity-based costing system:

Direct materials	$ 55,500
Direct labor (820 × $18)	14,760

Overhead activities costs:		
Engineering design (330 hours @ $30)	$ 9,900	
Machine setup (22 setups @ $200)	4,400	
Machining (732 machine hours @ $25)	18,300	
Assembly (1,500 subassemblies @ $8)	12,000	
Packaging and shipping (152 hours @ $15)	2,280	
Building occupancy (732 hours @ $6)	4,392	51,272
Total costs assigned to Slim-Way order		$121,532
Number of low-impact treadmills		150
Cost per unit		$810.21

(c) Precor Company will likely adopt ABC because of the difference in the cost per unit (which ABC found to be higher). More importantly, ABC provides greater insight into the sources and causes of the cost per unit. Managers are given greater insight into which activities to control in order to reduce costs. ABC will provide better product costing and greater profitability for the company.

SUMMARY OF STUDY OBJECTIVES

1 **Recognize the difference between traditional costing and activity-based costing.** A traditional costing system allocates overhead to products on the basis of predetermined plantwide or departmentwide volume of unit-based output rates such as direct labor or machine hours. An ABC system allocates overhead to identified activity cost pools, and then assigns costs to products using related cost drivers that measure the activities (resources) consumed.

2 **Identify the steps in the development of an activity-based costing system.** The development of an activity-based costing system involves four steps: (1) Identify and classify the major activities involved in the manufacture of specific products, and allocate manufacturing overhead costs to the appropriate cost pools. (2) Identify the cost driver that has a strong correlation to the costs accumulated in the cost pool. (3) Compute the overhead rate per cost driver. (4) Assign manufacturing overhead costs for each cost pool to products or services using the overhead rates.

3 **Know how companies identify the activity cost pools used in activity-based costing.** To identify activity cost pools, a company must perform an analysis of each operation or process, documenting and timing every task, action, or transaction.

4 **Know how companies identify and use cost drivers in activity-based costing.** Cost drivers identified for assigning activity cost pools must (a) accurately measure the actual consumption of the activity by the various products and (b) have related data easily available.

5 **Understand the benefits and limitations of activity-based costing.** Features of ABC that make it a more accurate product costing system include: (1) the increased number of cost pools used to assign overhead, (2) the enhanced control over overhead costs, and (3) the better management decisions it makes possible. The limitations of ABC are: (1) the higher analysis and measurement costs that accompany multiple activity centers and cost drivers, and (2) the necessity still to allocate some costs arbitrarily.

6 **Differentiate between value-added and non–value-added activities.** Value-added activities increase the worth of a product or service. Non–value-added activities simply add cost to or increase the time spent on a product or service without increasing its market value. Awareness of these classifications encourages managers to reduce or eliminate the time spent on non–value-added activities.

7 **Understand the value of using activity levels in activity-based costing.** Activities may be classified as unit-level, batch-level, product-level, and facility-level. Companies control overhead costs at unit-, batch-, product-, and facility-levels by modifying unit-, batch-, product-, and facility-level activities, respectively. Failure to recognize this classification of levels can result in distorted product costing.

8 **Apply activity-based costing to service industries.** The overall objective of using ABC in service industries is no different than for manufacturing industries—that is, improved costing of services provided (by job, service, contract, or customer). The general approach to costing is the same: analyze operations, identify activities, accumulate overhead costs by activity cost pools, and identify and use cost drivers to assign the cost pools to the services.

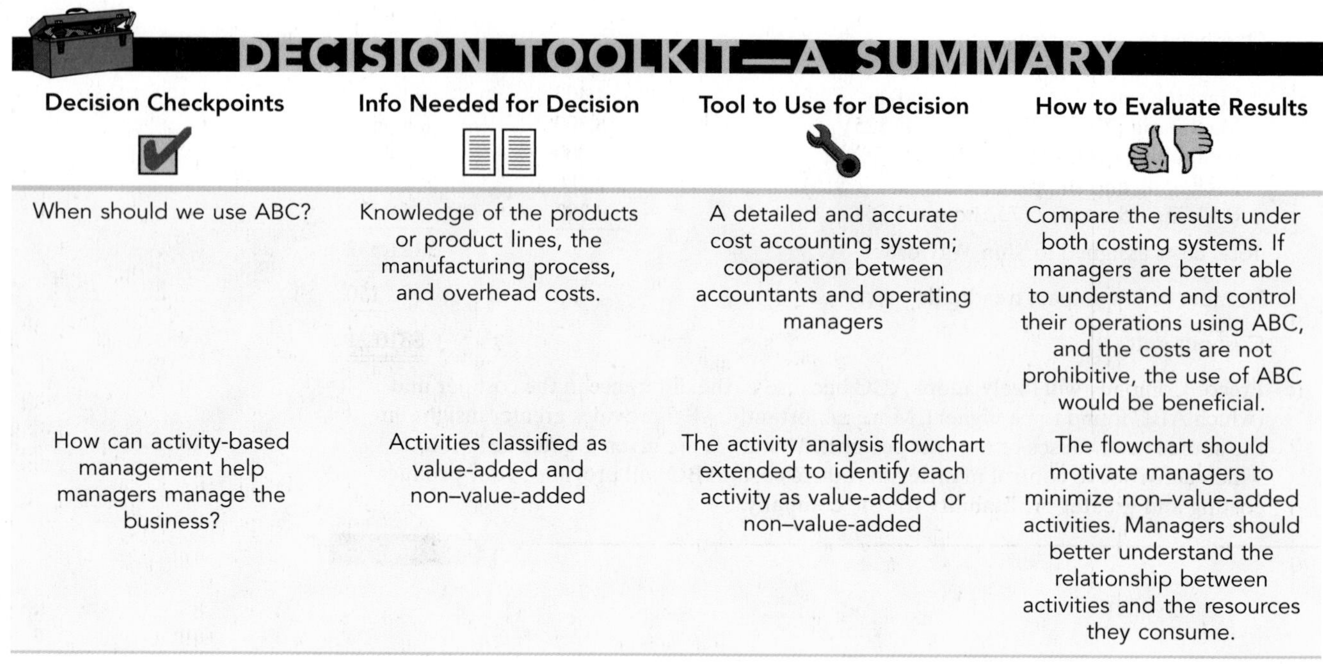

DECISION TOOLKIT—A SUMMARY

Decision Checkpoints	Info Needed for Decision	Tool to Use for Decision	How to Evaluate Results
When should we use ABC?	Knowledge of the products or product lines, the manufacturing process, and overhead costs.	A detailed and accurate cost accounting system; cooperation between accountants and operating managers	Compare the results under both costing systems. If managers are better able to understand and control their operations using ABC, and the costs are not prohibitive, the use of ABC would be beneficial.
How can activity-based management help managers manage the business?	Activities classified as value-added and non–value-added	The activity analysis flowchart extended to identify each activity as value-added or non–value-added	The flowchart should motivate managers to minimize non–value-added activities. Managers should better understand the relationship between activities and the resources they consume.

APPENDIX Just-in-Time Processing

STUDY OBJECTIVE 9

Explain just-in-time (JIT) processing.

Traditionally, continuous process manufacturing has been based on a **just-in-case** philosophy: Inventories of raw materials are maintained *just in case* some items are of poor quality or a key supplier is shut down by a strike. Similarly, subassembly parts are manufactured and stored *just in case* they are needed later in the manufacturing process. Finished goods are completed and stored *just in case* unexpected and rush customer orders are received. This philosophy often results in a **"push approach,"** in which raw materials and subassembly parts are pushed through each process. Traditional processing often results in the buildup of extensive manufacturing inventories.

Primarily in response to foreign competition, many U.S. firms have switched to **just-in-time (JIT) processing**. JIT manufacturing is dedicated to having the right amount of materials, parts, or products just as they are needed. JIT first hit the United States in the early 1980s when automobile companies adopted it to compete with foreign automakers. Many companies, including Dell, Caterpillar, and Harley-Davidson now successfully use JIT. Under JIT processing, companies receive raw materials **just in time** for use in production, they complete subassembly parts **just in time** for use in finished goods, and they complete finished goods **just in time** to be sold. Illustration 4A-1 (next page) shows the sequence of activities in just-in-time processing.

Objective of JIT Processing

A primary objective of JIT is to eliminate all manufacturing inventories. Inventories have an adverse effect on net income because they tie up funds and storage space that could be put to more productive uses. JIT strives to eliminate inventories by using a **"pull approach"** in manufacturing. This approach begins with the customer placing an order with the company, which starts the process of pulling the product through the manufacturing process. A computer at the final work station sends a signal to the preceding work station. This signal indicates the

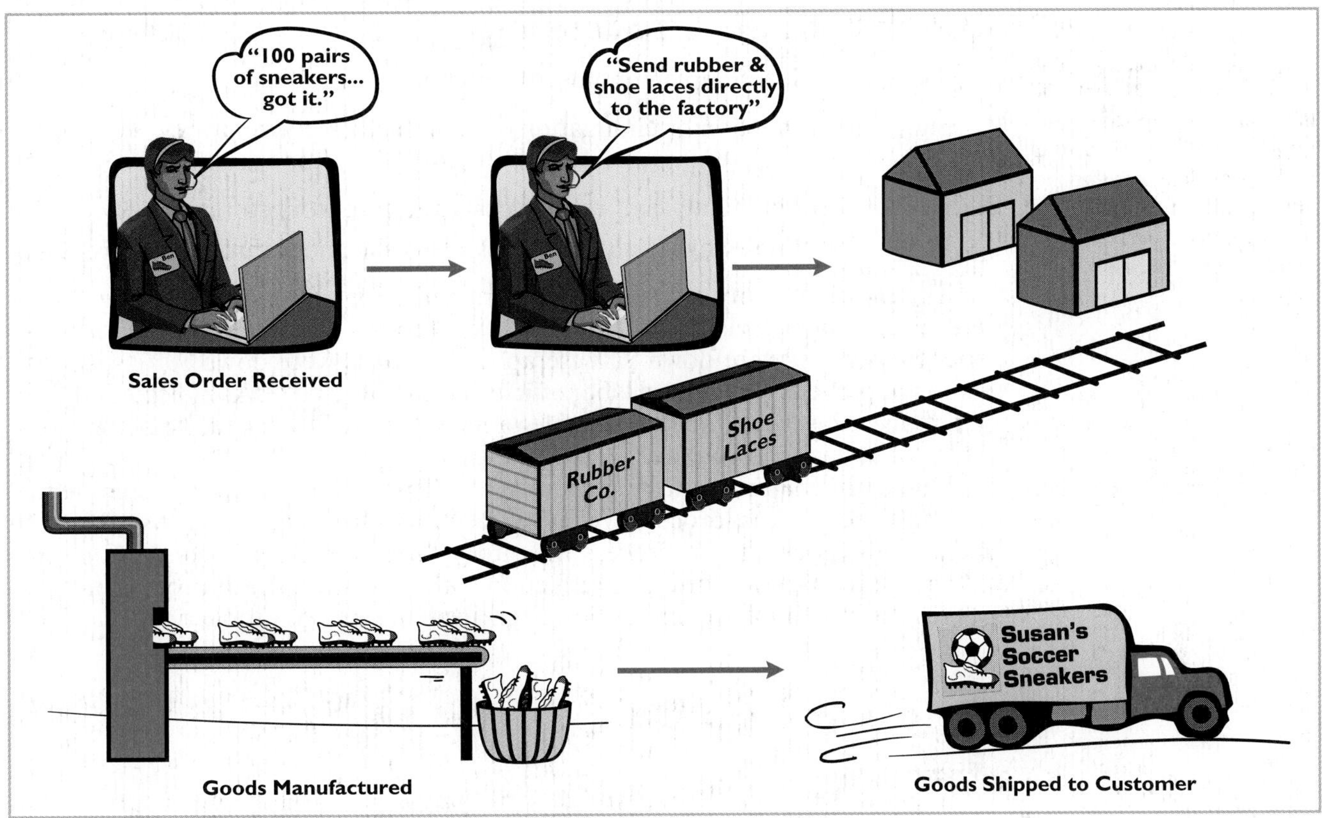

Illustration 4A-1
Just-in-time processing

exact materials (parts and subassemblies) needed to complete the production of a specified product for a specified time period, such as an eight-hour shift. The next-preceding process, in turn, sends its signal to other processes back up the line. The goal is a smooth continuous flow in the manufacturing process, with no buildup of inventories at any point.

Elements of JIT Processing

There are three important elements in JIT processing:

1. **Dependable suppliers.** Suppliers must be willing to deliver on short notice exact quantities of raw materials according to precise quality specifications (even including multiple deliveries within the same day). Suppliers must also be willing to deliver the raw materials at specified work stations rather than at a central receiving department. This type of purchasing requires constant and direct communication. Such communication is facilitated by an online computer linkage between the company and its suppliers.
2. A **multiskilled work force.** Under JIT, machines are often strategically grouped into work cells or work stations. Much of the work is automated. As a result, one worker may operate and maintain several different types of machines.
3. A **total quality control system.** The company must establish total quality control throughout the manufacturing operations. Total quality control means **no defects**. Since the pull approach signals only required quantities, any defects at any work station will shut down operations at subsequent work stations. Total quality control requires continuous monitoring by both line employees and supervisors at each work station.

HELPFUL HINT

Buyer leverage is important in finding dependable suppliers. Companies like GM and GE have more success than smaller companies.

Benefits of JIT Processing

HELPFUL HINT

Without its emphasis on quality control, JIT would be impractical or even impossible. In JIT, quality is engineered into the production process.

The major benefits of implementing JIT processing are:

1. Significant reduction or elimination of manufacturing inventories.
2. Enhanced product quality.
3. Reduction or elimination of rework costs and inventory storage costs.
4. Production cost savings from the improved flow of goods through the processes.

The effects in many cases have been dramatic. For example, after using JIT for two years, a major division of Hewlett-Packard found that work-in-process inventories (in dollars) were down 82%, scrap/rework costs were down 30%, space utilization improved by 40%, and labor efficiency improved 50%. As indicated, JIT not only reduces inventory but also enables a manufacturer to produce a better product faster and with less waste.

One of the major accounting benefits of JIT is the elimination of separate raw materials and work-in-process inventory accounts. These accounts are replaced by **one account,** Raw and In-Process Inventory. All materials and conversion costs are charged to this account. The reduction (or elimination) of in-process inventories results in a simpler computation of equivalent units of production.

Before You Go On...

REVIEW IT

1. What is the difference between the push approach and the pull approach to handling inventories in a manufacturing operation?
2. What are the major benefits of implementing JIT?
3. What are the principal accounting effects of just-in-time processing?

SUMMARY OF STUDY OBJECTIVE FOR APPENDIX

9 **Explain just-in-time (JIT) processing.** JIT is a processing system dedicated to having on hand the right materials and products just at the time they are needed, thereby reducing the amount of inventory and the time inventory is held. One of the principal accounting effects is that one account, Raw and In-Process Inventory, replaces both the raw materials and work-in-process inventory accounts.

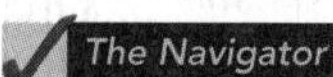

GLOSSARY

Activity Any event, action, transaction, or work sequence that incurs cost when producing a product or providing a service. (p. 149)

Activity-based costing (ABC) An overhead cost-allocation system that allocates overhead to multiple activity cost pools and assigns the activity cost pools to products or services by means of cost drivers that represent the activities used. (p. 149)

Activity-based management (ABM) Extends ABC from product costing to a comprehensive management tool that focuses on reducing costs and improving processes and decision making. (p. 159)

Activity cost pool The overhead cost attributed to a distinct type of activity or related activities. (p. 149)

Batch-level activities Activities performed for each batch of products. (p. 161)

Cost driver Any factor or activity that has a direct cause–effect relationship with the resources consumed. In ABC cost drivers are used to assign activity cost pools to products or services. (p. 149)

Facility-level activities Activities required to support or sustain an entire production process and not dependent on number of products, batches, or units produced. (p. 161)

***Just-in-time (JIT) processing** A processing system dedicated to having the right amount of materials, parts, or products arrive as they are needed, thereby reducing the amount of inventory. (p. 170)

Non–value-added activity An activity that adds cost to or increases the time spent on a product or service without increasing its market value. (p. 160)

Product-level activities Activities performed for and identifiable with an entire product line. (p. 161)

Unit-level activities Activities performed for each unit of production. (p. 161)

Value-added activity An activity that increases the worth of a product or service. (p. 159)

Demonstration Problem

Spreadwell Paint Company manufactures two high-quality base paints: an *oil-based* paint and a *latex* paint. Both are housepaints and are manufactured in neutral white color only. Spreadwell sells the white base paints to franchised retail paint and decorating stores where pigments are added to tint (color) the paint as the customer desires. The oil-based paint is made from, thinned, and cleaned with organic solvents (petroleum products) such as mineral spirits or turpentine. The latex paint is made from, thinned, and cleaned with water; synthetic resin particles are suspended in the water and dry and harden when exposed to the air.

Spreadwell uses the same processing equipment to produce both paints in different production runs. Between batches, the vats and other processing equipment must be washed and cleaned.

After analyzing the company's entire operations, Spreadwell's accountants and production managers have identified activity cost pools and accumulated annual budgeted overhead costs by pool as follows.

Activity Cost Pools	Estimated Overhead
Purchasing	$ 240,000
Processing (weighing and mixing, grinding, thinning and drying, straining)	1,400,000
Packaging (quarts, gallons, and 5-gallons)	580,000
Testing	240,000
Storage and inventory control	180,000
Washing and cleaning equipment	560,000
Total annual budgeted overhead	$3,200,000

Following further analysis, activity cost drivers were identified and their expected use by product and activity were scheduled as follows.

Activity Cost Pools	Cost Drivers	Expected Cost Drivers per Activity	Expected Use of Drivers per Product: Oil-based	Latex
Purchasing	Purchase orders	1,500 orders	800	700
Processing	Gallons processed	1,000,000 gals.	400,000	600,000
Packaging	Containers filled	400,000 containers	180,000	220,000
Testing	Number of tests	4,000 tests	2,100	1,900
Storing	Avg. gals. on hand	18,000 gals.	10,400	7,600
Washing	Number of batches	800 batches	350	450

Spreadwell has budgeted 400,000 gallons of oil-based paint and 600,000 gallons of latex paint for processing during the year.

Instructions

(a) Prepare a schedule showing the computations of the activity-based overhead rates.
(b) Prepare a schedule assigning each activity's overhead cost pool to each product.
(c) Compute the overhead cost per unit for each product.
(d) Classify each activity cost pool as value-added or non–value-added.

action plan

✔ Identify the major activities that pertain to the manufacture of specific products and allocate manufacturing overhead costs to activity cost pools.
✔ Identify the cost drivers that accurately measure each activity's contribution to the finished product.
✔ Compute the activity-based overhead rates.
✔ Assign manufacturing overhead costs for each activity cost pool to products, using the activity-based overhead rates.

Solution

(a) Computations of activity-based overhead rates:

Activity Cost Pools	Estimated Overhead	÷	Expected Use of Cost Drivers	=	Activity-Based Overhead Rates
Purchasing	$ 240,000		1,500 orders		$160 per order
Processing	1,400,000		1,000,000 gallons		$1.40 per gallon
Packaging	580,000		400,000 containers		$1.45 per container
Testing	240,000		4,000 tests		$60 per test
Storing	180,000		18,000 gallons		$10 per gallon
Washing	560,000		800 batches		$700 per batch
	$3,200,000				

(b) Assignment of activity cost pools to products:

	Oil-Based Paint			Latex Paint		
Activity Cost Pools	Expected Use of Drivers	Overhead Rates	Cost Assigned	Expected Use of Drivers	Overhead Rates	Cost Assigned
Purchasing	800	$160	$ 128,000	700	$160	$ 112,000
Processing	400,000	$1.40	560,000	600,000	$1.40	840,000
Packaging	180,000	$1.45	261,000	220,000	$1.45	319,000
Testing	2,100	$60	126,000	1,900	$60	114,000
Storing	10,400	$10	104,000	7,600	$10	76,000
Washing	350	$700	245,000	450	$700	315,000
Total overhead assigned			$1,424,000			$1,776,000

(c) Computation of overhead cost assigned per unit:

	Oil-Based Paint	Latex Paint
Total overhead cost assigned	$1,424,000	$1,776,000
Total gallons produced	400,000	600,000
Overhead cost per gallon	$3.56	$2.96

(d) Value-added activities: processing and packaging.
Non–value-added activities: purchasing, testing, storing, and washing.

Note: All asterisked Questions, Exercises, and Problems relate to material in the appendix to the chapter.

SELF-STUDY QUESTIONS

Answers are at the end of the chapter.

(SO 1) **1.** Activity-based costing (ABC):
a. can be used only in a process cost system.
b. focuses on units of production.
c. focuses on activities performed to produce a product.
d. uses only a single basis of allocation.

(SO 1) **2.** Activity-based costing:
a. is the initial phase of converting to a just-in-time operating environment.
b. can be used only in a job order costing system.
c. is a two-stage overhead cost allocation system that identifies activity cost pools and cost drivers.
d. uses direct labor as its primary cost driver.

3. Any activity that causes resources to be consumed is called a: (SO 1, 4)
a. just-in-time activity.
b. facility-level activity.
c. cost driver.
d. non–value-added activity.

4. The overhead rate for Machine Setups is $100 per setup. Products A and B have 80 and 60 setups, respectively. The overhead assigned to each product is: (SO 4)
a. Product A $8,000, Product B $8,000.
b. Product A $8,000, Product B $6,000.
c. Product A $6,000, Product B $6,000.
d. Product A $6,000, Product B $8,000.

(SO 4) **5.** Donna Crawford Co. has identified an activity cost pool to which it has allocated estimated overhead of $1,920,000. It has determined the expected use of cost drivers for that activity to be 160,000 inspections. Widgets require 40,000 inspections, Gadgets 30,000 inspections, and Targets, 90,000 inspections. The overhead assigned to each product is:

a. Widgets $40,000, Gadgets $30,000, Targets $90,000.
b. Widgets $480,000, Gadgets $360,000, Targets $108,000.
c. Widgets $360,000, Gadgets $480,000, Targets $1,080,000.
d. Widgets $480,000, Gadgets $360,000, Targets $1,080,000.

(SO 6) **6.** An activity that adds costs to the product but does not increase its market value is a:

a. value-added activity.
b. cost driver.
c. cost–benefit activity.
d. non–value-added activity.

(SO 6) **7.** The following activity is value-added:

a. Storage of raw materials.
b. Moving parts from machine to machine.
c. Shaping a piece of metal on a lathe.
d. All of the above.

8. A relevant facility-level cost driver for heating costs is: (SO 7)

a. machine hours.
b. direct material.
c. floor space.
d. direct labor cost.

***9.** Under just-in-time processing: (SO 9)

a. raw materials are received just in time for use in production.
b. subassembly parts are completed just in time for use in assembling finished goods.
c. finished goods are completed just in time to be sold.
d. All of the above.

***10.** The primary objective of just-in-time processing is to: (SO 9)

a. accumulate overhead in activity cost pools.
b. eliminate or reduce all manufacturing inventories.
c. identify relevant activity cost drivers.
d. identify value-added activities.

Go to the book's website, **www.wiley.com/college/weygandt,** for Additional Self-Study questions.

QUESTIONS

1. Under what conditions is direct labor a valid basis for allocating overhead?

2. What has happened in recent industrial history to reduce the usefulness of direct labor as the primary basis for allocating overhead to products?

3. In an automated manufacturing environment, what basis of overhead allocation is frequently more relevant than direct labor hours?

4. What is generally true about overhead allocation to high-volume products versus low-volume products under a traditional costing system?

5. (a) What are the principal differences between activity-based costing (ABC) and traditional product costing?
(b) What assumptions must be met for ABC costing to be useful?

6. What is the formula for computing activity-based overhead rates?

7. What steps are involved in developing an activity-based costing system?

8. Explain the preparation and use of a value-added/non–value-added activity flowchart in an ABC system.

9. What is an activity cost pool?

10. What is a cost driver?

11. What makes a cost driver accurate and appropriate?

12. What is the formula for assigning activity cost pools to products?

13. What are the benefits of activity-based costing?

14. What are the limitations of activity-based costing?

15. Under what conditions is ABC generally the superior overhead costing system?

16. What refinement has been made to enhance the efficiency and effectiveness of ABC for use in managing costs?

17. Of what benefit is classifying activities as value-added and non–value-added?

18. In what ways is the application of ABC to service industries the same as its application to manufacturing companies?

19. What is the relevance of the classification of levels of activity to ABC?

***20. (a)** Describe the philosophy and approach of just-in-time processing.
(b) Identify the major elements of JIT processing.

BRIEF EXERCISES

BE4-1 Infotrac Inc. sells a high-speed retrieval system for mining information. It provides the following information for the year.

Identify differences between costing systems.

(SO 1)

	Budgeted	Actual
Overhead cost	$1,000,000	$950,000
Machine hours	50,000	45,000
Direct labor hours	100,000	90,000

Overhead is applied on the basis of direct labor hours. (a) Compute the predetermined overhead rate. (b) Determine the amount of overhead applied for the year. (c) Explain how an activity-based costing system might differ in terms of computing a predetermined overhead rate.

Identify differences between costing systems.
(SO 1)

BE4-2 Sassafras Inc. has conducted an analysis of overhead costs related to one of its product lines using a traditional costing system (volume-based) and an activity-based costing system. Here are its results.

	Traditional Costing	ABC
Sales revenues	$600,000	$600,000
Overhead costs:		
Product RX3	$ 34,000	$ 50,000
Product Y12	36,000	20,000
	$ 70,000	$ 70,000

Explain how a difference in the overhead costs between the two systems may have occurred.

Identify cost drivers.
(SO 4)

BE4-3 Altex Co. identifies the following activities that pertain to manufacturing overhead: materials handling, machine setups, factory machine maintenance, factory supervision, and quality control. For each activity, identify an appropriate cost driver.

Identify cost drivers.
(SO 4)

BE4-4 Ayala Company manufactures four products in a single production facility. The company uses activity-based costing. The following activities have been identified through the company's activity analysis: (a) inventory control, (b) machine setups, (c) employee training, (d) quality inspections, (e) material ordering, (f) drilling operations, and (g) building maintenance.

For each activity, name a cost driver that might be used to assign overhead costs to products.

Compute activity-based overhead rates.
(SO 4)

BE4-5 Gomez Company identifies three activities in its manufacturing process: machine setups, machining, and inspections. Estimated annual overhead cost for each activity is $180,000, $325,000, and $87,500, respectively. The cost driver for each activity and the expected annual usage are: number of setups 2,500, machine hours 25,000, and number of inspections 1,750. Compute the overhead rate for each activity.

Compute activity-based overhead rates.
(SO 4)

BE4-6 Coats Galore, Inc. uses activity-based costing as the basis for information to set prices for its six lines of seasonal coats. Compute the activity-based overhead rates using the following budgeted data for each of the activity cost pools.

Activity Cost Pools	Estimated Overhead	Expected Use of Cost Drivers per Activity
Designing	$ 450,000	12,000 designer hours
Sizing and cutting	4,000,000	160,000 machine hours
Stitching and trimming	1,440,000	80,000 labor hours
Wrapping and packing	336,000	32,000 finished units

Compute activity-based overhead rates.
(SO 4)

BE4-7 Computer Parts, Inc., a manufacturer of computer chips, employs activity-based costing. The following budgeted data for each of the activity cost pools is provided below for the year 2008.

Activity Cost Pools	Estimated Overhead	Expected Use of Cost Drivers per Activity
Ordering and receiving	$ 90,000	15,000 orders
Etching	480,000	60,000 machine hours
Soldering	1,760,000	440,000 labor hours

For 2008, the company had 11,000 orders and used 50,000 machine hours, and labor hours totaled 500,000. What is the total overhead applied?

Classify activities as value- or non–value-added.
(SO 6)

BE4-8 Jerry Lewis Novelty Company identified the following activities in its production and support operations. Classify each of these activities as either value-added or non–value-added.

(a) Purchasing.
(b) Receiving.
(c) Design engineering.
(d) Storing inventory.
(e) Cost accounting.
(f) Moving work-in-process.
(g) Inspecting and testing.
(h) Painting and packing.

Classify service company activities as value- or non–value-added.
(SO 6, 8)

BE4-9 Rowan and Martin is an architectural firm that is contemplating the installation of activity-based costing. The following activities are performed daily by staff architects. Classify these activities as value-added or non–value-added: (1) designing and drafting, 3 hours; (2) staff meetings, 1 hour; (3) on-site supervision, 2 hours; (4) lunch, 1 hour; (5) consultation with client on specifications, 1.5 hours; (6) entertaining a prospective client for dinner, 2 hours.

Classify activities according to level.

(SO 7, 8)

BE4-10 Quick Pix is a large film developing and processing center that serves 130 outlets in grocery stores, service stations, camera and photo shops, and drug stores in 16 nearby towns. Quick Pix operates 24 hours a day, 6 days a week. Classify each of the following activity costs of Quick Pix as either unit-level, batch-level, product-level, or facility-level.

(a) Developing fluids.
(b) Photocopy paper.
(c) Depreciation of machinery.
(d) Setups for enlargements.
(e) Supervisor's salary.
(f) Ordering materials.
(g) Pickup and delivery.
(h) Commission to dealers.
(i) Insurance on building.
(j) Loading developing machines.

Classify activities according to level.

(SO 7)

BE4-11 Tool Time, Inc. operates 20 injection molding machines in the production of tool boxes of four different sizes, named the Apprentice, the Handyman, the Journeyman, and the Professional. Classify each of the following costs as unit-level, batch-level, product-level, or facility-level.

(a) First-shift supervisor's salary.
(b) Powdered raw plastic.
(c) Dies for casting plastic components.
(d) Depreciation on injection molding machines.
(e) Changing dies on machines.
(f) Moving components to assembly department.
(g) Engineering design.
(h) Employee health and medical insurance coverage.

Compute rates and activity levels.

(SO 4, 7)

BE4-12 Trek Cycle Company uses three activity pools to apply overhead to its products. Each activity has a cost driver used to allocate the overhead costs to the product. The activities and related overhead costs are as follows: Product design \$50,000; Machining \$300,000; and Material handling \$100,000. The cost drivers and expected use are as follows.

Activities	Cost Drivers	Expected Use of Cost Drivers per Activity
Product design	Number of product changes	10
Machining	Machine hours	150,000
Material handling	Number of set ups	100

(a) Compute the predetermined overhead rate for each activity. **(b)** Classify each of these activities as unit-level, batch-level, product-level, or facility-level.

EXERCISES

Assign overhead using traditional costing and ABC.

(SO 1, 4)

E4-1 Elle Inc. has two types of handbags: standard and custom. The controller has decided to use a plantwide overhead rate based on direct labor costs. The president has heard of activity-based costing and wants to see how the results would differ if this system were used. Two activity cost pools were developed: machining and machine setup. Presented below is information related to the company's operations.

	Standard	Custom
Direct labor costs	\$50,000	\$100,000
Machine hours	1,000	1,000
Setup hours	100	400

Total estimated overhead costs are \$300,000. Overhead cost allocated to the machining activity cost pool is \$200,000, and \$100,000 is allocated to the machine setup activity cost pool.

Instructions

(a) Compute the overhead rate using the traditional (plantwide) approach.
(b) Compute the overhead rates using the activity-based costing approach.
(c) Determine the difference in allocation between the two approaches.

Explain difference between traditional and activity-based costing.

(SO 1)

E4-2 Perdon Inc. has conducted the following analysis related to its product lines, using a traditional costing system (volume-based) and an activity-based costing system. Both the traditional and the activity-based costing systems include direct materials and direct labor costs.

		Total Costs	
Products	**Sales Revenue**	**Traditional**	**ABC**
Product 540X	$200,000	$55,000	$50,000
Product 137Y	160,000	50,000	35,000
Product 249S	80,000	15,000	35,000

Instructions

(a) For each product line, compute operating income using the traditional costing system.
(b) For each product line, compute operating income using the activity-based costing system.
(c) Using the following formula, compute the percentage difference in operating income for each of the product lines of Perdon: [Operating Income (ABC) − Operating Income (traditional cost)] ÷ Operating Income (traditional cost). (Round the percentage to two decimals.)
(d) Provide a rationale as to why the costs for Product 540X are approximately the same using either the traditional or activity-based costing system.

Assign overhead using traditional costing and ABC.

(SO 1, 4)

E4-3 International Fabrics has budgeted overhead costs of $900,000. It has allocated overhead on a plantwide basis to its two products (wool and cotton) using direct labor hours which are estimated to be 450,000 for the current year. The company has decided to experiment with activity-based costing and has created two activity cost pools and related activity cost drivers. These two cost pools are: Cutting (cost driver is machine hours) and Design (cost driver is number of setups). Overhead allocated to the Cutting cost pool is $300,000 and $600,000 is allocated to the Design cost pool. Additional information related to these pools is as follows.

	Wool	**Cotton**	**Total**
Machine hours	100,000	100,000	200,000
Number of setups	1,000	500	1,500

Instructions

(a) Determine the amount of overhead allocated to the wool product line and the cotton product line using activity-based costing.
(b) What is the difference between the allocation of overhead to the wool and cotton product lines using activity-based costing versus the traditional approach, assuming direct labor hours were incurred evenly between the wool and cotton?

Assign overhead using traditional costing and ABC.

(SO 1, 4)

E4-4 Alonzo Inc. manufactures two products: car wheels and truck wheels. To determine the amount of overhead to assign to each product line, the controller, YuYu Ortega, has developed the following information.

	Car	**Truck**
Estimated wheels produced	40,000	10,000
Direct labor hours per wheel	1	3

Total estimated overhead costs for the two product lines are $700,000.

Instructions

(a) Compute the overhead cost assigned to the car wheels and truck wheels, assuming that direct labor hours is used to allocate overhead costs.
(b) Ortega is not satisfied with the traditional method of allocating overhead because he believes that most of the overhead costs relate to the truck wheel product line because of its complexity. He therefore develops the following three activity cost pools and related cost drivers to better understand these costs.

Activity Cost Pools	**Expected Use of Cost Drivers**	**Estimated Overhead Costs**
Setting up machines	1,000 setups	$180,000
Assembling	70,000 labor hours	280,000
Inspection	1,200 inspections	240,000

Compute the activity-based overhead rates for these three cost pools.

(c) Compute the cost that is assigned to the car wheels and truck product lines using an activity-based costing system, given the following information.

Expected Use of Cost Drivers per Product		
	Car	**Truck**
Number of setups	200	800
Direct labor hours	40,000	30,000
Number of inspections	100	1,100

(d) What do you believe Ortega should do?

Assign overhead using traditional costing and ABC.

(SO 1, 4)

E4-5 Shady Lady sells window coverings to both commercial and residential customers. The following information relates to its budgeted operations for the current year.

		Commercial		**Residential**
Revenues		$300,000		$480,000
Direct material costs	$ 30,000		$ 50,000	
Direct labor costs	100,000		300,000	
Overhead costs	50,000	180,000	150,000	500,000
Operating income (loss)		$120,000		($ 20,000)

The controller, Wanda Lewis, is concerned about the residential product line. She cannot understand why this line is not more profitable given that the installations of window coverings are less complex to install for residential customers. In addition, the residential client base resides in close proximity to the company office, so travel costs are not as expensive on a per client visit for residential customers. As a result, she has decided to take a closer look at the overhead costs assigned to the two product lines to determine whether a more accurate product costing model can be developed. Here are the three activity cost pools and related information she developed:

Activity Cost Pools	**Estimated Overhead**	**Cost Drivers**
Scheduling and travel	$90,000	Hours of travel
Setup time	70,000	Number of setups
Supervision	40,000	Direct labor cost

Expected Use of Cost Drivers per Product		
	Commercial	**Residential**
Scheduling and travel	1,000	500
Setup time	450	250

Instructions

(a) Compute the activity-based overhead rates for each of the three cost pools, and determine the overhead cost assigned to each product line.

(b) Compute the operating income for the each product line, using the activity-based overhead rates.

(c) What do you believe Wanda Lewis should do?

Assign overhead using traditional costing and ABC.

(SO 1, 4)

E4-6 Wilkins Corporation manufactures safes—large mobile safes, and large walk-in stationary bank safes. As part of its annual budgeting process, Wilkins is analyzing the profitability of its two products. Part of this analysis involves estimating the amount of overhead to be allocated to each product line. The following information relates to overhead.

	Mobile Safes	**Walk-in Safes**
Units planned for production	200	50
Material moves per product line	300	200
Purchase orders per product line	450	350
Direct labor hours per product line	800	1,700

Instructions

(a) The total estimated manufacturing overhead was $235,000. Under traditional costing (which assigns overhead on the basis of direct-labor hours), what amount of manufacturing overhead costs are assigned to:

(1) One mobile safe?

(2) One walk-in safe?

(b) The total estimated manufacturing overhead of $235,000 was comprised of $150,000 for material-handling costs and $85,000 for purchasing activity costs. Under activity-based costing (ABC):

(1) What amount of material handling costs are assigned to:

(a) One mobile safe?

(b) One walk-in safe?

(2) What amount of purchasing activity costs are assigned to:

(a) One mobile safe?

(b) One walk-in safe?

(c) Compare the amount of overhead allocated to one mobile safe and to one walk-in safe under the traditional costing approach versus under ABC.

Identify activity cost pools.
(SO 3)

E4-7 Quik Prints Company is a small printing and copying firm with three high-speed offset printing presses, five copiers (two color and three black and white), one collator, one cutting and folding machine, and one fax machine. To improve its pricing practices, owner-manager Damon Hastings is installing activity-based accounting. Additionally, Damon employs five employees: two printers/designers, one receptionist/bookkeeper, one sales person/copy-machine operator, and one janitor/delivery clerk. Damon can operate any of the machines and, in addition to managing the entire operation, he performs the training, designing, selling, and marketing functions.

Instructions

As Quik Prints' independent accountant who prepares tax forms and quarterly financial statements, you have been asked to identify the activities that would be used to accumulate overhead costs for assignment to jobs and customers. Using your knowledge of a small printing and copying firm (and some imagination), identify at least twelve activity cost pools as the start of an activity-based costing system for Quik Prints Company.

Identify activity cost pools and cost drivers.
(SO 3, 4)

E4-8 Galavic Corporation manufactures snowmobiles in its Blue Mountain, Wisconsin plant. The following costs are budgeted for the first quarter's operations.

Machine setup, indirect materials	$ 4,000
Inspections	16,000
Tests	4,000
Insurance, plant	110,000
Engineering design	140,000
Depreciation, machinery	520,000
Machine setup, indirect labor	20,000
Property taxes	29,000
Oil, heating	19,000
Electricity, plant lighting	21,000
Engineering prototypes	60,000
Depreciation, plant	210,000
Electricity, machinery	36,000
Custodial (machine maintenance) wages	19,000

Instructions

Classify the above costs of Galavic Corporation into activity cost pools using the following: engineering, machinery, machine setup, quality control, factory utilities, maintenance. Next, identify a cost driver that may be used to assign each cost pool to each line of snowmobiles.

Identify activity cost drivers.
(SO 4)

E4-9 Peter Catalano's Verde Vineyards in Oakville, California produces three varieties of wine: Merlot, Viognier, and Pinot Noir. His winemaster, Kyle Ward, has identified the following activities as cost pools for accumulating overhead and assigning it to products.

1. Culling and replanting. Dead or overcrowded vines are culled, and new vines are planted or relocated. (Separate vineyards by variety.)
2. Tying. The posts and wires are reset, and vines are tied to the wires for the dormant season.
3. Trimming. At the end of the harvest the vines are cut and trimmed back in preparation for the next season.
4. Spraying. The vines are sprayed with chemicals for protection against insects and fungi.
5. Harvesting. The grapes are hand-picked, placed in carts, and transported to the crushers.
6. Stemming and crushing. Cartfuls of bunches of grapes of each variety are separately loaded into machines which remove stems and gently crush the grapes.

7. Pressing and filtering. The crushed grapes are transferred to presses which mechanically remove the juices and filter out bulk and impurities.
8. Fermentation. The grape juice, by variety, is fermented in either stainless-steel tanks or oak barrels.
9. Aging. The wines are aged in either stainless-steel tanks or oak barrels for one to three years depending on variety.
10. Bottling and corking. Bottles are machine-filled and corked.
11. Labeling and boxing. Each bottle is labeled, as is each nine-bottle case, with the name of the vintner, vintage, and variety.
12. Storing. Packaged and boxed bottles are stored awaiting shipment.
13. Shipping. The wine is shipped to distributors and private retailers.
14. Heating and air-conditioning of plant and offices.
15. Maintenance of buildings and equipment. Printing, repairs, replacements, and general maintenance are performed in the off-season.

Instructions
For each of Verde's fifteen activity cost pools, identify a probable cost driver that might be used to assign overhead costs to its three wine varieties.

Identify activity cost drivers.
(SO 4)

E4-10 Anna Bellatorre, Inc. manufactures five models of kitchen appliances at its Mesa plant. The company is installing activity-based costing and has identified the following activities performed at its Mesa plant.

1. Designing new models.
2. Purchasing raw materials and parts.
3. Storing and managing inventory.
4. Receiving and inspecting raw materials and parts.
5. Interviewing and hiring new personnel.
6. Machine forming sheet steel into appliance parts.
7. Manually assembling parts into appliances.
8. Training all employees of the company.
9. Insuring all tangible fixed assets.
10. Supervising production.
11. Maintaining and repairing machinery and equipment.
12. Painting and packaging finished appliances.

Having analyzed its Mesa plant operations for purposes of installing activity-based costing, Anna Bellatorre, Inc. identified its activity cost centers. It now needs to identify relevant activity cost drivers in order to assign overhead costs to its products.

Instructions
Using the activities listed above, identify for each activity one or more cost drivers that might be used to assign overhead to Anna Bellatorre's five products.

Compute overhead rates and assign overhead using ABC.
(SO 4, 5)

E4-11 Fontillas Instrument, Inc. manufactures two products: missile range instruments and space pressure gauges. During April, 50 range instruments and 300 pressure gauges were produced, and overhead costs of $89,500 were estimated. An analysis of estimated overhead costs reveals the following activities.

Activities	Cost Drivers	Total Cost
1. Materials handling	Number of requisitions	$35,000
2. Machine setups	Number of setups	27,500
3. Quality inspections	Number of inspections	27,000
		$89,500

The cost driver volume for each product was as follows.

Cost Drivers	Instruments	Gauges	Total
Number of requisitions	400	600	1,000
Number of setups	200	300	500
Number of inspections	200	400	600

Instructions

(a) Determine the overhead rate for each activity.

(b) Assign the manufacturing overhead costs for April to the two products using activity-based costing.

(c) Write a memorandum to the president of Fontillas Instrument explaining the benefits of activity-based costing.

Assign overhead using traditional costing and ABC; classify activities as value- or non–value-added.

(SO 1, 4, 6)

E4-12 Lim Clothing Company manufactures its own designed and labeled sports attire and sells its products through catalog sales and retail outlets. While Lim has for years used activity-based costing in its manufacturing activities, it has always used traditional costing in assigning its selling costs to its product lines. Selling costs have traditionally been assigned to Lim's product lines at a rate of 70% of direct material costs. Its direct material costs for the month of March for Lim's "high intensity" line of attire are $400,000. The company has decided to extend activity-based costing to its selling costs. Data relating to the "high intensity" line of products for the month of March are as follows.

Activity Cost Pools	Cost Drivers	Overhead Rate	Number of Cost Drivers Used per Activity
Sales commissions	Dollar sales	$0.05 per dollar sales	$930,000
Advertising—TV/Radio	Minutes	$300 per minute	250
Advertising—Newspaper	Column inches	$10 per column inch	2,000
Catalogs	Catalogs mailed	$2.50 per catalog	60,000
Cost of catalog sales	Catalog orders	$1 per catalog order	9,000
Credit and collection	Dollar sales	$0.03 per dollar sales	$930,000

Instructions

(a) Compute the selling costs to be assigned to the "high-intensity" line of attire for the month of March: (1) using the traditional product costing system (direct material cost is the cost driver), and (2) using activity-based costing.

(b) By what amount does the traditional product costing system undercost or overcost the "high-intensity" product line?

(c) Classify each of the activities as value-added or non–value-added.

Assign overhead using traditional costing and ABC; classify activities as value- or non–value-added.

(SO 1, 4, 6)

E4-13 Healthy Products, Inc., uses a traditional product costing system to assign overhead costs uniformly to all products. To meet Food and Drug Administration requirements and to assure its customers of safe, sanitary, and nutritious food, Healthy engages in a high level of quality control. Healthy assigns its quality-control overhead costs to all products at a rate of 17% of direct-labor costs. Its direct-labor cost for the month of June for its low-calorie dessert line is $55,000. In response to repeated requests from its financial vice president, Healthy's management agrees to adopt activity-based costing. Data relating to the low-calorie dessert line for the month of June are as follows.

Activity Cost Pools	Cost Drivers	Overhead Rate	Number of Cost Drivers Used per Activity
Inspections of material received	Number of pounds	$0.60 per pound	6,000 pounds
In-process inspections	Number of servings	$0.33 per serving	10,000 servings
FDA certification	Customer orders	$12.00 per order	420 orders

Instructions

(a) Compute the quality-control overhead cost to be assigned to the low-calorie dessert product line for the month of June: (1) using the traditional product costing system (direct labor cost is the cost driver), and (2) using activity-based costing.

(b) By what amount does the traditional product costing system undercost or overcost the low-calorie dessert line?

(c) Classify each of the activities as value-added or non–value-added.

Classify activities as value-added or non–value-added.

(SO 6)

E4-14 In an effort to expand the usefulness of its activity-based costing system, Peter Catalano's Verde Vineyards decides to adopt activity-based management techniques. One of these ABM techniques is classifying its activities as either value-added or non–value-added.

Instructions
Using Verde's list of fifteen activity cost pools in Exercise 4-9, classify each of the activities as either value-added or non–value-added.

E4-15 Anna Bellatorre, Inc. is interested in using its activity-based costing system to improve its operating efficiency and its profit margins by applying activity-based management techniques. As part of this undertaking, you have been asked to classify its Mesa plant activities as value-added or non–value-added.

Classify activities as value-added or non–value-added.
(SO 6)

Instructions
Using the list of activities identified in Exercise 4-10, classify each activity as either value-added or non–value-added.

E4-16 Dewey and Cheatam is a law firm that is initiating an activity-based costing system. Jim Dewey, the senior partner and strong supporter of ABC, has prepared the following list of activities performed by a typical attorney in a day at the firm.

Classify service company activities as value-added or non–value-added.
(SO 6, 8)

Activities	Hours
Writing contracts and letters	1.0
Attending staff meetings	0.5
Taking depositions	1.0
Doing research	1.0
Traveling to/from court	1.0
Contemplating legal strategy	1.0
Eating lunch	1.0
Litigating a case in court	2.5
Entertaining a prospective client	2.0

Instructions
Classify each of the activities listed by Jim Dewey as value-added or non–value-added and defend your classification. How much was value-added time and how much was non–value-added?

E4-17 Having itemized its costs for the first quarter of next year's budget, Galavic Corporation desires to install an activity-based costing system. First it identified the activity cost pools in which to accumulate factory overhead; second, it identified the relevant cost drivers. (This was done in Exercise 4-8.)

Classify activities by level.
(SO 7)

Instructions
Using the activity cost pools identified in Exercise 4-8, classify each of those cost pools as either unit-level, batch-level, product-level, or facility-level.

E4-18 Otto Dieffenbach & Sons, Inc. is a small manufacturing company in La Jolla that uses activity-based costing. Dieffenbach & Sons accumulates overhead in the following activity cost pools.

Classify activities by level.
(SO 7)

1. Hiring personnel.
2. Managing parts inventory.
3. Purchasing.
4. Testing prototypes.
5. Designing products.
6. Setting up equipment.
7. Training employees.
8. Inspecting machined parts.
9. Machining.
10. Assembling.

Instructions
For each activity cost pool, indicate whether the activity cost pool would be unit-level, batch-level, product-level, or facility-level.

Visit the book's website at **www.wiley.com/college/weygandt**, and choose the Student Companion site, to access Exercise Set B.

PROBLEMS: SET A

Assign overhead using traditional costing and ABC; compute unit costs; classify activities as value- or non–value-added.

(SO 1, 4, 6)

P4-1A FireOut, Inc. manufactures steel cylinders and nozzles for two models of fire extinguishers: (1) a home fire extinguisher and (2) a commercial fire extinguisher. The *home model* is a high-volume (54,000 units), half-gallon cylinder that holds 2 1/2 pounds of multipurpose dry chemical at 480 PSI. The *commercial model* is a low-volume (10,200 units), two-gallon cylinder that holds 10 pounds of multi-purpose dry chemical at 390 PSI. Both produts require 1.5 hours of direct labor for completion. Therefore, total annual direct labor hours are 96,300 or [1.5 hrs. × (54,000 + 10,200)]. Expected annual manufacturing overhead is $1,502,280. Thus, the predetermined overhead rate is $15.60 or ($1,502,280 ÷ 96,300) per direct labor hour. The direct materials cost per unit is $18.50 for the home model and $26.50 for the commercial model. The direct labor cost is $19 per unit for both the home and the commercial models.

The company's managers identified six activity cost pools and related cost drivers and accumulated overhead by cost pool as follows.

Activity Cost Pools	Cost Drivers	Estimated Overhead	Expected Use of Cost Drivers	Expected Use of Drivers by Product: Home	Commercial
Receiving	Pounds	$ 70,350	335,000	215,000	120,000
Forming	Machine hours	150,500	35,000	27,000	8,000
Assembling	Number of parts	390,600	217,000	165,000	52,000
Testing	Number of tests	51,000	25,500	15,500	10,000
Painting	Gallons	52,580	5,258	3,680	1,578
Packing and shipping	Pounds	787,250	335,000	215,000	120,000
		$1,502,280			

Instructions

(a) Unit cost—H.M. $60.90

(c) Cost assigned—H.M $1,031,300

(d) Cost/unit—H.M. $56.60

(a) Under traditional product costing, compute the total unit cost of each product. Prepare a simple comparative schedule of the individual costs by product (similar to Illustration 4-4).

(b) Under ABC, prepare a schedule showing the computations of the activity-based overhead rates (per cost driver).

(c) Prepare a schedule assigning each activity's overhead cost pool to each product based on the use of cost drivers. (Include a computation of overhead cost per unit, rounding to the nearest cent.)

(d) Compute the total cost per unit for each product under ABC.

(e) Classify each of the activities as a value-added activity or a non–value-added activity.

(f) Comment on (1) the comparative overhead cost per unit for the two products under ABC, and (2) the comparative total costs per unit under traditional costing and ABC.

Assign overhead to products using ABC and evaluate decision.

(SO 4)

P4-2A Jacobson Electronics manufactures two large-screen television models: the Royale which sells for $1,600, and a new model, the Majestic, which sells for $1,300. The production cost computed per unit under traditional costing for each model in 2008 was as follows.

Traditional Costing	Royale	Majestic
Direct materials	$ 700	$420
Direct labor ($20 per hour)	120	100
Manufacturing overhead ($38 per DLH)	228	190
Total per unit cost	$1,048	$710

In 2008, Jacobson manufactured 25,000 units of the Royale and 10,000 units of the Majestic. The overhead rate of $38 per direct labor hour was determined by dividing total expected manufacturing overhead of $7,600,000 by the total direct labor hours (200,000) for the two models.

Under traditional costing, the gross profit on the models was: Royale $552 or ($1,600 − $1,048), and Majestic $590 or ($1,300 − $710). Because of this difference, management is considering phasing out the Royale model and increasing the production of the Majestic model.

Before finalizing its decision, management asks Jacobson's controller to prepare an analysis using activity-based costing (ABC). The controller accumulates the following information about overhead for the year ended December 31, 2008.

Activities	Cost Drivers	Estimated Overhead	Expected Use of Cost Drivers	Activity-Based Overhead Rate
Purchasing	Number of orders	$1,200,000	40,000	$30/order
Machine setups	Number of setups	900,000	18,000	50/setup
Machining	Machine hours	4,800,000	120,000	40/hour
Quality control	Number of inspections	700,000	28,000	25/inspection

The cost drivers used for each product were:

Cost Drivers	Royale	Majestic	Total
Purchase orders	15,000	25,000	40,000
Machine setups	5,000	13,000	18,000
Machine hours	75,000	45,000	120,000
Inspections	9,000	19,000	28,000

Instructions

(a) Assign the total 2008 manufacturing overhead costs to the two products using activity-based costing (ABC).

(a) Royale $3,925,000

(b) What was the cost per unit and gross profit of each model using ABC costing?

(b) Cost/unit—Royale $977

(c) Are management's future plans for the two models sound? Explain.

Assign overhead costs using traditional costing and ABC; compare results.

(SO 1, 4)

P4-3A Stellar Stairs Co. of Poway designs and builds factory-made premium wooden stairs for homes. The manufactured stair components (spindles, risers, hangers, hand rails) permit installation of stairs of varying lengths and widths. All are of white oak wood. Its budgeted manufacturing overhead costs for the year 2009 are as follows.

Overhead Cost Pools	Amount
Purchasing	$ 57,000
Handling materials	82,000
Production (cutting, milling, finishing)	210,000
Setting up machines	85,000
Inspecting	90,000
Inventory control (raw materials and finished goods)	126,000
Utilities	180,000
Total budget overhead costs	$830,000

For the last 4 years, Stellar Stairs Co. has been charging overhead to products on the basis of machine hours. For the year 2009, 100,000 machine hours are budgeted.

Heather Fujar, owner-manager of Stellar Stairs Co., recently directed her accountant, Lindsay Baker, to implement the activity-based costing system that she has repeatedly proposed. At Heather Fujar's request, Lindsay and the production foreman identify the following cost drivers and their usage for the previously budgeted overhead cost pools.

Activity Cost Pools	Cost Drivers	Expected Use of Cost Drivers
Purchasing	Number of orders	600
Handling materials	Number of moves	8,000
Production (cutting, milling, finishing)	Direct labor hours	100,000
Setting up machines	Number of setups	1,250
Inspecting	Number of inspections	6,000
Inventory control (raw materials and finished goods)	Number of components	168,000
Utilities	Square feet occupied	90,000

Jason Dion, sales manager, has received an order for 280 stairs from Community Builders, Inc., a large housing development contractor. At Jason's request, Lindsay prepares cost estimates for producing components for 280 stairs so Jason can submit a contract price per stair to Community Builders. She accumulates the following data for the production of 280 stairways.

Direct materials	$103,600
Direct labor	$112,000
Machine hours	14,500
Direct labor hours	5,000
Number of purchase orders	60
Number of material moves	800
Number of machine setups	100
Number of inspections	450
Number of components	16,000
Number of square feet occupied	8,000

Instructions

(a) Compute the predetermined overhead rate using traditional costing with machine hours as the basis.

(b) Cost/stair $1,199.82

(b) What is the manufacturing cost per stairway under traditional costing? (Round to the nearest cent.)

(c) Cost/stair $1,055.54

(c) What is the manufacturing cost per stairway under the proposed activity-based costing? (Round to the nearest cent. Prepare all of the necessary schedules.)

(d) Which of the two costing systems is preferable in pricing decisions and why?

Assign overhead costs using traditional costing and ABC; compare results.

(SO 1, 4)

P4-4A Mendocino Corporation produces two grades of wine from grapes that it buys from California growers. It produces and sells roughly 3,000,000 liters per year of a low-cost, high-volume product called CoolDay. It sells this in 600,000 5-liter jugs. Mendocino also produces and sells roughly 300,000 liters per year of a low-volume, high-cost product called LiteMist. LiteMist is sold in 1-liter bottles. Based on recent data, the CoolDay product has not been as profitable as LiteMist. Management is considering dropping the inexpensive CoolDay line so it can focus more attention on the LiteMist product. The LiteMist product already demands considerably more attention than the CoolDay line.

Tyler Silva, president and founder of Mendocino, is skeptical about this idea. He points out that for many decades the company produced only the CoolDay line, and that it was always quite profitable. It wasn't until the company started producing the more complicated LiteMist wine that the profitability of CoolDay declined. Prior to the introduction of LiteMist, the company had simple equipment, simple growing and production procedures, and virtually no need for quality control. Because LiteMist is bottled in 1-liter bottles, it requires considerably more time and effort, both to bottle and to label and box than does CoolDay. The company must bottle and handle 5 times as many bottles of LiteMist to sell the same quantity as CoolDay. CoolDay requires 1 month of aging; LiteMist requires 1 year. CoolDay requires cleaning and inspection of equipment every 10,000 liters; LiteMist requires such maintenance every 600 liters.

Tyler has asked the accounting department to prepare an analysis of the cost per liter using the traditional costing approach and using activity-based costing. The following information was collected.

	CoolDay	LiteMist
Direct materials per liter	$0.40	$1.20
Direct labor cost per liter	$0.25	$0.50
Direct labor hours per liter	0.05	0.09
Total direct labor hours	150,000	27,000

Activity Cost Pools	Cost Drivers	Estimated Overhead	Expected Use of Cost Drivers	Expected Use of Cost Drivers per Product CoolDay	LiteMist
Grape processing	Cart of grapes	$ 145,860	6,600	6,000	600
Aging	Total months	396,000	6,600,000	3,000,000	3,600,000
Bottling and corking	Number of bottles	270,000	900,000	600,000	300,000
Labeling and boxing	Number of bottles	189,000	900,000	600,000	300,000
Maintain and inspect equipment	Number of inspections	240,800	800	350	450
		$1,241,660			

Instructions

Answer each of the following questions. (Round all calculations to three decimal places.)

(a) Under traditional product costing using direct labor hours, compute the total manufacturing cost per **liter** of both products.

(a) Cost/liter—C.D. $1.001

(b) Under ABC, prepare a schedule showing the computation of the activity-based overhead rates (per cost driver).

(c) Prepare a schedule assigning each activity's overhead cost pool to each product, based on the use of cost drivers. Include a computation of overhead cost per liter.

(c) Cost/liter—C.D. $.241

(d) Compute the total manufacturing cost per liter for both products under ABC.

(e) Write a memo to Tyler Silva discussing the implications of your analysis for the company's plans. In this memo provide a brief description of ABC, as well as an explanation of how the traditional approach can result in distortions.

P4-5A Hy and Lowe is a public accounting firm that offers two primary services, auditing and tax return preparation. A controversy has developed between the partners of the two service lines as to who is contributing the greater amount to the bottom line. The area of contention is the assignment of overhead. The tax partners argue for assigning overhead on the basis of 40% of direct labor dollars, while the audit partners argue for implementing activity-based costing. The partners agree to use next year's budgeted data for purposes of analysis and comparison. The following overhead data are collected to develop the comparison.

Assign overhead costs to services using traditional costing and ABC; compute overhead rates and unit costs; compare results.

(SO 1, 4, 6, 8)

Activity Cost Pools	Cost Drivers	Estimated Overhead	Expected Use of Cost Drivers	Expected Use of Cost Drivers per Service Audit	Tax
Employee training	Direct labor dollars	$216,000	$1,800,000	$1,000,000	$800,000
Typing and secretarial	Number of reports/ forms	76,200	2,500	600	1,900
Computing	Number of minutes	204,000	60,000	25,000	35,000
Facility rental	Number of employees	142,500	40	22	18
Travel	Per expense reports	81,300	Direct	56,000	25,300
		$720,000			

Instructions

(a) Using traditional product costing as proposed by the tax partners, compute the total overhead cost assigned to both services (audit and tax) of Hy and Lowe.

(b) (1) Using activity-based costing, prepare a schedule showing the computations of the activity-based overhead rates (per cost driver).

(2) Prepare a schedule assigning each activity's overhead cost pool to each service based on the use of the cost drivers.

(b) (2) Cost assigned—Tax $362,337

(c) Classify each of the activities as a value-added activity or a non-value-added activity.

(d) Comment on the comparative overhead cost for the two services under both traditional costing and ABC.

(d) Difference—Audit $42,337

PROBLEMS: SET B

Assign overhead using traditional costing and ABC; compute unit costs; classify activities as value- or non–value-added.

(SO 1, 4, 6)

P4-1B Waves Galore, Inc. manufactures hair curlers and blow-dryers. The handheld hair curler is Waves Galore's high volume product (80,000 units annually). It is a "large barrel," 20-watt, triple-heat appliance designed to appeal to the teenage market segment with its glow-in-the-dark handle. The handheld blow-dryer is Waves Galore's lower-volume product (40,000 units annually). It is a three-speed, 2,000 watt appliance with a "cool setting" and a removable filter. It also is designed for the teen market.

Both products require one hour of direct labor for completion. Therefore, total annual direct labor hours are 120,000, (80,000 + 40,000). Expected annual manufacturing overhead is $438,000. Thus, the predetermined overhead rate is $3.65 per direct labor hour. The direct materials cost per unit is $5.25 for the hair curler and $9.75 for the blow-dryer. The direct labor cost is $8.00 per unit for the hair curler and the blow-dryer.

Waves Galore purchases most of the parts from suppliers and assembles the finished product at its Fargo, North Dakota plant. It recently adopted activity-based costing, which after this year-end will totally replace its traditional direct labor-based cost accounting system. Waves Galore has identified the following six activity cost pools and related cost drivers and has assembled the following information.

Activity Cost Pools	Cost Drivers	Estimated Overhead	Expected Use of Cost Drivers	Expected Use of Cost Drivers per Product: Curlers	Dryers
Purchasing	Orders	$ 57,500	500	170	330
Receiving	Pounds	42,000	140,000	58,000	82,000
Assembling	Parts	166,000	830,000	415,000	415,000
Testing	Tests	52,000	130,000	82,000	48,000
Finishing	Units	60,000	120,000	80,000	40,000
Packing and shipping	Cartons	60,500	12,100	8,040	4,060
		$438,000			

Instructions

(a) Unit cost—Dryer $21.40

(c) Cost assigned—Dryer $205,050

(d) Cost/unit—Dryer $22.88

(a) Under traditional product costing, compute the total unit cost of each product. Prepare a simple comparative schedule of the individual costs by product (similar to Illustration 4-4).

(b) Under ABC, prepare a schedule showing the computations of the activity-based overhead rates per cost driver. (Round to the nearest cent.)

(c) Prepare a schedule assigning each activity's overhead cost pool to each product based on the use of cost drivers. (Include a computation of overhead cost per unit, rounding to the nearest cent.)

(d) Compute the total cost per unit for each product under ABC.

(e) Classify each of the activities as a value-added activity or a non-value-added activity.

(f) Comment on (1) the comparative overhead cost per unit for the two products under ABC, and (2) the comparative total costs per unit under traditional costing and ABC.

Assign overhead to products using ABC and evaluate decision.

(SO 4)

P4-2B Tough Thermos, Inc. manufactures two plastic thermos containers at its plastic molding facility in Bend, Oregon. Its large container, called the Ice House, has a volume of 5 gallons, side carrying handles, a snap-down lid, and a side drain and plug. Its smaller container, called the Cool Chest, has a volume of 2 gallons, an over-the-top carrying handle which is part of a tilting lid, and a removable shelf. Both containers and their parts are made entirely of hard-molded plastic. The Ice House sells for $35 and the Cool Chest sells for $24. The production costs computed per unit under traditional costing for each model in 2008 were as follows.

Traditional Costing	Ice House	Cool Chest
Direct materials	$ 9.50	$ 6.00
Direct labor ($10 per hour)	8.00	5.00
Manufacturing overhead ($17.08 per DLH)	13.66	8.54
Total per unit cost	$31.16	$19.54

In 2008, Tough Thermos manufactured 50,000 units of the Ice House and 20,000 units of the Cool Chest. The overhead rate of $17.08 per direct labor hour was determined by dividing total expected manufacturing overhead of $854,000 by the total direct labor hours (50,000) for the 2 models.

Under traditional costing, the gross profit on the two containers was: Ice House $3.84 or ($35 – $31.16), and Cool Chest $4.46 or ($24 – $19.54). The gross margin rates on cost are: Ice House 12% or ($3.84 ÷ $31.16), and Cool Chest 23% or ($4.46 ÷ $19.54). Because Tough Thermos can earn a gross margin rate on the Cool Chest that is nearly twice as great as that earned on the Ice House, with less investment in inventory and labor costs, its management is urging its sales staff to put its efforts into selling the Cool Chest over the Ice House.

Before finalizing its decision, management asks the controller Sven Meza to prepare a product costing analysis using activity-based costing (ABC). Meza accumulates the following information about overhead for the year ended December 31, 2008.

Activities	Cost Drivers	Estimated Overhead	Expected Use of Cost Drivers	Activity-Based Overhead Rate
Purchasing	Number of orders	$179,000	4,475	$40/order
Machine setups	Number of setups	195,000	780	$250/setup
Extruding	Machine hours	320,000	80,000	$4/machine hour
Quality control	Tests and inspections	160,000	8,000	$20/test

The cost drivers used for each product were:

Cost Drivers	Ice House	Cool Chest	Total
Purchase orders	2,500	1,975	4,475
Machine setups	480	300	780
Machine hours	60,000	20,000	80,000
Tests and inspections	5,000	3,000	8,000

Instructions

(a) Assign the total 2008 manufacturing overhead costs to the two products using activity-based costing (ABC).

(a) Ice House $560,000

(b) What was the cost per unit and gross profit of each model using ABC costing?

(b) Cost/unit—Ice $28.70

(c) Are management's future plans for the two models sound?

Assign overhead costs using traditional costing and ABC; compare results.

(SO 1, 4)

P4-3B Kitchen Kabinets Company designs and builds upscale kitchen cabinets for luxury homes. Many of the kitchen cabinet and counter arrangements are custom made, but occasionally the company does mass production on order. Its budgeted manufacturing overhead costs for the year 2009 are as follows.

Overhead Cost Pools	Amount
Purchasing	$ 114,400
Handling materials	164,320
Production (cutting, milling, finishing)	500,000
Setting up machines	174,480
Inspecting	184,800
Inventory control (raw materials and finished goods)	252,000
Utilities	360,000
Total budget overhead costs	$1,750,000

For the last 3 years, Kitchen Kabinets Company has been charging overhead to products on the basis of machine hours. For the year 2009, 100,000 machine hours are budgeted.

Ben Chen, the owner-manager, recently directed his accountant, John Kandy, to implement the activity-based costing system he has repeatedly proposed. At Ben's request, John and the production foreman identify the following cost drivers and their usage for the previously budgeted overhead cost pools.

Activity Cost Pools	Activity Cost Drivers	Expected Use of Cost Drivers
Purchasing	Number of orders	650
Handling materials	Numbers of moves	8,000
Production (cutting, milling, finishing)	Direct labor hours	100,000
Setting up machines	Number of setups	1,200
Inspecting	Number of inspections	6,000
Inventory control (raw materials and finished goods)	Number of components	36,000
Utilities	Square feet occupied	90,000

Sara Sosa, sales manager, has received an order for 50 kitchen cabinet arrangements from Bitty Builders, a housing development contractor. At Sara's request, John prepares cost estimates for producing components for 50 cabinet arrangements so Sara can submit a contract price per kitchen arrangement to Bitty Builders. He accumulates the following data for the production of 50 kitchen cabinet arrangements.

Direct materials	$180,000
Direct labor	$200,000
Machine hours	15,000
Direct labor hours	12,000
Number of purchase orders	50
Number of material moves	800
Number of machine setups	100
Number of inspections	450
Number of components (cabinets and accessories)	3,000
Number of square feet occupied	8,000

Instructions

(a) Compute the predetermined overhead rate using traditional costing with machine hours as the basis.

(b) Cost/Kitchen $12,850
(c) Cost/Kitchen $10,932.64

(b) What is the manufacturing cost per complete kitchen arrangement under traditional costing?

(c) What is the manufacturing cost per kitchen arrangement under the proposed activity-based costing? (Prepare all of the necessary schedules.)

(d) Which of the two costing systems is preferable in pricing decisions and why?

Assign overhead costs using traditional costing and ABC; compare results.

(SO 1, 4)

P4-4B Vino Verite Corporation produces two grades of wine from grapes that it buys from California growers. It produces and sells, in 1-gallon jugs, roughly 800,000 gallons per year of a low-cost, high-volume product called StarDew. It also produces and sells roughly 200,000 gallons per year of a low-volume, high-cost product called VineRose. VineRose is sold in 1-liter bottles; thus 200,000 gallons results in roughly 800,000 bottles. Based on recent data, the StarDew product has not been as profitable as VineRose. Management is considering dropping the inexpensive StarDew so it can focus more attention on the VineRose line product. VineRose already demands considerably more attention than StarDew.

Jorge Rojo, president and founder of Vino Verite, is skeptical about this idea. He points out that for many decades the company produced only the StarDew line, and that it was always quite profitable. It wasn't until the company started producing the more complicated VineRose wine that the profitability of StarDew declined. Prior to the introduction of VineRose the company had simple equipment, simple growing and production procedures, and virtually no need for quality control. Because VineRose is bottled in 1-liter bottles it requires considerably more time and effort, both to bottle and to label and box, than does StarDew. (There are roughly 4 liters in a gallon; thus the company must bottle and handle 4 bottles of VineRose to sell the same amount of wine as StarDew.) StarDew requires 1 month of aging; VineRose requires 1 year. StarDew requires cleaning and inspection of equipment every 5,000 gallons; VineRose requires such maintenance every 500 gallons.

Jorge has asked the accounting department to prepare an analysis of the cost per gallon using the traditional costing approach and using activity-based costing. The following information was collected.

	StarDew	VineRose
Direct materials per gallon	$1.10	$2.40
Direct labor cost per gallon	$0.50	$1.00
Direct labor hours per gallon	0.075	0.15
Total direct labor hours	60,000	30,000

				Expected Use of Cost Drivers per Product	
Activity Cost Pools	Cost Drivers	Estimated Overhead	Expected Use of Cost Drivers	StarDew	VineRose
Grape processing	Cart of grapes	$ 189,000	10,000	8,000	2,000
Aging	Total months	416,000	10,400,000	800,000	9,600,000
Bottling and corking	Number of bottles	360,000	1,600,000	800,000	800,000
Labeling and boxing	Number of bottles	240,000	1,600,000	800,000	800,000
Maintain and inspect equipment	Number of inspections	280,000	560	160	400
		$1,485,000			

Instructions

Answer each of the following questions. (Round all calculations to three decimal places.)

(a) Under traditional product costing using direct labor hours, compute the total manufacturing cost per **gallon** of both products.

(a) Cost/gal.—S.D. $2.838

(b) Under ABC, prepare a schedule showing the computation of the activity-based overhead rates (per cost driver).

(c) Prepare a schedule assigning each activity's overhead cost pool to each product, based on the use of cost drivers. Include a computation of overhead cost per unit.

(c) Cost/gal.—S.D. $0.704

(d) Compute the total manufacturing cost per gallon for both products under ABC.

(e) Write a memo to Jorge Rojo discussing the implications of your analysis for the company's plans. In this memo provide a brief description of ABC, as well as an explanation of how the traditional approach can result in distortions.

P4-5B Farm and Home Veterinary Clinic is a small-town partnership that offers two primary services, farm animal services and pet care services. Providing veterinary care to farm animals requires travel to the farm animal (house calls), while veterinary care to pets generally requires that the pet be brought into the clinic. As part of an investigation to determine the contribution that each of these two types of services makes to overall profit, one partner argues for allocating overhead using activity-based costing while the other partner argues for a more simple overhead cost allocation on the basis of direct labor hours. The partners agree to use next year's budgeted data, as prepared by their public accountant, for analysis and comparison purposes. The following overhead data are collected to develop the comparison.

Assign overhead costs to services using traditional costing and ABC; compute overhead rates and unit costs; compare results.

(SO 1, 4, 6, 8)

				Expected Use of Cost Drivers by Service	
Activity Cost Pools	Cost Drivers	Estimated Overhead	Expected Use of Cost Drivers	Farm Animals	Pets
Drug treatment	Treatments	$ 64,000	4,000	1,700	2,300
Surgery	Operations	70,000	800	200	600
Travel	Mileage	28,000	28,000	26,000	2,000
Consultation	Appointment/Calls	33,000	3,000	600	2,400
Accounting/office	Direct labor hours	30,000	5,000	2,000	3,000
Boarding and grooming	100% pets	40,000			
		$265,000			

Instructions

(a) Using traditional product costing as proposed by one partner, compute the total overhead cost assigned to both services of Farm and Home Veterinary Clinic.

(b) (1) Using activity-based costing, prepare a schedule showing the computations of the activity-based overhead rates (per cost driver).

(b) Cost assigned—Farm Animals $89,300

(2) Prepare a schedule assigning each activity's overhead cost pool to each service based on the use of the cost drivers.

(c) Classify each of the activities as a value-added activity or a non-value-added activity.

(d) ABC—Pets 66%

(d) Comment on the comparative overhead cost assigned to the two services under both traditional costing and ABC.

PROBLEMS: SET C

Visit the book's website at **www.wiley.com/college/weygandt,** and choose the Student Companion site, to access Problem Set C.

WATERWAYS CONTINUING PROBLEM

(*Note:* This is a continuation of the Waterways Problem from Chapters 1 through 3.)

WCP4 Waterways looked into ABC as a method of costing because of the variety of items they produce and the many different activities in which they are involved. This problem asks you to help Waterways use activity-based costing system to account for its production activities.

Go to the book's website, www.wiley.com/college/weygandt, to find the completion of this problem.

BROADENING YOUR PERSPECTIVE

DECISION MAKING ACROSS THE ORGANIZATION

BYP4-1 East Valley Hospital is a primary medical care facility and trauma center that serves 11 small, rural midwestern communities within a 40-mile radius. The hospital offers all the medical/surgical services of a typical small hospital. It has a staff of 18 full-time doctors and 20 part-time visiting specialists. East Valley has a payroll of 150 employees consisting of technicians, nurses, therapists, managers, directors, administrators, dieticians, secretaries, data processors, and janitors.

Instructions

With the class divided into groups, discuss and answer the following.

(a) Using your (limited, moderate, or in-depth) knowledge of a hospital's operations, identify as many **activities** as you can that would serve as the basis for implementing an activity-based costing system.

(b) For each of the activities listed in (a), identify a **cost driver** that would serve as a valid measure of the resources consumed by the activity.

MANAGERIAL ANALYSIS

BYP4-2 Ideal Manufacturing Company of Sycamore, Illinois has supported a research and development (R&D) department that has for many years been the sole contributor to the company's new farm machinery products. The R&D activity is an overhead cost center that provides services only to in-house manufacturing departments (four different product lines), all of which produce agricultural/farm/ranch related machinery products.

The department has never sold its services outside, but because of its long history of success, larger manufacturers of agricultural products have approached Ideal to hire its R&D department for special projects. Because the costs of operating the R&D department have been spiraling uncontrollably, Ideal's management is considering entertaining these outside approaches to absorb the increasing costs. But, (1) management doesn't have any cost basis for charging R&D services to outsiders, and (2) it needs to gain control of its R&D costs. Management decides to implement an activity-based costing system in order to determine the charges for both outsiders and the in-house users of the department's services.

R&D activities fall into four pools with the following annual costs.

Market analysis	$1,050,000
Product design	2,280,000
Product development	3,600,000
Prototype testing	1,400,000

Activity analysis determines that the appropriate cost drivers and their usage for the four activities are:

Activities	Cost Drivers	Total Estimated Drivers
Market analysis	Hours of analysis	15,000 hours
Product design	Number of designs	2,500 designs
Product development	Number of products	90 products
Prototype testing	Number of tests	700 tests

Instructions

(a) Compute the activity-based overhead rate for each activity cost pool.

(b) How much cost would be charged to an in-house manufacturing department that consumed 1,800 hours of market analysis time, was provided 280 designs relating to 10 products, and requested 92 engineering tests?

(c) How much cost would serve as the basis for pricing an R&D bid with an outside company on a contract that would consume 800 hours of analysis time, require 178 designs relating to 3 products, and result in 70 engineering tests?

(d) What is the benefit to Ideal Manufacturing of applying activity-based costing to its R&D activity for both in-house and outside charging purposes?

REAL-WORLD FOCUS

BYP4-3 Hewlett-Packard (H-P) is considered one of the best-managed and most innovative companies in the world. It continually has shown an ability to adapt to global competitive challenges through technical innovation and continual reassessment of its management and control mechanisms. Most applications of activity-based costing by Hewlett-Packard have been successful.

But, over the period August 1988 to August 1989, the Colorado Springs Division of Hewlett-Packard designed an activity-based costing system with the goal of providing for better product costing and inventory valuation. It began implementation in November 1989 but halted the process in the summer of 1992. Since then, the Colorado Springs Division has made no further attempts to re-implement a more expansive ABC approach.

Instructions

The March 1997 issue of *Management Accounting* contains an article by Steven P. Landry, Larry M. Wood, and Tim M. Linquist about the Colorado Springs Division titled "Can ABC Bring Mixed Results?" Read the article and answer the following questions.

(a) What went wrong at H-P's Colorado Springs Division in the design, development, and implementation of its activity-based costing system?

(b) What conclusions were drawn from H-P's Colorado Springs Division experience? What does successful ABC implementation require?

EXPLORING THE WEB

BYP4-4 Activity-based costing methods are constantly being improved upon, and many websites discuss suggestions for improvement. The article in this activity outlines an alternative perspective on activity-based costing.

Address: http://hbswk.hbs.edu/item/4587.html, or go to **www.wiley.com/college/weygandt**

Instructions

Read the article provided at the site and answer the following questions.

(a) What concerns do the authors say are raised by "real-world use" of ABC? According to the authors, what benefits have companies enjoyed from the use of ABC?

(b) What method do the authors suggest for estimating practical capacity? How important is it to be precise in this estimate?

(c) Describe the steps that are taken after practical capacity has been estimated.

(d) What is one of the primary benefits obtained by management in the report entitled "ABC, the Time-Driven Way"? What is an example of how this worked for a real company?

COMMUNICATION ACTIVITY

BYP4-5 In our Feature Story about Super Bakery, Inc., we described a virtual corporation as one that consists of a core unit that is supported by a network of outsourced activities. A virtual corporation minimizes investment in human resources, fixed assets, and working capital. The application of ABC to Super Bakery, Inc. is described in an article titled "ABC in a Virtual Corporation" by Tom Davis and Bruce Darling, in the October 1996 issue of *Management Accounting*.

Instructions

Assume you are the controller of a virtual corporation. Using the article as a basis for your communication, write a summary that answers the following questions.

(a) What unique strategies and tactics did Super Bakery's management implement that caused sales to take off and continue to grow at an average rate of 20%?

(b) Why did Super Bakery's management feel that it was necessary to install an ABC system?

(c) What is the main difference between Super Bakery's ABC system and other manufacturers' ABC systems?

ETHICS CASE

BYP4-6 Marcus Lim, the cost accountant for Hi-Power Mower Company, recently installed activity-based costing at Hi-Power's St. Louis lawn tractor (riding mower) plant where three models—the 8-horsepower Bladerunner, the 12-horsepower Quickcut, and the 18-horsepower Supercut—are manufactured. Marcus's new product costs for these three models show that the company's traditional costing system had been significantly undercosting the 18-horsepower Supercut. This was due primarily to the lower sales volume of the Supercut compared to the Bladerunner and the Quickcut.

Before completing his analysis and reporting these results to management, Marcus is approached by his friend Ray Pon, who is the production manager for the 18-horsepower Supercut model. Ray has heard from one of Marcus's staff about the new product costs and is upset and worried for his job because the new costs show the Supercut to be losing, rather than making, money.

At first Ray condemns the new cost system, whereupon Marcus explains the practice of activity-based costing and why it is more accurate than the company's present system. Even more worried now, Ray begs Marcus, "Massage the figures just enough to save the line from being discontinued. You don't want me to lose my job do you? Anyway, nobody will know."

Marcus holds firm but agrees to recompute all his calculations for accuracy before submitting his costs to management.

Instructions

(a) Who are the stakeholders in this situation?

(b) What, if any, are the ethical considerations in this situation?

(c) What are Marcus's ethical obligations to the company? To his friend?

"ALL ABOUT YOU" ACTIVITY

BYP4-7 There are many resources available on the Web to assist people in time management. Some of these resources are designed specifically for college students.

Instructions

Go to **http://www.dartmouth.edu/~acskills/video/video_tmcap.html.** Click on the Videos and the Time Management Video link. Watch the video and then answer the following questions.

(a) What are the main tools of time management for students, and what is each used for?
(b) At what time of day are students most inclined to waste time? What time of day is the best for studying complex topics?
(c) How can employing time-management practices be a "liberating" experience?
(d) Why is goal-setting important? What are the characteristics of good goals, and what steps should you take to help you develop your goals?

Answers to Insight and Accounting Across the Organization Questions

The Origins of ABC, p. 155

Q: Why does using direct labor as the basis for overhead allocation result in lower direct labor costs for Japanese companies?

A: *Managers want to minimize the amount of overhead that is allocated to their product. If overhead is allocated based upon the amount of direct labor used, then managers can minimize the amount of overhead allocated to their product by minimizing the amount of direct labor they use.*

Using ABC to Aid in Employee Evaluation, p. 158

Q: What positive implications does application of ABC have for the employees of this company?

A: *ABC will make these employees more aware of which activities cost the company more money. They will be motivated to reduce their use of these activities in order to improve their individual performance.*

What Does NASCAR Have to Do with Breakfast Cereal?, p. 161

Q: What are the benefits of reducing setup time?

A: *Setup time is a non–value-added activity. Customers are not willing to pay extra for more setup time. By reducing the time spent on setups, the company can reduce non–value-added costs. Also, by reducing setup time the company can switch from producing one product to producing a different product more quickly. This enables it to respond to customers' demands more quickly, thus avoiding stock-outs.*

Authors' Comments on *All About You*: Where Does the Time Go?, p. 167

In part, the response to this question depends on how broadly you apply the term "value-added activity" when looking at one's life. For example, some value-added activities relate to goals and objectives for school and work. It is important to try to manage your time effectively so as to maximize your chance of achieving these objectives. But it is also important to identify the other things in life that are important. These would include time with friends, family, your health, and hobbies and activities that you value.

When identifying personal value-added activities, it is important to identify all the things, school-related and otherwise, that matter most to you. In applying to your life the activity-based concepts that you learned in this chapter, try to eliminate the non-value-added activities that reduce your ability to focus on those aspects of life that are really important to you.

Answers to Self-Study Questions

1. c **2.** c **3.** c **4.** b **5.** d **6.** d **7.** c **8.** c ***9.** d ***10.** b

Remember to go back to the Navigator box on the chapter-opening page and check off your completed work.

Chapter 5

Cost-Volume-Profit

STUDY OBJECTIVES

After studying this chapter, you should be able to:

1 Distinguish between variable and fixed costs.
2 Explain the significance of the relevant range.
3 Explain the concept of mixed costs.
4 List the five components of cost-volume-profit analysis.
5 Indicate what contribution margin is and how it can be expressed.
6 Identify the three ways to determine the break-even point.
7 Give the formulas for determining sales required to earn target net income.
8 Define margin of safety, and give the formulas for computing it.

The Navigator

Scan **Study Objectives** ■
Read **Feature Story** ■
Read **Preview** ■
Read text and answer **Before You Go On** p. 205 ■ p. 211 ■ p. 214 ■
Work **Using the Decision Toolkit** ■
Review **Summary of Study Objectives** ■
Work **Demonstration Problem** ■
Answer **Self-Study Questions** ■
Complete **Assignments** ■

Feature Story

GROWING BY LEAPS AND LEOTARDS

When the last of her three children went off to school, Amy began looking for a job. At this same time, her daughter asked to take dance classes. The nearest dance studio was over 20 miles away, and Amy didn't know how she would balance a new job and drive her daughter to dance class. Suddenly it hit her—why not start her own dance studio?

Amy sketched out a business plan: A local church would rent its basement to her for $6 per hour. The size of the basement limited the number of students she could teach, but the rent was low. Insurance for a small studio was $50 per month. Initially she would teach only classes for young kids since that was all she felt qualified to do. She thought she could charge $2.50 for a one-hour class. There was room for eight students per class. She

wouldn't get rich—but at least it would be fun, and she didn't have much at risk.

Amy soon realized that the demand for dance classes far exceeded her capacity. She considered renting a bigger space that could serve 15 students per class. But her rent would also increase significantly. Also, rather than paying rent by the hour, she would have to pay $600 per month, even during the summer months when demand for dance classes was low. She also would have to pay utilities—roughly $70 per month.

However, with a bigger space Amy could offer classes for teens and adults. Teens and adults would pay a higher fee—$5 per hour—though the number of students per class would have to be smaller, probably only eight per class. She could hire a part-time instructor at about $18 per hour to teach advanced classes. Insurance costs could increase to $100 per month. In addition, she would need a part-time administrator at $100 per month to keep records. Amy also realized she could increase her income by selling dance supplies such as shoes, towels, and leotards.

Amy laid out a new business plan based on these estimates. If she failed, she stood to lose real money. Convinced she could make a go of it, she made the big plunge.

Her planning paid off: Within 10 years of starting her business in a church basement Amy had over 800 students, seven instructors, two administrators, and a facility with three separate studios.

✓ The Navigator

Inside Chapter 5

Preview of Chapter 5

As the Feature Story indicates, to manage any size business you must understand how costs respond to changes in sales volume and the effect of costs and revenues on profits. A prerequisite to understanding cost-volume-profit (CVP) relationships is knowledge of how costs behave. In this chapter, we first explain the considerations involved in cost behavior analysis. Then we discuss and illustrate CVP analysis.

The content and organization of Chapter 5 are as follows.

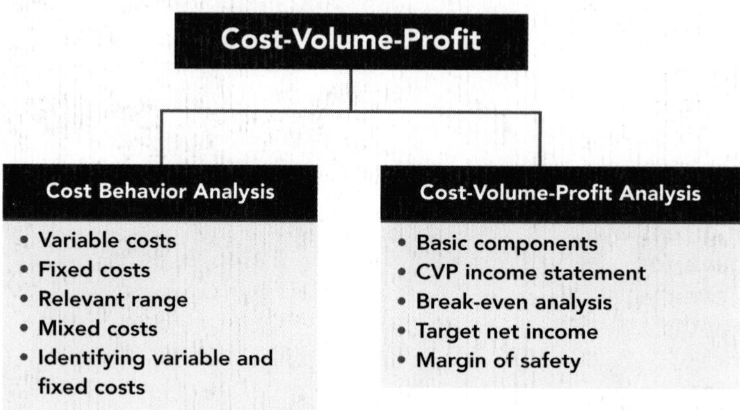

The Navigator

COST BEHAVIOR ANALYSIS

Cost behavior analysis is the study of how specific costs respond to changes in the level of business activity. As you might expect, some costs change, and others remain the same. For example, for an airline company such as Southwest or United, the longer the flight the higher the fuel costs. On the other hand, Massachusetts General Hospital's costs to staff the emergency room on any given night are relatively constant regardless of the number of patients treated. A knowledge of cost behavior helps management plan operations and decide between alternative courses of action. Cost behavior analysis applies to all types of entities, as the Feature Story about Amy's dance studio indicates.

The starting point in cost behavior analysis is measuring the key business activities. Activity levels may be expressed in terms of sales dollars (in a retail company), miles driven (in a trucking company), room occupancy (in a hotel), or dance classes taught (by a dance studio). Many companies use more than one measurement base. A manufacturer, for example, may use direct labor hours or units of output for manufacturing costs and sales revenue or units sold for selling expenses.

For an activity level to be useful in cost behavior analysis, changes in the level or volume of activity should be correlated with changes in costs. The activity level selected is referred to as the activity (or volume) index. The **activity index** identifies the activity that causes changes in the behavior of costs. With an appropriate activity index, companies can classify the behavior of costs in response to changes in activity levels into three categories: variable, fixed, or mixed.

Variable Costs

STUDY OBJECTIVE 1

Distinguish between variable and fixed costs.

Variable costs are costs that vary **in total** directly and proportionately with changes in the activity level. If the level increases 10%, total variable costs will increase 10%. If the level of activity decreases by 25%, variable costs will decrease 25%. Examples of variable costs include direct materials and direct labor for a manufacturer; cost of goods sold, sales commissions, and freight-out for a merchandiser; and gasoline in airline and trucking companies. A variable cost may also be defined as a cost that **remains the same *per unit* at every level of activity**.

To illustrate the behavior of a variable cost, assume that Damon Company manufactures radios that contain a $10 digital clock. The activity index is the number of radios produced. As Damon manufactures each radio, the total cost of the clocks increases by $10. As part (a) of Illustration 5-1 shows, total cost of the clocks will be $20,000 if Damon produces 2,000 radios, and $100,000 when it produces 10,000 radios. We also can see that a variable cost remains the same per unit as the level of activity changes. As part (b) of Illustration 5-1 shows, the unit cost of $10 for the clocks is the same whether Damon produces 2,000 or 10,000 radios.

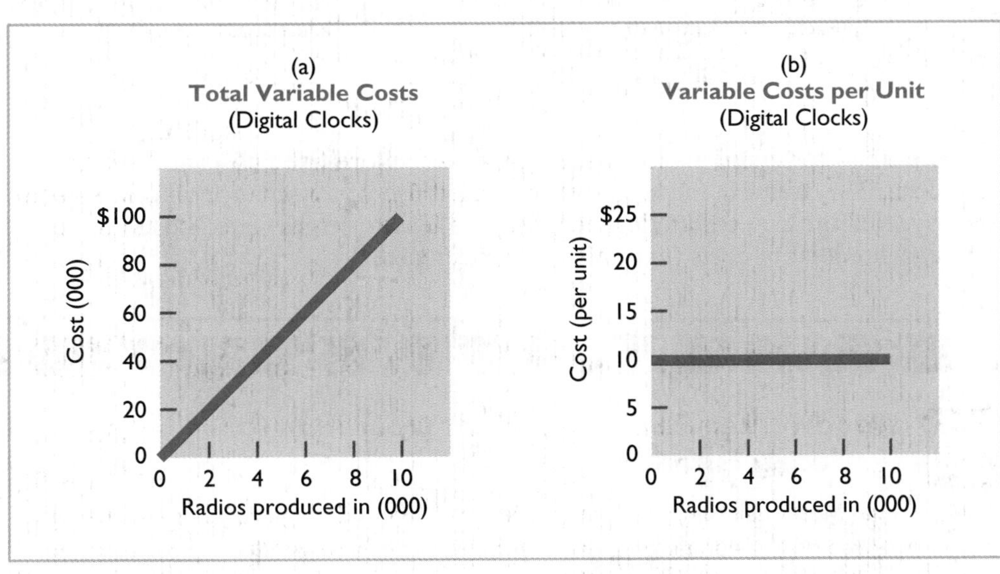

Illustration 5-1
Behavior of total and unit variable costs

HELPFUL HINT

True or false: **Variable cost per unit changes directly and proportionately with changes in activity.**
Answer: **False. Per unit cost remains constant at all levels of activity.**

Companies that rely heavily on labor to manufacture a product, such as Nike or Reebok, or to provide a service, such as Hilton or Marriott, are likely to have many variable costs. In contrast, companies that use a high proportion of machinery and equipment in producing revenue, such as AT&T or Duke Energy Co., may have few variable costs.

Fixed Costs

Fixed costs are costs that **remain the same in total** regardless of changes in the activity level. Examples include property taxes, insurance, rent, supervisory salaries, and depreciation on buildings and equipment. Because total fixed costs remain constant as activity changes, it follows that **fixed costs *per unit* vary inversely with activity: As volume increases, unit cost declines, and vice versa**.

To illustrate the behavior of fixed costs, assume that Damon Company leases its productive facilities at a cost of $10,000 per month. Total fixed costs of the facilities will remain constant at every level of activity, as part (a) of Illustration 5-2 (page 200) shows. But, on a per unit basis, the cost of rent will decline as activity increases, as part (b) of Illustration 5-2 shows. At 2,000 units, the unit cost is $5 ($10,000 ÷ 2,000). When Damon produces 10,000 radios, the unit cost is only $1 ($10,000 ÷ 10,000).

Illustration 5-2
Behavior of total and unit fixed costs

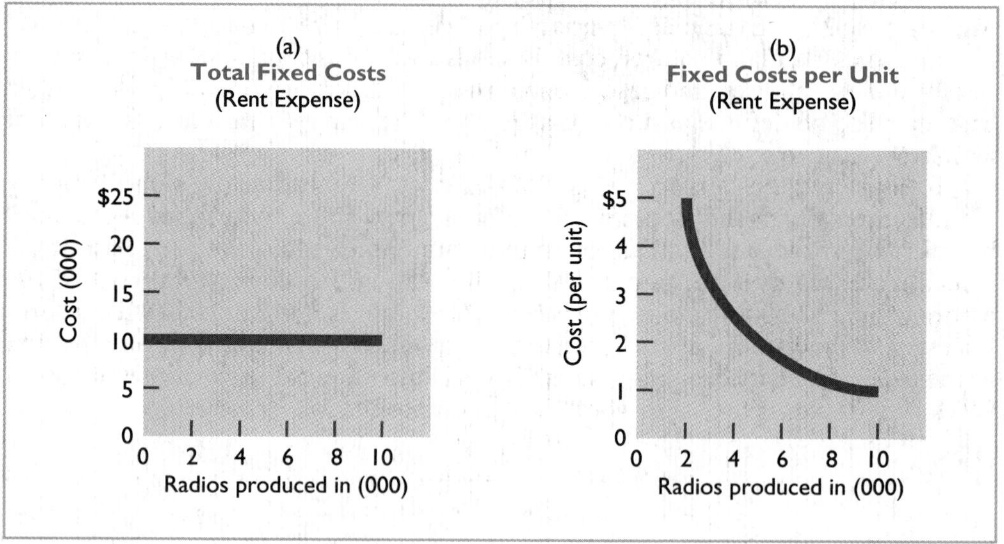

The trend for many manufacturers is to have more fixed costs and fewer variable costs. This trend is the result of increased use of automation and less use of employee labor. As a result, depreciation and lease charges (fixed costs) increase, whereas direct labor costs (variable costs) decrease.

Woodworker Runs an Efficient Operation for Producing Furniture

When Thomas Moser quit teaching communications at Bates College 25 years ago, he turned to what he loved doing—furniture woodworking. Today he has over 120 employees. In a business where profit margins are seldom thicker than wood shavings, cost control is everything. Moser keeps no inventory; he uses customers' 50% deposits on orders to buy the wood. Because computer-driven machines cut most of the standardized parts and joints, "we're free to be inefficient in assembly and finishing work, where the craft is most obviously expressed," says Moser. Direct labor costs are a manageable 30% of revenues. By keeping a tight lid on costs and running an efficient operation, Moser is free to spend most of his time doing what he enjoys most—designing furniture.

Source: Excerpts from "Out of the Woods," *Forbes*, April 5, 1999, p. 74.

Are the costs associated with use of the computer-driven cutting machines fixed or variable?

Relevant Range

STUDY OBJECTIVE 2
Explain the significance of the relevant range.

In Illustration 5-1, part (a) (page 199), a straight line is drawn throughout the entire range of the activity index for total variable costs. In essence, the assumption is that the costs are **linear**. If a relationship is linear (that is, straight-line), then changes in the activity index will result in a direct, proportional change in the variable cost. For example, if the activity level doubles, the cost doubles.

It is now necessary to ask: Is the straight-line relationship realistic? Does the linear assumption produce useful data for CVP analysis?

In most business situations, a straight-line relationship **does not exist** for variable costs throughout the entire range of possible activity. At abnormally low levels of activity, it may be impossible to be cost-efficient. Small-scale operations may not allow the company to obtain quantity discounts for raw materials or to use specialized labor. In contrast, at abnormally high levels of activity, labor costs may increase sharply because of overtime pay. Also at high activity levels, materials costs may jump significantly because of excess spoilage caused by worker fatigue.

As a result, in the real world, the relationship between the behavior of a variable cost and changes in the activity level is often **curvilinear**, as shown in part (a) of Illustration 5-3. In the curved sections of the line, a change in the activity index will not result in a direct, proportional change in the variable cost. That is, a doubling of the activity index will not result in an exact doubling of the variable cost. The variable cost may more than double, or it may be less than double.

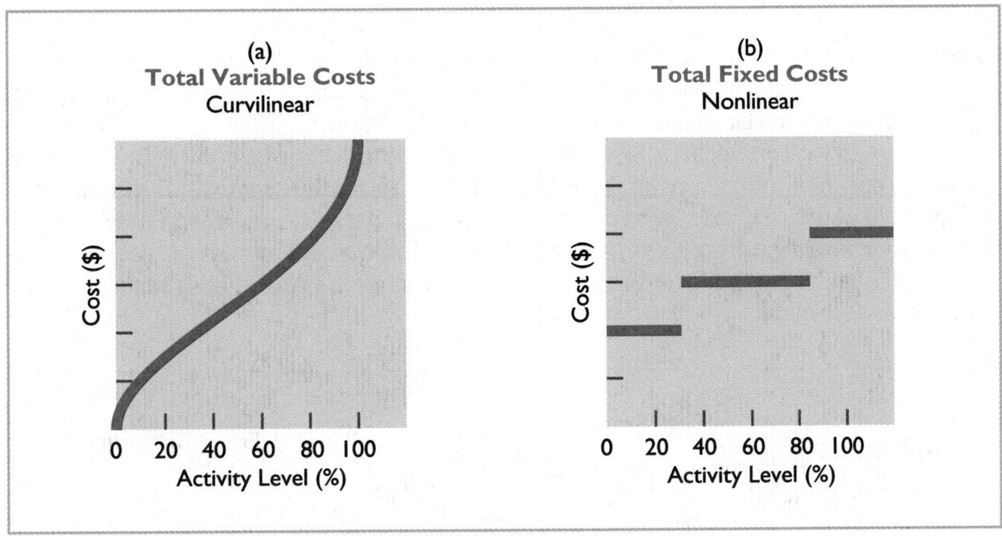

Illustration 5-3
Nonlinear behavior of variable and fixed costs

Total fixed costs also do not have a straight-line relationship over the entire range of activity. Some fixed costs will not change. But it is possible for management to change other fixed costs. For example, in the Feature Story the dance studio's rent was originally variable and then became fixed at a certain amount. It then increased to a new fixed amount when the size of the studio increased beyond a certain point. Illustration 5-3, part (b), shows an example of the behavior of total fixed costs through all potential levels of activity.

HELPFUL HINT
Fixed costs that may be changeable include research, such as new product development, and management training programs.

For most companies, operating at almost zero or at 100% capacity is the exception rather than the rule. Instead, companies often operate over a somewhat narrower range, such as 40–80% of capacity. The range over which a company expects to operate during a year is called the **relevant range** of the activity index. Within the relevant range, as both diagrams in Illustration 5-4 (page 202) show, a straight-line relationship generally exists for both variable and fixed costs.

ALTERNATIVE TERMINOLOGY
The relevant range is also called the *normal* or *practical range.*

Illustration 5-4
Linear behavior within relevant range

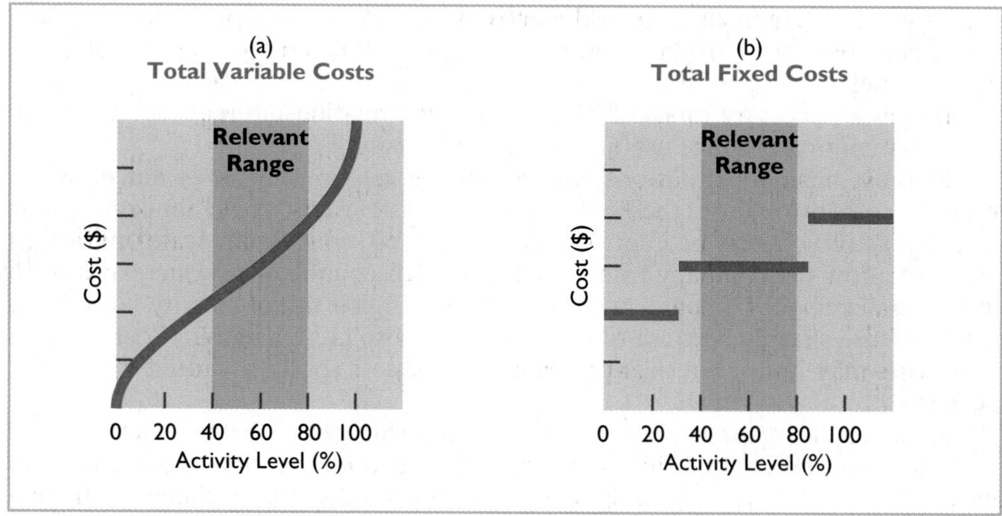

As you can see, although the linear (straight-line) relationship may not be completely realistic, **the linear assumption produces useful data for CVP analysis as long as the level of activity remains within the relevant range**.

Mixed Costs

STUDY OBJECTIVE 3
Explain the concept of mixed costs.

Mixed costs are costs that contain both a variable element and a fixed element. **Mixed costs, therefore, change in total but not proportionately with changes in the activity level.**

The rental of a U-Haul truck is a good example of a mixed cost. Assume that local rental terms for a 17-foot truck, including insurance, are $50 per day plus 50 cents per mile. When determining the cost of a one-day rental, the per day charge is a fixed cost (with respect to miles driven), whereas the mileage charge is a variable cost. The graphic presentation of the rental cost for a one-day rental is as follows.

Illustration 5-5
Behavior of a mixed cost

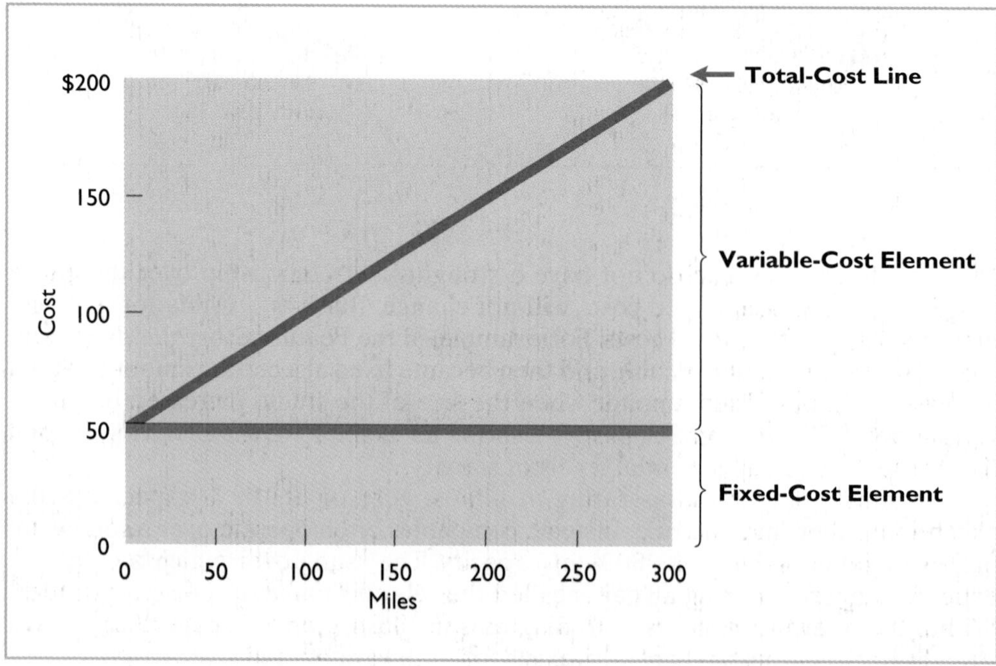

In this case, the fixed-cost element is the cost of having the service available. The variable-cost element is the cost of actually using the service. Another example of a mixed cost is utility costs (electric, telephone, and so on), where there is a flat service fee plus a usage charge.

For purposes of CVP analysis, **mixed costs must be classified into their fixed and variable elements**. How does management make the classification? One possibility is to determine the variable and fixed components each time a mixed cost is incurred. But because of time and cost constraints, this approach is rarely followed. Instead, the usual approach is to collect data on the behavior of the mixed costs at various levels of activity. Analysts then identify the fixed and variable cost components. Companies use various types of analysis. One type of analysis, called the **high-low method**, is discussed below. Other methods, such as the scatter diagram method and least squares regression analysis, are more appropriately explained in cost accounting courses.

HIGH-LOW METHOD

The **high-low method** uses the total costs incurred at the high and low levels of activity to classify mixed costs into fixed and variable components. The difference in costs between the high and low levels represents variable costs, since only the variable cost element can change as activity levels change.

The steps in computing fixed and variable costs under this method are as follows.

1. Determine variable cost per unit from the following formula.

Change in Total Costs	÷	High minus Low Activity Level	=	Variable Cost per Unit

Illustration 5-6
Formula for variable cost per unit using high-low method

To illustrate, assume that Metro Transit Company has the following maintenance costs and mileage data for its fleet of buses over a 4-month period.

Month	Miles Driven	Total Cost	Month	Miles Driven	Total Cost
January	**20,000**	**$30,000**	March	35,000	$49,000
February	40,000	48,000	April	**50,000**	**63,000**

Illustration 5-7
Assumed maintenance costs and mileage data

The high and low levels of activity are 50,000 miles in April and 20,000 miles in January. The maintenance costs at these two levels are $63,000 and $30,000, respectively. The difference in maintenance costs is $33,000 ($63,000 − $30,000), and the difference in miles is 30,000 (50,000 − 20,000). Therefore, for Metro Transit, variable cost per unit is $1.10, computed as follows.

$$\$33,000 \div 30,000 = \$1.10$$

2. Determine the fixed cost by subtracting the total variable cost at either the high or the low activity level from the total cost at that activity level.

For Metro Transit, the computations are shown in Illustration 5-8.

Illustration 5-8
High-low method computation of fixed costs

	A	B	C	D
1			METRO TRANSIT	
2				
3			Activity Level	
4			**High**	**Low**
5	Total cost		$63,000	$30,000
6	Less:	Variable costs		
7		50,000 × $1.10	55,000	
8		20,000 × $1.10		22,000
9	Total fixed costs		**$8,000**	**$8,000**
10				

Maintenance costs are therefore $8,000 per month plus $1.10 per mile. This is represented by the following formula:

Maintenance costs = Fixed costs + ($1.10 × Miles driven)

For example, at 45,000 miles, estimated maintenance costs would be $8,000 fixed and $49,500 variable ($1.10 × 45,000) for a total of $57,500.

The high-low method generally produces a reasonable estimate for analysis. However, it does not produce a precise measurement of the fixed and variable elements in a mixed cost because it ignores other activity levels in the computation.

Importance of Identifying Variable and Fixed Costs

Why is it important to segregate costs into variable and fixed elements? The answer may become apparent if we look at the following four business decisions.

1. If American Airlines is to make a profit when it reduces all domestic fares by 30%, what reduction in costs or increase in passengers will be required? **Answer**: To make a profit when it cuts domestic fares by 30%, American Airlines will have to increase the number of passengers or cut its variable costs for those flights. Its fixed costs will not change.
2. If Ford Motor Company meets workers' demands for higher wages, what increase in sales revenue will be needed to maintain current profit levels? **Answer**: Higher wages at Ford Motor Company will increase the variable costs of manufacturing automobiles. To maintain present profit levels, Ford will have to cut other variable costs or increase the price of its automobiles.
3. If United States Steel Corp.'s program to modernize plant facilities through significant equipment purchases reduces the work force by 50%, what will be the effect on the cost of producing one ton of steel?
   Answer: The modernizing of plant facilities at United States Steel Corp. changes the proportion of fixed and variable costs of producing one ton of steel. Fixed costs increase because of higher depreciation charges, whereas variable costs decrease due to the reduction in the number of steelworkers.
4. What happens if Kellogg Company increases its advertising expenses but cannot increase prices because of competitive pressure?
   Answer: Sales volume must be increased to cover the increase in fixed advertising costs.

Before You Go On...

REVIEW IT

1. What are the effects on (a) a variable cost and (b) a fixed cost due to a change in activity?
2. What is the relevant range, and how do costs behave within this range?
3. What are the steps in applying the high-low method to mixed costs?

DO IT

Helena Company reports the following total costs at two levels of production.

	10,000 units	20,000 units
Direct materials	$20,000	$40,000
Maintenance	8,000	10,000
Depreciation	4,000	4,000

Classify each cost as either variable, fixed, or mixed.

Action Plan

- Recall that a variable cost varies in total directly and proportionately with each change.
- Recall that a fixed cost remains the same in total with each change.
- Recall that a mixed cost changes in total but not proportionately with each change.

Solution Direct materials is a variable cost. Maintenance is a mixed cost. Depreciation is a fixed cost.

Related exercise material: *BE5-1, BE5-2, BE5-3, BE5-4, BE5-5, E5-1, E5-2, E5-3, E5-4, E5-5, and E5-6.*

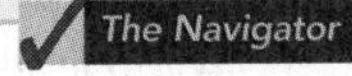

COST-VOLUME-PROFIT ANALYSIS

STUDY OBJECTIVE 4

List the five components of cost-volume-profit analysis.

Cost-volume-profit (CVP) analysis is the study of the effects of changes in costs and volume on a company's profits. CVP analysis is important in profit planning. It also is a critical factor in such management decisions as setting selling prices, determining product mix, and maximizing use of production facilities.

Basic Components

CVP analysis considers the interrelationships among the components shown in Illustration 5-9.

Illustration 5-9
Components of CVP analysis

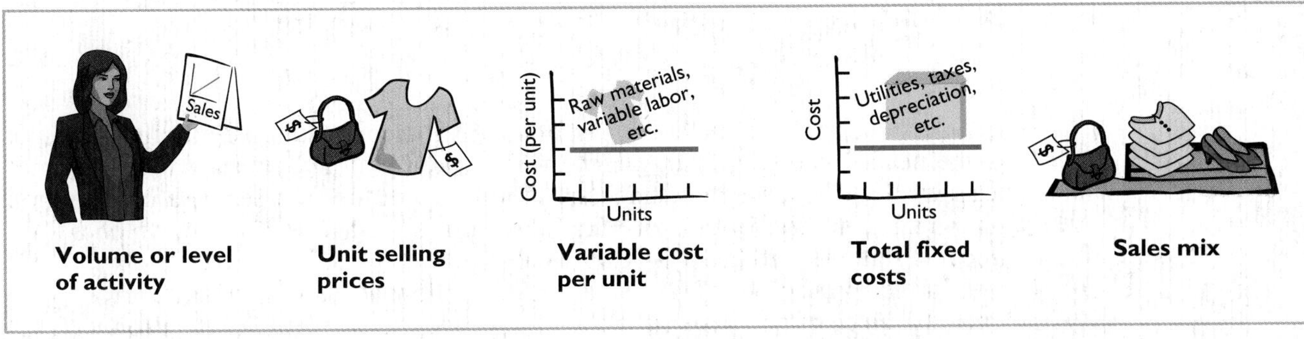

The following assumptions underlie each CVP analysis.

1. The behavior of both costs and revenues is linear throughout the relevant range of the activity index.
2. Costs can be classified accurately as either variable or fixed.
3. Changes in activity are the only factors that affect costs.
4. All units produced are sold.
5. When more than one type of product is sold, the sales mix will remain constant. That is, the percentage that each product represents of total sales will stay the same. Sales mix complicates CVP analysis because different products will have different cost relationships. In this chapter we assume a single product.

When these assumptions are not valid, the CVP analysis may be inaccurate.

CVP Income Statement

STUDY OBJECTIVE 5

Indicate what contribution margin is and how it can be expressed.

Because CVP is so important for decision making, management often wants this information reported in a **CVP income statement** format for internal use. The CVP income statement classifies costs as variable or fixed and computes a contribution margin. **Contribution margin (CM)** is the amount of revenue remaining after deducting variable costs. It is often stated both as a total amount and on a per unit basis.

We will use Vargo Video Company to illustrate a CVP income statement. Vargo Video produces a high-end, progressive-scan DVD player/recorder with up to 160-hour recording capacity and MP3 playback capability. Relevant data for the DVD players sold by this company in June 2008 are as follows.

Illustration 5-10
Assumed selling and cost data for Vargo Video

Unit selling price of DVD player	$500
Unit variable costs	$300
Total monthly fixed costs	$200,000
Units sold	1,600

The CVP income statement for Vargo Video therefore would be reported as follows.

Illustration 5-11
CVP income statement, with net income

VARGO VIDEO COMPANY
CVP Income Statement
For the Month Ended June 30, 2008

	Total	Per Unit
Sales (1,600 DVD players)	$800,000	$500
Variable costs	480,000	300
Contribution margin	320,000	$200
Fixed costs	200,000	
Net income	$120,000	

A traditional income statement and a CVP income statement both report the same net income of $120,000. However a traditional income statement does not classify costs as variable or fixed, and therefore it does not report a contribution margin. In addition, both a total and a per unit amount are often shown on a CVP income statement to facilitate CVP analysis.

In the applications of CVP analysis that follow, we assume that the term "cost" includes all costs and expenses related to production and sale of the product. That is, cost includes manufacturing costs plus selling and administrative expenses.

CONTRIBUTION MARGIN PER UNIT

Vargo Video's CVP income statement shows a contribution margin of $320,000, and a contribution margin per unit of $200 ($500 − $300). The formula for **contribution margin per unit** and the computation for Vargo Video are:

Illustration 5-12
Formula for contribution margin per unit

Unit Selling Price	−	Unit Variable Costs	=	Contribution Margin per Unit
$500	−	$300	=	**$200**

Contribution margin per unit indicates that for every DVD player sold, Vargo has $200 to cover fixed costs and contribute to net income. Because Vargo Video has fixed costs of $200,000, it must sell 1,000 DVD players ($200,000 ÷ $200) before it earns any net income. Vargo's CVP income statement, assuming a zero net income, is as follows.

Illustration 5-13
CVP income statement, with zero net income

VARGO VIDEO COMPANY
CVP Income Statement
For the Month Ended June 30, 2008

	Total	Per Unit
Sales (1,000 DVD players)	$500,000	$500
Variable costs	300,000	300
Contribution margin	**200,000**	**$200**
Fixed costs	200,000	
Net income	$ -0-	

It follows that for every DVD player sold above 1,000 units, net income increases by the amount of the contribution margin per unit, $200. For example, assume that Vargo sold one more DVD player, for a total of 1,001 DVD players sold. In this case Vargo reports net income of $200 as shown in Illustration 5-14.

Illustration 5-14
CVP income statement, with net income

VARGO VIDEO COMPANY
CVP Income Statement
For the Month Ended June 30, 2008

	Total	Per Unit
Sales (1,001 DVD players)	$500,500	$500
Variable costs	300,300	300
Contribution margin	**200,200**	**$200**
Fixed costs	200,000	
Net income	**$ 200**	

CONTRIBUTION MARGIN RATIO

Some managers prefer to use a contribution margin ratio in CVP analysis. The **contribution margin ratio** is the contribution margin per unit divided by the unit selling price. For Vargo Video, the ratio is as follows.

Illustration 5-15
Formula for contribution margin ratio

Contribution Margin per Unit	÷	Unit Selling Price	=	Contribution Margin Ratio
$200	÷	$500	=	**40%**

The contribution margin ratio of 40% means that $0.40 of each sales dollar ($1 × 40%) is available to apply to fixed costs and to contribute to net income.

This expression of contribution margin is very helpful in determining the effect of changes in sales on net income. For example, if sales increase $100,000, net income will increase $40,000 (40% × $100,000). Thus, by using the contribution margin ratio, managers can quickly determine increases in net income from any change in sales.

We can also see this effect through a CVP income statement. Assume that Vargo Video's current sales are $500,000 and it wants to know the effect of a $100,000 (200-unit) increase in sales. Vargo prepares a comparative CVP income statement analysis as follows.

Illustration 5-16
Comparative CVP income statements

VARGO VIDEO COMPANY
CVP Income Statements
For the Month Ended June 30, 2008

	No Change		With Change	
	Total	**Per Unit**	**Total**	**Per Unit**
Sales	$500,000	$500	$600,000	$500
Variable costs	300,000	300	360,000	300
Contribution margin	**200,000**	**$200**	**240,000**	**$200**
Fixed costs	200,000		200,000	
Net income	**$ -0-**		**$ 40,000**	

Study these CVP income statements carefully. The concepts presented in these statements are used extensively in this and later chapters.

DECISION TOOLKIT

Decision Checkpoints	Info Needed for Decision	Tool to Use for Decision	How to Evaluate Results
What was the contribution toward fixed costs and income from each unit sold?	Selling price per unit and variable cost per unit	Contribution margin per unit = Unit selling price − Unit variable cost	Every unit sold will increase income by the contribution margin.
What was the increase in income as a result of an increase in sales?	Contribution margin per unit and unit selling price	Contribution margin ratio = Contribution margin per unit ÷ Unit selling price	Every dollar of sales will increase income by the contribution margin ratio.

Break-even Analysis

STUDY OBJECTIVE 6
Identify the three ways to determine the break-even point.

A key relationship in CVP analysis is the level of activity at which total revenues equal total costs (both fixed and variable). This level of activity is called the **break-even point**. At this volume of sales, the company will realize no income but will suffer no loss. The process of finding the break-even point is called **break-even analysis**. Knowledge of the break-even point is useful to management when it decides whether to introduce new product lines, change sales prices on established products, or enter new market areas.

The break-even point can be:

1. Computed from a mathematical equation.
2. Computed by using contribution margin.
3. Derived from a cost-volume-profit (CVP) graph.

The break-even point can be expressed either in **sales units** or **sales dollars**.

MATHEMATICAL EQUATION

Illustration 5-17 shows a common equation used for CVP analysis.

Sales	=	Variable Costs	+	Fixed Costs	+	Net Income

Illustration 5-17
Basic CVP equation

Identifying the break-even point is a special case of CVP analysis. Because at the break-even point net income is zero, **break-even occurs where total sales equal variable costs plus fixed costs.**

We can compute the break-even point **in units** directly from the equation by **using unit selling prices** and **unit variable costs.** The computation for Vargo Video is:

Sales	=	Variable Costs	+	Fixed Costs	+	Net Income
\$500Q	=	\$300Q	+	\$200,000	+	\$0

$$\$200Q = \$200,000$$
$$Q = 1,000 \text{ units}$$

where

Q = sales volume in units
\$500 = selling price
\$300 = variable cost per unit
\$200,000 = total fixed costs

Illustration 5-18
Computation of break-even point in units

Thus, Vargo Video must sell 1,000 units to break even.

To find **sales dollars** required to break even, we multiply the units sold at the break-even point times the selling price per unit, as shown below.

$$1,000 \times \$500 = \$500,000 \text{ (break-even sales dollars)}$$

CONTRIBUTION MARGIN TECHNIQUE

We know that contribution margin equals total revenues less variable costs. It follows that at the break-even point, **contribution margin must equal total fixed costs.** On the basis of this relationship, we can compute the break-even point using either the contribution margin per unit or the contribution margin ratio.

When a company uses the contribution margin per unit, the formula to compute break-even point in units is fixed costs divided by contribution margin per unit. For Vargo Video the computation is as follows.

Fixed Costs	÷	Contribution Margin per Unit	=	Break-even Point in Units
\$200,000	÷	\$200	=	1,000 units

Illustration 5-19
Formula for break-even point in units using contribution margin

One way to interpret this formula is that Vargo Video generates \$200 of contribution margin with each unit that it sells. This \$200 goes to pay off fixed costs. Therefore, the company must sell 1,000 units to pay off \$200,000 in fixed costs.

When a company uses the contribution margin ratio, the formula to compute break-even point in dollars is fixed costs divided by the contribution margin ratio. We know that the contribution margin ratio for Vargo Video is 40% (\$200 ÷ \$500), which means that every dollar of sales generates 40 cents to pay off fixed costs. Thus, the break-even point in dollars is:

Illustration 5-20
Formula for break-even point in dollars using contribution margin ratio

Fixed Costs	÷	Contribution Margin Ratio	=	Break-even Point in Dollars
$200,000	÷	40%	=	$500,000

ACCOUNTING ACROSS THE ORGANIZATION

Charter Flights Offer a Good Deal

The Internet is wringing inefficiencies out of nearly every industry. While commercial aircraft spend roughly 4,000 hours a year in the air, chartered aircraft spend only 500 hours flying. That means that they are sitting on the ground—not making any money—about 90% of the time. One company, FlightServe, saw a business opportunity in that fact. For about the same cost as a first-class ticket, FlightServe decided to match up executives with charter flights in small "private jets." The executive would get a more comfortable ride and could avoid the hassle of big airports. FlightServe noted that the average charter jet has eight seats. When all eight seats were full, the company would have an 80% profit margin. It would break even at an average of 3.3 full seats per flight.

Source: "Jet Set Go," *The Economist*, March 18, 2000, p. 68.

? How did FlightServe determine that it would break even with 3.3 seats full per flight?

GRAPHIC PRESENTATION

An effective way to find the break-even point is to prepare a break-even graph. Because this graph also shows costs, volume, and profits, it is referred to as a **cost-volume-profit (CVP) graph**.

As the CVP graph in Illustration 5-21 (next page) shows, sales volume is recorded along the horizontal axis. This axis should extend to the maximum level of expected sales. Both total revenues (sales) and total costs (fixed plus variable) are recorded on the vertical axis.

The construction of the graph, using the data for Vargo Video, is as follows.

1. Plot the total-sales line, starting at the zero activity level. For every DVD player sold, total revenue increases by $500. For example, at 200 units, sales are $100,000. At the upper level of activity (1,800 units), sales are $900,000. The revenue line is assumed to be linear through the full range of activity.
2. Plot the total fixed cost using a horizontal line. For the DVD players, this line is plotted at $200,000. The fixed cost is the same at every level of activity.
3. Plot the total-cost line. This starts at the fixed-cost line at zero activity. It increases by the variable cost at each level of activity. For each DVD player, variable costs are $300. Thus, at 200 units, total variable cost is $60,000, and the total cost is $260,000. At 1,800 units total variable cost is $540,000, and total cost is $740,000. On the graph, the amount of the variable cost can be derived from the difference between the total cost and fixed cost lines at each level of activity.
4. Determine the break-even point from the intersection of the total-cost line and the total-revenue line. The break-even point in dollars is found by drawing a horizontal line from the break-even point to the vertical axis. The break-even point in units is found by drawing a vertical line from the break-even point to the horizontal axis. For the DVD players, the break-even point is $500,000 of sales, or 1,000 units. At this sales level, Vargo Video will cover costs but make no profit.

Illustration 5-21
CVP graph

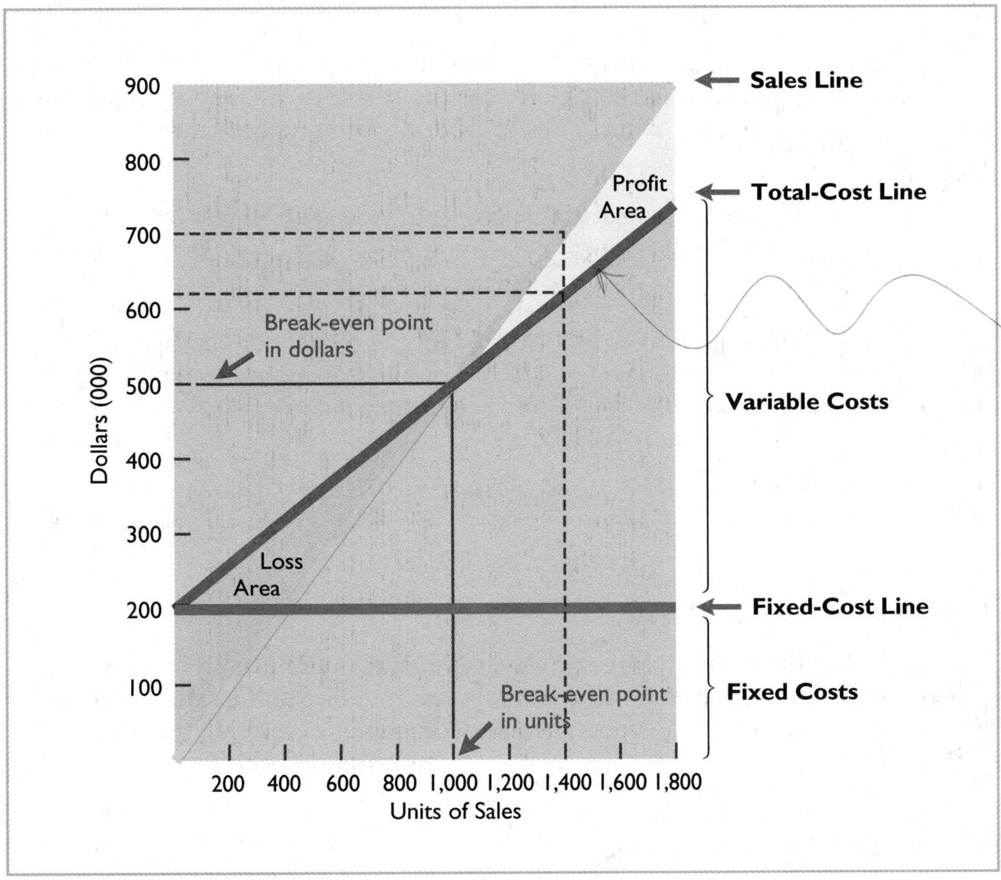

The CVP graph also shows both the net income and net loss areas. Thus, the amount of income or loss at each level of sales can be derived from the total sales and total cost lines.

A CVP graph is useful because the effects of a change in any element in the CVP analysis can be quickly seen. For example, a 10% increase in selling price will change the location of the total revenue line. Likewise, the effects on total costs of wage increases can be quickly observed.

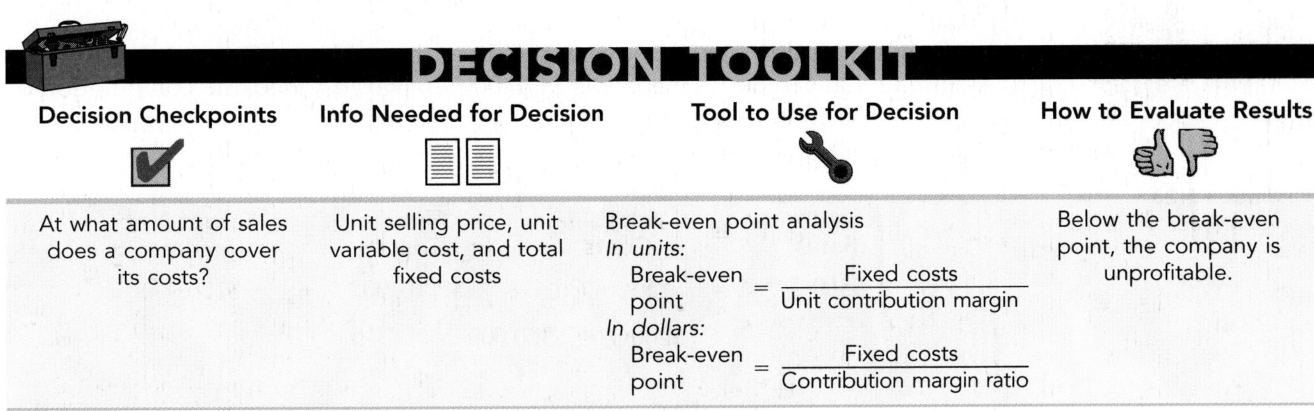

DECISION TOOLKIT

Decision Checkpoints	Info Needed for Decision	Tool to Use for Decision	How to Evaluate Results
At what amount of sales does a company cover its costs?	Unit selling price, unit variable cost, and total fixed costs	Break-even point analysis *In units:* Break-even point = Fixed costs / Unit contribution margin *In dollars:* Break-even point = Fixed costs / Contribution margin ratio	Below the break-even point, the company is unprofitable.

Before You Go On...

REVIEW IT

1. What are the assumptions that underlie each CVP application?
2. What is contribution margin, and how can it be expressed?
3. How can the break-even point be determined?

DO IT

Lombardi Company has a unit selling price of \$400, variable costs per unit of \$240, and fixed costs of \$180,000. Compute the break-even point in units using (a) a mathematical equation and (b) contribution margin per unit.

Action Plan

- Apply the formula: Sales = Variable costs + Fixed costs + Net income.
- Apply the formula: Fixed costs ÷ Contribution margin per unit = Break-even point in units.

Solution (a) The equation is \$400Q = \$240Q + \$180,000. The break-even point in units is 1,125 (\$180,000 ÷ \$160). (b) The contribution margin per unit is \$160 (\$400 − \$240). The formula therefore is \$180,000 ÷ \$160, and the break-even point in units is 1,125.

Related exercise material: *BE5-6, BE5-7, BE5-8, BE5-9, E5-8, E5-9, E5-10, E5-11, E5-12, and E5-13.*

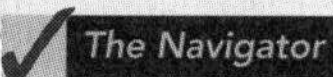

Target Net Income

STUDY OBJECTIVE 7

Give the formulas for determining sales required to earn target net income.

Rather than simply "breaking even," management usually sets an income objective often called **target net income.** It indicates the sales necessary to achieve a specified level of income. Companies determine the sales necessary to achieve target net income by using one of the three approaches discussed earlier.

MATHEMATICAL EQUATION

We know that at the break-even point no profit or loss results for the company. By adding an amount for target net income to the same basic equation, we obtain the following formula for determining required sales.

Illustration 5-22
Formula for required sales to meet target net income

$$\text{Required Sales} = \text{Variable Costs} + \text{Fixed Costs} + \text{Target Net Income}$$

Required sales may be expressed in either **sales units** or **sales dollars.** Assuming that target net income is \$120,000 for Vargo Video, the computation of required sales in units is as follows.

Illustration 5-23
Computation of required sales

Required Sales	=	Variable Costs	+	Fixed Costs	+	Target Net Income
\$500Q	=	\$300Q	+	\$200,000	+	\$120,000

\$200Q = \$320,000
Q = 1,600

where

Q = sales volume
\$500 = selling price
\$300 = variable costs per unit
\$200,000 = total fixed costs
\$120,000 = target net income

The sales dollars required to achieve the target net income is found by multiplying the units sold by the unit selling price [(1,600 × $500) = $800,000].

CONTRIBUTION MARGIN TECHNIQUE

As in the case of break-even sales, we can compute in either units or dollars the sales required to meet a target net income. The formula to compute required sales in units for Vargo Video using the contribution margin per unit is as follows.

Fixed Costs + Target Net Income	÷	Contribution Margin Per Unit	=	Required Sales in Units
($200,000 + $120,000)	÷	$200	=	1,600 units

Illustration 5-24
Formula for required sales in units using contribution margin per unit

This computation tells Vargo that to achieve its desired target net income of $120,000, it must sell 1,600 DVD players.

The formula to compute the required sales in dollars for Vargo Video using the contribution margin ratio is as follows.

Fixed Costs + Target Net Income	÷	Contribution Margin Ratio	=	Required Sales in Dollars
($200,000 + $120,000)	÷	40%	=	$800,000

Illustration 5-25
Formula for required sales in dollars using contribution margin ratio

This computation tells Vargo that to achieve its desired target net income of $120,000, it must generate sales of $800,000.

GRAPHIC PRESENTATION

We also can use the CVP graph in Illustration 5-21 (on page 211) to find the sales required to meet target net income. In the profit area of the graph, the distance between the sales line and the total cost line at any point equals net income. We can find required sales by analyzing the differences between the two lines until the desired net income is found.

For example, suppose Vargo Video sells 1,400 DVD players. Illustration 5-21 shows that a vertical line drawn at 1,400 units intersects the sales line at $700,000 and the total cost line at $620,000. The difference between the two amounts represents the net income (profit) of $80,000.

Margin of Safety

STUDY OBJECTIVE 8
Define margin of safety, and give the formulas for computing it.

The margin of safety is another relationship used in CVP analysis. **Margin of safety** is the difference between actual or expected sales and sales at the break-even point. This relationship measures the "cushion" that management has, allowing it to break even if expected sales fail to materialize. The margin of safety is expressed in dollars or as a ratio.

The formula for stating the **margin of safety in dollars** is actual (or expected) sales minus break-even sales. Assuming that actual (expected) sales for Vargo Video are $750,000, the computation is:

Actual (Expected) Sales	−	Break-even Sales	=	Margin of Safety in Dollars
$750,000	−	$500,000	=	$250,000

Illustration 5-26
Formula for margin of safety in dollars

Vargo's margin of safety is $250,000. Its sales must fall $250,000 before it operates at a loss.

The **margin of safety ratio** is the margin of safety in dollars divided by actual (or expected) sales. The formula and computation for determining the margin of safety ratio are:

Illustration 5-27
Formula for margin of safety ratio

Margin of Safety in Dollars	÷	Actual (Expected) Sales	=	Margin of Safety Ratio
$250,000	÷	$750,000	=	33%

This means that the company's sales could fall by 33% before it would be operating at a loss.

The higher the dollars or the percentage, the greater the margin of safety. Management continuously evaluates the adequacy of the margin of safety in terms of such factors as the vulnerability of the product to competitive pressures and to downturns in the economy.

MANAGEMENT INSIGHT

How a Rolling Stones' Tour Makes Money

Computation of break-even and margin of safety is important for service companies. Consider how the promoter for the Rolling Stones' tour used the break-even point and margin of safety. For example, one outdoor show should bring 70,000 individuals for a gross of $2.45 million. The promoter guarantees $1.2 million to the Rolling Stones. In addition, 20% of gross goes to the stadium in which the performance is staged. Add another $400,000 for other expenses such as ticket takers, parking attendants, advertising, and so on. The promoter also shares in sales of T-shirts and memorabilia for which the promoter will net over $7 million during the tour. From a successful Rolling Stones' tour, the promoter could make $35 million!

What amount of sales dollars are required for the promoter to break even?

Before You Go On...

REVIEW IT

1. What is the equation to compute target net income?
2. What is the formula for computing the margin of safety (a) in dollars and (b) as a ratio?

Be sure to read **ALL ABOUT YOU: *A Hybrid Dilemma*** on the next page for information on how topics in this chapter apply to you.

all about YOU

A Hybrid Dilemma

Have high gas prices got you down? Maybe you should consider a hybrid. These half-gas and half-electric vehicles are generating a lot of interest. They burn less fuel and therefore are easier on the environment. But are they easier on your pocketbook? Is a hybrid car at least a break-even investment, or is it more likely a money-losing proposition?

Some Facts

* Ford plans to sell at least seven different models of hybrid cars, about 250,000 vehicles annually, by the end of the decade.
* Hybrid vehicles typically cost $3,000 to $5,000 more than their conventional counterparts, although for some models the premium is higher.
* Bank of America and Timberland offer $3,000 to employees who purchase hybrids. Google offers $5,000 to employees who purchase cars that get at least 45 miles per gallon.
* The most fuel-efficient hybrids–the Toyota Prius and the Honda Civic–can save about $660 per year in fuel costs relative to a similar conventional car. However some other hybrids provide only slight fuel savings.
* Each gallon of gasoline that is not consumed reduces carbon dioxide emissions by 19 pounds. Many believe carbon dioxide contributes to global warming.
* The federal government initially provided tax credits of up to $3,400 to buyers of hybrids. These credits are to be phased out as automakers reach sales caps determined by the Internal Revenue Service (IRS).

About the Numbers

Sales of hybrid cars started very strong in 2005, but then tapered off. The following graph shows that sales of the Toyota Prius far exceed other brands.

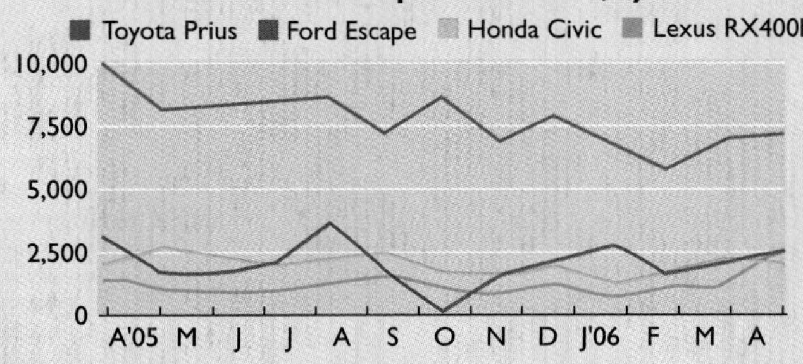

Source: J.D. Power and Associates, 2006, "Happening Hybrids," as reported in the *Wall Street Journal*, May 23, 2006.

What Do You Think?

Gas prices are depleting your wallet so fast that you might even have to give up your old car and resort to walking or riding your bike on occasion. Will making the investment in a hybrid slow the outflow from your wallet and spare your feet?

YES: At 44 miles per gallon, I can drive forever without ever having to fill up.

NO: Because of the premium price charged for hybrids, I will never drive enough miles to break even on my investment.

Sources: "The Dollars and Sense of Hybrids," *Consumer Reports*, April, 2006, pp. 18-22.; John D. Stoll and Gina Chon, "Consumer Drive for Hybrid Autos Is Slowing Down," *Wall Street Journal*, April 7, 2006, p. A2. Associated Press, "Bank Workers Get Hybrid Reward," *Wall Street Journal*, June 8, 2006, p. D2.

The authors' comments on this situation appear on page 232.

Using the Decision Toolkit

B.T. Hernandez Company, maker of high-quality flashlights, has experienced steady growth over the last 6 years. However, increased competition has led Mr. Hernandez, the president, to believe that an aggressive campaign is needed next year to maintain the company's present growth. The company's accountant has presented Mr. Hernandez with the following data for the current year, 2007, for use in preparing next year's advertising campaign.

COST SCHEDULES

Variable costs	
Direct labor per flashlight	$ 8.00
Direct materials	4.00
Variable overhead	3.00
Variable cost per flashlight	$15.00
Fixed costs	
Manufacturing	$ 25,000
Selling	40,000
Administrative	70,000
Total fixed costs	$135,000
Selling price per flashlight	$25.00
Expected sales, 2007 (20,000 flashlights)	$500,000

Mr. Hernandez has set the sales target for the year 2008 at a level of $550,000 (22,000 flashlights).

Instructions

(Ignore any income tax considerations.)

(a) What is the projected operating income for 2007?

(b) What is the contribution margin per unit for 2007?

(c) What is the break-even point in units for 2007?

(d) Mr. Hernandez believes that to attain the sales target in the year 2008, the company must incur an additional selling expense of $10,000 for advertising in 2008, with all other costs remaining constant. What will be the break-even point in sales dollars for 2008 if the company spends the additional $10,000?

(e) If the company spends the additional $10,000 for advertising in 2008, what is the sales level in dollars required to equal 2007 operating income?

Solution

(a)

Expected sales	$500,000
Less:	
Variable cost (20,000 flashlights × $15)	300,000
Fixed costs	135,000
Projected operating income	$ 65,000

(b)

Selling price per flashlight	$25
Variable cost per flashlight	15
Contribution margin per unit	$10

(c) Fixed costs ÷ Contribution margin per unit = Break-even point in units
$135,000 ÷ $10 = 13,500 units

(d) Fixed costs ÷ Contribution margin ratio = Break-even point in dollars
$145,000* ÷ 40%** = $362,500

*Fixed costs (from 2007)	$135,000
Additional advertising expense	10,000
Fixed costs (2008)	$145,000

**Contribution margin ratio = Contribution margin per unit ÷ Unit selling price
40% = $10 ÷ $25

(e) Required sales = (Fixed costs + Target net income) ÷ Contribution margin ratio

$525,000 = ($145,000 + $65,000) ÷ 40%

The Navigator

SUMMARY OF STUDY OBJECTIVES

1 **Distinguish between variable and fixed costs.** Variable costs are costs that vary in total directly and proportionately with changes in the activity index. Fixed costs are costs that remain the same in total regardless of changes in the activity index.

2 **Explain the significance of the relevant range.** The relevant range is the range of activity in which a company expects to operate during a year. It is important in CVP analysis because the behavior of costs is assumed to be linear throughout the relevant range.

3 **Explain the concept of mixed costs.** Mixed costs increase in total but not proportionately with changes in the activity level. For purposes of CVP analysis, mixed costs must be classified into their fixed and variable elements. One method that management may use to classify these costs is the high-low method.

4 **List the five components of cost-volume-profit analysis.** The five components of CVP analysis are (a) volume or level of activity, (b) unit selling prices, (c) variable cost per unit, (d) total fixed costs, and (e) sales mix.

5 **Indicate what contribution margin is and how it can be expressed.** Contribution margin is the amount of revenue remaining after deducting variable costs. It is identified in a CVP income statement, which classifies costs as variable or fixed. It can be expressed as a total amount, as a per unit amount, or as a ratio.

6 **Identify the three ways to determine the break-even point.** The break-even point can be (a) computed from a mathematical equation, (b) computed by using a contribution margin technique, and (c) derived from a CVP graph.

7 **Give the formulas for determining sales required to earn target net income.** The general formula for required sales is: Required sales = Variable costs + Fixed costs + Target net income. Two other formulas are: Required sales in units = (Fixed costs + Target net income) ÷ Contribution margin per unit, and Required sales in dollars = (Fixed costs + Target net income) ÷ Contribution margin ratio.

8 **Define margin of safety, and give the formulas for computing it.** Margin of safety is the difference between actual or expected sales and sales at the break-even point. The formulas for margin of safety are: Actual (expected) sales − Break-even sales = Margin of safety in dollars; Margin of safety in dollars ÷ Actual (expected) sales = Margin of safety ratio.

The Navigator

DECISION TOOLKIT—A SUMMARY

Decision Checkpoints	Info Needed for Decision	Tool to Use for Decision	How to Evaluate Results
What was the contribution toward fixed costs and income from each unit sold?	Selling price per unit and variable cost per unit	Contribution margin per unit = Unit selling price − Unit variable cost	Every unit sold will increase income by the contribution margin.
What was the increase in income as a result of an increase in sales?	Contribution margin per unit and unit selling price	Contribution margin ratio = Contribution margin per unit ÷ Unit selling price	Every dollar of sales will increase income by the contribution margin ratio.
At what amount of sales does a company cover its costs?	Unit selling price, unit variable cost, and total fixed costs	Break-even point analysis *In units:* $\text{Break-even point} = \dfrac{\text{Fixed costs}}{\text{Unit contribution margin}}$ *In dollars:* $\text{Break-even point} = \dfrac{\text{Fixed costs}}{\text{Contribution margin ratio}}$	Below the break-even point, the company is unprofitable.

GLOSSARY

Activity index The activity that causes changes in the behavior of costs. (p. 198).

Break-even point The level of activity at which total revenues equal total costs. (p. 208).

Contribution margin (CM) The amount of revenue remaining after deducting variable costs. (p. 206).

Contribution margin per unit The amount of revenue remaining per unit after deducting variable costs; calculated as unit selling price minus unit variable cost. (p. 207).

Contribution margin ratio The percentage of each dollar of sales that is available to apply to fixed costs and contribute to net income; calculated as contribution margin per unit divided by unit selling price. (p. 207).

Cost behavior analysis The study of how specific costs respond to changes in the level of business activity. (p. 198).

Cost-volume-profit (CVP) analysis The study of the effects of changes in costs and volume on a company's profits. (p. 205).

Cost-volume-profit (CVP) graph A graph showing the relationship between costs, volume, and profits. (p. 210).

Cost-volume-profit (CVP) income statement A statement for internal use that classifies costs as fixed or variable and reports contribution margin in the body of the statement. (p. 206).

Fixed costs Costs that remain the same in total regardless of changes in the activity level. (p. 199).

High-low method A mathematical method that uses the total costs incurred at the high and low levels of activity to classify mixed costs into fixed and variable components. (p. 203).

Margin of safety The difference between actual or expected sales and sales at the break-even point. (p. 213).

Mixed costs Costs that contain both a variable and a fixed cost element and change in total but not proportionately with changes in the activity level. (p. 202).

Relevant range The range of the activity index over which the company expects to operate during the year. (p. 201).

Target net income The income objective set by management. (p. 212).

Variable costs Costs that vary in total directly and proportionately with changes in the activity level. (p. 199).

Demonstration Problem

Mabo Company makes calculators that sell for $20 each. For the coming year, management expects fixed costs to total $220,000 and variable costs to be $9 per unit.

Instructions

(a) Compute break-even point in units using the mathematical equation.
(b) Compute break-even point in dollars using the contribution margin (CM) ratio.
(c) Compute the margin of safety percentage assuming actual sales are $500,000.
(d) Compute the sales required in dollars to earn net income of $165,000.

Solution

(a) Sales = Variable costs + Fixed costs + Net income
$20Q = $9Q + $220,000 + $0
$11Q = $220,000
Q = 20,000 units

(b) Contribution margin per unit = Unit selling price − Unit variable costs
$11 = $20 − $9
Contribution margin ratio = Contribution margin per unit ÷ Unit selling price
55% = $11 ÷ $20
Break-even point in dollars = Fixed cost ÷ Contribution margin ratio
= $220,000 ÷ 55%
= $400,000

(c) $\text{Margin of safety} = \dfrac{\text{Actual sales} - \text{Break-even sales}}{\text{Actual sales}}$

$= \dfrac{\$500,000 - \$400,000}{\$500,000}$

= 20%

(d) Required sales = Variable costs + Fixed costs + Net income
$20Q = $9Q + $220,000 + $165,000
$11Q = $385,000
Q = 35,000 units
35,000 units × $20 = $700,000 required sales

action plan

✓ Know the formulas.
✓ Recognize that variable costs change with sales volume; fixed costs do not.
✓ Avoid computational errors.

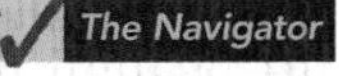

SELF-STUDY QUESTIONS

WILEY PLUS

Answers are at the end of the chapter.

(SO 1) **1.** Variable costs are costs that:
a. vary in total directly and proportionately with changes in the activity level.
b. remain the same per unit at every activity level.
c. Neither of the above.
d. Both (a) and (b) above.

(SO 2) **2.** The relevant range is:
a. the range of activity in which variable costs will be curvilinear.
b. the range of activity in which fixed costs will be curvilinear.
c. the range over which the company expects to operate during a year.
d. usually from zero to 100% of operating capacity.

(SO 3) **3.** Mixed costs consist of a:
a. variable cost element and a fixed cost element.
b. fixed cost element and a controllable cost element.
c. relevant cost element and a controllable cost element.
d. variable cost element and a relevant cost element.

(SO 3) **4.** Kendra Corporation's total utility costs during the past year were $1,200 during its highest month and $600 during its lowest month. These costs corresponded with 10,000 units of production during the high month and 2,000 units during the low month. What are the fixed and variable components of its utility costs using the high-low method?
a. $0.075 variable and $450 fixed.
b. $0.120 variable and $0 fixed.
c. $0.300 variable and $0 fixed.
d. $0.060 variable and $600 fixed.

5. One of the following is *not* involved in CVP analysis. That factor is: (SO 4)
a. sales mix.
b. unit selling prices.
c. fixed costs per unit.
d. volume or level of activity.

6. Contribution margin: (SO 5)
a. is revenue remaining after deducting variable costs.
b. may be expressed as contribution margin per unit.
c. is selling price less cost of goods sold.
d. Both (a) and (b) above.

7. Cournot Company sells 100,000 wrenches for $12 a unit. Fixed costs are $300,000, and net income is $200,000. What should be reported as variable expenses in the CVP income statement? (SO 5)
a. $700,000. **c.** $500,000.
b. $900,000. **d.** $1,000,000.

8. Gossen Company is planning to sell 200,000 pliers for $4 per unit. The contribution margin ratio is 25%. If Gossen will break even at this level of sales, what are the fixed costs? (SO 6)
a. $100,000. **c.** $200,000.
b. $160,000. **d.** $300,000.

9. The mathematical equation for computing required sales to obtain target net income is: Required sales = (SO 7)
a. Variable costs + Target net income.
b. Variable costs + Fixed costs + Target net income.

c. Fixed costs + Target net income.
d. No correct answer is given.

(SO 8) **10.** Marshall Company had actual sales of $600,000 when break-even sales were $420,000. What is the margin of safety ratio?
a. 25%. **c.** 33⅓%.
b. 30%. **d.** 45%.

Go to the book's website, **www.wiley.com/college/weygandt,** for Additional Self-Study questions.

QUESTIONS

1. **(a)** What is cost behavior analysis?
   (b) Why is cost behavior analysis important to management?
2. **(a)** Jenny Kent asks your help in understanding the term "activity index." Explain the meaning and importance of this term for Jenny.
   (b) State the two ways that variable costs may be defined.
3. Contrast the effects of changes in the activity level on total fixed costs and on unit fixed costs.
4. A. J. Hernandez claims that the relevant range concept is important only for variable costs.
   (a) Explain the relevant range concept.
   (b) Do you agree with A. J.'s claim? Explain.
5. "The relevant range is indispensable in cost behavior analysis." Is this true? Why or why not?
6. Ryan Ricketts is confused. He does not understand why rent on his apartment is a fixed cost and rent on a Hertz rental truck is a mixed cost. Explain the difference to Ryan.
7. How should mixed costs be classified in CVP analysis? What approach is used to effect the appropriate classification?
8. At the high and low levels of activity during the month, direct labor hours are 90,000 and 40,000, respectively. The related costs are $160,000 and $100,000. What are the fixed and variable costs at any level of activity?
9. "Cost-volume-profit (CVP) analysis is based entirely on unit costs." Do you agree? Explain.
10. Jill Nott defines contribution margin as the amount of profit available to cover operating expenses. Is there any truth in this definition? Discuss.
11. Kosko Company's Speedo calculator sells for $40. Variable costs per unit are estimated to be $28. What are the contribution margin per unit and the contribution margin ratio?
12. "Break-even analysis is of limited use to management because a company cannot survive by just breaking even." Do you agree? Explain.
13. Total fixed costs are $25,000 for Haag Inc. It has a contribution margin per unit of $15, and a contribution margin ratio of 25%. Compute the break-even sales in dollars.
14. Nancy Tobias asks your help in constructing a CVP graph. Explain to Nancy (a) how the break-even point is plotted, and (b) how the level of activity and dollar sales at the break-even point are determined.
15. Define the term "margin of safety." If Peine Company expects to sell 1,250 units of its product at $12 per unit, and break-even sales for the product are $12,000, what is the margin of safety ratio?
16. Ortega Company's break-even sales are $600,000. Assuming fixed costs are $180,000, what sales volume is needed to achieve a target net income of $60,000?
17. The traditional income statement for Mallon Company shows sales $900,000, cost of goods sold $500,000, and operating expenses $200,000. Assuming all costs and expenses are 70% variable and 30% fixed, prepare a CVP income statement through contribution margin.

BRIEF EXERCISES

Classify costs as variable, fixed, or mixed.

(SO 1, 3)

BE5-1 Monthly production costs in Pesavento Company for two levels of production are as follows.

Cost	3,000 units	6,000 units
Indirect labor	$10,000	$20,000
Supervisory salaries	5,000	5,000
Maintenance	4,000	7,000

Indicate which costs are variable, fixed, and mixed, and give the reason for each answer.

Diagram the behavior of costs within the relevant range.

(SO 2)

BE5-2 For Loder Company, the relevant range of production is 40–80% of capacity. At 40% of capacity, a variable cost is $4,000 and a fixed cost is $6,000. Diagram the behavior of each cost within the relevant range assuming the behavior is linear.

Diagram the behavior of a mixed cost.

(SO 3)

BE5-3 For Hunt Company, a mixed cost is $20,000 plus $16 per direct labor hour. Diagram the behavior of the cost using increments of 500 hours up to 2,500 hours on the horizontal axis and increments of $20,000 up to $80,000 on the vertical axis.

BE5-4 Deines Company accumulates the following data concerning a mixed cost, using miles as the activity level.

Determine variable and fixed cost elements using the high-low method.

(SO 3)

	Miles Driven	Total Cost		Miles Driven	Total Cost
January	8,000	$14,150	March	8,500	$15,000
February	7,500	13,600	April	8,200	14,490

Compute the variable and fixed cost elements using the high-low method.

BE5-5 Westerville Corp. has collected the following data concerning its maintenance costs for the past 6 months.

Determine variable and fixed cost elements using the high-low method.

(SO 3)

	Units Produced	Total Cost
July	18,000	$32,000
August	32,000	48,000
September	36,000	55,000
October	22,000	38,000
November	40,000	65,000
December	38,000	62,000

Compute the variable and fixed cost elements using the high-low method.

BE5-6 Determine the missing amounts.

Determine missing amounts for contribution margin.

(SO 5)

	Unit Selling Price	Unit Variable Costs	Contribution Margin per Unit	Contribution Margin Ratio
1.	$640	$384	(a)	(b)
2.	$300	(c)	$90	(d)
3.	(e)	(f)	$320	25%

BE5-7 Bruno Manufacturing Inc. had sales of $2,200,000 for the first quarter of 2008. In making the sales, the company incurred the following costs and expenses.

Prepare CVP income statement.

(SO 5)

	Variable	Fixed
Cost of goods sold	$920,000	$440,000
Selling expenses	70,000	45,000
Administrative expenses	86,000	98,000

Prepare a CVP income statement for the quarter ended March 31, 2008.

BE5-8 Larissa Company has a unit selling price of $520, variable costs per unit of $286, and fixed costs of $187,200. Compute the break-even point in units using **(a)** the mathematical equation and **(b)** contribution margin per unit.

Compute the break-even point.

(SO 6)

BE5-9 Turgro Corp. had total variable costs of $180,000, total fixed costs of $160,000, and total revenues of $300,000. Compute the required sales in dollars to break even.

Compute the break-even point.

(SO 6)

BE5-10 For MeriDen Company, variable costs are 60% of sales, and fixed costs are $195,000. Management's net income goal is $75,000. Compute the required sales in dollars needed to achieve management's target net income of $75,000. (Use the contribution margin approach.)

Compute sales for target net income.

(SO 7)

BE5-11 For Dousmann Company actual sales are $1,200,000 and break-even sales are $840,000. Compute **(a)** the margin of safety in dollars and **(b)** the margin of safety ratio.

Compute the margin of safety and the margin of safety ratio.

(SO 8)

BE5-12 PCB Corporation has fixed costs of $480,000. It has a unit selling price of $6, unit variable cost of $4.50, and a target net income of $1,500,000. Compute the required sales in units to achieve its target net income.

Compute the required sales in units for target net income.

(SO 7)

EXERCISES

Define and classify variable, fixed, and mixed costs.
(SO 1, 3)

E5-1 Dye Company manufactures a single product. Annual production costs incurred in the manufacturing process are shown below for two levels of production.

	Costs Incurred			
Production in Units	**5,000**		**10,000**	
Production Costs	**Total Cost**	**Cost/ Unit**	**Total Cost**	**Cost/ Unit**
Direct materials	$8,250	$1.65	$16,500	$1.65
Direct labor	9,500	1.90	19,000	1.90
Utilities	1,500	0.30	2,500	0.25
Rent	4,000	0.80	4,000	0.40
Maintenance	800	0.16	1,100	0.11
Supervisory salaries	1,000	0.20	1,000	0.10

Instructions

(a) Define the terms variable costs, fixed costs, and mixed costs.
(b) Classify each cost above as either variable, fixed, or mixed.

Diagram cost behavior, determine relevant range, and classify costs.
(SO 1, 2)

E5-2 Kozy Enterprises is considering manufacturing a new product. It projects the cost of direct materials and rent for a range of output as shown below.

Output in Units	Rent Expense	Direct Materials
1,000	$ 5,000	$ 4,000
2,000	5,000	6,000
3,000	5,000	7,800
4,000	7,000	8,000
5,000	7,000	10,000
6,000	7,000	12,000
7,000	7,000	14,000
8,000	7,000	16,000
9,000	7,000	18,000
10,000	10,000	23,000
11,000	10,000	28,000
12,000	10,000	36,000

Instructions

(a) Diagram the behavior of each cost for output ranging from 1,000 to 12,000 units.
(b) Determine the relevant range of activity for this product.
(c) Calculate the variable cost per unit within the relevant range.
(d) Indicate the fixed cost within the relevant range.

Determine fixed and variable costs using the high-low method and prepare graph.
(SO 1, 3)

E5-3 The controller of Dugan Industries has collected the following monthly expense data for use in analyzing the cost behavior of maintenance costs.

Month	Total Maintenance Costs	Total Machine Hours
January	$2,400	300
February	3,000	400
March	3,600	600
April	4,500	790
May	3,200	500
June	4,900	800

Instructions

(a) Determine the fixed and variable cost components using the high-low method.
(b) Prepare a graph showing the behavior of maintenance costs, and identify the fixed and variable cost elements. Use 200-hour increments and $1,000 cost increments.

Classify variable, fixed, and mixed costs.
(SO 1, 3)

E5-4 Black Brothers Furniture Corporation incurred the following costs.

1. Wood used in the production of furniture.
2. Fuel used in delivery trucks.

3. Straight-line depreciation on factory building.
4. Screws used in the production of furniture.
5. Sales staff salaries.
6. Sales commissions.
7. Property taxes.
8. Insurance on buildings.
9. Hourly wages of furniture craftsmen.
10. Salaries of factory supervisors.
11. Utilities expense.
12. Telephone bill.

Instructions

Identify the costs above as variable, fixed, or mixed.

Determine fixed and variable costs using the high-low method and prepare graph.

(SO 1, 3)

E5-5 The controller of Gutierrez Industries has collected the following monthly expense data for use in analyzing the cost behavior of maintenance costs.

Month	Total Maintenance Costs	Total Machine Hours
January	$2,800	3,000
February	3,000	4,000
March	3,600	6,000
April	4,500	7,900
May	3,200	5,000
June	5,000	8,000

Instructions

(a) Determine the fixed and variable cost components using the high-low method.

(b) Prepare a graph showing the behavior of maintenance costs, and identify the fixed and variable cost elements. Use 2,000-hour increments and $1,000 cost increments.

Determine fixed, variable, and mixed costs.

(SO 1, 3)

E5-6 Mozena Corporation manufactures a single product. Monthly production costs incurred in the manufacturing process are shown below for the production of 3,000 units. The utilities and maintenance costs are mixed costs. The fixed portions of these costs are $300 and $200, respectively.

Production in Units	3,000
Production Costs	
Direct materials	$ 7,500
Direct labor	15,000
Utilities	1,800
Property taxes	1,000
Indirect labor	4,500
Supervisory salaries	1,800
Maintenance	1,100
Depreciation	2,400

Instructions

(a) Identify the above costs as variable, fixed, or mixed.

(b) Calculate the expected costs when production is 5,000 units.

Explain assumptions underlying CVP analysis.

(SO 4)

E5-7 Jim Thome wants Thome Company to use CVP analysis to study the effects of changes in costs and volume on the company. Thome has heard that certain assumptions must be valid in order for CVP analysis to be useful.

Instructions

Prepare a memo to Jim Thome concerning the assumptions that underlie CVP analysis.

Compute break-even point in units and dollars.

(SO 5, 6)

E5-8 Green with Envy provides environmentally friendly lawn services for homeowners. Its operating costs are as follows.

Depreciation	$1,500 per month
Advertising	$200 per month
Insurance	$2,000 per month
Weed and feed materials	$13 per lawn
Direct labor	$12 per lawn
Fuel	$2 per lawn

Green with Envy charges $60 per treatment for the average single-family lawn.

Instructions

Determine the company's break-even point in **(a)** number of lawns serviced per month and **(b)** dollars.

Compute break-even point.
(SO 5, 6)

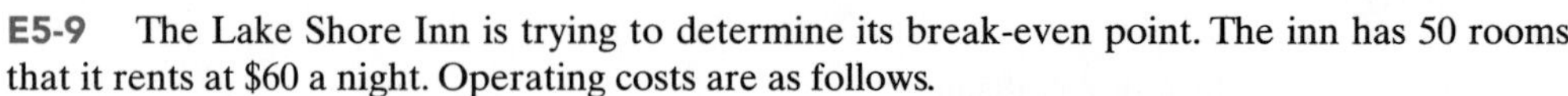

E5-9 The Lake Shore Inn is trying to determine its break-even point. The inn has 50 rooms that it rents at $60 a night. Operating costs are as follows.

Salaries	$7,200 per month
Utilities	$1,500 per month
Depreciation	$1,200 per month
Maintenance	$300 per month
Maid service	$8 per room
Other costs	$28 per room

Instructions

Determine the inn's break-even point in (1) number of rented rooms per month and (2) dollars.

Compute contribution margin and break-even point.
(SO 5, 6)

E5-10 In the month of March, New Day Spa services 570 clients at an average price of $120. During the month, fixed costs were $21,000 and variable costs were 65% of sales.

Instructions

(a) Determine the contribution margin in dollars, per unit, and as a ratio.
(b) Using the contribution margin technique, compute the break-even point in dollars and in units.

Compute break-even point.
(SO 5, 6)

E5-11 Airport Connection provides shuttle service between four hotels near a medical center and an international airport. Airport Connection uses two 10 passenger vans to offer 12 round trips per day. A recent month's activity in the form of a cost-volume-profit income statement is shown below.

Fare revenues (1,440 fares)		$36,000
Variable costs		
Fuel	$5,040	
Tolls and parking	3,100	
Maintenance	500	8,640
Contribution margin		27,360
Fixed costs		
Salaries	13,000	
Depreciation	1,300	
Insurance	1,128	15,428
Net income		$11,932

Instructions

(a) Calculate the break-even point in (1) dollars and (2) number of fares.
(b) Without calculations, determine the contribution margin at the break-even point.

Compute variable cost per unit, contribution margin ratio, and increase in fixed costs.
(SO 5, 6)

E5-12 In 2008, Hadicke Company had a break-even point of $350,000 based on a selling price of $7 per unit and fixed costs of $105,000. In 2009, the selling price and the variable cost per unit did not change, but the break-even point increased to $420,000.

Instructions

(a) Compute the variable cost per unit and the contribution margin ratio for 2008.
(b) Compute the increase in fixed costs for 2009.

Prepare CVP income statements.
(SO 5, 6)

E5-13 NIU Company has the following information available for September 2008.

Unit selling price of video game consoles	$ 400
Unit variable costs	$ 270
Total fixed costs	$52,000
Units sold	620

Instructions

(a) Prepare a CVP income statement that shows both total and per unit amounts.
(b) Compute NIU's break-even point in units.
(c) Prepare a CVP income statement for the break-even point that shows both total and per unit amounts.

E5-14 Lynn Company had $150,000 of net income in 2008 when the selling price per unit was $150, the variable costs per unit were $90, and the fixed costs were $570,000. Management expects per unit data and total fixed costs to remain the same in 2009. The president of Lynn Company is under pressure from stockholders to increase net income by $60,000 in 2009.

Compute various components to derive target net income under different assumptions.

(SO 6, 7)

Instructions

(a) Compute the number of units sold in 2008.

(b) Compute the number of units that would have to be sold in 2009 to reach the stockholders' desired profit level.

(c) Assume that Lynn Company sells the same number of units in 2009 as it did in 2008. What would the selling price have to be in order to reach the stockholders' desired profit level?

E5-15 Moran Company reports the following operating results for the month of August: Sales $350,000 (units 5,000); variable costs $210,000; and fixed costs $90,000. Management is considering the following independent courses of action to increase net income.

Compute net income under different alternatives.

(SO 7)

1. Increase selling price by 10% with no change in total variable costs.
2. Reduce variable costs to 55% of sales.

Instructions

Compute the net income to be earned under each alternative. Which course of action will produce the highest net income?

E5-16 Grissom Company estimates that variable costs will be 60% of sales, and fixed costs will total $800,000. The selling price of the product is $4.

Prepare a CVP graph and compute break-even point and margin of safety.

(SO 6, 8)

Instructions

(a) Prepare a CVP graph, assuming maximum sales of $3,200,000. (*Note*: Use $400,000 increments for sales and costs and 100,000 increments for units.)

(b) Compute the break-even point in (1) units and (2) dollars.

(c) Compute the margin of safety in (1) dollars and (2) as a ratio, assuming actual sales are $2.5 million.

EXERCISES: SET B

Visit the book's website at **www.wiley.com/college/weygandt**, and choose the Student Companion site, to access Exercise Set B.

PROBLEMS: SET A

P5-1A Matt Reiss owns the Fredonia Barber Shop. He employs five barbers and pays each a base rate of $1,000 per month. One of the barbers serves as the manager and receives an extra $500 per month. In addition to the base rate, each barber also receives a commission of $5.50 per haircut.

Determine variable and fixed costs, compute break-even point, prepare a CVP graph, and determine net income.

(SO 1, 3, 5, 6)

Other costs are as follows.

Advertising	$200 per month
Rent	$900 per month
Barber supplies	$0.30 per haircut
Utilities	$175 per month plus $0.20 per haircut
Magazines	$25 per month

Matt currently charges $10 per haircut.

Instructions

(a) Determine the variable cost per haircut and the total monthly fixed costs.

VC $6

(b) Compute the break-even point in units and dollars.

(c) Prepare a CVP graph, assuming a maximum of 1,800 haircuts in a month. Use increments of 300 haircuts on the horizontal axis and $3,000 on the vertical axis.

(d) Determine net income, assuming 1,900 haircuts are given in a month.

Prepare a CVP income statement, compute break-even point, contribution margin ratio, margin of safety ratio, and sales for target net income.

(SO 5, 6, 7, 8)

P5-2A Utech Company bottles and distributes Livit, a diet soft drink. The beverage is sold for 50 cents per 16-ounce bottle to retailers, who charge customers 75 cents per bottle. For the year 2008, management estimates the following revenues and costs.

Net sales	$1,800,000	Selling expenses—variable	$70,000
Direct materials	430,000	Selling expenses—fixed	65,000
Direct labor	352,000	Administrative expenses—variable	20,000
Manufacturing overhead—variable	316,000	Administrative expenses—fixed	60,000
Manufacturing overhead—fixed	283,000		

Instructions

(b) (1) 2,400,000 units

(c) CM ratio # 34%

(a) Prepare a CVP income statement for 2008 based on management's estimates.

(b) Compute the break-even point in (1) units and (2) dollars.

(c) Compute the contribution margin ratio and the margin of safety ratio. (Round to full percents.)

(d) Determine the sales dollars required to earn net income of $238,000.

Compute break-even point under alternative courses of action.

(SO 5, 6)

P5-3A Gorham Manufacturing's sales slumped badly in 2008. For the first time in its history, it operated at a loss. The company's income statement showed the following results from selling 600,000 units of product: Net sales $2,400,000; total costs and expenses $2,540,000; and net loss $140,000. Costs and expenses consisted of the amounts shown below.

	Total	Variable	Fixed
Cost of goods sold	$2,100,000	$1,440,000	$660,000
Selling expenses	240,000	72,000	168,000
Administrative expenses	200,000	48,000	152,000
	$2,540,000	$1,560,000	$980,000

Management is considering the following independent alternatives for 2009.

1. Increase unit selling price 20% with no change in costs, expenses, and sales volume.
2. Change the compensation of salespersons from fixed annual salaries totaling $210,000 to total salaries of $60,000 plus a 5% commission on net sales.

Instructions

(a) Compute the break-even point in dollars for 2008.

(b) Alternative 1 # $2,130,435

(b) Compute the break-even point in dollars under each of the alternative courses of action. (Round all ratios to nearest full percent.) Which course of action do you recommend?

Compute break-even point and margin of safety ratio, and prepare a CVP income statement before and after changes in business environment.

(SO 5, 6, 8)

P5-4A Alice Shoemaker is the advertising manager for Value Shoe Store. She is currently working on a major promotional campaign. Her ideas include the installation of a new lighting system and increased display space that will add $34,000 in fixed costs to the $270,000 currently spent. In addition, Alice is proposing that a 5% price decrease ($40 to $38) will produce a 20% increase in sales volume (20,000 to 24,000). Variable costs will remain at $22 per pair of shoes. Management is impressed with Alice's ideas but concerned about the effects that these changes will have on the break-even point and the margin of safety.

Instructions

(a) Compute the current break-even point in units, and compare it to the break-even point in units if Alice's ideas are used.

(b) Current margin of safety ratio # 25%

(b) Compute the margin of safety ratio for current operations and after Alice's changes are introduced. (Round to nearest full percent.)

(c) Prepare a CVP income statement for current operations and after Alice's changes are introduced. Would you make the changes suggested?

Compute contribution margin, fixed costs, break-even point, sales for target net income, and margin of safety ratio.

(SO 5, 6, 7, 8)

P5-5A Poole Corporation has collected the following information after its first year of sales. Net sales were $1,600,000 on 100,000 units; selling expenses $240,000 (40% variable and 60% fixed); direct materials $511,000; direct labor $285,000; administrative expenses $280,000 (20% variable and 80% fixed); manufacturing overhead $360,000 (70% variable and 30% fixed). Top management has asked you to do a CVP analysis so that it can make plans for the coming year. It has projected that unit sales will increase by 10% next year.

Instructions

(a) Compute (1) the contribution margin for the current year and the projected year, and (2) the fixed costs for the current year. (Assume that fixed costs will remain the same in the projected year.)

(b) Compute the break-even point in units and sales dollars for the current year. (b) 119,000 units

(c) The company has a target net income of $310,000. What is the required sales in dollars for the company to meet its target?

(d) If the company meets its target net income number, by what percentage could its sales fall before it is operating at a loss? That is, what is its margin of safety ratio?

PROBLEMS: SET B

Determine variable and fixed costs, compute break-even point, prepare a CVP graph, and determine net income.

(SO 1, 3, 5, 6)

P5-1B The Galena Barber Shop employs four barbers. One barber, who also serves as the manager, is paid a salary of $3,200 per month. The other barbers are paid $1,400 per month. In addition, each barber is paid a commission of $3 per haircut. Other monthly costs are: store rent $700 plus 60 cents per haircut, depreciation on equipment $500, barber supplies 40 cents per haircut, utilities $300, and advertising $100. The price of a haircut is $10.

Instructions

(a) Determine the variable cost per haircut and the total monthly fixed costs. (a) VC $ 4

(b) Compute the break-even point in units and dollars.

(c) Prepare a CVP graph, assuming a maximum of 1,800 haircuts in a month. Use increments of 300 haircuts on the horizontal axis and $3,000 increments on the vertical axis.

(d) Determine the net income, assuming 1,700 haircuts are given in a month.

Prepare a CVP income statement, compute break-even point, contribution margin ratio, margin of safety ratio, and sales for target net income.

(SO 5, 6, 7, 8)

P5-2B Wilks Company bottles and distributes No-FIZZ, a fruit drink. The beverage is sold for 50 cents per 16-ounce bottle to retailers, who charge customers 70 cents per bottle. For the year 2008, management estimates the following revenues and costs.

Net sales	$2,000,000	Selling expenses—variable	$ 100,000
Direct materials	360,000	Selling expenses—fixed	150,000
Direct labor	590,000	Administrative expenses—variable	40,000
Manufacturing overhead—variable	270,000	Administrative expenses—fixed	78,000
Manufacturing overhead—fixed	220,000		

Instructions

(a) Prepare a CVP income statement for 2008 based on management's estimates.

(b) Compute the break-even point in (1) units and (2) dollars. (b) (1) 2,800,000 units

(c) Compute the contribution margin ratio and the margin of safety ratio. (c) CM ratio # 32%

(d) Determine the sales dollars required to earn net income of $272,000.

Compute break-even point under alternative courses of action.

(SO 5, 6)

P5-3B Milner Manufacturing had a bad year in 2008. For the first time in its history it operated at a loss. The company's income statement showed the following results from selling 60,000 units of product: Net sales $1,500,000; total costs and expenses $1,660,000; and net loss $160,000. Costs and expenses consisted of the following.

	Total	Variable	Fixed
Cost of goods sold	$1,200,000	$780,000	$420,000
Selling expenses	340,000	65,000	275,000
Administrative expenses	120,000	55,000	65,000
	$1,660,000	$900,000	$760,000

Management is considering the following independent alternatives for 2009.

1. Increase unit selling price 20% with no change in costs, expenses, and sales volume.
2. Change the compensation of salespersons from fixed annual salaries totaling $200,000 to total salaries of $30,000 plus a 6% commission on net sales.

Instructions

(b) Alternative 1 # $1,520,000

(a) Compute the break-even point in dollars for 2008.

(b) Compute the break-even point in dollars under each of the alternative courses of action. (Round all ratios to nearest full percent.) Which course of action do you recommend?

Compute break-even point and margin of safety ratio, and prepare a CVP income statement before and after changes in business environment.

(SO 5, 6, 8)

P5-4B Anne Ogilvie is the advertising manager for Thrifty Shoe Store. She is currently working on a major promotional campaign. Her ideas include the installation of a new lighting system and increased display space that will add $51,000 in fixed costs to the $204,000 currently spent. In addition, Anne is proposing that a 6⅔% price decrease (from $30 to $28) will produce an increase in sales volume from 16,000 to 21,000 units. Variable costs will remain at $13 per pair of shoes. Management is impressed with Anne's ideas but concerned about the effects that these changes will have on the break-even point and the margin of safety.

Instructions

(a) Compute the current break-even point in units, and compare it to the break-even point in units if Anne's ideas are used.

(b) Current margin of safety ratio 25%

(b) Compute the margin of safety ratio for current operations and after Anne's changes are introduced. (Round to nearest full percent.)

(c) Prepare a CVP income statement for current operations and after Anne's changes are introduced. Would you make the changes suggested?

Compute contribution margin, fixed costs, break-even point, sales for target net income, and margin of safety ratio.

(SO 5, 6, 7, 8)

P5-5B Washington Corporation has collected the following information after its first year of sales. Net sales were $2,400,000 on 200,000 units; selling expenses $360,000 (30% variable and 70% fixed); direct materials $626,500; direct labor $507,500; administrative expenses $420,000 (40% variable and 60% fixed); manufacturing overhead $540,000 (50% variable and 50% fixed). Top management has asked you to do a CVP analysis so that it can make plans for the coming year. It has projected that unit sales will increase by 20% next year.

Instructions

(a) Compute (1) the contribution margin for the current year and the projected year, and (2) the fixed costs for the current year. (Assume that fixed costs will remain the same in the projected year.)

(b) 215,000 units

(b) Compute the break-even point in units and sales dollars for the current year.

(c) The company has a target net income of $620,000. What is the required sales in dollars for the company to meet its target?

(d) If the company meets its target net income number, by what percentage could its sales fall before it is operating at a loss? That is, what is its margin of safety ratio?

PROBLEMS: SET C

Visit the book's website at **www.wiley.com/college/weygandt**, and choose the Student Companion site, to access Problem Set C.

WATERWAYS CONTINUING PROBLEM

(*Note:* This is a continuation of the Waterways Problem from Chapters 1 through 4.)

WCP5 The Vice President for Sales and Marketing at Waterways Corporation is planning for production needs to meet sales demand in the coming year. He is also trying to determine how the company's profits might be increased in the coming year. This problem asks you to use cost-volume-profit concepts to help Waterways understand contribution margins of some of its products and to decide whether to mass-produce certain products.

Go to the book's website, ***www.wiley.com/college/weygandt,*** *to find the remainder of this problem.*

BROADENING YOUR PERSPECTIVE

DECISION MAKING ACROSS THE ORGANIZATION

BYP5-1 Gagliano Company has decided to introduce a new product. The new product can be manufactured by either a capital-intensive method or a labor-intensive method. The manufacturing method will not affect the quality of the product. The estimated manufacturing costs by the two methods are as follows.

	Capital-Intensive	Labor-Intensive
Direct materials	$5 per unit	$5.50 per unit
Direct labor	$6 per unit	$8.00 per unit
Variable overhead	$3 per unit	$4.50 per unit
Fixed manufacturing costs	$2,508,000	$1,538,000

Gagliano's market research department has recommended an introductory unit sales price of $30. The incremental selling expenses are estimated to be $502,000 annually plus $2 for each unit sold, regardless of manufacturing method.

Instructions

With the class divided into groups, answer the following.

(a) Calculate the estimated break-even point in annual unit sales of the new product if Gagliano Company uses the:

(1) capital-intensive manufacturing method.

(2) labor-intensive manufacturing method.

(b) Determine the annual unit sales volume at which Gagliano Company would be indifferent between the two manufacturing methods.

(c) Explain the circumstance under which Gagliano should employ each of the two manufacturing methods.

(CMA adapted)

MANAGERIAL ANALYSIS

BYP5-2 The condensed income statement for the Terri and Jerry partnership for 2008 is as follows.

TERRI AND JERRY COMPANY
Income Statement
For the Year Ended December 31, 2008

Sales (200,000 units)		$1,200,000
Cost of goods sold		800,000
Gross profit		400,000
Operating expenses		
Selling	$280,000	
Administrative	160,000	440,000
Net loss		($40,000)

A cost behavior analysis indicates that 75% of the cost of goods sold are variable, 50% of the selling expenses are variable, and 25% of the administrative expenses are variable.

Instructions

(Round to nearest unit, dollar, and percentage, where necessary. Use the CVP income statement format in computing profits.)

(a) Compute the break-even point in total sales dollars and in units for 2008.

(b) Terri has proposed a plan to get the partnership "out of the red" and improve its profitability. She feels that the quality of the product could be substantially improved by spending $0.25 more per unit on better raw materials. The selling price per unit could be increased to only $6.25 because of competitive pressures. Terri estimates that sales volume will increase by 30%. What effect would Terri's plan have on the profits and the break-even point in dollars of the partnership? (Round the contribution margin ratio to two decimal places.)

(c) Jerry was a marketing major in college. He believes that sales volume can be increased only by intensive advertising and promotional campaigns. He therefore proposed the following plan as an alternative to Terri's. (1) Increase variable selling expenses to $0.79 per unit, (2) lower the selling price per unit by $0.30, and (3) increase fixed selling expenses by $35,000. Jerry quoted an old marketing research report that said that sales volume would increase by 60% if these changes were made. What effect would Jerry's plan have on the profits and the break-even point in dollars of the partnership?

(d) Which plan should be accepted? Explain your answer.

REAL-WORLD FOCUS

BYP5-3 The Coca-Cola Company hardly needs an introduction. A line taken from the cover of a recent annual report says it all: If you measured time in servings of Coca-Cola, "a billion Coca-Cola's ago was yesterday morning." On average, every U.S. citizen drinks 363 8-ounce servings of Coca-Cola products each year. Coca-Cola's primary line of business is the making and selling of syrup to bottlers. These bottlers then sell the finished bottles and cans of Coca-Cola to the consumer.

In the annual report of Coca-Cola, the following information was provided.

THE COCA-COLA COMPANY
Management Discussion

Our gross margin declined to 61 percent this year from 62 percent in the prior year, primarily due to costs for materials such as sweeteners and packaging.

The increases [in selling expenses] in the last two years were primarily due to higher marketing expenditures in support of our Company's volume growth.

We measure our sales volume in two ways: (1) gallon shipments of concentrates and syrups and (2) unit cases of finished product (bottles and cans of Coke sold by bottlers).

Instructions

Answer the following questions.

(a) Are sweeteners and packaging a variable cost or a fixed cost? What is the impact on the contribution margin of an increase in the per unit cost of sweeteners or packaging? What are the implications for profitability?

(b) In your opinion, are marketing expenditures a fixed cost, variable cost, or mixed cost to The Coca-Cola Company? Give justification for your answer.

(c) Which of the two measures cited for measuring volume represents the activity index as defined in this chapter? Why might Coca-Cola use two different measures?

EXPLORING THE WEB

BYP5-4 Ganong Bros. Ltd., located in St. Stephen, New Brunswick, is Canada's oldest independent candy company. Its products are distributed worldwide. In 1885, Ganong invented the popular "chicken bone," a cinnamon flavored, pink, hard candy jacket over a chocolate center. The home page of Ganong, listed on the next page, includes information about the company and its products.

Address: www.ganong.com/retail/chicken_bones.html, or go to **www.wiley.com/college/weygandt**

Instructions

Read the description of "chicken bones," and answer the following.

(a) Describe the steps in making "chicken bones."

(b) Identify at least two variable and two fixed costs that are likely to affect the production of "chicken bones."

COMMUNICATION ACTIVITY

BYP5-5 Your roommate asks your help on the following questions about CVP analysis formulas.

(a) How can the mathematical equation for break-even sales show both sales units and sales dollars?

(b) How do the formulas differ for contribution margin per unit and contribution margin ratio?

(c) How can contribution margin be used to determine break-even sales in units and in dollars?

Instructions

Write a memo to your roommate stating the relevant formulas and answering each question.

ETHICS CASE

BYP5-6 Kenny Hampton is an accountant for Bartley Company. Early this year Kenny made a highly favorable projection of sales and profits over the next 3 years for Bartley's hot-selling computer PLEX. As a result of the projections Kenny presented to senior management, they decided to expand production in this area. This decision led to dislocations of some plant personnel who were reassigned to one of the company's newer plants in another state. However, no one was fired, and in fact the company expanded its work force slightly.

Unfortunately Kenny rechecked his computations on the projections a few months later and found that he had made an error that would have reduced his projections substantially. Luckily, sales of PLEX have exceeded projections so far, and management is satisfied with its decision. Kenny, however, is not sure what to do. Should he confess his honest mistake and jeopardize his possible promotion? He suspects that no one will catch the error because sales of PLEX have exceeded his projections, and it appears that profits will materialize close to his projections.

Instructions

(a) Who are the stakeholders in this situation?

(b) Identify the ethical issues involved in this situation.

(c) What are the possible alternative actions for Kenny? What would you do in Kenny's position?

"ALL ABOUT YOU" ACTIVITY

BYP5-7 In the "All About You" feature in this chapter, you learned that cost-volume-profit analysis can be used in making personal financial decisions. The purchase of a new car is one of your biggest personal expenditures. It is important that you carefully analyze your options.

Suppose that you are considering the purchase of a hybrid vehicle. Let's assume the following facts: The hybrid will initially cost an additional $3,000 above the cost of a traditional vehicle. The hybrid will get 40 miles per gallon of gas, and the traditional car will get 30 miles per gallon. Also, assume that the cost of gas is $3 per gallon.

Instructions

Using the facts above, answer the following questions.

(a) What is the variable gasoline cost of going one mile in the hybrid car? What is the variable cost of going one mile in the traditional car?

(b) Using the information in part (a), if "miles" is your unit of measure, what is the "contribution margin" of the hybrid vehicle relative to the traditional vehicle? That is, express the variable cost savings on a per-mile basis.

(c) How many miles would you have to drive in order to break even on your investment in the hybrid car?
(d) What other factors might you want to consider?

Answers to Insight and Accounting Across the Organization Questions

Woodworker Runs an Efficient Operation for Producing Furniture, p. 200

Q: Are the costs associated with use of the computer-driven cutting machines fixed or variable?
A: *The cost of the cutting machine that is recognized through depreciation expense is a fixed cost. The costs of operating (electricity) and maintaining the machine are variable.*

Charter Flights Offer a Good Deal, p. 210

Q: How did FlightServe determine that it would break even with 3.3 seats full per flight?
A: *FlightServe determined its break-even point with the following formula:*
Fixed costs ÷ Contribution margin per seat occupied = Break-even point in seats.

How a Rolling Stones' Tour Makes Money, p. 214

Q: What amount of sales dollars are required for the promoter to break even?
A: *Fixed costs = $1,200,000 + $400,000 = $1,600,000*
Contribution margin ratio = 80%
Break-even sales = $1,600,000 ÷ .80 = $2,000,000

Authors' Comments on *All About You:* A Hybrid Dilemma, p. 215

Just like the break-even analysis that a company would perform on an investment in a new piece of equipment, the break-even analysis of a hybrid car requires a lot of assumptions. After deciding on a car, you need to estimate how many miles you would drive each year and how many years you would own the car. If you trade cars every two or three years, it is unlikely, with the hybrids available today, that you will recoup your initial investment. Your chances of recouping the investment increase the longer you keep the car and the more miles you drive. You need to determine whether you will get a federal tax credit or a rebate from your employer. You also need to estimate what the car would be worth when you sell it. Based on assumed values for the average driver, *Consumer Reports* determined that only the most fuel-efficient hybrids save enough on fuel to cover their additional costs, but individual results will vary depending on the factors mentioned above.

Answers to Self-Study Questions

1. d **2.** c **3.** a **4.** a **5.** c **6.** d **7.** a **8.** c **9.** b **10.** b

Remember to go back to the Navigator box on the chapter-opening page and check off your completed work.

Chapter 6

Cost-Volume-Profit Analysis: Additional Issues

STUDY OBJECTIVES

After studying this chapter, you should be able to:

1. Describe the essential features of a cost-volume-profit income statement.
2. Apply basic CVP concepts.
3. Explain the term sales mix and its effects on break-even sales.
4. Determine sales mix when a company has limited resources.
5. Understand how operating leverage affects profitability.

The Navigator

Scan **Study Objectives**	☐
Read **Feature Story**	☐
Read **Preview**	☐
Read text and answer **Before You Go On** p. 244 ☐ p. 250 ☐	
Work **Using the Decision Toolkit**	☐
Review **Summary of Study Objectives**	☐
Work **Demonstration Problem**	☐
Answer **Self-Study Questions**	☐
Complete **Assignments**	☐

Feature Story

WHAT GOES UP (*FAST*), MUST COME DOWN (*FAST*)

During the late 1990s many people marveled at the efficiency of the so-called "New Economy," which uses digital technologies to improve business processes. Some managers were actually startled by their own success. The New Economy had created a new formula for profit. For example, David Peterschmidt, chief executive at software developer Inktomi, noted that the company had incurred considerable fixed costs in developing new software, but its variable costs were minor. As a consequence, once sales had covered the fixed costs, every additional sale was basically pure profit. When sales were booming, he happily stated, "Next to the federal government, this is the only business that's allowed to print money." But that was then. When the economy lagged, the new profit formula went sour. The company's sales disappeared, but its fixed costs did not. In no time, Inktomi went from record profits to staggering losses.

Many other companies have had similar experiences. As their manufacturing plants have become more automated, their fixed costs have become increasingly high. For example, during a five-year period, the average cost of a typical Intel semiconductor plant rose from $500 million to $2 billion as its manufacturing processes became increasingly sophisticated. These high fixed costs have made Intel very dependent on producing a high volume of computer chips. It needs high volume so that it can spread its fixed costs across a lot of units, thereby reducing the fixed cost per unit. As one Intel employee put it, "You have high fixed costs, so you want to minimize those fixed costs and keep factories running 24 hours a day."

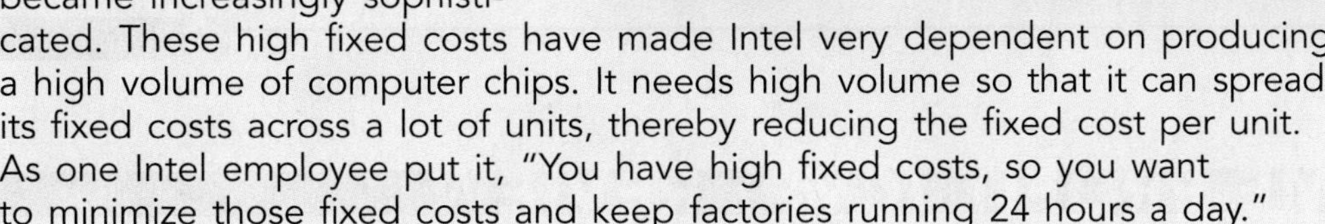

However, when management focuses too heavily on keeping volume high to reduce fixed costs per unit, it sometimes produces more inventory than the market wants. When this happens, companies have to cut prices sharply. High-tech firms, like Intel, whose products rapidly become obsolete, have occasionally been stuck with inventory that nobody wanted. Thus, while the huge outlays for new equipment have made these companies exceptionally efficient, such outlays have also increased their exposure to economic swings. In fact, because so many companies now have cost structures that rely heavily on fixed costs, many economists worry that swings in the entire economy will be more volatile than in the past.

Source: Greg Ip, "As Profits Swoon, Companies Blame A Marked Change in Cost Structure," *Wall Street Journal,* May 16, 2001.

Inside Chapter 6

Preview of Chapter 6

As the Feature Story about Inktomi and Intel suggests, the relationship between a company's fixed and variable costs can have a huge impact on its profitability. In particular, the trend toward cost structures dominated by fixed costs has significantly increased the volatility of many companies' net income. The purpose of this chapter is to demonstrate additional uses of cost-volume-profit analysis in making sound business decisions. The content and organization of this chapter are as follows.

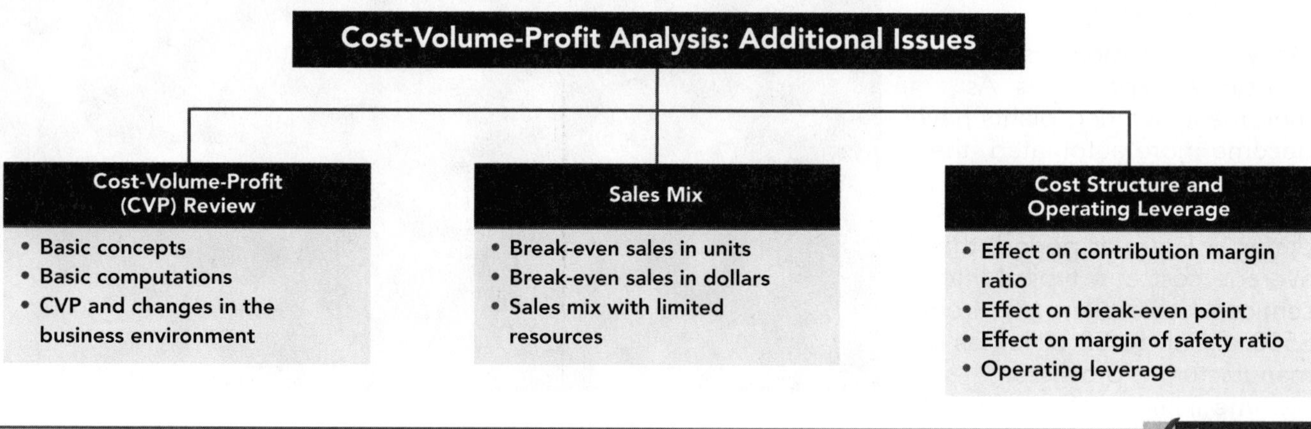

The Navigator

COST-VOLUME-PROFIT (CVP) REVIEW

As indicated in Chapter 5, cost-volume-profit (CVP) analysis is the study of the effects of changes in costs and volume on a company's profit. CVP analysis is important to profit planning. It is also a critical factor in such management decisions as determining product mix, maximizing use of production facilities, and setting selling prices.

Basic Concepts

Because CVP is so important for decision making, management often wants this information reported in a CVP income statement format for internal use. The CVP income statement classifies costs as *variable* or *fixed* and computes a contribution margin. **Contribution margin** is the amount of revenue remaining after deducting variable costs. It is often stated both as a total amount and on a per unit basis.

STUDY OBJECTIVE 1

Describe the essential features of a cost-volume-profit income statement.

Illustration 6-1 presents the CVP income statement for Vargo Video (which was shown in Illustration 5-11, on page 206). Note that Vargo's sales included 1,600 DVD players at $500 per unit.

Illustration 6-1
Basic CVP income statement

VARGO VIDEO COMPANY
CVP Income Statement
For the Month Ended June 30, 2008

	Total	Per Unit
Sales (1,600 DVD players)	$800,000	$ 500
Variable costs	480,000	300
Contribution margin	**320,000**	**$200**
Fixed costs	200,000	
Net income	**$120,000**	

Companies often prepare detailed CVP income statements. To illustrate, we use the same base information in Illustration 6-2 as that presented in Illustration 6-1.

Illustration 6-2
Detailed CVP income statement

VARGO VIDEO COMPANY
CVP Income Statement
For the Month Ended June 30, 2008

		Total	Per Unit
Sales		$800,000	$500
Variable expenses			
Cost of goods sold	$400,000		
Selling expenses	60,000		
Administrative expenses	20,000		
Total variable expenses		480,000	300
Contribution margin		**320,000**	**$200**
Fixed expenses			
Cost of goods sold	120,000		
Selling expenses	40,000		
Administrative expenses	40,000		
Total fixed expenses		200,000	
Net income		**$120,000**	

HELPFUL HINT
The appendix to this chapter provides additional discussion of income statements used for decision making.

In the applications of CVP analysis that follow, we assume that the term "cost" includes all costs and expenses related to production and sale of the product. That is, cost includes manufacturing costs plus selling and administrative expenses.

Basic Computations

STUDY OBJECTIVE 2
Apply basic CVP concepts.

Before we introduce additional issues of CVP analysis, let's review some of the basic concepts that you learned in Chapter 5, specifically break-even analysis, target net income, and margin of safety.

BREAK-EVEN ANALYSIS

Vargo Video's CVP income statement (Illustration 6-2) shows that total contribution margin (sales minus variable expenses) is $320,000, and the company's contribution margin per unit is $200. Recall that contribution margin can also be expressed in the form of the **contribution margin ratio** (contribution margin divided by sales), which in the case of Vargo is 40% ($200 ÷ $500).

Illustration 6-3 demonstrates how to compute Vargo's break-even point in units (using contribution margin per unit) or in dollars (using contribution margin ratio).

Illustration 6-3
Break-even point

Fixed Costs	÷	Contribution Margin per Unit	=	Break-even Point in Units
$200,000	÷	$200	=	1,000 units
Fixed Costs	÷	**Contribution Margin Ratio**	=	**Break-even Point in Dollars**
$200,000	÷	.40	=	$500,000

When a company is in its early stages of operation, its primary goal is to break even. Failure to break even will lead eventually to financial failure.

TARGET NET INCOME

Once a company achieves break-even, it then sets a sales goal that will generate a target net income. For example, assume that Vargo's management has a target net income of $250,000. Illustration 6-4 shows the required sales in units and dollars to achieve its target net income.

Illustration 6-4
Target net income

(Fixed Costs + Target Net Income)	÷	Contribution Margin per Unit	=	Required Sales in Units
($200,000 + $250,000)	÷	$200	=	2,250 units
(Fixed Costs + Target Net Income)	÷	**Contribution Margin Ratio**	=	**Required Sales in Dollars**
($200,000 + $250,000)	÷	.40	=	$1,125,000

In order to achieve net income of $250,000, Vargo has to sell 2,250 DVD players, for a total price of $1,125,000.

MARGIN OF SAFETY

Another measure managers use to assess profitability is the margin of safety. The **margin of safety** tells us **how far sales can drop** before the company will be operating at a loss. Managers like to have a sense of how much cushion they have between their current situation and operating at a loss. This can be expressed in dollars or as a ratio. In Illustration 6-2, for example, Vargo reported sales of $800,000. At that sales level, its margin of safety in dollars and as a ratio are as follows.

Illustration 6-5
Margin of safety

Actual (Expected) Sales	−	Break-even Sales	=	Margin of Safety in Dollars
$800,000	−	$500,000	=	$300,000
Margin of Safety in Dollars	÷	**Actual (Expected) Sales**	=	**Margin of Safety Ratio**
$300,000	÷	$800,000	=	37.5%

Thus, Vargo's sales could drop by $300,000, or 37.5%, before the company would operate at a loss.

CVP and Changes in the Business Environment

To better understand how CVP analysis works, let's look at three independent situations that might occur at Vargo Video. Each case uses the original DVD player sales and cost data, which were:

Illustration 6-6
Original DVD player sales and cost data

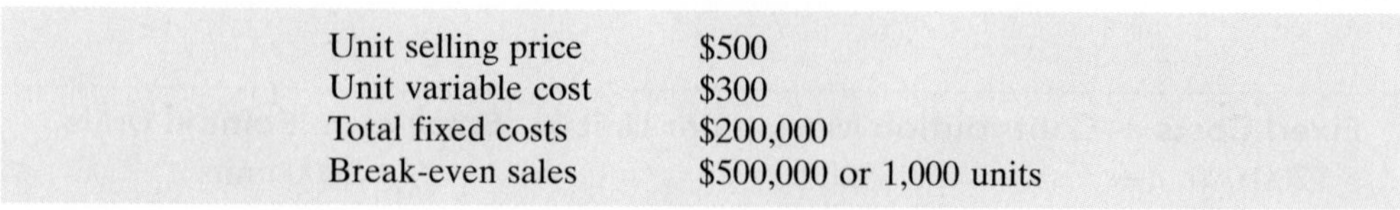

Unit selling price	$500
Unit variable cost	$300
Total fixed costs	$200,000
Break-even sales	$500,000 or 1,000 units

Case I. A competitor is offering a 10% discount on the selling price of its DVD players. Management must decide whether to offer a similar discount.

Question: What effect will a 10% discount on selling price have on the break-even point for DVD players?

Answer: A 10% discount on selling price reduces the selling price per unit to $450 [$500 − ($500 × 10%)]. Variable costs per unit remain unchanged at $300. Thus, the contribution margin per unit is $150. Assuming no change in fixed costs, break-even sales are 1,333 units, computed as follows.

Fixed Costs	÷	Contribution Margin per Unit	=	Break-even Sales
$200,000	÷	$150	=	1,333 units (rounded)

Illustration 6-7
Computation of break-even sales in units

For Vargo Video, this change requires monthly sales to increase by 333 units, or 33⅓%, in order to break even. In reaching a conclusion about offering a 10% discount to customers, management must determine how likely it is to achieve the increased sales. Also, management should estimate the possible loss of sales if the competitor's discount price is not matched.

Case II. To meet the threat of foreign competition, management invests in new robotic equipment that will lower the amount of direct labor required to make DVD players. The company estimates that total fixed costs will increase 30% and that variable cost per unit will decrease 30%.

Question: What effect will the new equipment have on the sales volume required to break even?

Answer: Total fixed costs become $260,000 [$200,000 + (30% × $200,000)]. The variable cost per unit becomes $210 [$300 − (30% × $300)]. The new break-even point is approximately 897 units, computed as follows.

Fixed Costs	÷	Contribution Margin per Unit	=	Break-even Sales
$260,000	÷	($500 − $210)	=	897 units (rounded)

Illustration 6-8
Computation of break-even sales in units

These changes appear to be advantageous for Vargo Video. The break-even point is reduced by 10%, or 100 units.

Case III. Vargo's principal supplier of raw materials has just announced a price increase. The higher cost is expected to increase the variable cost of DVD players by $25 per unit. Management decides to hold the line on the selling price of the DVD players. It plans a cost-cutting program that will save $17,500 in fixed costs per month. Vargo is currently realizing monthly net income of $80,000 on sales of 1,400 DVD players.

Question: What increase in units sold will be needed to maintain the same level of net income?

Answer: The variable cost per unit increases to $325 ($300 + $25). Fixed costs are reduced to $182,500 ($200,000 − $17,500). Because of the change in variable cost, the contribution margin per unit becomes $175 ($500 − $325). The required number of units sold to achieve the target net income is computed as follows.

Fixed Costs + Target Net Income	÷	Contribution Margin per Unit	=	Required Sales in Units
($182,500 + $80,000)	÷	$175	=	1,500

Illustration 6-9
Computation of required sales

To achieve the required sales, Vargo Video will have to sell 1,500 DVD players, an increase of 100 units. If this does not seem to be a reasonable expectation, management will either have to make further cost reductions or accept less net income if the selling price remains unchanged.

We hope that the concepts reviewed in this section are now familiar to you. We are now ready to examine additional ways that companies use CVP analysis to assess profitability and to help in making effective business decisions.

MANAGEMENT INSIGHT

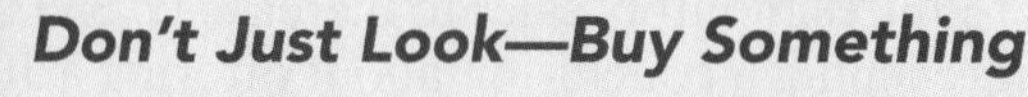

Don't Just Look—Buy Something

When analyzing an Internet business, analysts closely watch the so-called "conversion rate." This rate is calculated by dividing the number of people who actually take action at an Internet site (buy something) by the total number of people who visit the site. Average conversion rates are from 3% to 5%. A rate below 2% is poor, while a rate above 10% is great.

Conversion rates have an obvious effect on the break-even point. Suppose you spend $10,000 on your site, and you attract 5,000 visitors. If you get a 2% conversion rate (100 purchases), your site costs $100 per purchase ($10,000 ÷ 100). A 4% conversion rate gets you down to a cost of $50 per transaction, and an 8% conversion rate gets you down to $25. Studies show that conversion rates increase if the site has an easy-to-use interface, fast-performing screens, a convenient ordering process, and advertising that is both clever and clear.

Source: J. William Gurley, "The One Internet Metric That Really Counts," *Fortune,* March 6, 2000, p. 392.

Besides increasing their conversion rates, what steps can online merchants use to lower their break-even points?

DECISION TOOLKIT

Decision Checkpoints	Info Needed for Decision	Tool to Use for Decision	How to Evaluate Results
How can a company use CVP analysis to improve profitability?	Data on what effect a price change, a fixed-cost change, or a trade-off between fixed and variable costs would have on volume and costs	Measurement of income at new volume levels	If profitability increases under proposed change, adopt change.

SALES MIX

To this point our discussion of CVP analysis has assumed that a company sells only one product. However, most companies sell multiple products. When a company sells many products, it is important that management understand its sales mix.

STUDY OBJECTIVE 3

Explain the term sales mix and its effects on break-even sales.

Sales mix is the relative percentage in which a company sells its multiple products. For example, if 80% of Hewlett Packard's unit sales are printers and the other 20% are PCs, its sales mix is 80% to 20%.

Sales mix is important to managers because different products often have substantially different contribution margins. For example, Ford's SUVs and

F150 pickup trucks have higher contribution margins compared to its economy cars. Similarly, first-class tickets sold by United Airlines provide substantially higher contribution margins than coach-class tickets.

Break-even Sales in Units

Companies can compute break-even sales for a mix of two or more products by determining the **weighted-average unit contribution margin of all the products.** To illustrate, assume that Vargo Video sells not only DVD players but TV sets as well. Vargo sells its two products in the following amounts: 1,500 DVD players and 500 TVs. The sales mix, expressed as a function of total units sold is as follows.

Illustration 6-10
Sales mix as a function of units sold

DVD Players	TVs
1,500 units ÷ 2,000 units = 75%	500 units ÷ 2,000 units = 25%

That is, 75% of the units sold are DVD players and 25% of the units sold are TVs.

Illustration 6-11 shows additional information related to Vargo Video. The unit contribution margin for DVD players is $200, and for TVs it is $500. Vargo's fixed costs total $275,000.

Illustration 6-11
Per unit data—sales mix

Unit Data	DVD Players	TVs
Selling price	$500	$1,000
Variable costs	300	500
Contribution margin	$200	$500
Sales mix—units	75%	25%
Fixed costs = $275,000		

To compute break-even for Vargo, we then determine the weighted-average unit contribution margin for the two products. We use the weighted-average contribution margin because Vargo sells three times as many DVD players as TV sets, and therefore the DVD players must be counted three times for every TV set sold. The weighted-average contribution margin for a sales mix of 75% DVD players and 25% TVs is $275, which is computed as follows.

Illustration 6-12
Weighted-average unit contribution margin

DVD Players				TVs				
(Unit Contribution Margin	×	Sales Mix Percentage)	+	(Unit Contribution Margin	×	Sales Mix Percentage)	=	Weighted-Average Unit Contribution Margin
($200	×	.75)	+	($500	×	.25)	=	$275

We then use the weighted-average unit contribution margin of $275 to compute the break-even point in unit sales. The computation of break-even sales in units for Vargo Video, assuming $275,000 of fixed costs, is as follows.

Illustration 6-13
Break-even point in units

Fixed Costs	÷	Weighted-Average Unit Contribution Margin	=	Break-even Point in Units
$275,000	÷	$275	=	1,000 units

As shown in Illustration 6-13, the break-even point in units for Vargo Video is 1,000 units. Therefore, in order to break even, Vargo must sell 750 DVD players (.75 × 1,000 units) and 250 TVs (.25 × 1,000). This can be verified by the computations in Illustration 6-14, which shows that the total contribution margin is $275,000 when 1,000 units are sold, which equals the fixed costs of $275,000.

Illustration 6-14
Break-even proof—sales units

Product	Unit Sales	×	Unit Contribution Margin	=	Total Contribution Margin
DVD players	750	×	$200	=	$ 150,000
TVs	250	×	500	=	125,000
	1,000				$275,000

Management should continually review the company's sales mix. At any level of units sold, **net income will be greater if higher contribution margin units are sold, rather than lower contribution margin units.** For Vargo Video, the television sets produce the higher contribution margin. Consequently, if Vargo sells 300 TVs and 700 DVD players, net income would be higher than in the current sales mix, even though total units sold are the same.

An analysis of these relationships shows that a shift from low-margin sales to high-margin sales may increase net income, even though there is a decline in total units sold. Likewise, a shift from high- to low-margin sales may result in a decrease in net income, even though there is an increase in total units sold.

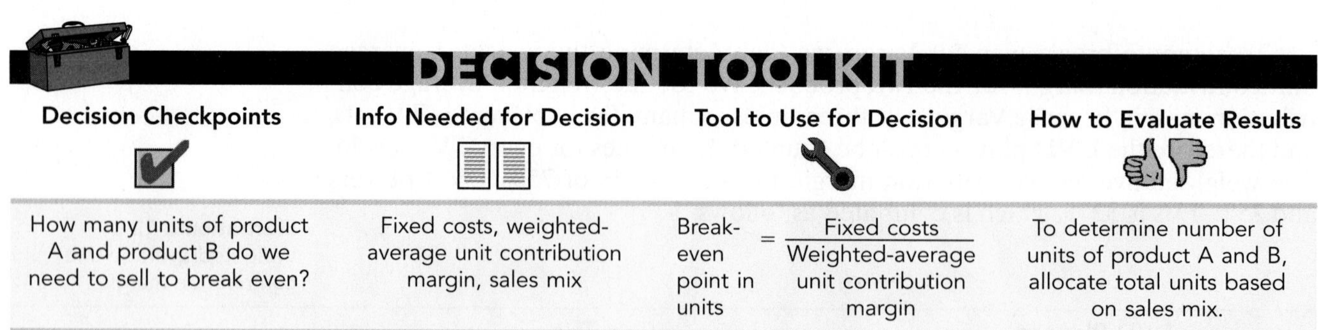
DECISION TOOLKIT

Decision Checkpoints	Info Needed for Decision	Tool to Use for Decision	How to Evaluate Results
How many units of product A and product B do we need to sell to break even?	Fixed costs, weighted-average unit contribution margin, sales mix	Break-even point in units = Fixed costs / Weighted-average unit contribution margin	To determine number of units of product A and B, allocate total units based on sales mix.

Break-even Sales in Dollars

The calculation of the break-even point presented for Vargo Video in the previous section works well if a company has only a *small number* of products. In contrast, consider 3M, the maker of Post-it Notes, which has more than 30,000 products. In order to calculate the break-even point for 3M using a weighted-average unit contribution margin, we would need to calculate 30,000 different unit contribution margins. That is not realistic.

Therefore, for a company like 3M, we calculate the break-even point in terms of sales dollars (rather than units sold), using sales information for divisions or product lines (rather than individual products). This approach requires that we compute sales mix as a percentage of total dollars sales (rather than units sold) and that we compute the contribution margin ratio (rather than contribution margin per unit).

To illustrate, suppose that Kale Garden Supply Company has two divisions—Indoor Plants and Outdoor Plants. Each division has hundreds of different types of plants and plant-care products. Illustration 6-15 provides information necessary for performing cost-volume-profit analysis for the two divisions of Kale Garden Supply.

Illustration 6-15
Cost-volume-profit data for Kale Garden Supply

	Indoor Plant Division		Outdoor Plant Division		Total	
Sales	$ 200,000		$ 800,000		$1,000,000	
Variable costs	120,000		560,000		680,000	
Contribution margin	$ 80,000		$ 240,000		$ 320,000	
Sales-mix percentage (Division sales ÷ Total sales)	$ 200,000 / $1,000,000	= .20	$ 800,000 / $1,000,000	= .80		
Contribution margin ratio (Contribution margin ÷ Sales)	$ 80,000 / $ 200,000	= .40	$ 240,000 / $ 800,000	= .30	$ 320,000 / $1,000,000	= .32
Total fixed costs = $300,000						

As shown in Illustration 6-15, the contribution margin ratio for the combined company is 32%, which is computed by dividing the total contribution margin by total sales. It is useful to note that the contribution margin ratio of 32% is a weighted average of the individual contribution margin ratios of the two divisions (40% and 30%). To illustrate, in Illustration 6-16 we multiply each division's contribution margin ratio by its sale-mix percentage, based on dollar sales, and then sum these amounts. As shown later, the calculation in Illustration 6-16 is useful because it enables us to determine how the break-even point changes when the sales mix changes.

Illustration 6-16
Calculation of weighted-average contribution margin

Indoor Plant Division				Outdoor Plant Division				
(Contribution Margin Ratio	×	Sales Mix Percentage)	+	(Contribution Margin Ratio	×	Sales Mix Percentage)	=	Weighted-Average Contribution Margin Ratio
(.40	×	.20)	+	(.30	×	.80)	=	.32

Kale Garden Supply's break-even point in dollars is then computed by dividing fixed costs by the weighted-average contribution margin ratio of 32%, as shown in Illustration 6-17.

Illustration 6-17
Calculation of break-even point in dollars

Fixed Costs	÷	Weighted-Average Contribution Margin Ratio	=	Break-even Point in Dollars
$300,000	÷	.32	=	$937,500

The break-even point is based on the sales mix of 20% to 80%. Of the company's total break-even sales of $937,500, a total of $187,500 (.20 × $937,500) will come from the Indoor Plant division, and \$750,000 (.80 × \$937,500) will come from the Outdoor Plant division.

What would be the impact on the break-even point if a higher percentage of Kale Garden Supply's sales were to come from the Indoor Plant division? Because the Indoor Plant division enjoys a higher contribution margin ratio, this change in the sales mix would result in a higher weighted-average contribution margin ratio, and consequently a lower break-even point in dollars. For example, if the sales mix changes to 50% for the Indoor Plant division and 50% for the Outdoor Plant division, the weighted-average contribution margin ratio would be 35% [(.40 × .50) + (.30 × .50)]. The new, lower, break-even point is \$857,143 (\$300,000 ÷ .35). The opposite would occur if a higher percentage of sales were expected from the Outdoor Plant division. As you can see, the information provided using CVP analysis can help managers better understand the impact of sales mix on profitability.

MANAGEMENT INSIGHT

Healthy for You, and Great for the Bottom Line

Zoom Kitchen, a chain of four restaurants in the Chicago area, is known for serving sizable portions of meat and potatoes. But the company's management is quite pleased with the fact that during the past four years salad sales have increased from 18% of its sales mix to 40%. Why are they pleased? Because the contribution margin on salads is much higher than on meat. The restaurant made a conscious effort to encourage people to buy more salads by offering an interesting assortment of salad ingredients including jicama, beets, marinated mushrooms, grilled tuna, and carved turkey. Management has to be very sensitive to contribution margin—it costs about \$600,000 to open up a new Zoom Kitchen restaurant.

Source: Amy Zuber, "Salad Sales 'Zoom' at Meat-and-Potatoes Specialist," *Nation's Restaurant News,* November 12, 2001, p. 26.

? Why do you suppose restaurants are so eager to sell beverages and desserts?

DECISION TOOLKIT

Decision Checkpoints 	Info Needed for Decision 	Tool to Use for Decision 	How to Evaluate Results 
How many dollars of sales are required from each division in order to break even?	Fixed costs, weighted-average contribution margin ratio, sales mix	Break-even point in dollars = $\frac{\text{Fixed costs}}{\text{Weighted-average contribution margin ratio}}$	To determine the sales dollars required from each division, allocate the total break-even sales using the sales mix.

Before You Go On...

REVIEW IT

1. What is meant by the term sales mix?
2. Why is sales mix important for break-even analysis?
3. How does the number of products that a company sells affect the method that is used to determine the break-even point?
4. What information is needed to compute break-even sales in units? Break-even sales in dollars?

DO IT

Manzeck Bicycles International produces and sells three different types of mountain bikes. Information regarding the three models is shown below.

	Pro	Intermediate	Standard	Total
Units sold	5,000	10,000	25,000	40,000
Selling price	$800	$500	$350	
Variable cost	$500	$300	$250	

The company's total fixed costs to produce the bicycles are $7,500,000.

Instructions

(a) Determine the sales mix as a function of units sold for the three products.

(b) Determine the weighted-average unit contribution margin.

(c) Determine the total number of units that the company must produce to break even.

(d) Determine the number of units of each model that the company must produce to break even.

Action Plan

- The sales mix is the relative percentage of each product sold in units.
- The weighted-average unit contribution margin is the sum of the per unit contribution margins multiplied by the respective sales mix percentage.
- Determine the break-even point in units by dividing the fixed costs by the weighted-average unit contribution margin.
- Determine the number of units of each model to produce by multiplying the total break-even units by the respective sales mix percentage for each product.

Solution

(a) The sales mix percentages as a function of units sold is:

Pro	Intermediate	Standard
5,000/40,000 = 12.5%	10,000/40,000 = 25%	25,000/40,000 = 62.5%

(b) The weighted-average unit contribution margin is:

$$[.125 \times (\$800 - \$500)] + [.25 \times (\$500 - \$300)] + [.625 \times (\$350 - \$250)] = \$150$$

(c) The break-even point in units is:

$$\$7{,}500{,}000 \div \$150 = 50{,}000 \text{ units}$$

(d) The break-even units to produce for each product are:

Pro:	50,000 units × 12.5%	=	6,250 units
Intermediate:	50,000 units × 25%	=	12,500 units
Standard	50,000 units × 62.5%	=	31,250 units
			50,000 units

Related exercise material: *BE6-7, BE6-8, BE6-9, BE6-10, E6-6, E6-7, E6-8, E6-9, and E6-10.*

The Navigator

Determining Sales Mix with Limited Resources

In the previous discussion we assumed a certain sales mix and then determined the break-even point given that sales mix. We now discuss how limited resources influence the sales-mix decision.

STUDY OBJECTIVE 4

Determine sales mix when a company has limited resources.

Everyone's resources are limited. For a company, the limited resource may be floor space in a retail department store, or raw materials, direct labor hours, or machine capacity in a manufacturing company. When a company has limited resources, management must decide which products to make and sell in order to maximize net income.

To illustrate, recall that Vargo manufactures DVD players and TVs. The limiting resource is machine capacity, which is 3,600 hours per month. Relevant data consist of the following.

Illustration 6-18
Contribution margin and machine hours

	DVD Players	TVs
Contribution margin per unit	$200	$500
Machine hours required per unit	.2	.625

HELPFUL HINT

CM alone is not enough to make this decision. The key factor is CM per unit of limited resource.

The TV sets may appear to be more profitable since they have a higher contribution margin per unit ($500) than the DVD players ($200). However, the DVD players take fewer machine hours to produce than the TV sets. Therefore, it is necessary to find the **contribution margin per unit of limited resource**—in this case, contribution margin per machine hour. This is obtained by dividing the contribution margin per unit of each product by the number of units of the limited resource required for each product, as shown in Illustration 6-19.

Illustration 6-19
Contribution margin per unit of limited resource

	DVD Players	TVs
Contribution margin per unit (a)	$200	$500
Machine hours required (b)	0.2	0.625
Contribution margin per unit of limited resource [(a) ÷ (b)]	**$1,000**	**$800**

The computation shows that the DVD players have a higher contribution margin per unit of limited resource. This would suggest that, given sufficient demand for DVD players, Vargo should shift the sales mix to produce more DVD players or increase machine capacity.

As indicated in Illustration 6-19, the constraint for the production of the TVs is the larger number of machine hours needed to produce them. In addressing this problem, we have taken the limited number of machine hours as a given, and have attempted to maximize the contribution margin given the constraint. One question that Vargo should ask, however, is whether this constraint can be reduced or eliminated. If Vargo is able to increase machine capacity from 3,600 hours to 4,200 hours, the additional 600 hours could be used to produce either the DVD players or TVs. The total contribution margin under each alternative is found by multiplying the machine hours by the contribution margin per unit of limited resource, as shown below.

Illustration 6-20
Incremental analysis—computation of total contribution margin

	DVD Players	TVs
Machine hours (a)	600	600
Contribution margin per unit of limited resource (b)	$ 1,000	$ 800
Contribution margin [(a) × (b)]	**$600,000**	**$480,000**

From this analysis, we can see that to maximize net income, all of the increased capacity should be used to make and sell the DVD players.

Vargo's manufacturing constraint might be due to a bottleneck in production or to poorly trained machine operators. In addition to finding ways to solve those problems, the company should consider other possible solutions, such as outsourcing part of the production, acquiring additional new equipment (discussed in Chapter 12), or striving to eliminate any non-value-added activities (see Chapter 4). As discussed in Chapter 1, this approach to evaluating constraints is referred to as the theory of constraints. The **theory of constraints** is a specific approach used to identify and manage constraints in order to achieve the company's goals. According to this theory, a company must continually identify its constraints and find ways to reduce or eliminate them, where appropriate.

MANAGEMENT INSIGHT

Something Smells

When fragrance sales recently went flat, retailers turned up the heat on fragrance manufacturers. They reduced the amount of floor space devoted to fragrances, leaving fragrance manufacturers fighting each other for the smaller space. The retailer doesn't just choose the fragrance with the highest contribution margin. Instead, it chooses the fragrance with the highest contribution margin per square foot. In this game, a product with a lower contribution margin, but a higher turnover, could well be the winner.

? What is the limited resource for a retailer, and what implications does this have for sales mix?

DECISION TOOLKIT

Decision Checkpoints 	Info Needed for Decision 	Tool to Use for Decision 	How to Evaluate Results 
How many units of product A and B should we produce in light of a limited resource?	Contribution margin per unit, limited resource required per unit	Contribution margin per unit of limited resource = Contribution margin per unit / Limited resource per unit	Any additional capacity of limited resource should be applied toward the product with higher contribution margin per unit of limited resource.

COST STRUCTURE AND OPERATING LEVERAGE

Cost structure refers to the relative proportion of fixed versus variable costs that a company incurs. Cost structure can have a significant effect on profitability. For example, computer equipment manufacturer Cisco Systems has substantially reduced its fixed costs by choosing to outsource much of its production. While this makes Cisco less susceptible to economic swings, it has also reduced its ability to experience the incredible profitability that it used to have during economic booms.

The choice of cost structure must be carefully considered. There are many ways that companies can influence their cost structure. For example, by acquiring sophisticated robotic equipment, many companies have reduced their use of manual labor. Similarly, some brokerage firms, such as E*Trade, have reduced their reliance on human brokers and have instead invested heavily in computers and online technology. In so doing, they have increased their reliance on fixed costs (through depreciation on the robotic equipment or computer equipment) and reduced their reliance on variable costs (the variable employee labor cost).

Alternatively, some companies have reduced their fixed costs and increased their variable costs by outsourcing their production. Nike, for example, does very little manufacturing, but instead outsources the manufacture of nearly all of its shoes. It has consequently converted many of its fixed costs into variable costs and therefore changed its cost structure.

STUDY OBJECTIVE 5

Understand how operating leverage affects profitability.

Consider the following example of Vargo Video and one of its competitors, New Wave Company. Both make DVD players. Vargo Video uses a traditional, labor-intensive manufacturing process. New Wave Company has invested in a completely automated system. The factory employees are involved only in setting up, adjusting, and maintaining the machinery. Illustration 6-21 shows CVP income statements for each company.

Illustration 6-21
CVP income statements for two companies

	Vargo Video	New Wave Company
Sales	$800,000	$800,000
Variable costs	480,000	160,000
Contribution margin	320,000	640,000
Fixed costs	200,000	520,000
Net income	$120,000	$120,000

Both companies have the same sales and the same net income. However, because of the differences in their cost structures, they differ greatly in the risks and rewards related to increasing or decreasing sales. Let's evaluate the impact of cost structure on the profitability of the two companies.

Effect on Contribution Margin Ratio

First let's look at the contribution margin ratio. Illustration 6-22 shows the computation of the contribution margin ratio for each company.

Illustration 6-22
Contribution margin ratio for two companies

	Contribution Margin	÷	Sales	=	Contribution Margin Ratio
Vargo Video	$320,000	÷	$800,000	=	.40
New Wave	$640,000	÷	$800,000	=	.80

New Wave has a contribution margin ratio of 80% versus only 40% for Vargo. That means that with every dollar of sales, New Wave generates 80 cents of contribution margin (and thus an 80 cent increase in net income), versus only 40 cents for Vargo. However, it also means that for every dollar that sales decline, New Wave loses 80 cents in net income, whereas Vargo will lose only 40 cents. New Wave's cost structure, which relies more heavily on fixed costs, makes it more sensitive to changes in sales revenue.

Effect on Break-even Point

The difference in cost structure also affects the break-even point. The break-even point for each company is calculated in Illustration 6-23.

Illustration 6-23
Computation of break-even point for two companies

	Fixed Costs	÷	Contribution Margin Ratio	=	Break-even Point in Dollars
Vargo Video	$200,000	÷	.40	=	$500,000
New Wave	$520,000	÷	.80	=	$650,000

New Wave needs to generate $150,000 ($650,000 − $500,000) more in sales than Vargo before it breaks even. This makes New Wave riskier than Vargo because a company cannot survive for very long unless it at least breaks even.

Effect on Margin of Safety Ratio

We can also evaluate the relative impact that changes in sales would have on the two companies by computing the margin of safety ratio. Illustration 6-24 shows the computation of the **margin of safety ratio** for the two companies.

	(Actual Sales	−	Break-even Sales)	÷	Actual Sales	=	Margin of Safety Ratio
Vargo Video	($800,000	−	$500,000)	÷	$800,000	=	.38
New Wave	($800,000	−	$650,000)	÷	$800,000	=	.19

Illustration 6-24
Computation of margin of safety ratio for two companies

The difference in the margin of safety ratio also reflects the difference in risk between the two companies. Vargo could sustain a 38% decline in sales before it would be operating at a loss. New Wave could sustain only a 19% decline in sales before it would be "in the red."

Operating Leverage

Operating leverage refers to the extent to which a company's net income reacts to a given change in sales. Companies that have higher fixed costs relative to variable costs have higher operating leverage. When a company's sales revenue is increasing, high operating leverage is a good thing because it means that profits will increase rapidly. But when sales are declining, too much operating leverage can have devastating consequences.

DEGREE OF OPERATING LEVERAGE

How can we compare operating leverage between two companies? The **degree of operating leverage** provides a measure of a company's earnings volatility and can be used to compare companies. Degree of operating leverage is computed by dividing contribution margin by net income. This formula is presented in Illustration 6-25 and applied to our two manufacturers of DVD players.

	Contribution Margin	÷	Net Income	=	Degree of Operating Leverage
Vargo Video	$320,000	÷	$120,000	=	2.67
New Wave	$640,000	÷	$120,000	=	5.33

Illustration 6-25
Computation of degree of operating leverage

New Wave's earnings would go up (or down) by about two times (5.33 ÷ 2.67 = 1.99) as much as Vargo's with an equal increase (or decrease) in sales. For example, suppose both companies experience a 10% decrease in sales. Vargo's net income will decrease by 26.7% (2.67 × 10%), while New Wave's will decrease by 53.3% (5.33 × 10%). Thus, New Wave's higher operating leverage exposes it to greater earnings volatility risk.

You should be careful not to conclude from this analysis that a cost structure that relies on higher fixed costs, and consequently has higher operating leverage, is necessarily bad. When used carefully, operating leverage can add considerably to a company's profitability. For example, computer equipment manufacturer Komag enjoyed a 66% increase in net income when its sales increased by only 8%. As one commentator noted, "Komag's fourth quarter illustrates the company's significant operating leverage; a small increase in sales leads to a big profit rise." However, as our illustration demonstrates, increased reliance on fixed costs increases a company's risk.

MANAGEMENT INSIGHT

The Cost of Experience

Cost structures vary considerably across industries, but they also vary considerably across companies within industries. For example, the airline industry is characterized by two types of companies—low-cost, low-fare airlines such as Southwest Airlines and JetBlue Airways, and the high-cost, high-fare airline giants such as United Airlines and American Airlines. One reason that airline giants have higher costs is that they are somewhat trapped in a flight system that they invented—the hub-and-spoke approach. Under this approach, passengers are flown from their city of origination to centralized hub cities and then flown to their ultimate destination. This results in high-fixed costs and high operating leverage. When air traffic was at peak volumes during the late 1990s, the large carriers enjoyed record profits. But when travel volume declined, this same cost structure resulted in massive losses and a series of bankruptcy declarations.

As a result of being in business for a long time, the established airline giants also must pay very large retirement payments, a cost the newer airlines do not face. What impact do these payments have on the break-even equation?

DECISION TOOLKIT

Decision Checkpoints	Info Needed for Decision	Tool to Use for Decision	How to Evaluate Results

How sensitive is the company's net income to changes in sales?	Contribution margin and net income	$\text{Degree of operating leverage} = \frac{\text{Contribution margin}}{\text{Net income}}$	Reports the change in net income that will occur with a given change in sales. A high degree of operating leverage means that the company's net income is very sensitive to changes in sales.

Before You Go On...

REVIEW IT

1. What is cost structure?
2. What impact does an increase in cost structure have on a company's contribution margin ratio? On a company's break-even point? On its margin of safety ratio?
3. What is operating leverage? What are the benefits and the drawbacks of operating leverage?
4. How can operating leverage be measured?

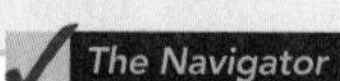

Be sure to read **ALL ABOUT YOU: *Big Decisions for Your Energy Future*** on the next page for information on how topics in this chapter apply to you.

all about YOU

Big Decisions for Your Energy Future

It seems that a day does not pass without some reminder that our use of energy, as we know it, is going to have to change, and change in a big way. Many politicians, scientists, economists, and businesspeople have become concerned about the potential implications of global warming. The largest source of the emissions thought to contribute to global warming is from coal-fired power plants. Alternative sources of energy have been available for many years, but due to their high cost relative to coal, their use has been limited. However, faced with rapidly growing energy needs and concerns over global warming, communities will soon have to make huge investments in alternative energy sources. The big question is, "What will be the best investments for the future?"

To answer this question, decision makers will employ the tools that you learned about in this and other chapters. The stakes are high, which is why it is important to make an informed decision.

Some Facts

* In 1980, wind-power electricity cost 80 cents per kilowatt hour. Using today's highly efficient turbines with rotor diameters of up to 125 meters, the cost can be as low as 3 to 4 cents (about the same as coal), or as much as 20 cents in places with less wind.
* It costs about $77,500 to install a residential solar-power system with a 10 kilowatt-capacity. Without subsidies, the system would take about 50 years to pay itself off; with subsidies, it would pay off in about 10 years.
* Industrial plants using solar panels have a cost per kilowatt hour of about 30 cents; with a new approach, called *concentrating solar power,* the cost is between 9 and 12 cents per kilowatt hour.
* Homes that use only products with the Environmental Protection Agency's Energy Star designation will use 30% less energy and save about $400 per year. In 2005 consumers saved $12 billion on utility bills using Energy Star products.
* Employing new materials and technologies, homes can now be built 70% more energy-efficient than homes of the past.
* The United States is the largest emitter of greenhouse gases, but projections suggest that it will soon be passed by China and probably India.

About the Numbers

This following drawing illustrates that only 13% of the world's energy is provided by renewable sources. Of that, almost 10% is provided by biomass, the conversion of plant matter to create energy, usually through burning. This often involves the burning of methane gas, a byproduct of decaying plant matter. Since methane is a powerful greenhouse gas, burning it has the additional desirable effect of reducing a greenhouse gas.

Going Green

Renewable energy sources–such as biomass, hydro, solar, wind, tide and geothermal–make up 13.1% of the world's primary energy supplies, according to the International Energy Agency (2004 data, the latest available)

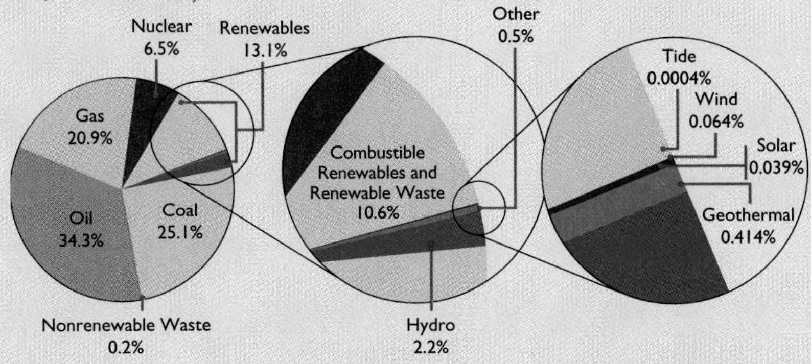

Note: Totals may not add-up due to rounding.
Source: IEA Energy Statistics (accessed September 2006).

What Do You Think?

Although renewable energy sources, such as solar and wind power, have been available for a long time, they have not been widely adopted because of their high cost relative to coal. Some people have recently suggested that conventional cost comparisons are not adequate, because they do not take environmental costs into account. For example, while coal is a very cheap energy source, it is also a significant contributor of greenhouse gases. Should environmental costs be incorporated into decision formulas when planners evaluate new power plants?

YES: As long as environmental costs are ignored, renewable energy will appear to be too expensive relative to coal.

NO: If one country decides to incorporate environmental costs into its decision process, but other countries do not, the country that does so will be at a competitive disadvantage because its products will cost more to produce.

Sources: Rebecca Smith, "The New Math of Alternative Energy," *Wall Street Journal Online,* February 12, 2007; Christine Burma, "How to Cut Energy Costs," *Wall Street Journal Online,* February 12, 2007; "The Heat Is On," *The Economist,* September 9, 2006, survey section, pp. 1–24.

The authors' comments on this situation appear on page 284.

Using the Decision Toolkit

Rexfield Corp. is contemplating a huge investment in automated mass-spectrometers for its medical laboratory testing services. Its current process relies heavily on the expertise of a high number of lab technicians. The new equipment would employ a computer expert system that integrates much of the decision process and knowledge base that is used by a skilled lab technician.

Rex Field, the company's CEO, has requested that an analysis of projected results using the old technology versus the new technology be done for the coming year. The accounting department has prepared the following CVP income statements for use in your analysis.

	Old	New
Sales revenue	$2,000,000	$2,000,000
Variable costs	1,400,000	600,000
Contribution margin	600,000	1,400,000
Fixed costs	400,000	1,200,000
Net income	$ 200,000	$ 200,000

Instructions

Use the information provided above to do the following.

(a) Compute the degree of operating leverage for the company under each scenario, and discuss your results.

(b) Compute the break-even point in dollars and margin of safety ratio for the company under each scenario, and discuss your results.

Solution

(a)

	Contribution Margin	÷	Net Income	=	Degree of Operating Leverage
Old	$600,000	÷	$200,000	=	3
New	$1,400,000	÷	$200,000	=	7

The degree of operating leverage measures the company's sensitivity to changes in sales. By switching to a cost structure dominated by fixed costs, the company would significantly increase its operating leverage. As a result, with a percentage change in sales, its percentage change in net income would be 2.33 times as much (7 ÷ 3) under the new structure as it would under the old.

(b) To compute the break-even point in sales dollars, we need first to compute the contribution margin ratio under each scenario. Under the old structure the contribution margin ratio would be .30 ($600,000 ÷ $2,000,000), and under the new it would be .70 ($1,400,000 ÷ $2,000,000).

	Fixed Costs	÷	Contribution Margin Ratio	=	Break-even point in dollars
Old	$400,000	÷	.30	=	$1,333,333
New	$1,200,000	÷	.70	=	$1,714,286

Because the company's fixed costs would be substantially higher under the new cost structure, its break-even point would increase significantly, from $1,333,333 to $1,714,286. A higher break-even point is riskier because it means that the company must generate higher sales to be profitable.

The margin of safety ratio tells how far sales can fall before the company is operating at a loss.

	(Actual Sales	−	Break-even Sales)	÷	Actual Sales	=	Margin of Safety Ratio
Old	($2,000,000	−	$1,333,333)	÷	$2,000,000	=	.33
New	($2,000,000	−	$1,714,286)	÷	$2,000,000	=	.14

Under the old structure, sales could fall by 33% before the company would be operating at a loss. Under the new structure, sales could fall by only 14%.

The Navigator

SUMMARY OF STUDY OBJECTIVES

1 **Describe the essential features of a cost-volume-profit income statement.** The CVP income statement classifies costs and expenses as variable or fixed and reports contribution margin in the body of the statement.

2 **Apply basic CVP concepts.** Contribution margin is the amount of revenue remaining after deducting variable costs. It can be expressed as a per unit amount or as a ratio. The break-even point in units is fixed costs divided by contribution margin per unit. The break-even point in dollars is fixed costs divided by the contribution margin ratio. These formulas can also be used to determine units or sales dollars needed to achieve target net income, simply by adding target net income to fixed costs before dividing by the contribution margin. Margin of safety indicates how much sales can decline before the company is operating at a loss. It can be expressed in dollar terms or as a percentage.

3 **Explain the term sales mix and its effects on break-even sales.** Sales mix is the relative proportion in which each product is sold when a company sells more than one product. For a company with a small number of products, break-even sales in units is determined by using the weighted-average unit contribution margin of all the products. If the company sells many different products, then calculating the break-even point using unit information is not practical. Instead, in a company with many products, break-even sales in dollars is calculated using the weighted-average contribution margin ratio.

4 **Determine sales mix when a company has limited resources.** When a company has limited resources, it is necessary to find the contribution margin per unit of limited resource. This amount is then multiplied by the units of limited resource to determine which product maximizes net income.

5 **Understand how operating leverage affects profitability.** Operating leverage refers to the degree to which a company's net income reacts to a change in sales. Operating leverage is determined by a company's relative use of fixed versus variable costs. Companies with high fixed costs relative to variable costs have high operating leverage. A company with high operating leverage will experience a sharp increase (decrease) in net income with a given increase (decrease) in sales. The degree of operating leverage can be measured by dividing contribution margin by net income.

DECISION TOOLKIT—A SUMMARY

Decision Checkpoints	Info Needed for Decision	Tool to Use for Decision	How to Evaluate Results
How can a company use CVP analysis to improve profitability?	Data on what effect a price change, a fixed-cost change, or a trade-off between fixed and variable costs would have on volume and costs	Measurement of income at new volume levels	If profitability increases under proposed change, adopt change.
How many units of product A and product B do we need to sell to break even?	Fixed costs, weighted-average unit contribution margin, sales mix	$\text{Break-even point in units} = \dfrac{\text{Fixed costs}}{\text{Weighted-average unit contribution margin}}$	To determine number of units of product A and B, allocate total units based on sales mix.
How many dollars of sales are required from each division in order to break even?	Fixed costs, weighted-average contribution margin ratio, sales mix	$\text{Break-even point in dollars} = \dfrac{\text{Fixed costs}}{\text{Weighted-average contribution margin ratio}}$	To determine the sales dollars required from each division, allocate the total break-even sales using the sales mix.
How many units of product A and B should we produce in light of a limited resource?	Contribution margin per unit, limited resource required per unit	$\text{Contribution margin per unit of limited resource} = \dfrac{\text{Contribution margin per unit}}{\text{Limited resource per unit}}$	Any additional capacity of limited resource should be applied toward the product with higher contribution margin per unit of limited resource.
How sensitive is the company's net income to changes in sales?	Contribution margin and net income	$\text{Degree of operating leverage} = \dfrac{\text{Contribution margin}}{\text{Net income}}$	Reports the change in net income that will occur with a given change in sales. A high degree of operating leverage means that the company's net income is very sensitive to changes in sales.

APPENDIX Absorption Costing versus Variable Costing

STUDY OBJECTIVE 6

Explain the difference between absorption costing and variable costing.

In the earlier chapters, we classified both variable and fixed manufacturing costs as product costs. In job order costing, for example, a job is assigned the costs of direct materials, direct labor, and **both** variable and fixed manufacturing overhead. This costing approach is referred to as **full** or **absorption costing**. It is so named because all manufacturing costs are charged to, or absorbed by, the product. Absorption costing is the approach used for external reporting under generally accepted accounting principles.

An alternative approach is to use **variable costing**. Under variable costing, only direct materials, direct labor, and variable manufacturing overhead costs are considered product costs. Companies recognize fixed manufacturing overhead costs as period costs (expenses) when incurred. The difference between absorption costing and variable costing is shown graphically as follows.

Illustration 6A-1
Difference between absorption costing and variable costing

Under both absorption and variable costing, selling and administrative expenses are period costs.

Companies may not use variable costing for external financial reports because generally accepted accounting principles require that fixed manufacturing overhead be accounted for as a product cost.

Example Comparing Absorption Costing with Variable Costing

To illustrate absorption and variable costing, assume that Premium Products Corporation manufactures a polyurethane sealant, called Fix-It, for car windshields. Relevant data for Fix-It in January 2008, the first month of production, are as follows.

Illustration 6A-2
Sealant sales and cost data for Premium Products Corporation

Selling price	$20 per unit.
Units	Produced 30,000; sold 20,000; beginning inventory zero.
Variable unit costs	Manufacturing $9 (direct materials $5, direct labor $3, and variable overhead $1).
	Selling and administrative expenses $2.
Fixed costs	Manufacturing overhead $120,000.
	Selling and administrative expenses $15,000.

The per unit manufacturing cost under each costing approach is computed in Illustration 6A-3.

Illustration 6A-3
Computation of per unit manufacturing cost

Type of Cost	Absorption Costing	Variable Costing
Direct materials	$ 5	$5
Direct labor	3	3
Variable manufacturing overhead	1	1
Fixed manufacturing overhead ($120,000 ÷ 30,000 units produced)	4	0
Manufacturing cost per unit	$13	$9

The manufacturing cost per unit is $4 higher ($13 − $9) for absorption costing. This occurs because fixed manufacturing overhead costs are a product cost under absorption costing. Under variable costing, they are, instead, a period cost, and so they are expensed. Based on these data, each unit sold and each unit remaining in inventory is costed under absorption costing at $13 and under variable costing at $9.

ABSORPTION COSTING EXAMPLE

Illustration 6A-4 shows the income statement for Premium Products using absorption costing. It shows that cost of goods manufactured is $390,000, computed by multiplying the 30,000 units produced times the manufacturing cost per unit of $13 (see Illustration 6A-3). Cost of goods sold is $260,000, after subtracting ending inventory of $130,000. Under absorption costing, $40,000 of the fixed overhead (10,000 units × $4) is deferred to a future period as part of the cost of ending inventory.

Illustration 6A-4
Absorption costing income statement

HELPFUL HINT
The income statement format in Illustration 6A-4 is the same as that used under generally accepted accounting principles.

PREMIUM PRODUCTS CORPORATION
Income Statement
For the Month Ended January 31, 2008
Absorption Costing

Sales (20,000 units × $20)		$400,000
Cost of goods sold		
Inventory, January 1	$ -0-	
Cost of goods manufactured (30,000 units × $13)	390,000	
Cost of goods available for sale	390,000	
Inventory, January 31 (10,000 units × $13)	**130,000**	
Cost of goods sold (20,000 units × $13)		260,000
Gross profit		140,000
Variable selling and administrative expenses (20,000 × $2)	40,000	
Fixed selling and administrative expenses	15,000	55,000
Net income		**$ 85,000**

VARIABLE COSTING EXAMPLE

As Illustration 6A-5 shows, companies use the cost-volume-profit format in preparing a variable costing income statement. The variable manufacturing cost of $270,000 is computed by multiplying the 30,000 units produced times variable manufacturing cost of $9 per unit (see Illustration 6A-3). As in absorption costing, both variable and fixed selling and administrative expenses are treated as period costs.

Illustration 6A-5
Variable costing income statement

HELPFUL HINT
Note the difference in the computation of the ending inventory: $9 per unit here, $13 per unit above.

PREMIUM PRODUCTS CORPORATION
Income Statement
For the Month Ended January 31, 2008
Variable Costing

Sales (20,000 units × $20)		$400,000
Variable cost of goods sold		
Inventory, January 1	$ -0-	
Variable cost of goods manufactured (30,000 units × $9)	270,000	
Variable cost of goods available for sale	270,000	
Inventory, January 31 (10,000 units × $9)	**90,000**	
Variable cost of goods sold	180,000	
Variable selling and administrative expenses (20,000 units × $2)	40,000	220,000
Contribution margin		180,000
Fixed manufacturing overhead	120,000	
Fixed selling and administrative expenses	15,000	135,000
Net income		**$ 45,000**

There is one primary difference between variable and absorption costing: Under variable costing, companies charge the fixed manufacturing overhead as an expense in the current period. Fixed manufacturing overhead costs of the current period, therefore, are not deferred to future periods through the ending inventory. As a result, absorption costing will show a **higher net income number** than variable costing **whenever units produced exceed units sold.** This difference can be seen in the income statements in Illustrations 6A-4 and 6A-5. There is a $40,000 difference in the ending inventories ($130,000 under absorption costing versus $90,000 under variable costing).

Under absorption costing, $40,000 of the fixed overhead costs (10,000 units × $4) has been deferred to a future period as part of inventory. In contrast, under variable costing, all fixed manufacturing costs are expensed in the current period.

As shown, when units produced exceed units sold, income under absorption costing is *higher.* When units produced are less than units sold, income under absorption costing is *lower.* When units produced and sold are the same, net income will be *equal* under the two costing approaches. In this case, there is no increase in ending inventory. So fixed overhead costs of the current period are not deferred to future periods through the ending inventory.

An Extended Example

STUDY OBJECTIVE 7

Discuss net income effects under absorption costing versus variable costing.

To further illustrate the concepts underlying absorption and variable costing, we will look at an extended example using Overbay Inc., a manufacturer of small airplane drones. We assume that production volume stays the same each year over the three-year period, but the number of units sold varies each year.

2008 RESULTS

As indicated in Illustration 6A-6 below, the variable manufacturing cost per drone is $240,000, and the fixed manufacturing cost per drone is $60,000. Total manufacturing cost per drone is therefore $300,000 ($240,000 + $60,000). Overbay also has variable selling and administrative expenses of $5,000 per drone, or $50,000 per year ($5,000 × 10 drones sold). The fixed selling and administrative expenses are $80,000.

Illustration 6A-6
Information for Overbay Inc.

	2008	2009	2010
Volume information			
Drones in beginning inventory	0	0	2
Drones produced	10	10	10
Drones sold	10	8	12
Drones in ending inventory	0	2	0
Financial information			
Selling price per drone	$400,000		
Variable manufacturing cost per drone	$240,000		
Fixed manufacturing overhead for the year	$600,000		
Fixed manufacturing overhead per drone	$ 60,000 ($600,000 ÷ 10)		
Variable selling and administrative expenses per drone	$ 5,000		
Fixed selling and administrative expenses	$ 80,000		

An absorption costing income statement for 2008 for Overbay Inc. is shown in Illustration 6A-7.

Illustration 6A-7
Absorption costing income statement—2008

OVERBAY INC.
Income Statement
For the Year Ended December 31, 2008
Absorption Costing

Sales (10 drones × $400,000)		$4,000,000
Cost of goods sold (10 drones × $300,000)		3,000,000
Gross profit		1,000,000
Variable selling and administrative expenses (10 drones × $5,000)	$50,000	
Fixed selling and administrative expenses	80,000	130,000
Net income		$ 870,000

Overbay reports net income of $870,000 under absorption costing.

Under a variable costing system the income statement follows a cost-volume-profit (CVP) format. In this case, the manufacturing cost is comprised solely of the variable manufacturing costs of $240,000 per drone. The fixed manufacturing costs of $600,000 for the year are expensed in 2008. As in absorption costing, the fixed and variable selling and administrative expenses are period costs expensed in 2008. A variable costing income statement for Overbay Inc. for 2008 is shown in Illustration 6A-8.

Illustration 6A-8
Variable costing income statement—2008

OVERBAY INC. Income Statement For the Year Ended December 31, 2008 Variable Costing		
Sales (10 drones × $400,000)		$4,000,000
Variable cost of goods sold		
(10 drones × $240,000)	$2,400,000	
Variable selling and administrative expenses		
(10 drones × $5,000)	50,000	2,450,000
Contribution margin		1,550,000
Fixed manufacturing overhead	600,000	
Fixed selling and administrative expenses	80,000	680,000
Net income		$ 870,000

As shown in Illustration 6A-8, the variable costing net income of $870,000 is the same as the absorption costing net income computed in Illustration 6A-7. **When the numbers of units produced and sold are the same, net income is equal under the two costing approaches.** Because no increase in ending inventory occurs, no fixed manufacturing overhead costs incurred in 2008 are deferred to future periods using absorption costing.

2009 RESULTS

In 2009, Overbay produced ten drones but sold only eight drones. As a result, there are two drones in ending inventory. The absorption costing income statement for 2009 is shown in Illustration 6A-9.

Illustration 6A-9
Absorption costing income statement—2009

OVERBAY INC. Income Statement For the Year Ended December 31, 2009 Absorption Costing		
Sales (8 drones × $400,000)		$3,200,000
Cost of goods sold (8 drones × $300,000)		2,400,000
Gross profit		800,000
Variable selling and administrative expenses		
(8 drones × $5,000)	$40,000	
Fixed selling and administrative expenses	80,000	120,000
Net income		$ 680,000

Under absorption costing, the ending inventory of two drones is $600,000 ($300,000 × 2). Each unit of ending inventory includes $60,000 of fixed manufacturing overhead. Therefore, fixed manufacturing overhead costs of $120,000 ($60,000 × 2 drones) are deferred until a future period.

The variable costing income statement for 2009 is shown in Illustration 6A-10.

Illustration 6A-10
Variable costing income statement—2009

OVERBAY INC. Income Statement For the Year Ended December 31, 2009 Variable Costing		
Sales (8 drones × $400,000)		$3,200,000
Variable cost of goods sold		
(8 drones × $240,000)	$1,920,000	
Variable selling and administrative expenses		
(8 drones × $5,000)	40,000	1,960,000
Contribution margin		1,240,000
Fixed manufacturing overhead	600,000	
Fixed selling and administrative expenses	80,000	680,000
Net income		$ 560,000

As shown, when units produced (10) exceeds units sold (8), net income under absorption costing ($680,000) is higher than net income under variable costing ($560,000). The reason: The cost of the ending inventory is higher under absorption costing than under variable costing. In 2009, under absorption costing, fixed manufacturing overhead of $120,000 is deferred and carried to future periods as part of inventory. Under variable costing, the $120,000 is expensed in the current period and, therefore the difference in the two net income numbers is $120,000 ($680,000 – $560,000).

2010 RESULTS

In 2010, Overbay produced ten drones and sold twelve (10 drones from the current year's production and 2 drones from the beginning inventory). As a result, there are no drones in ending inventory. The absorption costing income statement for 2010 is shown in Illustration 6A-11.

Illustration 6A-11
Absorption costing income statement—2010

OVERBAY INC. Income Statement For the Year Ended December 31, 2010 Absorption Costing		
Sales (12 drones × $400,000)		$4,800,000
Cost of goods sold (12 drones × $300,000)		3,600,000
Gross profit		1,200,000
Variable selling and administrative expenses		
(12 drones × $5,000)	$60,000	
Fixed selling and administrative expenses	80,000	140,000
Net income		$1,060,000

Fixed manufacturing costs of $720,000 are expensed as part of cost of goods sold in 2010. This $720,000 includes $120,000 of fixed manufacturing costs incurred during 2009 and included in beginning inventory, plus $600,000 of fixed manufacturing costs incurred during 2010. Given this result for the absorption costing statement, what would you now expect the result to be under variable costing? Let's take a look.

The variable costing income statement for 2010 is shown in Illustration 6A-12.

Illustration 6A-12
Variable costing income statement—2010

OVERBAY INC.
Income Statement
For the Year Ended December 31, 2010
Variable Costing

Sales (12 drones × $400,000)		$4,800,000
Variable cost of goods sold		
(12 drones × $240,000)	$2,880,000	
Variable selling and administrative expenses		
(12 drones × $5,000)	60,000	2,940,000
Contribution margin		1,860,000
Fixed manufacturing overhead	600,000	
Fixed selling and administrative expenses	80,000	680,000
Net income		$1,180,000

When Drones produced (10) are less than Drones sold (12), net income under absorption costing ($1,060,000) is less than net income under variable costing ($1,180,000). This difference of $120,000 ($1,180,000 − $1,060,000) results because $120,000 of fixed manufacturing overhead costs in beginning inventory are charged to 2010 under absorption costing. Under variable costing, there is no fixed manufacturing overhead cost in beginning inventory.

Illustration 6A-13 summarizes the results of the three years.

Illustration 6A-13
Comparison of net income under two costing approaches

	Net Income under Two Costing Approaches		
	2008 Production = Sales	**2009 Production > Sales**	**2010 Production < Sales**
Absorption costing	$ 870,000	$ 680,000	$1,060,000
Variable costing	870,000	560,000	1,180,000
Difference	**$ -0-**	**$120,000**	**$(120,000)**

This relationship between production and sales and its effect on net income under the two costing approaches is shown graphically in Illustration 6A-14.

Illustration 6A-14
Summary of income effects under absorption costing and variable costing

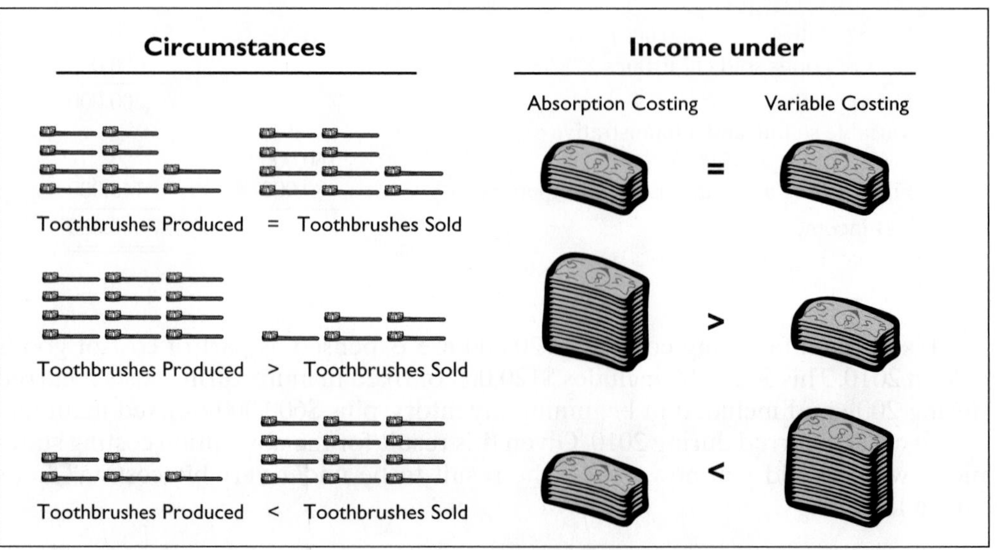

Decision-Making Concerns

STUDY OBJECTIVE 8

Discuss the merits of absorption versus variable costing for management decision making.

Generally accepted accounting principles require that absorption costing be used for the costing of inventory for external reporting purposes. Net income measured under GAAP (absorption costing) is often used internally to evaluate performance, justify cost reductions, or evaluate new projects. Some companies, however, have recognized that net income calculated using GAAP does not highlight differences between variable and fixed costs and may lead to poor business decisions. Consequently, these companies use variable costing for internal reporting purposes. The following discussion and example highlight a significant problem related to the use of absorption costing for decision-making purposes.

When production exceeds sales, absorption costing reports a higher net income than variable costing. The reason is that some fixed manufacturing costs are not expensed in the current period, but are deferred to future periods as part of inventory. As a result, management may be tempted to overproduce in a given period in order to increase net income. Although net income will increase, this decision to overproduce may not be in the company's best interest.

Suppose, for example, a division manager's compensation is based upon the division's net income. In such a case the manager may decide to meet the net income targets by increasing production. While this overproduction may increase the manager's compensation, the buildup of inventories in the long run will lead to additional costs to the company. Variable costing avoids this situation, because net income under variable costing is unaffected by changes in production levels, as the following illustration shows.

Warren Lund, a division manager of Walker Enterprises, is under pressure to boost the performance of the Lighting Division in 2008. Unfortunately, recent profits have not met expectations. The expected sales for this year are 20,000 units. As he plans for the year, Warren has to decide whether to produce 20,000 or 30,000 units. The following facts are available for the division.

Illustration 6A-15
Facts for Lighting Division—2008

Beginning inventory	0
Expected sales in units	20,000
Selling price per unit	$15
Variable manufacturing cost per unit	$6
Fixed manufacturing overhead cost (total)	$60,000
Fixed manufacturing overhead costs per unit	
Based on 20,000 units	$3 per unit ($60,000 ÷ 20,000 units)
Based on 30,000 units	$2 per unit ($60,000 ÷ 30,000 units)
Total manufacturing cost per unit	
Based on 20,000 units	$9 per unit ($6 variable + $3 fixed)
Based on 30,000 units	$8 per unit ($6 variable + $2 fixed)
Variable selling and administrative expenses per unit	$1
Fixed selling and administrative expenses	$15,000

Illustration 6A-16 (page 262) presents the division's results based upon the two possible levels of output under absorption costing.

If the Lighting Division produces 20,000 units, its net income under absorption costing is $85,000. If it produces 30,000 units, its net income is $105,000. By producing 30,000 units, the division has inventory of 10,000 units. This excess inventory causes net income to increase $20,000 because $20,000 of fixed costs (10,000 units × $2) are not charged to the current year, but are deferred to future periods.

What do you think Warren Lund might do in this situation? Given his concern about the profit numbers of the Lighting Division, he may be tempted to increase production. Although this increased production will increase 2008 net income, it may be costly to the company in the long run.

Illustration 6A-16
Absorption costing income statement—2008

LIGHTING DIVISION
Income Statement
For the Year Ended December 31, 2008
Absorption Costing

	20,000 Produced	30,000 Produced
Sales (20,000 units × \$15)	\$300,000	\$ 300,000
Cost of goods sold	180,000*	160,000**
Gross profit	120,000	140,000
Variable selling and administrative expenses (20,000 units × \$1)	20,000	20,000
Fixed selling and administrative expenses	15,000	15,000
Net income	\$ 85,000	\$105,000

*20,000 units × \$9
**20,000 units × \$8

Now let's evaluate the same situation under variable costing. A variable costing income statement is shown for production at both 20,000 and 30,000 units, using the information from Illustration 6A-15.

Illustration 6A-17
Variable costing income statement—2008

LIGHTING DIVISION
Income Statement
For the Year Ended December 31, 2008
Variable Costing

	20,000 Produced	30,000 Produced
Sales (20,000 units × \$15)	\$300,000	\$300,000
Variable cost of goods sold (20,000 units × \$6)	120,000	120,000
Variable selling and administrative expenses (20,000 units × \$1)	20,000	20,000
Contribution margin	160,000	160,000
Fixed manufacturing overhead	60,000	60,000
Fixed selling and administrative expenses	15,000	15,000
Net income	\$ 85,000	\$ 85,000

From this example we see that under variable costing, net income is not affected by the number of units produced. Net income is \$85,000 whether the division produces 20,000 or 30,000 units. Why? Because fixed manufacturing overhead is treated as a period expense. Unlike absorption costing, no fixed manufacturing overhead is deferred through inventory buildup. Therefore, under variable costing, production does not increase income; sales do. As a result, if the company uses variable costing, managers like Warren Lund cannot affect profitability by increasing production.

Potential Advantages of Variable Costing

Variable costing has a number of potential advantages relative to absorption costing:

1. Net income computed under variable costing is unaffected by changes in production levels. As a result, it is much easier to understand the impact of fixed and variable costs on the computation of net income when variable costing is used.

2. The use of variable costing is consistent with the cost-volume-profit material presented in Chapters 5 and 6.
3. Net income computed under variable costing is closely tied to changes in sales levels (not production levels), and therefore provides a more realistic assessment of the company's success or failure during a period.
4. The presentation of fixed and variable cost components on the face of the variable costing income statement makes it easier to identify these costs and understand their effect on the business. Under absorption costing, the allocation of fixed costs to inventory makes it difficult to evaluate the impact of fixed costs on the company's results.

Companies that use just-in-time processing techniques to minimize their inventories will not have significant differences between absorption and variable costing net income.

Before You Go On...

REVIEW IT

1. What is the primary distinction between absorption costing and variable costing?
2. Explain how a difference between the amount produced and amount sold creates a difference between net income under absorption costing and net income under variable costing.
3. What are the potential advantages of variable costing for decision making?

DO IT

Justin and Andrea Doll Company produces and sells tennis balls. The following costs are available for the year ended December 31, 2008. The company has no beginning inventory. In 2008, 8,000,000 units were produced, but only 7,500,000 units were sold. The unit selling price was $0.50 per ball. Costs and expenses were:

Variable costs per unit	
Direct materials	$0.10
Direct labor	0.05
Variable manufacturing overhead	0.08
Variable selling and administrative expenses	0.02
Annual fixed costs and expenses	
Manufacturing overhead	$500,000
Selling and administrative expenses	100,000

Instructions

(a) Compute the manufacturing cost of one unit of product using variable costing.

(b) Prepare a 2008 income statement for Justin and Andrea Doll Company using variable costing.

Action Plan

- Recall that under variable costing, only variable manufacturing costs are treated as manufacturing (product) costs.
- Subtract all fixed costs, both manufacturing overhead and selling and administrative expenses, as period costs.

Solution

(a) The cost of one unit of product under variable costing would be:

Direct materials	$0.10
Direct labor	0.05
Variable manufacturing overhead	0.08
	$0.23

(b) The variable costing income statement would be as follows.

JUSTIN AND ANDREA DOLL COMPANY
Income Statement
For the Year Ended December 31, 2008
Variable Costing

Sales (7,500,000 × $0.50)		$3,750,000
Variable cost of goods sold (7,500,000 × $0.23)	$1,725,000	
Variable selling and administrative expenses	150,000	1,875,000
Contribution margin		1,875,000
Fixed manufacturing overhead	500,000	
Fixed selling and administrative expenses	100,000	600,000
Net income		$1,275,000

Related exercise material: *BE6-16, BE6-17, BE6-18, BE6-19, E6-17, E6-18, and E6-19.*

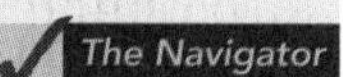

SUMMARY OF STUDY OBJECTIVES FOR APPENDIX

6 **Explain the difference between absorption costing and variable costing.** Under absorption costing, fixed manufacturing costs are product costs. Under variable costing, fixed manufacturing costs are period costs.

7 **Discuss net income effects under absorption costing versus variable costing.** If production volume exceeds sales volume, net income under absorption costing will exceed net income under variable costing by the amount of fixed manufacturing costs included in ending inventory that results from units produced but not sold during the period. If production volume is less than sales volume, net income under absorption costing will be less than under variable costing by the amount of fixed manufacturing costs included in the units sold during the period that were not produced during the period.

8 **Discuss the merits of absorption versus variable costing for management decision making.** The use of variable costing is consistent with cost–volume–profit analysis. Net income under variable costing is unaffected by changes in production levels. Instead, it is closely tied to changes in sales. The presentation of fixed costs in the variable costing approach makes it easier to identify fixed costs and to evaluate their impact on the company's profitability.

GLOSSARY

Absorption costing A costing approach in which all manufacturing costs are charged to the product. (p. 254)

Cost structure The relative proportion of fixed versus variable costs that a company incurs. (p. 247)

Degree of operating leverage A measure of the extent to which a company's net income reacts to a change in sales. It is calculated by dividing contribution margin by net income. (p. 249)

Operating leverage The extent to which a company's net income reacts to a change in sales. Operating leverage is determined by a company's relative use of fixed versus variable costs. (p. 249)

Sales mix The relative percentage in which a company sells its multiple products. (p. 240)

Theory of constraints A specific approach used to identify and manage constraints in order to achieve the company's goals. (p. 247)

Variable costing A costing approach in which only variable manufacturing costs are product costs, and fixed manufacturing costs are period costs (expenses). (p. 254)

Demonstration Problem

Carolina Corporation manufactures and sells three different types of high-quality sealed ball bearings. The bearings vary in terms of their quality specifications—primarily with respect to their smoothness and roundness. They are referred to as Fine, Extra-Fine, and Super-Fine bearings. Machine time is limited. More machine time is required to manufacture the Extra-Fine and Super-Fine bearings. Additional information is provided below.

	Product		
	Fine	**Extra-Fine**	**Super-Fine**
Selling price	$6.00	$10.00	$16.00
Variable costs and expenses	4.00	6.50	11.00
Contribution margin	$2.00	$ 3.50	$ 5.00
Machine hours required	0.02	0.04	0.08

Total fixed costs: $234,000

Instructions

Answer each of the following questions.

(a) Ignoring the machine time constraint, what strategy would appear optimal?
(b) What is the contribution margin per unit of limited resource for each type of bearing?
(c) If additional machine time could be obtained, how should the additional capacity be used?

Solution

(a) The Super-Fine bearings have the highest contribution margin per unit. Thus, ignoring any manufacturing constraints, it would appear that the company should shift toward production of more Super-Fine units.
(b) The contribution margin per unit of limited resource is calculated as:

	Fine	**Extra-Fine**	**Super-Fine**
$\frac{\text{Contribution margin per unit}}{\text{Limited resource consumed per unit}}$	$\frac{\$2}{.02} = \$100$	$\frac{\$3.5}{.04} = \$87.50$	$\frac{\$5}{.08} = \$62.50$

(c) The Fine bearings have the highest contribution margin per unit of limited resource, even though they have the lowest contribution margin per unit. Given the resource constraint, any additional capacity should be used to make Fine bearings.

action plan

✔ To determine how best to use a limited resource, calculate the contribution margin per unit of limited resource for each product type.

The Navigator

Note: All **asterisked** Questions, Exercises, and Problems relate to material contained in the appendix to the chapter.

SELF-STUDY QUESTIONS

Answers are at the end of the chapter.

(SO 1) **1.** Which one of the following is the format of a CVP income statement?
a. Sales − Variable costs = Fixed costs + Net income.
b. Sales − Fixed costs − Variable costs − Operating expenses = Net income.
c. Sales − Cost of goods sold − Operating expenses = Net income.
d. Sales − Variable costs − Fixed costs = Net income.

(SO 1, 2) **2.** Croc Catchers calculates its contribution margin to be less than zero. Which statement is true?
a. Its fixed costs are less than the variable cost per unit.
b. Its profits are greater than its total costs.
c. The company should sell more units.
d. Its selling price is less than its variable costs.

3. Which one of the following describes the break-even point? (SO 2)
a. It is the point where total sales equals total variable plus total fixed costs.
b. It is the point where the contribution margin equals zero.
c. It is the point where total variable costs equal total fixed costs.
d. It is the point where total sales equals total fixed costs.

(SO 1) 4. The following information is available for Chap Company.

Sales	$350,000
Cost of goods sold	$120,000
Total fixed expenses	$60,000
Total variable expenses	$100,000

Which amount would you find on Chap's CVP income statement?
a. Contribution margin of $250,000.
b. Contribution margin of $190,000.
c. Gross profit of $230,000.
d. Gross profit of $190,000.

(SO 2) 5. Gabriel Corporation has fixed costs of $180,000 and variable costs of $8.50 per unit. It has a target income of $268,000. How many units must it sell at $12 per unit to achieve its target net income?
a. 51,429 units **c.** 76,571 units
b. 128,000 units **d.** 21,176 units.

(SO 3) 6. Sales mix is:
a. important to sales managers but not to accountants.
b. easier to analyze on absorption costing income statements.
c. a measure of the relative percentage of a company's variable costs to its fixed costs.
d. a measure of the relative percentage in which a company's products are sold.

(SO 3) 7. Net income will be:
a. greater if more higher-contribution margin units are sold than lower-contribution margin units.
b. greater if more lower-contribution margin units are sold than higher-contribution margin units.
c. equal as long as total sales remain equal, regardless of which products are sold.
d. unaffected by changes in the mix of products sold.

(SO 4) 8. If the contribution margin per unit is $15 and it takes 3.0 machine hours to produce the unit, the contribution margin per unit of limited resource is:
a. $25. **c.** $4.
b. $5. **d.** No correct ansewr is given.

9. The degree of operating leverage: (SO 5)
a. can be computed by dividing total contribution margin by net income.
b. provides a measure of the company's earnings volatility.
c. affects a company's break-even point.
d. All of the above.

10. A high degree of operating leverage: (SO 5)
a. indicates that a company has a larger percentage of variable costs relative to its fixed costs.
b. is computed by dividing fixed costs by contribution margin.
c. exposes a company to greater earnings volatility risk.
d. exposes a company to less earnings volatility risk.

*11. Fixed manufacturing overhead costs are recognized as: (SO 6)
a. period costs under absorption costing.
b. product costs under absorption costs.
c. product costs under variable costing.
d. part of ending inventory costs under both absorption and variable costing.

*12. Net income computed under absorption costing will be: (SO 6)
a. higher than net income under variable costing in all cases.
b. equal to net income under variable costing in all cases.
c. higher than net income under variable costing when units produced are greater than units sold.
d. higher than net income under variable costing when units produced are less than units sold.

Go to the book's website, **www.wiley.com/college/weygandt**, for Additional Self-Study questions.

QUESTIONS

1. What is meant by CVP analysis?
2. Provide three examples of management decisions that benefit from CVP analysis.
3. Distinguish between a traditional income statement and a CVP income statement.
4. Describe the features of a CVP income statement that make it more useful for management decision making than the traditional income statement that is prepared for external users.
5. The traditional income statement for Rice Company shows sales $900,000, cost of goods sold $500,000, and operating expenses $200,000. Assuming all costs and expenses are 70% variable and 30% fixed, prepare a CVP income statement through contribution margin.
6. If management chooses to reduce its selling price to match that of a competitor, how will the break-even point be affected?
7. What is meant by the term sales mix? How does sales mix affect the calculation of the break-even point?
8. Radial Company sells two types of radial tires. The lower-priced model is guaranteed for only 40,000 miles; the higher-priced model is guaranteed for 100,000 miles. The unit contribution margin on the higher-priced tire is twice as high as that of the lower-priced tire. If the sales mix shifts so that the company begins to sell more units of the lower-priced tire, explain how the company's break-even point in units will change.
9. What approach should be used to calculate the break-even point of a company that has many products?
10. How is the contribution margin per unit of limited resource computed?
11. What is the theory of constraints? Provide some examples of possible constraints for a manufacturer.

12. What is meant by "cost structure?" Explain how a company's cost structure affects its break-even point.

13. What is operating leverage? How does a company increase its operating leverage?

14. How does the replacement of manual labor with automated equipment affect a company's cost structure? What implications does this have for its operating leverage and break-even point?

15. What is a measure of operating leverage, and how is it calculated?

16. Acorn Company has a degree of operating leverage of 8. Oak Company has a degree of operating leverage of 4. Interpret these measures.

*__17.__ Distinguish between absorption costing and variable costing.

*__18.__ **(a)** What is the major rationale for the use of variable costing?
(b) Discuss why variable costing may not be used for financial reporting purposes.

*__19.__ Flygt Corporation sells one product, its waterproof hiking boot. It began operations in the current year and had an ending inventory of 10,500 units. The company sold 20,000 units throughout the year. Fixed manufacturing overhead is $5 per unit, and total manufacturing cost per unit is $20 (including fixed manufacturing overhead costs). What is the difference in net income between absorption and variable costing?

*__20.__ If production equals sales, what, if any, is the difference between net income under absorption costing versus under variable costing?

*__21.__ If production is greater than sales, how does absorption costing net income differ from variable costing net income?

*__22.__ In the long run, will net income be higher or lower under variable costing compared to absorption costing?

BRIEF EXERCISES

BE6-1 Determine the missing amounts.

Determine missing amounts for contribution margin.
(SO 1, 2)

	Unit Selling Price	Unit Variable Costs	Contribution Margin per Unit	Contribution Margin Ratio
1.	$250	$170	(a)	(b)
2.	$500	(c)	$200	(d)
3.	(e)	(f)	$300	30%

BE6-2 Dilts Manufacturing Inc. has sales of $1,800,000 for the first quarter of 2008. In making the sales, the company incurred the following costs and expenses.

Prepare CVP income statement.
(SO 1, 2)

	Variable	Fixed
Cost of goods sold	$760,000	$540,000
Selling expenses	95,000	60,000
Administrative expenses	79,000	66,000

Prepare a CVP income statement for the quarter ended March 31, 2008.

BE6-3 Wesland Corp. had total variable costs of $170,000, total fixed costs of $120,000, and total revenues of $250,000. Compute the required sales in dollars to break even.

Compute the break-even point.
(SO 1, 2)

BE6-4 Hamby Company has a unit selling price of $400, variable costs per unit of $260, and fixed costs of $210,000. Compute the break-even point in units using (a) the mathematical equation and (b) contribution margin per unit.

Compute the break-even point.
(SO 1, 2)

BE6-5 For Markowis Company, variable costs are 70% of sales, and fixed costs are $210,000. Management's net income goal is $60,000. Compute the required sales needed to achieve management's target net income of $60,000. (Use the mathematical equation approach.)

Compute sales for target net income.
(SO 1, 2)

BE6-6 For Briggs Company actual sales are $1,200,000 and break-even sales are $900,000. Compute (a) the margin of safety in dollars and (b) the margin of safety ratio.

Compute the margin of safety and the margin of safety ratio.
(SO 1, 2)

BE6-7 Russell Corporation sells three different models of mosquito "zapper." Model A12 sells for $50 and has variable costs of $40. Model B22 sells for $100 and has variable costs of $70. Model C124 sells for $400 and has variable costs of $300. The sales mix of the three models is: A12, 60%; B22, 25%; and C124, 15%. What is the weighted-average unit contribution margin?

Compute weighted-average unit contribution margin based on sales mix.
(SO 3)

Compute break-even point in units for company with multiple products.
(SO 3)

BE6-8 Information for Russell Corporation is given in BE6-7. If the company has fixed costs of $199,500, how many units of each model must the company sell in order to break even?

Compute break-even point in dollars for company with multiple product lines.
(SO 3)

BE6-9 Presto Candle Supply makes candles. The sales mix (as a percent of total dollar sales) of its three product lines is: birthday candles 30%, standard tapered candles 50%, and large scented candles 20%. The contribution margin ratio of each candle type is shown below.

Candle Type	Contribution Margin Ratio
Birthday	10%
Standard tapered	20%
Large scented	45%

(a) What is the weighted-average contribution margin ratio?
(b) If the company's fixed costs are $440,000 per year, what is the dollar amount of each type of candle that must be sold to break even?

Determine weighted-average contribution margin.
(SO 3)

BE6-10 Family Furniture Co. consists of two divisions, Bedroom Division and Dining Room Division. The results of operations for the most recent quarter are:

	Bedroom Division	Dining Room Division	Total
Sales	$500,000	$750,000	$1,250,000
Variable costs	250,000	450,000	700,000
Contribution margin	$250,000	$300,000	$ 550,000

(a) Determine the company's sales mix.
(b) Determine the company's weighted-average contribution margin ratio.

Show allocation of limited resources.
(SO 4)

BE6-11 In Astoria Company, data concerning two products are: Contribution margin per unit—Product A $10, Product B $12; machine hours required for one unit—Product A 2, Product B 3. Compute the contribution margin per unit of limited resource for each product.

Compute degree of operating leverage.
(SO 5)

BE6-12 Ron's Shingle Corporation is considering the purchase of a new automated shingle-cutting machine. The new machine will reduce variable labor costs but will increase depreciation expense. Contribution margin is expected to increase from $160,000 to $240,000. Net income is expected to be the same at $40,000. Compute the degree of operating leverage before and after the purchase of the new equipment. Interpret your results.

Compute break-even point with change in operating leverage.
(SO 5)

BE6-13 Presented below are variable costing income statements for Finch Company and Sparrow Company. They are in the same industry, with the same net incomes, but different cost structures.

	Finch Co.	Sparrow Co.
Sales	$150,000	$150,000
Variable costs	60,000	15,000
Contribution margin	90,000	135,000
Fixed costs	50,000	95,000
Net income	$ 40,000	$ 40,000

Compute the break-even point in dollars for each company and comment on your findings.

Determine contribution margin from degree of operating leverage.
(SO 5)

BE6-14 The degree of operating leverage for Delta Corp. and Epsilon Co. are 1.4 and 5.6, respectively. Both have net incomes of $50,000. Determine their respective contribution margins.

Show allocation of limited resources.
(SO 4)

BE6-15 Logan Corporation manufactures two products with the following characteristics.

	Contribution Margin Per Unit	Machine Hours Required for Production
Product 1	$42	.14 hours
Product 2	$36	.10 hours

If Logan's machine hours are limited to 2,000 per month, determine which product it should produce.

***BE6-16** Large Orange Company produces basketballs. It incurred the following costs during the year.

Compute product costs under variable costing. (SO 6)

Direct materials	$14,490
Direct labor	$25,530
Fixed manufacturing overhead	$10,000
Variable manufacturing overhead	$32,420
Selling costs	$21,000

What are the total product costs for the company under variable costing?

***BE6-17** Information concerning Large Orange Company is provided in BE6-16. What are the total product costs for the company under absorption costing?

Compute product costs under absorption costing. (SO 6)

***BE6-18** Burns Manufacturing incurred the following costs during the year: direct materials $20 per unit; direct labor $12 per unit; variable manufacturing overhead $15 per unit; variable selling and administrative costs $8 per unit; fixed manufacturing overhead $120,000; and fixed selling and administrative costs $10,000. Burns produced 12,000 units and sold 10,000 units. Determine the manufacturing cost per unit under (a) absorption costing and (b) variable costing.

Determine manufacturing cost per unit under absorption and variable costing. (SO 6)

***BE6-19** Gore Company's fixed overhead costs are $3 per unit, and its variable overhead costs are $8 per unit. In the first month of operations, 50,000 units are produced, and 47,000 units are sold. Write a short memo to the chief financial officer explaining which costing approach will produce the higher income and what the difference will be.

Compute net income under absorption and variable costing. (SO 7)

EXERCISES

E6-1 The San Marcos Inn is trying to determine its break-even point. The inn has 75 rooms that are rented at $50 a night. Operating costs are as follows.

Compute break-even point and margin of safety. (SO 2)

Salaries	$8,500 per month
Utilities	2,000 per month
Depreciation	1,000 per month
Maintenance	500 per month
Maid service	5 per room
Other costs	33 per room

Instructions

(a) Determine the inn's break-even point in (1) number of rented rooms per month and (2) dollars.

(b) If the inn plans on renting an average of 50 rooms per day (assuming a 30-day month), what is (1) the monthly margin of safety in dollars and (2) the margin of safety ratio?

E6-2 In the month of June, Angela's Beauty Salon gave 3,500 haircuts, shampoos, and permanents at an average price of $30. During the month, fixed costs were $16,800 and variable costs were 80% of sales.

Compute contribution margin, break-even point, and margin of safety. (SO 2)

Instructions

(a) Determine the contribution margin in dollars, per unit, and as a ratio.

(b) Using the contribution margin technique, compute the break-even point in dollars and in units.

(c) Compute the margin of safety in dollars and as a ratio.

E6-3 Ger Company reports the following operating results for the month of August: Sales $300,000 (units 5,000); variable costs $210,000; and fixed costs $70,000. Management is considering the following independent courses of action to increase net income.

Compute net income under different alternatives. (SO 2)

1. Increase selling price by 10% with no change in total variable costs.
2. Reduce variable costs to 58% of sales.
3. Reduce fixed costs by $20,000.

Instructions

Compute the net income to be earned under each alternative. Which course of action will produce the highest net income?

Compute break-even point and prepare CVP income statement.

(SO 2)

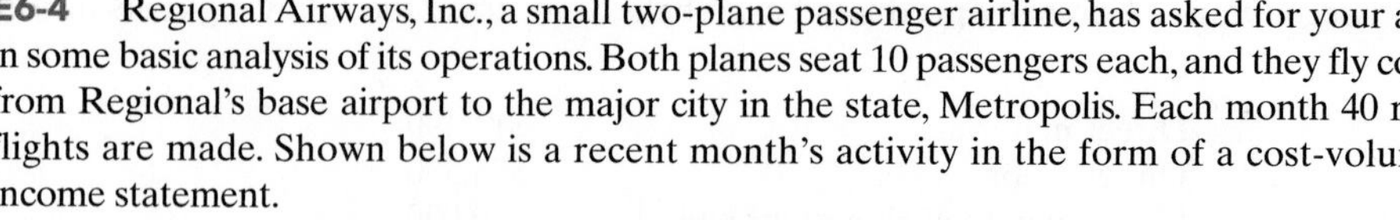

E6-4 Regional Airways, Inc., a small two-plane passenger airline, has asked for your assistance in some basic analysis of its operations. Both planes seat 10 passengers each, and they fly commuters from Regional's base airport to the major city in the state, Metropolis. Each month 40 round-trip flights are made. Shown below is a recent month's activity in the form of a cost-volume-profit income statement.

Fare revenues (300 fares)		$45,000
Variable costs		
Fuel	$14,000	
Snacks and drinks	800	
Landing fees	2,000	
Supplies and forms	1,200	18,000
Contribution margin		27,000
Fixed costs		
Depreciation	3,000	
Salaries	15,000	
Advertising	500	
Airport hanger fees	1,750	20,250
Net income		$ 6,750

Instructions

(a) Calculate the break-even point in (1) dollars and (2) number of fares.

(b) Without calculations, determine the contribution margin at the break-even point.

(c) If fares were decreased by 10%, an additional 100 fares could be generated. However, total variable costs would increase by 35%. Should the fare decrease be adopted?

Prepare a CVP income statement before and after changes in business environment.

(SO 2)

E6-5 Hall Company had sales in 2008 of $1,500,000 on 60,000 units. Variable costs totaled $720,000, and fixed costs totaled $400,000.

A new raw material is available that will decrease the variable costs per unit by 25% (or $3.00). However, to process the new raw material, fixed operating costs will increase by $150,000. Management feels that one-half of the decline in the variable costs per unit should be passed on to customers in the form of a sales price reduction. The marketing department expects that this sales price reduction will result in a 5% increase in the number of units sold.

Instructions

Prepare a CVP income statement for 2008, (a) assuming the changes have not been made, and (b) assuming that changes are made as described.

Compute break-even point in units for a company with more than one product.

(SO 3)

E6-6 Grass King manufactures lawnmowers, weed-trimmers, and chainsaws. Its sales mix and contribution margin per unit are as follows.

	Sales Mix	Contribution Margin per Unit
Lawnmowers	30%	$30
Weed-trimmers	50%	$20
Chainsaws	20%	$40

Grass King has fixed costs of $4,600,000.

Instructions

Compute the number of units of each product that Grass King must sell in order to break even under this product mix.

Compute service line break-even point and target net income in dollars for a company with more than one service.

(SO 3)

E6-7 Rapid Auto has over 200 auto-maintenance service outlets nationwide. It provides primarily two lines of service: oil changes and brake repair. Oil change–related services represent 65% of its sales and provide a contribution margin ratio of 20%. Brake repair represents 35% of its sales and provides a 60% contribution margin ratio. The company's fixed costs are $16,000,000 (that is, $80,000 per service outlet).

Instructions

(a) Calculate the dollar amount of each type of service that the company must provide in order to break even.

(b) The company has a desired net income of $60,000 per service outlet. What is the dollar amount of each type of service that must be provided by each service outlet to meet its target net income per outlet?

Compute break-even point in dollars for a company with more than one service.

(SO 3)

E6-8 Blazer Delivery is a rapidly growing delivery service. Last year 80% of its revenue came from the delivery of mailing "pouches" and small, standardized delivery boxes (which provides a 10% contribution margin). The other 20% of its revenue came from delivering non-standardized boxes (which provides a 60% contribution margin). With the rapid growth of Internet retail sales, Blazer believes that there are great opportunities for growth in the delivery of non-standardized boxes. The company has fixed costs of $12,000,000.

Instructions

(a) What is the company's break-even point in total sales dollars? At the break-even point, how much of the company's sales are provided by each type of service?

(b) The company's management would like to hold its fixed costs constant, but shift its sales mix so that 60% of its revenue comes from the delivery of non-standardized boxes and the remainder from pouches and small boxes. If this were to occur, what would be the company's break-even sales, and what amount of sales would be provided by each service type?

Compute break-even point in units for a company with multiple products.

(SO 3)

E6-9 Tiger Golf Accessories sells golf shoes, gloves, and a laser-guided range-finder that measures distance. Shown below are unit cost and sales data.

	Pairs of Shoes	Pairs of Gloves	Range-Finder
Unit sales price	$100	$30	$250
Unit variable costs	60	10	200
Unit contribution margin	$ 40	$20	$ 50
Sales mix	40%	50%	10%

Fixed costs are $620,000.

Instructions

(a) Compute the break-even point in units for the company.

(b) Determine the number of units to be sold at the break-even point for each product line.

(c) Verify that the mix of sales units determined in (b) will generate a zero net income.

Determine break-even point in dollars for two divisions.

(SO 3)

E6-10 Mega Electronix sells television sets and DVD players. The business is divided into two divisions along product lines. CVP income statements for a recent quarter's activity are presented below.

	TV Division	DVD Division	Total
Sales	$600,000	$400,000	$1,000,000
Variable costs	450,000	240,000	690,000
Contribution margin	$150,000	$160,000	310,000
Fixed costs			124,000
Net income			$ 186,000

Instructions

(a) Determine sales mix percentage and contribution margin ratio for each division.

(b) Calculate the company's weighted-average contribution margin ratio.

(c) Calculate the company's break-even point in dollars.

(d) Determine the sales level in dollars for each division at the break-even point.

Compute contribution margin and determine the product to be manufactured.

(SO 4)

E6-11 Spencer Company manufactures and sells three products. Relevant per unit data concerning each product are given below.

	Product		
	A	B	C
Selling price	$9	$ 12	$14
Variable costs and expenses	$3	$9.50	$12
Machine hours to produce	2	1	2

Instructions

(a) Compute the contribution margin per unit of the limited resource (machine hour) for each product.

(b) Assuming 1,500 additional machine hours are available, which product should be manufactured?

(c) Prepare an analysis showing the total contribution margin if the additional hours are (1) divided equally among the products, and (2) allocated entirely to the product identified in (b) above.

Compute contribution margin and determine the products to be manufactured.

(SO 4)

E6-12 Moctezuma Inc. produces and sells three products. Unit data concerning each product is shown below.

	Product		
	D	**E**	**F**
Selling price	$200	$300	$250
Direct labor costs	25	75	30
Other variable costs	105	90	148

The company has 2,000 hours of labor available to build inventory in anticipation of the company's peak season. Management is trying to decide which product should be produced. The direct labor hourly rate is $10.

Instructions

(a) Determine the number of direct labor hours per unit.

(b) Determine the contribution margin per direct labor hour.

(c) Determine which product should be produced and the total contribution margin for that product.

Compute contribution margin and determine the products to be manufactured.

(SO 4)

E6-13 Dalton Company manufactures and sells two products. Relevant per unit data concerning each product follow.

	Product	
	Basic	**Deluxe**
Selling price	$40	$52
Variable costs	$18	$24
Machine hours	.5	.7

Instructions

(a) Compute the contribution margin per machine hour for each product.

(b) If 1,000 additional machine hours are available, which product should Dalton manufacture?

(c) Prepare an analysis showing the total contribution margin if the additional hours are:

(1) Divided equally between the products.

(2) Allocated entirely to the product identified in part (b).

Compute degree of operating leverage and evaluate impact of alternative cost structures on net income.

(SO 5)

E6-14 The CVP income statements shown below are available for Billings Company and Bozeman Company.

	Billings Co.	**Bozeman Co.**
Sales revenue	$600,000	$600,000
Variable costs	280,000	80,000
Contribution margin	320,000	520,000
Fixed costs	170,000	370,000
Net income	$150,000	$150,000

Instructions

(a) Compute the degree of operating leverage for each company and interpret your results.

(b) Assuming that sales revenue increases by 10%, prepare a variable costing income statement for each company.

(c) Discuss how the cost structure of these two companies affects their operating leverage and profitability.

Compute degree of operating leverage and evaluate impact of alternative cost structures on net income and margin of safety.

(SO 5)

SERVICE

E6-15 Imagen Arquitectonica of Tijuana, Mexico is contemplating a major change in its cost structure. Currently, all of its drafting work is performed by skilled draftsmen. Alfredo Ayala, Imagen's owner, is considering replacing the draftsmen with a computerized drafting system.

However, before making the change Alfredo would like to know the consequences of the change, since the volume of business varies significantly from year to year. Shown below are CVP income statements for each alternative.

	Manual System	Computerized System
Sales	$1,500,000	$1,500,000
Variable costs	1,200,000	600,000
Contribution margin	300,000	900,000
Fixed costs	60,000	660,000
Net income	$ 240,000	$ 240,000

Instructions

(a) Determine the degree of operating leverage for each alternative.
(b) Which alternative would produce the higher net income if sales increased by $100,000?
(c) Using the margin of safety ratio, determine which alternative could sustain the greater decline in sales before operating at a loss.

Compute degree of operating leverage and impact on net income of alternative cost structures.
(SO 5)

E6-16 An investment banker is analyzing two companies that specialize in the production and sale of candied apples. Old-Fashion Apples uses a labor-intensive approach, and Mech-Apple uses a mechanized system. CVP income statements for the two companies are shown below.

	Old-Fashion Apples	Mech-Apple
Sales	$400,000	$400,000
Variable costs	320,000	160,000
Contribution margin	80,000	240,000
Fixed costs	20,000	180,000
Net income	$ 60,000	$ 60,000

The investment banker is interested in acquiring one of these companies. However, she is concerned about the impact that each company's cost structure might have on its profitability.

Instructions

(a) Calculate each company's degree of operating leverage. Determine which company's cost structure makes it more sensitive to changes in sales volume.
(b) Determine the effect on each company's net income if sales decrease by 10% and if sales increase by 5%. Do not prepare income statements.
(c) Which company should the investment banker acquire? Discuss.

Compute product cost and prepare an income statement under variable and absorption costing.
(SO 6)

***E6-17** Bob's Company builds custom fishing lures for sporting goods stores. In its first year of operations, 2008, the company incurred the following costs.

Variable Cost per Unit	
Direct materials	$7.50
Direct labor	$2.45
Variable manufacturing overhead	$5.75
Variable selling and administrative expenses	$3.90
Fixed Costs per Year	
Fixed manufacturing overhead	$234,650
Fixed selling and administrative expenses	$240,100

Bob's Company sells the fishing lures for $25. During 2008, the company sold 80,000 lures and produced 95,000 lures.

Instructions

(a) Assuming the company uses variable costing, calculate Bob's manufacturing cost per unit for 2008.
(b) Prepare a variable costing income statement for 2008.
(c) Assuming the company uses absorption costing, calculate Bob's manufacturing cost per unit for 2008.
(d) Prepare an absorption costing income statement for 2008.

Determine ending inventory under variable costing and determine whether absorption or variable costing would result in higher net income.

(SO 6, 7)

***E6-18** Ortiz Company produced 10,000 units during the past year, but only 9,000 of the units were sold. The following additional information is also available.

Direct materials used	$90,000
Direct labor incurred	$30,000
Variable manufacturing overhead	$24,000
Fixed manufacturing overhead	$50,000
Fixed selling and administrative expenses	$70,000
Variable selling and administrative expenses	$10,000

There was no work-in-process inventory at the beginning of the year, nor did Ortiz have any beginning finished goods inventory.

Instructions

(a) What would be Ortiz Company's finished goods inventory cost on December 31 under variable costing?

(b) Which costing method, absorption or variable costing, would show a higher net income for the year? By what amount?

Compute manufacturing cost under absorption and variable costing and explain difference.

(SO 6)

***E6-19** Hardwood Inc. produces wooden crates used for shipping products by ocean liner. In 2008, Hardwood incurred the following costs.

Wood used in crate production	$54,000
Nails (considered insignificant and a variable expense)	$ 340
Direct labor	$37,000
Utilities for the plant:	
$2,000 each month,	
plus $0.45 for each kilowatt-hour used each month	
Rent expense for the plant for the year	$21,400

Assume Hardwood used an average 500 kilowatt-hours each month over the past year.

Instructions

(a) What is Hardwood's total manufacturing cost if it uses a variable costing approach?

(b) What is Hardwood's total manufacturing cost if it uses an absorption costing approach?

(c) What accounts for the difference in manufacturing costs between these two costing approaches?

EXERCISES: SET B

Visit the book's website at **www.wiley.com/college/weygandt**, and choose the Student Companion site, to access Exercise Set B.

PROBLEMS: SET A

Compute break-even point under alternative courses of action.

(SO 1, 2)

P6-1A Cruz Manufacturing had a bad year in 2008. For the first time in its history it operated at a loss. The company's income statement showed the following results from selling 80,000 units of product: Net sales $1,600,000; total costs and expenses $1,740,000; and net loss $140,000. Costs and expenses consisted of the following.

	Total	Variable	Fixed
Cost of goods sold	$1,200,000	$780,000	$420,000
Selling expenses	420,000	75,000	345,000
Administrative expenses	120,000	45,000	75,000
	$1,740,000	$900,000	$840,000

Management is considering the following independent alternatives for 2009.

1. Increase unit selling price 25% with no change in costs and expenses.
2. Change the compensation of salespersons from fixed annual salaries totaling $200,000 to total salaries of $40,000 plus a 5% commission on net sales.

3. Purchase new high-tech factory machinery that will change the proportion between variable and fixed cost of goods sold to 50:50.

Instructions

(a) Compute the break-even point in dollars for 2008.
(b) Compute the break-even point in dollars under each of the alternative courses of action. (Round to the nearest dollar.) Which course of action do you recommend?

(b) (2) $1,754,839

P6-2A Poole Corporation has collected the following information after its first year of sales. Net sales were $1,600,000 on 100,000 units; selling expenses $240,000 (40% variable and 60% fixed); direct materials $511,000; direct labor $285,000; administrative expenses $280,000 (20% variable and 80% fixed); manufacturing overhead $360,000 (70% variable and 30% fixed). Top management has asked you to do a CVP analysis so that it can make plans for the coming year. It has projected that unit sales will increase by 10% next year.

Compute break-even point and margin of safety ratio, and prepare a CVP income statement before and after changes in business environment.

(SO 1, 2)

Instructions

(a) Compute (1) the contribution margin for the current year and the projected year, and (2) the fixed costs for the current year. (Assume that fixed costs will remain the same in the projected year.)
(b) Compute the break-even point in units and sales dollars for the first year.
(c) The company has a target net income of $310,000. What is the required sales in dollars for the company to meet its target?
(d) If the company meets its target net income number, by what percentage could its sales fall before it is operating at a loss? That is, what is its margin of safety ratio?
(e) The company is considering a purchase of equipment that would reduce its direct labor costs by $104,000 and would change its manufacturing overhead costs to 30% variable and 70% fixed (assume total manufacturing overhead cost is $360,000, as above). It is also considering switching to a pure commission basis for its sales staff. This would change selling expenses to 90% variable and 10% fixed (assume total selling expense is $240,000, as above). Compute (1) the contribution margin and (2) the contribution margin ratio, and recompute (3) the break-even point in sales dollars. Comment on the effect each of management's proposed changes has on the break-even point.

(b) 119,000 units

(e) (3) $1,515,152

P6-3A Manning Industries manufactures and sells three different models of wet-dry shop vacuum cleaners. Although the shop vacs vary in terms of quality and features, all are good sellers. Manning is currently operating at full capacity with limited machine time.

Sales and production information relevant to each model follows.

Determine sales mix with limited resources.

(SO 4)

	Product		
	Economy	Standard	Deluxe
Selling price	$30	$50	$100
Variable costs and expenses	$12	$18	$42
Machine hours required	.5	.8	1.6

Instructions

(a) Ignoring the machine time constraint, which single product should Manning Industries produce?
(b) What is the contribution margin per unit of limited resource for each product?
(c) If additional machine time could be obtained, how should the additional time be used?

(b) Economy $36

P6-4A The Creekside Inn is a restaurant in Tucson, Arizona. It specializes in southwestern style meals in a moderate price range. Terry Wilson, the manager of Creekside, has determined that during the last 2 years the sales mix and contribution margin ratio of its offerings are as follows.

Determine break-even sales under alternative sales strategies and evaluate results.

(SO 2, 3)

	Percent of Total Sales	Contribution Margin Ratio
Appetizers	10%	60%
Main entrees	60%	30%
Desserts	10%	50%
Beverages	20%	80%

Terry is considering a variety of options to try to improve the profitability of the restaurant. Her goal is to generate a target net income of $150,000. The company has fixed costs of $1,200,000 per year.

Instructions

(a) Total sales $3,000,000

(b) Total sales $3,750,000

(a) Calculate the total restaurant sales and the sales of each product line that would be necessary to achieve the desired target net income.

(b) Terry believes the restaurant could greatly improve its profitability by reducing the complexity and selling price of its entrees to increase the number of clients that it serves. It would then more heavily market its appetizers and beverages. She is proposing to drop the contribution margin ratio on the main entrees to 10% by dropping the average selling price. She envisions an expansion of the restaurant that would increase fixed costs by 50%. At the same time, she is proposing to change the sales mix to the following.

	Percent of Total Sales	Contribution Margin Ratio
Appetizers	20%	60%
Main entrees	30%	10%
Desserts	10%	50%
Beverages	40%	80%

Compute the total restaurant sales, and the sales of each product line that would be necessary to achieve the desired target net income.

(c) Suppose that Terry drops the selling price on entrees and increases fixed costs as proposed in part (b), but customers are not swayed by the marketing efforts and the sales mix remains what it was in part (a). Compute the total restaurant sales and the sales of each product line that would be necessary to achieve the desired target net income. Comment on the potential risks and benefits of this strategy.

Compute degree of operating leverage and evaluate impact of operating leverage on financial results.

(SO 5)

P6-5A The following CVP income statements are available for Old Company and New Company.

	Old Company	New Company
Sales	$400,000	$400,000
Variable costs	180,000	80,000
Contribution margin	220,000	320,000
Fixed costs	170,000	270,000
Net income	$ 50,000	$ 50,000

Instructions

(a) BE, Old $309,091
BE, New $337,500

(b) DOL, Old 4.4
DOL, New 6.4

(a) Compute the break-even point in dollars and the margin of safety ratio for each company.

(b) Compute the degree of operating leverage for each company and interpret your results.

(c) Assuming that sales revenue increases by 20%, prepare a CVP income statement for each company.

(d) Assuming that sales revenue decreases by 20%, prepare a CVP income statement for each company.

(e) Discuss how the cost structure of these two companies affects their operating leverage and profitability.

Prepare income statements under absorption costing and variable costing for a company with beginning inventory, and reconcile differences.

(SO 6, 7)

***P6-6A** AFN Company produces plastic that is used for injection-molding applications such as gears for small motors. In 2007, the first year of operations, AFN produced 4,000 tons of plastic and sold 3,000 tons. In 2008, the production and sales results were exactly reversed. In each year, the selling price per ton was $2,000, variable manufacturing costs were 15% of the sales price of units produced, variable selling expenses were 10% of the selling price of units sold, fixed manufacturing costs were $2,400,000, and fixed administrative expenses were $600,000.

Instructions

(a) 2008 $3,000,000

(b) 2008 $2,400,000

(a) Prepare income statements for each year using variable costing. (Use the format from Illustration 6A-5.)

(b) Prepare income statements for each year using absorption costing. (Use the format from Illustration 6A-4.)

(c) Reconcile the differences each year in net income under the two costing approaches.

(d) Comment on the effects of production and sales on net income under the two costing approaches.

***P6-7A** Basic Electric Motors is a division of Basic Electric Products Corporation. The division manufactures and sells an electric motor used in a wide variety of applications. During the coming year it expects to sell 50,000 units for $30 per unit. Esther Madonna is the division manager. She is considering producing either 50,000 or 80,000 units during the period. Other information is presented in the schedule.

Prepare absorption and variable costing income statements and reconcile differences between absorption and variable costing income statements when sales level and production level change. Discuss relative usefulness of absorption costing versus variable costing.

(SO 6, 7, 8)

Division Information for 2008	
Beginning inventory	0
Expected sales in units	50,000
Selling price per unit	$30
Variable manufacturing costs per unit	$12
Fixed manufacturing overhead costs (total)	$400,000
Fixed manufacturing overhead costs per unit:	
Based on 50,000 units	$8 per unit ($400,000 ÷ 50,000)
Based on 80,000 units	$5 per unit ($400,000 ÷ 80,000)
Manufacturing cost per unit:	
Based on 50,000 units	$20 per unit ($12 variable + $8 fixed)
Based on 80,000 units	$17 per unit ($12 variable + $5 fixed)
Variable selling and administrative expenses	$2
Fixed selling and administrative expenses (total)	$40,000

Instructions

(a) Prepare an absorption costing income statement, with one column showing the results if 50,000 units are produced and one column showing the results if 80,000 units are produced.

(a) 80,000 units: NI $510,000

(b) Prepare a variable costing income statement, with one column showing the results if 50,000 units are produced and one column showing the results if 80,000 units are produced.

(b) 80,000 units: NI $360,000

(c) Reconcile the difference in net incomes under the two approaches and explain what accounts for this difference.

(d) Discuss the relative usefulness of the variable costing income statements versus the absorption costing income statements for decision making and for evaluating the manager's performance.

PROBLEMS: SET B

P6-1B Griffey Manufacturing's sales slumped badly in 2008. For the first time in its history, it operated at a loss. The company's income statement showed the following results from selling 500,000 units of product: Net sales $2,500,000; total costs and expenses $2,600,000; and net loss $100,000. Costs and expenses consisted of the following.

Compute break-even point under alternative courses of action.

(SO 1, 2)

	Total	Variable	Fixed
Cost of goods sold	$2,100,000	$1,440,000	$ 660,000
Selling expenses	300,000	72,000	228,000
Administrative expenses	200,000	48,000	152,000
	$2,600,000	$1,560,000	$1,040,000

Management is considering the following independent alternatives for 2009.

1. Increase unit selling price 20% with no change in costs and expenses.
2. Change the compensation of salespersons from fixed annual salaries totaling $210,000 to total salaries of $70,000 plus a 4% commission on net sales.
3. Purchase new automated equipment that will change the proportion between variable and fixed cost of goods sold to 60% variable and 40% fixed.

Instructions

(a) Compute the break-even point in dollars for 2008.

(b) Compute the break-even point in dollars under each of the alternative courses of action. (Round to the nearest dollar.) Which course of action do you recommend?

(b) (1) $2,166,667

Compute break-even point and margin of safety ratio, and prepare a CVP income statement before and after changes in business environment.
(SO 1, 2)

P6-2B Washington Corporation has collected the following information after its first year of sales. Net sales were $2,400,000 on 200,000 units; selling expenses $360,000 (30% variable and 70% fixed); direct materials $626,500; direct labor $507,500; administrative expenses $420,000 (40% variable and 60% fixed); manufacturing overhead $540,000 (50% variable and 50% fixed). Top management has asked you to do a CVP analysis so that it can make plans for the coming year. It has projected that unit sales will increase by 20% next year.

Instructions

(a) Compute (1) the contribution margin for the current year and the projected year, and (2) the fixed costs for the current year. (Assume that fixed costs will remain the same in the projected year.)

(b) 215,000 units

(b) Compute the break-even point in units and sales dollars.

(c) The company has a target net income of $620,000. What is the required sales in dollars for the company to meet its target?

(d) If the company meets its target net income number, by what percentage could its sales fall before it is operating at a loss? That is, what is its margin of safety ratio?

(e) (3) $1,897,297

(e) The company is considering a purchase of equipment that would reduce its direct labor costs by $240,000 and would change its manufacturing overhead costs to 30% variable and 70% fixed (assume total manufacturing overhead cost is $540,000, as above). It is also considering switching to a pure commission basis for its sales staff. This would change selling expenses to 80% variable and 20% fixed (assume total selling expense is $360,000, as above). Compute (1) the contribution margin and (2) the contribution margin ratio, and recompute (3) the break-even point in sales dollars. Comment on the effect each of management's proposed changes has on the break-even point.

Determine sales mix with limited resources.
(SO 4)

P6-3B Simon Corporation manufactures and sells three different models of storm doors. Although the doors vary in terms of quality and features, all are good sellers. Simon is currently operating at full capacity with limited machine time.

Sales and production information relevant to each model follows.

	Product		
	Economy	**Standard**	**Deluxe**
Selling price	$180	$250	$430
Variable costs and expenses	$99	$150	$280
Machine hours required	.6	.9	1.2

Instructions

(a) Ignoring the machine time constraint, which single product should Simon produce?

(b) Economy $135

(b) What is the contribution margin per unit of limited resource for each product?

(c) If additional machine time could be obtained, how should the additional time be used?

Determine break-even sales under alternative sales strategies and evaluate results.
(SO 2, 3)

SERVICE

P6-4B The Bricktown Pub is a restaurant in Platteville, Wisconsin. It specializes in classic American fare in a moderate price range. Ben Borke, the manager of Bricktown, has determined that during the last 2 years the sales mix and contribution margin of its offerings are as follows.

	Percent of Total Sales	Contribution Margin Ratio
Appetizers	10%	50%
Main entrees	55%	30%
Desserts	10%	60%
Beverages	25%	75%

Ben is considering a variety of options to try to improve the profitability of the restaurant. His goal is to generate a target net income of $155,000. The company has fixed costs of $400,000 per year.

Instructions

(a) Total sales $1,200,000

(a) Calculate the total restaurant sales and the sales of each product line that would be necessary to achieve the desired target net income.

(b) Ben believes the restaurant could greatly improve its profitability if it were to reduce the complexity and selling price of its entrees to increase the number of clients that it serves, and then more heavily market its appetizers and beverages. He is proposing to drop the contribution margin on the main entrees to 15% by dropping the average selling price. He envisions an expansion of the restaurant that would increase fixed costs by 50%. At the same time, he is proposing to change the sales mix to the following.

	Percent of Total Sales	Contribution Margin Ratio
Appetizers	15%	50%
Main entrees	30%	15%
Desserts	15%	60%
Beverages	40%	75%

Compute the total restaurant sales, and the sales of each product line that would be necessary to achieve the desired target net income.

(c) Suppose that Ben drops the selling price on entrees, and increases fixed costs as proposed in part (b), but customers are not swayed by his marketing efforts, and the sales mix remains what it was in part (a). Compute the total restaurant sales and the sales of each product line that would be necessary to achieve the desired target net income. Comment on the potential risks and benefits of this strategy.

P6-5B The following CVP income statements are available for Retro Company and Modern Company.

Compute degree of operating leverage and evaluate impact of operating leverage on financial results.

(SO 5)

	Retro Company	Modern Company
Sales	$500,000	$500,000
Variable costs	300,000	100,000
Contribution margin	200,000	400,000
Fixed costs	140,000	340,000
Net income	$ 60,000	$ 60,000

Instructions

(a) Compute the break-even point in dollars and the margin of safety ratio for each company.

(b) Compute the degree of operating leverage for each company and interpret your results.

(c) Assuming that sales revenue increases by 25%, prepare a CVP income statement for each company.

(d) Assuming that sales revenue decreases by 25%, prepare a CVP income statement for each company.

(e) Discuss how the cost structure of these two companies affects their operating leverage and profitability.

(a) BE Retro $350,000
(b) DOL Retro 3.3

***P6-6B** Zaki Metal Company produces the steel wire that is used for the production of paper clips. In 2007, the first year of operations, Zaki produced 40,000 miles of wire and sold 30,000 miles. In 2008, the production and sales results were exactly reversed. In each year, the selling price per mile was $80, variable manufacturing costs were 25% of the sales price of units produced, variable selling expenses were $6 per mile sold, fixed manufacturing costs were $1,200,000, and fixed administrative expenses were $200,000.

Prepare income statements under absorption costing and variable costing for a company with beginning inventory, and reconcile differences.

(SO 6, 7)

Instructions

(a) Prepare income statements for each year using variable costing. (Use the format from Illustration 6A-5.)

(b) Prepare income statements for each year using absorption costing. (Use the format from Illustration 6A-4.)

(c) Reconcile the differences each year in net income under the two costing approaches.

(d) Comment on the effects of production and sales on net income under the two costing approaches.

(a) 2007 NI $220,000

(b) 2007 NI $520,000

***P6-7B** Harrison Pumps is a division of Liverpool Controls Corporation. The division manufactures and sells a pump used in a wide variety of applications. During the coming year it expects to sell 60,000 units for $20 per unit. Richard Starkey manages the division. He is considering producing either 60,000 or 100,000 units during the period. Other information is presented in the following schedule.

Prepare absorption and variable costing income statements and reconcile differences between absorption and variable costing income statements when sales level and production level change. Discuss relative usefulness of absorption costing versus variable costing.

(SO 6, 7, 8)

Division Information for 2008	
Beginning inventory	0
Expected sales in units	60,000
Selling price per unit	\$20.00
Variable manufacturing costs per unit	\$9.00
Fixed manufacturing overhead costs (total)	\$240,000
Fixed manufacturing overhead costs per unit:	
Based on 60,000 units	\$4.00 per unit (\$240,000 ÷ 60,000)
Based on 100,000 units	\$2.40 per unit (\$240,000 ÷ 100,000)
Manufacturing cost per unit:	
Based on 60,000 units	\$13.00 per unit (\$9.00 variable + \$4.00 fixed)
Based on 100,000 units	\$11.40 per unit (\$9.00 variable + \$2.40 fixed)
Variable selling and administrative expenses	\$1
Fixed selling and administrative expenses (total)	\$30,000

Instructions

(a) 100,000 produced: NI \$426,000

(b) 100,000 produced: NI \$330,000

(a) Prepare an absorption costing income statement, with one column showing the results if 60,000 units are produced and one column showing the results if 100,000 units are produced.
(b) Prepare a variable costing income statement, with one column showing the results if 60,000 units are produced and one column showing the results if 100,000 units are produced.
(c) Reconcile the difference in net incomes under the two approaches and explain what accounts for this difference.
(d) Discuss the relative usefulness of the variable costing income statements versus the absorption costing income statements for decision making and for evaluating the manager's performance.

PROBLEMS: SET C

Visit the book's website at **www.wiley.com/college/weygandt**, and choose the Student Companion site, to access Problem Set C.

WATERWAYS CONTINUING PROBLEM

(*Note:* This is a continuation of the Waterways Problem from Chapters 1 through 5.)

WCP6 This problem asks you to perform break-even analysis based on Waterways' sales mix and to make sales mix decisions related to Waterways' use of its productive facilities. An optional extension of the problem (related to the chapter appendix) also asks you to prepare a variable costing income statement and an absorption costing income statement.

Go to the book's website, **www.wiley.com/college/weygandt,** *to find the remainder of this problem.*

BROADENING YOUR PERSPECTIVE

DECISION MAKING ACROSS THE ORGANIZATION

BYP6-1 ComfortCraft manufactures swivel seats for customized vans. It currently manufactures 10,000 seats per year, which it sells for $480 per seat. It incurs variable costs of $180 per seat and fixed costs of $2,200,000. It is considering automating the upholstery process, which is now largely manual. It estimates that if it does so, its fixed costs will be $3,200,000, and its variable costs will decline to $80 per seat.

Instructions

With the class divided into groups, answer the following questions.

(a) Prepare a CVP income statement based on current activity.

(b) Compute contribution margin ratio, break-even point in dollars, margin of safety ratio, and degree of operating leverage based on current activity.

(c) Prepare a CVP income statement assuming that the company invests in the automated upholstery system.

(d) Compute contribution margin ratio, break-even point in dollars, margin of safety ratio, and degree of operating leverage assuming the new upholstery system is implemented.

(e) Discuss the implications of adopting the new system.

MANAGERIAL ANALYSIS

BYP6-2 For nearly 20 years Custom Coatings has provided painting and galvanizing services for manufacturers in its region. Manufacturers of various metal products have relied on the quality and quick turnaround time provided by Custom Coatings and its 20 skilled employees. During the last year, as a result of a sharp upturn in the economy, the company's sales have increased by 30% relative to the previous year. The company has not been able to increase its capacity fast enough, so Custom Coatings has had to turn work away because it cannot keep up with customer requests.

Top management is considering the purchase of a sophisticated robotic painting booth. The booth would represent a considerable move in the direction of automation versus manual labor. If Custom Coatings purchases the booth, it would most likely lay off 15 its skilled painters. To analyze the decision, the company compiled production information from the most recent year and then prepared a parallel compilation assuming that the company would purchase the new equipment and lay off the workers. Those data are shown below. As you can see, the company projects that during the last year it would have been far more profitable if it had used the automated approach.

	Current Approach	Automated Approach
Sales	$2,000,000	$2,000,000
Variable costs	1,200,000	400,000
Contribution margin	800,000	1,600,000
Fixed costs	200,000	600,000
Net income	$ 600,000	$1,000,000

Instructions

(a) Compute and interpret the contribution margin ratio under each approach.

(b) Compute the break-even point in sales dollars under each approach. Discuss the implications of your findings.

(c) Using the current level of sales, compute the margin of safety ratio under each approach and interpret your findings.

(d) Determine the degree of operating leverage for each approach at current sales levels. How much would the company's net income decline under each approach with a 10% decline in sales?

(e) At what level of sales would the company's net income be the same under either approach?

(f) Discuss the issues that the company must consider in making this decision.

REAL-WORLD FOCUS

BYP6-3 In its 2003 annual report the Del Monte Foods Company reported three separate operating segments: consumer products (which includes a variety of canned foods including tuna, fruit, and vegetables); pet products (which includes pet food and snacks and veterinary products); and soup and infant-feeding products (which includes soup, broth, and infant feeding and pureed products).

In its annual report Del Monte uses absorption costing. As a result, information regarding the relative composition of its fixed and variable costs is not available. We have assumed that $860.3 million of its total operating expenses of $1,920.3 million are fixed and have allocated the remaining variable costs across the three divisions. Sales data, along with assumed expense data, are provided below.

	(in millions)	
	Sales	**Variable Costs**
Consumer products	$1,031.8	$ 610
Pet products	837.3	350
Soup and infant-feeding products	302.0	100
	$2,171.1	$1,060

Instructions

(a) Compute each segment's contribution margin ratio and the sales mix.

(b) Using the information computed in part (a), compute the company's break-even point in dollars, and then determine the amount of sales that would be generated by each division at the break-even point.

EXPLORING THE WEB

BYP6-4 The external financial statements published by publicly traded companies are based on absorption cost accounting. As a consequence, it is very difficult to gain an understanding of the relative composition of the companies' fixed and variable costs. It is possible, however, to learn about a company's sales mix and the relative profitability of its various divisions. This exercise looks at the financial statements of FedEx Corporation.

Address: www.fedex.com/us/investorrelations, or go to **www.wiley.com/college/weygandt**

Steps

1. Go to the site above.
2. Under "Financial Information," choose "Annual Reports."
3. Choose "2006 Annual Report."

Instructions

(a) Read page 38 of the report under the heading "Description of Business." What are the three primary product lines of the company? What does the company identify as the key factors affecting operating results?

(b) Page 46 of the report lists the operating expenses of FedEx Ground. Assuming that rentals, depreciation, and "other" are all fixed costs, prepare a variable costing income statement for 2006, and compute the division's contribution margin ratio and the break-even point in dollars.

(c) Page 82, Note 14 ("Business segment information") provides additional information regarding the relative profitability of the three business segments.

(i) Calculate the sales mix for 2004 and 2006. (Note: Exclude Kinko's and "other" when you calculate total revenue.)

(ii) The company does not provide the contribution margin for each division, but it does provide "operating margin" (operating income divided by revenues) on pages 46, 48, and 49. List these for each division for 2004 and 2006.

(iii) Assuming that the "operating margin" (operating income divided by revenues) moves in parallel with each division's contribution margin, how has the shift in sales mix affected the company's profitability from 2004 to 2006?

COMMUNICATION ACTIVITY

BYP6-5 Westfield Corporation makes two different boat anchors—a traditional fishing anchor and a high-end yacht anchor—using the same production machinery. The contribution margin of the yacht anchor is three times as high as that of the other product. The company is currently operating at full capacity and has been doing so for nearly two years. Ralph Sampson, the company's CEO, want to cut back on production of the fishing anchor so that the company can make more yacht anchors. He says that this is a "no-brainer" because the contribution margin of the yacht anchor is so much higher.

Instructions

Write a short memo to Ralph Sampson describing the analysis that the company should do before it makes this decision and any other considerations that would affect the decision.

ETHICS CASE

***BYP6-6** Scott Bestor was hired during January 2008 to manage the home products division of Advanced Techno. As part of his employment contract, he was told that he would get $5,000 of additional bonus for every 1% increase that the division's profits exceeded those of the previous year.

Soon after coming on board, Scott met with his plant managers and explained that he wanted the plants to be run at full capacity. Previously the plant had employed just-in-time inventory practices and had consequently produced units only as they were needed. Scott stated that under previous management the company had missed out on too many sales opportunities because it didn't have enough inventory on hand. Because previous management had employed just-in-time inventory practices, when Scott came on board there was virtually no beginning inventory. The selling price and variable cost per unit remained the same from 2007 to 2008. Additional information is provided below.

	2007	2008
Net income	$ 400,000	$ 600,000
Units produced	20,000	25,000
Units sold	20,000	20,000
Fixed manufacturing overhead costs	$1,000,000	$1,000,000
Fixed manufacturing overhead costs per unit	$ 50	$ 40

Instructions

(a) Calculate Scott's bonus based upon the net income shown above.
(b) Recompute the 2007 and 2008 results using variable costing.
(c) Recompute Scott's 2008 bonus under variable costing.
(d) Were Scott's actions unethical? Do you think any actions need to be taken by the company?

"ALL ABOUT YOU" ACTIVITY

BYP6-7 Many of you will some day own your own business. One rapidly growing opportunity is no-frills workout centers. Such centers attract customers who want to take advantage of state-of-the-art fitness equipment but do not need the other amenities of full-service health clubs. One way to own your own fitness business is to buy a franchise. Snap Fitness is a Minnesota-based business that offers franchise opportunities. For a very low monthly fee ($26, without an annual contract) customers can access a Snap Fitness center 24 hours a day.

The Snap Fitness website (*www.snapfitness.com*) indicates that start-up costs range from $60,000 to $184,000. This initial investment covers the following pre-opening costs: franchise fee, grand opening marketing, leasehold improvements, utility/rent deposits, and training.

Instructions

(a) Suppose that Snap Fitness estimates that each location incurs $4,000 per month in fixed operating expenses plus $2,000 to lease equipment. A recent newspaper article describing no-frills fitness centers indicated that a Snap Fitness site might require only 300 members to break even. Using the information provided above, and your knowledge of CVP analysis, estimate the amount of variable costs. (When performing your analysis, assume that the only fixed costs are the estimated monthly operating expenses and the equipment lease.)

(b) Using the information from part (a), what would monthly sales in members and dollars have to be to achieve a target net income of $10,000 for the month ?

(c) Provide five examples of variable costs for a fitness center.

(d) Go to a fitness-business website such as Curves, Snap Fitness, or Anytime Fitness and find information about purchasing a franchise. Summarize the franchise information needed to decide whether entering into a franchise agreement would be a good idea.

Answers to Business Insight and Accounting Across the Organization Questions

Don't Just Look—Buy Something, p. 240

Q: Besides increasing their conversion rates, what steps can online merchants use to lower their break-even points?

A: *In theory, one of the principal advantages of online retailers is that they can minimize their investment in "bricks and mortar" and thus minimize their fixed costs. Some online merchants never even handle the merchandise they sell. Instead, they simply provide a centralized location for customers to view merchandise and to place orders. The online retailer then forwards the order to the supplier, and the supplier ships it directly to the customer.*

However, some online merchants who originally planned on employing this model have since found it necessary to build their own warehouses and distribution centers to ensure timely and dependable product delivery. This increases their fixed costs, and consequently increases their break-even point.

Healthy for You, and Great for the Bottom Line, p. 244

Q: Why do you suppose restaurants are so eager to sell beverages and desserts?

A: *There is a reason why servers at restaurants keep your beverage glass full, and why they wave the dessert tray in your face at the end of the meal. Both of these items traditionally have very high contribution margins and require very minimal investments in fixed costs. As a consequence they are a great mechanism by which a company can hit its break-even point.*

Something Smells, p. 247

Q: What is the limited resource for a retailer, and what implications does this have for sales mix?

A: *For retailers, the limited resource is not just shelf space, but shelf space per day. At first you might think that a product that is small and has a high contribution margin would be the product of choice. But you also have to factor in the amount of time that a product sits on the shelf.*

For example, suppose the following: Product A and B are the same size; product A has twice the contribution margin as product B, but A sits on the shelf five times as long as product B. In this case, once time spent on the shelf is taken into account, B's superior turnover more than makes up for its lower contribution margin.

The Cost of Experience, p. 250

Q: As a result of being in business for a long time, the established airline giants also must pay very large retirement payments, a cost the newer airlines do not face. What impact do these payments have on the break-even equation?

A: *The ongoing costs of retirement and health-care packages for retired employees represent a type of fixed cost. These so-called "legacy" costs can dramatically change the break-even equation. To cover these costs an old-line airline must fly many more passengers than a newer airline.*

Authors' Comments on *All About You:* Big Decisions for Your Energy Future, p. 251

If reduction of greenhouse gas emissions is a goal, then one step toward attainment of that goal is to assign a cost to greenhouse-gas emissions. One approach which is currently being used is the buying and selling of carbon-emission rights. As companies buy and sell emission rights, the price of polluting becomes a tangible factor in the formulations that will be used to make future energy-source decisions. This approach has been effective in addressing similar issues such as the reduction of sulfur emissions.

However, as suggested in the "No" response, many believe that, to be effective and fair, an enforceable international agreement on such an approach would be necessary. In the United

States, companies currently participate on a voluntary basis; in some other countries, participation is required.

Another factor to consider in these decisions is the timing of conversion to new technology. A gradual conversion to new technologies as existing power plants reach the end of their productive lives would be far less costly than a rapid conversion to new technologies that required scrapping existing plants before they are fully depreciated. Decisions about which plants to replace and when to replace them will require careful cost-benefit analyses.

Answers to Self-Study Questions

1. d **2.** d **3.** a **4.** a **5.** b **6.** d **7.** a **8.** b **9.** d **10.** c ***11.** b ***12.** c

Remember to go back to the Navigator box on the chapter-opening page and check off your completed work.

Chapter 7

Incremental Analysis

STUDY OBJECTIVES

After studying this chapter, you should be able to:

1. Identify the steps in management's decision-making process.
2. Describe the concept of incremental analysis
3. Identify the relevant costs in accepting an order at a special price.
4. Identify the relevant costs in a make-or-buy decision.
5. Identify the relevant costs in determining whether to sell or process materials further.
6. Identify the relevant costs to be considered in retaining or replacing equipment.
7. Identify the relevant costs in deciding whether to eliminate an unprofitable segment.

The Navigator

The Navigator

- Scan **Study Objectives**
- Read **Feature Story**
- Read **Preview**
- Read text and answer **Before You Go On** p. 299 p. 300
- Work **Using the Decision Toolkit**
- Review **Summary of Study Objectives**
- Work **Demonstration Problem**
- Answer **Self-Study Questions**
- Complete **Assignments**

Feature Story

MAKE IT OR BUY IT?

When is a manufacturer not a manufacturer? When it outsources. An extension of the classic "make or buy" decision, outsourcing involves hiring other companies to make all or part of a product or to perform services. Who is outsourcing? Nike, General Motors, Sara Lee, and Hewlett-Packard, to name a few. Even a recent trade journal article for small cabinet makers outlined the pros and cons of building cabinet doors and drawers internally, or outsourcing them to other shops.

Gibson Greetings, Inc., one of the country's largest sellers of greeting cards, has experienced both the pros and cons of outsourcing. In April one year it announced it would outsource the manufacturing of all of its cards and gift wrap. Gibson's stock price shot up quickly because investors believed the strategy could save the company $10 million a year, primarily by reducing manufacturing costs. But later in the same year Gibson got a taste of the negative side of outsourcing: When one of its suppliers was unable to meet its production schedule, about $20 million of Christmas cards went to stores a month later than scheduled.

Outsourcing is often a point of dispute in labor negotiations. Although many of the jobs lost to outsourcing go overseas, that is not always the case. In fact, a recent trend is to hire out work to vendors located close to the company. This reduces shipping costs and can improve coordination of efforts.

One company that has benefited from local outsourcing is Solectron Corporation in Silicon Valley. It makes things like cell phones, printers, and computers for high-tech companies in the region. To the surprise of many, it has kept thousands of people employed in California, rather than watching those jobs go overseas. What is its secret? It produces high-quality products efficiently. Solectron has to be efficient because it operates on a very thin profit margin—that is, it makes a tiny amount of money on each part—but it makes millions and millions of parts. It has proved the logic of outsourcing as a management decision, both for the companies for whom it makes parts and for its owners and employees.

✓ The Navigator

Inside Chapter 7

Preview of Chapter 7

An important purpose of management accounting is to provide managers with relevant information for decision making. Companies of all sorts must make product decisions. Philip Morris decided to cut prices to raise market share. Oral-B Laboratories opted to produce a new, higher priced ($5) toothbrush. General Motors discontinued making the Buick Riviera and announced the closure of its Oldsmobile Division. Quaker Oats decided to sell off a line of beverages, at a price more than one billion dollars less than it paid for that product line only a few years before. Ski manufacturers like Dynastar had to decide whether to use their limited resources to make snowboards instead of downhill skis.

This chapter explains management's decision-making process and a decision-making approach called incremental analysis. The use of incremental analysis is demonstrated in a variety of situations.

The content and organization of this chapter are as follows.

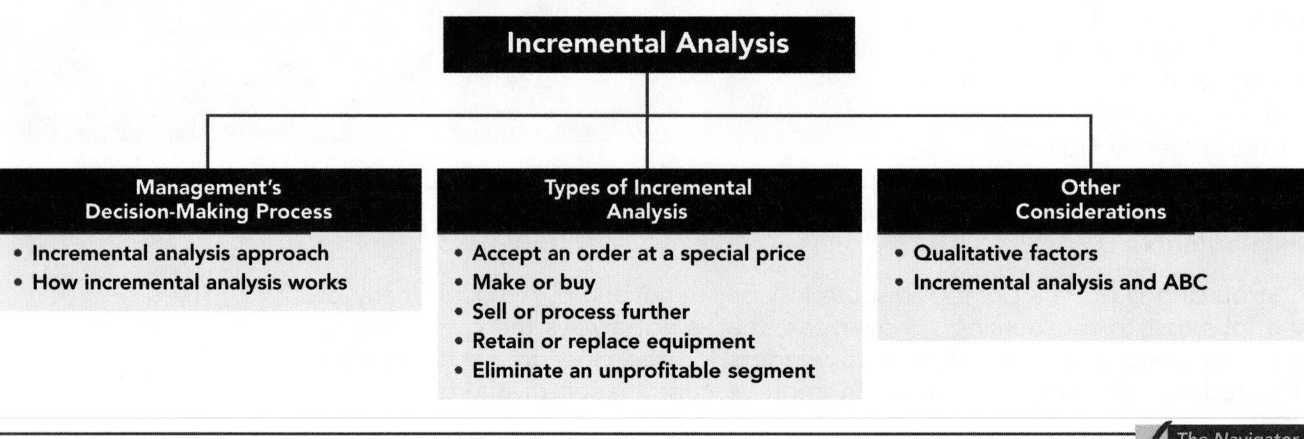

The Navigator

MANAGEMENT'S DECISION-MAKING PROCESS

STUDY OBJECTIVE 1

Identify the steps in management's decision-making process.

Making decisions is an important management function. Management's decision-making process does not always follow a set pattern because decisions vary significantly in their scope, urgency, and importance. It is possible, though, to identify some steps that are frequently involved in the process. These steps are shown in Illustration 7-1 below.

Accounting's contribution to the decision-making process occurs primarily in Steps 2 and 4—evaluating possible courses of action, and reviewing results. In Step 2, for each possible course of action, relevant revenue and cost data are

Illustration 7-1
Management's decision-making process

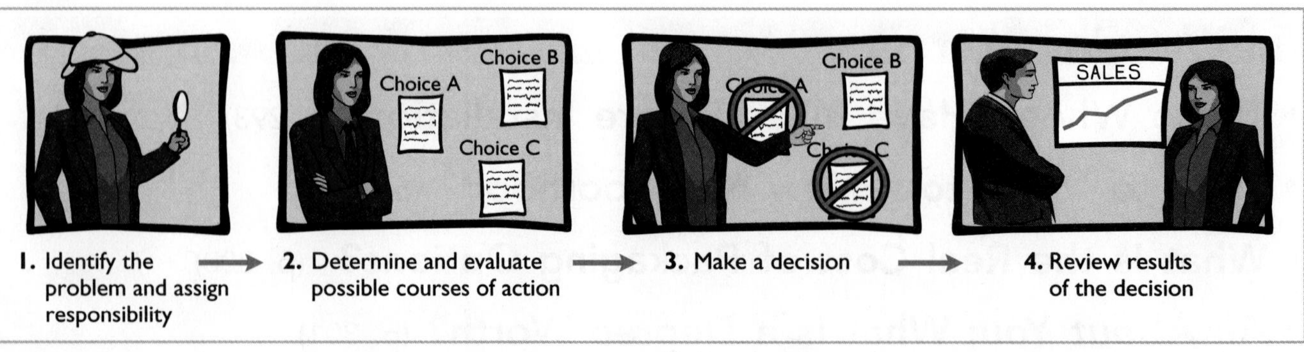

provided. These show the expected overall effect on net income. In Step 4, internal reports are prepared that review the actual impact of the decision.

In making business decisions, management ordinarily considers both financial and nonfinancial information. **Financial** information is related to revenues and costs and their effect on the company's overall profitability. **Nonfinancial** information relates to such factors as the effect of the decision on employee turnover, the environment, or the overall image of the company in the community. Although nonfinancial information can be as important as financial information, we will focus primarily on financial information that is relevant to the decision.

Incremental Analysis Approach

STUDY OBJECTIVE 2

Describe the concept of incremental analysis.

Decisions involve a choice among alternative courses of action. Suppose that you were deciding whether to purchase or lease a car. The financial data relate to the cost of leasing versus the cost of purchasing. For example, leasing would involve periodic lease payments; purchasing would require "up-front" payment of the purchase price. In other words, the financial data relevant to the decision are the data that would vary in the future among the possible alternatives. The process used to identify the financial data that change under alternative courses of action is called **incremental analysis**. In some cases, you will find that when you use incremental analysis, both costs **and** revenues will vary. In other cases, only costs **or** revenues will vary.

Just as your decision to buy or lease a car will affect your future financial situation, similar decisions, on a larger scale, will affect a company's future. Incremental analysis identifies the probable effects of those decisions on future earnings. Such analysis inevitably involves estimates and uncertainty. Gathering data for incremental analyses may involve market analysts, engineers, and accountants. In quantifying the data, the accountant is expected to produce the most reliable information available at the time the decision must be made.

ALTERNATIVE TERMINOLOGY

Incremental analysis is also called *differential analysis* because the analysis focuses on differences.

How Incremental Analysis Works

The basic approach in incremental analysis is illustrated in the following example.

Illustration 7-2 Basic approach in incremental analysis

Incremental Analysis.xls

File Edit View Insert Format Tools Data Window Help

	A	B	C	D
1		Alternative A	Alternative B	Net Income Increase (Decrease)
2	Revenues	$125,000	$110,000	$ (15,000)
3	Costs	100,000	80,000	20,000
4	Net income	$ 25,000	$ 30,000	$ 5,000
5				

This example compares alternative B with alternative A. The net income column shows the differences between the alternatives. In this case, incremental revenue will be $15,000 less under alternative B than under alternative A. But a $20,000 incremental cost saving will be realized.[1] Thus, alternative B will produce $5,000 more net income than alternative A.

In the following pages you will encounter three important cost concepts used in incremental analysis, as defined and discussed in Illustration 7-3 (page 290).

[1]Although income taxes are sometimes important in incremental analysis, they are ignored in the chapter for simplicity's sake.

- **Relevant cost** In incremental analysis, the only factors to be considered are those costs and revenues that differ across alternatives. Those factors are called **relevant costs.** Costs and revenues that do not differ across alternatives can be ignored when trying to choose between alternatives.

- **Opportunity cost** Often in choosing one course of action, the company must give up the opportunity to benefit from some other course of action. For example, if a machine is used to make one type of product, the benefit of making another type of product with that machine is lost. This lost benefit is referred to as **opportunity cost.**

- **Sunk cost** Costs that have already been incurred and will not be changed or avoided by any present or future decision are referred to as **sunk costs.** For example, if you have already purchased a machine, and now a new, more efficient machine is available, the book value of the original machine is a sunk cost. It should have no bearing on your decision whether to buy the new machine. **Sunk costs are not relevant costs.**

Illustration 7-3 Key cost concepts in incremental analysis

Incremental analysis sometimes involves changes that at first glance might seem contrary to your intuition. For example, sometimes variable costs **do not change** under the alternative courses of action. Also, sometimes fixed costs **do change**. For example, direct labor, normally a variable cost, is not an incremental cost in deciding between two new factory machines if each asset requires the same amount of direct labor. In contrast, rent expense, normally a fixed cost, is an incremental cost in a decision whether to continue occupancy of a building or to purchase or lease a new building.

TYPES OF INCREMENTAL ANALYSIS

A number of different types of decisions involve incremental analysis. The more common types of decisions are whether to:

1. Accept an order at a special price.
2. Make or buy component parts or finished products.
3. Sell products or process them further.
4. Retain or replace equipment.
5. Eliminate an unprofitable business segment.
6. Allocate limited resources.

We will consider each of these types of decisions in the following pages.

Accept an Order at a Special Price

STUDY OBJECTIVE 3

Identify the relevant costs in accepting an order at a special price.

Sometimes a company may have an opportunity to obtain additional business if it is willing to make a major price concession to a specific customer. To illustrate, assume that Sunbelt Company produces 100,000 automatic blenders per month, which is 80 percent of plant capacity. Variable manufacturing costs are $8 per unit. Fixed manufacturing costs are $400,000, or $4 per unit. The blenders are normally sold directly to retailers at $20 each. Sunbelt has an offer from Mexico Co. (a foreign wholesaler) to purchase an additional 2,000 blenders at $11 per unit. Acceptance of the offer would not affect normal sales of the product, and the additional units can be manufactured without increasing plant capacity. What should management do?

If management makes its decision on the basis of the total cost per unit of $12 ($8 + $4), the order would be rejected, because costs ($12) would exceed revenues ($11) by $1 per unit. However, since the units can be produced within existing plant capacity, the special order **will not increase fixed costs**. Let's identify the relevant data for the decision. First, the variable manufacturing costs will increase $16,000, ($8 × 2,000). Second, the expected revenue will increase $22,000, ($11 × 2,000). Thus, as shown in Illustration 7-4, Sunbelt will increase its net income by $6,000 by accepting this special order.

HELPFUL HINT

This is a good example of different costs for different purposes. In the long run all costs are relevant, but for this decision only costs that change are relevant.

Illustration 7-4
Incremental analysis—accepting an order at a special price

Accepting an order at a special price.xls

File Edit View Insert Format Tools Data Window Help

	A	B	C	D
1		Reject Order	Accept Order	Net Income Increase (Decrease)
2	Revenues	$0	$22,000	$ 22,000
3	Costs	0	16,000	(16,000)
4	Net income	$0	$ 6,000	$ 6,000
5				

Two points should be emphasized: First, we assume that sales of the product in other markets **would not be affected by this special order**. If other sales were affected, then Sunbelt would have to consider the lost sales in making the decision. Second, if Sunbelt is operating **at full capacity**, it is likely that the special order would be rejected. Under such circumstances, the company would have to expand plant capacity. In that case, the special order would have to absorb these additional fixed manufacturing costs, as well as the variable manufacturing costs.

Make or Buy

STUDY OBJECTIVE 4

Identify the relevant costs in a make-or-buy decision.

When a manufacturer assembles component parts in producing a finished product, management must decide whether to make or buy the components. The decision to buy parts or services is often referred to as outsourcing. For example, as discussed in the *Feature Story,* a company such as General Motors Corporation may either make or buy the batteries, tires, and radios used in its cars. Similarly, Hewlett-Packard Corporation may make or buy the electronic circuitry, cases, and printer heads for its printers. Boeing recently sold some of its commercial aircraft factories in an effort to cut production costs and focus instead on engineering and final assembly rather than manufacturing. The decision to make or buy components should be made on the basis of incremental analysis.

To illustrate the analysis, assume that Baron Company incurs the following annual costs in producing 25,000 ignition switches for motor scooters.

Illustration 7-5 Annual product cost data

Direct materials	$ 50,000
Direct labor	75,000
Variable manufacturing overhead	40,000
Fixed manufacturing overhead	60,000
Total manufacturing costs	$225,000
Total cost per unit ($225,000 ÷ 25,000)	**$9.00**

Or, instead of making its own switches, Baron Company might purchase the ignition switches from Ignition, Inc. at a price of $8 per unit. The question again is, "What should management do?"

At first glance, it appears that management should purchase the ignition switches for $8, rather than make them at a cost of $9. However, a review of operations indicates that if the ignition switches are purchased from Ignition, Inc., *all* of Baron's variable costs but only $10,000 of its fixed manufacturing costs will be eliminated (avoided). Thus, $50,000 of the fixed manufacturing costs will remain if the ignition switches are purchased. The relevant costs for incremental analysis, therefore, are as follows.

Illustration 7-6 Incremental analysis—make or buy

Incremental Analysis - Make or buy.xls

File Edit View Insert Format Tools Data Window Help

	A	B	C	D
1		**Make**	**Buy**	**Net Income Increase (Decrease)**
2	Direct materials	$ 50,000	$ 0	**$ 50,000**
3	Direct labor	75,000	0	**75,000**
4	Variable manufacturing costs	40,000	0	**40,000**
5	Fixed manufacturing costs	60,000	50,000	**10,000**
6	Purchase price (25,000 × $8)	0	200,000	**(200,000)**
7	Total annual cost	$225,000	$250,000	**$ (25,000)**
8				

ETHICS NOTE

In the make-or-buy decision it is important for management to take into account the social impact of its choice. For instance, buying may be the most economically feasible solution, but such action could result in the closure of a manufacturing plant that employs many good workers.

This analysis indicates that Baron Company will incur $25,000 of additional cost by buying the ignition switches. Therefore, Baron should continue to make the ignition switches, even though the total manufacturing cost is $1 higher than the purchase price. The reason is that if the company purchases the ignition switches, it will still have fixed costs of $50,000 to absorb.

OPPORTUNITY COST

The foregoing make-or-buy analysis is complete only if it is assumed that the productive capacity used to make the ignition switches cannot be converted to another purpose. If there is an opportunity to use this productive capacity in some other manner, then this opportunity cost must be considered. As indicated earlier, **opportunity cost** is the potential benefit that may be obtained by following an alternative course of action.

To illustrate, assume that through buying the switches, Baron Company can use the released productive capacity to generate additional income of $28,000 from producing a different product. This lost income is an additional cost of continuing to make the switches in the make-or-buy decision. This opportunity cost therefore is added to the "Make" column, for comparison. As shown, it is now advantageous to buy the ignition switches.

Incremental Analysis - Make or buy with opportunity cost.xls

	A	B	C	D
1		Make	Buy	Net Income Increase (Decrease)
2	Total annual cost	$225,000	$250,000	$(25,000)
3	**Opportunity cost**	**28,000**	0	**28,000**
4	Total cost	$253,000	$250,000	$ 3,000
5				

Illustration 7-7
Incremental analysis—make or buy, with opportunity cost

The qualitative factors in this decision include the possible loss of jobs for employees who produce the ignition switches. In addition, management must assess how well the supplier will be able to satisfy the company's quality control standards at the quoted price per unit.

INTERNATIONAL INSIGHT

These Wheels Have Miles before Installation

Consider the make-or-buy decision faced by Superior Industries International, Inc., a big aluminum-wheel maker in Van Nuys, California. For years, president Steve Borick had ignored the possibility of Chinese manufacturing. Then Mr. Borick started getting a blunt message from General Motors and Ford, with whom Superior does 85% of its business: Match the prices that they were seeing at Chinese wheel suppliers. If Superior did not want to agree to new terms at those lower prices, both auto makers said separately that they could go directly to Chinese manufacturers or could turn to another North American wheel-maker that would.

Stories like this, repeated in various industries, illustrate why manufacturers engage in overseas outsourcing. (Some refer to this as *off-shoring*.) For example, compare the relative labor costs in major auto-producing nations, in dollars per hour, to see why incremental analysis often leads to outsourcing production to countries like China.

Source: Norihiko Shirouzu, "Big Three's Outsourcing Plan: Make Parts Suppliers Do It," *Wall Street Journal* (June 10, 2004), p. A1.

What are the disadvantages of outsourcing to a foreign country?

Sell or Process Further

STUDY OBJECTIVE 5

Identify the relevant costs in determining whether to sell or process materials further.

Many manufacturers have the option of selling products at a given point in the production cycle or continuing to process with the expectation of selling them at a later point at a higher price. For example, a bicycle manufacturer such as Schwinn could sell its 10-speed bicycles to retailers either unassembled or assembled. A furniture manufacturer such as Ethan Allen could sell its dining room sets to furniture stores either unfinished or finished. The sell-or-process-further decision should be made on the basis of incremental analysis. The basic decision rule is: **Process further as long as the incremental revenue from such processing exceeds the incremental processing costs.**

SINGLE-PRODUCT CASE

Assume, for example, that Woodmasters Inc. makes tables. The cost to manufacture an unfinished table is $35, computed as follows.

Illustration 7-8 Per unit cost of unfinished table

Direct materials	$15
Direct labor	10
Variable manufacturing overhead	6
Fixed manufacturing overhead	4
Manufacturing cost per unit	**$35**

The selling price per unfinished unit is $50. Woodmasters currently has unused productive capacity that is expected to continue indefinitely. What are the relevant costs? Management concludes that some of this capacity may be used to finish the tables and sell them at $60 per unit. For a finished table, direct materials will increase $2 and direct labor costs will increase $4. Variable manufacturing overhead costs will increase by $2.40 (60% of direct labor). No increase is anticipated in fixed manufacturing overhead.

The incremental analysis on a per unit basis is as follows.

Illustration 7-9 Incremental analysis—sell or process further

Incremental Analysis - Sell or process further.xls

File Edit View Insert Format Tools Data Window Help

	A	B	C	D
1		**Sell**	**Process Further**	**Net Income Increase (Decrease)**
2	Sales per unit	$50.00	$60.00	**$10.00**
3	Cost per unit			
4	Direct materials	15.00	17.00	**(2.00)**
5	Direct labor	10.00	14.00	**(4.00)**
6	Variable manufacturing overhead	6.00	8.40	**(2.40)**
7	Fixed manufacturing overhead	4.00	4.00	**0.00**
8	Total	35.00	43.40	**(8.40)**
9	Net income per unit	$15.00	$16.60	**$ 1.60**
10				

HELPFUL HINT

Current net income is known. Net income from processing further is an estimate. In making its decision, management could add a "risk" factor for the estimate.

It would be advantageous for Woodmasters to process the tables further. The incremental revenue of $10.00 from the additional processing is $1.60 higher than the incremental processing costs of $8.40.

MULTIPLE-PRODUCT CASE

Sell-or-process-further decisions are particularly applicable to production processes that produce multiple products simultaneously. In many industries, a number of end-products are produced from a single raw material and a common production process. These multiple end-products are commonly referred to as **joint products**. For example, in the meat-packing industry, a single sheep produces meat, internal organs, hides, bones, and fat. In the petroleum industry, crude oil is refined to produce gasoline, lubricating oil, kerosene, paraffin, and ethylene.

Illustration 7-10 presents a joint product situation for Marais Creamery involving a decision **to sell or process further** cream and skim milk. Cream and skim milk are products that result from the processing of raw milk.

Illustration 7-10 Joint production process—Creamery

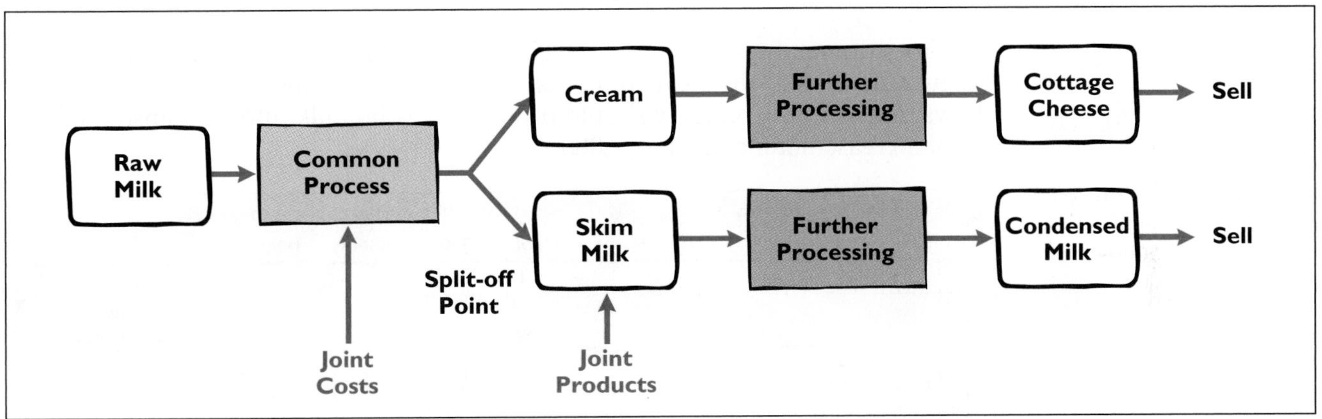

Marais incurs many costs prior to the manufacture of the cream and skim milk. All costs incurred prior to the point at which the two products are separately identifiable (the *split-off point*) are called **joint costs**. For purposes of determining the cost of each product, joint product costs must be allocated to the individual products. This is frequently done based on the relative sales value of the joint products. While this allocation is important for determination of product cost, it is irrelevant for any sell-or-process-further decisions. The reason is that these joint product costs are **sunk costs**. That is, they have already been incurred, and they cannot be changed or avoided by any subsequent decision.

Illustration 7-11 shows the daily cost and revenue data for Marais Creamery.

Illustration 7-11 Cost and revenue data per day

Costs (per day)	
Joint cost allocated to cream	$ 9,000
Joint cost allocated to skim milk	5,000
Processing cream into cottage cheese	10,000
Processing skim milk into condensed milk	8,000
Expected Revenues from Products (per day)	
Cream	$19,000
Skim milk	11,000
Cottage cheese	27,000
Condensed milk	26,000

From this information we can determine whether the company should simply sell the cream and skim milk, or process them further into cottage cheese and condensed milk. Illustration 7-12 (page 296) provides the analysis necessary to determine whether to sell the cream or process it further into cottage cheese.

Illustration 7-12 Analysis of whether to sell cream or process into cottage cheese

Incremental Analysis - Sell or process further - Cottage cheese.xls

	A	B	C	D
1		**Sell**	**Process Further**	**Net Income Increase (Decrease)**
2	Sales per day	$19,000	$27,000	$ 8,000
3	Cost per day			
4	Processing cream into cottage cheese	0	10,000	(10,000)
5		$19,000	$17,000	**$ (2,000)**
6				

From this analysis we can see that Marais should not process the cream further because it will sustain an incremental loss of $2,000. Illustration 7-13, however, shows that Marais Company should process the skim milk into condensed milk, as it will increase net income by $7,000.

Illustration 7-13 Analysis of whether to sell skim milk or process into condensed milk

Incremental Analysis - Sell or process further - Skim milk or process condensed milk.xls

	A	B	C	D
1		**Sell**	**Process Further**	**Net Income Increase (Decrease)**
2	Sales per day	$11,000	$26,000	$15,000
3	Cost per day			
4	Processing skim milk into condensed milk	0	8,000	(8,000)
5		$11,000	$18,000	**$ 7,000**
6				

Note that the amount of joint costs allocated to each product ($9,000 to the cream and $5,000 to the skim milk) is irrelevant in deciding whether to sell or process further. Why? The joint costs remain the same whether or not further processing is performed.

Retain or Replace Equipment

STUDY OBJECTIVE 6

Identify the relevant costs to be considered in retaining or replacing equipment.

Management often has to decide whether to continue using an asset or replace it. To illustrate, assume that Jeffcoat Company has a factory machine with a book value of $40,000 and a remaining useful life of four years. It is considering replacing this machine with a new machine. A new machine is available that costs $120,000. It is expected to have zero salvage value at the end of its four-year useful life. If the new machine is acquired, variable manufacturing costs are expected to decrease from $160,000 to $125,000 annually, and the old unit will be scrapped. The incremental analysis for the **four-year period** is as follows.

Illustration 7-14 Incremental analysis—retain or replace equipment

Incremental Analysis - Retain or replace equipment.xls

	A	B	C	D	E	F
1		**Retain Equipment**		**Replace Equipment**		**Net Income Increase (Decrease)**
2	Variable manufacturing costs	$640,000	a	$500,000	b	**$140,000**
3	New machine cost			120,000		**(120,000)**
4	Total	$640,000		$620,000		**$ 20,000**
5						
6	[a](4 years × $160,000)					
7	[b](4 years × $125,000)					
8						

In this case, it would be to the company's advantage to replace the equipment. The lower variable manufacturing costs due to replacement more than offset the cost of the new equipment.

One other point should be mentioned regarding Jeffcoat's decision: **The book value of the old machine does not affect the decision.** Book value is a **sunk cost,** which is a cost that cannot be changed by any present or future decision. **Sunk costs are not relevant in incremental analysis.** In this example, if the asset is retained, book value will be depreciated over its remaining useful life. Or, if the new unit is acquired, book value will be recognized as a loss of the current period. Thus, the effect of book value on current and future earnings is the same regardless of the replacement decision. **Any trade-in allowance or cash disposal value of the existing asset, however, is relevant** to the decision, because this value will not be realized if the asset remains in use.

Eliminate an Unprofitable Segment

STUDY OBJECTIVE 7

Identify the relevant costs in deciding whether to eliminate an unprofitable segment.

Management sometimes must decide whether to eliminate an unprofitable business segment. For example, in recent years many airlines have quit servicing certain cities or have cut back on the number of flights; and Goodyear recently quit producing several brands in the low-end tire market. Again, the key is to **focus on the relevant costs—the data that change under the alternative courses of action**. To illustrate, assume that Martina Company manufactures tennis racquets in three models: Pro, Master, and Champ. Pro and Master are profitable lines. Champ (highlighted in color in the table below) operates at a loss. Condensed income statement data are as follows.

Illustration 7-15 Segment income data

	Pro	Master	Champ	Total
Sales	$800,000	$300,000	$100,000	$1,200,000
Variable costs	520,000	210,000	90,000	820,000
Contribution margin	280,000	90,000	10,000	380,000
Fixed costs	80,000	50,000	30,000	160,000
Net income	$200,000	$ 40,000	$ (20,000)	$ 220,000

HELPFUL HINT

A decision to discontinue a segment based solely on the bottom line—net loss—is inappropriate.

It might be expected that total net income will increase by $20,000, to $240,000, if the unprofitable Champ line of racquets is eliminated. However, **net income may actually decrease if the Champ line is discontinued.** The reason is that the fixed costs allocated to the Champ racquets will have to be absorbed by the other products. To illustrate, assume that the $30,000 of fixed costs applicable to the unprofitable segment are allocated ⅔ to the Pro model and ⅓ to the Master model if the Champ model is eliminated. Fixed costs will increase to $100,000 ($80,000 + $20,000) in the Pro line and to $60,000 ($50,000 + $10,000) in the Master line. The revised income statement is:

Illustration 7-16 Income data after eliminating unprofitable product line

	Pro	Master	Total
Sales	$800,000	$300,000	$1,100,000
Variable costs	520,000	210,000	730,000
Contribution margin	280,000	90,000	370,000
Fixed costs	100,000	60,000	160,000
Net income	$180,000	$ 30,000	$ 210,000

Total net income has decreased $10,000 ($220,000 − $210,000). This result is also obtained in the following incremental analysis of the Champ racquets.

Illustration 7-17
Incremental analysis—eliminating an unprofitable segment

Incremental Analysis - Eliminating an unprofitable segment.xls

	A	B	C	D
1		**Continue**	**Eliminate**	**Net Income Increase (Decrease)**
2	Sales	$100,000	$ 0	**$(100,000)**
3	Variable costs	90,000	0	**90,000**
4	Contribution margin	10,000	0	**(10,000)**
5	Fixed costs	30,000	30,000	**0**
6	Net income	$ (20,000)	$(30,000)	**$ (10,000)**
7				

The loss in net income is attributable to the Champ line's contribution margin ($10,000) that will not be realized if the segment is discontinued.

In deciding on the future status of an unprofitable segment, management should consider the effect of elimination on related product lines. It may be possible for continuing product lines to obtain some or all of the sales lost by the discontinued product line. In some businesses, services or products may be linked—for example, free checking accounts at a bank, or coffee at a donut shop. In addition, management should consider the effect of eliminating the product line on employees who may have to be discharged or retrained.

MANAGEMENT INSIGHT

Time to Move to a New Neighborhood?

If you have ever moved, then you know how complicated and costly it can be. Now consider what it would be like for a manufacturing company with 260 employees and a 170,000-square foot facility to move from southern California to Idaho. That is what Buck Knives did in order to save its company from financial ruin. Electricity rates in Idaho were half those in California, workers' compensation was one-third the cost, and factory wages were 20% lower. Combined, this would reduce manufacturing costs by $600,000 per year. Moving the factory would cost about $8.5 million, plus $4 million to move key employees. Offsetting these costs was the estimated $11 million selling price of the California property. Based on these estimates, the move would pay for itself in three years.

Ultimately, the company received only $7.5 million for its California property, only 58 of 75 key employees were willing to move, construction was delayed by a year which caused the new plant to increase in price by $1.5 million, and wages surged in Idaho due to low unemployment. Despite all of these complications, though, the company considers the move a great success.

Source: Chris Lydgate, "The Buck Stopped," *Inc. Magazine*, May 2006, pp. 87–95.

What were some of the factors that complicated the company's decision to move? How should the company have incorporated such factors into its incremental analysis?

DECISION TOOLKIT

Decision Checkpoints	Info Needed for Decision	Tool to Use for Decision	How to Evaluate Results 
Which alternative should the company choose?	All relevant costs and opportunity costs	Compare relevant cost of each alternative.	Choose the alternative that maximizes net income.

Before You Go On...

REVIEW IT

1. Give three examples of how incremental analysis might be used.
2. What is the decision rule in deciding to sell or process products further?
3. How may the elimination of an unprofitable segment decrease the overall net income of a company?

DO IT

Cobb Company incurs a cost of $28 per unit, of which $18 is variable, to make a product that normally sells for $42. A foreign wholesaler offers to buy 5,000 units at $25 each. Cobb will incur shipping costs of $1 per unit. Compute the increase or decrease in net income Cobb will realize by accepting the special order, assuming Cobb has excess operating capacity.

Action Plan

- Identify all revenues that will change as a result of accepting the order.
- Identify all costs that will change as a result of accepting the order, and net this amount against the change in revenues.

Solution

	Reject	Accept	Net Income Increase (Decrease)
Revenues	$-0-	$125,000	$125,000
Costs	-0-	95,000*	(95,000)
Net income	$-0-	$ 30,000	$ 30,000

*(5,000 × $18) + (5,000 × $1)

Given the result of the analysis, Cobb Company should accept the special order.

Related exercise material: *BE7-3, E7-2, E7-3, and E7-4.*

OTHER CONSIDERATIONS IN DECISION MAKING

Qualitative Factors

In this chapter we have focused primarily on the quantitative factors that affect a decision—those attributes that can be easily expressed in terms of numbers or dollars. However, many of the decisions involving incremental analysis have important qualitative features; though not easily measured, they should not be ignored.

Consider, for example, the potential effects of the make-or-buy decision or of the decision to eliminate a line of business on existing employees and the community in which the plant is located. The cost savings that may be obtained from outsourcing or from eliminating a plant should be weighed against these qualitative attributes. One example would be the cost of lost morale that might result. Al "Chainsaw" Dunlap was a so-called "turnaround" artist who went into many companies, identified inefficiencies (using incremental analysis techniques), and tried to correct these problems to improve corporate profitability. Along the way he laid off thousands of employees at numerous companies. As head of Sunbeam, it was Al Dunlap who lost his job because his Draconian approach failed to improve Sunbeam's profitability. It was widely reported that Sunbeam's employees openly rejoiced for days after his departure. Clearly, qualitative factors can matter.

Relationship of Incremental Analysis and Activity-Based Costing

In Chapter 4 we noted that many companies have shifted to activity-based costing to allocate overhead costs to products. The primary reason for using activity-based costing is that it results in a more accurate allocation of overhead. The concepts presented in this chapter are completely consistent with the use of activity-based costing. In fact, activity-based costing will result in better identification of relevant costs and, therefore, better incremental analysis.

MANAGEMENT INSIGHT

What Is the Real Cost of Packaging Options?

The existence of excess plant capacity is frequently the incentive for management to add new products. Adding one new product may not add much incremental cost. But continuing to add products will at some point create new constraints, perhaps requiring additional investments in people, equipment, and facilities.

The effects of product and product line proliferation are generally understood. But the effect on incremental overhead costs of *changes in servicing customers* is less understood. For example, if a company newly offers its customers the option of product delivery by case or by pallet, the new service may appear to be simple and low in cost. But, if the manufacturing process must be realigned to package in two different forms; if two sets of inventory records must be maintained; and if warehousing, handling, and shipping require two different arrangements or sets of equipment, the additional costs of this new option could be as high as a whole new product. If the customer service option were adopted for all products, the product line could effectively be doubled—but so might many overhead costs.

Source: Elizabeth Haas Edersheim and Joan Wilson, "Complexity at Consumer Goods Companies: Naming and Taming the Beast," *Journal of Cost Management.*

If your marketing director suggests that, in addition to selling your cereal in a standard-size box, you should sell a jumbo size and an individual size, what issues must you consider?

Before You Go On...

REVIEW IT

1. What are some qualitative factors that should be considered in an incremental analysis decision?
2. What is the relationship between incremental analysis and activity-based costing?

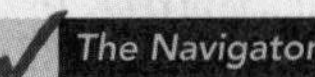

Be sure to read **ALL ABOUT YOU: *What Is a Degree Worth?*** on the next page for information on how topics in this chapter apply to you.

all about YOU

What Is a Degree Worth?

It may not have occurred to you at the time, but you already made a huge decision in your life that was ideally suited to managerial accounting. No, it's not your choice of whether to have pizza or Chinese food at lunch today. We are referring to your decision to pursue a post–high-school degree. If you weren't going to college, you could be working full-time. School costs money, which is an expenditure that you could have avoided. Also, if you did not go to college, many of you would avoid mountains of school-related debt. While you cannot go back and redo your initial decision, we can look at some facts to evaluate the wisdom of your decision.

Some Facts

* Over a lifetime of work, high-school graduates earn an average of $1.2 million, associate's degree holders earn an average of $1.6 million, and people with bachelor's degrees earn about $2.1 million.
* A year of tuition at a public four-year college costs about $8,655, and a year of tuition at a public two-year college costs about $1,359.
* There has also been considerable research on other, less-tangible benefits of post–high-school education. For example, some have suggested that there is a relationship between higher education and good health. Research also suggests that college-educated people are more optimistic.
* About 600,000 students drop out of four-year colleges each year.

About the Numbers

Tuition is very expensive. As a result, many students have high "unmet needs"—the portion of college expenses not provided by family or student aid. The graph below suggests that in the coming decade an increasing number of students with high "unmet" financial needs will decide not to pursue any form of post–high-school education. This has obvious implications for their long-term personal financial well-being. It also has significant implications for the well-being of the United States as a society. Research shows that people with post–high-school degrees pay more in taxes. Also, without adequate educational training of its citizenry, the United States will be less able to compete in a high-tech world.

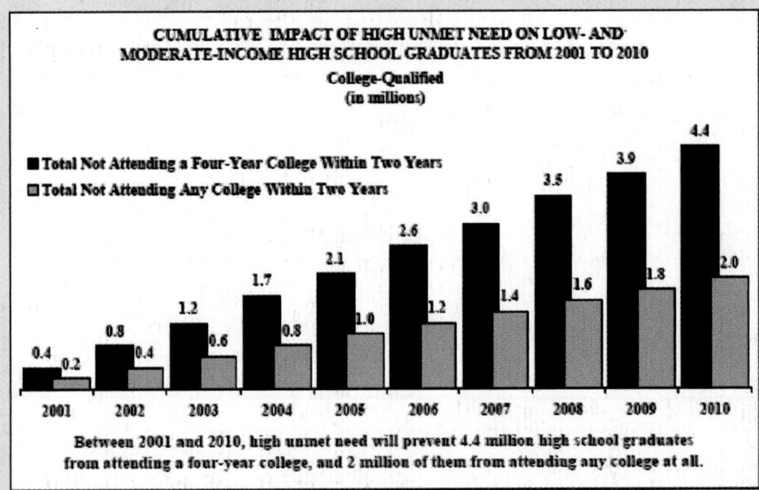

Source: "Empty Promises: The Myth of College Access in America," A Report of the Advisory Committee on Student Financial Assistance, June 2002, *www.ed.gov/about/bdscomm/list/acsfa/emptypromises.pdf*, p. 28 (accessed August 2006).

What Do You Think?

Each year many students decide to drop out of school. Many of them never return. Suppose that you are working two jobs and going to college and that you are not making ends meet. Your grades are suffering due to your lack of available study time. You feel depressed. Should you drop out of school?

YES: You can always go back to school. If your grades are bad, and you are depressed, what good is school doing you anyway?

NO: Once you drop out, it is very hard to get enough momentum to go back. Dropping out will dramatically reduce your long-term opportunities. It is better to stay in school, even if you take only one class per semester.

Sources: Kathleen Porter, "The Value of a College Degree," ERIC Clearinghouse on Higher Education, Washington DC, *www.ericdigests.org/2003-3/value.htm* (accessed August 2006).

The authors' comments on this situation appear on page 320.

Using the Decision Toolkit

Suppose Hewlett-Packard Company must decide whether to make or buy some of its components from Solectron Corp. The cost of producing 50,000 electrical connectors for its printers is $110,000, broken down as follows.

Direct materials	$60,000	Variable manufacturing overhead	$12,000
Direct labor	30,000	Fixed manufacturing overhead	8,000

Instead of making the electrical connectors at an average cost per unit of $2.20 ($110,000 ÷ 50,000), the company has an opportunity to buy the connectors at $2.15 per unit. If the connectors are purchased, all variable costs and one-half of the fixed costs will be eliminated.

Instructions

(a) Prepare an incremental analysis showing whether the company should make or buy the electrical connectors.

(b) Will your answer be different if the released productive capacity resulting from the purchase of the connectors will generate additional income of $25,000?

Solution

(a)

	Make	Buy	Net Income Increase (Decrease)
Direct materials	$ 60,000	$ -0-	$ 60,000
Direct labor	30,000	-0-	30,000
Variable manufacturing costs	12,000	-0-	12,000
Fixed manufacturing costs	8,000	4,000	4,000
Purchase price	-0-	107,500	(107,500)
Total cost	$110,000	$111,500	$ (1,500)

This analysis indicates that Hewlett-Packard will incur $1,500 of additional costs if it buys the electrical connectors. H-P therefore would choose to make the connectors.

(b)

	Make	Buy	Net Income Increase (Decrease)
Total cost	$110,000	$111,500	$ (1,500)
Opportunity cost	25,000	-0-	25,000
Total cost	$135,000	$111,500	$23,500

Yes, the answer is different. The analysis shows that if additional capacity is released, net income will be increased by $23,500 if the electrical connectors are purchased. In this case, H-P would choose to purchase the connectors.

SUMMARY OF STUDY OBJECTIVES

1 **Identify the steps in management's decision-making process.** Management's decision-making process consists of (a) identifying the problem and assigning responsibility for the decision, (b) determining and evaluating possible courses of action, (c) making the decision, and (d) reviewing the results of the decision.

2 **Describe the concept of incremental analysis.** Incremental analysis identifies financial data that change under alternative courses of action. These data are relevant to the decision because they will vary in the future among the possible alternatives.

3 **Identify the relevant costs in accepting an order at a special price.** The relevant costs are those that change if the order is accepted. These are typically variable manufacturing costs. The relevant information in accepting an order at a special price is the difference between the variable manufacturing costs to produce the special order and expected revenues.

4 **Identify the relevant costs in a make-or-buy decision.** In a make-or-buy decision, the relevant costs are (a) the variable manufacturing costs that will be saved, (b) the purchase price, and (c) opportunity costs.

5 **Identify the relevant costs in determining whether to sell or process materials further.** The decision rule for whether to sell or process materials further is: Process further as long as the incremental revenue from processing exceeds the incremental processing costs.

6 **Identify the relevant costs to be considered in retaining or replacing equipment.** The relevant costs to be considered in determining whether equipment should be retained or replaced are the effects on variable costs and the cost of the new equipment. Also, any disposal value of the existing asset must be considered.

7 **Identify the relevant costs in deciding whether to eliminate an unprofitable segment.** In deciding whether to eliminate an unprofitable segment, the relevant costs are the variable costs that drive the contribution margin, if any, produced by the segment. Disposition of the segment's fixed expenses must also be considered.

DECISION TOOLKIT—A SUMMARY

Decision Checkpoints 	Info Needed for Decision 	Tool to Use for Decision 	How to Evaluate Results 
Which alternative should the company choose?	All relevant costs and opportunity costs	Compare the relevant cost of each alternative.	Choose the alternative that maximizes net income.

GLOSSARY

Incremental analysis The process of identifying the financial data that change under alternative courses of action. (p. 289).

Joint costs For joint products, all costs incurred prior to the point at which the two products are separately identifiable (known as the *split-off point*). (p. 295).

Joint products Multiple end-products produced from a single raw material and a common production process. (p. 295).

Opportunity cost The potential benefit that is lost when one course of action is chosen rather than an alternative course of action. (p. 290).

Relevant costs Those costs and revenues that differ across alternatives. (p. 290).

Sunk cost A cost that cannot be changed by any present or future decision. (p. 290).

Demonstration Problem

Walston Company produces kitchen cabinets for homebuilders across the western United States. The cost of producing 5,000 cabinets is as follows.

Materials	$ 500,000
Labor	250,000
Variable overhead	100,000
Fixed overhead	400,000
Total	$1,250,000

Walston also incurs selling expenses of $20 per cabinet. Wellington Corp. has offered Walston $165 per cabinet for a special order of 1,000 cabinets. The cabinets would be sold to homebuilders in the eastern United States and thus would not conflict with Walston's current sales. Selling expenses per cabinet would be only $5 per cabinet. Walston has available capacity to do the work.

Instructions

(a) Prepare an incremental analysis for the special order.

(b) Should Walston accept the special order? Why or why not?

action plan

✓ Determine the relevant cost per unit of the special order.

✓ Identify the relevant costs and revenues for the units to be produced.

✓ Compare the results related to accepting the special order versus rejecting the special order.

Solution

(a) Relevant costs per unit would be:

Materials	$500,000/5,000 =	$100
Labor	250,000/5,000 =	50
Variable overhead	100,000/5,000 =	20
Selling expenses		5
Total relevant cost per unit		$175

	Reject Order	Accept Order	Net Income Increase (Decrease)
Revenues	$0	$ 165,000	$165,000
Costs	$0	$ 175,000	($175,000)
Net Income	$0	$ (10,000)	($ 10,000)

(b) Walston should reject the offer. The incremental benefit of $165 per cabinet is less than the incremental cost of $175. By accepting the order, Walston's net income would actually decline by $10,000.

SELF-STUDY QUESTIONS

Answers are at the end of the chapter.

(SO 1) **1.** Three of the steps in management's decision making process are (1) review results of decision, (2) determine and evaluate possible courses of action, and (3) make the decision. The steps are prepared in the following order:
a. (1), (2), (3).
b. (3), (2), (1).
c. (2), (1), (3).
d. (2), (3), (1).

(SO 2) **2.** Incremental analysis is the process of identifying the financial data that:
a. do not change under alternative courses of action.
b. change under alternative courses of action.
c. are mixed under alternative courses of action.
d. No correct answer is given.

(SO 3) **3.** It costs a company $14 of variable costs and $6 of fixed costs to produce product Z200 that sells for $30. A foreign buyer offers to purchase 3,000 units at $18 each. If the special offer is accepted and produced with unused capacity, net income will:
a. decrease $6,000.
b. increase $6,000.
c. increase $12,000.
d. increase $9,000.

(SO 3) **4.** It costs a company $14 of variable costs and $6 of fixed costs to produce product Z200. Product Z200 sells for $30. A buyer offers to purchase 3,000 units at $18 each. The seller will incur special shipping costs of $5 per unit. If the special offer is accepted and produced with unused capacity, net income will:
a. increase $3,000.
b. increase $12,000.
c. decrease $12,000.
d. decrease $3,000.

(SO 4) **5.** In a make-or-buy decision, relevant costs are:
a. manufacturing costs that will be saved.
b. the purchase price of the units.
c. opportunity costs.
d. all of the above.

6. The decision rule in a sell-or-process-further decision is: process further as long as the incremental revenue from processing exceeds: (SO 5)
a. incremental processing costs.
b. variable processing costs.
c. fixed processing costs.
d. No correct answer is given.

7. In a decision to retain or replace equipment, the book value of the old equipment is a (an): (SO 6)
a. opportunity cost.
b. sunk cost.
c. incremental cost.
d. marginal cost.

8. If an unprofitable segment is eliminated: (SO 7)
a. net income will always increase.
b. variable expenses of the eliminated segment will have to be absorbed by other segments.
c. fixed expenses allocated to the eliminated segment will have to be absorbed by other segments.
d. net income will always decrease.

9. A segment of Hazard Inc. has the following data. (SO 7)

Sales	$200,000
Variable expenses	140,000
Fixed expenses	100,000

If this segment is eliminated, what will be the effect on the remaining company? Assume that 50% of the fixed expenses will be eliminated and the rest will be allocated to the segments of the remaining company.
a. $120,000 increase.
b. $10,000 decrease.
c. $50,000 increase.
d. $10,000 increase.

Go to the book's website, **www.wiley.com/college/weygandt**, for Additional Self-Study questions.

QUESTIONS

1. What steps are frequently involved in management's decision-making process?
2. Your roommate, Mike Myer, contends that accounting contributes to most of the steps in management's decision-making process. Is your roommate correct? Explain.
3. "Incremental analysis involves the accumulation of information concerning a single course of action." Do you agree? Why?
4. Sara Gura asks for your help concerning the relevance of variable and fixed costs in incremental analysis. Help Sara with her problem.
5. What data are relevant in deciding whether to accept an order at a special price?
6. Son Ly Company has an opportunity to buy parts at $7 each that currently cost $10 to make. What manufacturing costs are relevant to this make-or-buy decision?
7. Define the term "opportunity cost." How may this cost be relevant in a make-or-buy decision?
8. What is the decision rule in deciding whether to sell a product or process it further?
9. What are joint products? What accounting issue results from the production process that creates joint products?
10. How are allocated joint costs treated when making a sell-or-process-further decision?
11. Your roommate, Vanessa Hunt, is confused about sunk costs. Explain to your roommate the meaning of sunk costs and their relevance to a decision to retain or replace equipment.
12. Erm Paris Inc. has one product line that is unprofitable. What circumstances may cause overall company net income to be lower if the unprofitable product line is eliminated?

BRIEF EXERCISES

Identify the steps in management's decision-making process. (SO 1)

BE7-1 The steps in management's decision-making process are listed in random order below. Indicate the order in which the steps should be executed.

____ Make a decision
____ Identify the problem and assign responsibility
____ Review results of the decision
____ Determine and evaluate possible courses of action

Determine incremental changes. (SO 2)

BE7-2 Anna Company is considering two alternatives. Alternative A will have revenues of $150,000 and costs of $100,000. Alternative B will have revenues of $185,000 and costs of $125,000. Compare Alternative A to Alternative B showing incremental revenues, costs, and net income.

Determine whether to accept a special order. (SO 3)

BE7-3 In Sydney Company it costs $30 per unit ($20 variable and $10 fixed) to make a product at full capacity that normally sells for $45. A foreign wholesaler offers to buy 3,000 units at $24 each. Sydney will incur special shipping costs of $2 per unit. Assuming that Sydney has excess operating capacity, indicate the net income (loss) Sydney would realize by accepting the special order.

Determine whether to make or buy a part. (SO 4)

BE7-4 Emil Manufacturing incurs unit costs of $7.50 ($4.50 variable and $3 fixed) in making a sub-assembly part for its finished product. A supplier offers to make 10,000 of the assembly part at $5 per unit. If the offer is accepted, Emil will save all variable costs but no fixed costs. Prepare an analysis showing the total cost saving, if any, Emil will realize by buying the part.

Determine whether to sell or process further. (SO 5)

BE7-5 Green Inc. makes unfinished bookcases that it sells for $60. Production costs are $35 variable and $10 fixed. Because it has unused capacity, Green is considering finishing the bookcases and selling them for $70. Variable finishing costs are expected to be $8 per unit with no increase in fixed costs. Prepare an analysis on a per unit basis showing whether Green should sell unfinished or finished bookcases.

Determine whether to sell or process further, joint products. (SO 5)

BE7-6 Each day, Dunham Corporation processes 1 ton of a secret raw material into two resulting products, AB1 and XY1. When it processes 1 ton of the raw material the company incurs joint processing costs of $60,000. It allocates $25,000 of these costs to AB1 and $35,000 of these costs to XY1. The resulting AB1 can be sold for $90,000. Alternatively, it can be processed further to make AB2 at an additional processing cost of $50,000, and sold for $150,000. Each day's batch of XY1 can be sold for $90,000. Alternatively, it can be processed further to create XY2, at an additional processing cost of $50,000, and sold for $130,000. Discuss what products Dunham Corporation should make.

Determine whether to retain or replace equipment. (SO 6)

BE7-7 Chudzick Company has a factory machine with a book value of $90,000 and a remaining useful life of 4 years. A new machine is available at a cost of $250,000. This machine will have a 4-year useful life with no salvage value. The new machine will lower annual variable manufacturing costs from $600,000 to $500,000. Prepare an analysis showing whether the old machine should be retained or replaced.

Determine whether to eliminate an unprofitable segment.
(SO 7)

BE7-8 Bitterman, Inc., manufactures golf clubs in three models. For the year, the Big Bart line has a net loss of $5,000 from sales $200,000, variable costs $175,000, and fixed costs $30,000. If the Big Bart line is eliminated, $20,000 of fixed costs will remain. Prepare an analysis showing whether the Big Bart line should be eliminated.

EXERCISES

Analyze statements about decision making and incremental analysis.
(SO 1, 2)

E7-1 Pender has prepared the following list of statements about decision making and incremental analysis.

1. The first step in management's decision-making process is, "Determine and evaluate possible courses of action."
2. The final step in management's decision-making process is to actually make the decision.
3. Accounting's contribution to management's decision-making process occurs primarily in evaluating possible courses of action and in reviewing the results.
4. In making business decisions, management ordinarily considers only financial information because it is objectively determined.
5. Decisions involve a choice among alternative courses of action.
6. The process used to identify the financial data that change under alternative courses of action is called incremental analysis.
7. Costs that are the same under all alternative courses of action sometimes affect the decision.
8. When using incremental analysis, some costs will always change under alternative courses of action, but revenues will not.
9. Variable costs will change under alternative courses of action, but fixed costs will not.

Instructions

Identify each statement as true or false. If false, indicate how to correct the statement.

Make incremental analysis for special-order decision.
(SO 3)

E7-2 Innova Company produces golf discs which it normally sells to retailers for $7 each. The cost of manufacturing 20,000 golf discs is:

Materials	$ 10,000
Labor	30,000
Variable overhead	20,000
Fixed overhead	40,000
Total	$100,000

Innova also incurs 5% sales commission ($0.35) on each disc sold.

Mudd Corporation offers Innova $4.75 per disc for 5,000 discs. Mudd would sell the discs under its own brand name in foreign markets not yet served by Innova. If Innova accepts the offer, its fixed overhead will increase from $40,000 to $45,000 due to the purchase of a new imprinting machine. No sales commission will result from the special order.

Instructions

(a) Prepare an incremental analysis for the special order.
(b) Should Innova accept the special order? Why or why not?
(c) What assumptions underlie the decision made in part (b)?

Use incremental analysis for special order.
(SO 3)

E7-3 Quick Company manufactures toasters. For the first 8 months of 2008, the company reported the following operating results while operating at 75% of plant capacity:

Sales (350,000 units)	$4,375,000
Cost of goods sold	2,500,000
Gross profit	1,875,000
Operating expenses	875,000
Net income	$1,000,000

Cost of goods sold was 70% variable and 30% fixed; operating expenses were also 70% variable and 30% fixed.

In September, Quick Company receives a special order for 15,000 toasters at $7.50 each from Ortiz Company of Mexico City. Acceptance of the order would result in an additional $3,000 of shipping costs but no increase in fixed operating expenses.

Instructions

(a) Prepare an incremental analysis for the special order.

(b) Should Quick Company accept the special order? Why or why not?

Use incremental analysis for special order.

(SO 3)

E7-4 Hardy Fiber Company is the creator of Y-Go, a technology that weaves silver into its fabrics to kill bacteria and odor on clothing while managing heat. Y-Go has become very popular as an undergarment for sports activities. Operating at capacity, the company can produce 1,000,000 undergarments of Y-Go a year. The per unit and the total costs for an individual garment when the company operates at full capacity are as follows.

	Per Undergarment	Total
Direct materials	$2.00	$2,000,000
Direct labor	0.50	500,000
Variable manufacturing overhead	1.00	1,000,000
Fixed manufacturing overhead	1.50	1,500,000
Variable selling expenses	0.25	250,000
Totals	$5.25	$5,250,000

The U.S. Army has approached Hardy Fiber and expressed an interest in purchasing 200,000 Y-Go undergarments for soldiers in extremely warm climates. The Army would pay the unit cost for direct materials, direct labor, and variable manufacturing overhead costs. In addition, the Army has agreed to pay an additional $1 per undergarment to cover all other costs and provide a profit. Presently, Hardy Fiber is operating at 70 percent capacity and does not have any other potential buyers for Y-Go. If Hardy Fiber accepts the Army's offer, it will not incur any variable selling expenses related to this order.

Instructions

Using incremental analysis, determine whether Hardy Fiber should accept the Army's offer.

Use incremental analysis for make-or-buy decision.

(SO 4)

E7-5 Stahl Inc. has been manufacturing its own shades for its table lamps. The company is currently operating at 100% of capacity, and variable manufacturing overhead is charged to production at the rate of 70% of direct labor cost. The direct materials and direct labor cost per unit to make the lamp shades are $5 and $6, respectively. Normal production is 30,000 table lamps per year.

A supplier offers to make the lamp shades at a price of $15.50 per unit. If Stahl Inc. accepts the supplier's offer, all variable manufacturing costs will be eliminated, but the $45,000 of fixed manufacturing overhead currently being charged to the lamp shades will have to be absorbed by other products.

Instructions

(a) Prepare the incremental analysis for the decision to make or buy the lamp shades.

(b) Should Stahl Inc. buy the lamp shades?

(c) Would your answer be different in (b) if the productive capacity released by not making the lamp shades could be used to produce income of $35,000?

Use incremental analysis for make-or-buy decision.

(SO 4)

E7-6 SY Telc has recently started the manufacture of RecRobo, a three-wheeled robot that can scan a home for fires and gas leaks and then transmit this information to a mobile phone. The cost structure to manufacture 20,000 RecRobo's is as follows.

	Cost
Direct materials ($40 per robot)	$ 800,000
Direct labor ($30 per robot)	600,000
Variable overhead ($6 per robot)	120,000
Allocated fixed overhead ($25 per robot)	500,000
Total	$2,020,000

SY Telc is approached by Chen Inc. which offers to make RecRobo for $90 per unit or $1,800,000.

Instructions

(a) Using incremental analysis, determine whether SY Telc should accept this offer under each of the following independent assumptions.

(1) Assume that $300,000 of the fixed overhead cost can be reduced (avoided).

(2) Assume that none of the fixed overhead can be reduced (avoided). However, if the robots are purchased from Chen Inc., SY Telc can use the released productive resources to generate additional income of $300,000.

(b) Describe the qualitative factors that might affect the decision to purchase the robots from an outside supplier.

Use incremental analysis for further processing of materials decision.

(SO 5)

E7-7 Wanda Sublette recently opened her own basketweaving studio. She sells finished baskets in addition to the raw materials needed by customers to weave baskets of their own. Wanda has put together a variety of raw material kits, each including materials at various stages of completion. Unfortunately, owing to space limitations, Wanda is unable to carry all varieties of kits originally assembled and must choose between two basic packages.

The basic introductory kit includes undyed, uncut reeds (with dye included) for weaving one basket. This basic package costs Wanda $14 and sells for $28. The second kit, called Stage 2, includes cut reeds that have already been dyed. With this kit the customer need only soak the reeds and weave the basket. Wanda is able to produce the second kit by using the basic materials included in the first kit and adding one hour of her own time, which she values at $20 per hour. Because she is more efficient at cutting and dying reeds than her average customer, Wanda is able to make two kits of the dyed reeds, in one hour, from one kit of undyed reeds. The Stage 2 kit sells for $35.

Instructions

Determine whether Wanda's basketweaving shop should carry the basic introductory kit with undyed and uncut reeds or the Stage 2 kit with reeds already dyed and cut. Prepare an incremental analysis to support your answer.

Determine whether to sell or process further, joint products.

(SO 5)

E7-8 Benson, Inc. produces three separate products from a common process costing $100,000. Each of the products can be sold at the split-off point or can be processed further and then sold for a higher price. Shown below are cost and selling price data for a recent period.

	Sales Value at Split-off Point	Cost to Process Further	Sales Value After Further Processing
Product 12	$50,000	$100,000	$190,000
Product 14	10,000	30,000	35,000
Product 16	60,000	150,000	220,000

Instructions

(a) Determine total net income if all products are sold at the split-off point.

(b) Determine total net income if all products are sold after further processing.

(c) Using incremental analysis, determine which products should be sold at the split-off point and which should be processed further.

(d) Determine total net income using the results from **(c)** and explain why the net income is different from that determined in **(b)**.

Determine whether to sell or process further, joint products.

(SO 5)

E7-9 Shynee Minerals processes materials extracted from mines. The most common raw material that it processes results in three joint products: Sarco, Barco, and Larco. Each of these products can be sold as is, or it can be processed further and sold for a higher price. The company incurs joint costs of $180,000 to process one batch of the raw material that produces the three joint products. The following cost and sales information is available for one batch of each product.

	Sales Value at Split-off Point	Allocated Joint Costs	Cost to Process Further	Sales Value of Processed Product
Sarco	$200,000	$40,000	$120,000	$300,000
Barco	300,000	60,000	89,000	400,000
Larco	400,000	80,000	250,000	800,000

Instructions

Determine whether each of the three joint products should be sold as is, or processed further.

E7-10 On January 2, 2008, Lucas Hospital purchased a $100,000 special radiology scanner from Faital Inc. The scanner has a useful life of 5 years and will have no disposal value at the end of its useful life. The straight-line method of depreciation is used on this scanner. Annual operating costs with this scanner are $105,000.

Use incremental analysis for retaining or replacing equipment decision.

(SO 6)

Approximately one year later, the hospital is approached by Alliant Technology salesperson, Becky Bishop, who indicated that purchasing the scanner in 2008 from Faital Inc. was a mistake. She points out that Alliant has a scanner that will save Lucas Hospital $27,000 a year in operating expenses over its 4-year useful life. She notes that the new scanner will cost $120,000 and has the same capabilities as the scanner purchased last year. The hospital agrees that both scanners are of equal quality. The new scanner will have no disposal value. Bishop agrees to buy the old scanner from Lucas Hospital for $30,000.

Instructions

(a) If Lucas Hospital sells its old scanner on January 2, 2009, compute the gain or loss on the sale.

(b) Using incremental analysis, determine if Lucas Hospital should purchase the new scanner on January 2, 2009.

(c) Explain why Lucas Hospital might be reluctant to purchase the new scanner, regardless of the results indicated by the incremental analysis in (b).

E7-11 Twyla Enterprises uses a computer to handle its sales invoices. Lately, business has been so good that it takes an extra 3 hours per night, plus every third Saturday, to keep up with the volume of sales invoices. Management is considering updating its computer with a faster model that would eliminate all of the overtime processing.

Use incremental analysis for retaining or replacing equipment decision.

(SO 6)

	Current Machine	New Machine
Original purchase cost	$15,000	$25,000
Accumulated depreciation	$ 6,000	—
Estimated annual operating costs	$24,000	$18,000
Useful life	5 years	5 years

If sold now, the current machine would have a salvage value of $5,000. If operated for the remainder of its useful life, the current machine would have zero salvage value. The new machine is expected to have zero salvage value after five years.

Instructions

Should the current machine be replaced?

E7-12 Maggie Sharrer, a recent graduate of Rolling's accounting program, evaluated the operating performance of Poway Company's six divisions. Maggie made the following presentation to Poway's Board of Directors and suggested the Erie Division be eliminated. "If the Erie Division is eliminated," she said, "our total profits would increase by $24,500."

Make incremental analysis concerning elimination of division.

(SO 7)

	The Other Five Divisions	Erie Division	Total
Sales	$1,664,200	$100,000	$1,764,200
Cost of goods sold	978,520	76,500	1,055,020
Gross profit	685,680	23,500	709,180
Operating expenses	527,940	48,000	575,940
Net income	$ 157,740	$ (24,500)	$ 133,240

In the Erie Division, cost of goods sold is $60,000 variable and $16,500 fixed, and operating expenses are $25,000 variable and $23,000 fixed. None of the Erie Division's fixed costs will be eliminated if the division is discontinued.

Instructions

Is Maggie right about eliminating the Erie Division? Prepare a schedule to support your answer.

Make incremental analysis for elimination of a product line.
(SO 7)

E7-13 Shatner Company makes three models of phasers. Information on the three products is given below.

	Stunner	Double-Set	Mega-Power
Sales	$300,000	$500,000	$200,000
Variable expenses	150,000	200,000	140,000
Contribution margin	150,000	300,000	60,000
Fixed expenses	120,000	225,000	90,000
Net income	$ 30,000	$ 75,000	$(30,000)

Fixed expenses consist of $300,000 of common costs allocated to the three products based on relative sales, and additional fixed expenses of $30,000 (Stunner), $75,000 (Double-Set), and $30,000 (Mega-Power). The common costs will be incurred regardless of how many models are produced. The other fixed expenses would be eliminated if a model is phased out.

Jim Kirk, an executive with the company, feels the Mega-Power line should be discontinued to increase the company's net income.

Instructions

(a) Compute current net income for Shatner Company.

(b) Compute net income by product line and in total for Shatner Company if the company discontinues the Mega-Power product line. (*Hint:* Allocate the $300,000 common costs to the two remaining product lines based on their relative sales.)

(c) Should Shatner eliminate the Mega-Power product line? Why or why not?

Identify relevant costs for different decisions.
(SO 3, 4, 5, 6, 7)

E7-14 The costs listed below relate to a variety of different decision situations.

Cost	Decision
1. Unavoidable fixed overhead	Eliminate an unprofitable segment
2. Direct labor	Make or buy
3. Original cost of old equipment	Equipment replacement
4. Joint production costs	Sell or process further
5. Opportunity cost	Accepting a special order
6. Segment manager's salary	Eliminate an unprofitable segment. Manager will be terminated.
7. Cost of new equipment	Equipment replacement
8. Incremental production costs	Sell or process further
9. Direct materials	Equipment replacement. The amount of materials required does not change.
10. Rent expense	Purchase or lease a building

Instructions

For each cost listed above, indicate if it is relevant or not to the related decision. For those costs determined to be irrelevant, briefly explain why.

EXERCISES: SET B

www.wiley.com/college/weygandt

Visit the book's website at **www.wiley.com/college/weygandt**, and choose the Student Companion site, to access Exercise Set B.

PROBLEMS: SET A

WILEY PLUS

Make incremental analysis for special order and identify non-financial factors in the decision.
(SO 3)

P7-1A Pro Sports Inc. manufactures basketballs for the National Basketball Association (NBA). For the first 6 months of 2008, the company reported the following operating results while operating at 90% of plant capacity and producing 112,500 units.

	Amount
Sales	$4,500,000
Cost of goods sold	3,600,000
Selling and administrative expenses	450,000
Net income	$ 450,000

Fixed costs for the period were: cost of goods sold $1,080,000, and selling and administrative expenses $225,000.

In July, normally a slack manufacturing month, Pro Sports receives a special order for 10,000 basketballs at $28 each from the Italian Basketball Association (IBA). Acceptance of the order would increase variable selling and administrative expenses $0.50 per unit because of shipping costs but would not increase fixed costs and expenses.

Instructions

(a) Prepare an incremental analysis for the special order.

(a) NI increase $31,000

(b) Should Pro Sports Inc. accept the special order? Explain your answer.

(c) What is the minimum selling price on the special order to produce net income of $4.10 per ball?

(d) What nonfinancial factors should management consider in making its decision?

Make incremental analysis related to make or buy, consider opportunity cost, and identify nonfinancial factors.

(SO 4)

P7-2A The management of Borealis Manufacturing Company is trying to decide whether to continue manufacturing a part or to buy it from an outside supplier. The part, called WISCO, is a component of the company's finished product.

The following information was collected from the accounting records and production data for the year ending December 31, 2008.

1. 7,000 units of WISCO were produced in the Machining Department.
2. Variable manufacturing costs applicable to the production of each WISCO unit were: direct materials $4.80, direct labor $4.30, indirect labor $0.43, utilities $0.40.
3. Fixed manufacturing costs applicable to the production of WISCO were:

Cost Item	Direct	Allocated
Depreciation	$2,100	$ 900
Property taxes	500	200
Insurance	900	600
	$3,500	$1,700

All variable manufacturing and direct fixed costs will be eliminated if WISCO is purchased. Allocated costs will have to be absorbed by other production departments.

4. The lowest quotation for 7,000 WISCO units from a supplier is $70,000.
5. If WISCO units are purchased, freight and inspection costs would be $0.40 per unit, and receiving costs totaling $1,250 per year would be incurred by the Machining Department.

Instructions

(a) Prepare an incremental analysis for WISCO. Your analysis should have columns for (1) Make WISCO, (2) Buy WISCO, and (3) Net Income Increase/(Decrease).

(a) NI (decrease) $(1,040)

(b) Based on your analysis, what decision should management make?

(c) Would the decision be different if Borealis Company has the opportunity to produce $5,000 of net income with the facilities currently being used to manufacture WISCO? Show computations.

(c) NI increase $3,960

(d) What nonfinancial factors should management consider in making its decision?

Determine if product should be sold or processed further.

(SO 5)

P7-3A Mesa Industrial Products Co. (MIPC) is a diversified industrial-cleaner processing company. The company's Verde plant produces two products: a table cleaner and a floor cleaner from a common set of chemical inputs (CDG). Each week 900,000 ounces of chemical input are processed at a cost of $210,000 into 600,000 ounces of floor cleaner and 300,000 ounces of table cleaner. The floor cleaner has no market value until it is converted into a polish with the trade name FloorShine. The additional processing costs for this conversion amount to $250,000.

FloorShine sells at $20 per 30-ounce bottle. The table cleaner can be sold for $25 per 30-ounce bottle. However, the table cleaner can be converted into two other products by adding 300,000 ounces of another compound (TCP) to the 300,000 ounces of table cleaner. This joint process will yield 300,000 ounces each of table stain remover (TSR) and table polish (TP). The additional processing costs for this process amount to $100,000. Both table products can be sold for $18 per 30-ounce bottle.

The company decided not to process the table cleaner into TSR and TP based on the following analysis.

	Table Cleaner	Process Further: Table Stain Remover (TSR)	Table Polish (TP)	Total
Production in ounces	(300,000)	300,000	300,000	
Revenue	$250,000	$180,000	$180,000	$360,000
Costs:				
CDG costs	70,000*	52,500	52,500	105,000**
TCP costs	0	50,000	50,000	100,000
Total costs	70,000	102,500	102,500	205,000
Weekly gross profit	$180,000	$ 77,500	$ 77,500	$155,000

*If table cleaner is not processed further it is allocated 1/3 of the $210,000 of CDG cost, which is equal to 1/3 of the total physical output.
**If table cleaner is processed further, total physical output is 1,200,000 ounces. TSR and TP combined account for 50% of the total physical output and are each allocated 25% of the CDG cost.

Instructions

(a) Determine if management made the correct decision to not process the table cleaner further by doing the following.
- (1) Calculate the company's total weekly gross profit assuming the table cleaner is not processed further.
- (2) Gross profit $200,000
- (2) Calculate the company's total weekly gross profit assuming the table cleaner is processed further.
- (3) Compare the resulting net incomes and comment on management's decision.

(b) Using incremental analysis, determine if the table cleaner should be processed further.

(CMA adapted)

Compute gain or loss, and determine if equipment should be replaced.
(SO 6)

P7-4A Last year (2008) Calway Condos installed a mechanized elevator for its tenants. The owner of the company, Cab Calway, recently returned from an industry equipment exhibition where he watched a computerized elevator demonstrated. He was impressed with the elevator's speed, comfort of ride, and cost efficiency. Upon returning from the exhibition, he asked his purchasing agent to collect price and operating cost data on the new elevator. In addition, he asked the company's accountant to provide him with cost data on the company's elevator. This information is presented below.

	Old Elevator	New Elevator
Purchase price	$120,000	$180,000
Estimated salvage value	0	0
Estimated useful life	6 years	5 years
Depreciation method	Straight-line	Straight-line
Annual operating costs other than depreciation:		
Variable	$ 35,000	$ 12,000
Fixed	23,000	8,400

Annual revenues are $240,000, and selling and administrative expenses are $29,000, regardless of which elevator is used. If the old elevator is replaced now, at the beginning of 2009, Calway Condos will be able to sell it for $25,000.

Instructions

(a) Determine any gain or loss if the old elevator is replaced.

(b)(2) NI $698,000

(b) Prepare a 5-year summarized income statement for each of the following assumptions:
- (1) The old elevator is retained.
- (2) The old elevator is replaced.

(c) NI increase $33,000

(c) Using incremental analysis, determine if the old elevator should be replaced.

(d) Write a memo to Cab Calway explaining why any gain or loss should be ignored in the decision to replace the old elevator.

P7-5A Lewis Manufacturing Company has four operating divisions. During the first quarter of 2008, the company reported aggregate income from operations of $176,000 and the following divisional results.

Compute contribution margin and prepare incremental analysis concerning elimination of divisions.

(SO 7)

	Division			
	I	II	III	IV
Sales	$250,000	$200,000	$500,000	$400,000
Cost of goods sold	200,000	189,000	300,000	250,000
Selling and administrative expenses	65,000	60,000	60,000	50,000
Income (loss) from operations	$ (15,000)	$ (49,000)	$140,000	$100,000

Analysis reveals the following percentages of variable costs in each division.

	I	II	III	IV
Cost of goods sold	70%	90%	80%	75%
Selling and administrative expenses	40	70	50	60

Discontinuance of any division would save 50% of the fixed costs and expenses for that division.

Top management is very concerned about the unprofitable divisions (I and II). Consensus is that one or both of the divisions should be discontinued.

Instructions

(a) Compute the contribution margin for Divisions I and II.

(a) I $84,000

(b) Prepare an incremental analysis concerning the possible discontinuance of (1) Division I and (2) Division II. What course of action do you recommend for each division?

(c) Prepare a columnar condensed income statement for Lewis Manufacturing, assuming Division II is eliminated. Use the CVP format. Division II's unavoidable fixed costs are allocated equally to the continuing divisions.

(c) Income III $133,850

(d) Reconcile the total income from operations ($176,000) with the total income from operations without Division II.

PROBLEMS: SET B

P7-1B Oakbrook Company is currently producing 18,000 units per month, which is 80% of its production capacity. Variable manufacturing costs are currently $13.20 per unit, and fixed manufacturing costs are $72,000 per month. Oakbrook pays a 9% sales commission to its sales people, has $30,000 in fixed administrative expenses per month, and is averaging $432,000 in sales per month.

Make incremental analysis for special order and identify nonfinancial factors in the decision.

(SO 3)

A special order received from a foreign company would enable Oakbrook Company to operate at 100% capacity. The foreign company offered to pay 80% of Oakbrook's current selling price per unit. If the order is accepted, Oakbrook will have to spend an extra $2.00 per unit to package the product for overseas shipping. Also, Oakbrook Company would need to lease a new stamping machine to imprint the foreign company's logo on the product, at a monthly cost of $5,000. The special order would require a sales commission of $4,000.

Instructions

(a) Compute the number of units involved in the special order and the foreign company's offered price per unit.

(b) What is the manufacturing cost of producing one unit of Oakbrook's product for regular customers?

(c) Prepare an incremental analysis of the special order. Should management accept the order?

(c) NI increase $9,000

(d) What is the lowest price that Oakbrook could accept for the special order to earn net income of $1.20 per unit?

(e) What nonfinancial factors should management consider in making its decision?

P7-2B The management of Dunham Manufacturing Company has asked for your assistance in deciding whether to continue manufacturing a part or to buy it from an outside supplier. The part, called Tropica, is a component of Dunham's finished product.

Make incremental analysis related to make or buy, consider opportunity cost, and identify nonfinancial factors.

(SO 4)

An analysis of the accounting records and the production data revealed the following information for the year ending December 31, 2008.

1. The Machinery Department produced 35,000 units of Tropica.
2. Each Tropica unit requires 10 minutes to produce. Three people in the Machinery Department work full time (2,000 hours per year) producing Tropica. Each person is paid $12 per hour.
3. The cost of materials per Tropica unit is $2.20.
4. Manufacturing costs directly applicable to the production of Tropica are: indirect labor, $6,000; utilities, $1,500; depreciation, $1,800; property taxes and insurance, $1,000. All of the costs will be eliminated if Tropica is purchased.
5. The lowest price for a Tropica from an outside supplier is $4 per unit. Freight charges will be $0.50 per unit, and a part-time receiving clerk at $8,500 per year will be required.
6. If Tropica is purchased, the excess space will be used to store Dunham's finished product. Currently, Dunham rents storage space at approximately $0.80 per unit stored per year. Approximately 5,000 units per year are stored in the rented space.

Instructions

(a) NI decrease $2,700

(a) Prepare an incremental analysis for the make or buy decision. Should Dunham make or buy the part? Why?

(b) NI increase $9,300

(b) Prepare an incremental analysis, assuming the released facilities can be used to produce $12,000 of net income in addition to the savings on the rental of storage space. What decision should now be made?

(c) What nonfinancial factors should be considered in the decision?

Determine if product should be sold or processed further.

(SO 5)

P7-3B Bonita Household Products Co. is a diversified household cleaner processing company. The company's Poway plant produces two products: a glass cleaner and a metal cleaner from a common set of chemical inputs, (TLC). Each week 1,000,000 ounces of chemical input are processed at a cost of $200,000 into 750,000 ounces of metal cleaner and 250,000 ounces of glass cleaner. The metal cleaner has no market value until it is converted into a polish with the trade name MetalShine. The additional processing costs for this conversion amount to $270,000. MetalShine sells at $15 per 25-ounce bottle.

The glass cleaner can be sold for $24 per 25-ounce bottle. However, the glass cleaner can be converted into two other products by adding 250,000 ounces of another compound (MST) to the 250,000 ounces of glass cleaner. This joint process will yield 250,000 ounces each of plastic cleaner (PC) and plastic polish (PP). The additional processing costs for this process amount to $140,000. Both plastic products can be sold for $20 per 25-ounce bottle.

The company decided not to process the glass cleaner into PC and PP based on the following analysis.

		Process Further		
	Glass Cleaner	Plastic Cleaner (PC)	Plastic Polish (PP)	Total
Production in ounces	(250,000)	(250,000)	(250,000)	
Revenue	$240,000	$200,000	$200,000	$400,000
Costs:				
TLC costs	50,000*	40,000	40,000	80,000**
MST costs	0	70,000	70,000	140,000
Total costs	50,000	110,000	110,000	220,000
Weekly gross profit	$190,000	$ 90,000	$ 90,000	$180,000

*If glass cleaner is not processed further it is allocated ¼ of the $200,000 of TLC cost, which is equal to ¼ of the total physical output.

**If glass cleaner is processed further, total physical output is 1,250,000 ounces. PC and PP combined account for 40% of the total physical output and are each allocated 20% of the TLC cost.

Instructions

(a) Determine if management made the correct decision to not process the glass cleaner further by doing the following.

(1) Calculate the company's total weekly gross profit assuming the glass cleaner is not processed further.

(2) Calculate the company's total weekly gross profit assuming the glass cleaner is processed further.

(3) Compare the resulting net incomes and comment on management's decision.

(b) Using incremental analysis, determine if the glass cleaner should be processed further.

(2) Gross profit $240,000

(CMA adapted)

P7-4B Quik Press Inc. offers one-day dry cleaning. At the beginning of 2008, the company purchased a mechanized pressing machine. The owner of the company, Jill Jabowski, recently returned from an industry equipment exhibition where she watched a computerized press demonstrated. She was impressed with the machine's speed, efficiency, and quality of output. Upon returning from the exhibition, she asked her purchasing agent to collect price and operating cost data on the new press. In addition, she asked the company's accountant to provide her with cost data on the company's press. This information is presented below.

Compute gain or loss, and determine if equipment should be replaced.

(SO 6)

	Old Press	New Press
Purchase price	$120,000	$150,000
Estimated salvage value	0	0
Estimated useful life	6 years	5 years
Depreciation method	Straight-line	Straight-line
Annual operating expenses other than depreciation:		
Variable	$30,000	$10,000
Fixed	20,000	7,000

Annual revenues are $200,000, and selling and administrative expenses are $24,000, regardless of which press is used. If the old press is replaced now, at the beginning of 2009, Quik Press will be able to sell it for $10,000.

Instructions

(a) Determine any gain or loss if the old press is replaced.

(b) Prepare a 5-year summarized income statement for each of the following assumptions:

(1) The old press is retained.

(2) The old press is replaced.

(c) Using incremental analysis, determine if the old press should be replaced.

(d) Write a memo to Jill Jabowski explaining why any gain or loss should be ignored in the decision to replace the old press.

(b)(2) NI $555,000

(c) NI increase $25,000

P7-5B Hindu Manufacturing Company has four operating divisions. During the first quarter of 2008, the company reported total income from operations of $36,000 and the following results for the divisions.

Compute contribution margin and prepare incremental analysis concerning elimination of divisions.

(SO 7)

	Division			
	Taos	Boseman	Salem	Olympia
Sales	$405,000	$730,000	$920,000	$500,000
Cost of goods sold	400,000	480,000	576,000	390,000
Selling and administrative expenses	100,000	207,000	246,000	120,000
Income (loss) from operations	$(95,000)	$ 43,000	$ 98,000	$(10,000)

Analysis reveals the following percentages of variable costs in each division.

	Taos	Boseman	Salem	Olympia
Cost of goods sold	90%	80%	90%	95%
Selling and administrative expenses	60	60	70	80

Discontinuance of any division would save 70% of the fixed costs and expenses for that division.

Top management is deeply concerned about the unprofitable divisions (Taos and Olympia). The consensus is that one or both of the divisions should be eliminated.

Instructions

(a) Compute the contribution margin for the two unprofitable divisions.

(b) Prepare an incremental analysis concerning the possible elimination of (1) the Taos Division and (2) the Olympia Division. What course of action do you recommend for each division?

(a) Olympia $33,500

(c) Income Salem $86,000

(c) Prepare a columnar condensed income statement using the CVP format for Hindu Manufacturing Company, assuming (1) the Taos Division is eliminated, and (2) the unavoidable fixed costs and expenses of the Taos Division are allocated 30% to Boseman, 50% to Salem, and 20% to Olympia.

(d) Compare the total income from operations with the Taos Division ($36,000) to total income from operations without this division.

PROBLEMS: SET C

Visit the book's website at **www.wiley.com/college/weygandt**, and choose the Student Companion site, to access Problem Set C.

WATERWAYS CONTINUING PROBLEM

(This is a continuation of the Waterways Problem from Chapters 1 through 6.)

WCP7 Waterways Corporation is considering various business opportunities. It wants to make best use of its production facilities to maximize income. This problem asks you to help Waterways do incremental analysis on these various opportunities.

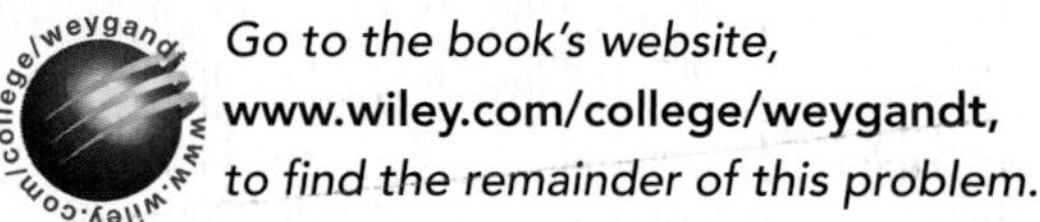

BROADENING YOUR PERSPECTIVE

DECISION MAKING ACROSS THE ORGANIZATION

BYP7-1 Castle Company is considering the purchase of a new machine. The invoice price of the machine is $125,000, freight charges are estimated to be $4,000, and installation costs are expected to be $6,000. Salvage value of the new equipment is expected to be zero after a useful life of 4 years. Existing equipment could be retained and used for an additional 4 years if the new machine is not purchased. At that time, the salvage value of the equipment would be zero. If the new machine is purchased now, the existing machine would have to be scrapped. Castle's accountant, Shaida Fang, has accumulated the following data regarding annual sales and expenses with and without the new machine.

1. Without the new machine, Castle can sell 12,000 units of product annually at a per unit selling price of $100. If the new machine is purchased, the number of units produced and sold would increase by 20%, and the selling price would remain the same.
2. The new machine is faster than the old machine, and it is more efficient in its usage of materials. With the old machine the gross profit rate will be 25% of sales, whereas the rate will be 30% of sales with the new machine.
3. Annual selling expenses are $180,000 with the current equipment. Because the new equipment would produce a greater number of units to be sold, annual selling expenses are expected to increase by 10% if it is purchased.
4. Annual administrative expenses are expected to be $100,000 with the old machine, and $113,000 with the new machine.
5. The current book value of the existing machine is $36,000. Castle uses straight-line depreciation.

Instructions

With the class divided into groups, prepare an incremental analysis for the 4 years showing whether Castle should keep the existing machine or buy the new machine. (Ignore income tax effects.)

MANAGERIAL ANALYSIS

BYP7-2 Technology Plus manufactures private-label small electronic products, such as alarm clocks, calculators, kitchen timers, stopwatches, and automatic pencil sharpeners. Some of the products are sold as sets, and others are sold individually. Products are studied as to their sales potential, and then cost estimates are made. The Engineering Department develops production plans, and then production begins. The company has generally had very successful product introductions. Only two products introduced by the company have been discontinued.

One of the products currently sold is a multi-alarm alarm clock. The clock has four alarms that can be programmed to sound at various times and for varying lengths of time. The company has experienced a great deal of difficulty in making the circuit boards for the clocks. The production process has never operated smoothly. The product is unprofitable at the present time, primarily because of warranty repairs and product recalls. Two models of the clocks were recalled, for example, because they sometimes caused an electric shock when the alarms were being shut off. The Engineering Department is attempting to revise the manufacturing process, but the revision will take another 6 months at least.

The clocks were very popular when they were introduced, and since they are private-label, the company has not suffered much from the recalls. Presently, the company has a very large order for several items from Kmart Stores. The order includes 5,000 of the multi-alarm clocks. When the company suggested that Kmart purchase the clocks from another manufacturer, Kmart threatened to rescind the entire order unless the clocks were included.

The company has therefore investigated the possibility of having another company make the clocks for them. The clocks were bid for the Kmart order based on an estimated $6.65 cost to manufacture:

Circuit board, 1 each @ $2.00	$2.00
Plastic case, 1 each @ $0.75	0.75
Alarms, 4 @ $0.10 each	0.40
Labor, 15 minutes @ $12/hour	3.00
Overhead, $2.00 per labor hour	0.50

Technology Plus could purchase clocks to fill the Kmart order for $11 from Silver Star, a Korean manufacturer with a very good quality record. Silver Star has offered to reduce the price to $7.50 after Technology Plus has been a customer for 6 months, placing an order of at least 1,000 units per month. If Technology Plus becomes a "preferred customer" by purchasing 15,000 units per year, the price would be reduced still further to $4.50.

Alpha Products, a local manufacturer, has also offered to make clocks for Technology Plus. They have offered to sell 5,000 clocks for $4 each. However, Alpha Products has been in business for only 6 months. They have experienced significant turnover in their labor force, and the local press has reported that the owners may face tax evasion charges soon. The owner of Alpha Products is an electronic engineer, however, and the quality of the clocks is likely to be good.

If Technology Plus decides to purchase the clocks from either Silver Star or Alpha, all the costs to manufacture could be avoided, except a total of $5,000 in overhead costs for machine depreciation. The machinery is fairly new, and has no alternate use.

Instructions

(a) What is the difference in profit under each of the alternatives if the clocks are to be sold for $14.50 each to Kmart?

(b) What are the most important nonfinancial factors that Technology Plus should consider when making this decision?

(c) What do you think Technology Plus should do in regard to the Kmart order? What should it do in regard to continuing to manufacture the multi-alarm alarm clocks? Be prepared to defend your answer.

REAL-WORLD FOCUS

BYP7-3 Founded in 1983, Beverly Hills Fan Company is located in Woodland Hills, California. With 23 employees and sales of less than $10 million, the company is relatively small. Management feels that there is potential for growth in the upscale market for ceiling fans and lighting. They are particularly optimistic about growth in Mexican and Canadian markets.

Presented below is information from the president's letter in the company's annual report.

> **BEVERLY HILLS FAN COMPANY**
> President's Letter
>
> An aggressive product development program was initiated during the past year resulting in new ceiling fan models planned for introduction this year. Award winning industrial designer Ron Rezek created several new fan models for the Beverly Hills Fan and L.A. Fan lines, including a new Showroom Collection, designed specifically for the architectural and designer markets. Each of these models has received critical acclaim, and order commitments for this year have been outstanding. Additionally, our Custom Color and special order fans continued to enjoy increasing popularity and sales gains as more and more customers desire fans that match their specific interior decors. Currently, Beverly Hills Fan Company offers a product line of over 100 models of contemporary, traditional, and transitional ceiling fans.

Instructions

(a) What points did the company management need to consider before deciding to offer the special-order fans to customers?

(b) How would incremental analysis be employed to assist in this decision?

EXPLORING THE WEB

BYP7-4 Outsourcing by both manufacturers and service companies is becoming increasingly common. There are now many firms that specialize in outsourcing consulting.

Address: www.trowbridgegroup.net, or go to **www.wiley.com/college/weygandt**

Instructions

Go to the Web page of The Trowbridge Group at the address shown above, and answer the following questions.

(a) What are some of the ways that outsourcing can "strengthen the overall performance of the company"?

(b) What are some of the potential problems that arise when companies outsource?

COMMUNICATION ACTIVITY

BYP7-5 Jeff Howell is a production manager at a metal fabricating plant. Last night he read an article about a new piece of equipment that would dramatically reduce his division's costs. Jeff was very excited about the prospect, and the first thing he did this morning was to bring the article to his supervisor, Nathan Peas, the plant manager. The following conversation occurred:

Jeff: Nathan, I thought you would like to see this article on the new PDD1130; they've made some fantastic changes that could save us millions of dollars.

Nathan: I appreciate your interest Jeff, but I actually have been aware of the new machine for two months. The problem is that we just bought a new machine last year. We spent $2 million on that machine, and it was supposed to last us 12 years. If we replace it now we would have to write its book value off of the books for a huge loss. If I go to top management now and say that I want a new machine, they will fire me. I think we should use our existing machine for a couple of years, and then when it becomes obvious that we have to have a new machine, I will make the proposal.

Instructions

Jeff just completed a course in managerial accounting, and he believes that Nathan is making a big mistake. Write a memo from Jeff to Nathan explaining Nathan's decision-making error.

ETHICS CASE

BYP7-6 Robert Buey became Chief Executive Officer of Phelps Manufacturing two years ago. At the time, the company was reporting lagging profits, and Robert was brought in to "stir things up." The company has three divisions, electronics, fiber optics, and plumbing supplies. Robert has no interest in plumbing supplies, and one of the first things he did was to put pressure on his accountants to reallocate some of the company's fixed costs away from the other two divisions to the plumbing division. This had the effect of causing the plumbing division to report losses during the last two years; in the past it had always reported low, but acceptable, net income. Robert felt that this reallocation would shine a favorable light on him in front of the board of directors because it meant that the electronics and fiber optics divisions would look like they were improving. Given that these are "businesses of the future," he believed that the stock market would react favorably to these increases, while not penalizing the poor results of the plumbing division. Without this shift in the allocation of fixed costs, the profits of the electronics and fiber optics divisions would not have improved. But now the board of directors has suggested that the plumbing division be closed because it is reporting losses. This would mean that nearly 500 employees, many of whom have worked for Phelps their whole lives, would lose their jobs.

Instructions

(a) If a division is reporting losses, does that necessarily mean that it should be closed?
(b) Was the reallocation of fixed costs across divisions unethical?
(c) What should Robert do?

"ALL ABOUT YOU" ACTIVITY

BYP7-7 Managerial accounting techniques can be used in a wide variety of settings. As we have frequently pointed out, you can use them in many personal situations. They also can be useful in trying to find solutions for societal issues that appear to be hard to solve.

Instructions

Read the *Fortune* article, "The Toughest Customers: How Hardheaded Business Metrics Can Help the Hard-core Homeless," by Cait Murphy, available at *http://money.cnn.com/magazines/fortune/fortune_archive/2006/04/03/8373067/index.htm.* Answer the following questions.

(a) How does the article define "chronic" homelessness?
(b) In what ways does homelessness cost a city money? What are the estimated costs of a chronic homeless person to various cities?
(c) What are the steps suggested to address the problem?
(d) What is the estimated cost of implementing this program in New York? What results have been seen?
(e) In terms of incremental analysis, frame the relevant costs in this situation.

Answers to Insight and Accounting Across the Organization Questions

These Wheels Have Miles Before Installation, p. 293

Q: What are the disadvantages of outsourcing to a foreign country?

A: *Possible disadvantages of outsourcing are that the supplier loses control over the quality of the product, as well as the timing of production. Also, the company exposes itself to price changes caused by changes in the value of the foreign currency. In addition, shipping large, heavy products such as tires is costly, and disruptions in shipping (due to strikes, weather, etc.) can cause delays in final assembly of vehicles. As a result of the outsourcing, the company will have to reassign, or even lay off, many skilled workers. Not only is this very disruptive to the lives of those employees, it also hurts morale of the remaining employees. As more U.S. employers begin to use robotic automation in their facilities, they are able to reduce the amount of labor required, and thus are beginning to be able to compete more favorably with foreign suppliers.*

Time to Move to a New Neighborhood? p. 298

Q: What were some of the factors that complicated the company's decision to move? How should the company have incorporated such factors into its incremental analysis?

A: *The company received only $7.5 million for its California property, only 58 of 75 key employees were willing to move, construction was delayed by a year which caused the new plant to increase in price by $1.5 million, and wages surged in Idaho due to low unemployment. In performing incremental analysis of the decision to move, a company should perform sensitivity analysis. This would include evaluating the impact on the decision if all costs were, for example, 10% higher than expected or if cost savings were 10% lower than expected.*

What Is the Real Cost of Packaging Options? p. 300

Q: If your marketing director suggests that, in addition to selling your cereal in a standard-size box, you should sell a jumbo size and an individual size, what issues must you consider?

A: *In evaluating this decision, you should identify the incremental revenues as well as incremental costs. The marketing manager is most likely focusing on the fact that by offering alternative packaging options, the company can market the product to a broader range of customers. However, alternative packaging options will also result in additional costs. It will increase the number of setups, require different types of storage and handling, and increase the need for additional storage space for the packages and the packaged products.*

Authors' Comments on *All About You*: What Is a Degree Worth? (p. 301)

This is a very difficult decision. All of the evidence suggests that your short-term and long-term prospects will be far greater with some form of post–high-school degree. Because of this, we feel strongly that you should make every effort to continue your education. Many of the discussions provided in this text present ideas on how to get control of your individual financial situation. We would encourage you to use these tools to identify ways to reduce your financial burden in order to continue your education. We also want to repeat that even taking only one course a semester is better than dropping out. Your instructors and advisors frequently provide advice to students who are faced with the decision about whether to continue with their education. If you are in this situation, we would encourage you to seek their advice since the implications of this decision can be long-lasting.

Answers to Self-Study Questions

1. d **2.** b **3.** c **4.** d **5.** d **6.** a **7.** b **8.** c **9.** b

Remember to go back to the Navigator box on the chapter-opening page and check off your completed work.

Chapter 8

Pricing

STUDY OBJECTIVES

After studying this chapter, you should be able to:

1 Compute a target cost when the market determines a product price.

2 Compute a target selling price using cost-plus pricing.

3 Use time-and-material pricing to determine the cost of services provided.

4 Determine a transfer price using the negotiated, cost-based, and market-based approaches.

5 Explain issues involved in transferring goods between divisions in different countries.

✓ The Navigator

✓ The Navigator

- Scan **Study Objectives** ☐
- Read **Feature Story** ☐
- Read **Preview** ☐
- Read text and answer **Before You Go On** p. 330 ☐ p. 333 ☐ p. 341 ☐
- Work **Using the Decision Toolkit** ☐
- Review **Summary of Study Objectives** ☐
- Work **Demonstration Problem** ☐
- Answer **Self-Study Questions** ☐
- Complete **Assignments** ☐

Feature Story

"I'LL CALL YOUR BLUFF, AND RAISE YOU 46%"

If you own a PC, then there is a roughly 85% chance that the microprocessor chip that runs your machine was made by Intel. For as long as most people can remember, Intel has had at least an 85% share of the market for PC computer chips. It isn't that nobody else makes computer chips; it's just that the competition can't seem to get a foothold.

Intel's primary competition comes from a scrappy company called Advanced Micro Devices (AMD). At one time, Intel made a couple of missteps that caused it to lose a few points of market share to AMD. First, Intel had two product recalls on its chips. Then it had problems meeting demand. In the meantime, AMD was boasting that it had a chip that was more powerful than Intel's, and that it had plenty of supply to meet demand. The result was that Intel's market share fell—to 82%.

To those familiar with Intel, its response was easily predicted. It cut prices by up to 26%. One analyst noted, "When Intel screws up, they can't send flowers, so they cut prices." Said another analyst, "Intel has drawn a line in the sand at 85% market share, and they will use price to regain that share."

AMD had little choice but to respond with price cuts of its own. It cut prices by up to 46% on some of its chips. In the past, price wars have typically hurt AMD worse since Intel's massive volume allows it to produce chips at a lower cost. In 2006 Intel's gross profit rate was about 50%, while AMD's was only about 36%. An all-out price war, however, would leave both companies battered and bruised. The stock price of both companies falls on the news of price cuts.

Source: Molly Williams, "Intel Cuts Prices, Prompts AMD to Answer the Call." *Wall Street Journal*, October 17, 2000.

The Navigator

Inside Chapter 8

Preview of Chapter 8

As the Feature Story about Intel and AMD indicates, few management decisions are more important than setting prices. Intel, for example, must sell computer chips at a price that is high enough to cover its costs and ensure a reasonable profit. But if the price is too high, the chips will not sell. In this chapter, we examine two types of pricing situations. The first part of the chapter addresses pricing for goods sold or services provided to external parties. The second part of the chapter addresses pricing decisions managers face when they sell goods to other divisions within the company.

The content and organization of this chapter are as follows.

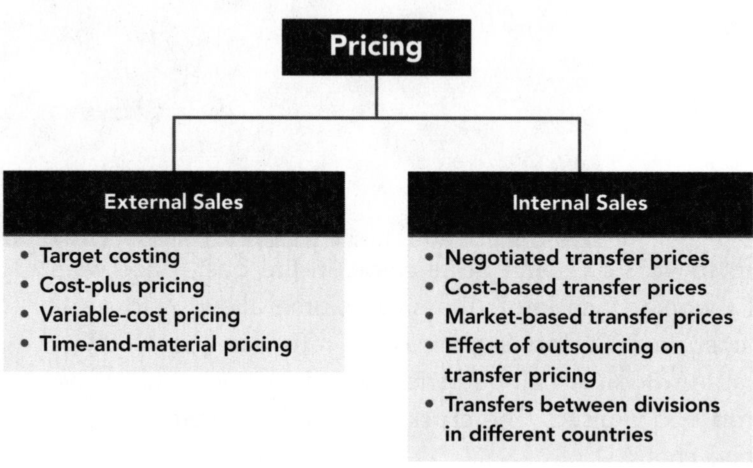

The Navigator

SECTION 1 External Sales

Establishing the price for any good or service is affected by many factors. Take the pharmaceutical industry as an example. Its approach to profitability has been to spend heavily on research and development in an effort to find and patent a few new drugs, price them high, and market them aggressively. Due to the AIDS crisis in Africa, the drug industry has been under considerable pressure recently to lower prices on drugs used to treat AIDS. For example, Merck Co. lowered the price of its AIDS drug Crixivan to $600 per patient in these countries. This compares with the $6,016 it typically charges in the United States.[1] As a consequence, individuals in the United States are questioning whether prices in the U.S. market are too high. The drug companies counter that to cover their substantial financial risks to develop these products, they need to set the prices high. Illustration 8-1 (next page) indicates the many factors that can affect pricing decisions.

In the long run a company must price its product to cover its costs and earn a reasonable profit. But to price its product appropriately, it must have a good understanding of market forces at work. In most cases, a company does not set the prices. Instead the price is set by the competitive market (the laws of supply and demand). For example, a company such as ChevronTexaco or ExxonMobil

[1] "AIDS Gaffes in Africa Come Back to Haunt Drug Industry at Home," *Wall Street Journal* (April 23, 2001), p. 1.

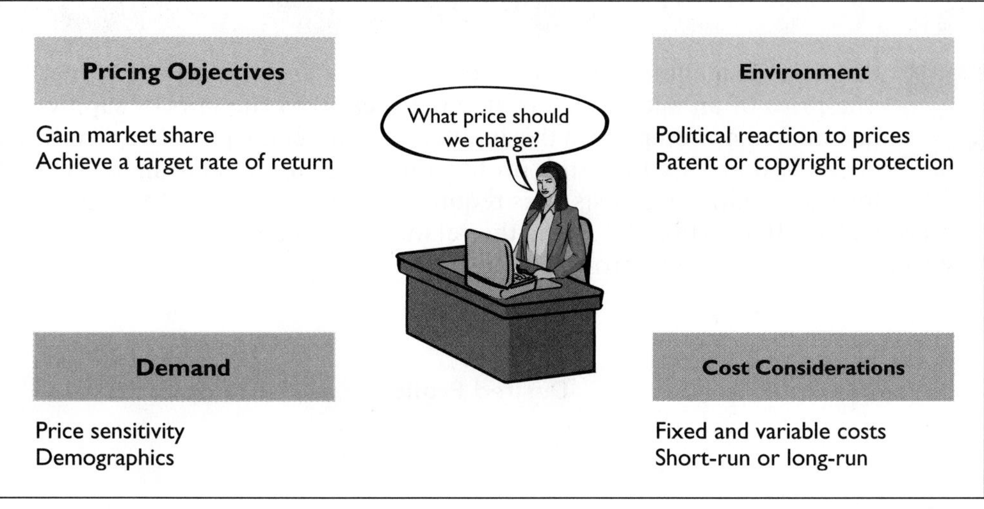

Illustration 8-1
Pricing factors

cannot set the price of gasoline by itself. These companies are called **price takers** because the price of gasoline is set by market forces (the supply of oil and the demand by customers). This is the case for any product that is not easily differentiated from competing products, such as farm products (corn or wheat) or minerals (coal or sand).

In other situations the company sets the prices. This would be the case where the product is specially made for a customer, as in a one-of-a-kind product such as a designer dress by Zoran or Armani. This also occurs when there are few or no other producers capable of manufacturing a similar item. An example would be a company that has a patent or copyright on a unique process, such as the case of computer chips by Intel. However, it is also the case when a company can effectively differentiate its product or service from others. Even in a competitive market like coffee, Starbucks has been able to differentiate its product and charge a premium for a cup of java.

MANAGEMENT INSIGHT

What's the Price on the Internet?

How has the Internet affected pricing? The answer isn't simple, because of two conflicting forces. On the one hand, the Internet allows customers to easily compare prices, thus driving prices down. In fact, many companies feared that the Internet would squeeze all profits out of their businesses. However, e-business has also allowed many businesses to more effectively target their customers and differentiate their products, thus allowing them to avoid severe price competition by striving to create customer-focused "markets of one." E-business technology conveniently provides up-to-date information about "buying behaviors and the level of real-time local demand. Also, e-businesses are able to customize offerings by rebundling related services and products—often from a number of different companies—into attractive 'baskets'."

Source: M. V. Deise et al., *Executive's Guide to E-Business: From Tactics to Strategy* (New York: John Wiley & Sons, Inc., 2000), p. 195.

How does the Internet affect product prices?

TARGET COSTING

STUDY OBJECTIVE 1

Compute a target cost when the market determines a product price.

Automobile manufacturers like Ford or Toyota face a competitive market. The price of an automobile is affected greatly by the laws of supply and demand, so no company in this industry can affect the price to a significant degree. Therefore, to earn a profit, companies in the auto industry must focus on controlling costs. This requires setting a **target cost** that provides a desired profit. Illustration 8-2 shows the relationship and importance of a target cost to the price and desired profit.

Illustration 8-2
Target cost as related to price and profit

Market Price	−	Desired Profit	=	Target Cost

If General Motors, for example, can produce its automobiles for the target cost (or less), it will meet its profit goal. If it cannot achieve its target cost, it will fail to produce the desired profit (and will most likely "get hammered" by stockholders and the market). In a competitive market, a company chooses the segment of the market it wants to compete in—that is, its market niche. For example, it may choose between selling luxury goods or economy goods in order to focus its efforts on one segment or the other.

Once the company has identified its segment of the market, it conducts market research to determine the target price. This target price is the price that the company believes would place it in the optimal position for its target audience. Once the company has determined this target price, it can determine its target cost by setting a desired profit. The difference between the target price and the desired profit is the target cost of the product. (This computation is shown in Illustration 8-2.) After the company determines the target cost, it assembles a team of employees with expertise in a variety of areas (production and operations, marketing, and finance). The team's task is to design and develop a product that can meet quality specifications while not exceeding the target cost. The target cost includes all product and period costs necessary to make and market the product or service.

MANAGEMENT INSIGHT

Wal-Mart Says the Price Is Too High

"And the price should be $19 per pair of jeans instead of $23," said the retailer Wal-Mart to jean maker Levi Strauss. What happened to Levi Strauss is what happens to many manufacturers who deal with Wal-Mart. Wal-Mart often sets the price, and the manufacturer has to find out how to make a profit, given that price. In Levi Strauss's case, it revamped its distribution and production to serve Wal-Mart and improve its overall record of timely deliveries. Producing a season of new jeans styles, from conception to store shelves, used to take Levi 12 to 15 months. Today it takes just 10 months for Levi Strauss signature jeans; for regular Levi's, the time is down to 7 1/2 months. As the chief executive of Levi Strauss noted, "We had to change people and practice. It's been somewhat of a D-Day invasion approach."

Source: "In Bow to Retailers' New Clout, Levi Strauss Makes Alterations," *Wall Street Journal*, June 17, 2004, p A1.

What are some issues that Levi should consider in deciding whether it should agree to meet Wal-Mart's target price?

DECISION TOOLKIT

Decision Checkpoints 	Info Needed for Decision 	Tool to Use for Decision 	How to Evaluate Results 
How does management use target costs to make decisions about manufacturing products or providing services?	Target selling price, desired profit, target cost	Target selling price less desired profit equals target cost	If actual cost exceeds target cost, the company will not earn desired profit. If desired profit is not achieved, company must evaluate whether to manufacture the product or provide the service.

COST-PLUS PRICING

STUDY OBJECTIVE 2

Compute a target selling price using cost-plus pricing.

As discussed, in a competitive, common-product environment the market price is already set, and the company instead must set a target cost. But, in a less competitive or noncompetitive environment, the company may be faced with the task of setting its own price. When the company sets the price, price is commonly a function of the cost of the product or service. That is, the typical approach is to use **cost-plus pricing**. This approach involves establishing a cost base and adding to this cost base a **markup** to determine a **target selling price**. The size of the markup (the "plus") depends on the desired return on investment (ROI = net income ÷ invested assets) for the product line, product, or service. In determining the proper markup, the company must also consider competitive and market conditions, political and legal issues, and other relevant risk factors. The cost-plus pricing formula is expressed as follows.

Illustration 8-3
Cost-plus pricing formula

Cost	+	Markup Percentage × Cost	=	Target Selling Price

To illustrate, assume that Cleanmore Products, Inc. is in the process of setting a selling price on its new top-of-the-line, 3-horsepower, 16-gallon, variable-speed wet/dry shop vacuum. The per unit variable cost estimates for the new shop vacuum are as follows.

Illustration 8-4
Variable costs per unit

	Per Unit
Direct materials	$23
Direct labor	17
Variable manufacturing overhead	12
Variable selling and administrative expenses	8
Variable cost per unit	**$60**

In addition, Cleanmore has the following (page 328) fixed costs per unit at a budgeted sales volume of 10,000 units.

Illustration 8-5
Fixed cost per unit, 10,000 units

	Total Costs	÷	Budgeted Volume	=	Cost Per Unit
Fixed manufacturing overhead	$280,000	÷	10,000	=	$28
Fixed selling and administrative expenses	240,000	÷	10,000	=	24
Fixed cost per unit					$52

Cleanmore has decided to price its new shop vacuum to earn a 20% return on its investment (ROI) of $1,000,000. Therefore, Cleanmore expects to receive income of $200,000 (20% × $1,000,000) on its investment. On a per unit basis, the desired ROI is $20 ($200,000 ÷ 10,000). Given the per unit costs shown above, Cleanmore then computes the sales price to be $132, as follows.

Illustration 8-6
Computation of selling price, 10,000 units

	Per Unit
Variable cost	$ 60
Fixed cost	52
Total cost	112
Desired ROI	20
Selling price per unit	$132

In most cases, companies like Cleanmore will use a percentage markup on cost to determine the selling price. The formula to compute the markup percentage to achieve a desired ROI of $20 per unit is as follows.

Illustration 8-7
Computation of markup percentage

Desired ROI Per Unit	÷	Total Unit Cost	=	Markup Percentage
$20	÷	$112	=	17.86%

Using a 17.86% markup on cost, Cleanmore Products would compute the target selling price as follows.

Illustration 8-8
Computation of selling price—markup approach

Total Unit Cost	+	(Total Unit Cost	×	Markup Percentage)	=	Target Selling Price Per Unit
$112	+	($112	×	17.86%)	=	$132

Cleanmore should set the price for its wet/dry vacuum at $132 per unit.

Limitations of Cost-Plus Pricing

The cost-plus pricing approach has a major advantage: It is simple to compute. However, the cost model does not give consideration to the demand side. That is, will customers pay the price Cleanmore computed for its vacuums? In addition, sales volume plays a large role in determining per unit costs. The lower the sales volume, for example, the higher the price Cleanmore must charge to meet its desired ROI. To illustrate, if the budgeted sales volume was 8,000 instead of 10,000, Cleanmore's variable cost per unit would remain the same. However, the fixed cost per unit would change as follows.

Illustration 8-9
Fixed cost per unit, 8,000 units

	Total Costs	÷	Budgeted Volume	=	Cost Per Unit
Fixed manufacturing overhead	$280,000	÷	8,000	=	$35
Fixed selling and administrative expenses	240,000	÷	8,000	=	30
Fixed cost per unit					$65

As indicated in Illustration 8-5, fixed costs per unit for 10,000 units were $52. However, at a lower sales volume of 8,000 units, fixed costs per unit increase to $65. Cleanmore's desired 20% ROI now results in a $25 ROI per unit [(20% × $1,000,000) ÷ 8,000]. Cleanmore computes the selling price at 8,000 units as follows.

Illustration 8-10
Computation of selling price, 8,000 units

	Per Unit
Variable cost	$ 60
Fixed cost	65
Total cost	125
Desired ROI	25
Selling price per unit	$150

As shown, the lower the budgeted volume, the higher the per unit price. The reason: Fixed costs and ROI are spread over fewer units, and therefore the fixed cost and ROI per unit increase. In this case, at 8,000 units, Cleanmore would have to mark up its total unit costs 20% to earn a desired ROI of $25 per unit, as shown below.

$$20\% = \frac{\$25 \text{ (desired ROI)}}{\$125 \text{ (total unit cost)}}$$

The target selling price would then be $150, as indicated earlier:

$$\$125 + (\$125 \times 20\%) = \$150$$

The opposite effect will occur if budgeted volume is higher (say, at 12,000 units) because fixed costs and ROI can be spread over more units. As a result, the cost-plus model of pricing will achieve its desired ROI only when Cleanmore sells the quantity it budgeted. If actual volume is much less than budgeted volume, Cleanmore may sustain losses unless it can raise its prices.

VARIABLE-COST PRICING

In determining the target price for Cleanmore's shop vacuum, we calculated the cost base by including all costs incurred. This approach is referred to as **full-cost pricing**. Instead of using full costs to set prices, some companies simply add a markup to their variable costs. Using **variable-cost pricing** as the basis for setting prices avoids the problem of using uncertain cost information (as shown in Illustration 8-9) related to fixed-cost-per-unit computations. Variable-cost pricing also is helpful in pricing special orders or when excess capacity exists.

The major disadvantage of variable-cost pricing is that managers may set the price too low and consequently fail to cover their fixed costs. In the long run, failure to cover fixed costs will lead to losses. As a result, companies that use variable-cost pricing must adjust their markups to make sure that the price set will provide a fair return. An example of how variable costs are used as the basis for setting prices is discussed in the appendix to this chapter.

MANAGEMENT INSIGHT

Losing Money with Every Sale

During 2006 the sale of high-definition television sets exploded. It would seem that this was good news for the makers of the flat-screens that are used in these televisions. But the reality was that those companies were losing money almost as fast as they were making TV screens. The problem is that there are a number of flat-screen manufacturers, and they all increased capacity because they expected sales volume to increase even more than it did. In order to avoid getting stuck with inventory, they then cut prices severely, so the companies actually had huge losses even as they were selling a record number of screens. The prices of high-definition TVs have continued to fall, which will make it unlikely that the flat-screen manufacturers will be able to increase their prices. Instead, they must look for ways to cut their costs by as much as 30%.

? If prices continue to tumble, and sales do not increase at a more rapid rate, what will probably happen to the manufacturers of flat-screen TVs?

DECISION TOOLKIT

Decision Checkpoints	Info Needed for Decision	Tool to Use for Decision	How to Evaluate Results
	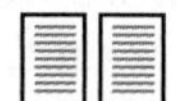		
What factors should be considered in determining selling price in a less competitive environment?	Total cost per unit and desired profit (cost-plus pricing)	Total cost per unit plus desired profit equals target selling price	Does company make its desired profit? If not, does the profit shortfall result from less volume?

Before You Go On...

REVIEW IT

1. What is a target cost, and how does management use it?
2. What is the general formula for determining the target selling price with cost-plus pricing?
3. How is the per unit return on investment determined?

DO IT

Air Corporation produces air purifiers. The following per unit cost information is available: direct materials $16; direct labor $18; variable manufacturing overhead $11; fixed manufacturing overhead $10; variable selling and administrative expenses $6; and fixed selling and administrative expenses $10. Using a 45% markup percentage on total per unit cost, compute the target selling price.

Action Plan

- Calculate the total cost per unit.
- Multiply the total cost per unit by the markup percentage, then add this amount to the total cost per unit to determine the target selling price.

Solution

Direct materials	$16
Direct labor	18
Variable manufacturing overhead	11
Fixed manufacturing overhead	10
Variable selling and administrative expenses	6
Fixed selling and administrative expenses	10
Total unit cost	$71

$$\text{Total unit cost} + \left(\text{Total unit cost} \times \text{Markup percentage}\right) = \text{Target selling price}$$

$$\$71 + (\$71 \times 45\%) = \$102.95$$

Related exercise material: *BE8-2, BE8-3, BE8-4, BE8-5, E8-3, E8-4, E8-5, E8-6, and E8-7.*

The Navigator

TIME-AND-MATERIAL PRICING

STUDY OBJECTIVE 3

Use time-and-material pricing to determine the cost of services provided.

Another variation on cost-plus pricing is called **time-and-material pricing**. Under this approach, the company sets two pricing rates—one for the **labor** used on a job and another for the **material**. The labor rate includes direct labor time and other employee costs. The material charge is based on the cost of direct parts and materials used and a **material loading charge** for related overhead costs. Time-and-material pricing is widely used in service industries, especially professional firms such as public accounting, law, engineering, and consulting firms, as well as construction companies, repair shops, and printers.

To illustrate a time-and-material pricing situation, assume the following data for Lake Holiday Marina, a boat and motor repair shop.

Illustration 8-11
Total annual budgeted time and material costs

LAKE HOLIDAY MARINA
Budgeted Costs for the Year 2008

	Time Charges	Material Loading Charges*
Mechanics' wages and benefits	$103,500	–
Parts manager's salary and benefits	–	$11,500
Office employee's salary and benefits	20,700	2,300
Other overhead (supplies, depreciation, property taxes, advertising, utilities)	26,800	14,400
Total budgeted costs	$151,000	$28,200

*The material loading charges exclude the invoice cost of the materials.

Using time-and-material pricing involves three steps: (1) calculate the per hour labor charge, (2) calculate the charge for obtaining and holding materials, and (3) calculate the charges for a particular job.

Step 1: Calculate the Labor Charge. The first step for time-and-material pricing is to determine a charge for labor time. The charge for labor time is expressed as a rate per hour of labor. This rate includes: (1) the direct labor cost of the employee, including hourly rate or salary and fringe benefits; (2) selling, administrative, and similar overhead costs; and (3) an allowance for a desired profit or ROI per hour of employee time. In some industries, such as auto, boat, and farm equipment repair shops, a company charges the same hourly labor rate regardless of which employee performs the work. In other industries, a company charges the rate according to classification or level of the employee. A public accounting firm, for example, would charge the services of an assistant, senior, manager, or partner at different rates; a law firm would charge different rates for the work of a paralegal, associate, or partner.

Illustration 8-12 shows computation of the hourly charges for Lake Holiday Marina during 2008. The marina budgets 5,000 hours of repair time in 2008, and it desires a profit margin of $8 per hour of labor.

Illustration 8-12
Computation of hourly time-charge rate

Lake Holiday Marina.xls

File Edit View Insert Format Tools Data Window Help

	A	B	C	D	E	F
1	**Per Hour**	**Total Cost**	÷	**Total Hours**	=	**Per Hour Charge**
2	Hourly labor rate for repairs					
3	Mechanics' wages and benefits	$103,500	÷	5,000	=	$20.70
4	Overhead costs					
5	Office employee's salary and benefits	20,700	÷	5,000	=	4.14
6	Other overhead	26,800	÷	5,000	=	5.36
7	Total hourly cost	$151,000	÷	5,000	=	30.20
8	Profit margin					8.00
9	Rate charged per hour of labor					**$38.20**
10						

The marina multiplies this rate of $38.20 by the number of hours of labor used on any particular job to determine the labor charge for that job.

Step 2: Calculate the Material Loading Charge. The charge for materials typically includes the invoice price of any materials used on the job plus a material loading charge. The **material loading charge** covers the costs of purchasing, receiving, handling, and storing materials, plus any desired profit margin on the materials themselves. The material loading charge is expressed as a **percentage** of the total estimated costs of parts and materials for the year. To determine this percentage, the company does the following: (1) It estimates its total annual costs for purchasing, receiving, handling, and storing materials. (2) It divides this amount by the total estimated cost of parts and materials. (3) It adds a desired profit margin on the materials themselves.

Illustration 8-13 shows computation of the material loading charge used by Lake Holiday Marina during 2008. The marina estimates that the total invoice cost

Illustration 8-13
Computation of material loading charge

Lake Holiday Marina.xls

File Edit View Insert Format Tools Data Window Help

	A	B	C	D	E	F
1		**Material Loading Charges**	÷	**Total Invoice Cost, Parts and Materials**	=	**Material Loading Percentage**
2	Overhead costs					
3	Parts manager's salary and benefits	$11,500				
4	Office employee's salary	2,300				
5		13,800	÷	$120,000	=	11.50%
6						
7	Other overhead	14,400	÷	120,000	=	12.00%
8		$28,200	÷	120,000	=	23.50%
9	Profit margin					20.00%
10	Material loading percentage					**43.50%**
11						

of parts and materials used in 2008 will be $120,000. The marina desires a 20% profit margin on the invoice cost of parts and materials.

The marina's material loading charge on any particular job is 43.50% multiplied by the cost of materials used on the job. For example, if the marina used $100 of parts, the additional material loading charge would be $43.50.

Step 3: Calculate Charges for a Particular Job. The charges for any particular job are the sum of (1) the labor charge, (2) the charge for the materials, and (3) the material loading charge. For example, suppose that Lake Holiday Marina prepares a price quotation to estimate the cost to refurbish a used 28-foot pontoon boat. Lake Holiday Marina estimates the job will require 50 hours of labor and $3,600 in parts and materials. Illustration 8-14 shows the marina's price quotation.

LAKE HOLIDAY MARINA
Time-and-Material Price Quotation

Job: Marianne Perino, repair of 28-foot pontoon boat		
Labor charges: 50 hours @ $38.20		$1,910
Material charges		
Cost of parts and materials	$3,600	
Material loading charge (43.5% × $3,600)	1,566	5,166
Total price of labor and material		$7,076

Illustration 8-14
Price quotation for time and material

Included in the $7,076 price quotation for the boat repair and refurbishment are charges for labor costs, overhead costs, materials costs, materials handling and storage costs, and a profit margin on both labor and parts. Lake Holiday Marina used labor hours as a basis for computing the time rate. Other companies, such as machine shops, plastic molding shops, and printers, might use machine hours.

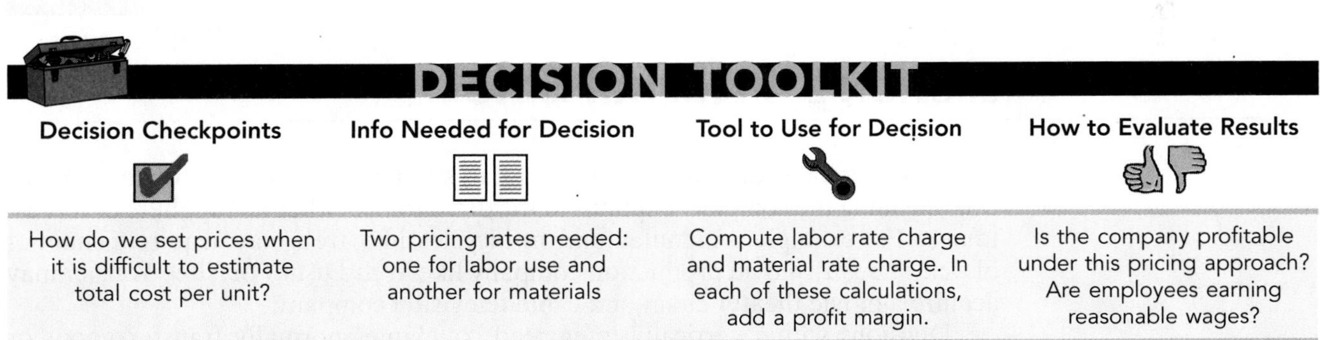
DECISION TOOLKIT

Decision Checkpoints	Info Needed for Decision	Tool to Use for Decision	How to Evaluate Results
How do we set prices when it is difficult to estimate total cost per unit?	Two pricing rates needed: one for labor use and another for materials	Compute labor rate charge and material rate charge. In each of these calculations, add a profit margin.	Is the company profitable under this pricing approach? Are employees earning reasonable wages?

Before You Go On...

REVIEW IT

1. What is time-and-material pricing? Where is it often used?
2. What is a material loading charge?

DO IT

Presented below are data for Harmon Electrical Repair Shop for next year.

Repair-technicians' wages	$130,000
Fringe benefits	30,000
Overhead	20,000

The desired profit margin per labor hour is $10. The material loading charge is 40% of invoice cost. Harman estimates that 8,000 labor hours will be worked next year. If Harmon repairs a TV that takes 4 hours to repair and uses parts of $50, compute the bill for this job.

Action Plan

- Calculate the labor charge.
- Calculate the material loading charge.
- Compute the bill for specific repair.

Solution

	Total Cost	÷	Total Hours	=	Per Hour Charge
Repair-technician's wages	$130,000	÷	8,000	=	$16.25
Fringe benefits	30,000	÷	8,000	=	3.75
Overhead	20,000	÷	8,000	=	2.50
	$180,000	÷	8,000	=	22.50
Profit margin					10.00
Rate charged per hour of labor					$32.50

Materials cost	$50
Materials loading charge ($50 × 40%)	20
Total materials cost	$70
Cost of TV repair	
Labor costs ($32.50 × 4)	$130
Materials cost	70
Total repair cost	$200

Related exercise material: *BE8-6, E8-8, E8-9, and E8-10.*

SECTION 2 Internal Sales

In today's global economy, growth is vital to survival. Frequently growth is "vertical," meaning the company expands in the direction of either its suppliers or its customers. For example, a manufacturer of bicycles, like Trek, may acquire a chain of bicycle shops. A movie production company like Walt Disney or Time Warner may acquire a movie theater chain or a cable television company.

Divisions within vertically integrated companies normally transfer goods or services to other divisions within the same company, as well as make sales to customers outside the company. When companies transfer goods internally, the price used to record the transfer between the two divisions is the **transfer price.** Illustration 8-15 (next page) highlights these transactions for Aerobic Bicycle Company. Aerobic Bicycle has a Bicycle Assembly Division and a Bicycle Component Division.

The pricing issues presented by transfer pricing are similar to those related to outside pricing issues. The objective is to maximize the return to the whole company. In addition, in the transfer-pricing situation, it is important that divisional performance not decline because of internal transfers. As a result, setting a transfer price is complicated because of competing interests among divisions within the company. For example, setting the transfer price high will benefit the Bicycle Component Division (the selling division), but will hurt the Bicycle Assembly Division (the purchasing division).

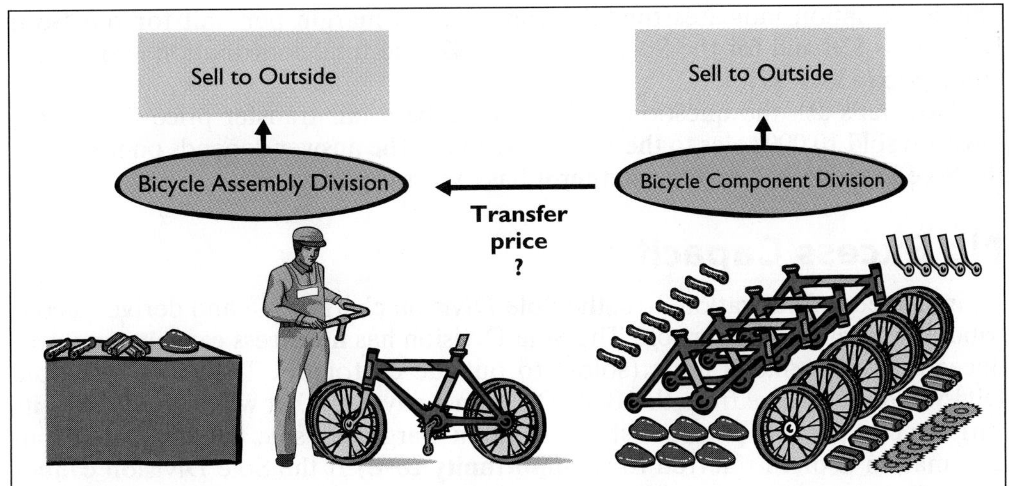

Illustration 8-15
Transfer-pricing example

There are three possible approaches for determining a transfer price:

1. Negotiated transfer prices.
2. Cost-based transfer prices.
3. Market-based transfer prices.

Conceptually, a negotiated transfer price should work best, but due to practical considerations, companies often use the other two methods.

NEGOTIATED TRANSFER PRICES

STUDY OBJECTIVE 4

Determine a transfer price using the negotiated, cost-based, and market-based approaches.

The **negotiated transfer price** is determined through agreement of division managers. To illustrate negotiated transfer pricing, we will examine Alberta Company. Until recently Alberta focused exclusively on making rubber soles for work boots and hiking boots. It sold these rubber soles to boot manufacturers. However, last year the company decided to take advantage of its strong reputation by expanding into the business of making hiking boots. As a consequence of this expansion, the company is now structured as two independent divisions, the Boot Division and the Sole Division. The company compensates the manager of each division based on achievement of profitability targets for his or her division.

The Sole Division continues to make rubber soles for both hiking boots and work boots and sells these soles to other boot manufacturers. The Boot Division manufactures leather uppers for hiking boots and attaches these uppers to rubber soles. During its first year the Boot Division purchased its rubber soles from *outside suppliers* so as not to disrupt the operations of the Sole Division. However, top management now wants the Sole Division to provide at least some of the soles used by the Boot Division. Illustration 8-16 shows the computation of the contribution margin per unit for each division when the Boot Division purchases soles from an outside supplier.

Boot Division		**Sole Division**	
Selling price of hiking boots	$90	Selling price of sole	$18
Variable cost of manufacturing boot (not including sole)	35	Variable cost per sole	11
Cost of sole purchased from outside suppliers	17		
Contribution margin per unit	**$38**	**Contribution margin per unit**	**$ 7**
Total contribution margin per unit		$45 ($38 + $7)	

Illustration 8-16
Computation of contribution margin for two divisions, when Boot Division purchases soles from an outside supplier

This information indicates that the contribution margin per unit for the Boot Division is $38 and for the Sole Division is $7. The total contribution margin per unit is $45 ($38 + $7).

Now let's ask the question, "What would be a fair transfer price if the Sole Division sold 10,000 soles to the Boot Division?" The answer depends on how busy the Sole Division is—that is, whether it has excess capacity.

No Excess Capacity

As indicated in Illustration 8-16, the Sole Division charges $18 and derives a contribution margin of $7 per sole. The Sole Division has **no excess capacity** and produces and sells 80,000 units (soles) to outside customers. Therefore, the Sole Division must receive from the Boot Division a payment that will at least cover its variable cost per sole **plus** its lost contribution margin per sole. (This lost contribution margin is often referred to as **opportunity cost**.) If the Sole Division cannot cover that amount—called the **minimum transfer price**—it should not sell its soles to the Boot Division. The minimum transfer price that would be acceptable to the Sole Division is $18, as shown below.

Illustration 8-17
Minimum transfer price—no excess capacity

Variable Cost	+	Opportunity Cost	=	Minimum Transfer Price
$11	+	$7	=	$18

From the perspective of the Boot Division (the buyer), the most it will pay is what the sole would cost from an outside supplier. In this case, therefore, the Boot Division would pay no more than $17. As shown in Illustration 8-18, an acceptable transfer price is not available in this situation.

Illustration 8-18
Transfer price negotiations—no deal

Excess Capacity

What happens if the Sole Division **has excess capacity?** For example, assume the Sole Division can produce 80,000 soles but can sell only 70,000 soles in the open market. As a result, it has available capacity of 10,000 units. In this situation, the Sole Division does not lose its contribution margin of $7 per unit and, therefore, the minimum price it would now accept is $11, as shown below.

Illustration 8-19
Minimum transfer price formula—excess capacity

Variable Cost	+	Opportunity Cost	=	Minimum Transfer Price
$11	+	$0	=	$11

In this case, the Boot Division and the Sole Division should negotiate a transfer price within the range of $11 to $17, as shown in Illustration 8-20.

Illustration 8-20
Transfer pricing negotiations—deal

Given excess capacity, Alberta Company will increase its overall net income if the Boot Division purchases the 10,000 soles internally. This is true as long as the Sole Division's variable cost is less than the outside price of $17. The Sole Division will receive a positive contribution margin from any transfer price above its variable cost of $11. The Boot Division will benefit from any price below $17. At any transfer price above $17 the Boot Division will go to an outside supplier, a solution that would be undesirable to both divisions, as well as to the company as a whole.

Variable Costs

In the minimum transfer price formula, **variable cost is defined as the variable cost of units sold *internally***. In some instances the variable cost of units sold internally will differ from the variable cost of units sold externally. For example, companies often reduce variable selling expenses when units are sold internally. In this case, the variable cost of units sold internally will be lower than that of units sold externally.

Alternatively, the variable cost of units sold internally could be higher if the internal division requests a special order that requires more expensive materials or additional labor. For example, assume that the Boot Division would like to make 5,000 new high-margin, heavy-duty boots. The sole required for this boot will be made of a denser rubber with an intricate lug design. Alberta Company is not aware of any supplier that currently makes such a sole, nor does it feel that any other supplier can meet the quality expectations. As a consequence, there is no available market price to use as the transfer price.

We can, however, still employ the formula for the minimum transfer price to assist in arriving at a reasonable solution. After evaluating the special sole, the Sole Division determines that its variable cost would be $19 per sole. The Sole Division is at full capacity. The Sole Division's opportunity cost at full capacity is the $7 ($18 − $11) per sole that it earns producing the standard sole and selling it to an outside customer. Therefore, the minimum transfer price that the Sole Division would be willing to accept for the special-order sole would be:

Illustration 8-21
Minimum transfer price formula—special order

Variable Cost	+	Opportunity Cost	=	Minimum Transfer Price
$19	+	$7	=	$26

The transfer price of $26 provides the Sole Division with enough revenue to cover its increased variable cost and its opportunity cost (contribution margin on its standard sole).

Summary of Negotiated Transfer Pricing

Under negotiated transfer pricing, the selling division establishes a minimum transfer price, and the purchasing division establishes a maximum transfer price. This system provides a sound basis for establishing a transfer price because both divisions are better off if the proper decision rules are used. However, companies often do not use negotiated transfer pricing because:

- Market price information is sometimes not easily obtainable.
- A lack of trust between the two negotiating divisions may lead to a breakdown in the negotiations.
- Negotiations often lead to different pricing strategies from division to division which is cumbersome and sometimes costly to implement.

Many companies, therefore, often use simple systems based on cost or market information to develop transfer prices.

COST-BASED TRANSFER PRICES

One method of determining transfer prices is to base the transfer price on the costs incurred by the division producing the goods or services. If the company uses a **cost-based transfer price**, the transfer price may be based on variable costs alone, or on variable costs plus fixed costs. The selling division may add a markup.

Under a cost-based approach, divisions sometimes use improper transfer prices. This leads to a loss of profitability for the company and unfair evaluations of division performance. To illustrate, assume that Alberta Company requires the division to use a transfer price based on the variable cost of the sole. With no excess capacity, the contribution margins per unit for the two divisions are:

Illustration 8-22
Cost-based transfer price—10,000 units

Boot Division		Sole Division	
Selling price of hiking boots	$90	Selling price of sole	$11
Variable cost of manufacturing boot (not including sole)	35	Variable cost per sole	11
Cost of sole purchased from sole division	11	**Contribution margin per unit**	**$ 0**
Contribution margin per unit	**$44**		
Total contribution margin per unit		**$44** ($44 + $0)	

This cost-based transfer system is a bad deal for the Sole Division, as it reports no profit on the transfer of 10,000 soles to the Boot Division. If the Sole Division could sell these soles to an outside customer, it would make $70,000 [10,000 × ($18 − $11)]. The Boot Division, on the other hand, is delighted: its contribution margin per unit increases from $38 to $44, or $6 per boot. The Sole Division lost a contribution margin per unit of $7 (Illustration 8-16, page 335), and the Boot Division experienced only a $6 increase in its contribution margin per unit. Overall, Alberta Company loses $10,000 [10,000 boots × ($7 − $6)]. Illustration 8-23 (page 339) illustrates this deficiency.

The overall results change if the Sole Division **has excess capacity**. In this case, the Sole Division continues to report a zero profit on these 10,000 units but does not lose the $7 per unit of contribution margin (because it had excess capacity). The Boot Division gains $6. So overall, the company is better off by $60,000 (10,000 × $6). However, with a cost-based system, the Sole Division continues to report a zero profit on these 10,000 units.

We can see that a cost-based system does not reflect the division's true profitability. What's more, it does not even provide adequate incentive for the Sole Division to control costs. The division's costs are simply passed on to the next division.

Illustration 8-23 Cost-based transfer price results—no excess capacity

Notwithstanding these disadvantages, the cost system is simple to understand and easy to use because the information is already available in the accounting system. In addition, market information is sometimes not available, so the only alternative is some type of cost-based system. As a result, it is the most common method used by companies to establish transfer prices.

MARKET-BASED TRANSFER PRICES

The **market-based transfer price** is based on existing market prices of competing goods or services. A market-based system is often considered the best approach because it is objective and generally provides the proper economic incentives. For example, if the Sole Division can charge the market price, it is indifferent as to whether soles are sold to outside customers or internally to the Boot Division—it does not lose any contribution margin. Similarly, the Boot Division pays a price for the soles that is at or reasonably close to market.

When the Sole Division has no excess capacity, the market-based system works reasonably well. The Sole Division receives market price, and the Boot Division pays market price.

If the Sole Division has excess capacity, however, the market-based system can lead to actions that are not in the best interest of the company. For example, the minimum transfer price that the Sole Division should receive is its variable cost plus opportunity cost. Given that the Sole Division has excess capacity, its opportunity cost is zero. However, under the market-based system, the Sole Division transfers the goods at the market price of $18, for a contribution margin per unit of $7. The Boot Division manager then has to accept the $18 sole price. The Boot Division must recognize, however, that this price is not the cost of the sole, given that the Sole Division had excess capacity. As a result, the Boot Division may overprice its boots in the market if it uses the market price of the sole plus a markup in setting the price of the boot. This action can lead to losses for Alberta overall.

As indicated earlier, in many cases, there simply is not a well-defined market for the good or service being transferred. As a result, a reasonable market value cannot be developed, and therefore companies resort to a cost-based system.

EFFECT OF OUTSOURCING ON TRANSFER PRICING

An increasing number of companies rely on **outsourcing**. Outsourcing involves contracting with an external party to provide a good or service, rather than performing the work internally. Some companies have taken outsourcing to the extreme by outsourcing all of their production. These so-called **virtual companies** have well-established brand names, though they do not manufacture any of their own products. Companies use incremental analysis (Chapter 7) to determine whether outsourcing is profitable. As companies increasingly rely on outsourcing, fewer components are transferred internally between divisions reducing the need for transfer prices.

TRANSFERS BETWEEN DIVISIONS IN DIFFERENT COUNTRIES

STUDY OBJECTIVE 5

Explain issues involved in transferring goods between divisions in different countries.

As more companies "globalize" their operations, an increasing number of transfers are between divisions that are located in different countries. For example, one estimate suggests that 60% of trade between countries is simply transfers between divisions. Differences in tax rates across countries can complicate the determination of the appropriate transfer price.

Companies must pay income tax in the country where they generate the income. In order to maximize income and minimize income tax, many companies prefer to report more income in countries with low tax rates, and less income in countries with high tax rates. They accomplish this by adjusting the transfer prices they use on internal transfers between divisions located in different countries. They allocate more contribution margin to the division in the low-tax-rate country, and allocate less to the division in the high-tax-rate country.

To illustrate, suppose that Alberta's Boot Division is located in a country with a corporate tax rate of 10%, and the Sole Division is located in a country with a tax rate of 30%. Illustration 8-24 demonstrates the after-tax contribution margin to the company as a whole assuming first, that the company transfers the soles at a transfer price of $18, and second, that it transfers them at a transfer price of $11.

Illustration 8-24
After-tax contribution margin per unit under alternative transfer prices

At $18 Transfer Price

Boot Division		Sole Division	
Selling price of hiking boots	$90.00	Selling price of sole	$18.00
Variable cost of manufacturing boot (not including sole)	35.00	Variable cost per sole	11.00
Cost of sole purchased internally	18.00		
Before-tax contribution margin	37.00	Before-tax contribution margin	7.00
Tax at 10%	3.70	Tax at 30%	2.10
After-tax contribution margin	$33.30	After-tax contribution margin	$ 4.90

Before-tax total contribution margin per unit to company = $37 + $7 = **$44**
After-tax total contribution margin per unit to company = $33.30 + $4.90 = **$38.20**

At $11 Transfer Price

Boot Division		Sole Division	
Selling price of hiking boots	$90.00	Selling price of sole	$11.00
Variable cost of manufacturing boot (not including sole)	35.00	Variable cost per sole	11.00
Cost of sole purchased internally	11.00		
Before-tax contribution margin	44.00	Before-tax contribution margin	0.00
Tax at 10%	4.40	Tax at 30%	0.00
After-tax contribution margin	$39.60	After-tax contribution margin	$ 0.00

Before-tax total contribution margin per unit to company = $44 + $0 = **$44**
After-tax total contribution margin per unit to company = $39.60 + $0 = **$39.60**

Note that the *before-tax* total contribution margin to Alberta Company is $44 regardless of whether the transfer price is $18 or $11. However, the *after-tax* total contribution margin to Alberta Company is $38.20 using the $18 transfer price, and

$39.60 using the $11 transfer price. The reason: When Alberta uses the $11 transfer price, more of the contribution margin is attributed to the division that is in the country with the lower tax rate.

As this analysis shows, Alberta Company would be better off using the $11 transfer price. However, this presents some concerns. First, the Sole Division manager won't be happy with an $11 transfer price. This price may lead to unfair evaluations of the Sole Division's manager. Second, the company must ask whether it is legal and ethical to use an $11 transfer price when the market price clearly is higher than that.

Additional consideration of international transfer pricing is presented in advanced accounting texts.

ETHICS INSIGHT

Transferring Profits and Reducing Taxes

International transfer pricing issues create a huge headache for the Internal Revenue Service. Some estimates suggest that the United States loses over $25 billion in underpaid taxes due to transfer price abuses. Occasionally violators are caught. Toyota, for example, reportedly paid a $1 billion dollar settlement. But enforcement is complicated and time-consuming, and many foreign firms are reluctant to give access to their records.

U.S. companies have also been accused of transfer pricing abuse. It has been noted that at one time U.S. giant Westinghouse booked over 25% of its profit in the tiny island of Puerto Rico. At the time, the corporate tax rate there was zero. The rules require that the transfer price be based on the current market price that a nonrelated party would pay for the goods. But often this current market price is difficult to determine.

? What are the implications for other taxpayers if companies reduce their taxes by using improper transfer prices to shift profits to lower-tax countries?

DECISION TOOLKIT

Decision Checkpoints 	Info Needed for Decision 	Tool to Use for Decision 	How to Evaluate Results 
What price should be charged for transfer of goods between divisions of a company?	Variable costs, opportunity costs, market prices	Variable cost plus opportunity cost provides minimum transfer price for seller.	If income of division provides fair evaluation of managers, then transfer price is useful. Also, income of the company overall should not be reduced due to the transfer pricing approach.

Before You Go On...

REVIEW IT

1. What are the objectives of transfer pricing?
2. What are the three approaches to transfer pricing? What are the advantages and disadvantages of each?
3. How do some companies reduce their tax payments through their choice of transfer price?

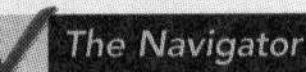

Be sure to read **ALL ABOUT YOU: *Is the Price Right?*** on page 342 for information on how topics in this chapter apply to you.

all about YOU

Is the Price Right?

The right price can make a big difference to companies. For example, at **Coca-Cola** a 4% increase in the price received for its products would increase net income significantly.

As indicated in the chapter, a company has to choose a price for its products that will cover its variable costs and make some contribution to fixed overhead in the short run. In the long run, the company must price its products to cover all costs. But pricing products to achieve these objectives is complex, given the nature of consumer behavior.

Some Facts

* Prices come in all forms such as tuition for school, fees for medical care, premiums for insurance, user fees for tolls. In some cases we can influence the price by our behavior (e.g., buying airplane tickets online rather than through a travel agent); in other cases, it is more difficult to influence price (e.g., the price of cable TV).
* In one survey, marketing managers rated pricing as their biggest problem. Other issues such as new competition, product differentiation, and selling expenses were not as stressful. Reasons for the stress are the importance of getting the price right to ensure overall profitability and the difficulty of getting it right.
* Do you buy products based on expected savings from rebates? If so, do you actually file for the rebate? Some 40% of rebates do not get redeemed. Many people do not bother to fill out the form and process the receipts. And some companies do not make it easy: They make up complex rules, demand original copies of bills, set short expiration periods, and delay sending checks. In some cases, the companies send the check with another company's name on the envelope in hope you will not recognize it and tear it up.
* Retailers use price-optimization software to assess difficult situations. For example: In a store with a variety of paintbrushes, the best seller was the cheapest one, at $1. But after inputting many variables, the store stopped selling the $1 brushes, which enabled it to sell more high-priced (and more profitable) paintbrushes. Why? The key factor in whether a customer bought a paintbrush was whether he or she was buying paint, not the price of the brush.

  Some useful sites for pricing information are *www.consumerreports.org, www.pricescan.com, www.consumerworld.org, www.consumer.gov,* and *www.ftc.gov.*

About the Numbers

At your local grocery store, you may see items that are identified as fair-traded. Fair-traded means that the retailer paid a minimum price to the producer to ensure a fair profit for the producer. Most individuals believe that by paying the fair-trade price, you are helping some struggling farmer, often in a less-developed country.

To better understand how pricing works in a fair-trade situation, here is an example of how the price is set for one pound of fair-trade coffee computed by wholesaler roaster **Dean's Beans**.

$1.41 Price paid to grower, includes 5-cent fair-trade premium
0.39 Administrative costs and shipping
0.36 Shrinkage during roasting
2.50 Operating and maintenance costs
0.14 Packaging and misc. cost
$4.80 Wholesale roaster cost

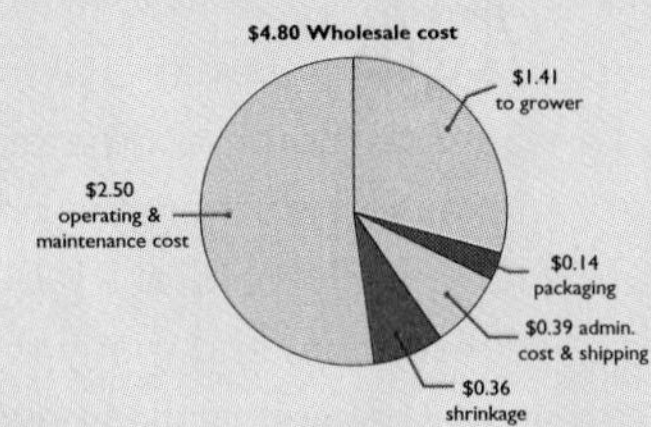

The price at which Dean's sells to the grocery store is $5.00, for a profit of $0.20 to the wholesaler. The retailer sells the pound of coffee to you for $8.49, for a profit of $3.49 profit before expenses. So next time you are considering a fair-traded product, you might ask, How much does that poor struggling farmer receive in relation to the markup that the retailer receives when the product is fair-traded?

Source: Steve Stecklow and Erin White, "What Price Virtue? At Some Retailers, 'Fair Trade' Carries a Very High Cost: Stores Charge Big Markups on Goods Intended to Help Farmers in Poor Countries; Bananas at $2.74 a Bunch," *Wall Street Journal,* June 8, 2004, p. Al.

What Do You Think?

One issue that always raises many questions is the pricing of medical drugs. For example, we often hear about the fact that certain drugs sold by U.S. companies cost much less overseas than in the United States. And there are certain drugs in the United States that seem extremely expensive. For example, Avantis is a cancer-reducing drug that costs patients $55,000 a year. Congress continues to study the issue of drug pricing. Do you think that high pricing of pharmaceuticals is fair?

YES: Drug companies have to spend substantial amounts of money to create new therapies. In addition to the heavy research and development costs involved, the lead time from discovery to actual use of new drugs on patients can exceed 10 years. In short, the drug companies must recover these costs by charging high prices.

NO: The drug companies are profitable. How can they expect individuals to pay very high prices for some of these live-saving drugs? Furthermore, how can a drug sold in the United States often sell for much less in another part of the world?

Sources: Brian Bergstein, "It's Buyer Beware in Stores," Wisconsin State Journal, April 28, 2007, p. A9; Marilyn Chase, "How Genentech Wins At Blockbuster Drugs," Wall Street Journal, June 6, 2007, p. B1; Brian Grow, "The Great Rebate Runaround,' Business Week, December 5, 2005.

The authors' comments on this situation appear on page 369.

Using the Decision Toolkit

Cedarburg Lumber specializes in building "high-end" playhouses for kids. It builds the components in its factory, and then ships the parts to the customer's home. It has contracted with carpenters across the country to do the final assembly. Each year the company introduces a new model. This year's model looks like a miniature castle, complete with spires and drawbridge. The accounting department provided the following cost estimates for this new product for a budgeted volume of 1,000 units.

	Per Unit	Total
Direct materials	$ 840	
Direct labor	$1,600	
Variable manufacturing overhead	$ 400	
Fixed manufacturing overhead		$540,000
Variable selling and administrative expenses	$ 510	
Fixed selling and administrative expenses		$320,000

Cedarburg Lumber uses cost-plus pricing to set its selling price. Management also directs that the target price be set to provide a 25% return on investment (ROI) on invested assets of $4,200,000.

Instructions

(a) Compute the markup percentage and target selling price on this new playhouse.

(b) Assuming that the volume is 1,500 units instead of 1,000 units, compute the markup percentage and target selling price that will allow Cedarburg Lumber to earn its desired ROI of 25%.

Solution

(a)

Variable cost per unit

	Per Unit
Direct materials	$ 840
Direct labor	1,600
Variable manufacturing overhead	400
Variable selling and administrative expenses	510
Variable cost per unit	$3,350

Fixed cost per unit

	Total Costs	÷	Budgeted Volume	=	Cost Per Unit
Fixed manufacturing overhead	$540,000	÷	1,000	=	$540
Fixed selling and administrative expenses	320,000	÷	1,000	=	320
Fixed cost per unit	$860,000				$860

Computation of selling price (1,000 units)

Variable cost per unit	$3,350
Fixed cost per unit	860
Total unit cost	4,210
Desired ROI per unit*	1,050
Selling price	$5,260

*($4,200,000 × .25) ÷ 1,000

The markup percentage is:

$$\frac{\text{Desired ROI per unit}}{\text{Total unit cost}} = \frac{\$1{,}050}{\$4{,}210} = 24.9\%$$

(b) If the company produces 1,500 units, its selling price and markup percentage would be:

Computation of selling price (1,500 units)

Variable cost per unit	$3,350
Fixed cost per unit ($860,000 ÷ 1,500)	573
Total unit cost	3,923
Desired ROI per unit*	700
Selling price	$4,623

*($4,200,000 × .25) ÷ 1,500

The markup percentage would be:

$$\frac{\text{Desired ROI per unit}}{\text{Total unit cost}} = \frac{\$700}{\$3{,}923} = 17.8\%$$

SUMMARY OF STUDY OBJECTIVES

1 **Compute a target cost when the market determines a product price.** To compute a target cost, the company determines its target selling price. Once the target selling price is set, it determines its target cost by setting a desired profit. The difference between the target price and desired profit is the target cost of the product.

2 **Compute a target selling price using cost-plus pricing.** Cost-plus pricing involves establishing a cost base and adding to this cost base a markup to determine a target selling price. The cost-plus pricing formula is expressed as follows: Target selling price = Cost + (Markup percentage × Cost).

3 **Use time-and-material pricing to determine the cost of services provided.** Under time-and-material pricing, two pricing rates are set—one for the labor used on a job and another for the material. The labor rate includes direct labor time and other employee costs. The material charge is based on the cost of direct parts and materials used and a material loading charge for related overhead costs.

4 **Determine a transfer price using the negotiated, cost-based, and market-based approaches.** The negotiated price is determined through agreement of division managers. Under a cost-based approach, the transfer price may be based on variable cost alone or on variable cost plus fixed costs. Companies may add a markup to these numbers. The cost-based approach often leads to poor performance evaluations and purchasing decisions. The advantage of the cost-based system is its simplicity. A market-based transfer price is based on existing competing market prices and services. A market-based system is often considered the best approach because it is objective and generally provides the proper economic incentives.

5 **Explain issues involved in transferring goods between divisions in different countries.** Companies must pay income tax in the country where they generate the income. In order to maximize income and minimize income tax, many companies prefer to report more income in countries with low tax rates, and less income in countries with high tax rates. This is accomplished by adjusting the transfer prices they use on internal transfers between divisions located in different countries.

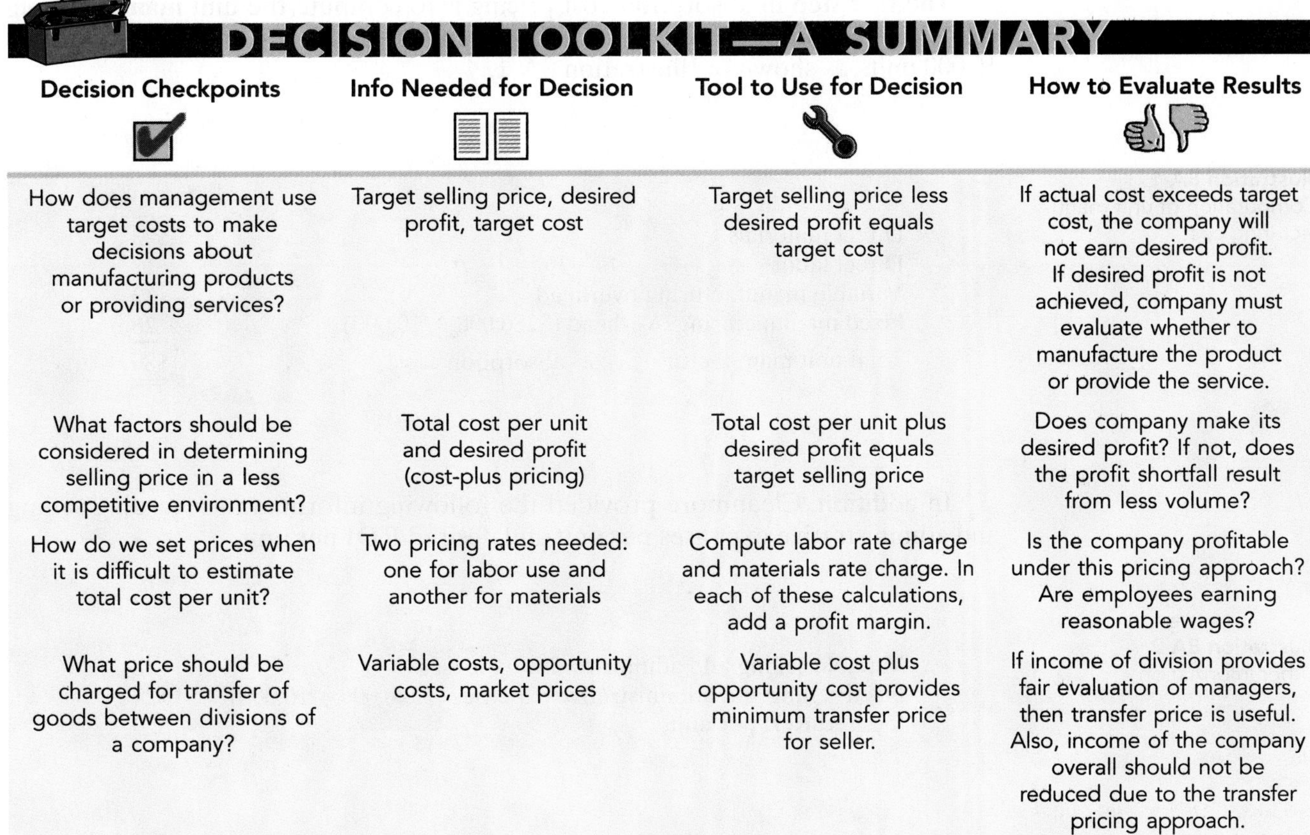

DECISION TOOLKIT—A SUMMARY

Decision Checkpoints	Info Needed for Decision	Tool to Use for Decision	How to Evaluate Results
How does management use target costs to make decisions about manufacturing products or providing services?	Target selling price, desired profit, target cost	Target selling price less desired profit equals target cost	If actual cost exceeds target cost, the company will not earn desired profit. If desired profit is not achieved, company must evaluate whether to manufacture the product or provide the service.
What factors should be considered in determining selling price in a less competitive environment?	Total cost per unit and desired profit (cost-plus pricing)	Total cost per unit plus desired profit equals target selling price	Does company make its desired profit? If not, does the profit shortfall result from less volume?
How do we set prices when it is difficult to estimate total cost per unit?	Two pricing rates needed: one for labor use and another for materials	Compute labor rate charge and materials rate charge. In each of these calculations, add a profit margin.	Is the company profitable under this pricing approach? Are employees earning reasonable wages?
What price should be charged for transfer of goods between divisions of a company?	Variable costs, opportunity costs, market prices	Variable cost plus opportunity cost provides minimum transfer price for seller.	If income of division provides fair evaluation of managers, then transfer price is useful. Also, income of the company overall should not be reduced due to the transfer pricing approach.

APPENDIX Other Cost Approaches to Pricing

STUDY OBJECTIVE 6

Determine prices using absorption-cost pricing and variable-cost pricing.

In determining the target price for Cleanmore's shop vacuum in the chapter, we calculated the cost base **by including all costs incurred**. This approach is referred to as **full-cost pricing**. Using total cost as the basis of the markup makes sense conceptually because in the long run the price must cover all costs and provide a reasonable profit. However, total cost is difficult to determine in practice. This is because period costs (selling and administrative expenses) are difficult to trace to a specific product. Activity-based costing can be used to overcome this difficulty to some extent.

In practice, companies use two other cost approaches: (1) absorption-cost pricing, and (2) variable-cost pricing. Absorption-cost pricing is more popular than variable-cost pricing.[1] We will illustrate both of them, though, because both have merit.

ABSORPTION-COST PRICING

Absorption-cost pricing is consistent with generally accepted accounting principles (GAAP). The reason: It includes both variable and fixed manufacturing costs as product costs. **It excludes from this cost base both variable and fixed selling and administrative costs**. Thus, companies must somehow provide for selling and administrative costs plus the target ROI, and they do this through the markup.

[1]For a discussion of cost-plus pricing, see Eunsup Skim and Ephraim F. Sudit, "How Manufacturers Price Products," *Management Accounting* (February 1995), pp. 37–39; and V. Govindarajan and R. N. Anthony, "How Firms Use Cost Data in Pricing Decisions," *Management Accounting,* 65, no. 1, pp. 30–36.

The **first step** in absorption-cost pricing is to compute the unit **manufacturing cost**. For Cleanmore Products, Inc., this amounts to $80 per unit at a volume of 10,000 units, as shown in Illustration 8A-1.

Illustration 8A-1
Computation of unit manufacturing cost

	Per Unit
Direct materials	$23
Direct labor	17
Variable manufacturing overhead	12
Fixed manufacturing overhead ($280,000 ÷ 10,000)	28
Total unit manufacturing cost (absorption cost)	$80

In addition, Cleanmore provided the following information regarding selling and administrative expenses per unit and desired ROI per unit.

Illustration 8A-2
Other information

Variable selling and administrative expenses	$8
Fixed selling and administrative expenses ($240,000 ÷ 10,000)	$24
Desired ROI per unit	$20

The **second step** in absorption-cost pricing is to compute the markup percentage using the formula in Illustration 8A-3. Note that when companies use manufacturing cost per unit as the cost base to compute the markup percentage, the **percentage must cover the desired ROI and also the selling and administrative expenses**.

Illustration 8A-3
Markup percentage—absorption-cost pricing

Desired ROI Per Unit	+	Selling and Administrative Expenses Per Unit	=	Markup Percentage	×	Manufacturing Cost Per Unit
$20	+	$32	=	**MP**	×	$80

Solving we find:

$$MP = (\$20 + \$32) \div \$80 = 65\%$$

The **third** and final **step** is to set the target selling price. Using a markup percentage of 65% and absorption cost pricing, Cleanmore computes the target selling price as shown in Illustration 8A-4.

Illustration 8A-4
Computation of target price—absorption-cost pricing

Manufacturing Cost per Unit	+	(Markup Percentage	×	Manufacturing Cost Per Unit)	=	Target Selling Price
$80	+	(65%	×	$80)	=	$132

Using a target price of $132 will produce the desired 20% return on investment for Cleanmore Products on its 3-horsepower, wet/dry shop vacuum at a volume level of 10,000 units, as shown in Illustration 8A-5.

Illustration 8A-5
Proof of 20% ROI—absorption-cost pricing

CLEANMORE PRODUCTS, INC.
Budgeted Absorption-Cost Income Statement

Revenue (10,000 units × $132)	$1,320,000
Cost of goods sold (10,000 units × $80)	800,000
Gross profit	520,000
Selling and administrative expenses [10,000 units × ($8 + $24)]	320,000
Net income	$ 200,000

Budgeted ROI

$$\frac{\text{Net income}}{\text{Invested assets}} = \frac{\$200,000}{\$1,000,000} = \mathbf{20\%}$$

Markup Percentage

$$\frac{\text{Net income + Selling and administrative expenses}}{\text{Cost of goods sold}} = \frac{\$200,000 + \$320,000}{\$800,000} = \mathbf{65\%}$$

Because of the fixed-cost element, if Cleanmore sells more than 10,000 units, the ROI will be greater than 20%. If it sells fewer than 10,000 units, the ROI will be less than 20%. The markup percentage is also verified by adding $200,000 (the net income) and $320,000 (selling and administrative expenses) and then dividing by $800,000 (the cost of goods sold or the cost base).

Most companies that use cost-plus pricing use either absorption cost or full cost as the basis. The reasons for this tendency are as follows.

1. Absorption-cost information is most readily provided by a company's cost accounting system. Because absorption-cost data already exist in general ledger accounts, it is cost-effective to use the data for pricing.
2. Basing the cost-plus formula on only variable costs could encourage managers to set too low a price to boost sales. There is the fear that if managers use only variable costs, they will substitute variable costs for full costs, which can lead to suicidal price cutting.
3. Absorption-cost or full-cost pricing provides the most defensible base for justifying prices to all interested parties—managers, customers, and government.

VARIABLE-COST PRICING

Under **variable-cost pricing**, the cost base consists of all of the **variable costs** associated with a product, including variable selling and administrative costs. **Because fixed costs are not included in the base, the markup must provide for fixed costs (manufacturing, and selling and administrative) and the target ROI.** Variable-cost pricing is more useful for making short-run decisions because it considers variable cost and fixed cost behavior patterns separately.

The **first step** in variable-cost pricing is to compute the unit variable cost. For Cleanmore Products, Inc., this amounts to $60 per unit as shown in Illustration 8A-6.

Illustration 8A-6
Computation of unit variable cost

	Per Unit
Direct materials	$23
Direct labor	17
Variable manufacturing overhead	12
Variable selling and administrative expense	8
Total unit variable cost	$60

The **second step** in variable-cost pricing is to compute the markup percentage. Illustration 8A-7 shows the formula for the markup percentage. For Cleanmore, fixed costs include fixed manufacturing overhead of \$28 per unit (\$280,000 ÷ 10,000) and fixed selling and administrative expenses of \$24 per unit (\$240,000 ÷ 10,000).

Illustration 8A-7
Computation of markup percentage—variable-cost pricing

Desired ROI Per Unit	+	Fixed Costs Per Unit	=	Markup Percentage	×	Variable Cost Per Unit
$20	+	($28 + $24)	=	**MP**	×	$60

Solving, we find:

$$MP = \frac{\$20 + (\$28 + \$24)}{\$60} = 120\%$$

The **third step** is to set the target selling price. Using a markup percentage of 120% and the contribution approach, Cleanmore computes the selling price as shown in Illustration 8A-8.

Illustration 8A-8
Computation of target price—variable-cost pricing

Variable Cost Per Unit	+	(Markup Percentage	×	Variable Cost Per Unit)	=	Target Selling Price
$60	+	(120%	×	$60)	=	$132

Using a target price of \$132 will produce the desired 20% return on investment for Cleanmore Products on its 3-horse power, wet/dry shop vacuum at a volume level of 10,000 units, as shown in Illustration 8A-9.

Illustration 8A-9
Proof of 20% ROI—contribution approach

CLEANMORE PRODUCTS, INC.
Budgeted Variable-Cost Income Statement

Revenue (10,000 vacuums × $132)		$1,320,000
Variable costs (10,000 vacuums × $60)		600,000
Contribution margin		720,000
Fixed manufacturing overhead (10,000 vacuums × $28)	$280,000	
Fixed selling and administrative expenses (10,000 vacuums × $24)	240,000	520,000
Net income		**$ 200,000**

Budgeted ROI

$$\frac{\text{Net income}}{\text{Invested assets}} = \frac{\$200{,}000}{\$1{,}000{,}000} = \mathbf{20\%}$$

Markup Percentage

$$\frac{\text{Net income} + \text{Fixed costs}}{\text{Variable costs}} = \frac{\$200{,}000 + \$520{,}000}{\$600{,}000} = \mathbf{120\%}$$

Under any of the three pricing approaches we have looked at (full-cost, absorption-cost, and variable-cost), the desired ROI will be attained only if the budgeted sales volume for the period is attained. None of these approaches guarantees a profit or a desired ROI. Achieving a desired ROI is the result of many factors, some of which are beyond the company's control, such as market conditions, political and legal issues, customers' tastes, and competitive actions.

Because absorption-cost pricing includes allocated fixed costs, it does not make clear how the company's costs will change as volume changes. To avoid blurring the effects of cost behavior on net income, some managers therefore prefer variable-cost pricing. The specific reasons for using variable-cost pricing, even though the basic accounting data are less accessible, are as follows.

1. Variable-cost pricing, being based on variable cost, is more consistent with cost-volume-profit analysis used by managers to measure the profit implications of changes in price and volume.
2. Variable-cost pricing provides the type of data managers need for pricing special orders. It shows the incremental cost of accepting one more order.
3. Variable-cost pricing avoids arbitrary allocation of common fixed costs (such as executive salaries) to individual product lines.

SUMMARY OF STUDY OBJECTIVE FOR APPENDIX

6 **Determine prices using absorption-cost pricing and variable-cost pricing.** Absorption-cost pricing uses total manufacturing cost as the cost base and provides for selling and administrative costs plus the target ROI through the markup. The target selling price is computed as: Manufacturing cost per unit + (Markup percentage × Manufacturing cost per unit).

Variable-cost pricing uses all of the variable costs, including selling and administrative costs, as the cost base and provides for fixed costs and target ROI through the markup. The target selling price is computed as: Variable cost per unit + (Markup percentage × Variable cost per unit).

GLOSSARY

Absorption-cost pricing An approach to pricing that defines the cost base as the manufacturing cost; it excludes both variable and fixed selling and administrative costs. (p. 345)

Cost-based transfer price A transfer price that uses as its foundation the costs incurred by the division producing the goods. (p. 338)

Cost-plus pricing A process whereby a product's selling price is determined by adding a markup to a cost base. (p. 327)

Full-cost pricing An approach to pricing that defines the cost base as all costs incurred. (p. 329)

Market-based transfer price A transfer price that is based on existing market prices of competing products. (p. 339)

Markup The percentage applied to a product's cost to determine the product's selling price. (p. 327)

Material loading charge A charge added to cover the cost of purchasing, receiving, handling, and storing materials, plus any desired profit margin on the materials themselves. (p. 332)

Negotiated transfer price A transfer price that is determined by the agreement of the division managers. (p. 335)

Outsourcing Contracting with an external party to provide a good or service, rather than performing the work internally. (p. 339)

Target cost The cost that will provide the desired profit on a product when the seller does not have control over the product's price. (p. 326)

Target selling price The selling price that will provide the desired profit on a product when the seller has the ability to determine the product's price. (p. 327)

Time-and-material pricing An approach to cost-plus pricing in which the company uses two pricing rates, one for the labor used on a job and another for the material. (p. 331)

Transfer price The price used to record the transfer of goods between two divisions of a company. (p. 334)

Variable-cost pricing An approach to pricing that defines the cost base as all variable costs; it excludes both fixed manufacturing and fixed selling and administrative costs. (pp. 329, 347)

Demonstration Problem

Revco Electronics is a division of International Motors, an automobile manufacturer. Revco produces car radio/CD players. Revco sells its products to International Motors, as well as to other car manufacturers and electronics distributors. The following information is available regarding Revco's car radio/CD player.

Selling price of car radio/CD player to external customers	\$49
Variable cost per unit	\$28
Capacity	200,000 units

Instructions

Determine whether the goods should be transferred internally or purchased externally and what the appropriate transfer price should be under each of the following **independent** situations.

(a) Revco Electronics is operating at full capacity. There is a saving of \$4 per unit for variable cost if the car radio is made for internal sale. International Motors can purchase a comparable car radio from an outside supplier for \$47.

(b) Revco Electronics has sufficient existing capacity to meet the needs of International Motors. International Motors can purchase a comparable car radio from an outside supplier for \$47.

(c) International Motors wants to purchase a special-order car radio/CD player that also includes a tape deck. It needs 15,000 units. Revco Electronics has determined that the additional variable cost would be \$12 per unit. Revco Electronics has no spare capacity. It will have to forgo sales of 15,000 units to external parties in order to provide this special order.

action plan

✓ Determine whether company is at full capacity or not.

✓ Find the minimum transfer price, using formulas.

✓ Compare maximum price the buyer would pay to the minimum price for the seller.

✓ Determine if a deal can be made.

Solution

(a) Revco Electronics' opportunity cost (its lost contribution margin) would be \$21 (\$49 − \$28). Using the formula for minimum transfer price, we determine:

Minimum transfer price	=	Variable cost	+	Opportunity cost
\$45	=	(\$28 − \$4)	+	\$21

Since this minimum transfer price is less than the \$47 it would cost if International Motors purchases from an external party, internal transfer should take place. Revco Electronics and International Motors should negotiate a transfer price between \$45 and \$47.

(b) Since Revco Electronics has available capacity, its opportunity cost (its lost contribution margin) would be \$0. Using the formula for minimum transfer price, we determine the following.

Minimum transfer price	=	Variable cost	+	Opportunity cost
\$28	=	\$28	+	\$0

Since International Motors can purchase the unit for \$47 from an external party, the most it would be willing to pay would be \$47. It is in the best interest of the company as a whole, as well as the two divisions, for a transfer to take place. The two divisions must reach a negotiated transfer price between \$28 and \$47 that recognizes the costs and benefits to each party and is acceptable to both.

(c) Revco Electronics' opportunity cost (its lost contribution margin per unit) would be \$21 (\$49 − \$28). Its variable cost would be \$40 (\$28 + \$12). Using the formula for minimum transfer price, we determine the following.

Minimum transfer price	=	Variable cost	+	Opportunity cost
\$61	=	\$40	+	\$21

Note that in this case Revco Electronics has no available capacity. Its management may decide that it does not want to provide this special order because to do so will require that it cut off the supply of the standard unit to some of its existing customers. This may anger those customers and result in the loss of customers.

The Navigator

*Note: All **asterisked** Questions, Exercises, and Problems relate to material in the appendix to the chapter.

SELF-STUDY QUESTIONS

Answers are at the end of the chapter.

(SO 2) **1.** Cost-plus pricing means that:
a. Selling price = Variable cost + (Markup percentage + Variable cost).
b. Selling price = Cost + (Markup percentage × Cost).
c. Selling price = Manufacturing cost + (Markup percentage + Manufacturing cost).
d. Selling price = Fixed cost + (Markup percentage × Fixed cost).

(SO 1) **2.** Target cost related to price and profit means that:
a. cost and desired profit must be determined before selling price.
b. cost and selling price must be determined before desired profit.
c. price and desired profit must be determined before costs.
d. costs can be achieved only if the company is at full capacity.

(SO 1) **3.** Classic Toys has examined the market for toy train locomotives. It believes there is a market niche in which it can sell locomotives at $80 each. It estimates that it could sell 10,000 of these locomotives annually. Variable costs to make a locomotive are expected to be $25. Classic anticipates a profit of $15 per locomotive. The target cost for the locomotive is:
a. $80. **c.** $40.
b. $65. **d.** $25.

(SO 2) **4.** Adler Company is considering developing a new product. The company has gathered the following information on this product.

Expected total unit cost	$25
Estimated investment for new product	$500,000
Desired ROI	10%
Expected number of units to be produced and sold	1,000

Given this information, the desired markup percentage and selling price are:
a. markup percentage 10%; selling price $55.
b. markup percentage 200%; selling price $75.
c. markup percentage 10%; selling price $50.
d. markup percentage 100%; selling price $55.

(SO 2) **5.** Mystique Co. provides the following information for the new product it recently introduced.

Total unit cost	$30
Desired ROI per unit	$10
Target selling price	$40

What would be Mystique Co.'s percentage markup on cost?
a. 125%. **c.** 33 ⅓%.
b. 75%. **d.** 25%.

(SO 3) **6.** Crescent Electrical Repair has decided to price its work on a time-and-material basis. It estimates the following costs for the year related to labor.

Technician wages and benefits	$100,000
Office employee's salary and benefits	$ 40,000
Other overhead	$ 80,000

Crescent desires a profit margin of $10 per labor hour and budgets 5,000 hours of repair time for the year. The office employee's salary, benefits, and other overhead costs should be divided evenly between time charges and material loading charges. Crescent labor charge per hour would be:
a. $42. **c.** $32.
b. $34. **d.** $30.

7. The Plastics Division of Weston Company manufactures plastic molds and then sells them to customers for $70 per unit. Its variable cost is $30 per unit, and its fixed cost per unit is $10. Management would like the Plastics Division to transfer 10,000 of these molds to another division within the company at a price of $40. The Plastics Division is operating at full capacity. What is the minimum transfer price that the Plastics Division should accept? (SO 4)
a. $10. **c.** $40.
b. $30. **d.** $70.

8. Assume the same information as question 7, except that the Plastics Division has available capacity of 10,000 units for plastic moldings. What is the minimum transfer price that the Plastics Division should accept? (SO 4)
a. $10. **c.** $40.
b. $30. **d.** $70.

***9.** AST Electrical provides the following cost information related to its production of electronic circuit boards. (SO 6)

	Per Unit
Variable manufacturing cost	$40
Fixed manufacturing cost	$30
Variable selling and administrative expenses	$8
Fixed selling and administrative expenses	$12
Desired ROI per unit	$15

What is its markup percentage assuming that AST Electrical uses absorption-cost pricing?
a. 16.67%. **c.** 54.28%.
b. 50%. **d.** 118.75%.

***10.** Assume the same information as question 9 and determine AST Electrical's markup percentage using variable-cost pricing. (SO 6)
a. 16.67%. **c.** 54.28%.
b. 50%. **d.** 118.75%.

Go to the book's website,
www.wiley.com/college/weygandt,
for Additional Self-Study questions.

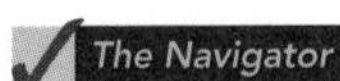

QUESTIONS

1. What are the two types of pricing environments for sales to external parties?
2. In what situation does a company place the greatest focus on its target cost? How is the target cost determined?
3. What is the basic formula to determine the target selling price in cost-plus pricing?
4. Stine Corporation produces a filter that has a per unit cost of $17. The company would like a 30% markup. Using cost-plus pricing, determine the per unit selling price.
5. What is the basic formula for the markup percentage?
6. What are some of the factors that affect a company's desired ROI?
7. Livingston Corporation manufactures an electronic switch for dishwashers. The cost base per unit, excluding selling and administrative expenses, is $60. The per unit cost of selling and administrative expenses is $20. The company's desired ROI per unit is $6. Calculate its markup percentage on total unit cost.
8. Estevan manufactures a standard cabinet for a DVD player. The variable cost per unit is $15. The fixed cost per unit is $9. The desired ROI per unit is $6. Compute the markup percentage on total unit cost and the target selling price for the cabinet.
9. In what circumstances is time-and-material pricing most often used?
10. What is the material loading charge? How is it expressed?
11. What is a transfer price? Why is determining a fair transfer price important to division managers?
12. When setting a transfer price, what objective(s) should the company have in mind?
13. What are the three approaches for determining transfer prices?
14. Describe the cost-based approach to transfer pricing. What is the strength of this approach? What are the weaknesses of this approach?
15. What is the general formula for determining the minimum transfer price that the selling division should be willing to accept?
16. When determining the minimum transfer price, what is meant by the "opportunity cost"?
17. In what circumstances will a negotiated transfer price be used instead of a market-based price?
18. Explain how companies use transfer pricing between divisions located in different countries to reduce tax payments, and discuss the propriety of this approach.

*19. What costs are excluded from the cost base when absorption-cost pricing is used to determine the markup percentage?

*20. Kay Corporation manufactures a fiber optic connector. The variable cost per unit is $15. The fixed cost per unit is $9. The company's desired ROI per unit is $3. Compute the markup percentage using variable-cost pricing.

BRIEF EXERCISES

Compute target cost. (SO 1)

BE8-1 Russell Company manufactures computer hard drives. The market for hard drives is very competitive. The current market price for a computer hard drive is $45. Russell would like a profit of $14 per drive. How can Russell Company accomplish this objective?

Use cost-plus pricing to determine selling price. (SO 2)

BE8-2 Gruner Corporation produces snowboards. The following per unit cost information is available: direct materials $12; direct labor $8; variable manufacturing overhead $6; fixed manufacturing overhead $14; variable selling and administrative expenses $4; and fixed selling and administrative expenses $12. Using a 32% markup percentage on total per unit cost, compute the target selling price.

Compute ROI per unit. (SO 2)

BE8-3 Travis Corporation produces high-performance rotors. It expects to produce 50,000 rotors in the coming year. It has invested $10,000,000 to produce rotors. The company has a required return on investment of 18%. What is its ROI per unit?

Compute markup percentage. (SO 2)

BE8-4 Shandling Corporation produces microwave units. The following per unit cost information is available: direct materials $36; direct labor $24; variable manufacturing overhead $18; fixed manufacturing overhead $42; variable selling and administrative expenses $14; and fixed selling and administrative expenses $28. Its desired ROI per unit is $30. Compute its markup percentage using a total-cost approach.

Compute ROI and markup percentage. (SO 2)

BE8-5 During the current year Bierko Corporation expects to produce 10,000 units and has budgeted the following: net income $300,000; variable costs $1,100,000; and fixed costs $100,000. It has invested assets of $1,500,000. The company's budgeted ROI was 20%. What was its budgeted markup percentage using a full-cost approach?

BE8-6 Swayze Small Engine Repair charges $45 per hour of labor. It has a material loading percentage of 40%. On a recent job replacing the engine of a riding lawnmower, Swayze worked 10.5 hours and used parts with a cost of $700. Calculate Swayze's total bill.

Use time-and-material pricing to determine bill.

(SO 3)

BE8-7 The Heating Division of ITA International produces a heating element that it sells to its customers for $42 per unit. Its variable cost per unit is $19, and its fixed cost per unit is $10. Top management of ITA International would like the Heating Division to transfer 15,000 heating units to another division within the company at a price of $29. The Heating Division is operating at full capacity. What is the minimum transfer price that the Heating Division should accept?

Determine minimum transfer price.

(SO 4)

BE8-8 Use the data from BE8-7, but assume that the Heating Division has sufficient excess capacity to provide the 15,000 heating units to the other division. What is the minimum transfer price that the Heating Division should accept?

Determine minimum transfer price with excess capacity.

(SO 4)

BE8-9 Use the data from BE8-7, but assume that the units being requested are special high-performance units, and that the division's variable cost would be $24 per unit (rather than $19). What is the minimum transfer price that the Heating Division should accept?

Determine minimum transfer price for special order.

(SO 4)

***BE8-10** Using the data in BE8-4, compute the markup percentage using absorption-cost pricing.

Compute markup percentage using absorption-cost pricing.

(SO 6)

***BE8-11** Using the data in BE8-4, compute the markup percentage using variable-cost pricing.

Compute markup percentage using variable-cost pricing.

(SO 6)

EXERCISES

WILEY PLUS

E8-1 Culver Cheese Company has developed a new cheese slicer called Slim Slicer. The company plans to sell this slicer through its catalog, which it issues monthly. Given market research, Culver believes that it can charge $15 for the Slim Slicer. Prototypes of the Slim Slicer, however, are costing $22. By using cheaper materials and gaining efficiencies in mass production Culver believes it can reduce Slim Slicer's cost substantially. Culver wishes to earn a return of 30% of the selling price.

Compute target cost.

(SO 1)

Instructions

(a) Compute the target cost for the Slim Slicer.
(b) When is target costing particularly helpful in deciding whether to produce a given product?

E8-2 LaserLook is involved in producing and selling high-end golf equipment. The company has recently been involved in developing various types of laser guns to measure yardages on the golf course. One small laser gun, called LittleLaser, appears to have a very large potential market. Because of competition, LaserLook does not believe that it can charge more than $90 for LittleLaser. At this price, LaserLook believes it can sell 100,000 of these laser guns. LittleLaser will require an investment of $8,500,000 to manufacture, and the company wants an ROI of 20%.

Compute target cost.

(SO 1)

Instructions

Determine the target cost for one LittleLaser.

E8-3 Mucky Duck makes swimsuits and sells these suits directly to retailers. Although Mucky Duck has a variety of suits, it does not make the All-Body suit used by highly skilled swimmers. The market research department believes that a strong market exists for this type of suit. The department indicates that the All-Body suit would sell for approximately $110. Given its experience, Mucky Duck believes the All-Body suit would have the following manufacturing costs.

Compute target cost and cost-plus pricing.

(SO 1, 2)

Direct materials	$ 25
Direct labor	30
Manufacturing overhead	45
Total costs	$100

Instructions

(a) Assume that Mucky Duck uses cost-plus pricing, setting the selling price 25% above its costs. (1) What would be the price charged for the All-Body swimsuit? (2) Under what circumstances might Mucky Duck consider manufacturing the All-Body swimsuit given this approach?

(b) Assume that Mucky Duck uses target costing. What is the price that Mucky Duck would charge the retailer for the All-Body swimsuit?

(c) What is the highest acceptable manufacturing cost Mucky Duck would be willing to incur to produce the All-Body swimsuit, if it desired a profit of $25 per unit? (Assume target costing.)

Use cost-plus pricing to determine selling price.

(SO 2)

E8-4 Selleck Corporation makes a commercial-grade cooking griddle. The following information is available for Selleck Corporation's anticipated annual volume of 30,000 units.

	Per Unit	Total
Direct materials	$17	
Direct labor	$8	
Variable manufacturing overhead	$11	
Fixed manufacturing overhead		$360,000
Variable selling and administrative expenses	$4	
Fixed selling and administrative expenses		$150,000

The company uses a 40% markup percentage on total cost.

Instructions

(a) Compute the total cost per unit.

(b) Compute the target selling price.

Use cost-plus pricing to determine various amounts.

(SO 2)

E8-5 Marlowe Corporation makes a mechanical stuffed alligator that sings the Martian national anthem. The following information is available for Marlowe Corporation's anticipated annual volume of 500,000 units.

	Per Unit	Total
Direct materials	$7	
Direct labor	$9	
Variable manufacturing overhead	$15	
Fixed manufacturing overhead		$3,300,000
Variable selling and administrative expenses	$14	
Fixed selling and administrative expenses		$1,500,000

The company has a desired ROI of 25%. It has invested assets of $24,000,000.

Instructions

(a) Compute the total cost per unit.

(b) Compute the desired ROI per unit.

(c) Compute the markup percentage using total cost per unit.

(d) Compute the target selling price.

Use cost-plus pricing to determine various amounts.

(SO 2)

E8-6 Roxy's Recording Studio rents studio time to musicians in 2-hour blocks. Each session includes the use of the studio facilities, a digital recording of the performance, and a professional music producer/mixer. Anticipated annual volume is 1,000 sessions. The company has invested $2,058,000 in the studio and expects a return on investment (ROI) of 20%. Budgeted costs for the coming year are as follows.

	Per Session	Total
Direct materials (tapes, CDs, etc)	$20	
Direct labor	$400	
Variable overhead	$50	
Fixed overhead		$950,000
Variable selling and administrative expenses	$40	
Fixed selling and administrative expenses		$500,000

Instructions

(a) Determine the total cost per session.

(b) Determine the desired ROI per session.

(c) Calculate the mark-up percentage on the total cost per session.

(d) Calculate the target price per session.

E8-7 Caan Corporation produces industrial robots for high-precision manufacturing. The following information is given for Caan Corporation.

Use cost-plus pricing to determine various amounts.

(SO 2)

	Per Unit	Total
Direct materials	$380	
Direct labor	$290	
Variable manufacturing overhead	$72	
Fixed manufacturing overhead		$1,800,000
Variable selling and administrative expenses	$55	
Fixed selling and administrative expenses		$327,000

The company has a desired ROI of 20%. It has invested assets of $49,600,000. It anticipates production of 3,000 units per year.

Instructions

(a) Compute the cost per unit of the fixed manufacturing overhead and the fixed selling and administrative expenses.

(b) Compute the desired ROI per unit. (Round to the nearest dollar.)

(c) Compute the target selling price.

E8-8 Padong Remanufacturing rebuilds spot welders for manufacturers. The following budgeted cost data for 2008 is available for Padong.

Use time-and-material pricing to determine bill.

(SO 3)

	Time Charges	Material Loading Charges
Technicians' wages and benefits	$228,000	–
Parts manager's salary and benefits	–	$42,500
Office employee's salary and benefits	38,000	9,000
Other overhead	15,200	24,000
Total budgeted costs	$281,200	$75,500

The company desires a $35 profit margin per hour of labor and a 25% profit margin on parts. It has budgeted for 7,600 hours of repair time in the coming year, and estimates that the total invoice cost of parts and materials in 2008 will be $400,000.

Instructions

(a) Compute the rate charged per hour of labor.

(b) Compute the material loading percentage. (Round to three decimal places.)

(c) Lindy Corporation has requested an estimate to rebuild its spot welder. Padong estimates that it would require 40 hours of labor and $2,500 of parts. Compute the total estimated bill.

E8-9 Justin's Custom Electronics (JCE) sells and installs complete security, computer, audio, and video systems for homes. On newly constructed homes it provides bids using time-and-material pricing. The following budgeted cost data are available.

Use time-and-material pricing to determine bill.

(SO 3)

	Time Charges	Material Loading Charges
Technicians' wages and benefits	$150,000	–
Parts manager's salary and benefits	–	$34,000
Office employee's salary and benefits	28,000	12,000
Other overhead	15,000	42,000
Total budgeted costs	$193,000	$88,000

The company has budgeted for 6,000 hours of technician time during the coming year. It desires a $38 profit margin per hour of labor and a 100% profit on parts. It estimates the total invoice cost of parts and materials in 2008 will be $700,000.

Instructions

(a) Compute the rate charged per hour of labor. (Round to two decimal places.)

(b) Compute the material loading percentage. (Round to two decimal places.)

(c) JCE has just received a request for a bid from R.J. Builders on a $1,200,000 new home. The company estimates that it would require 80 hours of labor and $40,000 of parts. Compute the total estimated bill.

Use time-and-material pricing to determine bill.

(SO 3)

E8-10 Karl's Klassic Kars restores classic automobiles to showroom status. Budgeted data for the current year are:

	Time Charges	Material Loading Charges
Restorers' wages and fringe benefits	$270,000	
Purchasing agent's salary and fringe benefits		$ 67,500
Administrative salaries and fringe benefits	54,000	21,960
Other overhead costs	21,600	75,600
Total budgeted costs	$345,600	$165,060

The company anticipated that the restorers would work a total of 12,000 hours this year. Expected parts and materials were $1,260,000.

In late January, the company experienced a fire in its facilities that destroyed most of the accounting records. The accountant remembers that the hourly labor rate was $68.80 and that the material loading charge was 93.10%.

Instructions

(a) Determine the profit margin per hour on labor.
(b) Determine the profit margin on materials.
(c) Determine the total price of labor and materials on a job that was completed after the fire that required 150 hours of labor and $60,000 in parts and materials.

Determine minimum transfer price.

(SO 4)

E8-11 Allied Company's Small Motor Division manufactures a number of small motors used in household and office appliances. The Household Division of Allied then assembles and packages such items as blenders and juicers. Both divisions are free to buy and sell any of their components internally or externally. The following costs relate to small motor LN233 on a per unit basis.

Fixed cost per unit	$5
Variable cost per unit	$8
Selling price per unit	$30

Instructions

(a) Assuming that the Small Motor Division has excess capacity, compute the minimum acceptable price for the transfer of small motor LN233 to the Household Division.
(b) Assuming that the Small Motor Division does not have excess capacity, compute the minimum acceptable price for the transfer of the small motor to the Household Division.
(c) Explain why the level of capacity in the Small Motor Division has an effect on the transfer price.

Determine effect on income from transfer price.

(SO 4)

E8-12 The Cycle Division of TravelVelocity Company has the following per unit data related to its most recent cycle called Roadbuster.

Selling price		$2,200
Variable cost of goods sold		
Body frame	$300	
Other variable costs	900	1,200
Contribution margin		$1,000

Presently, the Cycle Division buys its body frames from an outside supplier. However TravelVelocity has another division, FrameBody, that makes body frames for other cycle companies. The Cycle Division believes that FrameBody's product is suitable for its new Roadbuster cycle. Presently, FrameBody sells its frames for $350 per frame. The variable cost for FrameBody is $250. The Cycle Division is willing to pay $275 to purchase the frames from FrameBody.

Instructions

(a) Assume that FrameBody has excess capacity and is able to meet all of the Cycle Division's needs. If the Cycle Division buys 1,000 frames from FrameBody, determine the following:

(1) effect on the income of the Cycle Division; (2) effect on the income of FrameBody; and (3) effect on the income of TravelVelocity.

(b) Assume that FrameBody does not have excess capacity and therefore would lose sales if the frames were sold to the Cycle Division. If the Cycle Division buys 1,000 frames from FrameBody, determine the following: (1) effect on the income of the Cycle Division; (2) effect on the income of FrameBody; and (3) effect on the income of TravelVelocity.

Determine minimum transfer price.

(SO 4)

E8-13 NuVox Corporation manufactures car stereos. It is a division of RustBucket Motors, which manufactures vehicles. NuVox sells car stereos to RustBucket, as well as to other vehicle manufacturers and retail stores. The following information is available for NuVox's standard unit: variable cost per unit $34; fixed cost per unit $23; and selling price to outside customer $85. RustBucket currently purchases a standard unit from an outside supplier for $80. Because of quality concerns and to ensure a reliable supply, the top management of RustBucket has ordered NuVox to provide 200,000 units per year at a transfer price of $34 per unit. NuVox is already operating at full capacity. NuVox can avoid $4 per unit of variable selling costs by selling the unit internally.

Instructions

Answer each of the following questions.

(a) What is the minimum transfer price that NuVox should accept?
(b) What is the potential loss to the corporation as a whole resulting from this forced transfer?
(c) How should the company resolve this situation?

Compute minimum transfer price.

(SO 4)

E8-14 The Bathtub Division of Korey Plumbing Corporation has recently approached the Faucet Division with a proposal. The Bathtub Division would like to make a special "ivory" tub with gold-plated fixtures for the company's 50-year anniversary. It would make only 5,000 of these units. It would like the Faucet Division to make the fixtures and provide them to the Bathtub Division at a transfer price of $160. If sold externally, the estimated variable cost per unit would be $135. However, by selling internally the Faucet Division would save $6 per unit on variable selling expenses. The Faucet Division is currently operating at full capacity. Its standard unit sells for $50 per unit and has variable costs of $29.

Instructions

Compute the minimum transfer price that the Faucet Division should be willing to accept, and discuss whether it should accept this offer.

Determine minimum transfer price.

(SO 4)

E8-15 The Appraisal Department of Mega-Mortgage Bank performs appraisals of business properties for loans being considered by the bank and appraisals for home buyers that are financing their purchase through some other financial institution. The department charges $160 per home appraisal, and its variable costs are $126 per appraisal.

Recently, Mega-Mortgage Bank has opened its own Home-Loan Department and wants the Appraisal Department to perform 1,200 appraisals on all Mega-Mortgage Bank–financed home loans. Bank management feels that the cost of these appraisals to the Home-Loan Department should be $150. The variable cost per appraisal to the Home-Loan Department would be $6 less than those performed for outside customers due to savings in administrative costs.

Instructions

(a) Determine the minimum transfer price, assuming the Appraisal Department has excess capacity.
(b) Determine the minimum transfer price, assuming the Appraisal Department has no excess capacity.
(c) Assuming the Appraisal Department has no excess capacity, should management force the department to charge the Home-Loan Department only $150? Discuss.

Compute total cost per unit, ROI, and markup percentages using absorption-cost pricing and variable-cost pricing.

(SO 6)

***E8-16** Information for Marlowe Corporation is given in E8-5.

Instructions

Using the information given in E8-5, answer the following.

(a) Compute the total cost per unit.
(b) Compute the desired ROI per unit.
(c) Using absorption-cost pricing, compute the markup percentage.
(d) Using variable-cost pricing, compute the markup percentage.

Compute markup percentage using absorption-cost pricing and variable-cost pricing.
(SO 6)

***E8-17** Firefly Corporation produces outdoor portable fireplace units. The following per unit cost information is available: direct materials $21; direct labor $26; variable manufacturing overhead $16; fixed manufacturing overhead $22; variable selling and administrative expenses $9; and fixed selling and administrative expenses $15. The company's ROI per unit is $20.

Instructions

Compute Firefly Corporation's markup percentage using (a) absorption-cost pricing and (b) variable-cost pricing.

Compute various amounts using absorption-cost pricing and variable-cost pricing.
(SO 6)

***E8-18** Information for Caan Corporation is given in E8-7.

Instructions

Using the information given in E8-7, answer the following.

(a) Compute the cost per unit of the fixed manufacturing overhead and the fixed selling and administrative expenses.
(b) Compute the desired ROI per unit. (Round to the nearest dollar.)
(c) Compute the markup percentage and target selling price using absorption-cost pricing. (Round the markup percentage to three decimal places.)
(d) Compute the markup percentage and target selling price using variable-cost pricing. (Round the markup percentage to three decimal places.)

EXERCISES: SET B

Visit the book's website at **www.wiley.com/college/weygandt**, and choose Student Companion site, to access Exercise Set B.

PROBLEMS: SET A

Use cost-plus pricing to determine various amounts.
(SO 2)

P8-1A Lafluer Corporation needs to set a target price for its newly designed product M14–M16. The following data relate to this new product.

	Per Unit	Total
Direct materials	$20	
Direct labor	$42	
Variable manufacturing overhead	$10	
Fixed manufacturing overhead		$1,440,000
Variable selling and administrative expenses	$5	
Fixed selling and administrative expenses		$1,040,000

These costs are based on a budgeted volume of 80,000 units produced and sold each year. Lafluer uses cost-plus pricing methods to set its target selling price. The markup percentage on total unit cost is 30%.

Instructions

(a) Variable cost per unit $77

(a) Compute the total variable cost per unit, total fixed cost per unit, and total cost per unit for M14 – M16.
(b) Compute the desired ROI per unit for M14–M16.
(c) Compute the target selling price for M14–M16.
(d) Compute variable cost per unit, fixed cost per unit, and total cost per unit assuming that 60,000 M14 – M16s are sold during the year. (Round to two decimal places.)

Use cost-plus pricing to determine various amounts.
(SO 2)

P8-2A Bolus Computer Parts Inc. is in the process of setting a selling price on a new component it has just designed and developed. The following cost estimates for this new component have been provided by the accounting department for a budgeted volume of 50,000 units.

	Per Unit	Total
Direct materials	$50	
Direct labor	$25	
Variable manufacturing overhead	$20	
Fixed manufacturing overhead		$600,000
Variable selling and administrative expenses	$18	
Fixed selling and administrative expenses		$400,000

Bolus Computer Parts management requests that the total cost per unit be used in cost-plus pricing its products. On this particular product, management also directs that the target price be set to provide a 25% return on investment (ROI) on invested assets of $1,200,000.

Instructions

(Round all calculations to two decimal places.)

(a) Compute the markup percentage and target selling price that will allow Bolus Computer Parts to earn its desired ROI of 25% on this new component.

(b) Assuming that the volume is 40,000 units, compute the markup percentage and target selling price that will allow Bolus Computer Parts to earn its desired ROI of 25% on this new component.

(b) Target selling price $145.50

P8-3A Hawks Electronic Repair Shop has budgeted the following time and material for 2008.

Use time-and-material pricing to determine bill.

(SO 3)

HAWKS ELECTRONIC REPAIR SHOP
Budgeted Costs for the Year 2008

	Time Charges	Material Loading Charges
Shop employees' wages and benefits	$108,000	—
Parts manager's salary and benefits	—	$25,400
Office employee's salary and benefits	20,000	13,600
Overhead (supplies, depreciation, advertising, utilities)	26,000	18,000
Total budgeted costs	$154,000	$57,000

Hawks budgets 5,000 hours of repair time in 2008 and will bill a profit of $5 per labor hour along with a 30% profit markup on the invoice cost of parts. The estimated invoice cost for parts to be used is $100,000.

On January 5, 2008 Hawks is asked to submit a price estimate to fix a 72-inch big-screen TV. Hawks estimates that this job will consume 20 hours of labor and $500 in parts.

Instructions

(a) Compute the labor rate for Hawks Electronic Repair Shop for the year 2008.

(b) Compute the material loading charge percentage for Hawks Electronic Repair Shop for the year 2008.

(c) Prepare a time-and-material price quotation for fixing the big-screen TV.

(c) $1,651

P8-4A Wordsmith is a publishing company with a number of different book lines. Each line has contracts with a number of different authors. The company also owns a printing operation called Pronto Press. The book lines and the printing operation each operate as a separate profit center. The printing operation earns revenue by printing books by authors under contract with the book lines owned by Wordsmith, as well as authors under contract with other companies. The printing operation bills out at $0.01 per page, and a typical book requires 500 pages of print. A manager from Business Books, one of the Wordsmith's book lines, has approached the manager of the printing operation offering to pay $0.007 per page for 1,200 copies of a 500-page book. The book line pays outside printers $0.009 per page. The printing operation's variable cost per page is $0.006.

Determine minimum transfer price with no excess capacity and with excess capacity.

(SO 4)

Instructions

Determine whether the printing should be done internally or externally, and the appropriate transfer price, under each of the following situations.

(a) Assume that the printing operation is booked solid for the next 2 years, and it would have to cancel an obligation with an outside customer in order to meet the needs of the internal division.

(b) Assume that the printing operation has available capacity.

(c) The top management of Wordsmith believes that the printing operation should always do the printing for the company's authors. On a number of occasions it has forced the printing operation to cancel jobs with outside customers in order to meet the needs of its own lines. Discuss the pros and cons of this approach.

(d) Loss to company $600

(d) Calculate the change in contribution margin to each division, and to the company as a whole, if top management forces the printing operation to accept the $0.007 per page transfer price when it has no available capacity.

Determine minimum transfer price with no excess capacity.
(SO 4)

P8-5A Zapp Manufacturing Company makes various electronic products. The company is divided into a number of autonomous divisions that can either sell to internal units or sell externally. All divisions are located in buildings on the same piece of property. The Board Division has offered the Chip Division $20 per unit to supply it with chips for 40,000 boards. It has been purchasing these chips for $21 per unit from outside suppliers. The Chip Division receives $22.50 per unit for sales made to outside customers on this type of chip. The variable cost of chips sold externally by the Chip Division is $14. It estimates that it will save $4 per chip of selling expenses on units sold internally to the Board Division. The Chip Division has no excess capacity.

Instructions

(a) Calculate the minimum transfer price that the Chip Division should accept. Discuss whether it is in the Chip Division's best interest to accept the offer.

(b) Total loss to company $100,000

(b) Suppose that the Chip Division decides to reject the offer. What are the financial implications for each division, and for the company as a whole, of this decision?

Determine minimum transfer price under different situations.
(SO 4)

P8-6A Commcenter Manufacturing (CM) is a division of Worldwide Communications, Inc. CM produces pagers and other personal communication devices. These devices are sold to other Worldwide divisions, as well as to other communication companies. CM was recently approached by the manager of the Personal Communications Division regarding a request to make a special pager designed to receive signals from anywhere in the world. The Personal Communications Division has requested that CM produce 10,000 units of this special pager. The following facts are available regarding the Commcenter Manufacturing Division.

Selling price of standard pager	$95
Variable cost of standard pager	$50
Additional variable cost of special pager	$35

Instructions

For each of the following independent situations, calculate the minimum transfer price, and discuss whether the internal transfer should take place or whether the Personal Communications Division should purchase the pager externally.

(a) The Personal Communications Division has offered to pay the CM Division $105 per pager. The CM Division has no available capacity. The CM Division would have to forgo sales of 10,000 pagers to existing customers in order to meet the request of the Personal Communications Division.

(b) Minimum price $148

(b) The Personal Communications Division has offered to pay the CM Division $160 per pager. The CM Division has no available capacity. The CM Division would have to forgo sales of 14,000 pagers to existing customers in order to meet the request of the Personal Communications Division.

(c) The Personal Communications Division has offered to pay the CM Division $105 per pager. The CM Division has available capacity.

Compute the target price using absorption-cost pricing and variable-cost pricing.
(SO 6)

***P8-7A** Fast Buck Corporation needs to set a target price for its newly designed product EverReady. The following data relate to this new product.

	Per Unit	Total
Direct materials	$20	
Direct labor	$40	
Variable manufacturing overhead	$10	
Fixed manufacturing overhead		$1,400,000
Variable selling and administrative expenses	$5	
Fixed selling and administrative expenses		$1,120,000

The costs shown on page 360 are based on a budgeted volume of 80,000 units produced and sold each year. Fast Buck uses cost-plus pricing methods to set its target selling price. Because some managers prefer absorption-cost pricing and others prefer variable-cost pricing, the accounting department provides information under both approaches using a markup of 50% on absorption cost and a markup of 75% on variable cost.

Instructions

(a) Compute the target price for one unit of EverReady using absorption-cost pricing.

(b) Compute the target price for one unit of EverReady using variable-cost pricing.

(a) Markup $43.75
(b) Markup $56.25

***P8-8A** Weather Guard Windows Inc. is in the process of setting a target price on its newly designed tinted window. Cost data relating to the window at a budgeted volume of 4,000 units are as follows.

Compute various amounts using absorption-cost pricing and variable-cost pricing.

(SO 6)

	Per Unit	Total
Direct materials	$100	
Direct labor	$70	
Variable manufacturing overhead	$20	
Fixed manufacturing overhead		$120,000
Variable selling and administrative expenses	$10	
Fixed selling and administrative expenses		$102,000

Weather Guard Windows uses cost-plus pricing methods that are designed to provide the company with a 30% ROI on its tinted window line. A total of $700,000 in assets is committed to production of the new tinted window.

Instructions

(a) Compute the markup percentage under absorption-cost pricing that will allow Weather Guard Windows to realize its desired ROI.

(a) 40%

(b) Compute the target price of the window under absorption-cost pricing, and show proof that the desired ROI is realized.

(c) Compute the markup percentage under variable-cost pricing that will allow Weather Guard Windows to realize its desired ROI. (Round to three decimal places.)

(d) Compute the target price of the window under variable-cost pricing, and show proof that the desired ROI is realized.

(e) Since both absorption-cost pricing and variable-cost pricing produce the same target price and provide the same desired ROI, why do both methods exist? Isn't one method clearly superior to the other?

PROBLEMS: SET B

P8-1B Wamser Corporation needs to set a target price for its newly designed product E2-D2. The following data relate to this new product.

Use cost-plus pricing to determine various amounts.

(SO 2)

	Per Unit	Total
Direct materials	$18	
Direct labor	$30	
Variable manufacturing overhead	$8	
Fixed manufacturing overhead		$1,440,000
Variable selling and administrative expenses	$4	
Fixed selling and administrative expenses		$1,080,000

These costs are based on a budgeted volume of 90,000 units produced and sold each year. Wamser uses cost-plus pricing methods to set its target selling price. The markup percentage on total unit cost is 25%.

Instructions

(a) Compute total variable cost per unit, total fixed cost per unit, and total cost per unit for E2-D2.

(a) Variable cost per unit $60

(b) Compute the desired ROI per unit for E2-D2.

(c) Compute the target selling price for E2-D2.

(d) Compute variable cost per unit, fixed cost per unit, and total cost per unit assuming that 80,000 E2-D2s are sold during the year.

Use cost-plus pricing to determine various amounts.
(SO 2)

P8-2B Bosworth Electronics Inc. is in the process of setting a selling price on a new CDL component it has just developed. The following cost estimates for this component have been provided by the accounting department for a budgeted volume of 50,000 units.

	Per Unit	Total
Direct materials	$38	
Direct labor	$24	
Variable manufacturing overhead	$18	
Fixed manufacturing overhead		$450,000
Variable selling and administrative expenses	$12	
Fixed selling and administrative expenses		$360,000

Bosworth's management uses cost-plus pricing to set its selling price. Management also directs that the target price be set to provide a 20% return on investment (ROI) on invested assets of $1,500,000.

Instructions
(Round all calculations to two decimal places.)
(a) Compute the markup percentage and target selling price on this new CDL component.
(b) Target selling price $119.75
(b) Assuming that the volume is 40,000 units, compute the markup percentage and target selling price that will allow Bosworth Electronics to earn its desired ROI of 20%.

Use time-and-material pricing to determine bill.
(SO 3)

P8-3B Zip's Auto Body Shop has budgeted the following time and material for 2008.

ZIP'S AUTO BODY SHOP
Budgeted Costs for the Year 2008

	Time Charges	Material Loading Charges
Shop employees' wages and benefits	$111,000	—
Parts manager's salary and benefits	—	$26,600
Office employee's salary and benefits	21,000	12,000
Overhead (supplies, depreciation, advertising, utilities)	24,600	15,000
Total budgeted costs	$156,600	$53,600

Zip's budgets 6,000 hours of repair time in 2008. It will bill a profit of $7 per labor hour along with a 40% profit markup on the invoice cost of parts. Zip's anticipates using $200,000 of parts in 2008.

On January 10, 2008, Zip's is asked to submit a price estimate for the repair of a 2005 Chevrolet Blazer that was damaged in a head-on collision. Zip's estimates that this repair will consume 61 hours of labor and $4,200 in parts and materials.

Instructions
(a) Compute the labor rate for Zip's Auto Body Shop for the year 2008.
(b) Compute the material loading charge percentage for Zip's Auto Body Shop for the year 2008. (Round to three decimal places.)
(c) $9,024.70
(c) Prepare a time-and-material price quotation for the repair of the 2005 Blazer.

Determine minimum transfer price with no excess capacity and with excess capacity.
(SO 4)

P8-4B Cosmic Sounds is a record company with a number of record labels. Each record label has contracts with a number of recording artists. It also owns a recording studio called Blast Off. The record labels and the recording studio operate as separate profit centers. The studio earns revenue by recording artists under contract with the labels owned by Cosmic Sounds, as well as artists under contract with other companies. The studio bills out at $1,100 per hour, and a typical CD requires 80 hours of studio time. A manager from Big Bang, one of the Cosmic Sounds' record labels, has approached the manager of the recording studio offering to pay $800 per hour for an 80-hour session. The record label pays outside studios $1,000 per hour. The recording studio's variable cost per hour is $600.

Instructions
Determine whether the recording should be done internally or hired externally, and the appropriate transfer price, under each of the following situations.
(a) Assume that the recording studio is booked solid for the next 3 years, and it would have to cancel an obligation with an outside customer in order to meet the needs of the internal division.

(b) Assume that the recording studio has available capacity.

(c) The top management of Cosmic Sounds believes that the recording studio should always do the recording for the company's artists. On a number of occasions it has forced the recording studio to cancel jobs with outside customers in order to meet the needs of its own labels. Discuss the pros and cons of this approach.

(d) Calculate the change in contribution margin to each division, and to the company as a whole, if top management forces the recording studio to accept the $800 transfer price when it has no available capacity.

(d) Loss to company $8,000

P8-5B Chula Vista Pump Company makes irrigation pump systems. The company is divided into a number of autonomous divisions that can either sell to internal units or sell externally. All divisions are located in buildings on the same piece of property. The Pump Division has offered the Washer Division $4 per unit to supply it with the washers for 50,000 units. It has been purchasing these washers for $4.30 per unit from outside suppliers. The Washer Division receives $4.60 per unit for sales made to outside customers on this type of washer. The variable cost of units sold externally by the Washer Division is $3.20. It estimates that it will save 70 cents per unit of selling expenses on units sold internally to the Pump Division. The Washer Division has no excess capacity.

Determine minimum transfer price with no excess capacity.

(SO 4)

Instructions

(a) Calculate the minimum transfer price that the Washer Division should accept. Discuss whether it is in the Washer Division's best interest to accept the offer.

(b) Suppose that the Washer Division decides to reject the offer. What are the financial implications for each division, and the company as a whole, of the decision to reject the offer?

(b) Total loss to company $20,000

P8-6B Heartland Engines is a division of EverGreen Lawn Equipment Company. Heartland makes engines for lawn mowers, snow blowers, and other types of lawn and garden equipment. It sells its engines to the Lawn Mower Division and the Snow Blower Division of the company, as well as to other lawn equipment companies. It was recently approached by the manager of the Lawn Mower Division with a request to make a special, high-performance engine for a lawn mower designed to mow heavy brush. The Lawn Mower Division has requested that Heartland produce 8,500 units of this special engine. The following facts are available regarding the Heartland Engine Division.

Determine minimum transfer price under different situations.

(SO 4)

Selling price of standard lawn mower engine	$88
Variable cost of standard lawn mower engine	$55
Additional variable cost of special engine	$41

Instructions

For each of the following independent situations, calculate the minimum transfer price, and discuss whether the internal transfer should take place or whether the Lawn Mower Division should purchase its goods externally.

(a) The Lawn Mower Division has offered to pay the Heartland Engine Division $110 per engine. Heartland Engine has no available capacity. Heartland Engine would have to forgo sales of 8,500 units to existing customers in order to meet the request of the Lawn Mower Division.

(a) $129

(b) The Lawn Mower Division has offered to pay the Heartland Engine Division $170 per engine. Heartland has no available capacity. Heartland Engine would have to forgo sales of 12,000 units to existing customers in order to meet the request of the Lawn Mower Division. (Round to two decimal places.)

(b) $142.59

(c) The Lawn Mower division has offered to pay the Heartland Engine Division $110 per engine. Heartland Engine Division has available capacity.

(c) $96

***P8-7B** Wamser Corporation needs to set a target price for its newly designed product E2-D2. The following data relate to this new product.

Compute the target price using absorption-cost pricing and variable-cost pricing.

(SO 6)

	Per Unit	Total
Direct materials	$18	
Direct labor	$30	
Variable manufacturing overhead	$8	
Fixed manufacturing overhead		$1,440,000
Variable selling and administrative expenses	$4	
Fixed selling and administrative expenses		$1,080,000

The costs shown on page 363 are based on a budgeted volume of 90,000 units produced and sold each year. Wamser uses cost-plus pricing methods to set its target selling price. Because some managers prefer to work with absorption-cost pricing and other managers prefer variable-cost pricing, the accounting department provides information under both approaches using a markup of 50% on absorption cost and a markup of 80% on variable cost.

Instructions

(a) Markup $36
(b) Markup $48

(a) Compute the target price for one unit of E2-D2 using absorption-cost pricing.
(b) Compute the target price for one unit of E2-D2 using variable-cost pricing.

Compute various amounts using absorption-cost pricing and variable-cost pricing.
(SO 6)

***P8-8B** Santana Furniture Inc. is in the process of setting a target price on its newly designed leather recliner sofa. Cost data relating to the sofa at a budgeted volume of 3,000 units are as follows.

	Per Unit	Total
Direct materials	$140	
Direct labor	$80	
Variable manufacturing overhead	$40	
Fixed manufacturing overhead		$180,000
Variable selling and administrative expenses	$20	
Fixed selling and administrative expenses		$ 90,000

Santana Furniture uses cost-plus pricing methods that are designed to provide the company with a 30% ROI on its stuffed furniture line. A total of $700,000 in assets are committed to production of the new leather recliner sofa.

Instructions

(a) 37.5%

(a) Compute the markup percentage under absorption-cost pricing that will allow Santana Furniture to realize its desired ROI.
(b) Compute the target price of the sofa under absorption-cost pricing, and show proof that the desired ROI is realized.
(c) Compute the markup percentage under variable-cost pricing that will allow Santana Furniture to realize its desired ROI. (Round to three decimal places.)
(d) Compute the target price of the sofa under variable-cost pricing, and show proof that the desired ROI is realized.
(e) Since both absorption-cost pricing and variable-cost pricing produce the same target price and provide the same desired ROI, why do both methods exist? Isn't one method clearly superior to the other?

PROBLEMS: SET C

Visit the book's website at **www.wiley.com/college/weygandt**, and choose the Student Companion site, to access Problem Set C.

WATERWAYS CONTINUING PROBLEM

(This is a continuation of the Waterways Problem from Chapters 1 through 7.)

WCP8 Waterways Corporation competes in a market economy in which its products must be sold at market prices. Its emphasis is therefore on manufacturing its products at a cost that allows the company to earn its desired profit. This problem asks you to consider various pricing situations for Waterways' projects.

Go to the book's website,
www.wiley.com/college/weygandt,
to find the remainder of this problem.

BROADENING YOUR PERSPECTIVE

DECISION MAKING ACROSS THE ORGANIZATION

BYP8-1 Aurora Manufacturing has multiple divisions that make a wide variety of products. Recently the Bearing Division and the Wheel Division got into an argument over a transfer price. The Wheel Division needed bearings for garden tractor wheels. It normally buys its bearings from an outside supplier for $24 per set. The company's top management recently initiated a campaign to persuade the different divisions to buy their materials from within the company whenever possible. As a result, Steve Hamblin, the purchasing manager for the Wheel Division, received a letter from the vice president of Purchasing, ordering him to contact the Bearing Division to discuss buying bearings from this division.

To comply with this request, Steve from the Wheel Division called Terry Tompkin of the Bearing Division, and asked the price for 15,000 bearings. Terry responded that the bearings normally sell for $35 per set. However, Terry noted that the Bearing Division would save $3 on marketing costs by selling internally, and would pass this cost savings on to the Wheel Division. He further commented that they were at full capacity, and therefore would not be able to provide any bearings presently. In the future, if they had available capacity, they would be happy to provide bearings.

Steve responded indignantly, "Thanks but no thanks." He said, "We can get all the bearings we need from Falk Manufacturing for $24 per set." Terry snorted back, "Falk makes junk. It costs us $22 per set just to make our bearings. Our bearings can withstand heat of 2,000 degrees centigrade, and are good to within .00001 centimeters. If you guys are happy buying junk, then go ahead and buy from Falk."

Two weeks later, Steve's boss from the central office stopped in to find out whether he had placed an order with the Bearing Division. Steve responded that he would sooner buy his bearings from his worst enemy than from the Bearing Division.

Instructions

With the class divided into groups, prepare answers to the following questions.

(a) Why might the company's top management want the divisions to start doing more business with one another?

(b) Under what conditions should a buying division be forced to buy from an internal supplier? Under what conditions should a selling division be forced to sell to an internal division, rather than to an outside customer?

(c) The vice president of Purchasing thinks that this problem should be resolved by forcing the Bearing Division to sell to the Wheel Division at its cost of $22. Is this a good solution for the Wheel Division? Is this a good solution for the Bearing Division? Is this a good solution for the company?

(d) Provide at least two other possible solutions to this problem. Discuss the merits and drawbacks of each.

MANAGERIAL ANALYSIS

BYP8-2 Construction on the Atlantis Full-Service Car Wash is nearing completion. The owner is Jay Leer, a retired accounting professor. The car wash is strategically located on a busy street that separates an affluent suburban community from a middle-class community. It has two state-of-the-art stalls. Each stall can provide anything from a basic two-stage wash and rinse to a five-stage luxurious bath. It is all "touchless," that is, there are no brushes to potentially damage the car. Outside each stall there is also a 400 horse-power vacuum. Jay likes to joke that these vacuums are so strong that they will pull the carpet right out of your car if you aren't careful.

Jay has some important decisions to make before he can open the car wash. First, he knows that there is one drive-through car wash only a 10-minute drive away. It is attached to a gas station; it charges $5 for a basic wash, and $4 if you also buy at least 8 gallons of gas. It is a "brush"-type wash with rotating brush heads. There is also a self- serve "stand outside your car and spray until you are soaked" car wash a 15-minute drive away from Jay's location. He went over and tried this out. He went through $3 in quarters to get the equivalent of a basic wash. He knows that both of these locations always have long lines, which is one reason why he decided to build a new car wash.

Jay is planning to offer three levels of wash service—Basic, Deluxe, and Premium. The Basic is all automated; it requires no direct intervention by employees. The Deluxe is all automated except that at the end an employee will wipe down the car and will put a window treatment on the windshield that reduces glare and allows rainwater to run off more quickly. The Premium level is a "pampered" service. This will include all the services of the Deluxe, plus a special wax after the machine wax, and an employee will vacuum the car, wipe down the entire interior, and wash the inside of the windows. To provide the Premium service, Jay will have to hire a couple of "car wash specialists" to do the additional pampering.

Jay has pulled together the following estimates, based on data he received from the local Chamber of Commerce and information from a trade association.

	Per Unit	Total
Direct materials per Basic wash	$0.25	
Direct materials per Deluxe wash	$0.75	
Direct materials per Premium wash	$1.05	
Direct labor per Basic wash	na	
Direct labor per Deluxe wash	$0.40	
Direct labor per Premium wash	$2.40	
Variable overhead per Basic wash	$0.10	
Variable overhead per Deluxe and Premium washes	$0.20	
Fixed overhead		$112,500
Variable selling and administrative expenses all washes	$0.10	
Fixed selling and administrative expenses		$121,500

The total estimated number of washes of any type is 45,000. Jay has invested assets of $324,000. He would like a return on investment (ROI) of 25%.

Instructions

Answer each of the following questions.

(a) Identify the issues that Jay must consider in deciding on the price of each level of service of his car wash. Also discuss what issues he should consider in deciding on what levels of service to provide.

(b) Jay estimates that of the total 45,000 washes, 20,000 will be Basic, 20,000 will be Deluxe, and 5,000 will be Premium. Calculate the selling price, using cost-plus pricing, that Jay should use for each type of wash to achieve his desired ROI of 25%.

(c) During the first year, instead of selling 45,000 washes, Jay sold 43,000 washes. He was quite accurate in his estimate of first-year sales, but he was way off on the types of washes that he sold. He sold 3,000 Basic, 31,000 Deluxe, and 9,000 Premium. His actual total fixed expenses were as he expected, and his variable cost per unit was as estimated. Calculate Jay's actual net income and his actual ROI. (Round to two decimal places.)

(d) Jay is using a traditional approach to allocate overhead. As a consequence, he is allocating overhead equally to all three types of washes, even though the Basic wash is considerably less complicated and uses very little of the technical capabilities of the machinery. What should Jay do to determine more accurate costs per unit? How will this affect his pricing and, consequently, his sales?

REAL-WORLD FOCUS

BYP8-3 Merck & Co., Inc. is a global, research-driven pharmaceutical company that discovers, develops, manufactures, and markets a broad range of human and animal health products. The following are excerpts from the financial review section of the company's annual report.

MERCK & CO., INC.
Financial Review Section (partial)

In the United States, the Company has been working with private and governmental employers to slow the increase of health care costs.

Outside of the United States, in difficult environments encumbered by government cost containment actions, the Company has worked with payers to help them allocate scarce resources to optimize health care outcomes, limiting potentially detrimental effects of government actions on sales growth.

Several products face expiration of product patents in the near term.

The Company, along with other pharmaceutical manufacturers, received a notice from the Federal Trade Commission (FTC) that it was conducting an investigation into pricing practices.

Instructions

Answer each of the following questions.

(a) In light of the above excerpts from Merck's annual report, discuss some unique pricing issues faced by companies that operate in the pharmaceutical industry.

(b) What are some reasons why the same company often sells identical drugs for dramatically different prices in different countries? How can the same drug used for both humans and animals cost significantly different prices?

(c) Suppose that Merck has just developed a revolutionary new drug for the treatment of arthritis. Discuss the steps it would go through in setting a price. Include a discussion of the information it would need to gather, and the issues it would need to consider.

EXPLORING THE WEB

BYP8-4 Shopping "robots" have become very popular on the Web. These are sites that will find the price of a specified product that is listed by retailers on the Web ("e-tailers"). This allows the customer to search for the lowest possible price.

Address: www.dealtime.com or go to **www.wiley.com/college/weygandt**

Steps

1. Go to the Web page of DealTime.
2. Under the heading "**Electronics**," click on **DVD players**.
3. Choose one of the models.

Instructions

(a) Write down the name of the retailer and the price of the two lowest-priced units and the two highest-priced units.

(b) As a consumer, what concerns might you have in clicking on the "buy" button?

(c) Why might a consumer want to purchase a unit from a retailer that isn't offering the lowest price?

(d) What implications does the existence of these sites have for retailers?

COMMUNICATION ACTIVITY

BYP8-5 Judy Prest recently graduated from college with a degree in landscape architecture. Her father runs a tree, shrub, and perennial-flower nursery, and her brother has a business delivering topsoil, mulch, and compost. Judy has decided that she would like to start a landscape business. She believes that she can generate a nice profit for herself, while providing an opportunity for both her brother's and father's businesses to grow.

One potential problem that Judy is concerned about is that her father and brother tend to charge the highest prices of any local suppliers for their products. She is hoping that she can demonstrate that it would be in her interest, as well as theirs, for them to sell to her at a discounted price.

Instructions

Write a memo to Judy explaining what information she must gather, and what issues she must consider in working out an arrangement with her father and brother. In your memo, discuss how this situation differs from a "standard" transfer pricing problem, but also, how it has many of the characteristics of a transfer pricing problem.

ETHICS CASE

BYP8-6 Giant Airlines operates out of three main "hub" airports in the United States. Recently Mosquito Airlines began operating a flight from Reno, Nevada, into Giant's Metropolis hub for $190. Giant Airlines offers a price of $425 for the same route. The management of Giant is not happy about Mosquito invading its turf. In fact, Giant has driven off nearly every other competing airline from its hub, so that today 90% of flights into and out of Metropolis are Giant Airline flights. Mosquito is able to offer a lower fare because its pilots are paid less, it uses older planes, and it has lower overhead costs. Mosquito has been in business for only 6 months, and it services only two other cities. It expects the Metropolis route to be its most profitable.

Giant estimates that it would have to charge $210 just to break even on this flight. It estimates that Mosquito can break even at a price of $160. Within one day of Mosquito's entry into the market, Giant dropped its price to $140, whereupon Mosquito matched its price. They both maintained this fare for a period of 9 months, until Mosquito went out of business. As soon as Mosquito went out of business, Giant raised its fare back to $425.

Instructions

Answer each of the following questions.

(a) Who are the stakeholders in this case?
(b) What are some of the reasons why Mosquito's breakeven-point is lower than that of Giant?
(c) What are the likely reasons why Giant was able to offer this price for this period of time, while Mosquito couldn't?
(d) What are some of the possible courses of action available to Mosquito in this situation?
(e) Do you think that this kind of pricing activity is ethical? What are the implications for the stakeholders in this situation?

"ALL ABOUT YOU" ACTIVITY

BYP8-7 In the "All About You" feature in this chapter, you learned that pricing is a difficult and complex task both from the seller's and the consumer's sides. One issue that you will face is making sure that you receive a fair price for the goods that you are interested in buying. In some cases, price is not necessarily the deciding factor. Your wealth level, the quality of the product, the convenience of the product, the warranty, and the reputation of the manufacturer all may play an important role in your decision. As a result, it often is important to do solid research before you make your decision. Fortunately there are now a number of services that provide comparisons on price and quality for many products.

Instructions

Suppose you are interested in golf and want to buy a new driver and three dozen golf balls. (Hopefully that number of golf balls will last the season.) Go to *www.golfdigest.com/hotlist/* and see whether you can find any information that will help you make a decision on the driver and golf balls you might purchase.

Answers to Business Insight and Accounting Across the Organization Questions

What's the Price on the Internet? p. 325

Q: How does the Internet affect product prices?

A: *The Internet can result in lower product prices because it is easier for customers to compare prices across different retailers. However, the Internet also makes it possible for companies to offer a wider variety of products and to differentiate their products in a variety of ways. Providing customized alternatives allows retailers to offset some of the downward pressure on prices.*

Wal-Mart Says the Price Is Too High, p. 326

Q: What are some issues that Levi should consider in deciding whether it should agree to meet Wal-Mart's target price?

A: *Levi may be tempted to reduce the quality of its product, or it may be forced to move more of its operations to low-wage suppliers. A big concern is that other retailers may complain that Levi is selling its jeans to Wal-Mart at a price that is lower than they receive. Also, customers may no longer be willing to pay for Levi's other models of higher-priced jeans that it sells in other stores because they can get the low-price jeans (those with the lower gross margin) at Wal-Mart. All of these are issues that a manufacturer must consider in deciding whether to be a supplier to Wal-Mart.*

Losing Money with Every Sale, p. 330

Q: If prices continue to tumble, and sales do not increase at a more rapid rate, what will probably happen to the manufacturers of flat-screen TVs?

A: *Right now the industry has more capacity than is warranted by customer demand. As a consequence, suppliers are not able to build a sufficient return into their product price. If prices continue to fall, and sales volume does not increase at a more rapid pace, then the least-cost-efficient suppliers will eventually be forced out of business. As this occurs, there will be less downward price pressure on the remaining suppliers. Their increased efficiency, combined with less price pressure, should enable them to charge a price that provides a reasonable return.*

Transferring Profits and Reducing Taxes, p. 341

Q: What are the implications for other taxpayers if companies reduce their taxes by using improper transfer prices to shift profits to lower-tax countries?

A: *If companies reduce their taxes by using improper transfer prices, then more of the tax burden will fall on law-abiding companies or on individual taxpayers. As countries such as Ireland, for example, have drawn increased foreign investment by non-Irish companies, many other European countries have complained that Ireland is using unfair tax incentives. Many countries are beginning to scrutinize the transfer-pricing practices of multinational companies more closely in order to reduce cheating and increase tax revenues.*

Authors' Comments on *All About You*: Is the Price Right?, p. 342

*

The questions that Congress faces about pricing are difficult. Consumers (voters) are asking for relief from high drug prices. Many note that one reason for the high cost of the Medicare program is the cost of drugs, especially new ones. Others argue that Congress should permit the use of more generic drugs in the marketplace.

On the other hand, a company like Genentech argues that since 1976 the biotech industry has lost over $90 billion. Although Genentech has done well, most drug companies have not. The reason is that it takes a long time from creation of a new drug to use. For example, it took Genentech from 1982 untill 1999 to bring its breast cancer drug to market. Another way to look at the issue is to ask how much society is willing to invest in fighting disease. Consumers presently spend $15 billion a year on cancer drugs in the United States, which is 1/800th of the gross national product of the United States, spent on the leading cause of death for those under the age of 85.

There is no easy answer to the question posed here. Certainly, some people do not receive drugs because they cannot afford them. On the other hand, many are able to benefit from their use. As indicated in the story, the problem is even more complicated because some of these drugs are sold for lower prices overseas. Some argue that consumers are subsidizing individuals overseas. On the other hand, the prices have to be lower because some countries simply would not be able to afford these drugs, and the incremental revenue received does reduce the overall cost.

Answers to Self-Study Questions

1. b **2.** c **3.** b **4.** b **5.** c **6.** a **7.** d **8.** b **9.** b **10.** d

Remember to go back to the Navigator box on the chapter-opening page and check off your completed work.

Chapter 9

Budgetary Planning

STUDY OBJECTIVES

After studying this chapter, you should be able to:

1. Indicate the benefits of budgeting.
2. State the essentials of effective budgeting.
3. Identify the budgets that comprise the master budget.
4. Describe the sources for preparing the budgeted income statement.
5. Explain the principal sections of a cash budget.
6. Indicate the applicability of budgeting in nonmanufacturing companies.

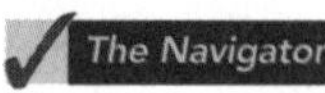

The Navigator

Scan **Study Objectives**	■
Read **Feature Story**	■
Read **Preview**	■
Read text and answer **Before You Go On** p. 377 ■ p. 381 ■ p. 388 ■ p. 391 ■	
Work **Using the Decision Toolkit**	■
Review **Summary of Study Objectives**	■
Work **Demonstration Problem**	■
Answer **Self-Study Questions**	■
Complete **Assignments**	■

Feature Story

THE NEXT AMAZON.COM? NOT QUITE

The bursting of the dot-com bubble resulted in countless stories of dot-com failures. Many of these ventures were half-baked, get-rich-quick schemes, rarely based on sound business practices. Initially they saw money flowing in faster than they knew what to do with—which was precisely the problem. Without proper planning and budgeting, much of the money went to waste. In some cases, failure was actually brought on by rapid, uncontrolled growth.

One such example was online discount bookseller, www.Positively-You.com. One of the website's co-founders, Lyle Bowline, had never run a business. However, his experience as an assistant director of an entrepreneurial center had provided him with knowledge about the do's and don'ts of small business. To minimize costs, he started the company small and simple. He invested $5,000 in computer equipment and ran the business out of his basement. In the early months, even though sales were only about $2,000 a month, the

company actually made a profit because it kept its costs low (a feat few other dot-coms could boast of).

Things changed dramatically when the company received national publicity in the financial press. Suddenly the company's sales increased to $50,000 a month—fully 25 times the previous level. The "simple" little business suddenly needed a business plan, a strategic plan, and a budget. It needed to rent office space and to hire employees.

Initially, members of a local book club donated time to help meet the sudden demand. Some put in so much time that eventually the company hired them. Quickly the number of paid employees ballooned. The sudden growth necessitated detailed planning and budgeting. The need for a proper budget was accentuated by the fact that the company's gross profit was only 16 cents on each dollar of goods sold. This meant that after paying for its inventory, the company had only 16 cents of every dollar to cover its remaining operating costs.

Unfortunately, the company never got things under control. Within a few months, sales had plummeted to $12,000 per month. At this level of sales the company could not meet the mountain of monthly expenses that it had accumulated in trying to grow. Ironically, the company's sudden success, and the turmoil it created, appears to have been what eventually caused the company to fail.

✓ The Navigator

Inside Chapter 9

Preview of Chapter 9

As the Feature Story about Positively-You.com indicates, budgeting is critical to financial well-being. As a student, you budget your study time and your money. Families budget income and expenses. Governmental agencies budget revenues and expenditures. Business enterprises use budgets in planning and controlling their operations.

Our primary focus in this chapter is budgeting—specifically, how budgeting is used as a *planning tool* by management. Through budgeting, it should be possible for management to maintain enough cash to pay creditors, to have sufficient raw materials to meet production requirements, and to have adequate finished goods to meet expected sales.

The content and organization of Chapter 9 are as follows.

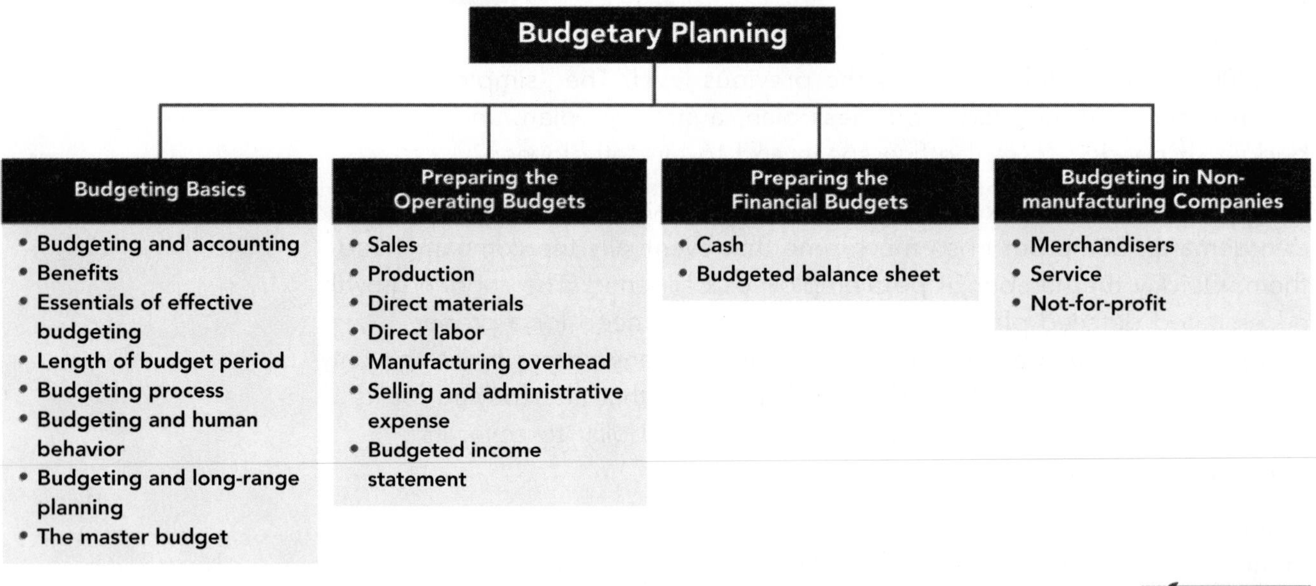

The Navigator

BUDGETING BASICS

One of management's major responsibilities is planning. As explained in Chapter 1, **planning** is the process of establishing enterprise-wide objectives. A successful organization makes both long-term and short-term plans. These plans set forth the objectives of the company and the proposed way of accomplishing them.

A **budget** is a formal written statement of management's plans for a specified future time period, expressed in financial terms. It normally represents the primary method of communicating agreed-upon objectives throughout the organization. Once adopted, a budget becomes an important basis for evaluating performance. It promotes efficiency and serves as a deterrent to waste and inefficiency. We consider the role of budgeting as a **control device** in Chapter 10.

Budgeting and Accounting

Accounting information makes major contributions to the budgeting process. From the accounting records, companies can obtain historical data on revenues, costs, and expenses. These data are helpful in formulating future budget goals.

Normally, accountants have the responsibility for presenting management's budgeting goals in financial terms. In this role, they translate management's plans and communicate the budget to employees throughout the company. They prepare periodic budget reports that provide the basis for measuring performance and comparing actual results with planned objectives. The budget itself, and the administration of the budget, however, are entirely management responsibilities.

The Benefits of Budgeting

The primary benefits of budgeting are:

STUDY OBJECTIVE 1
Indicate the benefits of budgeting.

1. It requires all levels of management to **plan ahead** and to formalize goals on a recurring basis.
2. It provides **definite objectives** for evaluating performance at each level of responsibility.
3. It creates an **early warning system** for potential problems so that management can make changes before things get out of hand.
4. It facilitates the **coordination of activities** within the business. It does this by correlating the goals of each segment with overall company objectives. Thus, the company can integrate production and sales promotion with expected sales.
5. It results in greater **management awareness** of the entity's overall operations and the impact on operations of external factors, such as economic trends.
6. It **motivates personnel** throughout the organization to meet planned objectives.

A budget is an aid to management; it is not a *substitute* for management. A budget cannot operate or enforce itself. Companies can realize the benefits of budgeting only when managers carefully administer budgets.

Essentials of Effective Budgeting

STUDY OBJECTIVE 2
State the essentials of effective budgeting.

Effective budgeting depends on a **sound organizational structure**. In such a structure, authority and responsibility for all phases of operations are clearly defined. Budgets based on **research and analysis** should result in realistic goals that will contribute to the growth and profitability of a company. And, the effectiveness of a budget program is directly related to its **acceptance by all levels of management**.

Once adopted, the budget is an important tool for evaluating performance. Managers should systematically and periodically review variations between actual and expected results to determine their cause(s). However, individuals should not be held responsible for variations that are beyond their control.

Length of the Budget Period

The budget period is not necessarily one year in length. **A budget may be prepared for any period of time.** Various factors influence the length of the budget period. These factors include the type of budget, the nature of the organization, the need for periodic appraisal, and prevailing business conditions. For example, cash may be budgeted monthly, whereas a plant expansion budget may cover a 10-year period.

The budget period should be long enough to provide an attainable goal under normal business conditions. Ideally, the time period should minimize the impact of seasonal or cyclical fluctuations. On the other hand, the budget period should not be so long that reliable estimates are impossible.

The **most common budget period is one year**. The annual budget, in turn, is often supplemented by monthly and quarterly budgets. Many companies use **continuous 12-month budgets**. These budgets drop the month just ended and add a future month. One advantage of continuous budgeting is that it keeps management planning a full year ahead.

The Budgeting Process

The development of the budget for the coming year generally starts several months before the end of the current year. The budgeting process usually begins with the collection of data from each organizational unit of the company. Past performance is often the starting point from which future budget goals are formulated.

The budget is developed within the framework of a **sales forecast**. This forecast shows potential sales for the industry and the company's expected share of such sales. Sales forecasting involves a consideration of various factors: (1) general economic conditions, (2) industry trends, (3) market research studies, (4) anticipated advertising and promotion, (5) previous market share, (6) changes in prices, and (7) technological developments. The input of sales personnel and top management is essential to the sales forecast.

In small companies like Positively-You.com, the budgeting process is often informal. In larger companies, a **budget committee** has responsibility for coordinating the preparation of the budget. The committee ordinarily includes the president, treasurer, chief accountant (controller), and management personnel from each of the major areas of the company, such as sales, production, and research. The budget committee serves as a review board where managers can defend their budget goals and requests. Differences are reviewed, modified if necessary, and reconciled. The budget is then put in its final form by the budget committee, approved, and distributed.

ACCOUNTING ACROSS THE ORGANIZATION

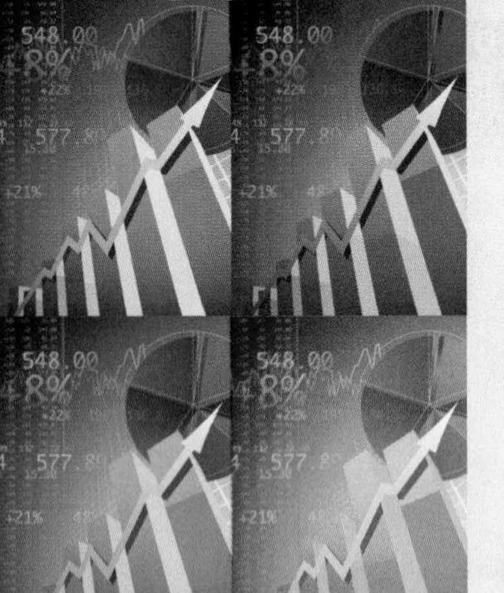

Businesses Often Feel Too Busy to Plan for the Future

A recent study by Willard & Shullman Group Ltd. found that fewer than 14% of businesses with fewer than 500 employees do an annual budget or have a written business plan. In all, nearly 60% of these businesses have no plans on paper at all. For many small businesses the basic assumption is that, "As long as I sell as much as I can, and keep my employees paid, I'm doing OK." A few small business owners even say that they see no need for budgeting and planning. Most small business owners, though, say that they understand that budgeting and planning are critical for survival and growth. But given the long hours that they already work addressing day-to-day challenges, they also say that they are "just too busy to plan for the future."

? Describe a situation in which a business "sells as much as it can" but cannot "keep its employees paid."

Budgeting and Human Behavior

A budget can have a significant impact on human behavior. It may inspire a manager to higher levels of performance. Or, it may discourage additional effort and pull down the morale of a manager. Why do these diverse effects occur? The answer is found in how the budget is developed and administered.

In developing the budget, each level of management should be invited to participate. This "bottom-to-top" approach is referred to as **participative budgeting**.

The advantages of participative budgeting are, first, that lower-level managers have more detailed knowledge of their specific area and thus are able to provide more accurate budgetary estimates. Second, when lower-level managers participate in the budgeting process, they are more likely to perceive the resulting budget as fair. The overall goal is to reach agreement on a budget that the managers consider fair and achievable, but which also meets the corporate goals set by top management. When this goal is met, the budget will provide positive motivation for the managers. In contrast, if the managers view the budget as being unfair and unrealistic, they may feel discouraged and uncommitted to budget goals. The risk of having unrealistic budgets is generally greater when the budget is developed from top management down to lower management than vice versa.

Participative budgeting does, however, have potential disadvantages. First, it is more time-consuming (and thus more costly) than a "top-down" approach, in which the budget is simply dictated to lower-level managers. A second disadvantage is that participative budgeting can foster budgetary "gaming" through budgetary slack. **Budgetary slack** occurs when managers intentionally underestimate budgeted revenues or overestimate budgeted expenses in order to make it easier to achieve budgetary goals. To minimize budgetary slack, higher-level managers must carefully review and thoroughly question the budget projections provided to them by employees whom they supervise. Illustration 9-1 graphically displays the appropriate flow of budget data from bottom to top in an organization.

Illustration 9-1
Flow of budget data from lower levels of management to top levels

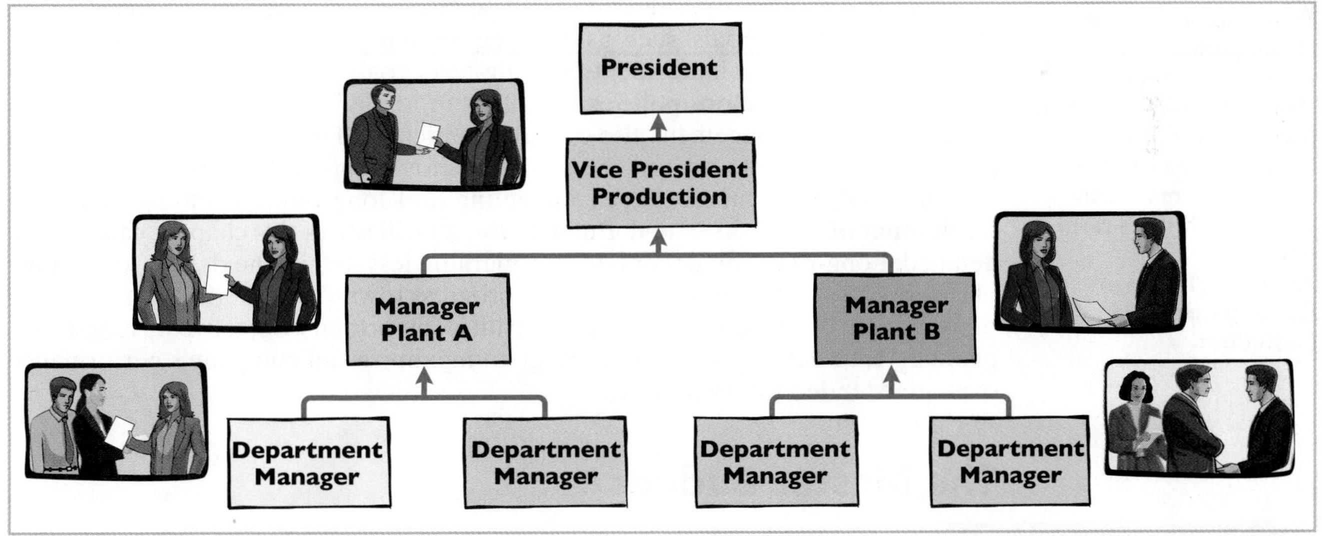

For the budget to be effective, top management must completely support the budget. The budget is an important basis for evaluating performance. It also can be used as a positive aid in achieving projected goals. The effect of an evaluation is positive when top management tempers criticism with advice and assistance. In contrast, a manager is likely to respond negatively if top management uses the budget exclusively to assess blame. A budget should not be used as a pressure device to force improved performance. In sum, a budget can be a manager's friend or a foe.

ETHICS NOTE

Unrealistic budgets can lead to unethical employee behavior such as cutting corners on the job or distorting internal financial reports.

ACCOUNTING ACROSS THE ORGANIZATION

Which Budget Approach Do You Prefer?

Not too long ago, in an effort to revive its plummeting stock, Time Warner's top management determined and publicly announced bold new financial goals for the coming year. Unfortunately, these goals were not reached.

The next year the company got a new CEO who promised, "We will not over promise, and we will deliver." The new budgets were developed with each operating unit setting what it felt were optimistic but attainable goals. In the words of one manager, using this approach created a sense of teamwork: "We're all going forward with our arms locked together."

Source: Carol J. Loomis, "AOL Time Warner's New Math," *Fortune*, February 4, 2002, pp. 98–102.

? What approach did Time Warner use to prepare the old budget? What approach did it use to prepare the new budget?

Budgeting and Long-Range Planning

Budgeting and long-range planning are not the same. One important difference is the **time period involved**. The maximum length of a budget is usually one year, and budgets are often prepared for shorter periods of time, such as a month or a quarter. In contrast, long-range planning usually encompasses a period of at least five years.

HELPFUL HINT

In comparing a budget with a long-range plan: (1) Which has more detail? (2) Which is done for a longer period of time? (3) Which is more concerned with short-term goals?
Answers: (1) Budget. (2) Long-range plan. (3) Budget.

A second significant difference is in **emphasis**. Budgeting focuses on achieving specific short-term goals, such as meeting annual profit objectives. **Long-range planning**, on the other hand, identifies long-term goals, selects strategies to achieve those goals, and develops policies and plans to implement the strategies. In long-range planning, management also considers anticipated trends in the economic and political environment and how the company should cope with them.

The final difference between budgeting and long-range planning relates to the **amount of detail presented**. Budgets, as you will see in this chapter, can be very detailed. Long-range plans contain considerably less detail. The data in long-range plans are intended more for a review of progress toward long-term goals than as a basis of control for achieving specific results. The primary objective of long-range planning is to develop the best strategy to maximize the company's performance over an extended future period.

The Master Budget

STUDY OBJECTIVE 3

Identify the budgets that comprise the master budget.

The term "budget" is actually a shorthand term to describe a variety of budget documents. All of these documents are combined into a master budget. The **master budget** is a set of interrelated budgets that constitutes a plan of action for a specified time period.

The master budget contains two classes of budgets. **Operating budgets** are the individual budgets that result in the preparation of the budgeted income statement. These budgets establish goals for the company's sales and production personnel. In contrast, **financial budgets** are the capital expenditure budget, the cash budget, and the budgeted balance sheet. These budgets focus primarily on the cash resources needed to fund expected operations and planned capital expenditures.

Illustration 9-2 pictures the individual budgets included in a master budget, and the sequence in which they are prepared. The company first develops the operating budgets, beginning with the sales budget. Then it prepares the financial budgets. We will explain and illustrate each budget shown in Illustration 9-2 except the capital expenditure budget. That budget is discussed under the topic of capital budgeting in Chapter 12.

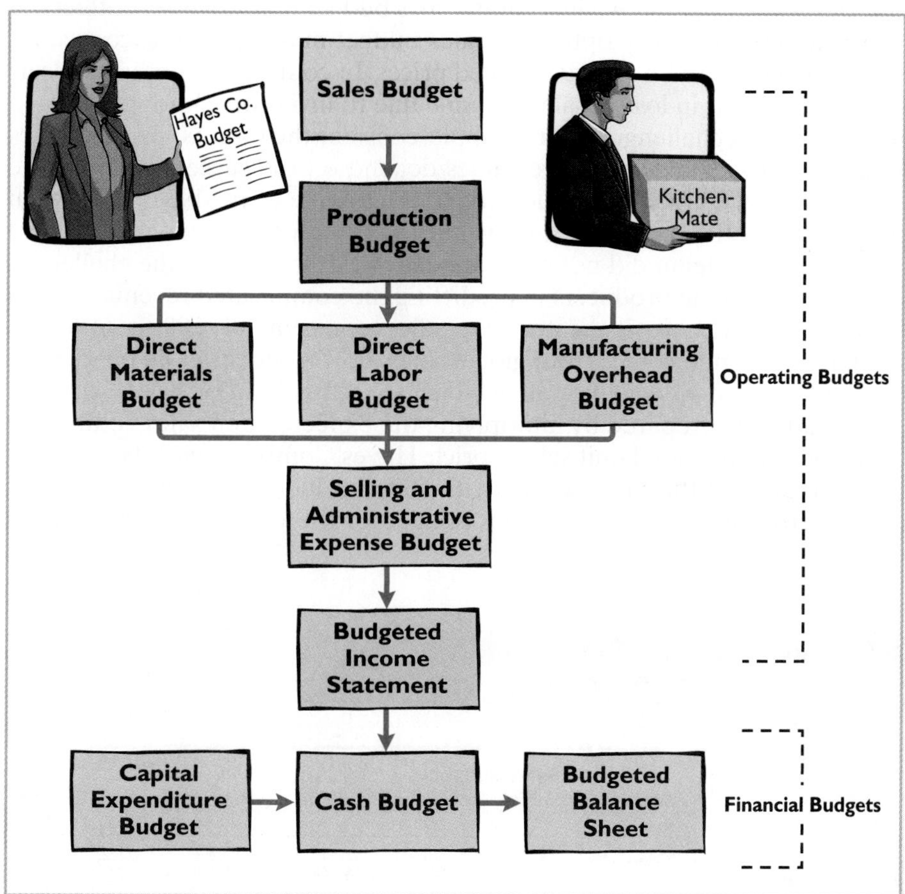

Illustration 9-2
Components of the master budget

Before You Go On...

REVIEW IT

1. What are the benefits of budgeting?
2. What are the factors essential to effective budgeting?
3. How does the budget process work?
4. How does budgeting differ from long-range planning?
5. What is a master budget?

PREPARING THE OPERATING BUDGETS

We use a case study of Hayes Company in preparing the operating budgets. Hayes manufactures and sells a single product, Kitchen-Mate. The budgets are prepared by quarters for the year ending December 31, 2008. Hayes Company begins its annual budgeting process on September 1, 2007, and it completes the budget for 2008 by December 1, 2007.

Sales Budget

HELPFUL HINT

For a retail or manufacturing company, what is the starting point in preparing the master budget, and why? Answer: The sales budget is the starting point for the master budget. It sets the level of activity for other functions such as production and purchasing.

As shown in the master budget in Illustration 9-2, **the sales budget is the first budget prepared**. Each of the other budgets depends on the sales budget. The **sales budget** is derived from the sales forecast. It represents management's best estimate of sales revenue for the budget period. An inaccurate sales budget may adversely affect net income. For example, an overly optimistic sales budget may result in excessive inventories that may have to be sold at reduced prices. In contrast, an unduly conservative budget may result in loss of sales revenue due to inventory shortages.

Forecasting sales is challenging. For example, consider the forecasting challenges faced by major sports arenas, whose revenues depend on the success of the home team. Madison Square Garden's revenues from April to June were $193 million when the Knicks made the NBA playoffs. But revenues were only $133.2 million a couple of years later when the team did not make the playoffs. Or consider the challenges faced by Hollywood movie producers in predicting the complicated revenue stream produced by a new movie. Movie theater ticket sales represent only 20% of total revenue. The bulk of revenue comes from global sales, DVDs, video-on-demand, merchandising products, and videogames, all of which are difficult to forecast.

The sales budget is prepared by multiplying the expected unit sales volume for each product by its anticipated unit selling price. Hayes Company expects sales volume to be 3,000 units in the first quarter, with 500-unit increases in each succeeding quarter. Illustration 9-3 shows the sales budget for the year, by quarters, based on a sales price of $60 per unit.

Illustration 9-3
Sales budget

Hayes Company Sales Budget.xls

File Edit View Insert Format Tools Data Window Help

	A	B	C	D	E	F
1			HAYES COMPANY			
2			Sales Budget			
3			For the Year Ending December 31, 2008			
4			Quarter			
5		1	2	3	4	Year
6	Expected unit sales	3,000	3,500	4,000	4,500	15,000
7	Unit selling price	× $60	× $60	× $60	× $60	× $60
8	Total sales	$180,000	$210,000	$240,000	$270,000	$900,000

Some companies classify the anticipated sales revenue as cash or credit sales and by geographical regions, territories, or salespersons.

Production Budget

The **production budget** shows the units to produce to meet anticipated sales. Production requirements are determined from the following formula.[1]

Illustration 9-4
Production requirements formula

Budgeted Sales Units	+	Desired Ending Finished Goods Units	−	Beginning Finished Goods Units	=	Required Production Units

[1]This formula ignores any work in process inventories, which are assumed to be nonexistent in Hayes Company.

A realistic estimate of ending inventory is essential in scheduling production requirements. Excessive inventories in one quarter may lead to cutbacks in production and employee layoffs in a subsequent quarter. On the other hand, inadequate inventories may result either in added costs for overtime work or in lost sales. Hayes Company believes it can meet future sales requirements by maintaining an ending inventory equal to 20% of the next quarter's budgeted sales volume. For example, the ending finished goods inventory for the first quarter is 700 units (20% × anticipated second-quarter sales of 3,500 units). Illustration 9-5 shows the production budget.

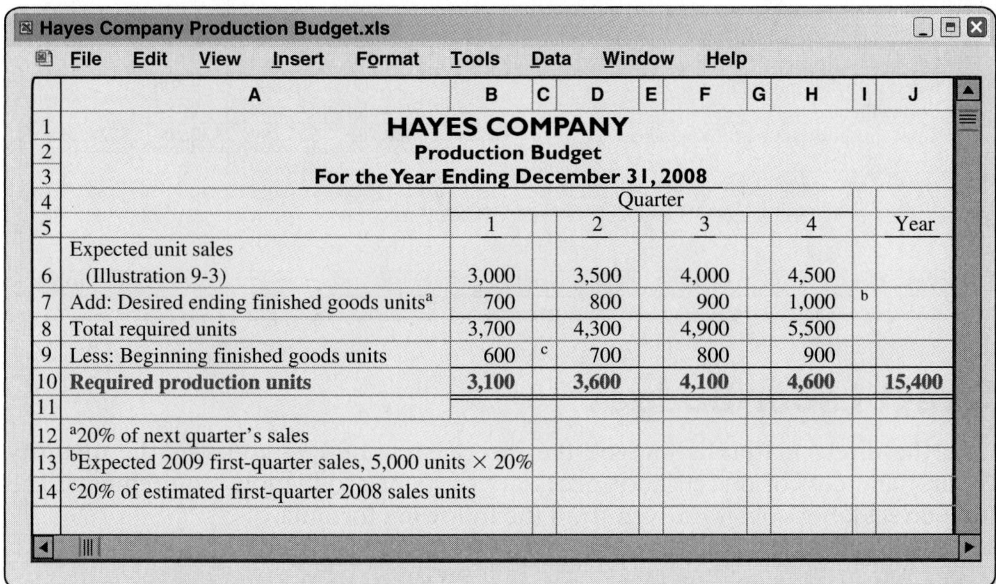

Hayes Company Production Budget.xls

HAYES COMPANY
Production Budget
For the Year Ending December 31, 2008

	Quarter 1	Quarter 2	Quarter 3	Quarter 4	Year
Expected unit sales (Illustration 9-3)	3,000	3,500	4,000	4,500	
Add: Desired ending finished goods units[a]	700	800	900	1,000[b]	
Total required units	3,700	4,300	4,900	5,500	
Less: Beginning finished goods units	600[c]	700	800	900	
Required production units	**3,100**	**3,600**	**4,100**	**4,600**	**15,400**

[a]20% of next quarter's sales
[b]Expected 2009 first-quarter sales, 5,000 units × 20%
[c]20% of estimated first-quarter 2008 sales units

Illustration 9-5
Production budget

The production budget, in turn, provides the basis for the budgeted costs for each manufacturing cost element, as explained in the following pages.

Direct Materials Budget

The **direct materials budget** shows both the quantity and cost of direct materials to be purchased. The quantities of direct materials are derived from the following formula.

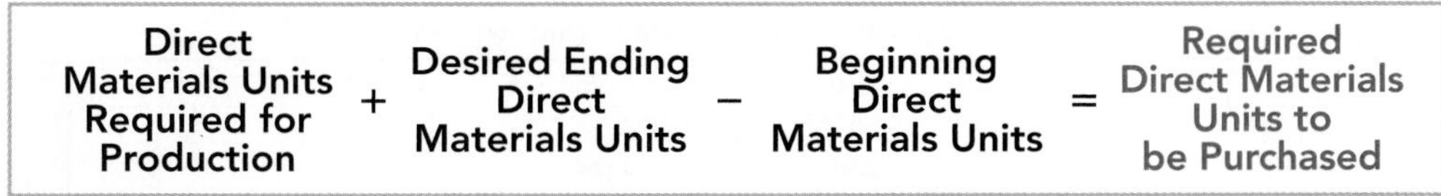

Illustration 9-6
Formula for direct materials quantities

The company then computes the budgeted cost of direct materials to be purchased by multiplying the required units of direct materials by the anticipated cost per unit.

The desired ending inventory is again a key component in the budgeting process. For example, inadequate inventories could result in temporary shutdowns of production. Because of its close proximity to suppliers, Hayes Company maintains an ending inventory of raw materials equal to 10% of the next quarter's production requirements. The manufacture of each Kitchen-Mate requires 2 pounds of raw materials, and the expected cost per pound is $4. Illustration 9-7 (page 380) shows the direct materials budget. Assume that the desired ending direct materials amount is 1,020 pounds for the fourth quarter of 2008.

Illustration 9-7
Direct materials budget

Hayes Company Direct Materials Budget.xls

File Edit View Insert Format Tools Data Window Help

HAYES COMPANY
Direct Materials Budget
For the Year Ending December 31, 2008

	Quarter 1	Quarter 2	Quarter 3	Quarter 4	Year
Units to be produced (Illustration 9-5)	3,100	3,600	4,100	4,600	
Direct materials per unit	× 2	× 2	× 2	× 2	
Total pounds needed for production	6,200	7,200	8,200	9,200	
Add: Desired ending direct materials (pounds)[a]	720	820	920	1,020	
Total materials required	6,920	8,020	9,120	10,220	
Less: Beginning direct materials (pounds)	620[b]	720	820	920	
Direct materials purchases	6,300	7,300	8,300	9,300	
Cost per pound	× $4	× $4	× $4	× $4	
Total cost of direct materials purchases	**$25,200**	**$29,200**	**$33,200**	**$37,200**	**$124,800**

[a]10% of next quarter's production requirements
[b]10% of estimated first-quarter pounds needed for production

Direct Labor Budget

Like the direct materials budget, the **direct labor budget** contains the quantity (hours) and cost of direct labor necessary to meet production requirements. The total direct labor cost is derived from the following formula.

Illustration 9-8
Formula for direct labor cost

Units to be Produced	×	Direct Labor Time per Unit	×	Direct Labor Cost per Hour	=	Total Direct Labor Cost

Direct labor hours are determined from the production budget. At Hayes Company, two hours of direct labor are required to produce each unit of finished goods. The anticipated hourly wage rate is $10. Illustration 9-9 shows these data.

Illustration 9-9
Direct labor budget

Hayes Company Direct Labor Budget.xls

File Edit View Insert Format Tools Data Window Help

HAYES COMPANY
Direct Labor Budget
For the Year Ending December 31, 2008

	Quarter 1	Quarter 2	Quarter 3	Quarter 4	Year
Units to be produced (Illustration 9-5)	3,100	3,600	4,100	4,600	
Direct labor time (hours) per unit	× 2	× 2	× 2	× 2	
Total required direct labor hours	6,200	7,200	8,200	9,200	
Direct labor cost per hour	× $10	× $10	× $10	× $10	
Total direct labor cost	**$62,000**	**$72,000**	**$82,000**	**$92,000**	**$308,000**

HELPFUL HINT
An important assumption in Illustration 9-9 is that the company can add to and subtract from its work force as needed so that the $10 per hour labor cost applies to a wide range of possible production activity.

The direct labor budget is critical in maintaining a labor force that can meet the expected levels of production.

Before You Go On...

REVIEW IT

1. What is the formula to determine required production units?
2. What are the inputs necessary to prepare the direct labor budget?
3. Which budget must be prepared before the direct materials budget?

DO IT

Becker Company estimates that 2008 unit sales will be 12,000 in quarter 1, 16,000 in quarter 2, and 20,000 in quarter 3, at a unit selling price of $30. Management desires to have ending finished goods inventory equal to 15% of the next quarter's expected unit sales. Prepare a production budget by quarter for the first 6 months of 2008.

Action Plan

- Begin with budgeted sales in units.
- Add desired ending finished goods inventory.
- Subtract beginning finished goods inventory.

Solution

BECKER COMPANY
Production Budget
For the Six Months Ending June 30, 2008

	Quarter		Six
	1	2	Months
Expected unit sales	12,000	16,000	
Add: Desired ending finished goods	2,400	3,000	
Total required units	14,400	19,000	
Less: Beginning finished goods inventory	1,800	2,400	
Required production units	12,600	16,600	29,200

Related exercise material: *BE9-3, E9-4, and E9-6.*

The Navigator

Manufacturing Overhead Budget

The **manufacturing overhead budget** shows the expected manufacturing overhead costs for the budget period. As Illustration 9-10 (page 382) shows, **this budget distinguishes between variable and fixed overhead costs.** Hayes Company expects variable costs to fluctuate with production volume on the basis of the following rates per direct labor hour: indirect materials $1.00, indirect labor $1.40, utilities $0.40, and maintenance $0.20. Thus, for the 6,200 direct labor hours to produce 3,100 units, budgeted indirect materials are $6,200 (6,200 × $1), and budgeted indirect labor is $8,680 (6,200 × $1.40). Hayes also recognizes that some maintenance is fixed. The amounts reported for fixed costs are assumed for our example. The accuracy of budgeted overhead cost estimates can be greatly improved by employing activity-based costing.

At Hayes Company, overhead is applied to production on the basis of direct labor hours. Thus, as Illustration 9-10 shows, the budgeted annual rate is $8 per hour ($246,400 ÷ 30,800).

Selling and Administrative Expense Budget

Hayes Company combines its operating expenses into one budget, the **selling and administrative expense budget**. This budget projects anticipated selling and

Illustration 9-10
Manufacturing overhead budget

Hayes Company Manufacturing Overhead Budget.xls

File Edit View Insert Format Tools Data Window Help

	A	B	C	D	E	F
1	**HAYES COMPANY**					
2	**Manufacturing Overhead Budget**					
3	**For the Year Ending December 31, 2008**					
4		Quarter				
5		1	2	3	4	Year
6	Variable costs					
7	Indirect materials ($1.00/hour)	$ 6,200	$ 7,200	$ 8,200	$ 9,200	$ 30,800
8	Indirect labor ($1.40/hour)	8,680	10,080	11,480	12,880	43,120
9	Utilities ($0.40/hour)	2,480	2,880	3,280	3,680	12,320
10	Maintenance ($0.20/hour)	1,240	1,440	1,640	1,840	6,160
11	Total variable costs	18,600	21,600	24,600	27,600	92,400
12	Fixed costs					
13	Supervisory salaries	20,000	20,000	20,000	20,000	80,000
14	Depreciation	3,800	3,800	3,800	3,800	15,200
15	Property taxes and insurance	9,000	9,000	9,000	9,000	36,000
16	Maintenance	5,700	5,700	5,700	5,700	22,800
17	Total fixed costs	38,500	38,500	38,500	38,500	154,000
18	**Total manufacturing overhead**	**$57,100**	**$60,100**	**$63,100**	**$66,100**	**$246,400**
19	**Direct labor hours (Illustration 9-9)**	**6,200**	**7,200**	**8,200**	**9,200**	**30,800**
20	**Manufacturing overhead rate per direct labor hour ($246,400 ÷ 30,800)**					**$8**
21						

administrative expenses for the budget period. This budget (Illustration 9-11) also classifies expenses as either variable or fixed. In this case, the variable expense rates per unit of sales are sales commissions $3 and freight-out $1. Variable expenses per quarter are based on the unit sales from the sales budget (Illustration 9-3, page 378). For example, Hayes expects sales in the first quarter to be 3,000 units. Thus, Sales Commissions Expense is $9,000 (3,000 × $3), and Freight-out is $3,000 (3,000 × $1). Fixed expenses are based on assumed data. Illustration 9-11 shows the selling and administrative expense budget.

Illustration 9-11
Selling and administrative expense budget

Hayes Company Manufacturing Selling and Administrative Expense Budget.xls

File Edit View Insert Format Tools Data Window Help

	A	B	C	D	E	F
1	**HAYES COMPANY**					
2	**Selling and Administrative Expense Budget**					
3	**For the Year Ending December 31, 2008**					
4		Quarter				
5		1	2	3	4	Year
6	Budgeted sales in units (Illustration 9-3)	3,000	3,500	4,000	4,500	15,000
7	Variable expenses					
8	Sales commissions ($3 per unit)	$ 9,000	$10,500	$12,000	$ 13,500	$ 45,000
9	Freight-out ($1 per unit)	3,000	3,500	4,000	4,500	15,000
10	Total variable expenses	12,000	14,000	16,000	18,000	60,000
11	Fixed expenses					
12	Advertising	5,000	5,000	5,000	5,000	20,000
13	Sales salaries	15,000	15,000	15,000	15,000	60,000
14	Office salaries	7,500	7,500	7,500	7,500	30,000
15	Depreciation	1,000	1,000	1,000	1,000	4,000
16	Property taxes and insurance	1,500	1,500	1,500	1,500	6,000
17	Total fixed expenses	30,000	30,000	30,000	30,000	120,000
18	**Total selling and administrative expenses**	**$42,000**	**$44,000**	**$46,000**	**$48,000**	**$180,000**
19						

Budgeted Income Statement

STUDY OBJECTIVE 4

Describe the sources for preparing the budgeted income statement.

The **budgeted income statement** is the important end-product of the operating budgets. This budget indicates the expected profitability of operations for the budget period. The budgeted income statement provides the basis for evaluating company performance. Budgeted income statements often act as a call to action. For example, a board member at XM Satellite Radio Holdings felt that budgeted costs were too high relative to budgeted revenues. When management refused to cut its marketing and programming costs, the board member resigned; he felt that without the cuts, the company risked financial crisis.

As you would expect, the budgeted income statement is prepared from the various operating budgets. For example, to find the cost of goods sold, it is first necessary to determine the total unit cost of producing one Kitchen-Mate, as follows.

Illustration 9-12
Computation of total unit cost

Cost of One Kitchen-Mate

Cost Element	Illustration	Quantity	Unit Cost	Total
Direct materials	9-7	2 pounds	$ 4.00	$ 8.00
Direct labor	9-9	2 hours	$10.00	20.00
Manufacturing overhead	9-10	2 hours	$ 8.00	16.00
Total unit cost				**$44.00**

Hayes Company then determines cost of goods sold by multiplying the units sold by the unit cost. Its budgeted cost of goods sold is $660,000 (15,000 × $44). All data for the income statement come from the individual operating budgets except the following: (1) interest expense is expected to be $100, and (2) income taxes are estimated to be $12,000. Illustration 9-13 shows the budgeted income statement.

Illustration 9-13
Budgeted income statement

HAYES COMPANY
Budgeted Income Statement
For the Year Ending December 31, 2008

Sales (Illustration 9-3)	$900,000
Cost of goods sold (15,000 × $44)	660,000
Gross profit	240,000
Selling and administrative expenses (Illustration 9-11)	180,000
Income from operations	60,000
Interest expense	100
Income before income taxes	59,900
Income tax expense	12,000
Net income	$ 47,900

DECISION TOOLKIT

Decision Checkpoints 	Info Needed for Decision 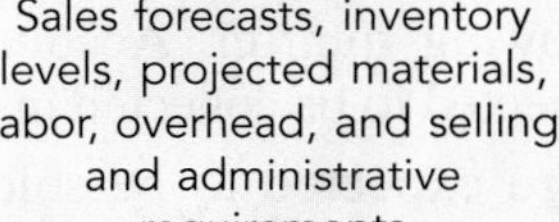	Tool to Use for Decision 	How to Evaluate Results 
Has the company met its targets for sales, production expenses, selling and administrative expenses, and net income?	Sales forecasts, inventory levels, projected materials, labor, overhead, and selling and administrative requirements	Master budget—a set of interrelated budgets including sales, production, materials, labor, overhead, and selling and administrative budgets	Results are favorable if revenues exceed budgeted amounts, or if expenses are less than budgeted amounts.

PREPARING THE FINANCIAL BUDGETS

As shown in Illustration 9-2 (page 377), the financial budgets consist of the capital expenditure budget, the cash budget, and the budgeted balance sheet. We will discuss the capital expenditure budget in Chapter 12; the other budgets are explained in the following sections.

Cash Budget

STUDY OBJECTIVE 5
Explain the principal sections of a cash budget.

The **cash budget** shows anticipated cash flows. Because cash is so vital, this budget is often considered to be the most important financial budget.

The cash budget contains three sections (cash receipts, cash disbursements, and financing) and the beginning and ending cash balances, as shown in Illustration 9-14.

Illustration 9-14
Basic form of a cash budget

ANY COMPANY Cash Budget	
Beginning cash balance	$X,XXX
Add: Cash receipts (Itemized)	X,XXX
Total available cash	X,XXX
Less: Cash disbursements (Itemized)	X,XXX
Excess (deficiency) of available cash over cash disbursements	X,XXX
Financing	X,XXX
Ending cash balance	$X,XXX

HELPFUL HINT
Why is the cash budget prepared after the other budgets are prepared? Answer: Because the information generated by the other budgets dictates the expected inflows and outflows of cash.

The **cash receipts section** includes expected receipts from the company's principal source(s) of revenue. These are usually cash sales and collections from customers on credit sales. This section also shows anticipated receipts of interest and dividends, and proceeds from planned sales of investments, plant assets, and the company's capital stock.

The **cash disbursements section** shows expected cash payments. Such payments include direct materials, direct labor, manufacturing overhead, and selling and administrative expenses. This section also includes projected payments for income taxes, dividends, investments, and plant assets.

The **financing section** shows expected borrowings and the repayment of the borrowed funds plus interest. Companies need this section when there is a cash deficiency or when the cash balance is below management's minimum required balance.

Data in the cash budget are prepared in sequence. The ending cash balance of one period becomes the beginning cash balance for the next period. Companies obtain data for preparing the cash budget from other budgets and from information provided by management. In practice, cash budgets are often prepared for the year on a monthly basis.

To minimize detail, we will assume that Hayes Company prepares an annual cash budget by quarters. Its cash budget is based on the following assumptions.

1. The January 1, 2008, cash balance is expected to be $38,000. Hayes wishes to maintain a balance of at least $15,000.
2. Sales (Illustration 9-3, page 378): 60% are collected in the quarter sold and 40% are collected in the following quarter. Accounts receivable of $60,000 at December 31, 2007, are expected to be collected in full in the first quarter of 2008.
3. Short-term investments are expected to be sold for $2,000 cash in the first quarter.

4. Direct materials (Illustration 9-7, page 380): 50% are paid in the quarter purchased and 50% are paid in the following quarter. Accounts payable of $10,600 at December 31, 2007, are expected to be paid in full in the first quarter of 2008.
5. Direct labor (Illustration 9-9, page 380): 100% is paid in the quarter incurred.
6. Manufacturing overhead (Illustration 9-10, page 382) and selling and administrative expenses (Illustration 9-11, page 382): All items except depreciation are paid in the quarter incurred.
7. Management plans to purchase a truck in the second quarter for $10,000 cash.
8. Hayes makes equal quarterly payments of its estimated annual income taxes.
9. Loans are repaid in the earliest quarter in which there is sufficient cash (that is, when the cash on hand exceeds the $15,000 minimum required balance).

In preparing the cash budget, it is useful to prepare schedules for collections from customers (assumption No. 2, previous page) and cash payments for direct materials (assumption No. 4, above). These schedules are shown in Illustrations 9-15 and 9-16.

Illustration 9-15
Collections from customers

HAYES COMPANY
Schedule of Expected Collections from Customers

	Quarter			
	1	2	3	4
Accounts receivable, 12/31/07	$ 60,000			
First quarter ($180,000)	108,000	$ 72,000		
Second quarter ($210,000)		126,000	$ 84,000	
Third quarter ($240,000)			144,000	$ 96,000
Fourth quarter ($270,000)				162,000
Total collections	$168,000	$198,000	$228,000	$258,000

Illustration 9-16
Payments for direct materials

HAYES COMPANY
Schedule of Expected Payments for Direct Materials

	Quarter			
	1	2	3	4
Accounts payable, 12/31/07	$10,600			
First quarter ($25,200)	12,600	$12,600		
Second quarter ($29,200)		14,600	$14,600	
Third quarter ($33,200)			16,600	$16,600
Fourth quarter ($37,200)				18,600
Total payments	$23,200	$27,200	$31,200	$35,200

Illustration 9-17 (page 386) shows the cash budget for Hayes Company. The budget indicates that Hayes will need $3,000 of financing in the second quarter to maintain a minimum cash balance of $15,000. Since there is an excess of available cash over disbursements of $22,500 at the end of the third quarter, the borrowing, plus $100 interest, is repaid in this quarter.

Hayes Company Cash Budget.xls

File Edit View Insert Format Tools Data Window Help

	A	B	C	D	E	G	I
1	**HAYES COMPANY**						
2	**Cash Budget**						
3	**For the Year Ending December 31, 2008**						
4			Quarter				
5		Assumption	1		2	3	4
6	Beginning cash balance	1	$ 38,000		$ 25,500	$ 15,000	$ 19,400
7	**Add: Receipts**						
8	Collections from customers	2	168,000		198,000	228,000	258,000
9	Sale of securities	3	2,000		0	0	0
10	Total receipts		170,000		198,000	228,000	258,000
11	Total available cash		208,000		223,500	243,000	277,400
12	**Less: Disbursements**						
13	Direct materials	4	23,200		27,200	31,200	35,200
14	Direct labor	5	62,000		72,000	82,000	92,000
15	Manufacturing overhead	6	53,300	a	56,300	59,300	62,300
16	Selling and administrative expenses	6	41,000	b	43,000	45,000	47,000
17	Purchase of truck	7	0		10,000	0	0
18	Income tax expense	8	3,000		3,000	3,000	3,000
19	Total disbursements		182,500		211,500	220,500	239,500
20	Excess (deficiency) of available cash over cash disbursements		25,500		12,000	22,500	37,900
21	**Financing**						
22	Borrowings		0		**3,000**	0	0
23	Repayments-plus $100 interest	9	0		0	**3,100**	0
24	Ending cash balance		$ 25,500		$ 15,000	$ 19,400	$ 37,900
25							
26	[a]$57,100-$3,800 depreciation						
27	[b]$42,000-$1,000 depreciation						

Illustration 9-17
Cash budget

MANAGEMENT INSIGHT

Without a Budget, Can the Games Begin?

Behind the grandeur of the Olympic Games lies a huge financial challenge—how to keep budgeted costs in line with revenues. For example, the 2006 Winter Olympics in Turin, Italy, narrowly avoided going into bankruptcy before the Games even started. In order for the event to remain solvent, organizers cancelled glitzy celebrations and shifted promotional responsibilities to an Italian state-run agency. Despite these efforts, after the Games were over, the Italian government created a lottery game to cover its financial losses.

As another example, organizers of the 2002 Winter Olympics in Salt Lake City cut budgeted costs by $200 million shortly before the events began. According to the chief operating and financial officer, the organizers went through every line item in the budget, sorting each one into "must have" versus "nice to have." As a result, the Salt Lake City Games produced a surplus of $100 million.

Source: Gabriel Kahn and Roger Thurow, "In Turin, Paying for Games Went Down to the Wire," *Wall Street Journal,* February 10, 2006.

Why does it matter whether the Olympic Games exceed their budget?

A cash budget contributes to more effective cash management. It shows managers when additional financing is necessary well before the actual need arises. And, it indicates when excess cash is available for investments or other purposes.

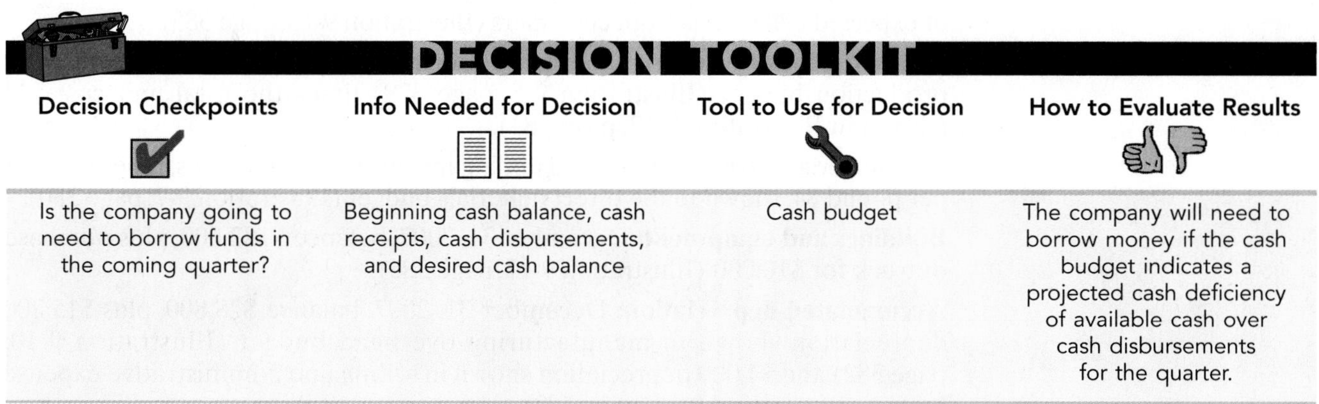

Decision Checkpoints	Info Needed for Decision	Tool to Use for Decision	How to Evaluate Results
Is the company going to need to borrow funds in the coming quarter?	Beginning cash balance, cash receipts, cash disbursements, and desired cash balance	Cash budget	The company will need to borrow money if the cash budget indicates a projected cash deficiency of available cash over cash disbursements for the quarter.

Budgeted Balance Sheet

The **budgeted balance sheet** is a projection of financial position at the end of the budget period. This budget is developed from the budgeted balance sheet for the preceding year and the budgets for the current year. Pertinent data from the budgeted balance sheet at December 31, 2007, are as follows.

Buildings and equipment	$182,000	Common stock	$225,000
Accumulated depreciation	$ 28,800	Retained earnings	$ 46,480

Illustration 9-18 show Hayes Company's budgeted balance sheet at December 31, 2008.

Illustration 9-18
Budgeted balance sheet

HAYES COMPANY
Budgeted Balance Sheet
December 31, 2008

Assets		
Cash		$ 37,900
Accounts receivable		108,000
Finished goods inventory		44,000
Raw materials inventory		4,080
Buildings and equipment	$192,000	
Less: Accumulated depreciation	48,000	144,000
Total assets		$337,980
Liabilities and Stockholders' Equity		
Accounts payable		$ 18,600
Common stock		225,000
Retained earnings		94,380
Total liabilities and stockholders' equity		$337,980

The computations and sources of the amounts are explained below.

Cash: Ending cash balance $37,900, shown in the cash budget (Illustration 9-17, page 386).

Accounts receivable: 40% of fourth-quarter sales $270,000, shown in the schedule of expected collections from customers (Illustration 9-15, page 385).

Finished goods inventory: Desired ending inventory 1,000 units, shown in the production budget (Illustration 9-5, page 379) times the total unit cost $44 (shown in Illustration 9-12, page 383).

Raw materials inventory: Desired ending inventory 1,020 pounds, times the cost per pound $4, shown in the direct materials budget (Illustration 9-7, page 380).

Buildings and equipment: December 31, 2007, balance $182,000, plus purchase of truck for $10,000 (Illustration 9-17, page 386).

Accumulated depreciation: December 31, 2007, balance $28,800, plus $15,200 depreciation shown in manufacturing overhead budget (Illustration 9-10, page 382) and $4,000 depreciation shown in selling and administrative expense budget (Illustration 9-11, page 382).

Accounts payable: 50% of fourth-quarter purchases $37,200, shown in schedule of expected payments for direct materials (Illustration 9-16, page 385).

Common stock: Unchanged from the beginning of the year.

Retained earnings: December 31, 2007, balance $46,480, plus net income $47,900, shown in budgeted income statement (Illustration 9-13, page 383).

After budget data are entered into the computer, Hayes prepares the various budgets (sales, cash, etc.), as well as the budgeted financial statements. Using spreadsheets, management can also perform "what if" (sensitivity) analyses based on different hypothetical assumptions. For example, suppose that sales managers project that sales will be 10% higher in the coming quarter. What impact does this change have on the rest of the budgeting process and the financing needs of the business? The impact of the various assumptions on the budget is quickly determined by the spreadsheet. Armed with these analyses, managers make more informed decisions about the impact of various projects. They also anticipate future problems and business opportunities. As seen in this chapter, budgeting is an excellent use of electronic spreadsheets.

Before You Go On...

REVIEW IT

1. What are the two classifications of the individual budgets in the master budget?
2. What is the sequence for preparing the budgets that comprise the operating budgets?
3. Identify some of the source documents that would be used in preparing each of the operating budgets.
4. What are the three principal sections of the cash budget?

DO IT

Martian Company management wants to maintain a minimum monthly cash balance of $15,000. At the beginning of March, the cash balance is $16,500, expected cash receipts for March are $210,000, and cash disbursements are expected to be $220,000. How much cash, if any, must be borrowed to maintain the desired minimum monthly balance?

Action Plan

- Write down the basic form of the cash budget, starting with the beginning cash balance, adding cash receipts for the period, deducting cash disbursements, and identifying the needed financing to achieve the desired minimum ending cash balance.
- Insert the data given into the outlined form of the cash budget.

Solution

MARTIAN COMPANY
Cash Budget
For the Month Ending March 31, 2008

Beginning cash balance	$ 16,500
Add: Cash receipts for March	210,000
Total available cash	226,500
Less: Cash disbursements for March	220,000
Excess of available cash over cash disbursements	6,500
Financing	8,500
Ending cash balance	$ 15,000

To maintain the desired minimum cash balance of $15,000, Martian Company must borrow $8,500 of cash.

Related exercise material: *BE9-9, E9-12, E9-13, E9-14, E9-15, and E9-16.*

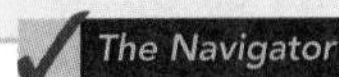

BUDGETING IN NONMANUFACTURING COMPANIES

Budgeting is not limited to manufacturers. Budgets are also used by merchandisers, service enterprises, and not-for-profit organizations.

STUDY OBJECTIVE 6

Indicate the applicability of budgeting in nonmanufacturing companies.

Merchandisers

As in manufacturing operations, the sales budget for a merchandiser is both the starting point and the key factor in the development of the master budget. The major differences between the master budgets of a merchandiser and a manufacturer are these:

1. A merchandiser **uses a merchandise purchases budget instead of a production budget**.
2. A merchandiser **does not use the manufacturing budgets (direct materials, direct labor, and manufacturing overhead)**.

The **merchandise purchases budget** shows the estimated cost of goods to be purchased to meet expected sales. The formula for determining budgeted merchandise purchases is:

Budgeted Cost of Goods Sold	+	Desired Ending Merchandise Inventory	−	Beginning Merchandise Inventory	=	Required Merchandise Purchases

Illustration 9-19
Merchandise purchases formula

To illustrate, assume that the budget committee of Lima Company is preparing the merchandise purchases budget for July 2008. It estimates that budgeted sales will be $300,000 in July and $320,000 in August. Cost of goods sold is expected to be 70% of sales—that is, $210,000 in July (.70 × $300,000) and $224,000 in August (.70 × $320,000). The company's desired ending inventory is 30% of the following month's cost of goods sold. Required merchandise purchases for July are $214,200, computed as follows.

Illustration 9-20
Merchandise purchases budget

LIMA COMPANY
Merchandise Purchases Budget
For the Month Ending July 31, 2008

Budgeted cost of goods sold ($300,000 × 70%)	$ 210,000
Add: Desired ending merchandise inventory ($224,000 × 30%)	67,200
Total	277,200
Less: Beginning merchandise inventory ($210,000 × 30%)	63,000
Required merchandise purchases for July	**$214,200**

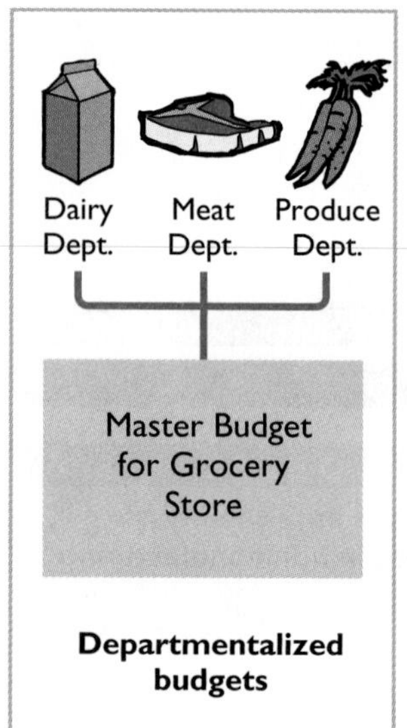

Departmentalized budgets

When a merchandiser is departmentalized, it prepares separate budgets for each department. For example, a grocery store prepares sales budgets and purchases budgets for each of its major departments, such as meats, dairy, and produce. The store then combines these budgets into a master budget for the store. When a retailer has branch stores, it prepares separate master budgets for each store. Then it incorporates these budgets into master budgets for the company as a whole.

Service Enterprises

In a service enterprise, such as a public accounting firm, a law office, or a medical practice, the critical factor in budgeting is **coordinating professional staff needs with anticipated services**. If a firm is overstaffed, several problems may result: Labor costs are disproportionately high. Profits are lower because of the additional salaries. Staff turnover sometimes increases because of lack of challenging work. In contrast, if a service enterprise is understaffed, it may lose revenue because existing and prospective client needs for service cannot be met. Also, professional staff may seek other jobs because of excessive work loads.

Service enterprises can obtain budget data for service revenue from **expected output** or **expected input**. When output is used, it is necessary to determine the expected billings of clients for services provided. In a public accounting firm, for example, output is the sum of its billings in auditing, tax, and consulting services. When input data are used, each professional staff member projects his or her billable time. The firm then applies billing rates to billable time to produce expected service revenue.

Not-for-Profit Organizations

Budgeting is just as important for not-for-profit organizations as for profit-oriented enterprises. The budget process, however, is different. In most cases, not-for-profit entities budget **on the basis of cash flows (expenditures and receipts), rather than on a revenue and expense basis**. Further, the starting point in the process is usually expenditures, not receipts. For the not-for-profit entity, management's task generally is to find the receipts needed to support the planned expenditures. The activity index is also likely to be significantly different. For example, in a not-for-profit entity, such as a university, budgeted faculty positions may be based on full-time equivalent students or credit hours expected to be taught in a department.

For some governmental units, voters approve the budget. In other cases, such as state governments and the federal government, legislative approval is required. After the budget is adopted, it must be followed. Overspending is often illegal. In governmental budgets, authorizations tend to be on a line-by-line basis. That is, the budget for a municipality may have a specified authorization for police and fire protection, garbage collection, street paving, and so on. The line-item authorization of governmental budgets significantly limits the amount of discretion management can exercise. The city manager often cannot use savings from one line item, such as street paving, to cover increased spending in another line item, such as snow removal.

Before You Go On...

REVIEW IT

1. What is the formula for computing required merchandise purchases?
2. How does budgeting in service and not-for-profit organizations differ from budgeting for manufacturers and merchandisers?

Be sure to read **ALL ABOUT YOU: *Avoiding Personal Financial Disaster*** on page 392 for information on how topics in this chapter apply to you.

all about YOU

Avoiding Personal Financial Disaster

You might hear people say that they "need to learn to live within a budget." The funny thing is that most people who say this haven't actually prepared a personal budget, nor do they intend to. Instead, what they are referring to is a vaguely defined, poorly specified, collection of rough ideas of how much they should spend on various aspects of their life. You can't live within or even outside of something that doesn't exist. With that in mind, let's take a look at personal budgets.

Some Facts

* The average American household income is $49,430, before taxes.
* The average family spends $5,375 on food each year. Of this, $3,099 is for food consumed at home, and $2,276 is for food consumed away from home.
* The average family spends $13,283 annually on housing costs. Of this amount, $7,829 is the actual cost of shelter, $2,684 is for utilities, and $1,518 is for furnishings and equipment.
* The average family spends $7,759 per year on transportation. Of this, $3,665 goes to vehicle purchase payments, and $1,235 is spent on fuel. The average family spends only $389 per year on public transportation.

About the Numbers

Obviously people spend their income in different ways. For example, the percentage of your income spent on necessities declines as your income increases. Nonetheless, it is interesting to see how the average family spends its money.

Average U.S. Household Expenditures

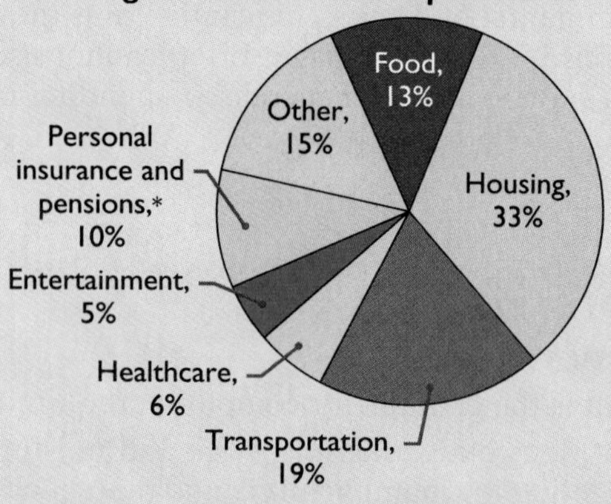

* This includes Social Security tax.

Source: "Consumer Expenditures in 2004," U.S. Department of Labor and U.S. Bureau of Labor Statistics, Report 992, April 2006.

What Do You Think?

Many worksheet templates that are provided for personal budgets for college students treat student loans as an income source. See, for example, the template provided at **http://financialplan.about.com/cs/budgeting/l/blmocolbud.htm**. Based on your knowledge of accounting, is this correct?

YES: Student loans provide a source of cash which can be used to pay costs. As the saying goes, "It all spends the same." Therefore student loans are income.

NO: Student loans must eventually be repaid; therefore they are not income. As the name suggests, they are loans.

The authors' comments on this situation appear on page 413.

Using the Decision Toolkit

The University of Wisconsin and its subunits must prepare budgets. One unique subunit of the University of Wisconsin is Babcock Ice Cream, a functioning producer of dairy products (and famous, at least on campus, for its delicious ice cream).

Assume that Babcock Ice Cream prepares monthly cash budgets. Relevant data from assumed operating budgets for 2008 are:

	January	February
Sales	$460,000	$412,000
Direct materials purchases	185,000	210,000
Direct labor	70,000	85,000
Manufacturing overhead	50,000	65,000
Selling and administrative expenses	85,000	95,000

Babcock sells its ice cream in shops on campus, as well as to local stores. Collections are expected to be 75% in the month of sale, and 25% in the month following sale. Babcock pays 60% of direct materials purchases in cash in the month of purchase, and the balance due in the month following the purchase. All other items above are paid in the month incurred. (Depreciation has been excluded from manufacturing overhead and selling and administrative expenses.)

Other data:

(1) Sales: December 2007, $320,000
(2) Purchases of direct materials: December 2007, $175,000
(3) Other receipts: January—Donation received, $2,000
February—Sale of used equipment, $4,000
(4) Other disbursements: February—Purchased equipment, $10,000
(5) Repaid debt: January, $30,000

The company's cash balance on January 1, 2008, is expected to be $50,000. The company wants to maintain a minimum cash balance of $45,000.

Instructions

(a) Prepare schedules for (1) expected collections from customers and (2) expected payments for direct materials purchases.
(b) Prepare a cash budget for January and February in columnar form.

Solution

(a) (1) Expected Collections from Customers

	January	February
December ($320,000)	$ 80,000	$ 0
January ($460,000)	345,000	115,000
February ($412,000)	0	309,000
Totals	$425,000	$424,000

(2) Expected Payments for Direct Materials

	January	February
December ($175,000)	$ 70,000	$ 0
January ($185,000)	111,000	74,000
February ($210,000)	0	126,000
Totals	$181,000	$200,000

(b)

BABCOCK ICE CREAM
Cash Budget
For the Two Months Ending February 28, 2008

	January	February
Beginning cash balance	$ 50,000	$ 61,000
Add: Receipts		
Collections from customers	425,000	424,000
Donations received	2,000	0
Sale of used equipment	0	4,000
Total receipts	427,000	428,000
Total available cash	477,000	489,000
Less: Disbursements		
Direct materials	181,000	200,000
Direct labor	70,000	85,000
Manufacturing overhead	50,000	65,000
Selling and administrative expenses	85,000	95,000
Purchase of equipment	0	10,000
Total disbursements	386,000	455,000
Excess (deficiency) of available cash over cash disbursements	91,000	34,000
Financing		
Borrowings	0	11,000
Repayments	30,000	0
Ending cash balance	$ 61,000	$ 45,000

The Navigator

SUMMARY OF STUDY OBJECTIVES

1 **Indicate the benefits of budgeting.** The primary advantages of budgeting are that it (a) requires management to plan ahead, (b) provides definite objectives for evaluating performance, (c) creates an early warning system for potential problems, (d) facilitates coordination of activities, (e) results in greater management awareness, and (f) motivates personnel to meet planned objectives.

2 **State the essentials of effective budgeting.** The essentials of effective budgeting are (a) sound organizational structure, (b) research and analysis, and (c) acceptance by all levels of management.

3 **Identify the budgets that comprise the master budget.** The master budget consists of the following budgets: (a) sales, (b) production, (c) direct materials, (d) direct labor, (e) manufacturing overhead, (f) selling and administrative expense, (g) budgeted income statement, (h) capital expenditure budget, (i) cash budget, and (j) budgeted balance sheet.

4 **Describe the sources for preparing the budgeted income statement.** The budgeted income statement is prepared from (a) the sales budget, (b) the budgets for direct materials, direct labor, and manufacturing overhead, and (c) the selling and administrative expense budget.

5 **Explain the principal sections of a cash budget.** The cash budget has three sections (receipts, disbursements, and financing) and the beginning and ending cash balances.

6 **Indicate the applicability of budgeting in nonmanufacturing companies.** Budgeting may be used by merchandisers for development of a merchandise purchases budget. In service enterprises budgeting is a critical factor in coordinating staff needs with anticipated services. In not-for-profit organizations, the starting point in budgeting is usually expenditures, not receipts.

DECISION TOOLKIT—A SUMMARY

Decision Checkpoints 	Info Needed for Decision 	Tool to Use for Decision 	How to Evaluate Results 
Has the company met its targets for sales, production expenses, selling and administrative expenses, and net income?	Sales forecasts, inventory levels, projected materials, labor, overhead, and selling and administrative requirements	Master budget — a set of interrelated budgets including sales, production, materials, labor, overhead, and selling and administrative budgets	Results are favorable if revenues exceed budgeted amounts, or if expenses are less than budgeted amounts.
Is the company going to need to borrow funds in the coming quarter?	Beginning cash balance, cash receipts, cash disbursements, and desired cash balance	Cash budget	The company will need to borrow money if the cash budget indicates a projected cash deficiency of available cash over cash disbursements for the quarter.

GLOSSARY

Budget A formal written statement of management's plans for a specified future time period, expressed in financial terms. (p. 372).

Budget committee A group responsible for coordinating the preparation of the budget. (p. 374).

Budgetary slack The amount by which a manager intentionally underestimates budgeted revenues or overestimates budgeted expenses in order to make it easier to achieve budgetary goals. (p. 375).

Budgeted balance sheet A projection of financial position at the end of the budget period. (p. 387).

Budgeted income statement An estimate of the expected profitability of operations for the budget period. (p. 383).

Cash budget A projection of anticipated cash flows. (p. 384).

Direct labor budget A projection of the quantity and cost of direct labor necessary to meet production requirements. (p. 380).

Direct materials budget An estimate of the quantity and cost of direct materials to be purchased. (p. 379).

Financial budgets Individual budgets that focus primarily on the cash resources needed to fund expected operations and planned capital expenditures. (p. 376).

Long-range planning A formalized process of selecting strategies to achieve long-term goals and developing policies and plans to implement the strategies. (p. 376).

Manufacturing overhead budget An estimate of expected manufacturing overhead costs for the budget period. (p. 381).

Master budget A set of interrelated budgets that constitutes a plan of action for a specific time period. (p. 376).

Merchandise purchases budget The estimated cost of goods to be purchased by a merchandiser to meet expected sales. (p. 389).

Operating budgets Individual budgets that result in a budgeted income statement. (p. 376).

Participative budgeting A budgetary approach that starts with input from lower-level managers and works upward so that managers at all levels participate. (p. 374).

Production budget A projection of the units that must be produced to meet anticipated sales. (p. 378).

Sales budget An estimate of expected sales revenue for the budget period. (p. 378).

Sales forecast The projection of potential sales for the industry and the company's expected share of such sales. (p. 374).

Selling and administrative expense budget A projection of anticipated selling and administrative expenses for the budget period. (p. 381).

Demonstration Problem

Soroco Company is preparing its master budget for 2008. Relevant data pertaining to its sales and production budgets are as follows:

Sales: Sales for the year are expected to total 1,200,000 units. Quarterly sales are 20%, 25%, 30%, and 25% respectively. The sales price is expected to be $50 per unit for the first three quarters and $55 per unit beginning in the fourth quarter. Sales in the first quarter of 2009 are expected to be 10% higher than the budgeted sales volume for the first quarter of 2008.

Production: Management desires to maintain ending finished goods inventories at 25% of the next quarter's budgeted sales volume.

Instructions

Prepare the sales budget and production budget by quarters for 2008.

action plan

- ✓ Know the form and content of the sales budget.
- ✓ Prepare the sales budget first as the basis for the other budgets.
- ✓ Determine the units that must be produced to meet anticipated sales.
- ✓ Know how to compute the beginning and ending finished goods units.

Solution

SOROCO COMPANY
Sales Budget
For the Year Ending December 31, 2008

	Quarter				
	1	2	3	4	Year
Expected unit sales	240,000	300,000	360,000	300,000	1,200,000
Unit selling price	× $50	× $50	× $50	× $55	—
Total sales	$12,000,000	$15,000,000	$18,000,000	$16,500,000	$61,500,000

SOROCO COMPANY
Production Budget
For the Year Ending December 31, 2008

	Quarter				
	1	2	3	4	Year
Expected unit sales	240,000	300,000	360,000	300,000	
Add: Desired ending finished goods units	75,000	90,000	75,000	66,000[1]	
Total required units	315,000	390,000	435,000	366,000	
Less: Beginning finished goods units	60,000[2]	75,000	90,000	75,000	
Required production units	255,000	315,000	345,000	291,000	1,206,000

[1]Estimated first-quarter 2009 sales volume 240,000 + (240,000 × 10%) = 264,000; 264,000 × 25%.
[2]25% of estimated first-quarter 2008 sales units (240,000 × 25%).

SELF-STUDY QUESTIONS

Answers are at the end of the chapter.

(SO 1) 1. Which of the following is not a benefit of budgeting?
- **a.** Management can plan ahead.
- **b.** An early warning system is provided for potential problems.
- **c.** It enables disciplinary action to be taken at every level of responsibility.
- **d.** The coordination of activities is facilitated.

(SO 2) 2. The essentials of effective budgeting do *not* include:
- **a.** top-down budgeting.
- **b.** management acceptance.
- **c.** research and analysis.
- **d.** sound organizational structure.

3. Compared to budgeting, long-range planning generally has the: (SO 2)
- **a.** same amount of detail.
- **b.** longer time period.
- **c.** same emphasis.
- **d.** same time period.

4. A sales budget is: (SO 3)
- **a.** derived from the production budget.
- **b.** management's best estimate of sales revenue for the year.

c. not the starting point for the master budget.
d. prepared only for credit sales.

(SO 3) 5. The formula for the production budget is budgeted sales in units plus:
a. desired ending merchandise inventory less beginning merchandise inventory.
b. beginning finished goods units less desired ending finished goods units.
c. desired ending direct materials units less beginning direct materials units.
d. desired ending finished goods units less beginning finished goods units.

(SO 3) 6. Direct materials inventories are kept in pounds in Byrd Company, and the total pounds of direct materials needed for production is 9,500. If the beginning inventory is 1,000 pounds and the desired ending inventory is 2,200 pounds, the total pounds to be purchased is:
a. 9,400.
b. 9,500.
c. 9,700.
d. 10,700.

(SO 3) 7. The formula for computing the direct labor budget is to multiply the direct labor cost per hour by the:
a. total required direct labor hours.
b. physical units to be produced.
c. equivalent units to be produced.
d. No correct answer is given.

8. Each of the following budgets is used in preparing the budgeted income statement *except* the: (SO 4)
a. sales budget.
b. selling and administrative budget.
c. capital expenditure budget.
d. direct labor budget.

9. Expected direct materials purchases in Read Company are $70,000 in the first quarter and $90,000 in the second quarter. Forty percent of the purchases are paid in cash as incurred, and the balance is paid in the following quarter. The budgeted cash payments for purchases in the second quarter are: (SO 5)
a. $96,000.
b. $90,000.
c. $78,000.
d. $72,000.

10. The budget for a merchandiser differs from a budget for a manufacturer because: (SO 6)
a. a merchandise purchases budget replaces the production budget.
b. the manufacturing budgets are not applicable.
c. None of the above.
d. Both (a) and (b) above.

Go to the book's website, **www.wiley.com/college/weygandt**, for Additional Self-Study questions.

QUESTIONS

1. **(a)** What is a budget?
(b) How does a budget contribute to good management?
2. Karen Bay and Frank Barone are discussing the benefits of budgeting. They ask you to identify the primary advantages of budgeting. Comply with their request.
3. Tina Haworth asks your help in understanding the essentials of effective budgeting. Identify the essentials for Tina.
4. **(a)** "Accounting plays a relatively unimportant role in budgeting." Do you agree? Explain.
(b) What responsibilities does management have in budgeting?
5. What criteria are helpful in determining the length of the budget period? What is the most common budget period?
6. Megan Pedigo maintains that the only difference between budgeting and long-range planning is time. Do you agree? Why or why not?
7. What is participative budgeting? What are its potential benefits? What are its potential shortcomings?
8. What is budgetary slack? What incentive do managers have to create budgetary slack?
9. Distinguish between a master budget and a sales forecast.
10. What budget is the starting point in preparing the master budget? What may result if this budget is inaccurate?
11. "The production budget shows both unit production data and unit cost data." Is this true? Explain.
12. Cali Company has 15,000 beginning finished goods units. Budgeted sales units are 160,000. If management desires 20,000 ending finished goods units, what are the required units of production?
13. In preparing the direct materials budget for Mast Company, management concludes that required purchases are 64,000 units. If 52,000 direct materials units are required in production and there are 7,000 units of beginning direct materials, what is the desired units of ending direct materials?
14. The production budget of Rooney Company calls for 80,000 units to be produced. If it takes 30 minutes to make one unit and the direct labor rate is $16 per hour, what is the total budgeted direct labor cost?
15. Morales Company's manufacturing overhead budget shows total variable costs of $198,000 and total fixed costs of $162,000. Total production in units is expected to be 160,000. It takes 15 minutes to make one unit, and the direct labor rate is $15 per hour. Express the manufacturing overhead rate as (a) a percentage of direct labor cost, and (b) an amount per direct labor hour.
16. Elbert Company's variable selling and administrative expenses are 10% of net sales. Fixed expenses are $50,000 per quarter. The sales budget shows expected sales of $200,000 and $250,000 in the first and second quarters, respectively. What are the total budgeted selling and administrative expenses for each quarter?

17. For Nolte Company, the budgeted cost for one unit of product is direct materials \$10, direct labor \$20, and manufacturing overhead 90% of direct labor cost. If 25,000 units are expected to be sold at \$69 each, what is the budgeted gross profit?
18. Indicate the supporting schedules used in preparing a budgeted income statement through gross profit for a manufacturer.
19. Identify the three sections of a cash budget. What balances are also shown in this budget?
20. Van Gundy Company has credit sales of \$500,000 in January. Past experience suggests that 45% is collected in the month of sale, 50% in the month following the sale, and 5% in the second month following the sale. Compute the cash collections from January sales in January, February, and March.
21. What is the formula for determining required merchandise purchases for a merchandiser?
22. How may expected revenues in a service enterprise be computed?

BRIEF EXERCISES

Prepare a diagram of a master budget. (SO 3)

BE9-1 Noble Manufacturing Company uses the following budgets: Balance Sheet, Capital Expenditure, Cash, Direct Labor, Direct Materials, Income Statement, Manufacturing Overhead, Production, Sales, and Selling and Administrative. Prepare a diagram of the interrelationships of the budgets in the master budget. Indicate whether each budget is an operating or a financial budget.

Prepare a sales budget. (SO 3)

BE9-2 Goody Company estimates that unit sales will be 10,000 in quarter 1; 12,000 in quarter 2; 14,000 in quarter 3; and 18,000 in quarter 4. Using a sales price of \$80 per unit, prepare the sales budget by quarters for the year ending December 31, 2008.

Prepare a production budget for 2 quarters. (SO 3)

BE9-3 Sales budget data for Goody Company are given in BE9-2. Management desires to have an ending finished goods inventory equal to 20% of the next quarter's expected unit sales. Prepare a production budget by quarters for the first 6 months of 2008.

Prepare a direct materials budget for 1 month. (SO 3)

BE9-4 Ortiz Company has 1,600 pounds of raw materials in its December 31, 2008, ending inventory. Required production for January and February of 2009 are 4,000 and 5,500 units, respectively. Two pounds of raw materials are needed for each unit, and the estimated cost per pound is \$6. Management desires an ending inventory equal to 20% of next month's materials requirements. Prepare the direct materials budget for January.

Prepare a direct labor budget for 2 quarters. (SO 3)

BE9-5 For Everly Company, units to be produced are 5,000 in quarter 1 and 6,000 in quarter 2. It takes 1.5 hours to make a finished unit, and the expected hourly wage rate is \$14 per hour. Prepare a direct labor budget by quarters for the 6 months ending June 30, 2008.

Prepare a manufacturing overhead budget. (SO 3)

BE9-6 For Justus Inc. variable manufacturing overhead costs are expected to be \$20,000 in the first quarter of 2008 with \$4,000 increments in each of the remaining three quarters. Fixed overhead costs are estimated to be \$35,000 in each quarter. Prepare the manufacturing overhead budget by quarters and in total for the year.

Prepare a selling and administrative expense budget. (SO 3)

BE9-7 Mize Company classifies its selling and administrative expense budget into variable and fixed components. Variable expenses are expected to be \$25,000 in the first quarter, and \$5,000 increments are expected in the remaining quarters of 2008. Fixed expenses are expected to be \$40,000 in each quarter. Prepare the selling and administrative expense budget by quarters and in total for 2008.

Prepare a budgeted income statement for the year. (SO 4)

BE9-8 Perine Company has completed all of its operating budgets. The sales budget for the year shows 50,000 units and total sales of \$2,000,000. The total unit cost of making one unit of sales is \$22. Selling and administrative expenses are expected to be \$300,000. Income taxes are estimated to be \$150,000. Prepare a budgeted income statement for the year ending December 31, 2008.

Prepare data for a cash budget. (SO 5)

BE9-9 Agee Industries expects credit sales for January, February, and March to be \$200,000, \$260,000, and \$310,000, respectively. It is expected that 70% of the sales will be collected in the month of sale, and 30% will be collected in the following month. Compute cash collections from customers for each month.

Determine required merchandise purchases for 1 month. (SO 6)

BE9-10 Palermo Wholesalers is preparing its merchandise purchases budget. Budgeted sales are \$400,000 for April and \$475,000 for May. Cost of goods sold is expected to be 60% of sales. The company's desired ending inventory is 20% of the following month's cost of goods sold. Compute the required purchases for April.

EXERCISES

E9-1 Black Rose Company has always done some planning for the future, but the company has never prepared a formal budget. Now that the company is growing larger, it is considering preparing a budget.

Explain the concept of budgeting.
(SO 1, 2, 3)

Instructions
Write a memo to Jack Bruno, the president of Black Rose Company, in which you define budgeting, identify the budgets that comprise the master budget, identify the primary benefits of budgeting, and discuss the essentials of effective budgeting.

E9-2 Zeller Electronics Inc. produces and sells two models of pocket calculators, XQ-103 and XQ-104. The calculators sell for $12 and $25, respectively. Because of the intense competition Zeller faces, management budgets sales semiannually. Its projections for the first 2 quarters of 2008 are as follows.

Prepare a sales budget for 2 quarters.
(SO 3)

	Unit Sales	
Product	**Quarter 1**	**Quarter 2**
XQ-103	20,000	25,000
XQ-104	12,000	15,000

No changes in selling prices are anticipated.

Instructions
Prepare a sales budget for the 2 quarters ending June 30, 2008. List the products and show for each quarter and for the 6 months, units, selling price, and total sales by product and in total.

E9-3 Roche and Young, CPAs, are preparing their service revenue (sales) budget for the coming year (2008). The practice is divided into three departments: auditing, tax, and consulting. Billable hours for each department, by quarter, are provided below.

Prepare a sales budget for four quarters.
(SO 3, 6)

Department	Quarter 1	Quarter 2	Quarter 3	Quarter 4
Auditing	2,200	1,600	2,000	2,400
Tax	3,000	2,400	2,000	2,500
Consulting	1,500	1,500	1,500	1,500

Average hourly billing rates are: auditing $80, tax $90, and consulting $100.

Instructions
Prepare the service revenue (sales) budget for 2008 by listing the departments and showing for each quarter and the year in total, billable hours, billable rate, and total revenue.

E9-4 Turney Company produces and sells automobile batteries, the heavy-duty HD-240. The 2008 sales budget is as follows.

Prepare quarterly production budgets.
(SO 3)

Quarter	HD-240
1	5,000
2	7,000
3	8,000
4	10,000

The January 1, 2008, inventory of HD-240 is 2,500 units. Management desires an ending inventory each quarter equal to 50% of the next quarter's sales. Sales in the first quarter of 2009 are expected to be 30% higher than sales in the same quarter in 2008.

Instructions
Prepare quarterly production budgets for each quarter and in total for 2008.

E9-5 Moreno Industries has adopted the following production budget for the first 4 months of 2009.

Prepare a direct materials purchases budget.
(SO 3)

Month	Units	Month	Units
January	10,000	March	5,000
February	8,000	April	4,000

Each unit requires 3 pounds of raw materials costing $2 per pound. On December 31, 2008, the ending raw materials inventory was 9,000 pounds. Management wants to have a raw materials inventory at the end of the month equal to 30% of next month's production requirements.

Instructions

Prepare a direct materials purchases budget by month for the first quarter.

Prepare production and direct materials budgets by quarters for 6 months.
(SO 3)

E9-6 On January 1, 2009 the Batista Company budget committee has reached agreement on the following data for the 6 months ending June 30, 2009.

Sales units:	First quarter 5,000; second quarter 6,000; third quarter 7,000
Ending raw materials inventory:	50% of the next quarter's production requirements
Ending finished goods inventory:	30% of the next quarter's expected sales units
Third-quarter production:	7,250 units

The ending raw materials and finished goods inventories at December 31, 2008, follow the same percentage relationships to production and sales that occur in 2009. Three pounds of raw materials are required to make each unit of finished goods. Raw materials purchased are expected to cost $4 per pound.

Instructions

(a) Prepare a production budget by quarters for the 6-month period ended June 30, 2009.
(b) Prepare a direct materials budget by quarters for the 6-month period ended June 30, 2009.

Prepare a direct labor budget.
(SO 3)

E9-7 Neely, Inc., is preparing its direct labor budget for 2008 from the following production budget based on a calendar year.

Quarter	Units	Quarter	Units
1	20,000	3	35,000
2	25,000	4	30,000

Each unit requires 1.6 hours of direct labor.

Instructions

Prepare a direct labor budget for 2008. Wage rates are expected to be $15 for the first 2 quarters and $16 for quarters 3 and 4.

Prepare a manufacturing overhead budget for the year.
(SO 3)

E9-8 Hardin Company is preparing its manufacturing overhead budget for 2008. Relevant data consist of the following.

Units to be produced (by quarters): 10,000, 12,000, 14,000, 16,000.

Direct labor: Time is 1.5 hours per unit.

Variable overhead costs per direct labor hour: Indirect materials $0.70; indirect labor $1.20; and maintenance $0.50.

Fixed overhead costs per quarter: Supervisory salaries $35,000; depreciation $16,000; and maintenance $12,000.

Instructions

Prepare the manufacturing overhead budget for the year, showing quarterly data.

Prepare a selling and administrative expense budget for 2 quarters.
(SO 3)

E9-9 Edington Company combines its operating expenses for budget purposes in a selling and administrative expense budget. For the first 6 months of 2008, the following data are available.

1. Sales: 20,000 units quarter 1; 22,000 units quarter 2.
2. Variable costs per dollar of sales: Sales commissions 5%, delivery expense 2%, and advertising 3%.
3. Fixed costs per quarter: Sales salaries $10,000, office salaries $6,000, depreciation $4,200, insurance $1,500, utilities $800, and repairs expense $600.
4. Unit selling price: $20.

Instructions

Prepare a selling and administrative expense budget by quarters for the first 6 months of 2008.

Prepare a production and a direct materials budget.
(SO 3)

E9-10 Tyson Chandler Company's sales budget projects unit sales of part 198Z of 10,000 units in January, 12,000 units in February, and 13,000 units in March. Each unit of part 198Z requires 2 pounds of materials, which cost $3 per pound. Tyson Chandler Company desires its ending raw materials inventory to equal 40% of the next month's production requirements, and its ending finished goods inventory to equal 25% of the next month's expected unit sales. These goals were met at December 31, 2007.

Instructions

(a) Prepare a production budget for January and February 2008.
(b) Prepare a direct materials budget for January 2008.

E9-11 Fuqua Company has accumulated the following budget data for the year 2008.

Prepare a budgeted income statement for the year.
(SO 3, 4)

1. Sales: 30,000 units, unit selling price $80.
2. Cost of one unit of finished goods: Direct materials 2 pounds at $5 per pound, direct labor 3 hours at $12 per hour, and manufacturing overhead $6 per direct labor hour.
3. Inventories (raw materials only): Beginning, 10,000 pounds; ending, 15,000 pounds.
4. Raw materials cost: $5 per pound.
5. Selling and administrative expenses: $200,000.
6. Income taxes: 30% of income before income taxes.

Instructions

(a) Prepare a schedule showing the computation of cost of goods sold for 2008.
(b) Prepare a budgeted income statement for 2008.

E9-12 Garza Company expects to have a cash balance of $46,000 on January 1, 2008. Relevant monthly budget data for the first 2 months of 2008 are as follows.

Prepare a cash budget for 2 months.
(SO 5)

Collections from customers: January $85,000, February $150,000.

Payments for direct materials: January $50,000, February $70,000.

Direct labor: January $30,000, February $45,000. Wages are paid in the month they are incurred.

Manufacturing overhead: January $21,000, February $25,000. These costs include depreciation of $1,000 per month. All other overhead costs are paid as incurred.

Selling and administrative expenses: January $15,000, February $20,000. These costs are exclusive of depreciation. They are paid as incurred.

Sales of marketable securities in January are expected to realize $10,000 in cash. Garza Company has a line of credit at a local bank that enables it to borrow up to $25,000. The company wants to maintain a minimum monthly cash balance of $20,000.

Instructions

Prepare a cash budget for January and February.

E9-13 Pink Martini Corporation is projecting a cash balance of $31,000 in its December 31, 2007, balance sheet. Pink Martini's schedule of expected collections from customers for the first quarter of 2008 shows total collections of $180,000. The schedule of expected payments for direct materials for the first quarter of 2008 shows total payments of $41,000. Other information gathered for the first quarter of 2008 is: sale of equipment $3,500; direct labor $70,000, manufacturing overhead $35,000, selling and administrative expenses $45,000; and purchase of securities $12,000. Pink Martini wants to maintain a balance of at least $25,000 cash at the end of each quarter.

Prepare a cash budget.
(SO 5)

Instructions

Prepare a cash budget for the first quarter.

E9-14 NIU Company's budgeted sales and direct materials purchases are as follows.

Prepare schedules of expected collections and payments.
(SO 5)

	Budgeted Sales	Budgeted D.M. Purchases
January	$200,000	$30,000
February	220,000	35,000
March	270,000	41,000

NIU's sales are 40% cash and 60% credit. Credit sales are collected 10% in the month of sale, 50% in the month following sale, and 36% in the second month following sale; 4% are uncollectible. NIU's purchases are 50% cash and 50% on account. Purchases on account are paid 40% in the month of purchase, and 60% in the month following purchase.

Instructions

(a) Prepare a schedule of expected collections from customers for March.
(b) Prepare a schedule of expected payments for direct materials for March.

Prepare schedules for cash receipts and cash payments, and determine ending balances for balance sheet.

(SO 5, 6)

E9-15 Environmental Landscaping Inc. is preparing its budget for the first quarter of 2008. The next step in the budgeting process is to prepare a cash receipts schedule and a cash payments schedule. To that end the following information has been collected.

Clients usually pay 60% of their fee in the month that service is provided, 30% the month after, and 10% the second month after receiving service.

Actual service revenue for 2007 and expected service revenues for 2008 are: November 2007, $90,000; December 2007, $80,000; January 2008, $100,000; February 2008, $120,000; March 2008, $130,000.

Purchases on landscaping supplies (direct materials) are paid 40% in the month of purchase and 60% the following month. Actual purchases for 2007 and expected purchases for 2008 are: December 2007, $14,000; January 2008, $12,000; February 2008, $15,000; March 2008, $18,000.

Instructions

(a) Prepare the following schedules for each month in the first quarter of 2008 and for the quarter in total:
(1) Expected collections from clients.
(2) Expected payments for landscaping supplies.

(b) Determine the following balances at March 31, 2008:
(1) Accounts receivable.
(2) Accounts payable.

Prepare a cash budget for two quarters.

(SO 5, 6)

E9-16 Donnegal Dental Clinic is a medium-sized dental service specializing in family dental care. The clinic is currently preparing the master budget for the first 2 quarters of 2008. All that remains in this process is the cash budget. The following information has been collected from other portions of the master budget and elsewhere.

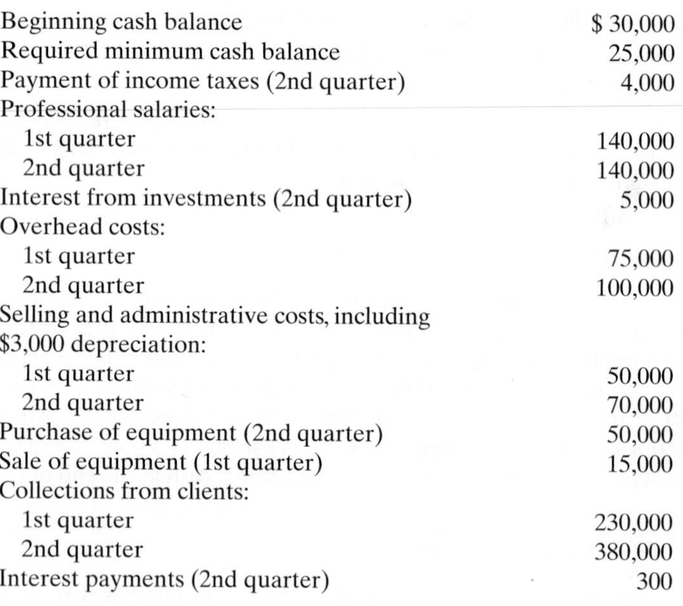

Beginning cash balance	$ 30,000
Required minimum cash balance	25,000
Payment of income taxes (2nd quarter)	4,000
Professional salaries:	
1st quarter	140,000
2nd quarter	140,000
Interest from investments (2nd quarter)	5,000
Overhead costs:	
1st quarter	75,000
2nd quarter	100,000
Selling and administrative costs, including $3,000 depreciation:	
1st quarter	50,000
2nd quarter	70,000
Purchase of equipment (2nd quarter)	50,000
Sale of equipment (1st quarter)	15,000
Collections from clients:	
1st quarter	230,000
2nd quarter	380,000
Interest payments (2nd quarter)	300

Instructions

Prepare a cash budget for each of the first two quarters of 2008.

Prepare a purchases budget and budgeted income statement for a merchandiser.

(SO 6)

E9-17 In May 2008, the budget committee of Dalby Stores assembles the following data in preparation of budgeted merchandise purchases for the month of June.

1. Expected sales: June $500,000, July $600,000.
2. Cost of goods sold is expected to be 70% of sales.
3. Desired ending merchandise inventory is 40% of the following (next) month's cost of goods sold.
4. The beginning inventory at June 1 will be the desired amount.

Instructions

(a) Compute the budgeted merchandise purchases for June.
(b) Prepare the budgeted income statement for June through gross profit.

EXERCISES: SET B

Visit the book's website at **www.wiley.com/college/weygandt**, and choose the Student Companion site, to access Exercise Set B.

PROBLEMS: SET A

Prepare budgeted income statement and supporting budgets.

(SO 3, 4)

P9-1A Danner Farm Supply Company manufactures and sells a pesticide called Snare. The following data are available for preparing budgets for Snare for the first 2 quarters of 2009.

1. Sales: Quarter 1, 28,000 bags; quarter 2, 42,000 bags. Selling price is $60 per bag.
2. Direct materials: Each bag of Snare requires 4 pounds of Gumm at a cost of $4 per pound and 6 pounds of Tarr at $1.50 per pound.
3. Desired inventory levels:

Type of Inventory	January 1	April 1	July 1
Snare (bags)	8,000	12,000	18,000
Gumm (pounds)	9,000	10,000	13,000
Tarr (pounds)	14,000	20,000	25,000

4. Direct labor: Direct labor time is 15 minutes per bag at an hourly rate of $14 per hour.
5. Selling and administrative expenses are expected to be 15% of sales plus $175,000 per quarter.
6. Income taxes are expected to be 30% of income from operations.

Your assistant has prepared two budgets: (1) The manufacturing overhead budget shows expected costs to be 150% of direct labor cost. (2) The direct materials budget for Tarr shows the cost of Tarr purchases to be $297,000 in quarter 1 and $439,500 in quarter 2.

Instructions

Prepare the budgeted income statement for the first 6 months and all required operating budgets by quarters. (*Note*: Use variable and fixed in the selling and administrative expense budget). Do not prepare the manufacturing overhead budget or the direct materials budget for Tarr.

Net income $600,250
Cost per bag $33.75

Prepare sales, production, direct materials, direct labor, and income statement budgets.

(SO 3, 4)

P9-2A LaRussa Inc. is preparing its annual budgets for the year ending December 31, 2009. Accounting assistants furnish the data shown below.

	Product JB 50	Product JB 60
Sales budget:		
Anticipated volume in units	400,000	200,000
Unit selling price	$20	$25
Production budget:		
Desired ending finished goods units	25,000	15,000
Beginning finished goods units	30,000	10,000
Direct materials budget:		
Direct materials per unit (pounds)	2	3
Desired ending direct materials pounds	30,000	15,000
Beginning direct materials pounds	40,000	10,000
Cost per pound	$3	$4
Direct labor budget:		
Direct labor time per unit	0.4	0.6
Direct labor rate per hour	$12	$12
Budgeted income statement:		
Total unit cost	$12	$21

An accounting assistant has prepared the detailed manufacturing overhead budget and the selling and administrative expense budget. The latter shows selling expenses of $660,000 for product JB 50 and $360,000 for product JB 60, and administrative expenses of $540,000 for product JB 50 and $340,000 for product JB 60. Income taxes are expected to be 30%.

(a) Total sales $13,000,000
(b) Required production units: JB 50, 395,000 JB 60, 205,000
(c) Total cost of direct materials purchases $4,820,000
(d) Total direct labor cost $3,372,000
(e) Net income $1,470,000

Instructions

Prepare the following budgets for the year. Show data for each product. Quarterly budgets should not be prepared.

(a) Sales
(b) Production
(c) Direct materials
(d) Direct labor
(e) Income statement (*Note*: Income taxes are not allocated to the products.)

Prepare sales and production budgets and compute cost per unit under two plans.

(SO 3, 4)

P9-3A Colt Industries had sales in 2008 of $6,400,000 and gross profit of $1,100,000. Management is considering two alternative budget plans to increase its gross profit in 2009.

Plan A would increase the selling price per unit from $8.00 to $8.40. Sales volume would decrease by 5% from its 2008 level. Plan B would decrease the selling price per unit by $0.50. The marketing department expects that the sales volume would increase by 150,000 units.

At the end of 2008, Colt has 40,000 units of inventory on hand. If Plan A is accepted, the 2009 ending inventory should be equal to 5% of the 2009 sales. If Plan B is accepted, the ending inventory should be equal to 50,000 units. Each unit produced will cost $1.80 in direct labor, $1.25 in direct materials, and $1.20 in variable overhead. The fixed overhead for 2009 should be $1,895,000.

(c) Unit cost: Plan A $6.75 Plan B $6.22
(d) Gross profit: Plan A $1,254,000 Plan B $1,216,000

Instructions

(a) Prepare a sales budget for 2009 under each plan.
(b) Prepare a production budget for 2009 under each plan.
(c) Compute the production cost per unit under each plan. Why is the cost per unit different for each of the two plans? (Round to two decimals.)
(d) Which plan should be accepted? (*Hint*: Compute the gross profit under each plan.)

Prepare cash budget for 2 months.

(SO 5)

P9-4A Haas Company prepares monthly cash budgets. Relevant data from operating budgets for 2009 are:

	January	February
Sales	$350,000	$400,000
Direct materials purchases	110,000	130,000
Direct labor	90,000	100,000
Manufacturing overhead	70,000	75,000
Selling and administrative expenses	79,000	86,000

All sales are on account. Collections are expected to be 50% in the month of sale, 30% in the first month following the sale, and 20% in the second month following the sale. Sixty percent (60%) of direct materials purchases are paid in cash in the month of purchase, and the balance due is paid in the month following the purchase. All other items above are paid in the month incurred except for selling and administrative expenses that include $1,000 of depreciation per month.

Other data:

1. Credit sales: November 2008, $260,000; December 2008, $320,000.
2. Purchases of direct materials: December 2008, $100,000.
3. Other receipts: January—Collection of December 31, 2008, notes receivable $15,000; February—Proceeds from sale of securities $6,000.
4. Other disbursements: February—Withdrawal of $5,000 cash for personal use of owner, Dewey Yaeger.

The company's cash balance on January 1, 2009, is expected to be $60,000. The company wants to maintain a minimum cash balance of $50,000.

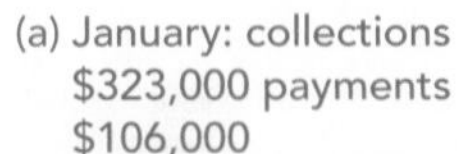

(a) January: collections $323,000 payments $106,000
(b) Ending cash balance: January $54,000 February $50,000

Instructions

(a) Prepare schedules for (1) expected collections from customers and (2) expected payments for direct materials purchases.
(b) Prepare a cash budget for January and February in columnar form.

Prepare purchases and income statement budgets for a merchandiser.

(SO 6)

P9-5A The budget committee of Deleon Company collects the following data for its San Miguel Store in preparing budgeted income statements for May and June 2009.

1. Sales for May are expected to be $800,000. Sales in June and July are expected to be 10% higher than the preceding month.
2. Cost of goods sold is expected to be 75% of sales.
3. Company policy is to maintain ending merchandise inventory at 20% of the following month's cost of goods sold.

4. Operating expenses are estimated to be:

Sales salaries	$30,000 per month
Advertising	5% of monthly sales
Delivery expense	3% of monthly sales
Sales commissions	4% of monthly sales
Rent expense	$5,000 per month
Depreciation	$800 per month
Utilities	$600 per month
Insurance	$500 per month

5. Income taxes are estimated to be 30% of income from operations.

Instructions

(a) Prepare the merchandise purchases budget for each month in columnar form.

(b) Prepare budgeted income statements for each month in columnar form. Show in the statements the details of cost of goods sold.

(a) Purchases:
May $612,000
June $673,200
(b) Net income:
May $46,970
June $54,250

P9-6A Glendo Industries' balance sheet at December 31, 2008, is presented below.

Prepare budgeted income statement and balance sheet.

(SO 4, 5)

GLENDO INDUSTRIES
Balance Sheet
December 31, 2008

Assets		
Current assets		
Cash		$ 7,500
Accounts receivable		82,500
Finished goods inventory (2,000 units)		30,000
Total current assets		120,000
Property, plant, and equipment		
Equipment	$40,000	
Less: Accumulated depreciation	10,000	30,000
Total assets		$150,000

Liabilities and Stockholders' Equity		
Liabilities		
Notes payable		$ 25,000
Accounts payable		45,000
Total liabilities		70,000
Stockholders' equity		
Common stock	$50,000	
Retained earnings	30,000	
Total stockholders' equity		80,000
Total liabilities and stockholders' equity		$150,000

Additional information accumulated for the budgeting process is as follows.

Budgeted data for the year 2009 include the following.

	4th Qtr. of 2009	**Year 2009 Total**
Sales budget (8,000 units at $35)	$84,000	$280,000
Direct materials used	17,000	69,400
Direct labor	12,500	56,600
Manufacturing overhead applied	10,000	54,000
Selling and administrative expenses	18,000	76,000

To meet sales requirements and to have 3,000 units of finished goods on hand at December 31, 2009, the production budget shows 9,000 required units of output. The total unit cost of production is expected to be $20. Glendo Industries uses the first-in, first-out (FIFO) inventory costing method. Selling and administrative expenses include $4,000 for depreciation on equipment. Interest expense is expected to be $3,500 for the year. Income taxes are expected to be 30% of income before income taxes.

All sales and purchases are on account. It is expected that 60% of quarterly sales are collected in cash within the quarter and the remainder is collected in the following quarter. Direct materials purchased from suppliers are paid 50% in the quarter incurred and the remainder in the following quarter. Purchases in the fourth quarter were the same as the materials used. In 2009, the company expects to purchase additional equipment costing $19,000. It expects to pay $8,000 on notes payable plus all interest due and payable to December 31 (included in interest expense $3,500, above). Accounts payable at December 31, 2009, includes amounts due suppliers (see above) plus other accounts payable of $5,700. In 2009, the company expects to declare and pay a $5,000 cash dividend. Unpaid income taxes at December 31 will be $5,000. The company's cash budget shows an expected cash balance of $7,950 at December 31, 2009.

Instructions

Net income $35,350
Total assets $146,550

Prepare a budgeted income statement for 2009 and a budgeted balance sheet at December 31, 2009. In preparing the income statement, you will need to compute cost of goods manufactured (direct materials + direct labor + manufacturing overhead) and finished goods inventory (December 31, 2009).

PROBLEMS: SET B

Prepare budgeted income statement and supporting budgets.
(SO 3, 4)

P9-1B Krause Farm Supply Company manufactures and sells a fertilizer called Basic II. The following data are available for preparing budgets for Basic II for the first 2 quarters of 2008.

1. Sales: Quarter 1, 40,000 bags; quarter 2, 60,000 bags. Selling price is $60 per bag.
2. Direct materials: Each bag of Basic II requires 6 pounds of Crup at a cost of $4 per pound and 10 pounds of Dert at $1.50 per pound.
3. Desired inventory levels:

Type of Inventory	January 1	April 1	July 1
Basic II (bags)	10,000	15,000	20,000
Crup (pounds)	9,000	12,000	15,000
Dert (pounds)	15,000	20,000	25,000

4. Direct labor: Direct labor time is 15 minutes per bag at an hourly rate of $12 per hour.
5. Selling and administrative expenses are expected to be 10% of sales plus $150,000 per quarter.
6. Income taxes are expected to be 30% of income from operations.

Your assistant has prepared two budgets: (1) The manufacturing overhead budget shows expected costs to be 100% of direct labor cost. (2) The direct materials budget for Dert which shows the cost of Dert purchases to be $682,500 in quarter 1 and $982,500 in quarter 2.

Instructions

Net income $420,000
Cost per bag $45.00

Prepare the budgeted income statement for the first 6 months of 2008 and all required operating budgets by quarters. (*Note*: Use variable and fixed in the selling and administrative expense budget.) Do not prepare the manufacturing overhead budget or the direct materials budget for Dert.

Prepare sales, production, direct materials, direct labor, and income statement budgets.
(SO 3, 4)

P9-2B Mercer Inc. is preparing its annual budgets for the year ending December 31, 2008. Accounting assistants furnish the following data.

	Product LN 35	Product LN 40
Sales budget:		
Anticipated volume in units	300,000	180,000
Unit selling price	$20	$30
Production budget:		
Desired ending finished goods units	30,000	25,000
Beginning finished goods units	20,000	15,000

Table continues on next page

	Product LN 35	Product LN 40
Direct materials budget:		
Direct materials per unit (pounds)	2	3
Desired ending direct materials pounds	50,000	20,000
Beginning direct materials pounds	40,000	10,000
Cost per pound	$2	$3
Direct labor budget:		
Direct labor time per unit	0.5	0.75
Direct labor rate per hour	$12	$12
Budgeted income statement:		
Total unit cost	$11	$20

An accounting assistant has prepared the detailed manufacturing overhead budget and the selling and administrative expense budget. The latter shows selling expenses of $560,000 for product LN 35 and $440,000 for product LN 40, and administrative expenses of $420,000 for product LN 35 and $380,000 for product LN 40. Income taxes are expected to be 30%.

Instructions

Prepare the following budgets for the year. Show data for each product. Quarterly budgets should not be prepared.

(a) Sales
(b) Production
(c) Direct materials
(d) Direct labor
(e) Income statement (*Note*: Income taxes are not allocated to the products.)

(a) Total sales $11,400,000
(b) Required production units: LN 35, 310,000
(c) Total cost of direct materials purchases $3,000,000
(d) Total direct labor cost $3,570,000
(e) Net income $1,890,000

P9-3B Litwin Industries has sales in 2008 of $4,900,000 (700,000 units) and gross profit of $1,187,500. Management is considering two alternative budget plans to increase its gross profit in 2009.

Prepare sales and production budgets and compute cost per unit under two plans.

(SO 3, 4)

Plan A would increase the selling price per unit from $7.00 to $7.60. Sales volume would decrease by 10% from its 2008 level. Plan B would decrease the selling price per unit by 5%. The marketing department expects that the sales volume would increase by 100,000 units.

At the end of 2008, Litwin has 70,000 units on hand. If Plan A is accepted, the 2009 ending inventory should be equal to 90,000 units. If Plan B is accepted, the ending inventory should be equal to 100,000 units. Each unit produced will cost $2.00 in direct materials, $1.50 in direct labor, and $0.50 in variable overhead. The fixed overhead for 2009 should be $975,000.

Instructions

(a) Prepare a sales budget for 2009 under (1) Plan A and (2) Plan B.
(b) Prepare a production budget for 2009 under (1) Plan A and (2) Plan B.
(c) Compute the cost per unit under (1) Plan A and (2) Plan B. Explain why the cost per unit is different for each of the two plans. (Round to two decimals.)
(d) Which plan should be accepted? (*Hint*: Compute the gross profit under each plan.)

(c) Unit cost: Plan A $5.50, Plan B $5.17
(d) Gross profit: Plan A $1,323,000 Plan B $1,184,000

P9-4B Orton Company prepares monthly cash budgets. Relevant data from operating budgets for 2009 are:

Prepare cash budget for 2 months.

(SO 5)

	January	February
Sales	$320,000	$400,000
Direct materials purchases	80,000	110,000
Direct labor	85,000	115,000
Manufacturing overhead	60,000	75,000
Selling and administrative expenses	75,000	80,000

All sales are on account. Collections are expected to be 60% in the month of sale, 30% in the first month following the sale, and 10% in the second month following the sale. Thirty percent (30%) of direct materials purchases are paid in cash in the month of purchase, and the balance due is paid in the month following the purchase. All other items above are paid in the month incurred. Depreciation has been excluded from manufacturing overhead and selling and administrative expenses.

Other data:

1. Credit sales: November 2008, $200,000; December 2008, $280,000.
2. Purchases of direct materials: December 2008, $90,000.

3. Other receipts: January—Collection of December 31, 2008, interest receivable $3,000; February—Proceeds from sale of securities $5,000.
4. Other disbursements: February—payment of $20,000 for land.

The company's cash balance on January 1, 2009, is expected to be $60,000. The company wants to maintain a minimum cash balance of $50,000.

(a) January: collections $296,000
payments $87,000
(b) Ending cash balance: January $52,000
February $50,000

Instructions

(a) Prepare schedules for (1) expected collections from customers and (2) expected payments for direct materials purchases.

(b) Prepare a cash budget for January and February in columnar form.

Prepare purchases and income statement budgets for a merchandiser.

(SO 6)

P9-5B The budget committee of Urbina Company collects the following data for its Westwood Store in preparing budgeted income statements for July and August 2008.

1. Expected sales: July $400,000, August $450,000, September $500,000.
2. Cost of goods sold is expected to be 64% of sales.
3. Company policy is to maintain ending merchandise inventory at 25% of the following month's cost of goods sold.
4. Operating expenses are estimated to be:

Sales salaries	$40,000 per month
Advertising	4% of monthly sales
Delivery expense	2% of monthly sales
Sales commissions	3% of monthly sales
Rent expense	$3,000 per month
Depreciation	$700 per month
Utilities	$500 per month
Insurance	$300 per month

5. Income taxes are estimated to be 30% of income from operations.

(a) Purchases: July $264,000
August $296,000
(b) Net income: July $44,450
August $53,900

Instructions

(a) Prepare the merchandise purchases budget for each month in columnar form.

(b) Prepare budgeted income statements for each month in columnar form. Show the details of cost of goods sold in the statements.

PROBLEMS: SET C

Visit the book's website at **www.wiley.com/college/weygandt**, and choose the Student Companion site, to access Problem Set C.

WATERWAYS CONTINUING PROBLEM

(This is a continuation of the Waterways Problem from Chapters 1 through 8.)

WCP9 Waterways Corporation is preparing its budget for the coming year, 2009. The first step is to plan for the first quarter of that coming year. The company has gathered information from its managers in preparation of the budgeting process. This problem asks you to prepare the various budgets that comprise the master budget for 2009.

*Go to the book's website, **www.wiley.com/college/weygandt**, to find the remainder of this problem.*

BROADENING YOUR PERSPECTIVE

DECISION MAKING ACROSS THE ORGANIZATION

BYP9-1 Lanier Corporation operates on a calendar-year basis. It begins the annual budgeting process in late August when the president establishes targets for the total dollar sales and net income before taxes for the next year.

The sales target is given first to the marketing department. The marketing manager formulates a sales budget by product line in both units and dollars. From this budget, sales quotas by product line in units and dollars are established for each of the corporation's sales districts. The marketing manager also estimates the cost of the marketing activities required to support the target sales volume and prepares a tentative marketing expense budget.

The executive vice president uses the sales and profit targets, the sales budget by product line, and the tentative marketing expense budget to determine the dollar amounts that can be devoted to manufacturing and corporate office expense. The executive vice president prepares the budget for corporate expenses. She then forwards to the production department the product-line sales budget in units and the total dollar amount that can be devoted to manufacturing.

The production manager meets with the factory managers to develop a manufacturing plan that will produce the required units when needed within the cost constraints set by the executive vice president. The budgeting process usually comes to a halt at this point because the production department does not consider the financial resources allocated to be adequate.

When this standstill occurs, the vice president of finance, the executive vice president, the marketing manager, and the production manager meet together to determine the final budgets for each of the areas. This normally results in a modest increase in the total amount available for manufacturing costs and cuts in the marketing expense and corporate office expense budgets. The total sales and net income figures proposed by the president are seldom changed. Although the participants are seldom pleased with the compromise, these budgets are final. Each executive then develops a new detailed budget for the operations in his or her area.

None of the areas has achieved its budget in recent years. Sales often run below the target. When budgeted sales are not achieved, each area is expected to cut costs so that the president's profit target can be met. However, the profit target is seldom met because costs are not cut enough. In fact, costs often run above the original budget in all functional areas (marketing, production, and corporate office).

The president is disturbed that Lanier has not been able to meet the sales and profit targets. He hired a consultant with considerable experience with companies in Lanier's industry. The consultant reviewed the budgets for the past 4 years. He concluded that the product line sales budgets were reasonable and that the cost and expense budgets were adequate for the budgeted sales and production levels.

Instructions

With the class divided into groups, answer the following.

(a) Discuss how the budgeting process employed by Lanier Corporation contributes to the failure to achieve the president's sales and profit targets.

(b) Suggest how Lanier Corporation's budgeting process could be revised to correct the problems.

(c) Should the functional areas be expected to cut their costs when sales volume falls below budget? Explain your answer. (CMA adapted.)

MANAGERIAL ANALYSIS

BYP9-2 Bedner & Flott Inc. manufactures ergonomic devices for computer users. Some of their more popular products include glare screens (for computer monitors), keyboard stands with wrist rests, and carousels that allow easy access to discs. Over the past 5 years, they experienced rapid growth, with sales of all products increasing 20% to 50% each year.

Last year, some of the primary manufacturers of computers began introducing new products with some of the ergonomic designs, such as glare screens and wrist rests, already built in. As a result, sales of Bedner & Flott's accessory devices have declined somewhat. The company believes that the disc carousels will probably continue to show growth, but that the other products will probably continue to decline. When the next year's budget was prepared, increases were built in to research and development so that replacement products could be developed or the company could expand into some other product line. Some product lines being considered are general-purpose ergonomic devices including back supports, foot rests, and sloped writing pads.

The most recent results have shown that sales decreased more than was expected for the glare screens. As a result, the company may have a shortage of funds. Top management has therefore asked that all expenses be reduced 10% to compensate for these reduced sales. Summary budget information is as follows.

Direct materials	$240,000
Direct labor	110,000
Insurance	50,000
Depreciation	90,000
Machine repairs	30,000
Sales salaries	50,000
Office salaries	80,000
Factory salaries (indirect labor)	50,000
Total	$700,000

Instructions

Using the information above, answer the following questions.

(a) What are the implications of reducing each of the costs? For example, if the company reduces direct materials costs, it may have to do so by purchasing lower-quality materials. This may affect sales in the long run.

(b) Based on your analysis in (a), what do you think is the best way to obtain the $70,000 in cost savings requested? Be specific. Are there any costs that cannot or should not be reduced? Why?

REAL-WORLD FOCUS

BYP9-3 Network Computing Devices Inc. was founded in 1988 in Mountain View, California. The company develops software products such as X-terminals, Z-mail, PC X-ware, and related hardware products. Presented below is a discussion by management in its annual report.

NETWORK COMPUTING DEVICES, INC.
Management Discussion

The Company's operating results have varied significantly, particularly on a quarterly basis, as a result of a number of factors, including general economic conditions affecting industry demand for computer products, the timing and market acceptance of new product introductions by the Company and its competitors, the timing of significant orders from large customers, periodic changes in product pricing and discounting due to competitive factors, and the availability of key components, such as video monitors and electronic subassemblies, some of which require substantial order lead times. The Company's operating results may fluctuate in the future as a result of these and other factors, including the Company's success in developing and introducing new products, its product and customer mix, and the level of competition which it experiences. The Company operates with a small backlog. Sales and operating results, therefore, generally depend on the volume and timing of orders received, which are difficult to forecast. The Company has experienced slowness in orders from some customers during the first quarter of each calendar year due to budgeting cycles common in the computer industry. In addition, sales in Europe typically are adversely affected in the third calendar quarter as many European customers reduce their business activities during the month of August.

Due to the Company's rapid growth rate and the effect of new product introductions on quarterly revenues, these seasonal trends have not materially impacted the Company's results of operations to date. However, as the Company's product lines mature and its rate of revenue growth declines, these seasonal factors may become more evident. Additionally, the Company's international sales are denominated in U.S. dollars, and an increase or decrease in the value of the U.S. dollar relative to foreign currencies could make the Company's products less or more competitive in those markets.

Instructions

(a) Identify the factors that affect the budgeting process at Network Computing Devices, Inc.

(b) Explain the additional budgeting concerns created by the international operations of the company.

EXPLORING THE WEB

BYP9-4 Information regarding many approaches to budgeting can be found on the Web. The following activity investigates the merits of "zero-based" budgeting as discussed by Michael LaFaive, Director of the Mackinac Center for Public Policy.

Address: www.mackinac.org/article.aspx?ID=5928, or go to **www.wiley.com/college/weygandt**

Instructions

Read the article at the website and answer the following questions.

(a) How does zero-based budgeting differ from standard budgeting procedures?

(b) What are some potential advantages of zero-based budgeting?

(c) What are some potential disadvantages of zero-based budgeting?

(d) How often do departments in Oklahoma undergo zero-based budgeting?

COMMUNICATION ACTIVITY

BYP9-5 In order to better serve their rural patients, Drs. Dan and Jack Fleming (brothers) began giving safety seminars. Especially popular were their "emergency-preparedness" talks given to farmers. Many people asked whether the "kit" of materials the doctors recommended for common farm emergencies was commercially available.

After checking with several suppliers, the doctors realized that no other company offered the supplies they recommended in their seminars, packaged in the way they described. Their wives, Julie and Amy, agreed to make a test package by ordering supplies from various medical supply companies and assembling them into a "kit" that could be sold at the seminars. When these kits proved a runaway success, the sisters-in-law decided to market them. At the advice of their accountant, they organized this venture as a separate company, called Life Protection Products (LPP), with Julie Fleming as CEO and Amy Fleming as Secretary-Treasurer.

LPP soon started receiving requests for the kits from all over the country, as word spread about their availability. Even without advertising, LPP was able to sell its full inventory every month. However, the company was becoming financially strained. Julie and Amy had about $100,000 in savings, and they invested about half that amount initially. They believed that this venture would allow them to make money. However, at the present time, only about $30,000 of the cash remains, and the company is constantly short of cash.

Julie has come to you for advice. She does not understand why the company is having cash flow problems. She and Amy have not even been withdrawing salaries. However, they have rented a local building and have hired two more full-time workers to help them cope with the increasing demand. They do not think they could handle the demand without this additional help.

Julie is also worried that the cash problems mean that the company may not be able to support itself. She has prepared the cash budget shown on page 412. All seminar customers pay for their products in full at the time of purchase. In addition, several large companies have ordered the kits for use by employees who work in remote sites. They have requested credit terms and have been allowed to pay in the month following the sale. These large purchasers amount to about 25% of the sales at the present time. LPP purchases the materials for the kits about 2 months ahead of time. Julie and Amy are considering slowing the growth of the company by simply purchasing less materials, which will mean selling fewer kits.

The workers are paid weekly. Julie and Amy need about $15,000 cash on hand at the beginning of the month to pay for purchases of raw materials. Right now they have been using cash from their savings, but as noted, only $30,000 is left.

Instructions

Write a response to Julie Fleming. Explain why LPP is short of cash. Will this company be able to support itself? Explain your answer. Make any recommendations you deem appropriate.

LIFE PROTECTION PRODUCTS
Cash Budget
For the Quarter Ending June 30, 2009

	April	May	June
Cash balance, beginning	$15,000	$15,000	$15,000
Cash received			
From prior month sales	5,000	7,500	12,500
From current sales	15,000	22,500	37,500
Total cash on hand	35,000	45,000	65,000
Cash payments			
To employees	3,000	3,000	3,000
For products	25,000	35,000	45,000
Miscellaneous expenses	5,000	6,000	7,000
Postage	1,000	1,000	1,000
Total cash payments	34,000	45,000	56,000
Cash balance	$ 1,000	$ 0	$ 9,000
Borrow from savings	$14,000	$15,000	$ 1,000
Borrow from bank?	$ 0	$ 0	$ 5,000

ETHICS CASE

BYP9-6 You are an accountant in the budgetary, projections, and special projects department of American Conductor, Inc., a large manufacturing company. The president, William Brown, asks you on very short notice to prepare some sales and income projections covering the next 2 years of the company's much heralded new product lines. He wants these projections for a series of speeches he is making while on a 2-week trip to eight East Coast brokerage firms. The president hopes to bolster American's stock sales and price.

You work 23 hours in 2 days to compile the projections, hand deliver them to the president, and are swiftly but graciously thanked as he departs. A week later you find time to go over some of your computations and discover a miscalculation that makes the projections grossly overstated. You quickly inquire about the president's itinerary and learn that he has made half of his speeches and has half yet to make. You are in a quandary as to what to do.

Instructions

(a) What are the consequences of telling the president of your gross miscalculations?
(b) What are the consequences of *not* telling the president of your gross miscalculations?
(c) What are the ethical considerations to you and the president in this situation?

"ALL ABOUT YOU" ACTIVITY

BYP9-7 The "All About You" feature in this chapter emphasizes that in order to get your personal finances under control, you need to prepare a personal budget. Assume that you have compiled the following information regarding your expected cash flows for a typical month.

Rent payment	$ 400	Miscellaneous costs	$110
Interest income	50	Savings	50
Income tax withheld	300	Eating out	150
Electricity bill	22	Telephone and Internet costs	90
Groceries	80	Student loan payments	275
Wages earned	2,000	Entertainment costs	250
Insurance	100	Transportation costs	150

Instructions

Using the information above, prepare a personal budget. In preparing this budget, use the format found at **http://financialplan.about.com/cs/budgeting/l/blbudget.htm**. Just skip any unused line items.

Answers to Insight and Accounting Across the Organization Questions

Business Often Feel Too Busy to Plan for the Future, p. 374

Q: Describe a situation in which a business "sells as much as it can" but cannot "keep its employees paid."

A: *If sales are made to customers on credit and collection is slow, the company may find that it does not have enough cash to pay employees or suppliers. Without these resources, the company will fail to survive.*

Which Budget Approach Do You Prefer?, p. 376

Q: What approach did Time Warner use to prepare the old budget? What approach did it use to prepare the new budget?

A: *Time Warner used a "top-down" approach to prepare the old budget since its goals were determined by top management. It used a participative approach to prepare the new budget since each operating unit set goals.*

Without a Budget, Can the Games Begin?, p. 386

Q: Why does it matter whether the Olympic Games exceed their budget?

A: *If the Olympic Games exceed their budget, taxpayers of the sponsoring community and country will end up footing the bill. Depending on the size of the losses, and the resources of the community, this could produce a substantial burden. As a result, other communities might be reluctant to host the Olympics in the future.*

Authors' Comments on *All About You:* Avoiding Personal Financial Disaster, p. 392

We are concerned that the personal budgets presented on websites and in financial planning textbooks often list student loans among the sources of income. This type of thinking can lead to an overreliance on debt during college, and will result in accumulation of large amounts of debt that must be repaid. We would prefer a format that lists non-debt sources of income, then subtracts expenses, then shows debt borrowed. This format emphasizes an important point: Just like a business, in the short run you can borrow money when your cash inflows are not sufficient to meet your outflows, but in the long run you need to learn to live within your income, and your budget.

Answers to Self-Study Questions

1. c **2.** a **3.** b **4.** b **5.** d **6.** d **7.** a **8.** c **9.** c **10.** d

Remember to go back to the Navigator box on the chapter-opening page and check off your completed work.

Chapter 10

Budgetary Control and Responsibility Accounting

STUDY OBJECTIVES

After studying this chapter, you should be able to:

1. Describe the concept of budgetary control.
2. Evaluate the usefulness of static budget reports.
3. Explain the development of flexible budgets and the usefulness of flexible budget reports.
4. Describe the concept of responsibility accounting.
5. Indicate the features of responsibility reports for cost centers.
6. Identify the content of responsibility reports for profit centers.
7. Explain the basis and formula used in evaluating performance in investment centers.

The Navigator

The Navigator

Scan **Study Objectives**	☐
Read **Feature Story**	☐
Read **Preview**	☐
Read text and answer **Before You Go On** p. 426 ☐ p. 434 ☐ p. 439	☐
Work **Using the Decision Toolkit**	☐
Review **Summary of Study Objectives**	☐
Work **Demonstration Problem**	☐
Answer **Self-Study Questions**	☐
Complete **Assignments**	☐

Feature Story

TRYING TO AVOID AN ELECTRIC SHOCK

Budgets are critical to evaluating an organization's success. They are based on management's expectations of what is most likely to happen in the future. In order to be useful, they must be accurate. But what if management's expectations are wrong? Estimates are never exactly correct, and

sometimes, especially in volatile industries, estimates can be "off by a mile."

In recent years the electric utility industry has become very volatile. Deregulation, volatile prices for natural gas, coal, and oil, changes in environmental regulations, and economic swings have all contributed to large changes in the profitability of electric utility companies. This means that for planning and budgeting purposes, utilities must plan and budget based on multiple "what if" scenarios that take into account factors beyond management's control. For example, in recent years, Duke Energy Corporation (*www.duke-energy.com*), headquartered in Charlotte, North Carolina, built budgeting and planning models based on three different scenarios of what the future might hold. One scenario assumes that the U.S. economy will slow considerably. A second scenario assumes that the company will experience "pricing pressure" as the market for energy becomes more efficient as a result of more energy being traded in Internet auctions. A third scenario assumes a continuation of the current environment of rapid growth, changing regulation, and large swings in the prices for the fuels the company uses to create energy.

Compounding this budgeting challenge is the fact that changes in many indirect costs can also significantly affect the company. For example, even a tiny change in market interest rates has a huge effect on the company because it has massive amounts of outstanding debt. And finally, as a result of the California energy crisis, there is mounting pressure for government intervention and regulation. This pressure has resulted in setting "rate caps" that limit the amount that utilities and energy companies can charge, thus lowering profits. The bottom line is that for budgeting and planning purposes, utility companies must remain alert and flexible.

✓ The Navigator

Inside Chapter 10

Preview of Chapter 10

In contrast to Chapter 9, we now consider how budgets are used by management to control operations. In the Feature Story on Duke Energy, we saw that budgeting must take into account factors beyond management's control. This chapter focuses on two aspects of management control: (1) budgetary control and (2) responsibility accounting.

The content and organization of Chapter 10 are as follows.

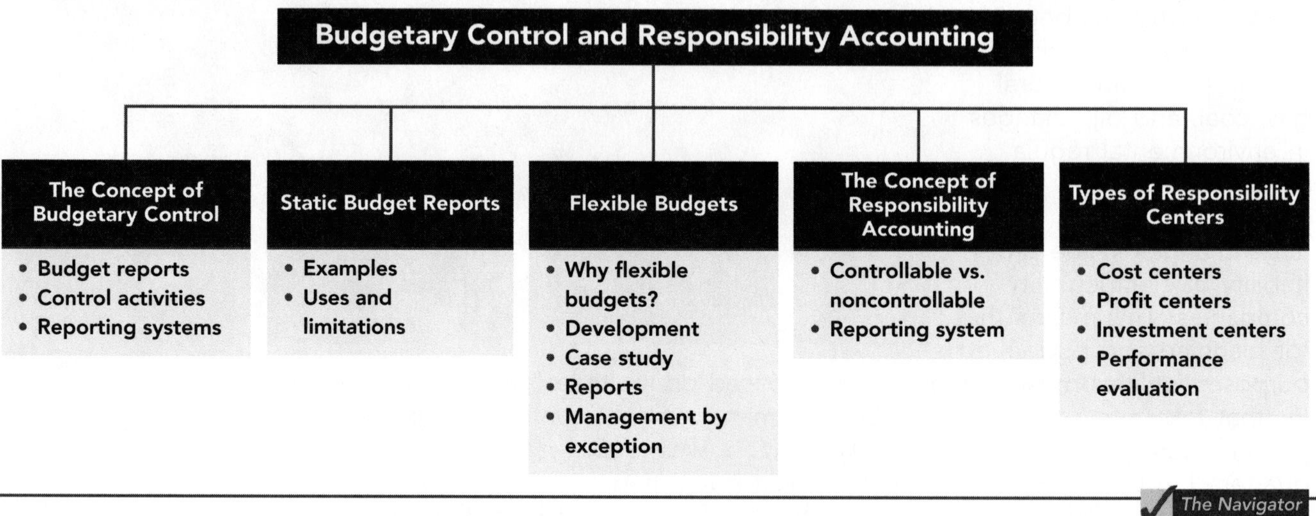

THE CONCEPT OF BUDGETARY CONTROL

STUDY OBJECTIVE 1

Describe the concept of budgetary control.

One of management's major functions is to control company operations. Control consists of the steps taken by management to see that planned objectives are met. We now ask: How do budgets contribute to control of operations?

The use of budgets in controlling operations is known as **budgetary control**. Such control takes place by means of **budget reports** that compare actual results with planned objectives. The use of budget reports is based on the belief that planned objectives lose much of their potential value without some monitoring of progress along the way. Just as your professors give midterm exams to evaluate your progress, so top management requires periodic reports on the progress of department managers toward their planned objectives.

Budget reports provide management with feedback on operations. The feedback for a crucial objective, such as having enough cash on hand to pay bills, may be made daily. For other objectives, such as meeting budgeted annual sales and operating expenses, monthly budget reports may suffice. Budget reports are prepared as frequently as needed. From these reports, management analyzes any differences between actual and planned results and determines their causes. Management then takes corrective action, or it decides to modify future plans.

Budgetary control involves activities shown in Illustration 10-1.

Illustration 10-1
Budgetary control activities

Budgetary control works best when a company has a formalized reporting system. The system does the following:

1. Identifies the name of the budget report, such as the sales budget or the manufacturing overhead budget.
2. States the frequency of the report, such as weekly or monthly.
3. Specifies the purpose of the report.
4. Indicates the primary recipient(s) of the report.

Illustration 10-2 provides a partial budgetary control system for a manufacturing company. Note the frequency of the reports and their emphasis on control. For example, there is a daily report on scrap and a weekly report on labor.

Illustration 10-2
Budgetary control reporting system

Name of Report	Frequency	Purpose	Primary Recipient(s)
Sales	Weekly	Determine whether sales goals are being met	Top management and sales manager
Labor	Weekly	Control direct and indirect labor costs	Vice president of production and production department managers
Scrap	Daily	Determine efficient use of materials	Production manager
Departmental overhead costs	Monthly	Control overhead costs	Department manager
Selling expenses	Monthly	Control selling expenses	Sales manager
Income statement	Monthly and quarterly	Determine whether income objectives are being met	Top management

STATIC BUDGET REPORTS

STUDY OBJECTIVE 2
Evaluate the usefulness of static budget reports.

You learned in Chapter 9 that the master budget formalizes management's planned objectives for the coming year. When used in budgetary control, each budget included in the master budget is considered to be static. A **static budget** is a projection of budget data **at one level of activity**. These budgets do not consider data for different levels of activity. As a result, companies always compare actual results with budget data at the activity level that was used in developing the master budget.

Examples

To illustrate the role of a static budget in budgetary control, we will use selected data prepared for Hayes Company in Chapter 9. Budget and actual sales data for the Kitchen-Mate product in the first and second quarters of 2008 are as follows.

Illustration 10-3
Budget and actual sales data

Sales	First Quarter	Second Quarter	Total
Budgeted	$180,000	$210,000	$390,000
Actual	179,000	199,500	378,500
Difference	$ 1,000	$ 10,500	$ 11,500

The sales budget report for Hayes Company's first quarter is shown below. The right-most column reports the difference between the budgeted and actual amounts.

Illustration 10-4
Sales budget report—first quarter

ALTERNATIVE TERMINOLOGY

The difference between budget and actual is sometimes called a *budget variance.*

HAYES COMPANY
Sales Budget Report
For the Quarter Ended March 31, 2008

Product Line	Budget	Actual	Difference Favorable F Unfavorable U
Kitchen-Mate[a]	$180,000	$179,000	**$1,000 U**

[a]In practice, each product line would be included in the report.

The report shows that sales are $1,000 under budget—an unfavorable result. This difference is less than 1% of budgeted sales ($1,000 ÷ $180,000 = .0056). Top management's reaction to unfavorable differences is often influenced by the materiality (significance) of the difference. Since the difference of $1,000 is immaterial in this case, we assume that Hayes Company management takes no specific corrective action.

Illustration 10-5 shows the budget report for the second quarter. It contains one new feature: cumulative year-to-date information. This report indicates that sales for the second quarter are $10,500 below budget. This is 5% of budgeted sales ($10,500 ÷ $210,000). Top management may now conclude that the difference between budgeted and actual sales requires investigation.

Illustration 10-5
Sales budget report—second quarter

HAYES COMPANY
Sales Budget Report
For the Quarter Ended June 30, 2008

	Second Quarter			Year-to-Date		
Product Line	Budget	Actual	Difference Favorable F Unfavorable U	Budget	Actual	Difference Favorable F Unfavorable U
Kitchen-Mate	$210,000	$199,500	**$10,500 U**	$390,000	$378,500	**$11,500 U**

Management's analysis should start by asking the sales manager the cause(s) of the shortfall. Managers should consider the need for corrective action. For example, management may decide to spur sales by offering sales incentives to customers or by increasing the advertising of Kitchen-Mates. Or, if management concludes that a downturn in the economy is responsible for the lower sales, it may modify planned sales and profit goals for the remainder of the year.

Uses and Limitations

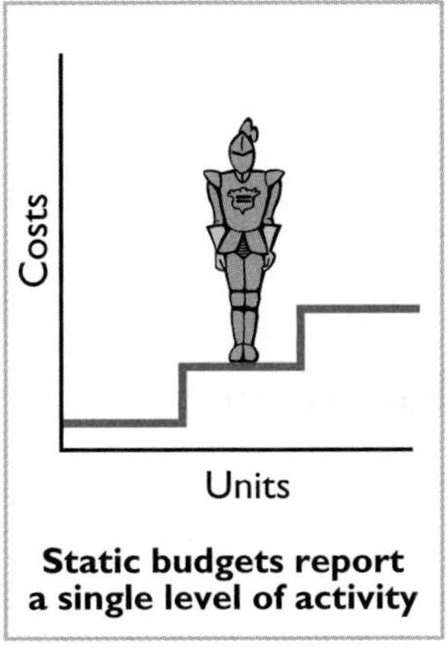

Static budgets report a single level of activity

From these examples, you can see that a master sales budget is useful in evaluating the performance of a sales manager. It is now necessary to ask: Is the master budget appropriate for evaluating a manager's performance in controlling costs? Recall that in a static budget, data are not modified or adjusted, regardless of changes in activity. It follows, then, that a static budget is appropriate in evaluating a manager's effectiveness in controlling costs when:

1. The actual level of activity closely approximates the master budget activity level, and/or
2. The behavior of the costs in response to changes in activity is fixed.

A static budget report is, therefore, appropriate for **fixed manufacturing costs** and for **fixed selling and administrative expenses**. But, as you will see shortly, static budget reports may not be a proper basis for evaluating a manager's performance in controlling variable costs.

FLEXIBLE BUDGETS

STUDY OBJECTIVE 3

Explain the development of flexible budgets and the usefulness of flexible budget reports.

In contrast to a static budget, which is based on one level of activity, a **flexible budget** projects budget data for various levels of activity. In essence, **the flexible budget is a series of static budgets at different levels of activity**. The flexible budget recognizes that the budgetary process is more useful if it is adaptable to changed operating conditions.

Flexible budgets can be prepared for each of the types of budgets included in the master budget. For example, Marriott Hotels can budget revenues and net income on the basis of 60%, 80%, and 100% of room occupancy. Similarly, American Van Lines can budget its operating expenses on the basis of various levels of truck miles driven. Likewise, in the Feature Story, Duke Energy can budget revenue and net income on the basis of estimated billions of kwh (kilowatt hours) of residential, commercial, and industrial electricity generated. In the following pages, we will illustrate a flexible budget for manufacturing overhead.

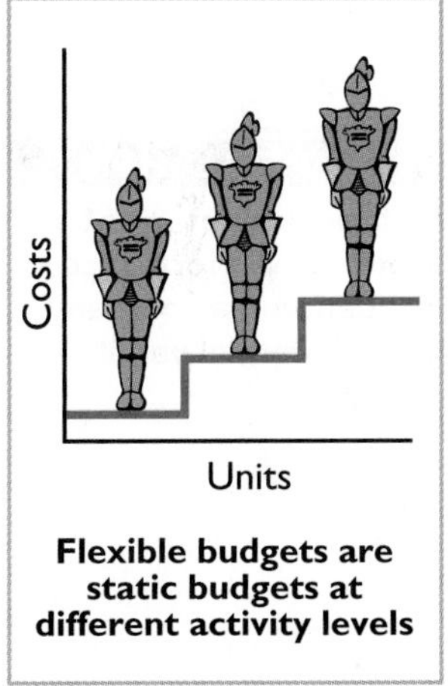

Flexible budgets are static budgets at different activity levels

Why Flexible Budgets?

Assume that you are the manager in charge of manufacturing overhead in the Forging Department of Barton Steel. In preparing the manufacturing overhead budget for 2008, you prepare the following static budget based on a production volume of 10,000 units of steel ingots.

Illustration 10-6
Static overhead budget

BARTON STEEL
Manufacturing Overhead Budget (Static)
Forging Department
For the Year Ended December 31, 2008

Budgeted production in units (steel ingots)	10,000
Budgeted costs	
Indirect materials	$ 250,000
Indirect labor	260,000
Utilities	190,000
Depreciation	280,000
Property taxes	70,000
Supervision	50,000
	$1,100,000

HELPFUL HINT
The master budget described in Chapter 9 is based on a static budget.

Fortunately for the company, the demand for steel ingots has increased, and Barton produces and sells 12,000 units during the year, rather than 10,000. You are elated: Increased sales means increased profitability, which should mean a bonus or a raise for you and the employees in your department. Unfortunately, a comparison of Forging Department actual and budgeted costs has put you on the spot. The budget report is shown below.

Illustration 10-7
Overhead static budget report

Barton Steel.xls

File Edit View Insert Format Tools Data Window Help

	A	B	C	D	E
1	BARTON STEEL				
2	Manufacturing Overhead Static Budget Report				
3	For the Year Ended December 31, 2008				
4				Difference	
5		Budget	Actual	Favorable - F Unfavorable - U	
6	Production in units	10,000	12,000		
7					
8	Costs				
9	Indirect materials	$ 250,000	$ 295,000	**$ 45,000**	U
10	Indirect labor	260,000	312,000	**52,000**	U
11	Utilities	190,000	225,000	**35,000**	U
12	Depreciation	280,000	280,000	**0**	
13	Property taxes	70,000	70,000	**0**	
14	Supervision	50,000	50,000	**0**	
15		$1,100,000	$1,232,000	**$132,000**	U
16					

HELPFUL HINT

A static budget is not useful for performance evaluation if a company has substantial variable costs.

This comparison uses budget data based on the original activity level (10,000 steel ingots). It indicates that the Forging Department is significantly **over budget** for three of the six overhead costs. And, there is a total unfavorable difference of $132,000, which is 12% over budget ($132,000 ÷ $1,100,000). Your supervisor is very unhappy! Instead of sharing in the company's success, you may find yourself looking for another job. What went wrong?

When you calm down and carefully examine the manufacturing overhead budget, you identify the problem: The budget data are not relevant! At the time the budget was developed, the company anticipated that only 10,000 units of steel ingots would be produced, **not** 12,000. Comparing actual with budgeted variable costs is meaningless. As production increases, the budget allowances for variable costs should increase proportionately. The variable costs in this example are indirect materials, indirect labor, and utilities.

Analyzing the budget data for these costs at 10,000 units, you arrive at the following per unit results.

Illustration 10-8
Variable costs per unit

Item	Total Cost	Per Unit
Indirect materials	$250,000	$25
Indirect labor	260,000	26
Utilities	190,000	19
	$700,000	$70

Illustration 10-9 calculates the budgeted variable costs at 12,000 units.

Item	Computation	Total
Indirect materials	$25 × 12,000	$300,000
Indirect labor	26 × 12,000	312,000
Utilities	19 × 12,000	228,000
		$840,000

Illustration 10-9
Budgeted variable costs, 12,000 units

Because fixed costs do not change in total as activity changes, the budgeted amounts for these costs remain the same. Illustration 10-10 shows the budget report based on the flexible budget for **12,000 units** of production. (Compare this with Illustration 10-7.)

Illustration 10-10
Overhead flexible budget report

Barton Steel.xls
File Edit View Insert Format Tools Data Window Help

	A	B	C	D	E
1	**BARTON STEEL**				
2	**Manufacturing Overhead Flexible Budget Report**				
3	**For the Year Ended December 31, 2008**				
4				Difference	
5		Budget	Actual	Favorable - F Unfavorable - U	
6	Production in units	12,000	12,000		
7					
8	Variable costs				
9	Indirect materials	$ 300,000	$ 295,000	$5,000	F
10	Indirect labor	312,000	312,000	0	
11	Utilities	228,000	225,000	3,000	F
12	Total variable costs	840,000	832,000	8,000	F
13					
14	Fixed costs				
15	Depreciation	280,000	280,000	0	
16	Property taxes	70,000	70,000	0	
17	Supervision	50,000	50,000	0	
18	Total fixed costs	400,000	400,000	0	
19	Total costs	$1,240,000	$1,232,000	$8,000	F
20					

This report indicates that the Forging Department's costs are *under budget*—a favorable difference. Instead of worrying about being fired, you may be in line for a bonus or a raise after all! As this analysis shows, the only appropriate comparison is between actual costs at 12,000 units of production and budgeted costs at 12,000 units. Flexible budget reports provide this comparison.

Developing the Flexible Budget

The flexible budget uses the master budget as its basis. To develop the flexible budget, management uses the following steps.

1. Identify the activity index and the relevant range of activity.
2. Identify the variable costs, and determine the budgeted variable cost per unit of activity for each cost.
3. Identify the fixed costs, and determine the budgeted amount for each cost.
4. Prepare the budget for selected increments of activity within the relevant range.

The activity index chosen should significantly influence the costs being budgeted. For manufacturing overhead costs, for example, the activity index is usually the same as the index used in developing the predetermined overhead rate—that is, direct labor hours or machine hours. For selling and administrative expenses, the activity index usually is sales or net sales.

The choice of the increment of activity is largely a matter of judgment. For example, if the relevant range is 8,000 to 12,000 direct labor hours, increments of 1,000 hours may be selected. The flexible budget is then prepared for each increment within the relevant range.

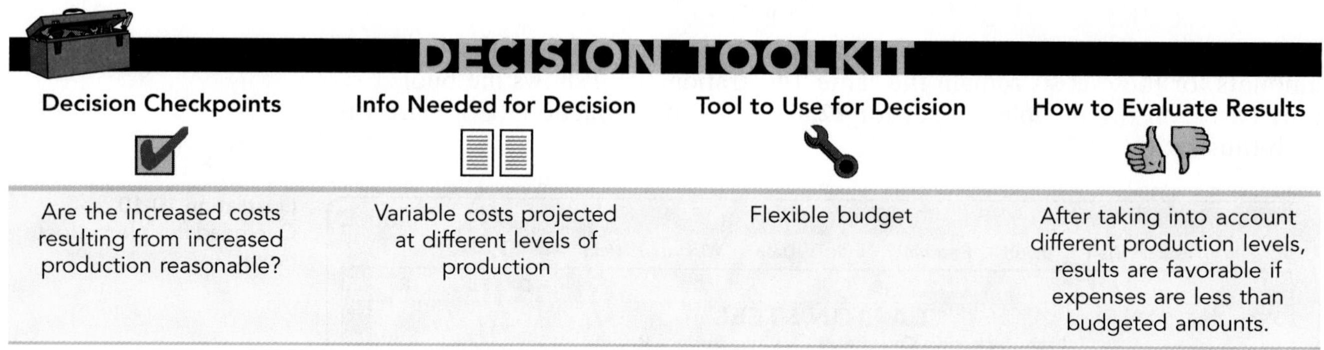

Flexible Budget—A Case Study

To illustrate the flexible budget, we use Fox Manufacturing Company. Fox's management uses a **flexible budget for monthly comparisons** of actual and budgeted manufacturing overhead costs of the Finishing Department. The master budget for the year ending December 31, 2008, shows expected annual operating capacity of 120,000 direct labor hours and the following overhead costs.

Illustration 10-11
Master budget data

Variable Costs		Fixed Costs	
Indirect materials	$180,000	Depreciation	$180,000
Indirect labor	240,000	Supervision	120,000
Utilities	60,000	Property taxes	60,000
Total	$480,000	Total	$360,000

The four steps for developing the flexible budget are applied as follows.

STEP 1. **Identify the activity index and the relevant range of activity.** The activity index is direct labor hours. The relevant range is 8,000–12,000 direct labor hours per month.

STEP 2. **Identify the variable costs, and determine the budgeted variable cost per unit of activity for each cost.** There are three variable costs. The variable cost per unit is found by dividing each total budgeted cost by the direct labor hours used in preparing the master budget (120,000 hours). For Fox Manufacturing, the computations are:

Illustration 10-12
Computation of variable costs per direct labor hour

Variable Cost	Computation	Variable Cost per Direct Labor Hour
Indirect materials	$180,000 ÷ 120,000	**$1.50**
Indirect labor	$240,000 ÷ 120,000	**2.00**
Utilities	$ 60,000 ÷ 120,000	**0.50**
Total		**$4.00**

STEP 3. **Identify the fixed costs, and determine the budgeted amount for each cost.** There are three fixed costs. Since Fox desires **monthly budget data,** it divides each annual budgeted cost by 12 to find the monthly amounts. For Fox Manufacturing, the monthly budgeted fixed costs are: depreciation $15,000, supervision $10,000, and property taxes $5,000.

STEP 4. **Prepare the budget for selected increments of activity within the relevant range.** Management prepares the budget in increments of 1,000 direct labor hours.

Illustration 10-13 shows Fox's flexible budget.

Fox Manufacturing Company.xls

File Edit View Insert Format Tools Data Window Help

FOX MANUFACTURING COMPANY
Monthly Manufacturing Overhead Flexible Budget
Finishing Department
For the Year 2008

	A	B	C	D	E	F
5	Activity level					
6	Direct labor hours	8,000	9,000	10,000	11,000	12,000
7	Variable costs					
8	Indirect materials	$12,000	$13,500	$15,000	$16,500	$18,000
9	Indirect labor	16,000	18,000	20,000	22,000	24,000
10	Utilities	4,000	4,500	5,000	5,500	6,000
11	Total variable costs	32,000	36,000	40,000	44,000	48,000
12	Fixed costs					
13	Depreciation	15,000	15,000	15,000	15,000	15,000
14	Supervision	10,000	10,000	10,000	10,000	10,000
15	Property taxes	5,000	5,000	5,000	5,000	5,000
16	Total fixed costs	30,000	30,000	30,000	30,000	30,000
17	Total costs	$62,000	$66,000	$70,000	$74,000	$78,000
18						

Illustration 10-13
Monthly overhead flexible budget

Fox uses the formula below to determine total budgeted costs at any level of activity.

Fixed Costs + **Variable Costs*** = **Total Budgeted Costs**

***Total variable cost per unit of activity × Activity level.**

Illustration 10-14
Formula for total budgeted costs

HELPFUL HINT
Using the data given for Fox, what amount of total costs would be budgeted for 10,600 direct labor hours? Answer: $30,000 fixed + $42,400 variable (i.e, 10,600 × $4) = $72,400 total.

For Fox, fixed costs are $30,000, and total variable cost per direct labor hour is $4. At 9,000 direct labor hours, total budgeted costs are $66,000 [$30,000 + ($4 × 9,000)]. At 8,622 direct labor hours, total budgeted costs are $64,488 [$30,000 + ($4 × 8,622)].

Total budgeted costs can also be shown graphically, as in Illustration 10-15 (page 424). In the graph, the horizontal axis represents the activity index, and costs are indicated on the vertical axis. The graph highlights two activity levels (10,000 and 12,000). As shown, total budgeted costs at these activity levels are $70,000 [$30,000 + ($4 × 10,000)] and $78,000 [$30,000 + ($4 × 12,000)], respectively.

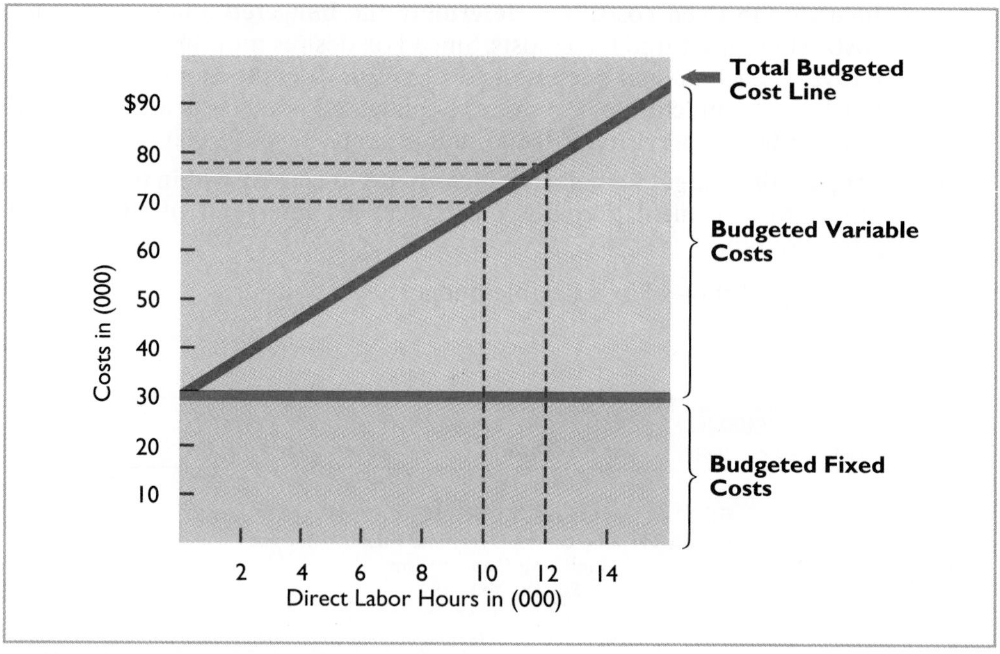

Illustration 10-15 Graphic flexible budget data highlighting 10,000 and 12,000 activity levels

Flexible Budget Reports

Flexible budget reports are another type of internal report. The flexible budget report consists of two sections: (1) production data for a selected activity index, such as direct labor hours, and (2) cost data for variable and fixed costs. The report provides a basis for evaluating a manager's performance in two areas: production control and cost control. Flexible budget reports are widely used in production and service departments.

Illustration 10-16 shows a budget report for the Finishing Department of Fox Company for the month of January. In this month, 9,000 hours are worked. The budget data are therefore based on the flexible budget for 9,000 hours in Illustration 10-13 (page 423). The actual cost data are assumed.

Illustration 10-16 Overhead flexible budget report

Fox Manufacturing Company.xls

FOX MANUFACTURING COMPANY
Manufacturing Overhead Flexible Budget Report
Finishing Department
For the Month Ended January 31, 2008

	Budget at	Actual costs at	Difference Favorable - F Unfavorable - U	
Direct labor hours (DLH)	9,000 DLH	9,000 DLH		
Variable costs				
Indirect materials	$13,500	$14,000	**$ 500**	U
Indirect labor	18,000	17,000	**1,000**	F
Utilities	4,500	4,600	**100**	U
Total variable costs	36,000	35,600	**400**	F
Fixed costs				
Depreciation	15,000	15,000	**0**	
Supervision	10,000	10,000	**0**	
Property taxes	5,000	5,000	**0**	
Total fixed costs	30,000	30,000	**0**	
Total costs	$66,000	$65,600	**$ 400**	F

How appropriate is this report in evaluating the Finishing Department manager's performance in controlling overhead costs? The report clearly provides a reliable basis. Both actual and budget costs are based on the activity level worked during January. Since variable costs generally are incurred directly by the department, the difference between the budget allowance for those hours and the actual costs is the responsibility of the department manager.

In subsequent months, Fox Manufacturing will prepare other flexible budget reports. For each month, the budget data are based on the actual activity level attained. In February that level may be 11,000 direct labor hours, in July 10,000, and so on.

Note that this flexible budget is based on a single cost driver. A more accurate budget often can be developed using the activity-based costing concepts explained in Chapter 4.

ACCOUNTING ACROSS THE ORGANIZATION

Budgets and the Exotic Newcastle Disease

Exotic Newcastle Disease, one of the most infectious bird diseases in the world, kills so swiftly that many victims die before any symptoms appear. When it broke out in Southern California in 2003, it could have spelled disaster for the San Diego Zoo. "We have one of the most valuable collections of birds in the world, if not *the* most valuable," says Paula Brock, CFO of the Zoological Society of San Diego, which operates the zoo.

Bird exhibits were closed to the public for several months (the disease, which is harmless to humans, can be carried on clothes and shoes). The tires of arriving delivery trucks were sanitized, as were the shoes of anyone visiting the zoo's nonpublic areas. Zookeeper uniforms had to be changed and cleaned daily. And ultimately, the zoo, with $150 million in revenues, spent almost half a million dollars on quarantine measures in 2003.

It worked: no birds got sick. Better yet, the damage to the rest of the zoo's budget was minimized by another protective measure: the monthly budget reforecast. "When we get a hit like this, we still have to find a way to make our bottom line," says Brock. Thanks to a new planning process Brock had introduced a year earlier, the zoo's scientists were able to raise the financial alarm as they redirected resources to ward off the disease. "Because we had timely awareness," she says, "we were able to make adjustments to weather the storm."

Budget reforecasting is nothing new. (The San Diego Zoo's annual static budget was behind the times before Brock took over as CFO in 2001.) But the reaction of the zoo's staff shows the benefits of Brock's immediate efforts to link strategy to the process. It's a move long touted by consultants as a key way to improve people's involvement in budgeting.

"To keep your company on a path, it has to have some kind of map," says Brock. "The budgeting-and-planning process is that map. I cannot imagine an organization feeling in control if it didn't have that sort of discipline."

Source: Tim Reason, "Budgeting in the Real World," *CFO Magazine*, July 12, 2005, *www.cfodirect.com/cfopublic.nsf/vContentPrint/649A82C8FF8AB06B85257037004* (accessed July 2005).

What is the major benefit of tying a budget to the overall goals of the company?

Management by Exception

Management by exception means that top management's review of a budget report is focused either entirely or primarily on differences between actual results and planned objectives. This approach enables top management to focus on problem areas. For example, many companies now use online reporting systems for employees to file their travel and entertainment expense reports. In addition to cutting reporting time in half, the online system enables managers to quickly analyze variances from travel budgets. This enables companies to cut down on expense account "padding" such as spending too much on meals or falsifying documents for costs that were never actually incurred.

Management by exception does not mean that top management will investigate every difference. For this approach to be effective, there must be guidelines for identifying an exception. The usual criteria are materiality and controllability.

MATERIALITY

Without quantitative guidelines, management would have to investigate every budget difference regardless of the amount. Materiality is usually expressed as a percentage difference from budget. For example, management may set the percentage difference at 5% for important items and 10% for other items. Managers will investigate all differences either over or under budget by the specified percentage. Costs over budget warrant investigation to determine why they were not controlled. Likewise, costs under budget merit investigation to determine whether costs critical to profitability are being curtailed. For example, if maintenance costs are budgeted at $80,000 but only $40,000 is spent, major unexpected breakdowns in productive facilities may occur in the future.

Alternatively, a company may specify a single percentage difference from budget for all items and supplement this guideline with a minimum dollar limit. For example, the exception criteria may be stated at 5% of budget or more than $10,000.

CONTROLLABILITY OF THE ITEM

Exception guidelines are more restrictive for controllable items than for items the manager cannot control. In fact, there may be no guidelines for noncontrollable items. For example, a large unfavorable difference between actual and budgeted property tax expense may not be flagged for investigation because the only possible causes are an unexpected increase in the tax rate or in the assessed value of the property. An investigation into the difference would be useless: the manager cannot control either cause.

Before You Go On...

REVIEW IT

1. What is the meaning of budgetary control?
2. When is a static budget appropriate for evaluating a manager's effectiveness in controlling costs?
3. What is a flexible budget?
4. How is a flexible budget developed?
5. What are the criteria used in management by exception?

DO IT

Your roommate asks your help in understanding how to compute total budgeted costs at any level of activity. Compute total budgeted costs at 30,000 direct labor hours, assuming that in the flexible budget graph, the fixed cost line and the total budgeted cost line intersect the vertical axis at $36,000 and that the total budget cost line is $186,000 at an activity level of 50,000 direct labor hours.

Action Plan

- Apply the formula: Fixed costs + Variable costs (Total variable costs per unit × Activity level) = Total budgeted costs.

Solution Using the graph, fixed costs are $36,000, and variable costs are $3 per direct labor hour [($186,000 − $36,000) ÷ 50,000]. Thus, at 30,000 direct labor hours, total budgeted costs are $126,000 [$36,000 + ($3 × 30,000)].

Related exercise material: *BE10-3, BE10-4, BE10-5, E10-3, E10-4, E10-5, E10-6, and E10-8.*

✓ The Navigator

THE CONCEPT OF RESPONSIBILITY ACCOUNTING

STUDY OBJECTIVE 4

Describe the concept of responsibility accounting.

Like budgeting, responsibility accounting is an important part of management accounting. **Responsibility accounting** involves accumulating and reporting costs (and revenues, where relevant) on the basis of the manager who has the authority to make the day-to-day decisions about the items. Under responsibility accounting, a manager's performance is evaluated on matters directly under that manager's control. Responsibility accounting can be used at every level of management in which the following conditions exist.

1. Costs and revenues can be directly associated with the specific level of management responsibility.
2. The costs and revenues can be controlled by employees at the level of responsibility with which they are associated.
3. Budget data can be developed for evaluating the manager's effectiveness in controlling the costs and revenues.

Illustration 10-17 depicts levels of responsibility for controlling costs.

Illustration 10-17
Responsibility for controllable costs at varying levels of management

Under responsibility accounting, any individual who controls a specified set of activities can be a responsibility center. Thus, responsibility accounting may extend from the lowest level of control to the top strata of management. Once responsibility is established, the company first measures and reports the effectiveness of the individual's performance for the specified activity. It then reports that measure upward throughout the organization.

HELPFUL HINT

All companies use responsibility accounting. Without some form of responsibility accounting, there would be chaos in discharging management's control function.

Responsibility accounting is especially valuable in a decentralized company. **Decentralization** means that the control of operations is delegated to many managers throughout the organization. The term **segment** is sometimes used to identify an area of responsibility in decentralized operations. Under responsibility accounting, companies prepare segment reports periodically, such as monthly, quarterly, and annually, to evaluate managers' performance.

Responsibility accounting is an essential part of any effective system of budgetary control. The reporting of costs and revenues under responsibility accounting differs from budgeting in two respects:

1. A distinction is made between controllable and noncontrollable items.
2. Performance reports either emphasize or include only items controllable by the individual manager.

Responsibility accounting applies to both profit and not-for-profit entities. For-profit entities seek to maximize net income. Not-for-profit entities wish to provide services as efficiently as possible.

MANAGEMENT INSIGHT

Competition versus Collaboration

Many compensation and promotion programs encourage competition among employees for pay raises. To get ahead you have to perform better than your fellow employees. While this may encourage hard work, it does not foster collaboration, and it can lead to distrust and disloyalty. Such results have led some companies to believe that cooperation and collaboration are essential in order to succeed in today's environment. For example, division managers might increase collaboration (and reduce costs) by sharing design and marketing resources or by jointly negotiating with suppliers. In addition, companies can reduce the need to hire and lay off employees by sharing employees across divisions as human resource needs increase and decrease.

As a consequence, many companies now explicitly include measures of collaboration in their performance measures. For example, Procter & Gamble measures collaboration in employees' annual performance reviews. At Cisco Systems the assessment of an employee's teamwork can affect the annual bonus by as much as 20%.

Source: Carol Hymowitz, "Rewarding Competitors Over Collaboration No Longer Makes Sense," *Wall Street Journal*, February 13, 2006.

How might managers of separate divisions be able to reduce division costs through collaboration?

Controllable versus Noncontrollable Revenues and Costs

HELPFUL HINT
Are there more or fewer controllable costs as you move to higher levels of management?
Answer: More.

All costs and revenues are controllable at some level of responsibility within a company. This truth underscores the adage by the CEO of any organization that "the buck stops here." Under responsibility accounting, the critical issue is **whether the cost or revenue is controllable at the level of responsibility with which it is associated.** A cost over which a manager has control is called a **controllable cost**. From this definition, it follows that:

1. All costs are controllable by top management because of the broad range of its authority.
2. Fewer costs are controllable as one moves down to each lower level of managerial responsibility because of the manager's decreasing authority.

In general, **costs incurred directly by a level of responsibility are controllable at that level**. In contrast, costs incurred indirectly and allocated to a responsibility level are **noncontrollable costs** at that level.

HELPFUL HINT
The longer the time span, the more likely that the cost becomes controllable.

Responsibility Reporting System

A **responsibility reporting system** involves the preparation of a report for each level of responsibility in the company's organization chart. To illustrate such a system, we use the partial organization chart and production departments of Francis Chair Company in Illustration 10-18.

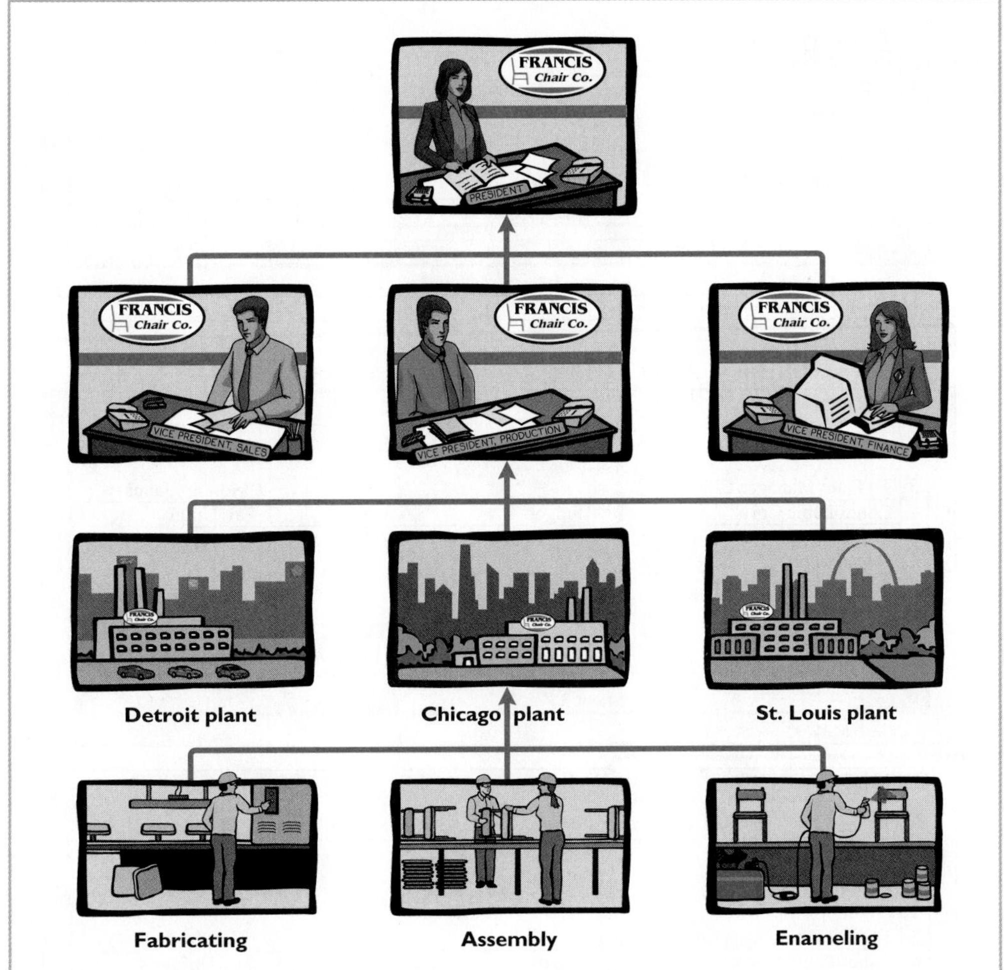

Illustration 10-18
Partial organization chart

Report A
President sees summary data of vice presidents.

Report B
Vice president sees summary of controllable costs in his/her functional area.

Report C
Plant manager sees summary of controllable costs for each department in the plant.

Report D
Department manager sees controllable costs of his/her department.

The responsibility reporting system begins with the lowest level of responsibility for controlling costs and moves upward to each higher level. Illustration 10-19 (page 430) details the connections between levels.

Illustration 10-19
Responsibility reporting system

Report A
President sees summary data of vice presidents.

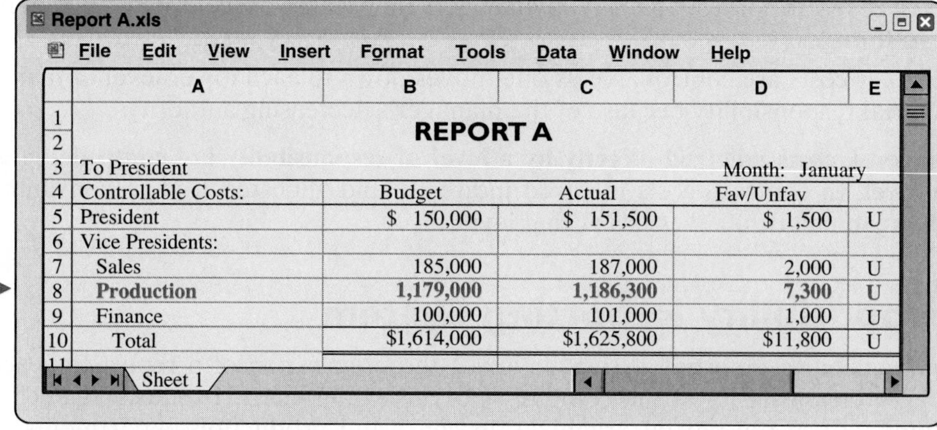

REPORT A

To President			Month: January	
Controllable Costs:	Budget	Actual	Fav/Unfav	
President	$ 150,000	$ 151,500	$ 1,500	U
Vice Presidents:				
Sales	185,000	187,000	2,000	U
Production	**1,179,000**	**1,186,300**	**7,300**	**U**
Finance	100,000	101,000	1,000	U
Total	$1,614,000	$1,625,800	$11,800	U

Report B
Vice president sees summary of controllable costs in his/her functional area.

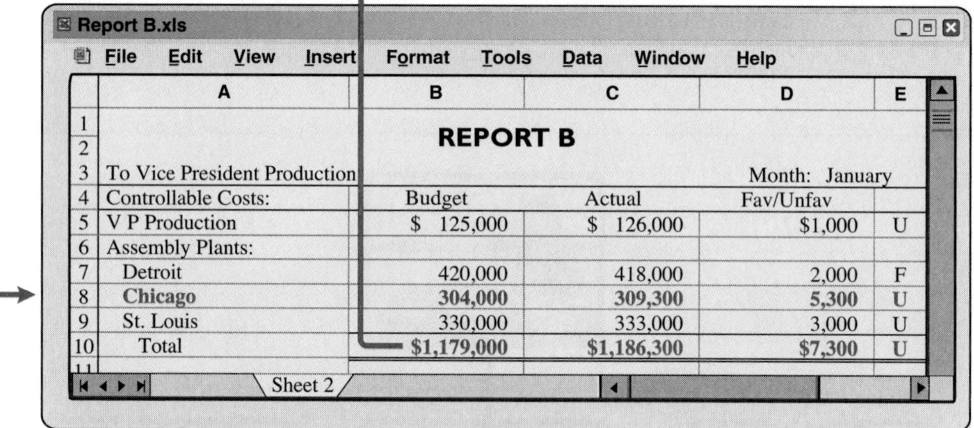

REPORT B

To Vice President Production			Month: January	
Controllable Costs:	Budget	Actual	Fav/Unfav	
V P Production	$ 125,000	$ 126,000	$1,000	U
Assembly Plants:				
Detroit	420,000	418,000	2,000	F
Chicago	**304,000**	**309,300**	**5,300**	**U**
St. Louis	330,000	333,000	3,000	U
Total	**$1,179,000**	**$1,186,300**	**$7,300**	**U**

Report C
Plant manager sees summary of controllable costs for each department in the plant.

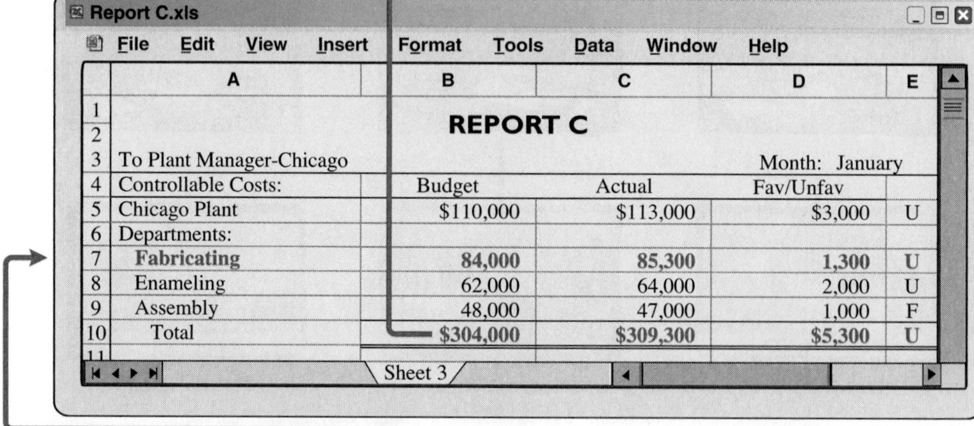

REPORT C

To Plant Manager-Chicago			Month: January	
Controllable Costs:	Budget	Actual	Fav/Unfav	
Chicago Plant	$110,000	$113,000	$3,000	U
Departments:				
Fabricating	**84,000**	**85,300**	**1,300**	**U**
Enameling	62,000	64,000	2,000	U
Assembly	48,000	47,000	1,000	F
Total	**$304,000**	**$309,300**	**$5,300**	**U**

Report D
Department manager sees controllable costs of his/her department.

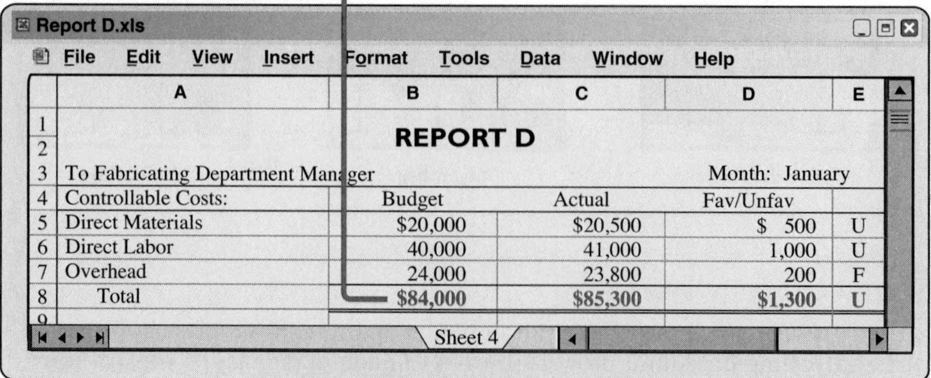

REPORT D

To Fabricating Department Manager			Month: January	
Controllable Costs:	Budget	Actual	Fav/Unfav	
Direct Materials	$20,000	$20,500	$ 500	U
Direct Labor	40,000	41,000	1,000	U
Overhead	24,000	23,800	200	F
Total	**$84,000**	**$85,300**	**$1,300**	**U**

A brief description of the four reports for Francis Chair Company is as follows.

1. **Report D** is typical of reports that go to department managers. Similar reports are prepared for the managers of the Fabricating, Assembly, and Enameling Departments.
2. **Report C** is an example of reports that are sent to plant managers. It shows the costs of the Chicago plant that are controllable at the second level of responsibility. In addition, Report C shows summary data for each department that is controlled by the plant manager. Similar reports are prepared for the Detroit and St. Louis plant managers.
3. **Report B** illustrates the reports at the third level of responsibility. It shows the controllable costs of the vice president of production and summary data on the three assembly plants for which this officer is responsible. Similar reports are prepared for the vice presidents of sales and finance.
4. **Report A** is typical of reports that go to the top level of responsibility—the president. It shows the controllable costs and expenses of this office and summary data on the vice presidents that are accountable to the president.

A responsibility reporting system permits management by exception at each level of responsibility. And, each higher level of responsibility can obtain the detailed report for each lower level of responsibility. For example, the vice president of production in the Francis Chair Company may request the Chicago plant manager's report because this plant is $5,300 over budget.

This type of reporting system also permits comparative evaluations. In Illustration 10-19, the Chicago plant manager can easily rank the department managers' effectiveness in controlling manufacturing costs. Comparative rankings provide further incentive for a manager to control costs.

TYPES OF RESPONSIBILITY CENTERS

There are three basic types of responsibility centers: cost centers, profit centers, and investment centers. These classifications indicate the degree of responsibility the manager has for the performance of the center.

A **cost center** incurs costs (and expenses) but does not directly generate revenues. Managers of cost centers have the authority to incur costs. They are evaluated on their ability to control costs. **Cost centers are usually either production departments or service departments.** Production departments participate directly in making the product. Service departments provide only support services. In a Ford Motor Company automobile plant, the welding, painting, and assembling departments are production departments. Ford's maintenance, cafeteria, and human resources departments are service departments. All of them are cost centers.

HELPFUL HINT

(1) Is the jewelry department of Macy's department store a profit center or a cost center? (2) Is the props department of a movie studio a profit center or a cost center? Answers: (1) Profit center. (2) Cost center.

A **profit center** incurs costs (and expenses) and also generates revenues. Managers of profit centers are judged on the profitability of their centers. Examples of profit centers include the individual departments of a retail store, such as clothing, furniture, and automotive products, and branch offices of banks.

Like a profit center, an **investment center** incurs costs (and expenses) and generates revenues. In addition, an investment center has control over decisions regarding the assets available for use. Investment center managers are evaluated on both the profitability of the center and the rate of return earned on the funds invested. Investment centers are often associated with subsidiary companies. Utility Duke Energy has operating divisions such as electric utility, energy trading, and natural gas. Investment center managers control or significantly influence investment decisions related to such matters as plant expansion and entry into new market areas. Illustration 10-20 (page 432) depicts the three types of responsibility centers.

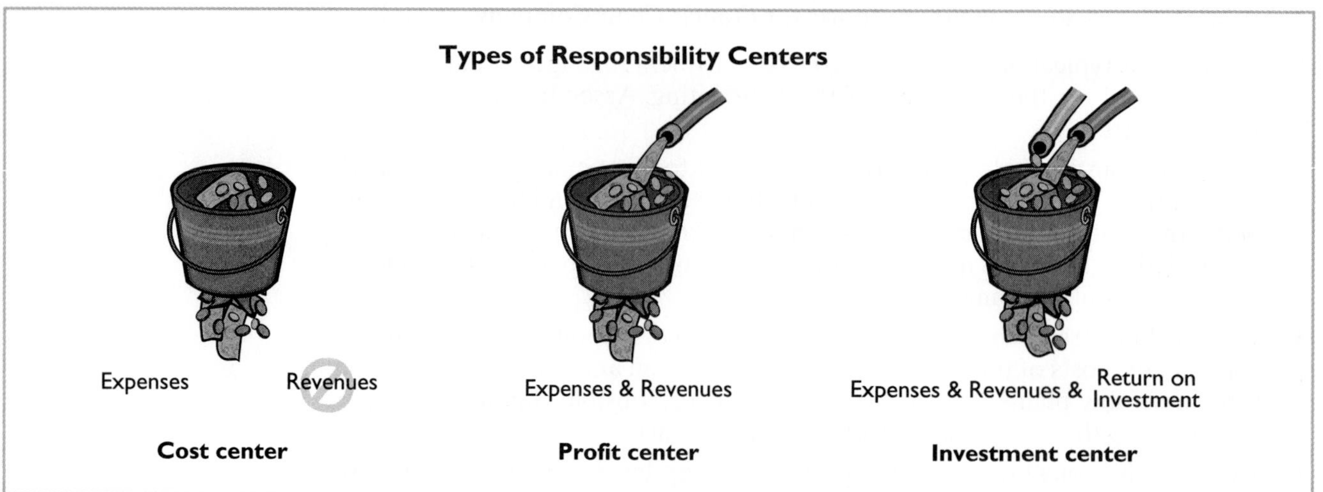

Illustration 10-20
Types of responsibility centers

Responsibility Accounting for Cost Centers

STUDY OBJECTIVE 5

Indicate the features of responsibility reports for cost centers.

The evaluation of a manager's performance for cost centers is based on his or her ability to meet budgeted goals for controllable costs. **Responsibility reports for cost centers compare actual controllable costs with flexible budget data.**

Illustration 10-21 shows a responsibility report. The report is adapted from the flexible budget report for Fox Manufacturing Company in Illustration 10-16 on page 424. It assumes that the Finishing Department manager is able to control all manufacturing overhead costs except depreciation, property taxes, and his own monthly salary of $6,000. The remaining $4,000 ($10,000 − $6,000) of supervision costs are assumed to apply to other supervisory personnel within the Finishing Department, whose salaries are controllable by the manager.

Illustration 10-21
Responsibility report for a cost center

Fox Manufacturing Company.xls

File Edit View Insert Format Tools Data Window Help

	A	B	C	D	E
1	**FOX MANUFACTURING COMPANY**				
2	**Finishing Department**				
3	**Responsibility Report**				
4	**For the Month Ended January 31, 2008**				
5				Difference	
6	Controllable Cost	Budget	Actual	Favorable - F Unfavorable - U	
7	Indirect materials	$13,500	$14,000	**$ 500**	U
8	Indirect labor	18,000	17,000	**$1,000**	F
9	Utilities	4,500	4,600	**100**	U
10	**Supervision**	**4,000**	**4,000**	**0**	
11		$40,000	$39,600	**$ 400**	F
12					

The report in Illustration 10-21 includes **only controllable costs**, and no distinction is made between variable and fixed costs. The responsibility report continues the concept of management by exception. In this case, top management may request an explanation of the $1,000 favorable difference in indirect labor and/or the $500 unfavorable difference in indirect materials.

Responsibility Accounting for Profit Centers

STUDY OBJECTIVE 6

Identify the content of responsibility reports for profit centers.

To evaluate the performance of a profit center manager, upper management needs detailed information about both controllable revenues and controllable costs. The operating revenues earned by a profit center, such as sales, are controllable by the manager. All variable costs (and expenses) incurred by the center are also controllable by the manager because they vary with sales. However, to determine the controllability of fixed costs, it is necessary to distinguish between direct and indirect fixed costs.

DIRECT AND INDIRECT FIXED COSTS

A profit center may have both direct and indirect fixed costs. **Direct fixed costs** relate specifically to one center and are incurred for the sole benefit of that center. Examples of such costs include the salaries established by the profit center manager for supervisory personnel and the cost of a timekeeping department for the center's employees. Since these fixed costs can be traced directly to a center, they are also called **traceable costs. Most direct fixed costs are controllable by the profit center manager.**

In contrast, **indirect fixed costs** pertain to a company's overall operating activities and are incurred for the benefit of more than one profit center. Management allocates indirect fixed costs to profit centers on some type of equitable basis. For example, property taxes on a building occupied by more than one center may be allocated on the basis of square feet of floor space used by each center. Or, the costs of a company's human resources department may be allocated to profit centers on the basis of the number of employees in each center. Because these fixed costs apply to more than one center, they are also called **common costs. Most indirect fixed costs are not controllable by the profit center manager.**

RESPONSIBILITY REPORT

The responsibility report for a profit center shows budgeted and actual **controllable revenues and costs**. The report is prepared using the cost-volume-profit income statement explained in Chapter 5. In the report:

1. Controllable fixed costs are deducted from contribution margin.
2. The excess of contribution margin over controllable fixed costs is identified as **controllable margin**.
3. Noncontrollable fixed costs are not reported.

HELPFUL HINT

Recognize that we are emphasizing *financial* measures of performance. These days companies are also making an effort to stress *nonfinancial* performance measures such as product quality, labor productivity, market growth, materials' yield, manufacturing flexibility, and technological capability.

Illustration 10-22 (page 434) shows the responsibility report for the manager of the Marine Division, a profit center of Mantle Manufacturing Company. For the year, the Marine Division also had $60,000 of indirect fixed costs that were not controllable by the profit center manager.

Controllable margin is considered to be the best measure of the manager's performance **in controlling revenues and costs**. The report in Illustration 10-22 shows that the manager's performance was below budgeted expectations by 10% ($36,000 ÷ $360,000). Top management would likely investigate the causes of this unfavorable result. Note that the report does not show the Marine Division's noncontrollable fixed costs of $60,000. These costs would be included in a report on the profitability of the profit center.

Management also may choose to see **monthly** responsibility reports for profit centers. In addition, responsibility reports may include cumulative year-to-date results.

Illustration 10-22
Responsibility report for profit center

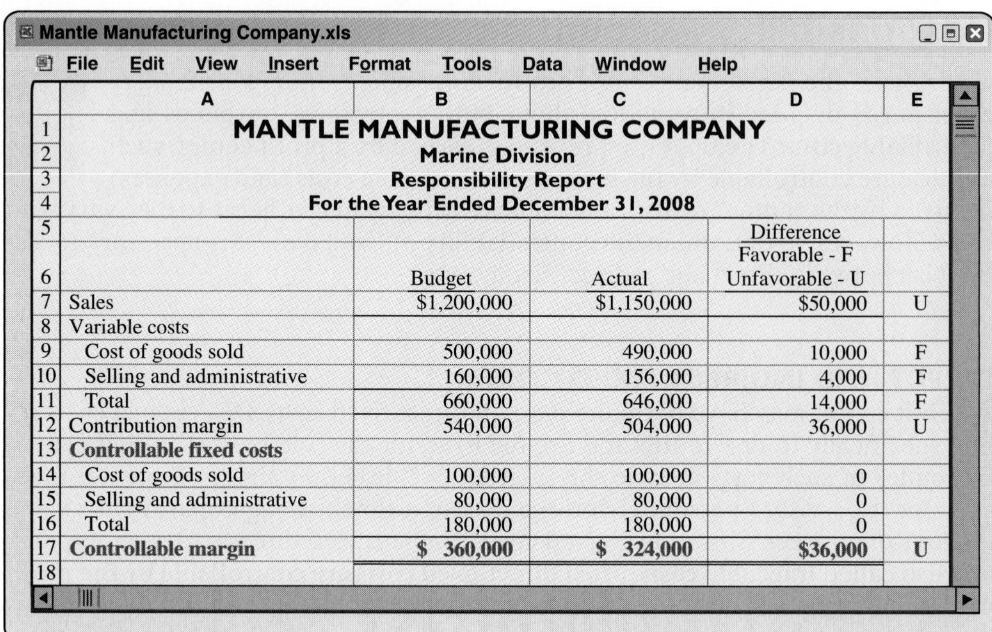

Mantle Manufacturing Company.xls

MANTLE MANUFACTURING COMPANY
Marine Division
Responsibility Report
For the Year Ended December 31, 2008

	Budget	Actual	Difference Favorable - F Unfavorable - U	
Sales	$1,200,000	$1,150,000	$50,000	U
Variable costs				
Cost of goods sold	500,000	490,000	10,000	F
Selling and administrative	160,000	156,000	4,000	F
Total	660,000	646,000	14,000	F
Contribution margin	540,000	504,000	36,000	U
Controllable fixed costs				
Cost of goods sold	100,000	100,000	0	
Selling and administrative	80,000	80,000	0	
Total	180,000	180,000	0	
Controllable margin	**$ 360,000**	**$ 324,000**	**$36,000**	U

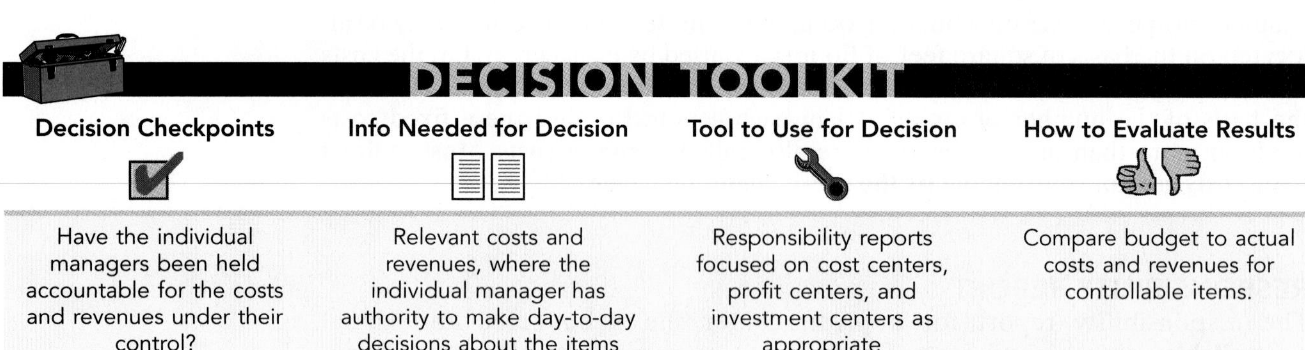

DECISION TOOLKIT

Decision Checkpoints	Info Needed for Decision	Tool to Use for Decision	How to Evaluate Results
Have the individual managers been held accountable for the costs and revenues under their control?	Relevant costs and revenues, where the individual manager has authority to make day-to-day decisions about the items	Responsibility reports focused on cost centers, profit centers, and investment centers as appropriate	Compare budget to actual costs and revenues for controllable items.

Before You Go On...

REVIEW IT

1. What conditions are essential for responsibility accounting?
2. What is involved in a responsibility reporting system?
3. What is the primary objective of a responsibility report for a cost center?
4. How does contribution margin differ from controllable margin in a responsibility report for a profit center?

DO IT

Midwest Division operates as a profit center. It reports the following for the year:

	Budgeted	**Actual**
Sales	$1,500,000	$1,700,000
Variable costs	700,000	800,000
Controllable fixed costs	400,000	400,000
Noncontrollable fixed costs	200,000	200,000

Prepare a responsibility report for the Midwest Division for December 31, 2008.

Action Plan

- Deduct variable costs from sales to show contribution margin.
- Deduct controllable fixed costs from the contribution margin to show controllable margin.
- Do not report noncontrollable fixed costs.

Solution

MIDWEST DIVISION
Responsibility Report
For the Year Ended December 31, 2008

	Budget	Actual	Difference Favorable F Unfavorable U
Sales	$1,500,000	$1,700,000	$200,000 F
Variable costs	700,000	800,000	100,000 U
Contribution margin	800,000	900,000	100,000 F
Controllable fixed costs	400,000	400,000	-0-
Controllable margin	$ 400,000	$ 500,000	$100,000 F

Related exercise material: *BE10-7 and E10-13.*

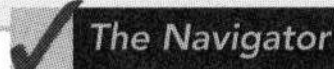

Responsibility Accounting for Investment Centers

STUDY OBJECTIVE 7

Explain the basis and formula used in evaluating performance in investment centers.

As explained earlier, an investment center manager can control or significantly influence the investment funds available for use. Thus, the primary basis for evaluating the performance of a manager of an investment center is **return on investment (ROI)**. The return on investment is considered to be a useful performance measurement because it shows the **effectiveness of the manager in utilizing the assets at his or her disposal**.

RETURN ON INVESTMENT (ROI)

The formula for computing ROI for an investment center, together with assumed illustrative data, is shown in Illustration 10-23.

Illustration 10-23
ROI formula

Controllable Margin	÷	Average Operating Assets	=	Return on Investment (ROI)
$1,000,000	÷	$5,000,000	=	20%

Both factors in the formula are controllable by the investment center manager. Operating assets consist of current assets and plant assets used in operations by the center and controlled by the manager. Nonoperating assets such as idle plant assets and land held for future use are excluded. Average operating assets are usually based on the cost or book value of the assets at the beginning and end of the year.

RESPONSIBILITY REPORT

The scope of the investment center manager's responsibility significantly affects the content of the performance report. Since an investment center is an independent entity for operating purposes, **all fixed costs are controllable by its manager**. For example, the manager is responsible for depreciation on investment center assets. Therefore, more fixed costs are identified as controllable in the performance report for an investment center manager than in a performance report for a profit center manager. The report also shows budgeted and actual ROI below controllable margin.

To illustrate this responsibility report, we will now assume that the Marine Division of Mantle Manufacturing Company is an investment center. It has budgeted and actual average operating assets of $2,000,000. The manager can control $60,000 of fixed costs that were not controllable when the division was a profit center. Illustration 10-24 shows the division's responsibility report.

Illustration 10-24
Responsibility report for investment center

Mantle Manufacturing Company.xls

File Edit View Insert Format Tools Data Window Help

MANTLE MANUFACTURING COMPANY
Marine Division
Responsibility Report
For the Year Ended December 31, 2008

	Budget	Actual	Difference Favorable - F Unfavorable - U	
Sales	$1,200,000	$1,150,000	$ 50,000	U
Variable costs				
Cost of goods sold	500,000	490,000	10,000	F
Selling and administrative	160,000	156,000	4,000	F
Total	660,000	646,000	14,000	F
Contribution margin	540,000	504,000	36,000	U
Controllable fixed costs				
Cost of goods sold	100,000	100,000	0	
Selling and administrative	80,000	80,000	0	
Other fixed costs	**60,000**	**60,000**	**0**	
Total	240,000	240,000	0	
Controllable margin	**$ 300,000**	**$ 264,000**	**$ 36,000**	U
Return on investment	**15.0%**	**13.2%**	**1.8%**	U
	(a)	(b)	(c)	

(a) $\frac{\$300{,}000}{\$2{,}000{,}000}$ (b) $\frac{\$264{,}000}{\$2{,}000{,}000}$ (c) $\frac{\$36{,}000}{\$2{,}000{,}000}$

The report shows that the manager's performance based on ROI was below budget expectations by 1.8% (15.0% versus 13.2%). Top management would likely want an explanation of the reasons for this unfavorable result.

JUDGMENTAL FACTORS IN ROI

The return on investment approach includes two judgmental factors:

1. **Valuation of operating assets.** Operating assets may be valued at acquisition cost, book value, appraised value, or market value. The first two bases are readily available from the accounting records.
2. **Margin (income) measure.** This measure may be controllable margin, income from operations, or net income.

Each of the alternative values for operating assets can provide a reliable basis for evaluating a manager's performance as long as it is consistently applied between reporting periods. However, the use of income measures other than controllable margin will not result in a valid basis for evaluating the performance of an investment center manager.

IMPROVING ROI

The manager of an investment center can improve ROI by increasing controllable margin, and/or reducing average operating assets. To illustrate, we will use the following assumed data for the Laser Division of Berra Manufacturing.

Sales	$2,000,000
Variable cost	1,100,000
Contribution margin (45%)	900,000
Controllable fixed costs	300,000
Controllable margin (a)	$ 600,000
Average operating assets (b)	$5,000,000
Return on investment (a) ÷ (b)	**12%**

Illustration 10-25
Assumed data for Laser Division

Increasing Controllable Margin. Controllable margin can be increased by increasing sales or by reducing variable and controllable fixed costs as follows.

1. **Increase sales 10%.** Sales will increase $200,000 ($2,000,000 × .10). Assuming no change in the contribution margin percentage of 45%, contribution margin will increase $90,000 ($200,000 × .45). Controllable margin will increase by the same amount because controllable fixed costs will not change. Thus, controllable margin becomes $690,000 ($600,000 + $90,000). The new ROI is 13.8%, computed as follows.

$$\text{ROI} = \frac{\text{Controllable margin}}{\text{Average operating assets}} = \frac{\$690{,}000}{\$5{,}000{,}000} = \mathbf{13.8\%}$$

Illustration 10-26
ROI computation—increase in sales

An increase in sales benefits both the investment center and the company if it results in new business. It would not benefit the company if the increase was achieved at the expense of other investment centers.

2. **Decrease variable and fixed costs 10%.** Total costs decrease $140,000 [($1,100,000 + $300,000) × .10]. This reduction results in a corresponding increase in controllable margin. Thus, controllable margin becomes $740,000 ($600,000 + $140,000). The new ROI is 14.8%, computed as follows.

$$\text{ROI} = \frac{\text{Controllable margin}}{\text{Average operating assets}} = \frac{\$740{,}000}{\$5{,}000{,}000} = \mathbf{14.8\%}$$

Illustration 10-27
ROI computation—decrease in costs

This course of action is clearly beneficial when waste and inefficiencies are eliminated. But, a reduction in vital costs such as required maintenance and inspections is not likely to be acceptable to top management.

Reducing Average Operating Assets. Assume that average operating assets are reduced 10% or $500,000 ($5,000,000 × .10). Average operating assets become $4,500,000 ($5,000,000 − $500,000). Since controllable margin remains unchanged at $600,000, the new ROI is 13.3%, computed as follows.

$$\text{ROI} = \frac{\text{Controllable margin}}{\text{Average operating assets}} = \frac{\$600{,}000}{\$4{,}500{,}000} = \mathbf{13.3\%}$$

Illustration 10-28
ROI computation—decrease in operating assets

Reductions in operating assets may or may not be prudent. It is beneficial to eliminate overinvestment in inventories and to dispose of excessive plant assets. However, it is unwise to reduce inventories below expected needs or to dispose of essential plant assets.

ACCOUNTING ACROSS THE ORGANIZATION

Does Hollywood Look at ROI?

If Hollywood were run like a real business, where things like return on investment mattered, there would be one unchallenged, sacred principle that studio chieftains would never violate: Make lots of G-rated movies.

No matter how you slice the movie business—by star vehicles, by budget levels, by sequels or franchises—by far the best return on investment comes from the not-so-glamorous world of G-rated films. The problem is, these movies represent only 3% of the total films made in a typical year.

Take 2003: According to Motion Picture Association of America statistics, of the 940 movies released that year, only 29 were G-rated. Yet the highest-grossing movie of the year, *Finding Nemo*, was G-rated. . . . On the flip side are the R-rated films, which dominate the total releases and yet yield the worst return on investment. A whopping 646 R-rated films were released in 2003—69% of the total output—but only four of the top-20 grossing movies of the year were R-rated films.

This trend—G-rated movies are good for business but underproduced; R-rated movies are bad for business, and yet overdone—is something that has been driving economists batty for the past several years.

Source: Grainger, David, "The Dysfunctional Family-Film Business," *Fortune*, January 10, 2005, pp. 20–21.

What might be the reason that movie studios do not produce G-rated movies as much as R-rated ones?

DECISION TOOLKIT

Decision Checkpoints	Info Needed for Decision	Tool to Use for Decision	How to Evaluate Results
Has the investment center performed up to expectations?	Controllable margin (contribution margin minus controllable fixed costs), and average investment center operating assets	Return on investment	Compare actual ROI to expected ROI.

Principles of Performance Evaluation

Performance evaluation is at the center of responsibility accounting. **Performance evaluation** is a management function that compares actual results with budget goals. It involves both behavioral and reporting principles.

BEHAVIORAL PRINCIPLES

The human factor is critical in evaluating performance. Behavioral principles include the following.

1. **Managers of responsibility centers should have direct input into the process of establishing budget goals of their area of responsibility.** Without such input, managers may view the goals as unrealistic or arbitrarily set by top management. Such views adversely affect the managers' motivation to meet the targeted objectives.
2. **The evaluation of performance should be based entirely on matters that are controllable by the manager being evaluated.** Criticism of a manager on matters outside his or her control reduces the effectiveness of the evaluation process. It leads to negative reactions by a manager and to doubts about the fairness of the company's evaluation policies.
3. **Top management should support the evaluation process.** As explained earlier, the evaluation process begins at the lowest level of responsibility and extends upward to the highest level of management. Managers quickly lose faith in the process when top management ignores, overrules, or bypasses established procedures for evaluating a manager's performance.
4. **The evaluation process must allow managers to respond to their evaluations.** Evaluation is not a one-way street. Managers should have the opportunity to defend their performance. Evaluation without feedback is both impersonal and ineffective.
5. **The evaluation should identify both good and poor performance.** Praise for good performance is a powerful motivating factor for a manager. This is especially true when a manager's compensation includes rewards for meeting budget goals.

REPORTING PRINCIPLES

Performance evaluation under responsibility accounting should be based on certain reporting principles. These principles pertain primarily to the internal reports that provide the basis for evaluating performance. Performance reports should:

1. Contain only data that are controllable by the manager of the responsibility center.
2. Provide accurate and reliable budget data to measure performance.
3. Highlight significant differences between actual results and budget goals.
4. Be tailor-made for the intended evaluation.
5. Be prepared at reasonable intervals.

In recent years companies have come under increasing pressure from influential shareholder groups to do a better job of linking executive pay to corporate performance. For example, software maker Siebel Systems unveiled a new incentive plan after lengthy discussions with the California Public Employees' Retirement System. One unique feature of the plan is that managers' targets will be publicly disclosed at the beginning of each year for investors to evaluate.

Before You Go On...

REVIEW IT

1. What is the formula for computing return on investment (ROI)?
2. Identify three actions a manager may take to improve ROI.

Be sure to read **ALL ABOUT YOU: *Budgeting for Housing Costs*** on page 440 for information on how topics in this chapter apply to you.

all about YOU

Budgeting for Housing Costs

In Chapter 9 you learned how to prepare a budget. Budgets are great planning tools, but planning is only one purpose of budgeting. As you learned in this chapter, budgets also are used as the basis of performance evaluation. That is, a company prepares the budget to lay out what it plans on doing, and then it compares its actual results with its plan to see how well it did.

It works the same way for individual budgets. Preparing a personal budget is a great first step. But the real benefit of budgeting comes from comparing your actual results with your personal budget and then making the necessary (and sometimes unpleasant) adjustments. Although unexpected bills can create problems, most financial problems are the result of not controlling routine expenses.

Some Facts

* Most experts encourage people to keep housing costs (mortgage, insurance, and taxes) at approximately 25% to 30% of pre-tax income.
* The U.S. Department of Agriculture estimates that it will cost between $127,080 and $254,400 to raise a child born in 2002 to the age of 18. That amount *does not* include college tuition. Married couples with children file for bankruptcy twice as often as married couples without children.
* Medical bills contribute to one out of five bankruptcies. One out of seven Americans has no health insurance.
* Approximately 40% of American households do not have even $1,000 in cash available for emergencies when unexpected expenses arise.
* Increases in interest rates are causing budget problems for people with adjustable-rate mortgages. As interest rates rose from 2005 to 2006, the number of adjustable-rate mortgages that were at least 90 days past due increased by more than 140%.

About the Numbers

Housing represents the largest cost for nearly all Americans. The cost of housing as a percentage of income varies considerably across the United States. The following graph shows the percentage of homeowners with mortgages in each state who spend more than 30% of household income on housing costs.

Figure 1. Mortgaged Owners Spending 30% or more of Household Income on Selected Monthly Owner Costs, 2004

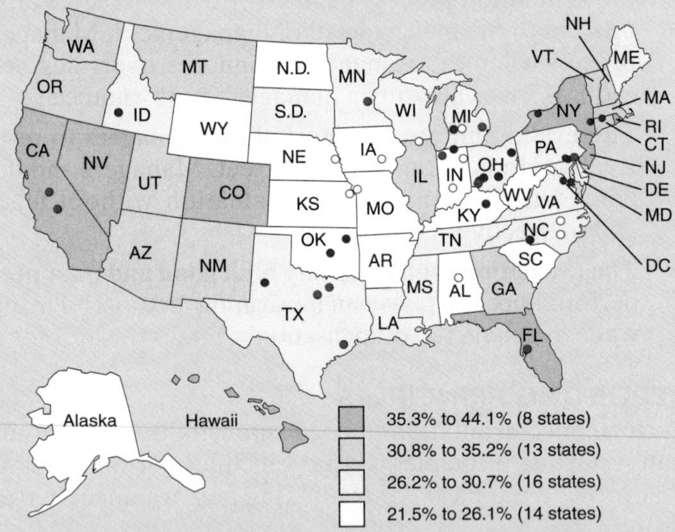

What Do You Think?

As noted above, housing is the greatest expense for most people. The percentage of people in the United States who own a home is high compared to many other countries. This is in part the result of U.S. government programs and incentives that encourage home ownership. For example, the interest on a home mortgage is deductible for tax purposes.

Suppose you have just graduated from college and are moving to a new community. Should you immediately buy a new home?

YES: The cost of housing continues to rise. By purchasing a home soon, I can make my housing cost more like a fixed cost, and thus reduce future cost increases. Also I will benefit from the appreciation in my home's value.

NO: I just moved to a new town, so I don't know the market. Also, it is likely that my income will increase in the next few years, so I will be able to afford a better house if I wait a few years. Also, house prices have increased a lot in recent years, but some experts think they may actually decline in some parts of the country. I don't want to get stuck with a house that I can't sell.

Sources: Liz Pullman Weston, "How to Survive 7 Budget Busters," *moneycentral.msn.com/content/Savinganddebt/Learntobudget/P58710.asp*; Amber Kostelac, "Housing Is Affordable in the Hoosier State," *www.incontext.indiana.edu/2005/october/pdfs/housing.pdf*, October 2005 (both accessed August 2006).

The authors' comments on this situation appear on page 467.

Using the Decision Toolkit

The manufacturing overhead budget for Reebles Company contains the following items.

Variable costs	
Indirect materials	$25,000
Indirect labor	12,000
Maintenance expenses	10,000
Manufacturing supplies	6,000
Total variable	$53,000
Fixed costs	
Supervision	$17,000
Inspection costs	1,000
Insurance expenses	2,000
Depreciation	15,000
Total fixed	$35,000

The budget was based on an estimated 2,000 units being produced. During November, 1,500 units were produced, and the following costs incurred.

Variable costs	
Indirect materials	$25,200
Indirect labor	13,500
Maintenance expenses	8,200
Manufacturing supplies	5,100
Total variable	$52,000
Fixed costs	
Supervision	$19,300
Inspection costs	1,200
Insurance expenses	2,200
Depreciation	14,700
Total fixed	$37,400

Instructions

(a) Determine which items would be controllable by Ed Lopat, the production manager. (Assume "supervision" excludes Lopat's own salary.)

(b) How much should have been spent during the month for the manufacture of the 1,500 units?

(c) Prepare a flexible manufacturing overhead budget report for Mr. Lopat.

(d) Prepare a responsibility report. Include only the costs that would have been controllable by Mr. Lopat. In an attached memo, describe clearly for Mr. Lopat the areas in which his performance needs to be improved.

Solution

(a) Ed Lopat should be able to control all the variable costs and the fixed costs of supervision and inspection. Insurance and depreciation ordinarily are not the responsibility of the department manager.

(b) The total variable cost per unit is $26.50 ($53,000 ÷ 2,000). The total budgeted cost during the month to manufacture 1,500 units is variable costs $39,750 (1,500 × $26.50) plus fixed costs ($35,000), for a total of $74,750 ($39,750 + $35,000).

(c)

REEBLES COMPANY
Production Department
Manufacturing Overhead Budget Report (Flexible)
For the Month Ended November 30, 2008

	Budget at 1,500 units	Actual at 1,500 units	Difference Favorable F Unfavorable U
Variable costs			
Indirect materials	$18,750	$25,200	$ 6,450 U
Indirect labor	9,000	13,500	4,500 U
Maintenance	7,500	8,200	700 U
Manufacturing supplies	4,500	5,100	600 U
Total variable	39,750	52,000	12,250 U
Fixed costs			
Supervision	17,000	19,300	2,300 U
Inspection	1,000	1,200	200 U
Insurance	2,000	2,200	200 U
Depreciation	15,000	14,700	300 F
Total fixed	35,000	37,400	2,400 U
Total costs	$74,750	$89,400	$14,650 U

(d) Because a production department is a cost center, the responsibility report should include only the costs that are controllable by the production manager. In this type of report, no distinction is made between variable and fixed costs. Budget data in the report should be based on the units actually produced.

REEBLES COMPANY
Production Department
Manufacturing Overhead Responsibility Report
For the Month Ended November 30, 2008

Controllable Cost	Budget	Actual	Difference Favorable F Unfavorable U
Indirect materials	$18,750	$25,200	$ 6,450 U
Indirect labor	9,000	13,500	4,500 U
Maintenance	7,500	8,200	700 U
Manufacturing supplies	4,500	5,100	600 U
Supervision	17,000	19,300	2,300 U
Inspection	1,000	1,200	200 U
Total	$57,750	$72,500	$14,750 U

To: Mr. Ed Lopat, Production Manager
From: ________________, Vice-President of Production
Subject: Performance Evaluation for the Month of November

Your performance in controlling costs that are your responsibility was very disappointing in the month of November. As indicated in the accompanying responsibility report, total costs were $14,750 over budget. On a percentage basis, costs were 26% over budget. As you can see, actual costs were over budget for every cost item. In three instances, costs were significantly over budget (indirect materials 34%, indirect labor 50%, and supervision 14%).

Ed, it is imperative that you get costs under control in your department as soon as possible.

I think we need to talk about ways to implement more effective cost control measures. I would like to meet with you in my office at 9 a.m. on Wednesday to discuss possible alternatives.

The Navigator

SUMMARY OF STUDY OBJECTIVES

1 **Describe the concept of budgetary control.** Budgetary control consists of (a) preparing periodic budget reports that compare actual results with planned objectives, (b) analyzing the differences to determine their causes, (c) taking appropriate corrective action, and (d) modifying future plans, if necessary.

2 **Evaluate the usefulness of static budget reports.** Static budget reports are useful in evaluating the progress toward planned sales and profit goals. They are also appropriate in assessing a manager's effectiveness in controlling costs when (a) actual activity closely approximates the master budget activity level, and/or (b) the behavior of the costs in response to changes in activity is fixed.

3 **Explain the development of flexible budgets and the usefulness of flexible budget reports.** To develop the flexible budget it is necessary to: (a) Identify the activity index and the relevant range of activity. (b) Identify the variable costs, and determine the budgeted variable cost per unit of activity for each cost. (c) Identify the fixed costs, and determine the budgeted amount for each cost. (d) Prepare the budget for selected increments of activity within the relevant range. Flexible budget reports permit an evaluation of a manager's performance in controlling production and costs.

4 **Describe the concept of responsibility accounting.** Responsibility accounting involves accumulating and reporting revenues and costs on the basis of the individual manager who has the authority to make the day-to-day decisions about the items. The evaluation of a manager's performance is based on the matters directly under the manager's control. In responsibility accounting, it is necessary to distinguish between controllable and noncontrollable fixed costs and to identify three types of responsibility centers: cost, profit, and investment.

5 **Indicate the features of responsibility reports for cost centers.** Responsibility reports for cost centers compare actual costs with flexible budget data. The reports show only controllable costs, and no distinction is made between variable and fixed costs.

6 **Identify the content of responsibility reports for profit centers.** Responsibility reports show contribution margin, controllable fixed costs, and controllable margin for each profit center.

7 **Explain the basis and formula used in evaluating performance in investment centers.** The primary basis for evaluating performance in investment centers is return on investment (ROI). The formula for computing ROI for investment centers is: Controllable margin ÷ Average operating assets.

DECISION TOOLKIT—A SUMMARY

Decision Checkpoints	Info Needed for Decision	Tool to Use for Decision	How to Evaluate Results
Are the increased costs resulting from increased production reasonable?	Variable costs projected at different levels of production	Flexible budget	After taking into account different production levels, results are favorable if expenses are less than budgeted amounts.
Have the individual managers been held accountable for the costs and revenues under their control?	Relevant costs and revenues, where the individual manager has authority to make day-to-day decisions about the items	Responsibility reports focused on cost centers, profit centers, and investment centers as appropriate	Compare budget to actual costs and revenues for controllable items.
Has the investment center performed up to expectations?	Controllable margin (contribution margin minus controllable fixed costs), and average investment center operating assets	Return on investment	Compare actual ROI to expected ROI.

APPENDIX Residual Income—Another Performance Measurement

STUDY OBJECTIVE 8

Explain the difference between ROI and residual income.

Although most companies use ROI in evaluating their investment performance, ROI has a significant disadvantage. To illustrate, let's look at the Electronics Division of Pujols Manufacturing Company. It has an ROI of 20% computed as follows.

Illustration 10A-1
ROI formula

Controllable Margin	÷	Average Operating Assets	=	Return on Investment (ROI)
$1,000,000	÷	$5,000,000	=	20%

The Electronics Division is considering producing a new product, a GPS satellite tracker (hereafter referred to as Tracker), for its boats. To produce Tracker, operating assets will have to increase $2,000,000. Tracker is expected to generate an additional $260,000 of controllable margin. Illustration 10A-2 shows how Tracker will effect ROI.

Illustration 10A-2
ROI comparison

	Without Tracker	Tracker	With Tracker
Controllable margin (a)	$1,000,000	$ 260,000	$1,260,000
Average operating assets (b)	$5,000,000	$2,000,000	$7,000,000
Return on investment [(a) ÷ (b)]	**20%**	**13%**	**18%**

The investment in Tracker reduces ROI from 20% to 18%.

Let's suppose that you are the manager of the Electronics Division and must make the decision to produce or not produce Tracker. If you were evaluated using ROI, you probably would not produce Tracker because your ROI would drop from 20% to 18%. The problem with this ROI analysis is that it ignores an important variable, the minimum rate of return on a company's operating assets. The **minimum rate of return** is the rate at which the Electronics Division can cover its costs and earn a profit. Assuming that the Electronics Division has a minimum rate of return of 10%, it should invest in Tracker because its ROI of 13% is greater than 10%.

Residual Income Compared to ROI

To evaluate performance using the minimum rate of return, companies use the residual income approach. **Residual income** is the income that remains after subtracting from the controllable margin the minimum rate of return on a company's average operating assets. The residual income for Tracker would be computed as follows.

Illustration 10A-3
Residual income formula

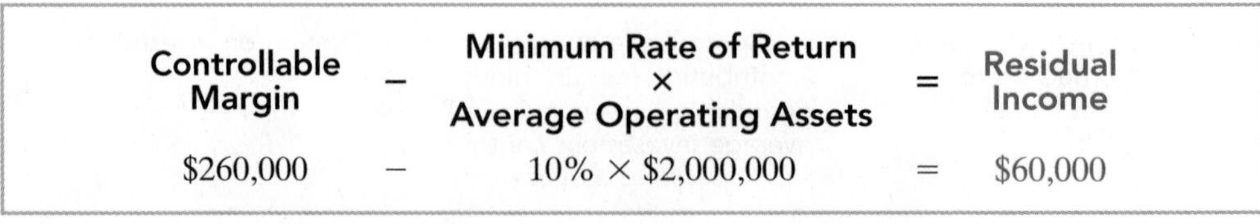

Controllable Margin	−	Minimum Rate of Return × Average Operating Assets	=	Residual Income
$260,000	−	10% × $2,000,000	=	$60,000

As shown, the residual income related to the Tracker investment is $60,000. Illustration 10A-4 indicates how residual income changes as the additional investment is made.

	Without Tracker	Tracker	With Tracker
Controllable margin (a)	$1,000,000	$260,000	$1,260,000
Average operating assets × 10% (b)	500,000	200,000	700,000
Residual income [(a) − (b)]	$ 500,000	$ 60,000	**$ 560,000**

Illustration 10A-4
Residual income comparison

This example illustrates how performance evaluation based on ROI can be misleading and can even cause managers to reject projects that would actually increase income for the company. As a result, many companies such as Coca-Cola, Briggs and Stratton, Eli Lilly, and Siemens AG use residual income (or a variant often referred to as economic value added) to evaluate investment alternatives and measure company performance.

Residual Income Weakness

It might appear from the above discussion that the goal of any company should be to maximize the total amount of residual income in each division. This goal, however, ignores the fact that one division might use substantially fewer assets to attain the same level of residual income as another division. For example, we know that to produce Tracker, the Electronics Division of Pujols Manufacturing used $2,000,000 of average operating assets to generate $260,000 of controllable margin. Now let's say a different division produced a product called SeaDog, which used $4,000,000 to generate $460,000 of controllable margin, as shown in Illustration 10A-5.

	Tracker	SeaDog
Controllable margin (a)	$260,000	$460,000
Average operating assets × 10% (b)	200,000	400,000
Residual income [(a) − (b)]	**$ 60,000**	**$ 60,000**

Illustration 10A-5
Comparison of two products

If the performance of these two investments were evaluated using residual income, they would be considered equal: Both products have the same total residual income. This ignores, however, the fact that SeaDog required **twice** as many operating assets to achieve the same level of residual income.

SUMMARY OF STUDY OBJECTIVE FOR APPENDIX

8 **Explain the difference between ROI and residual income.** ROI is controllable margin divided by average operating assets. Residual income is the income that remains after subtracting the minimum rate of return on a company's average operating assets. ROI sometimes provides misleading results because profitable investments are often rejected when the investment reduces ROI but increases overall profitability.

GLOSSARY

Budgetary control The use of budgets to control operations. (p. 416).

Controllable cost A cost over which a manager has control. (p. 428).

Controllable margin Contribution margin less controllable fixed costs. (p. 433).

Cost center A responsibility center that incurs costs but does not directly generate revenues. (p. 431).

Decentralization Control of operations is delegated to many managers throughout the organization. (p. 428).

Direct fixed costs Costs that relate specifically to a responsibility center and are incurred for the sole benefit of the center. (p. 433).

Flexible budget A projection of budget data for various levels of activity. (p. 419).

Indirect fixed costs Costs that are incurred for the benefit of more than one profit center. (p. 433).

Investment center A responsibility center that incurs costs, generates revenues, and has control over decisions regarding the assets available for use. (p. 431).

Management by exception The review of budget reports by top management focused entirely or primarily on differences between actual results and planned objectives. (p. 425).

Noncontrollable costs Costs incurred indirectly and allocated to a responsibility center that are not controllable at that level. (p. 429).

Profit center A responsibility center that incurs costs and also generates revenues. (p. 431).

Responsibility accounting A part of management accounting that involves accumulating and reporting revenues and costs on the basis of the manager who has the authority to make the day-to-day decisions about the items. (p. 427).

Responsibility reporting system The preparation of reports for each level of responsibility in the company's organization chart. (p. 429).

Residual income The income that remains after subtracting from the controllable margin the minimum rate of return on a company's average operating assets. (p. 444).

Return on investment (ROI) A measure of management's effectiveness in utilizing assets at its disposal in an investment center. (p. 435).

Segment An area of responsibility in decentralized operations. (p. 428).

Static budget A projection of budget data at one level of activity. (p. 417).

Demonstration Problem

Glenda Company uses a flexible budget for manufacturing overhead based on direct labor hours. For 2008 the master overhead budget for the Packaging Department based on 300,000 direct labor hours was as follows.

Variable Costs		Fixed Costs	
Indirect labor	$360,000	Supervision	$ 60,000
Supplies and lubricants	150,000	Depreciation	24,000
Maintenance	210,000	Property taxes	18,000
Utilities	120,000	Insurance	12,000
	$840,000		$114,000

During July, 24,000 direct labor hours were worked. The company incurred the following variable costs in July: indirect labor $30,200, supplies and lubricants $11,600, maintenance $17,500, and utilities $9,200. Actual fixed overhead costs were the same as monthly budgeted fixed costs.

Instructions

Prepare a flexible budget report for the Packaging Department for July.

Solution to Demonstration Problem

GLENDA COMPANY
Manufacturing Overhead Budget Report (Flexible)
Packaging Department
For the Month Ended July 31, 2008

Direct labor hours (DLH)	Budget 24,000 DLH	Actual Costs 24,000 DLH	Difference Favorable F Unfavorable U
Variable costs			
Indirect labor ($1.20)	$28,800	$30,200	$1,400 U
Supplies and lubricants ($0.50)	12,000	11,600	400 F
Maintenance ($0.70)	16,800	17,500	700 U
Utilities ($0.40)	9,600	9,200	400 F
Total variable	67,200	68,500	1,300 U
Fixed costs			
Supervision	$ 5,000	$ 5,000	-0-
Depreciation	2,000	2,000	-0-
Property taxes	1,500	1,500	-0-
Insurance	1,000	1,000	-0-
Total fixed	9,500	9,500	-0-
Total costs	$76,700	$78,000	$1,300 U

The Navigator

action plan

- Classify each cost as variable or fixed.
- Compute the budgeted cost per direct labor hour for all variable costs.
- Use budget data for actual direct labor hours worked.
- Determine the difference between budgeted and actual costs.
- Identify the difference as favorable or unfavorable.
- Determine the difference in total variable costs, total fixed costs, and total costs.

SELF-STUDY QUESTIONS

Answers are at the end of the chapter.

(SO 1) **1.** Budgetary control involves all but one of the following:
(a) modifying future plans.
(b) analyzing differences.
(c) using static budgets.
(d) determining differences between actual and planned results.

(SO 2) **2.** A static budget is useful in controlling costs when cost behavior is:
(a) mixed. **(c)** variable.
(b) fixed. **(d)** linear.

(SO 3) **3.** At zero direct labor hours in a flexible budget graph, the total budgeted cost line intersects the vertical axis at $30,000. At 10,000 direct labor hours, a horizontal line drawn from the total budgeted cost line intersects the vertical axis at $90,000. Fixed and variable costs may be expressed as:
(a) $30,000 fixed plus $6 per direct labor hour variable.
(b) $30,000 fixed plus $9 per direct labor hour variable.
(c) $60,000 fixed plus $3 per direct labor hour variable.
(d) $60,000 fixed plus $6 per direct labor hour variable.

(SO 3) **4.** At 9,000 direct labor hours, the flexible budget for indirect materials is $27,000. If $28,000 of indirect materials costs are incurred at 9,200 direct labor hours, the flexible budget report should show the following difference for indirect materials:
(a) $1,000 unfavorable.
(b) $1,000 favorable.
(c) $400 favorable.
(d) $400 unfavorable.

5. Under responsibility accounting, the evaluation of a manager's performance is based on matters that the manager: (SO 4)
(a) directly controls.
(b) directly and indirectly controls.
(c) indirectly controls.
(d) has shared responsibility for with another manager.

6. Responsibility centers include: (SO 4)
(a) cost centers.
(b) profit centers.
(c) investment centers.
(d) all of the above.

7. Responsibility reports for cost centers: (SO 5)
(a) distinguish between fixed and variable costs.
(b) use static budget data.
(c) include both controllable and noncontrollable costs.
(d) include only controllable costs.

8. In a responsibility report for a profit center, controllable fixed costs are deducted from contribution margin to show: (SO 6)
(a) profit center margin.
(b) controllable margin.
(c) net income.
(d) income from operations.

(SO 7) 9. In the formula for return on investment (ROI), the factors for controllable margin and operating assets are, respectively:
(a) controllable margin percentage and total operating assets.
(b) controllable margin dollars and average operating assets.
(c) controllable margin dollars and total assets.
(d) controllable margin percentage and average operating assets.

10. A manager of an investment center can improve ROI by: (SO 7)
(a) increasing average operating assets.
(b) reducing sales.
(c) increasing variable costs.
(d) reducing variable and/or controllable fixed costs.

Go to the book's website, **www.wiley.com/college/weygandt**, for Additional Self-Study questions.

QUESTIONS

1. (a) What is budgetary control?
   (b) Greg Gilligan is describing budgetary control. What steps should be included in Greg's description?
2. The following purposes are part of a budgetary reporting system: (a) Determine efficient use of materials. (b) Control overhead costs. (c) Determine whether income objectives are being met. For each purpose, indicate the name of the report, the frequency of the report, and the primary recipient(s) of the report.
3. How may a budget report for the second quarter differ from a budget report for the first quarter?
4. Joe Cey questions the usefulness of a master sales budget in evaluating sales performance. Is there justification for Joe's concern? Explain.
5. Under what circumstances may a static budget be an appropriate basis for evaluating a manager's effectiveness in controlling costs?
6. "A flexible budget is really a series of static budgets." Is this true? Why?
7. The static manufacturing overhead budget based on 40,000 direct labor hours shows budgeted indirect labor costs of $54,000. During March, the department incurs $65,000 of indirect labor while working 45,000 direct labor hours. Is this a favorable or unfavorable performance? Why?
8. A static overhead budget based on 40,000 direct labor hours shows Factory Insurance $6,500 as a fixed cost. At the 50,000 direct labor hours worked in March, factory insurance costs were $6,200. Is this a favorable or unfavorable performance? Why?
9. Kate Coulter is confused about how a flexible budget is prepared. Identify the steps for Kate.
10. Alou Company has prepared a graph of flexible budget data. At zero direct labor hours, the total budgeted cost line intersects the vertical axis at $25,000. At 10,000 direct labor hours, the line drawn from the total budgeted cost line intersects the vertical axis at $85,000. How may the fixed and variable costs be expressed?
11. The flexible budget formula is fixed costs $40,000 plus variable costs of $4 per direct labor hour. What is the total budgeted cost at (a) 9,000 hours and (b) 12,345 hours?
12. What is management by exception? What criteria may be used in identifying exceptions?
13. What is responsibility accounting? Explain the purpose of responsibility accounting.
14. Ann Wilkins is studying for an accounting examination. Describe for Ann what conditions are necessary for responsibility accounting to be used effectively.
15. Distinguish between controllable and noncontrollable costs.
16. How do responsibility reports differ from budget reports?
17. What is the relationship, if any, between a responsibility reporting system and a company's organization chart?
18. Distinguish among the three types of responsibility centers.
19. (a) What costs are included in a performance report for a cost center? (b) In the report, are variable and fixed costs identified?
20. How do direct fixed costs differ from indirect fixed costs? Are both types of fixed costs controllable?
21. Lori Quan is confused about controllable margin reported in an income statement for a profit center. How is this margin computed, and what is its primary purpose?
22. What is the primary basis for evaluating the performance of the manager of an investment center? Indicate the formula for this basis.
23. Explain the ways that ROI can be improved.
24. Indicate two behavioral principles that pertain to (a) the manager being evaluated and (b) top management.

*25. What is a major disadvantage of using ROI to evaluate investment and company performance?

*26. What is residual income, and what is one of its major weaknesses?

BRIEF EXERCISES

BE10-1 For the quarter ended March 31, 2008, Voorhees Company accumulates the following sales data for its product, Garden-Tools: $310,000 budget; $304,000 actual. Prepare a static budget report for the quarter.

Prepare static budget report.
(SO 2)

BE10-2 Data for Voorhees Company are given in BE10-1. In the second quarter, budgeted sales were $380,000, and actual sales were $383,000. Prepare a static budget report for the second quarter and for the year to date.

Prepare static budget report for 2 quarters.
(SO 2)

BE10-3 In Mussatto Company, direct labor is $20 per hour. The company expects to operate at 10,000 direct labor hours each month. In January 2008, direct labor totaling $203,000 is incurred in working 10,400 hours. Prepare (a) a static budget report and (b) a flexible budget report. Evaluate the usefulness of each report.

Show usefulness of flexible budgets in evaluating performance.
(SO 3)

BE10-4 Hannon Company expects to produce 1,200,000 units of Product XX in 2008. Monthly production is expected to range from 80,000 to 120,000 units. Budgeted variable manufacturing costs per unit are: direct materials $4, direct labor $6, and overhead $8. Budgeted fixed manufacturing costs per unit for depreciation are $2 and for supervision are $1. Prepare a flexible manufacturing budget for the relevant range value using 20,000 unit increments.

Prepare a flexible budget for variable costs.
(SO 3)

BE10-5 Data for Hannon Company are given in BE10-4. In March 2008, the company incurs the following costs in producing 100,000 units: direct materials $425,000, direct labor $590,000, and variable overhead $805,000. Prepare a flexible budget report for March. Were costs controlled?

Prepare flexible budget report.
(SO 3)

BE10-6 In the Assembly Department of Cobb Company, budgeted and actual manufacturing overhead costs for the month of April 2008 were as follows.

Prepare a responsibility report for a cost center.
(SO 5)

	Budget	Actual
Indirect materials	$15,000	$14,300
Indirect labor	20,000	20,600
Utilities	10,000	10,750
Supervision	5,000	5,000

All costs are controllable by the department manager. Prepare a responsibility report for April for the cost center.

BE10-7 Eckert Manufacturing Company accumulates the following summary data for the year ending December 31, 2008, for its Water Division which it operates as a profit center: sales—$2,000,000 budget, $2,080,000 actual; variable costs—$1,000,000 budget, $1,050,000 actual; and controllable fixed costs—$300,000 budget, $310,000 actual. Prepare a responsibility report for the Water Division.

Prepare a responsibility report for a profit center.
(SO 6)

BE10-8 For the year ending December 31, 2008, Kaspar Company accumulates the following data for the Plastics Division which it operates as an investment center: contribution margin—$700,000 budget, $715,000 actual; controllable fixed costs—$300,000 budget, $309,000 actual. Average operating assets for the year were $2,000,000. Prepare a responsibility report for the Plastics Division beginning with contribution margin.

Prepare a responsibility report for an investment center.
(SO 7)

BE10-9 For its three investment centers, Paige Company accumulates the following data:

Compute return on investment using the ROI formula.
(SO 7)

	I	II	III
Sales	$2,000,000	$3,000,000	$ 4,000,000
Controllable margin	1,200,000	2,000,000	3,200,000
Average operating assets	5,000,000	8,000,000	10,000,000

Compute the return on investment (ROI) for each center.

BE10-10 Data for the investment centers for Paige Company are given in BE10-9. The centers expect the following changes in the next year: (I) increase sales 15%; (II) decrease costs $200,000; (III) decrease average operating assets $400,000. Compute the expected return on investment (ROI) for each center. Assume center I has a contribution margin percentage of 75%.

Compute return on investment under changed conditions.
(SO 7)

Compute ROI and residual income.
(SO 8)

***BE10-11** Wasson, Inc. reports the following financial information.

Average operating assets	$3,000,000
Controllable margin	$ 600,000
Minimum rate of return	9%

Compute the return on investment and the residual income.

Compute ROI and residual income.
(SO 8)

***BE10-12** Presented below is information related to the Santa Clara Division of Cut Wood, Inc.

Contribution margin	$1,200,000
Controllable margin	$ 800,000
Average operating assets	$3,200,000
Minimum rate of return	16%

Compute the Santa Clara's return on investment and residual income.

EXERCISES

WILEY PLUS

Understand the concept of budgetary control.
(SO 1, 2, 3)

E10-1 Jim Thome has prepared the following list of statements about budgetary control.

1. Budget reports compare actual results with planned objectives.
2. All budget reports are prepared on a weekly basis.
3. Management uses budget reports to analyze differences between actual and planned results and determine their causes.
4. As a result of analyzing budget reports, management may either take corrective action or modify future plans.
5. Budgetary control works best when a company has an informal reporting system.
6. The primary recipients of the sales report are the sales manager and the vice-president of production.
7. The primary recipient of the scrap report is the production manager.
8. A static budget is a projection of budget data at one level of activity.
9. Top management's reaction to unfavorable differences is not influenced by the materiality of the difference.
10. A static budget is not appropriate in evaluating a manager's effectiveness in controlling costs unless the actual activity level approximates the static budget activity level or the behavior of the costs is fixed.

Instructions
Identify each statement as true or false. If false, indicate how to correct the statement.

Prepare and evaluate static budget report.
(SO 2)

E10-2 Pargo Company budgeted selling expenses of $30,000 in January, $35,000 in February, and $40,000 in March. Actual selling expenses were $31,000 in January, $34,500 in February, and $47,000 in March.

Instructions
(a) Prepare a selling expense report that compares budgeted and actual amounts by month and for the year to date.
(b) What is the purpose of the report prepared in (a), and who would be the primary recipient?
(c) What would be the likely result of management's analysis of the report?

Prepare flexible manufacturing overhead budget.
(SO 3)

E10-3 Raney Company uses a flexible budget for manufacturing overhead based on direct labor hours. Variable manufacturing overhead costs per direct labor hour are as follows.

Indirect labor	$1.00
Indirect materials	0.50
Utilities	0.40

Fixed overhead costs per month are: Supervision $4,000, Depreciation $1,500, and Property Taxes $800. The company believes it will normally operate in a range of 7,000–10,000 direct labor hours per month.

Instructions

Prepare a monthly manufacturing overhead flexible budget for 2008 for the expected range of activity, using increments of 1,000 direct labor hours.

Prepare flexible budget reports for manufacturing overhead costs, and comment on findings.

(SO 3)

E10-4 Using the information in E10-3, assume that in July 2008, Raney Company incurs the following manufacturing overhead costs.

Variable Costs		Fixed Costs	
Indirect labor	$8,700	Supervision	$4,000
Indirect materials	4,300	Depreciation	1,500
Utilities	3,200	Property taxes	800

Instructions

(a) Prepare a flexible budget performance report, assuming that the company worked 9,000 direct labor hours during the month.

(b) Prepare a flexible budget performance report, assuming that the company worked 8,500 direct labor hours during the month.

(c) Comment on your findings.

Prepare flexible selling expense budget.

(SO 3)

E10-5 Trusler Company uses flexible budgets to control its selling expenses. Monthly sales are expected to range from $170,000 to $200,000. Variable costs and their percentage relationship to sales are: Sales Commissions 5%, Advertising 4%, Traveling 3%, and Delivery 2%. Fixed selling expenses will consist of Sales Salaries $34,000, Depreciation on Delivery Equipment $7,000, and Insurance on Delivery Equipment $1,000.

Instructions

Prepare a monthly flexible budget for each $10,000 increment of sales within the relevant range for the year ending December 31, 2008.

Prepare flexible budget reports for selling expenses.

(SO 3)

E10-6 The actual selling expenses incurred in March 2008 by Trusler Company are as follows.

Variable Expenses		Fixed Expenses	
Sales commissions	$9,200	Sales salaries	$34,000
Advertising	7,000	Depreciation	7,000
Travel	5,100	Insurance	1,000
Delivery	3,500		

Instructions

(a) Prepare a flexible budget performance report for March using the budget data in E10-5, assuming that March sales were $170,000. Expected and actual sales are the same.

(b) Prepare a flexible budget performance report, assuming that March sales were $180,000. Expected sales and actual sales are the same.

(c) Comment on the importance of using flexible budgets in evaluating the performance of the sales manager.

Prepare flexible budget and responsibility report for manufacturing overhead.

(SO 3, 5)

E10-7 Pletcher Company's manufacturing overhead budget for the first quarter of 2008 contained the following data.

Variable Costs		Fixed Costs	
Indirect materials	$12,000	Supervisory salaries	$36,000
Indirect labor	10,000	Depreciation	7,000
Utilities	8,000	Property taxes and insurance	8,000
Maintenance	6,000	Maintenance	5,000

Actual variable costs were: indirect materials $13,800, indirect labor $9,600, utilities $8,700, and maintenance $4,900. Actual fixed costs equaled budgeted costs except for property taxes and insurance, which were $8,200. The actual activity level equaled the budgeted level.

All costs are considered controllable by the production department manager except for depreciation, and property taxes and insurance.

Instructions

(a) Prepare a manufacturing overhead flexible budget report for the first quarter.

(b) Prepare a responsibility report for the first quarter.

Prepare flexible budget report, and answer question.

(SO 2, 3)

E10-8 As sales manager, Terry Dewitt was given the following static budget report for selling expenses in the Clothing Department of Garber Company for the month of October.

GARBER COMPANY
Clothing Department
Budget Report
For the Month Ended October 31, 2008

	Budget	Actual	Difference Favorable F Unfavorable U
Sales in units	8,000	10,000	2,000 F
Variable expenses			
Sales commissions	$ 2,000	$ 2,600	$ 600 U
Advertising expense	800	850	50 U
Travel expense	3,600	4,000	400 U
Free samples given out	1,600	1,300	300 F
Total variable	8,000	8,750	750 U
Fixed expenses			
Rent	1,500	1,500	–0–
Sales salaries	1,200	1,200	–0–
Office salaries	800	800	–0–
Depreciation—autos (sales staff)	500	500	–0–
Total fixed	4,000	4,000	–0–
Total expenses	$12,000	$12,750	$ 750 U

As a result of this budget report, Terry was called into the president's office and congratulated on his fine sales performance. He was reprimanded, however, for allowing his costs to get out of control. Terry knew something was wrong with the performance report that he had been given. However, he was not sure what to do, and comes to you for advice.

Instructions

(a) Prepare a budget report based on flexible budget data to help Terry.
(b) Should Terry have been reprimanded? Explain.

Prepare and discuss a responsibility report.

(SO 3, 5)

E10-9 Pronto Plumbing Company is a newly formed company specializing in plumbing services for home and business. The owner, Paul Pronto, had divided the company into two segments: Home Plumbing Services and Business Plumbing Services. Each segment is run by its own supervisor, while basic selling and administrative services are shared by both segments.

Paul has asked you to help him create a performance reporting system that will allow him to measure each segment's performance in terms of its profitability. To that end, the following information has been collected on the Home Plumbing Services segment for the first quarter of 2008.

	Budgeted	Actual
Service revenue	$25,000	$26,000
Allocated portion of:		
Building depreciation	11,000	11,000
Advertising	5,000	4,200
Billing	3,500	3,000
Property taxes	1,200	1,000
Material and supplies	1,500	1,200
Supervisory salaries	9,000	9,400
Insurance	4,000	3,500
Wages	3,000	3,300
Gas and oil	2,700	3,400
Equipment depreciation	1,600	1,300

Instructions

(a) Prepare a responsibility report for the first quarter of 2008 for the Home Plumbing Services segment.

(b) Write a memo to Paul Pronto discussing the principles that should be used when preparing performance reports.

E10-10 Rensing Company has two production departments, Fabricating and Assembling. At a department managers' meeting, the controller uses flexible budget graphs to explain total budgeted costs. Separate graphs based on direct labor hours are used for each department. The graphs show the following.

State total budgeted cost formulas, and prepare flexible budget graph.

(SO 3)

1. At zero direct labor hours, the total budgeted cost line and the fixed cost line intersect the vertical axis at $40,000 in the Fabricating Department and $30,000 in the Assembling Department.
2. At normal capacity of 50,000 direct labor hours, the line drawn from the total budgeted cost line intersects the vertical axis at $150,000 in the Fabricating Department, and $110,000 in the Assembling Department.

Instructions

(a) State the total budgeted cost formula for each department.

(b) Compute the total budgeted cost for each department, assuming actual direct labor hours worked were 53,000 and 47,000, in the Fabricating and Assembling Departments, respectively.

(c) Prepare the flexible budget graph for the Fabricating Department, assuming the maximum direct labor hours in the relevant range is 100,000. Use increments of 10,000 direct labor hours on the horizontal axis and increments of $50,000 on the vertical axis.

E10-11 Lovell Company's organization chart includes the president; the vice president of production; three assembly plants—Dallas, Atlanta, and Tucson; and two departments within each plant—Machining and Finishing. Budget and actual manufacturing cost data for July 2008 are as follows:

Prepare reports in a responsibility reporting system.

(SO 4)

Finishing Department—Dallas: Direct materials $41,500 actual, $45,000 budget; direct labor $83,000 actual, $82,000 budget; manufacturing overhead $51,000 actual, $49,200 budget.

Machining Department—Dallas: Total manufacturing costs $220,000 actual, $216,000 budget.

Atlanta Plant: Total manufacturing costs $424,000 actual, $421,000 budget.

Tucson Plant: Total manufacturing costs $494,000 actual, $496,500 budget.

The Dallas plant manager's office costs were $95,000 actual and $92,000 budget. The vice president of production's office costs were $132,000 actual and $130,000 budget. Office costs are not allocated to departments and plants.

Instructions

Using the format on page 430, prepare the reports in a responsibility system for:

(a) The Finishing Department—Dallas.

(b) The plant manager—Dallas.

(c) The vice president of production.

E10-12 The Mixing Department manager of Crede Company is able to control all overhead costs except rent, property taxes, and salaries. Budgeted monthly overhead costs for the Mixing Department, in alphabetical order, are:

Prepare a responsibility report for a cost center.

(SO 5)

Indirect labor	$12,000	Property taxes	$ 1,000
Indirect materials	7,500	Rent	1,800
Lubricants	1,700	Salaries	10,000
Maintenance	3,500	Utilities	5,000

Actual costs incurred for January 2008 are indirect labor $12,200; indirect materials $10,200; lubricants $1,650; maintenance $3,500; property taxes $1,100; rent $1,800; salaries $10,000; and utilities $6,500.

Instructions

(a) Prepare a responsibility report for January 2008.

(b) What would be the likely result of management's analysis of the report?

Compute missing amounts in responsibility reports for three profit centers, and prepare a report.

(SO 6)

E10-13 Gonzales Manufacturing Inc. has three divisions which are operated as profit centers. Actual operating data for the divisions listed alphabetically are as follows.

Operating Data	Women's Shoes	Men's Shoes	Children's Shoes
Contribution margin	$240,000	(3)	$180,000
Controllable fixed costs	100,000	(4)	(5)
Controllable margin	(1)	$ 90,000	96,000
Sales	600,000	450,000	(6)
Variable costs	(2)	330,000	250,000

Instructions

(a) Compute the missing amounts. Show computations.

(b) Prepare a responsibility report for the Women's Shoe Division assuming (1) the data are for the month ended June 30, 2008, and (2) all data equal budget except variable costs which are $10,000 over budget.

Prepare a responsibility report for a profit center, and compute ROI.

(SO 6, 7)

E10-14 The Sports Equipment Division of Brandon McCarthy Company is operated as a profit center. Sales for the division were budgeted for 2008 at $900,000. The only variable costs budgeted for the division were cost of goods sold ($440,000) and selling and administrative ($60,000). Fixed costs were budgeted at $100,000 for cost of goods sold, $90,000 for selling and administrative and $70,000 for noncontrollable fixed costs. Actual results for these items were:

Sales	$880,000
Cost of goods sold	
Variable	409,000
Fixed	105,000
Selling and administrative	
Variable	61,000
Fixed	67,000
Noncontrollable fixed	80,000

Instructions

(a) Prepare a responsibility report for the Sports Equipment Division for 2008.

(b) Assume the division is an investment center, and average operating assets were $1,000,000. Compute ROI.

Compute ROI for current year and for possible future changes.

(SO 7)

E10-15 The Green Division of Frizell Company reported the following data for the current year.

Sales	$3,000,000
Variable costs	1,950,000
Controllable fixed costs	600,000
Average operating assets	5,000,000

Top management is unhappy with the investment center's return on investment (ROI). It asks the manager of the Green Division to submit plans to improve ROI in the next year. The manager believes it is feasible to consider the following independent courses of action.

1. Increase sales by $320,000 with no change in the contribution margin percentage.
2. Reduce variable costs by $100,000.
3. Reduce average operating assets by 4%.

Instructions

(a) Compute the return on investment (ROI) for the current year.

(b) Using the ROI formula, compute the ROI under each of the proposed courses of action. (Round to one decimal.)

Prepare a responsibility report for an investment center.

(SO 7)

E10-16 The Medina and Ortiz Dental Clinic provides both preventive and orthodontic dental services. The two owners, Martin Medina and Olga Ortiz, operate the clinic as two separate investment centers: Preventive Services and Orthodontic Services. Each of them is in charge of one of the centers: Martin for Preventive Services and Olga for Orthodontic Services. Each month they prepare an income statement for the two centers to evaluate performance and make decisions about how to improve the operational efficiency and profitability of the clinic.

Recently they have been concerned about the profitability of the Preventive Services operations. For several months it has been reporting a loss. Shown below is the responsibility report for the month of May 2008.

	Actual	Difference from Budget
Service revenue	$ 40,000	$1,000 F
Variable costs:		
Filling materials	5,000	100 U
Novocain	4,000	200 U
Supplies	2,000	250 F
Dental assistant wages	2,500	-0-
Utilities	500	50 U
Total variable costs	14,000	100 U
Fixed costs:		
Allocated portion of receptionist's salary	3,000	200 U
Dentist salary	10,000	500 U
Equipment depreciation	6,000	-0-
Allocated portion of building depreciation	15,000	1,000 U
Total fixed costs	34,000	1,700 U
Operating income (loss)	$ (8,000)	$ 800 U

In addition, the owners know that the investment in operating assets at the beginning of the month was $82,400, and it was $77,600 at the end of the month. They have asked for your assistance in evaluating their current performance reporting system.

Instructions

(a) Prepare a responsibility report for an investment center as illustrated in the chapter.

(b) Write a memo to the owners discussing the deficiencies of their current reporting system.

Prepare missing amounts in responsibility reports for three investment centers.

(SO 7)

E10-17 The Transamerica Transportation Company uses a responsibility reporting system to measure the performance of its three investment centers: Planes, Taxis, and Limos. Segment performance is measured using a system of responsibility reports and return on investment calculations. The allocation of resources within the company and the segment managers' bonuses are based in part on the results shown in these reports.

Recently, the company was the victim of a computer virus that deleted portions of the company's accounting records. This was discovered when the current period's responsibility reports were being prepared. The printout of the actual operating results appeared as follows.

	Planes	Taxis	Limos
Service revenue	$?	$500,000	$?
Variable costs	5,500,000	?	320,000
Contribution margin	?	200,000	480,000
Controllable fixed costs	1,500,000	?	?
Controllable margin	?	80,000	240,000
Average operating assets	25,000,000	?	1,600,000
Return on investment	12%	10%	?

Instructions

Determine the missing pieces of information above.

Compare ROI and residual income.
(SO 8)

***E10-18** Presented below is selected information for three regional divisions of Yono Company.

	Divisions		
	North	**West**	**South**
Contribution margin	$ 300,000	$ 500,000	$ 400,000
Controllable margin	$ 150,000	$ 400,000	$ 225,000
Average operating assets	$1,000,000	$2,000,000	$1,500,000
Minimum rate of return	13%	16%	10%

Instructions

(a) Compute the return on investment for each division.
(b) Compute the residual income for each division.
(c) Assume that each division has an investment opportunity that would provide a rate of return of 19%.
 (1) If ROI is used to measure performance, which division or divisions will probably make the additional investment?
 (2) If residual income is used to measure performance, which division or divisions will probably make the additional investment?

Fill in information related to ROI and residual income.
(SO 8)

***E10-19** Presented below is selected financial information for two divisions of Capital Brewery. You are to supply the missing information for the lettered items.

	Lager	**Lite Lager**
Contribution margin	$500,000	$ 300,000
Controllable margin	200,000	(c)
Average operating assets	(a)	$1,000,000
Minimum rate of return	(b)	13%
Return on investment	25%	(d)
Residual income	$ 90,000	$ 200,000

EXERCISES: SET B

Visit the book's website at **www.wiley.com/college/weygandt**, and choose the Student Companion site, to access Exercise Set B.

PROBLEMS: SET A

Prepare flexible budget and budget report for manufacturing overhead.
(SO 3)

P10-1A Malone Company estimates that 360,000 direct labor hours will be worked during the coming year, 2008, in the Packaging Department. On this basis, the following budgeted manufacturing overhead cost data are computed for the year.

Fixed Overhead Costs		**Variable Overhead Costs**	
Supervision	$ 90,000	Indirect labor	$126,000
Depreciation	60,000	Indirect materials	90,000
Insurance	30,000	Repairs	54,000
Rent	24,000	Utilities	72,000
Property taxes	18,000	Lubricants	18,000
	$222,000		$360,000

It is estimated that direct labor hours worked each month will range from 27,000 to 36,000 hours.

During October, 27,000 direct labor hours were worked and the following overhead costs were incurred.

Fixed overhead costs: Supervision $7,500, Depreciation $5,000, Insurance $2,470, Rent $2,000, and Property taxes $1,500.
Variable overhead costs: Indirect labor $10,360, Indirect materials, $6,400, Repairs $4,000, Utilities $5,700, and Lubricants $1,640.

Instructions

(a) Total costs: DLH 27,000, $45,500; DLH 36,000, $54,500

(a) Prepare a monthly manufacturing overhead flexible budget for each increment of 3,000 direct labor hours over the relevant range for the year ending December 31, 2008.

(b) Total $1,070 U

(b) Prepare a flexible budget report for October.
(c) Comment on management's efficiency in controlling manufacturing overhead costs in October.

Prepare flexible budget, budget report, and graph for manufacturing overhead.

(SO 3)

P10-2A Fultz Company manufactures tablecloths. Sales have grown rapidly over the past 2 years. As a result, the president has installed a budgetary control system for 2008. The following data were used in developing the master manufacturing overhead budget for the Ironing Department, which is based on an activity index of direct labor hours.

Variable Costs	Rate per Direct Labor Hour	Annual Fixed Costs	
Indirect labor	$0.40	Supervision	$42,000
Indirect materials	0.50	Depreciation	18,000
Factory utilities	0.30	Insurance	12,000
Factory repairs	0.20	Rent	24,000

The master overhead budget was prepared on the expectation that 480,000 direct labor hours will be worked during the year. In June, 42,000 direct labor hours were worked. At that level of activity, actual costs were as shown below.

Variable—per direct labor hour: Indirect labor $0.43, Indirect materials $0.49, Factory utilities $0.32, and Factory repairs $0.24.

Fixed: same as budgeted.

Instructions

(a) Total costs: 35,000 DLH, $57,000; 50,000 DLH, $78,000

(b) Budget $66,800 Actual $70,160

(a) Prepare a monthly manufacturing overhead flexible budget for the year ending December 31, 2008, assuming production levels range from 35,000 to 50,000 direct labor hours. Use increments of 5,000 direct labor hours.
(b) Prepare a budget report for June comparing actual results with budget data based on the flexible budget.
(c) Were costs effectively controlled? Explain.
(d) State the formula for computing the total budgeted costs for the Ironing Department.
(e) Prepare the flexible budget graph, showing total budgeted costs at 35,000 and 45,000 direct labor hours. Use increments of 5,000 direct labor hours on the horizontal axis and increments of $10,000 on the vertical axis.

State total budgeted cost formula, and prepare flexible budget reports for 2 time periods.

(SO 2, 3)

P10-3A Zelmer Company uses budgets in controlling costs. The August 2008 budget report for the company's Assembling Department is as follows.

ZELMER COMPANY
Budget Report
Assembling Department
For the Month Ended August 31, 2008

Manufacturing Costs	Budget	Actual	Difference Favorable F Unfavorable U
Variable costs			
Direct materials	$ 48,000	$ 47,000	$1,000 F
Direct labor	54,000	51,300	2,700 F
Indirect materials	24,000	24,200	200 U
Indirect labor	18,000	17,500	500 F
Utilities	15,000	14,900	100 F
Maintenance	9,000	9,200	200 U
Total variable	168,000	164,100	3,900 F
Fixed costs			
Rent	12,000	12,000	–0–
Supervision	17,000	17,000	–0–
Depreciation	7,000	7,000	–0–
Total fixed	36,000	36,000	–0–
Total costs	$204,000	$200,100	$3,900 F

The monthly budget amounts in the report were based on an expected production of 60,000 units per month or 720,000 units per year. The Assembling Department manager is pleased with the report and expects a raise, or at least praise for a job well done. The company president, however, is unhappy with the results for August, because only 58,000 units were produced.

Instructions

(a) State the total monthly budgeted cost formula.

(b) Budget $198,400

(b) Prepare a budget report for August using flexible budget data. Why does this report provide a better basis for evaluating performance than the report based on static budget data?

(c) Budget $215,200
Actual $216,510

(c) In September, 64,000 units were produced. Prepare the budget report using flexible budget data, assuming (1) each variable cost was 10% higher than its actual cost in August, and (2) fixed costs were the same in September as in August.

Prepare responsibility report for a profit center.

(SO 6)

P10-4A Jantzen Manufacturing Inc. operates the Patio Furniture Division as a profit center. Operating data for this division for the year ended December 31, 2008, are as shown below.

	Budget	Difference from Budget
Sales	$2,500,000	$60,000 F
Cost of goods sold		
Variable	1,300,000	41,000 F
Controllable fixed	200,000	6,000 U
Selling and administrative		
Variable	220,000	7,000 U
Controllable fixed	50,000	2,000 U
Noncontrollable fixed costs	70,000	4,000 U

In addition, Jantzen Manufacturing incurs $180,000 of indirect fixed costs that were budgeted at $175,000. Twenty percent (20%) of these costs are allocated to the Patio Furniture Division.

Instructions

(a) Contribution margin
$94,000 F
Controllable margin
$86,000 F

(a) Prepare a responsibility report for the Patio Furniture Division for the year.

(b) Comment on the manager's performance in controlling revenues and costs.

(c) Identify any costs excluded from the responsibility report and explain why they were excluded.

Prepare responsibility report for an investment center, and compute ROI.

(SO 7)

P10-5A Dinkle Manufacturing Company manufactures a variety of tools and industrial equipment. The company operates through three divisions. Each division is an investment center. Operating data for the Home Division for the year ended December 31, 2008, and relevant budget data are as follows.

	Actual	Comparison with Budget
Sales	$1,500,000	$100,000 favorable
Variable cost of goods sold	700,000	60,000 unfavorable
Variable selling and administrative expenses	125,000	25,000 unfavorable
Controllable fixed cost of goods sold	170,000	On target
Controllable fixed selling and administrative expenses	80,000	On target

Average operating assets for the year for the Home Division were $2,500,000 which was also the budgeted amount.

Instructions

(a) Controllable margin:
Budget $410;
Actual $425

(a) Prepare a responsibility report (in thousands of dollars) for the Home Division.

(b) Evaluate the manager's performance. Which items will likely be investigated by top management?

(c) Compute the expected ROI in 2009 for the Home Division, assuming the following independent changes to actual data.

   (1) Variable cost of goods sold is decreased by 6%.

   (2) Average operating assets are decreased by 10%.

   (3) Sales are increased by $200,000, and this increase is expected to increase contribution margin by $90,000.

Prepare reports for cost centers under responsibility accounting, and comment on performance of managers.

(SO 4)

P10-6A Nieto Company uses a responsibility reporting system. It has divisions in Denver, Seattle, and San Diego. Each division has three production departments: Cutting, Shaping, and Finishing. The responsibility for each department rests with a manager who reports to the division production manager. Each division manager reports to the vice president of production. There are also vice presidents for marketing and finance. All vice presidents report to the president.

In January 2008, controllable actual and budget manufacturing overhead cost data for the departments and divisions were as shown below.

Manufacturing Overhead	Actual	Budget
Individual costs—Cutting Department—Seattle		
Indirect labor	$ 73,000	$ 70,000
Indirect materials	47,700	46,000
Maintenance	20,500	18,000
Utilities	20,100	17,000
Supervision	22,000	20,000
	$183,300	$171,000
Total costs		
Shaping Department—Seattle	$158,000	$148,000
Finishing Department—Seattle	210,000	206,000
Denver division	676,000	673,000
San Diego division	722,000	715,000

Additional overhead costs were incurred as follows: Seattle division production manager—actual costs $52,500, budget $51,000; vice president of production—actual costs $65,000, budget $64,000; president—actual costs $76,400, budget $74,200. These expenses are not allocated.

The vice presidents who report to the president, other than the vice president of production, had the following expenses.

Vice president	Actual	Budget
Marketing	$133,600	$130,000
Finance	109,000	105,000

Instructions

(a) Using the format on page 430, prepare the following responsibility reports.
 (1) Manufacturing overhead—Cutting Department manager—Seattle division.
 (2) Manufacturing overhead—Seattle division manager.
 (3) Manufacturing overhead—vice president of production.
 (4) Manufacturing overhead and expenses—president.

(b) Comment on the comparative performances of:
 (1) Department managers in the Seattle division.
 (2) Division managers.
 (3) Vice presidents.

(a) (1) $12,300 U
(2) $27,800 U
(3) $38,800 U
(4) $48,600 U

Compare ROI and residual income.

(SO 8)

***P10-7A** Haniwall Industries has manufactured prefabricated houses for over 20 years. The houses are constructed in sections to be assembled on customers' lots. Haniwall expanded into the precut housing market when it acquired Orlando Company, one of its suppliers. In this market, various types of lumber are precut into the appropriate lengths, banded into packages, and shipped to customers' lots for assembly. Haniwall designated the Orlando Division as an investment center.

Haniwall uses return on investment (ROI) as a performance measure with investment defined as average operating assets. Management bonuses are based in part on ROI. All investments are expected to earn a minimum rate of return of 16%. Orlando's ROI has ranged from 20.1% to 23.5% since it was acquired. Orlando had an investment opportunity in 2008 that had an estimated ROI of 19%. Orlando's management decided against the investment because it believed the investment would decrease the division's overall ROI.

Selected financial information for Orlando are presented on the next page. The division's average operating assets were $12,300,000 for the year 2008.

ORLANDO DIVISION
Selected Financial Information
For the Year Ended December 31, 2008

Sales	$26,000,000
Contribution margin	9,100,000
Controllable margin	2,460,000

Instructions

(a) Calculate the following performance measures for 2008 for the Orlando Division.
  (1) Return on investment (ROI).
  (2) Residual income.

(b) Would the management of Orlando Division have been more likely to accept the investment opportunity it had in 2008 if residual income were used as a performance measure instead of ROI? Explain your answer.

(CMA, adapted)

PROBLEMS: SET B

Prepare flexible budget and budget report for manufacturing overhead.

(SO 3)

P10-1B Clarke Company estimates that 240,000 direct labor hours will be worked during 2008 in the Assembly Department. On this basis, the following budgeted manufacturing overhead data are computed.

Variable Overhead Costs		Fixed Overhead Costs	
Indirect labor	$ 72,000	Supervision	$ 72,000
Indirect materials	48,000	Depreciation	36,000
Repairs	24,000	Insurance	12,000
Utilities	50,400	Rent	9,000
Lubricants	9,600	Property taxes	6,000
	$204,000		$135,000

It is estimated that direct labor hours worked each month will range from 18,000 to 24,000 hours.

During January, 20,000 direct labor hours were worked and the following overhead costs were incurred.

Variable Overhead Costs		Fixed Overhead Costs	
Indirect labor	$ 6,200	Supervision	$ 6,000
Indirect materials	3,600	Depreciation	3,000
Repairs	1,600	Insurance	1,000
Utilities	3,300	Rent	800
Lubricants	830	Property taxes	500
	$15,530		$11,300

Instructions

(a) Total costs: 18,000 DLH, $26,550; 24,000 DLH, $31,650

(b) Budget, $28,250 Actual, $26,830

(a) Prepare a monthly manufacturing overhead flexible budget for each increment of 2,000 direct labor hours over the relevant range for the year ending December 31, 2008.

(b) Prepare a manufacturing overhead budget report for January.

(c) Comment on management's efficiency in controlling manufacturing overhead costs in January.

Prepare flexible budget, budget report, and graph for manufacturing overhead.

(SO 3)

P10-2B Flaherty Manufacturing Company produces one product, Kebo. Because of wide fluctuations in demand for Kebo, the Assembly Department experiences significant variations in monthly production levels.

The annual master manufacturing overhead budget is based on 300,000 direct labor hours. In July 27,500 labor hours were worked. The master manufacturing overhead budget for the year and the actual overhead costs incurred in July are as follows.

Overhead Costs	Master Budget (annual)	Actual in July
Variable		
Indirect labor	$ 360,000	$32,000
Indirect materials	210,000	17,000
Utilities	90,000	8,100
Maintenance	60,000	5,400
Fixed		
Supervision	150,000	12,500
Depreciation	120,000	10,000
Insurance and taxes	60,000	5,000
Total	$1,050,000	$90,000

Instructions

(a) Prepare a monthly overhead flexible budget for the year ending December 31, 2008, assuming monthly production levels range from 22,500 to 30,000 direct labor hours. Use increments of 2,500 direct labor hours.

(b) Prepare a budget report for the month of July 2008 comparing actual results with budget data based on the flexible budget.

(c) Were costs effectively controlled? Explain.

(d) State the formula for computing the total monthly budgeted costs in the Assembly Department.

(e) Prepare the flexible budget graph showing total budgeted costs at 25,000 and 27,500 direct labor hours. Use increments of 5,000 on the horizontal axis and increments of $10,000 on the vertical axis.

(a) Total costs: 22,500 DLH, $81,500; 30,000 DLH, $99,500

(b) Budget $93,500 Actual $90,000

P10-3B Hardesty Company uses budgets in controlling costs. The May 2008 budget report for the company's Packaging Department is as follows.

State total budgeted cost formula, and prepare flexible budget reports for 2 time periods.

(SO 2, 3)

HARDESTY COMPANY
Budget Report
Packaging Department
For the Month Ended May 31, 2008

Manufacturing Costs	Budget	Actual	Difference Favorable F Unfavorable U
Variable costs			
Direct materials	$ 45,000	$ 47,000	$2,000 U
Direct labor	50,000	53,000	3,000 U
Indirect materials	15,000	15,200	200 U
Indirect labor	12,500	13,000	500 U
Utilities	7,500	7,100	400 F
Maintenance	5,000	5,200	200 U
Total variable	135,000	140,500	5,500 U
Fixed costs			
Rent	8,000	8,000	–0–
Supervision	7,000	7,000	–0–
Depreciation	5,000	5,000	–0–
Total fixed	20,000	20,000	–0–
Total costs	$155,000	$160,500	$5,500 U

The monthly budget amounts in the report were based on an expected production of 50,000 units per month or 600,000 units per year.

The company president was displeased with the department manager's performance. The department manager, who thought he had done a good job, could not understand the unfavorable results. In May, 55,000 units were produced.

Instructions

(a) State the total budgeted cost formula.

(b) Budget $168,500

(b) Prepare a budget report for May using flexible budget data. Why does this report provide a better basis for evaluating performance than the report based on static budget data?

(c) Budget $128,000
Actual $132,400

(c) In June, 40,000 units were produced. Prepare the budget report using flexible budget data, assuming (1) each variable cost was 20% less in June than its actual cost in May, and (2) fixed costs were the same in the month of June as in May.

Prepare responsibility report for a profit center.
(SO 6)

P10-4B Grider Manufacturing Inc. operates the Home Appliance Division as a profit center. Operating data for this division for the year ended December 31, 2008, are shown below.

	Budget	Difference from Budget
Sales	$2,400,000	$90,000 U
Cost of goods sold		
Variable	1,200,000	40,000 U
Controllable fixed	200,000	8,000 F
Selling and administrative		
Variable	240,000	8,000 F
Controllable fixed	60,000	6,000 U
Noncontrollable fixed costs	50,000	2,000 U

In addition, Grider Manufacturing incurs $150,000 of indirect fixed costs that were budgeted at $155,000. Twenty percent (20%) of these costs are allocated to the Home Appliance Division. None of these costs are controllable by the division manager.

Instructions

(a) Contribution margin $122,000 U
Controllable margin $120,000 U

(a) Prepare a responsibility report for the Home Appliance Division (a profit center) for the year.

(b) Comment on the manager's performance in controlling revenues and costs.

(c) Identify any costs excluded from the responsibility report and explain why they were excluded.

Prepare responsibility report for an investment center, and compute ROI.
(SO 7)

P10-5B Jeffery Manufacturing Company manufactures a variety of garden and lawn equipment. The company operates through three divisions. Each division is an investment center. Operating data for the Lawnmower Division for the year ended December 31, 2008, and relevant budget data are as follows.

	Actual	Comparison with Budget
Sales	$2,800,000	$150,000 unfavorable
Variable cost of goods sold	1,400,000	80,000 unfavorable
Variable selling and administrative expenses	300,000	50,000 favorable
Controllable fixed cost of goods sold	270,000	On target
Controllable fixed selling and administrative expenses	130,000	On target

Average operating assets for the year for the Lawnmower Division were $5,000,000 which was also the budgeted amount.

Instructions

(a) Controllable margin:
Budget $880
Actual $700

(a) Prepare a responsibility report (in thousands of dollars) for the Lawnmower Division.

(b) Evaluate the manager's performance. Which items will likely be investigated by top management?

(c) Compute the expected ROI in 2009 for the Lawnmower Division, assuming the following independent changes.

(1) Variable cost of goods sold is decreased by 15%.

(2) Average operating assets are decreased by 20%.

(3) Sales are increased by $500,000 and this increase is expected to increase contribution margin by $200,000.

PROBLEMS: SET C

Visit the book's website at **www.wiley.com/college/weygandt**, and choose the Student Companion site, to access Problem Set C.

WATERWAYS CONTINUING PROBLEM

(*Note:* This is a continuation of the Waterways Problem from Chapters 1 through 9.)

WCP10 Waterways Corporation is continuing its budget preparations. This problem gives you static budget information as well as actual overhead costs and asks you to calculate amounts related to budgetary control and responsibility accounting.

Go to the book's website,
www.wiley.com/college/weygandt,
to find the completion of this problem.

BROADENING YOUR PERSPECTIVE

DECISION MAKING ACROSS THE ORGANIZATION

BYP10-1 G-Bar Pastures is a 400-acre farm on the outskirts of the Kentucky Bluegrass, specializing in the boarding of broodmares and their foals. A recent economic downturn in the thoroughbred industry has led to a decline in breeding activities, and it has made the boarding business extremely competitive. To meet the competition, G-Bar Pastures planned in 2008 to entertain clients, advertise more extensively, and absorb expenses formerly paid by clients such as veterinary and blacksmith fees.

The budget report for 2008 is presented below. As shown, the static income statement budget for the year is based on an expected 21,900 boarding days at $25 per mare. The variable expenses per mare per day were budgeted: Feed $5, Veterinary fees $3, Blacksmith fees $0.30, and Supplies $0.55. All other budgeted expenses were either semifixed or fixed.

During the year, management decided not to replace a worker who quit in March, but it did issue a new advertising brochure and did more entertaining of clients.[1]

G-BAR PASTURES
Static Budget Income Statement
Year Ended December 31, 2008

	Actual	Master Budget	Difference
Number of mares	52	60	8*
Number of boarding days	18,980	21,900	2,920*
Sales	$379,600	$547,500	$167,900*

Continued

[1]Data for this case are based on Hans Sprohge and John Talbott, "New Applications for Variance Analysis," *Journal of Accountancy* (AICPA, New York), April 1989, pp. 137–141.

	Actual	Master Budget	Difference
Less: Variable expenses			
Feed	104,390	109,500	5,110
Veterinary fees	58,838	65,700	6,862
Blacksmith fees	6,074	6,570	496
Supplies	10,178	12,045	1,867
Total variable expenses	179,480	193,815	14,335
Contribution margin	200,120	353,685	153,565*
Less: Fixed expenses			
Depreciation	40,000	40,000	-0-
Insurance	11,000	11,000	-0-
Utilities	12,000	14,000	2,000
Repairs and maintenance	10,000	11,000	1,000
Labor	88,000	96,000	8,000
Advertisement	12,000	8,000	4,000*
Entertainment	7,000	5,000	2,000*
Total fixed expenses	180,000	185,000	5,000
Net income	$ 20,120	$168,685	$148,565*

*Unfavorable.

Instructions

With the class divided into groups, answer the following.

(a) Based on the static budget report:

(1) What was the primary cause(s) of the loss in net income?

(2) Did management do a good, average, or poor job of controlling expenses?

(3) Were management's decisions to stay competitive sound?

(b) Prepare a flexible budget report for the year.

(c) Based on the flexible budget report, answer the three questions in part (a) above.

(d) What course of action do you recommend for the management of G-Bar Pastures?

MANAGERIAL ANALYSIS

BYP10-2 Fugate Company manufactures expensive watch cases sold as souvenirs. Three of its sales departments are: Retail Sales, Wholesale Sales, and Outlet Sales. The Retail Sales Department is a profit center. The Wholesale Sales Department is a cost center. Its managers merely take orders from customers who purchase through the company's wholesale catalog. The Outlet Sales Department is an investment center, because each manager is given full responsibility for an outlet store location. The manager can hire and discharge employees, purchase, maintain, and sell equipment, and in general is fairly independent of company control.

Jane Duncan is a manager in the Retail Sales Department. Richard Wayne manages the Wholesale Sales Department. Jose Lopez manages the Golden Gate Club outlet store in San Francisco. The following are the budget responsibility reports for each of the three departments.

	Budget		
	Retail Sales	Wholesale Sales	Outlet Sales
Sales	$ 750,000	$ 400,000	$200,000
Variable costs			
Cost of goods sold	150,000	100,000	25,000
Advertising	100,000	30,000	5,000
Sales salaries	75,000	15,000	3,000
Printing	10,000	20,000	5,000
Travel	20,000	30,000	2,000
Fixed costs			
Rent	50,000	30,000	10,000
Insurance	5,000	2,000	1,000
Depreciation	75,000	100,000	40,000
Investment in assets	$1,000,000	$1,200,000	$800,000

Actual Results	Retail Sales	Wholesale Sales	Outlet Sales
Sales	$ 750,000	$ 400,000	$200,000
Variable costs			
Cost of goods sold	195,000	120,000	26,250
Advertising	100,000	30,000	5,000
Sales salaries	75,000	15,000	3,000
Printing	10,000	20,000	5,000
Travel	15,000	20,000	1,500
Fixed costs			
Rent	40,000	50,000	12,000
Insurance	5,000	2,000	1,000
Depreciation	80,000	90,000	60,000
Investment in assets	$1,000,000	$1,200,000	$800,000

Instructions

(a) Determine which of the items should be included in the responsibility report for each of the three managers.

(b) Compare the budgeted measures with the actual results. Decide which results should be called to the attention of each manager.

REAL-WORLD FOCUS

BYP10-3 Computer Associates International, Inc., the world's leading business software company, delivers the end-to-end infrastructure to enable e-business through innovative technology, services, and education. CA has 19,000 employees worldwide and recently had revenue of over $6 billion.

Presented below is information from the company's annual report.

COMPUTER ASSOCIATES INTERNATIONAL
Management Discussion

The Company has experienced a pattern of business whereby revenue for its third and fourth fiscal quarters reflects an increase over first- and second-quarter revenue. The Company attributes this increase to clients' increased spending at the end of their calendar year budgetary periods and the culmination of its annual sales plan. Since the Company's costs do not increase proportionately with the third- and fourth-quarters' increase in revenue, the higher revenue in these quarters results in greater profit margins and income. Fourth-quarter profitability is traditionally affected by significant new hirings, training, and education expenditures for the succeeding year.

Instructions

(a) Why don't the company's costs increase proportionately as the revenues increase in the third and fourth quarters?

(b) What type of budgeting seems appropriate for the Computer Associates situation?

EXPLORING THE WEB

BYP10-4 There are many useful resources regarding budgeting available on websites. The following activity investigates the results of a comprehensive budgeting study performed by a very large international accounting firm.

Address: **www.pwc.com/extweb/pwcpublications.nsf/docid/C2D9FB96F792CFA3852572B10049C87D**, or go to **www.wiley.com/college/weygandt**

Steps
Go to the address on the previous page, click on the link to download the full report, and then register to receive the report. (Remove the checkmark to receive future reports.)

Instructions
Scan the report to answer the following questions.
(a) What percentage of respondents report that they are "very satisfied" with their financial planning process?
(b) What are the top six key elements that companies forecast?
(c) What is the percentage of total budget time spent on each of the following budgeting activities?
(1) Data collection/consolidation
(2) Analysis
(3) Strategy/target setting
(4) Review/approval
(5) Report preparation
(d) What percentage of firms spend more than four months to complete a budget?
(e) What percentage of surveyed firms update their forecasts on a monthly basis?

COMMUNICATION ACTIVITY

BYP10-5 The manufacturing overhead budget for Edmonds Company contains the following items.

Variable costs		Fixed costs	
Indirect materials	$24,000	Supervision	$18,000
Indirect labor	12,000	Inspection costs	1,000
Maintenance expense	10,000	Insurance expense	2,000
Manufacturing supplies	6,000	Depreciation	15,000
Total variable	$52,000	Total fixed	$36,000

The budget was based on an estimated 2,000 units being produced. During the past month, 1,500 units were produced, and the following costs incurred.

Variable costs		Fixed costs	
Indirect materials	$24,200	Supervision	$19,300
Indirect labor	13,500	Inspection costs	1,200
Maintenance expense	8,200	Insurance expense	2,200
Manufacturing supplies	5,100	Depreciation	14,700
Total variable	$51,000	Total fixed	$37,400

Instructions
(a) Determine which items would be controllable by Mark Farris, the production manager.
(b) How much should have been spent during the month for the manufacture of the 1,500 units?
(c) Prepare a flexible manufacturing overhead budget report for Mr. Farris.
(d) Prepare a responsibility report. Include only the costs that would have been controllable by Mr. Farris. Assume that the supervision cost above includes Mr. Farris's salary of $10,000, both at budget and actual. In an attached memo, describe clearly for Mr. Farris the areas in which his performance needs to be improved.

ETHICS CASE

BYP10-6 National Products Corporation participates in a highly competitive industry. In order to meet this competition and achieve profit goals, the company has chosen the decentralized form of organization. Each manager of a decentralized investment center is measured on the basis of profit contribution, market penetration, and return on investment. Failure to meet the objectives established by corporate management for these measures has not been acceptable and usually has resulted in demotion or dismissal of an investment center manager.

An anonymous survey of managers in the company revealed that the managers feel the pressure to compromise their personal ethical standards to achieve the corporate objectives. For example, at certain plant locations there was pressure to reduce quality control to a level which could not assure that all unsafe products would be rejected. Also, sales personnel were encouraged to use questionable sales tactics to obtain orders, including gifts and other incentives to purchasing agents.

The chief executive officer is disturbed by the survey findings. In his opinion such behavior cannot be condoned by the company. He concludes that the company should do something about this problem.

Instructions

(a) Who are the stakeholders (the affected parties) in this situation?
(b) Identify the ethical implications, conflicts, or dilemmas in the above described situation.
(c) What might the company do to reduce the pressures on managers and decrease the ethical conflicts?

(CMA adapted)

"ALL ABOUT YOU" ACTIVITY

BYP10-7 It is one thing to prepare a personal budget; it is another thing to stick to it. Financial planners have suggested various mechanisms to provide support for enforcing personal budgets. One approach is called "envelope budgeting."

Instructions

Read the article provided at **http://en.wikipedia.org/wiki/Envelope_budgeting**, and answer the following questions.

(a) Summarize the process of envelope budgeting.
(b) Evaluate whether you think you would benefit from envelope budgeting. What do you think are its strengths and weaknesses relative to your situation?

Answers to Insight and Accounting Across the Organization Questions

Budgets and the Exotic Newcastle Disease, p. 425

Q: What is the major benefit of tying a budget to the overall goals of the company?

A: *People working on a budgeting process that is clearly guided and focused by strategic goals spend less time arguing about irrelevant details and more time focusing on the items that matter.*

Competition versus Collaboration, p. 428

Q: How might managers of separate divisions be able to reduce division costs through collaboration?

A: *Division managers might reduce costs by sharing design and marketing resources or by jointly negotiating with suppliers. In addition, they can reduce the need to hire and lay off employees by sharing staff across divisions as human resource needs change.*

Does Hollywood Look at ROI?, p. 438

Q: What might be the reason that movie studios do not produce G-rated movies as much as R-rated ones?

A: *Perhaps Hollywood believes that big-name stars or large budgets, both of which are typical of R-rated movies, sell movies. However, one study recently concluded, "We can't find evidence that stars help movies, and we can't find evidence that bigger budgets increase return on investment." Some film companies are going out of their way to achieve at least a PG rating.*

Authors' Comments on *All About You:* Budgeting for Housing Costs, p. 440

In general, in past years it has been a wise decision to purchase a home rather than to rent. As noted, over time home prices have usually appreciated in most parts of the country. Mortgage interest provides some tax relief, and by purchasing a home you get some control over your housing costs. However, in the current environment the decision is a little more complicated. In some parts of the country, home prices have appreciated so much that some experts suggest that renting is actually a more financially prudent choice, at least in the short term.

If you do purchase a home, do not bite off more than you can chew. In addition to a higher mortgage payment, a more expensive house will result in increased maintenance and utility costs, more spent on insurance premiums, and higher property taxes. Make sure to factor all of these expenses into your budget.

Answers to Self-Study Questions

1. c **2.** b **3.** a **4.** d **5.** a **6.** d **7.** d **8.** b **9.** b **10.** d

Remember to go back to the Navigator box on the chapter-opening page and check off your completed work.

Chapter 11

Standard Costs and Balanced Scorecard

STUDY OBJECTIVES

After studying this chapter, you should be able to:

1 Distinguish between a standard and a budget.

2 Identify the advantages of standard costs.

3 Describe how companies set standards.

4 State the formulas for determining direct materials and direct labor variances.

5 State the formula for determining the total manufacturing overhead variance.

6 Discuss the reporting of variances.

7 Prepare an income statement for management under a standard costing system.

8 Describe the balanced scorecard approach to performance evaluation.

The Navigator

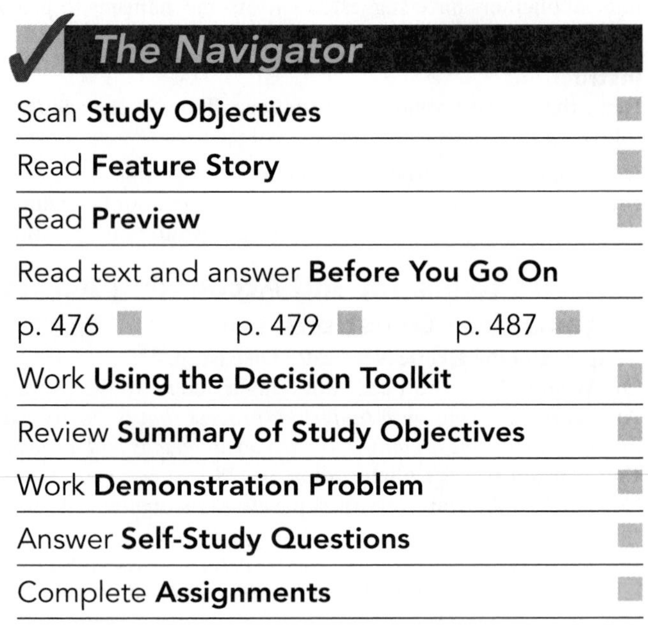

The Navigator

Scan **Study Objectives**

Read **Feature Story**

Read **Preview**

Read text and answer **Before You Go On**

p. 476 p. 479 p. 487

Work **Using the Decision Toolkit**

Review **Summary of Study Objectives**

Work **Demonstration Problem**

Answer **Self-Study Questions**

Complete **Assignments**

Feature Story

HIGHLIGHTING PERFORMANCE EFFICIENCY

There's a very good chance that the highlighter you're holding in your hand was made by Sanford (*www.sanfordcorp.com*), a maker of permanent markers and other writing instruments. Sanford, headquartered in Illinois, annually sells hundreds of millions of dollars' worth of Accent® highlighters, fine-point pens, Sharpie permanent markers, Expo dry-erase markers for overhead projectors, and other writing instruments.

Since Sanford makes literally billions of writing utensils per year, the company must keep tight control over manufacturing costs. A very important part of Sanford's manufacturing process is determining how much direct materials, labor, and overhead should cost. The company then compares these costs to actual costs to assess performance efficiency. Raw materials for Sanford's markers include a barrel, plug, cap, ink reservoir, and a nib (tip). Machines assemble these parts to produce thousands of units per hour. A major component of manufacturing overhead is machine maintenance—some fixed, some variable.

"Labor costs are associated with material handling and equipment maintenance functions. Although the assembly process is highly automated, labor is still required to move raw materials to the machine and to package the finished product. In addition, highly skilled technicians are required to service and maintain each piece of equipment," says Mike Orr, vice president, operations.

Labor rates are predictable because the hourly workers are covered by a union contract. The story is the same with the fringe benefits and some supervisory salaries. Even volume levels are fairly predictable—demand for the product is high—so fixed overhead is efficiently absorbed. Raw material standard costs are based on the previous year's actual prices plus any anticipated inflation. For the past several years, though, inflation had been so low that the company was considering any price increase in raw material to be unfavorable because its standards remained unchanged.

The Navigator

Inside Chapter 11

Preview of Chapter 11

Standards are a fact of life. You met the admission standards for the school you are attending. The vehicle that you drive had to meet certain governmental emissions standards. The hamburgers and salads you eat in a restaurant have to meet certain health and nutritional standards before they can be sold. As described in our Feature Story, Sanford Corp. has standards for the costs of its materials, labor, and overhead. The reason for standards in these cases is very simple: They help to ensure that overall product quality is high while keeping costs under control.

In this chapter we continue the study of controlling costs. You will learn how to evaluate performance using standard costs and a balanced scorecard.

The content and organization of Chapter 11 are as follows.

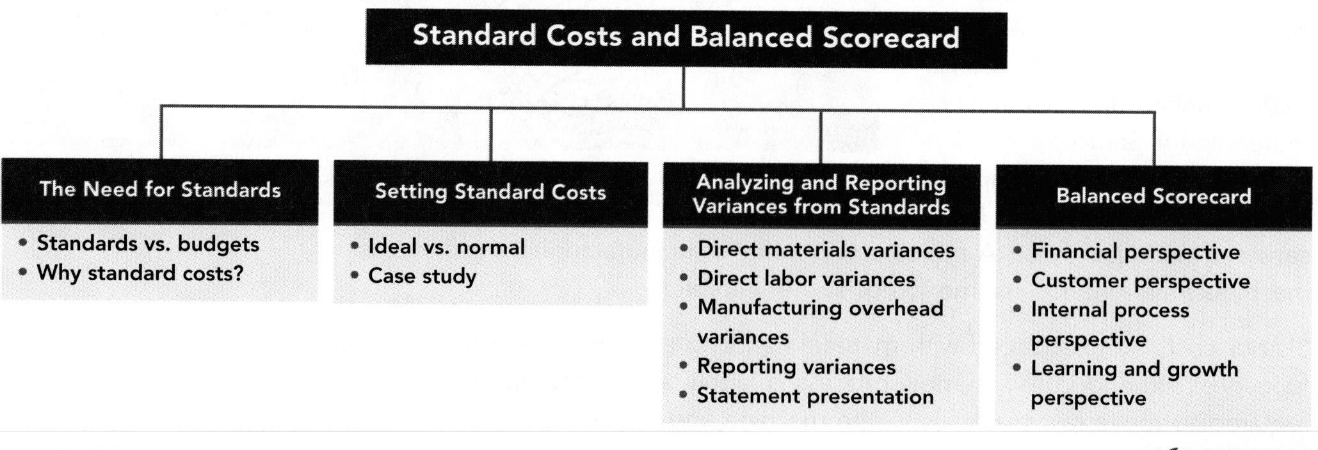

The Navigator

THE NEED FOR STANDARDS

Standards are common in business. Those imposed by government agencies are often called **regulations**. They include the Fair Labor Standards Act, the Equal Employment Opportunity Act, and a multitude of environmental standards. Standards established internally by a company may extend to personnel matters, such as employee absenteeism and ethical codes of conduct, quality control standards for products, and standard costs for goods and services. In managerial accounting, **standard costs** are predetermined unit costs, which companies use as measures of performance.

We will focus on manufacturing operations in this chapter. But you should also recognize that standard costs also apply to many types of service businesses as well. For example, a fast-food restaurant such as McDonald's knows the price it should pay for pickles, beef, buns, and other ingredients. It also knows how much time it should take an employee to flip hamburgers. If the company pays too much for pickles or if employees take too much time to prepare Big Macs, McDonald's notices the deviations and takes corrective action. Not-for-profit enterprises such as universities, charitable organizations, and governmental agencies also may use standard costs.

Distinguishing between Standards and Budgets

STUDY OBJECTIVE 1

Distinguish between a standard and a budget.

Both **standards** and **budgets** are predetermined costs, and both contribute to management planning and control. There is a difference, however, in the way the terms are expressed. A standard is a **unit** amount. A budget is a **total** amount. Thus, it is customary to state that the **standard cost** of direct labor for a unit of product is, say, $10. If the company produces 5,000 units of the product, the $50,000 of direct labor is the **budgeted** labor cost. A standard is the budgeted **cost per unit** of product. A standard is therefore concerned with each individual cost component that makes up the entire budget.

There are important accounting differences between budgets and standards. Except in the application of manufacturing overhead to jobs and processes, budget data are not journalized in cost accounting systems. In contrast, as we illustrate in the appendix to this chapter, standard costs may be incorporated into cost accounting systems. Also, a company may report its inventories at standard cost in its financial statements, but it would not report inventories at budgeted costs.

Why Standard Costs?

Standard costs offer a number of advantages to an organization, as shown in Illustration 11-1.

Illustration 11-1
Advantages of standard costs

Advantages of standard costs

Facilitate management planning

Promote greater economy by making employees more "cost-conscious"

Useful in setting selling prices

Contribute to management control by providing basis for evaluation of cost control

Useful in highlighting variances in management by exception

Simplify costing of inventories and reduce clerical costs

STUDY OBJECTIVE 2

Identify the advantages of standard costs.

The organization will realize these advantages only when standard costs are carefully established and prudently used. Using standards solely as a way to place blame can have a negative effect on managers and employees. To minimize this effect, many companies offer wage incentives to those who meet the standards.

SETTING STANDARD COSTS—A DIFFICULT TASK

STUDY OBJECTIVE 3

Describe how companies set standards.

The setting of standard costs to produce a unit of product is a difficult task. It requires input from all persons who have responsibility for costs and quantities. To determine the standard cost of direct materials, management consults purchasing agents, product managers, quality control engineers, and production supervisors. In setting the cost standard for direct labor, managers obtain pay rate data from the payroll department. Industrial engineers generally determine the labor time requirements. The managerial accountant provides important input for the standard-setting process by accumulating historical cost data and by knowing how costs respond to changes in activity levels.

To be effective in controlling costs, standard costs need to be current at all times. Thus, standards are under continuous review. They should change whenever managers determine that the existing standard is not a good measure of performance. Circumstances that warrant revision of a standard include changed wage rates resulting from a new union contract, a change in product specifications, or the implementation of a new manufacturing method.

Ideal versus Normal Standards

Companies set standards at one of two levels: ideal or normal. **Ideal standards** represent optimum levels of performance under perfect operating conditions. **Normal standards** represent efficient levels of performance that are attainable under expected operating conditions.

Some managers believe ideal standards will stimulate workers to ever-increasing improvement. However, most managers believe that ideal standards lower the morale of the entire workforce because they are difficult, if not impossible, to meet. Very few companies use ideal standards.

ETHICS NOTE

When standards are set too high, employees sometimes feel pressure to consider unethical practices to meet these standards.

Most companies that use standards set them at a normal level. Properly set, normal standards should be **rigorous but attainable**. Normal standards allow for rest periods, machine breakdowns, and other "normal" contingencies in the production process. In the remainder of this chapter we will assume that standard costs are set at a normal level.

ACCOUNTING ACROSS THE ORGANIZATION

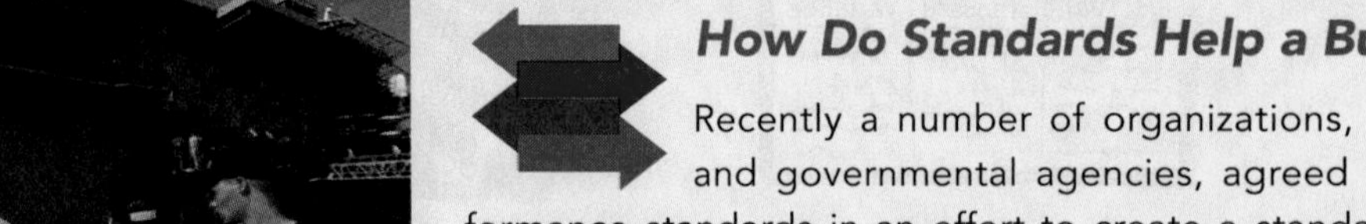

How Do Standards Help a Business?

Recently a number of organizations, including corporations, consultants, and governmental agencies, agreed to share information regarding performance standards in an effort to create a standard set of measures for thousands of business processes. The group, referred to as the Open Standards Benchmarking Collaborative, includes IBM, Procter and Gamble, the U.S. Navy, and the World Bank. Companies that are interested in participating can go to the group's Web site and enter their information.

Source: William M. Bulkeley, "Business, Agencies to Standardize Their Benchmarks," *Wall Street Journal,* May 19, 2004.

How will the creation of such standards help a business or organization?

A Case Study

To establish the standard cost of producing a product, it is necessary to establish standards for each manufacturing cost element—direct materials, direct labor, and manufacturing overhead. The standard for each element is derived from the standard price to be paid and the standard quantity to be used.

To illustrate, we look at a case study of how standard costs are set. In this extended example, we assume that Xonic, Inc. wishes to use standard costs to measure performance in filling an order for 1,000 gallons of Weed-O, a liquid weed killer.

DIRECT MATERIALS

The **direct materials price standard** is the cost per unit of direct materials that should be incurred. This standard should be based on the purchasing department's best estimate of the **cost of raw materials.** This cost is frequently based on current purchase prices. The price standard also includes an amount for related costs such as receiving, storing, and handling. The materials price standard per pound of material for Xonic's weed killer is:

Illustration 11-2
Setting direct materials price standard

Item	Price
Purchase price, net of discounts	$2.70
Freight	0.20
Receiving and handling	0.10
Standard direct materials price per pound	**$3.00**

The **direct materials quantity standard** is the quantity of direct materials that should be used per unit of finished goods. This standard is expressed as a physical measure, such as pounds, barrels, or board feet. In setting the standard, management considers both the quality and quantity of materials required to manufacture the product. The standard includes allowances for unavoidable waste and normal spoilage. The standard quantity per unit for Xonic, Inc. is as follows.

Illustration 11-3
Setting direct materials quantity standard

Item	Quantity (Pounds)
Required materials	3.5
Allowance for waste	0.4
Allowance for spoilage	0.1
Standard direct materials quantity per unit	**4.0**

The standard direct materials cost per unit is the standard direct materials price times the standard direct materials quantity. For Xonic, Inc., the standard direct materials cost per gallon of Weed-O is $12.00 ($3.00 × 4.0 pounds).

DIRECT LABOR

The **direct labor price standard** is the rate per hour that should be incurred for direct labor. This standard is based on current wage rates, adjusted for anticipated changes such as cost of living adjustments (COLAs). The price standard also generally includes employer payroll taxes and fringe benefits, such as paid holidays and vacations. For Xonic, Inc., the direct labor price standard is as follows.

ALTERNATIVE TERMINOLOGY

The direct labor price standard is also called the *direct labor rate standard.*

Illustration 11-4
Setting direct labor price standard

Item	Price
Hourly wage rate	$ 7.50
COLA	0.25
Payroll taxes	0.75
Fringe benefits	1.50
Standard direct labor rate per hour	**$10.00**

ALTERNATIVE TERMINOLOGY

The direct labor quantity standard is also called the *direct labor efficiency standard.*

The **direct labor quantity standard** is the time that should be required to make one unit of the product. This standard is especially critical in labor-intensive companies. Allowances should be made in this standard for rest periods, cleanup, machine setup, and machine downtime. For Xonic, Inc., the direct labor quantity standard is as follows.

Illustration 11-5
Setting direct labor quantity standard

Item	Quantity (Hours)
Actual production time	1.5
Rest periods and cleanup	0.2
Setup and downtime	0.3
Standard direct labor hours per unit	**2.0**

The standard direct labor cost per unit is the standard direct labor rate times the standard direct labor hours. For Xonic, Inc., the standard direct labor cost per gallon of Weed-O is $20 ($10.00 × 2.0 hours).

MANUFACTURING OVERHEAD

Calculating the overhead rate

Overhead ÷ Standard activity index

For manufacturing overhead, companies use a **standard predetermined overhead rate** in setting the standard. This overhead rate is determined by dividing budgeted overhead costs by an expected standard activity index. For example, the index may be standard direct labor hours or standard machine hours.

As discussed in Chapter 4, many companies employ activity-based costing (ABC) to allocate overhead costs. Because ABC uses multiple activity indices to allocate overhead costs, it results in a better correlation between activities and costs incurred than do other methods. As a result, the use of ABC can significantly improve the usefulness of standard costing for management decision making.

Xonic, Inc. uses standard direct labor hours as the activity index. The company expects to produce 13,200 gallons of Weed-O during the year at normal capacity. **Normal capacity** is the average activity output that a company should experience over the long run. Since it takes two direct labor hours for each gallon, total standard direct labor hours are 26,400 (13,200 gallons × 2 hours).

At normal capacity of 26,400 direct labor hours, overhead costs are expected to be $132,000. Of that amount, $79,200 are variable and $52,800 are fixed. Illustration 11-6 shows computation of the standard predetermined overhead rates for Xonic, Inc.

Illustration 11-6
Computing predetermined overhead rates

Budgeted Overhead Costs	Amount	÷	Standard Direct Labor Hours	=	Overhead Rate per Direct Labor Hour
Variable	$ 79,200		26,400		$3.00
Fixed	52,800		26,400		2.00
Total	$132,000		26,400		**$5.00**

The standard manufacturing overhead rate per unit is the predetermined overhead rate times the activity index quantity standard. For Xonic, Inc., which uses direct labor hours as its activity index, the standard manufacturing overhead rate per gallon of Weed-O is $10 ($5 × 2 hours).

TOTAL STANDARD COST PER UNIT

After a company has established the standard quantity and price per unit of product, it can determine the total standard cost. The total standard cost per unit is the sum of the standard costs of direct materials, direct labor, and manufacturing overhead. For Xonic, Inc., the total standard cost per gallon of Weed-O is $42, as shown on the following standard cost card.

Illustration 11-7
Standard cost per gallon of Weed-O

Product: Weed-O | **Unit Measure: Gallon**

Manufacturing Cost Elements	Standard Quantity	×	Standard Price	=	Standard Cost
Direct materials	4 pounds		$ 3.00		$12.00
Direct labor	2 hours		$10.00		$20.00
Manufacturing overhead	2 hours		$ 5.00		$10.00
					$42.00

The company prepares a standard cost card for each product. This card provides the basis for determining variances from standards.

MANAGEMENT INSIGHT

How Can We Make Susan's Chili Profitable?

Setting standards can be difficult. Consider Susan's Chili Factory, which manufactures and sells chili. The cost of manufacturing Susan's chili consists of the costs of raw materials, labor to convert the basic ingredients to chili, and overhead. We will use materials cost as an example. Managers need to develop three standards: (1) What should be the formula (mix) of ingredients for one gallon of chili? (2) What should be the normal wastage (or shrinkage) for the individual ingredients? (3) What should be the standard cost for the individual ingredients that go into the chili?

Susan's Chili Factory also illustrates how managers can use standard costs in controlling costs. Suppose that summer droughts have reduced crop yields. As a result, prices have doubled for beans, onions, and peppers. In this case, actual costs will be significantly higher than standard costs, which will cause management to evaluate the situation. Similarly, assume that poor maintenance caused the onion-dicing blades to become dull. As a result, usage of onions to make a gallon of chili tripled. Because this deviation is quickly highlighted through standard costs, managers can take corrective action promptly.

Source: Adapted from David R. Beran, "Cost Reduction Through Control Reporting," *Management Accounting*, April 1982, pp. 29–33.

How might management use this raw material cost information?

Before You Go On...

REVIEW IT

1. How do standards differ from budgets?
2. What are the advantages of standard costs to an organization?
3. Distinguish between normal standards and ideal standards. Which standard is more widely used? Why?

DO IT

The management of Arapahoe Company has decided to use standard costs. Management asks you to explain the components used in setting the standard cost per unit for direct materials, direct labor, and manufacturing overhead.

Action Plan

- Differentiate between the two components of each standard: price and quantity.

Solution The standard direct materials cost per unit is the standard direct materials price times the standard direct materials quantity. The standard direct labor cost per unit is the standard direct labor rate times the standard direct labor hours. The standard manufacturing overhead rate per unit is the standard predetermined overhead rate times the activity index quantity standard.

Related exercise material: *BE11-2, BE11-3, E11-1, E11-2, and E11-3.*

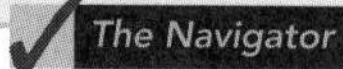

ANALYZING AND REPORTING VARIANCES FROM STANDARDS

ALTERNATIVE TERMINOLOGY

In business, the term *variance* is also used to indicate differences between total budgeted and total actual costs.

One of the major management uses of standard costs is to identify variances from standards. **Variances** are the differences between total actual costs and total standard costs.

To illustrate, we will assume that in producing 1,000 gallons of Weed-O in the month of June, Xonic, Inc. incurred the following costs.

Illustration 11-8
Actual production costs

Direct materials	$13,020
Direct labor	20,580
Variable overhead	6,500
Fixed overhead	4,400
Total actual costs	$44,500

Companies determine total standard costs by multiplying the units produced by the standard cost per unit. The total standard cost of Weed-O is $42,000 (1,000 gallons × $42). Thus, the total variance is $2,500, as shown below.

Illustration 11-9
Computation of total variance

Actual costs	$44,500
Less: Standard costs	42,000
Total variance	**$ 2,500**

Note that the variance is expressed in total dollars, and not on a per unit basis.

When actual costs exceed standard costs, the variance is **unfavorable**. The $2,500 variance in June for Weed-O is unfavorable. An unfavorable variance has a negative connotation. It suggests that the company paid too much for one or more of the manufacturing cost elements or that it used the elements inefficiently.

If actual costs are less than standard costs, the variance is **favorable**. A favorable variance has a positive connotation. It suggests efficiencies in incurring manufacturing costs and in using direct materials, direct labor, and manufacturing overhead.

However, be careful: A favorable variance could be obtained by using inferior materials. In printing wedding invitations, for example, a favorable variance could result from using an inferior grade of paper. Or, a favorable variance might be achieved in installing tires on an automobile assembly line by tightening only half of the lug bolts. A variance is not favorable if the company has sacrificed quality control standards.

Direct Materials Variances

STUDY OBJECTIVE 4
State the formulas for determining direct materials and direct labor variances.

In completing the order for 1,000 gallons of Weed-O, Xonic used 4,200 pounds of direct materials. These were purchased at a cost of $3.10 per unit. Illustration 11-10 shows the formula for the **total materials variance** and the calculation for Xonic, Inc.

Illustration 11-10
Formula for total materials variance

Actual Quantity × Actual Price (AQ) × (AP)	−	Standard Quantity × Standard Price (SQ) × (SP)	=	Total Materials Variance (TMV)
(4,200 × $3.10)	−	(4,000 × $3.00)	=	$1,020 U

Thus, for Xonic, the total materials variance is $1,020 ($13,020 − $12,000) unfavorable.

Next, the company analyzes the total variance to determine the amount attributable to price (costs) and to quantity (use). The **materials price variance** for Xonic, Inc. is computed from the following formula.[1]

Illustration 11-11
Formula for materials price variance

Actual Quantity × Actual Price (AQ) × (AP)	−	Actual Quantity × Standard Price (AQ) × (SP)	=	Materials Price Variance (MPV)
(4,200 × $3.10)	−	(4,200 × $3.00)	=	$420 U

For Xonic, the materials price variance is $420 ($13,020 − $12,600) unfavorable.

HELPFUL HINT
The alternative formula is:
AQ × AP − SP = MPV

The price variance can also be computed by multiplying the actual quantity purchased by the difference between the actual and standard price per unit. The computation in this case is 4,200 × ($3.10 − $3.00) = $420 U.

Illustration 11-12 (page 478) shows the formula for the **materials quantity variance** and the calculation for Xonic, Inc.

[1] We will assume that all materials purchased during the period are used in production and that no units remain in inventory at the end of the period.

Illustration 11-12
Formula for materials quantity variance

Actual Quantity × Standard Price (AQ) × (SP)	−	Standard Quantity × Standard Price (SQ) × (SP)	=	Materials Quantity Variance (MQV)
(4,200 × \$3.00)	−	(4,000 × \$3.00)	=	\$600 U

Thus, for Xonic, Inc., the materials quantity variance is \$600 (\$12,600 − \$12,000) unfavorable.

HELPFUL HINT
The alternative formula is:
SP × AQ − SQ = MQV

The price variance can also be computed by applying the standard price to the difference between actual and standard quantities used. The computation in this example is \$3.00 × (4,200 − 4,000) = \$600 U.

The total materials variance of \$1,020 U, therefore, consists of the following.

Illustration 11-13
Summary of materials variances

Materials price variance	\$ 420 U
Materials quantity variance	600 U
Total materials variance	**\$1,020 U**

Companies sometimes use a matrix to analyze a variance. **When the matrix is used, a company computes the formulas for each cost element first and then computes the variances.** Illustration 11-14 shows the completed matrix for the direct materials variance for Xonic, Inc. The matrix provides a convenient structure for determining each variance.

Illustration 11-14
Matrix for direct materials variances

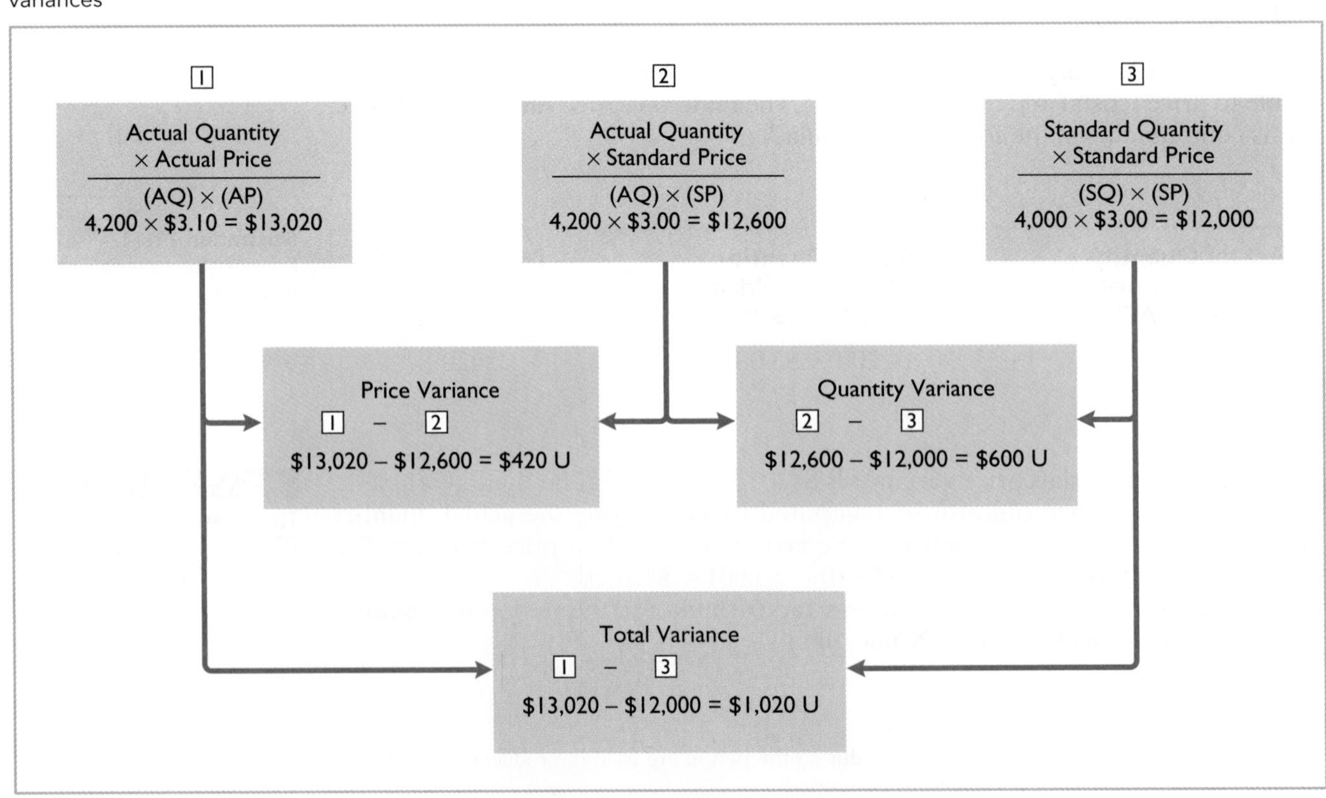

CAUSES OF MATERIALS VARIANCES

What are the causes of a variance? The causes may relate to both internal and external factors. The investigation of a **materials price variance usually begins in the purchasing department**. Many factors affect the price paid for raw materials. These include availability of quantity and cash discounts, the quality of the materials requested, and the delivery method used. To the extent that these factors are considered in setting the price standard, the purchasing department is responsible for any variances.

However, a variance may be beyond the control of the purchasing department. Sometimes, for example, prices may rise faster than expected. Moreover, actions by groups over which the company has no control, such as the OPEC nations' oil price increases, may cause an unfavorable variance. There are also times when a production department may be responsible for the price variance. This may occur when a rush order forces the company to pay a higher price for the materials.

The starting point for determining the cause(s) of an unfavorable **materials quantity variance is in the production department**. If the variances are due to inexperienced workers, faulty machinery, or carelessness, the production department is responsible. However, if the materials obtained by the purchasing department were of inferior quality, then the purchasing department is responsible.

DECISION TOOLKIT

Decision Checkpoints 	Info Needed for Decision 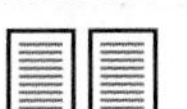	Tool to Use for Decision 	How to Evaluate Results 
Has management accomplished its price and quantity objectives regarding materials?	Actual cost and standard cost of materials	Materials price and materials quantity variances	Positive (favorable) variances suggest that price and quantity objectives have been met.

Before You Go On...

REVIEW IT

1. What are the three main components of the total variance from standard cost?
2. What are the formulas for computing the total, price, and quantity variances for direct materials?

DO IT

The standard cost of Product XX includes two units of direct materials at $8.00 per unit. During July, the company buys 22,000 units of direct materials at $7.50 and uses those materials to produce 10,000 units. Compute the total, price, and quantity variances for materials.

Action Plan

Use the formulas for computing each of the materials variances:

- Total materials variance $= (AQ \times AP) - (SQ \times SP)$
- Materials price variance $= (AQ \times AP) - (AQ \times SP)$
- Materials quantity variance $= (AQ \times SP) - (SQ \times SP)$

Solution Substituting amounts into the formulas, the variances are:

Total materials variance = (22,000 × $7.50) − (20,000 × $8.00) = $5,000 unfavorable.
Materials price variance = (22,000 × $7.50) − (22,000 × $8.00) = $11,000 favorable.
Materials quantity variance = (22,000 × $8.00) − (20,000 × $8.00) = $16,000 unfavorable.

Related exercise material: *BE11-4 and E11-5*

The Navigator

Direct Labor Variances

The process of determining direct labor variances is the same as for determining the direct materials variances. In completing the Weed-O order, Xonic, Inc. incurred 2,100 direct labor hours at an average hourly rate of $9.80. The standard hours allowed for the units produced were 2,000 hours (1,000 gallons × 2 hours). The standard labor rate was $10 per hour. Illustration 11-15 shows the formula for the **total labor variance** and its calculation for Xonic, Inc.

Illustration 11-15
Formula for total labor variance

Actual Hours × Actual Rate (AH) × (AR)	−	Standard Hours × Standard Rate (SH) × (SR)	=	Total Labor Variance (TLV)
(2,100 × $9.80)	−	(2,000 × $10.00)	=	$580 U

The total labor variance is $580 ($20,580 − $20,000) unfavorable.

The formula for the **labor price variance** and the calculation for Xonic, Inc. are as follows.

Illustration 11-16
Formula for labor price variance

Actual Hours × Actual Rate (AH) × (AR)	−	Actual Hours × Standard Rate (AH) × (SR)	=	Labor Price Variance (LPV)
(2,100 × $9.80)	−	(2,100 × $10.00)	=	$420 F

For Xonic, Inc., the labor price variance is $420 ($20,580 − $21,000) favorable.

HELPFUL HINT
The alternative formula is:
AH × AR − SR = LPV

The labor price variance can also be computed by multiplying actual hours worked by the difference between the actual pay rate and the standard pay rate. The computation in this example is 2,100 × ($10.00 − $9.80) = $420 F.

Illustration 11-17 shows the formula for the **labor quantity variance** and its calculation for Xonic, Inc.

Illustration 11-17
Formula for labor quantity variance

Actual Hours × Standard Rate (AH) × (SR)	−	Standard Hours × Standard Rate (SH) × (SR)	=	Labor Quantity Variance (LQV)
(2,100 × $10.00)	−	(2,000 × $10.00)	=	$1,000 U

Thus, for Xonic, the labor quantity variance is $1,000 ($21,000 − $20,000) unfavorable.

HELPFUL HINT
The alternative formula is:
SR × AH − SH = LQV

The same result can be obtained by multiplying the standard rate by the difference between actual hours worked and standard hours allowed. In this case the computation is $10.00 × (2,100 − 2,000) = $1,000 U.

The total direct labor variance of $580 U, therefore, consists of:

Illustration 11-18
Summary of labor variances

Labor price variance	$ 420 F
Labor quantity variance	1,000 U
Total direct labor variance	**$ 580 U**

These results can also be obtained from the matrix in Illustration 11-19.

Illustration 11-19
Matrix for direct labor variances

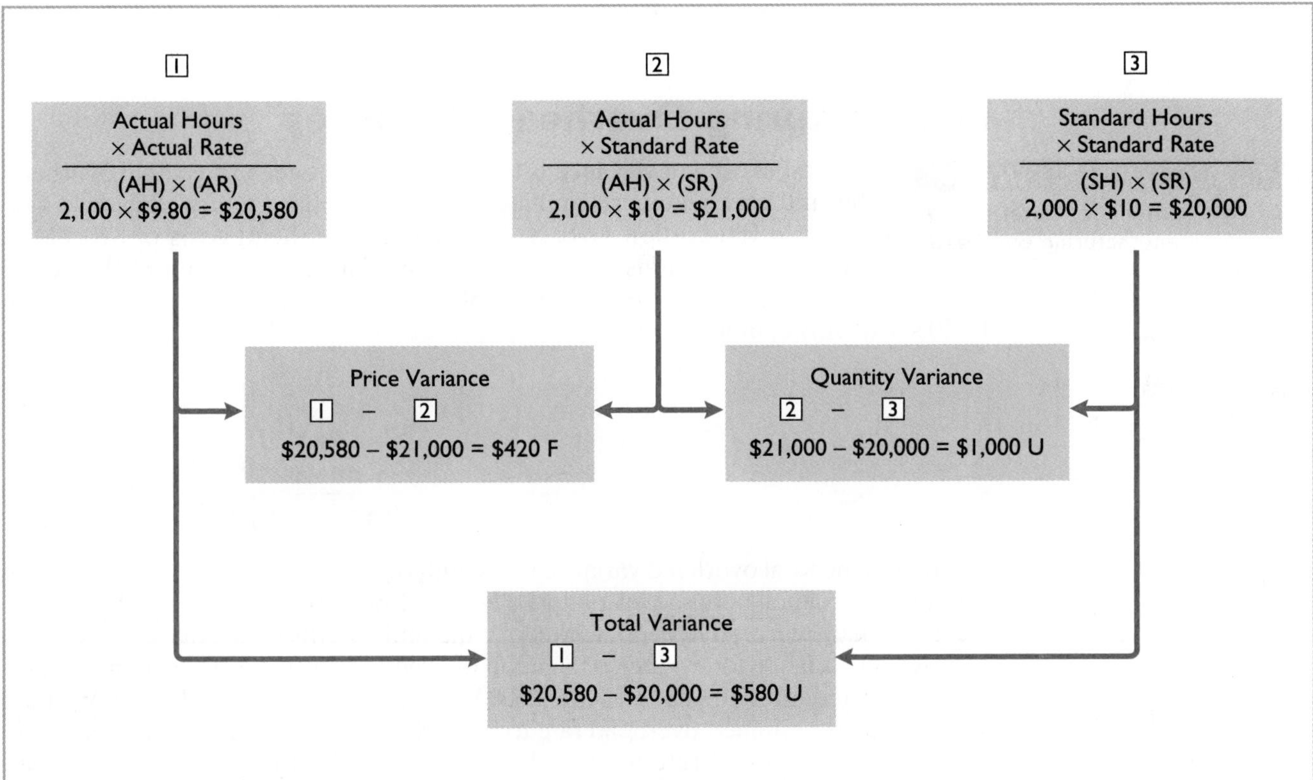

CAUSES OF LABOR VARIANCES

Labor price variances usually result from two factors: (1) paying workers **higher wages than expected**, and (2) **misallocation of workers**. In companies where pay rates are determined by union contracts, labor price variances should be infrequent. When workers are not unionized, there is a much higher likelihood of such variances. The responsibility for these variances rests with the manager who authorized the wage increase.

Misallocation of the workforce refers to using skilled workers in place of unskilled workers and vice versa. The use of an inexperienced worker instead of an experienced one will result in a favorable price variance because of the lower pay rate of the unskilled worker. An unfavorable price variance would result if a skilled worker were substituted for an inexperienced one. The production department generally is responsible for labor price variances resulting from misallocation of the workforce.

Labor quantity variances relate to the **efficiency of workers**. The cause of a quantity variance generally can be traced to the production department. The causes of an unfavorable variance may be poor training, worker fatigue, faulty machinery, or carelessness. These causes are the responsibility of the **production department**. However, if the excess time is due to inferior materials, the responsibility falls outside the production department.

DECISION TOOLKIT

Decision Checkpoints	Info Needed for Decision	Tool to Use for Decision	How to Evaluate Results

Has management accomplished its price and quantity objectives regarding labor?	Actual cost and standard cost of labor	Labor price and labor quantity variances	Positive (favorable) variances suggest that price and quantity objectives have been met.

Manufacturing Overhead Variances

STUDY OBJECTIVE 5

State the formula for determining the total manufacturing overhead variance.

The **total overhead variance** is the difference between the actual overhead costs and overhead costs applied based on standard hours allowed. As indicated in Illustration 11-8, Xonic incurred overhead costs of $10,900 to produce 1,000 gallons of Weed-O in June. The computation of the actual overhead is comprised of a variable and a fixed component. Illustration 11-20 shows this computation.

Illustration 11-20
Actual overhead costs

Variable overhead	$ 6,500
Fixed overhead	4,400
Total actual overhead	**$10,900**

To find the total overhead variance in a standard costing system, we determine the overhead costs applied based on standard hours allowed. **Standard hours allowed** are the hours that *should* have been worked for the units produced. Because it takes two hours of direct labor to produce one gallon of Weed-O, for the 1,000-gallon Weed-O order, the standard hours allowed are 2,000 hours (1,000 gallons × 2 hours). We then apply the predetermined overhead rate to the 2,000 standard hours allowed.

The predetermined rate for Weed-O is $5, comprised of a variable overhead rate of $3 and a fixed rate of $2. Recall from Illustration 11-6 that the amount of budgeted overhead costs at normal capacity of $132,000 was divided by normal capacity of 26,400 direct labor hours, to arrive at a predetermined overhead rate of $5 ($132,000 ÷ 26,400). The predetermined rate of $5 is then multiplied by the 2,000 standard hours allowed, to determine the overhead costs applied.

Illustration 11-21 shows the formula for the total overhead variance and the calculation for Xonic, Inc. for the month of June.

Illustration 11-21
Formula for total overhead variance

Actual Overhead	−	Overhead Applied*	=	Total Overhead Variance
$10,900 ($6,500 + $4,400)	−	$10,000 ($5 × 2,000 hours)	=	$900 U

***Based on standard hours allowed.**

Thus, for Xonic, Inc. the total overhead variance is $900 unfavorable.

The overhead variance is generally analyzed through a price and quantity variance. These computations are discussed in more detail in advanced courses. The name usually given to the price variance is the **overhead controllable variance**; the quantity variance is referred to as the **overhead volume variance**. Appendix 11B discusses how the total overhead volume variance can be broken down into these two variances.

CAUSES OF MANUFACTURING OVERHEAD VARIANCES

One reason for an overhead variance relates to over- or under-spending on overhead items. For example, overhead may include indirect labor for which a company paid wages higher than the standard labor price allowed. Or the price of electricity to run the company's machines increased, and the company did not anticipate this additional cost. Companies should investigate any spending variances, to determine whether they will continue in the future. Generally, the responsibility for these variances rests with the production department.

The overhead variance can also result from the inefficient use of overhead. For example, because of poor maintenance, a number of the manufacturing machines are experiencing breakdowns on a consistent basis, leading to reduced production. Or the flow of materials through the production process is impeded because of a lack of skilled labor to perform the necessary production tasks, due to a lack of planning. In both of these cases, the production department is responsible for the cause of these variances. On the other hand, overhead can also be underutilized because of a lack of sales orders. When the cause is a lack of sales orders, the responsibility rests outside the production department.

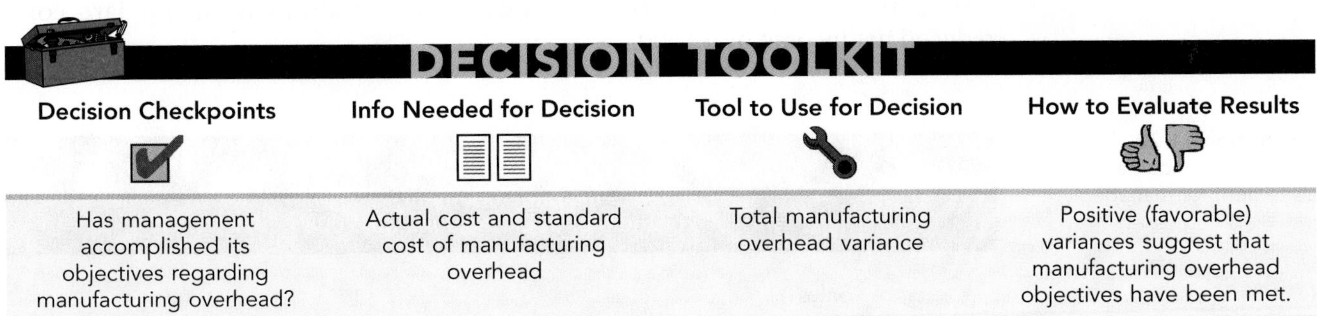

Decision Checkpoints	Info Needed for Decision	Tool to Use for Decision	How to Evaluate Results
Has management accomplished its objectives regarding manufacturing overhead?	Actual cost and standard cost of manufacturing overhead	Total manufacturing overhead variance	Positive (favorable) variances suggest that manufacturing overhead objectives have been met.

Reporting Variances

STUDY OBJECTIVE 6
Discuss the reporting of variances.

All variances should be reported to appropriate levels of management as soon as possible. The sooner managers are informed, the sooner they can evaluate problems and take corrective action.

The form, content, and frequency of variance reports vary considerably among companies. One approach is to prepare a weekly report for each department that has primary responsibility for cost control. Under this approach, materials price variances are reported to the purchasing department, and all other variances are reported to the production department that did the work. The following report for Xonic, Inc., with the materials for the Weed-O order listed first, illustrates this approach.

Illustration 11-22
Materials price variance report

XONIC, INC.
Variance Report — Purchasing Department
For Week Ended June 8, 2008

Type of Materials	Quantity Purchased	Actual Price	Standard Price	Price Variance	Explanation
X100	4,200 lbs.	$3.10	$3.00	$420 U	Rush order
X142	1,200 units	2.75	2.80	60 F	Quantity discount
A85	600 doz.	5.20	5.10	60 U	Regular supplier on strike
Total price variance				**$420 U**	

The explanation column is completed after consultation with the purchasing department manager.

Variance reports facilitate the principle of "management by exception" explained in Chapter 10. For example, the vice president of purchasing can use the report shown above to evaluate the effectiveness of the purchasing department manager. Or, the vice president of production can use production department variance reports to determine how well each production manager is controlling costs. In using variance reports, top management normally looks for **significant variances**. These may be judged on the basis of some quantitative measure, such as more than 10% of the standard or more than $1,000.

Statement Presentation of Variances

STUDY OBJECTIVE 7

Prepare an income statement for management under a standard costing system.

In income statements **prepared for management** under a standard cost accounting system, **cost of goods sold is stated at standard cost and the variances are disclosed separately**. Illustration 11-23 shows this format. Based entirely on the production and sale of Weed-O, it assumes selling and administrative costs of $3,000. Observe that each variance is shown, as well as the total net variance. In this example, variations from standard costs reduced net income by $2,500.

Illustration 11-23
Variances in income statement for management

XONIC, INC.
Income Statement
For the Month Ended June 30, 2008

Sales		$60,000
Cost of goods sold (at standard)		42,000
Gross profit (at standard)		18,000
Variances		
Materials price	**$ 420**	
Materials quantity	**600**	
Labor price	**(420)**	
Labor quantity	**1,000**	
Overhead	**900**	
Total variance unfavorable		**2,500**
Gross profit (actual)		15,500
Selling and administrative expenses		3,000
Net income		$12,500

Standard costs may be used in financial statements prepared for stockholders and other external users. The costing of inventories at standard costs is in accordance with generally accepted accounting principles when there are no significant differences between actual costs and standard costs. Hewlett-Packard and Jostens, Inc., for example, report their inventories at standard costs. However, if there are significant differences between actual and standard costs, the financial statements must report inventories and cost of goods sold at actual costs.

It is also possible to show the variances in an income statement prepared in the variable costing (CVP) format. To do so, it is necessary to analyze the overhead variances into variable and fixed components. This type of analysis is explained in cost accounting textbooks.

BALANCED SCORECARD

STUDY OBJECTIVE 8

Describe the balanced scorecard approach to performance evaluation.

Financial measures (measurement of dollars), such as variance analysis and return on investment (ROI), are useful tools for evaluating performance. However, many companies now supplement these financial measures with nonfinancial measures to better assess performance and anticipate future results. For example, airlines, like Delta, American, and United, use capacity utilization as an important measure to understand and predict future performance. Newspaper publishers, such as the *New York Times* and the *Chicago Tribune*, use circulation figures as another measure by which to assess performance. Illustration 11-24 lists some key nonfinancial measures used in various industries.

Illustration 11-24
Nonfinancial measures used in various industries

Industry	Measure
Automobiles	Capacity utilization of plants. Average age of key assets. Impact of strikes. Brand-loyalty statistics.
Computer Systems	Market profile of customer end-products. Number of new products. Employee stock ownership percentages. Number of scientists and technicians used in R&D.
Chemicals	Customer satisfaction data. Factors affecting customer product selection. Number of patents and trademarks held. Customer brand awareness.
Regional Banks	Number of ATMs by state. Number of products used by average customer. Percentage of customer service calls handled by interactive voice response units. Personnel cost per employee. Credit card retention rates.

Source: Financial Accounting Standards Board, *Business Reporting: Insights into Enhancing Voluntary Disclosures* (Norwalk, Conn.: FASB, 2001)

Most companies recognize that both financial and nonfinancial measures can provide useful insights into what is happening in the company. As a result, many companies now use a broad-based measurement approach, called the **balanced scorecard**, to evaluate performance. The balanced scorecard incorporates financial and nonfinancial measures in an integrated system that links performance measurement and a company's strategic goals. Nearly 50% of the largest companies in the United States including Unilever, Chase, and Wal-Mart, are using the balanced scorecard approach.

The balanced scorecard evaluates company performance from a series of "perspectives." The four most commonly employed perspectives are as follows.

1. The financial perspective is the most traditional view of the company. It employs financial measures of performance used by most firms.
2. The customer perspective evaluates how well the company is performing from the viewpoint of those people who buy and use its products or services. This view measures how well the company compares to competitors in terms of price, quality, product innovation, customer service, and other dimensions.

3. The **internal process perspective** evaluates the internal operating processes critical to success. All critical aspects of the value chain—including product development, production, delivery and after-sale service—are evaluated to ensure that the company is operating effectively and efficiently.
4. The **learning and growth perspective** evaluates how well the company develops and retains its employees. This would include evaluation of such things as employee skills, employee satisfaction, training programs, and information dissemination.

Within each perspective, the balanced scorecard identifies objectives that will contribute to attainment of strategic goals. Illustration 11-25 shows examples of objectives within each perspective.

Illustration 11-25
Examples of objectives within the four perspectives of balanced scorecard

Financial perspective
- Return on assets
- Net income
- Credit rating
- Share price
- Profit per employee

Customer perspective
- Percentage of customers who would recommend product
- Customer retention
- Response time per customer request
- Brand recognition
- Customer service expense per customer

Internal process perspective
- Percentage of defect-free products
- Stockouts
- Labor utilization rates
- Waste reduction
- Planning accuracy

Learning and growth perspective
- Percentage of employees leaving in less than one year
- Number of cross-trained employees
- Ethics violations
- Training hours
- Reportable accidents

The objectives are linked across perspectives in order to tie performance measurement to company goals. The financial objectives are normally set first, and then objectives are set in the other perspectives in order to accomplish the financial objectives.

For example, within the financial perspective, a common goal is to increase profit per dollars invested as measured by ROI. In order to increase ROI, a customer-perspective objective might be to increase customer satisfaction as measured by the percentage of customers who would recommend the product to a friend. In order to increase customer satisfaction, an internal business process perspective objective might be to increase product quality as measured by the percentage of defect-free units. Finally, in order to increase the percentage of defect-free units, the learning and growth perspective objective might be to reduce factory employee turnover as measured by the percentage of employees leaving in under one year.

Illustration 11-26 illustrates this linkage across perspectives.

Illustration 11-26
Linked process across balanced scorecard perspectives

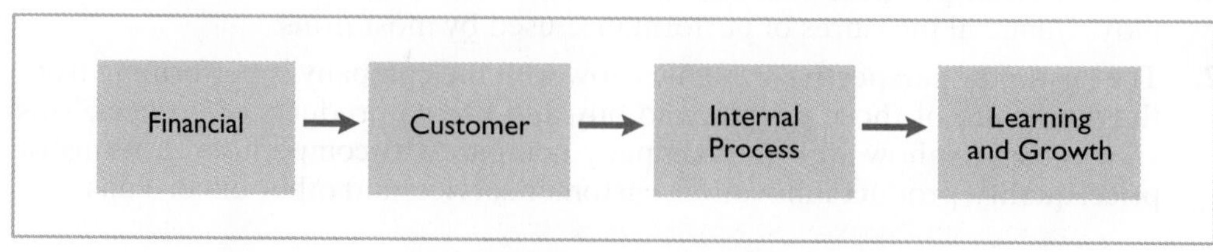

Through this linked process, the company can better understand how to achieve its goals and what measures to use to evaluate performance.

In summary, the balanced scorecard does the following:

1. Employs both financial and nonfinancial measures. (For example, ROI is a financial measure; employee turnover is a nonfinancial measure.)
2. Creates linkages so that high-level corporate goals can be communicated all the way down to the shop floor.
3. Provides measurable objectives for such nonfinancial measures as product quality, rather than vague statements such as "We would like to improve quality."
4. Integrates all of the company's goals into a single performance measurement system, so that an inappropriate amount of weight will not be placed on any single goal.

ACCOUNTING ACROSS THE ORGANIZATION

It May Be Time to Fly United Again

Many of the benefits of a balanced scorecard approach are evident in the improved operations at United Airlines. At the time it filed for bankruptcy in 2002, United had a reputation for some of the worst service in the airline business. But when Glenn Tilton took over as United's Chief Executive Officer in September 2002, he recognized that things had to change.

One thing he did was to implement an incentive program that allows all of United's 63,000 employees to earn a bonus of 2.5% or more of their wages if the company "exceeds its goals for on-time flight departures and for customer intent to fly United again." Since instituting this program the company's on-time departures are among the best, its customer complaints have been reduced considerably, and its number of customers who say that they would fly United again is at its highest level ever. While none of these things guarantees that United will survive, these improvements certainly increase its chances.

Source: Susan Carey, "Friendlier Skies: In Bankruptcy, United Airlines Forges a Path to Better Service," *Wall Street Journal*, June 15, 2004.

Which of the perspectives of a balanced scorecard were the focus of United's CEO?

Before You Go On...

REVIEW IT

1. What are the formulas for computing the total, price, and quantity variances for direct labor?
2. What is the formula for computing the total variance for manufacturing overhead?
3. How are standard costs and variances reported in income statements prepared for management?
4. What are the basic characteristics of the balanced scorecard?

Be sure to read **ALL ABOUT YOU: *Balancing Costs and Quality in Health Care*** on page 488 for information on how topics in this chapter apply to you.

Balancing Costs and Quality in Health Care

Do you think that standard costs are used only in making products like wheel bearings and hamburgers? Think again. Standards influence virtually every aspect of our lives. For example, the next time you call to schedule an appointment with your doctor, ask the receptionist how many minutes the appointment is scheduled for. Doctors are under increasing pressure to see more patients each day, which means the time spent with each patient is shorter. As insurance companies and employers push for reduced medical costs, every facet of medicine has been standardized and analyzed. Doctors, nurses, and other medical staff are evaluated in every part of their operations to ensure maximum efficiency.

While keeping medical treatment affordable seems like a worthy goal, what are the potential implications for the quality of health care? Does a focus on the bottom line result in a reduction in the quality of health care? Here are some facts to think about while you are sitting in the waiting room.

Some Facts

* Medical costs for a family of four hit $13,383 in 2006, a 9.6% increase over 2005. Of this amount, the employer typically pays about $8,363, and the employee pays about $5,020. Increases have averaged about 10% per year in recent years.
* During the 1990s many health-care facilities provided bonuses to doctors based on cost-based financial incentives. By the end of the 1990s critics began to question this approach because they felt it created perverse incentives for doctors. If a doctor is under pressure to reduce costs, he or she may feel compelled to not provide necessary care.
* Two reports, *To Err Is Human* in 1999 and *Crossing the Quality Chasm* in 2001, called attention to quality and patient-safety shortcomings. As a result, the new emphasis is to align compensation policies with quality improvement.
* Some health plans have adopted compensation systems that attempt to tie pay to performance. These systems offer higher pay for doctors who meet specific goals, such as preventive care, patient satisfaction, acquisition of information technology, and cost containment. In 2004, major California health plans paid physician organizations about $40 million in performance-based bonuses.

About the Numbers

As the following graph shows, the United States spends a huge amount on health care compared to other countries. Note that we spend more on a per person basis, and as a percentage of our gross domestic product (GDP) than every other listed country. This fact makes it even more frustrating that more than 40 million Americans have no health coverage, and that on many measures of health-care quality, America falls short.

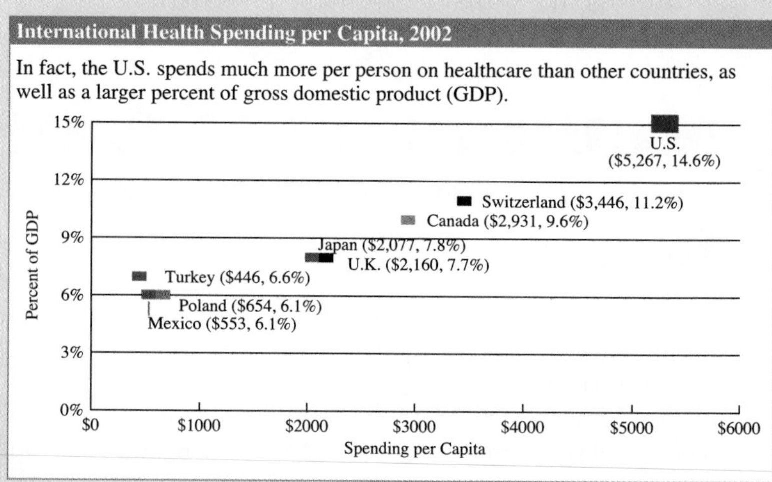

Source: BlueCross BlueShield Association, *www.bcbs.com/mcrg/chap1/ch1_Slide_4.html;* adapted from G. F. Anderson et al., *Health Affairs* (2005).

What Do You Think?

Eventually we all need to see a doctor. Therefore, we all have a vested interest in the quality of medical care. As medical costs have soared in recent years, many approaches have been tried to keep costs down. A simmering debate has centered on a very basic question: To what extent should accountants, through financial measures, influence the type of medical care that you receive?

Suppose that your local medical facility is in danger of closing because it has been losing money. Should the facility put in place incentives that provide bonuses to doctors if they meet certain standard-cost targets for the cost of treating specific ailments?

YES: If the facility is in danger of closing, then someone should take steps to change the medical practices to reduce costs. A closed medical facility is of no use to me, my family, or the community.

NO: I don't want an accountant deciding the right medical treatment for me. My family and I deserve the best medical care.

Source: Thomas Bodenheimer, et al., Can Money Buy Quality? Physician Response to Pay for Performance, Issue Brief No. 102, December 2005, *www.hschange.com/CONTENT/807/#ib1;* Bradley C. Strunk and Robert E. Hurley, "Paying for Quality: Health Plans Try Carrots Instead of Sticks, Issue Brief No. 82, May 2004.

The authors' comments on this situation appear on page 516.

Using the Decision Toolkit

Assume that during the past month Sanford produced 10,000 cartons of Liquid ACCENT® highlighters. Liquid ACCENT® offers a translucent barrel and cap with a visible ink supply for see-through color. The special fluorescent ink is fade- and water-resistant. Each carton contains 100 boxes of markers, and each box contains five markers. The markers come in boxes of one of five fluorescent colors—orange, blue, yellow, green, and pink—and in a five-color set.

Assume the following additional facts: The standard cost for one carton of 500 markers is as follows.

Manufacturing Cost Elements	Standard Quantity	×	Price	=	Cost
Direct materials					
Tips (boxes of 500)	500	×	$ 0.03	=	$ 15.00
Translucent barrels and caps (boxes of 500)	500	×	$ 0.09	=	45.00
Fluorescent ink (100 oz. containers)	100 oz.	×	$ 0.32	=	32.00
Total direct materials					92.00
Direct labor	0.25 hours	×	$ 9.00	=	2.25
Overhead	0.25 hours	×	$48.00	=	12.00
					$106.25

During the month, the following transactions occurred in manufacturing the 10,000 cartons of highlighters.

1. Purchased 10,000 boxes of tips for $148,000 ($14.80 per 500 tips); purchased 10,200 boxes of translucent barrels and caps for $453,900 ($44.50 per 500 barrels and caps); and purchased 9,900 containers of fluorescent ink for $328,185 ($33.15 per 100 ounces).
2. All materials purchased during the period were used to make markers during the period.
3. 2,300 direct labor hours were worked at a total labor cost of $20,240 (an average hourly rate of $8.80).
4. Variable manufacturing overhead incurred was $34,600, and fixed overhead incurred was $84,000.

The manufacturing overhead rate of $48.00 is based on a normal capacity of 2,600 direct labor hours. The total budget at this capacity is $83,980 fixed and $40,820 variable.

Instructions

Determine whether Sanford met its price and quantity objectives relative to materials, labor, and overhead.

Solution

To determine whether Sanford met its price and quantity objectives, compute the total variance and the variances for direct material and direct labor, and calculate the total variance for manufacturing overhead.

Total Variance	
Actual cost incurred:	
Direct materials	
Tips	$148,000
Translucent barrels and caps	453,900
Fluorescent ink	328,185

Total direct materials	$ 930,085
Direct labor	20,240
Overhead	118,600
Total actual costs	1,068,925
Standard cost (10,000 × $106.25)	1,062,500
Total variance	$ 6,425 U

Direct Materials Variances

Total	=	$930,085	−	$920,000 (10,000 × $92)	=	$10,085 U
Price (Tips)	=	$148,000 (10,000 × $14.80)	−	$150,000 (10,000 × $15.00)	=	$ 2,000 F
Price (Barrels and caps)	=	$453,900 (10,200 × $44.50)	−	$459,000 (10,200 × $45.00)	=	$ 5,100 F
Price (Ink)	=	$328,185 (9,900 × $33.15)	−	$316,800 (9,900 × $32.00)	=	$11,385 U
Quantity (Tips)	=	$150,000 (10,000 × $15.00)	−	$150,000 (10,000 × $15.00)	=	$ 0
Quantity (Barrels and caps)	=	$459,000 (10,200 × $45.00)	−	$450,000 (10,000 × $45.00)	=	$ 9,000 U
Quantity (Ink)	=	$316,800 (9,900 × $32.00)	−	$320,000 (10,000 × $32.00)	=	$ 3,200 F

Direct Labor Variances

Total	=	$20,240 (2,300 × $8.80)	−	$22,500 (2,500 × $9.00)	=	$ 2,260 F
Price	=	$20,240 (2,300 × $8.80)	−	$20,700 (2,300 × $9.00)	=	$ 460 F
Quantity	=	$20,700 (2,300 × $9.00)	−	$22,500 (2,500 × $9.00)	=	$ 1,800 F

Overhead Variance

Total	=	$118,600 ($84,000 + $34,600)	−	$120,000 (2,500 × $48)	=	$ 1,400 F

Sanford's total variance was an unfavorable $6,425. The unfavorable materials variance outweighed the favorable labor and overhead variances. The primary determinants were an unfavorable price variance for ink and an unfavorable quantity variance for barrels and caps.

The Navigator

SUMMARY OF STUDY OBJECTIVES

1 **Distinguish between a standard and a budget.** Both standards and budgets are predetermined costs. The primary difference is that a standard is a unit amount, whereas a budget is a total amount. A standard may be regarded as the budgeted cost per unit of product.

2 **Identify the advantages of standard costs.** Standard costs offer a number of advantages. They (a) facilitate management planning, (b) promote greater economy, (c) are useful in setting selling prices, (d) contribute to management control, (e) permit "management by exception," and (f) simplify the costing of inventories and reduce clerical costs.

3 **Describe how companies set standards.** The direct materials price standard should be based on the delivered cost of raw materials plus an allowance for receiving and handling. The direct materials quantity standard should establish the required quantity plus an allowance for waste and spoilage.

The direct labor price standard should be based on current wage rates and anticipated adjustments such as COLAs. It also generally includes payroll taxes and fringe benefits. Direct labor quantity standards should be based on required production time plus an allowance for rest periods, cleanup, machine setup, and machine downtime.

For manufacturing overhead, a standard predetermined overhead rate is used. It is based on an expected standard activity index such as standard direct labor hours or standard machine hours.

4 **State the formulas for determining direct materials and direct labor variances.** The formulas for the direct materials variances are:

$$\begin{pmatrix}\text{Actual quantity}\\ \times\text{ Actual price}\end{pmatrix} - \begin{pmatrix}\text{Standard quantity}\\ \times\text{ Standard price}\end{pmatrix} = \begin{matrix}\text{Total}\\ \text{materials}\\ \text{variance}\end{matrix}$$

$$\begin{pmatrix}\text{Actual quantity}\\ \times\text{ Actual price}\end{pmatrix} - \begin{pmatrix}\text{Actual quantity}\\ \times\text{ Standard price}\end{pmatrix} = \begin{matrix}\text{Materials}\\ \text{price}\\ \text{variance}\end{matrix}$$

$$\begin{pmatrix}\text{Actual quantity}\\ \times\text{ Standard price}\end{pmatrix} - \begin{pmatrix}\text{Standard quantity}\\ \times\text{ Standard price}\end{pmatrix} = \begin{matrix}\text{Materials}\\ \text{quantity}\\ \text{variance}\end{matrix}$$

The formulas for the direct labor variances are:

$$\begin{pmatrix}\text{Actual hours}\\ \times\text{ Actual rate}\end{pmatrix} - \begin{pmatrix}\text{Standard hours}\\ \times\text{ Standard rate}\end{pmatrix} = \begin{matrix}\text{Total}\\ \text{labor}\\ \text{variance}\end{matrix}$$

$$\begin{pmatrix}\text{Actual hours}\\ \times\text{ Actual rate}\end{pmatrix} - \begin{pmatrix}\text{Actual hours}\\ \times\text{ Standard rate}\end{pmatrix} = \begin{matrix}\text{Labor}\\ \text{price}\\ \text{variance}\end{matrix}$$

$$\begin{pmatrix}\text{Actual hours}\\ \times\text{ Standard rate}\end{pmatrix} - \begin{pmatrix}\text{Standard hours}\\ \times\text{ Standard rate}\end{pmatrix} = \begin{matrix}\text{Labor}\\ \text{quantity}\\ \text{variance}\end{matrix}$$

5 **State the formula for determining the total manufacturing overhead variance.** The formula for the total manufacturing overhead variance is:

$$\begin{pmatrix}\text{Actual}\\ \text{overhead}\end{pmatrix} - \begin{pmatrix}\text{Overhead}\\ \text{applied at}\\ \text{standard hours}\\ \text{allowed}\end{pmatrix} = \begin{matrix}\text{Total overhead}\\ \text{variance}\end{matrix}$$

6 **Discuss the reporting of variances.** Variances are reported to management in variance reports. The reports facilitate management by exception by highlighting significant differences.

7 **Prepare an income statement for management under a standard costing system.** Under a standard costing system, an income statement prepared for management will report cost of goods sold at standard cost and then disclose each variance separately.

8 **Describe the balanced scorecard approach to performance evaluation.** The balanced scorecard incorporates financial and nonfinancial measures in an integrated system that links performance measurement and a company's strategic goals. It employs four perspectives: financial, customer, internal processes, and learning and growth. Objectives are set within each of these perspectives that link to objectives within the other perspectives.

DECISION TOOLKIT—A SUMMARY

Decision Checkpoints	Info Needed for Decision	Tool to Use for Decision	How to Evaluate Results
Has management accomplished its price and quantity objectives regarding materials?	Actual cost and standard cost of materials	Materials price and materials quantity variances	Positive (favorable) variances suggest that price and quantity objectives have been met.
Has management accomplished its price and quantity objectives regarding labor?	Actual cost and standard cost of labor	Labor price and labor quantity variances	Positive (favorable) variances suggest that price and quantity objectives have been met.
Has management accomplished its objectives regarding manufacturing overhead?	Actual cost and standard cost of manufacturing overhead	Total manufacturing overhead variance	Positive (favorable) variances suggest that manufacturing overhead objectives have been met.

APPENDIX 11A Standard Cost Accounting System

STUDY OBJECTIVE 9

Identify the features of a standard cost accounting system.

A **standard cost accounting system** is a double-entry system of accounting. In this system, companies use standard costs in making entries, and they formally recognize variances in the accounts. Companies may use a standard cost system with either job order or process costing.

In this appendix, we will explain and illustrate a **standard cost, job order cost accounting system**. The system is based on two important assumptions:

(1) Variances from standards are recognized at the earliest opportunity.

(2) The Work in Process account is maintained exclusively on the basis of standard costs.

In practice, there are many variations among standard cost systems. The system described here should prepare you for systems you see in the "real world."

Journal Entries

We will use the transactions of Xonic, Inc. to illustrate the journal entries. Note as you study the entries that the major difference between the entries here and those for the job order cost accounting system in Chapter 2 is the **variance accounts**.

1. Purchase raw materials on account for $13,020 when the standard cost is $12,600.

	Debit	Credit
Raw Materials Inventory	12,600	
Materials Price Variance	420	
Accounts Payable		13,020
(To record purchase of materials)		

Xonic debits the inventory account for actual quantities at standard cost. This enables the perpetual materials records to show actual quantities. Xonic debits the price variance, which is unfavorable, to Materials Price Variance.

2. Incur direct labor costs of $20,580 when the standard labor cost is $21,000.

	Debit	Credit
Factory Labor	21,000	
Labor Price Variance		420
Wages Payable		20,580
(To record direct labor costs)		

Like the raw materials inventory account, Xonic debits Factory Labor for actual hours worked at the standard hourly rate of pay. In this case, the labor variance is favorable. Thus, Xonic credits Labor Price Variance.

3. Incur actual manufacturing overhead costs of $10,900.

	Debit	Credit
Manufacturing Overhead	10,900	
Accounts Payable/Cash/Acc. Depreciation		10,900
(To record overhead incurred)		

The controllable overhead variance (see Appendix 11B) is not recorded at this time. It depends on standard hours applied to work in process. This amount is not known at the time overhead is incurred.

4. Issue raw materials for production at a cost of $12,600 when the standard cost is $12,000.

	Debit	Credit
Work in Process Inventory	12,000	
Materials Quantity Variance	600	
Raw Materials Inventory		12,600
(To record issuance of raw materials)		

Xonic debits Work in Process Inventory for standard materials quantities used at standard prices. It debits the variance account because the variance is unfavorable. The company credits Raw Materials Inventory for actual quantities at standard prices.

5. Assign factory labor to production at a cost of $21,000 when standard cost is $20,000.

Account	Debit	Credit
Work in Process Inventory	20,000	
Labor Quantity Variance	1,000	
Factory Labor		21,000
(To assign factory labor to jobs)		

Xonic debits Work in Process Inventory for standard labor hours at standard rates. It debits the unfavorable variance to Labor Quantity Variance. The credit to Factory Labor produces a zero balance in this account.

6. Apply manufacturing overhead to production $10,000.

Account	Debit	Credit
Work in Process Inventory	10,000	
Manufacturing Overhead		10,000
(To assign overhead to jobs)		

Xonic debits Work in Process Inventory for standard hours allowed multiplied by the standard overhead rate.

7. Transfer completed work to finished goods $42,000.

Account	Debit	Credit
Finished Goods Inventory	42,000	
Work in Process Inventory		42,000
(To record transfer of completed work to finished goods)		

In this example, both inventory accounts are at standard cost.

8. Sell the 1,000 gallons of Weed-O for $60,000.

Account	Debit	Credit
Accounts Receivable	60,000	
Cost of Goods Sold	42,000	
Sales		60,000
Finished Goods Inventory		42,000
(To record sale of finished goods and the cost of goods sold)		

The company debits Cost of Goods Sold at standard cost. Gross profit, in turn, is the difference between sales and the standard cost of goods sold.

9. Recognize unfavorable total overhead variance:

Account	Debit	Credit
Overhead Variance	900	
Manufacturing Overhead		900
(To recognize overhead variances)		

Prior to this entry, a debit balance of $900 existed in Manufacturing Overhead. This entry therefore produces a zero balance in the Manufacturing Overhead account. The information needed for this entry is often not available until the end of the accounting period.

Ledger Accounts

Illustration 11A-1 (page 494) shows the cost accounts for Xonic, Inc., after posting the entries. Note that six variance accounts are included in the ledger. The remaining accounts are the same as those illustrated for a job order cost system in Chapter 2, in which only actual costs were used.

Illustration 11A-1
Cost accounts with variances

Raw Materials Inventory	
(1) 12,600	(4) 12,600

Materials Price Variance	
(1) 420	

Work in Process Inventory	
(4) 12,000	(7) 42,000
(5) 20,000	
(6) 10,000	

Factory Labor	
(2) 21,000	(5) 21,000

Materials Quantity Variance	
(4) 600	

Finished Goods Inventory	
(7) 42,000	(8) 42,000

Manufacturing Overhead	
(3) 10,900	(6) 10,000
	(9) 900

Labor Price Variance	
	(2) 420

Cost of Goods Sold	
(8) 42,000	

Labor Quantity Variance	
(5) 1,000	

Overhead Variance	
(9) 900	

HELPFUL HINT
All debit balances in variance accounts indicate unfavorable variances; all credit balances indicate favorable variances.

SUMMARY OF STUDY OBJECTIVE FOR APPENDIX 11A

9 **Identify the features of a standard cost accounting system.** In a standard cost accounting system, companies journalize and post standard costs, and they maintain separate variance accounts in the ledger.

APPENDIX 11B A Closer Look at Overhead Variances

STUDY OBJECTIVE 10
Compute overhead controllable and volume variance.

As indicated in the chapter, the total overhead variance is generally analyzed through a price variance and a quantity variance. The name usually given to the price variance is the **overhead controllable variance**; the quantity variance is referred to as the **overhead volume variance**.

OVERHEAD CONTROLLABLE VARIANCE

The **overhead controllable variance** shows whether overhead costs are effectively controlled. To compute this variance, the company compares actual overhead costs incurred with budgeted costs for the **standard hours allowed**. The budgeted costs are determined from a flexible manufacturing overhead budget. The concepts related to a flexible budget were discussed in Chapter 10.

For Xonic the budget formula for manufacturing overhead is variable manufacturing overhead cost of $3 per hour of labor plus fixed manufacturing overhead costs of $4,400. Illustration 11B-1 shows the flexible budget for Xonic, Inc.

Illustration 11B-1
Flexible budget using standard direct labor hours

	A	B	C	D	E
1	**XONIC, INC**				
2	**Flexible Manufacturing Overhead Budget**				
3	Activity Index				
4	Standard direct labor hours	1,800	**2,000**	2,200	2,400
5	Costs				
6	Variable costs				
7	Indirect materials	$1,800	**$ 2,000**	$ 2,200	$ 2,400
8	Indirect labor	2,700	**3,000**	3,300	3,600
9	Utilities	900	**1,000**	1,100	1,200
10	Total variable costs	5,400	**6,000**	6,600	7,200
11					
12	Fixed costs				
13	Supervision	3,000	**3,000**	3,000	3,000
14	Depreciation	1,400	**1,400**	1,400	1,400
15	Total fixed costs	4,400	**4,400**	4,400	4,400
16	Total costs	$9,800	**$10,400**	$11,000	$11,600
17					

As shown, the budgeted costs for 2,000 standard hours are $10,400 ($6,000 variable and $4,400 fixed).

Illustration 11B-2 shows the formula for the overhead controllable variance and the calculation for Xonic, Inc.

Illustration 11B-2
Formula for overhead controllable variance

Actual Overhead	–	Overhead Budgeted*	=	Overhead Controllable Variance
$10,900 ($6,500 + $4,400)	–	$10,400 ($6,000 + $4,400)	=	$500 U

*Based on standard hours allowed.

The overhead controllable variance for Xonic, Inc. is $500 unfavorable.

Most controllable variances are associated with variable costs, which are controllable costs. Fixed costs are often known at the time the budget is prepared and are therefore not as likely to deviate from the budgeted amount. In Xonic's case, all of the overhead controllable variance is due to the difference between the actual variable overhead costs ($6,500) and the budgeted variable costs ($6,000).

Management can compare actual and budgeted overhead for each manufacturing overhead cost that contributes to the controllable variance. In addition, management can develop cost and quantity variances for each overhead cost, such as indirect materials and indirect labor.

OVERHEAD VOLUME VARIANCE

The **overhead volume variance** is the difference between normal capacity hours and standard hours allowed times the fixed overhead rate. The overhead volume variance relates to whether fixed costs were under- or over-applied during the year. For example, the overhead volume variance answers the question of whether

Xonic effectively used its fixed costs. If Xonic produces less Weed-O than normal capacity would allow, an unfavorable variance results. Conversely, if Xonic produces more Weed-O than what is considered normal capacity, a favorable variance results.

The formula for computing the overhead volume variance is as follows.

Illustration 11B-3
Formula for overhead volume variance

Fixed Overhead Rate	×	(Normal Capacity Hours – Standard Hours Allowed)	=	Overhead Volume Variance

To illustrate the fixed overhead rate computation, recall that Xonic Inc. budgeted fixed overhead cost for the year of $52,800 (Illustration 11-6 on page 474). At normal capacity, 26,400 standard direct labor hours are required. The fixed overhead rate is therefore $2 ($52,800 ÷ 26,400 hours).

Xonic produced 1,000 units of Weed-O in June. The standard hours allowed for the 1,000 gallons produced in June is 2,000 (1,000 gallons × 2 hours). For Xonic, standard direct labor hours for June at normal capacity is 2,200 (26,400 annual hours ÷ 12 months). The computation of the overhead volume variance in this case is as follows.

Illustration 11B-4
Computation of overhead volume variance for Xonic Co.

Fixed Overhead Rate	×	(Normal Capacity Hours – Standard Hours Allowed)	=	Overhead Volume Variance
$2	×	(2,200 – 2,000)	=	$400 U

In Xonic's case, a $400 unfavorable volume variance results. The volume variance is unfavorable because Xonic produced only 1,000 gallons rather than the normal capacity of 1,100 gallons in the month of June. As a result, it underapplied fixed overhead for that period.

In computing the overhead variances, it is important to remember the following.

1. Standard hours allowed are used in each of the variances.
2. Budgeted costs for the controllable variance are derived from the flexible budget.
3. The controllable variance generally pertains to variable costs.
4. The volume variance pertains solely to fixed costs.

SUMMARY OF STUDY OBJECTIVE FOR APPENDIX 11B

10 Compute overhead controllable and volume variance. The total overhead variance is generally analyzed through a price variance and a quantity variance. The name usually given to the price variance is the overhead controllable variance. The quantity variance is referred to as the overhead volume variance.

GLOSSARY

Balanced scorecard An approach that incorporates financial and nonfinancial measures in an integrated system that links performance measurement and a company's strategic goals. (p. 485)

Customer perspective A viewpoint employed in the balanced scorecard to evaluate the company from the perspective of those people who buy and use its products or services. (p. 485)

Direct labor price standard The rate per hour that should be incurred for direct labor. (p. 473)

Direct labor quantity standard The time that should be required to make one unit of product. (p. 474)

Direct materials price standard The cost per unit of direct materials that should be incurred. (p. 473)

Direct materials quantity standard The quantity of direct materials that should be used per unit of finished goods. (p. 473)

Financial perspective A viewpoint employed in the balanced scorecard to evaluate a company's performance using financial measures. (p. 485)

Ideal standards Standards based on the optimum level of performance under perfect operating conditions. (p. 472)

Internal process perspective A viewpoint employed in the balanced scorecard to evaluate the effectiveness and efficiency of a company's value chain, including product development, production, delivery, and after-sale service. (p. 486)

Labor price variance The difference between the actual hours times the actual rate and the actual hours times the standard rate for labor. (p. 480)

Labor quantity variance The difference between actual hours times the standard rate and standard hours times the standard rate for labor. (p. 480)

Learning and growth perspective A viewpoint employed in the balanced scorecard to evaluate how well a company develops and retains its employees. (p. 486)

Materials price variance The difference between the actual quantity times the actual price and the actual quantity times the standard price for materials. (p. 477)

Materials quantity variance The difference between the actual quantity times the standard price and the standard quantity times the standard price for materials. (p. 477)

Normal capacity The average activity output that a company should experience over the long run. (p. 474)

Normal standards Standards based on an efficient level of performance that are attainable under expected operating conditions. (p. 472)

Overhead controllable variance The difference between actual overhead incurred and overhead budgeted for the standard hours allowed. (p. 494)

Overhead volume variance The difference between normal capacity hours and standard hours allowed times the fixed overhead rate. (p. 495)

Standard cost accounting system A double-entry system of accounting in which standard costs are used in making entries and variances are recognized in the accounts. (p. 491)

Standard costs Predetermined unit costs which companies use as measures of performance. (p. 470)

Standard hours allowed The hours that should have been worked for the units produced. (p. 482)

Standard predetermined overhead rate An overhead rate determined by dividing budgeted overhead costs by an expected standard activity index. (p. 474)

Total labor variance The difference between actual hours times the actual rate and standard hours times the standard rate for labor. (p. 480)

Total materials variance The difference between the actual quantity times the actual price and the standard quantity times the standard price of materials. (p. 477)

Total overhead variance The difference between actual overhead costs and overhead costs applied to work done, based on standard hours allowed. (p. 482)

Variances The difference between total actual costs and total standard costs. (p. 476)

Demonstration Problem

Manlow Company makes a cologne called Allure. The standard cost for one bottle of Allure is as follows.

	Standard				
Manufacturing Cost Elements	**Quantity**	×	**Price**	=	**Cost**
Direct materials	6 oz.	×	$ 0.90	=	$ 5.40
Direct labor	0.5 hrs.	×	$12.00	=	6.00
Manufacturing overhead	0.5 hrs.	×	$ 4.80	=	2.40
					$13.80

During the month, the following transactions occurred in manufacturing 10,000 bottles of Allure.

1. 58,000 ounces of materials were purchased at $1.00 per ounce.
2. All the materials purchased were used to produce the 10,000 bottles of Allure.
3. 4,900 direct labor hours were worked at a total labor cost of $56,350.
4. Variable manufacturing overhead incurred was $15,000 and fixed overhead incurred was $10,400.

The manufacturing overhead rate of $4.80 is based on a normal capacity of 5,200 direct labor hours. The total budget at this capacity is $10,400 fixed and $14,560 variable.

Instructions

(a) Compute the total variance and the variances for direct material and direct labor elements.

(b) Compute the total variance for manufacturing overhead.

Solution

action plan

- Check to make sure the total variance and the sum of the individual variances are equal.
- Find the price variance first, then the quantity variance.
- Base budgeted overhead costs on flexible budget data.
- Base overhead applied on standard hours allowed.
- Ignore actual hours worked in computing overhead variances.

(a)

Total Variance

Actual costs incurred	
Direct materials	$ 58,000
Direct labor	56,350
Manufacturing overhead	25,400
	139,750
Standard cost (10,000 × $13.80)	138,000
Total variance	$ 1,750 U

Direct Materials Variances

Total	=	$58,000 (58,000 × $1.00)	–	$54,000 (60,000 × $0.90)	=	$4,000 U
Price	=	$58,000 (58,000 × $1.00)	–	$52,200 (58,000 × $0.90)	=	$5,800 U
Quantity	=	$52,200 (58,000 × $0.90)	–	$54,000 (60,000 × $0.90)	=	$1,800 F

Direct Labor Variances

Total	=	$56,350 (4,900 × $11.50)	–	$60,000 (5,000 × $12.00)	=	$3,650 F
Price	=	$56,350 (4,900 × $11.50)	–	$58,800 (4,900 × $12.00)	=	$2,450 F
Quantity	=	$58,800 (4,900 × $12.00)	–	$60,000 (5,000 × $12.00)	=	$1,200 F

(b)

Overhead Variance

Total	=	$25,400 ($15,000 + $10,400)	–	$24,000 (5,000 × $4.80)	=	$ 1,400 U

The Navigator

Note: All asterisked Questions, Exercises, and Problems relate to material in the appendices to the chapter.

SELF-STUDY QUESTIONS

Answers are at the end of the chapter.

(SO 1) 1. Standards differ from budgets in that:
   a. budgets but not standards may be used in valuing inventories.
   b. budgets but not standards may be journalized and posted.
   c. budgets are a total amount and standards are a unit amount.
   d. only budgets contribute to management planning and control.

(SO 2) 2. The advantages of standard costs include all of the following *except:*
   a. management by exception may be used.
   b. management planning is facilitated.
   c. they may simplify the costing of inventories.
   d. management must use a static budget.

(SO 3) 3. The setting of standards is:
   a. a managerial accounting decision.
   b. a management decision.
   c. a worker decision.
   d. preferably set at the ideal level of performance.

(SO 4) 4. Each of the following formulas is correct except:
   a. Labor price variance = (Actual hours × Actual rate) − (Actual hours × Standard rate).
   b. Total overhead variance = Actual overhead − Overhead applied.
   c. Materials price variance = (Actual quantity × Actual price) − (Standard quantity × Standard price).
   d. Labor quantity variance = (Actual hours × Standard rate) − (Standard hours × Standard rate).

(SO 4) 5. In producing product AA, 6,300 pounds of direct materials were used at a cost of $1.10 per pound. The standard was 6,000 pounds at $1.00 per pound. The direct materials quantity variance is:
   a. $330 unfavorable.
   b. $300 unfavorable.
   c. $600 unfavorable.
   d. $630 unfavorable.

(SO 4) 6. In producing product ZZ, 14,800 direct labor hours were used at a rate of $8.20 per hour. The standard was 15,000 hours at $8.00 per hour. Based on these data, the direct labor:
   a. quantity variance is $1,600 favorable.
   b. quantity variance is $1,600 unfavorable.
   c. price variance is $2,960 favorable.
   d. price variance is $3,000 unfavorable.

7. Which of the following is *correct* about the total overhead variance? (SO 5)
   a. Budgeted overhead and budgeted overhead applied are the same.
   b. Total actual overhead is composed of variable overhead, fixed overhead, and period costs.
   c. Standard hours actually worked are used in computing the variance.
   d. Standard hours allowed for the work done is the measure used in computing the variance.

8. The formula for computing the total overhead variance is: (SO 5)
   a. actual overhead less overhead applied.
   b. overhead budgeted less overhead applied.
   c. actual overhead less overhead budgeted.
   d. No correct answer given.

9. Which of the following is *incorrect* about variance reports? (SO 6)
   a. They facilitate "management by exception."
   b. They should only be sent to the top level of management.
   c. They should be prepared as soon as possible.
   d. They may vary in form, content, and frequency among companies.

10. Which of the following would *not* be an objective used in the customer perspective of the balanced scorecard approach? (SO 8)
   a. Percentage of customers who would recommend product to a friend.
   b. Customer retention.
   c. Brand recognition.
   d. Earnings per share.

*11. Which of the following is *incorrect* about a standard cost accounting system? (SO 9)
   a. It is applicable to job order costing.
   b. It is applicable to process costing.
   c. It reports only favorable variances.
   d. It keeps separate accounts for each variance.

Go to the book's website, **www.wiley.com/college/weygandt**, for Additional Self-Study questions.

The Navigator

QUESTIONS

1. **(a)** "Standard costs are the expected total cost of completing a job." Is this correct? Explain.
   (b) "A standard imposed by a governmental agency is known as a regulation." Do you agree? Explain.
2. **(a)** Explain the similarities and differences between standards and budgets.
   (b) Contrast the accounting for standards and budgets.
3. Standard costs facilitate management planning. What are the other advantages of standard costs?
4. Contrast the roles of the management accountant and management in setting standard costs.
5. Distinguish between an ideal standard and a normal standard.

6. What factors should be considered in setting (a) the direct materials price standard and (b) the direct materials quantity standard?
7. "The objective in setting the direct labor quantity standard is to determine the aggregate time required to make one unit of product." Do you agree? What allowances should be made in setting this standard?
8. How is the predetermined overhead rate determined when standard costs are used?
9. What is the difference between a favorable cost variance and an unfavorable cost variance?
10. In each of the following formulas, supply the words that should be inserted for each number in parentheses.
    (a) (Actual quantity × (1)) − (Standard quantity × (2)) = Total materials variance
    (b) ((3) × Actual price) − (Actual quantity × (4)) = Materials price variance
    (c) (Actual quantity × (5)) − ((6) × Standard price) = Materials quantity variance
11. In the direct labor variance matrix, there are three factors: (1) Actual hours × Actual rate, (2) Actual hours × Standard rate, and (3) Standard hours × Standard rate. Using the numbers, indicate the formulas for each of the direct labor variances.
12. Greer Company's standard predetermined overhead rate is $8 per direct labor hour. For the month of June, 26,000 actual hours were worked, and 27,000 standard hours were allowed. How much overhead was applied?
13. How often should variances be reported to management? What principle may be used with variance reports?
14. What circumstances may cause the purchasing department to be responsible for both an unfavorable materials price variance and an unfavorable materials quantity variance?
15. What are the four perspectives used in the balanced scorecard? Discuss the nature of each, and how the perspectives are linked.
16. Tom Jones says that the balanced scorecard was created to replace financial measures as the primary mechanism for performance evaluation. He says that it uses only nonfinancial measures. Is this true?
17. What are some examples of nonfinancial measures used by companies to evaluate performance?
18. (a) How are variances reported in income statements prepared for management? (b) May standard costs be used in preparing financial statements for stockholders? Explain.

*19. (a) Explain the basic features of a standard cost accounting system. (b) What type of balance will exist in the variance account when (1) the materials price variance is unfavorable and (2) the labor quantity variance is favorable?

*20. If the $8 per hour overhead rate in question 12 includes $5 variable, and actual overhead costs were $218,000, what is the overhead controllable variance for June? The normal capacity hours were 28,000. Is the variance favorable or unfavorable?

*21. What is the purpose of computing the overhead volume variance? What is the basic formula for this variance?

*22. Janet Finney does not understand why the overhead volume variance indicates that fixed overhead costs are under- or overapplied. Clarify this matter for Janet.

*23. Nick Menke is attempting to outline the important points about overhead variances on a class examination. List four points that Nick should include in his outline.

BRIEF EXERCISES

Distinguish between a standard and a budget.
(SO 1)

BE11-1 Orasco Company uses both standards and budgets. For the year, estimated production of Product X is 500,000 units. Total estimated cost for materials and labor are $1,200,000 and $1,600,000. Compute the estimates for (a) a standard cost and (b) a budgeted cost.

Set direct materials standard.
(SO 3)

BE11-2 Asaki Company accumulates the following data concerning raw materials in making one gallon of finished product: (1) Price—net purchase price $2.20, freight-in $0.20 and receiving and handling $0.10. (2) Quantity—required materials 2.6 pounds, allowance for waste and spoilage 0.4 pounds. Compute the following.

(a) Standard direct materials price per gallon.
(b) Standard direct materials quantity per gallon.
(c) Total standard materials cost per gallon.

Set direct labor standard.
(SO 3)

BE11-3 Labor data for making one gallon of finished product in Asaki Company are as follows: (1) Price—hourly wage rate $12.00, payroll taxes $0.80, and fringe benefits $1.20. (2) Quantity—actual production time 1.2 hours, rest periods and clean up 0.25 hours, and setup and downtime 0.15 hours. Compute the following.

(a) Standard direct labor rate per hour.
(b) Standard direct labor hours per gallon.
(c) Standard labor cost per gallon.

Compute direct materials variances.
(SO 4)

BE11-4 Neville Company's standard materials cost per unit of output is $10 (2 pounds × $5). During July, the company purchases and uses 3,200 pounds of materials costing $16,160 in making 1,500 units of finished product. Compute the total, price, and quantity materials variances.

BE11-5 Wamser Company's standard labor cost per unit of output is $20 (2 hours × $10 per hour). During August, the company incurs 2,100 hours of direct labor at an hourly cost of $10.50 per hour in making 1,000 units of finished product. Compute the total, price, and quantity labor variances.

Compute direct labor variances.
(SO 4)

BE11-6 In October, Keane Company reports 21,000 actual direct labor hours, and it incurs $115,000 of manufacturing overhead costs. Standard hours allowed for the work done is 20,000 hours. The predetermined overhead rate is $6 per direct labor hour. Compute the total overhead variance.

Compute total overhead variance.
(SO 5)

BE11-7 The four perspectives in the balanced scorecard are (1) financial, (2) customer, (3) internal process, and (4) learning and growth. Match each of the following objectives with the perspective it is most likely associated with: (a) Plant capacity utilization. (b) Employee work days missed due to injury. (c) Return on assets. (d) Brand recognition.

Match balanced scorecard perspectives.
(SO 8)

***BE11-8** Journalize the following transactions for Orkin Manufacturing.

Journalize materials variances.
(SO 9)

(a) Purchased 6,000 units of raw materials on account for $11,100. The standard cost was $12,000.
(b) Issued 5,500 units of raw materials for production. The standard units were 5,800.

***BE11-9** Journalize the following transactions for Rogler Manufacturing.

Journalize labor variances.
(SO 9)

(a) Incurred direct labor costs of $24,000 for 3,000 hours. The standard labor cost was $25,200.
(b) Assigned 3,000 direct labor hours costing $24,000 to production. Standard hours were 3,100.

***BE11-10** Some overhead data for Keane Company are given in BE11-6. In addition, the flexible manufacturing overhead budget shows that budgeted costs are $4 variable per direct labor hour and $50,000 fixed. Compute the overhead controllable variance.

Compute the overhead controllable variance.
(SO 10)

***BE11-11** Using the data in BE11-6 and BE11-10, compute the overhead volume variance. Normal capacity was 25,000 direct labor hours.

Compute overhead volume variance.
(SO 10)

EXERCISES

WILEY PLUS

E11-1 Lovitz Company is planning to produce 2,000 units of product in 2008. Each unit requires 3 pounds of materials at $6 per pound and a half hour of labor at $14 per hour. The overhead rate is 70% of direct labor.

Compute budget and standard.
(SO 1, 2, 3)

Instructions

(a) Compute the budgeted amounts for 2008 for direct materials to be used, direct labor, and applied overhead.
(b) Compute the standard cost of one unit of product.
(c) What are the potential advantages to a corporation of using standard costs?

E11-2 Tony Rondeli manufactures and sells homemade wine, and he wants to develop a standard cost per gallon. The following are required for production of a 50-gallon batch.

Compute standard materials costs.
(SO 3)

3,000 ounces of grape concentrate at $0.04 per ounce
54 pounds of granulated sugar at $0.35 per pound
60 lemons at $0.60 each
50 yeast tablets at $0.25 each
50 nutrient tablets at $0.20 each
2,500 ounces of water at $0.004 per ounce

Tony estimates that 4% of the grape concentrate is wasted, 10% of the sugar is lost, and 20% of the lemons cannot be used.

Instructions

Compute the standard cost of the ingredients for one gallon of wine. (Carry computations to two decimal places.)

E11-3 Muhsin Company has gathered the information shown on page 502 about its product.

Compute standard cost per unit.
(SO 3)

Direct materials: Each unit of product contains 4.5 pounds of materials. The average waste and spoilage per unit produced under normal conditions is 0.5 pounds. Materials cost $4 per pound, but Muhsin always takes the 2% cash discount all of its suppliers offer. Freight costs average $0.25 per pound.

Direct labor: Each unit requires 2 hours of labor. Setup, cleanup, and downtime average 0.2 hours per unit. The average hourly pay rate of Muhsin's employees is $12. Payroll taxes and fringe benfits are an additional $3 per hour.

Manufacturing overhead: Overhead is applied at a rate of $6 per direct labor hour.

Instructions

Compute Muhsin's total standard cost per unit.

Compute labor quantity variance.
(SO 3, 4)

E11-4 Rapid Repair Services, Inc. is trying to establish the standard labor cost of a typical oil change. The following data have been collected from time and motion studies conducted over the past month.

Actual time spent on the oil change	1.0 hour
Hourly wage rate	$10
Payroll taxes	10% of wage rate
Setup and downtime	10% of actual labor time
Cleanup and rest periods	30% of actual labor time
Fringe benefits	25% of wage rate

Instructions

(a) Determine the standard direct labor hours per oil change.
(b) Determine the standard direct labor hourly rate.
(c) Determine the standard direct labor cost per oil change.
(d) If an oil change took 1.5 hours at the standard hourly rate, what was the direct labor quantity variance?

Compute materials price and quantity variances.
(SO 4)

E11-5 The standard cost of Product B manufactured by Mateo Company includes three units of direct materials at $5.00 per unit. During June, 28,000 units of direct materials are purchased at a cost of $4.70 per unit, and 28,000 units of direct materials are used to produce 9,000 units of Product B.

Instructions

(a) Compute the total materials variance and the price and quantity variances.
(b) Repeat (a), assuming the purchase price is $5.20 and the quantity purchased and used is 26,200 units.

Compute labor price and quantity variances.
(SO 4)

E11-6 Scheer Company's standard labor cost of producing one unit of Product DD is 4 hours at the rate of $12.00 per hour. During August, 40,800 hours of labor are incurred at a cost of $12.10 per hour to produce 10,000 units of Product DD.

Instructions

(a) Compute the total labor variance.
(b) Compute the labor price and quantity variances.
(c) Repeat (b), assuming the standard is 4.2 hours of direct labor at $12.25 per hour.

Compute materials and labor variances.
(SO 4)

E11-7 Haslett Inc., which produces a single product, has prepared the following standard cost sheet for one unit of the product.

Direct materials (8 pounds at $2.50 per pound)	$20
Direct labor (3 hours at $12.00 per hour)	$36

During the month of April, the company manufactures 230 units and incurs the following actual costs.

Direct materials purchased and used (1,900 pounds)	$4,940
Direct labor (700 hours)	$8,120

Instructions

Compute the total, price, and quantity variances for materials and labor.

Compute the materials and labor variances and list reasons for unfavorable variances.
(SO 4)

E11-8 The following direct materials and direct labor data pertain to the operations of Solario Manufacturing Company for the month of August.

Costs		Quantities	
Actual labor rate	$13 per hour	Actual hours incurred and used	4,200 hours
Actual materials price	$128 per ton	Actual quantity of materials purchased and used	1,225 tons
Standard labor rate	$12 per hour	Standard hours used	4,300 hours
Standard materials price	$130 per ton	Standard quantity of materials used	1,200 tons

Instructions

(a) Compute the total, price, and quantity variances for materials and labor.

(b) Provide two possible explanations for each of the unfavorable variances calculated above, and suggest where responsibility for the unfavorable result might be placed.

E11-9 During March 2008, Hinton Tool & Die Company worked on four jobs. A review of direct labor costs reveals the following summary data.

Prepare a variance report for direct labor.

(SO 4, 6)

Job Number	Actual Hours	Actual Costs	Standard Hours	Standard Costs	Total Variance
A257	220	$ 4,400	225	$4,500	$ 100 F
A258	450	9,900	430	8,600	1,300 U
A259	300	6,150	300	6,000	150 U
A260	115	2,070	110	2,200	130 F
Total variance					$1,220 U

Analysis reveals that Job A257 was a repeat job. Job A258 was a rush order that required overtime work at premium rates of pay. Job A259 required a more experienced replacement worker on one shift. Work on Job A260 was done for one day by a new trainee when a regular worker was absent.

Instructions

Prepare a report for the plant supervisor on direct labor cost variances for March. The report should have columns for (1) Job No., (2) Actual Hours, (3) Standard Hours, (4) Quantity Variance, (5) Actual Rate, (6) Standard Rate, (7) Price Variance, and (8) Explanation.

E11-10 Manufacturing overhead data for the production of Product H by Norland Company are as follows.

Compute overhead variance.

(SO 5)

Overhead incurred for 52,000 actual direct labor hours worked	$213,000
Overhead rate (variable $3; fixed $1) at normal capacity of 54,000 direct labor hours	$4
Standard hours allowed for work done	51,000

Instructions

Compute the total overhead variance.

E11-11 Jay Levitt Company produces one product, a putter called GO-Putter. Levitt uses a standard cost system and determines that it should take one hour of direct labor to produce one GO-Putter. The normal production capacity for this putter is 100,000 units per year. The total budgeted overhead at normal capacity is $800,000 comprised of $200,000 of variable costs and $600,000 of fixed costs. Levitt applies overhead on the basis of direct labor hours.

Compute overhead variances.

(SO 5)

During the current year, Levitt produced 90,000 putters, worked 94,000 direct labor hours, and incurred variable overhead costs of $186,000 and fixed overhead costs of $600,000.

Instructions

(a) Compute the predetermined variable overhead rate and the predetermined fixed overhead rate.

(b) Compute the applied overhead rate for Levitt for the year.

(c) Compute the total overhead variance.

E11-12 Buerhle Company purchased (at a cost of $10,900) and used 2,300 pounds of materials during May. Buerhle's standard cost of materials per unit produced is based on 2 pounds per unit at a cost $5 per pound. Production in May was 1,070 units.

Compute variances for materials.

(SO 4)

Instructions

(a) Compute the total, price, and quantity variances for materials.

(b) Assume Buerhle also had an unfavorable labor quantity variance. What is a possible scenario that would provide one cause for the variances computed in (a) and the unfavorable labor quantity variance?

Prepare a variance report.
(SO 4, 6)

E11-13 Imperial Landscaping plants grass seed as the basic landscaping for business campuses. During a recent month the company worked on three projects (Ames, Korman, and Stilles). The company is interested in controlling the material costs, namely the grass seed, for these plantings projects.

In order to provide management with useful cost control information, the company uses standard costs and prepares monthly variance reports. Analysis reveals that the purchasing agent mistakenly purchased poor-quality seed for the Ames project. The Korman project, however, received higher-than-standard-quality seed that was on sale. The Stilles project received standard-quality seed; however, the price had increased and a new employee was used to spread the seed.

Shown below are quantity and cost data for each project.

	Actual		Standard		Total
Project	**Quantity**	**Costs**	**Quantity**	**Costs**	**Variance**
Ames	500 lbs.	$1,175	460 lbs.	$1,150	$ 25 U
Korman	400	960	410	1,025	65 F
Stilles	500	1,300	480	1,200	100 U
Total variance					$ 60 U

Instructions

(a) Prepare a variance report for the purchasing department with the following columns: (1) Project, (2) Actual pounds purchased, (3) Actual price, (4) Standard price, (5) Price variance, and (6) Explanation.

(b) Prepare a variance report for the production department with the following columns: (1) Project, (2) Actual pounds, (3) Standard pounds, (4) Standard price, (5) Quantity variance, and (6) Explanation.

Complete variance report.
(SO 6)

E11-14 Archangel Corporation prepared the following variance report.

ARCHANGEL CORPORATION
Variance Report—Purchasing Department
for Week Ended January 9, 2009

Type of Materials	Quantity Purchased	Actual Price	Standard Price	Price Variance	Explanation
Rogue11	? lbs.	$5.20	$5.00	$5,200 ?	Price increase
Storm17	7,000 oz.	?	3.25	1,050 U	Rush order
Beast29	22,000 units	0.45	?	440 F	Bought larger quantity

Instructions

Fill in the appropriate amounts or letters for the question marks in the report.

Prepare income statement for management.
(SO 7)

E11-15 Cepeda Company uses a standard cost accounting system. During January, the company reported the following manufacturing variances.

Materials price variance	$1,250 U	Labor quantity variance	$ 725 U
Materials quantity variance	700 F	Overhead variance	800 U
Labor price variance	525 U		

In addition, 8,000 units of product were sold at $8.00 per unit. Each unit sold had a standard cost of $6.00. Selling and administrative expenses were $6,000 for the month.

Instructions

Prepare an income statement for management for the month ended January 31, 2008.

Identify performance evaluation terminology.
(SO 3, 8)

E11-16 The following is a list of terms related to performance evaluation.

(1) Balanced scorecard
(2) Variance
(3) Learning and growth perspective
(4) Nonfinancial measures
(5) Customer perspective
(6) Internal process perspective
(7) Ideal standards
(8) Normal standards

Instructions
Match each of the following descriptions with one of the terms above.

(a) The difference between total actual costs and total standard costs.
(b) An efficient level of performance that is attainable under expected operating conditions.
(c) An approach that incorporates financial and nonfinancial measures in an integrated system that links performance measurement and a company's strategic goals.
(d) A viewpoint employed in the balanced scorecard to evaluate how well a company develops and retains its employees.
(e) An evaluation tool that is not based on dollars.
(f) A viewpoint employed in the balanced scorecard to evaluate the company from the perspective of those people who buy and use its products or services.
(g) An optimum level of performance under perfect operating conditions.
(h) A viewpoint employed in the balanced scorecard to evaluate the efficiency and effectiveness of the company's value chain.

Journalize entries in a standard cost accounting system.
(SO 9)

***E11-17** Peyton Company installed a standard cost system on January 1. Selected transactions for the month of January are as follows.

1. Purchased 18,000 units of raw materials on account at a cost of $4.50 per unit. Standard cost was $4.30 per unit.
2. Issued 18,000 units of raw materials for jobs that required 17,600 standard units of raw materials.
3. Incurred 15,200 actual hours of direct labor at an actual rate of $4.80 per hour. The standard rate is $5.50 per hour. (Credit Wages Payable)
4. Performed 15,200 hours of direct labor on jobs when standard hours were 15,400.
5. Applied overhead to jobs at the rate of 100% of direct labor cost for standard hours allowed.

Instructions
Journalize the January transactions.

Answer questions concerning missing entries and balances.
(SO 4, 5, 9)

***E11-18** Cesar Company uses a standard cost accounting system. Some of the ledger accounts have been destroyed in a fire. The controller asks your help in reconstructing some missing entries and balances.

Instructions
Answer the following questions.

(a) Materials Price Variance shows a $2,000 favorable balance. Accounts Payable shows $128,000 of raw materials purchases. What was the amount debited to Raw Materials Inventory for raw materials purchased?
(b) Materials Quantity Variance shows a $3,000 unfavorable balance. Raw Materials Inventory shows a zero balance. What was the amount debited to Work in Process Inventory for direct materials used?
(c) Labor Price Variance shows a $1,500 unfavorable balance. Factory Labor shows a debit of $140,000 for wages incurred. What was the amount credited to Wages Payable?
(d) Factory Labor shows a credit of $140,000 for direct labor used. Labor Quantity Variance shows a $900 unfavorable balance. What was the amount debited to Work in Process for direct labor used?
(e) Overhead applied to Work in Process totaled $165,000. If the total overhead variance was $1,200 unfavorable, what was the amount of overhead costs debited to Manufacturing Overhead?

Journalize entries for materials and labor variances.
(SO 9)

***E11-19** Data for Haslett Inc. are given in E11-7.

Instructions
Journalize the entries to record the materials and labor variances.

Compute manufacturing overhead variances and interpret findings.
(SO 10)

***E11-20** The following information was taken from the annual manufacturing overhead cost budget of Granada Company.

Variable manufacturing overhead costs	$33,000
Fixed manufacturing overhead costs	$19,800
Normal production level in labor hours	16,500
Normal production level in units	4,125
Standard labor hours per unit	4

During the year, 4,000 units were produced, 16,100 hours were worked, and the actual manufacturing overhead was $54,000. Actual fixed manufacturing overhead costs equaled budgeted fixed manufacturing overhead costs. Overhead is applied on the basis of direct labor hours.

Instructions

(a) Compute the total, fixed, and variable predetermined manufacturing overhead rates.
(b) Compute the total, controllable, and volume overhead variances.
(c) Briefly interpret the overhead controllable and volume variances computed in (b).

Compute overhead variances.
(SO 10)

***E11-21** The loan department of Local Bank uses standard costs to determine the overhead cost of processing loan applications. During the current month a fire occurred, and the accounting records for the department were mostly destroyed. The following data were salvaged from the ashes.

Standard variable overhead rate per hour	$9
Standard hours per application	2
Standard hours allowed	2,000
Standard fixed overhead rate per hour	$6
Actual fixed overhead cost	$13,200
Variable overhead budget based on standard hours allowed	$18,000
Fixed overhead budget	$13,200
Overhead controllable variance	$ 1,500 U

Instructions

(a) Determine the following.
  (1) Total actual overhead cost.
  (2) Actual variable overhead cost.
  (3) Variable overhead cost applied.
  (4) Fixed overhead cost applied.
  (5) Overhead volume variance.
(b) Determine how many loans were processed.

Compute variances.
(SO 10)

***E11-22** Jackson Company's overhead rate was based on estimates of $200,000 for overhead costs and 20,000 direct labor hours. Jackson's standards allow 2 hours of direct labor per unit produced. Production in May was 900 units, and actual overhead incurred in May was $18,800. The overhead budgeted for 1,800 standard direct labor hours is $17,600 ($5,000 fixed and $12,600 variable).

Instructions

(a) Compute the total, controllable, and volume variances for overhead.
(b) What are possible causes of the variances computed in part (a)?

EXERCISES: SET B

Visit the book's website at **www.wiley.com/college/weygandt**, and choose the Student Companion site, to access Exercise Set B.

PROBLEMS: SET A

Compute variances.
(SO 4, 5)

P11-1A Putnam Corporation manufactures a single product. The standard cost per unit of product is shown below.

Direct materials—1 pound plastic at $7.00 per pound	$ 7.00
Direct labor—1.5 hours at $12.00 per hour	18.00
Variable manufacturing overhead	11.25
Fixed manufacturing overhead	3.75
Total standard cost per unit	$40.00

The predetermined manufacturing overhead rate is $10 per direct labor hour ($15.00 ÷ 1.5). It was computed from a master manufacturing overhead budget based on normal production of 7,500 direct labor hours (5,000 units) for the month. The master budget showed total variable costs of $56,250 ($7.50 per hour) and total fixed overhead costs of $18,750 ($2.50 per hour). Actual costs for October in producing 4,900 units were as follows.

Direct materials (5,100 pounds)	$ 37,230
Direct labor (7,000 hours)	87,500
Variable overhead	56,170
Fixed overhead	19,680
Total manufacturing costs	$200,580

The purchasing department buys the quantities of raw materials that are expected to be used in production each month. Raw materials inventories, therefore, can be ignored.

Instructions

(a) Compute all of the materials and labor variances.

(a) MPV $1,530 U

(b) Compute the total overhead variance.

Compute variances, and prepare income statement.

(SO 4, 5, 7)

P11-2A Dinkel Manufacturing Corporation accumulates the following data relative to jobs started and finished during the month of June 2008.

Costs and Production Data	Actual	Standard
Raw materials unit cost	$2.25	$2.00
Raw materials units used	10,600	10,000
Direct labor payroll	$122,400	$120,000
Direct labor hours worked	14,400	15,000
Manufacturing overhead incurred	$184,500	
Manufacturing overhead applied		$189,000
Machine hours expected to be used at normal capacity		42,500
Budgeted fixed overhead for June		$51,000
Variable overhead rate per hour		$3.00
Fixed overhead rate per hour		$1.20

Overhead is applied on the basis of standard machine hours. Three hours of machine time are required for each direct labor hour. The jobs were sold for $400,000. Selling and administrative expenses were $40,000. Assume that the amount of raw materials purchased equaled the amount used.

Instructions

(a) Compute all of the variances for (1) direct materials and (2) direct labor.

(a) LQV $4,800 F

(b) Compute the total overhead variance.

(c) Prepare an income statement for management. Ignore income taxes.

Compute and identify significant variances.

(SO 4, 5, 6)

P11-3A Rapache Clothiers is a small company that manufactures tall-men's suits. The company has used a standard cost accounting system. In May 2008, 11,200 suits were produced. The following standard and actual cost data applied to the month of May when normal capacity was 14,000 direct labor hours. All materials purchased were used.

Cost Element	Standard (per unit)	Actual
Direct materials	8 yards at $4.30 per yard	$371,050 for 90,500 yards ($4.10 per yard)
Direct labor	1.2 hours at $13.50 per hour	$201,630 for 14,300 hours ($14.10 per hour)
Overhead	1.2 hours at $6.00 per hour (fixed $3.50; variable $2.50)	$49,000 fixed overhead $37,000 variable overhead

Overhead is applied on the basis of direct labor hours. At normal capacity, budgeted fixed overhead costs were $49,000, and budgeted variable overhead was $35,000.

Instructions

(a) Compute the total, price, and quantity variances for (1) materials and (2) labor.

(a) MPV $18,100 F

(b) Compute the total overhead variance.

(c) Which of the materials and labor variances should be investigated if management considers a variance of more than 4% from standard to be significant?

Answer questions about variances.

(SO 4, 5)

P11-4A Dorantes Manufacturing Company uses a standard cost accounting system. In 2008, the company produced 28,000 units. Each unit took several pounds of direct materials and 1½ standard hours of direct labor at a standard hourly rate of $12.00. Normal capacity was 50,000 direct labor hours. During the year, 131,000 pounds of raw materials were purchased at $0.92 per pound. All materials purchased were used during the year.

Instructions

(a) If the materials price variance was $2,620 favorable, what was the standard materials price per pound?

(b) If the materials quantity variance was $4,700 unfavorable, what was the standard materials quantity per unit?

(c) What were the standard hours allowed for the units produced?

(d) If the labor quantity variance was $7,200 unfavorable, what were the actual direct labor hours worked?

(e) If the labor price variance was $10,650 favorable, what was the actual rate per hour?

(f) If total budgeted manufacturing overhead was $350,000 at normal capacity, what was the predetermined overhead rate?

(g) What was the standard cost per unit of product?

(h) How much overhead was applied to production during the year?

(i) Using one or more answers above, what were the total costs assigned to work in process?

Compute variances, prepare an income statement, and explain unfavorable variances.

(SO 4, 5, 7)

P11-5A Farm Labs, Inc. provides mad cow disease testing for both state and federal governmental agricultural agencies. Because the company's customers are governmental agencies, prices are strictly regulated. Therefore, Farm Labs must constantly monitor and control its testing costs. Shown below are the standard costs for a typical test.

Direct materials (2 test tubes @ $1.50 per tube)	$ 3
Direct labor (1 hour @ $25 per hour)	25
Variable overhead (1 hour @ $5 per hour)	5
Fixed overhead (1 hour @ $10 per hour)	10
Total standard cost per test	$43

The lab does not maintain an inventory of test tubes. Therefore, the tubes purchased each month are used that month. Actual activity for the month of November 2008, when 1,500 tests were conducted, resulted in the following:

Direct materials (3,050 test tubes)	$ 4,270
Direct labor (1,600 hours)	36,800
Variable overhead	7,400
Fixed overhead	14,000

Monthly budgeted fixed overhead is $14,000. Revenues for the month were $75,000, and selling and administrative expenses were $4,000.

Instructions

(a) LQV $2,500 U

(a) Compute the price and quantity variances for direct materials and direct labor.

(b) Compute the total overhead variance.

(c) Prepare an income statement for management.

(d) Provide possible explanations for each unfavorable variance.

Journalize and post standard cost entries, and prepare income statement.

(SO 4, 5, 7, 9)

***P11-6A** Adcock Corporation uses standard costs with its job order cost accounting system. In January, an order (Job No. 12) for 1,900 units of Product B was received. The standard cost of one unit of Product B is as follows.

Direct materials	3 pounds at $1.00 per pound	$ 3.00
Direct labor	1 hour at $8.00 per hour	8.00
Overhead	2 hours (variable $4.00 per machine hour; fixed $2.25 per machine hour)	12.50
Standard cost per unit		$23.50

Normal capacity for the month was 4,200 machine hours. During January, the following transactions applicable to Job No. 12 occurred.

1. Purchased 6,250 pounds of raw materials on account at $1.06 per pound.
2. Requisitioned 6,250 pounds of raw materials for Job No. 12.
3. Incurred 2,100 hours of direct labor at a rate of $7.75 per hour.
4. Worked 2,100 hours of direct labor on Job No. 12.
5. Incurred manufacturing overhead on account $25,800.
6. Applied overhead to Job No. 12 on basis of standard machine hours allowed.
7. Completed Job No. 12.
8. Billed customer for Job No. 12 at a selling price of $70,000.
9. Incurred selling and administrative expenses on account $2,000.

Instructions

(a) Journalize the transactions.
(b) Post to the job order cost accounts.
(c) Prepare the entry to recognize the total overhead variance.
(d) Prepare the January 2008 income statement for management.

Compute overhead controllable and volume variances.
(SO 10)

***P11-7A** Using the information in P11-1A, compute the overhead controllable variance and the overhead volume variance.

Compute overhead controllable and volume variances.
(SO 10)

***P11-8A** Using the information in P11-2A, compute the overhead controllable variance and the overhead volume variance.

Compute overhead controllable and volume variances.
(SO 10)

***P11-9A** Using the information in P11-3A, compute the overhead controllable variance and the overhead volume variance.

Compute overhead controllable and volume variances.
(SO 10)

***P11-10A** Using the information in P11-5A, compute the overhead controllable variance and the overhead volume variance.

PROBLEMS: SET B

Compute variances.
(SO 4, 5)

P11-1B Loper Corporation manufactures a single product. The standard cost per unit of product is as follows.

Direct materials—2 pounds of plastic at $5 per pound	$10
Direct labor—2 hours at $12 per hour	24
Variable manufacturing overhead	12
Fixed manufacturing overhead	6
Total standard cost per unit	$52

The master manufacturing overhead budget for the month based on normal productive capacity of 15,000 direct labor hours (7,500 units) shows total variable costs of $90,000 ($6 per labor hour) and total fixed costs of $45,000 ($3 per labor hour). Normal productive capacity is 15,000 direct labor hours. Overhead is applied on the basis of direct labor hours. Actual costs for November in producing 7,400 units were as follows.

Direct materials (15,000 pounds)	$ 73,500
Direct labor (14,900 hours)	181,780
Variable overhead	88,990
Fixed overhead	44,000
Total manufacturing costs	$388,270

The purchasing department normally buys the quantities of raw materials that are expected to be used in production each month. Raw materials inventories, therefore, can be ignored.

Instructions

(a) Compute all of the materials and labor variances.
(b) Compute the total overhead variance.

(a) MQV $1,000 U

Compute variances, and prepare income statement.
(SO 4, 5, 7)

P11-2B Orlanda Manufacturing Company uses a standard cost accounting system to account for the manufacture of exhaust fans. In July 2008, it accumulates the following data relative to 1,500 units started and finished.

Cost and Production Data	Actual	Standard
Raw materials		
Units purchased	17,500	
Units used	17,500	18,000
Unit cost	$3.40	$3.00
Direct labor		
Hours worked	2,900	3,000
Hourly rate	$11.80	$12.50
Manufacturing overhead		
Incurred	$87,500	
Applied		$93,000

Manufacturing overhead was applied on the basis of direct labor hours. Normal capacity for the month was 2,800 direct labor hours. At normal capacity, budgeted overhead costs were $20 per labor hour variable and $11 per labor hour fixed. Total budgeted fixed overhead costs were $30,800.

Jobs finished during the month were sold for $240,000. Selling and administrative expenses were $25,000.

Instructions

(a) LQV $1,250 F

(a) Compute all of the variances for (1) direct materials and (2) direct labor.
(b) Compute the total overhead variance.
(c) Prepare an income statement for management showing variances. Ignore income taxes.

Compute and identify significant variances.
(SO 4, 5, 6)

P11-3B Goltra Clothiers manufactures women's business suits. The company uses a standard cost accounting system. In March 2008, 11,800 suits were made. The following standard and actual cost data applied to the month of March when normal capacity was 15,000 direct labor hours. All materials purchased were used in production.

Cost Element	Standard (per unit)	Actual
Direct materials	5 yards at $6.80 per yard	$410,400 for 57,000 yards ($7.20 per yard)
Direct labor	1.0 hours at $11.50 per hour	$125,440 for 11,200 hours ($11.20 per hour)
Overhead	1.0 hours at $9.30 per hour (fixed $6.30; variable $3.00)	$90,000 fixed overhead $37,000 variable overhead

Overhead is applied on the basis of direct labor hours. At normal capacity, budgeted fixed overhead costs were $94,500, and budgeted variable overhead costs were $45,000.

Instructions

(a) MPV $22,800 U

(a) Compute the total, price, and quantity variances for (1) materials and (2) labor.
(b) Compute the total overhead variance.
(c) Which of the materials and labor variances should be investigated if management considers a variance of more than 5% from standard to be significant? Discuss the potential causes of this variance.

Answer questions about variances.
(SO 4, 5)

P11-4B Heath Manufacturing Company uses a standard cost accounting system. In 2008, the company produced 36,000 units. Each unit took several pounds of direct materials and $1\frac{1}{3}$ standard hours of direct labor at a standard hourly rate of $12.00. Normal capacity was 42,000 direct labor hours. During the year, 142,000 pounds of raw materials were purchased at $0.90 per pound. All materials purchased were used during the year.

Instructions

(a) If the materials price variance was $7,100 unfavorable, what was the standard materials price per pound?
(b) If the materials quantity variance was $4,760 favorable, what was the standard materials quantity per unit?
(c) What were the standard hours allowed for the units produced?
(d) If the labor quantity variance was $8,400 unfavorable, what were the actual direct labor hours worked?

(e) If the labor price variance was $9,740 favorable, what was the actual rate per hour?
(f) If total budgeted manufacturing overhead was $327,600 at normal capacity, what was the predetermined overhead rate per direct labor hour?
(g) What was the standard cost per unit of product?
(h) How much overhead was applied to production during the year?
(i) Using selected answers above, what were the total costs assigned to work in process?

P11-5B Hi-Tek Labs performs steroid testing services to high schools, colleges, and universities. Because the company deals solely with educational institutions, the price of each test is strictly regulated. Therefore, the costs incurred must be carefully monitored and controlled. Shown below are the standard costs for a typical test.

Compute variances, prepare an income statement, and explain unfavorable variances.

(SO 4, 5, 7)

Direct materials (1 petrie dish @ $2 per dish)	$ 2.00
Direct labor (0.5 hours @ $20 per hour)	10.00
Variable overhead (0.5 hours @ $8 per hour)	4.00
Fixed overhead (0.5 hours @ $3 per hour)	1.50
Total standard cost per test	$17.50

The lab does not maintain an inventory of petrie dishes. Therefore, the dishes purchased each month are used that month. Actual activity for the month of May 2008, when 2,000 tests were conducted, resulted in the following.

Direct materials (2,020 dishes)	$ 4,242
Direct labor (995 hours)	20,895
Variable overhead	8,100
Fixed overhead	3,400

Monthly budgeted fixed overhead is $3,600. Revenues for the month were $45,000, and selling and administrative expenses were $2,000.

Instructions

(a) Compute the price and quantity variances for direct materials and direct labor.
(b) Compute the total overhead variance.
(c) Prepare an income statement for management.
(d) Provide possible explanations for each unfavorable variance.

(a) LQV $100 F

***P11-6B** Gibsen Manufacturing Company uses standard costs with its job order cost accounting system. In January, an order (Job No. 84) was received for 4,100 units of Product D. The standard cost of 1 unit of Product D is as follows.

Journalize and post standard cost entries, and prepare income statement.

(SO 4, 5, 7, 9)

Direct materials—1.4 pounds at $4.00 per pound	$ 5.60
Direct labor—1 hour at $9.00 per hour	9.00
Overhead—1 hour (variable $7.40; fixed $10.00)	17.40
Standard cost per unit	$32.00

Overhead is applied on the basis of direct labor hours. Normal capacity for the month of January was 4,500 direct labor hours. During January, the following transactions applicable to Job No. 84 occurred.

1. Purchased 6,100 pounds of raw materials on account at $3.60 per pound.
2. Requisitioned 6,100 pounds of raw materials for production.
3. Incurred 3,800 hours of direct labor at $9.25 per hour.
4. Worked 3,800 hours of direct labor on Job No. 84.
5. Incurred $73,650 of manufacturing overhead on account.
6. Applied overhead to Job No. 84 on the basis of direct labor hours.
7. Transferred Job No. 84 to finished goods.
8. Billed customer for Job No. 84 at a selling price of $250,000.
9. Incurred selling and administrative expenses on account $61,000.

Instructions

(a) Journalize the transactions.
(b) Post to the job order cost accounts.
(c) Prepare the entry to recognize the total overhead variance.
(d) Prepare the income statement for management for January 2008.

Compute overhead controllable and volume variances.
(SO 10)

***P11-7B** Using the information in P11-1B, compute the overhead controllable variance and the overhead volume variance.

Compute overhead controllable and volume variances.
(SO 10)

***P11-8B** Using the information in P11-2B, compute the overhead controllable variance and the overhead volume variance.

Compute overhead controllable and volume variances.
(SO 10)

***P11-9B** Using the information in P11-3B, compute the overhead controllable variance and the overhead volume variance.

Compute overhead controllable and volume variances.
(SO 10)

***P11-10B** Using the information in P11-5B, compute the overhead controllable variance and the overhead volume variance.

PROBLEMS: SET C

Visit the book's website at **www.wiley.com/college/weygandt**, and choose the Student Companion site, to access Problem Set C.

WATERWAYS CONTINUING PROBLEM

(This is a continuation of the Waterways Problem from Chapters 1 through 10.)

WCP11 Waterways Corporation uses very stringent standard costs in evaluating its manufacturing efficiency. These standards are not "ideal" at this point, but the management is working toward that as a goal. This problem asks you to calculate and evaluate the company's variances.

Go to the book's website,
www.wiley.com/college/weygandt,
to find the remainder of this problem.

BROADENING YOUR PERSPECTIVE

DECISION MAKING ACROSS THE ORGANIZATION

BYP11-1 Colaw Professionals, a management consulting firm, specializes in strategic planning for financial institutions. Ken Comer and Mary Linden, partners in the firm, are assembling a new strategic planning model for use by clients. The model is designed for use on most personal computers and replaces a rather lengthy manual model currently marketed by the firm. To market the new model Ken and Mary will need to provide clients with an estimate of the number of labor hours and computer time needed to operate the model. The model is currently being test marketed at five small financial institutions. These financial institutions are listed below, along with the number of combined computer/labor hours used by each institution to run the model one time.

Financial Institutions	Computer/Labor Hours Required
Midland National	25
First State	45
Financial Federal	40
Pacific America	30
Lakeview National	30
Total	170
Average	34

Any company that purchases the new model will need to purchase user manuals for the system. User manuals will be sold to clients in cases of 20, at a cost of $300 per case. One manual must be used each time the model is run because each manual includes a nonreusable computer-accessed password for operating the system. Also required are specialized computer forms that are sold only by Colaw. The specialized forms are sold in packages of 250, at a cost of $50 per package. One application of the model requires the use of 50 forms. This amount includes two forms that are generally wasted in each application due to printer alignment errors. The overall cost of the strategic planning model to clients is $12,000. Most clients will use the model four times annually.

Colaw must provide its clients with estimates of ongoing costs incurred in operating the new planning model, and would like to do so in the form of standard costs.

Instructions

With the class divided into groups, answer the following.

(a) What factors should be considered in setting a standard for computer/labor hours?

(b) What alternatives for setting a standard for computer/labor hours might be used?

(c) What standard for computer/labor hours would you select? Justify your answer.

(d) Determine the standard materials cost associated with the user manuals and computer forms for each application of the strategic planning model.

MANAGERIAL ANALYSIS

***BYP11-2** Ed Widner and Associates is a medium-sized company located near a large metropolitan area in the Midwest. The company manufactures cabinets of mahogany, oak, and other fine woods for use in expensive homes, restaurants, and hotels. Although some of the work is custom, many of the cabinets are a standard size.

One such non-custom model is called Luxury Base Frame. Normal production is 1,000 units. Each unit has a direct labor hour standard of 5 hours. Overhead is applied to production based on standard direct labor hours. During the most recent month, only 900 units were produced; 4,500 direct labor hours were allowed for standard production, but only 4,000 hours were used. Standard and actual overhead costs were as follows.

	Standard (1,000 units)	Actual (900 units)
Indirect materials	$ 12,000	$ 12,300
Indirect labor	43,000	51,000
(Fixed) Manufacturing supervisors salaries	22,000	22,000
(Fixed) Manufacturing office employees salaries	13,000	11,500
(Fixed) Engineering costs	27,000	25,000
Computer costs	10,000	10,000
Electricity	2,500	2,500
(Fixed) Manufacturing building depreciation	8,000	8,000
(Fixed) Machinery depreciation	3,000	3,000
(Fixed) Trucks and forklift depreciation	1,500	1,500
Small tools	700	1,400
(Fixed) Insurance	500	500
(Fixed) Property taxes	300	300
Total	$143,500	$149,000

Instructions

(a) Determine the overhead application rate.

(b) Determine how much overhead was applied to production.

(c) Calculate the total overhead variance, controllable variance, and volume variance.

(d) Decide which overhead variances should be investigated.

(e) Discuss causes of the overhead variances. What can management do to improve its performance next month?

REAL-WORLD FOCUS

BYP11-3 Glassmaster Co. is organized as two divisions and one subsidiary. One division focuses on the manufacture of filaments such as fishing line and sewing thread; the other division manufactures antennas and specialty fiberglass products. Its subsidiary manufactures flexible steel wire controls and molded control panels.

The annual report of Glassmaster provides the following information.

> **GLASSMASTER COMPANY**
> Management Discussion
>
> Gross profit margins for the year improved to 20.9% of sales compared to last year's 18.5%. All operations reported improved margins due in large part to improved operating efficiencies as a result of cost reduction measures implemented during the second and third quarters of the fiscal year and increased manufacturing throughout due to higher unit volume sales. Contributing to the improved margins was a favorable materials price variance due to competitive pricing by suppliers as a result of soft demand for petrochemical-based products. This favorable variance is temporary and will begin to reverse itself as stronger worldwide demand for commodity products improves in tandem with the economy. Partially offsetting these positive effects on profit margins were competitive pressures on sales prices of certain product lines. The company responded with pricing strategies designed to maintain and/or increase market share.

Instructions

(a) Is it apparent from the information whether Glassmaster utilizes standard costs?

(b) Do you think the price variance experienced should lead to changes in standard costs for the next fiscal year?

EXPLORING THE WEB

BYP11-4 The Balanced Scorecard Institute *(www.balancedscorecard.org)* is a great resource for information about implementing the balanced scorecard. One item of interest provided at its website is an example of a balanced scorecard for a regional airline.

Address: http://www.balancedscorecard.org/files/Regional_Airline.pdf, or go to **www.wiley.com/college/weygandt**

Instructions

Go to the address above and answer the following questions.

(a) What are the objectives identified for the airline for each perspective?

(b) What measures are used for the objectives in the customer perspective?

(c) What initiatives are planned to achieve the objective in the learning perspective?

COMMUNICATION ACTIVITY

BYP11-5 The setting of standards is critical to the effective use of standards in evaluating performance.

Instructions

Explain the following in a memo to your instructor.

(a) The comparative advantages and disadvantages of ideal versus normal standards.

(b) The factors that should be included in setting the price and quantity standards for direct materials, direct labor, and manufacturing overhead.

ETHICS CASE

BYP11-6 At Camden Manufacturing Company, production workers in the Painting Department are paid on the basis of productivity. The labor time standard for a unit of production is established through periodic time studies conducted by the Lowery Management Department. In a time study, the actual time required to complete a specific task by a worker is observed. Allowances are then made for preparation time, rest periods, and clean-up time. Ron Orlano is one of several veterans in the Painting Department.

Ron is informed by Lowery Management that he will be used in the time study for the painting of a new product. The findings will be the basis for establishing the labor time standard for the next 6 months. During the test, Ron deliberately slows his normal work pace in an effort to obtain a labor time standard that will be easy to meet. Because it is a new product, the Lowery Management representative who conducted the test is unaware that Ron did not give the test his best effort.

Instructions

(a) Who was benefited and who was harmed by Ron's actions?
(b) Was Ron ethical in the way he performed the time study test?
(c) What measure(s) might the company take to obtain valid data for setting the labor time standard?

"ALL ABOUT YOU" ACTIVITY

BYP11-7 From the time you first entered school many years ago, instructors have been measuring and evaluating you by imposing standards. In addition, many of you will pursue professions that administer professional examinations to attain recognized certification. Recently a federal commission presented proposals suggesting all public colleges and universities should require standardized tests to measure their students' learning.

Instructions

Read the following article at **www.signonsandiego.com/uniontrib/20060811/news_1n11colleges.html**, and answer the following questions.

(a) What areas of concern did the panel's recommendations address?
(b) What are possible advantages of standard testing?
(c) What are possible disadvantages of standard testing?
(d) Would you be in favor of standardized tests?

Answers to Insight and Accounting Across the Organization Questions

How Do Standards Help a Business?, p. 472

Q: How will the creation of such standards help a business or organization?

A: *A business or organization may use the data to compare its performance relative to others with regard to common practices such as processing a purchase order or filling a sales order. Armed with this information, an organization can determine which areas to focus on with improvement campaigns.*

How Can We Make Susan's Chili Profitable?, p. 475

Q: How might management use this raw material cost information?

A: *Management might decide to increase the price of its chili. Or it might revise its recipes to use cheaper ingredients. Or it might eliminate some products until ingredients are available at costs closer to standard.*

It May Be Time to Fly United Again, p. 487

Q: Which of the perspectives of a balanced scorecard were the focus of United's CEO?

A: *Improving on-time flight departures is an objective within the internal process perspective. Customer intent to fly United again is an objective within the customer perspective.*

Authors' Comments on *All About You:* Balancing Costs and Quality in Health Care, p. 488

The practice of medicine holds an unusual place in society. On the one hand, it provides a critical, life-sustaining service. We expect and demand the highest-quality service. We measure its success in terms of health improvement and lives saved. On the other hand, it is a business, and like other businesses, it must operate profitably. Some health-care providers characterize this delicate balance as "The Business of Caring."

How should we balance providing quality health care and reducing costs? In recent years, managerial accounting has played an important, although not always successful, role in this issue. As noted earlier, in the 1990s health-care providers made extensive use of managerial accounting techniques to reduce costs. By the end of that decade, a number of important studies suggested that the quality of health care had suffered as a result of concentrating too much on cost-controlling efforts and not enough on maintaining quality.

Today many health-care organizations are implementing balanced scorecards in an effort to balance the dual (and in some ways competing) goals of quality health care and reduced costs. For example, by providing incentives for preventive medicine, health-care providers can reduce costs and at the same time improve patient health. It is likely that, in order to provide health care to more Americans, we will have to reduce costs. It is hoped that successful implementation of balanced scorecard programs will result in reduced costs through increased efficiency, while increasing the quality of health care.

Answers to Self-Study Questions

1. c **2.** d **3.** b **4.** c **5.** b **6.** a **7.** d **8.** a **9.** b **10.** d ***11.** c

Remember to go back to the Navigator box on the chapter-opening page and check off your completed work.

Chapter 12

Planning for Capital Investments

STUDY OBJECTIVES

After studying this chapter, you should be able to:

1 Discuss capital budgeting evaluation, and explain inputs used in capital budgeting.
2 Describe the cash payback technique.
3 Explain the net present value method.
4 Identify the challenges presented by intangible benefits in capital budgeting.
5 Describe the profitability index.
6 Indicate the benefits of performing a post-audit.
7 Explain the internal rate of return method.
8 Describe the annual rate of return method.

The Navigator

- Scan **Study Objectives**
- Read **Feature Story**
- Read **Preview**
- Read text and answer **Before You Go On** p. 528 p. 538
- Work **Using the Decision Toolkit**
- Review **Summary of Study Objectives**
- Work **Demonstration Problem**
- Answer **Self-Study Questions**
- Complete **Assignments**

Feature Story

SOUP IS GOOD FOOD

When you hear the word *Campbell,* what is the first thing that comes to mind? Soup. Campbell *is* soup. It sells 38% of all the soup—including homemade—consumed in the United States.

But can a company survive on soup alone? In an effort to expand its operations and to lessen its reliance on soup, Campbell Soup Company (*www.campbellsoup.com*) in 1990 began searching for an additional line of business. Campbell's management believed it saw an opportunity in convenient meals that were low in fat, nutritionally rich, and had therapeutic value for heart patients and diabetics. This venture would require a huge investment—but the rewards were potentially tremendous.

The initial investment required building food labs, hiring nutritional scientists, researching prototype products, constructing new production facilities, and marketing the new products. Management predicted that with an initial investment of roughly $55 million, the company might generate sales of $200 million per year.

By 1994 the company had created 24 meals, and an extensive field-study revealed considerable health benefits from the products. Unfortunately, initial sales of the new product line, called Intelligent Quisine, were less than stellar. In 1997 Campbell hired a consulting firm to evaluate whether to continue the project. Product development of the new line was costing $20 million per year—a sum that some managers felt could be better spent developing new products in other divisions or expanding overseas operations. In 1998 Campbell discontinued the project.

Campbell was not giving up on growth, but simply had decided to refocus its efforts on soup. The company's annual report stated management's philosophy: "Soup will be our growth engine." Campbell has sold off many of its nonsoup businesses, and in a recent year introduced 20 new soup products.

Source: Vanessa O'Connell, "Food for Thought: How Campbell Saw a Break-through Menu Turn into Leftovers," *Wall Street Journal,* October 6, 1998.

The Navigator

Inside Chapter 12

Preview of Chapter 12

Companies like Campbell Soup must constantly determine how to invest their resources. Other examples: Hollywood studios recently built 25 new sound stage projects to allow for additional filming in future years. Starwood Hotels and Resorts Worldwide, Inc. committed a total of $1 billion to renovate its existing hotel properties, while at roughly the same time, the hotel industry canceled about $2 billion worth of *new* construction. Union Pacific Resources Group Inc. announced that it would cut its planned capital expenditures by 19% in order to use the funds to reduce its outstanding debt.

The process of making such capital expenditure decisions is referred to as **capital budgeting**. Capital budgeting involves choosing among various capital projects to find the one(s) that will maximize a company's return on its financial investment. The purpose of this chapter is to discuss the various techniques used to make effective capital budgeting decisions.

The content and organization of this chapter are as follows.

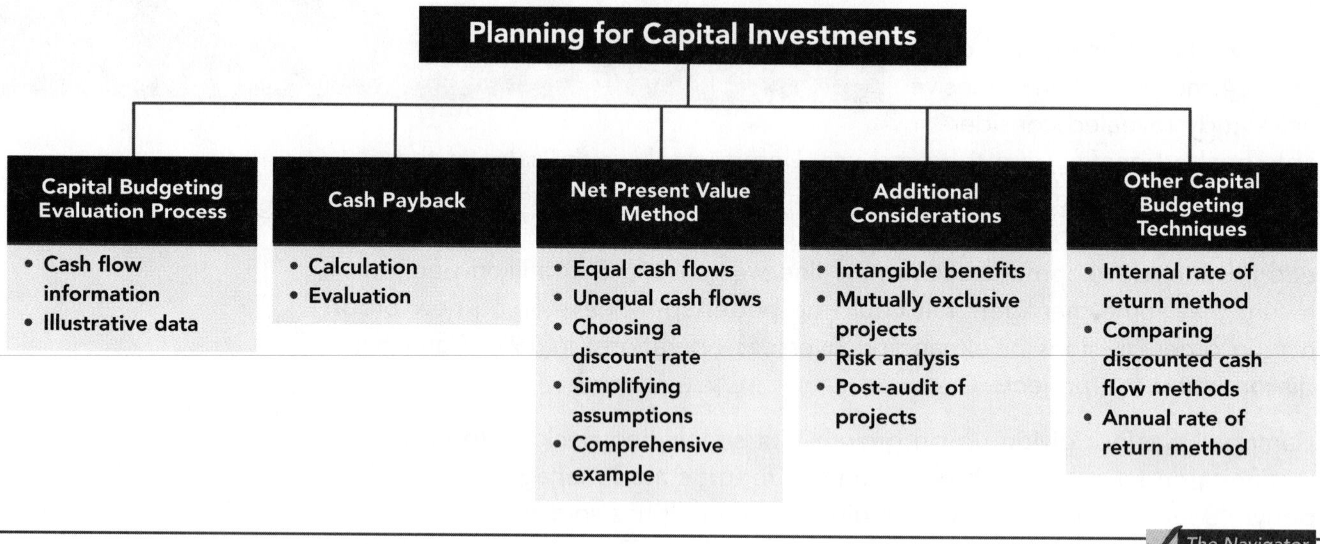

The Navigator

THE CAPITAL BUDGETING EVALUATION PROCESS

STUDY OBJECTIVE 1

Discuss capital budgeting evaluation, and explain inputs used in capital budgeting.

Many companies follow a carefully prescribed process in capital budgeting. At least once a year, top management requests proposals for projects from each department. A capital budgeting committee screens the proposals and submits its findings to the officers of the company. The officers, in turn, select the projects they believe to be most worthy of funding. They submit this list of projects to the board of directors. Ultimately, the directors approve the capital expenditure budget for the year. Illustration 12-1 (next page) shows this process.

The involvement of top management and the board of directors in the process demonstrates the importance of capital budgeting decisions. These decisions often have a significant impact on a company's future profitability. In fact, poor capital budgeting decisions can cost a lot of money, as the Campbell Soup Feature Story demonstrated. Such decisions have even led to the bankruptcy of some companies.

1. Project proposals are requested from departments, plants, and authorized personnel.

2. Proposals are screened by a capital budget committee.

3. Officers determine which projects are worthy of funding.

4. Board of directors approves capital budget.

Illustration 12-1
Corporate capital budget authorization process

MANAGEMENT INSIGHT

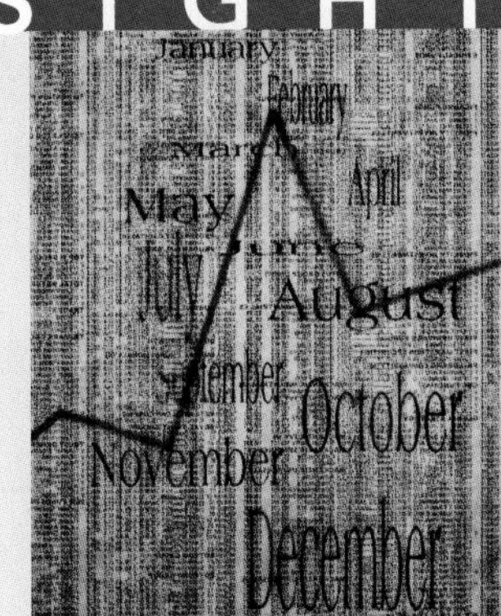

Investing for the Future

Monitoring capital expenditure amounts is one way to learn about a company's growth potential. Few companies can grow if they don't make significant capital investments. Here is a list of well-known companies and the amounts and types of their capital expenditures in a recent year.

Company Name	Amount	Type of Expenditures
Campbell Soup Company	$283 million	Acquisitions and plant expansions.
Barrick Gold Corporation	$228 million	Land acquisition and mine expansion.
Dell Computer Corporation	$329 million	Manufacturing and office facilities.
Sears, Roebuck and Co.	$925 million	New stores.
NIKE, Inc.	$186 million	Warehouse locations, management information systems.

Why is it important for top management to constantly monitor the nature, amount, and success of a company's capital expenditures?

Cash Flow Information

In this chapter we will look at several methods that help companies make effective capital budgeting decisions. Most of these methods employ **cash flow numbers**, rather than accrual accounting revenues and expenses. Remember from your financial accounting course that accrual accounting records *revenues* and *expenses*, rather than cash inflows and cash outflows. In fact, revenues and expenses measured during a period often differ significantly from their cash flow counterparts. Accrual accounting has advantages over cash accounting in many contexts. **For purposes of capital budgeting, though, estimated cash inflows and outflows are the preferred inputs**. Why? Because ultimately, the value of all financial investments is determined by the value of cash flows received and paid.

Sometimes cash flow information is not available. In this case, companies can make adjustments to accrual accounting numbers to estimate cash flow. Often, they estimate net annual cash flow by adding back depreciation expense to net income.

Depreciation expense is added back because it is an expense that does not require an outflow of cash. By adding back to net income the depreciation expense that was deducted in determining net income, companies determine net annual cash flow. Suppose, for example, that Reno Company's net income of $13,000 includes a charge for depreciation expense of $26,000. Its estimated net annual cash flow would be $39,000 ($13,000 + $26,000).

Illustration 12-2 lists some typical cash outflows and inflows related to equipment purchase and replacement.

Illustration 12-2
Typical cash flows relating to capital budgeting decisions

Cash Outflows

Initial investment
Repairs and maintenance
Increased operating costs
Overhaul of equipment

Cash Inflows

Sale of old equipment
Increased cash received from customers
Reduced cash outflows related to operating costs
Salvage value of equipment when project is complete

These cash flows are the inputs that are considered relevant in capital budgeting decisions.

The capital budgeting decision, under any technique, depends in part on a variety of considerations:

- **The availability of funds:** Does the company have unlimited funds, or will it have to ration capital investments?
- **Relationships among proposed projects:** Are proposed projects independent of each other, or does the acceptance or rejection of one depend on the acceptance or rejection of another?
- **The company's basic decision-making approach:** Does the company want to produce an accept-reject decision or a ranking of desirability among possible projects?
- **The risk associated with a particular project:** How certain are the projected returns? The certainty of estimates varies with such issues as market considerations or the length of time before returns are expected.

Illustrative Data

For our initial discussion of quantitative capital budgeting techniques, we will use a continuing example, which will enable us to compare the results of the various techniques. Assume that Stewart Soup Company is considering an investment of $130,000 in new equipment. The new equipment is expected to last 10 years. It will have a zero salvage value at the end of its useful life. The annual cash inflows are $200,000, and the annual cash outflows are $176,000. Illustration 12-3 summarizes these data.

Illustration 12-3
Investment information for Stewart Soup example

Initial investment	$130,000
Estimated useful life	10 years
Estimated salvage value	–0–
Estimated annual cash flows	
Cash inflows from customers	$200,000
Cash outflows for operating costs	176,000
Net annual cash flow	$ 24,000

In the following two sections we will examine two popular techniques for evaluating capital investments: cash payback and the net present value method.

CASH PAYBACK

The **cash payback technique** identifies the time period required to recover the cost of the capital investment from the net annual cash flow produced by the investment. Illustration 12-4 presents the formula for computing the cash payback period.

STUDY OBJECTIVE 2

Describe the cash payback technique.

Cost of Capital Investment	÷	Net Annual Cash Flow	=	Cash Payback Period

Illustration 12-4
Cash payback formula

The cash payback period in the Stewart Soup example is 5.42 years, computed as follows.

$$\$130{,}000 \div \$24{,}000 = 5.42 \text{ years}$$

HELPFUL HINT

Net annual cash flow can also be approximated by "Net cash provided by operating activities" from the statement of cash flows.

The evaluation of the payback period is often related to the expected useful life of the asset. For example, assume that at Stewart Soup a project is unacceptable if the payback period is longer than 60% of the asset's expected useful life. The 5.42-year payback period in this case is a bit over 50% of the project's expected useful life. Thus, the project is acceptable.

It follows that when the payback technique is used to decide among acceptable alternative projects, **the shorter the payback period, the more attractive the investment.** This is true for two reasons: First, the earlier the investment is recovered, the sooner the company can use the cash funds for other purposes. Second, the risk of loss from obsolescence and changed economic conditions is less in a shorter payback period.

The preceding computation of the cash payback period assumes **equal** net annual cash flows in each year of the investment's life. In many cases, this assumption is not valid. In the case of **uneven** net annual cash flows, the company determines the cash payback period when the cumulative net cash flows from the investment equal the cost of the investment.

To illustrate, assume that Chen Company proposes an investment in a new website that is estimated to cost $300,000. Illustration 12-5 shows the proposed investment cost, net annual cash flows, cumulative net cash flows, and the cash payback period.

Year	Investment	Net Annual Cash Flow	Cumulative Net Cash Flow
0	$300,000		
1		$ 60,000	$ 60,000
2		90,000	150,000
3		90,000	240,000
4		120,000	360,000
5		100,000	460,000
		Cash payback period = 3.5 years	

Illustration 12-5
Cash inflow schedule

As Illustration 12-5 shows, at the end of year 3, cumulative cash inflow of $240,000 is less than the investment cost of $300,000, but at the end of year 4 the cumulative cash inflow of $360,000 exceeds the investment cost. The cash inflow needed in year 4 to equal the investment cost is $60,000 ($300,000 − $240,000). Assuming the cash inflow occurred evenly during year 4, we then divide this amount by the net annual cash flow in year 4 ($120,000) to determine the point during the year when the cash payback occurs. Thus, we get 0.50 ($60,000/$120,000), or half of the year, and the cash payback period is 3.5 years.

The cash payback technique may be useful as an initial screening tool. It may be the most critical factor in the capital budgeting decision for a company that desires a fast turnaround of its investment because of a weak cash position. It also is relatively easy to compute and understand.

However, cash payback should not ordinarily be the only basis for the capital budgeting decision because it ignores the expected profitability of the project. To illustrate, assume that Projects A and B have the same payback period, but Project A's useful life is double the useful life of Project B. Project A's earning power, therefore, is twice as long as Project B's. A further—and major—disadvantage of this technique is that it ignores the time value of money.

NET PRESENT VALUE METHOD

STUDY OBJECTIVE 3

Explain the net present value method.

Recognition of the time value of money can make a significant difference in the long-term impact of the capital budgeting decision. For example, cash flows that occur early in the life of an investment will be worth more than those that occur later—because of the time value of money. Therefore it is useful to recognize the timing of cash flows when evaluating projects.

Capital budgeting techniques that take into account both the time value of money and the estimated net cash flow from an investment are called **discounted cash flow techniques**. They are generally recognized as the most informative and best conceptual approaches to making capital budgeting decisions. The expected net cash flow used in discounting cash flows consists of the annual net cash flows plus the estimated liquidation proceeds (salvage value) when the asset is sold for salvage at the end of its useful life.

The primary discounted cash flow technique is the **net present value method**. A second method, discussed later in the chapter, is the **internal rate of return**. At this point, before you read on, **we recommend that you examine Appendix A** at the end of the book to review time value of money concepts, upon which these methods are based.

The **net present value (NPV) method** involves discounting net cash flows to their present value and then comparing that present value with the capital outlay required by the investment. The difference between these two amounts is referred to as **net present value (NPV)**. Company management determines what interest rate to use in discounting the future net cash flows. This rate, often referred to as the **discount rate** or **required rate of return** is discussed in a later section.

The NVP decision rule is this: **A proposal is acceptable when net present value is zero or positive**. At either of those values, the rate of return on the investment equals or exceeds the required rate of return. When net present value is negative, the project is unacceptable. Illustration 12-6 (next page) shows the net present value decision criteria.

When making a selection among acceptable proposals, **the higher the positive net present value, the more attractive the investment**. The application of this method to two cases is described in the next two sections. In each case, we will assume that the investment has no salvage value at the end of its useful life.

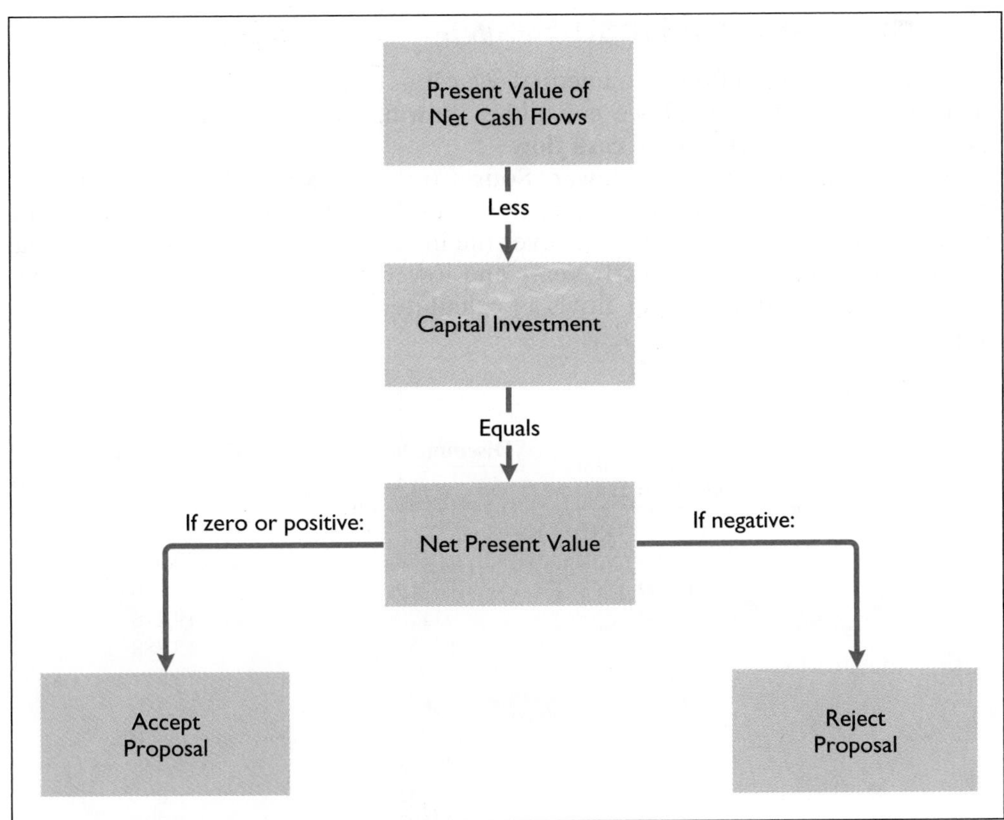

Illustration 12-6
Net present value decision criteria

Equal Annual Cash Flows

In our Stewart Soup Company example, the company's net annual cash flows are $24,000. If we assume this amount **is uniform over the asset's useful life**, we can compute the present value of the net annual cash flows by using the present value of an annuity of 1 for 10 periods (from Table 4, Appendix A). Assuming a discount rate of 12%, the present value of net cash flows are as shown in Illustration 12-7 (rounded to the nearest dollar).

HELPFUL HINT

The ABC Co. expects equal cash flows over an asset's 5-year useful life. What discount factor should it use in determining present values if management wants (1) a 12% return or (2) a 15% return? Answer: Using Table 4, the factors are (1) 3.60478 and (2) 3.35216.

Illustration 12-7
Computation of present value of equal net annual cash flows

	Present Value at 12%
Discount factor for 10 periods	5.65022
Present value of net cash flows:	
$24,000 × 5.65022	**$135,605**

The analysis of the proposal by the net present value method is as follows.

Illustration 12-8
Computation of net present value—equal net annual cash flows

	12%
Present value of net cash flows	$135,605
Capital investment	130,000
Net present value	**$ 5,605**

The proposed capital expenditure is acceptable at a required rate of return of 12% because the net present value is positive.

Unequal Annual Cash Flows

When net annual cash flows are unequal, we cannot use annuity tables to calculate their present value. Instead, we use tables showing the **present value of a single future amount for each annual cash flow.**

To illustrate, assume that Stewart Soup Company expects the same total net cash flows of $240,000 over the life of the investment. But because of a declining market demand for the new product over the life of the equipment, the net annual cash flows are higher in the early years and lower in the later years. The present value of the net annual cash flows is calculated as follows, using Table 3 in Appendix A.

HELPFUL HINT

Appendix A demonstrates the use of a financial calculator to solve time value of money problems.

Illustration 12-9
Computation of present value of unequal annual cash flows

Year	Assumed Net Annual Cash Flows	Discount Factor 12%	Present Value 12%
	(1)	(2)	(1) × (2)
1	$ 34,000	.89286	$ 30,357
2	30,000	.79719	23,916
3	27,000	.71178	19,218
4	25,000	.63552	15,888
5	24,000	.56743	13,618
6	22,000	.50663	11,146
7	21,000	.45235	9,499
8	20,000	.40388	8,078
9	19,000	.36061	6,852
10	18,000	.32197	5,795
	$240,000		**$ 144,367**

Therefore, the analysis of the proposal by the net present value method is as follows.

Illustration 12-10
Computation of net present value—unequal annual cash flows

	12%
Present value of net cash flows	$144,367
Capital investment	130,000
Net present value	**$ 14,367**

In this example, the present value of the net cash flows is greater than the $130,000 capital investment. Thus, the project is acceptable at a 12% required rate of return. The difference between the present values using the 12% rate under equal cash flows ($135,605) and unequal cash flows ($144,367) is due to the pattern of the flows. Since more money is received sooner under this particular uneven cash flow scenario, its present value is greater.

Choosing a Discount Rate

Now that you understand how companies apply the net present value method, it is logical to ask a related question: How is a discount rate (required rate of return) determined in real capital budgeting decisions? In most instances a company uses a required rate of return equal to its **cost of capital**—that is, the rate that it must pay to obtain funds from creditors and stockholders.

The cost of capital is a weighted average of the rates paid on borrowed funds as well as on funds provided by investors in the company's common stock and preferred stock. If management believes a project is riskier than the company's usual line of business, the discount rate should be increased. That is, the discount rate has two elements, a cost of capital element and a risk element. Often companies assume the risk element is equal to zero.

HELPFUL HINT
Cost of capital is the rate that management expects to pay on all borrowed and equity funds. It does not relate to the cost of funding a *specific* project.

Using an incorrect discount rate can lead to incorrect capital budgeting decisions. Consider again the Stewart Soup example in Illustration 12-8, where we used a discount rate of 12%. Suppose that this rate does not take into account the fact that this project is riskier than most of the company's investments. A more appropriate discount rate, given the risk, might be 15%. Illustration 12-11 compares the net present values at the two rates. At the higher, more appropriate discount rate of 15%, the net present value is negative, and the company should reject the project.

Illustration 12-11
Comparison of net present values at different discount rates

	Present Values at Different Discount Rates	
	12%	**15%**
Discount factor for 10 periods	5.65022	5.01877
Present value of net cash flows:		
$24,000 × 5.65022	$135,605	
$24,000 × 5.01877		$120,450
Capital investment	130,000	130,000
Positive (negative) net present value	**$ 5,605**	**$ (9,550)**

The discount rate is often referred to by alternative names, including the **required rate of return**, the **hurdle rate**, and the **cutoff rate**. Determination of the cost of capital varies somewhat depending on whether the entity is a for-profit or not-for-profit enterprise. Calculation of the cost of capital is discussed more fully in advanced accounting and finance courses.

Simplifying Assumptions

In our examples of the net present value method, we have made a number of simplifying assumptions:

- **All cash flows come at the end of each year.** In reality, cash flows will come at uneven intervals throughout the year. However, it is far simpler to assume that all cash flows come at the end (or in some cases the beginning) of the year. In fact, this assumption is frequently made in practice.
- **All cash flows are immediately reinvested in another project that has a similar return.** In most capital budgeting situations, companies receive cash flows during each year of a project's life. In order to determine the return on the investment, some assumption must be made about how the cash flows are reinvested in the year that they are received. It is customary to assume that cash flows received are reinvested in some other project of similar return until the end of the project's life.
- **All cash flows can be predicted with certainty.** The outcomes of business investments are full of uncertainty, as the Campbell Soup Feature Story shows. There is no way of knowing how popular a new product will be, how long a new machine will last, or what competitors' reactions might be to changes in a product. But, in order to make investment decisions, analysts must estimate future

outcomes. In this chapter we have assumed that future amounts are known with certainty.[1] In reality, little is known with certainty. More advanced capital budgeting techniques deal with uncertainty by considering the probability that various outcomes will occur.

Before You Go On...

REVIEW IT

1. What is the cash payback technique? What are its strengths and weaknesses?
2. What is the net present value decision rule to determine whether a project is acceptable?
3. What are common assumptions made in capital budgeting decisions?

DO IT

Watertown Paper Corporation is considering adding another machine for the manufacture of corrugated cardboard. The machine would cost $800,000. It would have an estimated life of 7 years and a salvage value of $40,000. The company estimates that annual cash inflows would increase by $400,000 and that annual cash outflows would increase by $190,000. Management believes a discount rate of 9% is appropriate. Using the net present value technique, should Watertown Paper accept the project?

Action Plan

- Use the NPV technique to calculate the difference between the present value of net cash flows and the initial investment.
- Accept the project if the net present value is positive.

Solution

Estimated annual cash inflows	$400,000
Estimated annual cash outflows	190,000
Net annual cash flow	$210,000

	Cash Flows	×	9% Discount Factor	=	Present Value
Present value of net annual cash flows	$210,000	×	5.03295[a]	=	$1,056,920
Present value of salvage value	$ 40,000	×	.54703[b]	=	21,881
Present value of net cash flows					1,078,801
Capital investment					800,000
Net present value					$ 278,801

[a]Table 4, Appendix A.
[b]Table 3, Appendix A.

Since the net present value is positive, the project is acceptable.

Related exercise material: *BE12-2, BE12-3, BE12-4, BE12-5, E12-1, E12-2, and E12-3.*

The Navigator

Comprehensive Example

Best Taste Foods is considering investing in new equipment to produce fat-free snack foods. Management believes that although demand for fat-free foods has leveled off, fat-free foods are here to stay. The following estimated costs, cost

[1]One exception is a brief discussion of sensitivity analysis later in the chapter.

of capital, and cash flows were determined in consultation with the marketing, production, and finance departments.

Initial investment	$1,000,000
Cost of equipment overhaul in 5 years	$200,000
Salvage value of equipment in 10 years	$20,000
Cost of capital (discount rate)	15%
Estimated annual cash flows	
Cash inflows received from sales	$500,000
Cash outflows for cost of goods sold	$200,000
Maintenance costs	$30,000
Other direct operating costs	$40,000

Illustration 12-12
Investment information for Best Taste Foods example

Remember that we are using cash flows in our analysis, not accrual revenues and expenses. Thus, for example, the direct operating costs would not include depreciation expense, since depreciation expense does not use cash. Illustration 12-13 presents the computation of the net annual cash flows of this project.

Cash inflows received from sales	$ 500,000
Cash outflows for cost of goods sold	(200,000)
Maintenance costs	(30,000)
Other direct operating costs	(40,000)
Net annual cash flow	**$ 230,000**

Illustration 12-13
Computation of net annual cash flow

Illustration 12-14 shows computation of the net present value for this proposed investment.

Event	Time Period	Cash Flow	×	15% Discount Factor	=	Present Value
Equipment purchase	0	$1,000,000		1.00000		$(1,000,000)
Equipment overhaul	5	200,000		.49718		(99,436)
Net annual cash flow	1–10	230,000		5.01877		1,154,317
Salvage value	10	20,000		.24719		4,944
Net present value						**$ 59,825**

Illustration 12-14
Computation of net present value for Best Taste Foods investment

Because the net present value of the project is positive, Best Taste should accept the project.

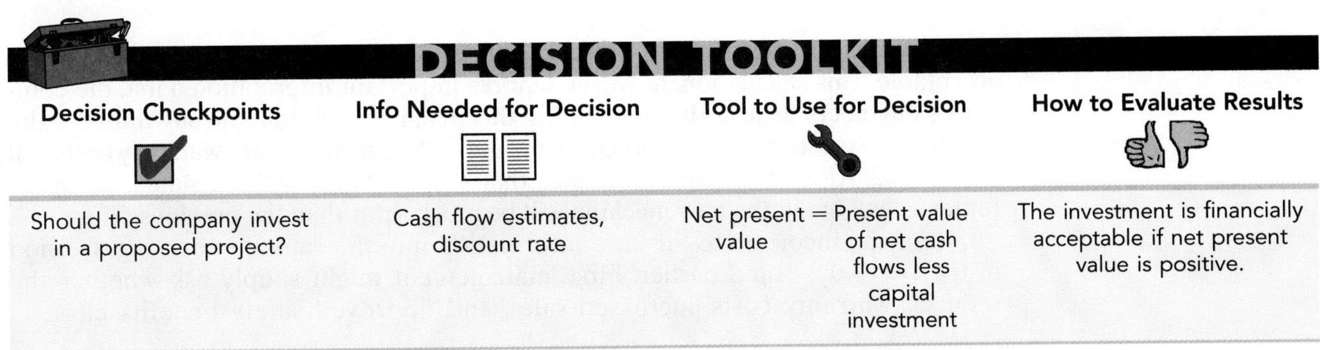

DECISION TOOLKIT

Decision Checkpoints	Info Needed for Decision	Tool to Use for Decision	How to Evaluate Results
Should the company invest in a proposed project?	Cash flow estimates, discount rate	Net present value = Present value of net cash flows less capital investment	The investment is financially acceptable if net present value is positive.

ADDITIONAL CONSIDERATIONS

Now that you understand how the net present value method works, we can add some "additional wrinkles." Specifically, these are: the impact of intangible benefits, a way to compare mutually exclusive projects, refinements that take risk into account, and the need to conduct post-audits of investment projects.

Intangible Benefits

STUDY OBJECTIVE 4

Identify the challenges presented by intangible benefits in capital budgeting.

The NPV evaluation techniques employed thus far rely on tangible costs and benefits that can be relatively easily quantified. Some investment projects, especially high-tech projects, fail to make it through initial capital budget screens because only the project's tangible benefits are considered. *Intangible benefits* might include increased quality, improved safety, or enhanced employee loyalty. By ignoring intangible benefits, capital budgeting techniques might incorrectly eliminate projects that could be financially beneficial to the company.

To avoid rejecting projects that actually should be accepted, analysts suggest two possible approaches:

1. Calculate net present value ignoring intangible benefits. Then, if the NPV is negative, ask whether the project offers any intangible benefits that are worth at least the amount of the negative NPV.
2. Project rough, conservative estimates of the value of the intangible benefits, and incorporate these values into the NPV calculation.

EXAMPLE

Assume that Berg Company is considering the purchase of a new mechanical robot to be used for soldering electrical connections. Illustration 12-15 shows the estimates related to this proposed purchase.

Illustration 12-15
Investment information for Berg Company example

Initial investment	$200,000				
Annual cash inflows	$ 50,000				
Annual cash outflows	20,000				
Net annual cash flow	**$ 30,000**				
Estimated life of equipment	10 years				
Discount rate	12%				

	Cash Flows	×	12% Discount Factor	=	Present Value
Present value of net cash flows	$30,000	×	5.65022	=	$169,507
Initial investment					200,000
Net present value					**$ (30,493)**

Based on the negative net present value of $30,493, the proposed project is not acceptable. This calculation, however, ignores important information. First, the company's engineers believe that purchasing this machine will dramatically improve the electrical connections in the company's products. As a result, future warranty costs will be reduced. Also, the company believes that higher quality will translate into higher future sales. Finally, the new machine will be much safer than the previous one.

Berg can incorporate this new information into the capital budgeting decision in the two ways listed earlier. First, management might simply ask whether the reduced warranty costs, increased sales, and improved safety benefits have an estimated total present value to the company of at least $30,493. If yes, then the project is acceptable.

Alternatively, analysts can estimate the annual cash flows of these benefits. In our initial calculation, we assumed each of these benefits to have a value of zero. It seems likely that their actual values are much higher than zero. Given the difficulty of estimating these benefits, however, conservative values should be assigned to them. If, after using conservative estimates, the net present value is positive, Berg should accept the project.

To illustrate, assume that Berg estimates that improved sales will increase cash inflows by $10,000 annually as a result of an increase in perceived quality. Berg also estimates that annual cost outflows would be reduced by $5,000 as a result of lower warranty claims, reduced injury claims, and missed work. Consideration of the intangible benefits results in the following revised NPV calculation.

Illustration 12-16
Revised investment information for Berg Company example, including intangible benefits

Initial investment	$200,000				
Annual cash inflows (revised)	$ 60,000				
Annual cash outflows (revised)	15,000				
Net annual cash flow	**$ 45,000**				
Estimated life of equipment	10 years				
Discount rate	12%				

	Cash Flows	×	12% Discount Factor	=	Present Value
Present value of net annual cash flows	$45,000	×	5.65022	=	$254,260
Initial investment					200,000
Net present value					**$ 54,260**

Using these conservative estimates of the value of the additional benefits, Berg should accept the project.

ETHICS INSIGHT

It Need Not Cost an Arm and a Leg

Most manufacturers say that employee safety matters above everything else. But how many back up this statement with investments that improve employee safety? Recently a woodworking hobbyist who also happens to be a patent attorney with a Ph.D. in physics invented a mechanism that automatically shuts down a power saw when the saw blade comes in contact with human flesh. The blade stops so quickly that only minor injuries result.

Power saws injure 40,000 Americans each year, and 4,000 of those injuries are bad enough to require amputation. Therefore, one might think that power-saw companies would be lined up to incorporate this mechanism into their saws. But, in the words of one power-tool company, "Safety doesn't sell." Since existing saw manufacturers were unwilling to incorporate the device into their saws, eventually the inventor started his own company to build the devices and sell them directly to businesses that use power saws.

Source: Melba Newsome, "An Edgy New Idea," *Time: Inside Business,* May 2006, p. A16.

? In addition to the obvious humanitarian benefit of reducing serious injuries, how else might the manufacturer of this product convince potential customers of its worth?

Mutually Exclusive Projects

In theory, companies should accept all projects with positive NPVs. However, companies rarely are able to adopt all positive-NPV proposals. First, proposals often are **mutually exclusive**. This means that if the company adopts one proposal, it would be impossible also to adopt the other proposal. For example, a company may be considering the purchase of a new packaging machine and is looking at various brands and models. It needs only one packaging machine. Once the company has determined which brand and model to purchase, the others will not be purchased—even though they also may have positive net present values.

Even in instances where projects are not mutually exclusive, managers often must choose between various positive-NPV projects because of **limited resources**. For example, the company might have ideas for two new lines of business, each of which has a projected positive NPV. However, both of these proposals require skilled personnel, and the company determines that it will not be able to find enough skilled personnel to staff both projects. Management will have to choose the project it thinks is a better option.

When choosing between alternative proposals, it is tempting simply to choose the project with the higher NPV. Consider the following example of two mutually exclusive projects. Each is assumed to have a 10-year life and a 12% discount rate.

Illustration 12-17 Investment information for mutually exclusive projects

	Project A	Project B
Initial investment	$40,000	$ 90,000
Net annual cash inflow	10,000	19,000
Salvage value	5,000	10,000
Present value of net cash flows		
($10,000 × 5.65022) + ($5,000 × .32197)	58,112	
($19,000 × 5.65022) + ($10,000 × .32197)		110,574

From the information in Illustration 12-17, we can compute the net present values of Project A and Project B as shown in Illustration 12-18.

Illustration 12-18 Net present value computation

	Project A	Project B
Present value of net cash flows	$58,112	$110,574
Initial investment	40,000	90,000
Net present value	$18,112	$ 20,574

Project B has the higher NPV, and so it would seem that the company should adopt B. Note, however, that Project B also requires more than twice the original investment of Project A. In choosing between the two projects, the company should also include in its calculations the amount of the original investment.

STUDY OBJECTIVE 5
Describe the profitability index.

One relatively simple method of comparing alternative projects is the **profitability index**. This method takes into account both the size of the original investment and the discounted cash flows. The profitability index is calculated by dividing the present value of net cash flows that occur after the initial investment by the amount of the initial investment.

Present Value of Net Cash Flows	÷	Initial Investment	=	Profitability Index

Illustration 12-19
Formula for profitability index

The profitability index allows comparison of the relative desirability of projects that require differing initial investments. Note that any project with a positive NPV will have a profitability index above 1. The profitability index for each of the mutually exclusive projects is calculated below.

$$\text{Profitability Index} = \frac{\text{Present Value of Net Cash Flows}}{\text{Initial Investment}}$$

Project A	Project B
$\frac{\$58,112}{\$40,000} = \mathbf{1.45}$	$\frac{\$110,574}{\$90,000} = \mathbf{1.23}$

Illustration 12-20
Calculation of profitability index

In this case the profitability index of Project A exceeds that of Project B. Thus, Project A is more desirable. Again, if these were not mutually exclusive projects, and if resources were not limited, then the company should invest in both projects, since both have positive NPVs. Additional considerations related to preference decisions are discussed in more advanced courses.

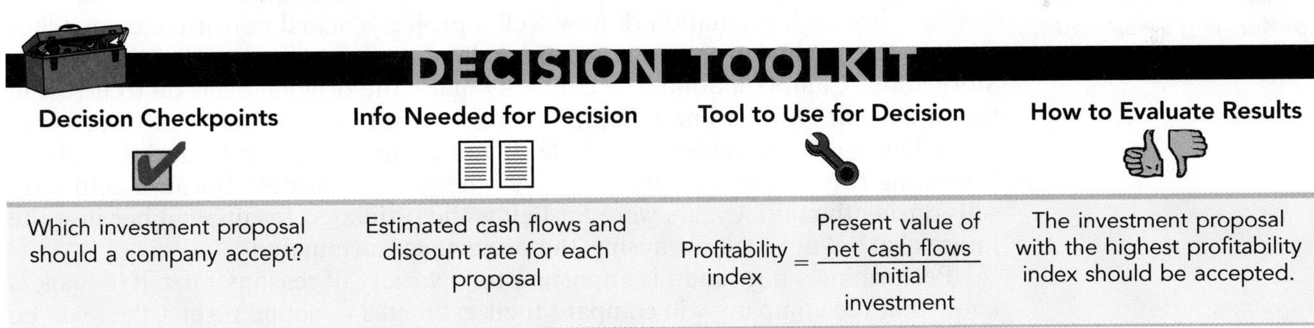

DECISION TOOLKIT

Decision Checkpoints	Info Needed for Decision	Tool to Use for Decision	How to Evaluate Results
Which investment proposal should a company accept?	Estimated cash flows and discount rate for each proposal	Profitability index = Present value of net cash flows / Initial investment	The investment proposal with the highest profitability index should be accepted.

Risk Analysis

A simplifying assumption made by many financial analysts is that projected results are known with certainty. In reality, projected results are only estimates based upon the forecaster's belief as to the most probable outcome. One approach for dealing with such uncertainty is **sensitivity analysis**. Sensitivity analysis uses a number of outcome estimates to get a sense of the variability among potential returns. An example of sensitivity analysis was presented in Illustration 12-11, where we illustrated the impact on NPV of different discount rate assumptions. A higher-risk project would be evaluated using a higher discount rate.

Similarly, to take into account that more distant cash flows are often more uncertain, a higher discount rate can be used to discount more distant cash flows. Other techniques to address uncertainty are discussed in advanced courses.

MANAGEMENT INSIGHT

Are You Ready for the 50-Inch Screen?

Building a new factory to produce 50-inch-plus TV screens can cost $4 billion at a time when prices for flat screens are tumbling. Now the makers of those giant liquid-crystal displays are wondering whether such investments are worth the gamble.

If LCD makers decide to hold off on building new factories, price declines for wide-screen TVs could slow in two or three years as production falls behind added consumer demand. Experts also say a slowdown in factory building could also bring welcome relief for the industry by reducing its volatile profit swings.

Since 2000, LCD makers have been on a nonstop construction binge, building new factories to produce the latest generation of screens arriving every 18 months or so. . . . Now, with the eighth generation of screens, the cost to build new factories is higher than ever—running between $3 billion to $4 billion each. And this generation of factories is optimized for screens measuring 50 inches or more diagonally, which so far is a much smaller potential market than that targeted by previous screen generations.

Source: Evan Ramstad, "The 50-Inch Screen Poses a Gamble," *Wall Street Journal*, June 8, 2006, p. B3.

In building factories to manufacture 50-inch TV screens, how might companies build risk factors into their financial analyses?

Post-Audit of Investment Projects

STUDY OBJECTIVE 6

Indicate the benefits of performing a post-audit.

Any well-run organization should perform an evaluation, called a **post-audit**, of its investment projects after their completion. A post-audit is a thorough evaluation of how well a project's actual performance matches the original projections. An example of a post-audit is seen in the Feature Story about Campbell Soup. The company made the original decision to invest in the Intelligent Quisine line based on management's best estimates of future cash flows. During the development phase of the project, Campbell hired an outside consulting firm to evaluate the project's potential for success. Because actual results during the initial years were far below the estimated results, and because the future also did not look promising, the project was terminated.

Performing a post-audit is important for a variety of reasons. First, if managers know that the company will compare their estimates to actual results, they will be more likely to submit reasonable and accurate data when they make investment proposals. This clearly is better for the company than for managers to submit overly optimistic estimates in an effort to get pet projects approved. Second, as seen with Campbell Soup, a post-audit provides a formal mechanism by which the company can determine whether existing projects should be supported or terminated. Third, post-audits improve future investment proposals because, by evaluating past successes and failures, managers improve their estimation techniques.

A post-audit involves the same evaluation techniques used in making the original capital budgeting decision—for example, use of the NPV method. The difference is that, in the post-audit, analysts insert actual figures, where known, and they revise estimates of future amounts based on new information. The managers responsible for the estimates used in the original proposal must explain the reasons for any significant differences between their estimates and actual results.

Post-audits are not foolproof. In the case of Campbell Soup, some observers suggested that the company was too quick to abandon the project. Industry analysts suggested that with more time and more advertising expenditures, the company might have enjoyed a success.

MANAGEMENT INSIGHT

Seeing the Big Picture

Inaccurate trend forecasting and market positioning are more detrimental to capital investment decisions than using the wrong discount rate. Ampex patented the VCR, but failed to see its market potential. Westinghouse made the same mistake with the flat-screen video display. More often, companies adopt projects or businesses only to discontinue them in response to market changes. Texas Instruments announced it would stop manufacturing computer chips, after it had made substantial capital investments that enabled it to become one of the world's leading suppliers. The company has dropped out of some 12 business lines in recent years.

Source: World Research Advisory Inc. (London, August 1998), p. 4.

? How important is the choice of discount rate in making capital budgeting decisions?

OTHER CAPITAL BUDGETING TECHNIQUES

Some companies use capital budgeting techniques other than, or in addition to, the cash payback and net present value methods. In this section we will briefly discuss these other approaches.

Internal Rate of Return Method

STUDY OBJECTIVE 7

Explain the internal rate of return method.

The **internal rate of return method** differs from the net present value method in that it finds the **interest yield of the potential investment**. The **internal rate of return (IRR)** is the interest rate that will cause the present value of the proposed capital expenditure to equal the present value of the expected net annual cash flows (that is, NPV equal to zero). Because it recognizes the time value of money, the internal rate of return method is (like the NPV method) a discounted cash flow technique.

How does one determine the internal rate of return? One way is to use a financial calculator (see Appendix A) or computerized spreadsheet to solve for this rate. Or, one can use a trial-and-error procedure.

To illustrate, assume that Stewart Soup Company is considering the purchase of a new front-end loader at a cost of $244,371. Net annual cash flows from this loader are estimated to be $100,000 a year for three years. To determine the internal rate of return on this front-end loader, the company finds the discount rate that results in a net present value of zero. As Illustration 12-21 below shows, at a rate of return of 10%, Stewart Soup has a positive net present value of $4,315. At a rate of return of

Illustration 12-21
Estimation of internal rate of return

Year	Net Annual Cash Flows	Discount Factor 10%	Present Value 10%	Discount Factor 11%	Present Value 11%	Discount Factor 12%	Present Value 12%
1	$100,000	.90909	$ 90,909	.90090	$ 90,090	.89286	$ 89,286
2	$100,000	.82645	82,645	.81162	81,162	.79719	79,719
3	$100,000	.75132	75,132	.73119	73,119	.71178	71,178
			248,686		244,371		240,183
Less: Initial investment			244,371		244,371		244,371
Net present value			$ 4,315		$ -0-		$ (4,188)

12%, it has a negative net present value of $4,188. At an 11% rate, the net present value is zero. Therefore 11% is the internal rate of return for this investment.

An easier approach to solving for the internal rate of return can be used if the net annual cash flows are **equal**, as in the Stewart Soup example. In this special case, we can find the internal rate of return using the following formula.

Illustration 12-22
Formula for internal rate of return—even cash flows

Applying this formula to the Stewart Soup example, we find:

$$\$244,371 \div \$100,000 = 2.44371$$

We then look up the factor 2.44371 in Table 4 of Appendix A in the three-period row and find it under 11%. Row 3 is reproduced below for your convenience.

TABLE 4 PRESENT VALUE OF AN ANNUITY OF 1

(*n*) Periods	4%	5%	6%	8%	9%	10%	11%	12%	15%
3	2.77509	2.72325	2.67301	2.57710	2.53130	2.48685	**2.44371**	2.40183	2.28323

Recognize that if the cash flows are **uneven**, then a trial-and-error approach or a financial calculator or computerized spreadsheet must be used.

Once managers know the internal rate of return, they compare it to the company's required rate of return (the discount rate). The IRR decision rule is as follows: **Accept the project when the internal rate of return is equal to or greater than the required rate of return. Reject the project when the internal rate of return is less than the required rate of return**. Illustration 12-23 shows these relationships. The internal rate of return method is widely used in practice, largely because most managers find the internal rate of return easy to interpret.

Illustration 12-23
Internal rate of return decision criteria

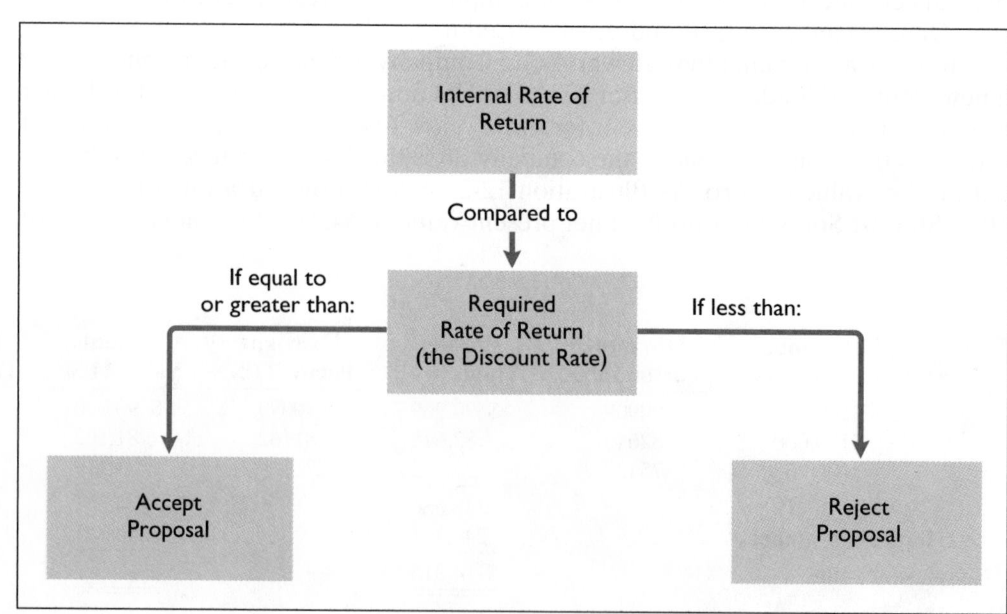

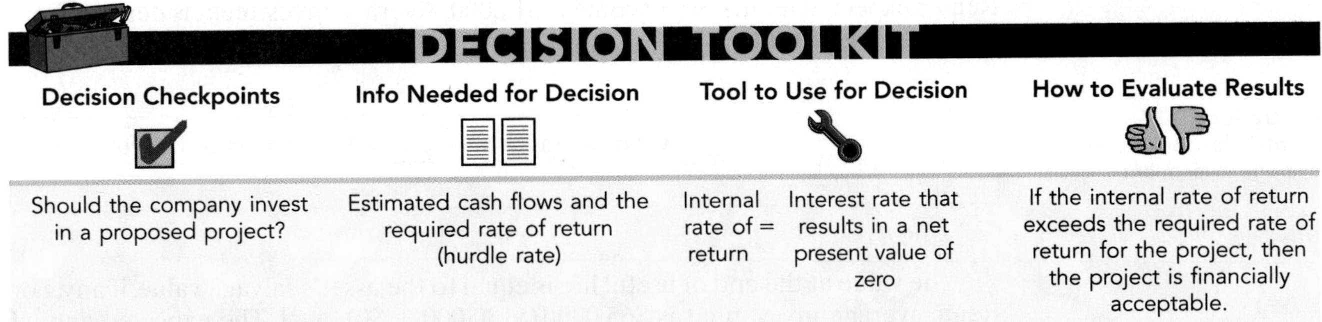

DECISION TOOLKIT

Decision Checkpoints	Info Needed for Decision	Tool to Use for Decision	How to Evaluate Results
Should the company invest in a proposed project?	Estimated cash flows and the required rate of return (hurdle rate)	Internal rate of return = Interest rate that results in a net present value of zero	If the internal rate of return exceeds the required rate of return for the project, then the project is financially acceptable.

Comparing Discounted Cash Flow Methods

Illustration 12-24 compares the two discounted cash flow methods—net present value and internal rate of return. When properly used, either method will provide management with relevant quantitative data for making capital budgeting decisions.

Illustration 12-24
Comparison of discounted cash flow methods

	Net Present Value	Internal Rate of Return
1. Objective	Compute net present value (a dollar amount).	Compute internal rate of return (a percentage).
2. Decision rule	If net present value is zero or positive, accept the proposal. If net present value is negative, reject the proposal.	If internal rate of return is equal to or greater than the required rate of return, accept the proposal. If internal rate of return is less than the required rate of return, reject the proposal.

Annual Rate of Return Method

STUDY OBJECTIVE 8
Describe the annual rate of return method.

The final capital budgeting technique we will look at is the **annual rate of return method**. It is based directly on accrual accounting data rather than on cash flows. It indicates **the profitability of a capital expenditure** by dividing expected annual net income by the average investment. Illustration 12-25 shows the formula for computing annual rate of return.

Illustration 12-25
Annual rate of return formula

Expected Annual Net Income	÷	Average Investment	=	Annual Rate of Return

Assume that Reno Company is considering an investment of $130,000 in new equipment. The new equipment is expected to last five years and have zero salvage value at the end of its useful life. Reno uses the straight-line method of depreciation for accounting purposes. The expected annual revenues and costs of the new product that will be produced from the investment are:

Illustration 12-26
Estimated annual net income from Reno Company's capital expenditure

Sales		$200,000
Less: Costs and expenses		
Manufacturing costs (exclusive of depreciation)	$132,000	
Depreciation expense ($130,000 ÷ 5)	26,000	
Selling and administrative expenses	22,000	180,000
Income before income taxes		20,000
Income tax expense		7,000
Net income		$ 13,000

Reno's expected annual net income is $13,000. Average investment is derived from the following formula.

Illustration 12-27
Formula for computing average investment

$$\text{Average Investment} = \frac{\text{Original Investment} + \text{Value at End of Useful Life}}{2}$$

The value at the end of useful life is equal to the asset's salvage value, if any. For Reno, average investment is $65,000 [($130,000 + $0) ÷ 2]. The expected annual rate of return for Reno's investment in new equipment is therefore 20%, computed as follows.

$$\$13{,}000 \div \$65{,}000 = 20\%$$

Management then compares the annual rate of return with its **required rate of return** for investments of similar risk. The required rate of return is generally based on the company's cost of capital. The decision rule is: **A project is acceptable if its rate of return is greater than management's required rate of return. It is unacceptable when the reverse is true.** When companies use the rate of return technique in deciding among several acceptable projects, **the higher the rate of return for a given risk, the more attractive the investment.**

The principal advantages of this method are the simplicity of its calculation and management's familiarity with the accounting terms used in the computation. A major limitation of the annual rate of return method is that it does not consider the time value of money. For example, no consideration is given as to whether cash inflows will occur early or late in the life of the investment. As explained in Appendix A, recognition of the time value of money can make a significant difference between the future value and the discounted present value of an investment. A second disadvantage is that this method relies on accrual accounting numbers rather than expected cash flows.

HELPFUL HINT
A capital budgeting decision based on only one technique may be misleading. It is often wise to analyze an investment from a number of different perspectives.

Before You Go On...

REVIEW IT

1. When is a proposal acceptable under (a) the net present value method and (b) the internal rate of return method?
2. How does the internal rate of return method differ from the net present value method?
3. What is the formula for and the decision rule in using the annual rate of return method? What are the drawbacks to the annual rate of return method?

Be sure to read **ALL ABOUT YOU: *The Risks of Adjustable Rates*** on the next page for information on how topics in this chapter apply to you.

all about YOU

The Risks of Adjustable Rates

It is likely that the biggest single capital expenditure decision you ever make will be the purchase of a home. As home prices rose rapidly between 2000 and 2005, many people found that they could not afford to buy a home using traditional fixed interest rate loans. Lenders encouraged some people to use less-conventional loans such as ARMs—adjustable-rate mortgages.

The lender periodically adjusts the interest rate on an ARM to reflect changes in market interest rates. The advantage of ARMs to home buyers is that the initial rate on an ARM is below the rate charged on a fixed-rate loan. This can enable the buyer to purchase a home that he or she otherwise could not afford. If market interest rates rise, however, the rate on the ARM can rise well above the initial rate. This will result in much higher mortgage payments. Rising rates can be a problem for homeowners who have not planned for them.

Some Facts

* 35% of people with ARMs do not know how much the rate could increase at one time, and 41% are not sure of the maximum rate they could face.
* 28% of people with ARMs do not know which index of interest rates is used to determine their adjustments.
* ARMs represented about one-third of all loans granted during 2004 and 2005, which was substantially higher than most previous years.
* Borrowers with less income or education were more likely not to know their mortgage terms. Borrowers with less income faced the largest change in their ARM payment, as a percentage of income, when interest rates changed.
* Subprime borrowers—people with weak credit histories—spend nearly 37% of their after-tax income on mortgage payments, insurance, and property taxes, whereas prime borrowers spend about 17% of after-tax income.
* Hundreds of thousands of families who purchased homes using adjustable-rate mortgages with low initial rates have lost their homes to foreclosure as interest rates increased and the mortgage rates readjusted. At the end of 2006 more than 450,000 loans were either in foreclosure or more than three months behind on payments.

About the Numbers

Although a high percentage of loans granted during 2004 and 2005 were adjustable-rate loans, these loans still represent a relatively small percentage of all loans outstanding. Many people who are initially granted an adjustable-rate loan subsequently refinance their loan to get a fixed-rate loan that will offer no unpleasant surprises in later years.

Mortgage Types

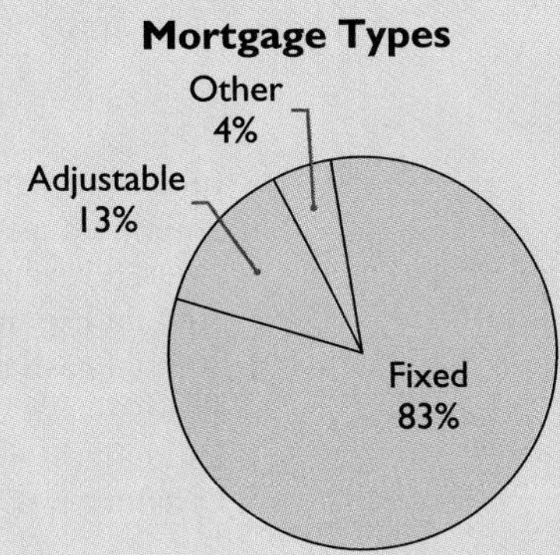

Source: Brian Bucks and Karen Pence, "Do Homeowners Know Their House Values and Mortgage Terms?," Federal Reserve Board of Governors, January 2006, *www.federalreserve.gov/pubs/feds/2006/200603/200603pap.pdf.*

What Do You Think?

Suppose that you are planning to buy your first home for $200,000. The payment on a 30-year, 7% fixed-rate loan of $180,000 (after a down payment of $20,000) would be $1,198 per month, which is more than you qualify for with the lender. The lender has suggested that you could instead use an ARM. The interest rate would be 5.5%, resulting in payments of $1,022 per month for the first three years. After that, the interest rate would be adjusted annually and could increase by as much as 2% each year, with an upper-end rate of 10.5%. Should you buy the home using adjustable-rate financing?

YES: House prices are just going to keep going up, up, up. If you don't get into the market now, you may never be able to.

NO: This nontraditional loan has too much uncertainty tied to it. If interest rates go up, your payment could get so high that you wouldn't be able to make the payment, in which case you would lose the house.

Sources: James R. Hagerty, "The Home-Mortgage Muddle; Some Borrowers Are Confused by Terms of Adjustable-Rate Loans," *Wall Street Journal*, March 11, 2006, p. B4; and Eduardo Porter and Vikas Bajaj, "Mortgage Trouble Clouds Homeownership Dream," *New York Times* (*nytimes.com*) March 17, 2007.

The authors' comments on this situation appear on page 555.

Using the Decision Toolkit

Campbell Soup is considering expanding its international presence. It sells 38% of the soup consumed in the United States, but only 2% of soup worldwide. Thus the company believes that it has great potential for international sales. Recently, 20% of Campbell's sales were in foreign markets (and nearly all of that was in Europe). Its goal is to have 30% of its sales be in foreign markets. In order to accomplish this goal, the company will have to invest heavily.

In recent years Campbell has spent between $300 and $400 million on capital expenditures. Suppose that Campbell is interested in expanding its South American presence by building a new production facility. After considering tax, marketing, labor, transportation, and political issues, Campbell has determined that the most desirable location is either in Buenos Aires or Rio de Janeiro. The following estimates have been provided. (All amounts are stated in U.S. dollars.)

	Buenos Aires	Rio de Janeiro
Initial investment	$2,500,000	$1,400,000
Estimated useful life	20 years	20 years
Annual revenues (accrual)	$500,000	$380,000
Annual expenses (accrual)	$200,000	$180,000
Annual cash inflows	$550,000	$430,000
Annual cash outflows	$222,250	$206,350
Estimated salvage value	$500,000	$0
Discount rate	9%	9%

Instructions

Evaluate each of these mutually exclusive proposals employing (a) cash payback, (b) net present value, (c) the profitability index, (d) the internal rate of return, and (e) annual rate of return. Discuss the implications of your findings.

Solution

	Buenos Aires	Rio de Janeiro
(a) Cash payback	$\frac{\$2,500,000}{\$327,750} = 7.63$ years	$\frac{\$1,400,000}{\$223,650} = 6.26$ years

(b) Net present value

Present value of net cash flows	Buenos Aires		Rio de Janeiro
	$327,750 × 9.12855 =	$2,991,882	$223,650 × 9.12855 = $2,041,600
	$500,000 × 0.17843 =	89,215	
		3,081,097	
Less: Initial investment		2,500,000	1,400,000
Net present value		$ 581,097	$ 641,600

	Buenos Aires	Rio de Janeiro
(c) Profitability index	$\frac{\$3,081,097}{\$2,500,000} = 1.23$	$\frac{\$2,041,600}{\$1,400,000} = 1.46$

(d) Internal rate of return: The internal rate of return can be approximated by experimenting with different discount rates to see which one comes the closest to resulting in a net present value of zero. Doing this, we find that Buenos Aires has an internal rate of return of approximately 12%, while the internal rate of return of the Rio de Janeiro location is approximately 15% as shown below. Rio, therefore, is preferable.

		Buenos Aires				Rio de Janeiro		
Internal rate of return								
Cash Flows	×	12% Discount Factor	=	Present Value	Cash Flows	×	15% Discount Factor	= Present Value
\$327,750	×	7.46944	=	\$2,448,109	\$223,650	×	6.25933	= \$1,399,899
\$500,000	×	0.10367	=	51,835				
				\$2,499,944				
Less: Capital investment				2,500,000				1,400,000
Net present value				\$ (56)				\$ (101)

(e) Annual rate of return

Average investment

$\frac{(\$2{,}500{,}000 + \$500{,}000)}{2} = \$1{,}500{,}000$ $\qquad$ $\frac{(\$1{,}400{,}000 + \$0)}{2} = \$700{,}000$

Annual rate of return $\frac{\$300{,}000}{\$1{,}500{,}000} = .20 = 20\%$ $\qquad$ $\frac{\$200{,}000}{\$700{,}000} = .286 = 28.6\%$

Implications: Although the annual rate of return is higher for Rio de Janeiro, this method has the disadvantage of ignoring time value of money, as well as using accrual numbers rather than cash flows. The cash payback of Rio de Janeiro is also shorter, but this method also ignores the time value of money. Thus, while these two methods can be used for a quick assessment, neither should be relied upon as the sole evaluation tool.

From the net present value calculation it would appear that the two projects are nearly identical in their acceptability. However, the profitability index indicates that the Rio de Janeiro investment is far more desirable because it generates its cash flows with a much smaller initial investment. A similar result is found by using the internal rate of return. Overall, assuming that the company will invest in only one project, it would appear that the Rio de Janeiro project should be chosen.

SUMMARY OF STUDY OBJECTIVES

1 **Discuss capital budgeting evaluation, and explain inputs used in capital budgeting.** Management gathers project proposals from each department; a capital budget committee screens the proposals and recommends worthy projects. Company officers decide which projects to fund, and the board of directors approves the capital budget. In capital budgeting, estimated cash inflows and outflows, rather than accrual-accounting numbers, are the preferred inputs.

2 **Describe the cash payback technique.** The cash payback technique identifies the time period required to recover the cost of the investment. The formula when net annual cash flows are equal is: Cost of capital investment ÷ Estimated net annual cash flow = Cash payback period. The shorter the payback period, the more attractive the investment.

3 **Explain the net present value method.** The net present value method compares the present value of future cash inflows with the capital investment to determine net present value. The NPV decision rule is: Accept the project if net present value is zero or positive. Reject the project if net present value is negative.

4 **Identify the challenges presented by intangible benefits in capital budgeting.** Intangible benefits are difficult to quantify, and thus are often ignored in capital budgeting decisions. This can result in incorrectly rejecting some projects. One method for considering intangible benefits is to calculate the NPV, ignoring intangible benefits; if the resulting NPV is below zero, evaluate whether the benefits are worth at least the amount of the negative net present value. Alternatively, intangible benefits can be incorporated into the NPV calculation, using conservative estimates of their value.

5 **Describe the profitability index.** The profitability index is a tool for comparing the relative merits of alternative capital investment opportunities. It is computed as: Present value of net cash flows ÷ Initial investment. The higher the index, the more desirable the project.

6 **Indicate the benefits of performing a post-audit.** A post-audit is an evaluation of a capital investment's actual performance. Post-audits create an incentive for managers to make accurate estimates. Post-audits also are useful for determining whether a company should continue, expand, or terminate a project. Finally, post-audits provide feedback that is useful for improving estimation techniques.

7 **Explain the internal rate of return method.** The objective of the internal rate of return method is to find the interest yield of the potential investment, which is expressed as a percentage rate. The IRR decision rule is: Accept the project when the internal rate of return is equal to or greater than the required rate of return. Reject the project when the internal rate of return is less than the required rate of return.

8 **Describe the annual rate of return method.** The annual rate of return uses accrual accounting data to indicate the profitability of a capital investment. It is calculated as: Expected annual net income ÷ Amount of the average investment. The higher the rate of return, the more attractive the investment.

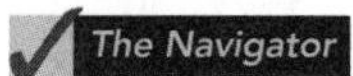

DECISION TOOLKIT—A SUMMARY

Decision Checkpoints	Info Needed for Decision	Tool to Use for Decision	How to Evaluate Results
Should the company invest in a proposed project?	Cash flow estimates, discount rate	Net present value = Present value of net cash flows less capital investment	The investment is financially acceptable if net present value is positive.
Which investment proposal should a company accept?	Estimated cash flows and discount rate for each proposal	Profitability index = Present value of net cash flows / Initial investment	The investment proposal with the highest profitability index should be accepted.
Should the company invest in a proposed project?	Estimated cash flows and the required rate of return (hurdle rate)	Internal rate of return = Interest rate that results in a net present value of zero	If the internal rate of return exceeds the required rate of return for the project, then the project is financially acceptable.

GLOSSARY

Annual rate of return method The determination of the profitability of a capital expenditure, computed by dividing expected annual net income by the average investment. (p. 537)

Capital budgeting The process of making capital expenditure decisions in business. (p. 520)

Cash payback technique A capital budgeting technique that identifies the time period required to recover the cost of a capital investment from the net annual cash flow produced by the investment. (p. 523)

Cost of capital The average rate of return that the firm must pay to obtain funds from creditors and stockholders. (p. 526)

Discounted cash flow technique A capital budgeting technique that considers both the estimated net cash flows from the investment and the time value of money. (p. 524)

Discount rate The interest rate used in discounting the future net cash flows to determine present value. (p. 524)

Internal rate of return (IRR) The interest rate that will cause the present value of the proposed capital expenditure to equal the present value of the expected net annual cash flows. (p. 535)

Internal rate of return (IRR) method A method used in capital budgeting that results in finding the interest yield of the potential investment. (p. 535)

Net present value (NPV) The difference that results when the original capital outlay is subtracted from the discounted net cash flows. (p. 524)

Net present value (NPV) method A method used in capital budgeting in which net cash flows are discounted to their present value and then compared to the capital outlay required by the investment. (p. 524)

Post-audit A thorough evaluation of how well a project's actual performance matches the original projections. (p. 534)

Profitability index A method of comparing alternative projects that takes into account both the size of the investment and its discounted future net cash flows. It is computed by dividing the present value of net future cash flows by the initial investment. (p. 532)

Required rate of return The rate of return management expects on investments; also called the *discount rate* or *cost of capital*. (p. 538)

Demonstration Problem

Sierra Company is considering a long-term capital investment project called ZIP. ZIP will require an investment of $120,000, and it will have a useful life of 4 years. Annual net income is expected to be $9,000 a year. Depreciation is computed by the straight-line method with no salvage value. The company's cost of capital is 12%. (*Hint:* Assume cash flows can be computed by adding back depreciation expense.)

Instructions

(Round all computations to two decimal places.)

(a) Compute the cash payback period for the project. (Round to two decimals.)
(b) Compute the net present value for the project. (Round to nearest dollar.)
(c) Compute the annual rate of return for the project.
(d) Should the project be accepted? Why?

Solution

(a) $120,000 ÷ $39,000, ($9,000 + $30,000), = 3.08 years

(b)

	Present Value at 12%
Discount factor for 4 periods	3.03735
Present value of net cash flows:	
$39,000 × 3.03735	$118,457
Capital investment	120,000
Negative net present value	$ (1,543)

(c) $9,000 ÷ $60,000 ($120,000 ÷ 2) = 15%

(d) The annual rate of return of 15% is good. However, the cash payback period is 77% of the project's useful life, and net present value is negative. The recommendation is to reject the project.

action plan

✓ Calculate the time it will take to pay back the investment: cost of the investment divided by net annual cash flows.

✓ When calculating NPV, remember that net annual cash flow equals annual net income plus annual depreciation expense.

✓ Be careful to use the correct discount factor in using the net present value method.

✓ Calculate the annual rate of return: expected annual net income divided by average investment.

The Navigator

SELF-STUDY QUESTIONS

Answers are at the end of the chapter.

(SO 1) **1.** Which of the following is *not* an example of a capital budgeting decision?
a. Decision to build a new plant.
b. Decision to renovate an existing facility.
c. Decision to buy a piece of machinery.
d. All of these are capital budgeting decisions.

(SO 1) **2.** What is the order of involvement of the following parties in the capital budgeting authorization process?
a. Plant managers, officers, capital budget committee, board of directors.
b. Board of directors, plant managers, officers, capital budget committee.
c. Plant managers, capital budget committee, officers, board of directors.
d. Officers, plant managers, capital budget committee, board of directors.

3. What is a weakness of the cash payback approach? (SO 2)
a. It uses accrual-based accounting numbers.
b. It ignores the time value of money.
c. It ignores the useful life of alternative projects.
d. Both (b) and (c) are true.

4. Which is a true statement regarding using a higher discount rate to calculate the net present value of a project? (SO 3)
a. It will make it less likely that the project will be accepted.
b. It will make it more likely that the project will be accepted.
c. It is appropriate to use a higher rate if the project is perceived as being less risky than other projects being considered.
d. It is appropriate to use a higher rate if the project will have a short useful life relative to other projects being considered.

(SO 3) **5.** A positive net present value means that the:
- **a.** project's rate of return is less than the cutoff rate.
- **b.** project's rate of return exceeds the required rate of return.
- **c.** project's rate of return equals the required rate of return.
- **d.** project is unacceptable.

(SO 3) **6.** Which of the following is *not* an alternative name for the discount rate?
- **a.** Hurdle rate.
- **b.** Required rate of return.
- **c.** Cutoff rate.
- **d.** All of these are alternative names for the discount rate.

(SO 4) **7.** If a project has intangible benefits whose value is hard to estimate, the best thing to do is:
- **a.** ignore these benefits, since any estimate of their value will most likely be wrong.
- **b.** include a conservative estimate of their value.
- **c.** ignore their value in your initial net present value calculation, but then estimate whether their potential value is worth at least the amount of the net present value deficiency.
- **d.** either (b) or (c) is correct.

8. A post-audit of an investment project should be performed: (SO 6)
- **a.** on all significant capital expenditure projects.
- **b.** on all projects that management feels might be financial failures.
- **c.** on randomly selected projects.
- **d.** only on projects that enjoy tremendous success.

9. A project should be accepted if its internal rate of return exceeds: (SO 7)
- **a.** zero.
- **b.** the rate of return on a government bond.
- **c.** the company's required rate of return.
- **d.** the rate the company pays on borrowed funds.

10. Which of the following is *incorrect* about the annual rate of return technique? (SO 8)
- **a.** The calculation is simple.
- **b.** The accounting terms used are familiar to management.
- **c.** The timing of the cash inflows is not considered.
- **d.** The time value of money is considered.

Go to the book's website, **www.wiley.com/college/weygandt**, for Additional Self-Study questions.

QUESTIONS

1. Describe the process a company may use in screening and approving the capital expenditure budget.
2. What are the advantages and disadvantages of the cash payback technique?
3. Walter Shea claims the formula for the cash payback technique is the same as the formula for the annual rate of return technique. Is Walter correct? What is the formula for the cash payback technique?
4. Two types of present value tables may be used with the discounted cash flow techniques. Identify the tables and the circumstance(s) when each table should be used.
5. What is the decision rule under the net present value method?
6. Discuss the factors that determine the appropriate discount rate to use when calculating the net present value.
7. What simplifying assumptions were made in the chapter regarding calculation of net present value?
8. What are some examples of potential intangible benefits of investment proposals? Why do these intangible benefits complicate the capital budgeting evaluation process? What might happen if intangible benefits are ignored in a capital budgeting decision?
9. What steps can be taken to incorporate intangible benefits into the capital budget evaluation process?
10. What advantages does the profitability index provide over direct comparison of net present value when comparing two projects?
11. What is a post-audit? What are the potential benefits of a post-audit?
12. Identify the steps required in using the internal rate of return method when the net annual cash flows are equal.
13. Waterville Company uses the internal rate of return method. What is the decision rule for this method?
14. What are the strengths of the annual rate of return approach? What are its weaknesses?
15. Your classmate, Kurt Snyder, is confused about the factors that are included in the annual rate of return technique. What is the formula for this technique?
16. Stella Waite is trying to understand the term "cost of capital." Define the term and indicate its relevance to the decision rule under the internal rate of return technique.

BRIEF EXERCISES

Compute the cash payback period for a capital investment.
(SO 2)

BE12-1 Marcus Company is considering purchasing new equipment for $450,000. It is expected that the equipment will produce net annual cash flows of $55,000 over its 10-year useful life. Annual depreciation will be $45,000. Compute the cash payback period.

BE12-2 Nien Company accumulates the following data concerning a proposed capital investment: cash cost $220,000, net annual cash flows $40,000, present value factor of cash inflows for 10 years 5.65 (rounded). Determine the net present value, and indicate whether the investment should be made.

Compute net present value of an investment.

(SO 3)

BE12-3 Timo Corporation, an amusement park, is considering a capital investment in a new exhibit. The exhibit would cost $136,000 and have an estimated useful life of 5 years. It will be sold for $70,000 at that time. (Amusement parks need to rotate exhibits to keep people interested.) It is expected to increase net annual cash flows by $25,000. The company's borrowing rate is 8%. Its cost of capital is 10%. Calculate the net present value of this project to the company.

Compute net present value of an investment.

(SO 3)

BE12-4 Michener Bottling Corporation is considering the purchase of a new bottling machine. The machine would cost $200,000 and has an estimated useful life of 8 years with zero salvage value. Management estimates that the new bottling machine will provide net annual cash flows of $35,000. Management also believes that the new bottling machine will save the company money because it is expected to be more reliable than other machines, and thus will reduce downtime. How much would the reduction in downtime have to be worth in order for the project to be acceptable? Assume a discount rate of 9%. (*Hint:* Calculate the net present value.)

Compute net present value of an investment and consider intangible benefits.

(SO 3, 4)

BE12-5 Harry Company is considering two different, mutually exclusive capital expenditure proposals. Project A will cost $395,000, has an expected useful life of 10 years, a salvage value of zero, and is expected to increase net annual cash flows by $70,000. Project B will cost $270,000, has an expected useful life of 10 years, a salvage value of zero, and is expected to increase net annual cash flows by $50,000. A discount rate of 9% is appropriate for both projects. Compute the net present value and profitability index of each project. Which project should be accepted?

Compute net present value and profitability index.

(SO 3, 5)

BE12-6 Martelle Company is performing a post-audit of a project completed one year ago. The initial estimates were that the project would cost $250,000, would have a useful life of 9 years, zero salvage value, and would result in net annual cash flows of $45,000 per year. Now that the investment has been in operation for 1 year, revised figures indicate that it actually cost $260,000, will have a useful life of 11 years, and will produce net annual cash flows of $38,000 per year. Evaluate the success of the project. Assume a discount rate of 10%.

Perform a post-audit.

(SO 6)

BE12-7 Frost Company is evaluating the purchase of a rebuilt spot-welding machine to be used in the manufacture of a new product. The machine will cost $170,000, has an estimated useful life of 7 years, a salvage value of zero, and will increase net annual cash flows by $33,740. What is its approximate internal rate of return?

Calculate internal rate of return.

(SO 7)

BE12-8 Vintech Corporation is considering investing in a new facility. The estimated cost of the facility is $2,045,000. It will be used for 12 years, then sold for $600,000. The facility will generate annual cash inflows of $400,000 and will need new annual cash outflows of $160,000. The company has a required rate of return of 7%. Calculate the internal rate of return on this project, and discuss whether the project should be accepted.

Calculate internal rate of return.

(SO 7)

BE12-9 Engles Oil Company is considering investing in a new oil well. It is expected that the oil well will increase annual revenues by $130,000 and will increase annual expenses by $80,000 including depreciation. The oil well will cost $490,000 and will have a $10,000 salvage value at the end of its 10-year useful life. Calculate the annual rate of return.

Compute annual rate of return.

(SO 8)

EXERCISES

E12-1 Dobbs Corporation is considering purchasing a new delivery truck. The truck has many advantages over the company's current truck (not the least of which is that it runs). The new truck would cost $56,000. Because of the increased capacity, reduced maintenance costs, and increased fuel economy, the new truck is expected to generate cost savings of $8,000. At the end of 8 years the company will sell the truck for an estimated $28,000. Traditionally the company has used a rule of thumb that a proposal should not be accepted unless it has a payback period that is less than 50% of the asset's estimated useful life. Hal Michaels, a new manager, has suggested that the company should not rely solely on the payback approach, but should also employ the net present value method when evaluating new projects. The company's cost of capital is 8%.

Compute cash payback and net present value.

(SO 2, 3)

Instructions

(a) Compute the cash payback period and net present value of the proposed investment.

(b) Does the project meet the company's cash payback criteria? Does it meet the net present value criteria for acceptance? Discuss your results.

Compute cash payback period and net present value.
(SO 2, 3)

E12-2 Jack's Custom Manufacturing Company is considering three new projects, each requiring an equipment investment of $21,000. Each project will last for 3 years and produce the following net annual cash flows.

Year	AA	BB	CC
1	$ 7,000	$ 9,500	$13,000
2	9,000	9,500	10,000
3	15,000	9,500	11,000
Total	$31,000	$28,500	$34,000

The equipment's salvage value is zero, and Jack uses straight-line depreciation. Jack will not accept any project with a cash payback period over 2 years. Jack's required rate of return is 12%.

Instructions

(a) Compute each project's payback period, indicating the most desirable project and the least desirable project using this method. (Round to two decimals and assume in your computations that cash flows occur evenly throughout the year.)

(b) Compute the net present value of each project. Does your evaluation change? (Round to nearest dollar.)

Compute net present value and profitability index.
(SO 3, 5)

E12-3 TLC Corp. is considering purchasing one of two new diagnostic machines. Either machine would make it possible for the company to bid on jobs that it currently isn't equipped to do. Estimates regarding each machine are provided below.

	Machine A	Machine B
Original cost	$78,000	$190,000
Estimated life	8 years	8 years
Salvage value	–0–	–0–
Estimated annual cash inflows	$20,000	$40,000
Estimated annual cash outflows	$5,000	$9,000

Instructions

Calculate the net present value and profitability index of each machine. Assume a 9% discount rate. Which machine should be purchased?

Determine internal rate of return.
(SO 7)

E12-4 Kendra Corporation is involved in the business of injection molding of plastics. It is considering the purchase of a new computer-aided design and manufacturing machine for $425,000. The company believes that with this new machine it will improve productivity and increase quality, resulting in an increase in net annual cash flows of $95,000 for the next 6 years. Management requires a 10% rate of return on all new investments.

Instructions

Calculate the internal rate of return on this new machine. Should the investment be accepted?

Determine internal rate of return.
(SO 7)

E12-5 Summer Company is considering three capital expenditure projects. Relevant data for the projects are as follows.

Project	Investment	Annual Income	Life of Project
22A	$240,000	$15,000	6 years
23A	270,000	24,400	9 years
24A	280,000	21,000	7 years

Annual income is constant over the life of the project. Each project is expected to have zero salvage value at the end of the project. Summer Company uses the straight-line method of depreciation.

Instructions

(a) Determine the internal rate of return for each project. Round the internal rate of return factor to three decimals.

(b) If Summer Company's required rate of return is 11%, which projects are acceptable?

E12-6 Mane Event is considering opening a new hair salon in Pompador, California. The cost of building a new salon is $300,000. A new salon will normally generate annual revenues of $70,000, with annual expenses (including depreciation) of $40,000. At the end of 15 years the salon will have a salvage value of $75,000.

Calculate annual rate of return.

(SO 8)

Instructions

Calculate the annual rate of return on the project.

E12-7 Alameda Service Center just purchased an automobile hoist for $41,000. The hoist has an 8-year life and an estimated salvage value of $3,000. Installation costs and freight charges were $3,300 and $700, respectively. Alameda uses straight-line depreciation.

The new hoist will be used to replace mufflers and tires on automobiles. Alameda estimates that the new hoist will enable his mechanics to replace five extra mufflers per week. Each muffler sells for $72 installed. The cost of a muffler is $34, and the labor cost to install a muffler is $12.

Compute cash payback period and annual rate of return.

(SO 2, 8)

Instructions

(a) Compute the cash payback period for the new hoist.

(b) Compute the annual rate of return for the new hoist. (Round to one decimal.)

E12-8 Morgan Company is considering a capital investment of $180,000 in additional productive facilities. The new machinery is expected to have a useful life of 6 years with no salvage value. Depreciation is by the straight-line method. During the life of the investment, annual net income and net annual cash flows are expected to be $20,000 and $50,000 respectively. Morgan has a 15% cost of capital rate which is the required rate of return on the investment.

Compute annual rate of return, cash payback period, and net present value.

(SO 2, 3, 8)

Instructions

(Round to two decimals.)

(a) Compute (1) the cash payback period and (2) the annual rate of return on the proposed capital expenditure.

(b) Using the discounted cash flow technique, compute the net present value.

EXERCISES: SET B

Visit the book's website at **www.wiley.com/college/weygandt**, and choose the Student Companion site, to access Exercise Set B.

PROBLEMS: SET A

WILEY PLUS

P12-1A The Three Stooges partnership is considering three long-term capital investment proposals. Each investment has a useful life of 5 years. Relevant data on each project are as follows.

Compute annual rate of return, cash payback, and net present value.

(SO 2, 3, 8)

	Project Moe	Project Larry	Project Curly
Capital investment	$150,000	$160,000	$200,000
Annual net income:			
Year 1	13,000	18,000	27,000
2	13,000	17,000	22,000
3	13,000	16,000	21,000
4	13,000	12,000	13,000
5	13,000	9,000	12,000
Total	$ 65,000	$ 72,000	$ 95,000

Depreciation is computed by the straight-line method with no salvage value. The company's cost of capital is 15%. (Assume that cash flows occur evenly throughout the year.)

Instructions

(b) L $(2,368); C $1,407

(a) Compute the cash payback period for each project. (Round to two decimals.)
(b) Compute the net present value for each project. (Round to nearest dollar.)
(c) Compute the annual rate of return for each project. (Round to two decimals.) (*Hint*: Use average annual net income in your computation.)
(d) Rank the projects on each of the foregoing bases. Which project do you recommend?

Compute annual rate of return, cash payback, and net present value.

(SO 2, 3, 8)

P12-2A Tony Siebers is an accounting major at a midwestern state university located approximately 60 miles from a major city. Many of the students attending the university are from the metropolitan area and visit their homes regularly on the weekends. Tony, an entrepreneur at heart, realizes that few good commuting alternatives are available for students doing weekend travel. He believes that a weekend commuting service could be organized and run profitably from several suburban and downtown shopping mall locations. Tony has gathered the following investment information.

1. Five used vans would cost a total of $75,000 to purchase and would have a 3-year useful life with negligible salvage value. Tony plans to use straight-line depreciation.
2. Ten drivers would have to be employed at a total payroll expense of $48,000.
3. Other annual out-of-pocket expenses associated with running the commuter service would include Gasoline $16,000, Maintenance $4,300, Repairs $5,000, Insurance $5,200, Advertising $2,500.
4. Tony has visited several financial institutions to discuss funding. The best interest rate he has been able to negotiate is 8%. Use this rate for cost of capital.
5. Tony expects each van to make ten round trips weekly and carry an average of six students each trip. The service is expected to operate 30 weeks each year, and each student will be charged $12.00 for a round-trip ticket.

Instructions

(a) (1) $2,000
(b) (1) 2.78 years

(a) Determine the annual (1) net income and (2) net annual cash flows for the commuter service.
(b) Compute (1) the cash payback period and (2) the annual rate of return. (Round to two decimals.)
(c) Compute the net present value of the commuter service. (Round to the nearest dollar.)
(d) What should Tony conclude from these computations?

Compute net present value, profitability index, and internal rate of return.

(SO 3, 5, 7)

P12-3A Carolina Clinic is considering investing in new heart monitoring equipment. It has two options: Option A would have an initial lower cost but would require a significant expenditure for rebuilding after 4 years. Option B would require no rebuilding expenditure, but its maintenance costs would be higher. Since the option B machine is of initial higher quality, it is expected to have a salvage value at the end of its useful life. The following estimates were made of the cash flows. The company's cost of capital is 11%.

	Option A	Option B
Initial cost	$160,000	$227,000
Annual cash inflows	$75,000	$80,000
Annual cash outflows	$35,000	$30,000
Cost to rebuild (end of year 4)	$60,000	$0
Salvage value	$0	$12,000
Estimated useful life	8 years	8 years

Instructions

(a) (1) NPV A $6,321
(3) IRR B 15%

(a) Compute the (1) net present value, (2) profitability index, and (3) internal rate of return for each option. (*Hint:* To solve for internal rate of return, experiment with alternative discount rates to arrive at a net present value of zero.)
(b) Which option should be accepted?

Compute net present value considering intangible benefits.

(SO 3, 4)

P12-4A Prestige Auto Care is considering the purchase of a new tow truck. The garage doesn't currently have a tow truck, and the $60,000 price tag for a new truck would represent a major expenditure. Jenna Lind, owner of the garage, has compiled the following estimates in trying to determine whether the tow truck should be purchased.

Initial cost	$60,000
Estimated useful life	8 years
Net annual cash flows from towing	$8,000
Overhaul costs (end of year 4)	$5,000
Salvage value	$15,000

Jenna's good friend, Reid Shaw, stopped by. He is trying to convince Jenna that the tow truck will have other benefits that Jenna hasn't even considered. First, he says, cars that need towing need to be fixed. Thus, when Jenna tows them to her facility her repair revenues will increase. Second, he notes that the tow truck could have a plow mounted on it, thus saving Jenna the cost of plowing her parking lot. (Reid will give her a used plow blade for free if Jenna will plow Reid's driveway.) Third, he notes that the truck will generate goodwill; people who are rescued by Jenna's tow truck will feel grateful and might be more inclined to use her service station in the future, or buy gas there. Fourth, the tow truck will have "Prestige Auto Care" on its doors, hood, and back tailgate — a form of free advertising wherever the tow truck goes. Reid estimates that, at a minimum, these benefits would be worth the following.

Additional annual net cash flows from repair work	$3,000
Annual savings from plowing	500
Additional annual net cash flows from customer "goodwill"	1,000
Additional annual net cash flows resulting from free advertising	500

The company's cost of capital is 9%.

Instructions

(a) Calculate the net present value, ignoring the additional benefits described by Reid. Should the tow truck be purchased? (a) NPV $(11,735)

(b) Calculate the net present value, incorporating the additional benefits suggested by Reid. Should the tow truck be purchased? (b) NPV $15,939

(c) Suppose Reid has been overly optimistic in his assessment of the value of the additional benefits. At a minimum, how much would the additional benefits have to be worth in order for the project to be accepted?

Compute net present value and internal rate of return with sensitivity analysis.

(SO 3, 7)

P12-5A Bonita Corp. is thinking about opening a soccer camp in southern California. To start the camp, Bonita would need to purchase land and build four soccer fields and a sleeping and dining facility to house 150 soccer players. Each year the camp would be run for 8 sessions of 1 week each. The company would hire college soccer players as coaches. The camp attendees would be male and female soccer players ages 12–18. Property values in southern California have enjoyed a steady increase in value. It is expected that after using the facility for 20 years, Bonita can sell the property for more than it was originally purchased for. The following amounts have been estimated.

Cost of land	$300,000
Cost to build soccer fields, dorm and dining facility	$600,000
Annual cash inflows assuming 150 players and 8 weeks	$950,000
Annual cash outflows	$840,000
Estimated useful life	20 years
Salvage value	$1,500,000
Discount rate	8%

Instructions

(a) Calculate the net present value of the project. (a) NPV $501,822

(b) To gauge the sensitivity of the project to these estimates, assume that if only 125 players attend each week, annual cash inflows will be $800,000 and annual cash outflows will be $770,000. What is the net present value using these alternative estimates? Discuss your findings.

(c) Assuming the original facts, what is the net present value if the project is actually riskier than first assumed, and a 11% discount rate is more appropriate?

(d) Assume that during the first 5 years the annual net cash flows each year were only $45,000. At the end of the fifth year the company is running low on cash, so management decides to sell the property for $1,300,000. What was the actual internal rate of return on the project? Explain how this return was possible given that the camp did not appear to be successful. (d) IRR 12%

PROBLEMS: SET B

P12-1B The partnership of Lou and Bud is considering three long-term capital investment proposals. Relevant data on each project are as follows.

Compute annual rate of return, cash payback, and net present value.

(SO 2, 3, 8)

	Project		
	Brown	Red	Yellow
Capital investment	$200,000	$225,000	$250,000
Annual net income:			
Year 1	25,000	20,000	26,000
2	16,000	20,000	24,000
3	13,000	20,000	23,000
4	10,000	20,000	22,000
5	8,000	20,000	20,000
Total	$ 72,000	$100,000	$115,000

Salvage value is expected to be zero at the end of each project. Depreciation is computed by the straight-line method. The company's required rate of return is the company's cost of capital which is 12%. (Assume that cash flows occur evenly throughout the year.)

Instructions

(b) NPV B $(584); Y $14,286

(a) Compute the cash payback period for each project. (Round to two decimals.)
(b) Compute the net present value for each project. (Round to nearest dollar.)
(c) Compute the annual rate of return for each project. (Round to two decimals.) (*Hint*: Use average annual net income in your computation.)
(d) Rank the projects on each of the foregoing bases. What project do you recommend?

Compute annual rate of return, cash payback, and net present value.

(SO 2, 3, 8)

P12-2B Jo Quick is managing director of the Tot Lot Day Care Center. Tot Lot is currently set up as a full-time child care facility for children between the ages of 12 months and 6 years. Jo Quick is trying to determine whether the center should expand its facilities to incorporate a newborn care room for infants between the ages of 6 weeks and 12 months. The necessary space already exists. An investment of $20,000 would be needed, however, to purchase cribs, high chairs, etc. The equipment purchased for the room would have a 5-year useful life with zero salvage value.

The newborn nursery would be staffed to handle 11 infants on a full-time basis. The parents of each infant would be charged $125 weekly, and the facility would operate 52 weeks of the year. Staffing the nursery would require two full-time specialists and five part-time assistants at an annual cost of $60,000. Food, diapers, and other miscellaneous supplies are expected to total $6,000 annually.

Instructions

(a) (1) 1,500
(b) (1) 3.64 years

(a) Determine (1) annual net income and (2) net annual cash flows for the new nursery.
(b) Compute (1) the cash payback period for the new nursery and (2) the annual rate of return. (Round to two decimals.)
(c) Compute the net present value of incorporating a newborn care room. (Round to the nearest dollar.) Tot Lot's cost of capital is 10%.
(d) What should Jo Quick conclude from these computations?

Compute net present value, profitability index, and internal rate of return.

(SO 3, 5, 7)

P12-3B Aqua Tech Testing is considering investing in a new testing device. It has two options: Option A would have an initial lower cost but would require a significant expenditure for rebuilding after 5 years. Option B would require no rebuilding expenditure, but its maintenance costs would be higher. Since the option B machine is of initial higher quality, it is expected to have a salvage value at the end of its useful life. The following estimates were provided. The company's cost of capital is 9%.

	Option A	Option B
Initial cost	$90,000	$170,000
Annual cash inflows	$180,000	$140,000
Annual cash outflows	$160,000	$108,000
Cost to rebuild (end of year 5)	$26,500	$0
Salvage value	$0	$27,500
Estimated useful life	8 years	8 years

Instructions

(a) (1) NPV A $3,473
(3) IRR B 12%

(a) Compute the (1) net present value, (2) profitability index, and (3) internal rate of return for each option. (*Hint:* To solve for internal rate of return, experiment with alternative discount rates to arrive at a net present value of zero.)
(b) Which option should be accepted?

P12-4B The Watertown Sanitation Company is considering the purchase of a garbage truck. The $77,000 price tag for a new truck would represent a major expenditure for the company. Kalia Vang, owner of the company, has compiled the following estimates in trying to determine whether the garbage truck should be purchased.

Compute net present value considering intangible benefits.

(SO 3, 4)

Initial cost	$77,000
Estimated useful life	10 years
Net annual cash flows	$12,000
Overhaul costs (end of year 5)	$7,000
Salvage value	$15,000

One of the employees is trying to convince Kalia that the truck has other merits that were not considered in the initial estimates. First, the new truck will be more efficient, with lower maintenance and operating costs. Second, it will be safer. Third, it has the ability to handle recycled materials at the same time as trash, thus offering a new revenue source. Estimates of the minimum value of these benefits are as follows.

Annual savings from reduced operating costs	$400
Annual savings from reduced maintenance costs	800
Additional annual net cash savings from reduced employee absence	500
Additional annual net cash inflows from recycling	300

The company's cost of capital is 10%.

Instructions

(a) Calculate the net present value, ignoring the additional benefits. Should the truck be purchased?

(a) NPV $(1,828)

(b) Calculate the net present value, incorporating the additional benefits. Should the truck be purchased?

(b) NPV $10,461

(c) Suppose management has been overly optimistic in the assessment of the value of the additional benefits. At a minimum, how much would the additional benefits have to be worth in order for the project to be accepted?

P12-5B Benjamin Corp. is thinking about opening an ice hockey camp in Idaho. In order to start the camp the company would need to purchase land and build two ice rinks and a dormitory-type sleeping and dining facility to house 200 players. Each year the camp would be run for 8 sessions of 1 week each. The company would hire college hockey players as coaches. The camp attendees would be male and female hockey players ages 12–18. Property values in Idaho have enjoyed a steady increase in recent years. Benjamin Corp. expects that after using the facility for 15 years, the rinks will have to be dismantled, but the land and buildings will be worth more than they were originally purchased for. The following amounts have been estimated.

Compute net present value and internal rate of return with sensitivity analysis.

(SO 3, 7)

Cost of land	$300,000
Cost to build ice rinks, dorm and dining hall	$600,000
Annual cash inflows assuming 200 players and 8 weeks	$920,000
Annual cash outflows	$760,000
Estimated useful life	15 years
Salvage value	$1,200,000
Discount rate	11%

Instructions

(a) Calculate the net present value of the project.

(a) NPV $501,339

(b) To gauge the sensitivity of the project to these estimates, assume that if only 150 players attend each week, annual cash inflows will be $700,000 and annual cash outflows will be $650,000. What is the net present value using these alternative estimates? Discuss your findings.

(c) Assuming the original facts, what is the net present value if the project is actually riskier than first assumed, and a 15% discount rate is more appropriate?

(d) Assume that during the first 6 years the annual net cash flows each year were only $84,000. At the end of the sixth year the company is running low on cash, so management decides to sell the property for $1,100,000. What was the actual internal rate of return on the project? Explain how this return was possible given that the camp did not appear to be successful.

(d) IRR 12%

PROBLEMS: SET C

Visit the book's website at **www.wiley.com/college/weygandt**, and choose the Student Companion site, to access Problem Set C.

WATERWAYS CONTINUING PROBLEM

(This is a continuation of the Waterways Problem from Chapters 1 through 11.)

WCP12 Waterways Corporation puts much emphasis on cash flow when it plans for capital investments. The company chose its discount rate of 8% based on the rate of return it must pay its owners and creditors. Using that rate, Waterways then uses different methods to determine the best decisions for making capital outlays. Waterways is considering buying five new backhoes to replace the backhoes it now has. This problem asks you to evaluate that decision, using various capital budgeting techniques.

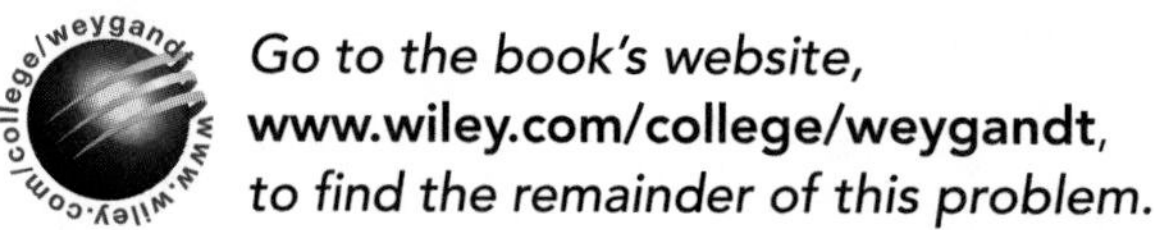

BROADENING YOUR PERSPECTIVE

DECISION MAKING ACROSS THE ORGANIZATION

BYP12-1 Migami Company is considering the purchase of a new machine. Its invoice price is $117,000, freight charges are estimated to be $3,000, and installation costs are expected to be $5,000. Salvage value of the new machine is expected to be zero after a useful life of 4 years. Existing equipment could be retained and used for an additional 4 years if the new machine is not purchased. At that time, the salvage value of the equipment would be zero. If the new machine is purchased now, the existing machine would be scrapped. Migami accountant, Caitlyn Lahr, has accumulated the following data regarding annual sales and expenses with and without the new machine.

1. Without the new machine, Migami can sell 10,000 units of product annually at a per unit selling price of $100. If the new unit is purchased, the number of units produced and sold would increase by 20%, and the selling price would remain the same.
2. The new machine is faster than the old machine, and it is more efficient in its usage of materials. With the old machine the gross profit rate will be 28.5% of sales, whereas the rate will be 30% of sales with the new machine.
3. Annual selling expenses are $160,000 with the current equipment. Because the new equipment would produce a greater number of units to be sold, annual selling expenses are expected to increase by 10% if it is purchased.
4. Annual administrative expenses are expected to be $100,000 with the old machine, and $112,000 with the new machine.
5. The current book value of the existing machine is $30,000. Migami uses straight-line depreciation.
6. Migami management has a required rate of return of 15% on its investment and a cash payback period of no more than 3 years.

Instructions

With the class divided into groups, answer the following. (Ignore income tax effects.)

(a) Calculate the annual rate of return for the new machine. (Round to two decimals.)
(b) Compute the cash payback period for the new machine. (Round to two decimals.)

(c) Compute the net present value of the new machine. (Round to the nearest dollar.)
(d) On the basis of the foregoing data, would you recommend that Migami buy the machine? Why?

MANAGERIAL ANALYSIS

BYP12-2 Tony Skateboards is considering building a new plant. James Bott, the company's marketing manager, is an enthusiastic supporter of the new plant. Alyssa Minh, the company's chief financial officer, is not so sure that the plant is a good idea. Currently the company purchases its skateboards from foreign manufacturers. The following figures were estimated regarding the construction of a new plant.

Cost of plant	$4,000,000	Estimated useful life	15 years
Annual cash inflows	4,000,000	Salvage value	$2,000,000
Annual cash outflows	3,550,000	Discount rate	11%

James Bott believes that these figures understate the true potential value of the plant. He suggests that by manufacturing its own skateboards the company will benefit from a "buy American" patriotism that he believes is common among skateboarders. He also notes that the firm has had numerous quality problems with the skateboards manufactured by its suppliers. He suggests that the inconsistent quality has resulted in lost sales, increased warranty claims, and some costly lawsuits. Overall, he believes sales will be $200,000 higher than projected above, and that the savings from lower warranty costs and legal costs will be $80,000 per year. He also believes that the project is not as risky as assumed above, and that a 9% discount rate is more reasonable.

Instructions

Answer each of the following.

(a) Compute the net present value of the project based on the original projections.
(b) Compute the net present value incorporating James' estimates of the value of the intangible benefits, but still using the 11% discount rate.
(c) Compute the net present value using the original estimates, but employing the 9% discount rate that James suggests is more appropriate.
(d) Comment on your findings.

REAL-WORLD FOCUS

BYP12-3 Tecumseh Products Company has its headquarters in Tecumseh, Michigan. It describes itself as "a global multinational corporation producing mechanical and electrical components essential to industries creating end-products for health, comfort, and convenience." The following was excerpted from the management discussion and analysis section of a recent annual report.

TECUMSEH PRODUCTS COMPANY
Management Discussion and Analysis

The company has invested approximately $50 million in a scroll compressor manufacturing facility in Tecumseh, Michigan. After experiencing setbacks in developing a commercially acceptable scroll compressor, the Company is currently testing a new generation of scroll product. The Company is unable to predict when, or if, it will offer a scroll compressor for commercial sale, but it does anticipate that reaching volume production will require a significant additional investment. Given such additional investment and current market conditions, management is currently reviewing its options with respect to scroll product improvement, cost reductions, joint ventures and alternative new products.

Instructions

Discuss issues the company should consider and techniques the company should employ to determine whether to continue pursuing this project.

EXPLORING THE WEB

BYP12-4 Campbell Soup Company is an international provider of soup products. Management is very interested in continuing to grow the company in its core business, while "spinning off" those businesses that are not part of its core operation.

Address: www.campbellsoups.com, or go to **www.wiley.com/college/weygandt**

Steps

1. Go to the home page of Campbell Soup Company at the address shown above.
2. Choose the current annual report.

Instructions

Review the financial statements and management's discussion and analysis, and answer the following questions.

(a) What was the total amount of capital expenditures in the current year, and how does this amount compare with the previous year?

(b) What interest rate did the company pay on new borrowings in the current year?

(c) Assume that this year's capital expenditures are expected to increase cash flows by $42 million. What is the expected internal rate of return (IRR) for these capital expenditures? (Assume a 10-year period for the cash flows.)

COMMUNICATION ACTIVITY

BYP12-5 Refer back to E12-7 to address the following.

Instructions

Prepare a memo to Mary Ann Griffin, your supervisor. Show your calculations from E12-7, (a) and (b). In one or two paragraphs, discuss important nonfinancial considerations. Make any assumptions you believe to be necessary. Make a recommendation based on your analysis.

ETHICS CASE

BYP12-6 Impro Company operates in a state where corporate taxes and workers' compensation insurance rates have recently doubled. Impro's president has just assigned you the task of preparing an economic analysis and making a recommendation relative to moving the entire operation to Missouri. The president is slightly in favor of such a move because Missouri is his boyhood home and he also owns a fishing lodge there.

You have just completed building your dream house, moved in, and sodded the lawn. Your children are all doing well in school and sports and, along with your spouse, want no part of a move to Missouri. If the company does move, so will you because the town is a one-industry community and you and your spouse will have to move to have employment. Moving when everyone else does will cause you to take a big loss on the sale of your house. The same hardships will be suffered by your coworkers, and the town will be devastated.

In compiling the costs of moving versus not moving, you have latitude in the assumptions you make, the estimates you compute, and the discount rates and time periods you project. You are in a position to influence the decision singlehandedly.

Instructions

(a) Who are the stakeholders in this situation?

(b) What are the ethical issues in this situation?

(c) What would you do in this situation?

"ALL ABOUT YOU" ACTIVITY

BYP12-7 Numerous articles have been written that identify early warning signs that you might be getting into trouble with your personal debt load. You can find many good articles on this topic on the Web.

Instructions

Find an article that identifies early warning signs of personal debt trouble. Write up a summary of the article and bring your summary and the article to class to share.

Answers to Insight and Accounting Across the Organization Questions

Investing for the Future, p. 521

Q: Why is it important for top management to constantly monitor the nature, amount, and success of a company's capital expenditures?

A: *In order to remain competitive, and to grow, companies must continually invest in new opportunities. However, not all projects will be successful, so management must continually monitor projects to ensure that continuation of the investment is in the company's best interest.*

It Need Not Cost an Arm and a Leg, p. 531

Q: In addition to the obvious humanitarian benefit of reducing serious injuries, how else might the manufacturer of this product convince potential customers of its worth?

A: *Serious injuries cost employers huge sums, which can sometimes force small companies out of business. In addition to the obvious humanitarian benefit, the manufacturer can demonstrate that this device is a sound financial investment in terms of reduced health-care and workers' compensation costs and fewer hours missed due to injury. Also, as the device gains wider acceptance, employers that do not have the device may ultimately be found negligent with regard to worker safety.*

Are You Ready for the 50-Inch Screen?, p. 534

Q: In building factories to manufacture 50-inch TV screens, how might companies build risk factors into their financial analyses?

A: *One approach is to use sensitivity analysis. Sensitivity analysis uses a number of outcome estimates to get a sense of the variability among potential returns. In addition, more distant cash flows can be discounted using a higher rate because of their high uncertainty.*

Seeing the Big Picture, p. 535

Q: How important is the choice of discount rate in making capital budgeting decisions?

A: *The point of this discussion is that errors in implementation, as well as the accuracy of the estimated future benefits and costs as measured by cash inflows and outflows, is what matters the most when making capital expenditure decisions. While the choice of discount rates will result in incremental differences in present value calculations, "missing the big picture" has the potential to cause much bigger decision errors. Underestimating potential future cash inflows can result in missed opportunities. Underestimating future costs can result in failed investments.*

Authors' Comments on *All About You*: The Risks of Adjustable Rates, p. 539

A big part of the American dream is home ownership. In the past, homes have enjoyed a relatively steady and safe increase in value; thus many people are eager to quit renting and become homeowners.

But home ownership is not without risks. In recent years home prices increased so much that economists expect that in some parts of the country home prices could fall by as much as 30%. In the example above, if the house lost 30% of its value it would be worth only $140,000—much less than the amount owed. Another risk is that, as interest rates increase, people with adjustable-rate mortgages can experience huge increases in their mortgage payments. In the example given here, if the loan rate hit the cap of 10.5%, the monthly payment would jump to $1,647. That represents a 61% increase. We don't want to discourage you from home ownership, but we do want to encourage you to get educated about mortgage terms.

Answers to Self-Study Questions

1. d **2.** c **3.** d **4.** a **5.** b **6.** d **7.** d **8.** a **9.** c **10.** d

Remember to go back to the Navigator box on the chapter-opening page and check off your completed work.

Chapter 13

Statement of Cash Flows

STUDY OBJECTIVES

After studying this chapter, you should be able to:

1. Indicate the usefulness of the statement of cash flows.
2. Distinguish among operating, investing, and financing activities.
3. Prepare a statement of cash flows using the indirect method.
4. Analyze the statement of cash flows.

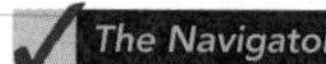

The Navigator

- Scan **Study Objectives**
- Read **Feature Story**
- Read **Preview**
- Read text and answer **Before You Go On** p. 562 p. 564 p. 572 p. 576
- Work **Using the Decision Toolkit**
- Work **Demonstration Problem 1**
- Review **Summary of Study Objectives**
- Work **Demonstration Problem 2**
- Answer **Self-Study Questions**
- Complete **Assignments**

Feature Story

GOT CASH?

In today's environment, companies must be ready to respond to changes quickly in order to survive and thrive. They need to produce new products and expand into new markets continually. To do this takes cash—lots and lots of cash. Keeping lots of cash available is a real challenge for a young company. It requires careful cash management and attention to cash flow.

One company that managed cash successfully in its early years was Microsoft (*www.microsoft.com*). During those years the company paid much of its payroll with stock options (rights to purchase company stock in the future at a given price) instead of cash. This strategy conserved cash, and turned more than a thousand of its employees into millionaires during the company's first 20 years of business.

In recent years Microsoft has had a different kind of cash problem. Now that it has reached a more "mature" stage in life, it generates so much cash—roughly $1 billion per month—that it cannot always figure out what to do with it. By 2004 Microsoft had accumulated $60 billion.

The company said it was accumulating cash to invest in new opportunities, buy other companies, and pay off pending lawsuits. But for years, the federal government has blocked attempts by Microsoft to buy anything other than small firms because it feared that purchase of a large firm would only increase Microsoft's monopolistic position. In addition, even the largest estimates of Microsoft's legal obligations related to pending lawsuits would use up only about $6 billion in cash.

Microsoft's stockholders have complained for years that holding all this cash was putting a drag on the company's profitability. Why? Because Microsoft had the cash invested in very low-yielding government securities. Stockholders felt that the company either should find new investment projects that would bring higher returns, or return some of the cash to stockholders.

Finally, in July 2004 Microsoft announced a plan to return cash to stockholders, by paying a special one-time $32 billion dividend in December 2004. This special dividend was so large that, according to the U.S. Commerce Department, it caused total personal income in the United States to rise by 3.7% in one month—the largest monthly increase ever recorded by the agency. (It also made the holiday season brighter, especially for retailers in the Seattle area.) Microsoft also doubled its regular annual dividend to $3.50 per share. Further, it announced that it would spend another $30 billion over the next four years buying treasury stock. These actions will help to deplete some of its massive cash horde, but as you will see in this chapter, for a cash-generating machine like Microsoft, the company will be anything but cash-starved.

Source: "Business: An End to Growth? Microsoft's Cash Bonanza," *The Economist*, July 23, 2005, p. 61.

The Navigator

Inside Chapter 13

Preview of Chapter 13

The balance sheet, income statement, and retained earnings statement do not always show the whole picture of the financial condition of a company or institution. In fact, looking at the financial statements of some well-known companies, a thoughtful investor might ask questions like these: How did Eastman Kodak finance cash dividends of $649 million in a year in which it earned only $17 million? How could United Airlines purchase new planes that cost $1.9 billion in a year in which it reported a net loss of over $2 billion? How did the companies that spent a combined fantastic $3.4 trillion on mergers and acquisitions in a recent year finance those deals? Answers to these and similar questions can be found in this chapter, which presents the statement of cash flows.

The content and organization of this chapter are as follows.

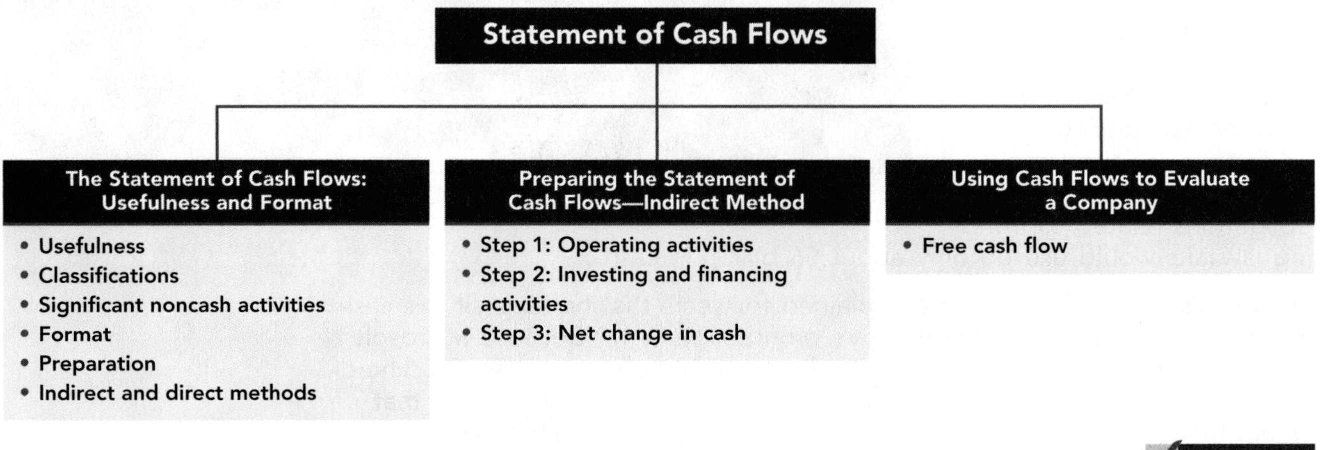

THE STATEMENT OF CASH FLOWS: USEFULNESS AND FORMAT

The balance sheet, income statement, and retained earnings statement provide only limited information about a company's cash flows (cash receipts and cash payments). For example, comparative balance sheets show the increase in property, plant, and equipment during the year. But they do not show how the additions were financed or paid for. The income statement shows net income. But it does not indicate the amount of cash generated by operating activities. The retained earnings statement shows cash dividends declared but not the cash dividends paid during the year. None of these statements presents a detailed summary of where cash came from and how it was used.

Usefulness of the Statement of Cash Flows

STUDY OBJECTIVE 1

Indicate the usefulness of the statement of cash flows.

The **statement of cash flows** reports the cash receipts, cash payments, and net change in cash resulting from operating, investing, and financing activities during a period. The information in a statement of cash flows should help investors, creditors, and others assess:

1. **The entity's ability to generate future cash flows.** By examining relationships between items in the statement of cash flows, investors can make predictions of the amounts, timing, and uncertainty of future cash flows better than they can from accrual basis data.

2. **The entity's ability to pay dividends and meet obligations.** If a company does not have adequate cash, it cannot pay employees, settle debts, or pay dividends. Employees, creditors, and stockholders should be particularly interested in this statement, because it alone shows the flows of cash in a business.
3. **The reasons for the difference between net income and net cash provided (used) by operating activities.** Net income provides information on the success or failure of a business enterprise. However, some financial statement users are critical of accrual-basis net income because it requires many estimates. As a result, users often challenge the reliability of the number. Such is not the case with cash. Many readers of the statement of cash flows want to know the reasons for the difference between net income and net cash provided by operating activities. Then they can assess for themselves the reliability of the income number.
4. **The cash investing and financing transactions during the period.** By examining a company's investing and financing transactions, a financial statement reader can better understand why assets and liabilities changed during the period.

ETHICS NOTE

Though we would discourage reliance on cash flows to the exclusion of accrual accounting, comparing cash from operations to net income can reveal important information about the "quality" of reported net income. Such a comparison can reveal the extent to which net income provides a good measure of actual performance.

Classification of Cash Flows

STUDY OBJECTIVE 2

Distinguish among operating, investing, and financing activities.

The statement of cash flows classifies cash receipts and cash payments as operating, investing, and financing activities. Transactions and other events characteristic of each kind of activity are as follows.

1. **Operating activities** include the cash effects of transactions that create revenues and expenses. They thus enter into the determination of net income.
2. **Investing activities** include (a) acquiring and disposing of investments and property, plant, and equipment, and (b) lending money and collecting the loans.
3. **Financing activities** include (a) obtaining cash from issuing debt and repaying the amounts borrowed, and (b) obtaining cash from stockholders, repurchasing shares, and paying dividends.

The operating activities category is the most important. It shows the cash provided by company operations. This source of cash is generally considered to be the best measure of a company's ability to generate sufficient cash to continue as a going concern.

Illustration 13-1 (page 560) lists typical cash receipts and cash payments within each of the three classifications. **Study the list carefully.** It will prove very useful in solving homework exercises and problems.

Note the following general guidelines:

1. Operating activities involve income statement items.
2. Investing activities involve cash flows resulting from changes in investments and long-term asset items.
3. Financing activities involve cash flows resulting from changes in long-term liability and stockholders' equity items.

Companies classify as operating activities some cash flows related to investing or financing activities. For example, receipts of investment revenue (interest and dividends) are classified as operating activities. So are payments of interest to lenders. Why are these considered operating activities? **Because companies report these items in the income statement, where results of operations are shown.**

Illustration 13-1
Typical receipt and payment classifications

TYPES OF CASH INFLOWS AND OUTFLOWS

Operating activities

Operating activities—Income statement items
Cash inflows:
From sale of goods or services.
From interest received and dividends received.
Cash outflows:
To suppliers for inventory.
To employees for services.
To government for taxes.
To lenders for interest.
To others for expenses.

Investing activities

Investing activities—Changes in investments and long-term assets
Cash inflows:
From sale of property, plant, and equipment.
From sale of investments in debt or equity securities of other entities.
From collection of principal on loans to other entities.
Cash outflows:
To purchase property, plant, and equipment.
To purchase investments in debt or equity securities of other entities.
To make loans to other entities.

Financing activities

Financing activities—Changes in long-term liabilities and stockholders' equity
Cash inflows:
From sale of common stock.
From issuance of long-term debt (bonds and notes).
Cash outflows:
To stockholders as dividends.
To redeem long-term debt or reacquire capital stock (treasury stock).

Significant Noncash Activities

Not all of a company's significant activities involve cash. Examples of significant noncash activities are:

1. Direct issuance of common stock to purchase assets.
2. Conversion of bonds into common stock.
3. Direct issuance of debt to purchase assets.
4. Exchanges of plant assets.

Companies do not report in the body of the statement of cash flows significant financing and investing activities that do not affect cash. Instead, they report these activities in either a **separate schedule** at the bottom of the statement of cash flows or in a **separate note or supplementary schedule** to the financial statements. The reporting of these noncash activities in a separate schedule satisfies the **full disclosure principle**.

HELPFUL HINT
Do not include noncash investing and financing activities in the body of the statement of cash flows. Report this information in a separate schedule.

In solving homework assignments you should present significant noncash investing and financing activities in a separate schedule at the bottom of the statement of cash flows. (See the last entry in Illustration 13-2, at the bottom of page 561, for an example.)

ACCOUNTING ACROSS THE ORGANIZATION

Net *What?*

Net income is not the same as net cash provided by operating activities. Below are some results from recent annual reports (dollars in millions). Note the wide disparity among these companies, all of which engaged in retail merchandising.

Company	Net Income	Net Cash Provided by Operating Activities
Kohl's Corporation	$ 730	$ 948
Wal-Mart Stores, Inc.	10,267	15,044
J. C. Penney Company, Inc.	524	61
Costco Wholesale Corp.	882	2,099
Target Corporation	3,198	3,195

In general, why do differences exist between net income and net cash provided by operating activities?

Format of the Statement of Cash Flows

The general format of the statement of cash flows presents the results of the three activities discussed previously—operating, investing, and financing—plus the significant noncash investing and financing activities. Illustration 13-2 shows a widely used form of the statement of cash flows.

Illustration 13-2
Format of statement of cash flows

COMPANY NAME
Statement of Cash Flows
Period Covered

Cash flows from operating activities		
(List of individual items)	XX	
Net cash provided (used) by operating activities		XXX
Cash flows from investing activities		
(List of individual inflows and outflows)	XX	
Net cash provided (used) by investing activities		XXX
Cash flows from financing activities		
(List of individual inflows and outflows)	XX	
Net cash provided (used) by financing activities		XXX
Net increase (decrease) in cash		XXX
Cash at beginning of period		XXX
Cash at end of period		XXX
Noncash investing and financing activities		
(List of individual noncash transactions)		XXX

The cash flows from operating activities section always appears first, followed by the investing activities section and then the financing activities section.

Before You Go On...

REVIEW IT

1. Why is the statement of cash flows useful?
2. What are the major classifications of cash flows on the statement of cash flows?
3. What are some examples of significant noncash activities?
4. What is the general format of the statement of cash flows? In what sequence are the three types of business activities presented?

DO IT

During its first week, Duffy & Stevenson Company had these transactions.

1. Issued 100,000 shares of $5 par value common stock for $800,000 cash.
2. Borrowed $200,000 from Castle Bank, signing a 5-year note bearing 8% interest.
3. Purchased two semi-trailer trucks for $170,000 cash.
4. Paid employees $12,000 for salaries and wages.
5. Collected $20,000 cash for services provided.

Classify each of these transactions by type of cash flow activity.

Action Plan

- Identify the three types of activities used to report all cash inflows and outflows.
- Report as operating activities the cash effects of transactions that create revenues and expenses and enter into the determination of net income.
- Report as investing activities transactions that (a) acquire and dispose of investments and productive long-lived assets and (b) lend money and collect loans.
- Report as financing activities transactions that (a) obtain cash from issuing debt and repay the amounts borrowed and (b) obtain cash from stockholders and pay them dividends.

Solution

1. Financing activity
2. Financing activity
3. Investing activity
4. Operating activity
5. Operating activity

Related exercise material: *BE13-1, BE13-2, E13-1, and E13-2.*

Preparing the Statement of Cash Flows

Companies prepare the statement of cash flows differently from the three other basic financial statements. First, it is not prepared from an adjusted trial balance. It requires detailed information concerning the changes in account balances that occurred between two points in time. An adjusted trial balance will not provide all of the necessary data. Second, the statement of cash flows deals with cash receipts and payments. As a result, the company **must adjust** the effects of the use of accrual accounting **to determine cash flows.**

The information to prepare this statement usually comes from three sources:

- **Comparative balance sheets.** Information in the comparative balance sheets indicates the amount of the changes in assets, liabilities, and stockholders' equities from the beginning to the end of the period.

- **Current income statement.** Information in this statement helps determine the amount of cash provided or used by operations during the period.
- **Additional information.** Such information includes transaction data that are needed to determine how cash was provided or used during the period.

Preparing the statement of cash flows from these data sources involves three major steps, explained in Illustration 13-3 below.

Illustration 13-3
Three major steps in preparing the statement of cash flows

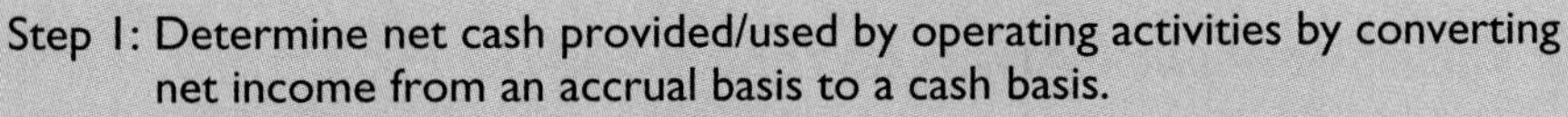
Step 1: Determine net cash provided/used by operating activities by converting net income from an accrual basis to a cash basis.

This step involves analyzing not only the current year's income statement but also comparative balance sheets and selected additional data.

Step 2: Analyze changes in noncurrent asset and liability accounts and record as investing and financing activities, or disclose as noncash transactions.

This step involves analyzing comparative balance sheet data and selected additional information for their effects on cash.

Step 3: Compare the net change in cash on the statement of cash flows with the change in the cash account reported on the balance sheet to make sure the amounts agree.

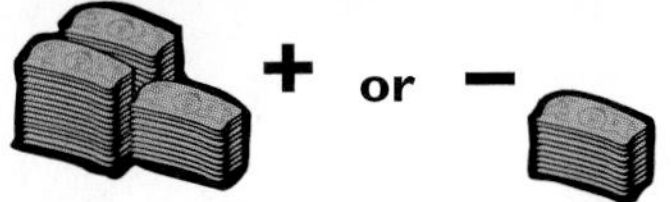

The difference between the beginning and ending cash balances can be easily computed from comparative balance sheets.

Indirect and Direct Methods

In order to perform step 1, a company **must convert net income from an accrual basis to a cash basis.** This conversion may be done by either of two methods: (1) the indirect method or (2) the direct method. **Both methods arrive at the same total amount** for "Net cash provided by operating activities." They differ in **how** they arrive at the amount.

The **indirect method** adjusts net income for items that do not affect cash. A great majority of companies (98.8%) use this method, as shown in the nearby chart.[1] Companies favor the indirect method for two reasons: (1) It is easier and less costly to prepare, and (2) it focuses on the differences between net income and net cash flow from operating activities.

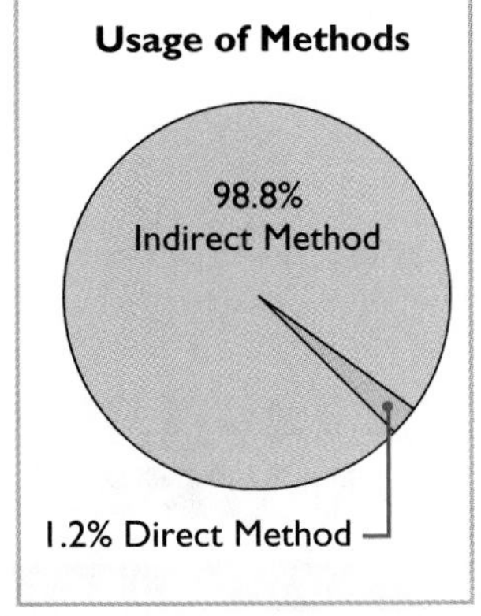

[1] *Accounting Trends and Techniques—2005* (New York: American Institute of Certified Public Accountants, 2005).

The **direct method** shows operating cash receipts and payments, making it more consistent with the objective of a statement of cash flows. The FASB has expressed a preference for the direct method, but allows the use of either method.

The next section illustrates the more popular indirect method. Appendix 13B illustrates the direct method.

MANAGEMENT INSIGHT

Cash Flow Isn't Always What It Seems

Some managers have taken actions that artificially increase cash flow from operating activities. They do this by moving negative amounts out of the operating section and into the investing or financing section.

For example, WorldCom, Inc. disclosed that it had improperly capitalized expenses: It had moved $3.8 billion of cash outflows from the "Cash from operating activities" section of the cash flow statement to the "Investing activities" section, thereby greatly enhancing cash provided by operating activities. Similarly, Dynegy, Inc. restated its cash flow statement because it had improperly included in operating activities, instead of in financing activities, $300 million from natural gas trading. The restatement resulted in a drop of 37% in cash flow from operating activities.

Source: Henny Sender, "Sadly, These Days Even Cash Flow Isn't Always What It Seems To Be," *Wall Street Journal*, May 8, 2002.

? For what reasons might managers at WorldCom and at Dynegy take the actions noted above?

Before You Go On...

REVIEW IT

1. What are the three major steps in preparing a statement of cash flows?
2. What is the primary difference between the indirect and direct approaches to the statement of cash flows?
3. Which method of preparing the statement of cash flows is more commonly used in practice?

PREPARING THE STATEMENT OF CASH FLOWS—INDIRECT METHOD

STUDY OBJECTIVE 3

Prepare a statement of cash flows using the indirect method.

To explain how to prepare a statement of cash flows using the indirect method, we use financial information from Computer Services Company. Illustration 13-4 presents Computer Services' current and previous-year balance sheets, its current-year income statement, and related financial information for the current year.

Illustration 13-4
Comparative balance sheets, income statement, and additional information for Computer Services Company

COMPUTER SERVICES COMPANY
Comparative Balance Sheets
December 31

Assets	2008	2007	Change in Account Balance Increase/Decrease
Current assets			
Cash	$ 55,000	$ 33,000	$ 22,000 Increase
Accounts receivable	20,000	30,000	10,000 Decrease
Merchandise inventory	15,000	10,000	5,000 Increase
Prepaid expenses	5,000	1,000	4,000 Increase
Property, plant, and equipment			
Land	130,000	20,000	110,000 Increase
Building	160,000	40,000	120,000 Increase
Accumulated depreciation—building	(11,000)	(5,000)	6,000 Increase
Equipment	27,000	10,000	17,000 Increase
Accumulated depreciation—equipment	(3,000)	(1,000)	2,000 Increase
Total assets	$398,000	$138,000	
Liabilities and Stockholders' Equity			
Current liabilities			
Accounts payable	$ 28,000	$ 12,000	$ 16,000 Increase
Income tax payable	6,000	8,000	2,000 Decrease
Long-term liabilities			
Bonds payable	130,000	20,000	110,000 Increase
Stockholders' equity			
Common stock	70,000	50,000	20,000 Increase
Retained earnings	164,000	48,000	116,000 Increase
Total liabilities and stockholders' equity	$398,000	$138,000	

COMPUTER SERVICES COMPANY
Income Statement
For the Year Ended December 31, 2008

Revenues		$507,000
Cost of goods sold	$150,000	
Operating expenses (excluding depreciation)	111,000	
Depreciation expense	9,000	
Loss on sale of equipment	3,000	
Interest expense	42,000	315,000
Income before income tax		192,000
Income tax expense		47,000
Net income		$145,000

Additional information for 2008:
1. The company declared and paid a $29,000 cash dividend.
2. Issued $110,000 of long-term bonds in direct exchange for land.
3. A building costing $120,000 was purchased for cash. Equipment costing $25,000 was also purchased for cash.
4. The company sold equipment with a book value of $7,000 (cost $8,000, less accumulated depreciation $1,000) for $4,000 cash.
5. Issued common stock for $20,000 cash.
6. Depreciation expense was comprised of $6,000 for building and $3,000 for equipment.

We will now apply the three steps to the information provided for Computer Services Company.

Step 1: Operating Activities

DETERMINE NET CASH PROVIDED/USED BY OPERATING ACTIVITIES BY CONVERTING NET INCOME FROM AN ACCRUAL BASIS TO A CASH BASIS

To determine net cash provided by operating activities under the indirect method, companies **adjust net income in numerous ways.** A useful starting point is to understand **why** net income must be converted to net cash provided by operating activities.

Under generally accepted accounting principles, most companies use the accrual basis of accounting. As you have learned, this basis requires that companies record revenue when earned and record expenses when incurred. Earned revenues may include credit sales for which the company has not yet collected cash. Expenses incurred may include some items that it has not yet paid in cash. Thus, under the accrual basis of accounting, net income is not the same as net cash provided by operating activities.

Therefore, under the **indirect method**, companies must adjust net income to convert certain items to the cash basis. The indirect method (or reconciliation method) starts with net income and converts it to net cash provided by operating activities. Illustration 13-5 lists the three types of adjustments.

Illustration 13-5
Three types of adjustments to convert net income to net cash provided by operating activities

Net Income	+/−	Adjustments	=	Net Cash Provided/ Used by Operating Activities
		• **Add back noncash expenses**, such as depreciation expense, amortization, or depletion. • **Deduct gains and add losses** that resulted from investing and financing activities. • **Analyze changes** to noncash current asset and current liability accounts.		

HELPFUL HINT

Depreciation is similar to any other expense in that it reduces net income. It differs in that it does not involve a current cash outflow; that is why it must be *added back* to net income to arrive at cash provided by operating activities.

We explain the three types of adjustments in the next three sections.

DEPRECIATION EXPENSE

Computer Services' income statement reports depreciation expense of $9,000. Although depreciation expense reduces net income, it does not reduce cash. In other words, depreciation expense is a noncash charge. The company must add it back to net income to arrive at net cash provided by operating activities. Computer Services reports depreciation expense as follows in the statement of cash flows.

Illustration 13-6
Adjustment for depreciation

Cash flows from operating activities	
Net income	$145,000
Adjustments to reconcile net income to net cash provided by operating activities:	
Depreciation expense	**9,000**
Net cash provided by operating activities	$154,000

As the first adjustment to net income in the statement of cash flows, companies frequently list depreciation and similar noncash charges such as amortization of intangible assets, depletion expense, and bad debt expense.

LOSS ON SALE OF EQUIPMENT

Illustration 13-1 states that the investing activities section should report cash received from the sale of plant assets. Sales of plant assets are not considered operating activities. Because of this, **companies must eliminate from net income all gains and losses related to the disposal of plant assets, to arrive at cash provided by operating activities.**

In our example, Computer Services' income statement reports a $3,000 loss on the sale of equipment (book value $7,000, less $4,000 cash received from sale of equipment). Illustration 13-7 shows that the $3,000 loss is eliminated by adding $3,000 back to net income to arrive at net cash provided by operating activities.

Illustration 13-7
Adjustment for loss on sale of equipment

Cash flows from operating activities		
Net income		$145,000
Adjustments to reconcile net income to net cash provided by operating activities:		
Depreciation expense	$9,000	
Loss on sale of equipment	**3,000**	12,000
Net cash provided by operating activities		$157,000

If a gain on sale occurs, the company deducts the gain from its net income in order to determine net cash provided by operating activities. **In the case of either a gain or a loss, companies report as a source of cash in the investing activities section of the statement of cash flows the actual amount of cash received from the sale.**

CHANGES TO NONCASH CURRENT ASSET AND CURRENT LIABILITY ACCOUNTS

A final adjustment in reconciling net income to net cash provided by operating activities involves examining all changes in noncash current asset and current liability accounts. The accrual accounting process records revenues in the period earned and expenses in the period incurred. For example, companies use Accounts Receivable to record amounts owed to the company for sales that have been made but for which cash collections have not yet been received. They use the Prepaid Insurance account to reflect insurance that has been paid for, but which has not yet expired, and therefore has not been expensed. Similarly, the Salaries Payable account reflects salaries expense that has been incurred by the company but has not been paid.

As a result, we need to adjust net income for these accruals and prepayments to determine net cash provided by operating activities. Thus we must analyze the change in each noncash current asset and current liability account to determine its impact on net income and cash.

CHANGES IN NONCASH CURRENT ASSETS. The adjustments required for changes in noncash current asset accounts are as follows: **Deduct from net income increases in current asset accounts, and add to net income decreases in current asset accounts, to arrive at net cash provided by operating activities.** We can observe these relationships by analyzing the accounts of Computer Services Company.

Decrease in Accounts Receivable. Computer Services Company's accounts receivable decreased by $10,000 (from $30,000 to $20,000) during the period. For Computer Services this means that cash receipts were $10,000 higher than revenues. The Accounts Receivable account in Illustration 13-8 shows that Computer Services Company had $507,000 in revenues (as reported on the income statement), but it collected $517,000 in cash. As shown in Illustration 13-9 (below), to adjust net income to net cash provided by operating activities, the company adds to net income the decrease of $10,000 in accounts receivable.

Illustration 13-8
Analysis of accounts receivable

Accounts Receivable

1/1/08	Balance	30,000	**Receipts from customers**	**517,000**
	Revenues	**507,000**		
12/31/08	Balance	20,000		

When the Accounts Receivable balance increases, cash receipts are lower than revenue earned under the accrual basis. Therefore, the company deducts from net income the amount of the increase in accounts receivable, to arrive at net cash provided by operating activities.

Increase in Merchandise Inventory. Computer Services Company's Merchandise Inventory balance increased $5,000 (from $10,000 to $15,000) during the period. The change in the Merchandise Inventory account reflects the difference between the amount of inventory purchased and the amount sold. For Computer Services this means that the cost of merchandise purchased exceeded the cost of goods sold by $5,000. As a result, cost of goods sold does not reflect $5,000 of cash payments made for merchandise. The company deducts from net income this inventory increase of $5,000 during the period, to arrive at net cash provided by operating activities (see Illustration 13-9). If inventory decreases, the company adds to net income the amount of the change, to arrive at net cash provided by operating activities.

Increase in Prepaid Expenses. Computer Services' prepaid expenses increased during the period by $4,000. This means that cash paid for expenses is higher than expenses reported on an accrual basis. In other words, the company has made cash payments in the current period, but will not charge expenses to income until future periods (as charges to the income statement). To adjust net income to net cash provided by operating activities, the company deducts from net income the $4,000 increase in prepaid expenses (see Illustration 13-9).

Illustration 13-9
Adjustments for changes in current asset accounts

Cash flows from operating activities		
Net income		$145,000
Adjustments to reconcile net income to net cash provided by operating activities:		
Depreciation expense	$ 9,000	
Loss on sale of equipment	3,000	
Decrease in accounts receivable	**10,000**	
Increase in merchandise inventory	**(5,000)**	
Increase in prepaid expenses	**(4,000)**	13,000
Net cash provided by operating activities		$158,000

If prepaid expenses decrease, reported expenses are higher than the expenses paid. Therefore, the company adds to net income the decrease in prepaid expenses, to arrive at net cash provided by operating activities.

CHANGES IN CURRENT LIABILITIES. The adjustments required for changes in current liability accounts are as follows: **Add to net income increases in current liability accounts, and deduct from net income decreases in current liability accounts, to arrive at net cash provided by operating activities.**

Increase in Accounts Payable. For Computer Services Company, Accounts Payable increased by $16,000 (from $12,000 to $28,000) during the period. That means the company received $16,000 more in goods than it actually paid for. As shown in Illustration 13-10 (below), to adjust net income to determine net cash provided by operating activities, the company adds to net income the $16,000 increase in Accounts Payable.

Decrease in Income Taxes Payable. When a company incurs income tax expense but has not yet paid its taxes, it records income tax payable. A change in the Income Tax Payable account reflects the difference between income tax expense incurred and income tax actually paid. Computer Services' Income Tax Payable account decreased by $2,000. That means the $47,000 of income tax expense reported on the income statement was $2,000 less than the amount of taxes paid during the period of $49,000. As shown in Illustration 13-10, to adjust net income to a cash basis, the company must reduce net income by $2,000.

Illustration 13-10
Adjustments for changes in current liability accounts

Cash flows from operating activities		
Net income		$145,000
Adjustments to reconcile net income to net cash provided by operating activities:		
Depreciation expense	$ 9,000	
Loss on sale of equipment	3,000	
Decrease in accounts receivable	10,000	
Increase in merchandise inventory	(5,000)	
Increase in prepaid expenses	(4,000)	
Increase in accounts payable	**16,000**	
Decrease in income tax payable	**(2,000)**	27,000
Net cash provided by operating activities		$172,000

Illustration 13-10 shows that, after starting with net income of $145,000, the sum of all of the adjustments to net income was $27,000. This resulted in net cash provided by operating activities of $172,000.

Summary of Conversion to Net Cash Provided by Operating Activities—Indirect Method

As shown in the previous illustrations, the statement of cash flows prepared by the indirect method starts with net income. It then adds or deducts items to arrive at net cash provided by operating activities. The required adjustments are of three types:

1. Noncash charges such as depreciation, amortization, and depletion.
2. Gains and losses on the sale of plant assets.
3. Changes in noncash current asset and current liability accounts.

Illustration 13-11 (page 570) provides a summary of these changes.

Illustration 13-11
Adjustments required to convert net income to net cash provided by operating activities

		Adjustment Required to Convert Net Income to Net Cash Provided by Operating Activities
Noncash Charges	Depreciation expense	Add
	Patent amortization expense	Add
	Depletion expense	Add
Gains and Losses	Loss on sale of plant asset	Add
	Gain on sale of plant asset	Deduct
Changes in Current Assets and Current Liabilities	Increase in current asset account	Deduct
	Decrease in current asset account	Add
	Increase in current liability account	Add
	Decrease in current liability account	Deduct

ACCOUNTING ACROSS THE ORGANIZATION

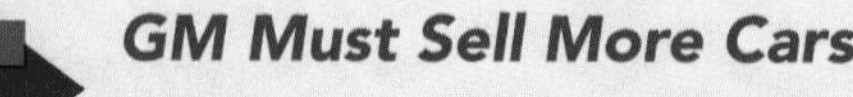

GM Must Sell More Cars

Market share matters—and it shows up in the accounting numbers. Just ask General Motors. In recent years GM has seen its market share erode until, at 25.6% of the market, the company reached the point where it actually consumed more cash than it generated. It isn't time to panic yet—GM has about $20 billion in cash on hand—but it is time to come up with a plan.

To address immediate cash needs, GM management may have to quit paying its $1.1 billion annual dividend, and it may have to sell off some assets and businesses. But in the long term, GM must either increase its market share, or shrink its manufacturing operations to fit its sales figures. The following table shows net income and cash provided by operating activities at various market-share levels.

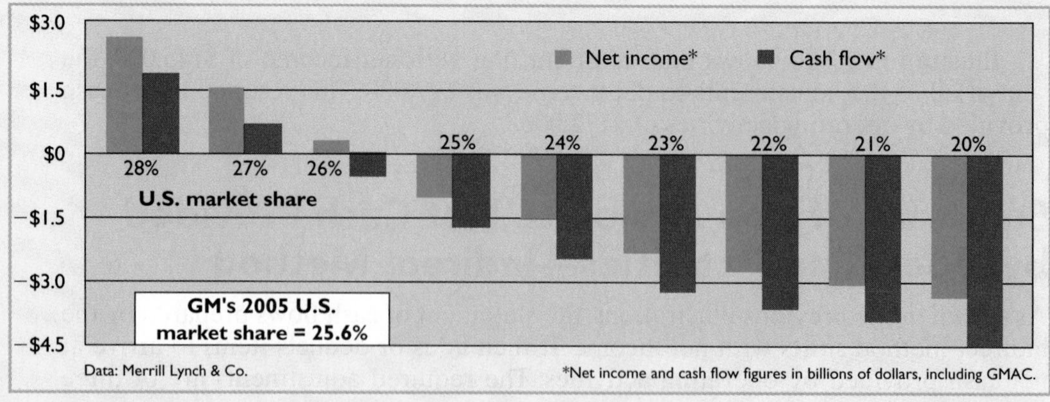

Source: David Welch and Dan Beucke, "Why GM's Plan Won't Work," *Business Week,* May 9, 2005, pp. 85–93.

? Why does GM's cash provided by operating activities drop so precipitously when the company's sales figures decline?

Step 2: Investing and Financing Activities

ANALYZE CHANGES IN NONCURRENT ASSET AND LIABILITY ACCOUNTS AND RECORD AS INVESTING AND FINANCING ACTIVITIES, OR DISCLOSE AS NONCASH TRANSACTIONS

Increase in Land. As indicated from the change in the Land account and the additional information, the company purchased land of $110,000 through the issuance of long-term bonds. The issuance of bonds payable for land has no effect on cash. But it is a significant noncash investing and financing activity that merits its disclosure in a separate schedule. (See Illustration 13-13 on page 572.)

HELPFUL HINT
The investing and financing activities are measured and reported in the same way under both the direct and indirect methods.

Increase in Building. As the additional data indicate, Computer Services Company acquired an office building for $120,000 cash. This is a cash outflow reported in the investing section. (See Illustration 13-13 on page 572.)

Increase in Equipment. The Equipment account increased $17,000. The additional information explains that this was a net increase that resulted from two transactions: (1) a purchase of equipment of $25,000, and (2) the sale for $4,000 of equipment costing $8,000. These transactions are investing activities. The company should report each transaction separately. The statement in Illustration 13-13 (page 572) reports the purchase of equipment as an outflow of cash for $25,000. It reports the sale as an inflow of cash for $4,000. The T account below shows the reasons for the change in this account during the year.

Illustration 13-12
Analysis of equipment

Equipment				
1/1/08	Balance	10,000	Cost of equipment sold	8,000
	Purchase of equipment	**25,000**		
12/31/08	Balance	27,000		

The following entry shows the details of the equipment sale transaction.

Cash	4,000	
Accumulated Depreciation	1,000	
Loss on Sale of Equipment	3,000	
Equipment		8,000

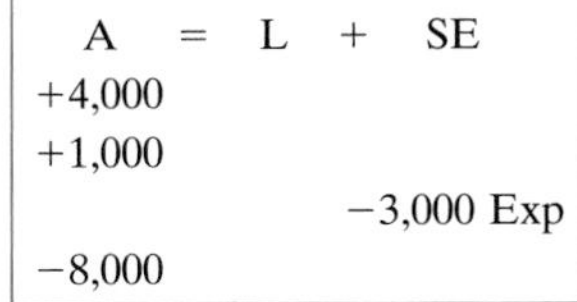

A	=	L	+	SE
+4,000				
+1,000				
				−3,000 Exp
−8,000				

Cash Flows
+4,000

Increase in Bonds Payable. The Bonds Payable account increased $110,000. As indicated in the additional information, the company acquired land from the issuance of these bonds. Illustration 13-13 reports this noncash transaction in a separate schedule at the bottom of the statement.

Increase in Common Stock. The balance sheet reports an increase in Common Stock of $20,000. The additional information section notes that this increase resulted from the issuance of new shares of stock. This is a cash inflow reported in the financing section in Illustration 13-13.

HELPFUL HINT
When companies issue stocks or bonds for cash, the actual proceeds will appear in the statement of cash flows as a financing inflow (rather than the par value of the stocks or face value of bonds).

Increase in Retained Earnings. Retained earnings increased $116,000 during the year. This increase can be explained by two factors: (1) Net income of $145,000 increased retained earnings. (2) Dividends of $29,000 decreased retained earnings. The company adjusts net income to net cash provided by operating activities in the operating activities section. Payment of the dividends (not the declaration) is a **cash outflow that the company reports as a financing activity** in Illustration 13-13.

STATEMENT OF CASH FLOWS—2008

Using the previous information, we can now prepare a statement of cash flows for 2008 for Computer Services Company as shown in Illustration 13-13.

Illustration 13-13
Statement of cash flows, 2008—indirect method

COMPUTER SERVICES COMPANY
Statement of Cash Flows—Indirect Method
For the Year Ended December 31, 2008

Cash flows from operating activities		
Net income		$145,000
Adjustments to reconcile net income to net cash provided by operating activities:		
Depreciation expense	$ 9,000	
Loss on sale of equipment	3,000	
Decrease in accounts receivable	10,000	
Increase in merchandise inventory	(5,000)	
Increase in prepaid expenses	(4,000)	
Increase in accounts payable	16,000	
Decrease in income tax payable	(2,000)	27,000
Net cash provided by operating activities		172,000
Cash flows from investing activities		
Purchase of building	(120,000)	
Purchase of equipment	(25,000)	
Sale of equipment	4,000	
Net cash used by investing activities		(141,000)
Cash flows from financing activities		
Issuance of common stock	20,000	
Payment of cash dividends	(29,000)	
Net cash used by financing activities		(9,000)
Net increase in cash		22,000
Cash at beginning of period		33,000
Cash at end of period		$ 55,000
Noncash investing and financing activities		
Issuance of bonds payable to purchase land		$110,000

HELPFUL HINT
Note that in the investing and financing activities sections, positive numbers indicate cash inflows (receipts), and negative numbers indicate cash outflows (payments).

Step 3: Net Change in Cash

COMPARE THE NET CHANGE IN CASH ON THE STATEMENT OF CASH FLOWS WITH THE CHANGE IN THE CASH ACCOUNT REPORTED ON THE BALANCE SHEET TO MAKE SURE THE AMOUNTS AGREE

Illustration 13-13 indicates that the net change in cash during the period was an increase of $22,000. This agrees with the change in Cash account reported on the balance sheet in Illustration 13-4 (page 565).

Before You Go On...

REVIEW IT

1. What is the format of the operating activities section?
2. Where is depreciation expense shown on a statement of cash flows?
3. Where are significant noncash investing and financing activities shown?

DO IT

Use the information provided below to prepare a statement of cash flows using the indirect method.

REYNOLDS COMPANY
Comparative Balance Sheets
December 31

Assets	2008	2007	Change Increase/Decrease
Cash	$ 54,000	$ 37,000	$ 17,000 Increase
Accounts receivable	68,000	26,000	42,000 Increase
Inventories	54,000	-0-	54,000 Increase
Prepaid expenses	4,000	6,000	2,000 Decrease
Land	45,000	70,000	25,000 Decrease
Buildings	200,000	200,000	-0-
Accumulated depreciation—buildings	(21,000)	(11,000)	10,000 Increase
Equipment	193,000	68,000	125,000 Increase
Accumulated depreciation—equipment	(28,000)	(10,000)	18,000 Increase
Totals	$569,000	$386,000	
Liabilities and Stockholders' Equity			
Accounts payable	$ 23,000	$ 40,000	$ 17,000 Decrease
Accrued expenses payable	10,000	-0-	10,000 Increase
Bonds payable	110,000	150,000	40,000 Decrease
Common stock ($1 par)	220,000	60,000	160,000 Increase
Retained earnings	206,000	136,000	70,000 Increase
Totals	$569,000	$386,000	

REYNOLDS COMPANY
Income Statement
For the Year Ended December 31, 2008

Revenues		$890,000
Cost of goods sold	$465,000	
Operating expenses	221,000	
Interest expense	12,000	
Loss on sale of equipment	2,000	700,000
Income before income taxes		190,000
Income tax expense		65,000
Net income		$125,000

Additional information:

1. Operating expenses include depreciation expense of $33,000 and charges from prepaid expenses of $2,000.
2. Land was sold at its book value for cash.
3. Cash dividends of $55,000 were declared and paid in 2008.
4. Interest expense of $12,000 was paid in cash.
5. Equipment with a cost of $166,000 was purchased for cash. Equipment with a cost of $41,000 and a book value of $36,000 was sold for $34,000 cash.
6. Bonds of $10,000 were redeemed at their book value for cash. Bonds of $30,000 were converted into common stock.

7. Common stock ($1 par) of $130,000 was issued for cash.
8. Accounts payable pertain to merchandise suppliers.

Action Plan

- Determine net cash provided/used by operating activities by adjusting net income for items that did not affect cash.
- Determine net cash provided/used by investing activities and financing activities.
- Determine the net increase/decrease in cash.

Solution

REYNOLDS COMPANY
Statement of Cash Flows—Indirect Method
For the Year Ended December 31, 2008

Cash flows from operating activities		
Net income		$125,000
Adjustments to reconcile net income to net cash provided by operating activities:		
Depreciation expense	$ 33,000	
Loss on sale of equipment	2,000	
Increase in accounts receivable	(42,000)	
Increase in inventories	(54,000)	
Decrease in prepaid expenses	2,000	
Decrease in accounts payable	(17,000)	
Increase in accrued expenses payable	10,000	(66,000)
Net cash provided by operating activities		59,000
Cash flows from investing activities		
Sale of land	25,000	
Sale of equipment	34,000	
Purchase of equipment	(166,000)	
Net cash used by investing activities		(107,000)
Cash flows from financing activities		
Redemption of bonds	(10,000)	
Sale of common stock	130,000	
Payment of dividends	(55,000)	
Net cash provided by financing activities		65,000
Net increase in cash		17,000
Cash at beginning of period		37,000
Cash at end of period		$ 54,000
Noncash investing and financing activities		
Conversion of bonds into common stock		$ 30,000

HELPFUL HINT

1. Determine net cash provided/used by operating activities, recognizing that operating activities generally relate to changes in current assets and current liabilities.
2. Determine net cash provided/used by investing activities, recognizing that investing activities generally relate to changes in noncurrent assets.
3. Determine net cash provided/used by financing activities, recognizing that financing activities generally relate to changes in long-term liabilities and stockholders' equity accounts.

Related exercise material: *BE13-4, BE13-5, BE13-6, BE13-7, E13-4, E13-5, and E13-6.*

The Navigator

USING CASH FLOWS TO EVALUATE A COMPANY

STUDY OBJECTIVE 4
Analyze the statement of cash flows.

Traditionally, investors and creditors have most commonly used ratios based on accrual accounting. These days, cash-based measures are gaining increased acceptance among analysts.

Free Cash Flow

In the statement of cash flows, cash provided by operating activities is intended to indicate the cash-generating capability of the company. Analysts have noted, however, that **cash provided by operating activities fails to take into account that a company must invest in new fixed assets** just to maintain its current level of operations. Companies also must at least **maintain dividends at current levels** to satisfy investors. The measurement of free cash flow provides additional insight regarding a company's cash-generating ability. **Free cash flow** describes the cash remaining from operations after adjustment for capital expenditures and dividends.

Consider the following example: Suppose that MPC produced and sold 10,000 personal computers this year. It reported $100,000 cash provided by operating activities. In order to maintain production at 10,000 computers, MPC invested $15,000 in equipment. It chose to pay $5,000 in dividends. Its free cash flow was $80,000 ($100,000 − $15,000 − $5,000). The company could use this $80,000 either to purchase new assets to expand the business or to pay an $80,000 dividend and continue to produce 10,000 computers. In practice, free cash flow is often calculated with the formula in Illustration 13-14. Alternative definitions also exist.

Illustration 13-14
Free cash flow

Free Cash Flow	=	Cash Provided by Operating Activities	−	Capital Expenditures	−	Cash Dividends

Illustration 13-15 provides basic information excerpted from the 2004 statement of cash flows of Microsoft Corporation.

Illustration 13-15
Microsoft cash flow information ($ in millions)

MICROSOFT CORPORATION
Statement of Cash Flows (partial)
2004

Cash provided by operating activities		$14,626
Cash flows from investing activities		
Additions to property and equipment	$ (1,109)	
Purchases of investments	(92,495)	
Sales of investments	85,302	
Acquisitions of companies	(4)	
Maturities of investments	5,561	
Cash used by investing activities		(2,745)
Cash paid for dividends		(1,729)

Microsoft's free cash flow is calculated as shown in Illustration 13-16.

Illustration 13-16
Calculation of Microsoft's free cash flow ($ in millions)

Cash provided by operating activities	$14,626
Less: Expenditures on property, plant, and equipment	1,109
Dividends paid	1,729
Free cash flow	$11,788

This is a tremendous amount of cash generated in a single year. It is available for the acquisition of new assets, the retirement of stock or debt, or the payment of dividends. Also note that this amount far exceeds Microsoft's 2004 net income of $8,168 million. This lends additional credibility to Microsoft's income number as an indicator of potential future performance. If anything, Microsoft's net income might understate its actual performance.

Oracle Corporation is one of the world's largest sellers of database software and information management services. Like Microsoft, its success depends on continuing to improve its existing products while developing new products to keep pace with rapid changes in technology. Oracle's free cash flow for 2004 was $2,988 million. This is impressive, but significantly less than Microsoft's amazing ability to generate cash.

DECISION TOOLKIT

Decision Checkpoints	Info Needed for Decision	Tool to Use for Decision	How to Evaluate Results
How much cash did the company generate to either expand operations or pay dividends?	Cash provided by operating activities, cash spent on fixed assets, and cash dividends	Free cash flow = Cash provided by operating activities − Capital expenditures − Cash dividends	Significant free cash flow indicates greater potential to finance new investment and pay additional dividends.

Before You Go On...

REVIEW IT

1. What is the difference between cash from operations and free cash flow?
2. What does it mean if a company has negative free cash flow?

Be sure to read **ALL ABOUT YOU: *Where Does the Money Go?*** on the next page for information on how topics in this chapter apply to you.

Where Does the Money Go?

When a company's cash flow from operating activities does not cover its cash needs, it must borrow money. In the short term this is OK, but in the long-term it can spell disaster. Sooner or later the company needs to increase its cash from operations or cut back on its expenditures, or it will go broke. Guess what? The same is true for you and me.

Where do you spend your cash? Most of us know how much we spend each month on rent and car payments. But how much do you spend each month on soda, coffee, pizza, video rentals, music downloads, and your cell phone service? Don't think it matters? Suppose you spend an average of only $4 per day on unneeded "incidentals." That's $120 a month, or almost $1,500 per year.

Some Facts

* College students spend about $200 billion per year on consumer products. Of that amount, $41 billion is "discretionary" in nature.
* More than 70% of college students own a cell phone, and 71% own a car.
* College students spend more than $8 billion per year purchasing DVDs, CDs, music downloads, and video games.
* Annual spending on travel by college students is about $4.6 billion.
* 78% of college students work, earning an average of $821 per month.

About the Numbers

College students spend an average of $287 per month on discretionary items (defined as anything other than tuition, room/board, rent, books, and school fees). A large chunk of that—more than $11 billion—is spent on beverages and snack foods. Maybe this would be a good place to start cutting your expenditures.

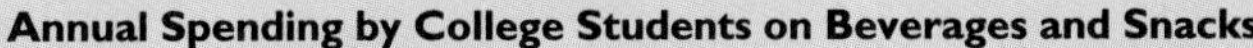

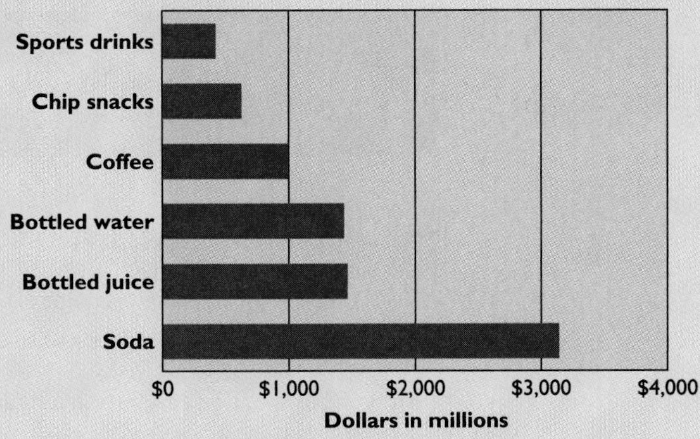

Source: "College Students Spend $200 Billion per Year," HarrisInteractive, *www.harrisinteractive.com/news/allnewsbydate.asp?NewsID=480* (accessed May 2006).

What Do You Think?

Let's say that you live on campus and own a car. You use the car for pleasure and to drive to a job that is three miles away. Suppose your annual cash flow statement includes the following items.

Cash inflows:	
Wages	$ 9,000
Student loans	5,000
Credit card debt	4,000
Cash outflows:	
Tuition, books, room, and board	13,000
Vehicle costs	2,000
Vacation	2,000
Cell phone service	500
Snacks and beverages	500

Should you get rid of your car and cell phone, quit eating snacks, and give up the idea of a vacation?

YES: At this rate you will accumulate nearly $40,000 in debts by the time you graduate. It is not fun to spend most of the paycheck of your post-graduation job paying off the debts you accumulated while in school.

NO: Give me a break. A person has to have some fun. Life wouldn't be worth living if I couldn't be drinking a Starbucks while cruising down the road talking on my cell phone.

Sources: Becky Ebenkamp, "College Communications 101," *Brandweek*, August 22-29, 2005, p. 16.

The authors' comments on this situation appear on page 617.

Using the Decision Toolkit

Intel Corporation is the leading producer of computer chips for personal computers. It makes the hugely successful Pentium chip. Its primary competitor is AMD (formerly Advanced Micro Devices). The two are vicious competitors, with frequent lawsuits filed between them. Financial statement data for Intel are provided below.

Instructions

Calculate free cash flow for Intel, and compare it with AMD's free cash flow, which was negative $354 million.

INTEL CORPORATION
Statements of Cash Flows
For the Years Ended December 31, 2004 and 2003
(in millions)

	2004	2003
Net cash provided by operating activities	$13,119	$11,515
Net cash used for investing activities	(5,032)	(7,090)
Net cash used for financing activities	(7,651)	(3,858)
Net increase (decrease) in cash and cash equivalents	$ 436	$ 567

Note. Cash spent on property, plant, and equipment in 2004 was $3,843. Cash paid for dividends was $1,022.

Solution

Intel's free cash flow is $8,254 million ($13,119 − $3,843 − $1,022). Compared to AMD's negative $354 million, this gives Intel a huge advantage in the ability to move quickly to invest in new projects.

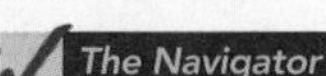

SUMMARY OF STUDY OBJECTIVES

1 **Indicate the usefulness of the statement of cash flows.** The statement of cash flows provides information about the cash receipts, cash payments, and net change in cash resulting from the operating, investing, and financing activities of a company during the period.

2 **Distinguish among operating, investing, and financing activities.** Operating activities include the cash effects of transactions that enter into the determination of net income. Investing activities involve cash flows resulting from changes in investments and long-term asset items. Financing activities involve cash flows resulting from changes in long-term liability and stockholders' equity items.

3 **Prepare a statement of cash flows using the indirect method.** The preparation of a statement of cash flows involves three major steps: (1) Determine net cash provided/used by operating activities by converting net income from an accrual basis to a cash basis. (2) Analyze changes in noncurrent asset and liability accounts and record as investing and financing activities, or disclose as noncash transactions. (3) Compare the net change in cash on the statement of cash flows with the change in the cash account reported on the balance sheet to make sure the amounts agree.

4 **Analyze the statement of cash flows.** Free cash flow indicates the amount of cash a company generated during the current year that is available for the payment of additional dividends or for expansion.

DECISION TOOLKIT—A SUMMARY

Decision Checkpoints	Info Needed for Decision	Tool to Use for Decision	How to Evaluate Results
How much cash did the company generate to either expand operations or pay dividends?	Cash provided by operating activities, cash spent on fixed assets, and cash dividends	Free cash flow = Cash provided by operating activities − Capital expenditures − Cash dividends	Significant free cash flow indicates greater potential to finance new investment and pay additional dividends.

GLOSSARY

Direct method A method of determining net cash provided by operating activities by adjusting each item in the income statement from the accrual basis to the cash basis. (p. 564)

Financing activities Cash flow activities that include (a) obtaining cash from issuing debt and repaying the amounts borrowed and (b) obtaining cash from stockholders, repurchasing shares, and paying dividends. (p. 559).

Free cash flow Cash provided by operating activities adjusted for capital expenditures and dividends paid. (p. 575).

Indirect method A method of preparing a statement of cash flows in which net income is adjusted for items that do not affect cash, to determine net cash provided by operating activities. (pp. 563, 566).

Investing activities Cash flow activities that include (a) acquiring and disposing of investments and property, plant, and equipment and (b) lending money and collecting the loans. (p. 559).

Operating activities Cash flow activities that include the cash effects of transactions that create revenues and expenses and thus enter into the determination of net income. (p. 559).

Statement of cash flows A basic financial statement that provides information about the cash receipts, cash payments, and net change in cash during a period, resulting from operating, investing, and financing activities. (p. 558).

Demonstration Problem 1

The income statement for the year ended December 31, 2008, for John Kosinski Manufacturing Company contains the following condensed information.

JOHN KOSINSKI MANUFACTURING COMPANY
Income Statement

Revenues		$6,583,000
Operating expenses (excluding depreciation)	$4,920,000	
Depreciation expense	880,000	5,800,000
Income before income taxes		783,000
Income tax expense		353,000
Net income		$ 430,000

Included in operating expenses is a $24,000 loss resulting from the sale of machinery for $270,000 cash. Machinery was purchased at a cost of $750,000.

The following balances are reported on Kosinski's comparative balance sheets at December 31.

JOHN KOSINSKI MANUFACTURING COMPANY
Comparative Balance Sheets (partial)

	2008	2007
Cash	$672,000	$130,000
Accounts receivable	775,000	610,000
Inventories	834,000	867,000
Accounts payable	521,000	501,000

Income tax expense of $353,000 represents the amount paid in 2008. Dividends declared and paid in 2008 totaled $200,000.

Instructions

Prepare the statement of cash flows using the indirect method.

action plan

- ✔ Determine net cash from operating activities. Operating activities generally relate to changes in current assets and current liabilities.
- ✔ Determine net cash from investing activities. Investing activities generally relate to changes in noncurrent assets.
- ✔ Determine net cash from financing activities. Financing activities generally relate to changes in long-term liabilities and stockholders' equity accounts.

Solution

JOHN KOSINSKI MANUFACTURING COMPANY
Statement of Cash Flows—Indirect Method
For the Year Ended December 31, 2008

Cash flows from operating activities		
Net income		$ 430,000
Adjustments to reconcile net income to net cash provided by operating activities:		
Depreciation expense	$ 880,000	
Loss on sale of machinery	24,000	
Increase in accounts receivable	(165,000)	
Decrease in inventories	33,000	
Increase in accounts payable	20,000	792,000
Net cash provided by operating activities		1,222,000
Cash flows from investing activities		
Sale of machinery	270,000	
Purchase of machinery	(750,000)	
Net cash used by investing activities		(480,000)
Cash flows from financing activities		
Payment of cash dividends		(200,000)
Net increase in cash		542,000
Cash at beginning of period		130,000
Cash at end of period		$ 672,000

✔ The Navigator

APPENDIX 13A Using a Worksheet to Prepare the Statement of Cash Flows—Indirect Method

STUDY OBJECTIVE 5

Explain how to use a worksheet to prepare the statement of cash flows using the indirect method.

When preparing a statement of cash flows, companies may need to make numerous adjustments of net income. In such cases, they often use **a worksheet to assemble and classify the data that will appear on the statement.** The worksheet is merely an aid in preparing the statement. Its use is optional. Illustration 13A-1 (next page) shows the skeleton format of the worksheet for preparation of the statement of cash flows.

The following guidelines are important in preparing a worksheet.

1. In the balance sheet accounts section, **list accounts with debit balances separately from those with credit balances.** This means, for example, that Accumulated Depreciation appears under credit balances and not as a contra account under debit balances. Enter the beginning and ending balances of each account in the appropriate columns. Enter as reconciling items in the two

Illustration 13A-1
Format of worksheet

XYZ Company.xls

File Edit View Insert Format Tools Data Window Help

XYZ COMPANY
Worksheet
Statement of Cash Flows For the Year Ended . . .

	A	B	C	D	E
5–8	**Balance Sheet Accounts**	**End of Last Year Balances**	**Reconciling Items Debit**	**Reconciling Items Credit**	**End of Current Year Balances**
9	Debit balance accounts	XX	XX	XX	XX
10		XX	XX	XX	XX
11	Totals	XXX			XXX
12	Credit balance accounts	XX	XX	XX	XX
13		XX	XX	XX	XX
14	Totals	XXX			XXX
15	**Statement of Cash**				
16	**Flows Effects**				
17	Operating activities				
18	Net income		XX		
19	Adjustments to net income		XX	XX	
20	Investing activities				
21	Receipts and payments		XX	XX	
22	Financing activities				
23	Receipts and payments		XX	XX	
24	Totals		XXX	XXX	
25	Increase (decrease) in cash		(XX)	XX	
26	Totals		XXX	XXX	
27					

middle columns the transactions that caused the change in the account balance during the year.

After all reconciling items have been entered, each line pertaining to a balance sheet account should "foot across." That is, the beginning balance plus or minus the reconciling item(s) must equal the ending balance. When this agreement exists for all balance sheet accounts, all changes in account balances have been reconciled.

2. The bottom portion of the worksheet consists of the operating, investing, and financing activities sections. It provides the information necessary to prepare the formal statement of cash flows. **Enter inflows of cash as debits in the reconciling columns. Enter outflows of cash as credits in the reconciling columns.** Thus, in this section, the sale of equipment for cash at book value appears as a debit under investing activities. Similarly, the purchase of land for cash appears as a credit under investing activities.
3. **The reconciling items shown in the worksheet are not entered in any journal or posted to any account.** They do not represent either adjustments or corrections of the balance sheet accounts. They are used only to facilitate the preparation of the statement of cash flows.

Preparing the Worksheet

Preparing a worksheet involves a series of prescribed steps. The steps in this case are:

1. Enter in the balance sheet accounts section the balance sheet accounts and their beginning and ending balances.

2. Enter in the reconciling columns of the worksheet the data that explain the changes in the balance sheet accounts other than cash and their effects on the statement of cash flows.
3. Enter on the cash line and at the bottom of the worksheet the increase or decrease in cash. This entry should enable the totals of the reconciling columns to be in agreement.

To illustrate the preparation of a worksheet, we will use the 2008 data for Computer Services Company. Your familiarity with these data (from the chapter) should help you understand the use of a worksheet. For ease of reference, the comparative balance sheets, income statement, and selected data for 2008 are presented in Illustration 13A-2 (on page 583).

DETERMINING THE RECONCILING ITEMS

Companies can use one of several approaches to determine the reconciling items. For example, they can first complete the changes affecting net cash provided by operating activities, and then can determine the effects of financing and investing transactions. Or, they can analyze the balance sheet accounts in the order in which they are listed on the worksheet. We will follow this latter approach for Computer Services, except for cash. As indicated in step 3, **cash is handled last**.

Accounts Receivable The decrease of $10,000 in accounts receivable means that cash collections from revenues are higher than the revenues reported in the income statement. To convert net income to net cash provided by operating activities, we add the decrease of $10,000 to net income. The entry in the reconciling columns of the worksheet is:

(a)	Operating—Decrease in Accounts Receivable	10,000	
	Accounts Receivable		10,000

Merchandise Inventory Computer Services Company's Merchandise Inventory balance increases $5,000 during the period. The Merchandise Inventory account reflects the difference between the amount of inventory that the company purchased and the amount that it sold. For Computer Services this means that the cost of merchandise purchased exceeds the cost of goods sold by $5,000. As a result, cost of goods sold does not reflect $5,000 of cash payments made for merchandise. We deduct this inventory increase of $5,000 during the period from net income to arrive at net cash provided by operating activities. The worksheet entry is:

(b)	Merchandise Inventory	5,000	
	Operating—Increase in Merchandise Inventory		5,000

Prepaid Expenses An increase of $4,000 in prepaid expenses means that expenses deducted in determining net income are less than expenses that were paid in cash. We deduct the increase of $4,000 from net income in determining net cash provided by operating activities. The worksheet entry is:

(c)	Prepaid Expenses	4,000	
	Operating—Increase in Prepaid Expenses		4,000

Illustration 13A-2
Comparative balance sheets, income statement, and additional information for Computer Services Company

Computer Services Company.xls

File Edit View Insert Format Tools Data Window Help

COMPUTER SERVICES COMPANY
Comparative Balance Sheets
December 31

	2008	2007	Change in Account Balance Increase/Decrease
Assets			
Current assets			
Cash	$ 55,000	$ 33,000	$ 22,000 Increase
Accounts receivable	20,000	30,000	10,000 Decrease
Merchandise inventory	15,000	10,000	5,000 Increase
Prepaid expenses	5,000	1,000	4,000 Increase
Property, plant, and equipment			
Land	130,000	20,000	110,000 Increase
Building	160,000	40,000	120,000 Increase
Accumulated depreciation—building	(11,000)	(5,000)	6,000 Increase
Equipment	27,000	10,000	17,000 Increase
Accumulated depreciation—equipment	(3,000)	(1,000)	2,000 Increase
Total	$398,000	$138,000	
Liabilities and Stockholders' Equity			
Current liabilities			
Accounts payable	$ 28,000	$ 12,000	$ 16,000 Increase
Income tax payable	6,000	8,000	2,000 Decrease
Long-term liabilities			
Bonds payable	130,000	20,000	110,000 Increase
Stockholders' equity			
Common stock	70,000	50,000	20,000 Increase
Retained earnings	164,000	48,000	116,000 Increase
Total liabilities and stockholders' equity	$398,000	$138,000	

Sheet 1 / Sheet 2

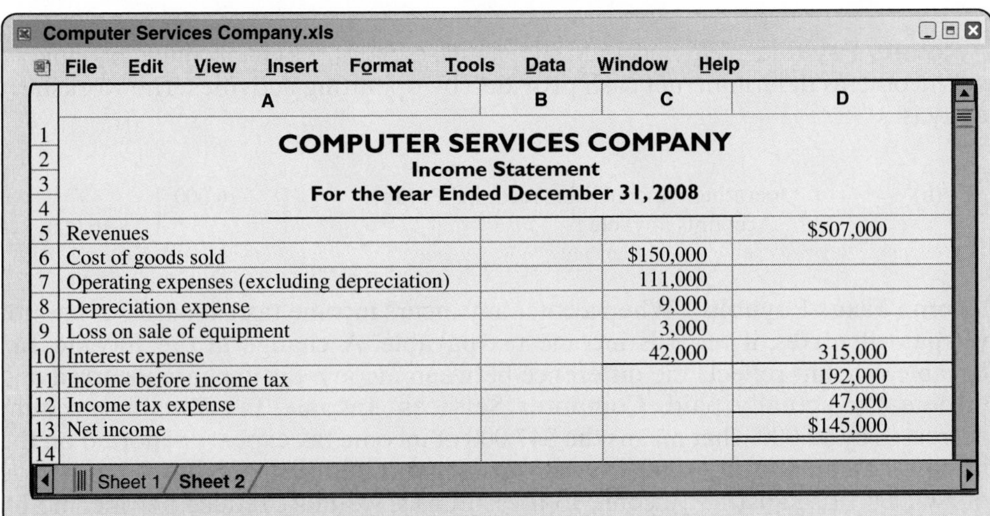

Computer Services Company.xls

File Edit View Insert Format Tools Data Window Help

COMPUTER SERVICES COMPANY
Income Statement
For the Year Ended December 31, 2008

Revenues			$507,000
Cost of goods sold		$150,000	
Operating expenses (excluding depreciation)		111,000	
Depreciation expense		9,000	
Loss on sale of equipment		3,000	
Interest expense		42,000	315,000
Income before income tax			192,000
Income tax expense			47,000
Net income			$145,000

Sheet 1 / Sheet 2

Additional information for 2008:

1. The company declared and paid a $29,000 cash dividend.
2. Issued $110,000 of long-term bonds in direct exchange for land.
3. A building costing $120,000 was purchased for cash. Equipment costing $25,000 was also purchased for cash.
4. The company sold equipment with a book value of $7,000 (cost $8,000, less accumulated depreciation $1,000) for $4,000 cash.
5. Issued common stock for $20,000 cash.
6. Depreciation expense was comprised of $6,000 for building and $3,000 for equipment.

HELPFUL HINT
These amounts are asterisked in the worksheet to indicate that they result from a significant noncash transaction.

Land The increase in land of $110,000 resulted from a purchase through the issuance of long-term bonds. The company should report this transaction as a significant noncash investing and financing activity. The worksheet entry is:

(d)	Land	110,000	
	Bonds Payable		110,000

Building The cash purchase of a building for $120,000 is an investing activity cash outflow. The entry in the reconciling columns of the worksheet is:

(e)	Building	120,000	
	Investing—Purchase of Building		120,000

Equipment The increase in equipment of $17,000 resulted from a cash purchase of $25,000 and the sale of equipment costing $8,000. The book value of the equipment was $7,000, the cash proceeds were $4,000, and a loss of $3,000 was recorded. The worksheet entries are:

(f)	Equipment	25,000	
	Investing—Purchase of Equipment		25,000
(g)	Investing—Sale of Equipment	4,000	
	Operating—Loss on Sale of Equipment	3,000	
	Accumulated Depreciation—Equipment	1,000	
	Equipment		8,000

Accounts Payable We must add the increase of $16,000 in accounts payable to net income to determine net cash provided by operating activities. The worksheet entry is:

(h)	Operating—Increase in Accounts Payable	16,000	
	Accounts Payable		16,000

Income Taxes Payable When a company incurs income tax expense but has not yet paid its taxes, it records income tax payable. A change in the Income Tax Payable account reflects the difference between income tax expense incurred and income tax actually paid. Computer Services' Income Tax Payable account decreases by $2,000. That means the $47,000 of income tax expense reported on the income statement was $2,000 less than the amount of taxes paid during the period of $49,000. To adjust net income to a cash basis, we must reduce net income by $2,000. The worksheet entry is:

(i)	Income Taxes Payable	2,000	
	Operating—Decrease in Income Taxes Payable		2,000

Bonds Payable The increase of $110,000 in this account resulted from the issuance of bonds for land. This is a significant noncash investing and financing activity. Worksheet entry (d) above is the only entry necessary.

Common Stock The balance sheet reports an increase in Common Stock of $20,000. The additional information section notes that this increase resulted from the issuance of new shares of stock. This is a cash inflow reported in the financing section. The worksheet entry is:

(j)	Financing—Issuance of Common Stock	20,000	
	Common Stock		20,000

Accumulated Depreciation—Building, and Accumulated Depreciation—Equipment Increases in these accounts of $6,000 and $3,000, respectively, resulted from depreciation expense. Depreciation expense is a **noncash charge that we must add to net income** to determine net cash provided by operating activities. The worksheet entries are:

(k)	Operating—Depreciation Expense—Building	6,000	
	Accumulated Depreciation—Building		6,000
(l)	Operating—Depreciation Expense—Equipment	3,000	
	Accumulated Depreciation—Equipment		3,000

Retained Earnings The $116,000 increase in retained earnings resulted from net income of $145,000 and the declaration and payment of a $29,000 cash dividend. Net income is included in net cash provided by operating activities, and the dividends are a financing activity cash outflow. The entries in the reconciling columns of the worksheet are:

(m)	Operating—Net Income	145,000	
	Retained Earnings		145,000
(n)	Retained Earnings	29,000	
	Financing—Payment of Dividends		29,000

Disposition of Change in Cash The firm's cash increased $22,000 in 2008. The final entry on the worksheet, therefore, is:

(o)	Cash	22,000	
	Increase in Cash		22,000

As shown in the worksheet, we enter the increase in cash in the reconciling credit column as a **balancing** amount. This entry should complete the reconciliation of the changes in the balance sheet accounts. Also, it should permit the totals of the reconciling columns to be in agreement. When all changes have been explained and the reconciling columns are in agreement, the reconciling columns are ruled to complete the worksheet. The completed worksheet for Computer Services Company is shown in Illustration 13A-3 (page 586).

Illustration 13A-3
Completed worksheet—indirect method

Computer Services Company.xls

File Edit View Insert Format Tools Data Window Help

COMPUTER SERVICES COMPANY
Worksheet
Statement of Cash Flows For the Year Ended December 31, 2008

	A	B	C	D	E
5		**Balance**	**Reconciling Items**		**Balance**
6	**Balance Sheet Accounts**	**12/31/07**	**Debit**	**Credit**	**12/31/08**
7	Debits				
8	Cash	33,000	(o) 22,000		55,000
9	Accounts Receivable	30,000		(a) 10,000	20,000
10	Merchandise Inventory	10,000	(b) 5,000		15,000
11	Prepaid Expenses	1,000	(c) 4,000		5,000
12	Land	20,000	(d) 110,000*		130,000
13	Building	40,000	(e) 120,000		160,000
14	Equipment	10,000	(f) 25,000	(g) 8,000	27,000
15	Total	144,000			412,000
16	Credits				
17	Accounts Payable	12,000		(h) 16,000	28,000
18	Income Taxes Payable	8,000	(i) 2,000		6,000
19	Bonds Payable	20,000		(d) 110,000*	130,000
20	Accumulated Depreciation—Building	5,000		(k) 6,000	11,000
21	Accumulated Depreciation—Equipment	1,000	(g) 1,000	(l) 3,000	3,000
22	Common Stock	50,000		(j) 20,000	70,000
23	Retained Earnings	48,000	(n) 29,000	(m) 145,000	164,000
24	Total	144,000			412,000
25	**Statement of Cash Flows Effects**				
26	Operating activities				
27	Net income		(m) 145,000		
28	Decrease in accounts receivable		(a) 10,000		
29	Increase in merchandise inventory			(b) 5,000	
30	Increase in prepaid expenses			(c) 4,000	
31	Increase in accounts payable		(h) 16,000		
32	Decrease in income taxes payable			(i) 2,000	
33	Depreciation expense—building		(k) 6,000		
34	Depreciation expense—equipment		(l) 3,000		
35	Loss on sale of equipment		(g) 3,000		
36	Investing activities				
37	Purchase of building			(e) 120,000	
38	Purchase of equipment			(f) 25,000	
39	Sale of equipment		(g) 4,000		
40	Financing activities				
41	Issuance of common stock		(j) 20,000		
42	Payment of dividends			(n) 29,000	
43	Totals		525,000	503,000	
44	Increase in cash			(o) 22,000	
45	Totals		525,000	525,000	
46					

* Significant noncash investing and financing activity.

SUMMARY OF STUDY OBJECTIVE FOR APPENDIX 13A

5 **Explain how to use a worksheet to prepare the statement of cash flows using the indirect method.** When there are numerous adjustments, a worksheet can be a helpful tool in preparing the statement of cash flows. Key guidelines for using a worksheet are: (1) List accounts with debit balances separately from those with credit balances. (2) In the reconciling columns in the bottom portion of the worksheet, show cash inflows as debits and cash outflows as credits. (3) Do not enter reconciling items in any journal or account, but use them only to help prepare the statement of cash flows.

The steps in preparing the worksheet are: (1) Enter beginning and ending balances of balance sheet accounts. (2) Enter debits and credits in reconciling columns. (3) Enter the increase or decrease in cash in two places as a balancing amount.

APPENDIX 13B Statement of Cash Flows—Direct Method

To explain and illustrate the direct method, we will use the transactions of Juarez Company for 2008 to prepare a statement of cash flows. Illustration 13B-1 presents information related to 2008 for Juarez Company.

STUDY OBJECTIVE 6

Prepare a statement of cash flows using the direct method.

Illustration 13B-1
Comparative balance sheets, income statement, and additional information for Juarez Company

JUAREZ COMPANY
Comparative Balance Sheets
December 31

Assets	2008	2007	Change Increase/Decrease
Cash	$191,000	$159,000	$ 32,000 Increase
Accounts receivable	12,000	15,000	3,000 Decrease
Inventory	170,000	160,000	10,000 Increase
Prepaid expenses	6,000	8,000	2,000 Decrease
Land	140,000	80,000	60,000 Increase
Equipment	160,000	-0-	160,000 Increase
Accumulated depreciation—equipment	(16,000)	-0-	16,000 Increase
Total	$663,000	$422,000	
Liabilities and Stockholders' Equity			
Accounts payable	$ 52,000	$ 60,000	$ 8,000 Decrease
Accrued expenses payable	15,000	20,000	5,000 Decrease
Income taxes payable	12,000	-0-	12,000 Increase
Bonds payable	130,000	-0-	130,000 Increase
Common stock	360,000	300,000	60,000 Increase
Retained earnings	94,000	42,000	52,000 Increase
Total	$663,000	$422,000	

JUAREZ COMPANY
Income Statement
For the Year Ended December 31, 2008

Revenues		$975,000
Cost of goods sold	$660,000	
Operating expenses (excluding depreciation)	176,000	
Depreciation expense	18,000	
Loss on sale of store equipment	1,000	855,000
Income before income taxes		120,000
Income tax expense		36,000
Net income		$ 84,000

Additional information:
1. In 2008, the company declared and paid a $32,000 cash dividend.
2. Bonds were issued at face value for $130,000 in cash.
3. Equipment costing $180,000 was purchased for cash.
4. Equipment costing $20,000 was sold for $17,000 cash when the book value of the equipment was $18,000.
5. Common stock of $60,000 was issued to acquire land.

Preparing the Statement of Cash Flows—Direct Method

To prepare a statement of cash flows under the direct approach, we will apply the three steps outlined in Illustration 13-3 (page 563).

STEP 1: OPERATING ACTIVITIES

DETERMINE NET CASH PROVIDED/USED BY OPERATING ACTIVITIES BY CONVERTING NET INCOME FROM AN ACCRUAL BASIS TO A CASH BASIS

Under the **direct method**, companies compute net cash provided by operating activities by **adjusting each item in the income statement** from the accrual basis to the cash basis. To simplify and condense the operating activities section, companies **report only major classes of operating cash receipts and cash payments**. For these major classes, the difference between cash receipts and cash payments is the net cash provided by operating activities. These relationships are as shown in Illustration 13B-2.

Illustration 13B-2
Major classes of cash receipts and payments

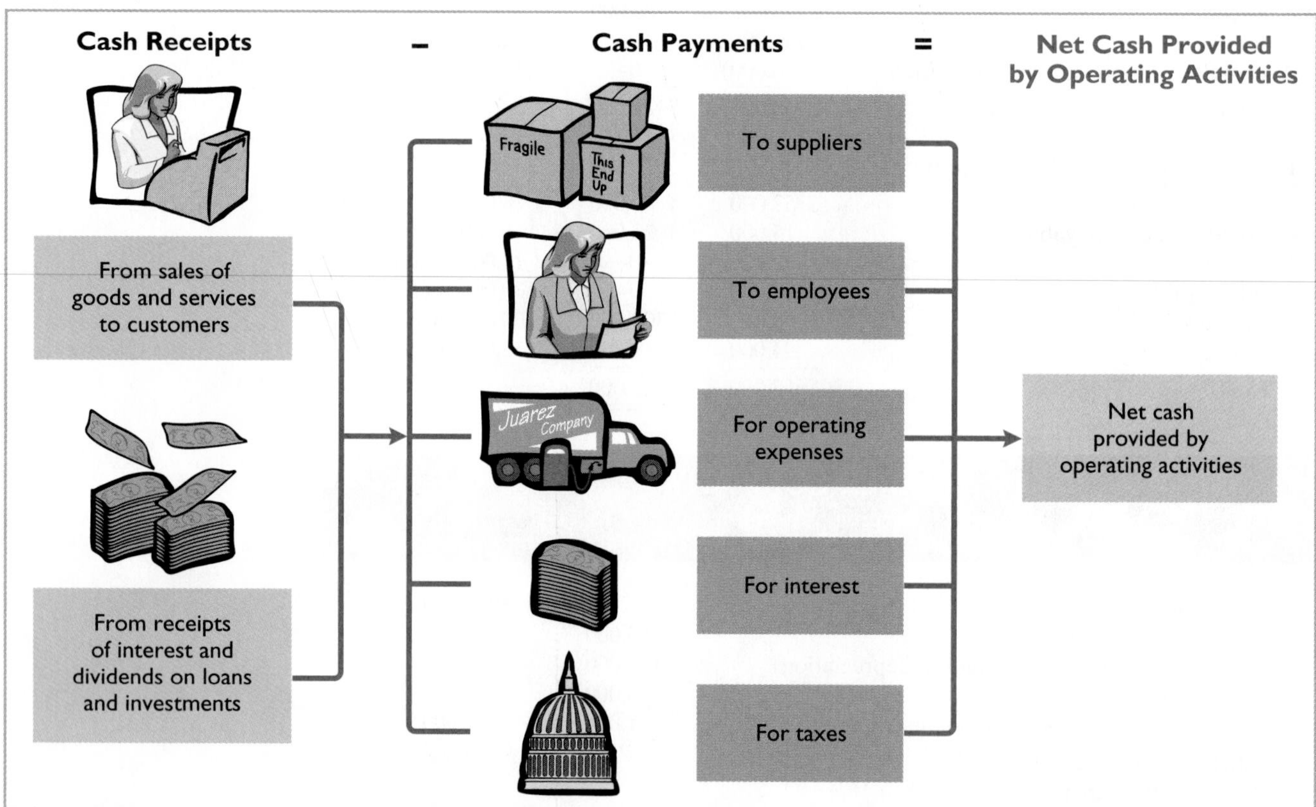

An efficient way to apply the direct method is to analyze the items reported in the income statement in the order in which they are listed. We then determine cash receipts and cash payments related to these revenues and expenses. The following pages present the adjustments required to prepare a statement of cash flows for Juarez Company using the direct approach.

Cash Receipts From Customers. The income statement for Juarez Company reported revenues from customers of $975,000. How much of that was cash receipts? To answer that, companies need to consider the change in accounts receivable during the year. When accounts receivable increase during the year, revenues on an accrual basis are higher than cash receipts from customers. Operations led to revenues, but not all of these revenues resulted in cash receipts.

To determine the amount of cash receipts, the company deducts from sales revenues the increase in accounts receivable. On the other hand, there may be a decrease in accounts receivable. That would occur if cash receipts from customers exceeded sales revenues. In that case, the company adds to sales revenues the decrease in accounts receivable.

For Juarez Company, accounts receivable decreased $3,000. Thus, cash receipts from customers were $978,000, computed as shown in Illustration 13B-3.

Illustration 13B-3
Computation of cash receipts from customers

Revenues from sales	$ 975,000
Add: Decrease in accounts receivable	3,000
Cash receipts from customers	**$ 978,000**

Juarez can also determine cash receipts from customers from an analysis of the Accounts Receivable account, as shown in Illustration 13B-4.

Illustration 13B-4
Analysis of accounts receivable

Accounts Receivable				
1/1/08	Balance	15,000	**Receipts from customers**	**978,000**
	Revenues from sales	975,000		
12/31/08	Balance	12,000		

HELPFUL HINT
The T account shows that revenue plus decrease in receivables equals cash receipts.

Illustration 13B-5 shows the relationships among cash receipts from customers, revenues from sales, and changes in accounts receivable.

Illustration 13B-5
Formula to compute cash receipts from customers—direct method

Cash Receipts from Customers	=	Revenues from Sales	+ Decrease in Accounts Receivable or − Increase in Accounts Receivable

Cash Payments to Suppliers. Juarez Company reported cost of goods sold of $660,000 on its income statement. How much of that was cash payments to suppliers? To answer that, it is first necessary to find purchases for the year. To find purchases, companies adjust cost of goods sold for the change in inventory. When inventory increases during the year, purchases for the year have exceeded cost of goods sold. As a result, to determine the amount of purchases, the company adds to cost of goods sold the increase in inventory.

In 2008, Juarez Company's inventory increased $10,000. It computes purchases as follows.

Illustration 13B-6
Computation of purchases

Cost of goods sold	$660,000
Add: Increase in inventory	10,000
Purchases	**$670,000**

After computing purchases, a company can determine cash payments to suppliers. This is done by adjusting purchases for the change in accounts payable.

When accounts payable increase during the year, purchases on an accrual basis are higher than they are on a cash basis. As a result, to determine cash payments to suppliers, a company deducts from purchases the increase in accounts payable. On the other hand, if cash payments to suppliers exceed purchases, there will be a decrease in accounts payable. In that case, a company adds to purchases the decrease in accounts payable.

For Juarez Company, cash payments to suppliers were $678,000, computed as follows.

Illustration 13B-7
Computation of cash payments to suppliers

Purchases	$670,000
Add: Decrease in accounts payable	8,000
Cash payments to suppliers	**$678,000**

Juarez also can determine cash payments to suppliers from an analysis of the Accounts Payable account, as shown in Illustration 13B-8.

Illustration 13B-8
Analysis of accounts payable

Accounts Payable

Payments to suppliers	**678,000**	1/1/08	Balance	60,000
			Purchases	670,000
		12/31/08	Balance	52,000

HELPFUL HINT
The T account shows that purchases plus decrease in accounts payable equals payments to suppliers.

Illustration 13B-9 shows the relationships among cash payments to suppliers, cost of goods sold, changes in inventory, and changes in accounts payable.

Illustration 13B-9
Formula to compute cash payments to suppliers—direct method

Cash Payments to Suppliers	=	Cost of Goods Sold	+ Increase in Inventory or − Decrease in Inventory	+ Decrease in Accounts Payable or − Increase in Accounts Payable

Cash Payments for Operating Expenses. Juarez reported on its income statement operating expenses of $176,000. How much of that amount was cash paid for operating expenses? To answer that, we need to adjust this amount for any changes in prepaid expenses and accrued expenses payable. For example, if prepaid expenses increased during the year, cash paid for operating expenses is higher than operating expenses reported on the income statement. To convert operating expenses to cash payments for operating expenses, a company adds the increase to operating expenses. On the other hand, if prepaid expenses decrease during the year, it deducts the decrease from operating expenses.

Companies must also adjust operating expenses for changes in accrued expenses payable. When accrued expenses payable increase during the year, operating expenses on an accrual basis are higher than they are in a cash basis. As a result, to determine cash payments for operating expenses, a company deducts from operating expenses an increase in accrued expenses payable. On the other hand, a company adds to operating expenses a decrease in accrued expenses payable because cash payments exceed operating expenses.

Juarez Company's cash payments for operating expenses were $179,000, computed as follows.

Operating expenses	$176,000
Deduct: Decrease in prepaid expenses	(2,000)
Add: Decrease in accrued expenses payable	5,000
Cash payments for operating expenses	**$179,000**

Illustration 13B-10
Computation of cash payments for operating expenses

Illustration 13B-11 shows the relationships among cash payments for operating expenses, changes in prepaid expenses, and changes in accrued expenses payable.

Illustration 13B-11
Formula to compute cash payments for operating expenses—direct method

Cash Payments for Operating Expenses = Operating Expenses { + Increase in Prepaid Expense or − Decrease in Prepaid Expense } { + Decrease in Accrued Expenses Payable or − Increase in Accrued Expenses Payable }

Depreciation Expense and Loss on Sale of Equipment. Companies show operating expenses exclusive of depreciation. Juarez's depreciation expense in 2008 was $18,000. Depreciation expense is not shown on a statement of cash flows because it is a noncash charge. If the amount for operating expenses includes depreciation expense, the company must reduce operating expenses by the amount of depreciation to determine cash payments for operating expenses.

The loss on sale of equipment of $1,000 is also a noncash charge. The loss on sale of equipment reduces net income, but it does not reduce cash. Thus, companies do not report on a statement of cash flows the loss on sale of equipment.

Other charges to expense that do not require the use of cash, such as the amortization of intangible assets, depletion expense, and bad debt expense, are treated in the same manner as depreciation.

Cash Payments For Income Taxes. Juarez reported income tax expense of $36,000 on the income statement. Income taxes payable, however, increased $12,000. This increase means that the company has not yet paid $12,000 of the income taxes. As a result, income taxes paid were less than income taxes reported in the income statement. Cash payments for income taxes were, therefore, $24,000 as shown below.

Income tax expense	$36,000
Deduct: Increase in income taxes payable	12,000
Cash payments for income taxes	**$24,000**

Illustration 13B-12
Computation of cash payments for income taxes

Illustration 13B-13 shows the relationships among cash payments for income taxes, income tax expense, and changes in income taxes payable.

Illustration 13B-13
Formula to compute cash payments for income taxes—direct method

Cash Payments for Income Taxes = Income Tax Expense { + Decrease in Income Taxes Payable or − Increase in Income Taxes Payable }

The operating activities section of the statement of cash flows of Juarez Company is shown in Illustration 13B-14.

Illustration 13B-14
Operating activities section of the statement of cash flows

Cash flows from operating activities		
Cash receipts from customers		$978,000
Less: Cash payments:		
To suppliers	$678,000	
For operating expenses	179,000	
For income taxes	24,000	881,000
Net cash provided by operating activities		$ 97,000

When a company uses the direct method, it must also provide in a **separate schedule** (not shown here) the net cash flows from operating activities as computed under the indirect method.

STEP 2: INVESTING AND FINANCING ACTIVITIES

ANALYZE CHANGES IN NONCURRENT ASSET AND LIABILITY ACCOUNTS AND RECORD AS INVESTING AND FINANCING ACTIVITIES, OR DISCLOSE AS NONCASH TRANSACTIONS

Increase in Land. Juarez's land increased $60,000. The additional information section indicates that the company issued common stock to purchase the land. The issuance of common stock for land has no effect on cash. But it is a **significant noncash investing and financing transaction.** This transaction requires disclosure in a separate schedule at the bottom of the statement of cash flows.

Increase in Equipment. The comparative balance sheets show that equipment increased $160,000 in 2008. The additional information in Illustration 13B-1 indicated that the increase resulted from two investing transactions: (1) Juarez purchased for cash equipment costing $180,000. And (2) it sold for $17,000 cash equipment costing $20,000, whose book value was $18,000. The relevant data for the statement of cash flows is the cash paid for the purchase and the cash proceeds from the sale. For Juarez Company, the investing activities section will show the following: The $180,000 purchase of equipment as an outflow of cash, and the $17,000 sale of equipment as an inflow of cash. The company **should not net** the two amounts. **Both individual outflows and inflows of cash should be shown.**

The analysis of the changes in equipment should include the related Accumulated Depreciation account. These two accounts for Juarez Company are shown in Illustration 13B-15.

Illustration 13B-15
Analysis of equipment and related accumulated depreciation

Equipment

1/1/08	Balance	–0–	Cost of equipment sold	20,000
	Cash purchase	**180,000**		
12/31/08	Balance	160,000		

Accumulated Depreciation—Equipment

Sale of equipment	2,000	1/1/08	Balance	–0–
			Depreciation expense	18,000
		12/31/08	Balance	16,000

Increase in Bonds Payable. Bonds Payable increased $130,000. The additional information in Illustration 13B-1 indicated that Juarez issued, for $130,000 cash, bonds with a face value of $130,000. The issuance of bonds is a financing activity. For Juarez Company, there is an inflow of cash of $130,000 from the issuance of bonds.

Increase in Common Stock. The Common Stock account increased $60,000. The additional information indicated that Juarez acquired land from the issuance of common stock. This transaction is a **significant noncash investing and financing transaction** which the company should report separately at the bottom of the statement.

Increase in Retained Earnings. The $52,000 net increase in Retained Earnings resulted from net income of $84,000 and the declaration and payment of a cash dividend of $32,000. Companies **do not report net income in the statement of cash flows under the direct method.** Cash dividends paid of $32,000 are reported in the financing activities section as an outflow of cash.

Statement of Cash Flows—2008 Illustration 13B-16 shows the statement of cash flows for Juarez.

Illustration 13B-16
Statement of cash flows, 2008—direct method

JUAREZ COMPANY Statement of Cash Flows—Direct Method For the Year Ended December 31, 2008		
Cash flows from operating activities		
Cash receipts from customers		$ 978,000
Less: Cash payments:		
To suppliers	$ 678,000	
For operating expenses	179,000	
For income taxes	24,000	881,000
Net cash provided by operating activities		97,000
Cash flows from investing activities		
Purchase of equipment	(180,000)	
Sale of equipment	17,000	
Net cash used by investing activities		(163,000)
Cash flows from financing activities		
Issuance of bonds payable	130,000	
Payment of cash dividends	(32,000)	
Net cash provided by financing activities		98,000
Net increase in cash		32,000
Cash at beginning of period		159,000
Cash at end of period		$ 191,000
Noncash investing and financing activities		
Issuance of common stock to purchase land		$ 60,000

STEP 3: NET CHANGE IN CASH

COMPARE THE NET CHANGE IN CASH ON THE STATEMENT OF CASH FLOWS WITH THE CHANGE IN THE CASH ACCOUNT REPORTED ON THE BALANCE SHEET TO MAKE SURE THE AMOUNTS AGREE

Illustration 13B-16 indicates that the net change in cash during the period was an increase of $32,000. This agrees with the change in balances in the cash account reported on the balance sheets in Illustration 13B-1 (page 587).

SUMMARY OF STUDY OBJECTIVE FOR APPENDIX 13B

6 **Prepare a statement of cash flows using the direct method.** The preparation of the statement of cash flows involves three major steps: (1) Determine net cash provided/used by operating activities by converting net income from an accrual basis to a cash basis. (2) Analyze changes in noncurrent asset and liability accounts and record as investing and financing activities, or disclose as noncash transactions. (3) Compare the net change in cash on the statement of cash flows with the change in the cash account reported on the balance sheet to make sure the amounts agree. The direct method reports cash receipts less cash payments to arrive at net cash provided by operating activities.

GLOSSARY FOR APPENDIX 13B

Direct method A method of determining net cash provided by operating activities by adjusting each item in the income statement from the accrual basis to the cash basis. (pp. 588)

Demonstration Problem 2

The income statement for Kosinski Manufacturing Company contains the following condensed information.

KOSINSKI MANUFACTURING COMPANY
Income Statement
For the Year Ended December 31, 2008

Revenues		$6,583,000
Operating expenses, excluding depreciation	$4,920,000	
Depreciation expense	880,000	5,800,000
Income before income taxes		783,000
Income tax expense		353,000
Net income		$ 430,000

Included in operating expenses is a $24,000 loss resulting from the sale of machinery for $270,000 cash. Machinery was purchased at a cost of $750,000. The following balances are reported on Kosinski's comparative balance sheet at December 31.

KOSINSKI MANUFACTURING COMPANY
Comparative Balance Sheets (partial)

	2008	2007
Cash	$672,000	$130,000
Accounts receivable	775,000	610,000
Inventories	834,000	867,000
Accounts payable	521,000	501,000

Income tax expense of $353,000 represents the amount paid in 2008. Dividends declared and paid in 2008 totaled $200,000.

Instructions

Prepare the statement of cash flows using the direct method.

Solution

KOSINSKI MANUFACTURING COMPANY
Statement of Cash Flows—Direct Method
For the Year Ended December 31, 2008

Cash flows from operating activities		
Cash collections from customers		$6,418,000*
Cash payments:		
For operating expenses	$4,843,000**	
For income taxes	353,000	5,196,000
Net cash provided by operating activities		1,222,000
Cash flows from investing activities		
Sale of machinery	270,000	
Purchase of machinery	(750,000)	
Net cash used by investing activities		(480,000)
Cash flows from financing activities		
Payment of cash dividends	(200,000)	
Net cash used by financing activities		(200,000)
Net increase in cash		542,000
Cash at beginning of period		130,000
Cash at end of period		$ 672,000

Direct-Method Computations:

*Computation of cash collections from customers:	
Revenues per the income statement	$6,583,000
Deduct: Increase in accounts receivable	(165,000)
Cash collections from customers	$6,418,000
**Computation of cash payments for operating expenses:	
Operating expenses per the income statement	$4,920,000
Deduct: Loss from sale of machinery	(24,000)
Deduct: Decrease in inventories	(33,000)
Deduct: Increase in accounts payable	(20,000)
Cash payments for operating expenses	$4,843,000

action plan

- ✓ Determine net cash from operating activities. Each item in the income statement must be adjusted to the cash basis.
- ✓ Determine net cash from investing activities. Investing activities generally relate to changes in noncurrent assets.
- ✓ Determine net cash from financing activities. Financing activities generally relate to changes in long-term liabilities and stockholders' equity accounts.

✓ The Navigator

Note: All Questions, Exercises, and Problems marked with an asterisk relate to material in the appendices to the chapter.

SELF-STUDY QUESTIONS

Answers are at the end of the chapter.

(SO 1) **1.** Which of the following is *incorrect* about the statement of cash flows?
a. It is a fourth basic financial statement.
b. It provides information about cash receipts and cash payments of an entity during a period.
c. It reconciles the ending cash account balance to the balance per the bank statement.
d. It provides information about the operating, investing, and financing activities of the business.

(SO 2) **2.** The statement of cash flows classifies cash receipts and cash payments by these activities:
a. operating and nonoperating.
b. investing, financing, and operating.
c. financing, operating, and nonoperating.
d. investing, financing, and nonoperating.

3. Which is an example of a cash flow from an operating activity? (SO 2)
a. Payment of cash to lenders for interest.
b. Receipt of cash from the sale of capital stock.
c. Payment of cash dividends to the company's stockholders.
d. None of the above.

4. Which is an example of a cash flow from an investing activity? (SO 2)
a. Receipt of cash from the issuance of bonds payable.
b. Payment of cash to repurchase outstanding capital stock.

c. Receipt of cash from the sale of equipment.
d. Payment of cash to suppliers for inventory.

(SO 2) 5. Cash dividends paid to stockholders are classified on the statement of cash flows as:
a. operating activities.
b. investing activities.
c. a combination of (a) and (b).
d. financing activities.

(SO 2) 6. Which is an example of a cash flow from a financing activity?
a. Receipt of cash from sale of land.
b. Issuance of debt for cash.
c. Purchase of equipment for cash.
d. None of the above

(SO 2) 7. Which of the following is *incorrect* about the statement of cash flows?
a. The direct method may be used to report cash provided by operations.
b. The statement shows the cash provided (used) for three categories of activity.
c. The operating section is the last section of the statement.
d. The indirect method may be used to report cash provided by operations.

Questions 8 and 9 apply only to the indirect method.

(SO 3) 8. Net income is $132,000, accounts payable increased $10,000 during the year, inventory decreased $6,000 during the year, and accounts receivable increased $12,000 during the year. Under the indirect method, what is net cash provided by operating activities?
a. $102,000. c. $124,000.
b. $112,000. d. $136,000.

(SO 3) 9. Items that are added back to net income in determining cash provided by operating activities under the indirect method do *not* include:
a. depreciation expense.
b. an increase in inventory.
c. amortization expense.
d. loss on sale of equipment.

10. The statement of cash flows should *not* be used to evaluate an entity's ability to: (SO 4)
a. earn net income.
b. generate future cash flows.
c. pay dividends.
d. meet obligations.

11. Free cash flow provides an indication of a company's ability to: (SO 4)
a. generate net income.
b. generate cash to pay dividends.
c. generate cash to invest in new capital expenditures.
d. both (b) and (c).

*12. In a worksheet for the statement of cash flows, a decrease in accounts receivable is entered in the reconciling columns as a credit to Accounts Receivable and a debit in the: (SO 5)
a. investing activities section.
b. operating activities section.
c. financing activities section.
d. None of the above.

Questions 13 and 14 apply only to the direct method.

*13. The beginning balance in accounts receivable is $44,000, the ending balance is $42,000, and sales during the period are $129,000. What are cash receipts from customers? (SO 6)
a. $127,000. c. $131,000.
b. $129,000. d. $141,000.

*14. Which of the following items is reported on a cash flow statement prepared by the direct method? (SO 6)
a. Loss on sale of building.
b. Increase in accounts receivable.
c. Depreciation expense.
d. Cash payments to suppliers.

Go to the book's website, **www.wiley.com/college/weygandt**, for Additional Self-Study questions.

The Navigator

QUESTIONS

1. (a) What is a statement of cash flows?
(b) John Norris maintains that the statement of cash flows is an optional financial statement. Do you agree? Explain.
2. What questions about cash are answered by the statement of cash flows?
3. Distinguish among the three types of activities reported in the statement of cash flows.
4. (a) What are the major sources (inflows) of cash in a statement of cash flows?
(b) What are the major uses (outflows) of cash?
5. Why is it important to disclose certain noncash transactions? How should they be disclosed?
6. Wilma Flintstone and Barny Rublestone were discussing the format of the statement of cash flows of Hart Candy Co. At the bottom of Hart Candy's statement of cash flows was a separate section entitled "Noncash investing and financing activities." Give three examples of significant noncash transactions that would be reported in this section.
7. Why is it necessary to use comparative balance sheets, a current income statement, and certain transaction data in preparing a statement of cash flows?
8. Contrast the advantages and disadvantages of the direct and indirect methods of preparing the statement of cash flows. Are both methods acceptable? Which method is preferred by the FASB? Which method is more popular?
9. When the total cash inflows exceed the total cash outflows in the statement of cash flows, how and where is this excess identified?
10. Describe the indirect method for determining net cash provided (used) by operating activities.

11. Why is it necessary to convert accrual-based net income to cash-basis income when preparing a statement of cash flows?
12. The president of Ferneti Company is puzzled. During the last year, the company experienced a net loss of $800,000, yet its cash increased $300,000 during the same period of time. Explain to the president how this could occur.
13. Identify five items that are adjustments to convert net income to net cash provided by operating activities under the indirect method.
14. Why and how is depreciation expense reported in a statement prepared using the indirect method?
15. Why is the statement of cash flows useful?
16. During 2008 Doubleday Company converted $1,700,000 of its total $2,000,000 of bonds payable into common stock. Indicate how the transaction would be reported on a statement of cash flows, if at all.

*17. Why is it advantageous to use a worksheet when preparing a statement of cash flows? Is a worksheet required to prepare a statement of cash flows?

*18. Describe the direct method for determining net cash provided by operating activities.

*19. Give the formulas under the direct method for computing (a) cash receipts from customers and (b) cash payments to suppliers.

*20. Garcia Inc. reported sales of $2 million for 2008. Accounts receivable decreased $200,000 and accounts payable increased $300,000. Compute cash receipts from customers, assuming that the receivable and payable transactions related to operations.

*21. In the direct method, why is depreciation expense not reported in the cash flows from operating activities section?

BRIEF EXERCISES

BE13-1 Each of these items must be considered in preparing a statement of cash flows for Kiner Co. for the year ended December 31, 2008. For each item, state how it should be shown in the statement of cash flows for 2008.

Indicate statement presentation of selected transactions. (SO 2)

(a) Issued bonds for $200,000 cash.
(b) Purchased equipment for $150,000 cash.
(c) Sold land costing $20,000 for $20,000 cash.
(d) Declared and paid a $50,000 cash dividend.

BE13-2 Classify each item as an operating, investing, or financing activity. Assume all items involve cash unless there is information to the contrary.

Classify items by activities. (SO 2)

(a) Purchase of equipment.
(b) Sale of building.
(c) Redemption of bonds.
(d) Depreciation.
(e) Payment of dividends.
(f) Issuance of capital stock.

BE13-3 The following T account is a summary of the cash account of Edmonds Company.

Identify financing activity transactions. (SO 2)

Cash (Summary Form)

Balance, Jan. 1	8,000		
Receipts from customers	364,000	Payments for goods	200,000
Dividends on stock investments	6,000	Payments for operating expenses	140,000
Proceeds from sale of equipment	36,000	Interest paid	10,000
Proceeds from issuance of bonds payable	300,000	Taxes paid	8,000
		Dividends paid	50,000
Balance, Dec. 31	306,000		

What amount of net cash provided (used) by financing activities should be reported in the statement of cash flows?

BE13-4 Martinez, Inc. reported net income of $2.5 million in 2008. Depreciation for the year was $160,000, accounts receivable decreased $350,000, and accounts payable decreased $280,000. Compute net cash provided by operating activities using the indirect method.

Compute cash provided by operating activities—indirect method. (SO 3)

BE13-5 The net income for Adcock Co. for 2008 was $280,000. For 2008 depreciation on plant assets was $70,000, and the company incurred a loss on sale of plant assets of $12,000. Compute net cash provided by operating activities under the indirect method.

Compute cash provided by operating activities—indirect method. (SO 3)

BE13-6 The comparative balance sheets for Goltra Company show these changes in noncash current asset accounts: accounts receivable decrease $80,000, prepaid expenses increase $28,000, and inventories increase $30,000. Compute net cash provided by operating activities using the indirect method assuming that net income is $200,000.

Compute net cash provided by operating activities—indirect method. (SO 3)

Determine cash received from sale of equipment.
(SO 3)

BE13-7 The T accounts for Equipment and the related Accumulated Depreciation for Pettengill Company at the end of 2008 are shown here.

Equipment			
Beg. bal.	80,000	Disposals	22,000
Acquisitions	41,600		
End. bal.	99,600		

Accumulated Depreciation			
Disposals	5,500	Beg. bal.	44,500
		Depr. exp.	12,000
		End. bal.	51,000

In addition, Pettengill Company's income statement reported a loss on the sale of equipment of $4,500. What amount was reported on the statement of cash flows as "cash flow from sale of equipment"?

Calculate free cash flow.
(SO 4)

BE13-8 In a recent year, Cypress Semiconductor Corporation reported cash provided by operating activities of $155,793,000, cash used in investing of $207,826,000, and cash used in financing of $33,372,000. In addition, cash spent for fixed assets during the period was $132,280,000. No dividends were paid. Calculate free cash flow.

Calculate free cash flow.
(SO 4)

BE13-9 Lott Corporation reported cash provided by operating activities of $360,000, cash used by investing activities of $250,000, and cash provided by financing activities of $70,000. In addition, cash spent for capital assets during the period was $200,000. No dividends were paid. Calculate free cash flow.

Calculate free cash flow.
(SO 4)

BE13-10 Alliance Atlantis Communications Inc. reported a $35.8 million increase in operating cash flow for its first quarter of 2005. Alliance reported cash provided by operating activities of $45,600,000 and revenues of $264,800,000. Cash spent on plant asset additions during the quarter was $1,600,000. No dividends were paid. Calculate free cash flow.

Calculate and analyze free cash flow.
(SO 4)

BE13-11 The management of Radar Inc. is trying to decide whether it can increase its dividend. During the current year it reported net income of $875,000. It had cash provided by operating activities of $734,000, paid cash dividends of $70,000, and had capital expenditures of $280,000. Compute the company's free cash flow, and discuss whether an increase in the dividend appears warranted. What other factors should be considered?

Indicate entries in worksheet.
(SO 5)

***BE13-12** During the year, prepaid expenses decreased $6,600, and accrued expenses increased $2,400. Indicate how the changes in prepaid expenses and accrued expenses payable should be entered in the reconciling columns of a worksheet. Assume that beginning balances were: Prepaid expenses $18,600 and Accrued expenses payable $8,200.

Compute receipts from customers—direct method.
(SO 6)

***BE13-13** Columbia Sportswear Company had accounts receivable of $206,024,000 at the beginning of a recent year, and $267,653,000 at year-end. Sales revenues were $1,095,307,000 for the year. What is the amount of cash receipts from customers?

Compute cash payments for income taxes—direct method.
(SO 6)

***BE13-14** Young Corporation reported income taxes of $340,000,000 on its 2008 income statement and income taxes payable of $277,000,000 at December 31, 2007, and $522,000,000 at December 31, 2008. What amount of cash payments were made for income taxes during 2008?

Compute cash payments for operating expenses—direct method.
(SO 6)

***BE13-15** Flynn Corporation reports operating expenses of $80,000 excluding depreciation expense of $15,000 for 2008. During the year prepaid expenses decreased $6,600 and accrued expenses payable increased $4,400. Compute the cash payments for operating expenses in 2008.

EXERCISES

Classify transactions by type of activity.
(SO 2)

E13-1 Pioneer Corporation had these transactions during 2008.

(a) Issued $50,000 par value common stock for cash.
(b) Purchased a machine for $30,000, giving a long-term note in exchange.
(c) Issued $200,000 par value common stock upon conversion of bonds having a face value of $200,000.
(d) Declared and paid a cash dividend of $18,000.
(e) Sold a long-term investment with a cost of $15,000 for $15,000 cash.
(f) Collected $16,000 of accounts receivable.
(g) Paid $18,000 on accounts payable.

Instructions

Analyze the transactions and indicate whether each transaction resulted in a cash flow from operating activities, investing activities, financing activities, or noncash investing and financing activities.

E13-2 An analysis of comparative balance sheets, the current year's income statement, and the general ledger accounts of Gagliano Corp. uncovered the following items. Assume all items involve cash unless there is information to the contrary.

Classify transactions by type of activity.

(SO 2)

(a) Payment of interest on notes payable.
(b) Exchange of land for patent.
(c) Sale of building at book value.
(d) Payment of dividends.
(e) Depreciation.
(f) Receipt of dividends on investment in stock.
(g) Receipt of interest on notes receivable.
(h) Issuance of capital stock.
(i) Amortization of patent.
(j) Issuance of bonds for land.
(k) Purchase of land.
(l) Conversion of bonds into common stock.
(m) Loss on sale of land.
(n) Retirement of bonds.

Instructions

Indicate how each item should be classified in the statement of cash flows using these four major classifications: operating activity (indirect method), investing activity, financing activity, and significant noncash investing and financing activity.

E13-3 Rachael Ray Corporation had the following transactions.

Prepare journal entry and determine effect on cash flows.

(SO 2)

1. Sold land (cost $12,000) for $15,000.
2. Issued common stock for $20,000.
3. Recorded depreciation of $17,000.
4. Paid salaries of $9,000.
5. Issued 1,000 shares of $1 par value common stock for equipment worth $8,000.
6. Sold equipment (cost $10,000, accumulated depreciation $7,000) for $1,200.

Instructions

For each transaction above, **(a)** prepare the journal entry, and **(b)** indicate how it would affect the statement of cash flows.

E13-4 Villa Company reported net income of $195,000 for 2008. Villa also reported depreciation expense of $45,000 and a loss of $5,000 on the sale of equipment. The comparative balance sheet shows a decrease in accounts receivable of $15,000 for the year, a $17,000 increase in accounts payable, and a $4,000 decrease in prepaid expenses.

Prepare the operating activities section—indirect method.

(SO 3)

Instructions

Prepare the operating activities section of the statement of cash flows for 2008. Use the indirect method.

E13-5 The current sections of Bellinham Inc.'s balance sheets at December 31, 2007 and 2008, are presented here.

Prepare the operating activities section—indirect method.

(SO 3)

Bellinham's net income for 2008 was $153,000. Depreciation expense was $24,000.

	2008	2007
Current assets		
Cash	$105,000	$ 99,000
Accounts receivable	110,000	89,000
Inventory	158,000	172,000
Prepaid expenses	27,000	22,000
Total current assets	$400,000	$382,000
Current liabilities		
Accrued expenses payable	$ 15,000	$ 5,000
Accounts payable	85,000	92,000
Total current liabilities	$100,000	$ 97,000

Instructions
Prepare the net cash provided by operating activities section of the company's statement of cash flows for the year ended December 31, 2008, using the indirect method.

Prepare partial statement of cash flows—indirect method.
(SO 3)

E13-6 The three accounts shown below appear in the general ledger of Cesar Corp. during 2008.

Equipment

Date		Debit	Credit	Balance
Jan. 1	Balance			160,000
July 31	Purchase of equipment	70,000		230,000
Sept. 2	Cost of equipment constructed	53,000		283,000
Nov. 10	Cost of equipment sold		49,000	234,000

Accumulated Depreciation—Equipment

Date		Debit	Credit	Balance
Jan. 1	Balance			71,000
Nov. 10	Accumulated depreciation on equipment sold	30,000		41,000
Dec. 31	Depreciation for year		28,000	69,000

Retained Earnings

Date		Debit	Credit	Balance
Jan. 1	Balance			105,000
Aug. 23	Dividends (cash)	14,000		91,000
Dec. 31	Net income		67,000	158,000

Instructions
From the postings in the accounts, indicate how the information is reported on a statement of cash flows using the indirect method. The loss on sale of equipment was $5,000. (*Hint:* Cost of equipment constructed is reported in the investing activities section as a decrease in cash of $53,000.)

Prepare statement of cash flows and compute free cash flow.
(SO 3, 4)

E13-7 Scully Corporation's comparative balance sheets are presented below.

SCULLY CORPORATION
Comparative Balance Sheets
December 31

	2008	2007
Cash	$ 14,300	$ 10,700
Accounts receivable	21,200	23,400
Land	20,000	26,000
Building	70,000	70,000
Accumulated depreciation	(15,000)	(10,000)
Total	$110,500	$120,100
Accounts payable	$12,370	$31,100
Common stock	75,000	69,000
Retained earnings	23,130	20,000
Total	$110,500	$120,100

Additional information:

1. Net income was $22,630. Dividends declared and paid were $19,500.
2. All other changes in noncurrent account balances had a direct effect on cash flows, except the change in accumulated depreciation. The land was sold for $4,900.

Instructions

(a) Prepare a statement of cash flows for 2008 using the indirect method.
(b) Compute free cash flow.

E13-8 Here are comparative balance sheets for Taguchi Company.

Prepare a statement of cash flows—indirect method.
(SO 3)

TAGUCHI COMPANY
Comparative Balance Sheets
December 31

Assets	2008	2007
Cash	$ 73,000	$ 22,000
Accounts receivable	85,000	76,000
Inventories	170,000	189,000
Land	75,000	100,000
Equipment	260,000	200,000
Accumulated depreciation	(66,000)	(32,000)
Total	$597,000	$555,000
Liabilities and Stockholders' Equity		
Accounts payable	$ 39,000	$ 47,000
Bonds payable	150,000	200,000
Common stock ($1 par)	216,000	174,000
Retained earnings	192,000	134,000
Total	$597,000	$555,000

Additional information:

1. Net income for 2008 was $103,000.
2. Cash dividends of $45,000 were declared and paid.
3. Bonds payable amounting to $50,000 were redeemed for cash $50,000.
4. Common stock was issued for $42,000 cash.
5. No equipment was sold during 2008.

Instructions

Prepare a statement of cash flows for 2008 using the indirect method.

E13-9 Muldur Corporation's comparative balance sheets are presented below.

Prepare statement of cash flows and compute free cash flow.
(SO 3, 4)

MULDUR CORPORATION
Comparative Balance Sheets
December 31

	2008	2007
Cash	$ 15,200	$ 17,700
Accounts receivable	25,200	22,300
Investments	20,000	16,000
Equipment	60,000	70,000
Accumulated depreciation	(14,000)	(10,000)
Total	$106,400	$116,000
Accounts payable	$ 14,600	$ 11,100
Bonds payable	10,000	30,000
Common stock	50,000	45,000
Retained earnings	31,800	29,900
Total	$106,400	$116,000

Additional information:

1. Net income was $18,300. Dividends declared and paid were $16,400.
2. Equipment which cost $10,000 and had accumulated depreciation of $1,200 was sold for $3,300.
3. All other changes in noncurrent account balances had a direct effect on cash flows, except the change in accumulated depreciation.

Instructions

(a) Prepare a statement of cash flows for 2008 using the indirect method.
(b) Compute free cash flow.

Prepare a worksheet.
(SO 5)

***E13-10** Comparative balance sheets for Eddie Murphy Company are presented below.

EDDIE MURPHY COMPANY
Comparative Balance Sheets
December 31

Assets	**2008**	**2007**
Cash	$ 63,000	$ 22,000
Accounts receivable	85,000	76,000
Inventories	180,000	189,000
Land	75,000	100,000
Equipment	260,000	200,000
Accumulated depreciation	(66,000)	(42,000)
Total	$597,000	$545,000
Liabilities and Stockholders' Equity		
Accounts payable	$ 34,000	$ 47,000
Bonds payable	150,000	200,000
Common stock ($1 par)	214,000	164,000
Retained earnings	199,000	134,000
Total	$597,000	$545,000

Additional information:

1. Net income for 2008 was $125,000.
2. Cash dividends of $60,000 were declared and paid.
3. Bonds payable amounting to $50,000 were redeemed for cash $50,000.
4. Common stock was issued for $50,000 cash.
5. Depreciation expense was $24,000.
6. Sales for the year were $978,000.

Instructions

Prepare a worksheet for a statement of cash flows for 2008 using the indirect method. Enter the reconciling items directly on the worksheet, using letters to cross-reference each entry.

Compute cash provided by operating activities—direct method.
(SO 6)

***E13-11** Hairston Company completed its first year of operations on December 31, 2008. Its initial income statement showed that Hairston had revenues of $192,000 and operating expenses of $78,000. Accounts receivable and accounts payable at year-end were $60,000 and $23,000, respectively. Assume that accounts payable related to operating expenses. Ignore income taxes.

Instructions

Compute net cash provided by operating activities using the direct method.

Compute cash payments—direct method.
(SO 6)

***E13-12** The 2004 income statement for McDonald's Corporation shows cost of goods sold $4,852.7 million and operating expenses (including depreciation expense of $1,201 million) $10,671.5 million. The comparative balance sheet for the year shows that inventory increased $18.1 million, prepaid expenses increased $56.3 million, accounts payable (merchandise suppliers) increased $136.9 million, and accrued expenses payable increased $160.9 million.

Instructions

Using the direct method, compute (a) cash payments to suppliers and (b) cash payments for operating expenses.

***E13-13** The 2008 accounting records of Verlander Transport reveal these transactions and events.

Compute cash flow from operating activities—direct method.

(SO 6)

Payment of interest	$ 10,000	Collection of accounts receivable	$182,000
Cash sales	48,000	Payment of salaries and wages	53,000
Receipt of dividend revenue	18,000	Depreciation expense	16,000
Payment of income taxes	12,000	Proceeds from sale of vehicles	12,000
Net income	38,000	Purchase of equipment for cash	22,000
Payment of accounts payable for merchandise	115,000	Loss on sale of vehicles	3,000
		Payment of dividends	14,000
Payment for land	74,000	Payment of operating expenses	28,000

Instructions

Prepare the cash flows from operating activities section using the direct method. (Not all of the items will be used.)

***E13-14** The following information is taken from the 2008 general ledger of Pierzynski Company.

Calculate cash flows—direct method.

(SO 6)

Rent	Rent expense	$ 40,000
	Prepaid rent, January 1	5,900
	Prepaid rent, December 31	9,000
Salaries	Salaries expense	$ 54,000
	Salaries payable, January 1	10,000
	Salaries payable, December 31	8,000
Sales	Revenue from sales	$170,000
	Accounts receivable, January 1	16,000
	Accounts receivable, December 31	7,000

Instructions

In each case, compute the amount that should be reported in the operating activities section of the statement of cash flows under the direct method.

EXERCISES: SET B

Visit the book's website at **www.wiley.com/college/weygandt**, and choose the Student Companion site, to access Exercise Set B.

PROBLEMS: SET A

WILEY PLUS

P13-1A You are provided with the following transactions that took place during a recent fiscal year.

Distinguish among operating, investing, and financing activities.

(SO 2)

Transaction	Where Reported on Statement	Cash Inflow, Outflow, or No Effect?
(a) Recorded depreciation expense on the plant assets.		
(b) Recorded and paid interest expense.		
(c) Recorded cash proceeds from a sale of plant assets.		
(d) Acquired land by issuing common stock.		
(e) Paid a cash dividend to preferred stockholders.		
(f) Distributed a stock dividend to common stockholders.		
(g) Recorded cash sales.		
(h) Recorded sales on account.		
(i) Purchased inventory for cash.		
(j) Purchased inventory on account.		

Instructions

Complete the table indicating whether each item (1) should be reported as an operating (O) activity, investing (I) activity, financing (F) activity, or as a noncash (NC) transaction reported in a separate schedule, and (2) represents a cash inflow or cash outflow or has no cash flow effect. Assume use of the indirect approach.

Determine cash flow effects of changes in equity accounts.
(SO 3)

P13-2A The following account balances relate to the stockholders' equity accounts of Gore Corp. at year-end.

	2008	2007
Common stock, 10,500 and 10,000 shares, respectively, for 2008 and 2007	$160,000	$140,000
Preferred stock, 5,000 shares	125,000	125,000
Retained earnings	300,000	260,000

A small stock dividend was declared and issued in 2008. The market value of the shares was $10,500. Cash dividends were $15,000 in both 2008 and 2007. The common stock has no par or stated value.

Instructions

(a) Net income $65,500

(a) What was the amount of net income reported by Gore Corp. in 2008?
(b) Determine the amounts of any cash inflows or outflows related to the common stock and dividend accounts in 2008.
(c) Indicate where each of the cash inflows or outflows identified in (b) would be classified on the statement of cash flows.

Prepare the operating activities section—indirect method.
(SO 3)

P13-3A The income statement of Elbert Company is presented here.

ELBERT COMPANY
Income Statement
For the Year Ended November 30, 2008

Sales		$7,700,000
Cost of goods sold		
Beginning inventory	$1,900,000	
Purchases	4,400,000	
Goods available for sale	6,300,000	
Ending inventory	1,400,000	
Total cost of goods sold		4,900,000
Gross profit		2,800,000
Operating expenses		
Selling expenses	450,000	
Administrative expenses	700,000	1,150,000
Net income		$1,650,000

Additional information:

1. Accounts receivable increased $250,000 during the year, and inventory decreased $500,000.
2. Prepaid expenses increased $150,000 during the year.
3. Accounts payable to suppliers of merchandise decreased $340,000 during the year.
4. Accrued expenses payable decreased $100,000 during the year.
5. Administrative expenses include depreciation expense of $90,000.

Cash from operations $1,400,000

Instructions

Prepare the operating activities section of the statement of cash flows for the year ended November 30, 2008, for Elbert Company, using the indirect method.

Prepare the operating activities section—direct method.
(SO 6)

***P13-4A** Data for Elbert Company are presented in P13-3A.

Instructions

Prepare the operating activities section of the statement of cash flows using the direct method.

Cash from operations $1,400,000

P13-5A Grania Company's income statement contained the condensed information below.

Prepare the operating activities section—indirect method.

(SO 3)

GRANIA COMPANY
Income Statement
For the Year Ended December 31, 2008

Revenues		$970,000
Operating expenses, excluding depreciation	$624,000	
Depreciation expense	60,000	
Loss on sale of equipment	16,000	700,000
Income before income taxes		270,000
Income tax expense		40,000
Net income		$230,000

Grania's balance sheet contained the comparative data at December 31, shown below.

	2008	2007
Accounts receivable	$75,000	$60,000
Accounts payable	41,000	28,000
Income taxes payable	11,000	7,000

Accounts payable pertain to operating expenses.

Instructions

Prepare the operating activities section of the statement of cash flows using the indirect method.

Cash from operations $308,000

***P13-6A** Data for Grania Company are presented in P13-5A.

Prepare the operating activities section—direct method.

(SO 6)

Cash from operations $308,000

Instructions

Prepare the operating activities section of the statement of cash flows using the direct method.

P13-7A Presented below are the financial statements of Weller Company.

Prepare a statement of cash flows—indirect method, and compute free cash flow.

(SO 3, 4)

WELLER COMPANY
Comparative Balance Sheets
December 31

Assets	**2008**	**2007**
Cash	$ 35,000	$ 20,000
Accounts receivable	33,000	14,000
Merchandise inventory	27,000	20,000
Property, plant, and equipment	60,000	78,000
Accumulated depreciation	(29,000)	(24,000)
Total	$126,000	$108,000
Liabilities and Stockholders' Equity		
Accounts payable	$ 29,000	$ 15,000
Income taxes payable	7,000	8,000
Bonds payable	27,000	33,000
Common stock	18,000	14,000
Retained earnings	45,000	38,000
Total	$126,000	$108,000

WELLER COMPANY
Income Statement
For the Year Ended December 31, 2008

Sales		$242,000
Cost of goods sold		175,000
Gross profit		67,000
Selling expenses	$18,000	
Administrative expenses	6,000	24,000
Income from operations		43,000
Interest expense		3,000
Income before income taxes		40,000
Income tax expense		8,000
Net income		$ 32,000

Additional data:

1. Dividends declared and paid were $25,000.
2. During the year equipment was sold for $8,500 cash. This equipment cost $18,000 originally and had a book value of $8,500 at the time of sale.
3. All depreciation expense, $14,500, is in the selling expense category.
4. All sales and purchases are on account.

Instructions

(a) Cash from operations $33,500

(a) Prepare a statement of cash flows using the indirect method.
(b) Compute free cash flow.

Prepare a statement of cash flows—direct method, and compute free cash flow.
(SO 4, 6)

***P13-8A** Data for Weller Company are presented in P13-7A. Further analysis reveals the following.

1. Accounts payable pertain to merchandise suppliers.
2. All operating expenses except for depreciation were paid in cash.

Instructions

(a) Cash from operations $33,500

(a) Prepare a statement of cash flows for Weller Company using the direct method.
(b) Compute free cash flow.

Prepare a statement of cash flows—indirect method.
(SO 3)

P13-9A Condensed financial data of Arma Inc. follow.

ARMA INC.
Comparative Balance Sheets
December 31

Assets	**2008**	**2007**
Cash	$ 90,800	$ 48,400
Accounts receivable	92,800	33,000
Inventories	112,500	102,850
Prepaid expenses	28,400	26,000
Investments	138,000	114,000
Plant assets	270,000	242,500
Accumulated depreciation	(50,000)	(52,000)
Total	$682,500	$514,750
Liabilities and Stockholders' Equity		
Accounts payable	$112,000	$ 67,300
Accrued expenses payable	16,500	17,000
Bonds payable	110,000	150,000
Common stock	220,000	175,000
Retained earnings	224,000	105,450
Total	$682,500	$514,750

ARMA INC.
Income Statement
For the Year Ended December 31, 2008

Sales		$392,780
Less:		
Cost of goods sold	$135,460	
Operating expenses, excluding depreciation	12,410	
Depreciation expense	46,500	
Income taxes	27,280	
Interest expense	4,730	
Loss on sale of plant assets	7,500	233,880
Net income		$158,900

Additional information:

1. New plant assets costing $85,000 were purchased for cash during the year.
2. Old plant assets having an original cost of $57,500 were sold for $1,500 cash.
3. Bonds matured and were paid off at face value for cash.
4. A cash dividend of $40,350 was declared and paid during the year.

Instructions

Prepare a statement of cash flows using the indirect method.

Cash from operations $185,250

***P13-10A** Data for Arma Inc. are presented in P13-9A. Further analysis reveals that accounts payable pertain to merchandise creditors.

Prepare a statement of cash flows—direct method.

(SO 6)

Instructions

Prepare a statement of cash flows for Arma Inc. using the direct method.

Cash from operations $185,250

P13-11A The comparative balance sheets for Ramirez Company as of December 31 are presented below.

Prepare a statement of cash flows—indirect method.

(SO 3)

RAMIREZ COMPANY
Comparative Balance Sheets
December 31

Assets	**2008**	**2007**
Cash	$ 71,000	$ 45,000
Accounts receivable	44,000	62,000
Inventory	151,450	142,000
Prepaid expenses	15,280	21,000
Land	105,000	130,000
Equipment	228,000	155,000
Accumulated depreciation—equipment	(45,000)	(35,000)
Building	200,000	200,000
Accumulated depreciation—building	(60,000)	(40,000)
Total	$709,730	$680,000
Liabilities and Stockholders' Equity		
Accounts payable	$ 47,730	$ 40,000
Bonds payable	260,000	300,000
Common stock, $1 par	200,000	160,000
Retained earnings	202,000	180,000
Total	$709,730	$680,000

Additional information:

1. Operating expenses include depreciation expense of $42,000 and charges from prepaid expenses of $5,720.
2. Land was sold for cash at book value.

3. Cash dividends of $15,000 were paid.
4. Net income for 2008 was $37,000.
5. Equipment was purchased for $95,000 cash. In addition, equipment costing $22,000 with a book value of $10,000 was sold for $6,000 cash.
6. Bonds were converted at face value by issuing 40,000 shares of $1 par value common stock.

Cash from operations $105,000

Instructions

Prepare a statement of cash flows for the year ended December 31, 2008, using the indirect method.

Prepare a worksheet—indirect method.

(SO 5)

***P13-12A** Condensed financial data of Oprah Company appear below.

OPRAH COMPANY
Comparative Balance Sheets
December 31

Assets	**2008**	**2007**
Cash	$ 92,700	$ 47,250
Accounts receivable	90,800	57,000
Inventories	121,900	102,650
Investments	84,500	87,000
Plant assets	250,000	205,000
Accumulated depreciation	(49,500)	(40,000)
	$590,400	$458,900
Liabilities and Stockholders' Equity		
Accounts payable	$ 57,700	$ 48,280
Accrued expenses payable	12,100	18,830
Bonds payable	100,000	70,000
Common stock	250,000	200,000
Retained earnings	170,600	121,790
	$590,400	$458,900

OPRAH COMPANY
Income Statement
For the Year Ended December 31, 2008

Sales		$297,500
Gain on sale of plant assets		8,750
		306,250
Less:		
Cost of goods sold	$99,460	
Operating expenses (excluding depreciation expense)	14,670	
Depreciation expense	49,700	
Income taxes	7,270	
Interest expense	2,940	174,040
Net income		$132,210

Additional information:

1. New plant assets costing $92,000 were purchased for cash during the year.
2. Investments were sold at cost.
3. Plant assets costing $47,000 were sold for $15,550, resulting in gain of $8,750.
4. A cash dividend of $83,400 was declared and paid during the year.

Reconciling items total $610,210

Instructions

Prepare a worksheet for the statement of cash flows using the indirect method. Enter the reconciling items directly in the worksheet columns, using letters to cross-reference each entry.

PROBLEMS: SET B

P13-1B You are provided with the following transactions that took place during a recent fiscal year.

Distinguish among operating, investing, and financing activities.

(SO 2)

Transaction	Where Reported on Statement	Cash Inflow, Outflow, or No Effect?
(a) Recorded depreciation expense on the plant assets.		
(b) Incurred a loss on disposal of plant assets.		
(c) Acquired a building by paying cash.		
(d) Made principal repayments on a mortgage.		
(e) Issued common stock.		
(f) Purchased shares of another company to be held as a long-term equity investment.		
(g) Paid dividends to common stockholders.		
(h) Sold inventory on credit. The company uses a perpetual inventory system.		
(i) Purchased inventory on credit.		
(j) Paid wages to employees.		

Instructions

Complete the table indicating whether each item (1) should be reported as an operating (O) activity, investing (I) activity, financing (F) activity, or as a noncash (NC) transaction reported in a separate schedule, and (2) represents a cash inflow or cash outflow or has no cash flow effect. Assume use of the indirect approach.

P13-2B The following selected account balances relate to the plant asset accounts of Zambia Inc. at year-end.

Determine cash flow effects of changes in plant asset accounts.

(SO 3)

	2008	2007
Accumulated depreciation—buildings	$337,500	$300,000
Accumulated depreciation—equipment	144,000	96,000
Buildings	750,000	750,000
Depreciation expense	101,500	85,500
Equipment	300,000	240,000
Land	100,000	70,000
Loss on sale of equipment	3,000	0

Additional information:

1. Zambia purchased $85,000 of equipment and $30,000 of land for cash in 2008.
2. Zambia also sold equipment in 2008.
3. Depreciation expense in 2008 was $37,500 on building and $64,000 on equipment.

Instructions

(a) Determine the amounts of any cash inflows or outflows related to the plant asset accounts in 2008.

(b) Indicate where each of the cash inflows or outflows identified in (a) would be classified on the statement of cash flows.

(a) Cash proceeds $6,000

P13-3B The income statement of Marquette Company is presented on page 610.

Prepare the operating activities section—indirect method.

(SO 3)

Additional information:

1. Accounts receivable decreased $520,000 during the year, and inventory increased $140,000.
2. Prepaid expenses increased $175,000 during the year.
3. Accounts payable to merchandise suppliers increased $50,000 during the year.
4. Accrued expenses payable increased $165,000 during the year.

MARQUETTE COMPANY
Income Statement
For the Year Ended December 31, 2008

Sales		$5,400,000
Cost of goods sold		
Beginning inventory	$1,780,000	
Purchases	3,430,000	
Goods available for sale	5,210,000	
Ending inventory	1,920,000	
Total cost of goods sold		3,290,000
Gross profit		2,110,000
Operating expenses		
Selling expenses	420,000	
Administrative expense	525,000	
Depreciation expense	105,000	
Amortization expense	20,000	1,070,000
Net income		$1,040,000

Instructions

Cash from operations $1,585,000

Prepare the operating activities section of the statement of cash flows for the year ended December 31, 2008, for Marquette Company, using the indirect method.

Prepare the operating activities section—direct method.

(SO 6)

Cash from operations $1,585,000

***P13-4B** Data for Marquette Company are presented in P13-3B.

Instructions

Prepare the operating activities section of the statement of cash flows using the direct method.

Prepare the operating activities section—indirect method.

(SO 3)

P13-5B The income statement of Shapiro Inc. reported the following condensed information.

SHAPIRO INC.
Income Statement
For the Year Ended December 31, 2008

Revenues	$545,000
Operating expenses	400,000
Income from operations	145,000
Income tax expense	47,000
Net income	$ 98,000

Shapiro's balance sheet contained these comparative data at December 31.

	2008	2007
Accounts receivable	$50,000	$75,000
Accounts payable	30,000	51,000
Income taxes payable	10,000	4,000

Shapiro has no depreciable assets. Accounts payable pertain to operating expenses.

Instructions

Cash from operations $108,000

Prepare the operating activities section of the statement of cash flows using the indirect method.

Prepare the operating activities section—direct method.

(SO 6)

Cash from operations $108,000

***P13-6B** Data for Shapiro Inc. are presented in P13-5B.

Instructions

Prepare the operating activities section of the statement of cash flows using the direct method.

P13-7B Presented below are the financial statements of Molina Company.

Prepare a statement of cash flows—indirect method, and compute free cash flow.

(SO 3, 4)

MOLINA COMPANY
Comparative Balance Sheets
December 31

Assets		**2008**		**2007**
Cash		$ 28,000		$ 33,000
Accounts receivable		23,000		14,000
Merchandise inventory		41,000		25,000
Property, plant, and equipment	$ 70,000		$ 78,000	
Less: Accumulated depreciation	(27,000)	43,000	(24,000)	54,000
Total		$135,000		$126,000
Liabilities and Stockholders' Equity				
Accounts payable		$ 31,000		$ 43,000
Income taxes payable		26,000		20,000
Bonds payable		20,000		10,000
Common stock		25,000		25,000
Retained earnings		33,000		28,000
Total		$135,000		$126,000

MOLINA COMPANY
Income Statement
For the Year Ended December 31, 2008

Sales		$286,000
Cost of goods sold		194,000
Gross profit		92,000
Selling expenses	$28,000	
Administrative expenses	9,000	37,000
Income from operations		55,000
Interest expense		7,000
Income before income taxes		48,000
Income tax expense		10,000
Net income		$ 38,000

Additional data:

1. Dividends of $33,000 were declared and paid.
2. During the year equipment was sold for $10,000 cash. This equipment cost $13,000 originally and had a book value of $10,000 at the time of sale.
3. All depreciation expense, $6,000, is in the selling expense category.
4. All sales and purchases are on account.
5. Additional equipment was purchased for $5,000 cash.

Instructions

(a) Prepare a statement of cash flows using the indirect method.
(b) Compute free cash flow.

(a) Cash from operations $13,000

***P13-8B** Data for Molina Company are presented in P13-7B. Further analysis reveals the following.

Prepare a statement of cash flows—direct method, and compute free cash flow.

(SO 4, 6)

(a) Cash from operations $13,000

1. Accounts payable pertains to merchandise creditors.
2. All operating expenses except for depreciation are paid in cash.

Instructions

(a) Prepare a statement of cash flows using the direct method.
(b) Compute free cash flow.

Prepare a statement of cash flows—indirect method.
(SO 3)

P13-9B Condensed financial data of Yaeger Company are shown below.

YAEGER COMPANY
Comparative Balance Sheets
December 31

Assets	**2008**	**2007**
Cash	$ 97,700	$ 33,400
Accounts receivable	70,800	37,000
Inventories	121,900	102,650
Investments	89,500	107,000
Plant assets	310,000	205,000
Accumulated depreciation	(49,500)	(40,000)
Total	$640,400	$445,050
Liabilities and Stockholders' Equity		
Accounts payable	$ 62,700	$ 48,280
Accrued expenses payable	15,100	18,830
Bonds payable	140,000	70,000
Common stock	250,000	200,000
Retained earnings	172,600	107,940
Total	$640,400	$445,050

YAEGER COMPANY
Income Statement
For the Year Ended December 31, 2008

Sales		$297,500
Gain on sale of plant assets		5,000
		302,500
Less:		
Cost of goods sold	$99,460	
Operating expenses, excluding depreciation expense	14,670	
Depreciation expense	35,500	
Income taxes	27,270	
Interest expense	2,940	179,840
Net income		$122,660

Additional information:

1. New plant assets costing $141,000 were purchased for cash during the year.
2. Investments were sold at cost.
3. Plant assets costing $36,000 were sold for $15,000, resulting in a gain of $5,000.
4. A cash dividend of $58,000 was declared and paid during the year.

Cash from operations $110,800

Instructions
Prepare a statement of cash flows using the indirect method.

Prepare a statement of cash flows—direct method.
(SO 6)

***P13-10B** Data for Yaeger Company are presented in P13-9B. Further analysis reveals that accounts payable pertain to merchandise creditors.

Cash from operations $110,800

Instructions
Prepare a statement of cash flows for Yaeger Company using the direct method.

P13-11B Presented below are the comparative balance sheets for Lewis Company at December 31.

Prepare a statement of cash flows—indirect method.

(SO 3)

LEWIS COMPANY
Comparative Balance Sheets
December 31

Assets	**2008**	**2007**
Cash	$ 31,000	$ 57,000
Accounts receivable	77,000	64,000
Inventory	192,000	140,000
Prepaid expenses	12,140	16,540
Land	100,000	150,000
Equipment	215,000	175,000
Accumulated depreciation—equipment	(70,000)	(42,000)
Building	250,000	250,000
Accumulated depreciation—building	(70,000)	(50,000)
Total	$737,140	$760,540
Liabilities and Stockholders' Equity		
Accounts payable	$ 58,000	$ 45,000
Bonds payable	235,000	265,000
Common stock, $1 par	280,000	250,000
Retained earnings	164,140	200,540
Total	$737,140	$760,540

Additional information:

1. Operating expenses include depreciation expense $65,000 and charges from prepaid expenses of $4,400.
2. Land was sold for cash at cost.
3. Cash dividends of $69,290 were paid.
4. Net income for 2008 was $32,890.
5. Equipment was purchased for $80,000 cash. In addition, equipment costing $40,000 with a book value of $23,000 was sold for $25,000 cash.
6. Bonds were converted at face value by issuing 30,000 shares of $1 par value common stock.

Instructions

Prepare a statement of cash flows for 2008 using the indirect method.

Cash from operations $48,290

PROBLEMS: SET C

Visit the book's website at **www.wiley.com/college/weygandt** and choose the Student Companion site to access Problem Set C.

WATERWAYS CONTINUING PROBLEM

(This is a continuation of the Waterways Problem from Chapters 1 through 12.)

WCP13 Waterways prepared the balance sheet and income statement for the irrigation installation division for 2008. Now the company also needs to prepare a cash flow statement for the same division. This problem asks you to prepare a statement of cash flows and to calculate cash-basis measures.

*Go to the book's website, **www.wiley.com/college/weygandt**, to find the completion of this problem.*

BROADENING YOUR PERSPECTIVE

Financial Reporting Problem

PepsiCo, Inc.

BYP13-1 The financial statements of PepsiCo are presented at the company's website, **www.pepsico.com.**

Instructions

Refer to PepsiCo's financial statements, and answer the following questions.

(a) What was the amount of net cash provided by operating activities for the year ended December 31, 2005? For the year ended December 25, 2004?
(b) What was the amount of increase or decrease in cash and cash equivalents for the year ended December 31, 2005? For the year ended December 25, 2004?
(c) Which method of computing net cash provided by operating activities does PepsiCo use?
(d) From your analysis of the 2005 statement of cash flows, did the change in accounts and notes receivable decrease or increase cash? Did the change in inventories decrease or increase cash? Did the change in accounts payable and other current liabilities decrease or increase cash?
(e) What was the net outflow or inflow of cash from investing activities for the year ended December 31, 2005?
(f) What was the amount of interest paid in the year ended December 31, 2005? What was the amount of income taxes paid in the year ended December 31, 2005? (See Note 14.)

Comparative Analysis Problem

PepsiCo, Inc. vs. The Coca-Cola Company

BYP13-2 The financial statements of PepsiCo and The Coca-Cola Company can be found at the companies' websites, **www.pepsico.com** and **www.coca-cola.com.**

Instructions

Refer to the financial statements, and answer the following questions.

(a) Based on the information contained in these financial statements, compute free cash flow for each company for 2005.
(b) What conclusions concerning the management of cash can be drawn from these data?

Decision Making Across the Organization

BYP13-3 Ron Nord and Lisa Smith are examining the following statement of cash flows for Carpino Company for the year ended January 31, 2008.

CARPINO COMPANY
Statement of Cash Flows
For the Year Ended January 31, 2008

Sources of cash	
From sales of merchandise	$380,000
From sale of capital stock	420,000
From sale of investment (purchased below)	80,000
From depreciation	55,000
From issuance of note for truck	20,000
From interest on investments	6,000
Total sources of cash	961,000

Uses of cash	
For purchase of fixtures and equipment	330,000
For merchandise purchased for resale	258,000
For operating expenses (including depreciation)	160,000
For purchase of investment	75,000
For purchase of truck by issuance of note	20,000
For purchase of treasury stock	10,000
For interest on note payable	3,000
Total uses of cash	856,000
Net increase in cash	$ 105,000

Ron claims that Carpino's statement of cash flows is an excellent portrayal of a superb first year with cash increasing $105,000. Lisa replies that it was not a superb first year. Rather, she says, the year was an operating failure, that the statement is presented incorrectly, and that $105,000 is not the actual increase in cash. The cash balance at the beginning of the year was $140,000.

Instructions
With the class divided into groups, answer the following.

(a) Using the data provided, prepare a statement of cash flows in proper form using the indirect method. The only noncash items in the income statement are depreciation and the gain from the sale of the investment.
(b) With whom do you agree, Ron or Lisa? Explain your position.

Exploring the Web

BYP13-4 Purpose: Learn about the SEC.

Address: www.sec.gov/index.html, or go to **www.wiley.com/college/weygandt**

From the SEC homepage, choose **About the SEC,** and then **What We Do**.

Instructions
Answer the following questions.

(a) How many enforcement actions does the SEC take each year against securities law violators? What are typical infractions?
(b) After the Depression, Congress passed the Securities Acts of 1933 and 1934 to improve investor confidence in the markets. What two "common sense" notions are these laws based on?
(c) Who was the President of the United States at the time of the creation of the SEC? Who was the first SEC Chairperson?

BYP13-5 Purpose: Use the Internet to view SEC filings.

Address: biz.yahoo.com/i, or go to **www.wiley.com/college/weygandt**

Steps
1. Type in a company name.
2. Choose **Profile**.
3. Choose **SEC Filings**. (This will take you to Yahoo-Edgar Online.)

Instructions
Answer the following questions.

(a) What company did you select?
(b) Which filing is the most recent? What is the date?
(c) What other recent SEC filings are available for your viewing?

Communication Activity

BYP13-6 Kyle Benson, the owner-president of Computer Services Company, is unfamiliar with the statement of cash flows that you, as his accountant, prepared. He asks for further explanation.

Instructions

Write him a brief memo explaining the form and content of the statement of cash flows as shown in Illustration 13-13 (page 572).

Ethics Case

BYP13-7 Tappit Corp. is a medium-sized wholesaler of automotive parts. It has 10 stockholders who have been paid a total of $1 million in cash dividends for 8 consecutive years. The board's policy requires that, for this dividend to be declared, net cash provided by operating activities as reported in Tappit's current year's statement of cash flows must exceed $1 million. President and CEO Willie Morton's job is secure so long as he produces annual operating cash flows to support the usual dividend.

At the end of the current year, controller Robert Jennings presents president Willie Morton with some disappointing news: The net cash provided by operating activities is calculated by the indirect method to be only $970,000. The president says to Robert, "We must get that amount above $1 million. Isn't there some way to increase operating cash flow by another $30,000?" Robert answers, "These figures were prepared by my assistant. I'll go back to my office and see what I can do." The president replies, "I know you won't let me down, Robert."

Upon close scrutiny of the statement of cash flows, Robert concludes that he can get the operating cash flows above $1 million by reclassifying a $60,000, 2-year note payable listed in the financing activities section as "Proceeds from bank loan—$60,000." He will report the note instead as "Increase in payables—$60,000" and treat it as an adjustment of net income in the operating activities section. He returns to the president, saying, "You can tell the board to declare their usual dividend. Our net cash flow provided by operating activities is $1,030,000." "Good man, Robert! I knew I could count on you," exults the president.

Instructions

(a) Who are the stakeholders in this situation?
(b) Was there anything unethical about the president's actions? Was there anything unethical about the controller's actions?
(c) Are the board members or anyone else likely to discover the misclassification?

"All About You" Activity

BYP13-8 In this chapter you learned that companies prepare a statement of cash flows in order to keep track of their sources and uses of cash and to help them plan for their future cash needs. Planning for your own short- and long-term cash needs is every bit as important as it is for a company.

Instructions

Read the article provided at **www.fool.com/savings/shortterm/02.htm**, and answer the following questions.

(a) Describe the three factors that determine how much money you should set aside for short-term needs.
(b) How many months of living expenses does the article suggest to set aside?
(c) Estimate how much you should set aside based upon your current situation. Are you closer to Cliff's scenario or to Prudence's?

Answers to Insight and Accounting Across the Organization Questions

Net *What*?, p. 561

Q: In general, why do differences exist between net income and net cash provided by operating activities?

A: *The differences are explained by differences in the timing of the reporting of revenues and expenses under accrual accounting versus cash. Under accrual accounting, companies report revenues when earned, even if cash hasn't been received, and they report expenses when incurred, even if cash hasn't been paid.*

Cash Flow Isn't Always What It Seems, p. 564

Q: For what reasons might managers at WorldCom and at Dynegy take the actions noted above?

A: *Analysts increasingly use cash-flow-based measures of income, such as cash flow provided by operations, in addition to net income. More investors now focus on cash flow from operations, and some compensation contracts now have bonuses tied to cash-flow numbers. Thus, some managers have taken actions that artificially increase cash flow from operations.*

GM Must Sell More Cars, p. 570

Q: Why does GM's cash provided by operating activities drop so precipitously when the company's sales figures decline?

A: *GM's cash inflow is directly related to how many cars it sells. But many of its cash outflows are not tied to sales—they are "fixed." For example, many of its employee payroll costs are very rigid due to labor contracts. Therefore, even though sales (and therefore cash inflows) fall, these cash outflows don't decline.*

Authors' Comments on *All About You*: Where Does the Money Go?, p. 577

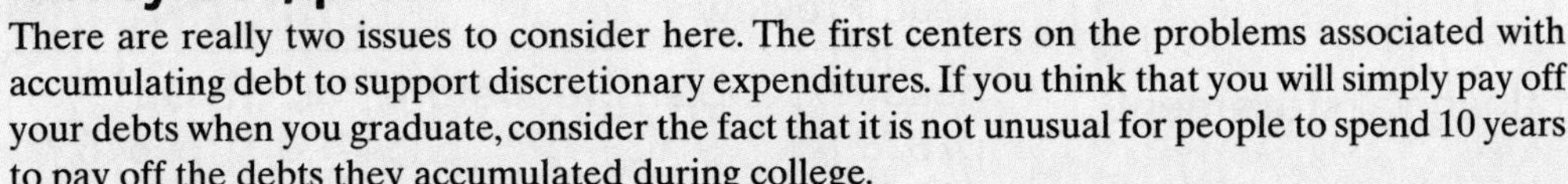

There are really two issues to consider here. The first centers on the problems associated with accumulating debt to support discretionary expenditures. If you think that you will simply pay off your debts when you graduate, consider the fact that it is not unusual for people to spend 10 years to pay off the debts they accumulated during college.

A second issue relates to the impact that working so many hours can have on your academic performance. Research shows that college students today spend more hours working at jobs and fewer hours studying than at any time in the past. This same research shows that academic performance declines when students work too many hours at their jobs. If you could cut back on your discretionary expenditures, you could quit working so many hours, which would mean that you would do better in school, which would mean that you would have a better shot at a good job after college.

The bottom line: While we think that borrowing to invest in yourself through your education makes good sense, we think that borrowing to support a Starbucks habit is a bad idea. For more ideas on how to get your cash flow under control, see *http://financialplan.about.com/cs/college/a/MoneyCollege.htm*.

Answers to Self-Study Questions

1. c 2. b 3. a 4. c 5. d 6. b 7. c 8. d 9. b 10. a 11. d *12. b *13. c *14. d

Remember to go back to the Navigator box on the chapter-opening page and check off your completed work.

Chapter 14

Financial Statement Analysis: The Big Picture

STUDY OBJECTIVES

After studying this chapter, you should be able to:

1 Discuss the need for comparative analysis.
2 Identify the tools of financial statement analysis.
3 Explain and apply horizontal analysis.
4 Describe and apply vertical analysis.
5 Identify and compute ratios used in analyzing a firm's liquidity, profitability, and solvency.
6 Understand the concept of earning power, and how irregular items are presented.
7 Understand the concept of quality of earnings.

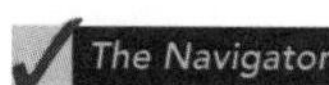

The Navigator

Scan **Study Objectives**	■
Read **Feature Story**	■
Read **Preview**	■
Read text and answer **Before You Go On** p. 628 ■ p. 639 ■ p. 644 ■ p. 646	■
Work **Using the Decision Toolkit**	■
Review **Summary of Study Objectives**	■
Work **Demonstration Problem**	■
Answer **Self-Study Questions**	■
Complete **Assignments**	■

Feature Story

"FOLLOW THAT STOCK!"

If you thought cab drivers with cell phones were scary, how about a cab driver with a trading desk in the front seat?

When a stoplight turns red or traffic backs up, New York City cabby Carlos Rubino morphs into a day trader, scanning real-time quotes of his favorite stocks as they spew across a PalmPilot mounted next to the steering wheel. "It's kind of stressful," he says, "but I like it."

Itching to know how a particular stock is doing? Mr. Rubino is happy to look up quotes for passengers. Yahoo and Amazon.com are two of the most requested ones. He even lets customers use his laptop computer to send urgent e-mails from the back seat. Aware of a local law prohibiting cabbies from using cell phones while they're driving, Mr. Rubino extends that rule to his trading. "I stop the cab at the side of the road if I have to make a trade," he says. "Safety first."

Originally from São Paulo, Brazil, Mr. Rubino has been driving his cab since 1987, and started trading stocks a few years ago. His curiosity grew as he began to educate himself by reading business publications. The Wall Street brokers he picks up are usually impressed with his knowledge, he says. But the feeling generally isn't mutual. Some of them "don't know much," he says. "They buy what people tell them to buy—they're like a toll collector."

Mr. Rubino is an enigma to his fellow cab drivers. A lot of his colleagues say they want to trade too. "But cab drivers are a little cheap," he says. "The [real-time] quotes cost $100 a month. The wireless Internet access is $54 a month."

Will he give up his brokerage firm on wheels for a stationary job? Not likely. Though he claims a 70% return on his investments in some months, he says he makes $1,300 and up a week driving his cab—more than he does trading. Besides, he adds, "Why go somewhere and have a boss?"

Source: Excerpted from Barbara Boydston, "With This Cab, People Jump in and Shout, 'Follow that Stock!'," *Wall Street Journal*, August 18, 1999, p. C1. Reprinted by permission of the Wall Street Journal

The Navigator

Inside Chapter 14

Preview of Chapter 14

We can learn an important lesson from the Feature Story: Experience is the best teacher. By now you have learned a significant amount about financial reporting by U.S. companies. Using some basic decision tools, you can perform a rudimentary analysis on any U.S. company and draw basic conclusions about its financial health. Although it would not be wise for you to bet your life savings on a company's stock relying solely on your current level of knowledge, we strongly encourage you to practice your new skills wherever possible. Only with practice will you improve your ability to interpret financial numbers.

Before unleashing you on the world of high finance, we will present a few more important concepts and techniques, as well as provide you with a comprehensive review of corporate financial statements. We use decision tools to analyze a single company—J.C. Penney Company, one of the country's oldest and largest retail store chains.

The content and organization of Chapter 14 are as follows.

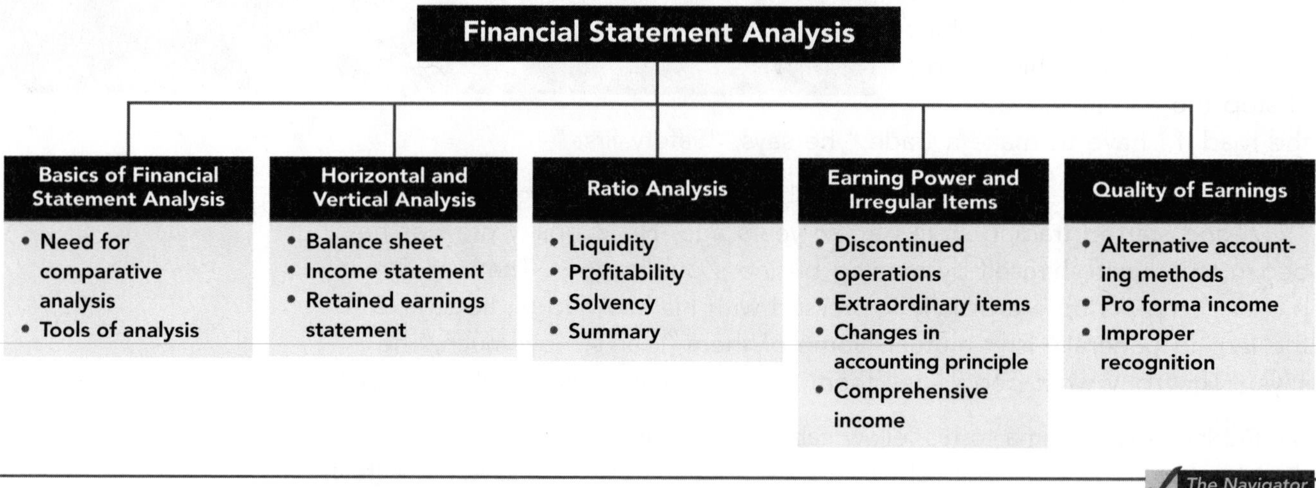

The Navigator

BASICS OF FINANCIAL STATEMENT ANALYSIS

Analyzing financial statements involves evaluating three characteristics: a company's liquidity, profitability, and solvency. A **short-term creditor**, such as a bank, is primarily interested in liquidity—the ability of the borrower to pay obligations when they come due. The liquidity of the borrower is extremely important in evaluating the safety of a loan. A **long-term creditor**, such as a bondholder, looks to profitability and solvency measures that indicate the company's ability to survive over a long period of time. Long-term creditors consider such measures as the amount of debt in the company's capital structure and its ability to meet interest payments. Similarly, **stockholders** look at the profitability and solvency of the company. They want to assess the likelihood of dividends and the growth potential of the stock.

Need for Comparative Analysis

STUDY OBJECTIVE 1

Discuss the need for comparative analysis.

Every item reported in a financial statement has significance. When J.C. Penney Company, Inc. reports cash of $3,016 million on its balance sheet, we know the company had that amount of cash on the balance sheet date. But, we do not know whether the amount represents an increase over prior years, or whether it is adequate in relation to the company's need for cash. To obtain such information, we need to compare the amount of cash with other financial statement data.

Comparisons can be made on a number of different bases. Three are illustrated in this chapter:

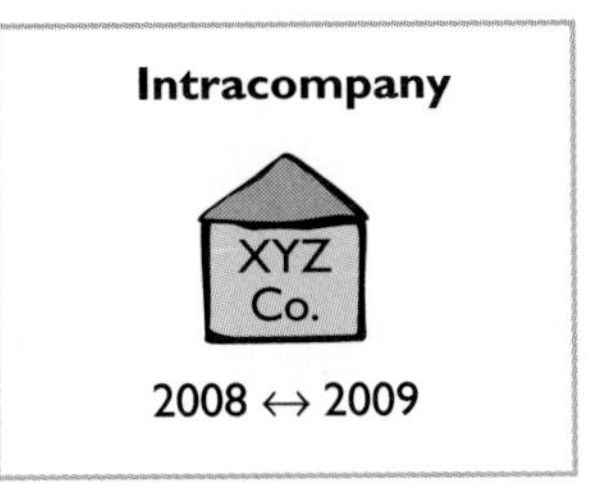

1. **Intracompany basis.** This basis compares an item or financial relationship **within a company** in the current year with the same item or relationship in one or more prior years. For example, J.C. Penney can compare its cash balance at the end of the current year with last year's balance to find the amount of the increase or decrease. Likewise, J.C. Penney can compare the percentage of cash to current assets at the end of the current year with the percentage in one or more prior years. Intracompany comparisons are useful in detecting changes in financial relationships and significant trends.

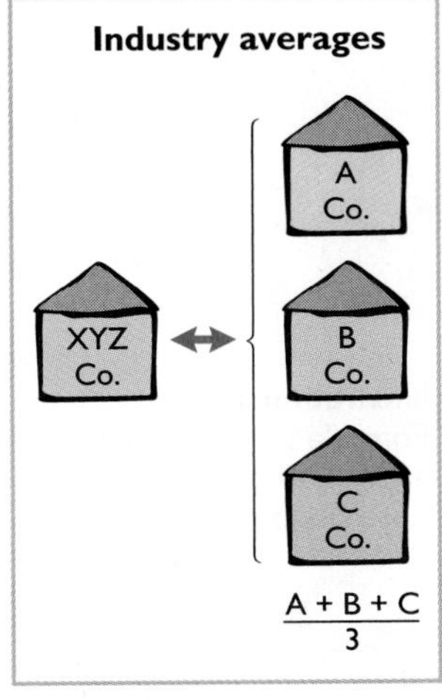

2. **Industry averages.** This basis compares an item or financial relationship of a company with **industry averages** (or **norms**) published by financial ratings organizations such as Dun & Bradstreet, Moody's, and Standard & Poor's. For example, J.C. Penney's net income can be compared with the average net income of all companies in the retail chain-store industry. Comparisons with industry averages provide information as to a company's relative performance within the industry.

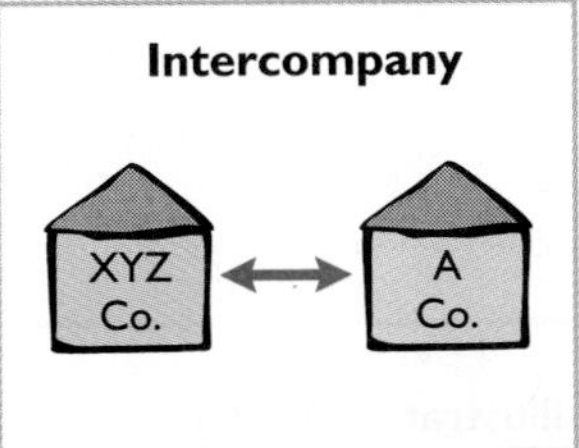

3. **Intercompany basis.** This basis compares an item or financial relationship of one company with the same item or relationship in **one or more competing companies**. Analysts make these comparisons on the basis of the published financial statements of the individual companies. For example, we can compare J.C. Penney's total sales for the year with the total sales of a major competitor such as Kmart. Intercompany comparisons are useful in determining a company's competitive position.

Tools of Analysis

STUDY OBJECTIVE 2

Identify the tools of financial statement analysis.

We use various tools to evaluate the significance of financial statement data. Three commonly used tools are these:

- **Horizontal analysis** evaluates a series of financial statement data over a period of time.
- **Vertical analysis** evaluates financial statement data by expressing each item in a financial statement as a percent of a base amount.
- **Ratio analysis** expresses the relationship among selected items of financial statement data.

Horizontal analysis is used primarily in intracompany comparisons. Two features in published financial statements facilitate this type of comparison: First, each of the basic financial statements presents comparative financial data for a minimum of two years. Second, a summary of selected financial data is presented for a series of five to ten years or more. *Vertical analysis* is used in both intra- and intercompany comparisons. *Ratio analysis* is used in all three types of comparisons. In the following sections, we explain and illustrate each of the three types of analysis.

HORIZONTAL ANALYSIS

STUDY OBJECTIVE 3

Explain and apply horizontal analysis.

Horizontal analysis, also called **trend analysis**, is a technique for evaluating a series of financial statement data over a period of time. Its purpose is to determine the increase or decrease that has taken place. This change may be expressed as either an amount or a percentage. For example, the recent net sales figures of J.C. Penney Company are as follows.

Illustration 14-1
J.C. Penney Company's net sales

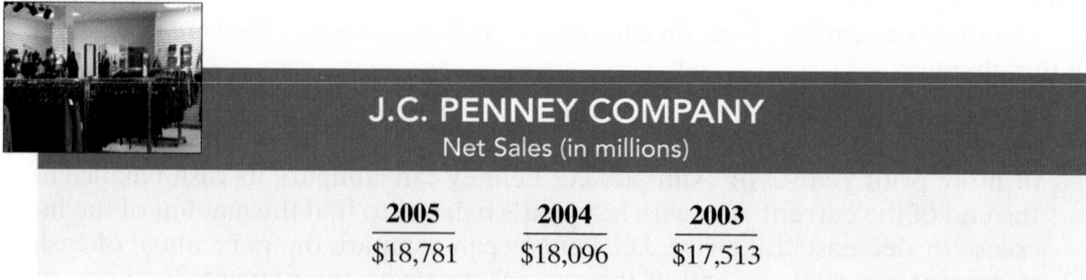

J.C. PENNEY COMPANY
Net Sales (in millions)

2005	2004	2003
$18,781	$18,096	$17,513

If we assume that 2003 is the base year, we can measure all percentage increases or decreases from this base period amount as follows.

Illustration 14-2
Formula for horizontal analysis of changes since base period

$$\text{Change Since Base Period} = \frac{\text{Current Year Amount} - \text{Base Year Amount}}{\text{Base Year Amount}}$$

For example, we can determine that net sales for J.C. Penney increased from 2003 to 2004 approximately 3.3% [($18,096 − $17,513) ÷ $17,513]. Similarly, we can determine that net sales increased from 2003 to 2005 approximately 7.2% [($18,781 − $17,513) ÷ $17,513].

Alternatively, we can express current year sales as a percentage of the base period. We do this by dividing the current year amount by the base year amount, as shown below.

Illustration 14-3
Formula for horizontal analysis of current year in relation to base year

$$\text{Current Results in Relation to Base Period} = \frac{\text{Current Year Amount}}{\text{Base Year Amount}}$$

Illustration 14-4 presents this analysis for J.C. Penney for a three-year period using 2003 as the base period.

Illustration 14-4
Horizontal analysis of J.C. Penney Company's net sales in relation to base period

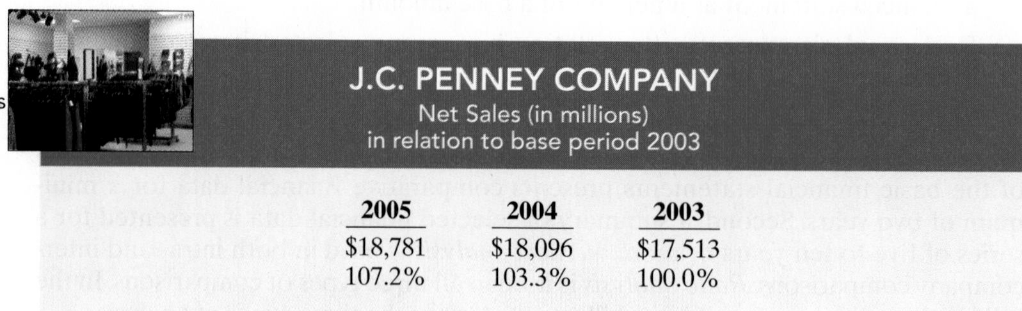

J.C. PENNEY COMPANY
Net Sales (in millions)
in relation to base period 2003

2005	2004	2003
$18,781	$18,096	$17,513
107.2%	103.3%	100.0%

Balance Sheet

To further illustrate horizontal analysis, we will use the financial statements of Quality Department Store Inc., a fictional retailer. Illustration 14-5 presents a horizontal analysis of its two-year condensed balance sheets, showing dollar and percentage changes.

Illustration 14-5
Horizontal analysis of balance sheets

QUALITY DEPARTMENT STORE INC.
Condensed Balance Sheets
December 31

	2005	2004	Increase or (Decrease) during 2005 Amount	Percent
Assets				
Current assets	$1,020,000	$ 945,000	$ 75,000	7.9%
Plant assets (net)	800,000	632,500	167,500	26.5%
Intangible assets	15,000	17,500	(2,500)	(14.3%)
Total assets	$1,835,000	$1,595,000	$240,000	15.0%
Liabilities				
Current liabilities	$ 344,500	$ 303,000	$ 41,500	13.7%
Long-term liabilities	487,500	497,000	(9,500)	(1.9%)
Total liabilities	832,000	800,000	32,000	4.0%
Stockholders' Equity				
Common stock, $1 par	275,400	270,000	5,400	2.0%
Retained earnings	727,600	525,000	202,600	38.6%
Total stockholders' equity	1,003,000	795,000	208,000	26.2%
Total liabilities and stockholders' equity	$1,835,000	$1,595,000	$240,000	15.0%

The comparative balance sheets in Illustration 14-5 show that a number of significant changes have occurred in Quality Department Store's financial structure from 2004 to 2005:

- In the assets section, plant assets (net) increased $167,500, or 26.5%.
- In the liabilities section, current liabilities increased $41,500, or 13.7%.
- In the stockholders' equity section, retained earnings increased $202,600, or 38.6%.

These changes suggest that the company expanded its asset base during 2005 and **financed this expansion primarily by retaining income** rather than assuming additional long-term debt.

Income Statement

Illustration 14-6 (page 624) presents a horizontal analysis of the two-year condensed income statements of Quality Department Store Inc. for the years 2005 and 2004. Horizontal analysis of the income statements shows the following changes:

- Net sales increased $260,000, or 14.2% ($260,000 ÷ $1,837,000).
- Cost of goods sold increased $141,000, or 12.4% ($141,000 ÷ $1,140,000).
- Total operating expenses increased $37,000, or 11.6% ($37,000 ÷ $320,000).

Overall, gross profit and net income were up substantially. Gross profit increased 17.1%, and net income, 26.5%. Quality's profit trend appears favorable.

Illustration 14-6
Horizontal analysis of income statements

QUALITY DEPARTMENT STORE INC.
Condensed Income Statements
For the Years Ended December 31

	2005	2004	Increase or (Decrease) during 2005 Amount	Percent
Sales	$2,195,000	$1,960,000	$235,000	12.0%
Sales returns and allowances	98,000	123,000	(25,000)	(20.3%)
Net sales	2,097,000	1,837,000	260,000	14.2%
Cost of goods sold	1,281,000	1,140,000	141,000	12.4%
Gross profit	816,000	697,000	119,000	17.1%
Selling expenses	253,000	211,500	41,500	19.6%
Administrative expenses	104,000	108,500	(4,500)	(4.1%)
Total operating expenses	357,000	320,000	37,000	11.6%
Income from operations	459,000	377,000	82,000	21.8%
Other revenues and gains				
Interest and dividends	9,000	11,000	(2,000)	(18.2%)
Other expenses and losses				
Interest expense	36,000	40,500	(4,500)	(11.1%)
Income before income taxes	432,000	347,500	84,500	24.3%
Income tax expense	168,200	139,000	29,200	21.0%
Net income	$ 263,800	$ 208,500	$ 55,300	26.5%

HELPFUL HINT
Note that though the amount column is additive (the total is $55,300), the percentage column is not additive (26.5% is not the total). A separate percentage has been calculated for each item.

Retained Earnings Statement

Illustration 14-7 presents a horizontal analysis of Quality Department Store's comparative retained earnings statements. Analyzed horizontally, net income increased $55,300, or 26.5%, whereas dividends on the common stock increased only $1,200, or 2%. We saw in the horizontal analysis of the balance sheet that ending retained earnings increased 38.6%. As indicated earlier, the company retained a significant portion of net income to finance additional plant facilities.

Illustration 14-7
Horizontal analysis of retained earnings statements

QUALITY DEPARTMENT STORE INC.
Retained Earnings Statements
For the Years Ended December 31

	2005	2004	Increase or (Decrease) during 2005 Amount	Percent
Retained earnings, Jan. 1	$525,000	$376,500	$148,500	39.4%
Add: Net income	263,800	208,500	55,300	26.5%
	788,800	585,000	203,800	
Deduct: Dividends	61,200	60,000	1,200	2.0%
Retained earnings, Dec. 31	$727,600	$525,000	$202,600	38.6%

Horizontal analysis of changes from period to period is relatively straightforward and is quite useful. But complications can occur in making the computations. If an item has no value in a base year or preceding year but does have a value in the next year, we cannot compute a percentage change. Similarly, if a negative amount appears in the base or preceding period and a positive amount exists the following year (or vice versa), no percentage change can be computed.

DECISION TOOLKIT

Decision Checkpoints	Info Needed for Decision	Tool to Use for Decision	How to Evaluate Results
	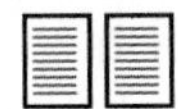		
How do the company's financial position and operating results compare with those of the previous period?	Income statement and balance sheet	Comparative financial statements should be prepared over at least two years, with the first year reported being the base year. Changes in each line item relative to the base year should be presented both by amount and by percentage. This is called horizontal analysis.	Significant changes should be investigated to determine the reason for the change.

VERTICAL ANALYSIS

STUDY OBJECTIVE 4

Describe and apply vertical analysis.

Vertical analysis, also called **common-size analysis**, is a technique that expresses each financial statement item as a percent of a base amount. On a balance sheet we might say that current assets are 22% of total assets—*total assets* being the base amount. Or on an income statement, we might say that selling expenses are 16% of net sales—*net sales* being the base amount.

Balance Sheet

Illustration 14-8 presents the vertical analysis of Quality Department Store Inc.'s comparative balance sheets. The base for the asset items is **total assets.** The base for the liability and stockholders' equity items is **total liabilities and stockholders' equity**.

Illustration 14-8
Vertical analysis of balance sheets

QUALITY DEPARTMENT STORE INC.
Condensed Balance Sheets
December 31

	2005		2004	
	Amount	**Percent**	**Amount**	**Percent**
Assets				
Current assets	$1,020,000	55.6%	$ 945,000	59.2%
Plant assets (net)	800,000	43.6%	632,500	39.7%
Intangible assets	15,000	0.8%	17,500	1.1%
Total assets	$1,835,000	100.0%	$1,595,000	100.0%
Liabilities				
Current liabilities	$ 344,500	18.8%	$ 303,000	19.0%
Long-term liabilities	487,500	26.5%	497,000	31.2%
Total liabilities	832,000	45.3%	800,000	50.2%
Stockholders' Equity				
Common stock, $1 par	275,400	15.0%	270,000	16.9%
Retained earnings	727,600	39.7%	525,000	32.9%
Total stockholders' equity	1,003,000	54.7%	795,000	49.8%
Total liabilities and stockholders' equity	$1,835,000	100.0%	$1,595,000	100.0%

HELPFUL HINT

The formula for calculating these balance sheet percentages is:

$$\frac{\text{Each item on B/S}}{\text{Total assets}} = \%$$

Vertical analysis shows the relative size of each category in the balance sheet. It also can show the **percentage change** in the individual asset, liability, and stockholders' equity items. For example, we can see that current assets decreased from 59.2% of total assets in 2004 to 55.6% in 2005 (even though the absolute dollar amount increased $75,000 in that time). Plant assets (net) have increased from 39.7% to 43.6% of total assets. Retained earnings have increased from 32.9% to 39.7% of total liabilities and stockholders' equity. These results reinforce the earlier observations that **Quality is choosing to finance its growth through retention of earnings rather than through issuing additional debt.**

Income Statement

Illustration 14-9 shows vertical analysis of Quality's income statements. Cost of goods sold as a percent of net sales declined 1% (62.1% vs. 61.1%), and total operating expenses as a percent of net sales declined 0.4% (17.4% vs. 17.0%). As a result, it is not surprising to see net income as a percent of net sales increase from 11.4% to 12.6%. Quality appears to be a profitable enterprise that is becoming even more successful.

Illustration 14-9
Vertical analysis of income statements

QUALITY DEPARTMENT STORE INC.
Condensed Income Statements
For the Years Ended December 31

	2005		2004	
	Amount	**Percent**	**Amount**	**Percent**
Sales	$2,195,000	104.7%	$1,960,000	106.7%
Sales returns and allowances	98,000	4.7%	123,000	6.7%
Net sales	2,097,000	100.0%	1,837,000	100.0%
Cost of goods sold	1,281,000	61.1%	1,140,000	62.1%
Gross profit	816,000	38.9%	697,000	37.9%
Selling expenses	253,000	12.0%	211,500	11.5%
Administrative expenses	104,000	5.0%	108,500	5.9%
Total operating expenses	357,000	17.0%	320,000	17.4%
Income from operations	459,000	21.9%	377,000	20.5%
Other revenues and gains				
Interest and dividends	9,000	0.4%	11,000	0.6%
Other expenses and losses				
Interest expense	36,000	1.7%	40,500	2.2%
Income before income taxes	432,000	20.6%	347,500	18.9%
Income tax expense	168,200	8.0%	139,000	7.5%
Net income	$ 263,800	12.6%	$ 208,500	11.4%

HELPFUL HINT
The formula for calculating these income statement percentages is:

$$\frac{\text{Each item on I/S}}{\text{Net sales}} = \%$$

An associated benefit of vertical analysis is that it enables you to compare companies of different sizes. For example, Quality's main competitor is a J.C. Penney store in a nearby town. Using vertical analysis, we can compare the condensed income statements of Quality Department Store Inc. (a small retail company) with J.C. Penney Company, Inc. (a giant international retailer), as shown in Illustration 14-10.

Illustration 14-10
Intercompany income statement comparison

CONDENSED INCOME STATEMENTS
(in thousands)

	Quality Department Store Inc.		J. C. Penney Company[1]	
	Dollars	**Percent**	**Dollars**	**Percent**
Net sales	$2,097	100.0%	$18,781,000	100.0%
Cost of goods sold	1,281	61.1%	11,405,000	60.7%
Gross profit	816	38.9%	7,376,000	39.3%
Selling and administrative expenses	357	17.0%	5,799,000	30.9%
Income from operations	459	21.9%	1,577,000	8.4%
Other expenses and revenues (including income taxes)	195	9.3%	489,000	2.6%
Net income	$ 264	12.6%	$ 1,088,000	5.8%

J.C. Penney's net sales are 8,956 times greater than the net sales of relatively tiny Quality Department Store. But vertical analysis eliminates this difference in size. The percentages show that Quality's and J.C. Penney's gross profit rates were comparable at 38.9% and 39.3%. However, the percentages related to income from operations were significantly different at 21.9% and 8.4%. This disparity can be attributed to Quality's selling and administrative expense percentage (17%) which is much lower than J.C. Penney's (30.9%). Although J.C. Penney earned net income more than 4,121 times larger than Quality's, J.C. Penney's net income as a **percent of each sales dollar** (5.8%) is only 46% of Quality's (12.6%).

DECISION TOOLKIT

Decision Checkpoints	Info Needed for Decision	Tool to Use for Decision	How to Evaluate Results
How do the relationships between items in this year's financial statements compare with those of last year or those of competitors?	Income statement and balance sheet	Each line item on the income statement should be presented as a percentage of net sales, and each line item on the balance sheet should be presented as a percentage of total assets or total liabilities and stockholders' equity. These percentages should be investigated for differences either across years in the same company or in the same year across different companies. This is called vertical analysis.	Any significant differences either across years or between companies should be investigated to determine the cause.

[1] *2005 Annual Report* J.C. Penney Company, Inc. (Dallas, Texas).

Before You Go On...

REVIEW IT

1. What are the different tools that might be used to compare financial information?
2. What is horizontal analysis?
3. What is vertical analysis?

DO IT

Summary financial information for Rosepatch Company is as follows.

	December 31, 2008	December 31, 2007
Current assets	$234,000	$180,000
Plant assets (net)	756,000	420,000
Total assets	$990,000	$600,000

Compute the amount and percentage changes in 2008 using horizontal analysis, assuming 2007 is the base year.

Action Plan

- Find the percentage change by dividing the amount of the increase by the 2007 amount (base year).

Solution

	Increase in 2008	
	Amount	Percent
Current assets	$ 54,000	30% [($234,000 − $180,000) ÷ $180,000]
Plant assets (net)	336,000	80% [($756,000 − $420,000) ÷ $420,000]
Total assets	$390,000	65% [($990,000 − $600,000) ÷ $600,000]

Related exercise material: *BE14-2, BE14-3, BE14-5, BE14-6, BE14-7, E14-1, E14-3, and E14-4.*

✓ The Navigator

RATIO ANALYSIS

STUDY OBJECTIVE 5

Identify and compute ratios used in analyzing a firm's liquidity, profitability, and solvency.

Ratio analysis expresses the relationship among selected items of financial statement data. A **ratio** expresses the mathematical relationship between one quantity and another. The relationship is expressed in terms of either a percentage, a rate, or a simple proportion. To illustrate, in 2005 Nike, Inc., had current assets of $6,351.1 million and current liabilities of $1,999.2 million. We can find the relationship between these two measures by dividing current assets by current liabilities. The alternative means of expression are:

Percentage: Current assets are 318% of current liabilities.
Rate: Current assets are 3.18 times current liabilities.
Proportion: The relationship of current assets to liabilities is 3.18:1.

To analyze the primary financial statements, we can use ratios to evaluate liquidity, profitability, and solvency. Illustration 14-11 describes these classifications.

Illustration 14-11
Financial ratio classifications

Revenues − Expenses = Net income

Founded in 1892
XYZ Co.

Liquidity Ratios

Measure short-term ability of the company to pay its maturing obligations and to meet unexpected needs for cash

Profitability Ratios

Measure the income or operating success of a company for a given period of time

Solvency Ratios

Measure the ability of the company to survive over a long period of time

Ratios can provide clues to underlying conditions that may not be apparent from individual financial statement components. However, a single ratio by itself is not very meaningful. Thus, in the discussion of ratios we will use the following types of comparisons.

1. **Intracompany comparisons** for two years for Quality Department Store.
2. **Industry average comparisons** based on median ratios for department stores.
3. **Intercompany comparisons** based on J.C. Penney Company as Quality Department Store's principal competitor.

Liquidity Ratios

Liquidity ratios measure the short-term ability of the company to pay its maturing obligations and to meet unexpected needs for cash. Short-term creditors such as bankers and suppliers are particularly interested in assessing liquidity. The ratios we can use to determine the enterprise's short-term debt-paying ability are the current ratio, the acid-test ratio, receivables turnover, and inventory turnover.

1. CURRENT RATIO

The **current ratio** is a widely used measure for evaluating a company's liquidity and short-term debt-paying ability. The ratio is computed by dividing current assets by current liabilities. Illustration 14-12 shows the 2005 and 2004 current ratios for Quality Department Store and comparative data.

Illustration 14-12
Current ratio

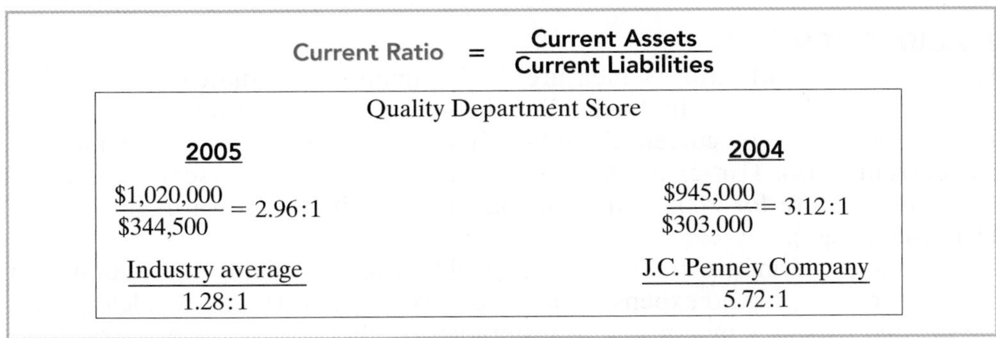

$$\text{Current Ratio} = \frac{\text{Current Assets}}{\text{Current Liabilities}}$$

Quality Department Store

2005	2004
$\frac{\$1{,}020{,}000}{\$344{,}500} = 2.96:1$	$\frac{\$945{,}000}{\$303{,}000} = 3.12:1$
Industry average	J.C. Penney Company
1.28:1	5.72:1

HELPFUL HINT

Can any company operate successfully without working capital? Yes, if it has very predictable cash flows and solid earnings. A number of companies (e.g., Whirlpool, American Standard, and Campbell's Soup) are pursuing this goal. The rationale: Less money tied up in working capital means more money to invest in the business.

What does the ratio actually mean? The 2005 ratio of 2.96:1 means that for every dollar of current liabilities, Quality has $2.96 of current assets. Quality's current ratio has decreased in the current year. But, compared to the industry average of 1.28:1, Quality appears to be reasonably liquid. J.C. Penney has a very high current ratio of 5.72 which indicates it has considerable current assets relative to its current liabilities.

The current ratio is sometimes referred to as the **working capital ratio**; **working capital** is current assets minus current liabilities. The current ratio is a more dependable indicator of liquidity than working capital. Two companies with the same amount of working capital may have significantly different current ratios.

The current ratio is only one measure of liquidity. It does not take into account the **composition** of the current assets. For example, a satisfactory current ratio does not disclose the fact that a portion of the current assets may be tied up in slow-moving inventory. A dollar of cash would be more readily available to pay the bills than a dollar of slow-moving inventory.

ACCOUNTING ACROSS THE ORGANIZATION

How to Manage the Current Ratio

The apparent simplicity of the current ratio can have real-world limitations. An addition of equal amounts to both the numerator and the denominator causes the ratio to change.

Assume, for example, that a company has $2,000,000 of current assets and $1,000,000 of current liabilities. Its current ratio is 2:1. If it purchases $1,000,000 of inventory on account, it will have $3,000,000 of current assets and $2,000,000 of current liabilities. Its current ratio will decrease to 1.5:1. If, instead, the company pays off $500,000 of its current liabilities, it will have $1,500,000 of current assets and $500,000 of current liabilities, and its current ratio will increase to 3:1. Thus, any trend analysis should be done with care, because the ratio is susceptible to quick changes and is easily influenced by management.

How might management influence the company's current ratio?

2. ACID-TEST RATIO

ALTERNATIVE TERMINOLOGY

The acid-test ratio is also called the *quick ratio*.

The **acid-test (quick) ratio** is a measure of a company's immediate short-term liquidity. We compute this ratio by dividing the sum of cash, short-term investments, and net receivables by current liabilities. Thus, it is an important complement to the current ratio. For example, assume that the current assets of Quality Department Store for 2005 and 2004 consist of the items shown in Illustration 14-13 (next page).

Cash, short-term investments, and receivables (net) are highly liquid compared to inventory and prepaid expenses. The inventory may not be readily saleable, and the prepaid expenses may not be transferable to others. Thus, the acid-test ratio

Illustration 14-13
Current assets of Quality Department Store

QUALITY DEPARTMENT STORE INC.
Balance Sheet (partial)

	2005	2004
Current assets		
Cash	$ 100,000	$155,000
Short-term investments	20,000	70,000
Receivables (net*)	230,000	180,000
Inventory	620,000	500,000
Prepaid expenses	50,000	40,000
Total current assets	$1,020,000	$945,000

*Allowance for doubtful accounts is $10,000 at the end of each year.

measures **immediate** liquidity. The 2005 and 2004 acid-test ratios for Quality Department Store and comparative data are as follows.

Illustration 14-14
Acid-test ratio

$$\text{Acid-Test Ratio} = \frac{\text{Cash + Short-Term Investments + Receivables (Net)}}{\text{Current Liabilities}}$$

Quality Department Store

2005	2004
$\frac{\$100,000 + \$20,000 + \$230,000}{\$344,500} = 1.02:1$	$\frac{\$155,000 + \$70,000 + \$180,000}{\$303,000} = 1.34:1$
Industry average	**J.C. Penney Company**
0.33:1	1.19:1

The ratio has declined in 2005. Is an acid-test ratio of 1.02:1 adequate? This depends on the industry and the economy. When compared with the industry average of 0.33:1 and Penney's of 1.19:1, Quality's acid-test ratio seems adequate.

3. RECEIVABLES TURNOVER

We can measure liquidity by how quickly a company can convert certain assets to cash. How liquid, for example, are the receivables? The ratio used to assess the liquidity of the receivables is **receivables turnover**. It measures the number of times, on average, the company collects receivables during the period. We compute receivables turnover by dividing net credit sales (net sales less cash sales) by the average net receivables. Unless seasonal factors are significant, average net receivables can be computed from the beginning and ending balances of the net receivables.[2]

Assume that all sales are credit sales. The balance of net receivables at the beginning of 2004 is $200,000. Illustration 14-15 (page 632) shows the receivables turnover for Quality Department Store and comparative data. Quality's receivables turnover improved in 2005. The turnover of 10.2 times is substantially lower than J.C. Penney's 69 times, but is similar to the department store industry's average of 10.8 times.

[2]If seasonal factors are significant, the average receivables balance might be determined by using monthly amounts.

Illustration 14-15
Receivables turnover

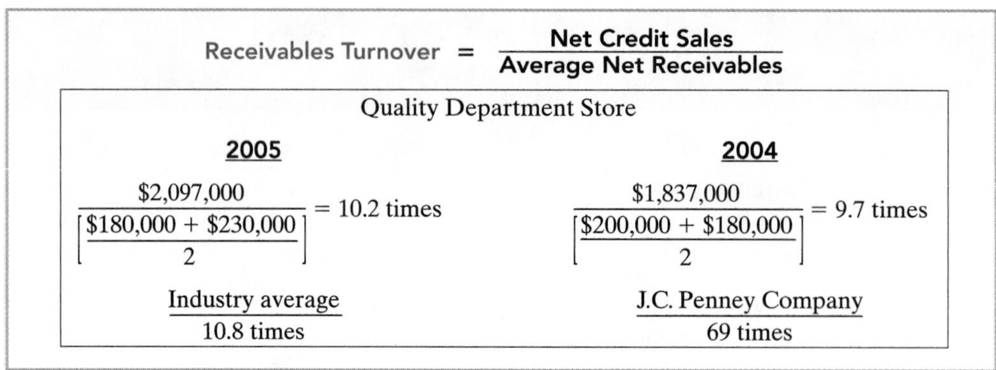

Average Collection Period. A popular variant of the receivables turnover ratio is to convert it to an **average collection period** in terms of days. To do so, we divide the receivables turnover ratio into 365 days. For example, the receivables turnover of 10.2 times divided into 365 days gives an average collection period of approximately 36 days. This means that receivables are collected on average every 36 days, or about every 5 weeks. Analysts frequently use the average collection period to assess the effectiveness of a company's credit and collection policies. The general rule is that the collection period should not greatly exceed the credit term period (the time allowed for payment).

4. INVENTORY TURNOVER

Inventory turnover measures the number of times, on average, the inventory is sold during the period. Its purpose is to measure the liquidity of the inventory. We compute the inventory turnover by dividing cost of goods sold by the average inventory. Unless seasonal factors are significant, we can use the beginning and ending inventory balances to compute average inventory.

Assuming that the inventory balance for Quality Department Store at the beginning of 2004 was $450,000, its inventory turnover and comparative data are as shown in Illustration 14-16. Quality's inventory turnover declined slightly in 2005. The turnover of 2.3 times is relatively low compared with the industry average of 6.7 and J.C. Penney's 3.6. Generally, the faster the inventory turnover, the less cash a company has tied up in inventory and the less the chance of inventory obsolescence.

Illustration 14-16
Inventory turnover

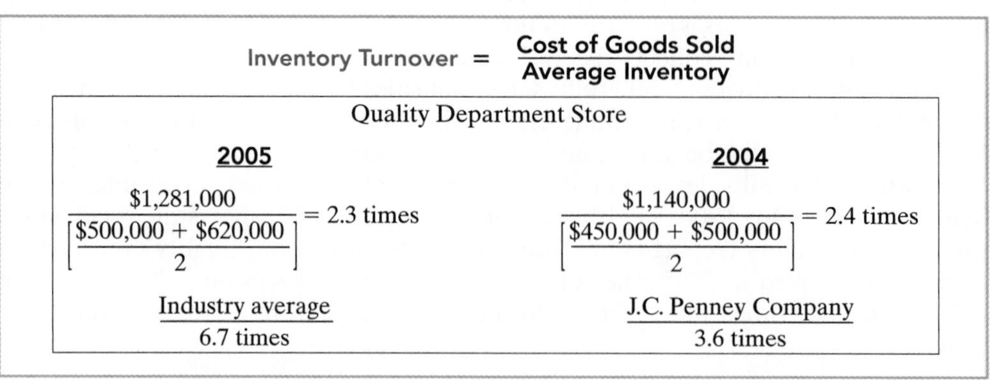

Days in Inventory. A variant of inventory turnover is the **days in inventory**. We calculate it by dividing the inventory turnover into 365. For example, Quality's 2005

inventory turnover of 2.3 times divided into 365 is approximately 159 days. An average selling time of 159 days is also relatively high compared with the industry average of 54.5 days (365 ÷ 6.7) and J.C. Penney's 101.4 days (365 ÷ 3.6).

Inventory turnover ratios vary considerably among industries. For example, grocery store chains have a turnover of 10 times and an average selling period of 37 days. In contrast, jewelry stores have an average turnover of 1.3 times and an average selling period of 281 days.

Profitability Ratios

Profitability ratios measure the income or operating success of a company for a given period of time. Income, or the lack of it, affects the company's ability to obtain debt and equity financing. It also affects the company's liquidity position and the company's ability to grow. As a consequence, both creditors and investors are interested in evaluating earning power—profitability. Analysts frequently use profitability as the ultimate test of management's operating effectiveness.

5. PROFIT MARGIN

Profit margin is a measure of the percentage of each dollar of sales that results in net income. We can compute it by dividing net income by net sales. Illustration 14-17 shows Quality Department Store's profit margin and comparative data.

ALTERNATIVE TERMINOLOGY

Profit margin is also called the *rate of return on sales*.

Illustration 14-17
Profit margin

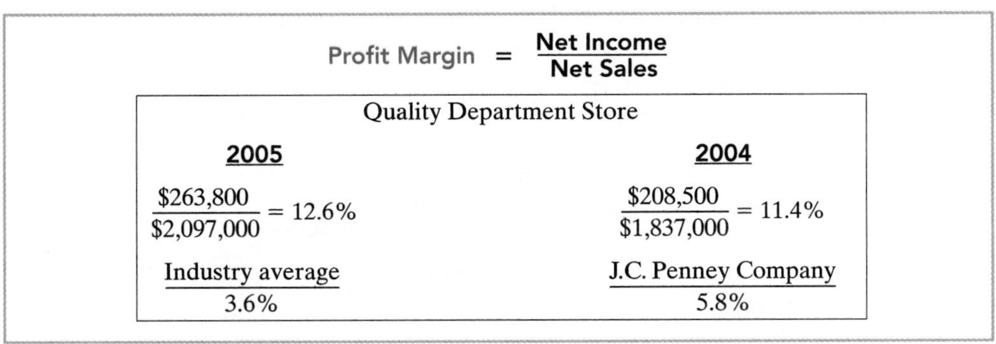

$$\text{Profit Margin} = \frac{\textbf{Net Income}}{\textbf{Net Sales}}$$

Quality Department Store

2005	2004
$\frac{\$263{,}800}{\$2{,}097{,}000} = 12.6\%$	$\frac{\$208{,}500}{\$1{,}837{,}000} = 11.4\%$
Industry average	J.C. Penney Company
3.6%	5.8%

Quality experienced an increase in its profit margin from 2004 to 2005. Its profit margin is unusually high in comparison with the industry average of 3.6% and J.C. Penney's 5.8%.

High-volume (high inventory turnover) enterprises such as grocery stores (Safeway or Kroger) and discount stores (Kmart or Wal-Mart) generally experience low profit margins. In contrast, low-volume enterprises such as jewelry stores (Tiffany & Co.) or airplane manufacturers (Boeing Co.) have high profit margins.

6. ASSET TURNOVER

Asset turnover measures how efficiently a company uses its assets to generate sales. It is determined by dividing net sales by average assets. The resulting number shows the dollars of sales produced by each dollar invested in assets. Unless seasonal factors are significant, we can use the beginning and ending balance of total assets to determine average total assets. Assuming that total assets at the beginning of 2004 were $1,446,000, the 2005 and 2004 asset turnover for Quality Department Store and comparative data are Shown in Illustration 14-18.

Illustration 14-18
Asset turnover

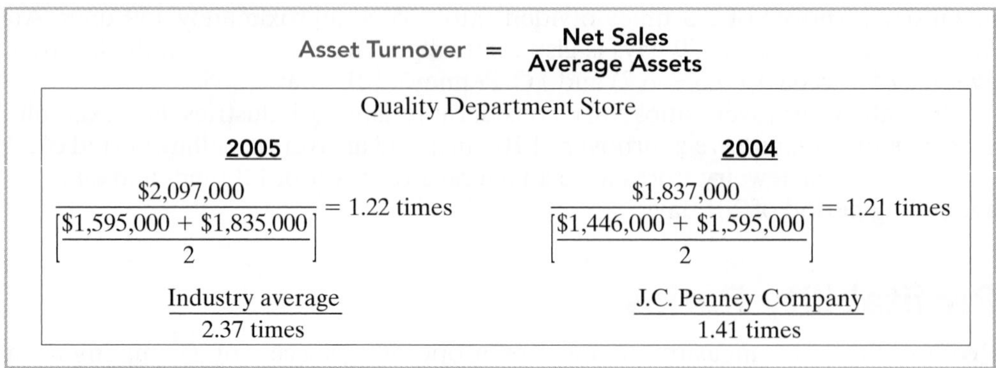

$$\text{Asset Turnover} = \frac{\text{Net Sales}}{\text{Average Assets}}$$

Quality Department Store

2005	2004
$\frac{\$2,097,000}{\left[\frac{\$1,595,000 + \$1,835,000}{2}\right]} = 1.22$ times	$\frac{\$1,837,000}{\left[\frac{\$1,446,000 + \$1,595,000}{2}\right]} = 1.21$ times
Industry average	J.C. Penney Company
2.37 times	1.41 times

Asset turnover shows that in 2005 Quality generated sales of $1.22 for each dollar it had invested in assets. The ratio changed little from 2004 to 2005. Quality's asset turnover is below the industry average of 2.37 times and J.C. Penney's ratio of 1.41 times.

Asset turnover ratios vary considerably among industries. For example, a large utility company like Consolidated Edison (New York) has a ratio of 0.49 times, and the large grocery chain Kroger Stores has a ratio of 4.34 times.

7. RETURN ON ASSETS

An overall measure of profitability is **return on assets**. We compute this ratio by dividing net income by average assets. The 2005 and 2004 return on assets for Quality Department Store and comparative data are shown below.

Illustration 14-19
Return on assets

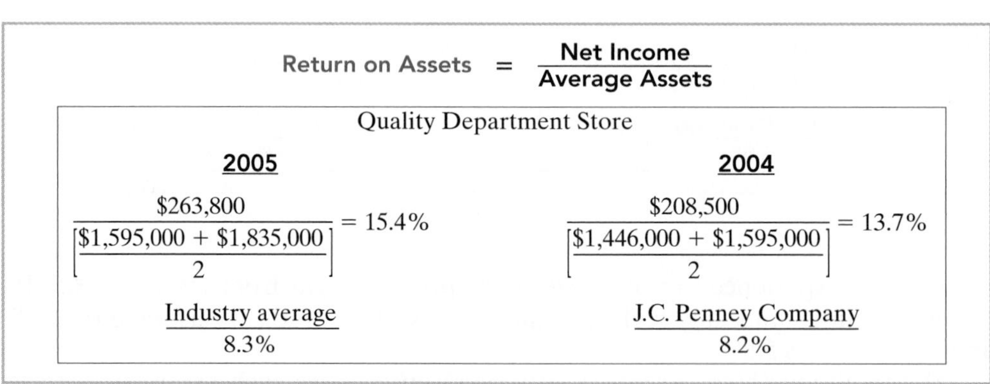

$$\text{Return on Assets} = \frac{\text{Net Income}}{\text{Average Assets}}$$

Quality Department Store

2005	2004
$\frac{\$263,800}{\left[\frac{\$1,595,000 + \$1,835,000}{2}\right]} = 15.4\%$	$\frac{\$208,500}{\left[\frac{\$1,446,000 + \$1,595,000}{2}\right]} = 13.7\%$
Industry average	J.C. Penney Company
8.3%	8.2%

Quality's return on assets improved from 2004 to 2005. Its return of 15.4% is very high compared with the department store industry average of 8.3% and J.C. Penney's 8.2%.

8. RETURN ON COMMON STOCKHOLDERS' EQUITY

Another widely used profitability ratio is **return on common stockholders' equity**. It measures profitability from the common stockholders' viewpoint. This ratio shows how many dollars of net income the company earned for each dollar invested by the owners. We compute it by dividing net income by average common stockholders' equity. Assuming that common stockholders' equity at the beginning of 2004 was $667,000, Illustration 14-20 shows the 2005 and 2004 ratios for Quality Department Store and comparative data.

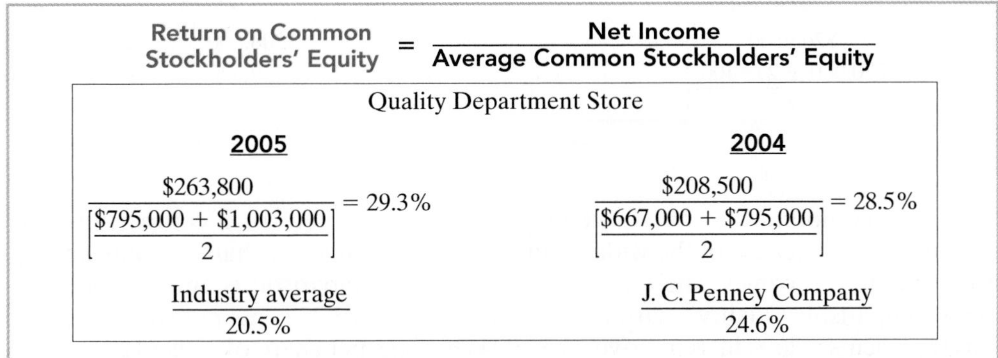

Illustration 14-20
Return on common stockholders' equity

Quality's rate of return on common stockholders' equity is high at 29.3%, considering an industry average of 20.5% and a rate of 24.6% for J.C. Penney. Note that Quality's rate of return on stockholders' equity (29.3%) is substantially higher than its rate of return on assets (15.4%). The reason is that Quality has made effective use of **leverage**. **Leveraging** or **trading on the equity** at a gain means that the company has borrowed money at a lower rate of interest than it is able to earn by using the borrowed money. Leverage enables Quality Department Store to use money supplied by nonowners to increase the return to the owners. A comparison of the rate of return on total assets with the rate of interest paid for borrowed money indicates the profitability of trading on the equity. Quality Department Store earns more on its borrowed funds than it has to pay in the form of interest. Thus the return to stockholders exceeds the return on the assets, due to benefits from the positive leveraging.

With Preferred Stock. When a company has preferred stock, we must deduct **preferred dividend** requirements from net income to compute income available to common stockholders. Similarly, we deduct the par value of preferred stock (or call price, if applicable) from total stockholders' equity to determine the amount of common stockholders' equity used in this ratio. The ratio then appears as follows.

$$\text{Return on Common Stockholders' Equity} = \frac{\text{Net Income} - \text{Preferred Dividends}}{\text{Average Common Stockholders' Equity}}$$

Illustration 14-21
Return on common stockholders' equity with preferred stock

9. EARNINGS PER SHARE (EPS)

Earnings per share (EPS) is a measure of the net income earned on each share of common stock. It is computed by dividing net income by the number of weighted average common shares outstanding during the year. A measure of net income earned on a per share basis provides a useful perspective for determining profitability. Assuming that there is no change in the number of outstanding shares during 2004 and that the 2005 increase occurred midyear, Illustration 14-22 (page 636) shows the net income per share for Quality Department Store for 2005 and 2004.

Illustration 14-22
Earnings per share

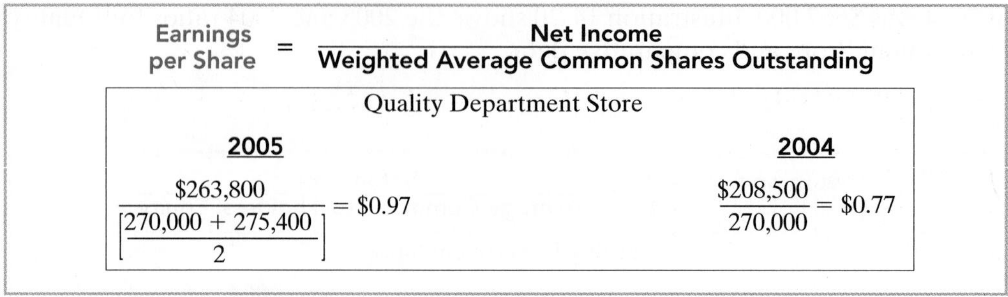

$$\text{Earnings per Share} = \frac{\text{Net Income}}{\text{Weighted Average Common Shares Outstanding}}$$

Quality Department Store

2005	2004
$\frac{\$263,800}{\left[\frac{270,000 + 275,400}{2}\right]} = \$0.97$	$\frac{\$208,500}{270,000} = \$0.77$

Note that no industry or J.C. Penney data are presented. Such comparisons are not meaningful because of the wide variations in the number of shares of outstanding stock among companies. The only meaningful EPS comparison is an intracompany trend comparison: Quality's earnings per share increased 20 cents per share in 2005. This represents a 26% increase over the 2004 earnings per share of 77 cents.

The terms "earnings per share" and "net income per share" refer to the amount of net income applicable to each share of **common stock**. Therefore, in computing EPS, if there are preferred dividends declared for the period, we must deduct them from net income to determine income available to the common stockholders.

10. PRICE-EARNINGS RATIO

The **price-earnings (P-E) ratio** is an oft-quoted measure of the ratio of the market price of each share of common stock to the earnings per share. The price-earnings (P-E) ratio reflects investors' assessments of a company's future earnings. We compute it by dividing the market price per share of the stock by earnings per share. Assuming that the market price of Quality Department Store Inc. stock is $8 in 2004 and $12 in 2005, the price-earnings ratio computation is as follows.

Illustration 14-23
Price-earnings ratio

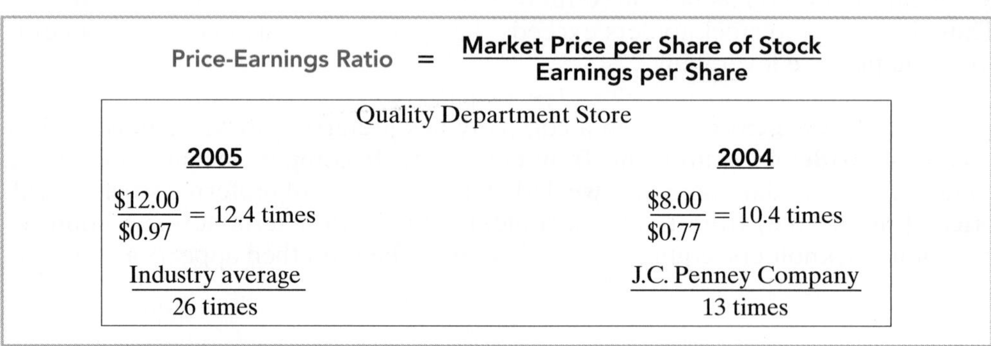

$$\text{Price-Earnings Ratio} = \frac{\text{Market Price per Share of Stock}}{\text{Earnings per Share}}$$

Quality Department Store

2005	2004
$\frac{\$12.00}{\$0.97} = 12.4$ times	$\frac{\$8.00}{\$0.77} = 10.4$ times
Industry average	J.C. Penney Company
26 times	13 times

In 2005 each share of Quality's stock sold for 12.4 times the amount that the company earned on each share. Quality's price-earnings ratio is lower than the industry average of 26 times, but almost the same as the ratio of 13 times for J.C. Penney. The average price-earnings ratio for the stocks that constitute the Standard and Poor's 500 Index (500 largest U.S. firms) in July 2007 was a little more than 20 times.

11. PAYOUT RATIO

The **payout ratio** measures the percentage of earnings distributed in the form of cash dividends. We compute it by dividing cash dividends by net income. Companies that have high growth rates generally have low payout ratios because they reinvest most of their net income into the business. The 2005 and 2004 payout ratios for Quality Department Store are computed as shown in Illustration 14-24.

Illustration 14-24
Payout ratio

$$\text{Payout Ratio} = \frac{\text{Cash Dividends}}{\text{Net Income}}$$

Quality Department Store	
2005	**2004**
$\frac{\$61,200}{\$263,800} = 23.2\%$	$\frac{\$60,000}{\$208,500} = 28.8\%$
Industry average	J.C. Penney Company
16.0%	12.0%

Quality's payout ratio is higher than J.C. Penney's payout ratio of 12.0%. As indicated earlier (page 626), Quality funded its purchase of plant assets through retention of earnings but still is able to pay dividends.

Solvency Ratios

Solvency ratios measure the ability of a company to survive over a long period of time. Long-term creditors and stockholders are particularly interested in a company's ability to pay interest as it comes due and to repay the face value of debt at maturity. Debt to total assets and times interest earned are two ratios that provide information about debt-paying ability.

12. DEBT TO TOTAL ASSETS RATIO

The **debt to total assets ratio** measures the percentage of the total assets that creditors provide. We compute it by dividing total debt (both current and long-term liabilities) by total assets. This ratio indicates the company's degree of leverage. It also provides some indication of the company's ability to withstand losses without impairing the interests of creditors. The higher the percentage of debt to total assets, the greater the risk that the company may be unable to meet its maturing obligations. The 2005 and 2004 ratios for Quality Department Store and comparative data are as follows.

Illustration 14-25
Debt to total assets ratio

$$\text{Debt to Total Assets Ratio} = \frac{\text{Total Debt}}{\text{Total Assets}}$$

Quality Department Store	
2005	**2004**
$\frac{\$832,000}{\$1,835,000} = 45.3\%$	$\frac{\$800,000}{\$1,595,000} = 50.2\%$
Industry average	J.C. Penney Company
40.1%	67.8%

A ratio of 45.3% means that creditors have provided 45.3% of Quality Department Store's total assets. Quality's 45.3% is above the industry average of 40.1%. It is considerably below the high 67.8% ratio of J.C. Penney. The lower the ratio, the more equity "buffer" there is available to the creditors. Thus, from the creditors' point of view, a low ratio of debt to total assets is usually desirable.

The adequacy of this ratio is often judged in the light of the company's earnings. Generally, companies with relatively stable earnings (such as public utilities) have higher debt to total assets ratios than cyclical companies with widely fluctuating earnings (such as many high-tech companies).

13. TIMES INTEREST EARNED

ALTERNATIVE TERMINOLOGY

Times interest earned is also called *interest coverage.*

Times interest earned provides an indication of the company's ability to meet interest payments as they come due. We compute it by dividing income before interest expense and income taxes by interest expense. Illustration 14-26 shows the 2005 and 2004 ratios for Quality Department Store and comparative data. Note that times interest earned uses income before income taxes and interest expense. This represents the amount available to cover interest. For Quality Department Store the 2005 amount of $468,000 is computed by taking the income before income taxes of $432,000 and adding back the $36,000 of interest expense.

Illustration 14-26
Times interest earned

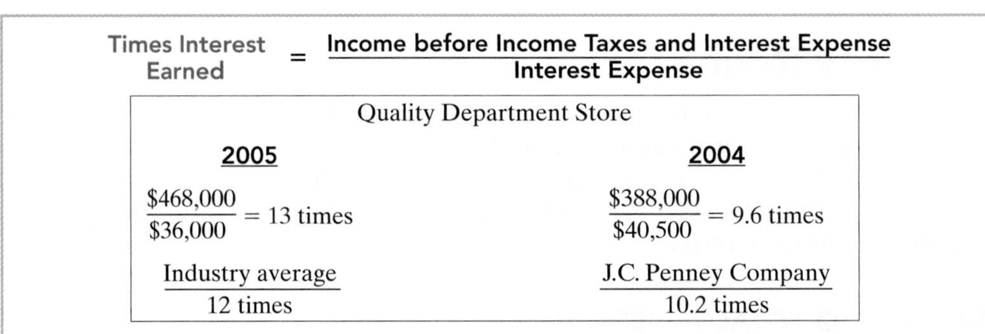

$$\text{Times Interest Earned} = \frac{\text{Income before Income Taxes and Interest Expense}}{\text{Interest Expense}}$$

Quality Department Store

2005	2004
$\frac{\$468,000}{\$36,000} = 13$ times	$\frac{\$388,000}{\$40,500} = 9.6$ times
Industry average	J.C. Penney Company
12 times	10.2 times

Quality's interest expense is well covered at 13 times, compared with the industry average of 12 times and J.C. Penney's 10.2 times.

ACCOUNTING ACROSS THE ORGANIZATION

Keeping Up to Date as an Investor

Today, investors have access to information provided by corporate managers that used to be available only to professional analysts. Corporate managers have always made themselves available to security analysts for questions at the end of every quarter. Now, because of a combination of new corporate disclosure requirements by the Securities and Exchange Commission and technologies that make communication to large numbers of people possible at a very low price, the average investor can listen in on these discussions. For example, one individual investor, Matthew Johnson, a Nortel Networks local area network engineer in Belfast, Northern Ireland, "stayed up past midnight to listen to Apple Computer's recent Internet conference call. Hearing the company's news 'from the dog's mouth,' he says 'gave me better information' than hunting through chat-rooms."

Source: Jeff D. Opdyke, "Individuals Pick Up on Conference Calls," *Wall Street Journal*, November 20, 2000.

? If you want to keep current with the financial and operating developments of a company in which you own shares, what are some ways you can do so?

Summary of Ratios

Illustration 14-27 summarizes the ratios discussed in this chapter. The summary includes the formula and purpose or use of each ratio.

Illustration 14-27
Summary of liquidity, profitability, and solvency ratios

Ratio	Formula	Purpose or Use
Liquidity Ratios		
1. Current ratio	$\frac{\text{Current assets}}{\text{Current liabilities}}$	Measures short-term debt-paying ability.
2. Acid-test (quick) ratio	$\frac{\text{Cash + Short-term investments + Receivables (net)}}{\text{Current liabilities}}$	Measures immediate short-term liquidity.
3. Receivables turnover	$\frac{\text{Net credit sales}}{\text{Average net receivables}}$	Measures liquidity of receivables.
4. Inventory turnover	$\frac{\text{Cost of goods sold}}{\text{Average inventory}}$	Measures liquidity of inventory.
Profitability Ratios		
5. Profit margin	$\frac{\text{Net income}}{\text{Net sales}}$	Measures net income generated by each dollar of sales.
6. Asset turnover	$\frac{\text{Net sales}}{\text{Average assets}}$	Measures how efficiently assets are used to generate sales.
7. Return on assets	$\frac{\text{Net income}}{\text{Average assets}}$	Measures overall profitability of assets.
8. Return on common stockholders' equity	$\frac{\text{Net income}}{\text{Average common stockholders' equity}}$	Measures profitability of owners' investment.
9. Earnings per share (EPS)	$\frac{\text{Net income}}{\text{Weighted average common shares outstanding}}$	Measures net income earned on each share of common stock.
10. Price-earnings (P-E) ratio	$\frac{\text{Market price per share of stock}}{\text{Earnings per share}}$	Measures the ratio of the market price per share to earnings per share.
11. Payout ratio	$\frac{\text{Cash dividends}}{\text{Net income}}$	Measures percentage of earnings distributed in the form of cash dividends.
Solvency Ratios		
12. Debt to total assets ratio	$\frac{\text{Total debt}}{\text{Total assets}}$	Measures the percentage of total assets provided by creditors.
13. Times interest earned	$\frac{\text{Income before income taxes and interest expense}}{\text{Interest expense}}$	Measures ability to meet interest payments as they come due.

Before You Go On...

REVIEW IT

1. What are liquidity ratios? Explain the current ratio, acid-test ratio, receivables turnover, and inventory turnover.
2. What are profitability ratios? Explain the profit margin, asset turnover ratio, return on assets, return on common stockholders' equity, earnings per share, price-earnings ratio, and payout ratio.
3. What are solvency ratios? Explain the debt to total assets ratio and times interest earned.

DO IT

Selected financial data for Drummond Company at December 31, 2008, are as follows: cash \$60,000; receivables (net) \$80,000; inventory \$70,000; current liabilities \$140,000. Compute the current and acid-test ratios.

Action Plan

- Use the formula for the current ratio: Current assets ÷ Current liabilities.
- Use the formula for the acid-test ratio: [Cash + Short-term investments + Receivables (net)] ÷ Current liabilities.

Solution The current ratio is 1.5:1 (\$210,000 ÷ \$140,000). The acid-test ratio is 1:1 (\$140,000 ÷ \$140,000).

Related exercise material: *BE14-9, BE14-10, BE14-11, BE14-12, BE14-13, E14-5, E14-6, E14-7, E14-8, E14-9, E14-10, and E14-11.*

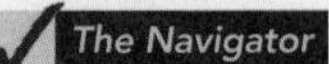

EARNING POWER AND IRREGULAR ITEMS

STUDY OBJECTIVE 6

Understand the concept of earning power, and how irregular items are presented.

Users of financial statements are interested in the concept of earning power. **Earning power** means the normal level of income to be obtained in the future. Earning power differs from actual net income by the amount of irregular revenues, expenses, gains, and losses. Users are interested in earning power because it helps them derive an estimate of future earnings without the "noise" of irregular items.

For users of financial statements to determine earning power or regular income, the "irregular" items are separately identified on the income statement. Companies report two types of "irregular" items.

1. Discontinued operations.
2. Extraordinary items.

These "irregular" items are reported net of income taxes. That is, the income statement first reports income tax on the income before "irregular" items. Then the amount of tax for each of the listed "irregular" items is computed. The general concept is "let the tax follow income or loss."

Discontinued Operations

Discontinued operations refers to the disposal of a **significant component** of a business. Examples involve stopping an entire activity or eliminating a major class of customers. For example, Kmart reported as discontinued operations its decision to terminate its interest in four business activities, including PACE Membership Warehouse and PayLess Drug Stores Northwest.

Following the disposal of a significant component, the company should report on its income statement both income from continuing operations and income (or loss) from discontinued operations. **The income (loss) from discontinued operations consists of two parts: the income (loss) from operations** and **the gain (loss) on disposal of the segment**.

To illustrate, assume that during 2008 Acro Energy Inc. has income before income taxes of \$800,000. During 2008 Acro discontinued and sold its unprofitable chemical division. The loss in 2008 from chemical operations (net of \$60,000 taxes) was \$140,000. The loss on disposal of the chemical division (net of \$30,000 taxes) was \$70,000. Assuming a 30% tax rate on income, Illustration 14-28 shows Acro's income statement presentation.

ACRO ENERGY INC. Income Statement (partial) For the Year Ended December 31, 2008		
Income before income taxes		$800,000
Income tax expense		240,000
Income from continuing operations		560,000
Discontinued operations		
Loss from operations of chemical division, net of $60,000 income tax saving	**$140,000**	
Loss from disposal of chemical division, net of $30,000 income tax saving	**70,000**	**210,000**
Net income		$350,000

Illustration 14-28
Statement presentation of discontinued operations

HELPFUL HINT

Observe the dual disclosures: (1) The results of operations of the discontinued division must be eliminated from the results of continuing operations. (2) The company must also report the disposal of the operation.

Note that the statement uses the caption "Income from continuing operations," and adds a new section "Discontinued operations". **The new section reports both the operating loss and the loss on disposal net of applicable income taxes.** This presentation clearly indicates the separate effects of continuing operations and discontinued operations on net income.

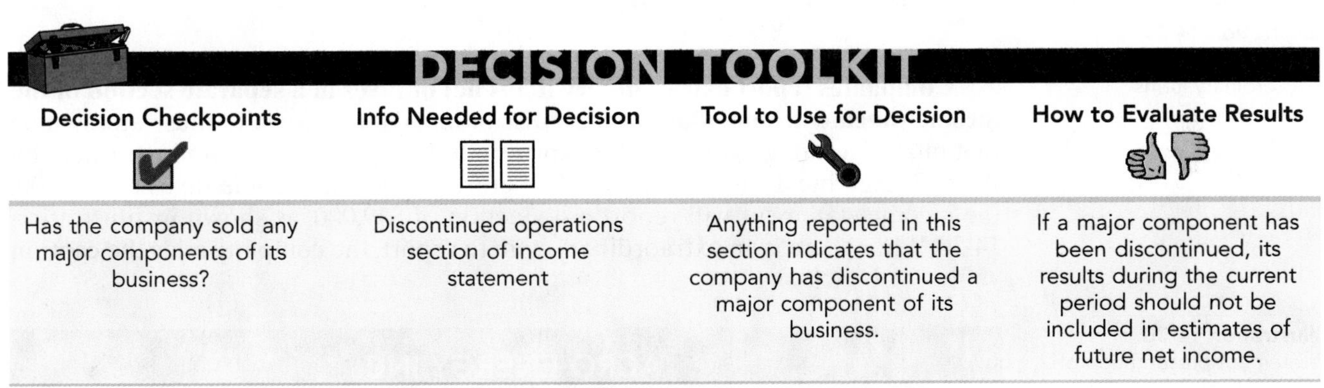

DECISION TOOLKIT

Decision Checkpoints	Info Needed for Decision	Tool to Use for Decision	How to Evaluate Results
Has the company sold any major components of its business?	Discontinued operations section of income statement	Anything reported in this section indicates that the company has discontinued a major component of its business.	If a major component has been discontinued, its results during the current period should not be included in estimates of future net income.

Extraordinary Items

Extraordinary items are events and transactions that meet two conditions: They are (1) **unusual in nature,** and (2) **infrequent in occurrence**. To be *unusual*, the item should be abnormal and only incidentally related to the company's customary activities. To be *infrequent*, the item should not be reasonably expected to recur in the foreseeable future.

A company must evaluate both criteria in terms of its operating environment. Thus, Weyerhaeuser Co. reported the $36 million in damages to its timberland caused by the volcanic eruption of Mount St. Helens as an extraordinary item. The eruption was both unusual and infrequent. In contrast, Florida Citrus Company does not report frost damage to its citrus crop as an extraordinary item, because frost damage is not infrequent. Illustration 14-29 (page 642) shows the classification of extraordinary and ordinary items.

Extraordinary items		Ordinary items	
1. Effects of major natural casualties, if rare in the area.		1. Effects of major natural casualties, not uncommon in the area.	
2. Expropriation (takeover) of property by a foreign government.		2. Write-down of inventories or write-off of receivables.	
3. Effects of a newly enacted law or regulation, such as a property condemnation action.		3. Losses attributable to labor strikes.	
		4. Gains or losses from sales of property, plant, or equipment.	

Illustration 14-29
Examples of extraordinary and ordinary items

Companies report extraordinary items net of taxes in a separate section of the income statement, immediately below discontinued operations. To illustrate, assume that in 2008 a foreign government expropriated property held as an investment by Acro Energy Inc. If the loss is $70,000 before applicable income taxes of $21,000, the income statement will report a deduction of $49,000, as shown in Illustration 14-30. When there is an extraordinary item to report, the company adds the caption

Illustration 14-30
Statement presentation of extraordinary items

ACRO ENERGY INC.
Income Statement (partial)
For the Year Ended December 31, 2008

Income before income taxes		$800,000
Income tax expense		240,000
Income from continuing operations		560,000
Discontinued operations		
Loss from operations of chemical division, net of $60,000 income tax saving	$140,000	
Loss from disposal of chemical division, net of $30,000 income tax saving	70,000	210,000
Income before extraordinary item		350,000
Extraordinary item		
Expropriation of investment, net of $21,000 income tax saving		**49,000**
Net income		$301,000

HELPFUL HINT
If there are no discontinued operations, the third line of the income statement would be labeled "Income before extraordinary item."

"Income before extraordinary item" immediately before the section for the extraordinary item. This presentation clearly indicates the effect of the extraordinary item on net income.

What if a transaction or event meets one (but not both) of the criteria for an extraordinary item? In that case the company reports it under either "Other revenues and gains" or "Other expenses and losses" at its gross amount (not net of tax). This is true, for example, of gains (losses) resulting from the sale of property, plant, and equipment. It is quite common for companies to use the label "Nonrecurring charges" for losses that do not meet the extraordinary item criteria.

MANAGEMENT INSIGHT

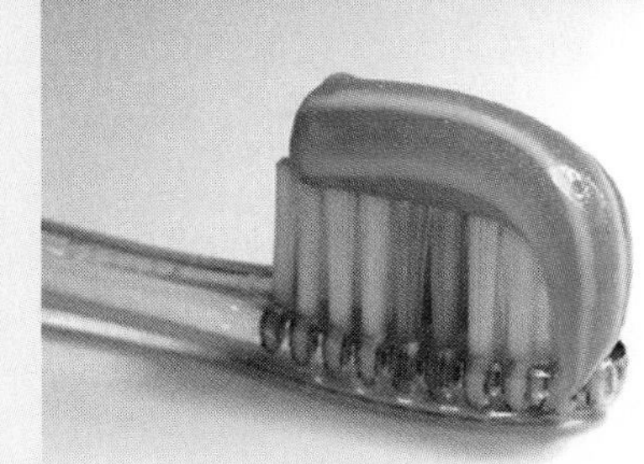

What Is Extraordinary?

Many companies these days are incurring restructuring charges as a result of attempting to reduce costs. Are these costs ordinary or extraordinary? Some companies report "one-time" restructuring charges over and over. Case in point: Toothpaste and diapers giant Procter & Gamble Co. reported a restructuring charge in 12 consecutive quarters, and Motorola had "special" charges 14 quarters in a row. On the other hand, some companies take a restructuring charge only once in five years. The one-size-fits-all classification therefore will not work. There appears to be no substitute for a careful analysis of the numbers that comprise net income.

If a company takes a large restructuring charge, what is the effect on the company's current income statement versus future ones?

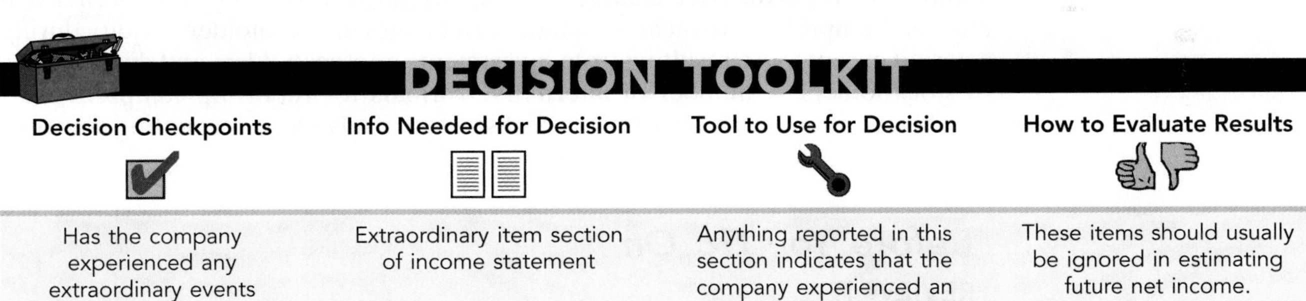

DECISION TOOLKIT

Decision Checkpoints	Info Needed for Decision	Tool to Use for Decision	How to Evaluate Results
Has the company experienced any extraordinary events or transactions?	Extraordinary item section of income statement	Anything reported in this section indicates that the company experienced an event that was both unusual and infrequent.	These items should usually be ignored in estimating future net income.

Changes in Accounting Principle

For ease of comparison, users of financial statements expect companies to prepare such statements on a basis **consistent** with the preceding period. A **change in accounting principle** occurs when the principle used in the current year is different from the one used in the preceding year. Accounting rules permit a change when management can show that the new principle is preferable to the old principle. An example is a change in inventory costing methods (such as FIFO to average cost).

Companies report most changes in accounting principle retroactively. That is, they report both the current period and previous periods using the new principle. As a result the same principle applies in all periods. This treatment improves the ability to compare results across years.

ETHICS NOTE

Changes in accounting principle should result in financial statements that are more informative for statement users. They should *not* be used to artificially improve the reported performance or financial position of the corporation.

DECISION TOOLKIT

Decision Checkpoints	Info Needed for Decision	Tool to Use for Decision	How to Evaluate Results

Has the company changed any of its accounting principles?	Effect of change in accounting principle on current and prior periods.	Management indicates that the new principle is preferable to the old principle.	Examine current and prior years reported, using new-principle basis to assess trends for estimating future income.

Comprehensive Income

The income statement reports most revenues, expenses, gains, and losses recognized during the period. However, over time, specific exceptions to this general practice have developed. Certain items now bypass income and are reported directly in stockholders' equity.

For example, companies do not include in income any unrealized gains and losses on available-for-sale securities. Instead, they report such gains and losses in the balance sheet as adjustments to stockholders' equity. Why are these gains and losses on available-for-sale securities excluded from net income? Because disclosing them separately (1) reduces the volatility of net income due to fluctuations in fair value, yet (2) informs the financial statement user of the gain or loss that would be incurred if the securities were sold at fair value.

Many analysts have expressed concern over the significant increase in the number of items that bypass the income statement. They feel that such reporting has reduced the usefulness of the income statement. To address this concern, in addition to reporting net income, a company must also report comprehensive income. **Comprehensive income** includes all changes in stockholders' equity during a period except those resulting from investments by stockholders and distributions to stockholders. A number of alternative formats for reporting comprehensive income are allowed. These formats are discussed in advanced accounting courses.

Before You Go On...

REVIEW IT

1. What are the similarities and differences in reporting material items not typical of regular operations?
2. What is included in comprehensive income?

DO IT

In its proposed 2008 income statement, AIR Corporation reports income before income taxes $400,000, extraordinary loss $100,000, income taxes (30%) $120,000, and net income $210,000. Prepare a correct income statement, beginning with income before income taxes.

Action Plan

- Recall that the loss is extraordinary because it meets the criteria of being both unusual and infrequent.
- Disclose the income tax effect of each component of income, beginning with income before any irregular items.
- Report irregular items net of any income tax effect.

Solution

AIR CORPORATION
Income Statement (partial)

Income before income taxes	$400,000
Income tax expense (30%)	120,000
Income before extraordinary item	280,000
Extraordinary loss net of $30,000 income tax saving	70,000
Net income	$210,000

Related exercise material: *BE14-14, BE14-15, E14-12, and E14-13.*

The Navigator

QUALITY OF EARNINGS

STUDY OBJECTIVE 7
Understand the concept of quality of earnings.

In evaluating the financial performance of a company, the quality of a company's earnings is of extreme importance to analysts. A company that has a high **quality of earnings** provides full and transparent information that will not confuse or mislead users of the financial statements.

The issue of quality of earnings has taken on increasing importance because recent accounting scandals suggest that some companies are spending too much time managing their income and not enough time managing their business. Here are some of the factors affecting quality of earnings.

Alternative Accounting Methods

Variations among companies in the application of generally accepted accounting principles may hamper comparability and reduce quality of earnings. For example, one company may use the FIFO method of inventory costing, while another company in the same industry may use LIFO. If inventory is a significant asset to both companies, it is unlikely that their current ratios are comparable. For example, if General Motors Corporation had used FIFO instead of LIFO for inventory valuation, its inventories in a recent year would have been 26% higher, which significantly affects the current ratio (and other ratios as well).

In addition to differences in inventory costing methods, differences also exist in reporting such items as depreciation, depletion, and amortization. Although these differences in accounting methods might be detectable from reading the notes to the financial statements, adjusting the financial data to compensate for the different methods is often difficult, if not impossible.

Pro Forma Income

Companies whose stock is publicly traded are required to present their income statement following generally accepted accounting principles (GAAP). In recent years, many companies have also reported a second measure of income, called pro forma income. **Pro forma income** usually excludes items that the company thinks are unusual or nonrecurring. For example, in a recent year, Cisco Systems (a high-tech company) reported a quarterly net loss under GAAP of $2.7 billion. Cisco reported pro forma income for the same quarter as a profit of $230 million. This large difference in profits between GAAP income numbers and pro forma income is not unusual these days. For example, during one recent 9-month period the 100 largest firms on the Nasdaq stock exchange reported a total pro forma income of $19.1 billion, but a total loss as measured by GAAP of $82.3 billion—a difference of about $100 billion!

To compute pro forma income, companies generally can exclude any items they deem inappropriate for measuring their performance. Many analysts and investors are critical of the practice of using pro forma income because these numbers often make companies look better than they really are. As the financial press noted, pro forma numbers might be called EBS, which stands for "earnings before bad stuff." Companies, on the other hand, argue that pro forma numbers more clearly indicate sustainable income because they exclude unusual and nonrecurring expenses. "Cisco's technique gives readers of financial statements a clear picture of Cisco's normal business activities," the company said in a statement issued in response to questions about its pro forma income accounting.

Recently, the SEC provided some guidance on how companies should present pro forma information. Stay tuned: Everyone seems to agree that pro forma numbers can be useful if they provide insights into determining a company's sustainable income. However, many companies have abused the flexibility that pro forma numbers allow and have used the measure as a way to put their companies in a good light.

Improper Recognition

Because some managers have felt pressure from Wall Street to continually increase earnings, they have manipulated the earnings numbers to meet these expectations. The most common abuse is the improper recognition of revenue. One practice that companies are using is *channel stuffing*: Offering deep discounts on their products to customers, companies encourage their customers to buy early (stuff the channel) rather than later. This lets the company report good earnings in the current period, but it often leads to a disaster in subsequent periods because customers have no need for additional goods. To illustrate, Bristol-Myers Squibb recently indicated that it used sales incentives to encourage wholesalers to buy more drugs than needed to meet patients' demands. As a result, the company had to issue revised financial statements showing corrected revenues and income.

Another practice is the improper capitalization of operating expenses. The classic case is WorldCom. It capitalized over $7 billion dollars of operating expenses so that it would report positive net income. In other situations, companies fail to report all their liabilities. Enron had promised to make payments on certain contracts if financial difficulty developed, but these guarantees were not reported as liabilities. In addition, disclosure was so lacking in transparency that it was impossible to understand what was happening at the company.

Before You Go On...

REVIEW IT

1. What is meant by *quality of earnings?*
2. Give examples of alternative accounting methods that hamper comparability.
3. What is pro forma income and why are analysts often critical of this number?

Be sure to read **ALL ABOUT YOU: *Should I Play the Market Yet?*** on the next page for information on how topics in this chapter apply to you.

all about YOU

Should I Play the Market Yet?

In this chapter you learned how to use many tools for performing a financial analysis of a company. Sometimes companies fail even though they have a good product and good sales growth. All too often the cause of failure is something that should have caused only momentary discomfort. But if a company lacks sufficient liquidity, a momentary hiccup can be fatal. This is true for individuals as well.

For example, the decision to invest in common stock can be risky. As a company's net income changes, its stock price can be volatile. You must take this into consideration when deciding whether to buy stock. You don't want to be in a situation where you have to sell a stock whose price has fallen in order to raise cash to pay your bills.

Some Facts

* 83.4 million Americans own stock investments, either through mutual funds or individual stocks; 89% of stock investors own stock mutual funds.
* 44% of the people who own stock bought their first stock before 1990.
* The typical equity investor is in his or her late 40s, is married, is employed, and has a household income in the low $60,000s.
* 58% of people who own stock said that they rely on professional financial advisors when making decisions regarding the purchase and sale of stock.
* 46% of people who own stock used the Internet to check stock prices, and 38% use it to read online financial publications.

About the Numbers

The percentage of Americans who buy stock, either through mutual funds or individual shares, has increased significantly in recent years. A big part of this increase is due to the increasing prevalence of employer-sponsored retirement plans, such as 401(k) plans.

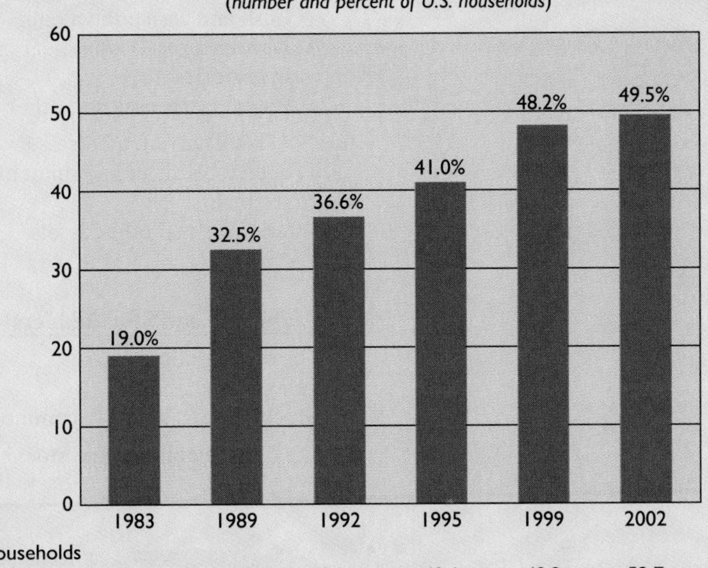

Source: "Equity Ownership in America," Investment Company Institute and the Securities Industry Association, 2002, p. 1.

What Do You Think?

Rachael West has been working at her new job for six months. She has a good salary, with lots of opportunities for growth. She has already accumulated $8,000 in savings, which right now is sitting in a bank savings account earning very little interest. She has decided to take $7,000 out of this savings account and buy common stock of her employer, a young company that has been in business for two years. Rachael's liquid assets, including her savings account, total $10,000. Her monthly expenses are approximately $3,000. Should Rachael make this investment?

YES: She has a good income, and this is a great opportunity for her to get in on the ground floor of her employer's fast-growing company.

NO: She shouldn't invest all of her money in one company, particularly the company at which she works.

The authors' comments on this situation appear on p. 671.

Using the Decision Toolkit

The condensed financial statements ot The Estée Lauder Companies, Inc., for the years ended June 30, 2005 and 2004, are presented below.

THE ESTÉE LAUDER COMPANIES, INC.
Balance Sheets
June 30

	(in millions)	
Assets	**2005**	**2004**
Current assets		
Cash and cash equivalents	$ 553.3	$ 611.6
Accounts receivable (net)	776.6	664.9
Inventories	768.3	653.5
Prepaid expenses and other current assets	204.4	269.2
Total current assets	2,302.6	2,199.2
Property, plant, and equipment (net)	694.2	647.0
Investments	12.3	12.6
Intangibles and other assets	876.7	849.3
Total assets	$3,885.8	$3,708.1
Liabilities and Stockholders' Equity		
Current liabilities	$1,497.7	$1,322.0
Long-term liabilities	679.5	637.1
Stockholders' equity—common	1,708.6	1,749.0
Total liabilities and stockholders' equity	$3,885.8	$3,708.1

THE ESTÉE LAUDER COMPANIES, INC.
Income Statements
For the Year Ended June 30

	(in millions)	
	2005	**2004**
Revenues	$6,336.3	$5,790.4
Costs and expenses		
Cost of goods sold	1,617.4	1,476.3
Selling and administrative expenses	4,007.6	3,679.0
Interest expense	13.9	27.1
Total costs and expenses	5,638.9	5,182.4
Income before income taxes	697.4	608.0
Income tax expense	291.3	232.6
Net income	$ 406.1	$ 375.4

Instructions

Compute the following ratios for 2005 and 2004.

(a) Current ratio.

(b) Inventory turnover. (Inventory on 6/30/03 was $599.0.)

(c) Profit margin ratio.
(d) Return on assets. (Assets on 6/30/03 were $3,349.9.)
(e) Return on common stockholders' equity. (Equity on 6/30/03 was $1,795.9.)
(f) Debt to total assets ratio.
(g) Times interest earned.

Solution

	2005	2004
(a) Current ratio:		
$2,302.6 ÷ $1,497.7 =	1.5:1	
$2,199.2 ÷ $1,322.0 =		1.7:1
(b) Inventory turnover:		
$1,617.4 ÷ [($768.3 + $653.5) ÷ 2] =	2.3 times	
$1,476.3 ÷ [($653.5 + $599.0) ÷ 2] =		2.4 times
(c) Profit margin:		
$406.1 ÷ $6,336.3	6.4%	
$375.4 ÷ $5,790.4		6.5%
(d) Return on assets:		
$406.1 ÷ [($3,885.8 + $3,708.1) ÷ 2] =	10.7%	
$375.4 ÷ [($3,708.1 + $3,349.9) ÷ 2] =		10.6%
(e) Return on common stockholders' equity:		
$406.1 ÷ [($1,708.6 + $1,749.0) ÷ 2] =	23.5%	
$375.4 ÷ [($1,749.0 + $1,795.9) ÷ 2] =		21.2%
(f) Debt to total assets ratio:		
($1,497.7 + $679.5) ÷ $3,885.8 =	56.0%	
($1,322.0 + $637.1) ÷ $3,708.1 =		52.8%
(g) Times interest earned:		
($406.1 + $291.3 + $13.9) ÷ $13.9 =	51.2 times	
($375.4 + $232.6 + $27.1) ÷ $27.1 =		23.4 times

The Navigator

SUMMARY OF STUDY OBJECTIVES

1 **Discuss the need for comparative analysis.** There are three bases of comparison: (1) Intracompany, which compares an item or financial relationship with other data within a company. (2) Industry, which compares company data with industry averages. (3) Intercompany, which compares an item or financial relationship of a company with data of one or more competing companies.

2 **Identify the tools of financial statement analysis.** Financial statements can be analyzed horizontally, vertically, and with ratios.

3 **Explain and apply horizontal analysis.** Horizontal analysis is a technique for evaluating a series of data over a period of time to determine the increase or decrease that has taken place, expressed as either an amount or a percentage.

4 **Describe and apply vertical analysis.** Vertical analysis is a technique that expresses each item within a financial statement in terms of a percentage of a relevant total or a base amount.

5 **Identify and compute ratios used in analyzing a firm's liquidity, profitability, and solvency.** The formula and purpose of each ratio was presented in Illustration 14-27 (page 639).

6 **Understand the concept of earning power, and how irregular items are presented.** Earning power refers to a company's ability to sustain its profits from operations. "Irregular items"—discontinued operations and extraordinary items—are presented net of tax below income from continuing operations to highlight their unusual nature.

7 **Understand the concept of quality of earnings.** A high quality of earnings provides full and transparent information that will not confuse or mislead users of the financial statements. Issues related to quality of earnings are (1) alternative accounting methods, (2) pro forma income, and (3) improper recognition.

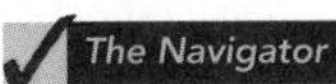

DECISION TOOLKIT—A SUMMARY

Decision Checkpoints	Info Needed for Decision	Tool to Use for Decision	How to Evaluate Results
How do the company's financial position and operating results compare with those of the previous period?	Income statement and balance sheet	Comparative financial statements should be prepared over at least two years, with the first year reported being the base year. Changes in each line item relative to the base year should be presented both by amount and by percentage. This is called horizontal analysis.	Significant changes should be investigated to determine the reason for the change.
How do the relationships between items in this year's financial statements compare with those of last year or those of competitors?	Income statement and balance sheet	Each line item on the income statement should be presented as a percentage of net sales, and each line item on the balance sheet should be presented as a percentage of total assets or total liabilities and stockholders' equity. These percentages should be investigated for differences either across years in the same company or in the same year across different companies. This is called vertical analysis.	Any significant differences either across years or between companies should be investigated to determine the cause.
Has the company sold any major components of its business?	Discontinued operations section of income statement	Anything reported in this section indicates that the company has discontinued a major component of its business.	If a major component has been discontinued, its results during the current period should not be included in estimates of future net income.
Has the company experienced any extraordinary events or transactions?	Extraordinary item section of income statement	Anything reported in this section indicates that the company experienced an event that was both unusual and infrequent.	These items should usually be ignored in estimating future net income.
Has the company changed any of its accounting principles?	Effect of change in accounting principle on current and prior periods.	Management indicates that the new principle is preferable to the old principle.	Examine current and prior years reported, using new-principle basis to assess trends for estimating future income.

GLOSSARY

Acid-test (quick) ratio A measure of a company's immediate short-term liquidity; computed by dividing the sum of cash, short-term investments, and net receivables by current liabilities. (p. 630).

Asset turnover A measure of how efficiently a company uses its assets to generate sales; computed by dividing net sales by average assets. (p. 633).

Change in accounting principle The use of a principle in the current year that is different from the one used in the preceding year. (p. 643).

Comprehensive income Includes all changes in stockholders' equity during a period except those resulting from investments by stockholders and distributions to stockholders. (p. 644).

Current ratio A measure used to evaluate a company's liquidity and short-term debt-paying ability; computed by dividing current assets by current liabilities. (p. 629).

Debt to total assets ratio Measures the percentage of total assets provided by creditors; computed by dividing total debt by total assets. (p. 637).

Discontinued operations The disposal of a significant component of a business. (p. 640).

Earnings per share (EPS) The net income earned on each share of common stock; computed by dividing net income by the number of weighted average common shares outstanding. (p. 635).

Extraordinary items Events and transactions that are unusual in nature and infrequent in occurrence. (p. 641).

Horizontal analysis A technique for evaluating a series of financial statement data over a period of time, to determine the increase (decrease) that has taken place, expressed as either an amount or a percentage. (p. 621).

Inventory turnover A measure of the liquidity of inventory; computed by dividing cost of goods sold by average inventory. (p. 632).

Leveraging See Trading on the equity.

Liquidity ratios Measures of the short-term ability of the company to pay its maturing obligations and to meet unexpected needs for cash. (p. 629).

Payout ratio Measures the percentage of earnings distributed in the form of cash dividends; computed by dividing cash dividends by net income. (p. 636).

Price-earnings (P-E) ratio Reflects investors' assessments of a company's future earnings; computed by dividing the market price of the stock by earnings per share. (p. 636).

Profit margin Measures the percentage of each dollar of sales that results in net income; computed by dividing net income by net sales. (p. 633).

Profitability ratios Measures of the income or operating success of a company for a given period of time. (p. 633).

Pro forma income A measure of income that usually excludes items that a company thinks are unusual or nonrecurring. (p. 645).

Quality of earnings Indicates the level of full and transparent information provided to users of the financial statements (p. 645).

Ratio An expression of the mathematical relationship between one quantity and another. The relationship may be expressed either as a percentage, a rate, or a simple proportion. (p. 628).

Ratio analysis A technique for evaluating financial statements that expresses the relationship between selected financial statement data. (p. 628).

Receivables turnover A measure of the liquidity of receivables; computed by dividing net credit sales by average net receivables. (p. 631).

Return on assets An overall measure of profitability; computed by dividing net income by average assets. (p. 634).

Return on common stockholders' equity Measures the dollars of net income earned for each dollar invested by the owners; computed by dividing net income by average common stockholders' equity. (p. 634).

Solvency ratios Measures of the ability of the company to survive over a long period of time. (p. 637).

Times interest earned Measures a company's ability to meet interest payments as they come due; computed by dividing income before interest expense and income taxes by interest expense. (p. 638).

Trading on the equity Borrowing money at a lower rate of interest than can be earned by using the borrowed money. (p. 635).

Vertical analysis A technique for evaluating financial statement data that expresses each item within a financial statement as a percent of a base amount. (p. 625).

Demonstration Problem

The events and transactions of Dever Corporation for the year ending December 31, 2008, resulted in the following data.

Cost of goods sold	$2,600,000
Net sales	4,400,000
Other expenses and losses	9,600
Other revenues and gains	5,600
Selling and administrative expenses	1,100,000
Income from operations of plastics division	70,000
Gain from disposal of plastics division	500,000
Loss from tornado disaster (extraordinary loss)	600,000

Analysis reveals that:

1. All items are before the applicable income tax rate of 30%.
2. The plastics division was sold on July 1.
3. All operating data for the plastics division have been segregated.

Instructions

Prepare an income statement for the year.

action plan

- ✔ Report material items not typical of operations in separate sections, net of taxes.
- ✔ Associate income taxes with the item that affects the taxes.
- ✔ Apply the corporate tax rate to income before income taxes to determine tax expense.

Solution

DEVER CORPORATION
Income Statement
For the Year Ended December 31, 2008

Net sales		$4,400,000
Cost of goods sold		2,600,000
Gross profit		1,800,000
Selling and administrative expenses		1,100,000
Income from operations		700,000
Other revenues and gains	$5,600	
Other expenses and losses	9,600	4,000
Income before income taxes		696,000
Income tax expense ($696,000 × 30%)		208,800
Income from continuing operations		487,200
Discontinued operations		
Income from operations of plastics division, net of $21,000 income taxes ($70,000 × 30%)	49,000	
Gain from disposal of plastics division, net of $150,000 income taxes ($500,000 × 30%)	350,000	399,000
Income before extraordinary item		886,200
Extraordinary item		
Tornado loss, net of $180,000 income tax saving ($600,000 × 30%)		420,000
Net income		$ 466,200

The Navigator

SELF-STUDY QUESTIONS

Answers are at the end of the chapter.

(SO 1) 1. Comparisons of data within a company are an example of the following comparative basis:
- a. Industry averages.
- b. Intracompany.
- c. Intercompany.
- d. Both (b) and (c).

(SO 3) 2. In horizontal analysis, each item is expressed as a percentage of the:
- a. net income amount.
- b. stockholders' equity amount.
- c. total assets amount.
- d. base year amount.

3. In vertical analysis, the base amount for depreciation expense is generally: (SO 4)
- a. net sales.
- b. depreciation expense in a previous year.
- c. gross profit.
- d. fixed assets.

4. The following schedule is a display of what type of analysis? (SO 4)

	Amount	Percent
Current assets	$200,000	25%
Property, plant, and equipment	600,000	75%
Total assets	$800,000	

a. Horizontal analysis.
b. Differential analysis.
c. Vertical analysis.
d. Ratio analysis.

(SO 3) 5. Sammy Corporation reported net sales of $300,000, $330,000, and $360,000 in the years, 2006, 2007, and 2008, respectively. If 2006 is the base year, what is the trend percentage for 2008?
a. 77%.
b. 108%.
c. 120%.
d. 130%.

(SO 5) 6. Which of the following measures is an evaluation of a firm's ability to pay current liabilities?
a. Acid-test ratio.
b. Current ratio.
c. Both (a) and (b).
d. None of the above.

(SO 5) 7. A measure useful in evaluating the efficiency in managing inventories is:
a. inventory turnover.
b. average days to sell inventory.
c. Both (a) and (b).
d. None of the above.

(SO 6) 8. In reporting discontinued operations, the income statement should show in a special section:
a. gains and losses on the disposal of the discontinued segment.
b. gains and losses from operations of the discontinued segment.
c. Both (a) and (b).
d. Neither (a) nor (b).

9. Scout Corporation has income before taxes of $400,000 and an extraordinary loss of $100,000. If the income tax rate is 25% on all items, the income statement should show income before extraordinary items and extraordinary items, respectively, of: (SO 6)
a. $325,000 and $100,000.
b. $325,000 and $75,000.
c. $300,000 and $100,000
d. $300,000 and $75,000.

10. Which situation below might indicate a company has a low quality of earnings? (SO 7)
a. The same accounting principles are used each year.
b. Revenue is recognized when earned.
c. Maintenance costs are expensed as incurred.
d. The company is continually reporting pro forma income numbers.

Go to the book's website, **www.wiley.com/college/weygandt**, for Additional Self-Study questions.

QUESTIONS

1. **(a)** Juan Marichal believes that the analysis of financial statements is directed at two characteristics of a company: liquidity and profitability. Is Juan correct? Explain.
   (b) Are short-term creditors, long-term creditors, and stockholders interested primarily in the same characteristics of a company? Explain.
2. **(a)** Distinguish among the following bases of comparison: (1) intracompany, (2) industry averages, and (3) intercompany.
   (b) Give the principal value of using each of the three bases of comparison.
3. Two popular methods of financial statement analysis are horizontal analysis and vertical analysis. Explain the difference between these two methods.
4. **(a)** If Leonard Company had net income of $360,000 in 2008 and it experienced a 24.5% increase in net income for 2009, what is its net income for 2009?
   (b) If six cents of every dollar of Leonard revenue is net income in 2008, what is the dollar amount of 2008 revenue?
5. What is a ratio? What are the different ways of expressing the relationship of two amounts? What information does a ratio provide?
6. Name the major ratios useful in assessing (a) liquidity and (b) solvency.
7. Raphael Ochoa is puzzled. His company had a profit margin of 10% in 2008. He feels that this is an indication that the company is doing well. Cindy Lore, his accountant, says that more information is needed to determine the firm's financial well-being. Who is correct? Why?
8. What do the following classes of ratios measure? (a) Liquidity ratios. (b) Profitability ratios. (c) Solvency ratios.
9. What is the difference between the current ratio and the acid-test ratio?
10. Donte Company, a retail store, has a receivables turnover of 4.5 times. The industry average is 12.5 times. Does Donte have a collection problem with its receivables?
11. Which ratios should be used to help answer the following questions?
    (a) How efficient is a company in using its assets to produce sales?
    (b) How near to sale is the inventory on hand?
    (c) How many dollars of net income were earned for each dollar invested by the owners?
    (d) How able is a company to meet interest charges as they fall due?
12. The price-earnings ratio of General Motors (automobile builder) was 8, and the price-earnings ratio of Microsoft (computer software) was 38. Which company did the stock market favor? Explain.

13. What is the formula for computing the payout ratio? Would you expect this ratio to be high or low for a growth company?
14. Holding all other factors constant, indicate whether each of the following changes generally signals good or bad news about a company.
    (a) Increase in profit margin.
    (b) Decrease in inventory turnover.
    (c) Increase in the current ratio.
    (d) Decrease in earnings per share.
    (e) Increase in price-earnings ratio.
    (f) Increase in debt to total assets ratio.
    (g) Decrease in times interest earned.
15. The return on assets for Tresh Corporation is 7.6%. During the same year Tresh's return on common stockholders' equity is 12.8%. What is the explanation for the difference in the two rates?
16. Which two ratios do you think should be of greatest interest to:
    (a) A pension fund considering the purchase of 20-year bonds?
    (b) A bank contemplating a short-term loan?
    (c) A common stockholder?
17. Why must preferred stock dividends be subtracted from net income in computing earnings per share?
18. (a) What is meant by trading on the equity?
    (b) How would you determine the profitability of trading on the equity?
19. Hillman Inc. has net income of $160,000, weighted average shares of common stock outstanding of 50,000, and preferred dividends for the period of $40,000. What is Hillman's earnings per share of common stock? Kate Hillman, the president of Hillman Inc., believes the computed EPS of the company is high. Comment.
20. Why is it important to report discontinued operations separately from income from continuing operations?
21. You are considering investing in Shawnee Transportation. The company reports 2008 earnings per share of $6.50 on income before extraordinary items and $4.75 on net income. Which EPS figure would you consider more relevant to your investment decision? Why?
22. STL Inc. reported 2007 earnings per share of $3.20 and had no extraordinary items. In 2008, EPS on income before extraordinary items was $2.99, and EPS on net income was $3.49. Is this a favorable trend?
23. Indicate which of the following items would be reported as an extraordinary item in Mordica Corporation's income statement.
    (a) Loss from damages caused by volcano eruption.
    (b) Loss from sale of temporary investments.
    (c) Loss attributable to a labor strike.
    (d) Loss caused when manufacture of a product was prohibited by the Food and Drug Administration.
    (e) Loss from flood damage. (The nearby Black River floods every 2 to 3 years.)
    (f) Write-down of obsolete inventory.
    (g) Expropriation of a factory by a foreign government.
24. Identify and explain factors that affect quality of earnings.

BRIEF EXERCISES

Follow the rounding procedures used in the chapter.

Discuss need for comparative analysis.
(SO 1)

BE14-1 You recently received a letter from your Uncle Frank. A portion of the letter is presented below.

> You know that I have a significant amount of money I saved over the years. I am thinking about starting an investment program. I want to do the investing myself, based on my own research and analysis of financial statements. I know that you are studying accounting, so I have a couple of questions for you. I have heard that different users of financial statements are interested in different characteristics of companies. Is this true, and, if so, why? Also, some of my friends, who are already investing, have told me that comparisons involving a company's financial data can be made on a number of different bases. Can you explain these bases to me?

Instructions

Write a letter to your Uncle Frank which answers his questions.

Identify and use tools of financial statement analysis.
(SO 2, 3, 4, 5)

BE14-2 Drew Carey Corporation reported the following amounts in 2007, 2008, and 2009.

	2007	2008	2009
Current assets	$200,000	$230,000	$240,000
Current liabilities	$160,000	$168,000	$184,000
Total assets	$500,000	$600,000	$620,000

Instructions

(a) Identify and describe the three tools of financial statement analysis. **(b)** Perform each of the three types of analysis on Drew Carey's current assets.

BE14-3 Using the following data from the comparative balance sheet of Rodenbeck Company, illustrate horizontal analysis.

Prepare horizontal analysis. (SO 3)

	December 31, 2009	December 31, 2008
Accounts receivable	$ 520,000	$ 400,000
Inventory	$ 840,000	$ 600,000
Total assets	$ 3,000,000	$2,500,000

BE14-4 Using the same data presented above in BE14-3 for Rodenbeck Company, illustrate vertical analysis.

Prepare vertical analysis. (SO 4)

BE14-5 Net income was $500,000 in 2007, $450,000 in 2008, and $522,000 in 2009. What is the percentage of change from **(a)** 2007 to 2008 and **(b)** 2008 to 2009? Is the change an increase or a decrease?

Calculate percentage of change. (SO 3)

BE14-6 If Soule Company had net income of $585,000 in 2009 and it experienced a 30% increase in net income over 2008, what was its 2008 net income?

Calculate net income. (SO 3)

BE14-7 Horizontal analysis (trend analysis) percentages for Epstein Company's sales, cost of goods sold, and expenses are shown below.

Determine change in net income. (SO 3)

Horizontal Analysis	2009	2008	2007
Sales	96.2	106.8	100.0
Cost of goods sold	102.0	97.0	100.0
Expenses	109.6	98.4	100.0

Did Epstein's net income increase, decrease, or remain unchanged over the 3-year period?

BE14-8 Vertical analysis (common size) percentages for Charles Company's sales, cost of goods sold, and expenses are shown below.

Calculate change in net income. (SO 4)

Vertical Analysis	2009	2008	2007
Sales	100.0	100.0	100.0
Cost of goods sold	59.2	62.4	64.5
Expenses	25.0	25.6	27.5

Did Charles's net income as a percent of sales increase, decrease, or remain unchanged over the 3-year period? Provide numerical support for your answer.

BE14-9 Selected condensed data taken from a recent balance sheet of Perkins Inc. are as follows.

Calculate liquidity ratios. (SO 5)

PERKINS INC.
Balance Sheet (partial)

Cash	$ 8,041,000
Short-term investments	4,947,000
Accounts receivable	12,545,000
Inventories	14,814,000
Other current assets	5,571,000
Total current assets	$45,918,000
Total current liabilities	$40,644,000

What are the **(a)** working capital, **(b)** current ratio, and **(c)** acid-test ratio?

BE14-10 McLaren Corporation has net income of $11.44 million and net revenue of $80 million in 2008. Its assets are $14 million at the beginning of the year and $18 million at the end of the year. What are McLaren's **(a)** asset turnover and **(b)** profit margin?

Calculate profitability ratios. (SO 5)

Evaluate collection of accounts receivable. (SO 5)

BE14-11 The following data are taken from the financial statements of Morino Company.

	2009	2008
Accounts receivable (net), end of year	$ 550,000	$ 520,000
Net sales on account	3,960,000	3,100,000

Terms for all sales are 1/10, n/60.

(a) Compute for each year (1) the receivables turnover and (2) the average collection period. At the end of 2007, accounts receivable (net) was $480,000.

(b) What conclusions about the management of accounts receivable can be drawn from these data?

Evaluate management of inventory. (SO 5)

BE14-12 The following data are from the income statements of Huntsinger Company.

	2009	2008
Sales	$6,420,000	$6,240,000
Beginning inventory	980,000	860,000
Purchases	4,340,000	4,661,000
Ending inventory	1,020,000	980,000

(a) Compute for each year (1) the inventory turnover and (2) the average days to sell the inventory.
(b) What conclusions concerning the management of the inventory can be drawn from these data?

Calculate profitability ratios. (SO 5)

BE14-13 Gladow Company has stockholders' equity of $400,000 and net income of $66,000. It has a payout ratio of 20% and a rate of return on assets of 15%. How much did Gladow pay in cash dividends, and what were its average assets?

Prepare income statement including extraordinary items. (SO 6)

BE14-14 An inexperienced accountant for Ming Corporation showed the following in the income statement: income before income taxes and extraordinary item $400,000, and extraordinary loss from flood (before taxes) $70,000. The extraordinary loss and taxable income are both subject to a 30% tax rate. Prepare a correct income statement.

Prepare discontinued operations section of income statement. (SO 6)

BE14-15 On June 30, Reeves Corporation discontinued its operations in Mexico. During the year, the operating loss was $300,000 before taxes. On September 1, Reeves disposed of the Mexico facility at a pretax loss of $120,000. The applicable tax rate is 30%. Show the discontinued operations section of the income statement.

EXERCISES

WILEY PLUS

Follow the rounding procedures used in the chapter.

Prepare horizontal analysis. (SO 3)

E14-1 Financial information for Blevins Inc. is presented below.

	December 31, 2009	December 31, 2008
Current assets	$125,000	$100,000
Plant assets (net)	396,000	330,000
Current liabilities	91,000	70,000
Long-term liabilities	133,000	95,000
Common stock, $1 par	161,000	115,000
Retained earnings	136,000	150,000

Instructions

Prepare a schedule showing a horizontal analysis for 2009 using 2008 as the base year.

Prepare vertical analysis. (SO 4)

E14-2 Operating data for Gallup Corporation are presented below.

	2009	2008
Sales	$750,000	$600,000
Cost of goods sold	465,000	390,000
Selling expenses	120,000	72,000
Administrative expenses	60,000	54,000
Income tax expense	33,000	24,000
Net income	72,000	60,000

Instructions

Prepare a schedule showing a vertical analysis for 2009 and 2008.

E14-3 The comparative condensed balance sheets of Conard Corporation are presented below.

Prepare horizontal and vertical analyses.

(SO 3, 4)

CONARD CORPORATION
Comparative Condensed Balance Sheets
December 31

	2009	2008
Assets		
Current assets	$ 74,000	$ 80,000
Property, plant, and equipment (net)	99,000	90,000
Intangibles	27,000	40,000
Total assets	$200,000	$210,000
Liabilities and stockholders' equity		
Current liabilities	$ 42,000	$ 48,000
Long-term liabilities	143,000	150,000
Stockholders' equity	15,000	12,000
Total liabilities and stockholders' equity	$200,000	$210,000

Instructions

(a) Prepare a horizontal analysis of the balance sheet data for Conard Corporation using 2008 as a base.

(b) Prepare a vertical analysis of the balance sheet data for Conard Corporation in columnar form for 2009.

E14-4 The comparative condensed income statements of Hendi Corporation are shown below.

Prepare horizontal and vertical analyses.

(SO 3, 4)

HENDI CORPORATION
Comparative Condensed Income Statements
For the Years Ended December 31

	2009	2008
Net sales	$600,000	$500,000
Cost of goods sold	483,000	420,000
Gross profit	117,000	80,000
Operating expenses	57,200	44,000
Net income	$ 59,800	$ 36,000

Instructions

(a) Prepare a horizontal analysis of the income statement data for Hendi Corporation using 2008 as a base. (Show the amounts of increase or decrease.)

(b) Prepare a vertical analysis of the income statement data for Hendi Corporation in columnar form for both years.

E14-5 Nordstrom, Inc. operates department stores in numerous states. Selected financial statement data for the year ending January 29, 2005, are as follows.

Compute liquidity ratios and compare results.

(SO 5)

NORDSTROM, INC.
Balance Sheet (partial)

(in millions)	End-of-Year	Beginning-of-Year
Cash and cash equivalents	$ 361	$ 340
Receivables (less allowance of 19 and 20)	646	667
Merchandise inventory	917	902
Prepaid expenses	53	46
Other current assets	595	570
Total current assets	$2,572	$2,525
Total current liabilities	$1,341	$1,123

For the year, net sales were $7,131, and cost of goods sold was $4,559 (in millions).

Instructions

(a) Compute the four liquidity ratios at the end of the year.

(b) Using the data in the chapter, compare Nordstrom's liquidity with (1) that of J.C. Penney Company, and (2) the industry averages for department stores.

Perform current and acid-test ratio analysis.

(SO 5)

E14-6 Leach Incorporated had the following transactions occur involving current assets and current liabilities during February 2008.

Feb.	3	Accounts receivable of $15,000 are collected.
	7	Equipment is purchased for $28,000 cash.
	11	Paid $3,000 for a 3-year insurance policy.
	14	Accounts payable of $12,000 are paid.
	18	Cash dividends of $5,000 are declared.

Additional information:

1. As of February 1, 2008, current assets were $130,000, and current liabilities were $50,000.
2. As of February 1, 2008, current assets included $15,000 of inventory and $2,000 of prepaid expenses.

Instructions

(a) Compute the current ratio as of the beginning of the month and after each transaction.

(b) Compute the acid-test ratio as of the beginning of the month and after each transaction.

Compute selected ratios.

(SO 5)

E14-7 Bennis Company has the following comparative balance sheet data.

BENNIS COMPANY
Balance Sheets
December 31

	2009	2008
Cash	$ 15,000	$ 30,000
Receivables (net)	70,000	60,000
Inventories	60,000	50,000
Plant assets (net)	200,000	180,000
	$345,000	$320,000
Accounts payable	$50,000	$60,000
Mortgage payable (15%)	100,000	100,000
Common stock, $10 par	140,000	120,000
Retained earnings	55,000	40,000
	$345,000	$320,000

Additional information for 2009:

1. Net income was $25,000.
2. Sales on account were $410,000. Sales returns and allowances were $20,000.
3. Cost of goods sold was $198,000.
4. The allowance for doubtful accounts was $2,500 on December 31, 2009, and $2,000 on December 31, 2008.

Instructions

Compute the following ratios at December 31, 2009.

(a) Current.

(b) Acid-test.

(c) Receivables turnover.

(d) Inventory turnover.

Compute selected ratios.

(SO 5)

E14-8 Selected comparative statement data for Willingham Products Company are presented on the next page. All balance sheet data are as of December 31.

	2009	2008
Net sales	$760,000	$720,000
Cost of goods sold	480,000	440,000
Interest expense	7,000	5,000
Net income	50,000	42,000
Accounts receivable	120,000	100,000
Inventory	85,000	75,000
Total assets	580,000	500,000
Total common stockholders' equity	430,000	325,000

Instructions

Compute the following ratios for 2009.

(a) Profit margin.
(b) Asset turnover.
(c) Return on assets.
(d) Return on common stockholders' equity.

E14-9 The income statement for Christensen, Inc., appears below.

Compute selected ratios.
(SO 5)

CHRISTENSEN, INC.
Income Statement
For the Year Ended December 31, 2008

Sales	$400,000
Cost of goods sold	230,000
Gross profit	170,000
Expenses (including $16,000 interest and $24,000 income taxes)	105,000
Net income	$ 65,000

Additional information:

1. The weighted average common shares outstanding in 2008 were 30,000 shares.
2. The market price of Christensen, Inc. stock was $13 in 2008.
3. Cash dividends of $26,000 were paid, $5,000 of which were to preferred stockholders.

Instructions

Compute the following ratios for 2008.

(a) Earnings per share.
(b) Price-earnings.
(c) Payout.
(d) Times interest earned.

E14-10 Rees Corporation experienced a fire on December 31, 2009, in which its financial records were partially destroyed. It has been able to salvage some of the records and has ascertained the following balances.

Compute amounts from ratios.
(SO 5)

	December 31, 2009	December 31, 2008
Cash	$ 30,000	$ 10,000
Receivables (net)	72,500	126,000
Inventory	200,000	180,000
Accounts payable	50,000	90,000
Notes payable	30,000	60,000
Common stock, $100 par	400,000	400,000
Retained earnings	113,500	101,000

Additional information:

1. The inventory turnover is 3.5 times.
2. The return on common stockholders' equity is 24%. The company had no additional paid-in capital.
3. The receivables turnover is 8.8 times.
4. The return on assets is 20%.
5. Total assets at December 31, 2008, were $605,000.

Instructions

Compute the following for Rees Corporation.

(a) Cost of goods sold for 2009.
(b) Net sales (credit) for 2009.
(c) Net income for 2009.
(d) Total assets at December 31, 2009.

Compute ratios.
(SO 5)

E14-11 Scully Corporation's comparative balance sheets are presented below.

SCULLY CORPORATION
Balance Sheets
December 31

	2008	2007
Cash	$ 4,300	$ 3,700
Accounts receivable	21,200	23,400
Inventory	10,000	7,000
Land	20,000	26,000
Building	70,000	70,000
Accumulated depreciation	(15,000)	(10,000)
Total	$110,500	$120,100
Accounts payable	$ 12,370	$ 31,100
Common stock	75,000	69,000
Retained earnings	23,130	20,000
Total	$110,500	$120,100

Scully's 2008 income statement included net sales of $100,000, cost of goods sold of $60,000, and net income of $15,000.

Instructions

Compute the following ratios for 2008.

(a) Current ratio.
(b) Acid-test ratio.
(c) Receivables turnover.
(d) Inventory turnover.
(e) Profit margin.
(f) Asset turnover.
(g) Return on assets.
(h) Return on common stockholders' equity.
(i) Debt to total assets ratio.

Prepare a correct income statement.
(SO 6)

E14-12 For its fiscal year ending October 31, 2008, Molini Corporation reports the following partial data.

Income before income taxes	$540,000
Income tax expense (30% × $390,000)	117,000
Income before extraordinary items	423,000
Extraordinary loss from flood	150,000
Net income	$273,000

The flood loss is considered an extraordinary item. The income tax rate is 30% on all items.

Instructions

(a) Prepare a correct income statement, beginning with income before income taxes.
(b) Explain in memo form why the income statement data are misleading.

Prepare income statement.
(SO 6)

E14-13 Yadier Corporation has income from continuing operations of $290,000 for the year ended December 31, 2008. It also has the following items (before considering income taxes).

1. An extraordinary loss of $80,000.
2. A gain of $30,000 on the discontinuance of a division.

3. A correction of an error in last year's financial statements that resulted in a $20,000 understatement of 2007 revenue.

Assume all items are subject to income taxes at a 30% tax rate.

Instructions

(a) Prepare an income statement, beginning with income from continuing operations.
(b) Indicate the statement presentation of any item not included in (a) above.

EXERCISES: SET B

Visit the book's website at **www.wiley.com/college/weygandt**, and choose the Student Companion site, to access Exercise Set B.

PROBLEMS

Follow the rounding procedures used in the chapter.

Prepare vertical analysis and comment on profitability.
(SO 4, 5)

P14-1 Comparative statement data for Douglas Company and Maulder Company, two competitors, appear below. All balance sheet data are as of December 31, 2009, and December 31, 2008.

	Douglas Company		Maulder Company	
	2009	**2008**	**2009**	**2008**
Net sales	$1,549,035		$339,038	
Cost of goods sold	1,080,490		241,000	
Operating expenses	302,275		79,000	
Interest expense	8,980		2,252	
Income tax expense	54,500		6,650	
Current assets	325,975	$312,410	83,336	$ 79,467
Plant assets (net)	521,310	500,000	139,728	125,812
Current liabilities	65,325	75,815	35,348	30,281
Long-term liabilities	108,500	90,000	29,620	25,000
Common stock, $10 par	500,000	500,000	120,000	120,000
Retained earnings	173,460	146,595	38,096	29,998

Instructions

(a) Prepare a vertical analysis of the 2009 income statement data for Douglas Company and Maulder Company in columnar form.
(b) Comment on the relative profitability of the companies by computing the return on assets and the return on common stockholders' equity ratios for both companies.

Compute ratios from balance sheet and income statement.
(SO 5)

P14-2 The comparative statements of Villa Tool Company are presented below.

VILLA TOOL COMPANY
Income Statement
For the Year Ended December 31

	2009	2008
Net sales	$1,818,500	$1,750,500
Cost of goods sold	1,011,500	996,000
Gross profit	807,000	754,500
Selling and administrative expense	516,000	479,000
Income from operations	291,000	275,500
Other expenses and losses		
Interest expense	18,000	14,000
Income before income taxes	273,000	261,500
Income tax expense	81,000	77,000
Net income	$ 192,000	$ 184,500

VILLA TOOL COMPANY
Balance Sheets
December 31

Assets	2009	2008
Current assets		
Cash	$ 60,100	$ 64,200
Short-term investments	69,000	50,000
Accounts receivable (net)	117,800	102,800
Inventory	123,000	115,500
Total current assets	369,900	332,500
Plant assets (net)	600,300	520,300
Total assets	$970,200	$852,800
Liabilities and Stockholders' Equity		
Current liabilities		
Accounts payable	$160,000	$145,400
Income taxes payable	43,500	42,000
Total current liabilities	203,500	187,400
Bonds payable	200,000	200,000
Total liabilities	403,500	387,400
Stockholders' equity		
Common stock ($5 par)	280,000	300,000
Retained earnings	286,700	165,400
Total stockholders' equity	566,700	465,400
Total liabilities and stockholders' equity	$970,200	$852,800

All sales were on account. The allowance for doubtful accounts was $3,200 on December 31, 2009, and $3,000 on December 31, 2008.

Instructions

Compute the following ratios for 2009. (Weighted average common shares in 2009 were 57,000.)

(a) Earnings per share.
(b) Return on common stockholders' equity.
(c) Return on assets.
(d) Current.
(e) Acid-test.
(f) Receivables turnover.
(g) Inventory turnover.
(h) Times interest earned.
(i) Asset turnover.
(j) Debt to total assets.

Perform ratio analysis, and evaluate financial position and operating results.
(SO 5)

P14-3 Condensed balance sheet and income statement data for Kersenbrock Corporation appear below.

KERSENBROCK CORPORATION
Balance Sheets
December 31

	2009	2008	2007
Cash	$ 25,000	$ 20,000	$ 18,000
Receivables (net)	50,000	45,000	48,000
Other current assets	90,000	95,000	64,000
Investments	75,000	70,000	45,000
Plant and equipment (net)	400,000	370,000	358,000
	$640,000	$600,000	$533,000
Current liabilities	$ 75,000	$ 80,000	$ 70,000
Long-term debt	80,000	85,000	50,000
Common stock, $10 par	340,000	310,000	300,000
Retained earnings	145,000	125,000	113,000
	$640,000	$600,000	$533,000

KERSENBROCK CORPORATION
Income Statement
For the Year Ended December 31

	2009	2008
Sales	$740,000	$700,000
Less: Sales returns and allowances	40,000	50,000
Net sales	700,000	650,000
Cost of goods sold	420,000	400,000
Gross profit	280,000	250,000
Operating expenses (including income taxes)	235,000	220,000
Net income	$ 45,000	$ 30,000

Additional information:

1. The market price of Kersenbrock's common stock was $4.00, $5.00, and $8.00 for 2007, 2008, and 2009, respectively.

2. All dividends were paid in cash.

Instructions

(a) Compute the following ratios for 2008 and 2009.
  (1) Profit margin.
  (2) Asset turnover.
  (3) Earnings per share. (Weighted average common shares in 2009 were 32,000 and in 2008 were 31,000.)
  (4) Price-earnings.
  (5) Payout.
  (6) Debt to total assets.

(b) Based on the ratios calculated, discuss briefly the improvement or lack thereof in financial position and operating results from 2008 to 2009 of Kersenbrock Corporation.

P14-4 Financial information for Hanshew Company is presented below.

Compute ratios, and comment on overall liquidity and profitability.
(SO 5)

HANSHEW COMPANY
Balance Sheets
December 31

Assets	2009	2008
Cash	$ 70,000	$ 65,000
Short-term investments	52,000	40,000
Receivables (net)	98,000	80,000
Inventories	125,000	135,000
Prepaid expenses	29,000	23,000
Land	130,000	130,000
Building and equipment (net)	180,000	175,000
	$684,000	$648,000
Liabilities and Stockholders' Equity		
Notes payable	$100,000	$100,000
Accounts payable	48,000	42,000
Accrued liabilities	50,000	40,000
Bonds payable, due 2012	150,000	150,000
Common stock, $10 par	200,000	200,000
Retained earnings	136,000	116,000
	$684,000	$648,000

HANSHEW COMPANY
Income Statement
For the Years Ended December 31

	2009	2008
Sales	$850,000	$790,000
Cost of goods sold	620,000	575,000
Gross profit	230,000	215,000
Operating expenses	187,000	173,000
Net income	$ 43,000	$ 42,000

Additional information:

1. Inventory at the beginning of 2008 was $118,000.
2. Receivables (net) at the beginning of 2008 were $88,000. The allowance for doubtful accounts was $4,000 at the end of 2009, $3,800 at the end of 2008, and $3,700 at the beginning of 2008.
3. Total assets at the beginning of 2008 were $630,000.
4. No common stock transactions occurred during 2008 or 2009.
5. All sales were on account.

Instructions

(a) Indicate, by using ratios, the change in liquidity and profitability of Hanshew Company from 2008 to 2009. (*Note*: Not all profitability ratios can be computed.)

(b) Given below are three independent situations and a ratio that may be affected. For each situation, compute the affected ratio (1) as of December 31, 2009, and (2) as of December 31, 2010, after giving effect to the situation. Net income for 2010 was $50,000. Total assets on December 31, 2010, were $700,000.

Situation	Ratio
(1) 18,000 shares of common stock were sold at par on July 1, 2010.	Return on common stockholders' equity
(2) All of the notes payable were paid in 2010. The only change in liabilities was that the notes payable were paid.	Debt to total assets
(3) Market price of common stock was $9 on December 31, 2009, and $12.80 on December 31, 2010.	Price-earnings ratio

Compute selected ratios, and compare liquidity, profitability, and solvency for two companies.

(SO 5)

P14-5 Selected financial data of Target and Wal-Mart for 2005 are presented here (in millions).

	Target Corporation	Wal-Mart Stores, Inc.
	Income Statement Data for Year	
Net sales	$45,682	$285,222
Cost of goods sold	31,445	219,793
Selling and administrative expenses	10,480	51,354
Interest expense	570	986
Other income (expense)	1,157	2,767
Income tax expense	1,146	5,589
Net income	$ 3,198	$ 10,267
	Balance Sheet Data (End of Year)	
Current assets	$13,922	$ 38,491
Noncurrent assets	18,371	81,732
Total assets	$32,293	$120,223
Current liabilities	$ 8,220	$ 42,888
Long-term debt	11,044	27,939
Total stockholders' equity	13,029	49,396
Total liabilities and stockholders' equity	$32,293	$120,223

	Beginning-of-Year Balances	
Total assets	$31,416	$105,405
Total stockholders' equity	11,132	43,623
Current liabilities	8,314	40,364
Total liabilities	20,284	61,782
	Other Data	
Average net receivables	$4,845	$ 1,485
Average inventory	4,958	28,030
Net cash provided by operating activities	3,821	15,044

Instructions

(a) For each company, compute the following ratios.

(1) Current.
(2) Receivables turnover.
(3) Average collection period.
(4) Inventory turnover.
(5) Days in inventory.
(6) Profit margin.
(7) Asset turnover.
(8) Return on assets.
(9) Return on common stockholders' equity.
(10) Debt to total assets.
(11) Times interest earned.

(b) Compare the liquidity, solvency, and profitability of the two companies.

P14-6 The comparative statements of Dillon Company are presented below.

Compute numerous ratios.
(SO 5)

DILLON COMPANY
Income Statement
For Year Ended December 31

	2009	2008
Net sales (all on account)	$600,000	$520,000
Expenses		
Cost of goods sold	415,000	354,000
Selling and administrative	120,800	114,800
Interest expense	7,800	6,000
Income tax expense	18,000	14,000
Total expenses	561,600	488,800
Net income	$ 38,400	$ 31,200

DILLON COMPANY
Balance Sheets
December 31

Assets	2009	2008
Current assets		
Cash	$ 21,000	$ 18,000
Short-term investments	18,000	15,000
Accounts receivable (net)	86,000	74,000
Inventory	90,000	70,000
Total current assets	215,000	177,000
Plant assets (net)	423,000	383,000
Total assets	$638,000	$560,000

Liabilities and Stockholders' Equity		
Current liabilities		
Accounts payable	$122,000	$110,000
Income taxes payable	23,000	20,000
Total current liabilities	145,000	130,000
Long-term liabilities		
Bonds payable	120,000	80,000
Total liabilities	265,000	210,000
Stockholders' equity		
Common stock ($5 par)	150,000	150,000
Retained earnings	223,000	200,000
Total stockholders' equity	373,000	350,000
Total liabilities and stockholders' equity	$638,000	$560,000

Additional data:

The common stock recently sold at $19.50 per share.
The year-end balance in the allowance for doubtful accounts was $3,000 for 2009 and $2,400 for 2008.

Instructions

Compute the following ratios for 2009.

(a) Current.
(b) Acid-test.
(c) Receivables turnover.
(d) Inventory turnover.
(e) Profit margin.
(f) Asset turnover.
(g) Return on assets.
(h) Return on common stockholders' equity.
(i) Earnings per share.
(j) Price-earnings.
(k) Payout.
(l) Debt to total assets.
(m) Times interest earned.

Compute missing information given a set of ratios.

(SO 5)

P14-7 Presented below is an incomplete income statement and an incomplete comparative balance sheet of Cotte Corporation.

COTTE CORPORATION
Income Statement
For the Year Ended December 31, 2009

Sales	$11,000,000
Cost of goods sold	?
Gross profit	?
Operating expenses	1,665,000
Income from operations	?
Other expenses and losses	
Interest expense	?
Income before income taxes	?
Income tax expense	560,000
Net income	$?

COTTE CORPORATION
Balance Sheets
December 31

Assets	2009	2008
Current assets		
Cash	$ 450,000	$ 375,000
Accounts receivable (net)	?	950,000
Inventory	?	1,720,000
Total current assets	?	3,045,000
Plant assets (net)	4,620,000	3,955,000
Total assets	$?	$7,000,000
Liabilities and Stockholders' Equity		
Current liabilities	$?	$ 825,000
Long-term notes payable	?	2,800,000
Total liabilities	?	3,625,000
Common stock, $1 par	3,000,000	3,000,000
Retained earnings	400,000	375,000
Total stockholders' equity	3,400,000	3,375,000
Total liabilities and stockholders' equity	$?	$7,000,000

Additional information:

1. The receivables turnover for 2009 is 10 times.
2. All sales are on account.
3. The profit margin for 2009 is 14.5%.
4. Return on assets is 22% for 2009.
5. The current ratio on December 31, 2009, is 3.0.
6. The inventory turnover for 2009 is 4.8 times.

Instructions
Compute the missing information given the ratios above. Show computations. (*Note*: Start with one ratio and derive as much information as possible from it before trying another ratio. List all missing amounts under the ratio used to find the information.)

Prepare income statement with discontinued operations and extraordinary loss.

(SO 6)

P14-8 Cheaney Corporation owns a number of cruise ships and a chain of hotels. The hotels, which have not been profitable, were discontinued on September 1, 2008. The 2008 operating results for the company were as follows.

Operating revenues	$12,850,000
Operating expenses	8,700,000
Operating income	$ 4,150,000

Analysis discloses that these data include the operating results of the hotel chain, which were: operating revenues $2,000,000 and operating expenses $2,400,000. The hotels were sold at a gain of $200,000 before taxes. This gain is not included in the operating results. During the year, Cheaney suffered an extraordinary loss of $800,000 before taxes, which is not included in the operating results. In 2008, the company had other revenues and gains of $100,000, which are not included in the operating results. The corporation is in the 30% income tax bracket.

Instructions
Prepare a condensed income statement.

Prepare income statement with nontypical items.

(SO 6)

P14-9 The ledger of LaRussa Corporation at December 31, 2008, contains the following summary data.

Net sales	$1,700,000	Cost of goods sold	$1,100,000
Selling expenses	120,000	Administrative expenses	150,000
Other revenues and gains	20,000	Other expenses and losses	28,000

Your analysis reveals the following additional information that is not included in the above data.

1. The entire puzzles division was discontinued on August 31. The income from operations for this division before income taxes was $20,000. The puzzles division was sold at a loss of $90,000 before income taxes.
2. On May 15, company property was expropriated for an interstate highway. The settlement resulted in an extraordinary gain of $120,000 before income taxes.
3. The income tax rate on all items is 30%.

Instructions

Prepare an income statement for the year ended December 31, 2008. Use the format illustrated in the Demonstration Problem (p. 652).

PROBLEMS: SET B

Visit the book's website at **www.wiley.com/college/weygandt**, and choose the Student Companion site, to access Problem Set B.

WATERWAYS CONTINUING PROBLEM

(This is a continuation of the Waterways Problem from Chapters 1 through 13.)

WCP14 Waterways Corporation has prepared comparative balance sheets and income statements for 2007 and 2008. This problem asks you to prepare horizontal and vertical analyses of the income statements and to calculate various ratios.

Go to the book's website,
***www.wiley.com/college/weygandt**,*
to find the completion of this problem.

BROADENING YOUR PERSPECTIVE

Financial Reporting Problem

PepsiCo, Inc.

BYP14-1 Your parents are considering investing in PepsiCo common stock. They ask you, as an accounting expert, to make an analysis of the company for them. The financial statements of PepsiCo can be found at the company's website, **www.pepsico.com.** Note that all dollar amounts are in millions.

Instructions

Refer to PepsiCo's financial statements, and answer the following questions. (Follow the approach in the chapter for rounding numbers.)

(a) Make a 5-year trend analysis, using 2001 as the base year, of (1) net sales and (2) net income. Comment on the significance of the trend results.

(b) Compute for 2005 and 2004 the (1) profit margin, (2) asset turnover, (3) return on assets, and (4) return on common stockholders' equity. How would you evaluate PepsiCo's profitability? Total assets at December 27, 2003, were $25,327, and total stockholders' equity at December 27, 2003, was $11,896.

(c) Compute for 2005 and 2004 the (1) debt to total assets and (2) times interest earned ratio. How would you evaluate PepsiCo's long-term solvency?

(d) What information outside the annual report may also be useful to your parents in making a decision about PepsiCo, Inc.?

Comparative Analysis Problem
PepsiCo, Inc. vs. The Coca-Cola Company

BYP14-2 The financial statements of PepsiCo and The Coca-Cola Company can be found at the companies' websites, **www.pepsico.com** and **www.coca-cola.com.**

Instructions
Refer to the financial statements, and answer the following questions.

(a) Based on the information contained in these financial statements, determine each of the following for each company.
  (1) The percentage increase (decrease) in (i) net sales and (ii) net income from 2004 to 2005.
  (2) The percentage increase in (i) total assets and (ii) total common stockholders' (shareholders') equity from 2004 to 2005.
  (3) The basic earnings per share and price-earnings ratio for 2005. (For Coca-Cola, use the basic earnings per share.) Coca-Cola's common stock had a market price of $43.60 at the end of fiscal-year 2005.

(b) What conclusions concerning the two companies can be drawn from these data?

Decision Making Across the Organization

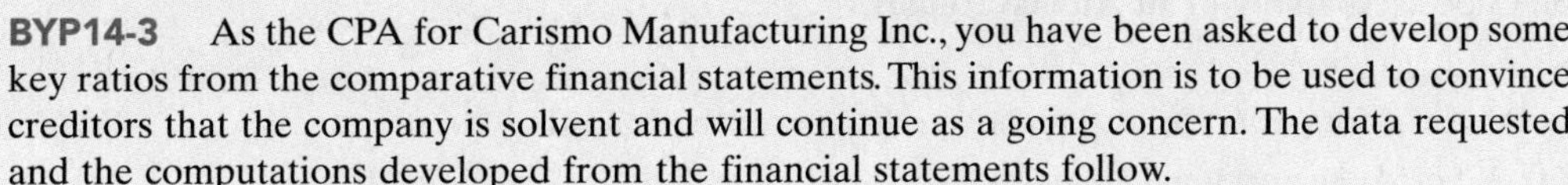

BYP14-3 As the CPA for Carismo Manufacturing Inc., you have been asked to develop some key ratios from the comparative financial statements. This information is to be used to convince creditors that the company is solvent and will continue as a going concern. The data requested and the computations developed from the financial statements follow.

	2008	**2007**
Current ratio	3.1 times	2.1 times
Acid-test ratio	.8 times	1.4 times
Asset turnover	2.8 times	2.2 times
Net income	Up 32%	Down 8%
Earnings per share	$3.30	$2.50

Instructions
With the class divided into groups, answer the following.

Carismo Manufacturing Inc. asks you to prepare a list of brief comments stating how each of these items supports the solvency and going-concern potential of the business. The company wishes to use these comments to support its presentation of data to its creditors. You are to prepare the comments as requested, giving the implications and the limitations of each item separately. Then prepare a collective inference that may be drawn from the individual items about Carismo's solvency and going-concern potential.

BYP14-4 General Dynamics develops, produces, and supports innovative, reliable, and highly sophisticated military and commercial products. In July of a recent year, the corporation announced that its Quincy Shipbuilding Division (Quincy) will be closed following the completion of the Maritime Prepositioning Ship construction program.

Prior to discontinuance, the operating results of Quincy were net sales $246.8 million, income from operations before income taxes $28.3 million, and income taxes $12.5 million. The corporation's loss on disposition of Quincy was $5.0 million, net of $4.3 million income tax benefits.

From its other operating activities, General Dynamics' financial results were net sales $8,163.8 million, cost of goods sold $6,958.8 million, and selling and administrative expenses $537.0 million. In addition, the corporation had interest expense of $17.2 million and interest revenue of $3.6 million. Income taxes were $282.9 million.

General Dynamics had an average of 42.3 million shares of common stock outstanding during the year.

Instructions

With the class divided into groups, answer the following.

(a) Prepare the income statement for the year, assuming that the year ended on December 31, 2008. Show earnings per share data on the income statement. All dollars should be stated in millions, except for per share amounts. (For example, $8 million would be shown as $8.0)

(b) In the preceding year, Quincy's earnings were $51.6 million before income taxes of $22.8 million. For comparative purposes, General Dynamics reported earnings per share of $0.61 from discontinued operations for Quincy in the preceding year.

(1) What was the average number of common shares outstanding during the preceding year?

(2) If earnings per share from continuing operations was $7.47, what was income from continuing operations during the preceding year? (Round to two decimals.)

Exploring the Web

BYP14-5 The Management Discussion and Analysis section of an annual report addresses corporate performance for the year, and sometimes uses financial ratios to support its claims.

Address: www.ibm.com/investor/tools/index.phtml or go to **www.wiley.com/college/weygandt**

Steps

1. From IBM's Investor Tools, choose **Investment Guides**.
2. Choose **Guide to Annual Reports**.
3. Choose **Anatomy of an Annual Report**.

Instructions

Using the information from the above site, answer the following questions.

(a) What are the optional elements that are often included in an annual report?
(b) What are the elements of an annual report that are required by the SEC?
(c) Describe the contents of the Management Discussion.
(d) Describe the contents of the Auditors' Report.
(e) Describe the contents of the Selected Financial Data.

Communication Activity

BYP14-6 Beth Harlan is the CEO of Lafferty's Electronics. Harlan is an expert engineer but a novice in accounting. She asks you to explain (1) the bases for comparison in analyzing Lafferty's financial statements, and (2) the factors affecting quality of earnings.

Instructions

Write a letter to Beth Harlan that explains the bases for comparison and factors affecting quality of earnings.

Ethics Case

BYP14-7 Jack McClintock, president of McClintock Industries, wishes to issue a press release to bolster his company's image and maybe even its stock price, which has been gradually falling. As controller, you have been asked to provide a list of twenty financial ratios along with some other operating statistics relative to McClintock Industries' first quarter financials and operations.

Two days after you provide the ratios and data requested, Jeremy Phelps, the public relations director of McClintock, asks you to prove the accuracy of the financial and operating data contained in the press release written by the president and edited by Jeremy. In the press release, the president highlights the sales increase of 25% over last year's first quarter and the positive change in the current ratio from 1.5:1 last year to 3:1 this year. He also emphasizes that production was up 50% over the prior year's first quarter.

You note that the press release contains only positive or improved ratios and none of the negative or deteriorated ratios. For instance, no mention is made that the debt to total assets ratio has increased from 35% to 55%, that inventories are up 89%, and that while the current ratio improved, the acid-test ratio fell from 1:1 to .5:1. Nor is there any mention that the reported profit for the quarter would have been a loss had not the estimated lives of McClintock's plant and machinery been increased by 30%. Jeremy emphasized, "The prez wants this release by early this afternoon."

Instructions

(a) Who are the stakeholders in this situation?
(b) Is there anything unethical in president McClintock's actions?
(c) Should you as controller remain silent? Does Jeremy have any responsibility?

"All About You" Activity

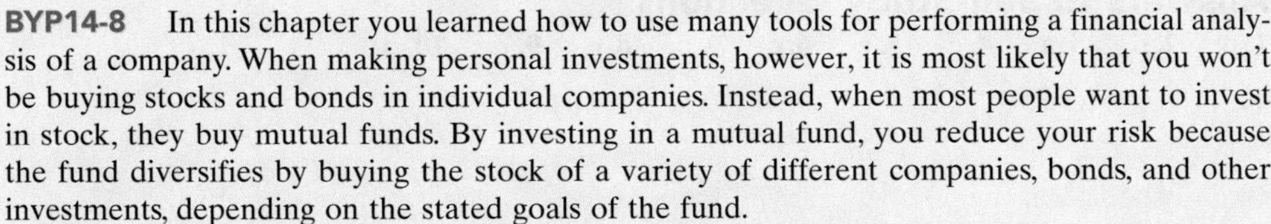

BYP14-8 In this chapter you learned how to use many tools for performing a financial analysis of a company. When making personal investments, however, it is most likely that you won't be buying stocks and bonds in individual companies. Instead, when most people want to invest in stock, they buy mutual funds. By investing in a mutual fund, you reduce your risk because the fund diversifies by buying the stock of a variety of different companies, bonds, and other investments, depending on the stated goals of the fund.

Before you invest in a fund, you will need to decide what type of fund you want. For example, do you want a fund that has the potential of high growth (but also high risk), or are you looking for lower risk and a steady stream of income? Do you want a fund that invests only in U.S. companies, or do you want one that invests globally? Many resources are available to help you with these types of decisions.

Instructions

Go to **http://web.archive.org/web/20050210200843/http://www.cnb1.com/invallocmdl.htm** and complete the investment allocation questionnaire. Add up your total points to determine the type of investment fund that would be appropriate for you.

Answers to Insight and Accounting Across the Organization Questions

How to Manage the Current Ratio, p. 630

Q: How might management influence the company's current ratio?

A: *Management can affect the current ratio by speeding up or withholding payments on accounts payable just before the balance sheet date. Management can alter the cash balance by increasing or decreasing long-term assets or long-term debt, or by issuing or purchasing equity shares.*

Keeping Up to Date as an Investor, p. 638

Q: If you want to keep current with the financial and operating developments of a company in which you own shares, what are some ways you can do so?

A: *You can obtain current information on your investments through a company's Web site, financial magazines, newspapers, and websites, CNBC television programs, investment letters, and a stockbroker.*

What Is Extraordinary?, p. 643

Q: If a company takes a large restructuring charge, what is the effect on the company's current income statement versus future ones?

A: *The current period's net income can be greatly diminished by a large restructuring charge, while the net income in future periods can be enhanced because they are relieved of costs (i.e., depreciation and labor expenses) that would have been charged to them.*

Authors' Comments on *All About You:* Should I Play the Market Yet?, p. 647

For a number of reasons, it is probably a bad idea for Rachael to buy her employer's stock. First, if Rachael is going to invest in the stock market, she should diversify her investments across a number of different companies. Second, you should never have more than a small portion of your total investment portfolio invested in your employer. Suppose that your employer starts to do poorly, the stock price falls, and you get laid off. You lose on two counts: You don't have income, and your net worth has been affected adversely by the drop in the stock price. (This exact situation happened to thousands of Enron employees, who not only lost their jobs, but their retirement savings as well, as Enron's stock plummeted.) Third, after purchasing her employer's stock, Rachael's liquidity would be negatively affected: She would have only $3,000 of remaining liquid assets.

If Rachel invests $7,000, she actually has only enough liquid assets to cover one month's worth of expenses. It is true that she could sell her stock, but if it has fallen in value, she will be reluctant to sell. In short, if she were to buy the stock, her financial flexibility would be very limited.

The bottom line is that we think that Rachael *should* invest in something that offers a higher return than her bank savings account, but we question whether she has enough liquidity to invest in individual stocks. We would recommend that she put some money in a stock mutual fund, some in a short-term CD, and the rest in a money-market fund.

Answers to Self-Study Questions

1. b **2.** d **3.** a **4.** c **5.** c **6.** c **7.** c **8.** c **9.** d **10.** d

Remember to go back to the Navigator box on the chapter-opening page and check off your completed work.

Appendix A

Time Value of Money

STUDY OBJECTIVES

After studying this appendix, you should be able to:

1 Distinguish between simple and compound interest.
2 Solve for future value of a single amount.
3 Solve for future value of an annuity.
4 Identify the variables fundamental to solving present value problems.
5 Solve for present value of a single amount.
6 Solve for present value of an annuity.
7 Compute the present values in capital budgeting situations.
8 Use a financial calculator to solve time value of money problems.

Would you rather receive $1,000 today or a year from now? You should prefer to receive the $1,000 today because you can invest the $1,000 and earn interest on it. As a result, you will have more than $1,000 a year from now. What this example illustrates is the concept of the **time value of money**. Everyone prefers to receive money today rather than in the future because of the interest factor.

NATURE OF INTEREST

STUDY OBJECTIVE 1
Distinguish between simple and compound interest.

Interest is payment for the use of another person's money. It is the difference between the amount borrowed or invested (called the principal) and the amount repaid or collected. The amount of interest to be paid or collected is usually stated as a rate over a specific period of time. The rate of interest is generally stated as an annual rate.

The amount of interest involved in any financing transaction is based on three elements:

1. **Principal (*p*)**: The original amount borrowed or invested.
2. **Interest Rate (*i*)**: An annual percentage of the principal.
3. **Time (*n*)**: The number of years that the principal is borrowed or invested.

Simple Interest

Simple interest is computed on the principal amount only. It is the return on the principal for one period. Simple interest is usually expressed as shown in Illustration A-1 (page A2).

Illustration A-1
Interest computation

Interest	=	Principal p	×	Rate i	×	Time n

For example, if you borrowed $5,000 for 2 years at a simple interest rate of 12% annually, you would pay $1,200 in total interest computed as follows:

$$\text{Interest} = p \times i \times n$$
$$= \$5{,}000 \times .12 \times 2$$
$$= \$1{,}200$$

Compound Interest

Compound interest is computed on principal **and** on any interest earned that has not been paid or withdrawn. It is the return on (or growth of) the principal for two or more time periods. Compounding computes interest not only on the principal but also on the interest earned to date on that principal, assuming the interest is left on deposit.

To illustrate the difference between simple and compound interest, assume that you deposit $1,000 in BankOne, where it will earn simple interest of 9% per year, and you deposit another $1,000 in CityCorp, where it will earn compound interest of 9% per year compounded annually. Also assume that in both cases you will not withdraw any interest until three years from the date of deposit. The computation of interest to be received and the accumulated year-end balances are indicated in Illustration A-2.

Illustration A-2
Simple vs. compound interest

BankOne

Simple Interest Calculation	Simple Interest	Accumulated Year-end Balance
Year 1 $1,000.00 × 9%	$ 90.00	$1,090.00
Year 2 $1,000.00 × 9%	90.00	$1,180.00
Year 3 $1,000.00 × 9%	90.00	$1,270.00
	$ 270.00	

CityCorp.

Compound Interest Calculation	Compound Interest	Accumulated Year-end Balance
Year 1 $1,000.00 × 9%	$ 90.00	$1,090.00
Year 2 $1,090.00 × 9%	98.10	$1,188.10
Year 3 $1,188.10 × 9%	106.93	$1,295.03
	$ 295.03	

$25.03 Difference

Note in the illustration above that simple interest uses the initial principal of $1,000 to compute the interest in all three years. Compound interest uses the accumulated balance (principal plus interest to date) at each year-end to compute interest in the succeeding year—which explains why your compound interest account is larger.

Obviously if you had a choice between investing your money at simple interest or at compound interest, you would choose compound interest, all other things—especially risk—being equal. In the example, compounding provides $25.03 of additional interest income. For practical purposes, compounding assumes that unpaid interest earned becomes a part of the principal, and the accumulated balance at the end of each year becomes the new principal on which interest is earned during the next year.

As can be seen in Illustration A-2, you should invest your money at CityCorp, which compounds interest annually. Compound interest is used in most business situations. Simple interest is generally applicable only to short-term situations of one year or less.

SECTION 1 Future Value Concepts

FUTURE VALUE OF A SINGLE AMOUNT

STUDY OBJECTIVE 2

Solve for future value of a single amount.

The **future value of a single amount** is the value at a future date of a given amount invested assuming compound interest. For example, in Illustration A-2, $1,295.03 is the future value of the $1,000 at the end of three years at 9% interest. The $1,295.03 could be determined more easily by using the following formula.

Illustration A-3
Future value computation

$$FV = p \times (1 + i)^n$$

where

FV = future value of a single amount
p = principal
i = interest rate for one period
n = number of periods

The future value of the CityCorp deposit in Illustration A-2 is computed as follows.

$$\begin{aligned} FV &= p \times (1 + i)^n \\ &= \$1{,}000 \times (1 + .09)^3 \\ &= \$1{,}000 \times 1.29503 \\ &= \$1{,}295.03 \end{aligned}$$

The 1.29503 is computed by multiplying (1.09 × 1.09 × 1.09). The amounts in this example can be depicted in the following time diagram.

Illustration A-4
Time diagram

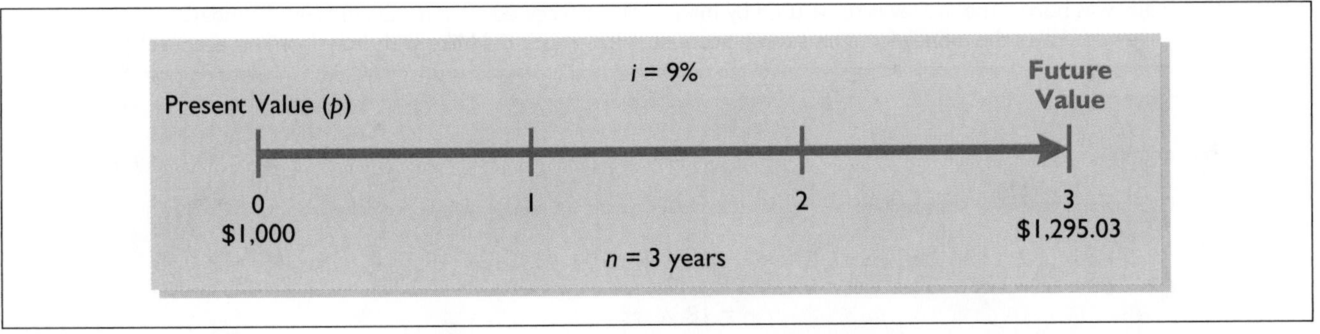

Another method that may be used to compute the future value of a single amount involves the use of a compound interest table. This table shows the future value of 1 for n periods. Table 1, shown at the top of the next page, is such a table.

TABLE 1
Future Value of 1

(n) Periods	4%	5%	6%	8%	9%	10%	11%	12%	15%
1	1.04000	1.05000	1.06000	1.08000	1.09000	1.10000	1.11000	1.12000	1.15000
2	1.08160	1.10250	1.12360	1.16640	1.18810	1.21000	1.23210	1.25440	1.32250
3	1.12486	1.15763	1.19102	1.25971	1.29503	1.33100	1.36763	1.40493	1.52088
4	1.16986	1.21551	1.26248	1.36049	1.41158	1.46410	1.51807	1.57352	1.74901
5	1.21665	1.27628	1.33823	1.46933	1.53862	1.61051	1.68506	1.76234	2.01136
6	1.26532	1.34010	1.41852	1.58687	1.67710	1.77156	1.87041	1.97382	2.31306
7	1.31593	1.40710	1.50363	1.71382	1.82804	1.94872	2.07616	2.21068	2.66002
8	1.36857	1.47746	1.59385	1.85093	1.99256	2.14359	2.30454	2.47596	3.05902
9	1.42331	1.55133	1.68948	1.99900	2.17189	2.35795	2.55803	2.77308	3.51788
10	1.48024	1.62889	1.79085	2.15892	2.36736	2.59374	2.83942	3.10585	4.04556
11	1.53945	1.71034	1.89830	2.33164	2.58043	2.85312	3.15176	3.47855	4.65239
12	1.60103	1.79586	2.01220	2.51817	2.81267	3.13843	3.49845	3.89598	5.35025
13	1.66507	1.88565	2.13293	2.71962	3.06581	3.45227	3.88328	4.36349	6.15279
14	1.73168	1.97993	2.26090	2.93719	3.34173	3.79750	4.31044	4.88711	7.07571
15	1.80094	2.07893	2.39656	3.17217	3.64248	4.17725	4.78459	5.47357	8.13706
16	1.87298	2.18287	2.54035	3.42594	3.97031	4.59497	5.31089	6.13039	9.35762
17	1.94790	2.29202	2.69277	3.70002	4.32763	5.05447	5.89509	6.86604	10.76126
18	2.02582	2.40662	2.85434	3.99602	4.71712	5.55992	6.54355	7.68997	12.37545
19	2.10685	2.52695	3.02560	4.31570	5.14166	6.11591	7.26334	8.61276	14.23177
20	2.19112	2.65330	3.20714	4.66096	5.60441	6.72750	8.06231	9.64629	16.36654

In Table 1, *n* is the number of compounding periods, the percentages are the periodic interest rates, and the decimal numbers in the respective columns are the future value of 1 factors. To use Table 1, multiply the principal amount by the future value factor for the specified number of periods and interest rate. For example, the future value factor for two periods at 9% is 1.18810. Multiplying this factor by $1,000 equals $1,188.10, which is the accumulated balance at the end of year 2 in the CityCorp example in Illustration A-2. The $1,295.03 accumulated balance at the end of the third year can be calculated from Table 1 by multiplying the future value factor for three periods (1.29503) by the $1,000.

The following demonstration problem illustrates how to use Table 1.

Illustration A-5
Demonstration Problem—
Using Table 1 for FV of 1

John and Mary Rich invested $20,000 in a savings account paying 6% interest at the time their son, Mike, was born. The money is to be used by Mike for his college education. On his 18th birthday, Mike withdraws the money from his savings account. How much did Mike withdraw from his account?

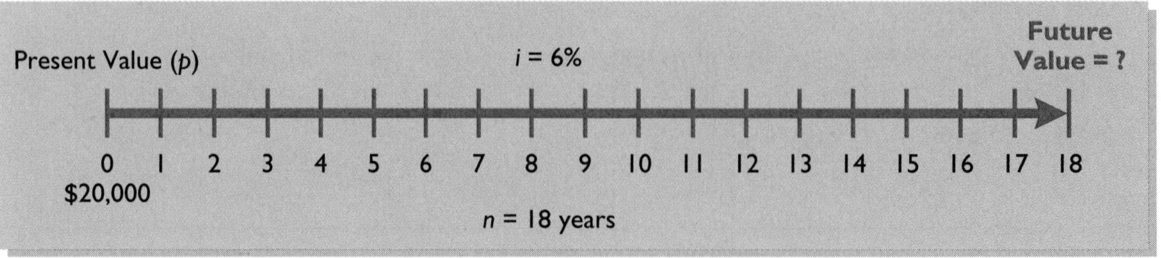

Answer: The future value factor from Table 1 is 2.85434 (18 periods at 6%). The future value of $20,000 earning 6% per year for 18 years is **$57,086.80** ($20,000 × 2.85434).

FUTURE VALUE OF AN ANNUITY

STUDY OBJECTIVE 3

Solve for future value of an annuity.

The preceding discussion involved the accumulation of only a single principal sum. Individuals and businesses frequently encounter situations in which a series of equal dollar amounts are to be paid or received periodically, such as loans or lease (rental) contracts. Such payments or receipts of equal dollar amounts are referred to as **annuities.** The **future value of an annuity** is the sum of all the payments (receipts) plus the accumulated compound interest on them. In computing the future value of an annuity, it is necessary to know (1) the interest rate, (2) the number of compounding periods, and (3) the amount of the periodic payments or receipts.

To illustrate the computation of the future value of an annuity, assume that you invest $2,000 at the end of each year for three years at 5% interest compounded annually. This situation is depicted in the time diagram in Illustration A-6.

Illustration A-6
Time diagram for a three-year annuity

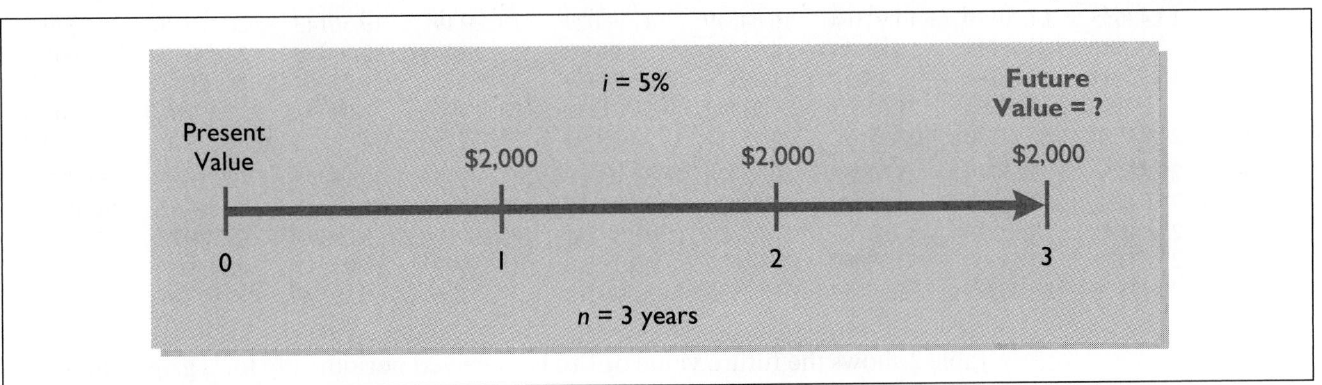

As can be seen in Illustration A-6, the $2,000 invested at the end of year 1 will earn interest for two years (years 2 and 3), and the $2,000 invested at the end of year 2 will earn interest for one year (year 3). However, the last $2,000 investment (made at the end of year 3) will not earn any interest. The future value of these periodic payments could be computed using the future value factors from Table 1 as shown in Illustration A-7.

Illustration A-7
Future value of periodic payments

Year Invested	Amount Invested	×	Future Value of 1 Factor at 5%	=	Future Value
1	$2,000	×	1.10250	=	$ 2,205
2	$2,000	×	1.05000	=	2,100
3	$2,000	×	1.00000	=	2,000
			3.15250		$6,305

The first $2,000 investment is multiplied by the future value factor for two periods (1.1025) because two years' interest will accumulate on it (in years 2 and 3). The second $2,000 investment will earn only one year's interest (in year 3) and therefore is multiplied by the future value factor for one year (1.0500). The final $2,000 investment is made at the end of the third year and will not earn any interest. Consequently, the future value of the last $2,000 invested is only $2,000 since it does not accumulate any interest.

This method of calculation is required when the periodic payments or receipts are not equal in each period. However, when the periodic payments (receipts) are the same in each period, the future value can be computed by using a future value of an annuity of 1 table. Table 2, shown on page A6, is such a table.

TABLE 2
Future Value of an Annuity of 1

(*n*) Periods	4%	5%	6%	8%	9%	10%	11%	12%	15%
1	1.00000	1.00000	1.00000	1.00000	1.00000	1.00000	1.00000	1.00000	1.00000
2	2.04000	2.05000	2.06000	2.08000	2.09000	2.10000	2.11000	2.12000	2.15000
3	3.12160	3.15250	3.18360	3.24640	3.27810	3.31000	3.34210	3.37440	3.47250
4	4.24646	4.31013	4.37462	4.50611	4.57313	4.64100	4.70973	4.77933	4.99338
5	5.41632	5.52563	5.63709	5.86660	5.98471	6.10510	6.22780	6.35285	6.74238
6	6.63298	6.80191	6.97532	7.33592	7.52334	7.71561	7.91286	8.11519	8.75374
7	7.89829	8.14201	8.39384	8.92280	9.20044	9.48717	9.78327	10.08901	11.06680
8	9.21423	9.54911	9.89747	10.63663	11.02847	11.43589	11.85943	12.29969	13.72682
9	10.58280	11.02656	11.49132	12.48756	13.02104	13.57948	14.16397	14.77566	16.78584
10	12.00611	12.57789	13.18079	14.48656	15.19293	15.93743	16.72201	17.54874	20.30372
11	13.48635	14.20679	14.97164	16.64549	17.56029	18.53117	19.56143	20.65458	24.34928
12	15.02581	15.91713	16.86994	18.97713	20.14072	21.38428	22.71319	24.13313	29.00167
13	16.62684	17.71298	18.88214	21.49530	22.95339	24.52271	26.21164	28.02911	34.35192
14	18.29191	19.59863	21.01507	24.21492	26.01919	27.97498	30.09492	32.39260	40.50471
15	20.02359	21.57856	23.27597	27.15211	29.36092	31.77248	34.40536	37.27972	47.58041
16	21.82453	23.65749	25.67253	30.32428	33.00340	35.94973	39.18995	42.75328	55.71747
17	23.69751	25.84037	28.21288	33.75023	36.97351	40.54470	44.50084	48.88367	65.07509
18	25.64541	28.13238	30.90565	37.45024	41.30134	45.59917	50.39593	55.74972	75.83636
19	27.67123	30.53900	33.75999	41.44626	46.01846	51.15909	56.93949	63.43968	88.21181
20	29.77808	33.06595	36.78559	45.76196	51.16012	57.27500	64.20283	72.05244	102.44358

Table 2 shows the future value of 1 to be received periodically for a given number of end-of-period payments. You can see from Table 2 that the future value of an annuity of 1 factor for three periods at 5% is 3.15250. The future value factor is the total of the three individual future value factors as shown in Illustration A-7. Multiplying this amount by the annual investment of $2,000 produces a future value of $6,305.

The demonstration problem in Illustration A-8 illustrates how to use Table 2.

Illustration A-8 Demonstration Problem— Using Table 2 for FV of an annuity of 1

Henning Printing Company knows that in four years it must replace one of its existing printing presses with a new one. To ensure that some funds are available to replace the machine in four years, the company is depositing $25,000 in a savings account at the end of each of the next four years (4 deposits in total). The savings account will earn 6% interest compounded annually. How much will be in the savings account at the end of four years when the new printing press is to be purchased?

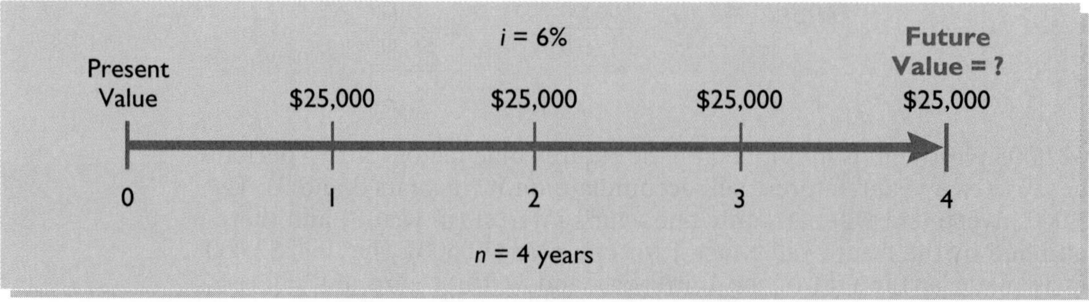

Answer: The future value factor from Table 2 is 4.37462 (4 periods at 6%). The future value of $25,000 invested at the end of each year for four years at 6% interest is **$109,365.50** ($25,000 × 4.37462).

SECTION 2 Present Value Concepts

PRESENT VALUE VARIABLES

STUDY OBJECTIVE 4

Identify the variables fundamental to solving present value problems.

The **present value** is the value now of a given amount to be received in the future, assuming compound interest. Like the future value, it is based on three variables: (1) the dollar amount to be received (future amount), (2) the length of time until the amount is received (number of periods), and (3) the interest rate (the discount rate). The process of determining the present value is referred to as **discounting the future amount**.

In this textbook, present value computations are used in measuring several items. For example, capital budgeting and other investment proposals are evaluated using present value computations. All rate of return and internal rate of return computations involve present value techniques.

PRESENT VALUE OF A SINGLE AMOUNT

STUDY OBJECTIVE 5

Solve for present value of a single amount.

To illustrate present value concepts, assume that you want to invest a sum of money today that will provide $1,000 at the end of one year. What amount would you need to invest today to have $1,000 one year from now? If you want a 10% rate of return, the investment or present value is $909.09 ($1,000 ÷ 1.10). The computation of this amount is shown in Illustration A-9.

Illustration A-9
Present value computation—$1,000 discounted at 10% for one year

$$\text{Present Value} = \textbf{Future Value} \div (1 + i)^1$$

$$PV = FV \div (1 + .10)^1$$
$$PV = \$1{,}000 \div 1.10$$
$$PV = \$909.09$$

The future amount ($1,000), the discount rate (10%), and the number of periods (1) are known. The variables in this situation can be depicted in the following time diagram.

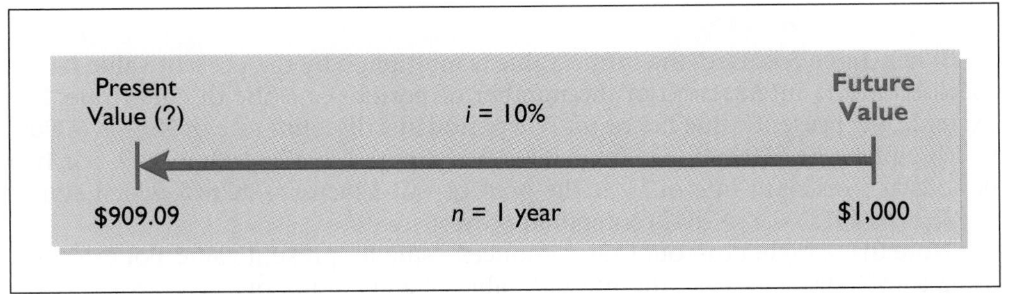

Illustration A-10
Finding present value if discounted for one period

If the single amount of $1,000 is to be received **in two years** and discounted at 10% [PV = $1,000 ÷ $(1 + .10)^2$], its present value is $826.45 [($1,000 ÷ 1.10) ÷ 1.10], as shown in Illustration A-11 (page A8).

Illustration A-11
Finding present value if discounted for two periods

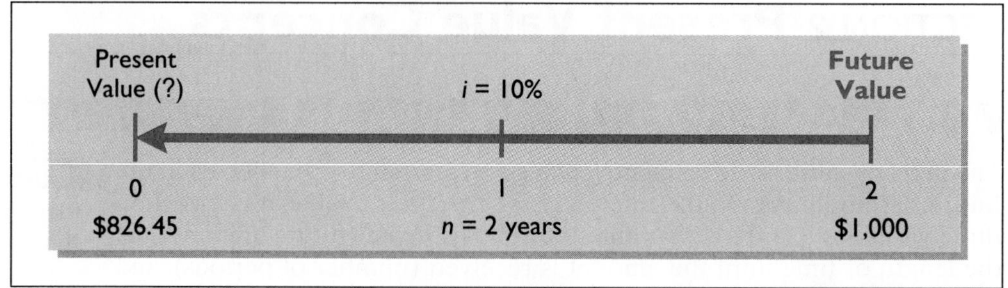

The present value of 1 may also be determined through tables that show the present value of 1 for *n* periods. In Table 3, *n* is the number of discounting periods involved. The percentages are the periodic interest rates or discount rates, and the five-digit decimal numbers in the respective columns are the present value of 1 factors.

TABLE 3
Present Value of 1

(*n*) Periods	4%	5%	6%	8%	9%	10%	11%	12%	15%
1	.96154	.95238	.94340	.92593	.91743	.90909	.90090	.89286	.86957
2	.92456	.90703	.89000	.85734	.84168	.82645	.81162	.79719	.75614
3	.88900	.86384	.83962	.79383	.77218	.75132	.73119	.71178	.65752
4	.85480	.82270	.79209	.73503	.70843	.68301	.65873	.63552	.57175
5	.82193	.78353	.74726	.68058	.64993	.62092	.59345	.56743	.49718
6	.79031	.74622	.70496	.63017	.59627	.56447	.53464	.50663	.43233
7	.75992	.71068	.66506	.58349	.54703	.51316	.48166	.45235	.37594
8	.73069	.67684	.62741	.54027	.50187	.46651	.43393	.40388	.32690
9	.70259	.64461	.59190	.50025	.46043	.42410	.39092	.36061	.28426
10	.67556	.61391	.55839	.46319	.42241	.38554	.35218	.32197	.24719
11	.64958	.58468	.52679	.42888	.38753	.35049	.31728	.28748	.21494
12	.62460	.55684	.49697	.39711	.35554	.31863	.28584	.25668	.18691
13	.60057	.53032	.46884	.36770	.32618	.28966	.25751	.22917	.16253
14	.57748	.50507	.44230	.34046	.29925	.26333	.23199	.20462	.14133
15	.55526	.48102	.41727	.31524	.27454	.23939	.20900	.18270	.12289
16	.53391	.45811	.39365	.29189	.25187	.21763	.18829	.16312	.10687
17	.51337	.43630	.37136	.27027	.23107	.19785	.16963	.14564	.09293
18	.49363	.41552	.35034	.25025	.21199	.17986	.15282	.13004	.08081
19	.47464	.39573	.33051	.23171	.19449	.16351	.13768	.11611	.07027
20	.45639	.37689	.31180	.21455	.17843	.14864	.12403	.10367	.06110

When Table 3 is used, the future value is multiplied by the present value factor specified at the intersection of the number of periods and the discount rate. For example, the present value factor for one period at a discount rate of 10% is .90909, which equals the $909.09 ($1,000 × .90909) computed in Illustration A-9. For two periods at a discount rate of 10%, the present value factor is .82645, which equals the $826.45 ($1,000 × .82645) computed previously.

Note that a higher discount rate produces a smaller present value. For example, using a 15% discount rate, the present value of $1,000 due one year from now is $869.57 versus $909.09 at 10%. It should also be recognized that the further removed from the present the future value is, the smaller the present value. For example, using the same discount rate of 10%, the present value of $1,000 due in **five** years is $620.92 versus $1,000 due in **one** year is $909.09.

The following two demonstration problems (Illustrations A-12, A-13) illustrate how to use Table 3.

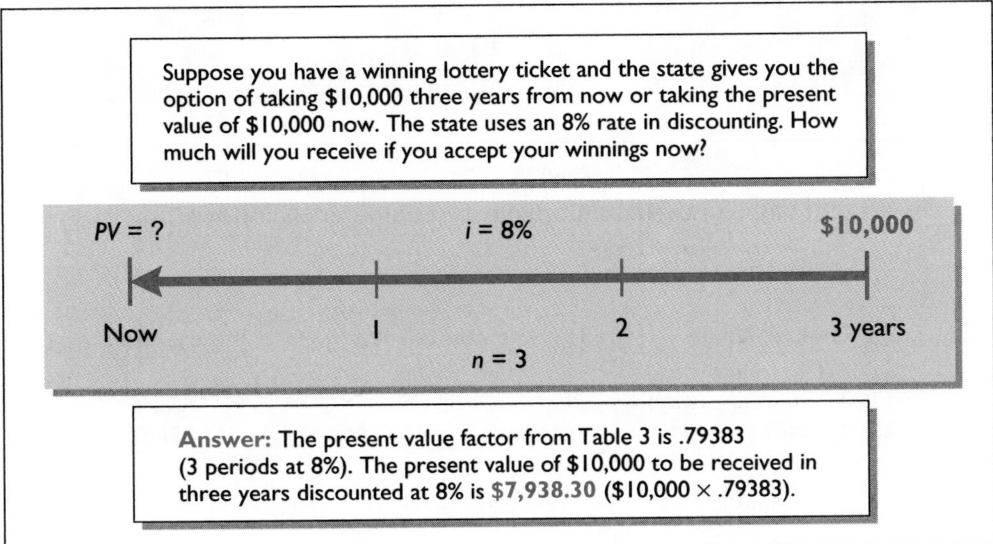

Illustration A-12
Demonstration Problem—
Using Table 3 for PV of 1

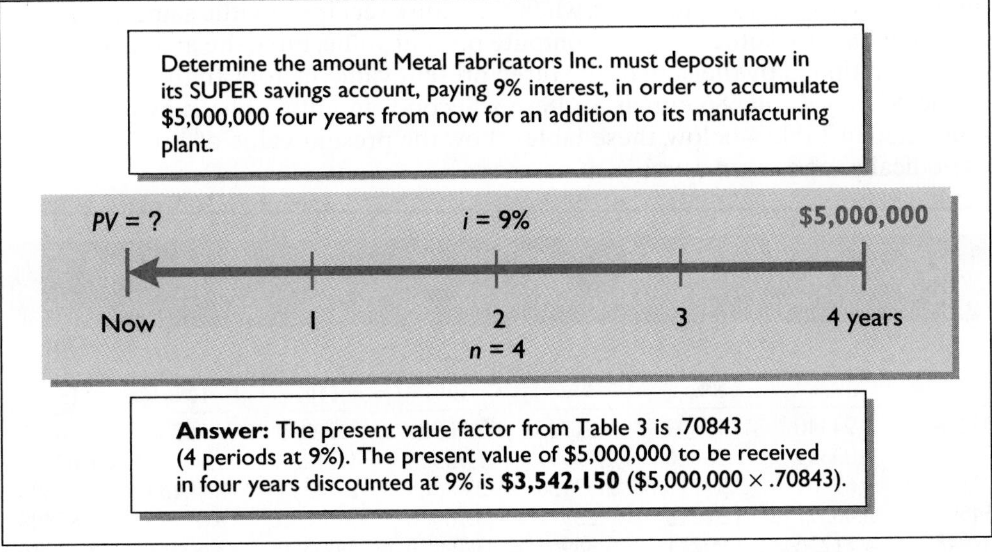

Illustration A-13
Demonstration Problem—
Using Table 3 for PV of 1

PRESENT VALUE OF AN ANNUITY

STUDY OBJECTIVE 6
Solve for present value of an annuity.

The preceding discussion involved the discounting of only a single future amount. Businesses and individuals frequently engage in transactions in which a series of equal dollar amounts are to be received or paid periodically. Examples of a series of periodic receipts or payments are loan agreements, installment sales, mortgage notes, lease (rental) contracts, and pension obligations. These series of periodic receipts or payments are called **annuities**. The **present value of an annuity** is the value now of a series of future receipts or payments, assuming compound interest. In computing the present value of an annuity, it is necessary to know (1) the discount rate, (2) the number of discount periods, and (3) the amount of the periodic receipts or payments.

To illustrate the computation of the present value of an annuity, assume that you will receive $1,000 cash annually for three years at a time when the discount rate is 10%. This situation is depicted in the time diagram in Illustration A-14 (page A10).

Illustration A-14
Time diagram for a three-year annuity

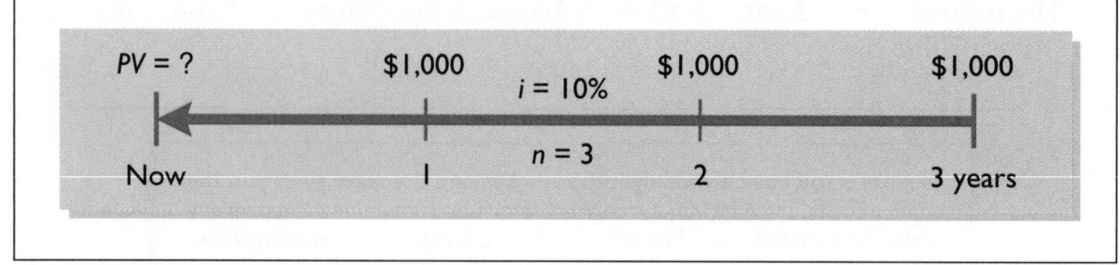

The present value in this situation may be computed as follows.

Illustration A-15
Present value of a series of future amounts computation

Future Amount	×	Present Value of 1 Factor at 10%	=	Present Value
$1,000 (One year away)	×	.90909	=	$ 909.09
1,000 (Two years away)	×	.82645	=	826.45
1,000 (Three years away)	×	.75132	=	751.32
		2.48686		**$2,486.86**

This method of calculation is required when the periodic cash flows are not uniform in each period. However, when the future receipts are the same in each period, there are two other ways to compute present value. First, the annual cash flow can be multiplied by the sum of the three present value factors. In the previous example, $1,000 × 2.48686 equals $2,486.86. Second, annuity tables may be used. As illustrated in Table 4 below, these tables show the present value of 1 to be received periodically for a given number of periods.

TABLE 4
Present Value of an Annuity of 1

(n) Periods	4%	5%	6%	8%	9%	10%	11%	12%	15%
1	.96154	.95238	.94340	.92593	.91743	.90909	.90090	.89286	.86957
2	1.88609	1.85941	1.83339	1.78326	1.75911	1.73554	1.71252	1.69005	1.62571
3	2.77509	2.72325	2.67301	2.57710	2.53130	2.48685	2.44371	2.40183	2.28323
4	3.62990	3.54595	3.46511	3.31213	3.23972	3.16986	3.10245	3.03735	2.85498
5	4.45182	4.32948	4.21236	3.99271	3.88965	3.79079	3.69590	3.60478	3.35216
6	5.24214	5.07569	4.91732	4.62288	4.48592	4.35526	4.23054	4.11141	3.78448
7	6.00205	5.78637	5.58238	5.20637	5.03295	4.86842	4.71220	4.56376	4.16042
8	6.73274	6.46321	6.20979	5.74664	5.53482	5.33493	5.14612	4.96764	4.48732
9	7.43533	7.10782	6.80169	6.24689	5.99525	5.75902	5.53705	5.32825	4.77158
10	8.11090	7.72173	7.36009	6.71008	6.41766	6.14457	5.88923	5.65022	5.01877
11	8.76048	8.30641	7.88687	7.13896	6.80519	6.49506	6.20652	5.93770	5.23371
12	9.38507	8.86325	8.38384	7.53608	7.16073	6.81369	6.49236	6.19437	5.42062
13	9.98565	9.39357	8.85268	7.90378	7.48690	7.10336	6.74987	6.42355	5.58315
14	10.56312	9.89864	9.29498	8.24424	7.78615	7.36669	6.98187	6.62817	5.72448
15	11.11839	10.37966	9.71225	8.55948	8.06069	7.60608	7.19087	6.81086	5.84737
16	11.65230	10.83777	10.10590	8.85137	8.31256	7.82371	7.37916	6.97399	5.95424
17	12.16567	11.27407	10.47726	9.12164	8.54363	8.02155	7.54879	7.11963	6.04716
18	12.65930	11.68959	10.82760	9.37189	8.75563	8.20141	7.70162	7.24967	6.12797
19	13.13394	12.08532	11.15812	9.60360	8.95012	8.36492	7.83929	7.36578	6.19823
20	13.59033	12.46221	11.46992	9.81815	9.12855	8.51356	7.96333	7.46944	6.25933

You can see from Table 4 that the present value of an annuity of 1 factor for three periods at 10% is 2.48685.[1] This present value factor is the total of the three individual present value factors as shown in Illustration A-15. Applying this amount to the annual cash flow of $1,000 produces a present value of $2,486.85.

The following demonstration problem (Illustration A-16) illustrates how to use Table 4.

Illustration A-16
Demonstration Problem—
Using Table 4 for PV of an annuity of 1

Steel Products Company has just signed an agreement to purchase equipment for installment payments of $6,000 each, to be paid at the end of each of the next five years. In setting the amount of the payments, the seller used a discount rate of 12%. What is the present value of the installment payments–that is, how much is Steel Products paying for the equipment, and how much is it paying in total interest over the term of the installment contract?

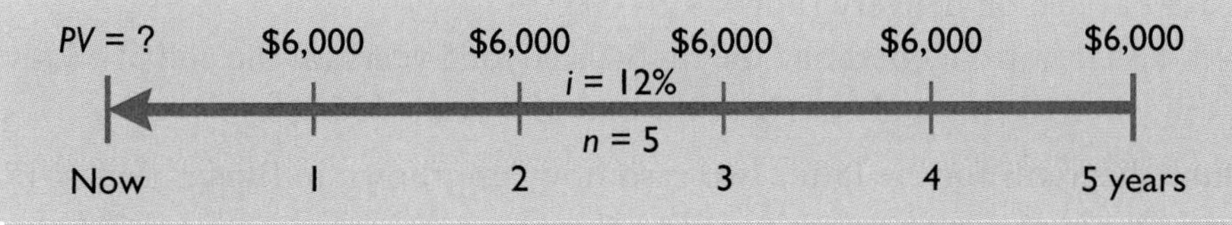

Answer: The present value factor fromTable 4 is 3.60478 (5 periods at 12%). The present value of five payments of $6,000 each discounted at 12% is **$21,628.68** ($6,000 × 3.60478). Therefore, the cost of the equipment to Steel Products is $21,628.68 and the financing charge (interest) is $8,371.32 [($6,000 × 5) – $21,628.68].

TIME PERIODS AND DISCOUNTING

In the preceding calculations, the discounting has been done on an annual basis using an annual interest rate. Discounting may also be done over shorter periods of time such as monthly, quarterly, or semiannually. When the time frame is less than one year, it is necessary to convert the annual interest rate to the applicable time frame.

Assume, for example, that the investor in Illustration A-15 received $500 **semiannually** for three years instead of $1,000 annually. In this case, the number of periods becomes six (3 × 2), the discount rate is 5% (10% ÷ 2), the present value factor from Table 4 is 5.07569 (6 periods at 5%), and the present value of the future cash flows is $2,537.85 (5.07569 × $500). This amount is slightly higher than the $2,486.86 computed in Illustration A-15 because interest is computed twice during the same year. That is, interest is earned on the first half year's interest.

[1] The difference of .00001 between 2.48686 and 2.48685 is due to rounding.

COMPUTING THE PRESENT VALUES IN A CAPITAL BUDGETING DECISION

STUDY OBJECTIVE 7

Compute the present values in capital budgeting situations.

The decision to make long-term capital investments is best evaluated using discounting techniques that recognize the time value of money. To do this, many companies calculate the present value of the cash flows involved in a capital investment.

To illustrate, Nagel-Siebert Trucking Company, a cross-country freight carrier in Montgomery, Illinois, is considering adding another truck to its fleet because of a purchasing opportunity. Navistar Inc., Nagel-Siebert's primary supplier of overland rigs, is overstocked and offers to sell its biggest rig for $154,000 cash payable upon delivery. Nagel-Siebert knows that the rig will produce a net cash flow per year of $40,000 for five years (received at the end of each year), at which time it will be sold for an estimated salvage value of $35,000. Nagel-Siebert's discount rate in evaluating capital expenditures is 10%. Should Nagel-Siebert commit to the purchase of this rig?

The cash flows that must be discounted to present value by Nagel-Siebert are as follows.

Cash payable on delivery (now): $154,000.

Net cash flow from operating the rig: $40,000 for 5 years (at the end of each year).

Cash received from sale of rig at the end of 5 years: $35,000.

The time diagrams for the latter two cash flows are shown in Illustration A-17.

Illustration A-17
Time diagrams for Nagel-Siebert Trucking Company

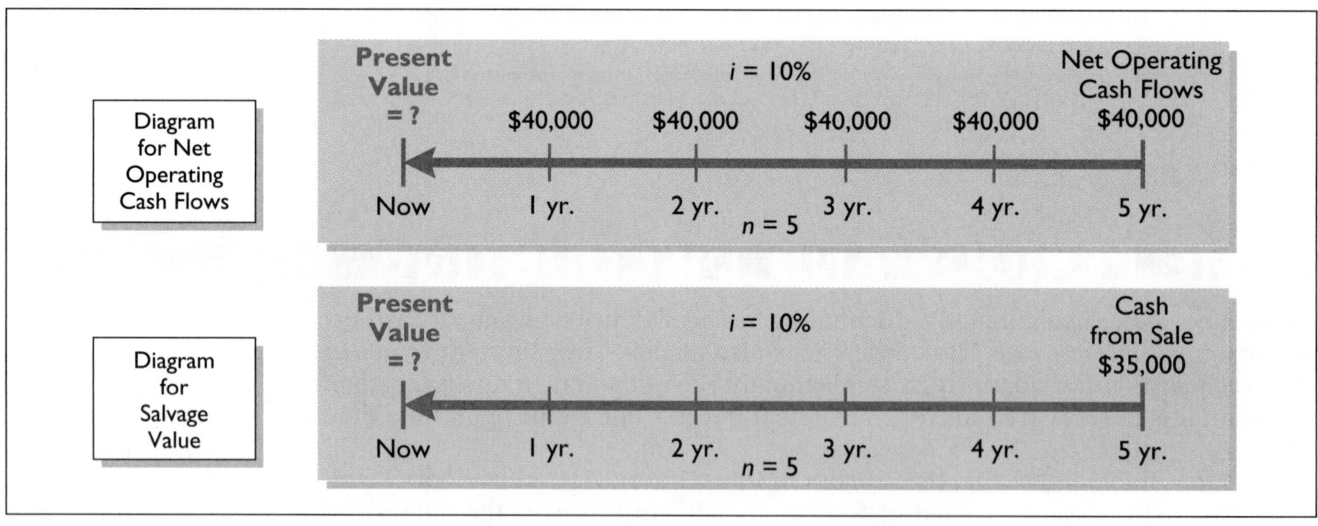

Notice from the diagrams that computing the present value of the net operating cash flows ($40,000 at the end of each year) is **discounting an annuity** (Table 4), while computing the present value of the $35,000 salvage value is **discounting a single sum** (Table 3). The computation of these present values is shown in Illustration A-18 (next page).

Because the present value of the cash receipts (inflows) of $173,363.80 ($151,631.60 + $21,732.20) exceeds the present value of the cash payments

Illustration A-18
Present value computations at 10%

Present Values Using a 10 Percent Discount Rate	
Present value of net operating cash flows received annually over 5 years:	
$40,000 × PV of 1 received annually for 5 years at 10%	
$40,000 × 3.79079 =	$151,631.60
Present value of salvage value (cash) to be received in 5 years	
$35,000 × PV of 1 received in 5 years at 10%	
$35,000 × .62092 =	21,732.20
Present value of cash **inflows**	173,363.80
Present value cash **outflows** (purchase price due now at 10%):	
$154,000 × PV of 1 due now	
$154,000 × 1.00000 =	154,000.00
Net present value	**$ 19,363.80**

(outflows) of $154,000.00, the net present value of $19,363.80 is positive, and **the decision to invest should be accepted.**

Now assume that Nagel-Siebert uses a discount rate of 15%, not 10%, because it wants a greater return on its investments in capital assets. The cash receipts and cash payments by Nagel-Siebert are the same. The present values of these receipts and cash payments discounted at 15% are shown in Illustration A-19.

Illustration A-19
Present value computations at 15 percent

Present Values Using a 15 Percent Discount Rate	
Present value of net operating cash flows received annually over 5 years at 15%:	
$40,000 × 3.35216	$134,086.40
Present value of salvage value (cash) to be received in 5 years at 15%	
$35,000 × .49718	17,401.30
Present value of cash **inflows**	$151,487.70
Present value of cash **outflows** (purchase price due now at 15%):	
$154,000 × 1.00000	154,000.00
Net present value	**$ (2,512.30)**

Because the present value of the cash payments (outflows) of $154,000 exceeds the present value of the cash receipts (inflows) of $151,487.70 ($134,086.40 + $17,401.30), the net present value of $2,512.30 is negative, and **the investment should be rejected.**

The above discussion relied on present value tables in solving present value problems. As we show in the next section, calculators may also be used to compute present values without the use of these tables. Some calculators, especially the "business" or financial calculators, have present value (PV) functions that allow you to calculate present values by merely identifying the proper amount, discount rate, periods, and pressing the PV key.

SECTION 3 Using Financial Calculators

STUDY OBJECTIVE 8

Use a financial calculator to solve time value of money problems.

Business professionals, once they have mastered the underlying concepts in sections 1 and 2, often use a financial (business) calculator to solve time value of money problems. In many cases, they must use calculators if interest rates or time periods do not correspond with the information provided in the compound interest tables.

To use financial calculators, you enter the time value of money variables into the calculator. Illustration A-20 shows the five most common keys used to solve time value of money problems.[2]

Illustration A-20
Financial calculator keys

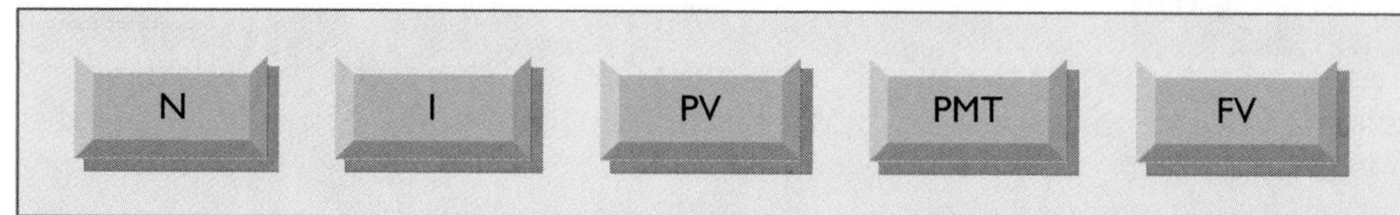

where

N = number of periods

I = interest rate per period (some calculators use I/YR or i)

PV = present value (occurs at the beginning of the first period)

PMT = payment (all payments are equal, and none are skipped)

FV = future value (occurs at the end of the last period)

In solving time value of money problems in this appendix, you will generally be given three of four variables and will have to solve for the remaining variable. The fifth key (the key not used) is given a value of zero to ensure that this variable is not used in the computation.

PRESENT VALUE OF A SINGLE SUM

To illustrate how to solve a present value problem using a financial calculator, assume that you want to know the present value of $84,253 to be received in five years, discounted at 11% compounded annually. Illustration A-21 pictures this problem.

Illustration A-21
Calculator solution for present value of a single sum

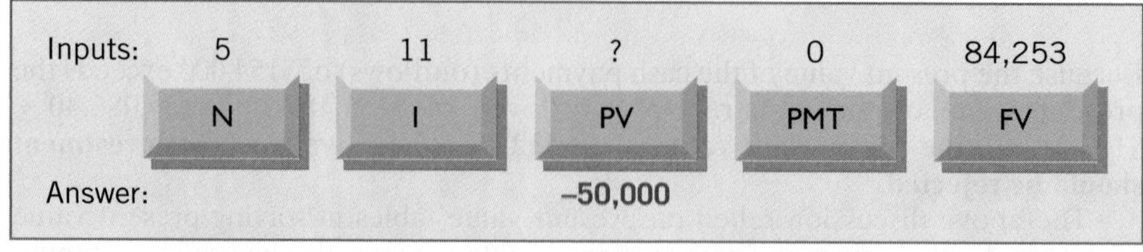

[2]On many calculators, these keys are actual buttons on the face of the calculator; on others they appear on the display after the user accesses a present value menu.

The diagram shows you the information (inputs) to enter into the calculator: N = 5, I = 11, PMT = 0, and FV = 84,253. You then press PV for the answer: −$50,000. As indicated, the PMT key was given a value of zero because a series of payments did not occur in this problem.

Plus and Minus

The use of plus and minus signs in time value of money problems with a financial calculator can be confusing. Most financial calculators are programmed so that the positive and negative cash flows in any problem offset each other. In the present value problem above, we identified the $84,253 future value initial investment as a positive (inflow); the answer −$50,000 was shown as a negative amount, reflecting a cash outflow. If the 84,253 were entered as a negative, then the final answer would have been reported as a positive 50,000.

Hopefully, the sign convention will not cause confusion. If you understand what is required in a problem, you should be able to interpret a positive or negative amount in determining the solution to a problem.

Compounding Periods

In the problem above, we assumed that compounding occurs once a year. Some financial calculators have a default setting, which assumes that compounding occurs 12 times a year. You must determine what default period has been programmed into your calculator and change it as necessary to arrive at the proper compounding period.

Rounding

Most financial calculators store and calculate using 12 decimal places. As a result, because compound interest tables generally have factors only up to five decimal places, a slight difference in the final answer can result. In most time value of money problems, the final answer will not include more than two decimal places.

PRESENT VALUE OF AN ANNUITY

To illustrate how to solve a present value of an annuity problem using a financial calculator, assume that you are asked to determine the present value of rental receipts of $6,000 each to be received at the end of each of the next five years, when discounted at 12%, as pictured in Illustration A-22.

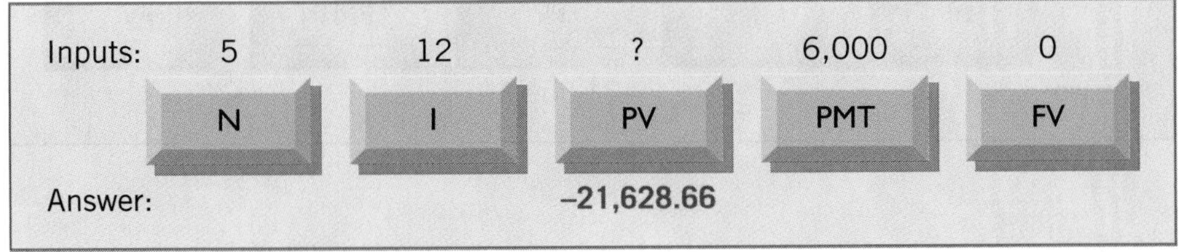

Illustration A-22 Calculator solution for present value of an annuity

In this case, you enter N = 5, I = 12, PMT = 6,000, FV = 0, and then press PV to arrive at the answer of $21, 628.66.

USEFUL APPLICATIONS OF THE FINANCIAL CALCULATOR

With a financial calculator you can solve for any interest rate or for any number of periods in a time value of money problem. Here are some examples of these applications.

Auto Loan

Assume you are financing a car with a three-year loan. The loan has a 9.5% nominal annual interest rate, compounded monthly. The price of the car is \$6,000, and you want to determine the monthly payments, assuming that the payments start one month after the purchase. This problem is pictured in Illustration A-23.

Illustration A-23
Calculator solution for auto loan payments

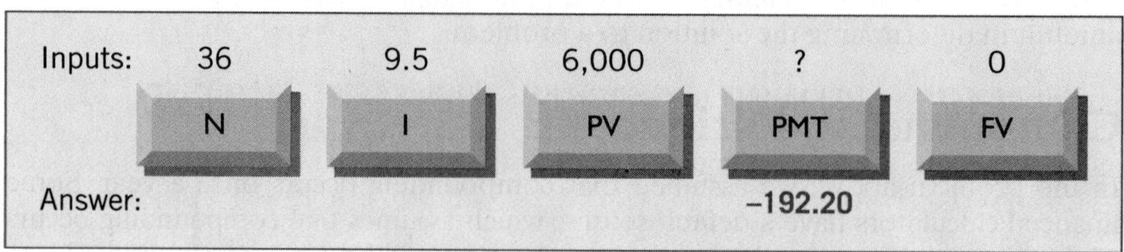

To solve this problem, you enter N = 36 (12 × 3), I = 9.5, PV = 6,000, FV = 0, and then press PMT. You will find that the monthly payments will be \$192.20. Note that the payment key is usually programmed for 12 payments per year. Thus, you must change the default (compounding period) if the payments are other than monthly.

Mortgage Loan Amount

Let's say you are evaluating financing options for a loan on a house. You decide that the maximum mortgage payment you can afford is \$700 per month. The annual interest rate is 8.4%. If you get a mortgage that requires you to make monthly payments over a 15-year period, what is the maximum purchase price you can afford? Illustration A-24 depicts this problem.

Illustration A-24
Calculator solution for mortgage amount

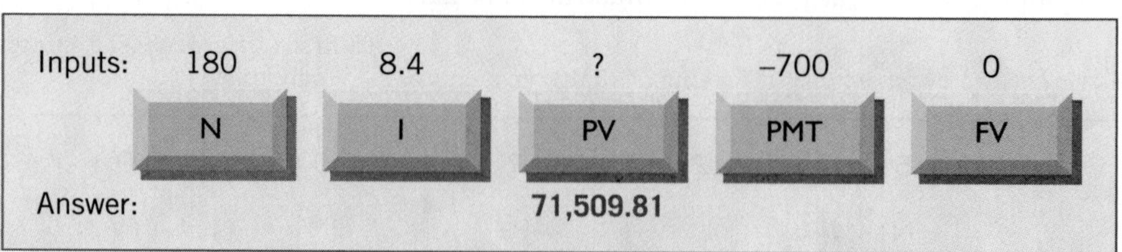

You enter N = 180 (12 × 15 years), I = 8.4, PMT = −700, FV = 0, and press PV. With the payments-per-year key set at 12, you find a present value of \$71,509.81—the maximum house price you can afford, given that you want to keep your mortgage payments at \$700. Note that by changing any of the variables, you can quickly conduct "what-if" analyses for different situations.

SUMMARY OF STUDY OBJECTIVES

1 **Distinguish between simple and compound interest.** Simple interest is computed on the principal only while compound interest is computed on the principal and any interest earned that has not been withdrawn.

2 **Solve for future value of a single amount.** Prepare a time diagram of the problem. Identify the principal amount, the number of compounding periods, and the interest rate. Using the future value of 1 table, multiply the principal amount by the future value factor specified at the intersection of the number of periods and the interest rate.

3 **Solve for future value of an annuity.** Prepare a time diagram of the problem. Identify the amount of the periodic payments (annuities), the number of compounding periods, and the interest rate. Using the future value of an annuity of 1 table, multiply the amount of the annuity by the future value factor specified at the intersection of the number of periods and the interest rate.

4 **Identify the variables fundamental to solving present value problems.** The following three variables are fundamental to solving present value problems: (1) the future amount, (2) the number of periods, and (3) the interest rate (the discount rate).

5 **Solve for present value of a single amount.** Prepare a time diagram of the problem. Identify the future amount, the number of discounting periods, and the discount (interest) rate. Using the present value of 1 table, multiply the future amount by the present value factor specified at the intersection of the number of periods and the discount rate.

6 **Solve for present value of an annuity.** Prepare a time diagram of the problem. Identify the future amounts (annuities), the number of discounting periods, and the discount (interest) rate. Using the present value of an annuity of 1 table, multiply the amount of the annuity by the present value factor specified at the intersection of the number of periods and the interest rate.

7 **Compute the present values in capital budgeting situations.** Compute the present values of all cash inflows and all cash outflows related to the capital budgeting proposal (an investment-type decision). If the **net** present value is positive, accept the proposal (make the investment). If the **net** present value is negative, reject the proposal (do not make the investment).

8 **Use a financial calculator to solve time value of money problems.** Financial calculators can be used to solve the same and additional problems as those solved with time value of money tables. One enters into the financial calculator the amounts for all of the known elements of a time value of money problem (periods, interest rate, payments, future or present value) and solves for the unknown element. Particularly useful situations involve interest rates and compounding periods not presented in the tables.

GLOSSARY

Annuity A series of equal dollar amounts to be paid or received periodically. (p. A5)

Compound interest The interest computed on the principal and any interest earned that has not been paid or withdrawn. (p. A2)

Discounting the future amount(s) The process of determining present value. (p. A7)

Future value of a single amount The value at a future date of a given amount invested assuming compound interest. (p. A3)

Future value of an annuity The sum of all the payments or receipts plus the accumulated compound interest on them. (p. A5)

Interest Payment for the use of another's money. (p. A1)

Present value The value now of a given amount to be received in the future, assuming compound interest. (p. A7)

Present value of an annuity The value now of a series of future receipts or payments, assuming compound interest. (p. A9)

Principal The amount borrowed or invested. (p. A1)

Simple interest The interest computed on the principal only. (p. A1)

BRIEF EXERCISES

Use tables to solve Brief Exercises 1 through 23.
Use a financial calculator to solve Brief Exercises 24 through 28.

BEA-1 Don Smith invested $5,000 at 6% annual interest, and left the money invested without withdrawing any of the interest for 10 years. At the end of the 10 years, Don withdrew the accumulated amount of money.

Compute the future value of a single amount.
(SO 2)

(a) What amount did Don withdraw assuming the investment earns simple interest?
(b) What amount did Don withdraw assuming the investment earns interest compounded annually?

Use future value tables.
(SO 2, 3)

BEA-2 For each of the following cases, indicate (a) to what interest rate columns and (b) to what number of periods you would refer in looking up the future value factor.

1. In Table 1 (future value of 1):

	Annual Rate	Number of Years Invested	Compounded
(a)	6%	5	Annually
(b)	8%	4	Semiannually

2. In Table 2 (future value of an annuity of 1):

	Annual Rate	Number of Years Invested	Compounded
(a)	5%	10	Annually
(b)	4%	6	Semiannually

Compute the future value of a single amount.
(SO 2)

BEA-3 Porter Company signed a lease for an office building for a period of 10 years. Under the lease agreement, a security deposit of $10,000 is made. The deposit will be returned at the expiration of the lease with interest compounded at 4% per year. What amount will Porter receive at the time the lease expires?

Compute the future value of an annuity.
(SO 3)

BEA-4 Gordon Company issued $1,000,000, 10-year bonds and agreed to make annual sinking fund deposits of $75,000. The deposits are made at the end of each year into an account paying 6% annual interest. What amount will be in the sinking fund at the end of 10 years?

Compute the future value of a single amount and of an annuity.
(SO 2, 3)

BEA-5 David and Kathy Hatcher invested $5,000 in a savings account paying 6% annual interest when their daughter, Sue, was born. They also deposited $500 on each of her birthdays until she was 18 (including her 18th birthday). How much will be in the savings account on her 18th birthday (after the last deposit)?

Compute the future value of a single amount.
(SO 2)

BEA-6 Ron Watson borrowed $20,000 on July 1, 2000. This amount plus accrued interest at 8% compounded annually is to be repaid on July 1, 2008. How much will Ron have to repay on July 1, 2008?

Use present value tables.
(SO 5, 6)

BEA-7 For each of the following cases, indicate (a) to what interest rate columns and (b) to what number of periods you would refer in looking up the discount rate.

1. In Table 3 (present value of 1):

	Annual Rate	Number of Years Involved	Discounts Per Year
(a)	12%	5	Semiannually
(b)	10%	15	Annually
(c)	8%	8	Semiannually

2. In Table 4 (present value of an annuity of 1):

	Annual Rate	Number of Years Involved	Number of Payments Involved	Frequency of Payments
(a)	12%	20	20	Annually
(b)	10%	5	5	Annually
(c)	8%	4	8	Semiannually

Determine present values.
(SO 5, 6)

BEA-8 (a) What is the present value of $10,000 due 4 periods from now, discounted at 8%? (b) What is the present value of $10,000 to be received at the end of each of 6 periods, discounted at 9%?

BEA-9 Smolinski Company is considering an investment which will return a lump sum of $500,000, 5 years from now. What amount should Smolinski Company pay for this investment to earn a 12% return?

Compute the present value of a single amount investment.
(SO 5)

BEA-10 Pizzeria Company earns 9% on an investment that will return $600,000, 8 years from now. What is the amount Pizzeria should invest now to earn this rate of return?

Compute the present value of a single amount investment.
(SO 5)

BEA-11 Kilarny Company is considering investing in an annuity contract that will return $20,000 annually at the end of each year for 18 years. What amount should Kilarny Company pay for this investment if it earns a 6% return?

Compute the present value of an annuity investment.
(SO 6)

BEA-12 Zarita Enterprises earns 8% on an investment that pays back $110,000 at the end of each of the next 4 years. What is the amount Zarita Enterprises invested to earn the 8% rate of return?

Compute the present value of an annuity investment.
(SO 6)

BEA-13 Hernandez Railroad Co. is about to issue $100,000 of 10-year bonds paying a 10% interest rate, with interest payable semiannually. The discount rate for such securities is 8%. How much can Hernandez expect to receive from the sale of these bonds?

Compute the present value of bonds.
(SO 5, 6)

BEA-14 Assume the same information as BEA-13 except that the discount rate was 10% instead of 8%. In this case, how much can Hernandez expect to receive from the sale of these bonds?

Compute the present value of bonds.
(SO 5, 6)

BEA-15 Caledonian Taco Company receives a $50,000, 6-year note bearing interest of 8% (paid annually) from a customer at a time when the discount rate is 9%. What is the present value of the note received by Caledonian?

Compute the present value of a note.
(SO 5, 6)

BEA-16 Galway Bay Enterprises issued 10%, 7-year, $2,000,000 par value bonds that pay interest semiannually on October 1 and April 1. The bonds are dated April 1, 2008, and are issued on that date. The discount rate of interest for such bonds on April 1, 2008, is 12%. What cash proceeds did Galway Bay receive from issuance of the bonds?

Compute the present value of bonds.
(SO 5, 6)

BEA-17 Barney Googal owns a garage and is contemplating purchasing a tire retreading machine for $14,280. After estimating costs and revenues, Barney projects a net cash flow from the retreading machine of $2,900 annually for 8 years. Barney hopes to earn a return of 11% on such investments. What is the present value of the retreading operation? Should Barney Googal purchase the retreading machine?

Compute the present value of a machine for purposes of making a purchase decision.
(SO 7)

BEA-18 Hung-Chao Yu Company issues an 8%, 6-year mortgage note on January 1, 2008 to obtain financing for new equipment. Land is used as collateral for the note. The terms provide for semiannual installment payments of $85,242. What were the cash proceeds received from the issuance of the note?

Compute the present value of a note.
(SO 6)

BEA-19 Ramos Company is considering purchasing equipment. The equipment will produce the following cash flows: Year 1, $30,000; Year 2, $40,000; Year 3, $50,000. Ramos requires a minimum rate of return of 12%. What is the maximum price Ramos should pay for this equipment?

Compute the maximum price to pay for a machine.
(SO 7)

BEA-20 Kerry Rodriguez invests $3,555.40 now and will receive $10,000 at the end of 12 years. What annual rate of interest will Kerry earn on her investment? (*Hint:* Use Table 3.)

Compute the interest rate on a single amount.
(SO 5)

BEA-21 Maloney Cork has been offered the opportunity of investing $20,462 now. The investment will earn 12% per year and will at the end of that time return Maloney $100,000. How many years must Maloney wait to receive $100,000? (*Hint:* Use Table 3.)

Compute the number of periods of a single amount.
(SO 5)

BEA-22 Annie Dublin purchased an investment of $9,818.15. From this investment, she will receive $1,000 annually for the next 20 years starting one year from now. What rate of interest will Annie's investment be earning for her? (*Hint:* Use Table 4.)

Compute the interest rate on an annuity.
(SO 6)

BEA-23 Andy Sanchez invests $8,863.25 now for a series of $1,000 annual returns beginning one year from now. Andy will earn a return of 5% on the initial investment. How many annual payments of $1,000 will Andy receive? (*Hint:* Use Table 4.)

Compute the number of periods of an annuity.
(SO 6)

BEA-24 Reba McEntire wishes to invest $19,000 on July 1, 2008, and have it accumulate to $49,000 by July 1, 2018.

Determine interest rate.
(SO 8)

Instructions

Use a financial calculator to determine at what exact annual rate of interest Reba must invest the $19,000.

Determine interest rate.
(SO 8)

BEA-25 On July 17, 2008, Tim McGraw borrowed $42,000 from his grandfather to open a clothing store. Starting July 17, 2009, Tim has to make 10 equal annual payments of $6,500 each to repay the loan.

Instructions

Use a financial calculator to determine what interest rate Tim is paying.

Determine interest rate.
(SO 8)

BEA-26 As the purchaser of a new house, Patty Loveless has signed a mortgage note to pay the Memphis National Bank and Trust Co. $14,000 every 6 months for 20 years, at the end of which time she will own the house. At the date the mortgage is signed the purchase price was $198,000, and Loveless made a down payment of $20,000. The first payment will be made 6 months after the date the mortgage is signed.

Instructions

Using a financial calculator, compute the exact rate of interest earned on the mortgage by the bank.

Various time value of money situations.
(SO 8)

BEA-27 Using a financial calculator, solve for the unknowns in each of the following situations.

(a) On June 1, 2008, Shelley Long purchases lakefront property from her neighbor, Joey Brenner, and agrees to pay the purchase price in seven payments of $16,000 each, the first payment to be payable June 1, 2009. (Assume that interest compounded at an annual rate of 7.35% is implicit in the payments.) What is the purchase price of the property?

(b) On January 1, 2008, Cooke Corporation purchased 200 of the $1,000 face value, 8% coupon, 10-year bonds of Howe Inc. The bonds mature on January 1, 2018, and pay interest annually beginning January 1, 2009. Cooke purchased the bonds to yield 10.65%. How much did Cooke pay for the bonds?

Various time value of money situations.
(SO 8)

BEA-28 Using a financial calculator, provide a solution to each of the following situations.

(a) Bill Schroeder owes a debt of $35,000 from the purchase of his new sport utility vehicle. The debt bears annual interest of 9.1% compounded monthly. Bill wishes to pay the debt and interest in equal monthly payments over 8 years, beginning one month hence. What equal monthly payments will pay off the debt and interest?

(b) On January 1, 2008, Sammy Sosa offers to buy Mark Grace's used snowmobile for $8,000, payable in five equal annual installments, which are to include 8.25% interest on the unpaid balance and a portion of the principal. If the first payment is to be made on December 31, 2008, how much will each payment be?

Appendix B

Standards of Ethical Conduct for Management Accountants

Management accountants have an obligation to the organizations they serve, their profession, the public, and themselves to maintain the highest standards of ethical conduct. In recognition of this obligation, the **Institute of Management Accountants** has published and promoted the following standards of ethical conduct for management accountants.

IMA STATEMENT OF ETHICAL PROFESSIONAL PRACTICE

Members of IMA shall behave ethically. A commitment to ethical professional practice includes: overarching principles that express our values, and standards that guide our conduct.

Principles

IMA's overarching ethical principles include: Honesty, Fairness, Objectivity, and Responsibility. Members shall act in accordance with these principles and shall encourage others within their organizations to adhere to them.

Standards

A member's failure to comply with the following standards may result in disciplinary action.

I. COMPETENCE

Each member has a responsibility to:

1. Maintain an appropriate level of professional expertise by continually developing knowledge and skills.
2. Perform professional duties in accordance with relevant laws, regulations, and technical standards.
3. Provide decision support information and recommendations that are accurate, clear, concise, and timely.
4. Recognize and communicate professional limitations or other constraints that would preclude responsible judgment or successful performance of an activity.

II. CONFIDENTIALITY

Each member has a responsibility to:

1. Keep information confidential except when disclosure is authorized or legally required.
2. Inform all relevant parties regarding appropriate use of confidential information. Monitor subordinates' activities to ensure compliance.
3. Refrain from using confidential information for unethical or illegal advantage.

III. INTEGRITY

Each member has a responsibility to:

1. Mitigate actual conflicts of interest. Regularly communicate with business associates to avoid apparent conflicts of interest. Advise all parties of any potential conflicts.
2. Refrain from engaging in any conduct that would prejudice carrying out duties ethically.
3. Abstain from engaging in or supporting any activity that might discredit the profession.

IV. CREDIBILITY

Each member has a responsibility to:

1. Communicate information fairly and objectively.
2. Disclose all relevant information that could reasonably be expected to influence an intended user's understanding of the reports, analyses, or recommendations.
3. Disclose delays or deficiencies in information, timeliness, processing, or internal controls in conformance with organization policy and/or applicable law.

Resolution of Ethical Conflict

In applying the Standards of Ethical Professional Practice, you may encounter problems identifying unethical behavior or resolving an ethical conflict. When faced with ethical issues, you should follow your organization's established policies on the resolution of such conflict. If these policies do not resolve the ethical conflict, you should consider the following courses of action:

1. Discuss the issue with your immediate supervisor except when it appears that the supervisor is involved. In that case, present the issue to the next level. If you cannot achieve a satisfactory resolution, submit the issue to the next management level. If your immediate superior is the chief executive officer or equivalent, the acceptable reviewing authority may be a group such as the audit committee, executive committee, board of directors, board of trustees, or owners. Contact with levels above the immediate superior should be initiated only with your superior's knowledge, assuming he or she is not involved. Communication of such problems to authorities or individuals not employed or engaged by the organization is not considered appropriate, unless you believe there is a clear violation of the law.
2. Clarify relevant ethical issues by initiating a confidential discussion with an IMA Ethics Counselor or other impartial advisor to obtain a better understanding of possible courses of action.
3. Consult your own attorney as to legal obligations and rights concerning the ethical conflict.

Source: Institute of Management Accountants, *www.imanct.org/pdf/981.pdf*. Reprinted by permission.

CASES FOR
Management Decision Making

Case	Overview
CASE 1 *Greetings Inc.: Job Order Costing*	This case is the first in a series of four cases that presents a business situation in which a traditional retailer decides to employ Internet technology to expand its sales opportunities. It requires the student to employ traditional job order costing techniques and then requests an evaluation of the resulting product costs. (Related to Chapter 2, Job Order Costing.)
CASE 2 *Greetings Inc.: Activity-Based Costing*	This case focuses on decision-making benefits of activity-based costing relative to the traditional approach. It also offers an opportunity to discuss the cost/benefit trade-off between simple ABC systems versus refined systems, and the potential benefit of using capacity rather than expected sales when allocating fixed overhead costs. (Related to Chapter 4, Activity-Based Costing.)
CASE 3 *Greetings Inc.: Transfer Pricing Issues*	This case illustrates the importance of proper transfer pricing for decision making as well as performance evaluation. The student is required to evaluate profitability using two different transfer pricing approaches and comment on the terms of the proposed transfer pricing agreement. (Related to Chapter 8, Pricing.)
CASE 4 *Greetings Inc.: Capital Budgeting*	This case is set in an environment in which the company is searching for new opportunities for growth. It requires evaluation of a proposal based on initial estimates as well as sensitivity analysis. It also requires evaluation of the underlying assumptions used in the analysis. (Related to Chapter 12, Planning for Capital Investments.)
CASE 5 *Auburn Circular Club Pro Rodeo Roundup*	This comprehensive case is designed to be used as a capstone activity at the end of the course. It deals with a not-for-profit service company. The case involves many managerial accounting issues that would be common for a start-up business. (Related to Chapter 5, Cost-Volume-Profit; Chapter 7, Incremental Analysis; and Chapter 9, Budgetary Planning.)
CASE 6 *Sweats Galore*	This case focuses on setting up a new business. In planning for this new business, the preparation of budgets is emphasized. In addition, an understanding of cost-volume-profit relationships is required. (Related to Chapter 5, Cost-Volume-Profit, and Chapter 9, Budgetary Planning.)
CASE 7 *Armstrong Helmet Company*	This comprehensive case involves finding the cost for a given product. In addition, it explores cost-volume-profit relationships. It requires the preparation of a set of budgets. (Related to Chapter 1, Managerial Accounting; Chapter 5, Cost-Volume-Profit; Chapter 9, Budgetary Planning; Chapter 10, Budgetary Control and Responsibility Accounting; Chapter 11, Standard Costs and Balanced Scorecard; and Chapter 12, Planning for Capital Investments.)

Greetings Inc.

Greetings Inc.: Job Order Costing

Developed by Thomas L. Zeller, Loyola University Chicago, and Paul D. Kimmel, University of Wisconsin–Milwaukee

The Business Situation

Greetings Inc. has operated for many years as a nationally recognized retailer of greeting cards and small gift items. It has 1,500 stores throughout the United States located in high-traffic malls.

As the stock price of many other companies soared, Greetings' stock price remained flat. As a result of a heated 2007 shareholders' meeting, the president of Greetings, Robert Burns, came under pressure from shareholders to grow Greetings' stock value. As a consequence of this pressure, in 2008 Mr. Burns called for a formal analysis of the company's options with regard to business opportunities.

Location was the first issue considered in the analysis. Greetings stores are located in high-traffic malls where rental costs are high. The additional rental cost was justified, however, by the revenue that resulted from these highly visible locations. In recent years, though, the intense competition from other stores in the mall selling similar merchandise has become a disadvantage of the mall locations.

Mr. Burns felt that to increase revenue in the mall locations, Greetings would need to attract new customers and sell more goods to repeat customers. In order to do this, the company would need to add a new product line. However, to keep costs down, the product line should be one that would not require much additional store space. In order to improve earnings, rather than just increase revenues, Greetings would have to carefully manage the costs of this new product line.

After careful consideration of many possible products, the company's management found a product that seemed to be a very good strategic fit for its existing products: high-quality unframed and framed prints. The critical element of this plan was that customers would pick out prints by viewing them on wide-screen computer monitors in each store. Orders would be processed and shipped from a central location. Thus, store size would not have to increase at all. To offer these products, Greetings established a new e-business unit called Wall Décor. Wall Décor is a "profit center"; that is, the manager of the new business unit is responsible for decisions affecting both revenues and costs.

Wall Décor was designed to distribute unframed and framed print items to each Greetings store on a just-in-time (JIT) basis. The system works as follows: The Wall Décor website allows customers to choose from several hundred prints. The print can be purchased in various forms: unframed, framed with a metal frame and no matting, or framed with a wood frame and matting. When a customer purchases an unframed print, it is packaged and shipped the same day from Wall Décor. When a customer purchases a framed print, the print is framed at Wall Décor and shipped within 48 hours.

Each Greetings store has a computer linked to Wall Décor's Web server so Greetings customers can browse the many options to make a selection. Once a selection is made, the customer can complete the order immediately. Store employees are trained to help customers use the website and complete the purchase. The advantage to this approach is that each Greetings store, through the Wall Décor website, can offer a wide variety of prints, yet the individual Greetings stores do not have to hold any inventory of prints or framing materials. About the only cost to the individual store is the computer and high-speed line connection to Wall Décor. The advantage to the customer is the wide variety of unframed and framed print items that can be conveniently purchased and delivered to the home or business, or to a third party as a gift.

Wall Décor uses a traditional job-order costing system. Operation of Wall Décor would be substantially less complicated, and overhead costs would be substantially less, if it sold only unframed prints. Unframed prints require no additional processing, and they can be easily shipped in simple protective tubes. Framing and matting requires the company to have multiple matting colors and frame styles, which requires considerable warehouse space. It also requires skilled employees to assemble the products and more expensive packaging procedures.

Manufacturing overhead is allocated to each unframed or framed print, based on the cost of the print. This overhead allocation approach is based on the assumption that more expensive prints will usually be framed and therefore more overhead costs should be assigned to these items. The predetermined overhead rate is the total expected manufacturing overhead divided by the total expected cost of prints. This method of allocation appeared reasonable to the accounting team and distribution floor manager. Direct labor costs for unframed prints consist of picking the prints off the shelf and packaging them for shipment. For framed prints, direct labor costs consist of picking the prints, framing, matting, and packaging.

The information in Illustration CA 1-1 on the next page for unframed and framed prints was collected by the accounting and production teams. The manufacturing overhead budget is presented in Illustration CA 1-2.

Instructions

Use the information in the case and your reading from Chapters 1 and 2 of the text to answer each of the following questions.

1. Define and explain the meaning of a predetermined manufacturing overhead rate that is applied in a job-order costing system.

2. What are the advantages and disadvantages of using the cost of each print as a manufacturing overhead cost driver?

3. Using the information on the next page, compute and interpret the predetermined manufacturing overhead rate for Wall Décor.

	Unframed Print	Steel-Framed Print, No Matting	Wood-Framed Print, with Matting
Volume—expected units sold	80,000	15,000	7,000
Cost Elements			
Direct materials			
Print (expected average cost for each of the three categories)	$12	$16	$20
Frame and glass		$4	$6
Matting			$4
Direct labor			
Picking time	10 minutes	10 minutes	10 minutes
Picking labor rate/hour	$12	$12	$12
Matting and framing time		20 minutes	30 minutes
Matting and framing rate/hour		$21	$21

Illustration CA 1-1 Information about prints and framed items for Wall Décor

Manufacturing Overhead Budget	
Supervisory salaries	$100,000
Factory rent	130,200
Equipment rent (framing and matting equipment)	50,000
Utilities	20,000
Insurance	10,000
Information technology	50,000
Building maintenance	11,000
Equipment maintenance	4,000
Budgeted total manufacturing overhead costs	$375,200

Illustration CA 1-2 Manufacturing overhead budget for Wall Décor

4. Compute the product cost for the following three items.
   (a) Lance Armstrong unframed print (base cost of print $12).
   (b) John Elway print in steel frame, no mat (base cost of print $16).
   (c) Lambeau Field print in wood frame with mat (base cost of print $20).
5. **(a)** How much of the total overhead cost is expected to be allocated to unframed prints?
   (b) How much of the total overhead cost is expected to be allocated to steel framed prints?
   (c) How much of the total overhead cost is expected to be allocated to wood framed prints?
   (d) What percentage of the total overhead cost is expected to be allocated to unframed prints?
6. Do you think the amount of overhead allocated to the three product categories is reasonable? Relate your response to this question to your findings in previous questions.
7. Anticipate business problems that may result from allocating manufacturing overhead based on the cost of the prints.

Case 2

Greetings Inc.

Greetings Inc.: Activity-Based Costing

Developed by Thomas L. Zeller, Loyola University Chicago, and Paul D. Kimmel, University of Wisconsin–Milwaukee

The Business Situation

Mr. Burns, president of Greetings Inc., created the Wall Décor unit of Greetings three years ago to increase the company's revenue and profits. Unfortunately, even though Wall Décor's revenues have grown quickly, Greetings appears to be losing money on Wall Décor. Mr. Burns has hired you to provide consulting services to Wall Décor's management. Your assignment is to make Wall Décor a profitable business unit.

Your first step is to talk with the Wall Décor work force. From your conversations with store managers you learn that the individual Greetings stores are very happy with the Wall Décor arrangement. The stores are generating additional sales revenue from the sale of unframed and framed prints. They are especially enthusiastic about this revenue source because the online nature of the product enables them to generate revenue without the additional cost of carrying inventory. Wall Décor sells unframed and framed prints to each store at product cost plus 20%. A 20% mark-up on products is a standard policy of all Greetings intercompany transactions. Each store is allowed to add an additional mark-up to the unframed and framed print items according to market pressures. That is, the selling price charged by each store for unframed and framed prints is determined by each store manager. This policy ensures competitive pricing in the respective store locations, an important business issue because of the intense mall competition.

While the store managers are generally happy with the Wall Décor products, they have noted a significant difference in the sales performance of the unframed prints and the framed prints. They find it difficult to sell unframed prints at a competitive price. The price competition in the malls is very intense. On average, stores find that the profits on unframed prints are very low because the cost for unframed prints charged by Wall Décor to the Greetings stores is only slightly below what competing stores charge their customers for unframed prints. As a result, the profit margin on unframed prints is very low, and the overall profit earned is small, even with the large volume of prints sold. In contrast, stores make a very good profit on framed prints and still beat the nearest competitor's price by about 15%. That is, the mall competitors cannot meet at a competitive price the quality of framed prints provided by the Greetings stores. As a result, store managers advertise the lowest prices in town for high-quality framed prints. One store manager referred to

Wall Décor's computer on the counter as a "cash machine" for framed prints and a "lemonade stand" for unframed prints.

In a conversation with the production manager you learned that she believes that the relative profitability of framed and unframed prints is distorted because of improper product costing. She feels that the costs provided by the company's traditional job-order costing system are inaccurate. From the very beginning, she has carefully managed production and distribution costs. She explains, "Wall Décor is essentially giving away expensive framed prints, and it appears that it is charging the stores too much for unframed prints." In her office she shows you her own product costing system, which supports her point of view.

Your tour of the information technology (IT) department provided additional insight as to why Wall Décor is having financial problems. You discovered that to keep the website running requires separate computer servers and several information technology professionals. Two separate activities are occurring in the technology area. First, purchasing professionals and IT professionals spend many hours managing thousands of prints and frame and matting materials. Their tasks include selecting the prints and the types of framing material to sell. They also must upload, manage, and download prints and framing material onto and off of the website. The IT staff tells you much of their time is spent with framing and matting material. Only a highly skilled IT professional can properly scan a print and load it up to the site so that it graphically represents what the print will look like when properly matted and framed.

In addition, you discover that a different team of IT professionals is dedicated to optimizing the operating performance of the website. These costs are classified as manufacturing overhead because a substantial amount of work is required to keep the site integrated with purchasing and production and to safeguard Wall Décor's assets online. Most time-consuming is the effort to develop and maintain the site so that customers can view the prints as they would appear either unframed or framed and matted.

A discussion with the IT professionals suggests that the time spent developing and maintaining the site for the unframed prints is considerably less than that required for the framed prints and in particular for the framed and matted prints. Developing and maintaining a site that can display the unframed prints is relatively straightforward. It becomes more complicated when the site must allow the customer to view every possible combination of print with every type of steel frame, and immensely more complicated when one considers all of the possible wood frames and different matting colors. Obviously, a very substantial portion of the IT professionals' time and resources is required to present the over 1,000 different framing and matting options.

Based on your preliminary findings, you have decided that the company's ability to measure and evaluate the profitability of individual products would be improved if the company employed an activity-based costing (ABC) system. As a first step in this effort, you compiled a list of costs, activities, and values. Your work consisted of taking the original manufacturing overhead cost ($375,200, provided in Case 1) and allocating the costs to activities. You identified four activities: picking prints; inventory selection and management (includes general management and overhead); website optimization; and framing and matting cost (includes equipment, insurance, rent, and supervisor's salary).

The first activity is picking prints. The estimated overhead related to this activity is $30,600. The cost driver for this activity is the number of prints. It is expected that the total number of prints will be 102,000. This is the sum of 80,000 unframed, 15,000 steel-framed, and 7,000 wood-framed.

Illustration CA 2-1
Information for activity 1

Activity	Cost Driver	Estimated Overhead	Expected Use of Cost Driver
Picking prints	Number of prints	$30,600	(80,000 + 15,000 + 7,000) = 102,000 prints

The second activity is inventory selection and management. The estimated overhead related to this activity is $91,700. The cost driver for this activity is the number of components per print item. An unframed print has one component, a steel-framed print has two components (the print and the frame), and a wood-framed print has three components (the print, the mat, and the frame). The total number of components is expected to be 131,000.

Illustration CA 2-2
Information for activity 2

Activity	Cost Driver	Estimated Overhead	Expected Use of Cost Driver
Inventory selection and management	Number of components: Print (1) Print and frame (2) Print, mat, and frame (3)	$91,700	Prints: 80,000 components Print and frame: 15,000 × 2 = 30,000 components Print, mat, and frame: 7,000 × 3 = 21,000 components Total = 131,000 components

The third activity is website optimization. The total overhead cost related to website optimization is expected to be $129,000. It was difficult to identify a cost driver that directly related website optimization to the products. In order to reflect the fact that the majority of the time spent on this activity related to framed prints, you first split the cost of website optimization between unframed prints and framed prints. Based on your discussion with the IT professionals, you determined that they spend roughly one-fifth of their time developing and maintaining the site for unframed prints, and the other four-fifths of their time on framed prints, even though the number of framed prints sold is substantially less than the number of unframed prints. As a consequence, you allocated $25,800 of the overhead costs related to website optimization to unframed prints and $103,200 to framed prints. You contemplated having three categories (unframed, steel-framed, and wood-framed with matting), but chose not to add this additional refinement.

Illustration CA 2-3
Information for activity 3

Activity	Cost Driver	Estimated Overhead	Expected Use of Cost Driver
Web-site optimization:			
Unframed	Number of prints at capacity	$25,800	Unframed prints: 100,000 print capacity
Framed	Number of prints at capacity	$103,200	Framed and/or matted prints: 25,000 print capacity (16,000 steel; 9,000 wood)

Once the $129,000 of the third activity was allocated across the two broad product categories, the number of prints at *operating capacity* was used as the cost driver. Note that operating capacity was used instead of expected units sold. The overhead costs related to website optimization are relatively fixed because the employees are salaried. If a fixed cost is allocated using a value that varies from period to period (like expected sales), then the cost per unit will vary from period to period. When allocating fixed costs it is better to use a base that does not vary as much, such as operating capacity. The advantage of using operating capacity as the base is that it keeps the fixed costs per unit stable over time.

The final activity is framing and matting. The expected overhead costs related to framing and matting are $123,900. None of this overhead cost should be allocated to unframed prints. The costs related to framing and matting are relatively fixed because the costs relate to equipment and other costs that do not vary with sales volume. As a consequence, like website optimization, you chose to base the cost driver on levels at operating *capacity*, rather than at the expected sales level. The cost driver is the number of components. Steel-framed prints have two components (the print and frame), and wood-framed prints have three components (the print, mat, and frame). The total components at operating capacity would be steel frame 32,000 or (16,000 × 2) and wood frame 27,000 or (9,000 × 3,000).

Illustration CA 2-4
Information for activity 4

Activity	Cost Driver	Estimated Overhead	Expected Use of Cost Driver
Framing and matting cost (equipment, insurance, rent, and supervisory labor)	Number of components at capacity	$123,900	Print and frame: 16,000 × 2 = 32,000 components at capacity Print, mat, and frame: 9,000 × 3 = 27,000 components at capacity Total = 59,000 components

To summarize, the overhead costs and cost drivers used for each product are expected to be:

Illustration CA 2-5
Summary of overhead costs and cost drivers

Activity	Cost Driver	Unframed	Steel-Framed, No Matting	Wood-Framed, with Matting	Total	Overhead Cost
1. Picking prints	Number of prints	80,000	15,000	7,000	102,000	$ 30,600
2. Inventory selection and management	Number of components	80,000	30,000	21,000	131,000	91,700
3. Website optimization	Number of prints at capacity	100,000			100,000	25,800
			16,000	9,000	25,000	103,200
4. Framing and matting	Number of components at capacity	na	32,000	27,000	59,000	123,900
						$375,200

Instructions

Answer the following questions.

1. Identify two reasons why an activity-based costing system may be appropriate for Wall Décor.
2. Compute the activity-based overhead rates for each of the four activities.
3. Compute the product cost for the following three items using ABC. (Review Case 1 for additional information that you will need to answer this question.)
   (a) Lance Armstrong unframed print (base cost of print $12)
   (b) John Elway print in steel frame, no mat (base cost of print $16)
   (c) Lambeau Field print in wood frame with mat (base cost of print $20)
4. In Case 1 for Greetings, the overhead allocations using a traditional volume-based approach were $3.36 for Lance Armstrong, $4.48 for John Elway, and $5.60 for Lambeau Field. The total product costs from Case 1 were Lance Armstrong $17.36, John Elway $33.48, and Lambeau Field $48.10. The overhead allocation rate for unframed prints, such as the unframed Lance Armstrong print in question 3, decreased under ABC compared to the amount of overhead that was allocated under the traditional approach in Case 1. Why is this the case? What are the potential implications for the company?
5. Explain why the overhead cost related to website optimization was first divided into two categories (unframed prints and framed prints) and then allocated based on number of prints.
6. When allocating the cost of website optimization, the decision was made to initially allocate the cost across two categories (unframed prints and framed prints) rather than three categories (unframed prints, steel-framed prints, and wood-framed prints with matting). Discuss the pros and cons of splitting the cost between two categories rather than three.
7. Discuss the implications of using operating *capacity* as the cost driver rather than the expected units sold when allocating fixed overhead costs.
8. **(a)** Allocate the overhead to the three product categories (unframed prints, steel-framed prints, and wood-framed prints with matting), assuming that the estimate of the expected units sold is correct and the actual amount of overhead incurred equaled the estimated amount of $375,200.
   (b) Calculate the total amount of overhead allocated. Explain why the total overhead of $375,200 was not allocated, even though the estimate of sales was correct. What are the implications of this for management?

Greetings Inc.

Greetings Inc.: Transfer Pricing Issues

Developed by Thomas L. Zeller, Loyola University Chicago, and Paul D. Kimmel, University of Wisconsin–Milwaukee

The Business Situation

Two years ago, prior to a major capital-budgeting decision (see Case 4), Robert Burns, the president of Greetings Inc., faced a challenging transfer pricing issue. He knew that Greetings store managers had heard about the ABC study (see Case 2) and that they knew a price increase for framed items would soon be on the way. In an effort to dissuade him from increasing the transfer price for framed prints, several store managers e-mailed him with detailed analyses showing how framed-print sales had given stores a strong competitive position and had increased revenues and profits. The store managers mentioned, however, that while they were opposed to an increase in the cost of framed prints, they were looking forward to a price decrease for unframed prints.

Management at Wall Décor was very interested in changing the transfer pricing strategy. You had reported to them that setting the transfer price based on the product costs calculated by using traditional overhead allocation measures had been a major contributing factor to its non-optimal performance.

Here is a brief recap of what happened during your presentation to Mr. Burns and the Wall Décor managers. Mr. Burns smiled during your presentation and graciously acknowledged your excellent activity-based costing (ABC) study and analysis. He even nodded with approval as you offered the following suggestions.

1. Wall Décor should decrease the transfer price for high-volume, simple print items.
2. Wall Décor should increase the transfer price for low-volume, complex framed print items.
3. Your analysis points to a transfer price that maintains the 20% markup over cost.
4. Adoption of these changes will provide Wall Décor with an 11% return on investment (ROI), beating the required 10% expected by Greetings' board of directors.
5. Despite the objections of the store managers, the Greetings stores must accept the price changes.

Finishing your presentation, you asked the executive audience, "What questions do you have?" Mr. Burns responded as follows.

> "Your analysis appears sound. However, it focuses almost exclusively on Wall Décor. It appears to tell us little about how to move forward and benefit the entire company, especially the Greetings retail stores. Let me explain.
>
> I am concerned about how individual store customers will react to the price changes, assuming the price increase of framed-print items is passed along to the customer. Store managers will welcome a decrease in the transfer price of unframed prints. They have complained about the high cost of prints from the beginning. With a decrease in print cost, store managers will be able to compete against mall stores for print items at a competitive selling price. In addition, the increase in store traffic for prints should increase the sales revenue for related items, such as cards, wrapping paper, and more. These are all low-margin items, but with increased sales volume of prints and related products, revenues and profits should grow for each store.
>
> Furthermore, store managers will be upset with the increase in the cost of framed prints. Framed prints have generated substantial revenues and profits for the stores. Increasing the cost of framed prints to the stores could create one of three problems: First, a store manager may elect to keep the selling price of framed-print items the same. The results of this would be no change in revenues, but profits would decline because of the increase in cost of framed prints.
>
> Second, a store manager may elect to increase the selling price of the framed prints to offset the cost increase. In this case, sales of framed prints would surely decline and so would revenues and profits. In addition, stores would likely see a decline in related sales of other expensive, high-quality, high-margin items. This is because sales data indicate that customers who purchase high-quality, high-price framed prints also purchase high-quality, high-margin items such as watches, jewelry, and cosmetics.
>
> Third, a store manager may elect to search the outside market for framed prints."

Mr. Burns offered you the challenge of helping him bring change to the company's transfer prices so that both business units, Greetings stores and Wall Décor, win. From his explanation, you could see and appreciate that setting the transfer price for unframed and framed prints impacts sale revenues and profits for related items and for the company overall. You immediately recognized the error in your presentation by simply providing a solution for Wall Décor alone.

You drove home that night thinking about the challenge. You recognized the need and importance of anticipating the reaction of Greetings store customers to changes in the prices of unframed and framed prints. The next day, the marketing team provided you with the following average data.

- For every unframed print sold (assume one print per customer), that customer purchases related products resulting in $4 of additional profit.
- For every framed print sold (assume one print per customer), that customer purchases related products resulting in $8 of additional profit.
- Each Greetings store sets its own selling price for unframed and framed prints. Store managers need this type of flexibility to be responsive to competitive pressures. On average the pricing for stores is as follows: unframed prints $21, steel-framed without matting $50, wood-framed with matting $70.

Instructions

Answer each of the following questions.

1. Prepare for class discussion what you think were the critical challenges for Mr. Burns. Recognize that Wall Décor is a profit center and each Greetings store is a profit center.
2. After lengthy and sometimes heated negotiations between Wall Décor and the store managers, a new transfer price was determined that calls for the stores and Wall Décor to split the profits on unframed prints 30/70 (30% to the store, 70% to Wall Décor) and the profits on framed prints 50/50. The following additional terms were also agreed to:

   - "Profits" are defined as the store selling price less the ABC cost.
   - Stores do not share the profits from related products with Wall Décor.
   - Wall Décor will not seek to sell unframed and framed print items through anyone other than Greetings.
   - Wall Décor will work to decrease costs.
   - Greetings stores will not seek suppliers of prints other than Wall Décor.
   - Stores will keep the selling price of framed prints as it was before the change in transfer price. On average, stores will decrease the selling price of unframed prints to $20, with an expected increase in volume to 100,000 prints.

   Analyze how Wall Décor and the stores benefited from this new agreement. In your analysis, first **(a)** compute the profits of the stores and Wall Décor using traditional amounts related to pricing, cost, and a 20% mark-up on Wall Décor costs. Next, **(b)** compute the profits of the stores and Wall Décor using the ABC cost and negotiated transfer price approach. Finally, **(c)** explain your findings, linking the overall profits for stores and Wall Décor.
   The following data apply to this analysis. (Round all calculations to three decimal places.)

	Unframed print	**Steel-framed, no matting**	**Wood-framed, with matting**
Average selling price by stores before transfer pricing study	$21	$50	$70
Average selling price by stores after transfer pricing study	$20	$50	$70
Volume at traditional selling price	80,000	15,000	7,000
Volume at new selling price	100,000	15,000	7,000
Wall Décor cost (traditional)	$17.36	$33.48	$48.10
ABC cost	$15.258	$39.028	$55.328

3. Review the additional terms of the agreement listed in instruction 2, above. In each case, state whether the item is appropriate, unnecessary, ineffective, or potentially harmful to the overall company.

Case 4

Greetings Inc.

Greetings Inc.: Capital Budgeting

Developed by Thomas L. Zeller, Loyola University Chicago, and Paul D. Kimmel, University of Wisconsin–Milwaukee

The Business Situation

Greetings Inc. stores, as well as the Wall Décor division, have enjoyed healthy profitability during the last two years. Although the profit margin on prints is often thin, the volume of print sales has been substantial enough to generate 15% of Greetings's store profits. In addition, the increased customer traffic resulting from the prints has generated significant additional sales of related non-print products. As a result, the company's rate of return has exceeded the industry average during this two-year period. Greetings's store managers likened the e-business leverage created by Wall Décor to a "high-octane" fuel to supercharge the stores' profitability.

This high rate of return (ROI) was accomplished even though Wall Décor's venture into e-business proved to cost more than originally budgeted. Why was it a profitable venture even though costs exceeded estimates? Greetings stores were able to generate a considerable volume of business for Wall Décor. This helped spread the high e-business operating costs, many of which were fixed, across many unframed and framed prints. This experience taught top management that maintaining an e-business structure and making this business model successful are very expensive and require substantial sales as well as careful monitoring of costs.

Wall Décor's success gained widespread industry recognition. The business press documented Wall Décor's approach to using information technology to increase profitability. The company's CEO, Robert Burns, has become a frequent business-luncheon speaker on the topic of how to use information technology to offer a great product mix to the customer and increase shareholder value. From the outside looking in, all appears to be going very well for Greetings stores and Wall Décor.

However, the sun is not shining as brightly on the inside at Greetings. The mall stores that compete with Greetings have begun to offer prints at very competitive prices. Although Greetings stores enjoyed a selling price advantage for a few years, the competition eventually responded, and now the pressure on selling price is as intense as ever. The pressure on the stores is heightened by the fact that the company's recent success has led shareholders to expect the stores to generate an above-average rate of return. Mr. Burns is very concerned about how the stores and Wall Décor can continue on a path of continued growth.

Fortunately, more than a year ago, Mr. Burns anticipated that competitors would eventually find a way to match the selling price of prints. As a consequence, he formed a committee to explore ways to employ technology to further reduce costs and to increase revenues and profitability. The committee is comprised of store managers and staff members from the information technology, marketing, finance, and accounting departments. Early in the group's discussion, the focus turned to the most expensive component of the existing business model—the large inventory of prints that Wall Décor has in its centralized warehouse. In addition, Wall Décor incurs substantial costs for shipping the prints from the centralized warehouse to customers across the country. Ordering and maintaining such a large inventory of prints consumes valuable resources.

One of the committee members suggested that the company should pursue a model that music stores have experimented with, where CDs are burned in the store from a master copy. This saves the music store the cost of maintaining a large inventory and increases its ability to expand its music offerings. It virtually guarantees that the store can always provide the CDs requested by customers.

Applying this idea to prints, the committee decided that each Greetings store could invest in an expensive color printer connected to its online ordering system. This printer would generate the new prints. Wall Décor would have to pay a royalty on a per print basis. However, this approach does offer certain advantages. First, it would eliminate all ordering and inventory maintenance costs related to the prints. Second, shrinkage from lost and stolen prints would be reduced. Finally, by reducing the cost of prints for Wall Décor, the cost of prints to Greetings stores would decrease, thus allowing the stores to sell prints at a lower price than competitors. The stores are very interested in this option because it enables them to maintain their current customers and to sell prints to an even wider set of customers at a potentially lower cost. A new set of customers means even greater related sales and profits.

As the accounting/finance expert on the team, you have been asked to perform a financial analysis of this proposal. The team has collected the information presented in Illustration CA 4-1.

Available Data	Amount
Cost of equipment (zero residual value)	$800,000
Cost of ink and paper supplies (purchase immediately)	100,000
Annual cash flow savings for Wall Décor	175,000
Annual additional store cash flow from increased sales	100,000
Sale of ink and paper supplies at end of 5 years	50,000
Expected life of equipment	5 years
Cost of capital	12%

Illustration CA 4-1
Information about the proposed capital investment project

Instructions

Mr. Burns has asked you to do the following as part of your analysis of the capital investment project.

1. Calculate the net present value using the numbers provided. Assume that annual cash flows occur at the end of the year.
2. Mr. Burns is concerned that the original estimates may be too optimistic. He has suggested that you do a sensitivity analysis assuming all costs are 10% higher than expected and that all inflows are 10% less than expected.
3. Identify possible flaws in the numbers or assumptions used in the analysis, and identify the risk(s) associated with purchasing the equipment.
4. In a one-page memo, provide a recommendation based on the above analysis. Include in this memo: **(a)** a challenge to store and Wall Décor management and **(b)** a suggestion on how Greetings stores could use the computer connection for related sales.

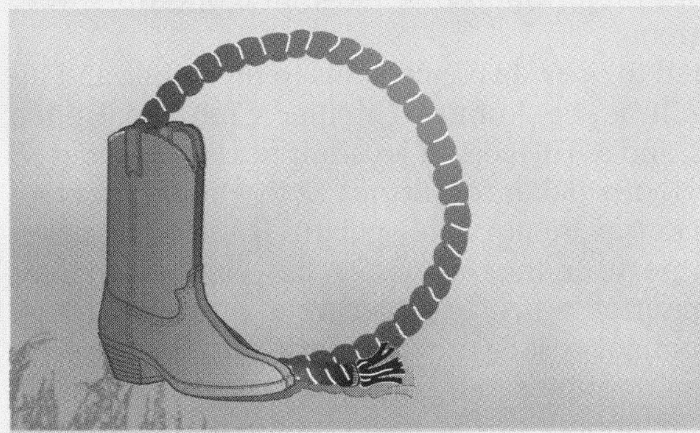

Auburn Circular Club Pro Rodeo Roundup

Developed by Jessica Johnson Frazier, Eastern Kentucky University, and Patricia H. Mounce, Mississippi College

The Business Situation

When Shelley Jones became president-elect of the Circular Club of Auburn, Kansas, she was asked to suggest a new fund-raising activity for the club. After a considerable amount of research, Shelley proposed that the Circular Club sponsor a professional rodeo. In her presentation to the club, Shelley said that she wanted a fund-raiser that would (1) continue to get better each year, (2) give back to the community, and (3) provide the club a presence in the community. Shelley's goal was to have an activity that would become an "annual community event" and that would break even the first year and raise $5,000 the following year. In addition, based on the experience of other communities, Shelley believed that a rodeo could grow in popularity so that the club would eventually earn an average of $20,000 annually.

A rodeo committee was formed. Shelley contacted the world's oldest and largest rodeo-sanctioning agency to apply to sponsor a professional rodeo. The sanctioning agency requires a rodeo to consist of the following five events: Bareback Riding, Bronco Riding, Steer Wrestling, Bull Riding, and Calf Roping. Because there were a number of team ropers in the area and because they wanted to include females in the competition, members of the rodeo committee added Team Roping and Women's Barrels. Prize money of $3,000 would be paid to winners in each of the seven events.

Members of the rodeo committee contracted with RJ Cattle Company, a livestock contractor on the rodeo circuit, to provide bucking stock, fencing, and chutes. Realizing that costs associated with the rodeo were tremendous and that ticket sales would probably not be sufficient to cover the costs, the rodeo committee sent letters to local businesses soliciting contributions in exchange for various sponsorships. Exhibiting Sponsors would contribute $1,000 to exhibit their products or services, while Major Sponsors would contribute $600. Chute Sponsors would contribute $500 to have the name of their business on one of the six bucking chutes. For a contribution of $100, individuals would be included in a Friends of Rodeo list found in the rodeo programs. At each performance the rodeo announcer would repeatedly mention the names of the businesses and individuals at each level of sponsorship. In addition, large signs and banners with the names of the businesses of the Exhibiting Sponsors, Major Sponsors, and Chute Sponsors were to be displayed prominently in the arena.

A local youth group was contacted to provide concessions to the public and divide the profits with the Circular Club. The Auburn Circular Club Pro Rodeo Roundup would be held on June 1, 2, and 3. The cost of an adult ticket was set at $8 in advance or $10 at the gate; the cost of a ticket for a child 12 or younger was set at $6 in advance or $8 at the gate. Tickets were not date-specific. Rather, one ticket would admit an individual to one performance of his or her choice—Friday, Saturday, or Sunday. The rodeo committee was able to secure a location through the county supervisors board at a nominal cost to the Circular Club. The arrangement allowed the use of the county fair grounds and arena for a one-week period. Several months prior to the rodeo, members of the rodeo committee had been assured that bleachers at the arena would hold 2,500 patrons. However, on Saturday night there were 1,663 in attendance and all seats were filled. Attendance was 898 Friday and 769 on Sunday.

The following revenue and expense figures relate to the first year of the rodeo.

Illustration CA 5-1
Revenue and expense data, year 1

Receipts		
Contributions from sponsors	$22,000	
Receipts from ticket sales	28,971	
Share of concession profits	1,513	
Sale of programs	600	
Total receipts		$53,084
Expenses		
Livestock contractor	26,000	
Prize money	21,000	
Contestant hospitality	3,341*	
Sponsor signs for arena	1,900	
Insurance	1,800	
Ticket printing	1,050	
Sanctioning fees	925	
Entertainment	859	
Judging fees	750	
Port-a-potties	716	
Rent	600	
Hay for horses and sand for arena	538	
Programs	500	
Western hats to first 500 children	450	
Hotel rooms for stock contractor	325	
Utilities	300	
Interest expense	251	
Miscellaneous fixed costs	105	
Total expenses		61,410
Net loss		$(8,326)

*The club contracted with a local caterer to provide a tent and food for the contestants. The cost of the food was contingent on the number of contestants each evening. Information concerning the number of contestants and the costs incurred are as follows:

	Contestants	Total Cost
Friday	68	$ 998
Saturday	96	1,243
Sunday	83	1,100

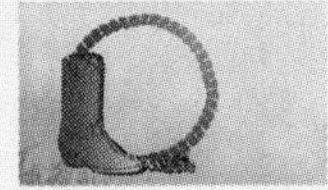

On Wednesday after the rodeo, members of the rodeo committee met to discuss and critique the rodeo. Jonathan Edmunds, CPA and President of the Circular Club, commented that the club did not lose money. Rather, Jonathan said, "The club made an investment in the rodeo."

Instructions

Answer each of the following questions.

1. Do you think it was necessary for Shelley Jones to stipulate that she wanted a fund-raiser that would (1) continue to get better each year, (2) give back to the community, and (3) provide the club a presence in the community? Why or why not?

2. What did Jonathan Edmunds mean when he said the club had made an investment in the rodeo?

3. Is Jonathan's comment concerning the investment consistent with Shelley's idea that the club should have a fund-raiser that would (1) continue to get better each year, (2) give back to the community, and (3) provide the club a presence in the community? Why or why not?

4. What do you believe is the behavior of the rodeo expenditures in relation to ticket sales?

5. Determine the fixed and variable cost components of the catering costs using the high-low method.

6. Assume you are elected chair of the rodeo committee for next year. What steps would you suggest the committee take to make the rodeo profitable?

7. Shelley, Jonathan, and Adrian Stein, the Fundraising Chairperson, are beginning to make plans for next year's rodeo. Shelley believes that by negotiating with local feed stores, innkeepers, and other business owners, costs can be cut dramatically. Jonathan agrees. After carefully analyzing costs, Jonathan has estimated that the fixed expenses can be pared to approximately $51,000. In addition, Jonathan has determined that variable costs are 4% of total gross receipts.

After talking with business owners who attended the rodeo, Adrian is confident that funds solicited from sponsors will increase. Adrian is comfortable in budgeting revenue from sponsors at $25,600. The local youth group is unwilling to provide concessions to the audience unless they receive all of the profits. Not having the personnel to staff the concession booth, members of the Circular Club reluctantly agree to let the youth group have 100% of the profits from the concessions. In addition, members of the rodeo committee, recognizing that the net income from programs was only $100, decide not to sell rodeo programs next year. Compute the break-even point in dollars of ticket sales assuming Adrian and Jonathan are correct in their assumptions.

8. Shelley has just learned that you are calculating the break-even point in ticket sales. She is still convinced that the Club can make a profit using the assumptions in number 7 above.

(a) Calculate the dollars of ticket sales needed in order to earn a target profit of $6,000.

(b) Calculate the dollars of ticket sales needed in order to earn a target profit of $12,000.

9. Are the facilities at the fairgrounds adequate to handle crowds needed to generate ticket revenues calculated in number 8 above to earn a $6,000 profit? Show calculations to support your answers.

10. Prepare a budgeted income statement for next year using the estimated revenues from sponsors and other assumptions in number 7 above. In addition, use ticket sales based on the - target profit of $12,000 estimated in 8(b). The cost of the livestock contractor, prize money, sanctioning fees, entertainment, judging fees, rent, and utilities will remain the same next year.

Changes in expenses include the following: Members of the Club have decided to eliminate all costs related to contestant hospitality by soliciting a tent and food for the contestants and taking care of the "Contestant Hospitality Tent" themselves. The county has installed permanent restrooms at the arena, eliminating the need to rent port-a-potties. The rodeo committee intends to pursue arrangements to have hotel rooms, hay and sand, and children's hats provided at no charge in exchange for sponsorships. The cost of banners varies with the number of sponsors. Signs and More charged the Circular Club $130 for each Exhibiting Sponsor banner and $48 for each Major Sponsor banner. At this time there is no way to know whether additional sponsors will be Exhibiting Sponsors or Major Sponsors. Therefore, for budgeting purposes you should increase the cost of the banners by the percentage increase in sponsor contributions. (*Hint*: Round all calculations to three decimal places.) By checking prices, the Circular Club will be able to obtain insurance providing essentially the same amount of coverage as this year for only $600. For the first rodeo the Club ordered 10,000 tickets. Realizing the constraints on available seating, the Club is ordering only 5,000 tickets for next year, and therefore its costs are reduced 50%. The interest expense for next year will be $300, and miscellaneous fixed costs are to be budgeted at $100.

11. A few members in the Circular Club do not want to continue with the annual rodeo. However, Shelley is insistent that the Club must continue to conduct the rodeo as an annual fund-raiser. Shelley argues that she has spent hundreds of dollars on western boots, hats, and other items of clothing to wear to the rodeo. Are the expenses related to Shelley's purchases of rodeo clothing relevant costs? Why or why not?

12. Rather than hire the local catering company to cater the Contestant Hospitality Tent, members of the Circular Club are considering asking Shady's Bar-B-Q to cater the event in exchange for a $600 Major Sponsor spot. In addition, The Fun Shop, a local party supply business, will be asked to donate a tent to use for the event. The Fun Shop will also be given a $600 Major Sponsor spot. Several members of the Club are opposed to this consideration, arguing that the two Major Sponsor spots will take away from the money to be earned through other sponsors. Adrian Stein has explained to the members that the Major Sponsor signs for the arena cost only $48 each. In addition, there is more than enough room to display two additional sponsor signs. What would you encourage the Club to do concerning the Contestant Hospitality Tent? Would your answer be different if the arena were limited in the number of additional signs that could be displayed? What kind of cost would we consider in this situation that would not be found on a financial statement?

Sweats Galore

Developed by Jessica Johnson Frazier, Eastern Kentucky University, and Patricia H. Mounce, Mississippi College

The Business Situation

After graduating with a degree in business from Eastern University in Campus Town, USA, Michael Woods realized that he wanted to remain in Campus Town. After a number of unsuccessful attempts at getting a job in his discipline, Michael decided to go into business for himself. In thinking about his business venture, Michael determined that he had four criteria for the new business:

1. He wanted to do something that he would enjoy.
2. He wanted a business that would give back to the community.
3. He wanted a business that would grow and be more successful every year.
4. Realizing that he was going to have to work very hard, Michael wanted a business that would generate a minimum net income of $25,000 annually.

While reflecting on the criteria he had outlined, Michael, who had been president of his fraternity and served as an officer in several other student organizations, realized that there was no place in Campus Town to have custom sweatshirts made using a silk-screen process. When student organizations wanted sweatshirts to give to their members or to market on campus, the officers had to make a trip to a city 100 miles away to visit "Shirts and More."

Michael had worked as a part-time employee at Shirts and More while he was in high school and had envisioned owning such a shop. He realized that a sweatshirt shop in Campus Town had the potential to meet all four of his criteria. Michael set up an appointment with Jayne Stoll, the owner of Shirts and More, to obtain information useful in getting his shop started. Because Jayne liked Michael and was intrigued by his entrepreneurial spirit, she answered many of Michael's questions.

In addition, Jayne provided information concerning the type of equipment Michael would need for his business and its average useful life. Jayne knows a competitor who is retiring and would like to sell his equipment. Michael can purchase the equipment at the beginning of 2008, and the owner is willing to give him terms of 50% due upon purchase and 50% due the quarter following the purchase. Michael decided to purchase the following equipment as of January 1, 2008.

	Cost	Useful Life
Hand-operated press that applies ink to the shirt	$7,500	5 yrs.
Light-exposure table	1,350	10 yrs.
Dryer conveyer belt that makes ink dry on the shirts	2,500	10 yrs.
Computer with graphics software and color printer	3,500	4 yrs.
Display furniture	2,000	10 yrs.
Used cash register	500	5 yrs.

Michael has decided to use the sweatshirt supplier recommended by Jayne. He learned that a gross of good-quality sweatshirts to be silk-screened would cost $1,440. Jayne has encouraged Michael to ask the sweatshirt supplier for terms of 40% of a quarter's purchases to be paid in the quarter of purchase, with the remaining 60% of the quarter's purchases to be paid in the quarter following the purchase.

Michael also learned from talking with Jayne that the ink used in the silk-screen process costs approximately $0.75 per shirt.

Knowing that the silk-screen process is somewhat labor intensive, Michael plans to hire six college students to help with the process. Each one will work an average of 20 hours per week for 50 weeks during the year. Michael estimates total annual wages for the workers to be $72,000.

In addition, Michael will need one person to take orders, bill customers, and operate the cash register. Cary Sue Smith, who is currently Director of Student Development at Eastern University, has approached Michael about a job in sales. Cary Sue knows the officers of all of the student organizations on campus. In addition, she is very active in the community. Michael thinks Cary Sue can bring in a lot of business. In addition she also has the clerical skills needed for the position. Because of her contacts, Michael is willing to pay Cary Sue $1,200 per month plus a commission of 10 percent of sales. Michael estimates Cary Sue will spend 50% of the workday focusing on sales, and the remaining 50% will be spent on clerical and administrative duties.

Michael realizes that he will have difficulty finding a person skilled in computer graphics to generate the designs to be printed on the shirts. Jayne recently hired a graphics designer in that position for Shirts and More at a rate of $500 per month plus $0.10 for each shirt printed. Michael believes he can find a university graphics design student to work for the same rate Jayne is paying her designer.

Michael was fortunate to find a commercial building for rent near the university and the downtown area. The landlord requires a one-year lease. Although the monthly rent of $1,000 is more than Michael had anticipated paying, the building is nice, has adequate parking, and there is room for expansion. Michael anticipates that 75% of the building will be used in the silk-screen process and 25% will be used for sales.

Michael's fraternity brothers have encouraged him to advertise weekly in the Eastern University student newspaper. Upon inquiring, Michael found that a 3″ × 3″ ad would cost $25 per week. Michael also plans to run a weekly ad in the local newspaper that will cost him $75 per week.

Michael wants to sell a large number of quality shirts at a reasonable price. He estimates the selling price of each customized shirt to be $16. Jayne has suggested that he should ask customers to pay for 70% of their purchases in the quarter purchased and pay the additional 30% in the quarter following the purchases.

After talking with the insurance agent and the property valuation administrator in his municipality, Michael estimates that the property taxes and insurance on the machinery will cost $2,240 annually; property tax and insurance on display furniture and cash register will total $380 annually.

Jayne reminded Michael that maintenance of the machines is required for the silk-screen process. In addition, Michael realizes that he must consider the cost of utilities. The building Michael wants to rent is roughly the same size as the building occupied by Shirts and More. In addition, Shirts and More sells approximately the same number of shirts Michael plans to sell in his store. Therefore, Michael is confident that the maintenance and utility costs for his shop will be comparable to the maintenance and utility costs for Shirts and More, which are as follows within the relevant range of zero to 8,000 shirts.

	Shirts Sold	Maintenance Costs	Utility Costs
January	2,000	$1,716	$1,100
February	2,110	1,720	1,158
March	2,630	1,740	1,171
April	3,150	1,740	1,198
May	5,000	1,758	1,268
June	5,300	1,818	1,274
July	3,920	1,825	1,205
August	2,080	1,780	1,117
September	8,000	1,914	1,400
October	6,810	1,860	1,362
November	6,000	1,855	1,347
December	3,000	1,749	1,193

Michael estimates the number of shirts to be sold in the first five quarters, beginning January 2008, to be:

First quarter, year 1	8,000
Second quarter, year 1	10,000
Third quarter, year 1	20,000
Fourth quarter, year 1	12,000
First quarter, year 2	18,000

Seeing how determined his son was to become an entrepreneur, Michael's father offered to co-sign a note for an amount up to $20,000 to help Michael open his sweatshirt shop, Sweats Galore. However, when Michael and his father approached the loan officer at First Guarantee Bank, the loan officer asked Michael to produce the following budgets for 2008.

Sales budget
Schedule of expected collections from customers
Shirt purchases budget
Schedule of expected payments for purchases
Silk-screen labor budget
Selling and administrative expenses budget
Silk-screen overhead expenses budget
Budgeted income statement
Cash budget
Budgeted balance sheet

The loan officer advised Michael that the interest rate on a 12-month loan would be 8%. Michael expects the loan to be taken out as of January 1, 2008.

Michael has estimated that his income tax rate will be 20%. He expects to pay the total tax due when his returns are filed in 2009.

Instructions

Answer the following questions.

1. Do you think it was important for Michael to stipulate his four criteria for the business (see page CA-21), including the goal of generating a net income of at least $25,000 annually? Why or why not?

2. If Michael has sales of $12,000 during January of his first year of business, determine the amount of variable and fixed costs associated with utilities and maintenance using the high-low method for each.
3. Using the format below, prepare a sales budget for the year ending 2008.

SWEATS GALORE
Sales Budget
For the Year Ending December 31, 2008

	Quarter				
	1	2	3	4	Year
Expected unit sales					
Unit selling price	x				
Budgeted sales revenue	$				

4. Prepare a schedule of expected collections from customers.

SWEATS GALORE
Schedule of Expected Collections from Customers
For the Year Ending December 31, 2008

	Quarter			
	1	2	3	4
Accounts receivable 1/1/08	–0–			
First quarter				
Second quarter				
Third quarter				
Fourth quarter				
Total collections				

5. Michael learned from talking with Jayne that the supplier is so focused on making quality sweatshirts that many times the shirts are not available for several days. She encouraged Michael to maintain an ending inventory of shirts equal to 25% of the next quarter's sales. Prepare a shirt purchases budget for shirts using the format provided.

SWEATS GALORE
Shirt Purchases Budget
For the Year Ending December 31, 2008

	Quarter				
	1	2	3	4	Year
Shirts to be silk-screened					
Plus: Desired ending inventory					
Total shirts required					
Less: Beginning inventory					
Total shirts needed					
Cost per shirt					
Total cost of shirt purchases					

6. Prepare a schedule of expected payments for purchases.

SWEATS GALORE
Schedule of Expected Payments for Purchases
For the Year Ending December 31, 2008

	Quarter			
	1	2	3	4
Accounts payable 1/1/08	–0–			
First quarter				
Second quarter				
Third quarter				
Fourth quarter				
Total payments				

7. Prepare a silk-screen labor budget.

SWEATS GALORE
Silk-Screen Labor Budget
For the Year Ending December 31, 2008

	Quarter 1	2	3	4	Year
Units to be produced					
Silk-screen labor hours per unit					
Total required silk-screen labor hours					
Silk-screen labor cost per hour					
Total silk-screen labor cost					

8. Prepare a selling and administrative expenses budget for Sweats Galore for the year ending December 31, 2008.

SWEATS GALORE
Selling and Administrative Expenses Budget
For the Year Ending December 31, 2008

	Quarter 1	2	3	4	Year
Variable expenses:					
Sales commissions					
Total variable expenses					
Fixed expenses:					
Advertising					
Rent					
Sales salaries					
Office salaries					
Depreciation					
Property taxes and insurance					
Total fixed expenses					
Total selling and administrative expenses					

9. Prepare a silk-screen overhead expenses budget for Sweats Galore for the year ending December 31, 2008.

SWEATS GALORE
Silk-Screen Overhead Expenses Budget
For the Year Ending December 31, 2008

	Quarter 1	2	3	4	Year
Variable expenses:					
Ink					
Maintenance					
Utilities					
Graphics design					
Total variable expenses					
Fixed expenses:					
Rent					
Maintenance					
Utilities					
Graphics design					
Property taxes and insurance					
Depreciation					
Total fixed expenses					
Total silk-screen overhead					
Direct silk-screen hours					
Overhead rate per silk-screen hour					

10. Using the information found in the case and the previous budgets, prepare a budgeted income statement for Sweats Galore for the year ended December 31, 2008.

SWEATS GALORE
Budgeted Income Statement
For the Year Ending December 31, 2008

Sales
Cost of goods sold
Gross profit
Selling and administrative expenses
Income from operations
Interest expense
Income before income taxes
Income tax expense
Net income

11. Using the information found in the case and the previous budgets, prepare a cash budget for Sweats Galore for the year ended December 31, 2008.

SWEATS GALORE
Cash Budget
For the Year Ending December 31, 2008

	Quarter			
	1	2	3	4
Beginning cash balance				
Add: Receipts				
Collections from customers				
Total available cash				
Less: Disbursements				
Payments for shirt purchases				
Silk-screen labor				
Silk-screen overhead				
Selling and administrative expenses				
Payment for equipment purchase				
Total disbursements				
Excess (deficiency) of available cash over disbursements				
Financing				
Borrowings				
Ending cash balance				

12. Using the information contained in the case and the previous budgets, prepare a budgeted balance sheet for Sweats Galore for the year ended December 31, 2008.

SWEATS GALORE
Budgeted Balance Sheet
December 31, 2008

Assets

Cash
Accounts receivable
Sweatshirt inventory
Equipment
Less: Accumulated depreciation
Total assets

Liabilities and Owner's Equity

Accounts payable
Notes payable
Interest payable
Taxes payable
Total liabilities
Michael Woods, Capital
Total liabilities and owner's equity

13. (a) Using the information contained in the case and the previous budgets, calculate the estimated contribution margin per unit for 2008. (*Hint:* Silk-screened labor and the taxes are both fixed costs.)

(b) Calculate the total estimated fixed costs for 2008 (including interest and taxes).

(c) Compute the break-even point in units and dollars for 2008.

14. (a) Michael is very disappointed that he did not have an income of $25,000 for his first year of budgeted operations as he had wanted. How many shirts would Michael have had to sell in order to have had a profit of $25,000? (Ignore changes in income-tax expense.)

(b) Why does Michael's net income differ from his ending cash balance?

15. Do you think it was a good idea to offer Cary Sue a salary plus 10% of sales? Why or why not?

Case 7

Armstrong Helmet Company

Developed by Dick Wasson, Southwestern College

The Business Situation

Armstrong Helmet Company manufactures a unique model of bicycle helmet. The company began operations December 1, 2008. Its accountant quit the second week of operations, and the company is searching for a replacement. The company has decided to test the knowledge and ability of all candidates interviewing for the position. Each candidate will be provided with the information below and then asked to prepare a series of reports, schedules, budgets, and recommendations based on that information. The information provided to each candidate is as follows.

Cost Items and Account Balances	
Administrative salaries	$15,500
Advertising for helmets	11,000
Cash, December 1	–0–
Depreciation on factory building	1,500
Depreciation on office equipment	800
Insurance on factory building	1,500
Miscellaneous expenses—factory	1,000
Office supplies expense	300
Professional fees	500
Property taxes on factory building	400
Raw materials used	70,000
Rent on production equipment	6,000
Research and development	10,000
Sales commissions	40,000
Utility costs—factory	900
Wages—factory	70,000
Work in process, December 1	–0–
Work in process, December 31	–0–
Raw materials inventory, December 1	–0–
Raw materials inventory, December 31	–0–
Raw material purchases	70,000
Finished goods inventory, December 1	–0–

Production and Sales Data

Number of helmets produced	10,000
Expected sales in units for December ($40 unit sales price)	8,000
Expected sales in units for January	10,000
Desired ending inventory	20% of next month's sales
Direct materials per finished unit	1 kilogram
Direct materials cost	$7 per kilogram
Direct labor hours per unit	.35
Direct labor hourly rate	$20

Cash Flow Data

Cash collections from customers: 75% in month of sale and 25% the following month.
Cash payments to suppliers: 75% in month of purchase and 25% the following month.
Income tax rate: 45%.
Cost of proposed production equipment: $720,000.
Manufacturing overhead and selling and administrative costs are paid as incurred.
Desired ending cash balance: $30,000.

Instructions

Using the data presented above (including data on page CA-28), do the following.

1. Classify the costs as either product costs or period costs using a five-column table as shown below. Enter the dollar amount of each cost in the appropriate column and total each classification.

	Product Costs			
Item	**Direct Materials**	**Direct Labor**	**Manufacturing Overhead**	**Period Costs**

2. Classify the costs as either variable or fixed costs. Assume there are no mixed costs. Enter the dollar amount of each cost in the appropriate column and total each classification. Use the format shown below. Assume that Utility costs—Factory are a fixed cost.

Item	**Variable Costs**	**Fixed Costs**	**Total Costs**

3. Prepare a schedule of cost of goods manufactured for the month of December 2008.
4. Determine the cost of producing a helmet.
5. Identify the type of cost accounting system that Armstrong Helmet Company is probably using at this time. Explain.
6. Under what circumstances might Armstrong use a different cost accounting system?
7. Compute the unit variable cost for a helmet.
8. Compute the unit contribution margin and the contribution margin ratio.
9. Calculate the break-even point in units and in sales dollars.
10. Prepare the following budgets for the month of December 2008.
    (a) Sales.
    (b) Production.
    (c) Direct materials.
    (d) Direct labor.
    (e) Selling and administrative expenses.
    (f) Cash.
    (g) Budgeted income statement.

11. Prepare a flexible budget for manufacturing costs for activity levels between 8,000 and 10,000 units, in 1,000 unit increments.
12. Identify one potential cause of materials, direct labor, and manufacturing overhead variances in the production of the helmet.
13. Determine the cash payback period on the proposed production equipment purchase, assuming a monthly cash flow as indicated in the cash budget (requirement 10f).

COMPANY INDEX

SUBJECT INDEX